STANLEY W. JACOB, M.D., F.A.C.S.

Associate Professor of Surgery
Oregon Health Sciences University
Portland, Oregon

First Kemper Foundation Research Scholar
American College of Surgeons
Markle Scholar in Medical Sciences

The Late
CLARICE ASHWORTH FRANCONE

Medical Illustrator
Formerly, Head of the Department of Medical Illustrations
Oregon Health Sciences University
Portland, Oregon

WALTER J. LOSSOW, Ph.D.

Formerly Physiologist, Department of Physiology
and Donner Laboratory,
University of California, Berkeley
Formerly Lecturer in Human Anatomy and Physiology,
California State College at Hayward;
Merritt College, Oakland, California;
and Lassen College, Susanville, California
Formerly Member, Editorial Board,
Physiological Chemistry and Physics

STRUCTURE AND FUNCTION IN MAN

FIFTH EDITION

1982

W. B. SAUNDERS COMPANY

Philadelphia London Toronto Mexico City Rio de Janeiro Sydney Tokyo

W. B. Saunders Company: West Washington Square
Philadelphia, PA 19105

1 St. Anne's Road
Eastbourne, East Sussex BN21 3UN, England

1 Goldthorne Avenue
Toronto, Ontario M8Z 5T9, Canada

Apartado 26370 — Cedro 512
Mexico 4, D.F., Mexico

Rua Coronel Cabrita, 8
Sao Cristovao Caixa Postal 21176
Rio de Janeiro, Brazil

9 Waltham Street
Artarmon, N.S.W. 2064, Australia

Ichibancho, Central Bldg., 22-1 Ichibancho
Chiyoda-Ku, Tokyo 102, Japan

Library of Congress Cataloging in Publication Data

Jacob, Stanley W.

Structure and function in man.

Bibliography: p.

Includes index.

1. Human physiology.   2. Anatomy, Human.   I. Francone,
   Clarice Ashworth.   II. Lossow, Walter J.   III. Title.

QP34.5.J3 1982   612   81–51191

ISBN 0–7216–5094–5   AACR2

Listed here is the latest translated edition of this book together
with the language of the translation and the publisher.

Spanish (*3rd Edition*) — Editora Interamericana S.A. Mexico 4 D.F., Mexico

Portuguese (*4th Edition*) — Editora Interamericana Ltda. Rio de Janerio, Brazil

Cover drawing from *Anatomy of the Artist*, by Jenö Barcsay.
London: Octopus Books, Ltd., 1973.
Budapest: Corvina Press, 1973.

Structure and Function in Man   ISBN 0-7216-5094-5

Last digit is the print number: 9   8   7   6   5   4   3   2   1

IN MEMORIAM

The fifth edition of *Structure and Function in Man* is published in memory of our co-author Clarice Ashworth Francone, who died late last year. We were fortunate that she was able to complete work on this edition and its artwork, which, as in previous editions, excels in accuracy, clarity, and beauty. She will be deeply missed by both of us.

STANLEY W. JACOB

WALTER J. LOSSOW

To my father, without whose encouragement
this would not have been possible.

STANLEY W. JACOB

To my son Don.

CLARICE ASHWORTH FRANCONE

To my students.

WALTER J. LOSSOW

Preface
to the Fifth Edition

The past few years have seen the emergence of several new career opportunities to join the already existing professions of nursing and other paramedical disciplines. *Structure and Function in Man* originally was written in 1965 to fulfill the need for a unified understanding of anatomy and physiology on the part of those students preparing for health-related careers. Today, it is in its fifth edition, indicating its continuing sound background in the basic foundations needed by these students. At the same time, it is enjoying increasing acceptance abroad, with foreign translations taking it to the students of other countries.

This edition features a larger, more open format and relabeling of all anatomic illustrations, using a modern, clear typeface. Four colors have been used in the printed illustrations, with more color added in some figures to aid student comprehension. A second color is being used within the text to simplify textual organization for the reader.

The fifth edition of *Structure and Function in Man* contains a totally new chapter, "Basic Chemistry and the Chemical Constituents of Living Matter." New material on basic physiology has been incorporated into almost all chapters. To reinforce the discussion of fundamental physiologic concepts, practical treatments of disorders are discussed to help the student, who today will be given a greater responsibility in patient care. In addition, with the help of a reader who has never taken a course in anatomy and physiology, revisions have been made throughout the text so that it can be easily read and understood by the beginning student. Multiple teaching aids include chapter objectives at the beginning of each chapter and an outlined summary at the end. Additionally, there are review questions at the end of each chapter; a full glossary; an appendix with prefixes, suffixes, and combining forms; and an updated list of Suggested Additional Reading. Visual aids featured in this fifth edition include

1. Twenty-six new illustrations, to bring the total to 525.
2. Thirty-five revised illustrations.
3. Thirty new or revised Tables.

In addition, some of the textual changes include the addition to the chapter on the muscular system of a narrative describing muscle actions; completely revised descriptions of neurons, the nerve impulse, the neuromuscular junction, and synapses; a more thorough discussion of the organization of the cerebral cortex; added material on electroencephalograms, sleep, and seizure disorders; more detailed descriptions of sensory and motor pathways and the autonomic nervous system; amplification of the descriptions of the physiology of vision, equilibrium, and hearing; rewritten sections on the circulation that describe in greater detail the cardiac cycle, the regulation of blood pressure, and shock; extensive revision of the chapter on the lymphatic system, including an updating of the section on the B and T cell immune systems; completely revised sections on the transport of oxygen and carbon dioxide and the regulation of respiration; more detailed descriptions of the digestion of major foodstuffs and metabolism; a completely rewritten discussion of temperature regulation; considerable additional data on the endocrine glands and the mechanisms of hormone action; a new section on the development of the mammary glands and lactation, and added material on dysmenorrhea, menopause, the functions of androgens, and venereal disease.

STANLEY W. JACOB, M.D.
WALTER J. LOSSOW, PH.D.

Acknowledgments

If this text receives any measure of success many individuals will have made this possible.

We wish to express our appreciation to Barbara Weber, Terry Bristol, Beverly Methvin, Karen Clement, Anna Conley, Joel Cruz, Marilyn Jacob, Lois Locke, Blanche Palmer, Frances Kemper, Paula Burnett, Frank Weber, William Weaver, Ph.D., Helyn Galash, Robert Brooks, Ph.D., Marilyn Underdahl, Rebecca Meyer, and Bonnie Marble.

The authors wish to acknowledge the editorial and production assistance of the W. B. Saunders Company. A particular note of gratitude goes to Ms. Katherine Pitcoff and Ms. Elizabeth Cobbs, whose advice and encouragement contributed significantly to the completion of this manuscript.

Preface
to the First Edition

Many centuries ago anatomy and physiology were taught in a single course—not so much for the benefit of the student, but because the two fields of knowledge were not really separate even in the minds of researchers and educators. At the time there was insufficient knowledge of either science to warrant separate treatment. As the years passed, intensive studies were completed by methodically curious scientists in both fields. These investigations were aided by the progressive development of the physical and chemical sciences and by advances in technology providing more refined methods for observation and experimentation.

Gradually, the accumulation of facts and the elucidation of general concepts made specialization necessary; so anatomy and physiology were taught as individual sciences. Recent years have witnessed a return to the older philosophy of treating them as one integrated subject in the hope that students would more readily understand life as the truly integrated process it is.

One cannot appreciate the subject matter of physiology without first learning the basic concepts of anatomy. One cannot realize the full significance of human structure without also understanding the complex functions associated with it. Thus, while specialization is still necessary for advanced students, beginning and reviewing students at every educational level benefit from an integrated presentation of anatomy and physiology.

Structure and Function in Man is designed for use by the beginning student. This book emphasizes physiology without neglecting anatomy, an accomplishment due to the incorporation of approximately 300 new half-tone drawings depicting the anatomy of the entire body. The text employs the Nomina Anatomica (N.A.) terminology, replacing such words as *Eustachian* with *auditory* and *pituitary* with *hypophysis*. A brief survey of each organ system is presented; chapters are comprehensively summarized and study questions included. Complete lists of references have not been added; to do so in a field as wide as anatomy and physiology would have created a book of inordinate length. Clues to further reading are provided in a special section at the end of the text. This book is only a beginning.

"The hardest conviction to get into the mind of the beginner is that the education he is receiving in college is not a medical course but a life course for which the work of a few years under teachers is but a preparation."—Sir William Osler.

STANLEY W. JACOB

Portland, Oregon
CLARICE A. FRANCONE

Visual Aids

To supplement the text and laboratory manual by Jacob, Francone, and Lossow, certain illustrations have been made into visual teaching aids that can be purchased directly from the W. B. Saunders Company, West Washington Square, Philadelphia, Pa., 19105. These aids consist of a set of acetate overlays in two colors for use with an overhead projector. The overlays are based on illustrations from the text and cover the structure and function of important body systems. More information can be obtained by contacting the W. B. Saunders Company or one of its local representatives.

Contents

UNIT 4 □ Reproduction

Unit 1 □ INTRODUCTION

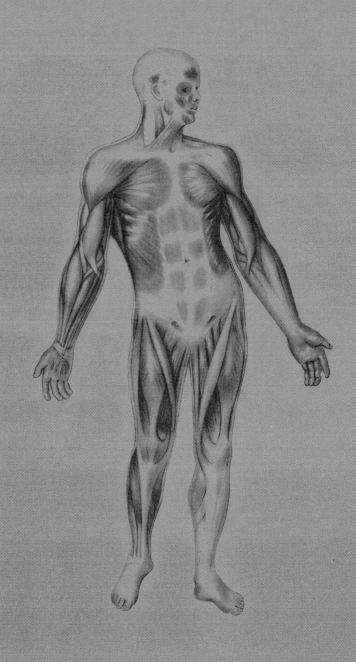

The Body As A Whole

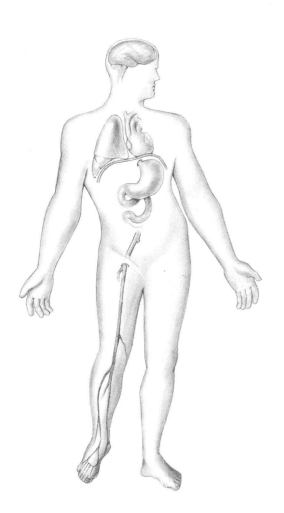

Objectives

The aim of this chapter is to enable the student to:

☐ Describe the distribution of body fluids.

☐ Describe the basic mechanism for maintaining homeostasis.

☐ Identify the major homeostatic organs and systems of the body.

☐ Identify the two major types of communication mechanisms involved in the coordination of the body.

☐ Construct a diagram of the body and label it with respect to anatomical directions, planes and cavities.

☐ Define and relate the cell, tissue, organ, and system as structural units.

☐ List the major systems of the human body.

THE HUMAN BODY

The order and plan of creation have challenged man throughout history. His world is organized into a solar system, the solar system into a galaxy, and the galaxy into a universe. In the opposite direction, his world is divided into civilizations, civilizations into societies, societies into human individuals, and these human individuals into chemical elements. Man finds himself, like Huxley, overcome at the "wonderful unity of plan in the thousands and thousands of living constructions, and the modifications of similar apparatuses to serve diverse ends." Such is the human body.

The Complex Organism

Man as a living organism may be viewed as an assemblage of minute units, called cells, which are marvelously integrated both structurally and functionally. Cells eventually specialize or differentiate to a greater or lesser extent. An aggregate of similarly differentiated cells composes a tissue, such as the fat cells of adipose tissue. Tissues, in turn, form organs; organs form systems. Ultimately, systems combine in an intricate manner to create a thinking, acting human being. When viewing the human body in this fashion, one stands in awe at the complexity of the organization of the body and the fine balance and interdependence of the various parts. Anatomy and physiology describe this interdependence of structure and function.

Scientific Study

Anatomy Defined. *Human anatomy* is the science of the shape and structure of the body and its parts. *Gross anatomy* deals with the macroscopic structures uncovered by dissection and visible to the unaided eye. *Microscopic anatomy* employs the use of the light microscope. The most detailed studies involve the methods of *electron microscopy*.

Physiology Defined. *Human physiology* is the study of the functions of the body and its parts. *Cellular physiology* is the most prominent specialized branch and is concerned with the study of the activities of individual cells and their parts.

The division between *anatomy* and *physiology* is not always clear, and the use of these terms is best considered an indication of emphasis rather than a sharp division of subject matter. In many areas, the interplay between these two approaches of inquiry has become so close that scientists have tended to specialize in the study of particular *organs* and *organ systems*, the definitions of which involve both structural and functional aspects. *Cardiology*, for example, is the study of the heart and related elements.

-ology: The Study of. On a more detailed level, the fields of *cytology*, study of the structure and function of the individual cells, and *histology*, study of tissue structure and function, have both become generally recognized disciplines.

Two other perspectives deserve special mention in a survey of the approaches to studying the structure and function of the human body. These are *pathology* and *embryology*. Pathology is the study of abnormal or disease states in the body, and is distinct from the more general inquiry into the normal structure and functioning of the organism. Embryology is the study of the development of the fertilized egg into the mature organism. The techniques of the anatomist, as well as those of the physiologist, are employed in both pathology and embryology.

Development of the Electron Microscope

Since the discovery and identification of atoms and molecules by 19th century physiologists, the single most impressive development in the study of biological structures has been the construction of the first electron microscope in the 1930's (Fig. 1–1). Electron microscopy is still a rapidly developing discipline, and it will perhaps be several decades before we have progressed sufficiently in our experimentation to reach the limits of its applicability. The impact of this instrument has been to multiply many times over our potential source of information about the fine details of cellular organization. In fact, it is the slowness of the development of physiological techniques of analysis on the molecular level that most severely retards our ability to interpret meaningfully what the electron microscope reveals.

The physiological side of analysis on the molecular level is termed *molecular biology*, and is based primarily on the use of sophisti-

Figure 1–1. The electron microscope is now being employed to study structures at a magnification of 200,000×.

cated biochemical techniques to study the structure of the basic molecular units of the cell and the mechanisms by which they function. Further categorization or specialization on this level of detail does not occur, since there are common objectives in the study of molecules, molecular structures and mechanisms.

Body Fluids

Body fluids are found within the cells (*intracellular*), or outside the cells in the *extracellular* space. The extracellular space is further divided into a *vascular,* or *plasma, compartment* and an *interstitial compartment* (between cells). In adults *plasma* accounts for about 5 per cent of the body weight; *interstitial fluid,* 15 per cent; and *intracellular fluid,* 45 per cent. Hence, approximately 65 per cent of the body weight consists of water, three-fourths of which is intracellular. Three-fourths of the water in the extracellular space is in the interstitial

compartment. (See Chapter 17 for additional information.)

Homeostasis

To function properly, cells require a constant environment. The environment of the body cells, the interstitial fluid medium (derived from the blood stream) immediately surrounding each cell, is called the internal environment of the body. From the time the cell was identified as the basic structural and functional unit of life, physiologists have recognized the importance of maintaining a constant internal environment. Claude Bernard, the famous French physiologist who introduced the term "internal environment" *(milieu intérieur),* is chiefly responsible for this basic concept. The American physiologist Walter Cannon developed a more general concept of constant internal body conditions and coined the term *homeostasis* (G. *homoios,* like; G. *stasis,* position) for the "steady state" conditions (holding within normal ranges despite continuous change) that are maintained by coordinated physiological processes. Among the homeostatic control mechanisms now understood are those maintaining normal concentrations of blood constituents, body temperature, volume and pH of body fluids, blood pressure, and heart rate.

All the homeostatic control mechanisms of the body operate by a process of **negative feedback.** The feedback is, in effect, an informational signal that tells the *driving mechanism* (or functional unit) how well it is doing at establishing or maintaining some variable at the desired level. The feedback is called negative because the change induced is negative to the initial change and counterbalances it. For example, if an individual's breathing becomes too shallow and slow, the removal of carbon dioxide from the body will be reduced and the concentration of carbon dioxide in the blood will rise. The rise in carbon dioxide concentration becomes an informational signal that is fed back to the center in the brain that controls breathing. Breathing will be stimulated and the elimination of carbon dioxide from the body will be increased, thereby reducing the concentration of carbon dioxide toward the normal value. If breathing becomes too deep and rapid, the concentration of carbon dioxide in the blood will fall and feedback responses

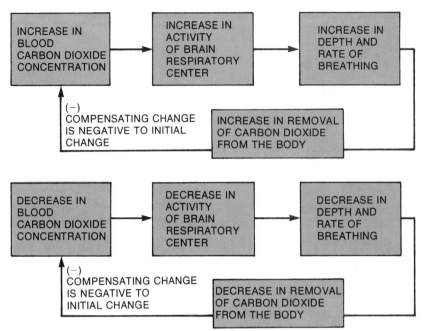

Figure 1–2. Negative feedback system for regulating the concentration of carbon dioxide in the blood. (This control system also functions as a regulator of breathing.) *Top.* An increase in the carbon dioxide concentration stimulates the respiratory center in the brain (in the medulla), which responds by transmitting impulses more rapidly to the muscles involved in breathing (the diaphragm and external intercostals). The resulting increase in depth and rate of breathing removes more carbon dioxide from the body, lowering its concentration in the blood. *Bottom.* A decrease in carbon dioxide concentration reduces the stimulation of the respiratory center; impulses are transmitted less rapidly to the muscles involved in breathing; breathing becomes shallower and slower, and the concentration of carbon dioxide in the blood rises.

will be initiated (opposite to those caused by an increase in carbon dioxide concentration) that will raise the concentration of carbon dioxide in the blood. Figure 1–2 illustrates the negative feedback system regulating the concentration of carbon dioxide in the blood. It should be noted that in this system breathing is, in turn, regulated by the concentration of carbon dioxide.

Coordination of the Body

It is perhaps apparent from the foregoing that the human body is not simply an aggregate or collection of substances or parts, but a highly organized and precisely coordinated unit that functions as an integrated whole. This structural and functional unity is achieved by means of structural organization and numerous interrelated control mechanisms. Each portion of the body — cell, tissue, organ, etc. — while retaining some degree of independence (autonomy) through self-control, is affected by and in turn affects

other areas of the body. Similarly, the body as a whole is partly independent of environmental influence and yet is still affected by and affects its environment. For instance, such factors limit the performance of the long-distance runner; and it is important to note that training or conditioning can broaden this range of activity.

Several of the organs of the body can best be understood as homeostatic organs, since their primary function is directed toward maintenance of homeostasis; these organs include the heart, lungs, kidneys, liver, gastrointestinal tract, and skin. These organs have developed into distinct units precisely because a unitary structure has proved most advantageous for performance of the function involved; that is, the "fittest" structures have presumably best withstood the evolutionary tests of survival.

The coordination of bodily functions occurs through internal regulating mechanisms. These can be distinguished into two general types: the nervous and the hormonal. The central nervous system acts as a sort of hierarchical integrator, receiving messages from its network of sensory nerves and putting out messages through its motor nerves to compensate for any detected imbalance or disturbance.

The hormonal system is composed of eight major endocrine glands that secrete chemical substances called *hormones*. Hormones are transported in the extracellular fluids to all parts of the body to help regulate function. For instance, thyroid hormone increases the rate of almost all chemical reactions in all cells. In this way thyroid hormone helps to set the tempo of body activity.

Understanding Complex Behavior

It will be instructive to consider briefly a few of the diverse functions and control mechanisms which operate in the apparently simple behavior of eating. The activities implicated in ingesting food range at one end of the scale from mastication, swallowing, and salivation, which stimulate digestive processes, to the activities employed in the search for food, prey capture, begging, etc. at the other. Among the variables which regulate feeding behavior are the concentration of circulating nutrients, e.g., blood sugar, which in turn is under hormonal control; the body reserve and weight; sensations in the muscles of the stomach and other parts of the digestive tract; the odor, taste (flavor), and visual aspects of food; and many other less obvious factors.

Social, cultural, and personal influences in a person's life are by no means irrelevant to the physiological functioning of the body. The formation of habits, the impact of psychological conflict, and numerous other aspects of human experience have time and again been shown to have radical effects on the health of the body. Physicians estimate that between 40 and 70 per cent of all physiological disorders have psychosomatic features traceable to the patient's personal and social life.

ORGANIZATION OF THE BODY

Anatomic reference systems have been adopted to facilitate uniformity of description of the body. Four basic reference systems of organization are considered: direction, planes, cavities, and structural units.

Direction

The body in the anatomic position is erect, facing forward with the arms at the sides and the palms toward the front, as shown in Figure 1–3. All descriptions of location or position assume the body to be in this posture. The following directions are usually considered:

Superior — uppermost or above; for example, the head is superior to the neck.

Inferior — lowermost or below; the foot is inferior to the ankle.

Anterior — toward the front, ventral; the breast is on the anterior chest wall.

Posterior — toward the back, dorsal; the vertebral column is posterior to the digestive tract.

Cephalad — toward the head; the thoracic cavity lies cephalad (or superior) to the abdominal cavity.

Medial — nearest the midline of the body; the ulna is on the medial side of the forearm.

Lateral — toward the side; that is, away from the medial side; the radius is lateral to the ulna.

Proximal — nearest the point of attachment or origin; the elbow is proximal to the wrist.

Distal — away from the point of attachment or origin; the wrist is distal to the elbow.

Planes (Fig. 1–3)

The body is also discussed with respect to planes passing through it.

Midsagittal — the plane vertically dividing the body through the midline into right and left halves.

Sagittal — any plane parallel to the midsagittal line vertically dividing the body into right and left portions.

Horizontal (transverse) — any plane dividing the body into superior and inferior portions.

Frontal (coronal) — any plane dividing the body into anterior (or ventral) and posterior (or dorsal) portions at right angles to the sagittal plane.

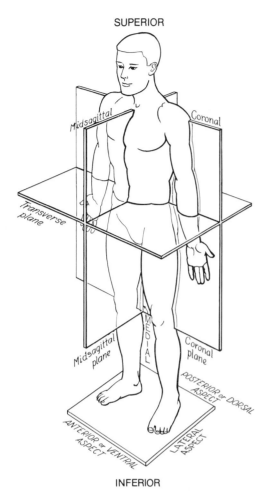

SUPERIOR

INFERIOR

Figure 1–3. Anatomic position of body (anterior view, palms forward) with reference systems.

Cavities

Cavity is a term used to describe the third organizational reference system. The body has two major cavities, each subdivided into two lesser cavities (Fig. 1–4). The organs of a cavity are collectively referred to as viscera.

1. Ventral cavity
   A. Thoracic — pleural and pericardial cavities
   B. Abdominopelvic
2. Dorsal cavity
   A. Cranial
   B. Spinal

VENTRAL CAVITY. Organs of the ventral cavity are involved in maintaining a constant internal environment, or homeostasis.

The thoracic cavity is divided into the pericardial cavity, housing the heart, and the pleural cavities, surrounding each lung. The mediastinum is a space between the pleural cavities containing, in addition to the pericardial cavity and the heart, such structures as the esophagus, trachea, thymus, great blood vessels, lymph vessels, and nerves.

The abdominopelvic cavity contains those organs inferior to the respiratory diaphragm but above the urogenital diaphragm, including the kidneys, stomach, large and small intestine, spleen, liver, gallbladder, ovaries, uterus, and pancreas.

DORSAL CAVITY. The dorsal cavity contains structures of the nervous system serving to coordinate the body's functions in a unified manner. It is divided into a cranial portion, containing the brain, and a spinal portion, containing the spinal cord.

The term *parietal* refers to the walls of a cavity; for example, the parietal peritoneum lines the abdominal wall. The term *visceral* refers to the covering of the organs; the visceral peritoneum covers the abdominal organs.

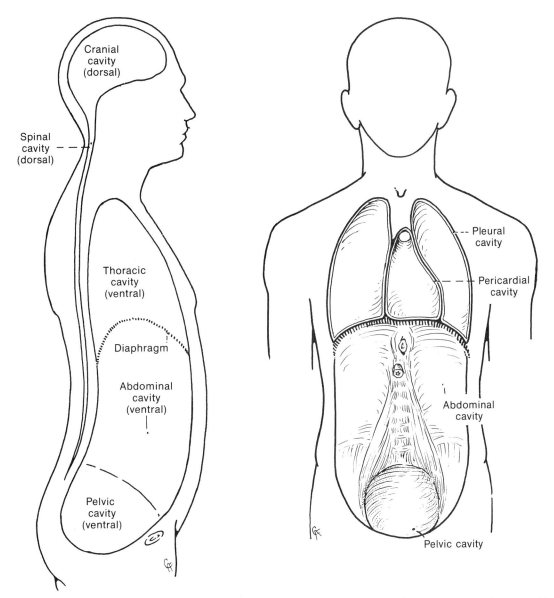

Figure 1–4. *Left.* The body has two major cavities, dorsal and ventral, each subdivided into two lesser cavities. For convenience the abdominal and pelvic cavities pictured here are referred to simply as the abdominopelvic cavity. *Right.* Frontal view of body cavities.

Structural Units

The fourth and final system of reference is the structural unit, subdivided into cells, tissues, organs, and systems.

Cells. All living matter is composed of cells. The basic constituent of the cell is protoplasm, an aqueous colloidal solution of protein, lipid, carbohydrate, and inorganic salts surrounded by a limiting membrane. This "ground substance of life" performs all the activities necessary to maintain life, including metabolism, respiration, digestion, assimilation, excretion, and reproduction. Each different kind of cell, taken as a group, constitutes a tissue (for example, muscle and bone). The tissues in turn compose the organs (such as the stomach and kidneys), each organ being fabricated of several different tissues. Finally, the organs themselves are grouped into organ systems (such as the digestive system or the nervous system).

Tissues. Tissues are composed of cells and intercellular substance, or matrix. Generally, tissues contain cells similar in appearance, function, and embryonic origin.

All the diverse tissues of the body can be grouped under one of the following categories: epithelial, connective, muscle, or nervous tissue.

Epithelial tissue covers surfaces, forms glands, and lines most cavities of the body. It consists of one or more layers of cells with only little intercellular material. Muscle tissue is characterized by elongated cells, or fibers, which generate movement by shortening or contracting in a forcible manner. Nerve tissue is composed of nerve cells forming a coordinating system of fibers connecting the many sensory and motor structures of the body. Connective tissue binds together and supports other tissues and organs. It has a

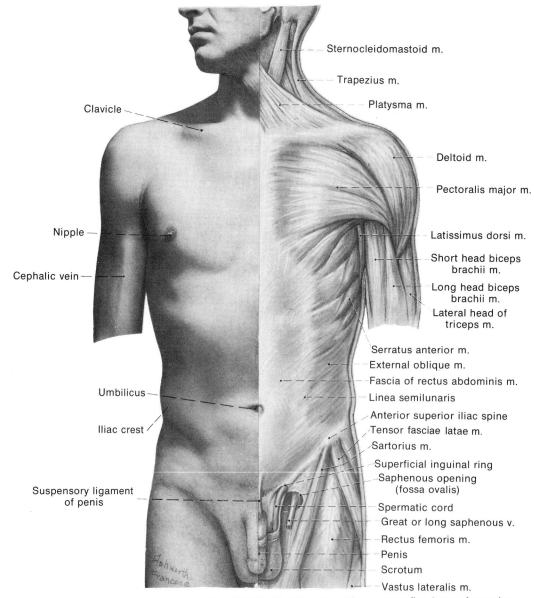

Figure 1–5. Anterior surface of male, left half with skin removed to expose first layer of muscles.

Labels in figure:

Sternocleidomastoid m.
Trapezius m.
Platysma m.
Clavicle
Deltoid m.
Pectoralis major m.
Nipple
Latissimus dorsi m.
Short head biceps brachii m.
Cephalic vein
Long head biceps brachii m.
Lateral head of triceps m.
Serratus anterior m.
External oblique m.
Fascia of rectus abdominis m.
Umbilicus
Linea semilunaris
Anterior superior iliac spine
Iliac crest
Tensor fasciae latae m.
Sartorius m.
Superficial inguinal ring
Saphenous opening (fossa ovalis)
Suspensory ligament of penis
Spermatic cord
Great or long saphenous v.
Rectus femoris m.
Penis
Scrotum
Vastus lateralis m.

matrix (intercellular matter) consisting of various kinds of fibers embedded in nonfibrous substances. The matrix is far more conspicuous than the cells by which this matrix is secreted. In fact, the character of the matrix mainly determines the properties of the particular kind of connective tissue in question (Chapter 4).

Organs. An organ is composed of cells integrated into tissues serving a common function. Examples of organs are the spleen, liver, heart, lungs, and skin.

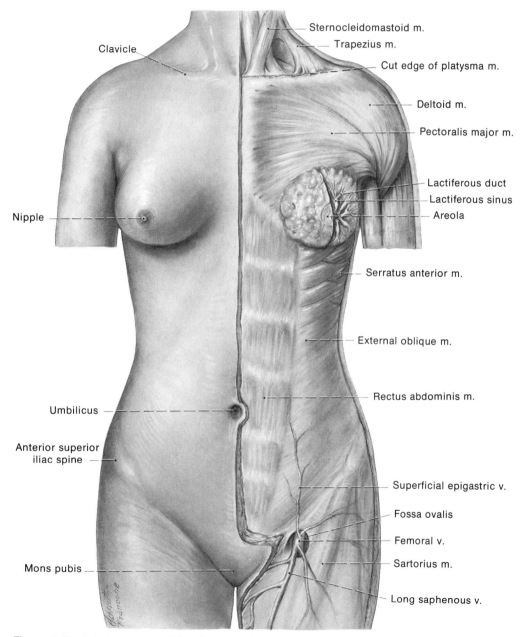

Figure 1–6. Anterior surface of female, left half with skin removed to expose first layer of muscles.

Systems. Cells are grouped together to form tissues; tissues combine to form organs. A *system* is a group of organs. The system is the basis for the general structural plan of the body. Brief mention will be made of the various systems to give an idea of the general organization of the body shown in the figures of the human torso (Figs. 1–5 to 1–14).

The *skin* is made up of the epidermal and dermal layers and, as a system, includes the hair, nails, and sebaceous and sweat glands. Its primary functions are insulation of the body from various environmental hazards and temperature and water regulation.

The *skeletal system* is composed of bones and the cartilaginous and membranous

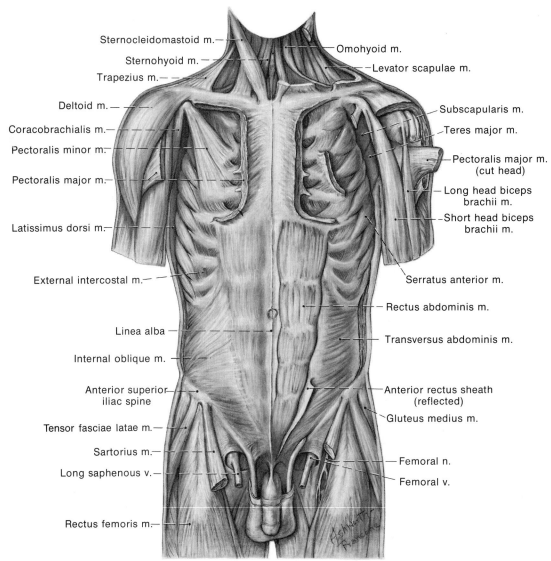

Sternocleidomastoid m.—

Sternohyoid m. —

Trapezius m. — —

Deltoid m. — —

Coracobrachialis m.—

Pectoralis minor m.—

Pectoralis major m.—

Latissimus dorsi m.—

External intercostal m.—

Linea alba —

Internal oblique m. —

Anterior superior iliac spine

Tensor fasciae latae m.—

Sartorius m.—

Long saphenous v. —

Rectus femoris m.—

Omohyoid m.

Levator scapulae m.

Subscapularis m.

Teres major m.

Pectoralis major m. (cut head)

Long head biceps brachii m.

Short head biceps brachii m.

Serratus anterior m.

Rectus abdominis m.

Transversus abdominis m.

Anterior rectus sheath (reflected)

Gluteus medius m.

Femoral n.

Femoral v.

Figure 1–7. Pectoralis major muscle removed on right side, pectoralis minor on left side; second and third layers of abdominal muscles exposed.

structures associated with them. This system protects and supports the soft parts of the body and supplies levers for body movement. Connective tissue predominates in this area. Articulations (joints) will be described separately.

The *muscular system* is composed of muscles, fasciae, tendon sheaths, and bursae.

The three types of muscles are: striated, moving the skeleton; smooth, such as along the alimentary tract; and cardiac, found in the heart.

The *nervous system* consists of the brain, the spinal cord, cranial nerves, peripheral nerves, and sensory and motor terminals. It is the correlating and controlling system of the

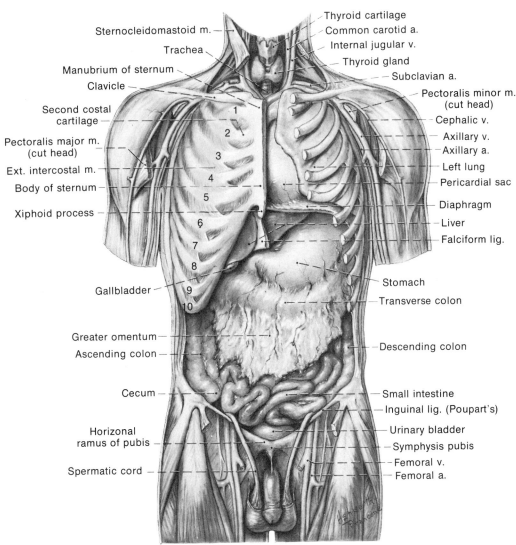

Figure 1–8. Anterior muscles of chest and abdomen removed, showing underlying viscera.

body, intimately connected with the other systems and with the outside world. Special senses include vision, hearing, taste, and smell.

The *circulatory system* comprises the heart, arteries, veins, lymph vessels, and capillaries. It pumps and distributes the blood carrying oxygen, nutrients, and wastes. The lymphatic system, which drains tissue spaces and carries absorbed fat into the blood, will be considered separately.

The *respiratory system* is composed of the air sinuses, pharynx, larynx, trachea, bronchi, and lungs. It is involved in bringing oxygen to and in eliminating carbon dioxide from the blood.

The *digestive system* includes the alimentary tract, with the associated glands, from the lips to the anus. It converts food into simpler substances that can be absorbed and utilized by the body.

The *urinary system* comprises the kid-

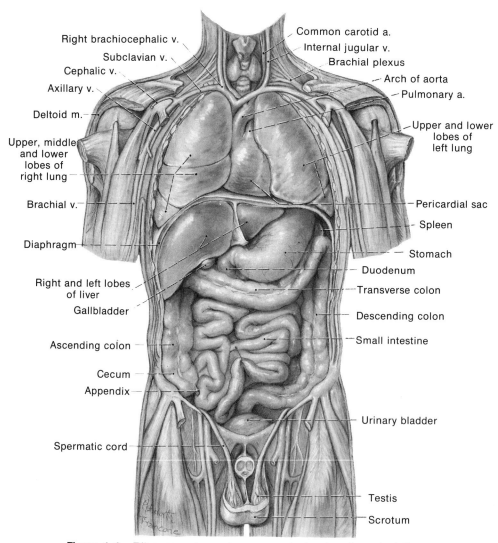

Figure 1–9. Rib cage and omentum removed, showing visceral relations.

neys, ureters, urinary bladder, and urethra. Its chief functions are the formation and elimination of urine and the maintenance of homeostasis.

The *endocrine system* includes the hypophysis (pituitary), thyroid, parathyroids, suprarenals, pancreatic islets in the pancreas, ovaries, testes, pineal body, and placenta (during pregnancy). The endocrine glands are involved in the chemical regulation of body functions.

The *reproductive system* consists of the ovaries, uterine tubes, uterus, vagina, and vulva in the female, and the testes, seminal vesicles, penis, prostate, and urethra in the male.

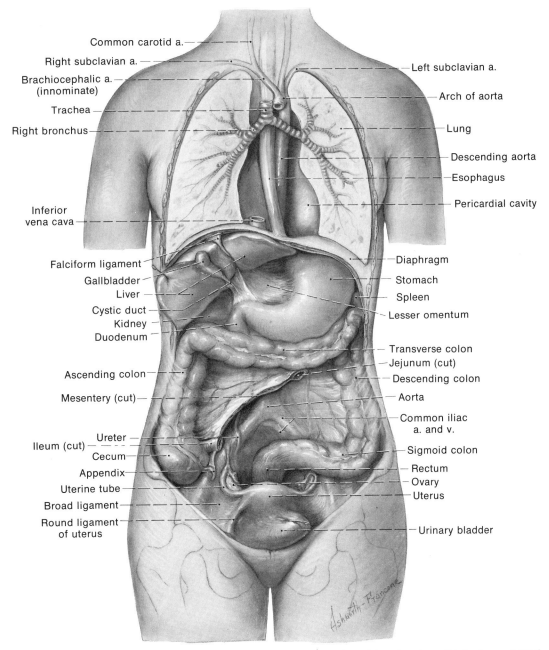

Figure 1–10. Female, demonstrating visceral relations; lungs sectioned, heart and small intestine removed.

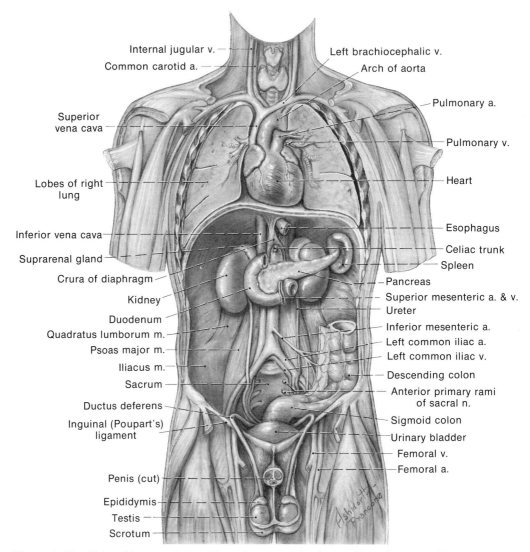

Internal jugular v.
Common carotid a.
Superior vena cava
Lobes of right lung
Inferior vena cava
Suprarenal gland
Crura of diaphragm
Kidney
Duodenum
Quadratus lumborum m.
Psoas major m.
Iliacus m.
Sacrum
Ductus deferens
Inguinal (Poupart's) ligament
Penis (cut)
Epididymis
Testis
Scrotum

Left brachiocephalic v.
Arch of aorta
Pulmonary a.
Pulmonary v.
Heart
Esophagus
Celiac trunk
Spleen
Pancreas
Superior mesenteric a. & v.
Ureter
Inferior mesenteric a.
Left common iliac a.
Left common iliac v.
Descending colon
Anterior primary rami of sacral n.
Sigmoid colon
Urinary bladder
Femoral v.
Femoral a.

Figure 1–11. Male, with stomach, small intestine, most of colon, and anterior parts of lungs removed.

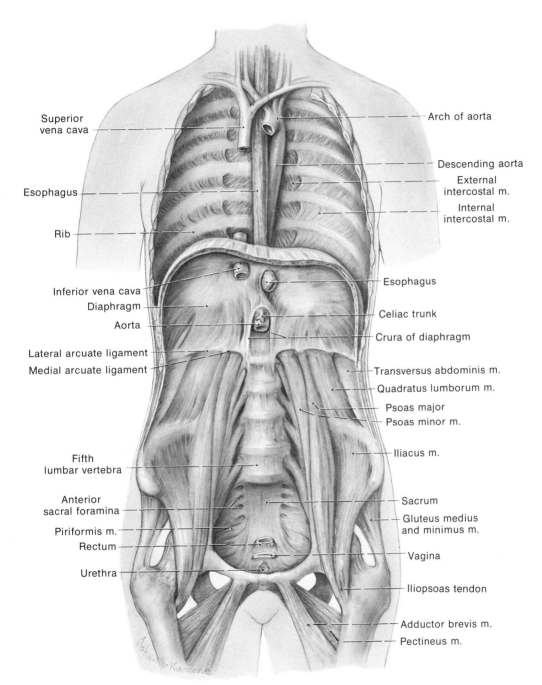

Figure 1–12. Female, with all the viscera removed, exposing the internal posterior walls of chest and abdominal and pelvic cavities.

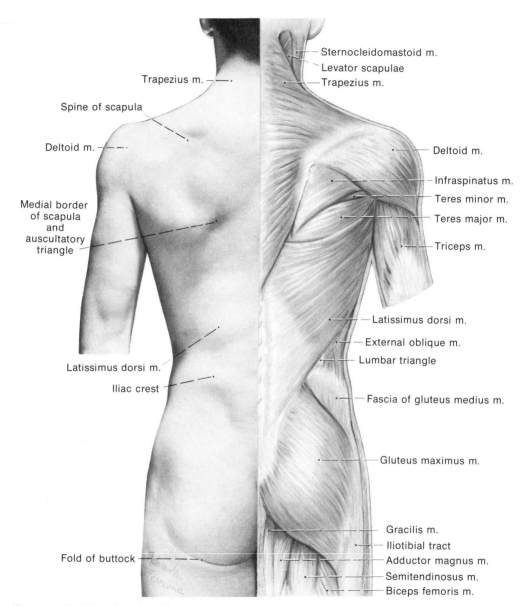

Trapezius m.

Spine of scapula

Deltoid m.

Medial border
of scapula
and
auscultatory
triangle

Latissimus dorsi m.

Iliac crest

Fold of buttock

Sternocleidomastoid m.

Levator scapulae

Trapezius m.

Deltoid m.

Infraspinatus m.

Teres minor m.

Teres major m.

Triceps m.

Latissimus dorsi m.

External oblique m.

Lumbar triangle

Fascia of gluteus medius m.

Gluteus maximus m.

Gracilis m.

Iliotibial tract

Adductor magnus m.

Semitendinosus m.

Biceps femoris m.

Figure 1–13. Posterior view of male, with skin removed on right side to expose first layer of muscles.

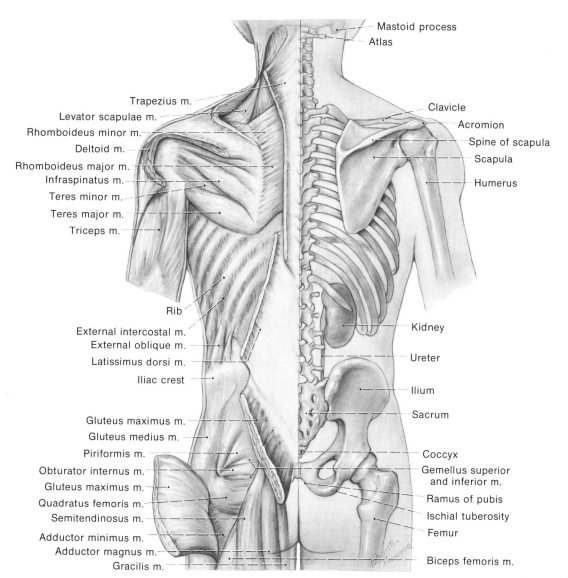

Mastoid process
Atlas
Trapezius m.
Levator scapulae m.
Rhomboideus minor m.
Deltoid m.
Rhomboideus major m.
Infraspinatus m.
Teres minor m.
Teres major m.
Triceps m.
Clavicle
Acromion
Spine of scapula
Scapula
Humerus
Rib
External intercostal m.
External oblique m.
Latissimus dorsi m.
Iliac crest
Kidney
Ureter
Ilium
Sacrum
Gluteus maximus m.
Gluteus medius m.
Piriformis m.
Obturator internus m.
Gluteus maximus m.
Quadratus femoris m.
Semitendinosus m.
Adductor minimus m.
Adductor magnus m.
Gracilis m.
Coccyx
Gemellus superior
  and inferior m.
Ramus of pubis
Ischial tuberosity
Femur
Biceps femoris m.

Figure 1–14. Most of the superficial muscles have been removed on the left side to expose the deep layers. All the muscles have been removed on the right side, exposing the skeletal framework.

SUMMARY

THE BODY AS A WHOLE

The Human Body

Specialized cells are structurally and functionally integrated to form an organism.

1. Anatomy: the study of the structure of the living organism.

2. Physiology: the study of the function of the living organism.

    a. Development of the electron microscope greatly enhanced the study of molecular biology.

    b. Water, the fluid medium of the body, accounts for about 65 per cent of the body weight. Three-fourths is within cells (intracellular fluid) and most of the remainder is between cells (interstitial fluid). The smallest proportion is in the circulatory system.

    c. Homeostasis refers to maintaining the "steady state" conditions of the body by coordinated physiological processes.

        (1) Among the homeostatic control mechanisms are those maintaining normal concentrations of blood constituents, body temperature, volume and pH of body fluids, blood pressure, and heart rate.

        (2) All homeostatic control mechanisms operate by negative feedback.

    d. Coordination of the body is primarily under nervous and hormonal control.

Organization of the Body

1. Four basic reference systems of organization are described:

    a. Direction: All descriptions of location or position assume the body to be erect and facing forward, with the arms at the side and the palms anterior. This is the so-called anatomic position. Directions include superior, inferior, anterior, posterior, cephalad, medial, lateral, proximal, and distal. Definitions of parietal and visceral are given.

    b. Planes: The body is discussed with respect to planes passing through it; these are the midsagittal, sagittal, horizontal, and frontal planes.

    c. Cavities

        (1) Ventral cavity, subdivided into the thoracic (further divided into the pleural and pericardial) and the abdominopelvic cavities.

        (2) Dorsal cavity, divided into the cranial and spinal cavities; the dorsal cavity contains structures of the nervous system.

    d. Structural units

        (1) The cell: All living matter is composed of cells and cell products. The cell carries out all activities essential for maintaining life.

        (2) Tissue: Composed of cells and intercellular substance. Cells of a tissue are similar in appearance, function, and embryonic origin. The four types of tissues are epithelial, connective, muscle, and nervous.

        (3) Organs: A group of tissues serving a common function brought together to form a single structure, such as the heart or lungs.

        (4) System: Cells, tissues, and organs combine to form a system. The body contains the following major systems: skin, skeletal, articular, muscular, nervous, circulatory, respiratory, digestive, urinary, endocrine, and reproductive.

REVIEW QUESTIONS

1. What percentage of the body weight is water? Is the greater proportion of the body water intracellular or extracellular? Where is most of the water in the extracellular space?

2. What is the internal environment of the body? Explain the terms homeostasis and negative feedback.

3. Define the following directions: superior, inferior, anterior, posterior, cephalad, medial, lateral, proximal, and distal.

4. Describe the four planes into which the body is divided.

5. Differentiate between parietal and visceral.

6. List the four types of tissues. Define an organ and a system.

Basic Chemistry and the Chemical Constituents of Living Matter

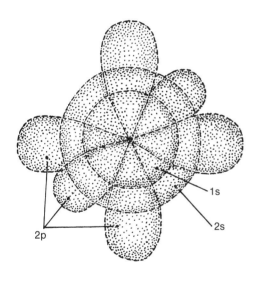

Objectives

The aim of this chapter is to enable the student to:

□ Explain the relationship between atoms and elements and between molecules and compounds.

□ Describe the structure of the atom.

□ Explain how the octet rule predicts the combining properties of elements.

□ Distinguish between covalent and ionic bonds.

□ Define molar and equivalent concentrations.

□ Distinguish between electrolytes and nonelectrolytes.

□ Define the terms acid and base.

□ Describe the pH scale.

□ Explain oxidation-reduction reactions, condensation reactions, and hydrolysis.

□ Describe the three kinds of radiation emitted by naturally occurring radioisotopes.

□ Discuss the significance of ionizing radiation to living organisms.

□ Describe the structures and important functions of the major organic chemical constituents of living matter, namely, (1) proteins, (2) carbohydrates, (3) lipids, and (4) nucleic acids and nucleotides.

□ Discuss the unique chemical properties of water that make it indispensable for life.

□ List some of the important functions of the inorganic chemical constituents of living matter other than water.

The first part of this chapter, an introduction to some basic chemistry applicable to the study of human anatomy and physiology, is intended for those students who have no background in chemistry; the second part is a description of the major chemical constituents of living matter.

ELEMENTS, ATOMS, COMPOUNDS, AND MOLECULES

All matter is composed of basic units called **elements.** There are 92 naturally occurring elements (more than a dozen others have been created artificially in the laboratory) and each is designated by one or two letters of its name. Thus, the symbols for carbon, oxygen, hydrogen, and nitrogen are C, O, H, and N, respectively. The symbol for chlorine is Cl; for sodium, Na (*natrium* is the Latin word for sodium); and for potassium, K (*kalium* is the Latin word for potassium). The relative abundance of the elements in living matter is quite different from their relative abundance in the earth's crust. The four most abundant elements in the human body, for example, hydrogen, oxygen, carbon, and nitrogen, represent 98 per cent of the total number of atoms. The four most abundant elements in the earth's crust, on the other hand, are oxygen, silicon, aluminum, and iron, with oxygen and silicon constituting 75 per cent of the total number of atoms.

Each element is a collection of a particular kind of discrete particle of matter, called the **atom.** Any amount of an element contains identical atoms, and one element is distinguished from another by the nature of its atoms. This "atomic theory" of matter was elaborated by the English chemist John Dalton in the 18th century. The use of the term "atom," however, dates back to the 4th century B.C., when a group of Greek philosophers, principally Democritus, intuitively theorized that matter was composed of individual particles, which they called atoms. Both Democritus and Dalton pictured atoms as indivisible particles (G. *atomos,* uncut, indivisible). However, discoveries made at the end of the 18th and beginning of the 19th century established that atoms are not the simple, indivisible particles they were thought to be but that they contain subatomic particles. Although atoms are divisible as chemical units, they are in another sense indivisible, since they are the smallest particles that embody the properties of an element. By the chemical combination of two or more atoms of different elements in fixed proportions, innumerable new substances, called *compounds,* are formed. Each compound has characteristic properties that differ from the properties of each of its elements. The smallest unit into which a compound can be divided and still retain its properties is called a *molecule.* The *molecular formula* of a compound gives the number of atoms of each element in its molecules. Water, a compound composed of the elements hydrogen and oxygen, has a molecular formula of H_2O; that is to say, each molecule of water has two atoms of hydrogen and one atom of oxygen.

The Structure of the Atom

Atoms consist of a dense inner core, or **nucleus,** containing positively charged particles called **protons** and neutral particles called **neutrons,** and a space surrounding the nucleus occupied by negatively charged particles in motion called **electrons** (the one exception to this description is the hydrogen atom, which consists of one proton in the nucleus and one electron in the surrounding space). Although electrons occupy most of the space of an atom, essentially all of the atom's mass is concentrated in the nucleus. Both protons and neutrons have masses of approximately 1, a relative unit based on a scale in which the most common form (or isotope — see below) of carbon is assigned a value of 12, and the sum of the number of protons and neutrons of an atom is its **mass number.**

Protons bear a charge of $+1$, electrons -1. The number of protons in an atom, called the **atomic number,** is its unique identifying characteristic. It determines the number of surrounding electrons (equal to the number of protons) and the chemical properties of the element. The mass number of an element, on the other hand, may vary. More than three-fourths of the chlorine atoms, for example, contain 17 protons and 18 neutrons; the remainder have 17 protons and 20 neutrons. Such different forms of an element are called **isotopes.** The isotopes of chlorine are written $^{35}_{17}Cl$ and $^{37}_{17}Cl$ (or, more simply, without the subscript). Most elements have at least two isotopes, and the **atomic weight** of any element listed in a table of atomic weights is an average value of the mass numbers of the isotopes found in naturally occurring mixtures. For instance, the atomic weight of chlorine is 35.5.

The motions of electrons do not follow fixed paths, but can be described in terms of probable positions, called **orbitals.** Each orbital can hold as many as two electrons, and different orbital types (each designated by a specific letter) represent unique spatial distributions and energy states of electrons. Orbitals are grouped together in what are called *energy levels* (numbered consecutively, beginning with 1). The first, or lowest, energy level holds one orbital containing a maximum of two electrons. The number of electrons and orbital types increase as the energy level increases, and the higher the energy level, the greater the average distance of its orbital electrons from the nucleus. For our purposes, the important consideration is the number of electrons in orbital types designated by the letters s and p, because the number of electrons in these orbitals determines the combining property of an element. This is so because atoms tend to form combinations by sharing or transferring electrons in one or more of these orbitals so as to acquire an outer octet of electrons (the number of electrons corresponding to one s orbital and three p orbitals filled to capacity). This statement, which predicts the combining properties of most of the commonly occurring elements, is known as the **octet rule.** The rare gases neon, argon, and krypton, which have octets of electrons in their outer s and p orbitals, are stable in their uncombined states and are, therefore, inert. Figure 2–1 illustrates the distribution of neon's 10 electrons: in the first energy level, a pair in an s orbital; in the second energy level, a pair in an s orbital and three pairs in three p orbitals (note that the s orbitals are spherical, the p orbitals bilobed). An atom of helium, which has a single s orbital filled to capacity, is also stable and inert.

The Covalent Bond

A tabulation of the electrons in each orbital of an atom is its *electron configuration.* The electron configurations of hydrogen, carbon, nitrogen, and oxygen are given

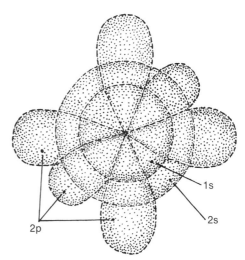

Figure 2–1. Schematic representation of neon's five orbitals. The letters s and p designate orbital types; the numbers preceding the letters designate energy levels. The s orbitals are spherical (the 2s electrons dispersed throughout a larger sphere); the p orbitals are bilobed, with one lobe on either side of the nucleus. Ten electrons, two in each orbital, completely fill the 1s, 2s, and 2p orbitals. Each electron in a p orbital occupies one lobe, and the three p orbitals are arranged in space so that each is perpendicular to the other.

in Table 2–1. Note that carbon, nitrogen, and oxygen require four, three, and two electrons, respectively, to achieve stable states with octets of electrons in their outer energy levels, and that hydrogen needs another electron in its first energy level to attain a stable configuration. These stable states may be arrived at by *electron sharing.* For example, in the methane molecule (CH_4), four pairs of electrons are shared, each pair between a carbon atom and one of four hydrogen atoms. The carbon acquires the four electrons it needs for an outer octet, and each hydrogen acquires the necessary electron for a pair.

Table 2–1 **ELECTRON CONFIGURATIONS OF HYDROGEN, CARBON, NITROGEN, AND OXYGEN**

ENERGY LEVEL	1	2	
ORBITAL TYPE	s	s	p
Hydrogen	1		
Carbon	2	2	1 1
Nitrogen	2	2	1 1 1
Oxygen	2	2	2 1 1

The electron sharing in methane is illustrated below, using dots to represent the outer electrons.

$$H:\overset{\displaystyle H}{\underset{\displaystyle H}{\overset{..}{C}}}:H$$

(The geometry of the methane molecule — with each hydrogen atom at the apex of a figure with four surfaces — is best explained by the formation of four molecular hybrid orbitals, designated sp^3 orbitals, each resembling a p orbital but having lobes of unequal size.) In a molecule of ammonia (NH_3), three pairs of electrons are shared, each between a nitrogen atom and one of three hydrogen atoms (the geometry of the ammonia molecule is also best accounted for by the formation of sp^3 hybrid orbitals). In the ammonia molecule, diagrammed below (the dots representing shared and unshared outer electrons), it can be seen that the electron sharing provides the nitrogen atom with the three electrons it requires for an outer octet.

$$H:\overset{\displaystyle H}{\underset{\displaystyle H}{\overset{..}{N}}}:$$

In the carbon dioxide molecule (CO_2), illustrated below, each of two oxygen atoms shares two pairs of electrons with a single carbon atom, each oxygen thereby obtaining the necessary two electrons for an octet, the carbon four electrons for its octet.

$$:\overset{..}{O}::C::\overset{..}{O}:$$

(This combination of atoms is pictured as a complex arrangement of molecular orbitals formed by overlapping p orbitals and overlapping sp hybrid orbitals.)

The joining of two atoms by sharing electrons is known as a **covalent bond.** Sharing one pair of electrons is called a *single bond* and is generally represented by a dash drawn between the two atoms. Two dashes drawn between two atoms signify a *double bond,* or two pairs of shared electrons; three dashes indicate a *triple bond,* or three pairs of shared electrons. In the illustrations below, on the left, ethyl alcohol and the amino acid glycine (amino acids, the building blocks of proteins, are described later in this chapter) are drawn with dashes to show the bonding arrangements. On the right the dot representation is used to show all of the shared and unshared outer electrons.

$$H-\overset{\displaystyle H}{\underset{\displaystyle H}{C}}-\overset{\displaystyle H}{\underset{\displaystyle H}{C}}-O-H$$

$$H\cdot\overset{\displaystyle H}{\overset{..}{C}}\cdot\overset{\displaystyle H}{\underset{\displaystyle \text{ı. } H}{\overset{..}{C}}}:\overset{..}{O}:H$$

Ethyl alcohol

$$H-\overset{\displaystyle H}{\underset{\displaystyle H}{N}}-\overset{\displaystyle O}{\overset{\|}{C}}-C-O-H$$

$$H:\overset{\displaystyle H}{\underset{\displaystyle H}{\overset{..}{N}}}:\overset{..}{C}:\overset{\displaystyle H\overset{..}{O}:}{\overset{..}{C}}:\overset{..}{O}:H$$

Glycine

It should be apparent from the foregoing that hydrogen, oxygen, nitrogen, and carbon form 1, 2, 3, and 4 covalent bonds, respectively. The term used to indicate the bonding capacity of any element is **valence.** Hence, the valence of hydrogen is 1, oxygen 2, nitrogen 3, and carbon 4.

When a covalent bond is formed between two like atoms, as in molecular hydrogen (H_2) and molecular oxygen (O_2), the electron pairs are shared equally between the atoms. In covalent bonds formed between unlike atoms, on the other hand, unequal sharing of electrons is quite common. In the water molecule (H_2O) the electrons are more strongly attracted to the oxygen atom than to the hydrogen atoms; consequently, the oxygen has a negative charge and each hydrogen a positive charge. A molecule of water can be represented as follows:

$$\overset{\displaystyle \uparrow}{\underset{\displaystyle H \quad + \quad H}{\overset{\displaystyle O}{\diagup \diagdown}}}$$

Water molecule, showing direction of dipole moment

As a result of the unequal charge distribution and bent structure, the water molecule is a **dipole,** i.e., it is oppositely charged at two ends, with the oxygen end negative and the hydrogen end positive. The molecule is said to have a **dipole moment,** represented by the symbol $\longmapsto$, in which the arrow points to the negatively charged end of the dipole. In the carbon dioxide molecule, although each bond is a dipole (oxygen has a stronger attraction for electrons than carbon), the molecule as a whole is not a dipole because the bonds are arranged in a straight line facing opposite directions.

$$\overset{\leftarrow}{O}=\overset{\leftrightarrow}{C}=\vec{O}$$

Carbon dioxide molecule,
showing no net dipole moment

As we shall see, the dipole nature of the water molecule is responsible for a number of its special properties.

The Ionic Bond

Another way for an atom to attain a stable electron configuration with an octet of electrons in the outer energy level is by *giving up or accepting electrons*. The electron configurations of the sodium and chlorine atoms are given in Table 2–2. When sodium combines with chlorine to form sodium chloride, the single electron in sodium's third energy level is transferred to chlorine. As a result, both atoms have outer electron octets. Such a union between atoms involving electron transfer is called an **ionic bond.** When sodium chloride is dissolved in water, it dissociates, but the transferred electron remains with chlorine. As a result, *sodium ions*, bearing a charge of +1, and *chloride ions*, bearing a charge of −1, are released into the solution (these ions are written Na^+ and Cl^-).

Moles; Equivalents; Molar and Equivalent Concentrations

The molecular formula of glucose is $C_6H_{12}O_6$. The sum of the atomic weights of all of the atoms in a compound is its *molecular weight;* the molecular weight of glucose, therefore, is 6(12) + 12(1) + 6(16), or 180. The molecular weight of a compound, ex-

pressed in grams, represents one **mole** of that substance. Thus, 1 mole of glucose contains 180 grams of glucose. The concentration of a compound in solution, expressed as the number of moles in 1 liter (M/L), is its *molar concentration,* or *molarity.* A 1 molar solution of glucose contains 180 grams of glucose per liter, a 0.1 molar (100 millimolar, or 100 mM/L) solution contains 18 grams per liter.

Frequently the concentration of ions in body fluids is given as the *equivalent concentration,* the number of equivalents or milliequivalents per liter (Eq/L, mEq/L). An *equivalent* of an atom is the amount that replaces or combines with 1 gram of hydrogen (hence, called equivalent, equivalent weight, or combining weight). It is calculated as the atomic weight divided by the valence. If the valence of each atom in a compound is 1, 1 mole of that compound contains 1 equivalent of each atom. Hence, the equivalent concentration of each ion in solution is given by the molar concentration of the compound. Thus, a 100 millimolar solution of sodium chloride (NaCl) contains 100 mEq/L of Na^+ and 100 mEq/L of Cl^-. On the other hand, in the case of calcium chloride ($CaCl_2$), since calcium has a valence of 2 and, therefore, an equivalent of calcium is one-half its atomic weight (or, to put it another way, its atomic weight represents 2 equivalents), each mole of $CaCl_2$ contains 2 equivalents of calcium (and 2 equivalents of chlorine). Therefore, the equivalent concentration of each ion in calcium chloride in solution is twice the molar concentration of calcium chloride. A 100 millimolar solution of calcium chloride, therefore, contains 200 mEq/L of Ca^{++} and 200 mEq/L of Cl^-.

Electrolytes

When a salt such as sodium chloride is dissolved in water and releases ions into the solution, the solution will conduct an electric current. Substances whose solutions conduct an electric current are classified as *electrolytes.* Substances whose solutions do not contain ions and, therefore, do not conduct an electric current are classified as *nonelectrolytes.* Free ions in solution are formed when electrolytes that are placed in water either dissociate into ions (ionize) or react with water to generate ions. Ions may be monoatomic, for example, sodium ions (Na^+) and chloride ions (Cl^-); or polyatomic, for exam-

Table 2–2   ELECTRON CONFIGURATIONS
OF SODIUM AND CHLORINE

ENERGY LEVEL	1	2		3	
ORBITAL TYPE	s	s	p	s	p
Sodium	2	2	2 2 2	1	
Chlorine	2	2	2 2 2	2	2 2 1

ple, nitrate ions (NO_3^-) and hydroxide ions (OH^-). The atoms of polyatomic ions are generally held together by covalent bonds. Electrolytes are described as strong or weak, depending on how completely they ionize. *Strong electrolytes* ionize almost completely; *weak electrolytes* ionize only slightly (the degree of ionization can be measured quantitatively with an apparatus consisting of a pair of electrodes in the solution connected to a battery and an ammeter).

Free ions are present in solutions of acids and bases as well as in solutions of salts. According to the concept most widely used to describe acids and bases (Brønsted-Lowry concept), an *acid* is a proton (hydrogen ion) donor and a *base* is a proton acceptor. The almost complete ionization of hydrochloric acid, a strong electrolyte, may be represented as follows:

$$HCl \longrightarrow H^+ + Cl^-$$

Since the chloride ion, Cl^-, has a slight tendency to accept protons, it is said to be the weak conjugate base of the strong acid, HCl, the two forming what is called a *conjugate acid-base pair*. (It should be noted that, although it is the convention to use the symbol H^+ for hydrogen ions, "bare" hydrogen ions do not exist in water. The hydrogen ions are hydrated, that is, attached to water molecules as hydronium ions, H_3O^+.) Acetic acid and carbonic acid are weak electrolytes. Their ionizations can be expressed as follows:

$$CH_3COOH \rightleftharpoons H^+ + CH_3COO^-$$
Acetic acid

$$H_2CO_3 \rightleftharpoons H^+ + HCO_3^-$$
Carbonic acid

Note that these ionizations, in contrast to the one given for hydrochloric acid, are reversible. An equilibrium is maintained between these weak acids and their ions, and only a small proportion of the molecules of each acid are dissociated at any instant. In these equilibriums, the acetate ion is the conjugate base of acetic acid, and the bicarbonate ion is the conjugate base of carbonic acid. The strongest proton acceptor, or base, in aqueous (L. *aqua*, water) solutions is the hydroxide ion, OH^- (according to an older concept, a base was defined as a substance that produces hydroxide ions in aqueous solutions,

and a strong electrolyte such as sodium hydroxide, NaOH, which yields hydroxide ions in aqueous solutions, would be called a strong base).

Most salts are strong electrolytes. *Salts* are defined in various ways. One useful way of viewing a salt is as a compound formed by replacing the hydrogen ion (or ions) in an acid with another positive ion. Some common salts, in addition to sodium chloride, are ammonium chloride (NH_4Cl), calcium carbonate ($CaCO_3$), sodium bicarbonate ($NaHCO_3$), and magnesium sulphate ($MgSO_4$).

pH

pH is a convenient expression of the hydrogen ion concentration of a solution, which uses whole numbers rather than cumbersome decimals or fractions. Pure water dissociates very slightly, releasing hydrogen and hydroxide ions — the concentration of each is 10^{-7} (.0000001) mole per liter (the product of the two is a constant, 10^{-14}, at 25°C). pH is defined as the *negative logarithm of the hydrogen ion concentration*. The logarithm of 10^{-7} is -7; the negative logarithm is 7. Hence, the pH of pure water is 7. This is the neutral condition. The hydrogen ion concentration is raised by the addition of an acid to pure water and lowered by the addition of a base (the product of the two concentrations remaining 10^{-14}). If, by the addition of an acid to water, the hydrogen ion concentration is increased from 10^{-7} to 10^{-4}

Table 2–3 THE pH SCALE

H^+ (Mole/Liter)	pH	OH^- (Mole/Liter)
10^0	0	10^{-14}
10^{-1}	1	10^{-13}
10^{-2}	2	10^{-12}
10^{-3}	3	10^{-11}
10^{-4}	4	10^{-10}
10^{-5}	5	10^{-9}
10^{-6}	6	10^{-8}
10^{-7}	7	10^{-7}
10^{-8}	8	10^{-6}
10^{-9}	9	10^{-5}
10^{-10}	10	10^{-4}
10^{-11}	11	10^{-3}
10^{-12}	12	10^{-2}
10^{-13}	13	10^{-1}
10^{-14}	14	10^0

Table 2–4 pH OF SOME LIQUIDS AND
BODY FLUIDS

FLUID	pH
Lemon juice	2.3
Orange juice	3.0–4.0
Cow's milk	6.3–6.6
Carbonated drinks	2.0–4.0
Sea water	7.5–8.3
Blood plasma	7.35–7.45
Interstitial fluid	7.4
Intracellular fluids	
Muscle	6.1
Liver	6.9
Gastric juice	1.2–3.0
Urine	5.5–7.0
Saliva	6.35–6.85
Pancreatic juice	7.8–8.0
Bile	7.8–8.6

(.0001) mole per liter, the pH of the solution will be reduced to 4. If, by the addition of a base, the hydrogen ion concentration is lowered to 10^{-10} (.0000000001) mole per liter, the pH of the solution will be raised to 10. The pH of an acidic solution, then, is less than 7; of a basic solution, greater than 7. The entire range of the pH scale is given in Table 2–3. Table 2–4 lists the pH of some common liquids and body fluids.

Body fluids must be maintained within narrow limits for normal physiological function. For example, pH of blood plasma below 7.0 or above 7.8 is life threatening. Buffer systems in body fluids play an essential role in preventing excessive changes in pH. A buffer is a substance that causes a resistance to any change in pH when added to a solution. The major buffer systems in body fluids and how they function are described in Chapter 17.

Chemical Reactions

Chemical reactions involve, among other things, the synthesis of a new substance from simpler ones, the degradation of a substance into two or more different substances, the transfer of a component from one substance to another, and the exchange of components between interacting substances. Among the terms used to describe chemical reactions, one of the most useful is **oxidation-reduction.** The loss of electrons (or, in more general terms, an increase in charge) is an *oxidation;* the gain of electrons (or decrease in charge) is

a *reduction* (in any given reaction, oxidation is always accompanied by reduction). In covalent compounds the charges, or oxidation numbers, assigned to atoms are based on the unequal sharing of electrons between atoms (see earlier discussion of the covalent bond). Hydrogen almost always has an oxidation number of $+1$ and oxygen almost always has an oxidation number of -2. In glucose, $C_6H_{12}O_6$, the oxidation numbers of the hydrogen and oxygen atoms cancel one another, leaving carbon with an oxidation number of 0. The overall reaction for the degradation of glucose to carbon dioxide and water in the presence of oxygen may be written as follows:

$$C_6H_{12}O_6 + 6O_2 \longrightarrow 6CO_2 + 6H_2O$$

Glucose is oxidized because the oxidation number of the carbon atoms increases from 0 in glucose to $+4$ in carbon dioxide. Oxygen is reduced, since its oxidation number decreases from 0 in molecular oxygen to -2 in water. As a general rule, it can be stated that removal of hydrogens is equivalent to oxidation and that accepting hydrogens is equivalent to reduction.

In many of the synthetic reactions carried out by the body's cells, the joining together of two molecules involves the removal of a molecule of water between them. A reaction in which two molecules are joined with the splitting out of a small molecule between them is called a **condensation reaction.** When water is split out, it is also called a *dehydration reaction.* Reactions of this type are illustrated later in this chapter in the section describing the synthesis of proteins, complex carbohydrates, and certain lipids. When these substances are degraded into their constituents, which were linked together by condensation reactions, water is added in a reaction called **hydrolysis.**

Radioactivity

The isotopes of some elements are *radioactive;* that is, their nuclei are unstable and emit radiation that transforms them into the stable isotopes of other elements. This transformation process is called *radioactive decay.* Three kinds of radiation are emitted by naturally occurring radioisotopes: (1) **alpha (α) particles** (also called alpha rays), the bare nuclei of helium atoms (two protons and two neutrons); (2) **beta (β) particles** (also called beta rays), high energy electrons; and (3) **gamma (γ) rays,** radiant energy similar to x-rays, but on the average having a shorter wave length and higher energy. Uranium 238 (^{238}U), thorium 232 (^{232}Th), and potassium 40 (^{40}K) are the three principal naturally occurring radioisotopes. In some cases radioactive decay occurs in a series of steps which produce a family of radioisotopes. There are 14 steps, for example, in the transformation of ^{238}U to the stable isotope of lead (^{206}Pb). A number of radioisotopes are produced in the upper atmosphere by the action of cosmic rays, the high energy radiation from outer space. One of these is carbon 14 (^{14}C), which is continuously being produced as cosmic rays induce nuclear reactions that release neutrons which may eventually react with nitrogen atoms to produce carbon 14 and a proton. The production of carbon 14 may be represented as follows:

$$^{1}_{0}n \ + \ ^{14}_{7}N \ \longrightarrow \ ^{14}_{6}C \ + \ ^{1}_{1}H$$

| Neutron | Nitrogen atom | Carbon isotope | Proton |

Carbon 14 decays into nitrogen 14 through the emission of a beta particle. The rate of radioactive decay, which varies considerably from one element to another, is expressed as the half-life of the element. **Half-life** is defined as the time required for half of the nuclei of a given isotope to decay. Carbon 14 has a half-life of 5730 years.

Radioisotopes can also be produced artificially by bombarding the nuclei of isotopes with alpha particles, protons, neutrons, or electrons. Oxygen 17 was the first *man-made radioisotope* so formed. This pioneering experiment was performed in 1919 by Ernest Rutherford, using radium as a source of alpha particles. Subsequent studies established that, when an alpha particle combines with a nitrogen nucleus, a proton is emitted and oxygen 17 formed:

$$^{14}_{7}N \ + \ ^{4}_{2}He \ \longrightarrow \ ^{1}_{1}H \ + \ ^{17}_{8}O$$

| Nitrogen atom | Alpha particle | Proton | Oxygen isotope |

Modern atom-smashing techniques utilize accelerators (in which magnetic and electric fields accelerate atomic particles) and nuclear reactors. Cobalt 60, for example, used in medicine as a powerful source of gamma rays, is manufactured by exposing rods of cobalt to neutrons inside a reactor.

The principal property of high energy radiation (which includes as its principal forms x-rays and the alpha, beta, and gamma rays of naturally occurring radioisotopes) is its ability to ionize atoms and molecules by ejecting orbital electrons. For this reason, such radiation is generally referred to as **ionizing radiation.** Specialized structures in living cells, especially the genetic matter, can be damaged by ionizing radiation by direct hits or interaction with unstable chemical products of ionizing radiation (especially of water). Alpha and beta particles do not readily penetrate the surface of the human body and exert their effects for the most part when radioisotopes are inhaled or ingested in food or drinking water. Most susceptible to damage from ionizing radiation are tissues with rapidly dividing cells, such as the lining of the intestine and the red bone marrow tissue that manufactures oxygen-carrying red blood cells, white blood cells (which combat invading microorganisms), and platelets (essential agents in blood clotting). The major threat immediately after overexposure to ionizing radiation is infection and uncontrolled bleeding. The principal long-term effect is a higher than normal risk of leukemia and other forms of cancer.

Radiation is measured in terms of the rate of nuclear disintegrations or its capacity to affect living organisms. The following are the units of measurement:

1. **Curie** (abbreviated c). A measure of the rate of nuclear disintegrations based on radium as a standard. One curie equals 37 billion disintegrations per second (almost exactly the activity of one gram of radium).

2. **Rad.** A measure of energy absorbed by irradiated tissue. One rad represents the absorption of 100 ergs per gram (420,000 rads would be equivalent to one calorie — that is, would raise the temperature of one gram of water by one degree centigrade — if all of the absorbed energy is converted to heat).

3. **Roentgen** (abbreviated r). A measure of the ionizing effect of radiation. One roentgen produces approximately 2 billion each of positive and negative ions (one electrostatic unit) in one cc of air. This unit is useful only for x-rays and gamma rays. One roentgen of

such radiation of medium or low intensity is very nearly equal to one rad.

4. **Rem.** A measure of the biological effect of absorbed radiation which takes into account the comparative effectiveness of the type of radiation. One rad of x-rays, gamma rays, or beta rays is equivalent to one rem. One rad of alpha rays is equivalent to about 10 rems.

The Environmental Protection Agency (EPA) has estimated that about half of the radiation to which the general population is exposed is **background radiation** from natural sources. Approximately one-third of this is in the form of cosmic rays. The remainder has its origin largely from minerals in the soil and rock deposits, which may be received externally or internally if radioisotopes find their way into water or food supplies (radium 226 and lead 210 of the uranium series, radium 228 of the thorium series, and potassium 40 enter food cycles following uptake by plants). The average annual exposure to an individual from natural radiation amounts to about 100 millirems. **Medical and dental procedures,** principally diagnostic x-rays, account for another 45 per cent of the radiation exposure (a chest x-ray exposes a person to approximately 25 millirems). Among other medical uses of radiation are the treatment of certain types of cancer with x-rays and gamma rays and diagnostic procedures involving the use of radioisotopes (the uptake of iodine 131 by the thyroid gland, for example, to detect hyperthyroidism or hypothyroidism). The third largest source of radiation exposure (about 3 per cent of the total) is **radioactive fallout** from past nuclear weapon tests (mainly between 1945 and 1962). Some of the radioisotopes in this fallout have long half-lives and are still present in the environment and our bodies (strontium 90, for example, makes its way through food cycles into the bodies of humans and, since it is chemically similar to calcium, concentrates in bone, especially in rapidly growing children). The EPA has the responsibility for establishing radiation exposure limits. For the general public, it recommends a maximum of 500 millirems (five times the natural background radiation).

The isotopes of any element, whether stable or radioactive, have essentially the same chemical properties. Radioisotopes, therefore, are widely used in research as **tracers** to study the metabolism of living organisms (metabolism is the term used for all of the chemical reactions carried out by living cells). In these experiments, individual radioisotopes or radioactively labeled compounds (synthesized with radioisotopes replacing one or more atoms of a given molecule) are administered to intact animals or added to isolated organs, preparations of tissues, cells, or extracts of cells. Because of the presence of the radioisotope, the administered substance and its transformation products can be detected and measured. The use of radioisotopes in tracer experiments has provided an extraordinary range of information about the chemical processes that occur in living cells.

CHEMICAL CONSTITUENTS OF LIVING MATTER

Protoplasm (G. *prōtos,* first; G. *plasma,* anything formed) is the name given collectively to the numerous substances that make up the living cell. When chemists first began to study the chemical compounds found in living matter, they observed that most of them are composed of just a few elements, including carbon, hydrogen, oxygen, and nitrogen and lesser amounts of sulphur and phosphorus. It was generally believed that these "organic" compounds were produced by a "vital force" in living cells and could not be manufactured in the laboratory. In 1828, however, Friedrich Wöhler, a German chemist, produced urea from an inorganic substance, and subsequently many other organic compounds were synthesized in the laboratory. The "vital force" theory had to be discarded, and the term "organic," originally applied to "natural products" isolated from animal and plant sources, became the name of a separate branch of chemistry, organic chemistry, which is defined as the chemistry of carbon compounds. Because carbon atoms can form multiple covalent bonds with themselves, carbon atoms linked together in straight and branched chains or ring structures can form the backbone of an extraordinary number and variety of organic compounds. Millions of natural and man-made organic compounds are known today. Far fewer inorganic compounds are known, and these are, as a rule, smaller and simpler (a number of the simple compounds containing carbon, such as carbon dioxide, carbon monoxide, and carbonic acid, are classified as inorganic).

The greater number of organic compounds found in living matter can be placed in four general classes: (1) proteins, (2) carbohydrates, (3) lipids, and (4) nucleic acids and nucleotides. Inorganic substances in living organisms include water (the most abundant compound, either inorganic or organic, in living matter); acids, bases, and salts dissolved in body fluids; and salts deposited in bones and teeth. Described here are the major classes of organic compounds in living matter followed by an account of the inorganic substances.

Proteins

The most prevalent substance in most cells, next to water, is protein, constituting 10 to 20 per cent of the cell mass. Proteins are also major constituents of blood plasma and intercellular matter. Proteins serve many essential functions. They are, among other things: (1) *enzymes* — biological catalysts with remarkable powers of speeding up the rate of specific chemical reactions, thereby making possible chemical reactions that could not otherwise occur at body temperature (enzymatic action is discussed in Chapter 3, page 63); (2) one of the major *components of cell membranes;* (3) the *contractile elements of muscle;* (4) *hormones;* (5) *receptors* on the cell surface and within the cell to which substances acting on cells, such as hormones, can become bound; (6) *antibodies;* (7) *buffers;* (8) *oxygen carriers* (hemoglobin in red blood cells) and *oxygen storers* (myoglobin in skeletal muscle); (9) blood constituents which *maintain the osmotic pressure of blood plasma* (principally albumin, the most abundant one; a discussion of osmotic pressure appears in Chapter 3, page 56), (10) *blood clotting factors;* (11) a *source of energy* (by degradation into their constituent amino acids, which, for the most part, are converted to glucose); and (12) an important *component of the intercellular fabric of connective tissues,* such as tendons, bone, supporting tissue around internal organs, and the dermis, the principal layer of the skin (*collagen,* the major fibrous protein of the connective tissue matrix, constitutes about 40 per cent of the body protein).

Proteins are constructed from **amino acids** linked together to form long chains, often coiled (helix structure), which may wind around one another, as in some fibrous proteins, or fold into compact shapes, as in globular proteins. Twenty standard amino acids are the building blocks of proteins. Common to all amino acids are an acid, or carboxyl ($-COOH$), group and an amino ($-NH_2$) group attached to the carbon next to the carboxyl group, called the alpha carbon (in one exception, proline, the alpha carbon is part of a nitrogen-containing ring). Their general structural formula is:

$$
\begin{array}{c}
H \\
| \\
R-C-COOH \\
| \\
NH_2
\end{array}
$$

The side chain, represented by the letter R, distinguishes one amino acid from another. Six amino acids are illustrated in Figure 2–2. Note that lysine has a second amino group in its side chain. Since the amino group is basic (the ion form, $-NH_3{}^+$, predominating between pH 6.0 and 7.0), lysine is classified as a basic amino acid. Glutamic acid, which has a second carboxyl group (the ion form, $-COO^-$, predominating between pH 6.0 and 7.0), is classified as acidic. Serine and cysteine are two of several amino acids with polar groups (having oppositely charged ends — see page 24) in their side chains, which in serine is the hydroxyl ($-OH$) group and in cysteine is the sulfhydryl ($-SH$) group. Frequently two cysteines are joined by a disulphide ($-S-S-$) bond, and the union of the two is called cystine. Of the 20 standard amino acids, three are basic (two having nonamino basic groups), two acidic, seven polar, and eight nonpolar and neutral. Amino acids with acidic, basic, and polar groups in their side chains are more water soluble than the others (the solvent properties of water are discussed later in this chapter), and their proportion in a given protein affects its solubility properties.

The linkage between two amino acids is called a **peptide bond,** a bond formed by a condensation reaction in which water is split out between the amino group of one amino acid and the carboxyl group of the other (Fig. 2–3). Two amino acids joined together are called a *dipeptide,* three a *tripeptide.* A prefix is often used for a peptide with a longer chain: *tetra-, penta-, hexa-, hepta-, octa-, nona-,* or *decapeptide.* On the other hand, it may simply be referred to as a peptide. There are a number of biologically active peptides.

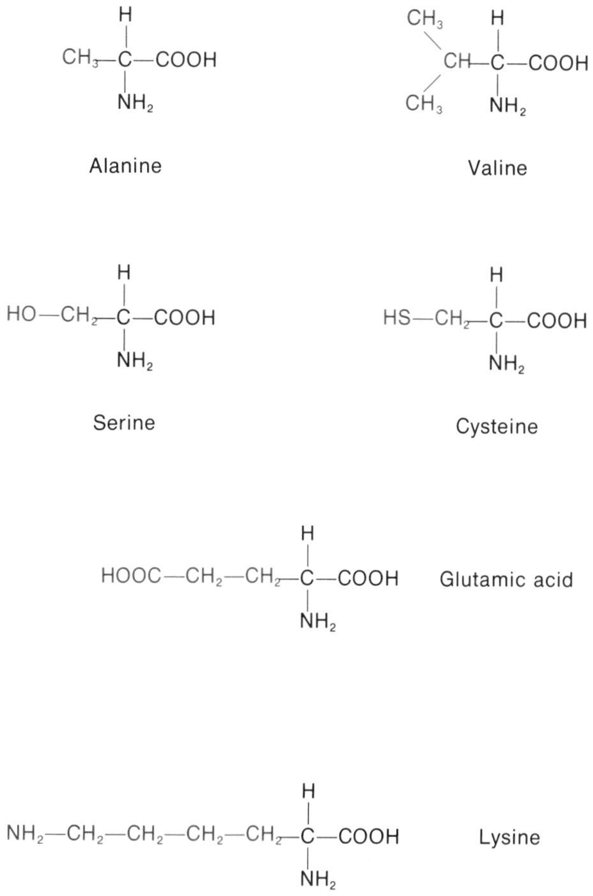

$$CH_3-\overset{\overset{\displaystyle H}{|}}{\underset{\underset{\displaystyle NH_2}{|}}{C}}-COOH$$

Alanine

$$\overset{\displaystyle CH_3}{\underset{\displaystyle CH_3}{\diagdown}}CH-\overset{\overset{\displaystyle H}{|}}{\underset{\underset{\displaystyle NH_2}{|}}{C}}-COOH$$

Valine

$$HO-CH_2-\overset{\overset{\displaystyle H}{|}}{\underset{\underset{\displaystyle NH_2}{|}}{C}}-COOH$$

Serine

$$HS-CH_2-\overset{\overset{\displaystyle H}{|}}{\underset{\underset{\displaystyle NH_2}{|}}{C}}-COOH$$

Cysteine

$$HOOC-CH_2-CH_2-\overset{\overset{\displaystyle H}{|}}{\underset{\underset{\displaystyle NH_2}{|}}{C}}-COOH$$ Glutamic acid

Figure 2–2. Six of 20 standard amino acids, the building blocks of proteins. All have in common a carboxyl group and, on the carbon next to the carboxyl carbon (the alpha carbon), an amino group. The side chains, which differ from one amino acid to another, are lettered in color.

$$NH_2-CH_2-CH_2-CH_2-CH_2-\overset{\overset{\displaystyle H}{|}}{\underset{\underset{\displaystyle NH_2}{|}}{C}}-COOH$$ Lysine

Some are produced by splitting off a portion of a protein. *Angiotensin II*, for example, a regulator of blood volume, is an octapeptide derived (in a two-step sequence) from a serum protein. Other peptides, for example, the hormones of the neurohypophysis (posterior pituitary gland), namely, *oxytocin* and the *antidiuretic hormone (ADH)*, both octapeptides, are not derived from proteins.

The term *polypeptide* (G. *polys*, many) refers to a chain of many amino acids. A protein consists of one or more polypeptide chains, each having a specific number and sequence of amino acids and a characteristic shape. (The shape of a polypeptide chain or of a protein is referred to as its conformation.) The biological activity of a protein is determined by its shape, which in turn is determined by the amino acid sequence of its one or more polypeptide chains. The two major types of proteins, based on shape, are fibrous and globular. In **fibrous proteins** the chains are linear. In two common proteins of this type, collagen, mentioned above, and keratin, which is present in hair and the surface layer of the skin, the chains are wound around one another in threadlike or ropelike fashion. In **globular proteins** (L. *globulus*, little ball) the polypeptide chains are folded into compact shapes, often spherical. The numerous globular proteins serve diverse functions. Most of the approximately 2000 known enzymes are globular proteins, as are antibodies, hemoglobin, myoglobin, albumin, and many hormones.

In the hierarchy of the structural organization of a protein, the number and sequence of amino acids in a polypeptide chain is called its *primary structure*. Often all or part of a chain has a regular arrangement, most commonly a coiling. The coiling of a chain, a structural form known as a *helix* (helix is the Greek word for spiral), is an example of a *secondary structure* of a protein. Secondary structure also refers to how polypeptide chains wind around one another in some fibrous proteins. Illustrated in Figure 2–4 is the secondary structure of the basic collagen molecule (called tropocollagen), which consists of three helical polypeptide chains

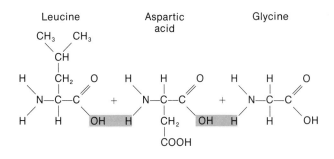

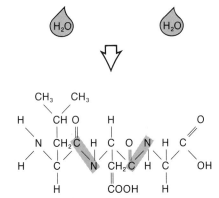

Figure 2–3. Peptide bonds between amino acids are formed by a condensation reaction in which water is split out between the carboxyl group of one amino acid and the amino group of another. Illustrated is the linking of three amino acids into a tripeptide.

wound around each other to form a triple helix. This basic molecule is assembled into fibrils, and aggregates of fibrils form collagen fibers that can be seen under the light microscope. The *tertiary structure* of a protein is the way polypeptide chains are bent and folded in globular proteins. Illustrated in Figure 2–4 is the tertiary structure of myoglobin. The *quaternary structure* of a protein refers to the arrangement of polypeptide chains in proteins having more than one chain.

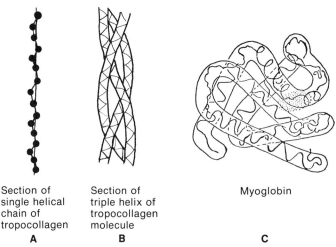

Section of single helical chain of tropocollagen

A

Section of triple helix of tropocollagen molecule

B

Myoglobin

C

Figure 2–4. Secondary structure of tropocollagen, the basic molecule of collagen, and the tertiary structure of myoglobin. The tropocollagen molecule consists of three polypeptide chains, each twisted into a coiled form, called a helix, wound around each other to form a triple helix. In the first drawing (A) the circles represent individual amino acids linked together in a short section of a single helical chain. In the second drawing (B) a short section of the triple helix of a tropocollagen molecule, the lines drawn to enclose each helical chain show how the three chains wind around one another. In the most common form of collagen, each chain has about 1000 amino acids and the molecule is 3000 Å long. In the drawing of myoglobin (C) the lines enclosing the 153 amino acid chain outline the folded tertiary structure of the molecule.

Stabilization of the structure of proteins involves several types of bonds or interactions. The coils of helices are held together by what are known as *hydrogen bonds*. These are weak bonds formed between an electronegative atom and a hydrogen atom covalently bonded to another electronegative atom; in this case, the hydrogen atom forms a link between the electronegative nitrogen and oxygen atoms of peptide groups on successive coils, as illustrated below:

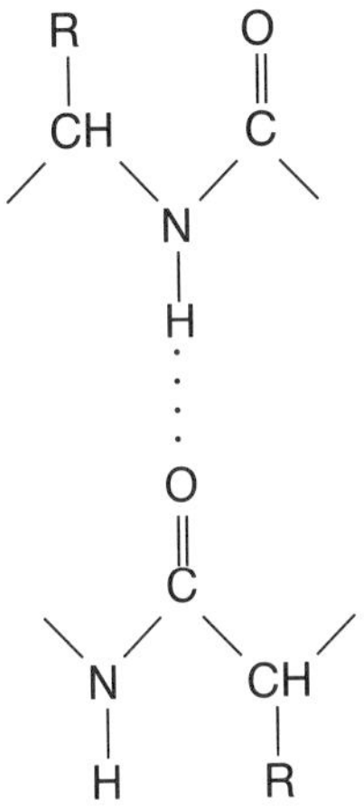

Hydrogen bonds also help stabilize the folded tertiary structure of globular proteins (these may be between side chain groups as well as peptide groups). Also holding together folded polypeptide chains are: *disulphide bridges* between cysteines, the *attraction between oppositely charged acidic and basic groups*, and so-called *hydrophobic interactions* — those between water-insoluble side chains (containing no acidic, basic, or polar groups), which cluster internally and mutually repel water.

Many proteins have nonprotein components. The most numerous of these are the **glycoproteins** (G. *glykys*, sweet), which have side chains of sugar linked to amino acids in the polypeptide chains. Most proteins secreted by cells, such as collagen, antibodies, and various digestive enzymes, are glycoproteins. Another large group of proteins containing a nonprotein component are the **heme proteins**, which have an iron-containing pigment, heme (Fig. 2–5), wrapped around by the protein's polypeptide chain. Among the heme proteins are myoglobin, hemoglobin (which has a quaternary structure consisting of four polypeptide chains, each enfolding a heme group), and the cytochromes. The latter

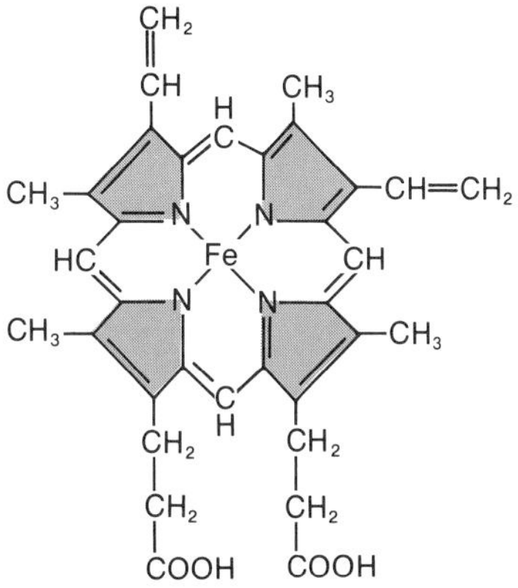

Figure 2–5. The structure of a typical heme, a red pigment present in heme proteins, such as myoglobin, hemoglobin, and the cytochromes. A heme characteristically has iron in the center of a ring structure, called protoporphyrin IX, which consists of four nitrogen-containing rings (pyrroles) joined by carbon bridges.

include, among others, several involved in the end phase of respiration carried out by all cells, in organelles called mitochondria (see Chapter 3), and one in liver cells involved in the oxidative detoxification of a number of drugs.

As mentioned earlier in this chapter, when proteins are degraded, the peptide bonds are split by a reaction involving the addition of water, called hydrolysis. When ingested proteins are digested in the gastrointestinal tract, the products are derived proteins (proteoses and peptones), polypeptides, peptides, dipeptides, and amino acids; when digestion is completed, amino acids, the final products, are absorbed into the blood stream, taken up principally by skeletal muscle and the liver, and rebuilt into proteins.

Carbohydrates

Carbohydrates, which include among them sugars and starches, were so named because, in those originally studied, the hydrogen and oxygen atoms attached to the carbon chain were in the same proportion as in water and could be represented as $C_x(H_2O)_y$. Subsequent studies, however, established that, although this description applies to a great many carbohydrates, it does not apply to all of them. Carbohydrates serve principally as a source of energy and as a major component of the intercellular "ground substance" of connective tissues, in which

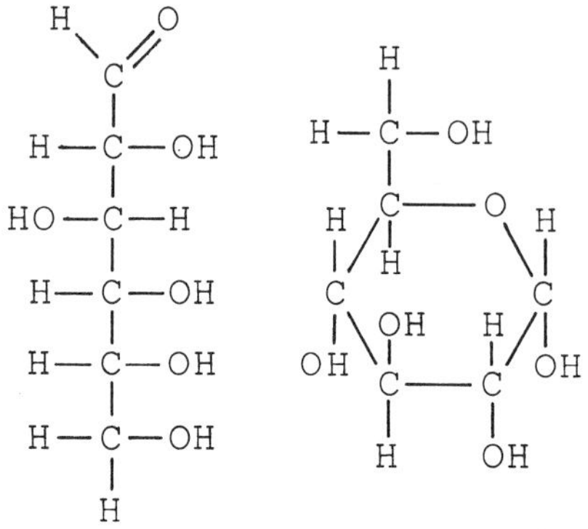

Figure 2–6. Glucose, a simple sugar, is represented in the open chain form on the left and the ring structure (the predominant form) on the right.

fibrous proteins, such as collagen, are embedded.

The principal classes of carbohydrates are *monosaccharides* (G. *monos*, alone; G. *sakchar*, sugar), or simple sugars; *disaccharides*, composed of two monosaccharides; and *polysaccharides*, complex carbohydrates composed of many monosaccharides. Disaccharides and polysaccharides are synthesized by condensation reactions in which two monosaccharides are joined following the removal of water between a hydroxyl group on each one. Conversely, they are degraded into their constituents by hydrolysis, i.e., splitting with the addition of water.

Glucose (Fig. 2–6), a 6-carbon sugar, or *hexose*, is one of the body's major fuels. It circulates in the blood stream and is the building block of **glycogen** (Fig. 2–7), a storage polysaccharide found mainly in the liver and skeletal muscle. During the absorption of a digested meal into the blood stream, glucose furnishes most of the energy needs of the body. The excess is converted to glycogen and fat (discussed below). Glucose is also the building block of **starch**, the storage polysaccharide of plants, and a component of two common disaccharides, namely, **sucrose**, found in many plants (most familiar as "table sugar"), and **lactose** (milk sugar). Sucrose is composed of glucose and another 6-carbon monosaccharide, *fructose*; lactose is composed of glucose and *galactose*, also a 6-carbon monosaccharide.

Ribose and deoxyribose, two 5-carbon monosaccharides, or *pentoses*, are biologically important as constituents of another major group of organic compounds, namely, nucleic acids and their building blocks, called nucleotides (described later in this chapter and in Chapter 3).

Mention was made earlier of the importance of carbohydrates as the major components of the "ground substance" of connective tissues. This ground substance and the fibrous proteins embedded in it constitute the connective tissue matrix (intercellular matter). The ground substance carbohydrates, known as **mucopolysaccharides**, are heteropolysaccharides (G. *heteros*, other); that is, they are composed of two different monosaccharide units. These sugar units are of two types: those having an acid group (acid sugars) and those having an amino group (amino sugars). The most abundant muco-

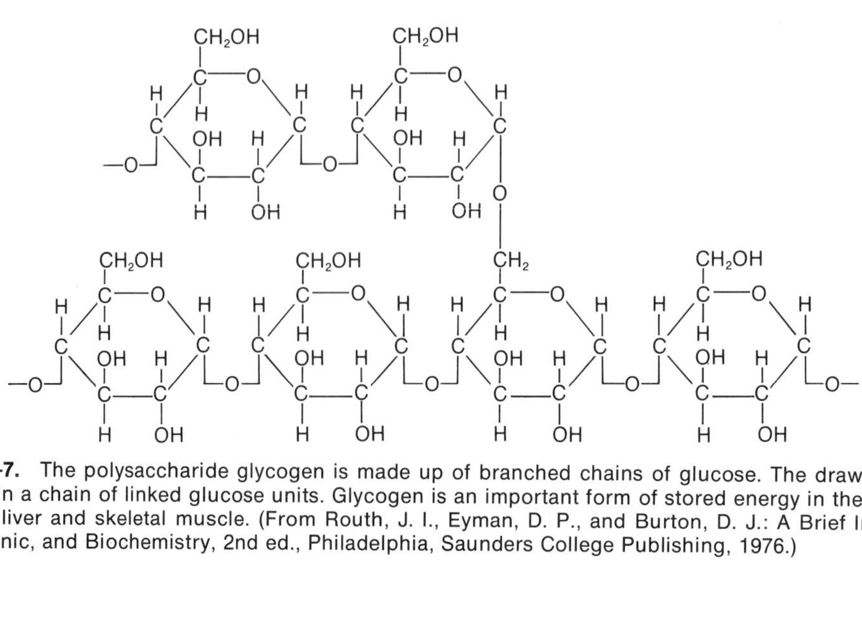

Figure 2–7. The polysaccharide glycogen is made up of branched chains of glucose. The drawing shows the branch point in a chain of linked glucose units. Glycogen is an important form of stored energy in the body, located chiefly in the liver and skeletal muscle. (From Routh, J. I., Eyman, D. P., and Burton, D. J.: A Brief Introduction to General, Organic, and Biochemistry, 2nd ed., Philadelphia, Saunders College Publishing, 1976.)

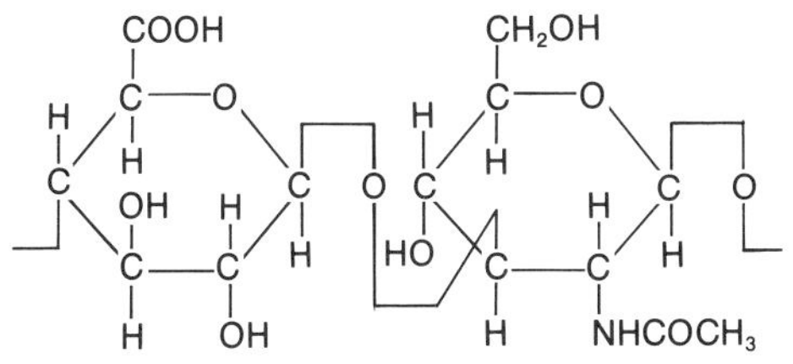

COOH CH₂OH

Glucuronic   N-acetylglucosamine
acid

Figure 2–8. In hyaluronic acid, the most abundant mucopolysaccharide in the body, glucuronic acid and N-acetylglucosamine, drawn here linked together, alternate regularly in an unbranched chain. Mucopolysaccharides are, among other things, the chief constituents of the "ground substance" of connective tissue matrices.

polysaccharide is **hyaluronic acid,** in which *glucuronic acid* and *N-acetylglucosamine* (having an acetyl group, -$COCH_3$, combined with the amino group) alternate regularly in an unbranched chain (Fig. 2–8). (This mucopolysaccharide is found not only in connective tissue matrices, but also in synovial fluid — a lubricating fluid in joints — and in the vitreous humor of the eye.) Other important mucopolysaccharides are the **chondroitin sulphates,** found principally in the ground substance of cartilage matrices. In the chains of these mucopolysaccharides, *galactosamine* containing a sulphate group alternates with glucuronic acid. Mucopolysaccharides may be complexed with small amounts of protein, a combination referred to as *mucoproteins* or *proteoglycans* (glycan is another name for polysaccharide).

Lipids

Lipid is the general term used to identify substances that do not readily dissolve in water but are soluble in organic solvents such as ether, chloroform, and alcohol. There is no agreed upon system for classifying them. In this section the more commonly used terms are used to describe lipids of major importance in four categories: (1) *triglycerides* (fats), (2) *phospholipids*, (3) *sphingolipids*, and (4) *steroids.*

Triglycerides

Triglycerides, also called fats, are a combination of three *fatty acids* and the alcohol *glycerol* (Fig. 2–9). Triglycerides are the major reserve form of energy in the body. Whereas the capacity to store carbohydrates as glycogen is limited, the capacity to store fat in adipose (L. *adeps*, fat) tissue (in the subcutaneous layer of the skin, the abdomen, and other regions) is virtually unlimited. The bulk of any excess ingested calories is converted to fat, which supplies most of the energy needs of the body after a meal is completely absorbed (except for the brain, which, under normal conditions, uses glucose only). Subcutaneous adipose tissue also provides a layer of insulation and protective padding on the surface of the body, and adipose tissue surrounding vital organs provides them with support and protection. The most abundant fatty acids in adipose tissue fat depots have 16 or 18 carbons and are saturated; that is, they have the maximum number of hydrogen atoms attached to the carbon atoms, so that there are no carbon-carbon double bonds. The names of the two most common fatty acids are *palmitic acid*, a 16-carbon saturated fatty acid, and *stearic acid*, an 18-carbon saturated fatty acid. Of the unsaturated fatty acids (having one or more double bonds with less than the maximum number of attached hydrogen atoms), *oleic acid*, an 18-carbon fatty acid with one double bond is the most common. In plant triglycerides, 16- and 18-carbon unsaturated fatty acids predominate. Butterfat has a high proportion of short-chain fatty acids, principally butyric acid (containing four carbons) and caproic acid (containing six carbons).

Phospholipids

Some biochemists divide phospholipids into two groups — phosphoglycerides and phosphosphingosides. Others classify the latter as a subdivision of the sphingolipids. The second classification system, the one followed here, seems more appropriate because it places in one group compounds that have the same backbone unit and that are found principally in the nervous system.

Phospholipids resemble triglycerides; they differ by having one of the fatty acids replaced by a phosphate group combined with another group, usually a nitrogen-containing base, which together form the electrically charged, water-soluble, so-called *hydrophilic* (G. *hydōr*, water; G. *philein*, to love) head of the phospholipid molecule

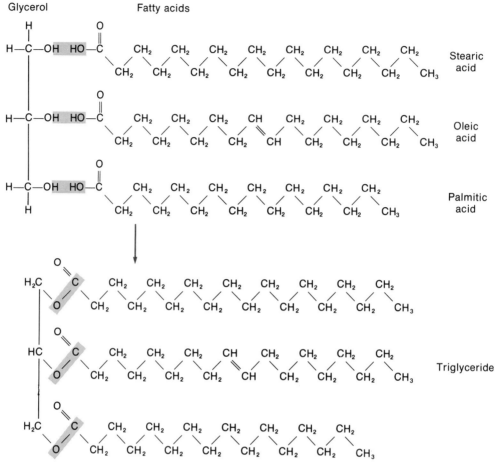

Figure 2–9. Synthesis of a triglyceride from glycerol and three fatty acids. Water is removed in condensation reactions between the carboxyl group of each fatty acid and an alcohol group of glycerol (the bonds formed by these reactions are called ester bonds). Triglycerides, also called fats, are the principal energy reservoir in the body.

(Fig. 2–10). The long fatty acid chains represent the water-insoluble *hydrophobic* (G. *phobos,* fear) tail. Molecules of this type, having hydrophilic and hydrophobic ends, are called *amphipathic* (G. *amphi,* on both sides). (See page 39 for a discussion of the solubility properties of amphipathic substances.) The most common phospholipids

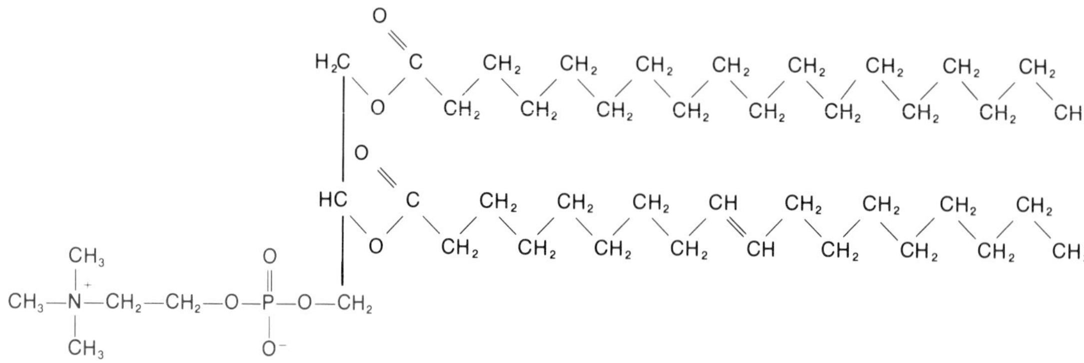

Figure 2–10. A typical phospholipid. Phospholipids are similar to triglycerides, differing by having one of the three fatty acids replaced by a phosphate group combined with another component, usually a nitrogen-containing base. These two components form the molecule's hydrophilic "head." The phospholipid illustrated is a lecithin, characterized by having choline as part of the head. Phospholipids are a major constituent of cell membranes.

are the *lecithins*, which contain choline as the nitrogen-containing base, and the *cephalins*, which contain ethanolamine as the nitrogen-containing base.

Phospholipids, along with proteins, are the major constituents of cell membranes. These include the membrane surrounding the cell (called the cell, or plasma, membrane) and internal membranes enclosing the nucleus and certain organelles inside the cell (the arrangement of phospholipids and proteins in cell membranes is illustrated in Figure 3–3).

Sphingolipids

Sphingolipids have as a common backbone a long tail consisting of *sphingosine* (an amino alcohol) or a derivative of sphingosine combined with a long-chain fatty acid (this tail structure is called a *ceramide*). Sphingolipids can be subdivided into the *phosphosphingolipids* and the *glycosphingolipids* on the basis of the composition of their head groups. In the phosphosphingolipids, also referred to as the *sphingomyelins*, the head has a phosphate group combined with either choline or ethanolamine (Fig. 2–11). The head of a glycosphingolipid has one or more monosaccharides. In the simplest of these, the *cerebrosides*, a single monosaccharide forms the head. In the nervous system, the cerebrosides are mainly galactocerebrosides; that is, galactose forms the head. The most

complex glycosphingolipids, the *gangliosides*, are characterized by the presence of sialic acid (a sugar acid derivative) in a head containing several sugar units.

Sphingolipids are components of the external membranes of cells and, as indicated earlier, are found mainly in the nervous system. They are one of the major constituents of myelin, the insulating wrapping around nerve cell fibers. Myelin, which is derived from the cell membranes of certain accessory cells of the nervous system (see Chapter 9), has a much higher proportion of lipids than do cell surface membranes (about 75 per cent of the dry weight, compared with the usually less than 50 per cent in cell membranes). The galactocerebrosides, the principal sphingolipids in myelin, represent 20 per cent of its dry weight. Some sphingolipids, namely, the gangliosides, appear to be concentrated at receptor sites in cell surface membranes, binding and interacting with substances that induce changes in cellular processes.

The accumulation of certain sphingolipids occurs in a number of genetic diseases as a consequence of a deficiency of an enzyme required for the degradation of an individual sphingolipid or a type of sphingolipid. These disorders are called **lipid-storage diseases**. In *Tay-Sachs disease*, for example, which has a high incidence among Jews of Eastern European extraction, a ganglioside (GM$_2$) accumulates in the brain. Its symptoms progress from muscular weakness to re-

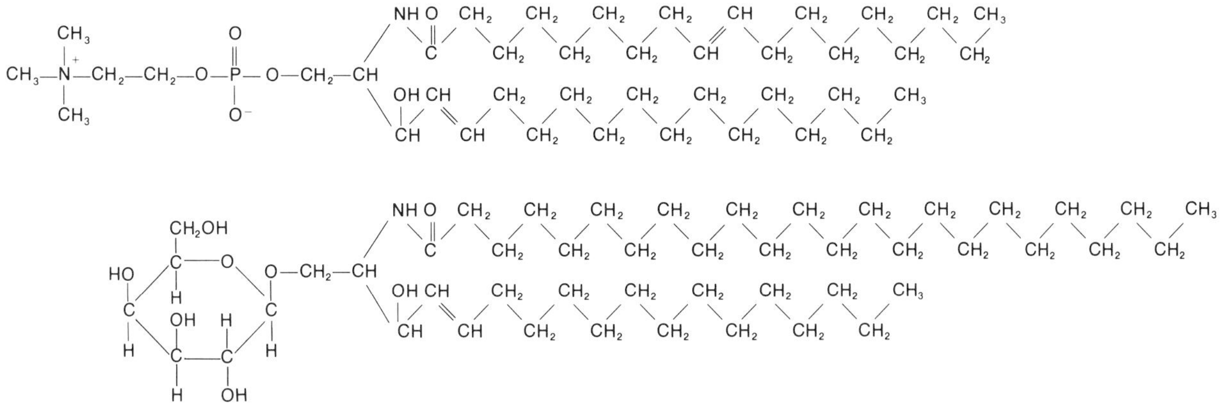

Figure 2–11. Sphingolipids have a characteristic long tail containing sphingosine (an amino alcohol) or a derivative of sphingosine combined with a long-chain fatty acid (the combination of the two is known as a ceramide). The top drawing is a typical phosphosphingolipid (also called a sphingomyelin), in which the head portion of the molecule is formed by a phosphate group linked to either choline or ethanolamine. The bottom drawing is a glycosphingolipid, which has one or more monosaccharides in the head portion. The glycosphingolipid in the drawing is a cerebroside, the simplest type, having a head formed by one monosaccharide (the head of this particular cerebroside is galactose; hence, it is called a galactocerebroside). Sphingolipids are components of cell surface membranes and are found chiefly in the nervous system.

tarded mental development, seizures, and blindness, with death occurring before the age of four. Other inheritable lipid-storage diseases include *Niemann-Pick disease* (accumulation of sphingomyelins, especially in the liver and spleen) and *Gaucher's disease* (accumulation of glucocerebrosides, mainly in the spleen). Mental retardation occurs in Niemann-Pick disease and in the infantile form of Gaucher's disease. In general, mental retardation and neurological dysfunction are major symptoms of almost all lipid-storage diseases.

Steroids

Steroids contain a basic structural unit of four rings of carbon, which can be seen in the illustration of cholesterol (Fig. 2–12), the most common steroid in the body. Cholesterol is an important component of external cell membranes (intracellular membranes have very little cholesterol) and is also the precursor of a number of other essential steroids, such as estrogens (female sex hormones), androgens (male sex hormones), hormones of the adrenal glands, vitamin D, and bile acids (substances secreted by the liver that aid lipid digestion and absorption). The structures of the major steroid hormones are given in Figure 16–13. When cholesterol is transported in the blood stream as part of lipid-protein complexes, called plasma lipoproteins, the greater proportion of the cholesterol is combined with a long-chain fatty acid as *esterified cholesterol* (in which an ester bond is formed in a condensation reaction involving the removal of water between the

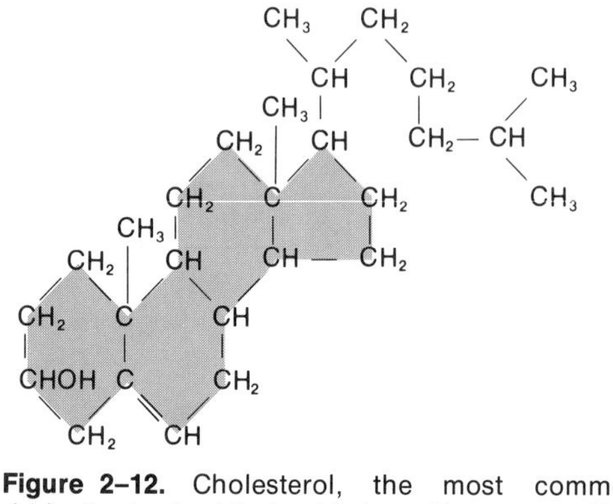

Figure 2–12. Cholesterol, the most common steroid in the body. All steroids have the same unit of four rings as cholesterol. Cholesterol is a component of cell surface membranes and is a precursor of a number of other important steroids, such as vitamin D and the steroid hormones.

carboxyl group of the fatty acid and the hydroxyl group of cholesterol). In the adrenal glands, cholesterol is stored chiefly in the esterified form, and hydrolysis of these esters occurs as a first step in the synthesis of adrenal hormones.

Nucleic Acids and Nucleotides

Nucleic acids consist of long chains built up from *nucleotides*. A nucleotide has three components: a 5-carbon sugar, a phosphate group, and one of four nitrogen-containing bases. The nucleic acid **DNA (deoxyribonucleic acid)** is the genetic matter of the cell — it contains coded information for the synthesis of proteins, including enzymes (since enzymes function as biological catalysts that make it possible for chemical reactions to occur in the cell, the instructions for the synthesis of specific enzymes determine the cell's and the organism's structure and function). DNA is so named because the 5-carbon sugar in its nucleotide unit is deoxyribose (the components of nucleotides and the double-stranded helix structure of DNA, generally referred to as the "double helix," are illustrated in Figures 3–21, 3–22, and 3–23). **RNA (ribonucleic acid)**, on the other hand, contains the 5-carbon sugar ribose as a nucleotide component. Three types of RNA — messenger RNA, transfer RNA, and ribosomal RNA — are involved in the transfer and translation of genetic information in the process of synthesizing proteins from instructions coded in DNA. Messenger RNA carries the coded information from DNA to the site of protein synthesis, transfer RNA acts as a transporting vehicle for amino acids, and ribosomal RNA is complexed with protein in cell organelles called ribosomes, mechanical devices that serve as the site of protein synthesis (the synthesis of a protein from information coded in a gene, a segment of DNA, is summarized in Figure 3–24).

Certain nucleotides are in themselves biologically active. **ATP (adenosine triphosphate)**, for example, a nucleotide with two additional phosphate groups (Fig. 2–13), is the direct source of energy for most of the work performed by cells. When nutrients are degraded, the energy released is used to manufacture ATP, and the energy contained in its two high-energy phosphate bonds, principally the terminal one, provides the power for most of the energy-requiring processes in

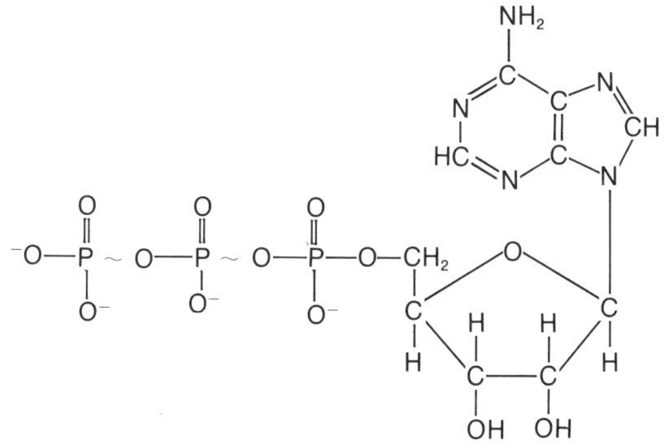

Figure 2–13. ATP (adenosine triphosphate) is a nucleotide (nitrogen-containing base, 5-carbon sugar, and a phosphate group) with two additional phosphate groups. (In ATP the base is adenine, the sugar ribose.) The wavy lines represent high-energy bonds. ATP functions as a carrier of chemical energy derived from the degradation of nutrients to cellular processes requiring energy input. Its high-energy phosphate bonds, chiefly the terminal one, provide the direct source of energy for most of the work done by cells.

the cell, such as biochemical synthesis and muscular contraction. It is estimated that cleavage of the terminal high-energy bond of ATP, splitting off a phosphate group and leaving ADP (adenosine diphosphate), releases between 7000 and 8000 calories (one calorie is the amount of heat required to raise the temperature of one gram of water 1°C). (The discovery of the energy-carrying function of ATP and its synthesis during the degradation of glucose and fatty acids are described in Chapter 3, page 58.)

Cyclic AMP (adenosine monophosphate, with the phosphate group arranged in a ring — Fig. 2–14) plays a key role in mediat-

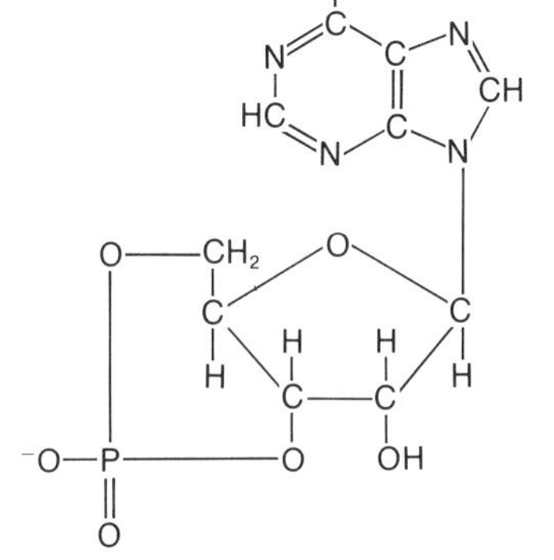

Figure 2–14. Cyclic AMP, a biologically active nucleotide, plays a central role in mediating many cellular activities, often operating as a "second messenger" between the "first messenger," such as a hormone, and its effects upon the cell.

ing various cellular processes. In many cases — for example, in mediating the effects of certain hormones — cyclic AMP is called the "second messenger." The hormone, the first messenger, stimulates the formation of cyclic AMP, which in turn brings about a change in some cellular process (for a diagrammatic representation of how cyclic AMP mediates the stimulation of the breakdown of glycogen by glucagon or epinephrine, see Figure 16–2).

Water

Water, the most prevalent substance in the body, represents about 60 to 70 per cent of its weight. This water is by no means inert and unimportant. It has unique chemical properties which make it indispensable for life. Water is, among other things, a most efficient dispersing medium, and in its absence most of the chemical reactions occurring in the body could not take place. The highly effective solvent properties of water are accounted for by its dipole structure, in which the two hydrogen atoms form an electropositive end and the oxygen atom forms an electronegative end (see page 24). Ionic compounds are dissolved because of the strong attraction between an electrically charged ion and the oppositely charged end of a water dipole. The ions are pulled apart and surrounded by water molecules. These "hydrated" ions remain in solution.

Water also readily dissolves substances that have many polar groups (the hydroxyl groups of sugars, for example) because these groups tend to form hydrogen bonds with water molecules. In the hydrogen bond (described earlier in this chapter in the section on proteins), an electropositive hydrogen atom links two electronegative atoms. In the hydrogen bond illustrated below between a hydroxyl group and water, the link is between two oxygen atoms:

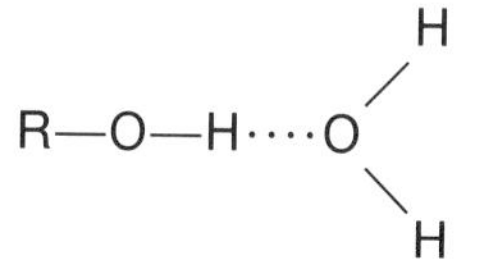

$$R—O—H \cdots O \begin{matrix} H \\ \\ H \end{matrix}$$

Water is also able to form solutions of amphipathic substances — those having hydrophobic tails and hydrophilic heads (page 36). In these solutions, called **micellar solutions**, the molecules form tail-to-tail aggregates, usually spherical, called **micelles**, in which only the hydrophilic heads are in contact with water. Micelles form only when the concentration of the amphipathic substance reaches a critical level, the so-called *critical micellar concentration* (which becomes evident when the solution suddenly clears). Complex micellar solutions are formed in the small intestine during digestion from the products of lipid degradation (some of which are amphipathic) in the presence of bile salts, an amphipathic substance secreted by the liver. It is from this micellar solution that the products of the digestion of lipids are absorbed. Bile salts are required for the formation of these micelles; in their absence, fat absorption is depressed and no cholesterol is absorbed.

Water, in addition to being an exceptionally good solvent, has a number of other properties that are biologically important. It has, for example, a high *specific heat* (the specific heat is the amount of heat required to raise the temperature of one gram of a substance 1°C). This property serves to keep the temperature of the organism relatively stable when rapid changes occur in the temperature of the environment. Coupled with this is its *heat conductivity*, which is high (for fluids) and which facilitates temperature homeostasis, since even small changes in internal temperature in one area are quickly dispersed over large areas. Water also has a high *heat of vaporization* — it takes 540 calories to change one gram of liquid water to water vapor. This provides an effective cooling mechanism through the evaporation of perspiration from body surfaces. These unusual properties of water, as well as its high boiling point, high surface tension (the tendency of the surface to contract into a spherical shape, presenting the smallest possible surface), and its capillary action (causing water to rise in a continuous column in a fine-bore tube), are explained by the internal cohesion of liquid water resulting from the formation of hydrogen bonds between water molecules:

In the most common crystalline form of ice, each water molecule is hydrogen-bonded with four other water molecules in a regular lattice. Although in liquid water most of the water molecules are also hydrogen-bonded, these bonds are continuously being rapidly broken and made.

Inorganic Substances Other Than Water

The inorganic substances in living matter other than water include electrolytes in body fluids and salt deposits in bone and the dentin of teeth. The ions of electrolytes dissolved in body fluids are of considerable importance to living organisms. The electrical excitability of nerve and muscle tissue, for example, depends upon the distribution of sodium ions (Na^+) and potassium ions (K^+) across cell membranes (giving rise to the so-called "membrane potential"), and impulses traveling along nerve and muscle fibers result from sudden shifts in the concentrations of these ions on the internal and external membrane surfaces. Calcium ions (Ca^{++}) regulate a number of cell functions (including the triggering of muscle contraction) by becoming reversibly bound to specialized proteins. Ions, especially sodium ions, are involved in regulating the volume of body fluids. Although the greater number of inorganic substances in the body are dissolved in body fluids, calcium salts deposited in the matrices of bone and the dentin of teeth account for at least 65 per cent of the weight of these tissues and contribute to their unique properties.

SUMMARY

BASIC CHEMISTRY AND THE CHEMICAL CONSTITUENTS OF LIVING MATTER

Elements, Atoms, Compounds, and Molecules

1. All matter is composed of elements, each of which is a collection of atoms, an atom representing the smallest particle that retains the element's properties.

2. Combinations of two or more atoms of different elements form compounds. The smallest unit retaining the properties of a compound is a molecule.

Structure of the Atom

1. Atoms consist of (a) a dense inner core accounting for essentially all of the atom's mass, called the nucleus, which contains particles bearing a charge of +1, called protons, and neutral particles, called neutrons; and (b) a region surrounding the nucleus accounting for most of the space of the atom occupied by particles bearing a charge of −1, called electrons.

    a. The atomic number of an atom, the number of protons, determines the number of surrounding electrons.

    b. The mass number of an atom is the sum of the number of protons and neutrons, each of which has a mass of approximately 1.

        (1) Different forms of an element, called isotopes, have a different number of neutrons and hence a different mass number. The atomic weight of an element is the average value of the mass numbers of its isotopes.

    c. The probable positions of electrons are described in terms of orbitals, each orbital holding as many as two electrons and representing a unique spatial distribution and energy state.

    d. The number of electrons in the outer s and p orbitals predicts the combining properties of an atom because atoms tend to form combinations by sharing or transferring electrons in these orbitals so as to form an outer octet of electrons (octet rule).

    e. The joining of two atoms by sharing electrons is called a covalent bond. The bonding capacity, or valence, of hydrogen is 1, oxygen 2, nitrogen 3, and carbon 4.

    f. An ionic bond is formed when two atoms join with a transfer of electrons from one to the other.

Moles; Equivalents; Molar and Equivalent Concentrations

1. One mole of a compound is equal to its molecular weight expressed in grams.

2. The number of moles per liter of a compound in solution is its molar concentration.

3. An equivalent of an atom, the amount that replaces or combines with 1 gram of hydrogen, is calculated as the atomic weight divided by the valence.

4. The number of equivalents per liter of an ion in solution is its equivalent concentration.

Electrolytes

1. An electrolyte is a substance whose solution contains ions and conducts electricity.

2. Strong electrolytes ionize almost completely; weak electrolytes ionize only slightly.

3. Free ions are present in solutions of salts, acids, and bases.

4. An acid is a proton (hydrogen ion) donor; a base is a proton acceptor.

pH

1. pH is defined as the negative logarithm of the hydrogen ion concentration of a solution.

2. A solution with a pH of 7 is neutral. An acidic solution has a pH of less than 7; a basic solution has a pH of greater than 7.

Chemical Reactions

1. In oxidation-reduction reactions, the loss of electrons (or increase in oxidation number) is an oxidation and the gain of electrons (or decrease in oxidation number) is a reduction.

    a. Removal of hydrogens is equivalent to oxidation; accepting hydrogens is equivalent to reduction.

2. A reaction joining two molecules in which a small molecule, such as water, is split out between them is called a condensation reaction.

3. Degrading substances with the addition of water is called hydrolysis.

Radioactivity

1. A radioisotope has an unstable nucleus that emits radiation which transforms the radioisotope into the stable isotope of another element (a process called radioactive decay).

2. The three kinds of radiation emitted by naturally occurring radioisotopes are:

    a. Alpha particles (or rays), the bare nuclei of helium atoms (2 protons and 2 neutrons).

b. Beta particles (or rays), high energy electrons.
c. Gamma rays, radiant energy of shorter wave length and higher energy than x-rays.

3. The radiation of naturally occurring radioisotopes and x-rays are the chief forms of ionizing radiation.

4. The units of measurement of radiation are the curie, rad, roentgen, and rem.

5. The major sources of radiation exposure to the general population are background radiation (about 50 per cent), medical and dental procedures (about 45 per cent) and radioactive fallout from past nuclear weapons tests (about 3 per cent).

6. Radioisotopes are used in research as tracers to study metabolic pathways in living organisms.

CHEMICAL CONSTITUENTS OF LIVING MATTER

The most common organic compounds are classified as (a) proteins, (b) carbohydrates, (c) lipids, and (d) nucleic acids and nucleotides. Inorganic substances include water; acids, bases, and salts dissolved in body fluids; and salts deposited in bones and teeth.

Proteins

1. They serve, among other things, as enzymes, major components of cell membranes, the contractile elements of muscle, hormones, receptors, antibodies, oxygen carriers, blood clotting factors, a source of energy, and part of the intercellular fabric of connective tissues.

2. They are composed of amino acids linked together into long chains.

3. The peptide bond, which links two amino acids, is formed by a condensation reaction in which water is split out between the amino group of one amino acid and the carboxyl group of another.

4. Proteins may have one or more polypeptide chains, each having a specific number and sequence of amino acids and characteristic shape.

5. The major protein types, based on shape, are fibrous, in which the chains are linear, and globular, in which the chains are folded into compact shapes.

6. The primary structure of a protein is the number and sequence of amino acids in its one or more polypeptide chains; secondary structure is some regular arrangement of the chain, most commonly a coiling (helix); tertiary structure is the way polypeptide chains are bent and folded in globular proteins; quaternary structure is the arrangement of chains in globular proteins if there are two or more chains.

7. Most proteins secreted by cells, such as collagen and antibodies, are glycoproteins.

8. Myoglobin, hemoglobin, and the cytochromes are examples of heme proteins.

Carbohydrates

1. They include sugars and starches and were so named because in those originally studied hydrogen and oxygen atoms were linked to carbon atoms in the same ratio as in water.

2. The monosaccharide glucose is an important nutrient and supplies most of the energy needs of the body during the absorption of a meal.

a. Glucose is the building block of glycogen, a polysaccharide stored principally in the liver and skeletal muscle.

3. Mucopolysaccharides, heteropolysaccharides constructed from two different monosaccharide units, are the major components of the ground substance of connective tissue matrices.

a. The most abundant mucopolysaccharide is hyaluronic acid.
b. Mucopolysaccharides combined with small amounts of protein are called mucoproteins or proteoglycans.

Lipids

1. Lipids are substances that readily dissolve in organic solvents such as ether. Those of major importance can be described in four groups: triglycerides, phospholipids, sphingolipids, and steroids.

a. *Triglycerides* (fats): A combination of three fatty acids and glycerol. They are the major energy reservoir in the body.

b. *Phospholipids:* Resemble triglycerides, differing by having one of the fatty acids replaced by a hydrophilic head consisting of a phosphate group combined with another group, generally a nitrogen-containing base. They are major components of cell membranes.

c. *Sphingolipids*: Have in common a long tail containing sphingosine (or a derivative) combined with a long-chain fatty acid. Are components of cell surface membranes and are found principally in the central nervous system.

d. *Steroids*: Constructed from a unit of four carbon rings.

　(1) Cholesterol, the major one, is a component of cell surface membranes and a precursor of vitamin D, bile acids, and the sex and adrenal hormones.

Nucleic Acids and Nucleotides

1. Nucleic acids consist of nucleotides linked together as long chains. Each nucleotide is composed of a 5-carbon sugar, a phosphate group, and one of four nitrogen-containing bases.

2. DNA is the genetic matter of the cell.

3. Messenger RNA, transfer RNA, and ribosomal RNA participate in transferring information coded in DNA into the synthesis of proteins.

4. Two biologically active nucleotides are ATP and cyclic AMP.

Water

1. Its solvent properties are accounted for by its dipole structure.

2. A number of other biologically important properties of water, including a high specific heat and high heat of vaporization, are explained by internal cohesion due to the formation of hydrogen bonds between water molecules.

Inorganic Substances Other Than Water

1. Ions of electrolytes dissolved in body fluids serve important functions. For example, the distribution of and shifts in the concentration of sodium and potassium ions give rise to the resting membrane potential and propagated impulses in nerve and mus-cle tissue. Calcium ions regulate various cell functions by becoming reversibly bound to specialized proteins.

2. Calcium salts deposited in the matrices of bone and the dentin of teeth contribute to the unique properties of these tissues.

REVIEW QUESTIONS

1. What is the smallest particle of an element that retains its properties? What is the smallest unit into which a compound can be divided and still retain its properties? What information does the formula for water, H_2O, give?
2. Define the following terms used to describe atoms: mass number, atomic number, isotope, atomic weight, and orbital.
3. Explain the octet rule. Distinguish between covalent and ionic bonds.
4. Define the following terms: mole, molar concentration, equivalent, equivalent concentration, electrolyte, nonelectrolyte, acid, base, pH, oxidation-reduction, radioisotope, half-life, and ionizing radiation.
5. List four functions of proteins. What are the building blocks of proteins? How is a peptide bond formed? Distinguish between the primary, secondary, tertiary, and quaternary structures of proteins. Describe the secondary structure of collagen.
6. List an important function of each of the following: glucose, glycogen, and mucopolysaccharides. What is the most abundant mucopolysaccharide?
7. How does the structure of a triglyceride differ from that of phospholipid? What is the structural unit of (a) steroids and (b) the tail of sphingolipids? List at least one function each of triglycerides, phospholipids, sphingolipids, and cholesterol.
8. What is the relationship between nucleotides and nucleic acids? What are the three components of nucleotides? Of what importance to the cell is each of the following: DNA, RNA, ATP, and cyclic AMP?
9. Explain how the dipole structure of water and the formation of hydrogen bonds between water molecules account for some of water's chemical properties.
10. List two functions of ions in body fluids.

3
The Cell

Objectives

The aim of this chapter is to enable the student to:

- Explain the origin of the cell theory and the emergence of an understanding of how the genetic substance of the cell determines the nature of the cell.

- List the principal functions of each cellular organelle.

- Identify the major mechanisms of movement of substances across the cell membrane and explain how they work.

- Distinguish between the aerobic and anaerobic breakdown of glucose and describe how the aerobic process produces more ATP than does the anaerobic process.

- Describe how the breakdown of fatty acids yields more energy than does the breakdown of glucose.

- Explain what is meant by the cell cycle in populations of dividing cells.

- Describe the four stages of mitosis and explain the difference between mitosis and meiosis.

- Describe how the structure of DNA explains how an exact copy can be made prior to cell division and how it carries coded information for the synthesis of proteins.

- Describe how proteins are synthesized from information coded in genes.

- Explain how genetic diseases can be detected by amniocentesis.

- Describe the production of medically useful proteins by recombinant DNA technology.

- Explain how cancer cells differ from normal cells.

- Describe how cellular differentiation takes place.

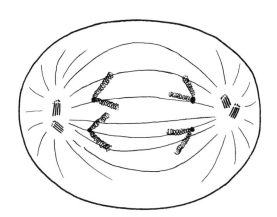

IMPORTANCE OF THE CELL

The human body is composed of cells, matrices (intercellular material), and body fluids. Of the three, only the cells are living, possessing the characteristics of growth, metabolism, irritability, and reproduction.

The cell is the structural, or morphologic, unit of the body, as well as its functional, or physiologic unit. The human body develops from a single cell, the *fertilized ovum.* Repeated divisions of the ovum result in many types of cells differing from one another in composition and function; however, most of the basic structures of the cell are common to all cells.

The cell is regarded as a highly organized unit ceaselessly engaged in dynamic biochemical activities. Keeping the cell environment (the fluid medium surrounding each cell) constant within a relatively narrow range is essential for optimum cell functioning.

All the organs, structures, and systems of the body can be viewed as designed to afford each individual cell its optimum environment. However, the nature of the living organism is more truly revealed when this is coupled with the recognition that, in the final analysis, it is the cells themselves which do the work to provide this optimum environment. The mutually cooperative interactions among cells are essential for maintaining the structural and functional integrity of the human organism.

HISTORY OF THE CELL

The word *cell* was introduced as a biological term in 1665 by Robert Hooke, an English scientist, to describe what reminded him of the cells of a honeycomb when he examined a section of cork with his 30-power microscope. Hooke came to the conclusion, after many years of study, that these boxlike compartments were fundamental to the structure of all living plants. However, a formal statement of what is known as the *cell theory* did not appear until the publication in 1838 and 1839 of monographs by M. J. Schleiden, a botanist, and Theodor Schwann, a zoologist. This generalization, a summary of their own findings and those of their contemporaries, described cells as the fundamental units of structure and function of all living things,

capable of carrying out all of the processes of life as independent entities and, collectively, as complex systems. The origin of cells remained a matter of dispute until the writings of Rudolf Virchow in 1858 led to the general acceptance of the view that cells arise by division of preexisting ones. *"Omnis cellula e cellula"* (all cells come from cells) is Virchow's widely quoted dictum. In 1882 Walther Flemming published remarkable drawings of cell division showing that discrete bodies, called *chromosomes,* which take form during cell division, appeared to be split lengthwise prior to cell division to form double strands. The strands separated and each daughter cell received a complete set of chromosomes. The inheritance of these bodies provides continuity from one cell generation to the next. A year later Edouard van Beneden observed that the sperm and egg cells of Ascaris, a parasitic worm, contained one-half as many chromosomes (haploid number) as nonsexual cells and that when a sperm cell fertilized an egg the sperm and egg nuclei fused to restore the full (diploid) number. Chromosomes, therefore, are the agents for continuity in sexual reproduction of the whole organism. At that time a number of leading biologists believed that a substance called nuclein (now known as nucleic acids), which had been isolated from the nucleus of human white blood cells by Friedrich Miescher, was responsible for the transmission of hereditary characteristics, but this idea was soon discarded, partly because of the prevailing belief that only nuclear protein was complex enough to carry genetic information. However, during the 1940's new observations proved that DNA, the nucleic acid component of chromosomes, rather than the protein component, is the hereditary substance. An intense search in laboratories all over the world for the exact chemical structure of DNA culminated in the publication by James Watson and Francis Crick of the celebrated double helix model of DNA (described on page 68). This model explained how coded information could be built into DNA, and not many years after its publication the code itself was broken. The code and how it operates is described later in this chapter. For the present, all that needs to be said is that DNA resembles a tape subdivided into units (called *genes*) which contain instructions for the manufacture of proteins, including *enzymes.* Enzymes govern cellular processes by acting as biological catalysts, promoting chemical reactions but remaining intact at the end of the reaction. Without enzymes, cellular reactions could not occur and the constituents of the cell could be neither assembled nor broken down. Thus, the nature of a cell is determined ultimately by the genetic instructions for the synthesis of its enzymes.

Tissue culture studies begun in 1912 have tested and confirmed the thesis that each (potentially or actually) independent cell, so long as it retains its capacity for growth and multiplication, must be considered an integral living unit.

The most dramatic advances in cytology (the study of cell structure) have occurred in the past 40 years, since the development of the electron microscope and increasingly sophisticated biochemical techniques and instruments. Although there has been some discussion recently about whether or not some substructures found within the cell should be considered independent living units and, further, whether some viruses are alive apart from a host cell, the general consensus seems to be that in the most obvious and relevant sense the cell is clearly the smallest living unit of which all definitely living things are composed (Fig. 3–1).

STRUCTURE OF THE CELL

The cell may be defined structurally as an organized unit mass of protoplasm consisting of two complementary, mutually dependent parts: (1) the *nucleus*, a more or less central part; and (2) the *cytoplasm* (G. *kytos*, cell), a surrounding part. The nucleus is delineated from the surrounding cytoplasm by a delicate *nuclear membrane;* the cytoplasm is bounded externally by a specialized layer, also very thin and delicate, which is called the *cell*, or *plasma, membrane* (Fig. 3–2).

Listed below are the structural functional parts of the cell:
1. Cell membranes
2. Nucleus
   a. Chromosomes
   b. Nucleoli
3. Cytoplasm
   a. Cytoplasmic organelles
      (1) Endoplasmic reticulum
      (2) Ribosomes
      (3) Golgi apparatus
      (4) Mitochondria
      (5) Lysosomes
      (6) Centrioles
   b. Cytoplasmic inclusions

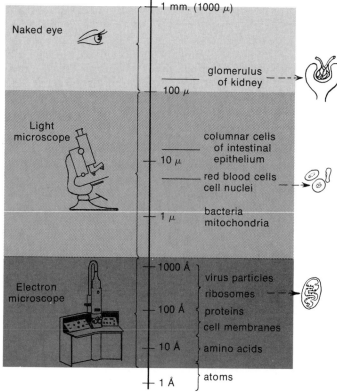

Figure 3–1. The limits of resolution of the electron microscope as contrasted to those of the eye and the light microscope. A millimeter, mm., is equal to 1/1000 meter, or 0.03937 inch; a micrometer, μm, 1/1000 millimeter; an angstrom, Å, 1/10,000 micrometer.

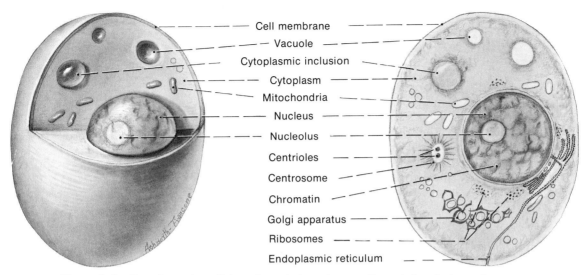

Cell membrane
Vacuole
Cytoplasmic inclusion
Cytoplasm
Mitochondria
Nucleus
Nucleolus
Centrioles
Centrosome
Chromatin
Golgi apparatus
Ribosomes
Endoplasmic reticulum

Figure 3–2. Two views of a cell, based on what can be seen through the electron microscope.

Cell Membranes

On all protoplasmic surfaces, a specialized layer, or membrane, is found that is denser than the rest of the protoplasm. In the cell, these membranes include the internal membranes enclosing the various organelles and the nucleus, as well as the external membrane, or *plasma membrane,* which forms the exterior layer.

The plasma membrane acts to regulate interchange between the cell and its environment and is a site for receiving signals from the immediate environment or from a distance that prompt adaptive changes essential for maintaining homeostasis of the cell and organism. Many hormones, for example, initiate their effects by becoming bound to specific receptors on the cell surface and activating enzymes in the cell membrane. Of equal importance is the action of internal membranes. The mitochondrial membrane (see page 51), for example, is the major site for the synthesis of ATP.

Phospholipids and proteins are the principal constituents of cell membranes. The former form the basic structure of the membrane; the latter are in large measure responsible for its functional properties. Analysis of x-ray data of membrane fragments indicates that the phospholipids form two parallel layers (referred to as the bilayer) with their *hydrophilic* heads (see Chapter 2, page 35) facing the aqueous medium on the mem-

Figure 3–3. *A,* Schematic drawing of a cell membrane. Phospholipids form a double layer with their so-called hydrophobic tails facing inward, meeting at the center of the membrane, and their so-called hydrophilic heads facing away from the interior of the membrane. Membrane proteins are represented in various shapes partially or completely penetrating the phospholipid bilayer. Bending of some of the phospholipid tails is caused by the presence of unsaturated fatty acids and creates a more fluid condition in the membrane. *B,* Enlarged diagrammatic representations of phospholipids illustrate how a double bond of an unsaturated fatty acid, shown on the left, introduces a bend in the carbon chain.

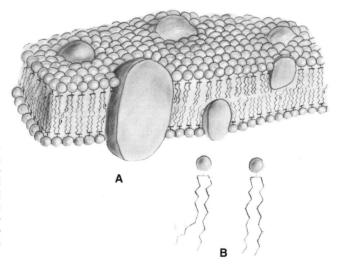

A

B

brane surfaces and their *hydrophobic* tails facing the interior of the membrane. Interdispersed proteins partially or completely penetrate the phospholipid bilayer (Fig. 3–3). The technique known as freeze-etch electron microscopy has aided considerably in constructing the present picture of cell membranes. In this procedure a suspension of membranes in water is rapidly frozen (to liquid nitrogen temperature) and fractured with a sharp blade in a vacuum. The membrane is split in the plane between the two phospholipid layers. In the electron micrographs particles are revealed (presumed to be protein) along the inner surface of the bilayer 5 to 8.5 nanometers in diameter. In order for membrane proteins to function normally, the membrane must be in a fluid state, since many activities of membranes involve changes in protein structure or arrangement. Fluidity is made possible by the presence of unsaturated fatty acids, which cause structural deformity of the phospholipid bilayer (Fig. 3–3).

The Nucleus

The nucleus, which contains the genetic material of the cell, is a specialized spherical mass of protoplasm, usually located in the center of the cell. Each cell begins its existence with a nucleus, which on occasion can be lost when the cell reaches its mature form, as with the red blood cell, which extrudes its nucleus prior to entering the blood. A few cell types, such as the megakaryocyte (G. *megas*, large; G. *karyon*, nut or kernel) of bone marrow (which fragments to form platelets, essential factors in blood clotting), possess multiple nuclei.

The genetic substance, deoxyribonucleic acid (DNA), is located in structures called **chromosomes,** which can be seen as separate bodies during mitosis (cell division). Each species has a constant number of chromosomes, and in humans there are 46 in each cell, except in the sperm and ovum, which contain half that number (for more details, see page 65). Genes, the hereditary units occupying specific positions on chromosomes, are segments of DNA containing coded information for the synthesis of proteins. Chromosomal DNA is packaged by association with certain small, highly basic proteins (histones) into particles called **nucleosomes.** As pictured in the current model of a nucleosome (Fig. 3–4), eight histones,

Figure 3–4. Schematic drawing of three nucleosomes connected by spacer regions. Each nucleosome, according to the current model, consists of eight closely packed histones (basic proteins) wrapped around with DNA. Straight segments of DNA, containing a single bound histone, occupy the spacer regions. Nucleosomes, strung together like beads on a string, form chromatin.

closely packed in the center of the particle, are wrapped around by 1¾ turns of DNA. The nucleosomes are connected by straight (spacer) segments of DNA, each of which contains a single bound histone, and are stretched out like beads on a string to form what is called **chromatin.** Nuclear protoplasm, called *nucleoplasm,* is typically colorless and transparent, but when a cell is stained with certain dyes, especially hematoxylin, which display a distinct affinity for nuclear materials, the chromatin appears in the light microscope as thin, elongated threads looped and massed together in such a way as to give the appearance of a network. Only during cell division is chromatin coiled and folded into the form of chromosomes — the often-pictured rodlike bodies.

Closely associated with the chromatin material can usually be found one to several larger masses, the *nucleoli.* At different times a nucleus may possess one, several, or no nucleoli. However, the number is usually fixed and definite for each type of cell. The nucleoli are sites for the synthesis of the RNA (ribonucleic acid) component of ribosomes (cytoplasmic organelles described below) and generally become enlarged during periods when a cell is actively synthesizing proteins.

In electron micrographs the nuclear membrane is revealed as a double-membrane structure, and it appears to be continuous at points with the endoplasmic reticulum (a cytoplasmic organelle described below). During mitosis, the nuclear membrane disappears and a new one re-forms later in each daughter cell.

Cytoplasm

Protoplasm outside the nucleus is called *cytoplasm.* It makes up the general storage and working area of the cell. Under the light microscope, the main body of cytoplasm gives the appearance of an optically clear fluid in which a variety of visible bodies are suspended. Prior to the development of the electron microscope, this was termed the "clean cytoplasmic matrix." However, such an expression is misleading, for electron micrographs have since shown that this so-called "clean" cytoplasm possesses a complex, ultramicroscopic structure. The struc-

tures which are contained in or compose the cytoplasm are of two general types: *organelle* and *inclusion* (Fig. 3–5). Organelles are active, organized, living material, converting energy and usually possessing a surrounding membrane. Inclusions are passive, often very temporary materials such as pigment, secretory granules, and aggregates of stored protein, lipid, or carbohydrate, which will be utilized by the cell in its life processes.

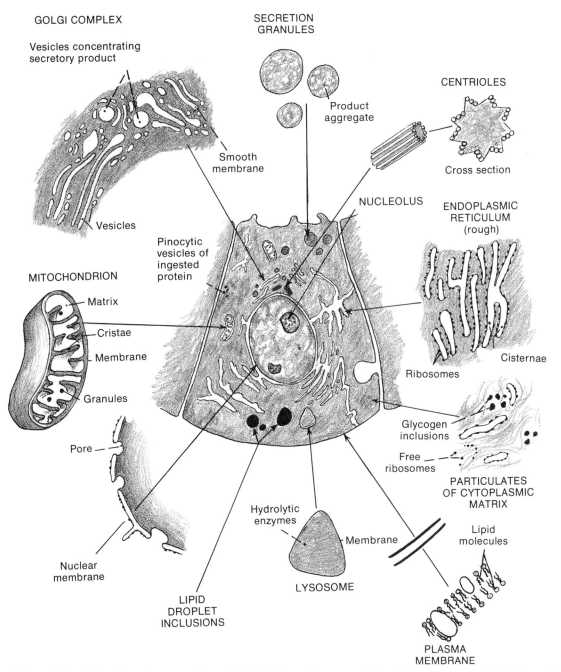

Figure 3–5. Parts of a cell as seen through the electron microscope. (After Bloom and Fawcett: *A Textbook of Histology,* 8th edition. Philadelphia, W. B. Saunders Co., 1962.)

Cytoplasmic Organelles

Endoplasmic Reticulum

From a structural point of view, the most impressive organelle is the network of channels or tubules pervading the entire cytoplasm, called the *endoplasmic reticulum.* Two distinct varieties, *smooth* and *rough,* can be seen, each with different functions. The rough type derives its name from the numerous granular *ribosomes* (see following paragraph) scattered over its surface, giving it a rough appearance (Fig. 3–6). It functions in the synthesis of proteins (on the attached ribosomes — see below) that will be exported from the cell (such as digestive enzymes, hormones, antibodies, and collagen) or packaged by the cell as organelles known as *lysosomes* (described below), which contain digestive enzymes. Most of the proteins incorporated into the cell membrane are probably also synthesized in the rough endoplasmic reticulum. The smooth endoplasmic reticulum, lacking attached ribosomes, is the site of various chemical transformations, including the synthesis of certain nonprotein substances, such as steroid hormones in cells of the adrenal gland and gonads, and the detoxification of foreign substances in liver

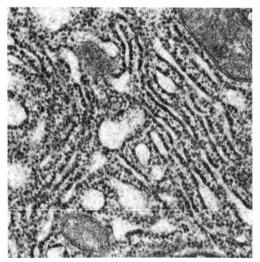

Figure 3–6. Electron micrograph of rough endoplasmic reticulum of a rabbit exocrine pancreatic cell (specialized for the synthesis of precursors of digestive enzymes). The attachment of numerous ribosomes (small, irregular, spheroidal bodies) to the external surface of the membranes of the endoplasmic reticulum (network of channels) gives rise to the term rough endoplasmic reticulum. Free ribosomes can also be seen in the cytoplasm between channels. (Magnification 41,000×.)

cells. In muscle cells the smooth endoplasmic reticulum, called the *sarcoplasmic reticulum* (G. *sarx,* flesh), sequesters and releases calcium ions, which act as the triggering agents for contraction.

Ribosomes

These dense aggregates of RNA (ribonucleic acid) and protein are the site of protein synthesis. As mentioned, when they are attached to the membrane of the endoplasmic reticulum to form the so-called rough endoplasmic reticulum, the proteins synthesized are mainly those destined to be packaged for secretion or as organelles called lysosomes. When packaging occurs, the proteins synthesized on the ribosomes are segregated from the cytoplasm of the cell in the cisternal space (cavity; L. *cisterna,* reservoir) of the rough endoplasmic reticulum and are transported to the *Golgi apparatus* (described in the following paragraph) for final processing. According to George Palade and colleagues, pioneers in the study of secretory proteins, transport from the rough endoplasmic reticulum to the Golgi apparatus is probably accomplished by "shuttling vesicles" moving between the two organelles.

Golgi Apparatus

The *Golgi complex* or *apparatus* is named after the Italian microscopist, Camillo Golgi, who discovered these bodies in 1898 using a special silver stain of his own. The Spanish histologist Ramón y Cajal was the first person to suggest that these bodies take part in the production of a substance to be secreted from cells. He drew this conclusion in 1914 upon observing droplets of mucus in the region of the Golgi apparatus in cells of the small intestine called *goblet cells,* which secrete a mucus that forms a protective coating on the free surface of the intestine. As indicated in the foregoing paragraphs, the Golgi apparatus is involved in the last stages of the production of and in the packaging of proteins to be secreted or retained in lysosomes. Most secretory proteins are glycoproteins. Side chains of sugars, called the core carbohydrate, are added in the rough endoplasmic reticulum, but one of the specific functions of the Golgi apparatus is to modify the core carbohydrate by the removal of some sugars and the addition of others. Various other chemical transformations in the Golgi apparatus produce a finished product. When the secretory proteins are digestive enzymes or hormones, concentration of the product is carried out in the Golgi apparatus with the formation of what are known as *secretory granules* — dense bodies enclosed by a membrane derived from the Golgi apparatus. Enzymes stored in secretory granules are in an inactive form called *proenzymes*. Release of the contents of secretory granules to the exterior of the cell at the appropriate time occurs by a process called *exocytosis* (G. *exo*, outside). This involves fusion of the membrane of the secretory granule with the plasma membrane and discharge of the product from an open pocket in the membrane.

Much of our knowledge of the assembly line production and packaging of secretory proteins has been gained from studies that combine the techniques of electron microscopy and radioautography. In this procedure, sections of tissues are prepared at intervals after administering a radioactively labeled amino acid, sugar, or other substance that will be incorporated into the new protein. Each section is coated with a photographic emulsion and stored in a light-tight box to allow the radioactivity to darken the film. Examination of the specimen in the electron microscope reveals the location of the newly synthesized protein in the cell. Figure 3–7 illustrates the course of events, as studied with this procedure, in the synthesis and secretion of digestive proenzymes by the pancreatic cell (which pass to the intestinal tract via the pancreatic duct).

Mitochondria

The "powerhouses" of the cell, *mitochondria*, contain the oxidative enzymes for the complete breakdown of fatty acids and for the terminal phase of the breakdown of glucose (described on page 58). In addition, they contain the enzyme system that accounts for the production of most of the ATP in the cell. ATP, as pointed out in Chapter 2, is the cell's primary energy-carrying molecule. When nutrients are degraded, the energy released is invested in the manufacture of ATP, which, in turn, by virtue of its energy-rich phosphate bonds, chiefly the terminal one, provides the power for the cell's many activities.

In electron micrographs, mitochondria exhibit a double membrane arrangement, with the inner membrane lifted into folds

Figure 3–7. Schematic diagram of the synthesis, packaging, and secretion of precursors of digestive enzymes (proenzymes) by a pancreatic cell following the administration of a radioactively labeled amino acid. The solid red line follows the sequence of events. The amino acids pass into the cell from a blood vessel. Proteins manufactured on ribosomes move up inside the endoplasmic reticulum and are transported to the Golgi apparatus. The final stages of the synthesis take place here and the concentration of the secretory product begins. Concentration continues in condensing vacuoles, presumably derived from the Golgi apparatus. The concentration process ends with the formation of secretory granules (also called zymogen granules) in which the enzymes are temporarily stored. Release of the secretory product from the cell is brought about by fusion of the granule membrane with the cell membrane and discharge of the granule contents from an open pocket.

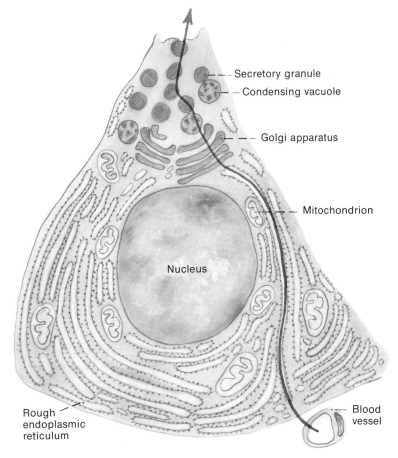

Secretory granule
Condensing vacuole
Golgi apparatus
Mitochondrion
Nucleus
Blood vessel
Rough endoplasmic reticulum

called *cristae* (Fig. 3–8). The enzymes breaking down fatty acids and most of those participating in the *Krebs cycle,* which carry out the final phase of the oxidation of fatty acids and glucose (see page 59), are located in the interior soluble portion of mitochondria known as the *matrix space.* The inner membrane is the site of ATP synthesis. It contains a series of electron carrier compounds, called the *respiratory,* or *electron transport, chain* (see Fig. 3–15), which release energy as electrons pass through the system. This energy is used for the phosphorylation (adding a phosphate group) of ADP (adenosine diphosphate), thereby forming ATP. The explanation now generally accepted for how electron transport is coupled to ATP synthesis is the **chemiosmotic theory** proposed by Peter Mitchell, who won the 1978 Nobel prize in chemistry for formulating it and providing much of the experimental proof. According to this theory (which was fiercely resisted for

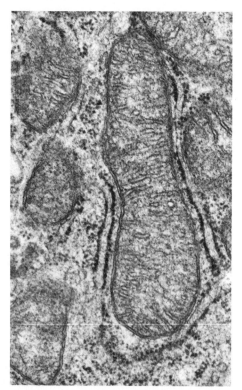

Figure 3–8. Electron micrograph of mitochondria from a human kidney tubule cell. Note the double membrane with invaginations of the inner one forming slender projections into the interior, called cristae. The interior portion of a mitochondrion is known as the matrix space. The space between the inner and outer membranes and between the cristal membranes is referred to as the intracristal space. (Magnification 41,000×.)

many years because most biochemists believed energy coupling involved high-energy chemical intermediates), the transfer of electrons through the respiratory chain drives protons (hydrogen ions) outward across the inner membrane, creating stored energy in the form of an electrochemical gradient. The reverse flow of protons is used by an enzyme complex (ATPase) to synthesize ATP. Several models have been proposed to explain how the proton gradient interacts with the enzyme complex to generate ATP, but none has been generally accepted.

Lysosomes

The name of this organelle (G. *lysis,* a loosening; G. *soma,* body) suggests its nature — a body containing digestive enzymes. The enzymes present in these structures are described as hydrolytic (G. *hydōr,* water) since they break down organic compounds by the addition of water. More than a dozen such enzymes, acting on virtually all classes of organic substances, have been identified in lysosomes.

Lysosomes were isolated in the early 1950's by Christian de Duve and associates. Their presence in the cell was suggested by the apparent leakage of a specific enzyme from a cell fraction containing mitochondria. De Duve and colleagues were using the newly developed procedure of centrifugal fractionation to isolate cell fractions. In this procedure the cells are disrupted in a homogenizer and centrifuged at successively higher speeds; each centrifugation yields a pellet containing a specific cell fraction (Fig. 3–9, *sequence A*). When de Duve *et al.* realized that the enzyme they were studying was not of a type associated with mitochondria and, therefore, must be in an unknown organelle of similar density and size, they had to modify the final step of the fractionation by introducing a density gradient in order to separate the two organelle fractions. A density gradient is formed by layering solutions of decreasing density from bottom to top in a centrifuge tube. During centrifugation the organelles of similar size come to rest in bands according to their densities (Fig. 3–9, *sequence B*).

Lysosomes are responsible for a number of cellular functions, including the following: (1) Digestion of bulky substances taken into the cell following *phagocytosis* (G. *phagein,* to eat), a process in which a section of the cell membrane forms a pocket enclosing the par-

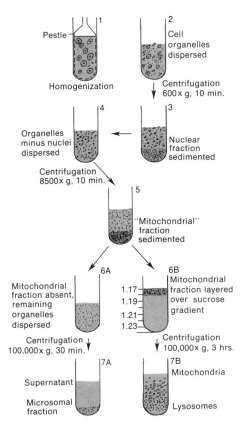

Figure 3–9. Isolation of cell organelles by centrifugation following disruption of the cell by homogenization is illustrated in these drawings. The sequence through 7A shows the recovery of nuclear, "mitochondrial," and microsomal (containing ribosomes) fractions. A modification of the procedure (6B and 7B), introduced by de Duve and colleagues, separates lysosomes from mitochondria in the "mitochondrial" fraction.

ticle, which pinches free and then fuses with a lysosome (Fig. 3–10). The digested particle may be a source of nutrition, but more commonly is a potentially harmful agent. Lysosomes are especially prominent in certain types of white blood cells and in macrophages, large phagocytic cells located outside the blood stream (Fig. 3–11). (2) *Autolysis* (G. *autos*, self), the self-destruction of cells after rupture of lysosomes. An example of this is the destruction of a structure formed during each menstrual cycle (the corpus luteum) that secretes female sex hormones. (3) *Autophagy* (self-eating), the digestion of organelles or parts of organelles taken into lysosomes during starvation. (4) Destruction of extracellular matter by discharging lysosomal enzymes to the outside of cells. An example of this is the release by bone cells of

enzymes that break down limited areas of bone matrix. This releases calcium from the bone and is one mechanism for maintaining normal levels of blood calcium (low blood calcium causes muscular irritability and, in extreme cases, convulsions). Release of lysosomal enzymes to the exterior of cells sometimes has harmful consequences. In arthritis, for example, the inflammation and tissue damage are caused by lysosomal enzymes. Aspirin and cortisone, drugs used to treat arthritis, stabilize lysosomal enzymes.

Centrioles

These are a pair of small, hollow, cylindrical structures, usually oriented at right angles to one another, located just outside the nucleus. Two pairs are seen in dividing cells. At the onset of cell division the centriole pairs move apart and become the poles of the cell to which each set of chromosomes migrates (for further details of cell division, see page 64).

Cytoplasmic Inclusions

These are various aggregations of material in the cell. They may be nutrients formed in the cell (such as glycogen granules, especially noticeable in liver and muscle cells, or fat droplets, which almost completely fill the fat cells of adipose tissue), pigments (such as melanin in cells of the skin), digestive vacuoles formed following phagocytosis, or the secretory granules described in the preceding paragraphs.

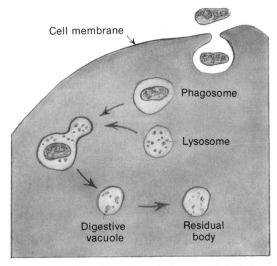

Figure 3–10. Digestion of a large particle by lysosomal enzymes following phagocytosis, showing fusion of a lysosome with the vesicle (phagosome) containing the particle to form a digestive vacuole.

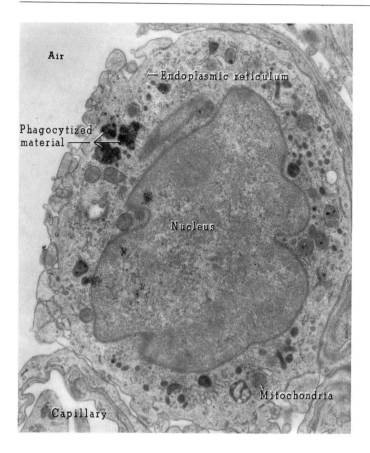

Air

—Endoplasmic reticulum

Phagocytized material —

Nucleus

Mitochondria

Capillary

Figure 3–11. Electron micrograph of a lung macrophage (alveolar macrophage) magnified 18,000×.

The Shape and Size of Cells

Different varieties of cells assume a wide spectrum of shapes. For example, nerve cells tend to be elongated and branched, while epithelial cells take the form of overlapping tiles, as in the skin, or of variously shaped bricks, as in the lining of the digestive tract. Generally speaking, the form of each cell bears a distinct relation to its particular function.

If a cell is removed from the restraining factors of its normal environment, it will tend strongly to a spherical shape as do all liquid particles because of the physics of the surface forces. For similar reasons, many cells are rounded and droplike when they first form by cell division and must expend energy to develop a desired shape. However, after a cell has assumed its final form, it may retain this shape in a variety of ways. It may secrete a rigid or semirigid nonliving coating that serves to hold the protoplasm in a definite mold; it may construct a delicate internal skeleton that supports the protoplasm; or it may, alternatively or in addition, stabilize its shape by a gelatinizing of the protoplasm or by pressure from surrounding cells.

As with shape, the size of the cell is related to its function. To support internal metabolism the cell must be able to obtain an adequate supply of oxygen and other nutrients and to give off carbon dioxide and other wastes. These necessary exchanges between the cell and the environment can occur only at the surface of the cell. Consequently, the surface of the cell must be adequately large in proportion to the protoplasmic volume. As the cell grows larger, the proportion of surface to volume steadily diminishes, with the surface area increasing as the square and the volume increasing as the cube of the diameter (Fig. 3–12).

This upper limit on size varies according to each particular cell shape and according to the intensity of its metabolism. Generally speaking, human cells with basically symmetrical shapes range between 1 and 100 micrometers (0.001 and 0.1 mm). There are, of course, exceptions. The total length of a

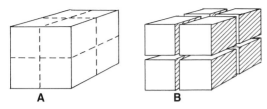

Figure 3–12. Illustrates increased surface area with fragmentation. *A* indicates lines of separation; *B* shows actual separation with increased surface area.

spinal sensory nerve fiber may reach from the toe to the medulla, but again the diameter is probably less than 10 micrometers, thus preserving a good surface-to-volume ratio.

The second physical limitation — the lower limit of size — seems to rest most critically on the physical properties of molecules and atoms. The specifics of this lower limit are still quite open to a variety of hypotheses because relevant data are scarce, primarily owing to the limitations, or lack, of instruments to probe at this level.

PHYSIOLOGY OF THE CELL

The human body is composed of about one hundred trillion cells which are arranged in tissues to carry out remarkably specialized functions, such as skeletal support, muscular contraction, and conduction of electrical impulses. Besides these specialized functions, most cells carry out vital general functions, three of which will be considered here. The three are movement of substances across the cell membranes, energy metabolism, and enzymatic action.

Movement Across the Cell Membrane

In order to maintain life activities and perform a diversity of tasks, cells must have rather precise control over their internal concentrations of various chemical substances. To regulate these concentrations, the cells must continually take in and expel substances involved in cellular functioning.

Cell physiologists have long considered an understanding of the exchange mechanisms between the cell and its environment to be fundamental to understanding the overall physiology of the cell and the integration of many cells to form higher organisms. Any exchange, of course, must occur at the surface of the cell, across the cell membrane. Mechanisms by which this exchange occurs include diffusion, osmosis, active transport, pinocytosis, and phagocytosis.

Physiochemical Basis of Diffusion. *Diffusion* may be described as a *net* transport of particles from a region in which they are more concentrated to a region in which they are less concentrated. This occurs because of the random motion of particles, which tends to bring about equal concentration of particles throughout a closed system. Characteristic of all matter is its kinetic or thermal (heat) motion; that is, the motion of atoms or molecules as units in relation to one another. At absolute zero ($-273°$ C) movement ceases. It increases as the temperature increases.

If two salt solutions of different concentrations are placed in a closed container and separated by a membrane that does not present a barrier to the salt, the salt on both sides of the membrane will disperse throughout the chamber. In time, the concentration of salt on each side of the membrane will be equal, and a net movement of salt from the region of high to the region of low concentration will have occurred.

The equilibrium, once achieved, is not an idle one in which thermal motion and exchange of molecules between the two solutions ceases in any sense. Rather, it is dynamic, involving a continuous rearrangement of the relative positions of the molecules. Equilibrium is simply the point at which the exchanges are equivalent, producing no change in concentrations.

Diffusion Through the Cell Membrane. As mentioned earlier, the structural fabric of the cell membrane consists of a bilayer of phospholipids, with their hydrophilic heads facing the aqueous medium on the membrane surfaces and their hydrophobic tails facing the interior of the membane. The incompatibility of the interior of the membrane with water and small, water-soluble substances, such as metal ions, simple sugars, and amino acids, creates a barrier through which they cannot freely diffuse (see Table 3–1). But the diffusion rates of these substances through biological membranes are greater than would be expected from the foregoing or from studies of their passage through artificial phospholipid membranes (phospholipids spontaneously form bilayer films in water). This has led to the concept that membrane proteins provide channels and act as carriers to facilitate the flow of

Table 3-1   TABLE OF PERMEABILITIES (PASSIVE)

VERY RAPID	RAPID	SLOW	VERY SLOW	VIRTUALLY NO PENETRATION
Gases	Water	(Simple	Strong electrolytes	Complex (colloidal)
Carbon dioxide		organic	Inorganic salts	compounds
Oxygen		substances)	Acids	Proteins
Nitrogen		Glucose	Bases	Polysaccharides
Fat solvents		Amino acids	Disaccharides	Phospholipids
Alcohol		Glycerol	Sucrose	
Ether		Fatty acids	Maltose	
Chloroform			Lactose	

From Marsland: *Principles of Modern Biology.* P. 116, Table 6–1.

these substances through cell membranes. Studies making use of compounds such as the antibiotic valomycin, which functions as a carrier for potassium, increasing its rate of diffusion through biological and artificial membranes, have provided experimental support for the carrier hypothesis. A carrier, it is assumed, binds a substance at one surface of the membrane, then migrates to the opposite surface and releases it. Carrier-aided transport is usually referred to as *facilitated diffusion* and is an important mechanism for controlling the permeability of membranes.

Osmosis is a special case of diffusion. It refers to the diffusion of water through membranes where a difference between the concentration of solutes (dissolved substances) is maintained on opposite sides of the membrane by the impermeability of the membrane to the solute or by active transport (discussed below) of the solute from one side to the other. Under this circumstance only the water molecules equilibrate. As a result there is a net transfer of water from the dilute solution (where the water molecules are more highly concentrated) to the concentrated solution. The force with which a solution draws water into it is called *osmotic pressure.* The higher the concentration of a solution, the greater is its osmotic pressure. Osmotic pressure can be conveniently measured in a *mercury osmometer* (Fig. 3–13). In it a semipermeable membrane (allowing only water to pass through it) separates distilled water from the solution to be tested. Water will flow into the test solution until the pressure of the column of mercury balances the osmotic pressure of the test solution. The osmotic pressure of a solution is expressed as mm of mercury.

Cells in a *hypertonic* solution (one whose osmotic pressure is greater than that of the cell) will shrink. They will swell in a

hypotonic solution (osmotic pressure lower than the cell's). No change will occur in an *isotonic* solution (osmotic pressure the same as the cell's).

Active Transport. Diffusion and osmosis are referred to as passive transport processes because the driving force for transport is provided not by the membrane but by the *concentration gradient,* which causes the net

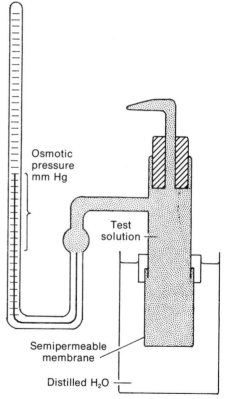

Osmotic
pressure
mm Hg

Test
solution

Semipermeable
membrane

Distilled H$_2$O

Figure 3–13. Measurement of osmotic pressure with a Pfeffer mercury osmometer. Distilled water passes through the semipermeable membrane into the test solution until the pressure of the column of mercury counterbalances the osmotic pressure of the test solution.

movement of substances from regions of high concentration to regions of low. In active transport the cell uses energy to transport substances against a concentration gradient; that is, from a region of low concentration to one of high. For example, all cells maintain a high external concentration of sodium compared with the internal concentration; the reverse is true of potassium. If the production of ATP is blocked by metabolic poisons, the tendency of sodium and potassium to equilibrate will cause cell death. Active transport mechanisms exist for a number of other substances in addition to sodium and potassium. For example, the cells of the thyroid gland actively concentrate iodine (a component of the hormone thyroxine). In fact, practically all of the iodine in the body is inside these cells. Cells lining the intestines and kidney tubules transport various ions and certain sugars and amino acids against concentration gradients from their lumens (tubular interiors) to the blood stream. Active transport of glucose and certain other simple sugars appears to be coupled to the active transport of sodium. If active sodium transport (the so-called sodium pump) is blocked, active transport of these sugars will not occur.

Various models have been proposed to explain active transport. All assume that protein carriers which become mobile by changes in shape are involved. In one such model, illustrated in Figure 3–14, binding of the substance to be transported changes the shape of the carrier, enabling it to rotate. The carrier assumes an immobile form after releasing the substance on the opposite side of the membrane. Return to the mobile form requires the expenditure of metabolic energy.

Importance of Changes in the Permeability of Membranes. It should be emphasized that it is essential for the special functions of some cells for changes in permeability to occur in response to specific stimuli. In the membranes of nerve and muscle fibers, for example, changes in the permeability to sodium and potassium following excitation are responsible for the initiation and propagation of the electrical impulse. Regulation of the volume of body fluids by the kidneys depends, in part, upon changes in the permeability of cells of the kidney tubules to water in response to ADH, the antidiuretic hormone.

Pinocytosis and Phagocytosis. Pinocytosis (G. *pinein,* to drink; G. *kytos,* cell) and

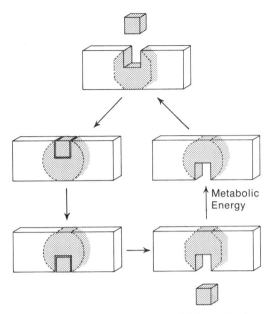

Figure 3–14. A suggested model for active transport. A protein carrier changes shape to a form that can rotate after binding a substance to be transported across the membrane. It returns to an immobile form after releasing the substance. To enable the carrier to return the binding site to its original position, energy input is required to change the shape of the protein to the mobile form. After rotating, it is again in an immobile form.

phagocytosis (G. *phagein,* to eat) are energy-dependent, active processes of ingestion by the cell of substances present in the extracellular fluid. The two processes are quite similar, each involving an incupping, or invagination, of the cell membrane and subsequent closure of the external opening to form a vesicle containing materials from the extracellular fluids. The term phagocytosis is applied to the ingestion of large particulate matter such as bacteria, coagulated organic matter, and some other cells, whereas pinocytosis is the ingestion of dissolved molecular substances. Phagocytic vesicles (phagosomes) are easily seen through the light microscope and were observed in white blood cells as long ago as the end of the 19th century by Elie Metchnikoff of the Pasteur Institute. However, pinocytic vesicles are considerably smaller and were first detected with time-lapse photography in tissue-culture cells in 1931 by the American physiologist Warren Lewis. Pinocytosis was largely ignored until it was widely observed with the electron microscope in the 1950's.

Phagocytosis, like pinocytosis, is an auxiliary means by which the cells may take in various substances needed for metabolic processes. Phagocytosis more commonly serves a further specialized function of great significance in the disease and infection treatment systems of the body. Certain types of white blood cells, generally known as phagocytes, are highly specialized to deal with foreign substances, including bacteria and small parasites, that enter the body and are potential causes of various harmful actions. Almost immediately after a vesicle moves toward the interior of the cell, it fuses with a lysosome to form a *digestive vacuole* (see Fig. 3–10, illustrating lysosome function). Indigestible matter remains in *residual bodies*, which are usually retained for a long time but may fuse with the cell membrane and excrete their contents. Phagocytic white blood cells die after accumulating excessive amounts of debris in this manner. The gradual accumulation of residues in other cells of the body is believed to contribute to their aging.

Energy Metabolism

Metabolism is a general term used to describe all the chemical reactions occurring in living matter. Energy metabolism, an aspect of metabolism that is of fundamental importance to all cells, refers to the chemical degradation of nutrients by the cell to produce the energy it needs to perform such functions as active transport, muscular contraction, and biochemical synthesis. As mentioned earlier in this chapter and in Chapter 2, the energy released by the degradation of nutrient substances is not utilized directly by the cell for the performance of its work. Rather, the energy is used to generate ATP (adenosine triphosphate) from ADP (adenosine diphosphate), and the energy contained in the high-energy bonds of ATP is in turn directly utilized by the cell for functions requiring energy input (see Figure 2–13, page 39, for the structure of ATP). Studies with isolated frog muscles in the 1930's led to the discovery of ATP's energy-carrying role in the cell. At that time it was generally believed that the breakdown of glycogen to lactic acid provided the direct source of energy for muscular contraction. However, this belief was contradicted by the observation that a muscle could contract when stimulated even though treated with poisons that block

the breakdown of glycogen to lactic acid. Subsequent studies over a period of years proved that ATP is the immediate source of energy for the contraction. By the 1940's it was generally acknowledged that ATP is not only the direct source of energy for muscular contraction, but serves as what has been called a general "energy currency" for use by the cell in performing its work.

How the chemical energy of ATP is utilized by cells has been the subject of considerable study and speculation. It was originally postulated that energy transfer involves the donation of the terminal phosphate of ATP to specific acceptor molecules to energize them. Although this seems to be an important mechanism for making ATP's energy available to the cell, it is not the only one. For one thing, in many cases the two terminal phosphate groups are split off as a unit, leaving a molecule of AMP (adenosine monophosphate). This occurs, for example, during the activation of fatty acids (to form a combination of the fatty acid with coenzyme A), with a fatty acid-AMP complex apparently becoming bound to an enzyme in an intermediate step. Furthermore, even when only the terminal phosphate of ATP is split off to yield ADP in ATP-utilizing systems, the sequence of events may be more involved than the donation of a phosphate to an acceptor molecule. The contraction of muscle may be one such case. It has been proposed that during the cycle of contraction and relaxation ATP binds to the protein myosin, and following the cleavage of ATP to ADP an energized complex of myosin, ADP, and phosphate is formed.

Most of the ATP in the cell is generated by the addition of a phosphate to ADP during the breakdown of glucose and the fatty acid component of fat. The initial phase of the breakdown of glucose (to pyruvic or lactic acid) takes place in the cytoplasm of the cell. The remaining reactions occur in mitochondria. All of the enzymes involved in the degradation of fatty acid are located in mitochondria. The breakdown of fatty acids occurs under aerobic conditions only — that is, only in the presence of oxygen. The fatty acids are completely disrupted to carbon dioxide and water. Under most circumstances glucose, too, is aerobically degraded to carbon dioxide and water. The utilization of glucose in the absence of oxygen does occur, however, and is especially important during strenuous exercise, when active muscles cannot be adequately supplied with oxygen. Under these (anaerobic) conditions the breakdown of glucose ends with the formation of lactic acid (a process called *glycolysis*). Much less ATP is produced by the anaerobic breakdown of glucose than by the aerobic breakdown. Maximum ATP production comes from the oxidative breakdown of fatty acids. Oxidation of a gram of fatty acid to carbon dioxide and water yields about two and one half times as much ATP as oxidation of a gram of glucose to carbon dioxide and water.

Figures 3–15 and 3–16 illustrate ATP formation during the breakdown of glucose and palmitic acid, a 16-carbon fatty acid. These illustrations are not meant to be an exercise in the study of biochemical pathways (subject matter for a course in biochemistry) but to show why the yield of ATP is maximal when fatty acids are oxidized to carbon dioxide and minimal when glucose is anaerobically degraded to lactic acid.

Let us follow first the **ATP yields from the anaerobic and aerobic breakdown of glucose.** The anaerobic degradation of glucose, called *glycolysis,* yields lactic acid as the final product. ATP is produced in just two steps (6 and 8) by the *transfer of phosphate groups to ADP from high energy phosphate compounds* formed during the glycolytic sequence. Since in step 4 a hexose is split into two trioses (3-carbon sugars), one an intermediate in the glycolytic pathway, the other converted to it, the formation of one ATP per triose molecule in steps 6 and 8 results in the formation of two molecules of ATP per glucose molecule in each of these steps. Hence, four molecules of ATP are generated and, after subtracting two molecules of ATP used up in priming steps (1 and 3), the net yield is two molecules of ATP per molecule of glucose. During the aerobic breakdown of glucose to carbon dioxide and water, ATP is also produced in steps 6 and 8, but, in addition, a far greater number of ATP molecules are produced by what is known as *oxidative phosphorylation,* a process in which the synthesis of ATP from ADP and inorganic phosphate is coupled to the transfer of electrons from chemical intermediates to oxygen via the mitochondrial *respiratory chain* (the generally accepted theory accounting for the coupling of electron transfer to the synthesis of ATP is described on page 52 of this chap-

ter). When glucose is degraded anaerobically, electrons taken up by NAD^+ (the oxidized form of nicotinamide adenine dinucleotide — the reduced form, carrying electrons, written $NADH + H^+$) in step 5 are released in step 9a, in which pyruvic acid is reduced to lactic acid. When the aerobic pathway is operating, however, lactic acid is not formed, and electrons picked up in step 5 are delivered to the respiratory chain, as are electrons removed in step 9b (the conversion of pyruvic acid to acetyl-CoA) and in steps 12, 13, 15, and 17 following the entry of acetyl-CoA into the Krebs, or citric acid, cycle (also called the tricarboxylic acid cycle). NAD^+ is the electron acceptor in all steps but 15, in which FAD (flavin adenine dinucleotide, the reduced form, carrying electrons, written $FADH_2$) is the electron acceptor. The experimental evidence has generally been interpreted as indicating that in NAD-linked electron transport in mitochondria three molecules of ATP are synthesized from ADP and inorganic phosphate for each pair of electrons transferred to oxygen (one at each of three sites in the respiratory chain) and that in FAD-linked electron transport two molecules of ATP are synthesized per pair of electrons (bypassing the first energy-coupling site in the respiratory chain). Electron transfer from step 5, which takes place not in mitochondria but in the cytoplasm of the cell, is a special case. The electrons cannot directly enter the respiratory chain because reduced NAD cannot penetrate the inner membrane of mitochondria; therefore, the electrons are "shuttled" into mitochondria via chemical intermediates. In some tissues the entry of these electrons into the respiratory chain is NAD linked; in others it is not. Hence, in some tissues the theoretical ATP yield per electron pair in this step is three and in others two. If we accept these ATP/electron pair ratios for oxidative phosphorylation, the net yield of ATP per molecule of glucose aerobically oxidized to carbon dioxide and water may be calculated as follows: six each in steps 9b, 12, 13, and 17; four in step 15; either four or six in step 5; and an additional two each in steps 6, 8, and 14 (step 14, like steps 6 and 8, does not involve oxidative phosphorylation, and ATP is formed when a phosphate group is transferred from guanosine triphosphate, abbreviated GTP, to ADP). This adds up to 38 or 40 molecules of ATP, and, after subtracting the

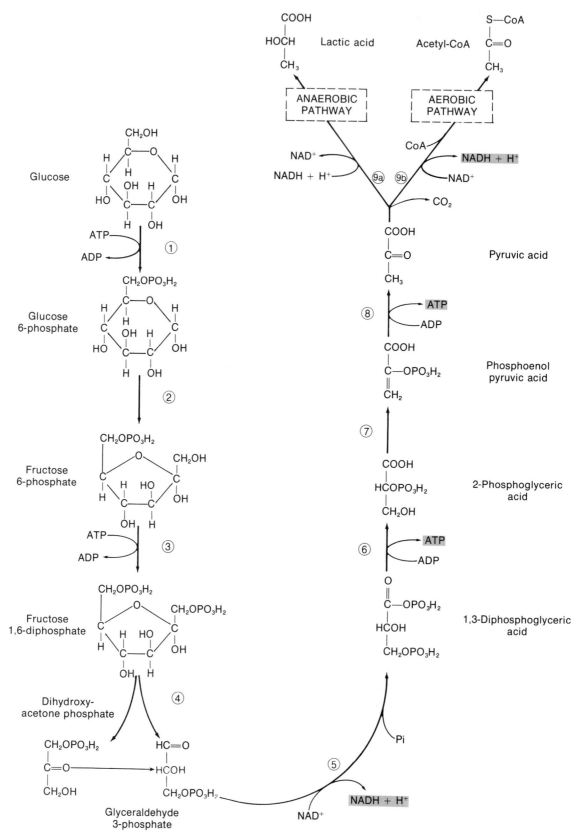

Figure 3–15. *See legend on opposite page*

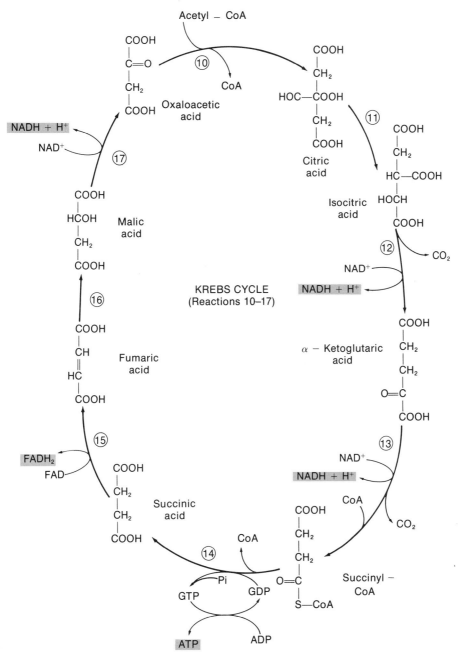

Figure 3–15. The breakdown of glucose anaerobically to lactic acid (glycolysis) and aerobically to carbon dioxide and water. When glucose is degraded anaerobically, ATP is produced only at reactions 6 and 8 by the transfer of phosphate from high energy phosphate compounds to ADP. Most of the ATP produced during the aerobic breakdown of glucose is accounted for by oxidative phosphorylation, that is, the coupling of the synthesis of ATP from ADP and inorganic phosphate to the transfer of pairs of electrons (removed in steps 5 and 9b in the sequence leading to the formation of acetyl-CoA and in steps 12, 13, 15, and 17 in the Krebs cycle) to oxygen via the mitochondrial respiratory chain. NAD^+ and FAD are the abbreviations for the oxidized forms of the electron carriers nicotinamide adenine dinucleotide and flavin adenine dinucleotide; the reduced forms, carrying electrons, are written $NADH + H^+$ and $FADH_2$. Pi is inorganic phosphate.

Illustration continued on following page

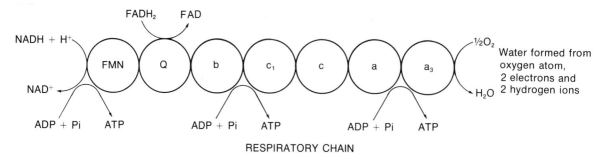

RESPIRATORY CHAIN

Figure 3–15 *Continued.* In the respiratory chain the abbreviations for the components are as follows: FMN, flavin mononucleotide; Q, the lipid-soluble coenzyme Q, or ubiquinone; and b, c_1, c, a, a_3, the series of cytochromes (heme proteins). The experimental evidence has generally been considered to indicate that in mitochondrial NAD-linked electron transfer three molecules of ATP are synthesized (each at a specific energy-coupling site in the respiratory chain) for each pair of electrons transferred to oxygen and that two molecules of ATP are synthesized for each electron pair in FAD-linked electron transfer (because the first energy-coupling site in the chain is bypassed).

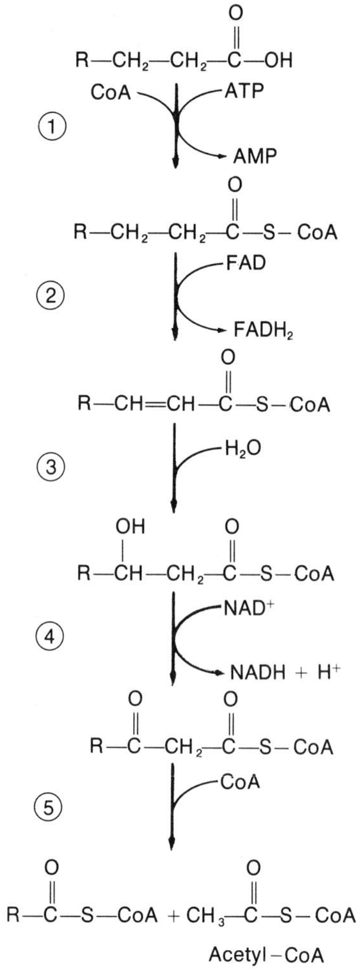

$$R—CH_2—CH_2—\overset{\overset{\displaystyle O}{\|}}{C}—OH$$

CoA ⟍ ⟋ATP

①

→ AMP

$$R—CH_2—CH_2—\overset{\overset{\displaystyle O}{\|}}{C}—S—CoA$$

⟋FAD

②

→ FADH$_2$

$$R—CH{=}CH—\overset{\overset{\displaystyle O}{\|}}{C}—S—CoA$$

⟋H$_2$O

③

$$R—\overset{\overset{\displaystyle OH}{|}}{CH}—CH_2—\overset{\overset{\displaystyle O}{\|}}{C}—S—CoA$$

⟋NAD$^+$

④

→ NADH + H$^+$

$$R—\overset{\overset{\displaystyle O}{\|}}{C}—CH_2—\overset{\overset{\displaystyle O}{\|}}{C}—S—CoA$$

⟋CoA

⑤

$$R—\overset{\overset{\displaystyle O}{\|}}{C}—S—CoA + CH_3—\overset{\overset{\displaystyle O}{\|}}{C}—S—CoA$$

Acetyl–CoA

Figure 3–16. Sequence of reactions leading to the splitting off of the terminal two carbons of a fatty acid with the formation of acetyl-CoA. R represents the remainder of the fatty acid chain. Reactions 2 through 5 are repeated until the fatty acid is completely cleaved. Since each cleavage is preceded by oxidation of the β carbon (second from the carboxyl carbon), the degradation of fatty acids is often called β oxidation. In the case of palmitic acid, a 16-carbon fatty acid, cleavage occurs seven times, and eight molecules of acetyl-CoA are formed.

two molecules of ATP used in steps 1 and 3, the net yield is 36 or 38 molecules of ATP per molecule of glucose, 18 or 19 times the yield from glycolysis. (Since some investigators have recently suggested that the ratio of three molecules of ATP per electron pair in NAD-linked electron transport is too high, this calculation may represent the upper limit of the net ATP yield from the aerobic degradation of glucose.)

ATP formation from the breakdown of the 16-carbon fatty acid, palmitic acid, can be considered in two stages: (1) disruption to eight acetyl-CoA units by a stepwise sequence which removes 2-carbon fragments one at a time, and (2) entry of the acetyl-CoA's into the Krebs cycle. The second stage, of course, is common to the oxidation of glucose and fatty acids. Since fatty acids contain more hydrogen atoms per carbon atom than glucose, more electrons and hydrogen ions can be removed from fatty acids than from glucose and delivered to the respiratory chain.

As illustrated in Figure 3–16, each time a 2-carbon fragment is split off the fatty acid chain to form acetyl-CoA, electron pairs are removed in two of the steps of the reaction sequence. Since in one of the steps FAD is the electron carrier and in the other NAD is the electron carrier, each cleavage generates five molecules of ATP (again, assuming that the ATP/electron pair ratio is three in mitochondrial NAD-linked electron transport and two in FAD-linked electron transport). Since palmitic acid is cleaved seven times, this produces 35 molecules of ATP. The passage of each molecule of acetyl-CoA through the Krebs cycle yields 12 molecules of ATP (three each in steps 12, 13, and 17; one in step 14; and two in step 15). Hence, 96 ATP's are produced when the eight acetyl-CoA's derived from the breakdown of palmitic acid pass through the Krebs cycle. The complete oxidation of a molecule of palmitic acid, therefore, yields 96 + 35, or 131, molecules of ATP. Subtracting the two ATP's used in the initial activation step (in which adenosine monophosphate, abbreviated AMP, is formed during an intermediate sequence), the net yield is 129 molecules of ATP per molecule of palmitic acid. This is about $3\frac{1}{2}$ times the ATP yield per molecule of glucose. Since the molecular weights of palmitic acid and glucose are 256 and 180, respectively, the net yield of ATP per gram of palmitic acid comes to about $2\frac{1}{2}$ times the yield per gram of glucose.

Enzymatic Action

As we have indicated, the cell is able to carry out chemical reactions under the limited physical and chemical conditions necessary for its existence (low temperature and pressure, and almost neutral pH) because of the presence of enzymes, the large protein molecules that act as catalysts to speed up the rates of chemical reactions. Without enzymes, reactions would proceed so slowly that life could not exist. Most enzymes are highly specific in their activity, each type being involved in only one reaction.

The word *enzyme* was coined from two Greek words meaning "in yeast." Subsequent to Pasteur's discovery that the souring of milk and wine and fermentation of sugars depend upon the presence of contaminating yeast cells, it was found that yeast juice could also ferment sugars. Eventually, the study of these so-called cell-free extracts led to the discovery of enzymes, all of which were found to be proteins. The protein chains in enzymes are coiled and folded into various globular shapes. How enzymes function has been a subject of intense study by biochemists. For a long time it was believed that the *substrate* (substance acted upon by the enzyme) and the enzyme fitted together rigidly, as a key fits a lock, at a part of the enzyme called the active site. Interaction of substrate and enzyme at this site, it was thought, reduced the energy needed for chemical change. However, several lines of evidence, including x-ray analysis, which has revealed that parts of the enzyme molecule move with respect to one another when the substrate is bound to the active site, suggest that the lock and key model is inaccurate. A more acceptable model, the "induced fit" model, formulated largely by Daniel Koshland and colleagues, proposes that the shape of the active site is not exactly complementary to that of the substrate, but is induced to take a complementary shape in the same way a glove takes the shape of a hand. This interaction between enzyme and substrate causes distortions and changes in orientation of the substrate, atomic rearrangements, and other changes which lead to the activation or rupture of the substrate. The "induced fit" model of enzyme action is consistent with the growing recognition that many actions of proteins, including, as already discussed, their action as carriers for active transport in cell membranes, involve changes in protein shape.

CELL REPRODUCTION

In the introductory history of the cell principle (page 45) it was pointed out that since the latter part of the 19th century biologists have agreed that new cells arise from preexisting parent cells. From their original formation, cells are continually growing and, eventually, reach a size (usually about double) at which they must either stop growing or divide. In the human body all populations of cells, except highly differentiated cells, such as nerve cells, are capable of undergoing cell division. In some regions of the body, such as in the skin, the lining of the intestines, and the blood-cell–forming system of the red bone marrow, cell division proceeds continuously under precise control so that the renewal rate exactly compensates for the death rate. Some parts of the body, such as the liver and kidneys, have been described as "discontinuous replicators." Cells in these organs divide at a low "wear and tear" replacement rate. Cells of the immunological defense system are an interesting special case. They multiply rapidly in response to contact with specific, harmful microorganisms or other foreign matter. Although the mechanism by which the rate of cell division is controlled is still not well understood, one widely discussed theory has received some experimental support. This theory proposes a negative feedback system in which the release of an inhibitor of cell division by mature cells of a given tissue controls cell proliferation of immature cells in that tissue. Substances that inhibit cell division, called **chalones** (a term derived from a Greek word meaning to slack off the main sheet of a sloop to slow it down), have been extracted from a variety of tissues. Chalones act only on the tissues from which they have been isolated. It is generally believed that the tissue specificity depends upon interaction between the chalones and the outer surface of the cell membrane. Loss of chalones, by wounds or surgical removal of large portions of an organ such as the liver, it is assumed, stimulates cell division until repair or replacement is accomplished.

The Cell Cycle

In populations of dividing cells, the sequence of growth and cell division is generally referred to as the *cell cycle*. The period of cell division is called *mitosis;* the period of growth between divisions is known as *interphase*. During one phase of the latter period DNA replicates. This phase of the cell cycle (typically lasting about six hours) is designated the *S phase*, to signify that DNA synthesis is taking place. Periods of growth prior to and following the S phase are designated G_1 and G_2, respectively. G_1 usually lasts about eight hours, but in a long cell cycle lasts much longer. G_2 usually lasts about five hours. Mitosis, designated *M*, lasts about one hour.

Stages of Mitosis (Fig. 3–17)

Prophase. 1. Chromosome: The DNA protein complex (chromatin network of threads) becomes coiled, and chromosomes can easily be seen on stained sections. As the chromosomes become larger, they can be seen to be duplicated into two highly coiled strands (chromatids) which are attached to one another by a centromere.

2. Nucleolus: During the last part of prophase, the nucleolus disappears.

3. Nuclear membrane: The nuclear membrane disappears during the late prophase period.

4. Centrioles: Each pair of centrioles migrates to the opposite side of the cell and a figure called the *mitotic spindle* is formed which extends from one centriole pair to the other. The spindle is composed of thin fibrils, or *astral rays.*

Metaphase. 1. Chromosomes: The chromosomes move toward the center of the cell and arrange themselves in a plane perpendicular to a line connecting the two centrioles. This plane is called the equatorial plate.

2. Nucleolus: Absent.

3. Nuclear membrane: Absent.

4. Centrioles and spindle: The thin fibrils from the centrioles appear to be attached to the chromosomes at the centromere.

Anaphase. 1. Chromosomes: The centromere divides, releasing the members of the chromatid pair from each other.

2. Nucleolus: Absent

3. Nuclear membrane: Absent.

4. Centrioles and spindle: The astral ray fibrils give the appearance of pulling the chromatids toward the opposite centrioles by

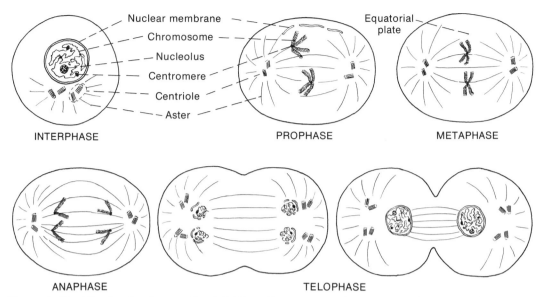

Figure 3–17. Mitosis, showing details of division. Shown are a pair of identical (homologous) chromosomes. Prior to the onset of mitosis, DNA replicates, giving rise to the double-stranded chromosomes that become apparent during mitosis. In prophase the two strands of each chromosome, attached to a common centromere, can be clearly seen. In metaphase the centromeres of the double-stranded chromosomes are lined up along the equatorial plate. The centromeres divide and, during anaphase, the single strands move toward the centrioles at opposite poles of the cell. The end results of mitosis are two daughter cells with the same genetic composition as the original parent cell.

their attachments to the centromeres. When the chromatids have been separated from each other, they are again called chromosomes. The significant feature of this stage is that one chromatid from each chromosome finds its way into each daughter cell, giving each cell an identical complement of chromosomes.

Telophase. 1. Chromosomes: The chromosomes reach the general location of the centrioles and begin to uncoil.

2. Nucleolus: A nucleolus appears in each cell.

3. Nuclear membrane: The nuclear membrane re-forms around each group of chromosomes.

4. Centrioles and spindle: As the chromosomes uncoil the spindle disappears.

5. Cell membrane: The cell membrane indents at the point of the equatorial plate, dividing the cytoplasm into two parts.

Mitosis permits perpetuation. There is a duplication of all cell parts with provision for transmitting a controlling mechanism into each of the cells produced. The details of the process are obscure, but the task is obviously performed with efficiency and accuracy, considering that it occurs more than a billion times during human development.

Chromosome Number

Number of Chromosomes in the Human Cell. There are 23 pairs, or 46 chromosomes, in human somatic, or body, cells and 23 in the gametes (sperm or ovum). In Figure 3–18, illustrating the chromosomes of human body cells, note that the members of 22 of these pairs are exactly alike, that these identical pairs can be distinguished from one another by overall length and the position of the centromeres, and that they are numbered from 1 to 22 in order of decreasing size. The 22 *homologous* (G. *homos*, one and the same) pairs, called *autosomes*, bear genes for the same traits. The 23rd pair, designated X and Y, are the sex chromosomes. Females have two X chromosomes, males one X and one Y. Genes present only on the larger X chromosome (the genes for red-green color blindness, for example) are called sex-linked genes.

Meiosis

Body cells containing two of each type of chromosomes are described as diploid. Gametes, containing only one type of each, are called haploid cells. Meiosis is a special

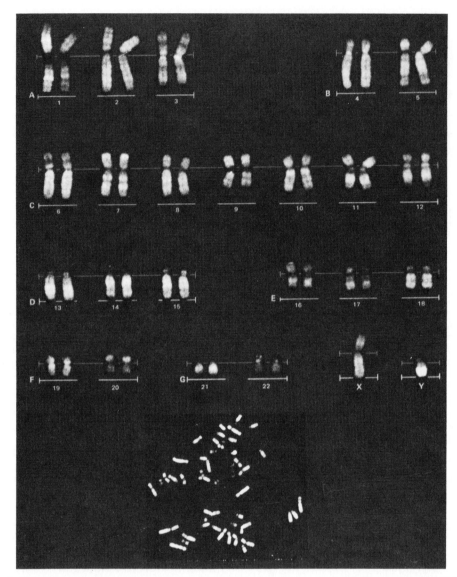

Figure 3–18. Normal human male karyotype stained with quinacrine mustard dihydrochloride (Q-banded). The term karyotype refers to this standard arrangement, in which homologous chromosomes are identified by their length and the position of the centromere joining the separate strands of each chromosome and numbered in order of decreasing size. Chromosomes X and Y are the sex chromosomes. (Courtesy of Douglas Hepburn, Clinical Cytogenetics Laboratory, University of Oregon Health Sciences Center.)

two-step sequence of cell division, occurring during the maturation of sex cells, in which the diploid number of chromosomes is reduced to the haploid number. The first division of the sequence is called the reduction division. At metaphase of the reduction division, double-stranded homologous chromosomes line up as pairs (synaptic pairs), rather than individually, in a row (Fig. 3–19). Each member of the pair is pulled to the opposite pole of the cell. Thus, reduction division

gives rise to two cells containing one set of double-stranded chromosomes. The second division, mitotic division of the two daughter cells, will produce (if all cells formed survive) four haploid gametes. In humans, four mature sperm cells but only one mature ovum (one cell surviving each division) are produced from each parent cell by the process of meiosis. The production of sex cells will be discussed in greater detail in Chapter 18.

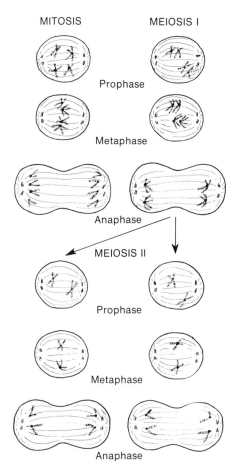

MITOSIS   MEIOSIS I

Prophase

Metaphase

Anaphase

MEIOSIS II

Prophase

Metaphase

Anaphase

Figure 3–19. Prophase, metaphase, and anaphase compared in mitosis and the two divisions of meiosis. Parent cells containing two pairs of chromosomes are shown to illustrate both processes. In prophase, each chromosome can be seen as a double strand (each strand called a chromatid). The four chromosomes lie apart in mitosis and as two pairs (synaptic pairs) in meiosis I (the reduction division). During mitosis the four chromosomes are lined up in a single row along the equatorial plate in metaphase, and in anaphase the individual strands of each separate and are pulled to opposite poles. Completion of cell division results in two daughter cells, each containing two pairs of single-stranded chromosomes. In the reduction division of meiosis, the synaptic pairs line up along the equatorial plate during metaphase, and in anaphase one member of each pair (still double-stranded) is pulled to the opposite pole. Reduction division gives rise to two cells, each containing one double-stranded member of each pair of chromosomes. When the second (mitotic) division of meiosis takes place and the double strands separate, each daughter cell receives one single-stranded member of each chromosome pair and thus contains half as many (haploid number) chromosomes as the parent cell. In humans, meiosis reduces the number of chromosomes from 46 in nonsexual cells to 23 in sperm and egg cells.

CELLULAR GENETICS

The Gene

The science of genetics began over a hundred years ago when an Austrian monk, Gregor Mendel, watched successive generations of peas grow. Noting the specific gross characteristics of successive generations of plants, Mendel came to conceive the genetic information in terms of *units,* now called **genes** (from the Greek "to be born"). Thus, there is a gene for each characteristic — such as weight, color of flower, etc. — contributed to the fertilized seed by each parent. He also developed the ideas of dominant and recessive genes to explain the greater frequency of regular occurrence of one parent's trait over the other's. For instance, the gene determining a white flower was dominant and the gene for a red flower was recessive, so that the offspring of parents, each with a long ancestral history of only one of these genes, would tend to have more white flowers than

red. Figure 3–20 illustrates this basic principle in the case of the inheritance of black (dominant) and white (recessive) coat colors in rabbits. Note that the recessive trait is visible *only* in the paired recessive condition. Absence of a dominant gene for black causes expression of white coat color.

Mendel published his findings in 1866, but they did not become known to the scientific world until about 1900. At that time they were "rediscovered," principally by the Dutch biologist Hugo De Vries, who was searching for a theoretical explanation for the phenomenon of *mutation,* a sudden change in the character of a species, now ascribed to a change in a gene. Mendel's principles are now, of course, an established part of the science of genetics. Experimental proof in the 1940's that DNA is the genetic matter of chromosomes marked the beginning of modern *molecular genetics,* the biochemical approach to understanding genic activity, distinct from the traditional Mendelian analysis using breeding experiments.

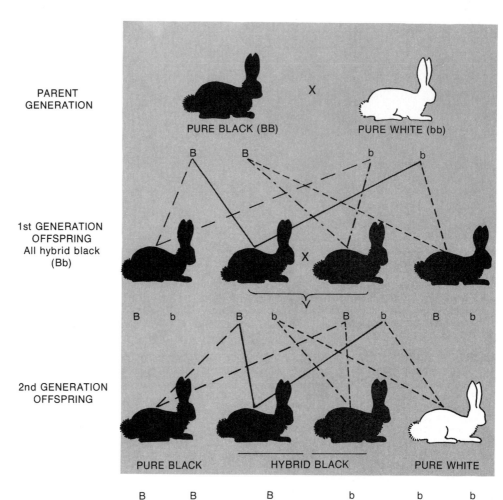

PARENT GENERATION

PURE BLACK (BB)   X   PURE WHITE (bb)

B   B   b   b

1st GENERATION OFFSPRING
All hybrid black (Bb)

X

B   b   B   b   B   b   B   b

2nd GENERATION OFFSPRING

PURE BLACK   HYBRID BLACK   PURE WHITE

B   B   B   b   b   b

Figure 3–20. Simple Mendelian inheritance in coat color in rabbits, showing dominance of black coat color.

DNA and the Genetic Code

Proof that DNA (deoxyribonucleic acid) is the genetic substance of chromosomes is generally credited to Oswald T. Avery and colleagues. In 1944 Avery, in collaboration with Colin M. MacLeod and Maclyn McCarty, reported that a mutant strain of pneumococcus that had lost the ability to manufacture a polysaccharide capsule which protected it against the body's defenses and was, therefore, unable to cause pneumonia (in mammals) could be transformed into a normal virulent type by adding to the culture of the mutant strain a "transforming principle" identified as DNA that had been extracted from the virulent strain. This work was not widely appreciated when it was published because it did not fit into the accepted body of knowledge of the time. The chief stumbling block was the belief that DNA was a uniform structure composed of a single repeating unit (a tetranucleotide) and was, therefore, incapable of containing coded ge-

netic information. By the late 1940's it was apparent from accumulated data that DNA was not a uniform structure. In the early 1950's it was reported that when a bacteriophage, a bacterial virus, infected a host bacterium most of the DNA of the virus entered the cell whereas most of its protein remained behind. These findings, among others, led to the general acceptance of the belief that DNA was, indeed, the genetic substance.

The publication by Watson and Crick in 1954 of the *double helix model* of DNA was certainly one of the most exciting events in the history of science. DNA, as we have already mentioned, is one type of nucleic acid (substances composed of units called nucleotides). In DNA the nucleotide components are a 5-carbon sugar called *deoxyribose*, a phosphate group, and one of four nitrogenous bases, namely, *adenine, guanine, thymine,* or *cytosine* (Fig. 3–21). Thus, four different nucleotides, each containing a different nitrogenous base, are the constituent units of DNA. In the **double helix** model formulated by Watson and Crick, the molecule has the appearance of a chain ladder twisted into the shape of a spiral staircase. Two linear chains formed by alternating units of phosphate and sugar are linked by pairs of bases (attached to the sugar units) which form the rungs of the ladder (Figs. 3–22 and 3–23). The **base pairing** is quite specific: adenine is always linked to thymine, guanine always to cytosine. The specific base pairing is an essential feature of the molecule. Thus, a sequence of bases attached to one strand, for example, one denoted by the letters G-A-A-C-T-G, is matched by a **complementary** sequence, C-T-T-G-A-C, on the other. The nucleotide units in the DNA polymer are held together by strong (covalent) bonds between the phosphate and sugar units in each chain. Weak hydrogen bonds (described in Chapter 2, page 33) between base pairs link the two chains.

As Watson and Crick pointed out in their original description of the double helix, the model can explain how DNA functions; that is to say, the model can explain how DNA can be replicated (a necessary event before cell division to provide each daughter cell with a copy of the genetic substance) and how coded information for the synthesis of enzymes and other proteins can be built into its structure (the very nature of a cell, remember, depends upon the kinds of enzymes it possesses).

Let us first consider **DNA replication.** Note that each half of double-stranded DNA is a complement of the other half. If the two chains are separated (by severing the weak hydrogen bonds joining base pairs), one half of the molecule can serve as a template for the synthesis of the other half. The specific pairing of bases during synthesis will ensure that the nucleotides are lined up in a se-

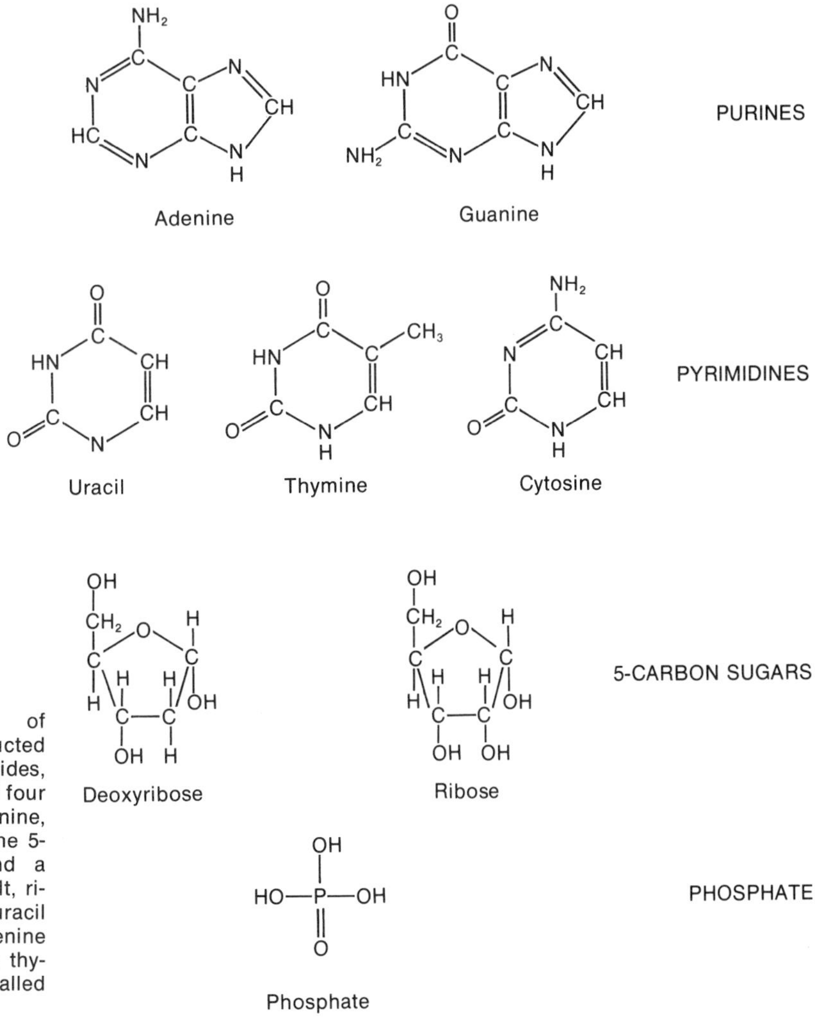

PURINES

Adenine

Guanine

PYRIMIDINES

Uracil

Thymine

Cytosine

5-CARBON SUGARS

Deoxyribose

Ribose

PHOSPHATE

Phosphate

Figure 3–21. Components of DNA and RNA. DNA is constructed from basic units called nucleotides, each of which consists of one of four nitrogen-containing bases, adenine, guanine, thymine, or cytosine, the 5-carbon sugar deoxyribose, and a phosphate. In RNA, similarly built, ribose replaces deoxyribose and uracil replaces thymine. The bases adenine and guanine are called purines; thymine, cytosine, and uracil are called pyrimidines.

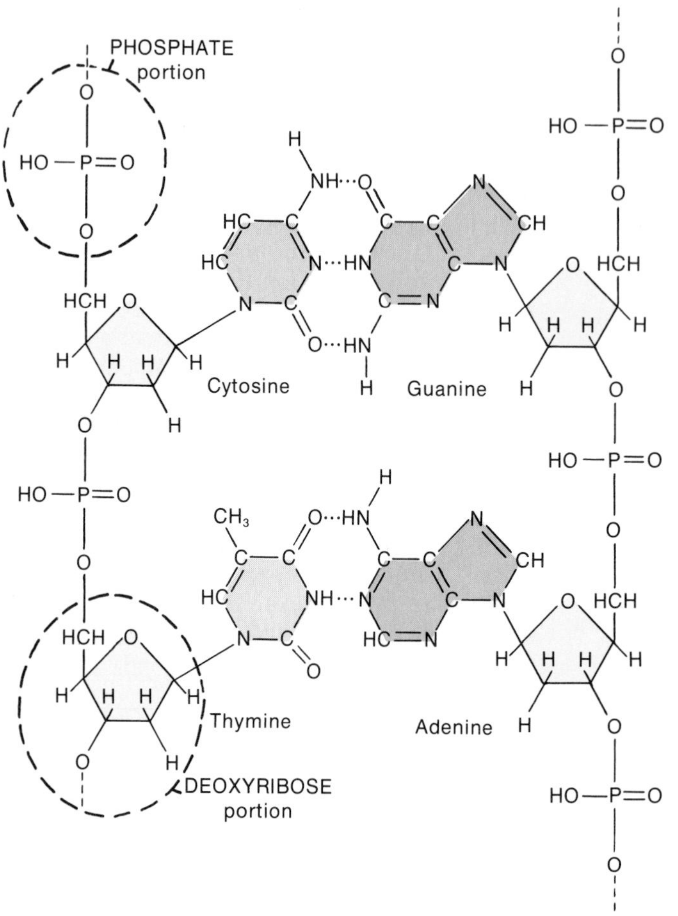

PHOSPHATE portion

Cytosine   Guanine

DEOXYRIBOSE portion

Thymine   Adenine

Figure 3–22. Chemical structure and diagrammatic representation of a segment of a DNA molecule and its components. (Courtesy of Richard Lyons, M.D.)

quence exactly complementary to that of the template. The newly synthesized complementary chains can then join to form an exact copy of the original double helix.

Now let us consider the process of **direct-ing protein synthesis.** A protein, as mentioned earlier, consists of amino acids linked together in long chains that are coiled and twisted into various shapes. There are 20 different amino acids; the order in which

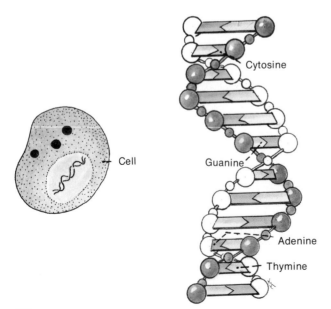

Cell

Cytosine

Guanine

Adenine

Thymine

Figure 3–23. Diagrammatic representation of DNA helix.

they are joined is unique for each protein and determines its shape and function. If a section of the double strand of DNA is parted, a sequence of bases will be exposed on each chain. The first letter of the four bases on the exposed chain, A-G-C-T, can be thought of as a four-letter alphabet from which words can be constructed, each word representing a specific amino acid. A gene is defined as a DNA segment with a sufficient number of word sequences to code for the synthesis of a protein (or one polypeptide of a protein consisting of two or more polypeptide chains). Experiments conducted in the 1960's established that a specific sequence of three consecutive bases is a code word for a single amino acid.

As mentioned in the section describing cell organelles, proteins are synthesized on cytoplasmic bodies called ribosomes. To carry the base sequences specifying the order of amino acids in a protein to the site of protein synthesis, the code of a gene is copied into a type of nucleic acid called appropriately enough, **messenger RNA,** which migrates to the ribosomes (Fig. 3–24). In the copying process (known as **transcription**) the base sequence of the gene serves as a template for the synthesis of a complementary chain of messenger RNA. Messenger RNA is a single strand and, in distinction to DNA, contains the 5-carbon sugar *ribose* instead of deoxyribose (hence ribonucleic acid, abbreviated RNA) and the nitrogenous base *uracil*

instead of thymine (Fig. 3–21). In the genetic code dictionary each word (a sequence of three bases), called a **codon,** is given with the letters representing the bases in messenger RNA. Since, in transcription, uracil rather than thymine is the complement of adenine, the letters of codons are U, C, A, and G (Table 3–2).

In the late 1970's molecular biologists made the surprising discovery that most genes in mammals, birds, and amphibians are discontinuous; that is, base sequences in DNA that code for amino acids are separated by intervening, noncoding base sequences, called **introns.** The cell makes a complete RNA copy of a segment of DNA containing both the coding sequences and introns and makes messenger RNA by cutting out the introns and splicing the coding sequences together. Why genes are in pieces is still somewhat of a mystery. According to one theory, it has an advantage from the standpoint of evolution because fragmented genes are more easily shuffled to form new combinations than are genes all in one piece. It is believed that each gene fragment codes for a functioning part of a protein.

As a protein is synthesized, the placement of amino acids in the sequence dictated by the codon sequence in messenger RNA is made possible by the action of another type of RNA, called **transfer RNA.** Transfer RNA's combine with specific amino acids and bring them to the site of protein synthesis. There is

Table 3–2   AMINO ACIDS AND THEIR RNA CODE WORDS

AMINO ACIDS	RNA CODE WORDS				
Alanine (Ala)	GCU	GCC	GCA	GCG		
Arginine (Arg)	CGU	CGC	CGA	CGG	AGA	AGG
Asparagine (Asn)	AAU	AAC				
Aspartic acid (Asp)	GAU	GAC				
Cysteine (Cys)	UGU	UGC				
Glutamic acid (Glu)	GAA	GAG				
Glutamine (Gln)	CAA	CAG				
Glycine (Gly)	GGU	GGC	GGA	GGG		
Histidine (His)	CAU	CAC				
Isoleucine (Ile)	AUU	AUC	AUA			
Leucine (Leu)	CUU	CUC	CUA	CUG	UUA	UUG
Lysine (Lys)	AAA	AAG				
Methionine (Met)	AUG					
Phenylalanine (Phe)	UUU	UUC				
Proline (Pro)	CCU	CCC	CCA	CCG		
Serine (Ser)	UCU	UCC	UCA	UCG	AGU	AGC
Threonine (Thr)	ACU	ACC	ACA	ACG		
Tryptophan (Tryp)	UGG					
Tyrosine (Tyr)	UAU	UAC				
Valine (Val)	GUU	GUC	GUA	GUG		

The above listing of codons accounts for 61 of 64 possible triplet combinations. The remaining three, UGA, UAA, and UAG, are signals for ending protein chains.

a specific transfer RNA for each of the 20 amino acids incorporated into proteins, and associated with each is an activating enzyme (aminoacyl-tRNA synthetase) that promotes capture of the proper amino acid. Each transfer RNA has a triplet sequence, called an **anticodon,** appropriate for the amino acid it is transporting, that recognizes the relevant codon on messenger RNA. A temporary codon-anticodon linkage places the amino acids in the proper order as the protein is synthesized. Ribosomes apparently play a role as mechanical devices that hold in place both the growing polypeptide chain and each newly arrived transfer RNA with its bound amino acid (Fig. 3–24).

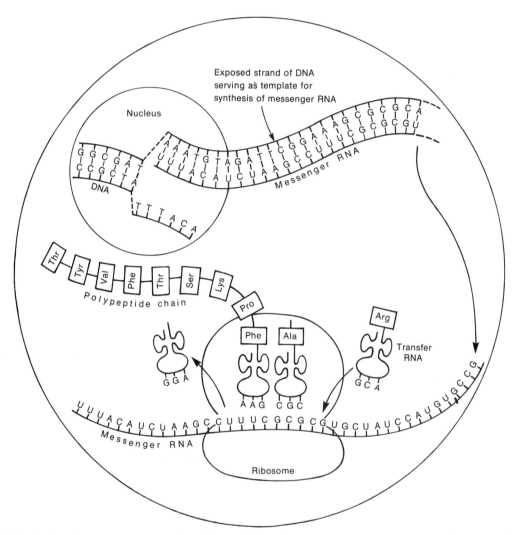

Figure 3–24. Schematic representation of the synthesis of a protein from instructions coded in a gene. The base sequence of a segment of one strand of DNA is transcribed in the nucleus into a complementary sequence in messenger RNA. (In the complete segment to be transcribed, coding base sequences are separated by noncoding, intervening sequences, called "introns," and messenger RNA is synthesized in two steps: first, all sequences are transcribed, then the noncoding sequences are cut out and the coding sequences are spliced together.) Specific base triplets in messenger RNA, called codons, represent words for 20 amino acids, from which a protein is constructed. Messenger RNA passes from the nucleus to a ribosome in the cytoplasm. The code is "read" by transfer RNA's, each of which contains a triplet called an anticodon, complementary to a codon. A transfer RNA picks up a particular amino acid (each amino acid has one or more of its own transfer RNA's), carries it to the ribosome, and engages briefly in an anticodon-codon linkage. The illustration shows phenylalanine transfer RNA at the end of a short polypeptide chain connected to a complementary codon. Alanine transfer RNA is alongside it. Alanine is added to the chain when phenylalanine disengages from its transfer RNA and links to alanine. Then, as the ribosome moves to the right, the alanine transfer RNA, carrying the growing chain, displaces the phenylalanine transfer RNA, and the arginine transfer RNA shown coming in on the right occupies the ribosomal site vacated by the alanine transfer RNA.

Genic Mutations

The mechanics of mutations are not well understood, but at this point it seems they all result from one or more structural changes in the genic DNA. Such changes may involve (1) substitution in one or more of the base pairs, (2) subtraction of one or more base pairs, (3) addition of one or more base pairs, or (4) combinations of the foregoing. These changes are heritable, provided they are not lethal, because each segment of a DNA molecule (gene) is capable of duplicating itself.

Since the code for a specific protein starts at one end of the gene, if a single addition or subtraction occurs near the start of a genic series, the whole code is disrupted and the entire gene becomes inoperative. If, however, a subtraction occurs near the beginning and is *balanced* by an addition nearby, most of the gene triplets will be unchanged. The gene will then continue to function with slightly altered characteristics. Changes resulting in the alteration of one triplet, assuming it remains a triplet, might summon a single different amino acid into a protein change. This, indeed, appears to be the case in certain heritable diseases. For instance, in sickle cell anemia the hemoglobin molecule differs from the normal one by substitution of one amino acid, namely, valine for glutamic acid. From the genetic code dictionary on page 71 it can be seen that this substitution can be accounted for by a single base change, A to U in the middle position of either codon for glutamic acid.

Genetic Biology

What does genetic biology mean to medicine? Scientists are becoming increasingly aware that a number of clinical conditions are the result of an abnormally functioning or absent enzyme or other protein caused by a defective gene. Sickle cell anemia, mentioned above, is one example of such a disorder. Cystic fibrosis, characterized by abnormal secretion of certain glands and respiratory tract blockage that can lead to death by pneumonia, is the most common inborn error of metabolism. It is believed to be the product of a single defective gene. Scientists have succeeded in identifying more than a thousand diseases related to genetic factors and the list is still growing —

to name a few: myopia, astigmatism, retinoblastoma (cancer of the retina), psoriasis, polydactyly (extra toes or fingers), muscular dystrophy, spastic paraplegia, diabetes, and hemophilia.

Using the principles of Mendelian genetics, one can predict the mathematical odds by which two people will conceive a child with a genetic defect, *given* a good history of the conditions suffered by their ancestors and relations. For instance, if both parents carry the trait for sickle cell anemia, which is recessive, the odds are one in four that each of their children will have the disease. If only one parent carries the trait, he or she can pass the trait but not the disease itself to the offspring. If the gene involved is dominant (Fig. 3–20), the chances of passing it on are much greater. Huntington's chorea is a degenerative nerve disease that strikes its victims around age 40 and is always fatal. If one parent carries the defective gene, there is a 50 per cent chance that each of his children will inherit it.

Amniocentesis. Amniocentesis is a technique which gives doctors the ability to test for some genetic defects early in pregnancy, giving parents the option of therapeutic abortion if the results show definite deformity. The procedure involves inserting a long needle through the pregnant mother's abdomen and drawing off a small sample of amniotic fluid, the liquid in which the fetus floats. Diverse cells of fetal origin which slough off into the amniotic fluid during development are then placed in a nutrient bath, where they continue to grow. By examining these cells microscopically for chromosomal abnormalities and analyzing them chemically for metabolic defects, it is possible to detect the presence of many genetic diseases. New procedures for detecting structural abnormalities in genes, involving the use of restriction enzymes (see page 74) to cut DNA into a characteristic pattern of fragments (which is altered by a gene abnormality), has made possible the prenatal diagnosis of a number of inherited disorders of hemoglobin, such as sickle cell anemia, which in the past could be detected only by obtaining samples of fetal blood, a hazardous procedure.

Amniocentesis is generally performed during the 15th to 16th week of pregnancy, at which time there is at least 175 ml of amniotic fluid (the fluid that is withdrawn, usually 24 ml, is rapidly replaced). A large clinical study under the auspices of the National

Institutes of Health indicates that the procedure involves no significant risk to either mother or child. Down's syndrome (mongolism), which occurs once in every 600 births and is caused by the presence of an extra chromosome 21, is one of the most easily detected defects by amniocentesis. Since it is known to be far more prevalent in pregnancies of older women than younger it has been suggested that all pregnant women over the age of 35 be screened and offered therapeutic abortion when the test is positive. It is estimated that this policy could reduce the incidence of Down's syndrome by about 50 per cent.

Recombinant DNA Technology

Recombinant DNA is a procedure which allows molecular biologists to transplant genes from one cell to another. For example, genes have been transplanted from mammals into bacteria and from one mammalian species into another. The occurrence of genetic recombination in bacteria was first revealed by O. T. Avery and colleagues when they transformed a nonvirulent strain of pneumococci into a virulent one (page 68). Two discoveries were largely responsible for launching recombinant DNA as a well-organized technology, namely, (1) "restriction enzymes," bacterial enzymes which cleave DNA into fragments; and (2) a way to use plasmids, which are small, circular, self-replicating, extrachromosomal DNA in bacteria, as vehicles for transplanting genes into bacteria.

Restriction enzymes cleave DNA at specific recognition base sequences, so that each enzyme produces a distinct pattern of fragments. Their normal function is to protect bacteria against foreign DNA (hence the term "restriction"). Isolated from bacteria, they have been used in recombinant DNA experiments to prepare genes from various sources for transplantation. Plasmids move about naturally in the microbial world, transferring genes between bacteria. To use as a vehicle for deliberate gene transplantation, a plasmid is opened at a unique site by a restriction enzyme and the gene is inserted into it. (This process is aided by the way restriction enzymes cleave the double strands of DNA — leaving staggered, complementary, "sticky" ends. Permanent linkage of the gene and plasmid is achieved by an enzyme

that forms covalent bonds between the ends of DNA strands.) The recombinant DNA molecule so formed is then introduced into a "host" bacterial cell (uptake of hybrid plasmids from the medium is promoted by treatment with calcium chloride). Genes for transplantation have also been synthesized chemically or biochemically. Biochemical synthesis is accomplished by making use of the enzyme "reverse transcriptase" (obtained from RNA tumor viruses — see discussion of cancer on page 76 to copy the genetic instructions for a protein in messenger RNA into a complementary single strand of DNA (called copy DNA), which serves as a template for synthesizing (by the enzyme DNA polymerase) the normal double-stranded form of DNA.

Recombinant DNA technology has spawned a multimillion dollar industry established, among other things, to introduce human genes into bacteria, which then become factories for the production of medically useful proteins, such as hormones and enzymes. A number of hormones, including insulin, as well as the antiviral agent interferon, have already been produced with this technology. In the production of insulin, plasmids are used as vehicles for incorporating synthetic genes for the two chains of insulin into a strain of the *Escherichia coli* bacterium, and the two chains manufactured by the bacteria are joined to make the complete insulin molecule.

The most ambitious aim of recombinant DNA technology is **gene therapy** — the replacement of defective genes in humans. Just one of the many problems that must be solved before this can become a reality is finding a safe vehicle for incorporating genes into the DNA of mammalian cells. In the first successful transplantation of a gene into a mammalian cell, a virus (which under some circumstances will incorporate its genes in a dormant state into the DNA of a host cell) was used to transfer the rabbit gene coding for one of the polypeptide chains of hemoglobin into a cultured line of monkey cells. However, the use of a virus to transplant genes into human cells would be hazardous because of the possibility of tumor induction. High molecular weight DNA has been used as a vehicle for transplanting genes into a variety of mammalian species. This procedure was used to perform the first gene transfer into living animals. Genes obtained from mice resistant to an anticancer drug were transplanted into bone marrow cells removed from susceptible mice, and the altered cells were successfully reintroduced into living animals, where they withstood drug treatment. (The drug, methotrexate, like many anticancer drugs, can also kill normal cells, especially rapidly dividing cells, including bone marrow cells.) As promising as these experiments sound, there are, unfortunately, unanswered questions to resolve which indicate that there remain formidable barriers to surmount before gene replacement therapy can be achieved. It is not known, for example, whether genes transplanted in this way are incorporated into a chromosome or are simply floating around free in the cell. If they are free, they could leak out of the cell or run wild and produce an excess of gene products. Even if genes are incorporated into chromosomes, there is no assurance that they will be under normal control by the cell. The problem is to get genes into the right chromosomes at specific sites where they will be subject to normal regulation. However, it has been suggested that a more limited application of the methods used to transfer genes conferring drug resistance into bone marrow cells might be as an aid to cancer chemotherapy, since the harmful effects of many anticancer drugs on bone marrow cells often limit the dosages and the period of time they can be used.

CANCER: ITS NATURE AND CAUSE

Cancer is a disease of the cell that is recognized and measured by the extent to which the cell deviates from its normal behavior. The ultimate understanding of malignant disease will depend on an equal degree of understanding of the function of the normal cell. This is not yet adequate.

During recent years attention has been given to the growth patterns of cancer cells, for knowledge of cell growth could be the basis of effective treatment. Although development of cancer may require a certain preexisting set of conditions, such as failure of the normal immunologic defenses of the body, it is believed that the initial causative event is a change in a single cell. The cell presumably undergoes permanent changes in its genetic structure, and then in multiplying gives rise to billions of similarly altered cells.

Cancer cells differ from normal cells in a characteristic way. The cancer cell has escaped from the usual mechanisms by which the body controls cell multiplication. In normal, continuously renewing tissues, such as the intestines and the skin, only one of the two daughter cells arising from division of a parent cell will retain the capacity to divide. The other will differentiate, replace a lost cell, die, and be shed. In cancer, on the other hand, differentiation apparently does not occur, and virtually all cells of the population grow and divide without restraint. We have mentioned the importance of chalones in regulating cell division in normal cell populations (see page 64). Control of cell division by chalones does not occur in cancer. A perhaps related phenomenon may be the absence of what is known as "contact inhibition" in cancer cell populations. It has been observed, for example, that normal skin cells cultured outside the body grow in a well-ordered monolayer and that cell division ceases when there is no longer a free surface. Tumor cells, in contrast, grow and move about randomly with no evidence of contact inhibition.

Tumors are either *benign* or *malignant*, depending upon whether or not the proliferating cells can invade surrounding tissues. The cells of benign tumors cannot do so, and therefore remain local growths. The cells of malignant tumors, or cancers, on the other hand, can leave the original tissue and create new growths (*metastases*) in new body locations. Cancers arising from epithelial tissues (see Chapter 4) are called **carcinomas**. Those derived from connective tissues (or other tissues which also take their origin from the embryonal mesoderm) are referred to as **sarcomas.** *Lymphomas* (arising in lymphoid tissue) and *leukemias* (abnormal proliferation of white blood cells in bone marrow or lymph nodes) may be regarded as subgroups of sarcomas.

Current research supports the view that multiple causative agents, acting singly or in combination, are responsible for the development of cancer. Certain chemicals, called carcinogens, and exposure to radiation are known to be potential cancer-causing agents. It is possible that these environmental or physical agents in some way damage DNA. Some investigators suspect that viruses are a cancer-triggering mechanism, acting alone or in combination with environmental agents or other factors, such as immunological defects and genetic predisposition. Convincing evidence links viruses with some human cancers (Burkitt's lymphoma, nasopharyngeal carcinoma, and cervical cancer). Considerable basic cancer research has focused upon the transformation of normal cells to cancer cells by viruses in tissue culture. From such studies the following picture has emerged: The usual result of viral infection — multiplication of the virus, cell destruction, and release of viruses into the blood stream — is suppressed, and all or part of the DNA of the virus becomes incorporated into the DNA of the host cell. (If the genetic matter of the virus is RNA rather than DNA, a copy of the viral DNA is first synthesized by an enzyme present in cancer-causing RNA viruses called "reverse transcriptase.") Synthesis of virus-coded proteins leads to progressive changes in the control of cell growth and is responsible for the transformation.

Cell Differentiation

In the beginning of this chapter it was pointed out that an individual develops from a single cell, the fertilized ovum (zygote), and that, as cell division proceeds, a stage of development is reached at which cells become differentiated; that is, they come to differ in structure and function. Specialized cell types become organized as tissues, each performing its unique functions. How cells differentiate is a question that has intrigued biologists for centuries. In the 1960's, nuclear transplant experiments carried out with frogs settled one aspect of this question — differentiation is not caused by a loss of genes. This had to be the case, since it was demonstrated that normal frogs could develop from an ovum from which the nucleus had been removed and replaced with one taken from a differentiated intestinal (epithelial) cell of a tadpole. Since the differentiated cell had to have a full complement of genes for this to happen, it became apparent that differentiation is accomplished by *switching genes off and on*. This switching continues in differentiated cells throughout the lifetime of an organism as the activities of cells undergo continuous change.

It has been clearly demonstrated that in bacteria, gene activity (that is, the transcription of its base sequence into a complementary sequence in messenger RNA) is regulated by the binding and release of proteins at specific sites on DNA. Some of these **regula-tory proteins** have been isolated and identified. Although specific regulatory proteins have not been identified in higher forms of life, there is considerable evidence that such gene regulators do function in higher organisms.

SUMMARY

THE CELL

Importance of the Cell

1. The cell is the structural and functional unit of the body.

    a. The human body develops from a single cell, the fertilized ovum.

History of the Cell

1. Robert Hooke introduced the word *cell* as a biological term in 1665 to describe the box-like compartments he recognized as basic structural units of plants.

2. In 1838 and 1839 M. J. Schleiden and Theodor Schwann formulated what is known as the cell theory.

    a. Described cells as the fundamental units of structure and function of all living things, capable of carrying out all the processes of life as independent entities and, collectively, as complex systems.

3. Before the end of the 19th century it became understood that

    a. Cells arise by division from preexisting ones
    b. Chromosomes, discrete bodies which take form during cell division, replicate prior to division and serve as the carriers of hereditary traits from one cell generation to the next.

4. In the 1940's DNA, the nucleic acid of chromosomes, was unequivocally identified as the hereditary substance.

    a. Not long afterward the publication of the double helix model of DNA explained how the genetic substance could carry a code in the form of instructions for the synthesis of enzymes and other proteins.
    (1) Since all cellular reactions depend upon the presence of specific en-

zymes and in their absence the constituents of the cell could be neither manufactured nor broken down, it became clear that the nature of a cell is determined by the genetic instructions for the synthesis of enzymes.

Structure of the Cell

The principal components of a cell are a **nucleus,** containing the genetic matter, enclosed by a nuclear membrane; **cytoplasm,** the substance outside the nucleus, containing various organelles; and a **cell membrane** enclosing the entire cell.

1. The cell membrane: composed principally of a phospholipid bilayer penetrated partially or completely by interdispersed proteins.

a. Regulates interchange between the cell and its environment.
b. Serves as a receptive surface for substances initiating adaptive changes within the cell.

2. The *cytoplasmic organelles*, each enclosed by its own membrane, include the following:

a. *Ribosomes:* dense aggregates of RNA and protein, serving as the site of protein synthesis.
b. *Endoplasmic reticulum:* a network of tubules.
 (1) The rough type, with ribosomes scattered over the surface, functions in the synthesis of proteins that are packaged for secretion or incorporation into lysosomes.
 (2) The smooth type functions in the synthesis of nonprotein substances.
c. The *Golgi apparatus:* saclike vesicles usually found in stacked piles. Completes the synthesis of and packages proteins to be secreted or retained in lysosomes.
d. *Lysosomes:* bodies containing digestive enzymes, which function, among other things, in the destruction of harmful microorganisms following phagocytosis and the breakdown of extracellular matter, as in bone, to release stored calcium.
e. *Mitochondria:* the so-called "powerhouses," where most of the cell's ATP is synthesized.
f. *Centrioles:* paired structures that become the poles of the cell to which chromosomes migrate during cell division.

Physiology of the Cell

1. Movement of substances across cell membranes is accomplished by

a. Diffusion
b. Osmosis
c. Active transport
d. Pinocytosis
e. Phagocytosis

2. *Energy Metabolism:* the degradation of nutrients by the cell, principally glucose and fatty acids, to produce the energy needed to perform such functions as muscular contraction, biochemical synthesis and active transport.

a. The energy released by degrading nutrients is not utilized directly but is used to synthesize ATP from ADP, and the energy contained in the high-energy bonds of ATP, principally the terminal one, is the direct source of energy for work performed by the cell.
b. Glucose can be degraded either aerobically to carbon dioxide and water or anaerobically to lactic acid, whereas fatty acids are degraded aerobically only.
c. Maximum ATP yield is obtained by the breakdown of fatty acids, minimum by the anaerobic breakdown of glucose.
d. During the anaerobic breakdown of glucose, ATP is produced in only two steps, in which phosphate is transferred from high energy compounds to ADP. When glucose is degraded aerobically, most of the ATP is produced by oxidative phosphorylation, in which the synthesis of ATP is coupled to the transfer of pairs of electrons (removed from chemical intermediates in several steps) to oxygen via the mitochondrial respiratory chain.

3. Chemical reactions under the conditions of temperature, pressure, and pH existing in cells can take place because of *enzyme action.*

a. Enzymes act as biological catalysts, speeding the rates of reactions but remaining unchanged at the end of the reaction.

Cell Reproduction

1. *Cell cycle:* readily observed in populations of continuously dividing cells, such as the skin and the intestines. A period of growth (*interphase*) is followed by cell division (*mitosis*).

   a. During an interval of interphase known as the S phase, DNA replicates.
      (1) Periods of growth occur prior to (called G_1) and following (called G_2) the S phase.
   b. Mitosis, the shortest period, can be divided into four stages: prophase, metaphase, anaphase, and telophase.
      (1) As a result of DNA synthesis during the S phase of interphase, each chromosome can be seen during prophase to be duplicated into two coiled strands.
      (2) The strands separate and, during anaphase, migrate to opposite sides of the cell so that each daughter cell receives the same number of chromosomes as the original parent cell.
   c. *Meiosis* is the two-stage sequence of cell divisions that produces haploid sex cells. There are 23 pairs of chromosomes in human body cells (diploid number) and half as many (haploid number) in sperm and egg cells.

Cellular Genetics

1. A *gene* can be described as a section of DNA containing coded information for the synthesis of a protein or a polypeptide of a protein made up of more than one polypeptide chain.

   a. The concept that genetic traits are transmitted from parent to offspring by discrete units (genes), each parent contributing one for each trait, was introduced by Gregor Mendel over a century ago.

2. DNA consists of two long strands, formed by alternating units of phosphate and deoxyribose, linked by complementary pairs of bases (adenine joined to thymine, guanine to cytosine) spiraled to form the so-called double helix.

   a. The order of bases in an individual DNA strand determines the sequence of *amino acids* in proteins. Sequences of three bases (triplets) code for each of the 20 amino acids constituting the building blocks of proteins.
   b. The code is carried from DNA to a ribosome in the cytoplasm by "messenger RNA."
   c. A code-reading vehicle, transfer RNA, binds and escorts specific amino acids to the ribosome so as to place each amino acid in the order dictated by the triplet sequence in messenger RNA.

Genetic Biology

1. Many clinical disorders result from a malfunctioning or missing enzyme or other protein caused by a defective gene.

2. Some genetic diseases can be detected in early pregnancy by amniocentesis.

3. Gene therapy, the replacement of defective genes in humans, is the long-range aim of recombinant DNA technology.

Cancer

Cancer cells have escaped the usual mechanism for controlling cell division. Whereas in normal continuously renewing tissues only one of two daughter cells retains the capacity to divide (the other, after replacing a dead cell, in turn dies), in cancer populations all of the cells divide without restraint.

Cell Differentiation

1. During embryological development, cells come to differ in structure and function, and specialized types become organized into tissues.

   a. Differentiation is accomplished by switching genes off and on as a result of the binding and release of regulatory proteins at specific sites on DNA.

REVIEW QUESTIONS

1. Discuss the contributions of the following individuals to our understanding of the cell: Robert Hooke, M. J. Schleiden and Theodor Schwann, Rudolf Virchow, Walther Flemming, Edouard van Beneden, Friedrich Miescher, and James Watson and Francis Crick.
2. Describe and list the functions of the following parts of the cell: (a) plasma

membrane, (b) nucleus, and (c) each of these organelles: ribosomes, endoplasmic reticulum, Golgi apparatus, mitochondria, lysosomes, and centrioles.

3. Distinguish between passive and active transport. Define diffusion, osmosis, pinocytosis, and phagocytosis.

4. Briefly explain why (a) the aerobic breakdown of glucose produces more ATP than its anaerobic breakdown and (b) the oxidation of fatty acids produces more ATP than the oxidation of glucose.

5. Describe the cell cycle. Name the three phases of interphase. In which phase does DNA replicate? Describe the four stages of mitosis. How does meiosis differ from mitosis?

6. How does the Watson-Crick model of DNA explain how DNA (a) replicates before cell division and (b) codes genetic information? Explain how ribosomes, messenger RNA, and transfer RNA cooperate in synthesizing a protein.

4
Tissues

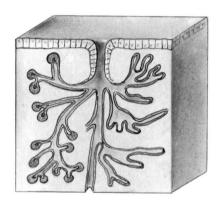

Objectives

The aim of this chapter is to enable the student to:

□ Identify the four basic types of tissue and describe their functions.

□ Classify epithelial tissues according to cell shape, cell arrangement, and function.

□ List the various types of specialized connective tissue and distinguish their functions.

□ Define the four types of transplantation of tissue and give examples of each.

□ Evaluate the three general methods of tissue preservation with respect to longevity and potential future transplant.

Tissues compose all organs and, in turn, all organ systems. It is important to understand these components before individual organs are studied. Even prior to the discovery of the microscope, the integrated pattern of tissues could be seen.

The basic unit of the tissue is the cell. Cells are either tightly packed or separated by interstitial (L. *interstitium,* a place between) material. Tissues are subdivided into four major categories: *epithelial, connective, muscular,* and *nervous.*

EPITHELIAL TISSUE

Epithelial tissue functions in protection, absorption, secretion, and excretion. When serving a protective or absorbent function, epithelial tissue is found in sheets covering a surface, such as the skin. In its secretory function, the epithelial cells involute from the surface into the underlying tissues to form gland structures, specialized for secretion. Only a minimal amount of intercellular substance is found in epithelial tissue, which is closely knit and not so readily penetrated as other tissues. Epithelial tissues are avascular (lack blood vessels). Nutrition and waste removal are provided by the network of blood vessels in underlying connective tissue. The epidermis and associated derivatives will be discussed in Chapter 5.

In general, epithelial cells are anchored to a specialized structure called the **basement membrane.** The basement membrane is important, since it serves as an anchor for the inner (attached) side of cells, affording protection to the underlying connective tissue. It is frequently used as a landmark delineating invasion of epithelial tumors. If the tumor has invaded the basement membrane, the outlook for the patient is poor. In the electron microscope the basement membrane can be seen to consist of two layers: (1) the *basal lamina* (the more conspicuous layer), composed largely of filamentous collagen fibrils which border (and are apparently secreted by) the epithelial cells; and (2) delicate, branching, reticular fibers (described below) embedded in a protein-polysaccharide ground substance, both products of fibroblasts, the connective tissue cells.

An epithelial tissue is named according to the outer (free) layer of cells, consisting of either one layer or several layers of different cell types. The free surface of an epithelial cell can be plain or can have definite structures, such as **cilia,** motile hairlike processes which, by synchronized, wavelike movements (resembling a windblown field of grain), either move mucus or propel substances along a tract, and **microvilli,** cylindrical cell processes which greatly increase membrane surface (especially of cells serving an absorptive function).

Unique structures along the lateral surface of epithelial cells, called **intercellular junctions,** play essential functional roles in various kinds of epithelial tissues. Three distinct types of junctions have been identified: *tight junctions,* which govern permeability; *gap junctions,* which make possible intercellular communication by exchange of chemical substances; and *desmosomes* (G. *desmos,* band), which maintain mechanical linkages that tend to resist disruptive forces.

In **tight junctions** the membranes are fused at their apical ends by contact between rows of membrane proteins that form what are called "sealing strands." The sealing strands are arranged in the form of a network, and the number of strands is the principal determinant of how tight these junctions are. So-called "leaky-tight" junctions, which have relatively few sealing strands, are generally found in parts of the body (such as the epithelium of the proximal convoluted tubules of the kidneys and the small intestine) where coupling of the copious passive transport of water between cells to the active transport of solute (dissolved substances) by the cell results in what is referred to as isotonic absorption. "Tight-tight" junctions in some parts of the body, the epithelium lining the distal convoluted tubules of the kidneys, for example, make possible hypertonic absorption, in which a steep gradient of active transport of solutes through the cell (with no significant leakage through intercellular spaces in the opposite direction) is independent of passive water transport. "Tight-tight" junctions in other locations, such as the epithelial linings of the trachea and bronchi, provide a highly impenetrable surface layer for a body tract.

Gap junctions permit free cell-to-cell passage of ions and other substances via communicating channels formed by the alignment of a disc-shaped array of proteins on adjacent membranes. These junctions, which enable epithelial cells to coordinate and regulate their activities, were serendipitously discovered when it was observed that, if an electric current was passed into a cell, the resulting voltage shift could be detected not only in the cell into which the current had been introduced, but also in the adjacent cell.

Desmosomes, also called adhering junctions, provide strong mechanical linkage between cells, thereby preventing tissue disruption from stretching. In these junctions, adjacent cells are linked by filamentous material. Two types can be distinguished: (1) *belt desmosomes,* in which filaments in the intercellular space form a band just below the tight junction; and (2) *spot desmosomes,* in which networks of filaments arising from disc-shaped plaques on the inner surfaces of the cell membranes of adjacent cells form points of contact at various levels. Two sets of intracellular filaments are associated with belt desmosomes, one a bundle running along the inside of the cell membrane, the other extending in a flat configuration into the cell interior. In spot desmosomes the intracellular filaments (somewhat thicker than the intercellular filaments and called tonofilaments) form a network throughout the cell and are also attached to the disc-shaped plaques. This arrangement tends to distribute disruptive forces to the tissue as a whole, and spot desmosomes are especially numerous in tissues subject to severe mechanical stress, such as the epithelium of the skin, mouth cavity, esophagus, and vagina. In a variation of spot desmosomes, called *hemidesmosomes,* the arrangement of filaments is similar, but these junctions link epithelial cells to underlying connective tissue rather than to each other.

Classification

Cells composing epithelial tissues are classified according to their shape, arrangement of cell layers, and function.

Shape. Epithelial cells are classified as squamous, cuboidal, and columnar. **Squamous cells** (L. *squamosus,* scaly) are flat and often serve as a protective layer. Other epithelial cells can become squamous if subjected to repeated irritation. **Cuboidal cells,** resembling small cubes, are found in five regions of the body and include lining tissue for ducts, secretory glands, renal tubules, germinal coverings for the ovaries, and the pigmented layer of the retina of the eye.

Columnar cells are tall and often rectangular. They line ducts such as the urethra and are found in mucus-secreting tissues, including the mucosa of the stomach, bile ducts, villi (fingerlike projections) of the intestines, uterine tubes, and upper respiratory tract.

Arrangement. Four of the most common arrangements of epithelial cells are simple, stratified, pseudostratified, and transitional epithelium (Fig. 4–1). The **simple** arrangement has one cell layer. The **stratified** arrangement has multiple layers (with rare exceptions, the superficial layers are flat and the tissue is classified as stratified squamous epithelium). The **pseudostratified** arrangement seems to consist of several layers, but is actually a single layer with all cells resting on the basement membrane. The basal, or stem, cells (cells which give rise to various mature cell types), however, do not reach the free (outer) surface and vary so much in shape and in the position of their nuclei that they give the tissue a stratified appearance. **Transitional** epithelium consists of several layers of closely packed, soft, pliable, and easily stretched cells. When the surface is stretched, the cells are flat; but they appear sawtoothed when the epithelium is relaxed, as in a recently emptied bladder. The descriptive term for this type of epithelium arose from the belief that it was in transition between stratified squamous and columnar epithelium. The changing appearance, however, is merely a reflection of the distended and relaxed conditions. Transitional epithelium lines the pelves of the kidneys, the ureters, the urinary bladder, and the upper part of the urethra.

Function. In addition to the epidermal layer of the skin (which is described in Chapter 5, a separate chapter on the skin), epithelial tissue consists of four major types: (1) the surface layer of mucous membranes, (2) glandular epithelium, (3) endothelium, and (4) mesothelium, the surface layer of serous membranes (Fig. 4–2).

MUCOUS MEMBRANE. Mucous membrane lines the digestive, respiratory, urinary, and reproductive tracts; it also lines the conjunctiva and the middle ear. These membranes consist of a surface layer of epithelial cells and an underlying layer of connective tissue (the lamina propria). The digestive tract includes the buccal cavity, pharynx, esophagus, stomach, small intestine, large intestine, and anal canal. The buccal cavity, lower pharynx, and esophagus are lined with

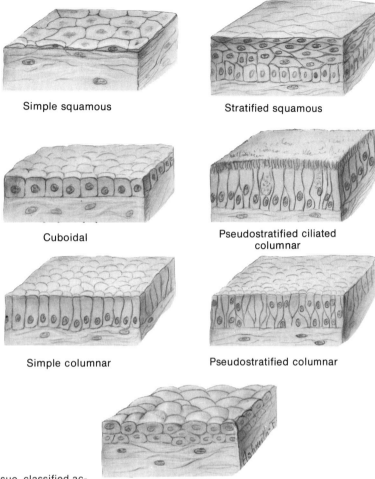

Figure 4–1. Types of epithelial tissue, classified according to shape and arrangement of cell layers.

Simple squamous

Stratified squamous

Cuboidal

Pseudostratified ciliated columnar

Simple columnar

Pseudostratified columnar

Transitional

TYPES OF EPITHELIUM

Endothelium

Mesothelium

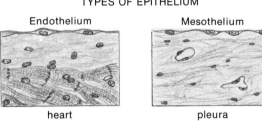

heart

pleura

Glandular

Mucous membrane

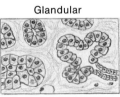

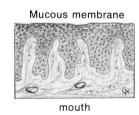

salivary gland

mouth

Figure 4–2. Epithelial tissue types include endothelium, mesothelium (the surface layer of serous membranes, which consist of the mesothelial cell layer and underlying layer of connective tissue), glandular tissue, and the surface layer of mucous membranes (which consist of the surface layer of epithelium and underlying layer of connective tissue). Endothelium and mesothelium, classified according to cell shape and arrangement, are simple squamous epithelium. Glandular epithelium is often simple cuboidal or columnar. The epithelium of mucous membranes is varied. In the mouth it is stratified squamous epithelium, shown (darker region in drawing) receiving projections into it from the underlying connective tissue.

stratified squamous epithelium. Simple columnar epithelium is found in the remainder of the digestive tract from the stomach to the rectum. The anal canal is lined with stratified squamous epithelium.

In the respiratory tract the nasopharynx, trachea, large bronchi, and parts of the larynx are lined with pseudostratified ciliated columnar epithelium. As the basal cells become less common peripherally, the pseudostratified appearance gradually disappears, and in the bronchioles it is characteristically simple ciliated columnar epithelium. These cells change to cuboidal ciliated and nonciliated epithelium in the smallest bronchioles. Vocal cords are covered by patches of stratified squamous epithelium.

In the urinary system, Bowman's capsule and the thin segment of the loop of Henle are lined with thin squamous epithelium, and the remaining tubules with cuboidal epithelium. The cuboidal epithelium becomes columnar as it approaches the pelves of the kidneys, which are lined with transitional epithelium continuing into the ureters, bladder, and upper portion of the urethra.

In the reproductive tract, the epididymis and ductus deferens of the male are lined with pseudostratified columnar epithelium, in the female the uterine tube and the uterus itself with ciliated and nonciliated columnar epithelium. The entire mucosa of the uterus contains tubular glands extending down to and sometimes entering the muscular layer. A change to stratified squamous epithelium occurs at the point at which the cervix opens into the vagina.

Mucous membranes serve four general functions: protection, support for associated structures, absorption of nutrients into the body, and secretion of mucus, enzymes, and salts.

GLANDULAR EPITHELIUM. Glands arise as involutions of epithelial cells, specializing in synthesizing and secreting certain special compounds. The epithelial cells constitute the *parenchymal* (functional as opposed to supportive) tissue of a gland. Glands can be divided into two types: *exocrine* (with excretory ducts) and *endocrine* (ductless). Exocrine glands have excretory ducts through which the secretory products pass to the surface and can be further divided into numerous gland types (Fig. 4–3). Simple or

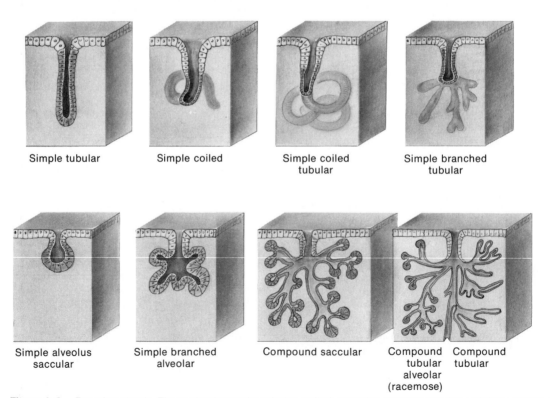

| Simple tubular | Simple coiled | Simple coiled tubular | Simple branched tubular |

| Simple alveolus saccular | Simple branched alveolar | Compound saccular | Compound tubular alveolar (racemose) | Compound tubular |

Figure 4–3. Exocrine glands. These glands may be tubular, coiled, saccular, or racemose (resembling a bunch of grapes on a stalk).

simple, branched glands, such as sweat glands, sebaceous glands, and most glands of the alimentary tract, have single ducts or branches arising from a single duct. Compound glands have several component lobules and a complex system of branching ducts and are found in the pancreas, mammary glands, and large salivary glands. The shape of the gland is either tubular or saccular (see Fig. 4–3), and glands may secrete either mucous or serous material.

ENDOTHELIUM. Endothelium is found in lymphatic vessels, blood vessels, and the lining of the heart (endocardium). The interior of the circulatory system is lined with a thin layer of endothelial cells, extending from the heart through the arteries into the capillaries and back again through the veins. The cells are a single layer of the squamous type.

MESOTHELIUM. The fourth general type of epithelial tissue is the mesothelium, the *surface epithelial layer of serous membranes* (the peritoneum, the pleura and the pericardium) that line the closed cavities of the body. Serous membranes have a simple squamous mesothelial cell layer overlying a supporting layer of connective tissue. These membranes include a parietal (L. *paries*, wall) portion lining the cavity wall and a visceral portion covering the organs. The **pleura** is the serous membrane lining the thoracic cavity and enveloping the lungs, the **pericardium** is the serous membrane covering the heart and lining the inner surface of the pericardial sac, and the **peritoneum** is the serous membrane lining the abdominal cavity and covering many abdominal organs. Serous membranes perform functions such as protection and reduction of friction (the space between the visceral and parietal layers contains a lubricant secreted by the mesothelial cells).

CONNECTIVE TISSUE

The second major subdivision of tissue, connective tissue, which includes connective tissue proper and a number of specialized tissues (such as bone and cartilage), performs many functions, including support and nourishment for other tissues, packing material in the spaces between organs, and defense for the body by phagocytosis and antibody production. Tendons, which connect muscle to bone, allow movement to take place. In this tissue there is an abundance of intercellular material called **matrix,** which is variable in type and amount and is one of the main sources of difference between types of connective tissue. The vascularity of connective tissues varies considerably. Loose connective tissues (described below) have a rich supply of blood vessels; some dense connective tissues have few blood vessels. Cartilage is avascular. The connective tissue matrix consists of varying proportions of three types of glycoprotein **fibers,** collagenous, elastic, and reticular, embedded in an amorphous **ground substance** composed principally of *mucopolysaccharides* (see Chapter 2, page 34), which may be combined with small amounts of protein as mucoproteins. Occasionally the fibers are not apparent (for example, in hyaline cartilage) but often they are quite obvious (tendon). *Collagenous fibers,* the most widespread, are highly inelastic and are responsible for the enormous tensile strength of tissues such as tendons. These fibers are composed of aggregates of fibrils (Fig. 4–4) assembled from collagen molecules. The basic collagen molecule (called tropocollagen) consists of three helical polypeptide chains coiled into a triple helix (Fig. 2–4). Although collagen fibrils are commonly packed in bundles, other looser weaves of fibrils occur. Collagen is rich in hydroxylated lysine and proline, and the stability of the triple helix depends upon linkages involving these hydroxylated amino acids. A deficiency in hydroxylation during synthesis, one of the consequences of a dietary insufficiency of vitamin C, disrupts the normal assembly of collagen. This accounts for poor wound healing in scurvy. *Elastic fibers* give stretchability and resiliency to tissues. This is especially important in structures that must expand and contract to function normally, such as the walls of large arteries. Elastic fibers are composed principally of an amorphous protein called elastin, shaped into a fibrous configuration by small amounts of surrounding microfibrils. *Reticular fibers* are constructed from one of several types of tropocollagen molecules, but are characteristically arranged in thin, delicate networks. These fibers, as mentioned, form part of the basement membrane to which epithelial cells are anchored. They are present in abundance in loose connective tissues, especially the reticular tissues (see below). Reticular fibers are not seen

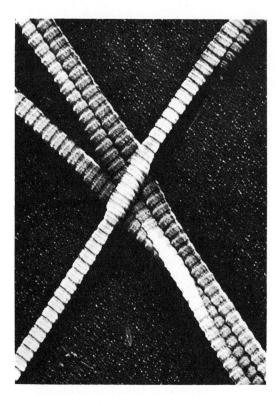

Figure 4–4. Electron micrograph of collagen fibrils from human skin. (From Bloom, W., and Fawcett, D. W.: A Textbook of Histology, 9th ed., Philadelphia, W. B. Saunders Co., 1968.)

in standard histological sections, but can be made visible by selective staining (silver impregnation).

Loose Connective Tissue

The fibers of loose connective tissue are not tightly woven. The tissue, filling spaces between and penetrating into the organs, is of three types: areolar, adipose, and reticular.

Areolar Tissue. The most widely distributed connective tissue is pliable and crossed by many delicate threads; yet, the tissue resists tearing and is somewhat elastic. Areolar tissue contains fibroblasts, histiocytes (macrophages), and mast and mesenchymal cells.

Fibroblasts are small, flattened, somewhat irregular cells with large nuclei and reduced cytoplasm. The term fibroblast refers to the ability of a cell to form fibrils. Fibroblasts are active in repair of injury. It is generally believed that suprarenal steroids inhibit and growth hormones stimulate fibroblastic activity. *Macrophages,* also called *histiocytes,* are phagocytic cells similar to leukocytes in blood; however, they perform phagocytic activity outside the vascular system. The histiocyte is irregular in shape and contains cytoplasmic granules. The cell is often stationary (or "fixed"), attached to fibers of the matrix. *Mast cells,* located adjacent to small blood vessels, are round or polygonal in shape and possess a cytoplasm filled with metachromatic granules. Mast cells function in the manufacture of heparin (an anticoagulant) and histamine (an inflammatory substance responsible for changes in allergic tissue). Depression in mast cell activity results from the administration of cortisol to patients. *Mesenchymal cells,* undifferentiated (embryonic) cells resembling fibroblasts in appearance, but smaller, have also been identified in loose connective tissue. Present principally along the walls of blood vessels, they can develop into the mature cell types of loose connective tissue. Areolar tissue is the basic supporting substance around organs, muscles, blood vessels, and nerves, forming the delicate membranes around the brain and spinal cord and composing the superficial fascia, or sheet of connective tissue, found deep in the skin.

Adipose Tissue. Adipose (L. *adeps*, fat) tissue is specialized areolar tissue with fat-containing cells. The fat cell, like other cells, has a nucleus, endoplasmic reticulum, cell membrane, mitochondria, and, in addition, a large fat droplet. The cytoplasmic fat occupies most of the space, and the displacement of the nucleus to the edge of the cell gives the adipocyte the appearance of a signet ring. Adipose tissue acts as a firm yet resilient packing around and between organs, bundles of muscle fibers, nerves, and supporting blood vessels. Since fat is a poor conductor of heat, adipose tissue protects the body from excessive heat loss or excessive rises in temperature.

Reticular Tissue. Reticular fibers are widespread in the body, but the term *reticular tissue* is restricted to sites where these fibers are associated with so-called *primitive reticular cells*, which can apparently give rise to large phagocytic cells (macrophages), also abundant in most reticular tissue. Reticular tissue forms the framework of lymphoid tissue (see below), the liver, and the bone marrow.

Dense Connective Tissue

Dense connective tissue is composed of closely arranged tough collagenous and elastic fibers with fewer cells than loose connective tissue. It can be classified according to the arrangement of the fibers and the proportion of elastin and collagen present. Examples of dense connective tissue having a regular arrangement of fibers are tendons, aponeuroses, fasciae, and ligaments. Examples of dense connective tissue having an irregular arrangment of fibers are capsules, muscle sheaths, and the dermis, the principal layer of the skin. Where elastic fibers predominate, dense connective tissue is referred to as elastic tissue. The walls of hollow structures, such as the trachea and the bronchi, have large amounts of elastic tissue.

Specialized Connective Tissue

Cartilage. Cartilage has a firm matrix. Cells of cartilage, called *chondrocytes* (G. *chondros*, cartilage), are large and rounded with spherical nuclei and are clustered in small cavities called lacunae. Collagenous and elastic fibers are embedded in the matrix, increasing the elastic and resistive properties of this tissue. Cartilage is covered with a dense connective tissue called the *perichondrium* (G. *peri*, around), except where it is the articular surface of a bone at synovial (fluid) joints. Since, as mentioned, cartilage is avascular, chondrocytes are nourished by diffusion through the matrix of substances from perichondrial blood vessels. Synovial fluid nourishes articular cartilage. The three types of cartilage are hyaline, fibrous, and elastic.

In utero, hyaline (G. *hyalos*, glass) *cartilage* is the precursor of much of the skeletal system. It is translucent with a clear matrix caused by abundant collagenous fibers (not visible as such) and cells scattered throughout the matrix. Hyaline cartilage is gradually replaced by bone in many parts of the body through the process of ossification; however, some remains as a covering on the articular surfaces. The hyaline costal cartilages attach the anterior ends of the upper seven pairs of ribs to the sternum. The trachea is kept open by incomplete rings of surrounding hyaline cartilage. This type of cartilage is also found in the nose.

Fibrous cartilage contains dense masses of unbranching collagenous fibers lying in the matrix. Cells of fibrous cartilage are present in rows between bundles of the matrix. Fibrocartilage is dense and resistant to stretching; it is less flexible and less resilient than hyaline cartilage. Fibrous cartilage, interposed between the vertebrae in the spinal column, is also present in the symphysis pubis, permitting a minimal range of movement.

Elastic cartilage, which is more resilient than either the hyaline or the fibrous type because of a predominance of elastic fibers impregnated in its ground substance, is found in the auricle of the external ear, the auditory tube, the epiglottis, and portions of the larynx.

Bone. Bone is a firm tissue formed by impregnation of the intercellular material with inorganic salts. It is living tissue supplied by blood vessels and nerves and is constantly being remodeled. The two common types are *compact*, forming the dense outer layer, and *cancellous*, forming the inner, lighter tissue (Fig. 6–1).

Dentin. The dentin of teeth is closely related to bone. The crown of the tooth is covered by enamel, the hardest substance in the body. Enamel is secreted onto the dentin by the epithelial cells of the enamel organ before the teeth are extruded through the gums. Dentin resembles bone but is harder and denser (see Fig. 14–3).

Blood and Hematopoietic Tissue. Red bone marrow is the blood-forming (hematopoietic) tissue. The red blood cells (erythrocytes) and white blood cells (leukocytes) originate in the capillary sinusoids of bone marrow.

Blood is a fluid tissue circulating through the body, carrying nutrients to cells and removing waste products (see Fig. 11–2).

Lymphoid Tissue. Lymphoid tissue is found in the lymph nodes, thymus, spleen, and tonsils. Reticular tissue forms its framework, and lymphocytes lie within the reticular tissue. A diffuse form of lymphoid tissue, not sharply delineated from the surrounding connective tissue, is found in mucous membranes, especially in the digestive and respiratory tracts. Lymphoid tissue plays a role in immunity.

Reticuloendothelial System. Connective tissue cells carrying on the process of phagocytosis are frequently referred to as the reticuloendothelial system or the macrophage system. The most frequently cited components of this system are the following: (1) macrophages distributed throughout loose connective tissues, which are especially numerous in mucous membranes of the digestive and respiratory tracts and in association with small blood vessels and lymphatics of subserous connective tissue of the pleura and

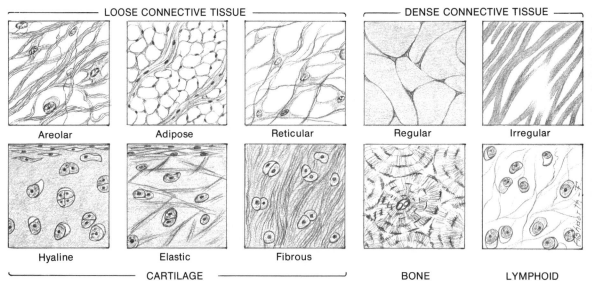

Figure 4–5. *Loose connective tissue:*
Areolar: loosely arranged fibroelastic connective tissue.
Adipose: regions of connective tissue dominated by aggregations of fat cells.
Reticular: makes delicate connecting and supporting frameworks, enters into the composition of basement membranes, produces macrophages, and plays important roles as scavenger and agent of defense against bacteria.
Dense connective tissue:
Regular: fibers that are oriented so as to withstand tension exerted in one direction.
Irregular: fibers that are arranged so as to withstand tensions exerted from different directions.
Cartilage:
Hyaline: the most fundamental kind of cartilage, consisting of a seemingly homogeneous matrix permeated with fine white fibers.
Elastic: specialized cartilage with elastic fibers in the matrix.
Fibrous: specialized cartilage emphasizing collagenous fibers in its matrix.
Bone: a tissue consisting of cells, fibers, and a ground substance, the distinguishing feature of which is the presence of a ground substance of inorganic salts.
Lymphoid tissue: a tissue consisting of two primary tissue elements—reticular tissue and cells, chiefly lymphocytes—intermingling in intimate association in the reticular interstices.

Table 4-1 TISSUES

TISSUE	LOCATION
Epithelial tissue	
Simple squamous	Body cavities (mesothelium), cardiovascular and lymphatic vessels (endothelium), alveoli, Bowman's capsule and thin segment of loop of Henle of kidney
Simple cuboidal	Many glands, pigmented epithelium of the retina, tubules of kidney
Simple columnar	Digestive tract from the esophagogastric junction to the anal canal, gallbladder
Simple ciliated columnar	Small bronchi, bronchioles, uterus, uterine tubes, efferent ductules of testes
Stratified squamous	Epidermis (skin), mouth and tongue, esophagus, anus, vagina, cornea
Pseudostratified columnar	Epididymis, ductus deferens, excretory duct of parotid gland
Pseudostratified ciliated columnar	Nasopharynx, trachea, large bronchi
Transitional epithelium	Urinary tract from renal pelvis to urethra
Connective tissue proper	
Loose connective tissue	
Areolar	Loosely arranged fibroelastic tissue between organs and muscles; supports blood vessels and nerves
Adipose	Subcutaneous fat, breast, yellow bone marrow
Reticular	Framework of liver, lymphoid tissues, bone marrow
Dense connective tissue	
Regular	Tendons, aponeuroses, ligaments
Irregular	Dermis, capsules, sheaths, septa
Specialized connective tissue	
Cartilage	
Hyaline	Articular surfaces of bones, costal cartilages, rings of trachea, tip of nose, larynx, fetal skeleton
Fibrous	Discs between vertebrae; symphysis pubis; knee and hip joints
Elastic	Auricle of external ear, auditory tube, epiglottis, cartilages of larynx
Bone	Skeleton
Dentin	Teeth
Hematopoietic	Red marrow of bones
Lymphoid	Lymph nodes, thymus, spleen, tonsils, mucous membranes of digestive and respiratory tracts (diffuse form)
Muscular tissue	
Striated (voluntary)	Skeletal muscles; muscles of the tongue, pharynx, larynx; extrinsic muscles of the eye
Smooth (involuntary)	Muscular walls of the digestive, respiratory, and urinary tracts, blood vessels, iris; ciliary muscles; erector pili muscles
Cardiac	Heart
Nervous tissue	
Nervous tissue proper	Neurons and nerve fibers
Neuroglia	Supportive tissue in central nervous system

peritoneum; (2) macrophages lining the alveoli (terminal air sacs) of the lungs; (3) monocytes in the blood stream; (4) macrophages lining the blood sinuses of the liver (Kupffer cells) and bone marrow; (5) macrophages lining the sinuses of lymph nodes and the spleen (in these locations also called large reticular cells); and (6) microglia of the central nervous system.

Synovial Membranes. Synovial membranes line the cavities of the freely moving joints and form tendon sheaths and bursae.

MUSCLE TISSUE

There are three types of muscle tissue: striated (voluntary), smooth (involuntary), and cardiac. *Striated,* or voluntary, muscle has cross-striations and can be controlled at will. *Involuntary* muscle is smooth, without striations, and is under the control of the autonomic nervous system. *Cardiac* muscle, although striated, is found exclusively in the heart and is not under voluntary control (see Fig. 8–1).

NERVOUS TISSUE

The fourth type of tissue is *nervous tissue,* divided into nervous tissue proper and accessory cells (neuroglia). Nervous tissue is the most highly organized tissue in the body, initiating, controlling, and coordinating the body's ability to adapt to its environment. In nervous tissue proper, the specialized conducting cells are *neurons,* linked together to form nerve pathways (see Chapter 9).

The various types of tissue are sum-marized in Table 4–1 and Figures 4–5 and 4–6.

TISSUE TRANSPLANTATION

During the last two decades, an active interest has been taken in methods and mechanisms of tissue transplantation. The following should prove useful to the student embarking on a medical or paramedical career.

Definitions

Autotransplant. A transplant to the same individual from whom the tissue was removed. For example, a skin graft from the thigh to a burned surface of the hand of the same person.

Isotransplant. A transplant between individuals of the same genetic background (identical twins) or between animals of nearly the same genetic background (inbred strains).

Homotransplant. A transplant between two individuals of the same species with a different genetic background, as from one patient to another (not his identical twin).

Heterotransplant. A transplant between members of two different species, as from a rat to a dog.

When any tissue is grafted between two individuals who are not identical twins, the graft is usually rejected because the immune system of the recipient recognizes proteins on the surfaces of cells of the grafted tissue as foreign, and attacks and destroys the graft. The proteins that are recognized as foreign are called *histocompatibility antigens,*

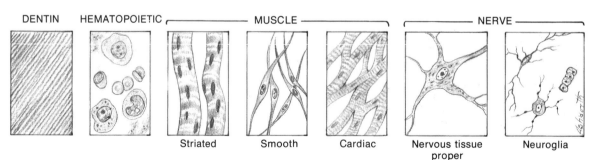

DENTIN HEMATOPOIETIC ⎯⎯⎯⎯ MUSCLE ⎯⎯⎯⎯ ⎯⎯⎯ NERVE ⎯⎯⎯

Striated Smooth Cardiac Nervous tissue proper Neuroglia

Figure 4–6. *Dentin,* like bone, consists of a collagenous mesh and calcified ground substance; unlike bone, it contains neither vessels nor total cells. *Hematopoietic tissue:* blood-forming tissues; i.e., red bone marrow. *Muscle tissue* has the properties of contractility and excitability (see Chapter 8). *Nervous tissue* has the properties of excitability and conductivity (see Chapter 9).

which by definition are cell membrane proteins that differ from one individual to another and stimulate an immune response that leads to graft rejection (for a description of the immune response, see Chapter 12).

Nature provides at least four exceptions to the concept that skin grafts between individuals are invariably destroyed: (1) Identical twins accept grafts. Inbred animal strains develop such a high degree of genetic similarity as to behave as identical twins and thus accept grafts. (2) Embryos accept grafts from each other. (3) Patients with certain disease states, such as thymic aplasia, will tolerate skin grafts. (4) Chimeras (organisms with two genetically different types of tissue) will accept skin grafts. The phenomenon of natural tolerance (chimerism) occurs in cattle twins and has been reported in nonidentical human twins. The possibility of tolerance to grafts between a mother and a child has been reported. Transplantation of kidneys is now a well-accepted routine in several medical centers.

In general, three approaches are being evaluated to prolong the life of homografts: (1) irradiation of the cells which have been sensitized by the antigens produced as a result of the graft; (2) transplanting the graft to a privileged site, such as the anterior chamber of the eye, in which not only the cornea will be accepted but other tissues as well; and (3) altering or lessening host response. Currently, drugs suppressing the cellular immune response are being employed; Imuran, cortisone, and antilymphocytic serum have proved effective. The approach of altering host response offers the greatest promise.

Grafting of Specific Tissues

Blood Vessels. Homografts of arteries can be transplanted. This type of graft degenerates over a period of several years; however, the homologous arterial transplant functions as a so-called "homostatic" tissue. This means that viability is not necessary for successful transplantation, but the tissue acts as a foundation around which the individual's own cells can produce tissue. Today, plastics are used for replacement of arteries.

Bone. Osteocytes in autologous bone grafts survive as living entities. Osteocytes in homologous or heterologous grafts die after transfer. Homologous and heterologous bone form a foundation for bone cells from the host to grow inward and replace the grafted tissue.

Cartilage. Both autologous and homologous cartilage survive transplantation. Possible explanations for survival of homografts of cartilage include the lack of blood vessels in the graft itself and the fact that the protein-polysaccharide (mucopolysaccharide) matrix can act as a barrier against host cell infiltration.

Endocrine Tissues. An impressive group of studies indicates that homotransplants of certain endocrine tissues do not provoke the usual rejection reaction. Endocrine tissue may be less highly antigenic than other tissues.

Teeth. Dental reimplantation is the procedure of reinserting into the alveolar socket a tooth accidentally extracted or dislodged. Studies are underway in some institutions on homotransplantation of teeth.

PRESERVATION OF TISSUES

There are three general methods of tissue preservation: preservation in a nutrient medium at temperatures above freezing; preservation in a nonviable state by freeze-drying or chemical fixation (applicable to homologous grafts of blood vessels, since they do not have to remain alive to provide satisfactory function); and preservation by freezing, or depressing the freezing point with the tissue remaining viable. The best long-term method of preservation is probably freezing. Cells like spermatozoa and red blood cells will survive freezing with the use of protective agents such as glycerol.

SUMMARY

TISSUES

Types of Tissues

The four basic tissues of the body are
a. Epithelial
b. Connective
c. Muscular
d. Nervous

Epithelial Tissue

a. Classified according to *shape*
  (1) Squamous (flat)
  (2) Cuboidal
  (3) Columnar
b. Classified according to *arrangement*
  (1) Simple, one cell layer
  (2) Stratified, several layers
  (3) Pseudostratified, apparently several layers, but actually all cells attached to basement membrane
  (4) Transitional, several layers of closely packed cells, easily stretched
c. Named according to the layer on the free surface
  (1) Simple squamous (surface layer of serous membranes, endothelial lining of heart and blood vessels, and respiratory surface of lungs)
  (2) Simple cuboidal (many glands and ducts, kidney tubules, germinal covering for ovaries, and pigmented layer of retina of eye)
  (3) Simple columnar (digestive tract)
  (4) Simple ciliated columnar (bronchioles)
  (5) Stratified squamous (epidermis)
  (6) Pseudostratified columnar (ductus deferens)
  (7) Pseudostratified ciliated columnar (nasopharynx, trachea, and large bronchi)
  (8) Transitional (urinary tract)
d. Classified according to *function*
  (1) Surface layer of mucous membranes (overlying a layer of connective tissue) lining digestive, respiratory, urinary, and reproductive tracts
  (2) Glandular epithelium
  (3) Endothelium, lining heart, blood vessels, and lymphatics
  (4) Mesothelium, the surface layer of serous membranes (overlying a sheet of connective tissue), lining the great cavities of the body, peritoneum, pericardium, and pleura; they include a parietal portion (lining cavity wall) and visceral layer (covering organs). Epithelial tissues function in protection, absorption, secretion, and excretion.

Connective Tissue

1. **Characterized by widely separated cells and abundance of intercellular material consisting of glycoprotein fibers and an amorphous ground substance composed principally of mucopolysaccharides.**

  a. Supportive function, to provide nourishment for overlying epithelial tissues, link muscle and bone as tendons, allowing movement.
  b. Special functions in bone, teeth, and reticuloendothelial (macrophage) system.

2. **Loose Connective Tissue**

  a. Areolar tissue: The most widely dispersed connective tissue — fine, pliable, resistant, elastic; contains fibroblasts, macrophages, and mast cells. Areolar tissue is the basic supporting substance around organs, muscles, blood vessels, and nerves. It forms membranes around the brain and spinal cord; it composes superficial fascia.
  b. Adipose tissue: Specialized areolar tissue with many fat-containing cells; adipose tissue acts as a firm, resilient packing around and between organs and between bundles of muscle fibers. In its subcutaneous location, it protects the body from excessive heat loss or excessive increases in temperature.
  c. Reticular tissue: A framework of delicate, branching fibrils, found in lymphoid organs, bone marrow, and the liver.

3. **Dense Connective Tissue**

  a. Contains closely packed collagenous and elastic fibers in regular array (tendons and ligaments) or irregular array (the dermis).
  b. Where elastic fibers predominate (as in the walls of large arteries, the trachea, and bronchi), they are referred to as elastic tissue.

4. **Specialized Connective Tissue**

  a. Cartilage: Yields a firm matrix between cells; cells of cartilage are called chondrocytes. There are three types of cartilage:

(1) Hyaline: The precursor of the skeletal system; during embryonic development much of it is gradually replaced by bone through the process of ossification. At termination of bone growth, it remains on articular surfaces. Also found in trachea, bronchi, larynx, costal cartilages, and nose.

(2) Fibrous: Contains dense masses of unbranching collagenous fibers lying in bundles. It is dense and resistant to stretching. The cells are located in rows between the collagenous bundles.

(3) Elastic: The most resilient type of cartilage; found in the auricles of the ear, auditory tube, epiglottis, and larynx.

b. Bone: Firm structure of living tissue formed by impregnation of the intercellular material with inorganic salts. Bone is constantly being remodeled.

c. Dentin: Dentin of the teeth is similar to bone. It is covered by enamel.

d. Blood: A fluid tissue circulating through the body, carrying nutrients to cells and removing waste products.

e. Hematopoietic tissue: Red bone marrow is the blood-forming (hematopoietic) tissue.

f. Lymphoid tissue: Found in lymph nodes, thymus, spleen, tonsils, and adenoids; functions in immunity.

g. Reticuloendothelial system: Composed of connective tissue cells carrying on the process of phagocytosis. Strong line of defense against infection.

Muscle Tissue

1. Three Types of Muscle

a. Voluntary, or striated
b. Involuntary, or smooth
c. Cardiac

Nervous Tissue

1. Division of Nervous Tissue

a. Nervous tissue proper, consisting of neurons, the specialized conducting cells

b. Tissue composed of various accessory cells (neuroglia)

Tissue Transplantation

1. Types of Transplants

a. Autotransplant
b. Isotransplant
c. Homotransplant
d. Heterotransplant

2. Transplanted tissues are usually rejected because the immune system recognizes proteins on the surfaces of cells of the grafted tissue as foreign ("histocompatibility antigens") and destroys the graft.

3. Nature provides at least four exceptions to the concept that the skin grafts between individuals are invariably destroyed:

a. Identical twins accept grafts.
b. Grafts between embryos are accepted.
c. Patients with certain diseases accept grafts from each other.
d. Chimeras accept grafts.

4. Three approaches are being evaluated to prolong the life of homografts:

a. Irradiation on effector side
b. Transplanting the graft to a privileged site
c. Altering or lessening host resistance by immunosuppressive agents

5. Grafting of Specific Tissues

a. Homografts of arteries can be transplanted.
b. Osteocytes in autologous bone grafts survive transplantation.
c. Possibly certain endocrine tissues do not elicit rejection.
d. A tooth which has been accidentally extracted or dislodged can be reinserted into the alveolar socket.

Preservation of Tissue (Three General Methods)

1. In a nutrient medium at a temperature above freezing.

2. In a nonviable state by freeze-drying or chemical fixation.

3. By freezing or by depressing the freezing point with the tissue remaining viable.

REVIEW QUESTIONS

1. List the four basic types of tissues.
2. List and define the terms used to classify the cells of epithelial tissues according to shape and arrangement. What type of tissue, classified by cell shape and arrangement, is found in the interior lining of each of the following: (1) small intestine, (2) heart, (3) trachea, (4) mouth, and (5) kidney tubules?
3. Define and give the locations of (1) mucous membrane, (2) mesothelium, and (3) endothelium.
4. Distinguish between epithelial and connective tissues with respect to (1) amount of matrix, (2) vascularity, and (3) functions.
5. List three types of cartilage and give one location of each.
6. Compare autotransplant, isotransplant, homotransplant, and heterotransplant.

Unit 2 □ FRAMEWORK OF THE BODY

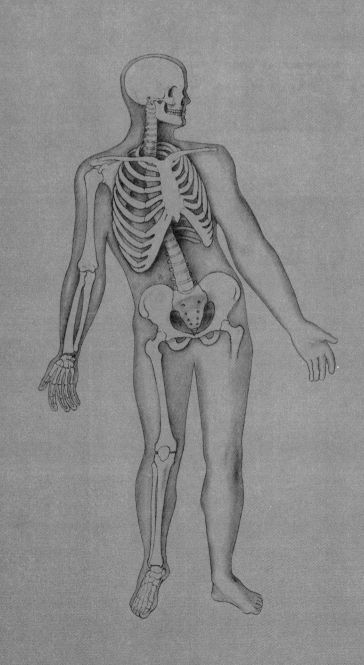

5
The Skin

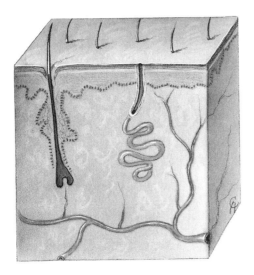

Objectives

The aim of this chapter is to enable the student to:

- Distinguish between the epidermal and dermal layers of the skin.
- Describe the important features of the layers of the epidermis.
- Explain the functions of melanocytes of the epidermis.
- Describe the appendages of the skin: hair, nails, sebaceous glands and sweat glands.
- Describe hair growth.
- List the functions of the skin.
- Describe some of the common disorders of skin.

IMPORTANCE OF THE SKIN

The skin of an average adult covers over 3000 square inches of surface area, weighs approximately 6 pounds (nearly twice the weight of the liver or brain) and receives about one-third of all blood circulating through the body. It is elastic, rugged, and, under ordinary conditions, self-regenerating. The skin is almost entirely waterproof, providing an efficient, closely regulated thermal barrier and participating in the dissipation of water and in the temperature-regulatory functions of the body.

LAYERS OF THE SKIN

Epidermis

The outer, or epidermal (G, *epi*, upon; G. *derma*, skin), layer of the skin is composed of stratified squamous epithelial cells. It consists of five layers, from superficial to deep (Fig. 5–1). They are the stratum corneum (horny layer), stratum lucidum (clear layer), stratum granulosum (granular layer), stratum spinosum (prickly layer), and stratum germinativum (regenerative layer).

The **stratum corneum** (L. *corneus*, horny) forms the outermost layer of the epidermis and consists of dead cells completely filled with a protein called keratin (G. *keras*, horn). They are commonly called keratinized cells and are continuously shed, requiring replacement. The stratum corneum consists of 20 per cent water, as compared with 70 per cent water in the stratum germinativum. The stratum corneum is composed of flattened cells resembling scales. It serves as a physical barrier to light and heat waves, microorganisms, and most chemicals. The thickness of

this layer is determined by the amount of stimulation of the surface by abrasion and weight bearing — hence thick palms and soles and the development of calluses (Fig. 5–2).

The **stratum lucidum,** lying directly beneath the stratum corneum, is not seen in thinner skin. It is a layer of one to five cells thick, consisting of transparent, flattened, dead or dying cells, usually lacking nuclei.

The **stratum granulosum,** two to five layers of flattened cells, provides a transition into the subjacent layers. Granules accumulate in the cells, giving the layer its name; however, the granules do not contribute to skin color. The stratum granulosum is thought to be active in keratinization, a process in which cells manufacture keratin and lose their nuclei, becoming more compact and brittle.

The **stratum spinosum** consists of several rows of "prickly" cells, polyhedral in shape. The cell outlines are spiny, hence the name, prickle cells. In some classifications this layer is included with the stratum germinativum as the Malpighian layer.

The **stratum germinativum,** the deepest and most important layer of the skin, contains cells capable of mitotic division. When new cells are formed, they undergo morphologic and nuclear changes as they move toward the most superficial layer. Simultaneously, these cells *give rise to all outer layers of the epidermis.* The epidermis will regenerate only so long as the stratum germinativum remains intact. The basal layer of these generative cells rests on a basement membrane which offers further protection from the environment.

Melanin, the principal pigment of the skin, is formed in the stratum germinativum by cells called **melanocytes** and is transferred from melanocyte processes to surrounding

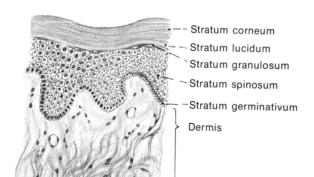

Stratum corneum
Stratum lucidum
Stratum granulosum
Stratum spinosum
Stratum germinativum

Dermis

Epidermis

Figure 5–1. The epidermis (consisting of five distinct layers) and the dermis compose the protective covering of the body.

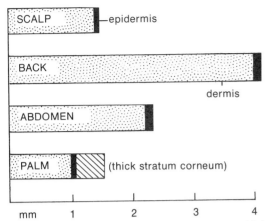

Figure 5–2. Graphic representation of skin thicknesses from various body sites.

epithelial cells. The presence of carotene is in part responsible for the yellow color of skin. The darker color of the skin is due to melanin; the pink tint is caused by vessels in the dermis (there are no vessels in the epidermis). The strongest factor in increasing pigmentation is the sun's stimulating effect on melanocytes. Melanin is capable of cross-linking with protein to form a tough, resistant compound; hence, heavily pigmented skin is more resistant to external irritation.

A variation in melanin content is the principal factor responsible for color differences among races. Certain population groups have more active melanocytes in their skin. This causes black, yellow, brown, and white races. Darkly pigmented skin does not contain a greater number of melanocytes, but the melanocytes present are more active.

Dermis (Corium)

The dermis, or corium, lying directly beneath the epidermis, is often called the true skin. It consists of connective tissue containing white collagenous and yellow elastic fibers. Blood vessels, nerves, lymph vessels, hair follicles, and sweat glands are embedded in the dermis. The dermis is divided into an upper layer, the *papillary layer,* so named because it forms projections into corresponding depressions in the overlying epidermis (papilla is the Latin word for nipple), and a lower layer, the *reticular layer,* lying between the papillary layer and the subcutaneous (L. *sub,* under; L. *cutis, skin*) tissue.

Subcutaneous Tissue

A sheet of areolar tissue containing fat, known as subcutaneous adipose tissue or superficial fascia, attaches the dermis to the underlying structures.

APPENDAGES OF THE SKIN

The appendages associated with the skin include hair, nails, sebaceous glands, and sweat glands (Figs. 5–3 and 5–4).

Hair

Hair is found on nearly every part of the surface of the body. Each hair is composed of three parts — the cuticle, cortex, and medulla. The *cuticle*, the outermost portion, contains several layers of overlapping, scalelike cells. The *cortex*, or principal portion of the hair, consists of elongated cells united to make flattened fibers. In dark hair, the fibers contain pigment granules. The central axis of the hair, known as the *medulla*, is composed of many-sided cells with air spaces between them. The medulla is not present in very thin hair. The visible portion of the hair is the *shaft*. The cells embedded in the skin form the *root*. Enclosing the root is the **hair follicle,** a tubular invagination of epidermis surrounded by a sheath of connective tissue (the dermal root sheath). The epidermal portion of the follicle is divided into two parts, the external and internal root sheaths. At its base the follicle expands into the *bulb*, into which dermal tissue, the *papilla* of the hair, projects from below (Figs. 5–3 and 5–4). The papilla contains blood vessels, which provide nutrition for the hair, and nerve endings. When the arrector pili muscles (bundles of smooth muscle fibers attached to the hair follicles) contract, the skin assumes a so-called "goose flesh" appearance where hair is sparse and results in a certain degree of "hair standing on end" where the hair is prominent.

Hair growth is similar to growth of the epidermis, with the deeper cell layers responsible for production of new cells. The epithelial matrix cells at the base of the bulb of the hair follicle divide mitotically. Daughter cells move upward, keratinize, and form the horny layer of the shaft. When hair stops growing (resting phase), it forms a clublike

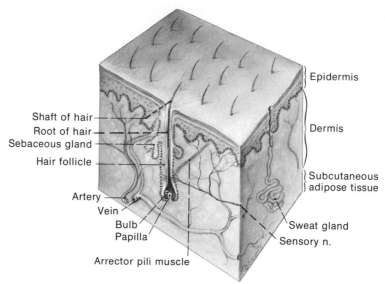

Figure 5–3. Three-dimensional view of the skin.

base (club hair) that becomes firmly anchored to a shrunken follicle by fine filaments of keratin. New hair growth loosens the old hair, which is shed. Men, women, and children have approximately the same number of hair follicles, but in women and children the hairs in many parts of the body are more rudimentary.

The keratin of the cortex is polymerized and crosslinked in a characteristic folded configuration (alpha keratin) rendering the fibers elastic. When stretched, the keratin chain is drawn out into a more linear form (beta keratin). Unless it is greatly distended or altered by chemical agents, it returns immediately to its normal configuration. When hair is wet, it can be elongated to one and one-half times its normal length. This is possible because keratin can be readily stretched in the direction of the long axis of the molecular chains of amino acids. Permanent wave sets act on this principle. After the

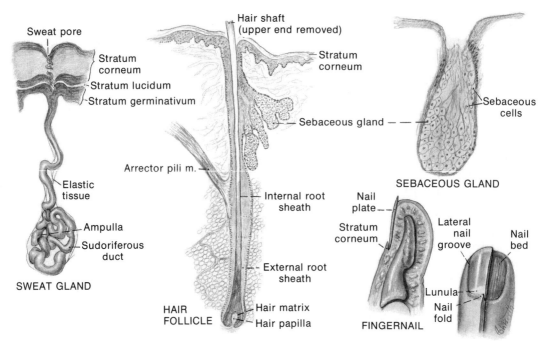

Figure 5–4. The appendages associated with the skin.

hair has been stretched and molded into a desired wave, reducing agents rupture the disulfide bonds of the hair. Oxidizing agents are then applied, reestablishing the stabilizing crosslinks in a new position.

Hair Color. Hair color is determined by complex genetic factors. Gray hair occurs when pigment is absent. White hair results from an absence of pigment plus the formation of air bubbles in the hair shaft. Heredity and other unknown factors determine the graying of hair. The hair of a black cat will turn gray from a diet deficient in pantothenic acid. Restoring this substance to the diet causes the hair to return to its normal color. This fact is of interest but has not proved to be of importance in man.

Nails

The nails, a modification of the horny epidermal cells, are composed of hard keratin. Air mixed in the keratin matrix forms the white crescent, the *lunula,* at the proximal end of each nail. The nail plate arising from the proximal nail fold and attached to the nail bed grows approximately 1 mm per week unless inhibited by disease. Regeneration of a lost fingernail occurs in 3½ to 5½ months; regeneration of a lost toenail occurs in 6 to 8 months.

Glands

Sebaceous Glands

Sebaceous glands generally arise from the walls of hair follicles and produce sebum, the oily substance primarily responsible for lubrication of the surface of the skin. Sebaceous secretion consists of entire cells containing sebum. When the cell disintegrates, sebum is secreted along the hair shaft onto the surface of the skin, providing a cosmetic gloss. In the few parts of the body where the glands are not associated with hair follicles, such as at the corners of the mouth, the glans penis, and the labia minora, the ducts open directly upon the surface of the skin. Sebaceous glands are absent on the palms and soles.

Sebaceous secretion is under the control of the endocrine system, increasing at puberty and in late pregnancy and decreasing with advancing age. The pubertal increase con-

tributes to the problem of acne in adolescents, and diminution is responsible for the relative dryness of the skin in later life.

The orifice of the sebaceous gland can become discolored as a result of oxidation of fatty material by the air, producing a "blackhead." Secretions retained in the gland provide a medium for growth of the pus-producing bacteria responsible for pimples and boils.

Sweat Glands

Sweat glands are simple tubular glands found in most parts of the skin except the lips and the glans penis, and most (*eccrine type*) are not associated with hair follicles. They are most numerous in the palms and soles. It has been estimated that there are 3000 sweat glands per square inch on the palm. Each consists of a secretory portion and an excretory duct. The secretory portion, located in the dermis tissue, is a blind tube twisted and coiled on itself. From the coiled secretory portion, the excretory duct spirals toward the surface. Each glandular tube is lined with secretory epithelium continuous with the epidermis. The secretory epithelium consists of two types of cells: (1) spindle-shaped, contractile, myoepithelial (G. *mys,* muscle) cells attached to the basement membrane, and (2) pyramidal cells that secrete sweat, resting on top of the myoepithelial cells.

Pure sweat contains the same inorganic constituents as blood but in lower concentration. The chief salt is sodium chloride. Organic constituents in sweat include urea, uric acid, amino acids, ammonia, sugar, lactic acid, and ascorbic acid. Sweat itself is practically odorless. The odor is produced by the action of bacteria on sweat. Ceruminous glands, which secrete wax, are found in the external meatus of the ear; ciliary glands, in the eyelids, secrete ocular fluid. Both are considered to be modified sweat glands.

Sweating leads to loss of heat in the body owing to the fact that heat is required to evaporate the water in the sweat; thus, sweating helps to lower the body temperature. Sweating is initiated by the effect of elevated blood temperature on cerebral centers. Denervated skin (without nerves) does not respond to temperature changes by sweating. Some individuals have congenital absence of sweat glands. Such persons can die of heat stroke if exposed to high temperatures even for brief periods. In some areas of the body, especially friction surfaces (palms and soles), sweat glands readily respond to stressful stimuli.

In contrast to the ordinary sweat glands (eccrine type) described above, sweat glands in certain regions of the body (known as the *apocrine type*), such as the armpits, anogenital area, navel, and nipples, are connected to hair follicles and reach deeply into the subcutaneous layer of the skin. Beginning with puberty, these glands secrete a viscous, odorous fluid and respond to emotional, especially sexual, stimulation.

FUNCTIONS OF THE SKIN

The skin functions in *sensation, protection, thermoregulation,* and *secretion.* Located in the skin are specific receptors sensitive to the four basic sensations of pain, touch, temperature, and pressure. Upon stimulation of a receptor, a nerve impulse is sent to the cerebral cortex of the brain, where the impulse is interpreted. The brain must interpret among degrees of stimulation and among combinations of stimulations, the latter of which result in sensations such as burning, tickling, and itching.

The skin forms an elastic, resistant covering that protects man from his complex environment. It prevents the passage of harmful physical and chemical agents and inhibits excessive loss of water and electrolytes.

The acid mantle of skin helps protect its surface from irritants and bacteria. Some skin diseases destroy the acidity of certain areas, impairing the self-sterilizing ability of the skin. In this condition, the skin is prone to bacterial invasion.

Experimental evidence indicates that the normal intact human skin is usually impermeable to water, carbohydrate, fat, and protein. All true gases and many volatile substances will pass through the epidermis. For example, many deaths have resulted from absorption of large quantities of organic pesticide sprays through the skin. Sex hormones are readily absorbed when applied in a proper vehicle. Mercury, lead, and copper penetrate the skin under certain conditions. The numerous follicular orifices serve as channels for absorption. Substances passing through normal skin are soluble in fat and water.

Heat is lost from the body by conduction, convection, radiation, and evaporation. These processes are regulated by nervous and chemical activation of the sweat glands and by dilation and constriction of the cutaneous vessels (see Chapter 14). As the body needs to dissipate heat, blood vessels of the skin dilate, allowing more blood to come to the surface, with a resulting heat loss.

The skin plays a part in the secretory functions of the body. Sebum secreted by sebaceous glands has antifungal and antibacterial properties and helps maintain the texture of the skin. Sweat is a secretion.

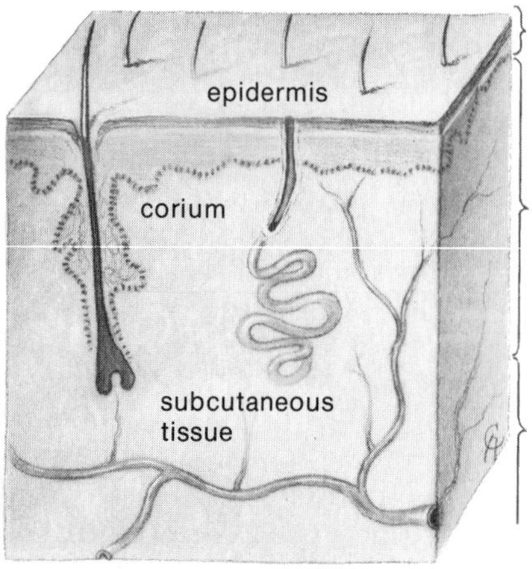

	Degree	Surface	Color	Pain
	1st	dry no blisters	erythematous	painful hyperesthetic
	2nd	moist blisters	mottled red	painful hyperesthetic
	3rd	dry	pearly white or charred	little pain anesthetic

Figure 5–5. Extent of burn injury — first, second, and third degree. In a first degree burn only the epidermis is injured (as in sunburn); a second degree burn extends into the dermis; a third degree burn involves the full thickness of skin, epidermis, dermis, extending into subcutaneous tissue. (Courtesy of Parke, Davis.)

TRANSPLANTATION OF SKIN

The skin has a great capacity for regeneration and repair. If the epidermis is removed, the skin will regenerate, provided that isolated patches of the stratum germinativum remain. In a deeper wound, a new covering of epidermis is formed over the denuded area by active division of epidermal cells at the margin. In some cases, this natural process of repair is inadequate to secure an efficient return of function to the damaged tissue, as in third degree burns (Fig. 5–5), and transplantation of the skin offers a solution.

WOUND HEALING

Wound healing involves the reaction of the entire body to trauma, as well as local changes in the wound itself. The body responds *clinically* to injury by a temporary elevation of temperature and pulse rate. Chemically, loss of nitrogen and potassium is followed by nitrogen and potassium retention.

During wound healing, bleeding into the wound results in clot formation, and vasodilation permits circulating cells, oxygen, and nutrients to be carried to the wound area. Debris in the wound is removed by phagocytes, and endothelial capillary buds appear in the clot by the second day. The clot is composed of a network of threads of a protein substance called fibrin, which is enmeshed in bodies called platelets. In this network the blood corpuscles are entangled.

Fibroblasts multiply in the wound and migrate from the periphery to combine with endothelial tissue and young blood vessels. These constitute *granulation tissue.* Fibroblasts release precursors of collagen into the interstitial spaces which form collagen fibers in the wound itself.

The *epidermis* is capable of rapid regeneration. Cell migration begins a few hours after an epidermal incision. A small defect will be covered completely after about 48 hours.

Factors interfering with wound healing. Many factors interfere with wound healing: inadequate nutrition; necrotic tissue (dead or dying tissue); foreign bodies; bacteria; interference with blood supply; blockage of lymphatics; systemic disease, such as diabetes mellitus; psychological factors.

Figure 5–6 illustrates various abnormalities of the skin.

Clinical Aspects

The appearance of the skin can be an important sign in diagnosis of various disorders. For instance, the skin may be red in hypertension (high blood pressure) and in other conditions in which the blood vessels of the skin are dilated. A pale skin suggests anemia (too few red corpuscles or too little hemoglobin). The color of the skin may be blue or purple (cyanosis) in severe heart

Figure 5–6. Terms used in connection with abnormalities of the skin. *Macule:* a discolored (especially reddened), unelevated spot on the skin. *Papule:* a solid elevation of the skin. *Nodule:* a small node which is solid and irregular in form. *Wheal:* a flat, edematous (containing an excessive accumulation of fluid) elevation of the skin, frequently accompanied by itching. *Polyp:* a pedunculated (attached by a narrow base) growth extending into the lumen of a body cavity or appearing on the skin. *Pustule:* an elevation filled with pus. *Ulcer:* a loss of substance on a cutaneous or mucous surface. *Cyst:* any sac, normal or otherwise, especially one which contains a liquid or semisolid substance without pus. *Fissure:* any cleft or groove.

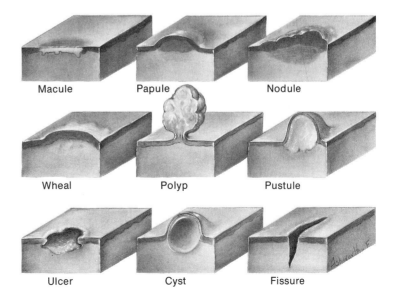

Macule Papule Nodule

Wheal Polyp Pustule

Ulcer Cyst Fissure

disease and in such pulmonary diseases as pneumonia (in which the blood is not being adequately supplied with oxygen). A yellow skin (jaundice) indicates the presence of bile pigments in the blood in larger than normal amounts.

Acne (pimples) is caused by infection and subsequent inflammation of sebaceous glands.

Hives (urticaria) is a skin condition characterized by the sudden appearance of raised patches which are white in the center and itch severely. Hives occur when an individual takes medication or certain foods to which he is sensitive.

Psoriasis is a chronic inflammatory disease which is neither infectious nor contagious, characterized by dry, whitish scales on reddish patches caused by excessive multiplication of epidermal cells. Although psoriasis has been considered incurable, a promising new treatment is available which combines high-intensity ultraviolet light with the ingestion of a photosensitizing drug (methoxsalen).

Decubitus ulcers (bed sores) occur where there are areas of pressure on the body. Frequent turning and alcohol rubs help to prevent this distressing condition.

Sunburn is a condition in which the skin is swollen and red after excessive exposure to the sun, especially ultraviolet rays, and can occur even on a cloudy day. It is thought to be due to the production of a histaminelike substance that dilates the capillaries and leads to the swelling, or edema. Further damage may be caused by the release of hydrolytic enzymes from disrupted lysosomes. Other consequences of overexposure to sunlight include an increase in melanin formation, which darkens the skin, and an impairment in feedback control of cell division (see page 64), which results in thickening of the skin.

Boils (furuncles) are circumscribed inflammations of the corium and subcutaneous tissue due to bacteria which enter through the hair follicles.

SUMMARY

THE SKIN

1. The skin receives about one-third of the blood circulating through the body. It is elastic, regenerates, and functions in sensation, protection, thermoregulation, and secretion.

2. **The skin consists of two layers.**

   a. The *epidermis,* composed of stratified squamous epithelium, has the following layers (beginning with the outermost):
   (1) Stratum corneum
   (2) Stratum lucidum
   (3) Stratum granulosum
   (4) Stratum spinosum
   (5) Stratum germinativum
   The cells of the stratum germinativum divide and give rise to the upper layers. As the cells move upward, they undergo morphologic changes, become keratinized, and gradually die. The flat, dead cells of the stratum corneum are continuously shed.
   The principal pigment, melanin, is formed in the melanocytes of the stratum germinativum and injected into the surrounding epithelial cells. Melanocytes are more active in the darker races.

   b. The *dermis,* a dense, vascular connective tissue divided into the papillary layer, close to the epidermis, and the reticular layer, between the papillary layer and underlying subcutaneous tissue.

3. **The subcutaneous tissue (superficial fascia), a loose connective tissue with variable amounts of fat, attaches the dermis to the underlying structures.**

Appendages of the Skin

1. **Hair**

   a. Consists of an outer, scalelike cuticle, central cortex (the principal portion), and inner medulla. The visible portion is the shaft; the root is the portion embedded in the skin.

   b. Hair growth occurs by division of matrix cells at the base of the hair follicle (a tubular invagination of the epidermis). Daughter cells move upward and keratinize.
   (1) When hair growth ceases, a clublike base becomes anchored to a shrunken follicle. The old hair is shed when loosened by new growth.

   c. Contraction of arrector pili muscles

(bundles of smooth muscle fibers attached to hair follicles) causes "goose flesh."

2. Nails

a. Composed of hard keratin; a modification of the horny epidermal cells.
b. Arise from the proximal nail fold.
c. Grow at the rate of approximately 1 mm per week.

3. Glands

a. *Sebaceous:* Most open into hair follicles.
  (1) The secretion (sebum) consists of the oily substance and cellular debris of disintegrated cells. Secretion increases at puberty and late in pregnancy, declining with advanced age.
b. *Sweat glands:* Simple coiled tubular glands. The ducts of the most common (eccrine) type open directly onto the surface of the skin. The ducts of the less common (apocrine) type open into hair follicles; these glands are found in the armpits, anogenital area, navel, and nipples.
  (1) The eccrine type secretes a watery fluid (containing the same inorganic constituents as in blood but in lower concentration) in response to elevated temperature. Eccrine glands on friction surfaces (palms and soles) also readily respond to emotional stimuli.
  (2) Apocrine sweat glands secrete a viscous, odorous fluid at the onset of puberty and respond to emotional stimuli.
  (3) Ceruminous glands in outer parts of the external auditory meatus and ciliary glands of the eyelids are modified sweat glands.

REVIEW QUESTIONS

1. List the five layers of the epidermis. In which layer are the cells dividing? Which layer consists of keratinized dead cells?
2. Name the principal pigment of the skin. Explain how epithelial cells become pigmented. What accounts for color differences among races?
3. List three appendages of the skin.
4. Describe the growth of hair.
5. How do apocrine sweat glands differ from eccrine sweat glands in location and composition of their secretions?
6. List four functions of the skin.

6
The Skeletal System

Objectives

The aim of this chapter is to enable the student to:

☐ Describe the functions of bone.

☐ Distinguish between the functions of osteoblasts, osteoclasts, and osteocytes.

☐ Describe the Haversian system, the microscopic functional unit of bone.

☐ Identify the types of bones.

☐ Describe the formation and growth of bone.

☐ List the vitamins and hormones that regulate bone formation and growth and describe how each functions.

☐ Explain the roles of the parathyroid hormone and calcitonin in regulating the release of calcium from bone.

☐ List and describe the various types of bone fractures and outline the stages of healing.

☐ Identify the bones of the axial and appendicular skeletons.

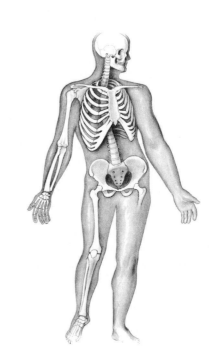

FUNCTIONS

The supporting structure of the body is a joined framework of bones called the *skeleton*. It enables man to stand erect and to accomplish extraordinary feats of artistic grace, athletic endeavor, and physical endurance.

Contrary to appearance, the individual bones of the skeleton are indeed living tissues. Five general functions are ascribed to the skeleton as a whole.

1. It *supports* the surrounding tissues.

2. It *protects* vital organs and other soft tissues of the body.

3. It assists in *body movement*, giving attachment to the muscles and providing leverage.

4. It manufactures blood cells. This *hematopoietic* function occurs in the red bone marrow.

5. It provides a *storage* area for mineral salts, especially phosphorus and calcium, to supply body needs.

Leonardo da Vinci is credited with being the first anatomist to correctly illustrate the skeleton with its 206 bones. The Belgian physician Andreas Vesalius (1514–1564) reconstructed a human skeleton that is still in existence today as the oldest anatomic specimen. Current investigation centers on actual function of the cells of bone in health and disease.

COMPOSITION OF BONE

Bone is a form of connective tissue and, as such, consists of cells and a matrix of fibers and ground substance. The distinguishing feature of bone is that the ground substance is calcified and, therefore, rigid. The collagenous fibers of the matrix are responsible for its resilience when tension is applied, whereas the calcium salts deposited in the matrix (accounting for 65 per cent of the weight of bone) prevent crushing when pressure is applied. A substance closely resembling the structure of *hydroxyapatite* $[Ca_3(PO_4)_2]_3 \cdot Ca(OH)_2$ makes up the major portion of salts present in bone. Small amounts of calcium carbonate ($CaCO_3$) are also present.

Bone Cells

Three types of cells exist in bone: osteoblasts (active in bone formation), osteoclasts (associated with bone resorption), and osteocytes (the principal cells of mature bone). Although each type is readily identified, especially in growing bone, reversible transformation from one to the other apparently occurs.

Deposition of Bone by Osteoblasts. Bone develops from spindle-shaped cells called *osteoblasts* (G. *osteon*, bone; G. *blastos*, germ). This occurs not only when bone is initially formed, but also in the remodeling and repair of fully formed bone. The first function of the osteoblasts is to secrete the organic matrix components, namely, the constituents of the ground substance, principally mucopolysaccharides (see Chapter 2), and a precursor of the fibrous protein collagen, which, following chemical alteration, polymerizes into fibrils. A geometric array of collagenous fibers (which has been described as resembling the struts and girders of a bridge) embedded in the amorphous ground substance takes form to give the matrix a leatherlike consistency. Calcium salts are then precipitated within the matrix, giving the bone its characteristic quality of hardness. For these salts to be deposited it is necessary that calcium first combine with phosphate, producing calcium phosphate ($CaHPO_4$); this substance is slowly converted over a period of several weeks into a hydroxyapatite pattern.

REGULATION OF DEPOSITION. Deposition of bone is regulated partially by the amount of strain on the bone — the more strain the greater the deposition. Bones in casts, therefore, will waste away, whereas continued and excessive strain will cause the bone to grow thick and strong. In addition, a break in the bone will stimulate injured osteoblasts to proliferate, secreting large quantities of matrix for the deposition of new bone.

Resorption of Bone by Osteoclasts. Large cells called *osteoclasts* are present in almost all cavities of bone, and they function to cause resorption (L. *resorbere*, to suck back) of bone. This is brought about by the release of enzymes from lysosomes that digest the protein portion of bone and split the salts. These phosphate and calcium salts are then absorbed into the surrounding extracellular fluid in the bone canaliculi (described under Histology).

The strength and, in some instances, the size of the skeletal bone will depend on the comparative activity of the bone. For example, it is obvious that during the growth period deposition is more active than resorption. The *osteoclasts* are associated with the removal of dead bone from the inner side during remodeling. As a result, the bone is prevented from becoming overly thick and heavy. Osteoblastic deposition continues to counteract the never-ending process of resorption, even when the bones are no longer capable of growth.

It is possible for crooked bones to become straight because of this continual process. A broken bone that has healed crookedly in a child will straighten in a matter of a few years.

During the four-day flight of Gemini IV in 1965, one of the astronauts lost between 1 and 12 per cent of his bone mass, as measured by x-ray of his hands and feet. The flight of Gemini V, which lasted eight days, caused losses of more than 20 per cent. As a result of these findings, exercises in flight were prescribed which were found to reduce this loss.

Osteocytes

Osteocytes, which are osteoblasts that have become surrounded by bone matrix as bone is formed, are the principal cells of fully formed bone. Although the mature osteocyte no longer forms bone matrix at a rapid pace, it is presumed to be involved in the maintenance of the matrix. In addition, osteocytes apparently participate in bone resorption under the influence of the parathyroid hormone (see discussion on calcium homeostasis on page 113).

Types of Bone Tissue

There are two types of bone tissue, **compact** and **cancellous**, also called spongy (Fig. 6–1). Compact bone tissue is dense and strong. Cancellous bone tissue, on the other hand, has many open (marrow) spaces, giving the tissue a spongy appearance even without the aid of a microscope. The plates of bone forming the open network of cancellous bone are called *trabeculae* (Latin for little beams).

CLASSIFICATION OF BONES

Individual bones of the skeleton are divided according to shape into five types: long, short, flat, irregular, and sesamoid.

1. **Long bones** (for example, humerus, radius, tibia, and fibula) consist of a shaft, or diaphysis, and two extremities, each called an epiphysis (Fig. 6–1). The shaft is formed primarily of compact tissue, which is thickest in the middle of the bone, where strain on it is the greatest. Strength of a long bone is further insured by a slight curvature of the shaft. The interior of the shaft is the *marrow cavity*, also called the *medullary canal*. The flared portions at each end of the diaphysis and each epiphysis are composed of a central core of cancellous bone surrounded by a thin layer of compact bone. In growing bone the epiphysis and diaphysis are separated by the cartilaginous epiphyseal, or growth, plate, where longitudinal growth occurs. The extremities are generally broad and expanded, as compared with the shaft, to facilitate articulation with other bones and provide a larger surface for muscle attachment. The articular surfaces are covered with a layer of hyaline cartilage.

2. **Short bones**, exemplified by the *carpal* bones of the wrist and the *tarsal* bones of the ankle, have a somewhat irregular shape and are not merely shorter versions of a long bone type. Only a thin layer of compact tissue covers the cancellous tissue of a typical short bone.

3. **Flat bones** are found wherever there is a need for protection of soft body parts or for a provision for extensive muscle attachment. The *ribs*, the *scapula*, parts of the *pelvic girdle*, and the bones of the *skull* are all examples of flat bones. These bones consist of two flat plates of compact tissue enclosing a layer of spongy bone.

4. **Irregular bones** have the same basic structure as short and flat bones; however, this last group comprises bones of peculiar and differing shape, such as the vertebrae and the ossicles of the ear.

5. **Sesamoid bones** are generally considered a separate type, since they are small and rounded. Sesamoid bones are enclosed in tendon and fascial tissue and are found adjacent to joints. They appear to function in increasing the lever function of muscles. The patella, or kneecap, is included among the 206 bones of the skeleton. It is the largest and most definitive of the sesamoid bones.

Membranes of Bone

The **periosteum** (G. *peri*, around; G. *osteon*, bone) is the connective tissue sheath

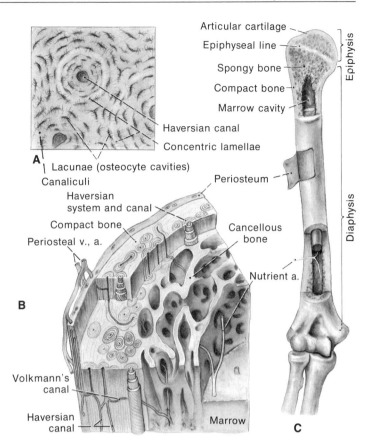

Figure 6–1. *A,* Cross section of bone, showing relation of osteocytes to Haversian system. *B,* This section has been magnified out of proportion to show Haversian system and lamellae. (Note communication between periosteal vessels and Haversian canal vessels by way of Volkmann's canals.) *C,* Diagram of the structure of a long bone. (After Lockhart.)

that covers the outer surface of bone except at the articular surfaces (which are layered with hyaline cartilage). The outer layer of the periosteum is relatively acellular, dense, and vascular; the inner layer is loose and, during growth, contains osteoblasts. In the adult, the inner layer contains an abundance of spindle-shaped connective tissue cells which, when stimulated by normal mechanical stress or injury, assume the appearance and bone-forming activity of osteoblasts. The periosteum is achored to bone by collagenous fibers (Sharpey's fibers) that penetrate the underlying matrix.

The **endosteum** (G. *endon,* within) is a thin, delicate membrane that lines all of the cavities of bone, including the marrow cavity of long bone (where it is most prominent), the marrow spaces of cancellous bone, and the Haversian canals (described below). It has both osteogenic and hematopoietic capabilities.

Marrow

The many spaces within the cancellous bone of the ribs, vertebrae, sternum, and pelvis are, in normal adults, filled with **red bone marrow**. This marrow, which is richly supplied with blood, consists mainly of blood cells and their precursors. Its primary function, referred to as hematopoiesis, is the formation of red and white blood cells and megakaryocytes, which fragment to form platelets (necessary for blood clotting). Therefore, cells in all stages of development are found within it. Red marrow is plentiful inside the ends of the humerus and femur at birth but gradually decreases in amount throughout the years.

Yellow marrow is connective tissue that consists chiefly of fat cells and is found primarily in the shafts of long bones, within the marrow cavity.

HISTOLOGY OF BONE

The **Haversian system,** named for Clopton Havers, the English anatomist who first described it, is a prominent histologic feature of compact bone. This system permits effective metabolism of bone cells and has several components (Fig. 6–1). Running parallel to the surface of the bone are many small canals containing blood vessels (generally one or two capillaries) that bring in oxygen and food and remove waste products. These canals, called **Haversian canals**, are surrounded by concentric rings of bone, each layer of which is called a **lamella**. Between two lamellae of compact bone are several tiny cavities called **lacunae**. The lacunae are connected to each other and ultimately to the larger, central Haversian canals by small canals, or **canaliculi.**

Each lacuna contains an osteocyte, or mature bone cell, suspended in tissue fluid. It is this fluid that circulates through compact bone via the Haversian system. The Haversian system functions to keep osteocytes alive and healthy.

In summary, the Haversian system consists of lacunae and their contained osteocytes, the canaliculi, a central Haversian canal with blood vessels and the surrounding lamellae.

Blood vessels in the Haversian canals interconnect by way of transverse and oblique canals and occasionally communicate through *Volkmann's canals* with the blood vessels of the surface periosteum and the endosteum lining the marrow cavity. The Haversian systems of compact bone are closely arranged, with interstitial lamellae filling the spaces between Haversian systems.

In the trabeculae of cancellous bone, the osteocytes also reside in lacunae between lamellae and are interconnected by canaliculi. But the Haversian systems are not complete, since Haversian blood vessels are absent. The osteocytes are nourished by direct communication between the network of canaliculi and the endosteum of the marrow spaces.

Bone Formation and Growth

Intramembranous Ossification. There are two types of ossification. The first of these, intramembranous ossification, is a process involving the direct mineralization of richly vascular dense connective tissue membrane, thus forming bone. The membrane itself becomes the *periosteum*, while immediately within the periosteum can be found compact bone with an inner core of *cancellous bone.*

Only the flat bones of the cranium form completely by this process.

Endochondral Ossification. Most bones form by the process of *endochondral ossification*, the replacement of a "scale model" of hyaline cartilage by bone. The cartilage skeleton is completely formed at the end of three months of pregnancy. During subsequent months of gestation, ossification and growth occur.

In long bones, endochondral bone formation starts at the center of the diaphysis of the cartilage model (Fig. 6–2). A number of events occur, more or less simultaneously, including the following: (1) Enlargement of cartilage cells and calcification of the matrix in the region of growth, which interferes with the nutrition of the hypertrophied cells. (2) Differentiation of cells in the perichondrium into osteoblasts (signaling the transformation of the perichondrium into periosteum), which deposit a collar of bone around the center of the shaft. (3) Invasion of the region of enlarged cartilage cells by osteoblasts and blood vessels through openings in the bone collar. (4) Replacement of dying cartilage cells by cancellous bone in what is known as the *primary center of ossification*. After the primary center of ossification is established, growth of the cartilage model, principally in length, occurs at each epiphysis. Cartilage cells multiply and enlarge, and toward the diaphyseal end of the region of growth calcification, death of cells and ossification take place. Expansion of the primary center of ossification in the diaphysis is accompanied by resorption of primary bone, its replacement by compact bone and continuous reconstruction. In addition, the shaft is hollowed to form the marrow cavity. At about the time of birth, secondary centers of ossification are established in each epiphysis, in which cancellous bone is formed. All of the cartilage in each epiphysis is gradually replaced by bone except at the articular surfaces and between the epiphysis and diaphysis as a transverse disc known as the **epiphyseal,** or **growth, plate**, where subsequent lengthening of long bone occurs. When bone lengthens, proliferation of cartilage cells temporarily widens the plate, and cancellous bone replaces cartilage in essentially the same manner as during earlier periods of bone formation. As long bone increases in length, there is a proportional increase in diameter brought about by the deposition of compact bone beneath the

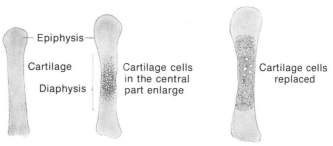

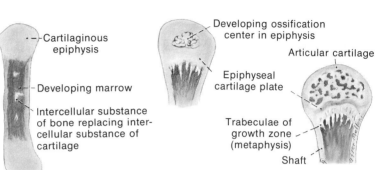

Figure 6–2. The bony deposit laid down around the diaphysis spreads toward the epiphysis, where ossification is also occurring. Gradual replacement of cartilage by bone occurs, and an increase in lengthwise direction of the bone accompanies this process. Growth in diameter of the bone occurs primarily with the deposit of bony tissue beneath the periosteum.

periosteum (subperiosteal intramembranous ossification) and enlargement of the marrow cavity by resorption of bone. Bone resorption also elongates the marrow cavity as growth in length proceeds at the growth plate.

Longitudinal growth of bones continues in a definite sequence until approximately 15 years of age in the female and 16 in the male. As the growing period comes to an end, proliferation of cartilage cells at the growth plate slows. When these sites are replaced by bone (an event called *closure of the epiphyses*), growth of bone ceases. A dense zone, called the **epiphyseal line**, is visible in adult bone at the site of union of the epiphysis and diaphysis. The relative contribution of the proximal and distal growth plate to bone elongation varies from bone to bone. The femur, for example, grows in length principally at the distal epiphysis. The tibia, on the other hand, lengthens principally at the proximal epiphysis.

The initial shape assumed by a bone during its formation is genetically determined. Extrinsic factors such as muscle strength, mechanical stress, and biochemical environment assume a function in determining the shape of a bone. *Wolff's law* reflects the role of mechanical forces acting on bone and, briefly stated, suggests that every change in use of a bone leads to a change not only in the internal structure but also in its external form and function.

Regulation of Bone Formation and Growth by Vitamins and Hormones

Vitamin D. One disease resulting in physiologic changes in the bone is a manifestation of vitamin D deficiency. This clinical condition, in which the calcification of bone is inadequate because absorption of calcium from the small intestine is subnormal, is called **rickets** in children and **osteomalacia** in adults. The essential defect in rickets, failure of the bone to ossify, produces soft bones. When a baby with this condition begins to walk, the bones bend in response to mechanical stresses; various deformities, such as bowed legs, result.

Rickets was first described in England about 1650, when the use of soft coal had become prevalent. It was caused, it is now known, by a deficiency in the ultraviolet radiation of sunlight in factory towns, where coal smoke and dark alleys created a sunless environment. Ultraviolet radiation activates the conversion of a natural substance in the skin (7-dehydrocholesterol) to vitamin D_3. Vitamin D_3 must be further modified by chemical reactions (hydroxylations) in the liver and kidneys before it can carry out its essential function of increasing the absorption of calcium from the small intestine. The active substance (**1,25-dihydroxyvitamin D_3**), now called a hormone, is secreted by the kidneys in response to a need by bone for calcium.

The intracellular action of dihydroxyvitamin D_3 in the small intestine is analogous to that of other steroid hormones (Chapter 16): after entering the intestinal cell it is bound by a receptor protein, which then can enter the nucleus and activate gene transcription. This results, in the case of dihydroxyvitamin D_3, in the synthesis of a calcium-binding protein that facilitates calcium transport. If a child is fed a balanced diet and exposed to sufficient sunlight, cod liver oil or other sources of vitamin D are not necessary. Cod liver oil is a good source of vitamin D_3 and therefore a useful antirachitic medicine because fish are able to synthesize the vitamin without benefit of ultraviolet light.

Growth Hormone. Growth hormone, also called somatotropic hormone or somatotropin, secreted by the hypophysis (pituitary gland), has a number of actions throughout the body. Its effect on bone is brought about by inducing the liver to release into the blood stream a substance called *somatomedin*, which stimulates the proliferation of cartilage cells at the growth plate. The consequence of a deficiency of growth hormone is inadequate lengthening of bone; excess of the hormone causes above-normal lengthening.

Vitamin C. Vitamin C is required for hydroxylation of the amino acid proline, an essential step in the synthesis of collagen (see Chapter 4, page 85). Deficiency during the period of bone formation and growth results in a weak bone matrix.

Thyroxine. One of the actions of thyroxine, a hormone secreted by the thyroid gland, is to increase the rate of replacement of cartilage by bone at the growth plate. A normal balance between growth hormone and thyroxine is important during the growth period. Administration of an excess of thyroxine to animals, for example, causes premature closure of the epiphyses. Thyroxine is also essential for the normal functioning of cells of the hypophysis that manufacture growth hormone. The stunted growth of severely hypothyroid children, called cretins, is in part the result of insufficient synthesis of growth hormone.

Estrogens and Androgens. The male and female sex hormones, among other things, promote the deposition of bone during growth and are essential for the normal maintenance of bone throughout life. These hormones accelerate closure of the epiphyses, and their absence in eunuchs leads to the excessive lengthening of bone seen in these individuals.

One of the serious consequences of estrogen deficiency following menopause is the predisposition of postmenopausal women to **osteoporosis**, a thinning and weakening of bone caused by the loss of abnormally large amounts of calcium salts. The weakened bone is subject to fracture by stresses that would not break normal bones. Hip fracture from minor trauma, for example, frequently occurs. Another major feature is loss of height and a humped back caused by so-called "crush fractures," in which the vertebrae collapse simply from carrying the weight of the body. Theoretically, osteoporosis could be caused by a decrease in bone deposition, by an increase in bone resorption without a compensating increase in deposition, or by some combination of the two. Recent findings suggest that a deficiency in estrogens increases the sensitivity of bone to the parathyroid hormone, which is secreted in response to low blood calcium levels and stimulates bone resorption (see discussion below of calcium homeostasis). Some physiologists believe, therefore, that an increase in bone resorption is a major contributor to the development of osteoporosis in postmenopausal women.

Vitamin A. Vitamin A stimulates the release of enzymes from lysosomes that are responsible for bone resorption. Deficiency can hamper the hollowing and reshaping of bone. In an extreme case of vitamin A deficiency produced experimentally in growing dogs, the insufficient widening of openings in the skull through which cranial nerves pass caused degeneration of pinched nerves. An excess of vitamin A may weaken bone or erode epiphyseal cartilage and prematurely halt growth.

Role of Bone in Calcium Homeostasis

Ninety-nine per cent of the total calcium of the body exists in the bone. The small but important remainder is present in the blood plasma and in the interstitial fluid, where the ionized form of calcium participates in vital chemical reactions.

Calcium has several functions that are best understood by viewing the effects of a severe calcium deficiency. Lack of calcium results in the following: (1) Excitation of nerve fiber membranes with transmission of uncontrolled impulses; under these conditions *tetany*, or spasm of the skeletal musculature, occurs. (2) Weakness of cardiac muscle with a consequent inadequate supply of blood to the total body circulation. (3) Interference with the process of blood coagulation (see Chapter 11).

Hormonal regulation of the release of calcium from the bone matrix is one of the important homeostatic regulatory mechanisms for maintaining normal blood calcium. (Two other control mechanisms, which involve governing the rate of calcium absorption from the small intestine and reabsorption from the kidneys, are described in Chapter 16). Two hormones, one secreted by the parathyroid gland, the other (calcitonin) by the thyroid gland, regulate the release of calcium from bone. A below-normal concentration of blood calcium increases the release of the **parathyroid hormone**, which increases bone resorption, raising the concentration of blood calcium. Although an above-normal calcium concentration decreases the release of the parathyroid hormone, protection against the effects of high blood calcium (impairment of kidney function, for example) depends upon the release of **calcitonin** (also called thyrocalcitonin). Calcitonin lowers blood calcium by inhibiting bone resorption. Bone resorption initiated by the parathyroid gland apparently involves not only the activity of osteoclasts but also of osteocytes. Microradiographs of sheep bone, for example, have revealed that treatment with the parathyroid hormone causes the matrix to dissolve away around each osteocyte.

FRACTURES

The breaking of a bone or cartilage is known as a fracture. A fracture is usually accompanied by an injury in the surrounding soft tissue. The resultant injury can be comparatively minor — for example, torn skin or bruised muscles — however, it can be even more serious than the fracture itself, as when the broken bone divides an artery or punctures a lung. The various types of fractures are given proper descriptive terms. A fracture can be open (compound) if the broken bone protrudes through the skin, or closed (simple) if it does not. Because of the greater possibility of infection, a compound fracture is the more dangerous of the two.

Types of Fractures (Fig. 6–3). A fracture is either *complete* or *incomplete*, depending on whether or not the fracture line extends partially or entirely through the substance of the bone. Fractures are classified according to the location or direction of the fracture line in the bone, and are then named *transverse, oblique, longitudinal*, or *spiral*.

In addition to these general terms, one common specific type is the comminuted fracture, in which the bone is divided into more than two fragments by more than one fracture line. A pathologic fracture occurs at the site of a local disease in a bone without external violence. A compression fracture, commonly found in vertebral bodies, occurs when two opposite faces of a bone are driven together. An incomplete fracture of a long bone, generally seen in children, is called a greenstick fracture. A fracture of the metatarsal bones without obvious trauma is known as a fatigue or march fracture.

Healing of Fracture

At the time of injury, bleeding occurs from damaged structures, and a blood clot forms between and around the bone fragments. The clot is invaded by fibroblasts and new capillaries. The mixture of fibroblasts and new capillaries, called *granulation tissue*, becomes transformed into a dense fibrous tissue, which in turn is transformed into the *temporary callus*, a fibrocartilaginous mass that knits the fracture. Osteoblasts, proliferating from the periosteum and endosteum, deposit the *bony callus*, a cancellous bone that gradually replaces the temporary callus. Healing is completed by reconstruction of the bony callus into compact bone.

Prompt medical attention is required in even the simplest of fractures to prevent serious complications. Optimal bone healing occurs when there is close and accurate approximation of the fracture ends. Provision for this by applying a splint or cast or by inserting a bone pin so that the structures are effectively immobilized and properly aligned is usually necessary for optimal repair.

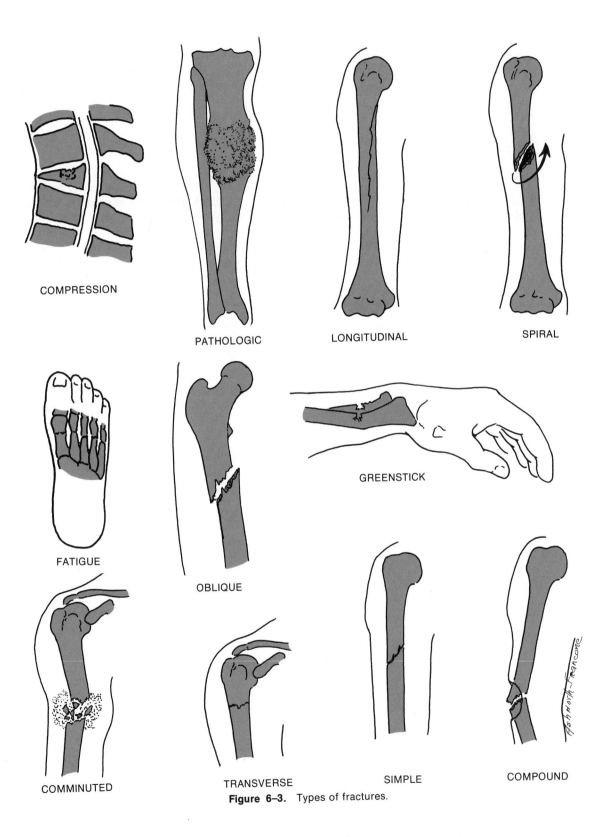

COMPRESSION

PATHOLOGIC

LONGITUDINAL

SPIRAL

FATIGUE

OBLIQUE

GREENSTICK

COMMINUTED

TRANSVERSE

SIMPLE

COMPOUND

Figure 6–3. Types of fractures.

BONE MARKINGS

The surface of a typical bone exhibits certain projections *(processes)* or depressions *(fossae)*. These markings are functional in the sense that they help to join one bone to another or serve as a passageway for blood vessels and nerves. They also provide attachment for muscles. The following terms will often be encountered in any discussion of bone.

process — any marked, bony prominence

spine — any sharp, slender projection, such as spinous process

condyle — a rounded or knucklelike prominence, usually found at the point of articulation with another bone

tubercle — a small, rounded process

tuberosity — a large, rounded process

trochanter — a large process for attachment of muscle, such as the trochanter of the femur

trochlea — a process shaped like a pulley

crest — a narrow ridge of bone

line — a less prominent ridge of bone than the crest

head — a terminal enlargement

fossa — a depression or cavity in or on a bone

fissure — a narrow slit, often between two bones

foramen — an orifice through which blood vessels, nerves, and ligaments pass

meatus or *canal* — a long, tubelike passage

sinus or *antrum* — a cavity with a bone

sulcus — a furrow or groove

DIVISIONS OF THE SKELETON

There are 206 bones in the skeleton. The *axial part* consists of the *skull* (28 bones, including those of the face), the *hyoid bone*, the *vertebrae* (26 bones), the *ribs* (24 bones), and the *sternum*. The *appendicular part* of the skeleton consists of the *upper extremities* (64 bones, including the *shoulder girdle*), and the *lower extremities* (62 bones, including the *pelvic girdle*). Components of the axial skeleton will be discussed first.

Text continued on page 120

Table 6–1   BONES

BONE	NUMBER	LOCATION
1. *Skull*	28 bones	
Cranium	8 bones	
Occipital	1	Posterior cranial floor and walls
Parietal	2	Forms the greater part of the superior lateral aspect and roof of the skull between frontal and occipital bones
Frontal	1	Forms forehead, most of orbital roof, and anterior cranial floor
Temporal	2	Inferior lateral aspect and base of the skull, housing middle and inner ear structures
Sphenoid	1	Mid-anterior base of the skull; forms part of floor and sides of orbit
Ethmoid	1	Between nasal bones and sphenoid, forming part of anterior cranial floor, medial wall of orbits, part of nasal septum, and roof
Face	14 bones	
Nasal	2	Upper bridge of nose
Maxillary	2	Upper jaw
Zygomatic (malar)	2	Prominence of cheeks and part of the lateral wall and floor of the orbits
Mandible	1	Lower jaw
Lacrimal	2	Anterior medial wall of the orbit
Palatine	2	Posterior nasal cavity between maxillae and the pterygoid processes of sphenoid
Vomer	1	Posterior nasal cavity, forming a portion of the nasal septum
Inferior nasal conchae (inferior turbinates)	2	Lateral wall of nasal cavity

Table continued on the following page

Table 6–1 BONES *(Continued)*

BONE	NUMBER	LOCATION
Auditory Ossicles	6 bones	
Malleus (hammer)	2	Small bones in inner ear in temporal bone, connecting the tympanic membrane to the inner ear and functioning in sound transmission
Incus (anvil)	2	
Stapes (stirrup)	2	
2. *Hyoid*	1 bone	Horseshoe-shaped, suspended from styloid process of temporal bone
3. *Trunk*	51 bones	
Vertebrae	26 bones	
Cervical	7	Neck
Thoracic	12	Thorax
Lumbar	5	Between thorax and pelvis
Sacrum	1 (5 fused)	Pelvis—fixed, or false, vertebrae
Coccyx	1 (4 fused)	Terminal vertebrae in pelvis—fixed, or false, vertebrae
Ribs	24	True ribs—upper seven pairs fastened to sternum by costal cartilages; false ribs—lower five pairs; eighth, ninth, and tenth pairs attached indirectly to the seventh rib by costal cartilages; last two pairs do not attach and are called floating ribs
Sternum	1	Flat, narrow bone situated in median line anteriorly in chest
4. *Upper Extremity*	64 bones	
Clavicle	2	Together, clavicles and scapulae form the shoulder girdle; the clavicle articulates with the sternum
Scapula	2	
Humerus	2	Long bone of upper arm
Ulna	2	The ulna is the longest bone of forearm, on medial side of radius
Radius	2	Lateral to ulna, shorter than ulna, but styloid process is larger
Carpals	16	Two rows of bones composing the wrist
Scaphoid		
Lunate		
Triangular		
Pisiform		
Capitate		
Hamate		
Trapezium		
Trapezoid		
Metacarpals	10	Long bones of the palm of the hand
Phalanges	28	Three in each finger and two in each thumb
5. *Lower Extremity*	62 bones	
Pelvic	2	Fusion of ilium, ischium, and pubis
Femur (thighbone)	2	Longest bone in body
Patella	2	Kneecap; located in quadriceps femoris tendon; a sesamoid bone
Tibia	2	Shinbone; anteromedial side of the leg
Fibula	2	Lateral to tibia
Tarsals	14	Form heel, ankle (with distal tibia and fibula), and proximal part of the foot
Calcaneus		
Talus		
Navicular		
Cuboid		
First cuneiform (medial)		
Second cuneiform (intermediate)		
Third cuneiform (lateral)		
Metatarsals	10	Long bones of the foot
Phalanges	28	Three in each lesser toe and two in each great toe

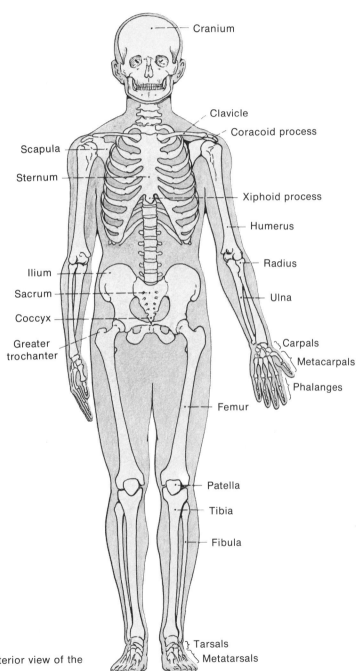

Figure 6–4. Anterior view of the skeleton.

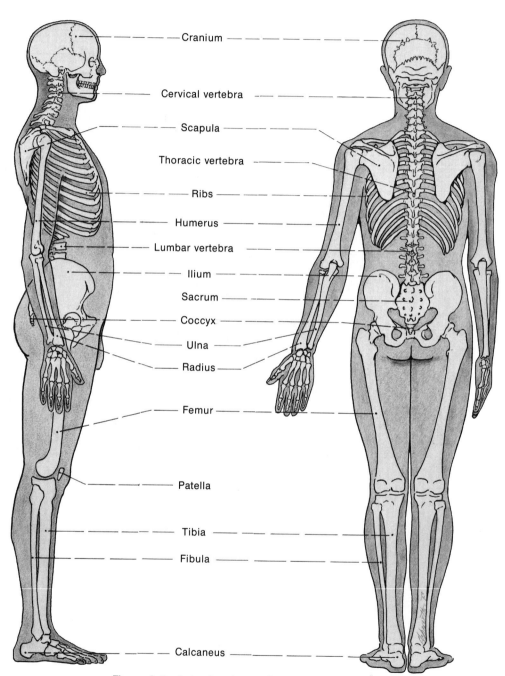

Cranium

Cervical vertebra

Scapula

Thoracic vertebra

Ribs

Humerus

Lumbar vertebra

Ilium

Sacrum

Coccyx

Ulna

Radius

Femur

Patella

Tibia

Fibula

Calcaneus

Figure 6–5. Lateral and posterior views of the skeleton.

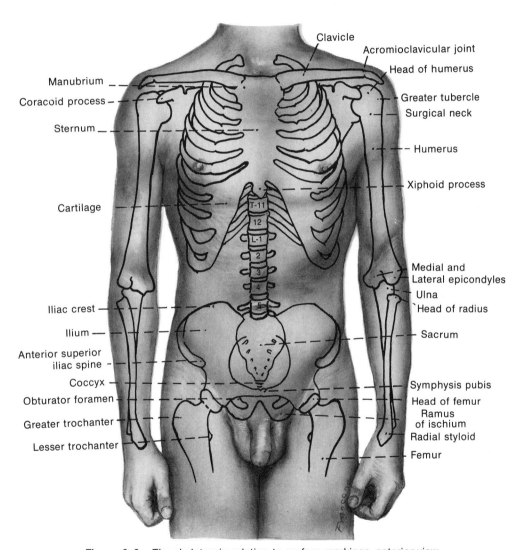

Figure 6–6. The skeleton in relation to surface markings, anterior view.

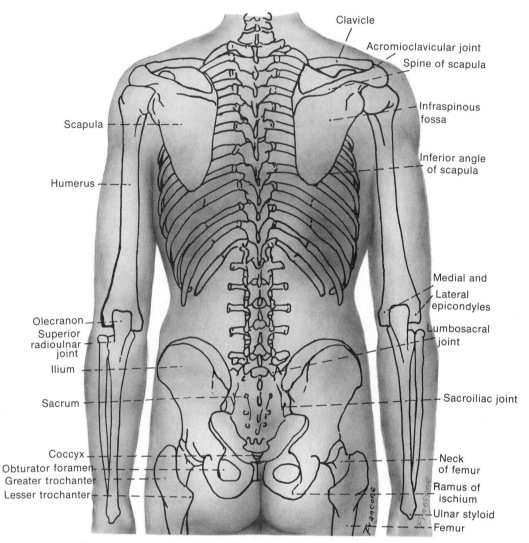

Figure 6–7. The skeleton in relation to surface markings, posterior view.

THE AXIAL SKELETON

The Skull

Cranial Bones. The skull, in the proper use of the term, includes both the *facial* and *cranial* bones (Figs. 6–8 to 6–16 and Table 6–1). The bones of the cranium enclose and protect the brain and its associated structures, the special sense organs. The muscles of mastication as well as the muscles for head movements are attached to the cranium. At certain locations within the cranium, cavities, or *air sinuses*, are present (Fig. 6–17). These communicate with the nasal cavity.

The individual bones of the cranium are immovably united at *sutures*, or juncture lines. During infancy and early childhood, the articulation is formed by sheets of fibrocartilaginous tissue which gradually ossify. Union of the cranial bones continues as the bone itself grows by increments at its outside edges; thus, the bones grow toward each other, so to speak, and eventually meet at suture lines.

FRONTAL BONE. The frontal bone forms the forehead, roof of the nasal cavity, and orbits, the bony sockets which contain the eyes. It develops in two halves which fuse by the end of the second year of life.

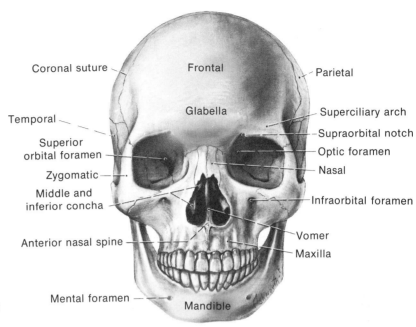

Figure 6–8. Frontal aspect of the skull.

Paired cavities, the *frontal sinuses,* are present above the orbits near the midline. The notable markings of the frontal bone are the *supraorbital margins,* the sharp, curved upper borders of the orbits, and the *superciliary arches,* ridges giving prominence to the eyebrows, situated above the margins and overlying the frontal sinuses. The arches join medially to form a smooth elevation, the *glabella.*

PARIETAL BONE. The two parietal bones form the sides and roof of the cranium and are joined at the *sagittal suture* in the midline. The line of articulation between the frontal bone and the two parietal bones is called the *coronal suture.* Like other parts of the cranium, the parietal bones exhibit a variety of grooves and depressions on their inner surfaces, lodging the venous sinuses and convolutions of the brain.

OCCIPITAL BONE. The occipital bone forms the back and base of the cranium and joins the parietal bones anteriorly at the *lambdoid suture.* The inferior portion of the

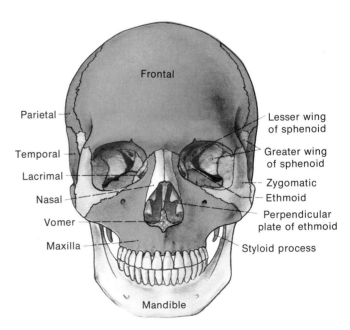

Figure 6–9. Bones of the face.

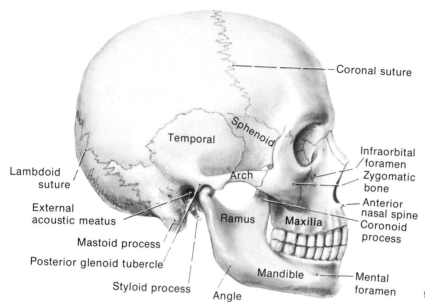

Figure 6–10. Right side of the skull.

bone has a large opening, the *foramen magnum* (literally, great opening), through which the spinal cord passes. It is at the level of the foramen magnum that the spinal cord joins the medulla oblongata of the brain. On each lower side of the occipital bone is a process called the *occipital condyle* for articulation with the first vertebra. Other obvious projections are the *external occipital crest* and the *external occipital protuberance*. These can be felt through the scalp at the base of the neck. Several ligaments and muscles are attached in this region.

TEMPORAL BONE.   The paired temporal bones help to form the sides and base of the cranium. Each encloses an ear and bears a fossa for articulation with the lower jaw. The temporal bone is irregular in shape and consists of the *squamous, petrous, mastoid,* and *tympanic* parts. The *squamous* portion is the largest and most superior of the four. It is a thin, flat plate of bone forming the temple. Projecting forward from the lower part of the squamous is the *zygomatic process*, forming the lateral part of the zygomatic arch, or cheek bone. The *petrous* part, shaped roughly like a three-sided pyramid with its apex directed medially, is located deep within the

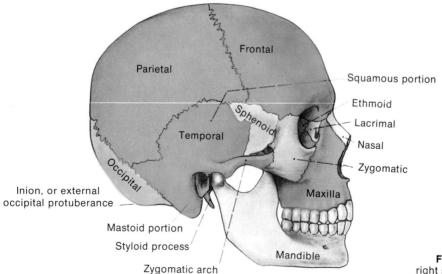

Figure 6–11. Bones of the right side of the skull.

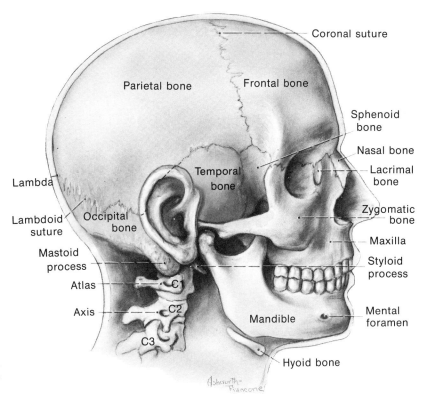

Figure 6-12. Relationship of skull and cervical vertebrae to face.

base of the skull between the sphenoid and occipital bones. The petrous contains the inner ear within its complexly fashioned cavities and also bounds a part of the middle ear. The *mastoid* portion is located behind and below the meatus, or opening, of the ear. In the adult, it contains a number of air spaces called *mastoid cells* or *sinuses*, separated from the brain only by thin, bony partitions. Inflammation of the cells of the mastoid (mastoiditis) is not uncommon and is a potentially dangerous source of infection which may invade the brain or its outer membranes.

The *mastoid process* is a rounded projec-

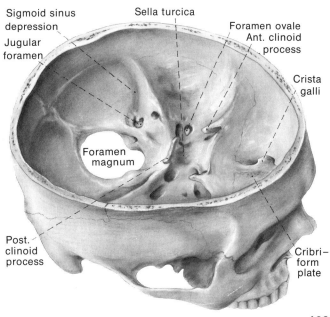

Figure 6-13. Interior of the brain case.

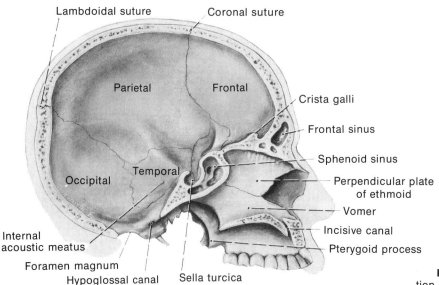

Lambdoidal suture · Coronal suture

Parietal · Frontal

Crista galli

Frontal sinus

Sphenoid sinus

Temporal

Occipital

Perpendicular plate of ethmoid

Vomer

Incisive canal

Pterygoid process

Internal acoustic meatus

Foramen magnum

Hypoglossal canal · Sella turcica

Figure 6–14. Sagittal section of skull.

tion of the temporal bone easily found behind the external ear. Several muscles of the neck are attached to the mastoid process. The *tympanic plate* forms the floor and anterior wall of the *external auditory meatus* and lies below the squamous portion anterior to the mastoid process. The long, slender *styloid process* is seen extending from the under surface of the tympanic plate but is attached for the most part to the petrous portion of the temporal bone.

SPHENOID BONE. The sphenoid bone forms the anterior portion of the base of the cranium. It is a single, wedge-shaped bone having a central body and two expanded wings that articulate with the temporal bones on either side. The sphenoid is joined an-

teriorly to both the ethmoid and frontal bones and posteriorly to the occipital bone. Thus, it serves as a kind of anchor, binding the cranial bones together. A septum, or partition, projects downward from the body of the sphenoid bone toward the nasal cavity and divides the two sphenoidal sinuses. Superiorly, there is a marked depression, the *sella turcica,* which is occupied by the *hypophysis* (pituitary gland). Medial and lateral plates extend from the base of the sphenoid to form a part of the walls of the orbit. These are perforated by several foramina, or passages, through which pass important nerves and blood vessels.

ETHMOID BONE. The ethmoid is the principal supporting structure of the nasal cavity and contributes to the formation of the

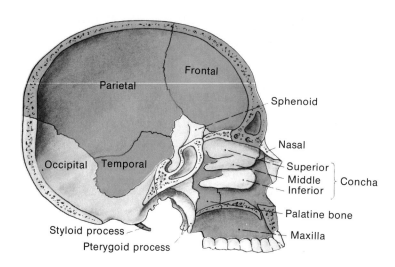

Frontal

Parietal

Sphenoid

Nasal

Occipital · Temporal

Superior
Middle
Inferior

Concha

Palatine bone

Styloid process

Maxilla

Pterygoid process

Figure 6–15. Sagittal view showing bones of skull.

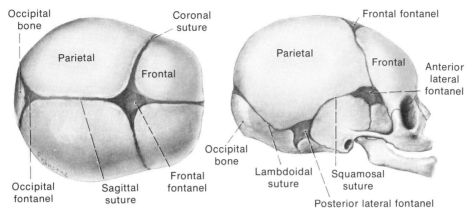

Figure 6–16. Fetal skull, demonstrating that ossification is not complete at birth. The occipital, or posterior, fontanel closes about six to eight weeks after birth; the anterior lateral, or sphenoid, fontanel closes at about three months after birth; the frontal, or anterior, fontanel closes at about 18 months of age; and the posterior lateral, or mastoid, fontanel closes at about two years of age.

orbits. It is the lightest of the cranial bones and consists predominantly of *cancellous tissue*. The *horizontal*, or *cribriform, plate* of the ethmoid forms the roof of the nasal cavity and unites the two lateral masses of air cells, the *ethmoidal labyrinths*. (The outer walls of these small air spaces are completed by various bones of the face.) Each labyrinth exhibits two or three bony plates, the nasal conchae, or *turbinate bones*, which project into the nasal cavity and allow for circulation and filtration of inhaled air before it passes to the lungs. The *perpendicular plate* of the eth-

moid forms the upper part of the nasal septum.

AUDITORY OSSICLES. Three bones of the ear — the *malleus, incus*, and *stapes* — are highly specialized in both structure and function. They will be discussed in detail in Chapter 10.

WORMIAN BONES. The so-called *Wormian bones* are located within the sutures of the cranium. These bones are inconstant in number. They are small and irregular in shape, and are not included in the total number of bones in the body. In summary,

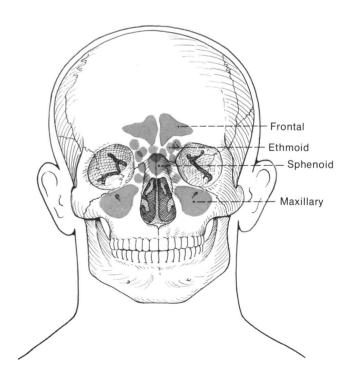

Figure 6–17. Sinuses of the skull.

then, the cranial portion of the skull consists of the following bones:

1 frontal
2 parietal
1 occipital
2 temporal
1 sphenoid
1 ethmoid
6 auditory ossicles
Wormian bones (variable number)

Facial Bones. Like those of the cranium, the bones of the face are immovably united by sutures, with a single exception — the mandible. The lower jaw is capable of movement in several directions and can be depressed or elevated, as in talking. It can also protrude or retract and move from side to side, as in chewing.

NASAL BONE. The paired nasal bones join to form the bridge of the nose. Superiorly, these flat bones articulate with the frontal bone and constitute a small portion of the *nasal septum.*

PALATINE BONE. The two palatine bones form the posterior part of the roof of the mouth, or *hard palate.* This area is the same as the floor of the nose. Extensions of the palatine bones extend upward and help to form the outer wall of the nasal cavity. Each palatine bone is somewhat L-shaped with *perpendicular* and *horizontal plates.* The horizontal plate contributes to the palate and joins the maxillary bone anteriorly.

MAXILLARY BONE. The two maxillae constitute the upper jaw. Between the ages of 7 and 12, maxillary growth is responsible for vertical elongation of the face. Each maxillary bone consists of a *body,* a *zygomatic process,* a *frontal process,* a *palatine process,* and an *alveolar process.*

The massive *body* of the maxilla forms part of the floor and outer wall of the nasal cavity, the greater part of the floor of the orbit, and much of the anterior face below the temple. This part of the bone, covered by several facial muscles, also contains a large maxillary sinus located lateral to the nose.

The *zygomatic process* extends laterally to participate in the formation of the cheek. The *frontal process* extends superiorly to the forehead. The *palatine process* passes posteriorly in a horizontal plane to articulate with the palatine bone and to form the greater portion of the bony palate anteriorly.

The *alveolar process* bears the teeth of the upper jaw and its border is covered by gum (the mucous membrane surrounding the neck and lower part of the crown of a tooth). Each tooth is embedded in a socket, or alveolus (G. *alveolus,* little hollow). In a preserved *edentulous* (without teeth) maxilla, vertical ridges may be seen on the more anterior (external) surface corresponding to the roots of the teeth.

The two maxillary bones are joined at the *intermaxillary suture* in the median plane. This fusion is normally completed before birth. When the two bones do not unite to form a continuous bone, the resulting defect is known as a *cleft palate* and is usually associated with a *cleft lip.*

ZYGOMATIC BONE. The two bones forming the prominence of the cheek are also called *malar* bones and rest upon the maxillae, articulating with their zygomatic processes. The *orbital surface* of the zygomatic bone forms part of the lateral wall and floor of the orbit. The *malar surface* of each bone is broad and flat and is seen from both the lateral and anterior views of the face. The zygomatic bone has a *frontal process* extending upward to articulate with the frontal bone and a smaller *temporal process* articulating laterally with the temporal bone, thus forming the easily identified zygomatic arch.

LACRIMAL BONE. The paired lacrimal bones make up part of the orbit at the inner angle of the eye. These small, thin bones lie directly behind the frontal process of the maxilla. The lateral surface of the bone presents a *fossa* which lodges the *lacrimal sac* and provides a groove for the passage of the *nasolacrimal duct.* One side of this groove is formed by a portion of the maxilla. Tears are directed from this point to the inferior meatus of the nasal cavity after cleansing the eye.

INFERIOR TURBINATE BONE. The two nasal conchae, or turbinate bones, are similar to those described with the ethmoid; the conchae of the ethmoid, however, occupy superior and middle portions. The inferior turbinate bones are larger, individual bones lying immediately below — one in each nostril on the lateral side. They are thin and fragile and consist of cancellous tissue covered by a thin layer of compact bone tissue in a scroll-like shape.

VOMER. The single, flat vomer constitutes the lower posterior portion of the nasal septum. The superior part of the bone has two lips, called *alae*, which articulate with the sphenoid superiorly. The word vomer is Latin for "ploughshare," to which the bone presumably bears a resemblance.

MANDIBLE (Fig. 6–18). Although the mandible (L. *mandibula,* jaw) develops in two parts, the intervening cartilage ossifies in early childhood and the bone becomes fused into a single, continuous structure, the lower jaw. The mandible, also called the *inferior maxillary bone,* is the strongest and longest bone of the face. In the upper border of the U-shaped *body* of the mandible are the alveoli containing the lower teeth. Gum covers the crest of this alveolar part. On either side of the body are the *rami,* which extend perpendicularly upward. Each ramus presents a *condyloid process* posteriorly for articulation with the mandibular fossa of the temporal bone. At the upper, anterior end of the ramus is the *coronoid process* (L. *corona,* crow or crown; G. *eidos,* form) for attachment of the temporalis muscle. The angle of the jaw is the area where the ramus meets the body of the mandible, rather than the region where the mandible articulates with the cranium.

The maxilla articulates with the cranium by the way of the frontal bone and with the mandible by way of the temporal bone; thus, the upper and lower jaws are not connected to each other. In the elderly, the alveolar portion of the mandible ceases to grow. When the teeth are finally lost, the alveoli become absorbed by the body of the bone, and the chin develops an angle and appears more prominent.

In summary, then, the facial portion of the skull consists of the following bones:

    1 mandible
    1 vomer
    2 maxillary
    2 zygomatic
    2 nasal
    2 lacrimal
    2 inferior nasal conchae
    2 palatine

Orbits. The orbits are the two deep cavities in the upper portion of the face that serve to protect the eyes. To summarize, one orbit consists of the following bones (Fig. 6–19):

Area of Orbit	Participating Bones
roof	frontal (primary bone)
	lesser wing of sphenoid
floor	maxilla
	zygoma
lateral wall	zygoma
rear wall	greater wing of sphenoid
medial wall	maxilla
	lacrimal
	ethmoid
upper margin	frontal
lateral margin	zygoma
medial margin	maxilla

Nasal Cavities. The bony framework of the nose bounding the two nasal fossae is located in the middle of the face between the palate inferiorly and the frontal bone above. To summarize, the nose is formed by the following bones:

Area of Nose	Participating Bones
roof	ethmoid
	frontal bone
floor	maxilla
	palatine
lateral wall	maxilla
	palatine
septum or medial wall	ethmoid
	vomer (primary bone)
	nasal bone
bridge	nasal bone
conchae	ethmoid (superior and middle)
	inferior nasal conchae

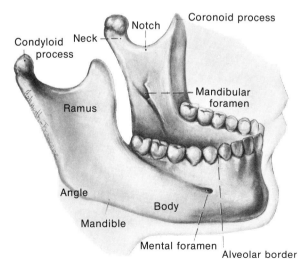

Figure 6–18. Mandible.

Condyloid process · Neck · Notch · Coronoid process · Mandibular foramen · Ramus · Angle · Body · Mandible · Mental foramen · Alveolar border

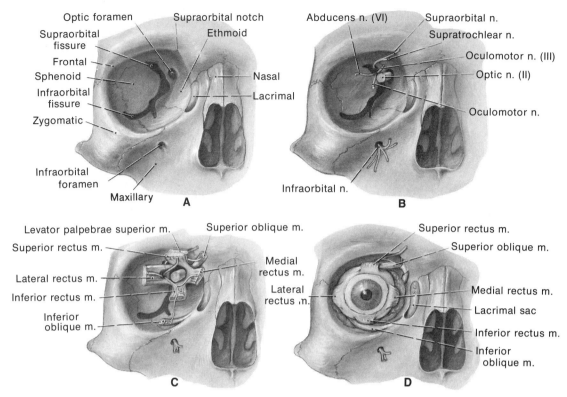

Figure 6–19. *A*, Skeletal structure of orbit. *B*, Innervation to eye muscles. *C*, Muscles of the eye with associated nerves. *D*, Attachment of muscles to eye.

Foramina of the Skull. When viewing the floor of the cranial cavity from above, one observes the large foramen magnum and a number of considerably smaller foramina penetrating the individual bones. These openings are passageways for blood vessels and nerves (Figs. 6–20 to 6–23 and Table 6–2).

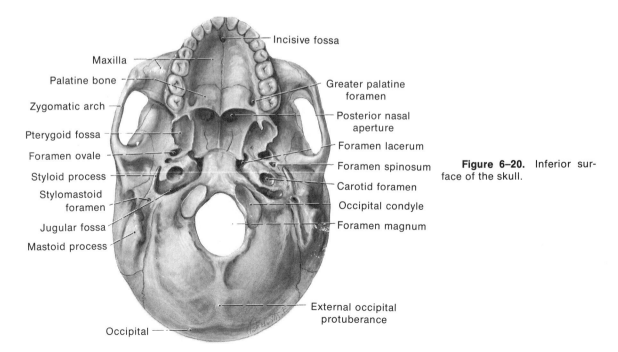

Figure 6–20. Inferior surface of the skull.

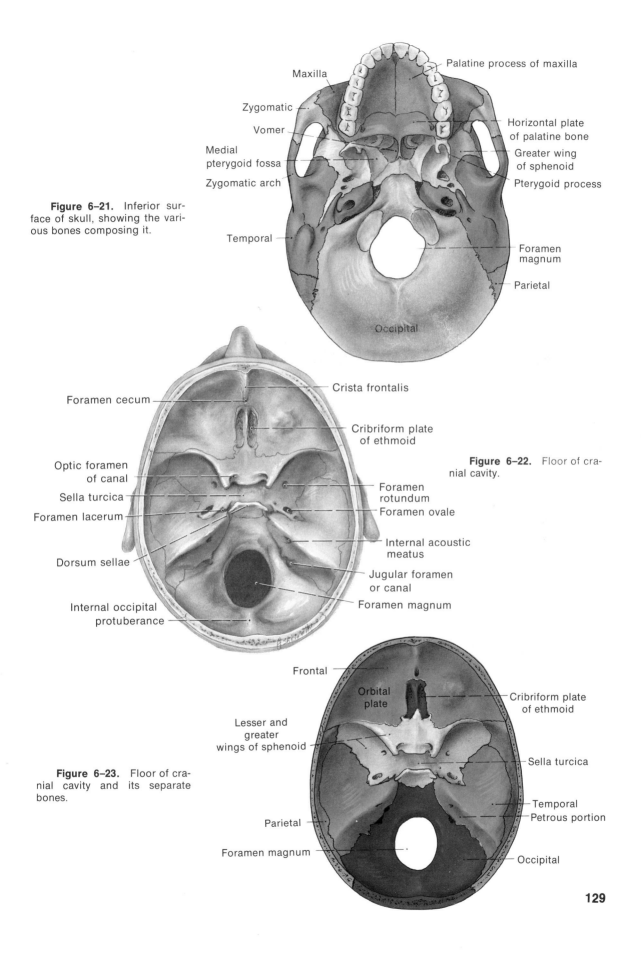

Figure 6–21. Inferior surface of skull, showing the various bones composing it.

Maxilla

Zygomatic

Vomer

Medial pterygoid fossa

Zygomatic arch

Temporal

Palatine process of maxilla

Horizontal plate of palatine bone

Greater wing of sphenoid

Pterygoid process

Foramen magnum

Parietal

Occipital

Figure 6–22. Floor of cranial cavity.

Foramen cecum

Optic foramen of canal

Sella turcica

Foramen lacerum

Dorsum sellae

Internal occipital protuberance

Crista frontalis

Cribriform plate of ethmoid

Foramen rotundum

Foramen ovale

Internal acoustic meatus

Jugular foramen or canal

Foramen magnum

Figure 6–23. Floor of cranial cavity and its separate bones.

Frontal

Orbital plate

Lesser and greater wings of sphenoid

Parietal

Foramen magnum

Cribriform plate of ethmoid

Sella turcica

Temporal
Petrous portion

Occipital

129

Table 6–2

FORAMEN	LOCATION	TRANSMITTED STRUCTURE(S)
Carotid canal or carotid foramen	Petrous portion, temporal bone	Internal carotid artery
Infraorbital foramen	Maxillary bone at lower rim of orbit	Maxillary division of fifth cranial nerve
Jugular foramen	Suture between petrous portion of temporal and occipital bones	Ninth, tenth, and eleventh cranial nerves
Mandibular foramen of mandible	Inner ramus of mandible	Nerves and vessels to lower teeth
Mental foramen of mandible	Outer body of mandible	Terminal branches of nerves from mandibular foramen
Optic foramen	Lesser wing of sphenoid	Second cranial nerve (optic)
Foramen ovale	Greater wing of sphenoid	Mandibular division of fifth cranial nerve
Foramen rotundum	Greater wing of sphenoid	Maxillary division of fifth cranial nerve
Superior orbital fissure	Within sphenoid, opening into orbital cavity	Third, fourth, and part of fifth cranial nerve
Stylomastoid foramen	Between styloid and mastoid processes of temporal bone	Facial nerve (seventh cranial) leaves cranial cavity
Supraorbital foramen	Frontal bone at orbital margin	Supraorbital nerve and blood vessels

The Hyoid Bone

The single hyoid bone is the unique component of the axial skeleton, since it has no articulations. Rather, it is suspended from the styloid process of the temporal bone by two *stylohyoid ligaments.* Externally, its position is noted in the neck, between the mandible and the larynx. It is shaped like a horseshoe, consisting of a *central body* with two lateral projections, the *greater* and *lesser cornua.* The hyoid bone functions as a primary support for the tongue and provides attachment for some of its mucles.

The Torso, or Trunk

The vertebrae, sternum, and ribs constitute the *trunk portion* of the axial skeleton. The *vertebral column* displays a remarkable combination of structural qualities, making it a highly versatile mechanism (Figs. 6–24 and 6–25). It is rigid enough to provide adequate support for the body, yet the discs between the vertebrae permit a high degree of flexibility. The vertebral column provides *protection* for the delicate and vital spinal cord contained within its articulated channel.

The spinal column is formed by a series of 26 vertebrae, separated and cushioned by intervertebral discs, or cartilages. The inner (spinal) canal is formed by successive foramina of the individual vertebrae and by the ligaments and discs connecting them.

Vertebrae. All the vertebrae are constructed on the same basic plan, although they do exhibit characteristic specializations in the different anatomic regions. A typical vertebra is characterized by the following features:

1. A *body* — the thick, disc-shaped anterior portion. The upper and lower surfaces are roughened for attachment of intervening discs of fibrocartilage, and the anterior edge is pierced by small holes for vessels nurturing the bone.

2. The *arch* is formed by two posteriorly projecting *pedicles*, is completed by two *laminae*, and encloses a space (the vertebral foramen) for passage of the spinal cord. The arch bears three processes for muscle attachment: a *spinous process*, directed backward from the junction of the two laminae, and two *transverse processes*, one on either side at the junction of a lamina and pedicle.

3. *Articular processes* — four in number (two superior and two inferior), arising on either side where a lamina and pedicle join, with smooth, slightly curved surfaces for articulation with the vertebrae immediately above and below.

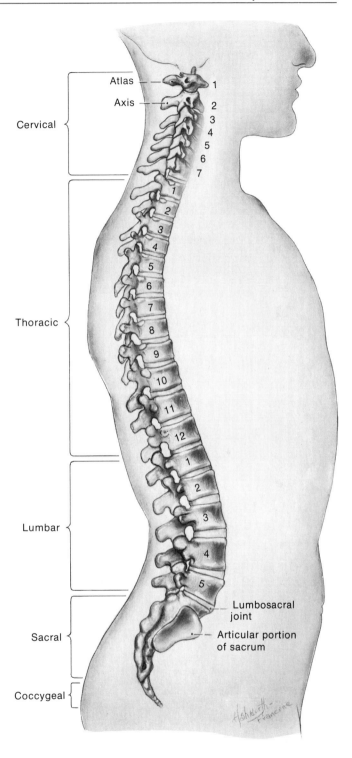

Figure 6-24. Vertebral column in relation to body outline.

4. The two pedicles are notched above and below, so that the articulated column has an opening, the *intervertebral foramen*, on each side. These foramina permit passage of nerves to and from the spinal cord. Frequent-ly, several laminae, which form the posterior wall of the vertebral column, must be re-moved surgically after injury to the vertebral column to relieve pressure on the spinal cord.

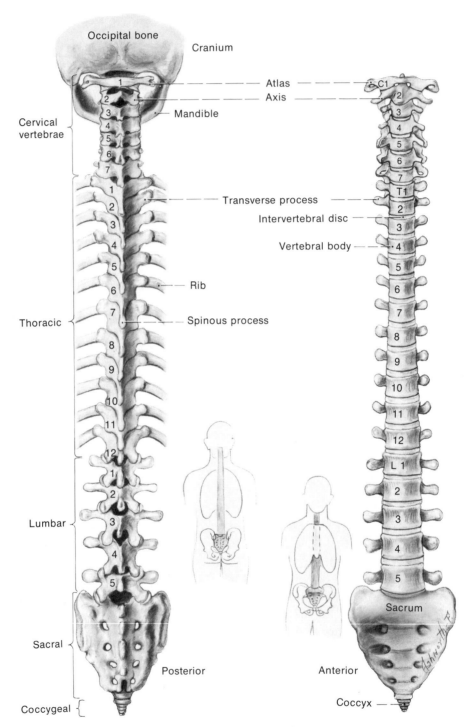

Figure 6–25. Posterior and anterior views of vertebral column.

The vertebrae are named and numbered regionally from above downward. There are seven *cervical*, twelve *thoracic*, and five *lumbar vertebrae* (Fig. 6–25). These remain separate throughout life and are called movable vertebrae. In addition, there are five sacral vertebrae, which become fused in adult life to form the single sacrum, and four coccygeal vertebrae, which unite firmly into the single coccyx. These last two are called *fixed* vertebrae; consequently, the vertebrae are referred to as being 26 in number, rather than 33. (Since the sacrum and coccyx, along with the two pelvic bones, form the pelvis, or pelvic girdle, they are actually part of the appendicular as well as of the axial skeleton.) Regardless of the individual's body height,

the adult vertebral column measures approximately 60 to 70 cm in length (24 to 28 inches).

CERVICAL VERTEBRAE. The cervical vertebrae are the smallest vertebrae, having somewhat oblong bodies and being broader from side to side than from front to back. The spinous processes of all but the first and seventh cervical vertebrae are *bifid*, or forked, to cradle the strong ligaments supporting the head. The transverse process is pierced by a foramen to allow passage of the vertebral artery (Fig. 6–26).

The first two cervical vertebrae are unique (Fig. 6–27). The *atlas* (first vertebra) supports the head by articulation with the condyles of the occipital bone. There is no

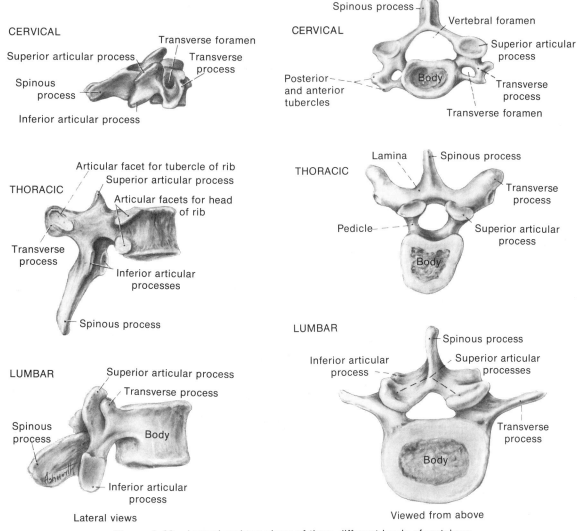

Figure 6–26. Lateral and top views of three different levels of vertebrae.

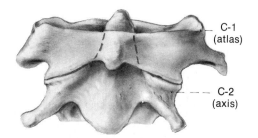

Figure 6–27. Atlas and axis.

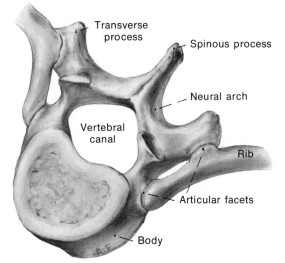

Figure 6–28. Vertebra showing articulation with rib.

typical body in the atlas, since it is a complete ring of bone having anterior and posterior arches and two lateral masses.

The *axis* (second vertebra) does have a body, from which the *dens* (odontoid process) projects up through the ring of the atlas to make a pivot on which the atlas and head rotate. There are flattened sides of the bone, *articular facets*, on each lateral mass of the axis for articulation with corresponding facets on the atlas.

Cervical vertebrae numbers 3, 4, 5, and 6 follow the typical patterns previously described. The seventh differs in that it has a long, undivided spinous process with a tubercle at its tip. The bone is called the *vertebra prominens*, since it can be seen and felt at the base of the neck.

THORACIC VERTEBRAE. The bodies of the thoracic vertebrae are longer and more rounded than those of the cervical region. The thoracic vertebrae have two distinguishing characteristics — the long *spinous process*, pointed and directed downward, and *facets* on either side for articulation with the ribs (Figs. 6–26 and 6–28). The facets on either side of the bodies articulate with the heads of ribs. (The articulations for the heads of the second through ninth ribs are formed by facets on the superior and inferior edges of the bodies of adjacent vertebrae.) The transverse processes of all but the eleventh and twelfth vertebrae carry a facet for the tubercle of the rib.

LUMBAR VERTEBRAE. The lumbar vertebrae are the largest and strongest of the different types. They have short pedicles, the transverse processes of all but the fifth vertebra are thin, and the spinous processes are thickened along their posterior and inferior borders. In a side view the spinous processes appear almost square.

Sacrum (Fig. 6–29). The sacrum is a triangular, slightly curved bone positioned at the base of the pelvic cavity between the two innominate bones. Its base articulates above with the fifth lumbar vertebra, and the anterior surface of this broad base forms the *sacral promontory*. The sacrum has a cavity which is a continuation of the spinal canal.

COCCYX. The coccyx articulates with the tip, or apex, of the sacrum. Slight movement is possible at this joint, serving to increase the size of the birth canal during delivery.

Vertebral Column as a Whole. In the embryo, the vertebral column shows a single C-shaped curve with the convex surface of the curve directed posteriorly. After birth, raising of the head creates an anteriorly directed curve in the neck; at the age of about one year the assumption of an erect posture creates an anteriorly directed curve in the lumbar area (Fig. 6–24). These anteriorly directed convex curves are referred to as *secondary curves*, and the oppositely directed curves in the thoracic and sacral regions, facing the same direction as the original single curve, are called *primary curves*.

The normal curves of the spine can become exaggerated as a result of injury, poor body posture, or disease. When the posterior curvature is accentuated in the thoracic area, the condition is called **kyphosis** or, more commonly, hunchback. When the anterior curvature in the lumbar region is accentuated, it is known as **lordosis**. A lateral curvature associated with rotation of the vertebrae is termed **scoliosis**.

In addition to its functions of body sup-

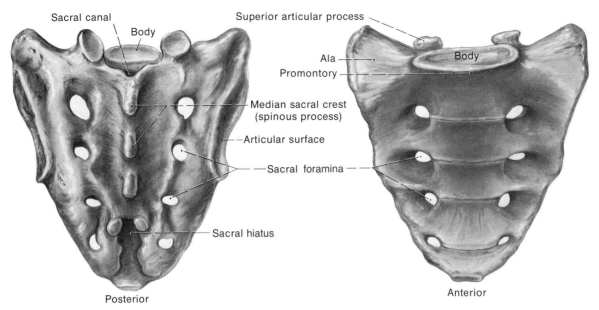

Figure 6–29. Posterior and anterior views of sacrum.

port and movement, as well as protection of the spinal cord, the vertebral column is built to withstand forces of compression many times the weight of the body. The intervertebral discs of cartilage act as cushions, so that landing on the feet after a jump or fall will be less likely to fracture the vertebrae. The discs also act as shock absorbers to reduce a transmitted jarring or pressure on the brain. The very thick discs in the lumbar region are the most effective shock absorbers.

INJURIES TO THE SPINAL COLUMN. When the spinal column is subjected to violence, fractures or dislocations can result. The most frequent fracture is a crush injury to the vertebral body. Sometimes a combined flexion and hyperextension injury dislocates one vertebra over another, causing locking of the articular processes. This occurs most frequently in diving accidents.

HERNIATED INTERVERTEBRAL DISC. The intervertebral disc acts as a cushion between adjacent vertebral bodies. It is a fibrocartilaginous structure with a tough outer layer called the *annulus fibrosus* (L. *anulus*, ring) and a soft, resilient interior remnant of the notochord, the *nucleus pulposus*. If the annulus becomes injured, the pressure within the disc is decreased and the nucleus can protrude (Fig. 6–30). The herniated portion sometimes causes pressure on a spinal nerve, resulting in nerve root irritation, a frequent cause of leg pain. Disc pa-

thology can result from injury but is most commonly (80 per cent of the instances) due to attrition caused by a lack of blood supply during adult life.

The Thorax (Figs. 6–31 and 6–32). That portion of the trunk consisting of the *sternum*, the *costal cartilages* (L. *costa*, rib), the *ribs*, and the bodies of the *thoracic vertebrae* is properly called the thorax. This bony cage encloses and protects the lungs and other structures of the chest cavity. The thorax also provides support for the bones of the shoulder girdle and upper extremities. In adult life, it is cone-shaped with a broad base.

STERNUM (Fig. 6–31). The "breastbone" (G. *sternon*, breast) develops in three parts—from above downward, the *manubrium*, the *gladiolus*, or body, and the *xiphoid process*. The parts are named for their resemblance to a sword (L. *manubrium*, a handle; L. *gladiolus*, small sword; G. *xiphoeidēs*, sword-shaped). There are no ribs attached to the xiphoid, but the manubrium and gladiolus exhibit notches on either side for attachment of the first seven costal cartilages. At the upper and outer aspects, the manubrium of the sternum articulates with the clavicle. Between the two points of articulation is the *suprasternal*, or *jugular, notch*, easily felt through the skin. The diaphragm, linea alba, and rectus abdominis muscle are attached to the xiphoid.

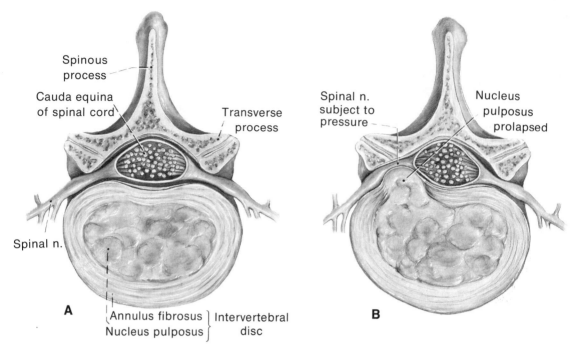

Spinous process

Cauda equina of spinal cord

Transverse process

Spinal n.

Annulus fibrosus ⎱ Intervertebral
Nucleus pulposus ⎰ disc

A

Spinal n. subject to pressure

Nucleus pulposus prolapsed

B

Figure 6–30. *A,* Normal relations of intervertebral disc to the spinal cord and nerve branches. *B,* Prolapsed pulposus of intervertebral disc impinging on the nerve. (After Netter.)

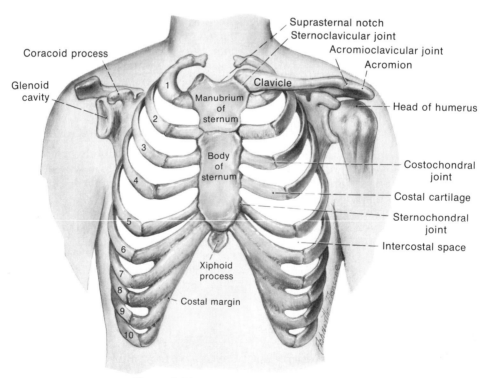

Coracoid process

Suprasternal notch
Sternoclavicular joint
Acromioclavicular joint
Acromion

Glenoid cavity

Clavicle

Manubrium of sternum

Head of humerus

Body of sternum

Costochondral joint

Costal cartilage

Sternochondral joint

Intercostal space

Xiphoid process

Costal margin

Figure 6–31. Anterior view of the rib cage.

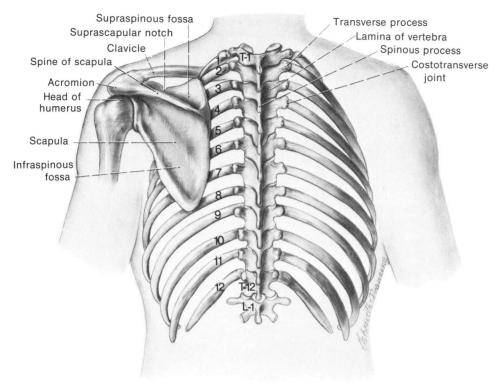

Figure 6–32. Posterior view of the rib cage and scapula.

RIBS. The 12 pairs of ribs (costae) are named according to their anterior attachments. The upper seven pairs articulate directly with the sternum and are called **true ribs.** The lower five pairs join with the sternum only indirectly or not at all and are called **false ribs.** The indirect attachments are those of the eighth, ninth, and tenth ribs, where the costal cartilage of each rib is attached to the cartilage of the rib above. Completely unattached at their anterior ends are the eleventh and twelfth ribs, which have a second name, **floating ribs.** A typical rib has a posterior, or vertebral, end containing a *head* and *neck*; an anterior end with a cup-shaped depression for attachment of a costal cartilage; and an intervening curved portion, called the *shaft* or *body*, which has a distinct bend in it, the *angle*, a short distance from the tubercle (Fig. 6–33). The heads of ribs numbered 2 through 9 have two facets for articulation with facets on the bodies of thoracic vertebrae. Each head articulates between the adjacent bodies of two vertebrae — its lower facet articulates with a vertebra having a corresponding number; the upper one articulates with the vertebra above. The heads of ribs numbered 1, 10, 11, and 12 have a single facet and each articulates with the body of a numerically corresponding vertebra (see Table 6–3).

A lateral bulge, or tubercle, is located at the junction of the neck and shaft except on the eleventh and twelfth ribs, which have neither a neck nor a tubercle. Each tubercle bears a facet which articulates with the transverse process of a correspondingly numbered thoracic vertebra. From their posterior verte-

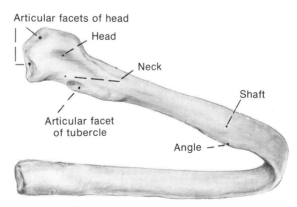

Figure 6–33. Detail of single rib.

Table 6–3 ARTICULATION OF RIBS WITH THORACIC VERTEBRAE

RIB NUMBER	HEAD OF RIB	TUBERCLE OF RIB
1	With body of a single, correspondingly numbered vertebra	With transverse process of a correspondingly numbered vertebra
2–9	Between bodies of two adjacent vertebrae, the lower vertebra having a corresponding number	With transverse process of a correspondingly numbered vertebra
10	With body of a single, correspondingly numbered vertebra	With transverse process of a correspondingly numbered vertebra
11,12	With body of a single, correspondingly numbered vertebra	None

bral attachments, the curved ribs slope downward as well as outward, thus increasing the size of the thoracic cavity; however, the anterior margin of the cavity is considerably higher than the posterior margin because the lower edge of the sternum is at the level of the tenth thoracic vertebra rather than the twelfth and because the costal cartilages of the false ribs are necessarily directed upward toward the sternum (Fig. 6–31).

APPENDICULAR SKELETON

Bones of the Upper Extremities

Included are the bones of the shoulder girdle, arm, forearm, wrist, hand, and fingers.

The *clavicle* (collar bone) is a long, slim bone located at the root of the neck just below the skin and anterior to the first rib (Fig. 6–34). The medial two-thirds of the clavicle is bowed forward, while the lateral one-third is bowed backward. The medial end articulates with the manubrium of the sternum and the lateral end with the acromion of the scapula. The joint between the clavicle and the sternum is the only bony articulation between the upper extremity and the thorax.

The *scapula* is a large, flat, triangular bone located on the dorsal portion of the thorax, covering the area from the second to the seventh rib (Fig. 6–35). The *coracoid process* of the scapula is a projection originating from the anterior surface of the superior border. It serves as the origin for some muscles that move the arm. The *acromion* is the point of the shoulder articulating with the lateral end of the clavicle. Below the acromion is the *glenoid cavity,* which articulates with the head of the humerus.

The *humerus* is the long bone of the upper arm. Its head is rounded and joined to the rest of the bone by the *anatomic neck.* The upper part of the bone has two prominences, the *greater* and *lesser tubercles,* serving as insertions for many of the muscles of the upper extremity. The *bicipital,* or *intertubercular, groove* is located between the tubercles and contains the tendon of one of the heads of the biceps muscle.

The surgical neck of the humerus — so called because it is the site of the most common fracture in the elderly — lies below the tubercles. Inferior to the neck on the shaft is the *deltoid tuberosity* on the lateral side.

The distal end of the bone becomes flattened and terminates in the *medial* and *lateral epicondyles.* The articular surface of the distal end of the humerus is formed by the *capitulum,* a smooth knob articulating with the radius, and the *trochlea,* a pulley-shaped area articulating with the trochlear notch of the ulna. The anterior surface of the distal end is the *coronoid fossa;* the posterior surface of the distal end is the *olecranon fossa.* Both fossae serve to receive the processes of the same name on the ulna.

The *ulna* (Latin for elbow) is the longer, medial bone of the forearm (Figs. 6–36 and 6–37). The *olecranon* is a prominent process forming the uppermost part of the ulna. Its anterior surface forms the upper part of the *trochlear notch,* which articulates with the trochlea of the humerus. Projecting below the olecranon is the *coronoid process,* which

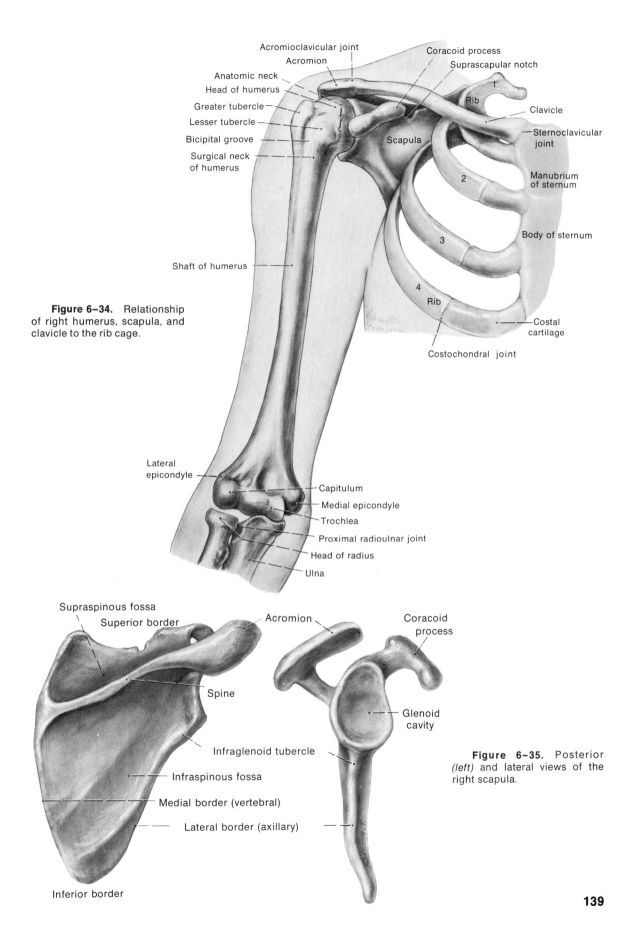

Acromioclavicular joint
Acromion
Coracoid process
Suprascapular notch
Anatomic neck
Head of humerus
Greater tubercle
Lesser tubercle
Bicipital groove
Surgical neck
of humerus
1
Rib
Clavicle
Sternoclavicular
joint
Scapula
2
Manubrium
of sternum
Body of sternum
3
Shaft of humerus
4
Rib
Costal
cartilage
Costochondral joint

Figure 6–34. Relationship of right humerus, scapula, and clavicle to the rib cage.

Lateral
epicondyle
Capitulum
Medial epicondyle
Trochlea
Proximal radioulnar joint
Head of radius
Ulna

Supraspinous fossa
Superior border
Acromion
Coracoid
process
Spine
Glenoid
cavity
Infraglenoid tubercle
Infraspinous fossa
Medial border (vertebral)
Lateral border (axillary)

Figure 6–35. Posterior *(left)* and lateral views of the right scapula.

Inferior border

139

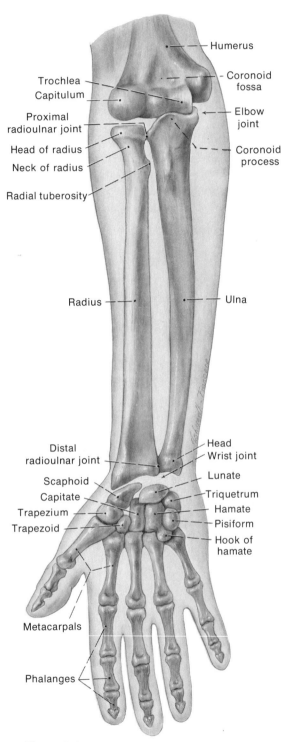

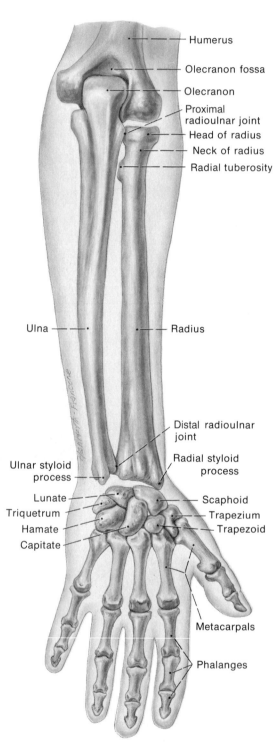

Figure 6–36. Anterior view of bones of the right forearm and hand.

Figure 6–37. Posterior view of bones of the right forearm and hand.

forms on its upper surface the lower portion of the trochlear notch. The shaft of the ulna is triangular and the lower (distal) end of the bone is known as the *head.* The head articulates with the ulnar notch of the radius and a fibrocartilaginous disc that prevents the ulna from articulating with the wrist bones. Posterior to the head can be found the *styloid process.*

The *radius* joins with the ulna along its length by the interosseous membrane traversing the area between the shafts of the two bones. It is located lateral to the ulna. The radial head, at the proximal end, articulates with the capitulum of the humerus and the radial notch of the ulna. The shaft has a tuberosity on the medial side which serves for insertion of the biceps. The styloid process of the radius is larger than the styloid process of the ulna and articulates with the bones of the wrist.

The bones of the wrist are called *carpals,* and are situated in two rows of four each. In the proximal row from medial to lateral are the *pisiform, triquetrum, lunate,* and *scaphoid.* In the distal row from medial to lateral are the *hamate, capitate, trapezoid,* and *trapezium.*

The palm of the hand consists of five *metacarpal* bones, each with a base, shaft, and head. The metacarpals radiate from the wrist like spokes from a wheel, rather than being parallel, and articulate with the proximal phalanges of the four fingers and the thumb. Each finger has three *phalanges* — a *proximal,* a *middle,* and a *terminal,* or *distal, phalanx.* The thumb has only two phalanges.

Bones of the Lower Extremities

The pelvic girdle, formed by the two pelvic bones, the sacrum and the coccyx, supports the trunk and provides attachment for the legs. The paired os coxae (pelvic bone or "hipbone") originally consists of three separate bones, the *ilium, ischium,* and *pubis.* These names are retained as descriptive regions for areas of the fused adult pelvic bone.

The *femur* is the bone of the thigh (Fig. 6–38). It is the longest and heaviest bone in the body. The *patella,* or "kneecap," is the largest sesamoid bone. Forming the lower portion of the leg are the *tibia* ("shinbone")

and *fibula* ("calfbone"). The ankle and foot are composed of the *tarsal* and *metatarsal* bones as well as the *phalanges.*

Pelvic Bone (Fig. 6–39).   The two "hipbones" articulate with each other anteriorly at the pubic symphysis. Posteriorly, they articulate with the sacrum. The ring of bone thus formed and the coccyx compose the pelvic girdle, also known as the pelvis.

ILIUM.   The uppermost and largest portion of the pelvic bone is the ilium, forming the expanded prominence of the upper hip. Its crest (where hands rest when on hips) is projected into the *anterior superior iliac spine,* below which is the *anterior inferior iliac spine.* The former is used as a convenient anatomic and surgical landmark, and both provide attachment to the muscles of the abdominal wall.

ISCHIUM.   The strongest portion of the pelvic bone is the *ischium.* Its curved edge is seen from the front as the lowermost margin of the pelvis. It consists of a *body* and a *ramus.* The body bears the *ischial tuberosity,* a large, roughened surface on its lower dorsal and inferior portion which takes the weight of the body in the sitting position. The ramus passes from the ischial tuberosity upward, forward, and medially to unite with the descending inferior ramus of the pubis.

PUBIS.   The pubis is superior and slightly anterior to the ischium. Between the pubis and ischium is the large *obturator foramen,* the largest foramen in the body. It is filled with fibrous areolar tissue, nerves, and blood vessels, and is functional only in the sense that it lightens the weight of the "hipbone." The pubis consists of a *body* with a rounded upper part, the *pubic crest,* and two *rami* (the superior and inferior pubic rami). The two pubic bones meet to form a joint called the *pubic symphysis.* The converging of the *ischiopubic rami* (each formed by the union of an inferior pubic ramus and a ramus of the ischium) at the lower border of the pubis symphysis forms what is known as the *pubic arch* or *pubic angle* (Fig. 6–40).

ACETABULUM.   On the lateral aspect of the "hipbone," just above the obturator foramen, is a deep socket called the acetabulum. All three portions of the pelvic bone meet and unite in this depression. The acetabulum receives the head of the femur to form the hip joint. The roughened, nonarticulating floor of the acetabulum is called the *acetabular fossa.*

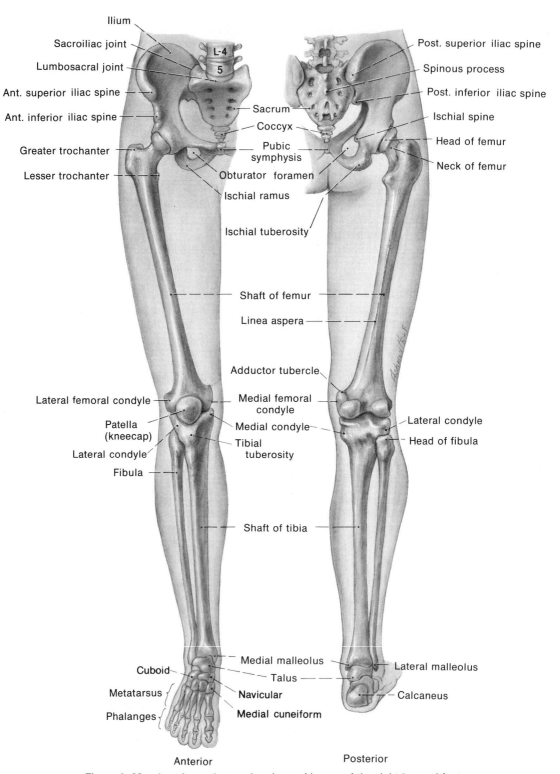

Ilium
Sacroiliac joint
Lumbosacral joint
Ant. superior iliac spine
Ant. inferior iliac spine
Greater trochanter
Lesser trochanter

L-4
5

Sacrum
Coccyx
Pubic symphysis
Obturator foramen
Ischial ramus

Ischial tuberosity

Post. superior iliac spine
Spinous process
Post. inferior iliac spine
Ischial spine
Head of femur
Neck of femur

Shaft of femur
Linea aspera

Adductor tubercle
Medial femoral condyle
Medial condyle
Tibial tuberosity

Lateral femoral condyle
Patella (kneecap)
Lateral condyle
Fibula

Lateral condyle
Head of fibula

Shaft of tibia

Cuboid
Metatarsus
Phalanges

Medial malleolus
Talus
Navicular
Medial cuneiform

Lateral malleolus
Calcaneus

Anterior

Posterior

Figure 6–38. Anterior and posterior views of bones of the right leg and foot.

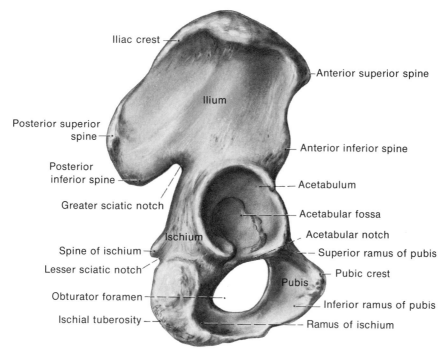

Figure 6-39. Lateral view of the right pelvic bone.

True and False Pelves. As mentioned, the term pelvis (the Latin word for basin) is used to designate the bony ring formed by the two pelvic bones, the sacrum and the coccyx. The term also refers to the cavity bounded by the bony pelvis. This cavity consists of two parts, the true pelvis (below) and the false pelvis (above), separated by the *pelvic brim,* an aperture formed by the prom-ontory of the sacrum, the *iliopectineal line* of each pelvic bone (a ridge on the ilium and pubis portions just below the iliac fossa ex-tending to the pubic crest), and the two pubic crests. (See Fig. 6–40.) The pelvic brim forms what is called the *inlet* of the true pelvis. The lower circumference of the true pelvis, called the *outlet,* is bounded by the tip of the coccyx and the two ischial tuberosities. The true (or

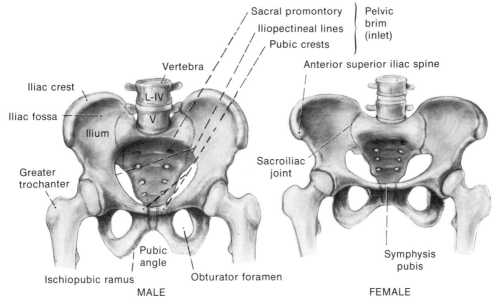

Figure 6-40. Comparison in proportions of the male and female pelves.

lesser) pelvis contains the rectum, bladder, and, between these two organs in the female, the uterus and vagina. The false (or greater) pelvis provides support for the intestines. The pelvis of the female shows characteristic differences relating to adaptations for pregnancy and parturition. The male and female pelves are compared in Table 6–4 and Figure 6–40.

Femur. The Latin word for "thigh" is femur. This single, large bone of the upper leg is *not* in a vertical line with the axis of the erect body. Rather, it is positioned at an angle, slanting downward and inward. From the point of view of the skeleton, the two femurs appear as a "V." Because of the greater pelvic breadth, the angle of inclination of the femurs is greater in the female than in the male.

The *upper extremity* of the femur bears a rounded *head* which projects medially upward to rest in the acetabulum, forming the hip joint. Below this is a constricted neck with greater and lesser trochanters. On the posterior aspect of the long shaft is a ridge called the *linea aspera*, the area of attachment for several muscles of the hip and leg.

The lower extremity of the femur is widened into a large *lateral condyle* and even larger *medial condyle*, separated by the *intercondyloid fossa*. The femur articulates distally with the tibia. The knee joint thus formed approximates the line of gravity of the body.

Patella. The "kneecap" is a small, flat, somewhat triangular sesamoid bone lying in front of the knee joint and enveloped within the tendon of the quadriceps femoris muscle. The only articulation is with the femur. The patella is movable and serves to increase leverage of muscles that straighten the knee.

Tibia. The tibia is the larger of the two

bones forming the lower leg. The upper end consists of two broad eminences, the *medial* and *lateral condyles.* Their concave surface articulates with the corresponding condyle of the femur. The lower extremity is smaller and prolonged as the *medial malleolus,* which forms the inner ankle bone. Slightly lateral to this projection is the surface for articulation with the talus, forming the ankle joint. The tibia also articulates with the fibula laterally at both upper and lower extremities.

Fibula. In proportion to its length, the fibula is the slenderest bone in the body, lying parallel with and on the lateral side of the tibia. Its upper extremity does not reach the knee joint but articulates by means of an expanded head with the tibia. The lower extremity terminates in a pointed process, the *lateral malleolus,* or "outer ankle bone," to which are attached the outer ankle ligaments. The fibula articulates distally with both the tibia and the talus.

Bones of the Foot

TARSUS (Fig. 6–41). The bones of the tarsus consist of a group of seven short bones which resemble the carpal bones of the wrist but are larger. The tarsal bones are the *calcaneus, talus, navicular, cuboid, medial cuneiform* (first), *intermediate cuneiform* (second), and *lateral cuneiform* (third). The calcaneus is the largest bone of the group and forms the prominence of the heel. The *talus* lies above the calcaneus obliquely. Its head projects forward and medially in the general direction of the great toe. The head of the talus articulates with the *navicular joint,* or medial compartment of the midtarsal joint.

METATARSAL BONES. There are five metatarsal bones in the foot. Each is a long bone with a base, shaft, and head. The *bases* of the first, second, and third metatarsals articulate with the three cuneiforms; the

Table 6–4 COMPARISON OF MALE AND FEMALE PELVES

	MALE (ANDROID)	FEMALE (GYNECOID)
Bone of pelvis	Heavy and rough	Small and slender
Sacrum	Narrow and curved	Broad, with a lesser curvature
False pelvis	Narrow	Wide
True pelvis	Deep but narrow, with less capacity	Shallow, wide, with greater capacity
Pelvic inlet	Heart-shaped	Oval, larger than in male
Greater sciatic notch	Narrow	Wide
Obturator foramen	Oval	Triangular
Pubic angle	Narrow, pointed	Wide, rounded
Direction	Tilted backward	Tilted forward

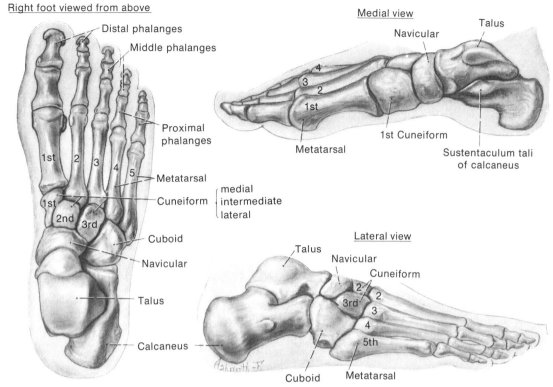

Figure 6–41. Three views of bones of the right foot.

fourth and fifth metatarsals articulate with the cuboid. These joints are named the *tarsometatarsal* joints. The intrinsic muscles of the toes are attached to the shafts of the metatarsals. The heads articulate with the proximal row of the phalanges of the toe at the metatarsophalangeal joints. The first metatarsal is larger than the others, owing to its weight-bearing function.

PHALANGES OF THE TOES. Bones of the toes are classified as long bones in spite of their being short in length. Like the bones of the fingers, they are called phalanges. There are two phalanges in the great toe and three in each of the four lesser toes — a total of 14.

Arches of the Foot (Fig. 6–42). The bones of the foot form *two longitudinal arches* and a *transverse arch,* enabling the foot to bear *weight* and provide *leverage.*

The calcaneus, talus, navicular, cuneiforms, and first, second, and third metatarsals compose the *medial longitudinal arch.* This arch is supported by the calcaneus posteriorly and by the heads of the three metatarsals anteriorly. The "keystone" of the medial longitudinal arch is the talus.

The *lateral longitudinal arch* is shallower and consists of the calcaneus, cuboid, and fourth and fifth metatarsals. The "keystone" of the lateral longitudinal arch is the cuboid.

Figure 6–42. The three arches of the foot.

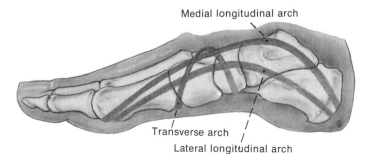

The second and third cuneiforms are considered to be the "keystone" of the *transverse arch*.

FLATFOOT. The term *pes planus*, or flatfoot, indicates a decreased height of longitudinal arches. This can be inherited or can result from muscle weakness in the foot. It is rarely a cause of pain.

SUMMARY

THE SKELETAL SYSTEM

Functions of the Skeletal System

a. Providing a support for the body
b. Protecting vital organs
c. Assisting in accomplishing body movement
d. Hematopoiesis
e. Providing a storage area for calcium

Organization of the Skeletal System

1. **There are 206 bones in the skeleton.**

a. The axial skeleton consists of the skull (facial and cranial bones), hyoid bone, vertebral column, ribs, and sternum
b. The appendicular skeleton consists of
   (1) The shoulder girdle and the bones of the upper arm, forearm, wrist, and hands
   (2) The pelvic girdle and the bones of the thighs, legs, ankles, and feet

Composition of Bone

Bone is a connective tissue consisting of cells and a matrix composed of collagenous fibers embedded in a calcified ground substance of which the principal constituents are mucopolysaccharides and salts which closely resemble the structure of hydroxyapatite.

Bone Cells

1. **Three types of cells are found in bone:**

a. Osteoblasts, active in synthesizing the bone matrix
b. Osteoclasts, functioning in bone resorption (breakdown of the matrix)
c. Osteocytes, the principal cells of mature bone
   (1) Osteoblasts and osteoclasts are responsible for the formation and growth of bone but remain active throughout life in remodeling and repairing fully formed bone.
   (2) Osteocytes are osteoblasts that have become surrounded by matrix during bone formation.
      (a) Although osteocytes no longer rapidly synthesize matrix constituents, they are apparently involved in maintenance of the matrix.
      (b) Osteocytes also participate in bone resorption upon stimulation by the parathyroid hormone (part of the regulatory mechanism for maintaining normal blood calcium).

Types of Bone

1. **Two types of bone are seen:**

a. **Compact bone:** dense and strong.
b. **Cancellous (spongy) bone:** consists of plates of bone, called trabeculae, which form open networks. The open (marrow) spaces give the tissue a spongy appearance without the aid of a microscope.

Classification of Bones

1. **Bones are identified as five types according to shape:**

a. **Long bones** (such as the humerus and tibia) consist of a shaft (diaphysis) and two extremities, each called an *epiphysis*:
   (1) The interior of the shaft has a marrow cavity (medullary canal). The shaft is composed largely of compact bone.
   (2) The flared ends of the shaft and each epiphysis, as well as the other bone types, consist of a central core of cancellous bone surrounded by a thin layer of compact bone.
b. **Short bones** (such as the carpals and tarsals): not only shorter, but also somewhat irregular in shape.
c. **Flat bones** (such as the ribs, scapula, parietal bones, and pelvic bones).
d. **Irregular bones** (such as the vertebrae).
e. **Sesamoid bones** (such as the patella): small, rounded bones enclosed in tendon and fascial tissue, found adjacent to joints.

Membranes of Bone

1. Periosteum, a fibrous connective tissue, covers the outer surface of bone except at articular surfaces (which are layered with hyaline cartilage).

2. Endosteum, a delicate connective tissue, lines all the cavities of bone, including the marrow spaces, marrow cavities, and Haversian canals.

3. Both contain osteoblast precursor cells and therefore have osteogenic potential.

Bone Marrow

1. In adults, the marrow spaces of the ribs, vertebrae, sternum, and pelvis contain *red bone marrow*.

  a. Functions in hematopoiesis — the formation of red and white blood cells and megakaryocytes (which disintegrate to form platelets).

2. The marrow cavities (medullary canals) of long bones are filled with *yellow bone marrow* (essentially adipose tissue).

Histology of Bone

1. The microscopic, functional unit of compact bone is known as the *Haversian system*.

  a. In each system a central Haversian canal containing blood vessels is surrounded by concentric rings of bone matrix called *lamellae*.
  b. Osteocytes lie between the lamellae, each in a space called a *lacuna*.
  c. *Canaliculi* connect lacunae with each other and with the central Haversian canal.

2. The structure of cancellous bone is sometimes called an incomplete Haversian system, since osteocytes in the bony plates reside in lacunae between lamellae and are interconnected by canaliculi.

  a. Haversian blood vessels are absent.
  b. The canaliculi communicate directly with blood vessels of the endosteum.

Bone Formation and Growth

1. There are two types of bone formation.

  a. **Intermembranous ossification:** bone forms directly in the embryonic connective tissue.

  b. **Endochondral ossification:** a "scale model" of hyaline cartilage is replaced by bone.

2. Most bones are formed by endochondral ossification. Only the cranial bones are formed completely by intermembranous ossification.

  a. In the endochondral process, the cartilage skeleton is formed in the embryo at the end of three months.
  b. During subsequent months ossification and growth occur.
  c. When endochondral bone formation is completed, growth in length occurs at the epiphyseal, or growth, plate (a transverse disc of cartilage remaining between the epiphysis and diaphysis).
  d. The plate is widened by multiplication of cartilage cells, and cancellous bone replaces dying cartilage cells.
  e. Growth in width occurs by the deposition of compact bone beneath the periosteum and enlargement of the marrow cavity by bone resorption.
  f. Bone growth ceases when the growth plate is replaced by bone (closure of the epiphysis).

Regulation of Bone Formation and Growth by Vitamins and Hormones

1. Vitamin D (now called a hormone) increases the rate of calcium absorption from the intestine.

  a. In the deficiency conditions, *rickets* in children and *osteomalacia* in adults, calcification of bone is inadequate.
  b. The active substance (1,25-dihydroxyvitamin D_3) is formed by the action of ultraviolet radiation on a precursor in the skin, followed by subsequent changes in the liver and kidneys.

2. Growth hormone: secreted by the hypophysis.

  a. Induces the liver to release a substance which stimulates proliferation of cartilage cells at the epiphyseal disc.

3. Vitamin C is required for the synthesis of collagen.

4. *Thyroxine:* secreted by the thyroid gland.
  a. Increases the rate of replacement of bone at the growth plate.

b. Also required for the synthesis of growth hormone.

5. Estrogens and androgens promote ossification and the maintenance of bone matrix throughout life.

6. Vitamin A stimulates the resorption of bone.

Calcium Release from Bone

1. Severe reductions in blood concentrations of calcium can cause:

a. Muscular spasms (tetany)
b. Weakened cardiac muscle
c. Deficiency in blood clotting

2. Two hormones, the parathyroid hormone and calcitonin (secreted by the thyroid gland), regulate the release of calcium from bone.

a. Low blood calcium increases the release of parathyroid hormone, which increases bone resorption, thereby raising the concentration of blood calcium.
b. High blood calcium stimulates the release of calcitonin. This hormone lowers blood calcium concentration by inhibiting bone resorption.

Fractures

1. A break in a bone or cartilage is termed a fracture.

2. A fracture can be compound or simple depending on whether or not the skin is broken.

3. It is described as complete or incomplete depending on whether or not the fracture line extends partially or entirely through the bone.

4. Classified according to direction, a fracture is transverse, oblique, longitudinal, or spiral.

5. In a comminuted fracture, the bone is divided into more than two fragments.

6. The stages of fracture healing include:

a. Clot formation.
b. Formation of dense fibrous tissue, which is converted to a fibrocartilaginous mass (temporary callus).
c. This in turn is converted to a bony callus.
d. Reconstruction of the bony callus into compact bone.

Bone Markings

1. A projection is called a process and a depression is called a fossa. The following have been defined in the text:

process	trochlea	fossa
spine	crest	fissure
condyle	line	foramen
tubercle	head	meatus
tuberosity	sinus	canal
trochanter	sulcus	antrum

Vertebral Column Injuries

1. Exaggerations of the spinal curvature are termed

a. *Kyphosis* when the posterior curvature is accentuated in the thoracic area.
b. *Lordosis* when the anterior curvature is accentuated in the lumbar region.
c. *Scoliosis* when there is a lateral curvature and rotation of the vertebrae.

2. The vertebral disc can become herniated when the outer covering (the annulus fibrosus) ruptures owing to trauma and the inner core (the nucleus pulposus) protrudes.

The table of bones lists the nature of each bone of the body.

REVIEW QUESTIONS

1. List the functions of the skeletal system.
2. Explain the functions of osteoblasts, osteocytes, and osteoclasts.
3. Distinguish between intramembranous and endochondral ossification. Describe the process of lengthening of bone and what occurs when growth in length ceases. Discuss the effect of a deficiency of ultraviolet radiation on ossification. Explain the role of growth hormone in bone lengthening.
4. Describe the Haversian system and explain its functional significance.
5. What condition in elderly women is responsible for bone fractures from stress that would not break normal bones? Discuss the probable origin of this condition.
6. List the components of the thorax. Describe the articulation between a typical rib and the vertebral column. Explain the meaning of the terms "true ribs," "false ribs," and "floating ribs."

The Articular System

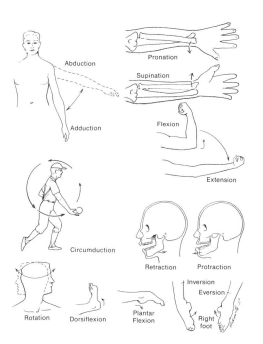

Objectives

The aim of this chapter is to enable the student to:

☐ Distinguish between the major types of joints and give examples of each.

☐ Identify the different types of synovial joints and the actions of each.

☐ Describe the anatomy of bursae.

☐ Discuss the major disorders of joints.

☐ Construct and label diagrams showing the gross anatomy of the knee joint.

An articulation (L. *articulare*, to divide into joints) is a place of union between two or more bones—regardless of the degree of movement permitted by this junction. Thus, the sutures between the skull are considered as much a part of the articular system as the elbow or the knee joint. Following a general discussion of the anatomy and physiology of joints, special consideration will be given to the largest and most complex joint in the body, the knee joint.

CLASSIFICATION OF JOINTS

Traditional classification places joints into three groups according to the degree of movement they permit: (1) *synarthroses* (G. *syn*, with, together; G. *arthrōsis*, jointing), immovable; (2) *amphiarthroses*, slightly movable; and (3) *diarthroses*, freely movable. Another name for joints classified as diarthroses is *synovial*, which identifies them as having an enclosed cavity filled with synovial fluid, a lubricant. Movement in synovial joints occurs as opposed, lubricated surfaces slide over one another. This mechanical property distinguishes synovial joints from the other two groups, in which movement occurs between bone connected by fibrous tissue or cartilage. Since many anatomists recognize that such a distinction provides a more natural and a simpler basis for classifying joints, in this chapter joints are described under two general headings: (1) *Fibrous and Cartilaginous Nonsynovial Joints* and (2) *Synovial Joints*. (See Fig. 7–1.) Conventional terms are used for the subclasses of each group.

Fibrous and Cartilaginous Nonsynovial Joints

Sutures (L. *sutura*, a sewing together) are articulations in which sawlike, toothlike,

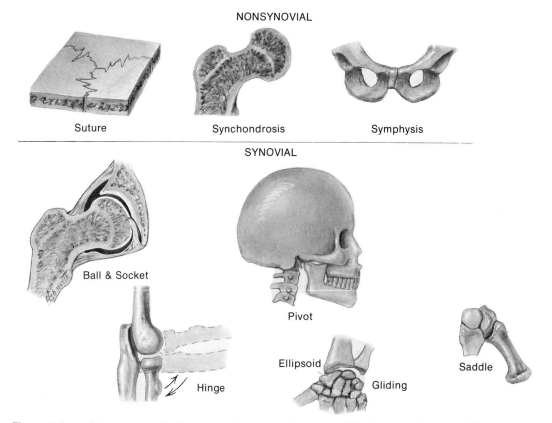

NONSYNOVIAL

Suture   Synchondrosis   Symphysis

SYNOVIAL

Ball & Socket   Pivot

Hinge   Ellipsoid   Gliding   Saddle

Figure 7–1. Joints are placed in two general groups on the basis of their mechanical properties — nonsynovial and synovial. Nonsynovial joints are subdivided primarily on the basis of the type of connective tissue that joins the articulating surfaces. Synovial joints are classified on the basis of the shapes of the articulating surfaces and the kinds of movements that occur.

or otherwise irregular, complementary edges of bones are united by a thin layer of fibrous connective tissue (the sutural ligament or membrane). These are immovable joints and are limited to the suture joints of the skull. Beginning in the late twenties, the fibrous tissue is slowly transformed into bone (completely ossified joints are called *synostoses*).

Synchondroses (G. *chondros,* cartilage) are joints in which two surfaces are connected by cartilage. These include temporary junctions, such as between the epiphysis and diaphysis of long bones, in which the cartilage is replaced by bone during the period of growth. Another joint classified as this type is the first sternocostal joint (between a concave surface on the sternum and the costal cartilage of the first rib).

Symphyses are joints in which the bones are connected by a disc of fibrocartilage. These are slightly movable articulations. Examples are the joint between the two pubic bones (pubic symphysis) and the joint between the bodies of two adjacent vertebrae.

Syndesmoses (G. *desmos,* band) are joints in which the bones are connected by ligaments. These joints are slightly movable. Examples are the distal tibiofibular joint and the joint between the shafts of the radius and ulna.

Synovial Joints

Anatomy. Synovial joints are freely movable articulations with a **joint cavity** enclosed by a **joint capsule** of dense fibrous connective tissue lined with a vascular connective tissue, known as the **synovial membrane,** which is responsible for the production of a viscous **synovial fluid.** The opposing surfaces of bone are covered with cartilage (usually hyaline cartilage, occasionally fibrocartilage), and this **articular cartilage,** lubricated by synovial fluid, provides a smooth sliding surface. (See Fig. 7–12, illustrating the knee joint.)

Articular cartilage receives its nourishment from synovial fluid as well as from a small network of blood vessels in the synovial membrane near its periphery, and from blood vessels in the underlying marrow spaces. Synovial fluid, however, is the major source of nutrition for the cartilage and in itself is able to sustain the viability of cartilage.

Articular discs are located between the articular cartilages of some synovial joints. The disc, composed of fibrocartilage, joins with the capsular ligament peripherally. It is thought that the articular disc functions as a buffer to minimize the impact of shock. Articular discs are supplied with nerve fibers providing sensory function and permitting the joints to respond more promptly and with precision to pressure changes within the joint cavity.

Collagenous fibers running directly from one bone to another compose the major element of the fibrous capsule enclosing a synovial joint. Well-defined bands of fibers that are distinguishable as local thickenings of the capsule and referred to as intrinsic, or capsular, ligaments further strengthen joints and play a part in restraining movements in certain directions (Fig. 7–2). Ligaments are usually arranged so that they remain taut while the joint is in the position of greatest stability. The range of joint motion is influenced by the laxity of the capsule. In the shoulder joint, for instance, which has the greatest range of motion in the body, the capsule is loose enough to permit the head of

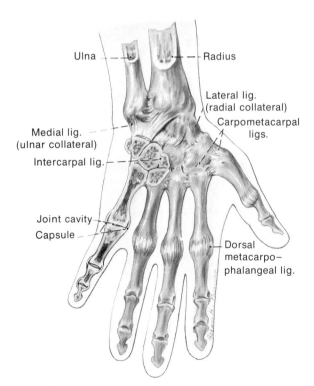

Ulna

Radius

Lateral lig.
(radial collateral)

Carpometacarpal ligs.

Medial lig.
(ulnar collateral)

Intercarpal lig.

Joint cavity

Capsule

Dorsal metacarpo-phalangeal lig.

Figure 7–2. Ligaments of the hand with cross-sectional view of a synovial joint showing the joint cavity and capsule.

the humerus to be drawn away from the articular surface of the scapula. If one were actually to sever the muscles at the shoulder joint, while leaving the fibrous capsule still intact, the humerus would be drawn as much as 1 inch away from the scapula. On the other hand, in the hip joint, the range of motion is more limited in relation to the requirements of greater strength, and the capsule is thicker and shorter.

Muscles provide an important mechanism for maintaining the stability of joints. They possess many advantages over ligaments, since during relaxation and contraction they maintain the articular surfaces in firm contact at every position of the joint. The importance of the musculature can be seen in paralysis, in which the related joints allow much greater range of motion than is normal.

In summary, joints serve the purposes of bearing weight and providing motion. They are so constructed as to afford stability. The joint capsule, ligaments, tendons, muscles, and articular discs (when present) provide stability. Viscous, synovial fluid functions in lubricating the joints and nourishing the cartilage.

Synovial Fluid. As mentioned, the connective tissue lining the inner surface of the joint capsule is known as the synovial membrane. (It also lines nonarticulating bone surfaces and any tendons or ligaments that may be inside the capsule.) The synovial membrane varies structurally in different regions of a joint, but generally consists of a loose, vascular connective tissue covered by fibroblasts (called synovial cells) varying in shape from flattened to polyhedral (having many surfaces). The membrane sometimes projects into the joint cavity as folds or fingerlike protrusions (synovial villi). This tissue functions to produce the lubrication of the joint.

Synovial fluid is usually slightly alkaline (pH 7.4), colorless to deep yellow, 95 per cent water and viscous. Its similarity in viscosity to egg white (G. *syn*, like; L. *ovum*, egg) accounts for the origin of the term. The mucopolysaccharide, hyaluronic acid (see Chapter 2), appears to be the chief lubricating substance of synovial fluid and is responsible for its viscosity and stickiness.

Physiology of Synovial Joint. Synovial joint mechanisms of lubrication function to minimize friction on articular cartilages to such an extent that normally, during movement, less friction is created than ice sliding on ice.

Various theories for the lubrication of synovial joints have been proposed. The first suggested a type of hydrodynamic lubrication, with an incompressible fluid circulating through the joint during movement. No two joint surfaces fit together perfectly; therefore, a cushion effect must be provided. The synovial fluid, it was suggested, maintains pressure at necessary points within the joint to keep the surfaces apart. This cushioning effect, it was later proposed, is complemented by a kind of weeping lubrication as synovial fluid oozes from the porous and fluid-filled articular cartilage under pressure. More recently it has been suggested that, where compression traps pools of fluid in valleys of irregular surfaces, only the small-moleculed mobile fraction passes into the cartilage and hyaluronic acid becomes more concentrated, making the fluid more viscous and therefore a more effective coat for protecting and lubricating the surfaces.

Movements. The following movements occur at synovial joints (Fig. 7–3):

1. *Flexion* — bending; decreasing the angle between two bones.

2. *Extension* — straightening out; increasing the angle between two bones.

3. *Abduction* — moving the bone away from the midline.

4. *Adduction* — moving the bone toward the midline.

5. *Rotation* — moving the bone around a central axis; the plane of motion is perpendicular to the axis.

6. *Circumduction* — moving the bone so that the end of it describes a circle and the sides of it describe a cone.

7. *Supination* — moving the bones of the forearm so that the radius and ulna are parallel; if the arm is at the side of the body the palm is moved from a posterior to an anterior postion (Fig. 7–4).

8. *Pronation* — moving the bones of the forearm so that the radius and ulna are not parallel; if the arm is at the side of the body the palm is moved from an anterior to a posterior position (Fig. 7–4).

9. *Eversion* — moving the sole of the foot outward at the ankle and intertarsal joints.

10. *Inversion* — moving the sole of the foot inward at the ankle and intertarsal joints.

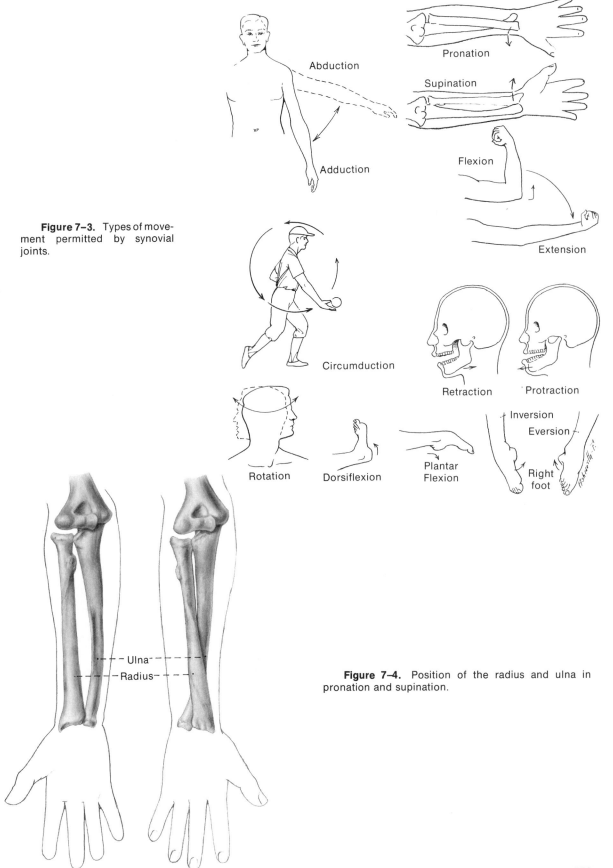

Abduction

Adduction

Pronation

Supination

Flexion

Extension

Figure 7–3. Types of movement permitted by synovial joints.

Circumduction

Retraction

Protraction

Rotation

Dorsiflexion

Plantar Flexion

Inversion

Eversion

Right foot

Ulna

Radius

Figure 7–4. Position of the radius and ulna in pronation and supination.

Supination

Pronation

153

11. *Protraction* — moving a part of the body forward on a plane parallel to the ground.

12. *Retraction* — moving a part of the body backward on a plane parallel to the ground.

13. *Elevation* — raising a part of the body.

14. *Depression* — lowering a part of the body.

Types.   Most joints in the body are of the synovial type. These, in turn, are classified according to the shape of the articulating ends of the involved bones. The shapes include the following:

1. *Ball and socket joint.* The ball-shaped head fits into a concave socket. This type of joint provides the widest range of motion, with movement in all planes in addition to rotation. An example of the ball and socket is the hip (Fig. 7–5).

2. *Hinge joint.* A convex surface fits into a concavity, and motion is limited to flexion and extension in a single plane. An example is the elbow joint.

3. *Pivot joint.* In the pivot joint, motion is limited to rotation; the joint is formed by a pivotlike process which rotates within a bony fossa around a longitudinal axis. An example is the atlas and the axis.

4. *Ellipsoid.* An oval-shaped surface fits into an elliptical cavity. Motion is possible in two planes at right angles to each other. Circumduction can be accomplished by combinations of flexion, abduction, extension, and adduction. This type of joint does not permit radial rotation. An example is the wrist joint between the radius and carpal bones.

5. *Saddle joint.* This is a unique joint between the carpus and first metacarpal (which articulates with the thumb). In it the articular surface is concave in one direction and convex in the other; the other articular surface is reciprocally convex-concave so that the two bones fit together. Movements are similar to those of an ellipsoid joint, but freer. Although this type of joint does not permit axial rotation, all movements, including some rotation, are possible.

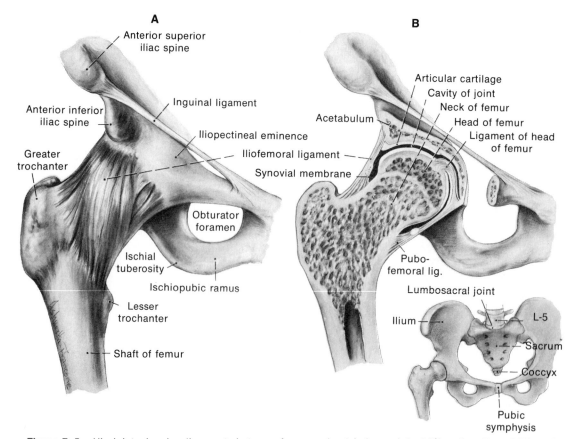

Figure 7–5. Hip joint, showing ligaments between femur and pelvic bone; intact (*A*) and sectioned (*B*) to show attachments.

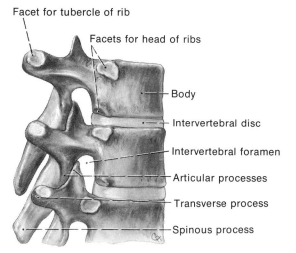

Figure 7–6. Articulations between vertebrae. The joints between the articular processes are synovial gliding; between the bodies they are nonsynovial symphyses.

6. *Gliding joint.* A gliding joint is formed by the opposing plane surfaces or slightly convex and concave surfaces, permitting only gliding movement. An example is between the superior and inferior articular processes of the vertebrae (Fig. 7–6).

A tabulation of all types of joints appears on page 160.

BURSAE

Bursae (G. *byrsa,* wineskin) are closed sacs with a synovial membrane lining similar

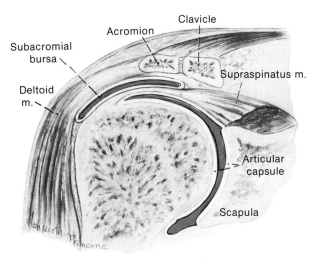

Figure 7–7. Subacromial bursa of the shoulder, cross sectioned to show attachments of muscles.

to that of a true joint. A bursa can be found in the spaces of connective tissue between tendons, ligaments, and bones, or, generally, where friction would otherwise develop. Bursae facilitate the gliding of muscles or tendons over bony or ligamentous surfaces. *Subcutaneous bursae* are found between the skin and underlying bony processes, such as the olecranon in the elbow and the patella in the knee. *Subfascial bursae* are located beneath the deep fascia. *Subtendinous bursae* are found in locations where one tendon overlies another or overlies a bony projection. The walls of subtendinous bursae may be continuous with the synovial membrane of a joint through an opening in the capsular wall (Fig. 7–7).

DISORDERS OF JOINTS

Bursitis

Bursitis is an inflammation of the synovial bursa which may result from excess stress or tension placed on the bursa, or from some local or systemic inflammatory process. It may occur in any of the periarticular bursae; the most frequent location is the subacromial bursa. The subacromial bursa lies close to the shoulder joint; consequently, in inflammation of this bursa, movement of the shoulder joint is limited and painful. Since the supraspinatus tendon, the major tendon involved in initiating the abduction of the humerus, forms the floor of the subacromial bursa, the patient with subacromial bursitis has limited abduction at the shoulder joint. Eventually, with inflammation, deposits of calcium occur in the supraspinatus tendon and further interfere with shoulder motion. If bursitis persists, the muscles eventually atrophy or degenerate. With chronic bursitis the shoulder can actually become stiff, even though the joint itself is not diseased. Inflammation of bursae located about the elbows, knees, ischial tuberosities, and attachment of the tendo calcaneus (Achilles' tendon) causes similar changes.

Arthritis

Arthritis (G. *arthron,* joint; G. *-itis,* inflammation) is one of the most common and painful abnormalities of the articular system.

Fifty varieties of arthritis are known. Three common types are rheumatoid arthritis, gouty arthritis, and degenerative joint disease.

Rheumatoid Arthritis. Rheumatoid arthritis is a chronic inflammatory disorder mainly attacking joints and their surrounding connective tissue structures. (Although the prime target is the joints, rheumatoid arthritis is usually considered a systemic disease because it can attack other parts of the body, such as the heart, lungs, and kidneys.) It occurs almost three times more often in men than in women. Among the many theories proposed to account for the development of rheumatoid arthritis, the one that has received the most support describes the condition as an autoimmune disease (in which the immune system responds to substances derived from one's own cells as it does to foreign substances). Frequently cited as evidence for the autoimmune theory is the observation that an antibody, the so-called "rheumatoid factor," is found in the blood of 70 to 80 per cent of the individuals suffering from rheumatoid arthritis. The proponents of this theory recognize, however, that some unknown triggering event (such as a viral infection, which might convert a normal substance into an abnormal one) precedes the autoimmune response. The earliest stage in rheumatoid arthritis is an inflammation of the synovial membrane in which the tissue becomes thickened. This thickened synovial tissue (*pannus*) grows inward along the surface of the articular cartilage. Growth of the pannus actually damages the cartilage. Next, the inflammatory tissue becomes invaded with tough fibrous material which is adherent and prevents motion of the joint. This stage is known as *fibrous ankylosis* (ankylosis means immobility of a joint). The fibrous tissue may ultimately become calcified and undergo changes to osseous tissue, resulting in a firm bony union, *bony ankylosis*. Rheumatoid arthritis, then, develops in four stages: inflammation of the synovial membrane, invasion of the articular cartilage by the pannus, fibrous ankylosis, and, finally, bony ankylosis. Alterations in the microcirculation of the joint give rise to characteristic clinical expressions of heat, redness, swelling, and pain. The tissue damage is believed to be caused by enzymes released from ruptured lysosomes in the proliferating synovial membrane cells and white blood cells. Most drugs, such as aspirin, used to treat rheumatoid arthritis have the property of stabilizing lysosomal membranes.

Gouty Arthritis. Gout is a metabolic disorder, the major clinical manifestation of which is arthritis. It is a disturbance of purine metabolism usually associated with an elevated uric acid in the blood. Attacks of gouty arthritis occur when deposits of urate crystals in and about joints lead to the inflammation of joint tissue, damage to articular cartilage, and severe pain. The pain of an attack of gouty arthritis, which has been described as comparable to being "crushed with a clamp of steel" or "exposed to hot coals," is generally considered to be more intense than the pain of rheumatoid arthritis. About 90 to 95 per cent of the victims are men. One or more genetic defects in males apparently lead to an increase in the formation of urates and to a decrease in the binding of urate by a blood protein (which it is believed increases the tendency of urate to precipitate in joints and other tissues).

Degenerative Joint Disease (Arthrosis). This disease is a noninflammatory disorder of movable joints characterized by deterioration of articular cartilage and the formation of new bone at the joint surfaces. (Since inflammation does not occur, many clinicians prefer not to describe the condition as a form of arthritis.) Degenerative joint disease is far more prevalent than rheumatoid arthritis but is not likely to cause the severe crippling sometimes produced by rheumatoid arthritis. Joints are subject to a great deal of wear and tear. After years of use, degenerative changes are to be expected. Some evidence of degenerative joint disease is found in many individuals over the age of 45. The weight-bearing joints of the lower extremities and spine are particularly subject to wear and tear and often show early degenerative changes. In many cases specific joints are affected depending upon a person's occupation. Baseball pitchers may develop the condition in the elbow, ballet dancers in the ankles, pneumatic drill operators in the wrists. There is initially a softening of the articular cartilage, followed by a separation of fibers and, later, actual disintegration of the cartilage. The normally smooth cartilage becomes pitted and frayed, and whole segments of cartilage may be lost. Bony outgrowths form on the degenerating articular surface, and protruding bony ridges at the joint margins may extend into nearby tendons and joints. These changes make movement of the joint more difficult. It is the presence of the bony outgrowths that gave the disease its outdated names "hypertrophic arthritis" and "osteoarthritis."

Rheumatic Fever

The musculoskeletal system may be involved in rheumatic fever, a disease characterized by inflammation of the synovial tissues, tendons, and other connective tissues about joints. Rheumatic fever begins abruptly with an intense inflammatory reaction of joints and then tends to subside after a brief period. No pannus occurs in rheumatic fever, so the cartilage and bone are not damaged. The functional disturbances of rheumatic fever can be attributed to active inflammation similar to changes noted in the early stages of rheumatoid arthritis. The symptoms of rheumatic fever are generally observed two to three weeks after an acute streptococcal sore throat and are believed to be due to the sensitivity of some individuals to antibodies produced in response to the streptococcal bacteria. During epidemics of streptococcal sore throat, the incidence of rheumatic fever is usually about three per cent of the infected individuals. It is considerably lower in sporadic infections because of the lesser severity of this type of infection. When the disease subsides, the patient usually does not show any residual functional damage of the articular system but frequently has permanent damage to the heart valves (especially the mitral and aortic valves), which manifests itself in later life as rheumatic heart disease.

Primary Fibrositis

Primary fibrositis, sometimes called "rheumatism" by the layman, is an inflammation of fibrous connective tissue more than a disease of muscles. Fibrositis occurring in the low back is referred to in nonscientific circles as "lumbago." Chronic fibrositis either involves many structures simultaneously or migrates from one part of the body to another. The involved portions of the body are usually tender and stiff. Since movement of the joints depends on function of periarticular and connective tissue and muscles, irritation of these structures leads to limitation of movement. Since the joints themselves are healthy, no permanent damage occurs. As soon as the connective tissue changes are relieved, the locomotor system again functions normally.

Tenosynovitis

Tendon sheaths may become inflamed, interfering with the free passage of the enclosed tendon. Function of joints moved by these tendons will then be impaired. If the inflammation occurs along the sheaths of the flexor tendons of the fingers, the finger frequently cannot be extended by the flexor apparatus without assistance — a so-called "trigger finger." In many instances, inflammation of the flexor tendon sheaths and palmar fascia may cause adhesions so strong that movement of the fingers is completely prevented. The fingers then become deformed and remain in positions of flexion. Dupuytren's contracture is an inflammation of the palmar fascia resulting in flexion deformities of the third, fourth, and fifth fingers.

THE KNEE JOINT

Anatomy (Figs. 7–8 to 7–13)

There are two *semilunar cartilages* (menisci) involved in the knee joint: the *medial semilunar cartilage* and the *lateral semilunar cartilage*. The *medial semilunar cartilage* is nearly semicircular, attaches by short fibers to the tibia, and is relatively fixed in position. It functions to deepen the socket for the medial femoral condyle. The *lateral semilunar cartilage* is a nearly complete ring and is attached to the tibia, with its long fibers permitting gliding of the cartilage. It functions to insure smooth articulation.

Two sets of ligaments are involved in movement of the knee joint. These are the *anterior* and *posterior cruciate ligaments* and the *medial* and *lateral collateral ligaments*.

The anterior cruciate ligament limits extension and rotation. The posterior cruciate ligament prevents forward dislocation of the femur. The winding and unwinding of the cruciate ligaments are particularly important in stabilizing the knee joint during rotation. Although the principal movements are flexion and extension, some rotation is essential during walking, as the joint flexes, to return the center of gravity toward the medial position.

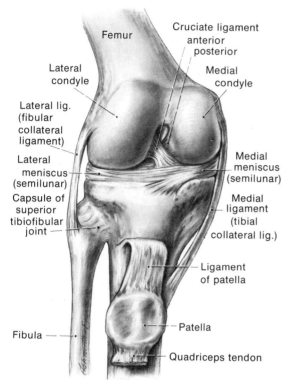

Figure 7–8. Anterior view of the right knee joint, slightly flexed. The patella has been severed from the quadriceps muscle and pulled down, exposing the ligaments between the femur and tibia.

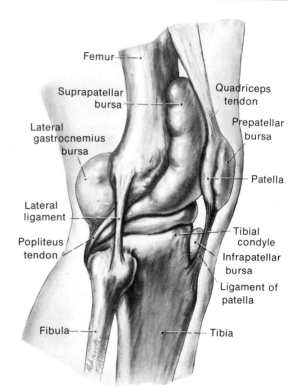

Figure 7–10. Lateral view of the right knee joint. The bursae have been expanded for clarity.

The collateral ligaments prevent lateral dislocation of the knee. These extend from the lateral condyle of the femur to the head of the fibula (*lateral ligament*) and from the medial condyle of the femur to the capsule and medial surface of the tibia (*medial liga-*

ment). The synovial membrane of the knee has deep, fat-filled folds which form flexible cushions and fill in irregularities and any spaces in the joint cavity where the small amount of synovial fluid may be absent. Several subcutaneous bursae are associated with

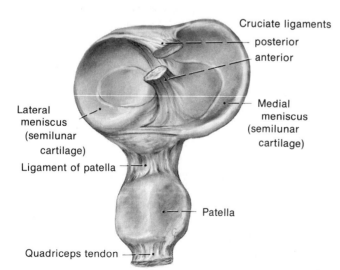

Figure 7–9. Superior aspect of the right tibia (with the attached patella drawn forward) showing the menisci and the tibial attachments of the cruciate ligaments.

Figure 7–11. Posterior view of the right knee joint.

Femur

Intercondylar notch

Medial epicondyle

Medial femoral condyle

Medial meniscus

Medial tibial condyle

Medial ligament (tibial collateral ligament)

Cruciate ligament
posterior
anterior

Lateral epicondyle

Lat. femoral condyle

Lateral meniscus

Lat. tibial condyle

Lateral ligament (fibular collateral ligament)

Fibula

Tibia

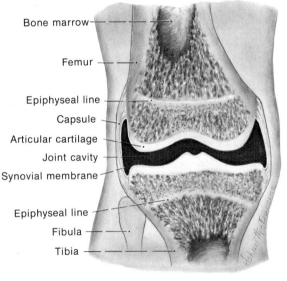

Bone marrow

Femur

Epiphyseal line

Capsule

Articular cartilage

Joint cavity

Synovial membrane

Epiphyseal line

Fibula

Tibia

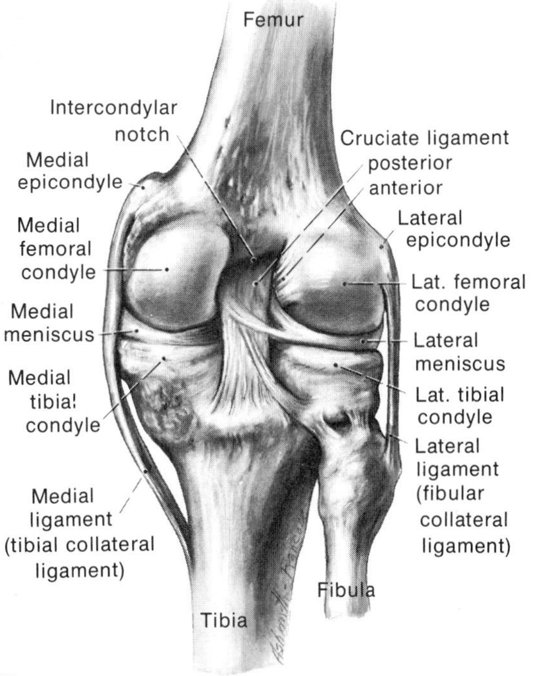

Figure 7–12. Frontal section through the right knee joint. The joint cavity is expanded for clarity.

Figure 7–13. Lateral view of the right knee joint in sagittal section.

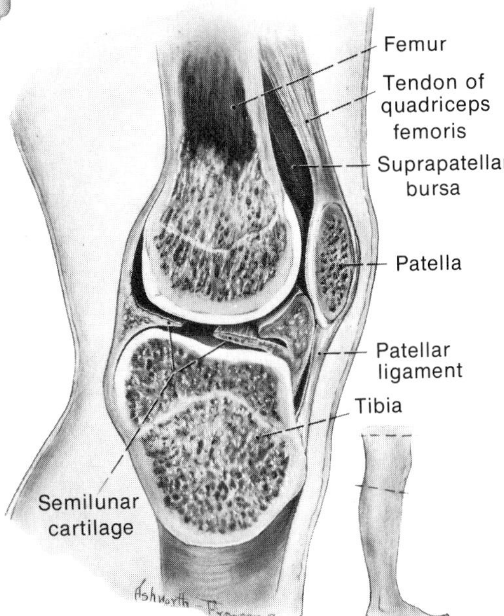

Femur

Tendon of quadriceps femoris

Suprapatellar bursa

Patella

Patellar ligament

Tibia

Semilunar cartilage

Table 7–1 JOINTS

JOINT	TYPE	MOVEMENT
Atlanto-occipital (Superior articular process of atlas and condyle of occipital bone)	Synovial, ellipsoid	Flexion and extension (nodding of head); abduction and adduction (lateral tilting of head); circumduction
Central atlantoaxial (Anterior arch of atlas and odontoid process of axis)	Synovial, pivot	Rotation of the atlas and head upon the axis
Vertebral		
Between bodies of vertebrae	Nonsynovial, symphyses	Restricted between any two vertebrae, but wide ranging for
Between articular processes	Synovial, gliding	vertebral column as a whole— flexion, extension, lateral flexion (bending to one side), circumduction and rotation (twisting)
Temporomandibular (Condyloid process of mandible and mandibular fossa of temporal bone)	Synovial, hinge and gliding (placed in a special category— condylar—by some anatomists)	Depression, elevation, protraction, retraction, and lateral displacement of mandible
Costovertebral (Heads of ribs and bodies of vertebrae; tubercles of first 10 ribs and transverse processes of vertebrae)	Synovial, gliding	Slight gliding movements which rotate ribs upward or downward
Costochondral (Anterior ends of ribs and costal cartilages)	Nonsynovial, synchondroses	Minimal
Sternocostal (Sternum and first seven costal cartilages)		
First	Nonsynovial, synchondrosis	Minimal
Two through seven	Although classified as synovial, gliding, the joint cavity is often absent, especially in lower joints.	Slight, gliding, but sufficient to provide mobility during breathing
Sternoclavicular (Manubrium of sternum and clavicle)	Synovial, gliding	Gliding
Acromioclavicular (Acromion of scapula and clavicle)	Synovial, gliding	Gliding, principally scapula sliding forward and backward and rotating on clavicle
Shoulder (Head of humerus and glenoid cavity of scapula)	Synovial, ball and socket	Flexion, extension, abduction, adduction, circumduction, and rotation
Elbow (Trochlea of humerus and trochlear notch of ulna; capitulum of humerus and head of radius)	Synovial, hinge	Flexion and extension
Radioulnar		
Proximal (Head of radius and radial notch of ulna)	Synovial, pivot	Pronation and supination
Middle (Along length of shafts)	Nonsynovial, syndesmosis	Slight
Distal (Head of ulna and ulnar notch of radius)	Synovial, gliding	Slight, gliding
Wrist (Radius and carpals)	Synovial, ellipsoid	Flexion, extension, abduction, adduction, and circumduction
Intercarpal	Synovial, gliding	Occurs in conjunction with movement of wrist
Carpometacarpal		
1. Carpus and first metacarpal (which articulates with thumb)	Synovial, saddle	Flexion, extension, abduction, adduction, circumduction, and rotation
2. Carpus and 2nd, 3rd, 4th, and 5th metacarpals	Synovial, gliding	Slight gliding, principally in grasping
Metacarpophalangeal	Synovial, ellipsoid	Flexion, extension, abduction, adduction, and circumduction

Table 7–1 **JOINTS** (*Continued*)

JOINT	TYPE	MOVEMENT
Interphalangeal	Synovial, hinge	Flexion and extension
Sacroiliac	Synovial, gliding (often resembles nonsynovial syndesmosis in late life after invasion by fibrous tissue)	Slight during flexion and extension of the trunk (increasing temporarily in pregnancy when ligaments relax)
Pubic symphysis	Nonsynovial, symphysis	Limited
Hip (Head of femur, acetabulum of pelvic ["hip"] bone)	Synovial, ball and socket	Flexion, extension, abduction, adduction, circumduction, and rotation
Knee (Concave surfaces of medial and lateral condyles of tibia and corresponding condyles of femur)	Synovial, hinge	Flexion, extension, and some rotation
Tibiofibular		
Proximal (Lateral condyle of tibia and head of fibula)	Synovial, gliding	Very slight
Distal	A synovial, gliding part is sometimes formed by extension of the ankle joint. The other part is nonsynovial, syndesmosis.	Very slight
Ankle (Tibia and fibula with the talus of tarsus)	Synovial, hinge	Principally dorsiflexion and plantar flexion; side-to-side gliding; inversion and eversion
Intertarsal	Synovial, gliding	Inversion and eversion; flattening and accentuating arches
Tarsometatarsal	Synovial, gliding	Slight, gliding
Metatarsophalangeal	Synovial, ellipsoid	Similar to metacarpophalangeal, but differing in range (for example, range of extension exceeds flexion)
Interphalangeal	Synovial, hinge	Flexion and extension

the knee joint. These are found in front of and to the side of the joint and between the patella and the skin. Inflammation of these bursae may be the cause of so-called "housemaid's knee."

Internal Derangement of the Knee

The knee joint depends on strong ligaments and strong muscles of the thigh for its stability. The condyles of the femur and tibia are held in contact by these structures during flexion and extension. An *internal derangement* is a mechanical derangement of the function of the joint caused by some abnormality which eliminates the supporting strength of the major ligaments or prevents the contact and smooth gliding of the condyles during flexion and extension of the knee. The most common derangement of the knee is a tear of the semilunar cartilage,

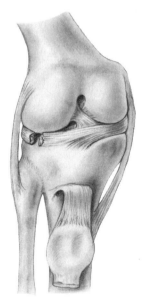

Figure 7–14. Lateral tear of the semilunar cartilage.

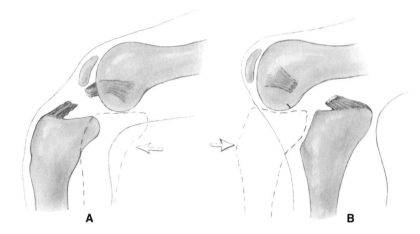

Figure 7–15. Cruciate ligament tear. *A,* Posterior; *B,* anterior.

which usually results from a twisting injury (Fig. 7–14). Normally, the cartilage buffers rotary grinding action of the condyles of the femur on the tibia. When the medial semilunar cartilage is torn, the patient presents a history of a twisting injury with a snapping sensation on the inner side of the knee. A patient with a torn lateral semilunar cartilage, on the other hand, also presents a history of a twisting injury, but with a snapping sensation on the outer side of the knee. The medial semilunar cartilage, which can be torn in a fall without additional trauma, is more fre-

quently damaged than the lateral one, which is usually torn in a sports or other injury where great force is exerted against the leg.

A patient with a torn semilunar cartilage experiences painful locking of the knee joint with tenderness at the site of injury. Usually a torn semilunar cartilage does not heal, since cartilage has a poor blood supply. Surgical removal of the torn cartilage or torn portion of the cartilage is the only definitive treatment of this condition.

Major violence is necessary to completely rupture a ligament. More often than not there occurs only a partial tearing of the fibers of the ligament. The direction of force applied to the knee determines which ligament is most likely to be injured by the impact (Figs. 7–15 and 7–16).

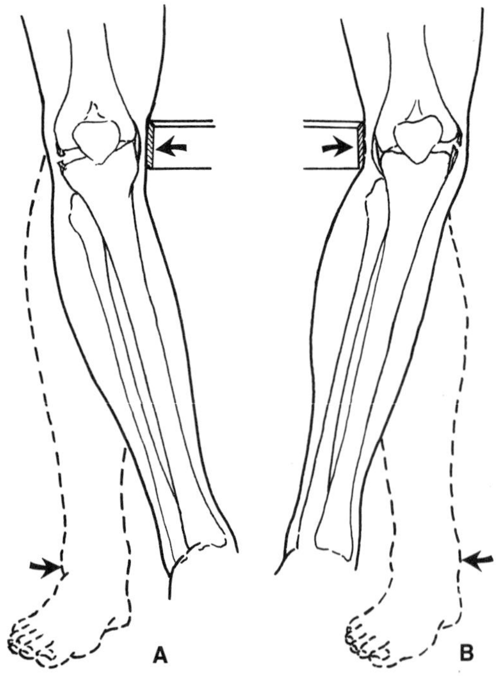

SUMMARY

THE ARTICULAR SYSTEM

Classification of Joints

1. Traditionally, joints are grouped according to the degree of movement permitted:
   a. Synarthroses: immovable
   b. Amphiarthroses: slightly movable
   c. Diarthroses: freely movable

2. On the basis of mechanical properties, the third group can be distinguished from the first two. In diarthroses, also called synovial joints, the joint is enclosed by a fibrous capsule lined with a membrane (the synovial membrane) that secretes a lubricant (synovial fluid), and the lubricated articulating surfaces slide over one another. Movement in the

Figure 7–16. Collateral ligament tear. *A,* Fibular collateral ligament; *B,* tibial collateral ligament.

other two types of joints, on the other hand, occurs between bones connected by fibrous tissue or cartilage.

3. Fibrous and Cartilaginous Nonsynovial Joints

a. Sutures: fibrous tissue unites bones.
b. Synchondroses: cartilage joins bones.
c. Symphyses: a fibrocartilage disc connects bones.
d. Syndesmoses: ligaments link bones.

4. Synovial Joints

a. Anatomy of synovial joints
 (1) *Joint cavity* enclosed by fibrous connective tissue, the *joint capsule.*
 (2) A vascular connective tissue, the *synovial membrane,* lining the capsule secretes a viscous lubricant, the *synovial fluid.*
 (3) *Articular cartilage* covering the opposing surfaces of bone is lubricated with synovial fluid and provides a smooth sliding surface.
 (4) Capsular *ligaments* strengthen joints and restrain motion.
 (5) *Muscles* maintain stability of joints by relaxation and contraction to keep articular surfaces in firm contact.
 (6) *Articular discs,* when present within the joint, serve to buffer shock.
b. Movements of synovial joints
 (1) Flexion
 (2) Extension
 (3) Abduction
 (4) Adduction
 (5) Rotation
 (6) Circumduction
 (7) Supination
 (8) Pronation
 (9) Eversion
 (10) Inversion
 (11) Protraction
 (12) Retraction
 (13) Elevation
 (14) Depression
c. Types of synovial joints
 (1) Ball and socket
 (2) Hinge
 (3) Pivot
 (4) Ellipsoid
 (5) Saddle
 (6) Gliding

Bursae

1. Bursae are found in close proximity to joints and are usually associated with spaces between connective tissue.

2. Bursae are closed sacs with a synovial membrane lining.

Disorders of Joints

1. Bursitis is the inflammation of the synovial bursa; it may result from excess stress, local inflammation, or systemic disease.

2. Arthritis is the general term for inflammation of joints.

 a. The stages of rheumatoid arthritis are inflammation of the synovial membrane, inward growth of the pannus (thickened synovial tissue) along the surface of articular cartilage, fibrous ankylosis, and bony ankylosis.
 b. Gouty arthritis is a metabolic disorder in purine metabolism which leads to the depositing of urate crystals in and around joints.

3. Degenerative joint disease comes from prolonged wear and tear on joints. The articular cartilage degenerates, becoming pitted, frayed, and eroded, and outgrowths of bone form on the degenerating articular surfaces.

4. Rheumatic fever is a disease in which the synovial tissues become inflamed and then rapidly return to normal.

5. Primary fibrositis ("rheumatism" or "lumbago") in the lower back region is an inflammation of the fibrous connective tissue of joints.

6. Tenosynovitis: The tendon sheaths become inflamed and may deter movement of the involved joints.

The Knee Joint

1. Anatomy

a. The knee joint is the largest and most complex joint in the body.
b. Two semilunar cartilages are found in the knee joint.
c. Two pairs of ligaments are found; the cruciate and collateral ligaments provide stability and necessary limitation of motion.

2. Internal derangement of the knee

   a. The most common internal derangement of the knee is a tear of the medial
   semilunar cartilage. The torn part or the
   entire cartilage should be removed,
   since cartilage has a poor blood supply
   and will not heal.

REVIEW QUESTIONS

1. Discuss the basis for the distinction between synovial and nonsynovial joints.

2. Distinguish between sutures, synchondroses, symphyses, and syndesmoses, and
   give an example of each.
3. Describe the anatomy of a synovial joint.
4. Give an example of each of the following
   types of synovial joints: ball and socket,
   hinge, pivot, ellipsoid, saddle, and gliding, and describe the action of each.
5. Describe the principal characteristics of
   rheumatoid arthritis, gouty arthritis, and
   degenerative joint disease.
6. Describe the anatomy and disorders of
   bursae.

8

The Muscular System

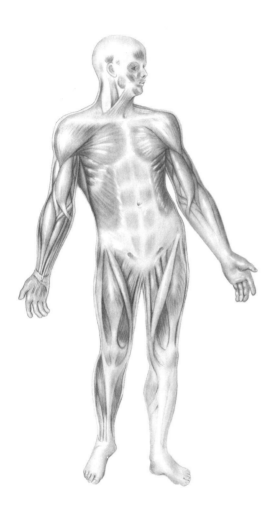

Objectives

The aim of this chapter is to enable the student to:

☐ Describe the structure of a whole skeletal muscle, muscle fiber, and myofibril.

☐ Explain how the arrangement of thick and thin filaments in a myofibril gives rise to the striated appearance of the myofibril.

☐ Describe the sliding filament model of muscular contraction and the associated structural changes seen in the electron microscope.

☐ Explain how the release of calcium from the sarcoplasmic reticulum triggers the muscular contraction.

☐ Describe how the nerve impulse is transmitted to the muscle fiber and how the impulse reaches the sarcoplasmic reticulum.

☐ List the sources of energy for muscular contraction during moderate and strenuous exercise.

☐ Identify the factors determining the strength of muscular contraction.

☐ Describe the differences between rapidly contracting and slowly contracting motor units.

☐ Identify the distinguishing characteristics of smooth and cardiac muscle.

☐ Describe how skeletal muscles are named according to action, shape, and their origins and insertions.

☐ Describe how a system of levers produces movement when muscles contract across joints.

☐ Describe the actions of the major muscles in different parts of the body.

Knowledge of the anatomy and physiology of the muscular system was uncertain and vague through the Renaissance. A few attempts to theorize the nature of muscular action were made by Hippocrates and Galen, but no real progress occurred until the seventeenth century, when Anton van Leeuwenhoek made the initial observations of muscle under the microscope. These observations laid the foundation for today's knowledge of the structure and function of muscle.

Muscles compose 40 to 50 per cent of the body's weight. When they contract, they effect movement of the body as a whole; of blood (circulation); of food through the digestive tract; of urine through the urinary tract; and of the chest, diaphragm, and abdomen during respiration. The two key words, then, are *contraction* and *movement*.

TYPES OF MUSCLE

The three types of muscle are *skeletal, smooth,* and *cardiac* (Fig. 8–1). Each is described below.

Skeletal Muscle

Skeletal muscle, as the name suggests, is usually associated with the skeletal system. It is also called *striated* muscle because of the presence of alternating dark and light bands along the length of its fibers and *voluntary* muscle because it is subject to voluntary control (although, of course, involuntary, reflex contractions and spontaneous, automatic movements, such as those expressing emotion, regularly occur, and even most voluntary movements appear to be built upon a base of reflex activity).

Mature skeletal muscle cells are long and slender; they range from 10 to 60 micrometers in diameter and may extend from one end of a muscle to the other, in some cases reaching a length of as great as 30 centimeters. Since their length is much greater than their width, these cells are called fibers. Each muscle fiber is multinucleated and is surrounded by an electrically polarized membrane — the *sarcolemma* (G. *sarx,* flesh; G. *lemma,* husk). The nuclei are usually located just under the sarcolemma.

The entire muscle consists of a number of bundles of muscle fibers known as *fasciculi* (Fig. 8–2). Surrounding each fiber and filling in the space between fibers within a fasciculus is a delicate connective tissue called the **endomysium** (G. *endon,* within; G. *mys,* muscle). Each fasciculus is bounded by a stronger connective tissue sheath, the **perimysium** (G. *peri,* around), which in turn is continuous with a tough connective tissue, the **epimysium** (G. *epi,* upon), enveloping the whole muscle. The *superficial fascia* (subcutaneous adipose tissue) forms a covering over the entire muscle trunk, and various arrangements of connective tissue, some having specific names, others generally referred to as *deep fascia,* surround or penetrate between individual muscles or groups of muscles. When viewed under the microscope, the skeletal muscle fiber is seen to have regular striations. These striations are due to transverse alternating dark and light bands on the **myofibrils,** which are parallel, threadlike structures in the *sarcoplasm* (muscle cytoplasm) of a muscle fiber (Fig. 8–3). Myofibrils, the smallest elements of the muscle fiber visible under the light microscope, are the contractile units of the fiber. With the electron microscope the striations on the myofibrils can be seen to arise from the arrangement of its subunits, **thick** and **thin filaments.** The former are composed largely

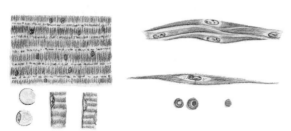

Striated, or voluntary (skeletal m.)

Smooth muscle

Cardiac muscle

Figure 8–1. Types of muscle.

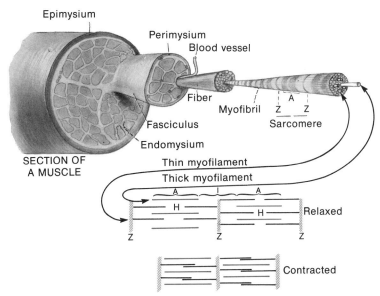

Figure 8-2. Detail of muscle showing structure and mechanics of muscular contraction.

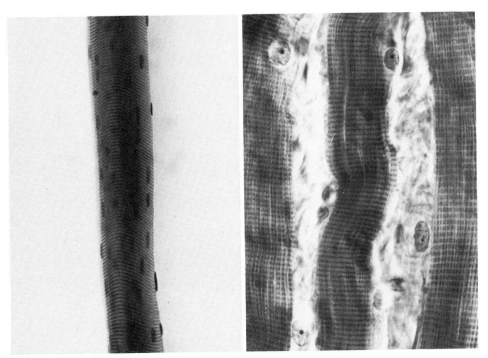

Figure 8-3. Photomicrographs of human skeletal muscle. *Left.* Portion of single intact fiber separated from the human gastrocnemius muscle. Note striations and numerous nuclei. (×275.) *Right.* Longitudinal section from lip showing portions of three fibers with connective tissue between them. In each fiber individual myofibrils with alternating dark and light bands can be seen. (×400.) (From Leeson, C. R., and Leeson, T. S.: Histology. 4th ed., Philadelphia, W. B. Saunders Co., 1981.)

of the protein *myosin,* the latter of three proteins — *actin* (the principal one), *tropomyosin,* and *troponin.* The **dark,** or **A, band** of the myofibril corresponds to the thick filaments, overlapped on either end with thin filaments; the **light,** or **I, band** corresponds to the region where there are only thin filaments (Fig. 8–4).

Two additional markings are of importance — the **Z line,** a narrow band in the central region of the I band representing a structure to which the thin filaments are attached on either side, and the **H zone,** a lighter region, located in the central portion of each A band, into which the thin filaments do not penetrate. The area between two adjacent Z lines, called a *sarcomere,* represents the repeating unit of a myofibril, each about 2.5 micrometers long in resting muscle. The shortening of a sarcomere during muscular contraction is described below under Mechanism of Contraction.

Sarcotubular Systems. Electron photomicrographs show myofibrils to be surrounded by structures made up of membranes in the form of vesicles and tubules. These structures form two systems (Fig. 8–5). One consists of what are called *T* (for transverse) *tubules,* which are actually invaginations of the membrane of the muscle fiber. The other, the principal system, called the *sarcoplasmic reticulum,* consists of tubules running parallel to the myofibrils. Each T tubule runs between a pair of sacs formed by fusion of the sarcoplasmic reticulum. These three transverse structures make up what is known as a

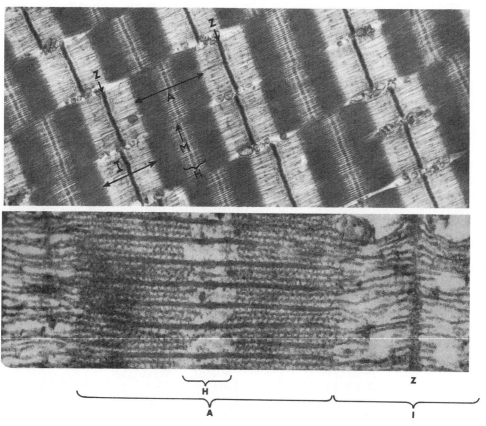

Figure 8–4. Electron micrographs of skeletal muscle of the rabbit. *Top.* Each diagonal strip is a longitudinal section of a myofibril magnified 13,000 ×. *Bottom.* Very thin section of a myofibril magnified 74,000 ×. The A bands represent the thick filaments overlapped in the darker regions with thin filaments. The lighter, H, zones in the centers of the A bands are regions free of thin filaments. The I bands represent nonoverlapping segments of thin filaments attached to both sides of the Z lines. In the bottom micrograph two thin filaments can be seen between thick filaments extending into the A band as far as the H zone. Swellings in the center of the thick filament give rise to the dense M line seen in the top micrograph. (From Leeson, C. R., and Leeson, T. S.: Histology. 4th ed., Philadelphia, W. B. Saunders Co., 1981.)

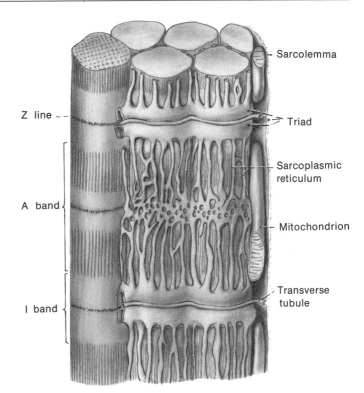

Z line

A band

I band

Sarcolemma

Triad

Sarcoplasmic
reticulum

Mitochondrion

Transverse
tubule

Figure 8–5. Diagrammatic representation of sarcoplasmic reticulum surrounding myofibrils of a fiber and of transverse tubules (invaginations of the sarcolemma). (Modified from Bloom and Fawcett: Textbook of Histology. 9th ed., Philadelphia, W. B. Saunders Co., 1968.)

triad. The triad is important functionally because, although there is no open continuity between the sarcoplasmic reticulum and the T tubules at the triad, the close association of the two systems at this site enables the T tubules to function as a conduit for transmission of the electrical impulse, the normal muscle stimulus, to the sarcoplasmic reticulum. The arrival of the electrical impulse activates the release from the sarcoplasmic reticulum of calcium, the triggering agent for muscle contraction (the action of calcium is described below under Mechanism of Contraction).

Physiology of Contraction

Motor Unit. As a result of terminal branching, a single nerve fiber innervates, on the average, about 150 muscle fibers. All of these fibers and the single nerve fiber innervating them are called a *motor unit* because the muscle fibers of the unit are always excited simultaneously and contract in unison.

It is important to note that terminal divisions of a motor neuron are distributed throughout the muscle belly. Stimulation of a single motor unit, therefore, causes weak contraction in a broad area of muscle rather than a strong contraction at one specific point.

Muscles controlling fine movements are characterized by the presence of a few muscle fibers in each motor unit; that is, the ratio of nerve fibers to muscle fibers is high. For instance, each motor unit present in the ocular muscle contains less than 10 muscle fibers. On the other hand, gross movements, for example, by major limb muscles, may be governed by motor units containing 1000 or more muscle fibers.

EXCITATION OF SKELETAL MUSCLE. Muscle fibers possess the property of being excitable. Any force affecting this excitability is called a stimulus, which, in muscle tissue, is usually conveyed by nerve fibers. The stimulus is an electrical impulse transmitted from a nerve fiber branch to muscle fiber at a junctional region called the **neuromuscular junction.** At the junction a gap, the *synaptic cleft*, exists between a nerve branch terminal and a recess on the surface of the muscle fiber. A nerve impulse reaching the neuromuscular junction causes a sharp increase in the release of acetylcholine, a chemical mediator stored in vesicles of the nerve terminal. Acetylcholine crosses the gap and acts on the membrane of the muscle fiber, causing it to generate its own impulse, which travels along the muscle fiber in both directions at a rate of about 5 meters per second and, as mentioned, is conducted to the sarcoplasmic reticulum via the T system. (A discussion of the origin of the electrical impulse in nerve and muscle fibers and a more complete description of the neuromuscular function appear in Chapter 9, The Nervous System.)

MECHANISM OF CONTRACTION. The generally accepted conception of how muscle contacts, the "sliding filament" model, is based on elegant electron microscopy studies relating structural changes to functional events when a muscle shortens during contraction. According to this model, the contraction is brought about by the *sliding of the thin filaments at each end of a sarcomere toward each other between the stationary thick filaments*. This draws the Z lines closer together, shortening the sarcomere (Fig. 8–2). In sections of muscle, prepared at sequential stages of contraction, it can be seen that, as a sarcomere shortens, the I band of each myofibril (the region containing only thin filaments bisected by a Z line) narrows as the thin filaments move toward the center of the sarcomere, while the A band (representing the length of the thick filaments) is unaltered. The H zone of the A band, the lighter, central region not penetrated by thin filaments in relaxed muscle, disappears as thin filaments come to completely overlap the thick filaments in the contracted state. When contraction is marked, a dense zone appears in the center of the A band as a result of overlap of thin filaments from opposite ends of a sarcomere. In cross section this overlap is identified as a doubling (over the relaxed condition) of the ratio of thin to thick filaments.

The movement of the thin filaments can be accounted for by cross-bridges extending from thick to thin filaments, which are utilized as mechanical pulling devices. **Myosin molecules,** from which thick filaments are constructed, have a globular head and linear tail. They can be readily split enzymatically (with trypsin) into two subunits. One, called *heavy meromyosin* (G. *meros,* part), contains the globular head and a linear tail section; the other, called *light meromyosin,* is an all-linear tail segment. The head of heavy meromyosin, which can be enzymatically separated from the tail section, has the property of combining with actin and contains

ATP-splitting enzymes. The linear light meromyosin subunits have a self-combining property. Thick filaments are assembled by tail-to-tail aggregation of myosin molecules so that in each half of the filaments the heads, which form the ends of the cross-bridges, face opposite directions (Fig. 8–6). This built-in directionality explains how thin filaments at opposite ends of a sarcomere can be pulled inward toward the center of the thick filaments.

The thin filament is an assembly of three proteins: **actin,** the principal one, **tropomyosin,** and **troponin.** Actin consists of two strands of spherical molecules coiled around one another (Fig. 8–6). On the surface of each strand of actin is a filamentous tropomyosin. Troponin is a complex of three globular subunits positioned at regular intervals (about 400 A apart) along the thin filament. The largest subunit of troponin, designated Tn-T, binds to tropomyosin. Another, Tn-I (the inhibitory subunit), reversibly binds to actin; when bound, the troponin complex, linked to tropomyosin and actin, seems to act as a "latch," holding tropomyosin in a position that blocks the myosin binding site on actin. The "latch" is released when calcium binds the smallest subunit, Tn-C, causing the troponin complex to undergo a change in conformation which breaks the link between the Tn-I subunit and actin.

The sequence of events leading to the contraction of muscle may be summarized as follows: The electrical impulse traveling along the membrane of a muscle fiber reaches the sarcoplasmic reticulum via the T tubules. This stimulates the release of *calcium,* which combines with the Tn-C subunits of troponin and induces a change in the conformation of the troponin molecules. Tropomyosin moves away from the myosin binding sites on actin, and the myosin heads, charged with ATP, combine with actin (it has been postulated that the energized, force-generating state of the myosin heads is a complex of myosin with ADP and phosphate formed following the cleavage of ATP by myosin ATPase). When actin and myosin interact, the energized myosin complex breaks down, providing the energy for the propulsive force (probably a swiveling of the myosin heads) for pulling the thin filaments toward the center of the sarcomere. Successive cycles, involving binding of ATP to myosin heads, detachment of myosin heads from

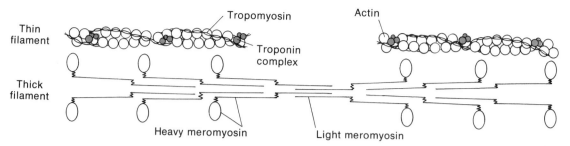

Figure 8-6. Schematic representation of the arrangement of the constituents in thick and thin filaments. Thick filaments are constructed from molecules of myosin, a protein that can be divided enzymatically into two parts, one (heavy meromyosin) consisting of a globular head and a linear tail section, the other (light meromyosin) consisting of an all-linear tail segment. The filaments assemble by tail-to-tail aggregation of myosin molecules so that the heads face opposite ends of the sarcomere. There are about 400 myosin molecules in a single thick filament. The protein action, the principal component of thin filaments, consists of two strands of spheroidal molecules twisted into a double helix. Tropomyosin is a filamentous protein on the surface of each actin strand. Troponin complexes, each composed of three globular protein subunits, are positioned at regular intervals along the thin filament and appear to act as "latches" by holding tropomyosin in a position that blocks the myosin binding site on actin (in the illustration, troponin complexes on only one side of actin are shown). When calcium, the triggering agent of contraction, is released into the sarcoplasmic reticulum, it is bound by the smallest subunit of troponin. This causes the troponin complex to undergo a change in conformation, the consequence of which is a movement of tropomyosin that exposes the myosin binding site on actin. The binding of ATP-charged myosin heads to actin begins a sequence of events that results in the propulsion by myosin of actin filaments from both ends of the sarcomere toward the center of the sarcomere, presumably by a swiveling motion of the myosin heads.

actin, and reattachment in a new position on actin, followed by the power stroke that moves the thin filaments, result in the continued sliding of the thin filaments. Contraction ends when calcium returns to the sarcoplasmic reticulum.

RIGOR COMPLEX. The detachment of the myosin cross-bridges from actin after ATP is split can take place only after a new ATP binds to the myosin heads. The low energy complex between actin and myosin without bound ATP is called a *rigor complex.* Rigor complexes, unlike active actin-myosin complexes, can form in either the absence or presence of calcium. The depletion of ATP after death results in the formation of rigor complexes and accounts for the development of *rigor mortis.*

ENERGY SOURCES. In the chapter on the cell we described the role of ATP as a direct source of energy for the variety of work, including muscular contraction, performed by cells. Described also was the synthesis of ATP during the aerobic (in the presence of oxygen) breakdown of glucose and the fatty acid component of fat to carbon dioxide and water and, during glycolysis, the anaerobic (in the absence of oxygen) break-

down of glucose (or glycogen) to lactic acid. ATP must be continuously resynthesized in muscle, since its reserves are meager. Muscle contains a small auxiliary source of high energy phosphate in the form of **creatine phosphate.** Creatine phosphate can be utilized during muscular contraction for the rapid resynthesis of ATP by phosphate transfer to ADP. When muscle is at rest, the reverse reaction, phosphate transfer from ATP to creatine, rebuilds the reserves of creatine phosphate. Muscle also has its own glycogen stores. Calculations based largely upon measurements of oxygen consumption and lactic acid production in human subjects suggest that during **moderate exercise** the energy is initially supplied by stored ATP and ATP resynthesized from creatine phosphate. Within a few seconds, the oxidation of fatty acids and glucose, taken up from the blood stream, provides an additional source of ATP. Oxygen consumption rises rapidly as increased amounts of fatty acids and glucose are oxidized. If any anaerobic breakdown of glycogen occurs under these conditions, it is too small to be detected. When the exercise is **strenuous,** a point is reached when the oxygen supply is insufficient to meet the energy needs of active muscle. When this occurs (estimated as an energy expenditure of approximately 220 calories per minute per kilogram of body weight), glycolysis provides a sizable portion of the energy needs. As discussed in the chapter on the cell (page 59), far less ATP is produced by the anaerobic than by the aerobic processes. The lactic acid produced during glycolysis is released from the muscles into the blood stream to be subsequently taken up by the liver (where it is converted to glucose and glycogen). A reasonably accurate measure of the extent of glycolysis can be obtained by determining the concentration of lactic acid in a blood sample drawn two to three minutes after a strenuous exercise trial lasting up to a few minutes. Exercising to a state of exhaustion is associated with a steep and continuous rise in blood lactic acid. Reducing the effort or introducing rest intervals is reflected in a leveling off of blood lactic acid concentrations.

OYXGEN DEBT. The depletion of energy stores during exercise represents a debt that is paid after exercise during a period when oxygen consumption returns gradually to normal. The oxygen debt is defined as the amount of oxygen consumed above the resting level during the postexercise period. If the exercise was moderate, the oxygen consumption returns to normal within a few minutes and the debt is small. Oxidation of fatty acids and glucose during this brief period replenishes the approximately half-depleted stores of ATP and creatine phosphate. Strenuous exercise results in a large oxygen debt, and the return to a resting oxygen consumption is slow (requiring an hour or more). The large debt is incurred because a portion of the glycogen stores as well as possibly all of the stores of ATP and creatine phosphate must be replaced. Furthermore, glycolysis continues during the recovery period in order to contribute to the replenishment of ATP and creatine phosphate. Since the glycogen used during this period must also be replaced, this adds to the debt.

ALL-OR-NONE LAW. The weakest stimulus that will initiate contraction of the fibers of a motor unit (or of an individual, isolated fiber) is known as the *threshold, liminal,* or *minimal stimulus*. To be effective the stimulus must also be applied for a minimum duration. A stimulus strong enough to elicit a response will produce maximal contraction. The contraction is either all or none. Increas-

ing the strength of the stimulus will not increase the response. If the stimulus is of lesser intensity, it is called *subthreshold, subliminal,* or *subminimal*. The combination of two subminimal stimuli, when applied in rapid succession, may be equivalent to the minimal stimulus, causing contraction of the cell. This is known as *summation of stimuli*.

CONTRACTION OF ISOLATED SKELETAL MUSCLE. Contraction of a muscle can be recorded in the laboratory by attachment of a tendon to a moving lever. In common practice, the gastrocnemius muscle of the frog is used in such preparations. A single, brief contraction is called a *muscle twitch*. Analysis of such a contraction of skeletal muscle shows a brief period after stimulation before contraction occurs. This *latent period* is followed by a *period of contraction* and, finally, by a *period of relaxation* (Fig. 8–7).

The response depends on (1) the strength of a stimulus, (2) the speed of application of a stimulus, (3) the number of stimulations, (4) the initial length of the muscle, and (5) the temperature.

If a muscle is subjected to successive stimuli of increasing strength, nerve fibers with higher thresholds will respond and activate the fibers of their respective motor units and the force of the muscle twitch will increase progressively as increasing numbers of motor units are recruited.

It is also possible to increase the magnitude of the response by stimulating a muscle while a twitch is still in progress. This *summation of twitches* is believed to result in part from the release by the initial contraction of elastic elements (attributed, among other things, to connective tissue components of muscle and its tendinous attachments) which resist the shortening. A volley of stimuli at low frequency will produce a succession of rising peaks of contraction, a response known as *clonus* or *incomplete tetanus* (Fig. 8–8). Stimulation at a high frequency will cause the fusion of summated twitches, resulting in a sustained contraction called *tetanus*.

It is perhaps apparent that the distinct muscle twitch is a laboratory phenomenon. In normal function smooth contractions are maintained by tetanization or, if the stimulation frequency is too low for tetanization, by asynchronous excitation of motor units by nerve impulses.

A curious phenomenon observed at the

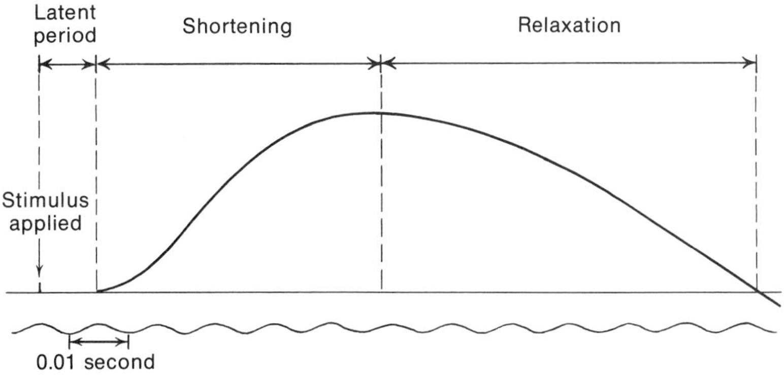

Latent period   Shortening   Relaxation

Stimulus applied

0.01 second

Figure 8–7. A single twitch recorded by attachment of a muscle to a moving lever. The rise in the lever records the shortening of the muscle. As the muscle relaxes, the fall in the lever records the return of the muscle to its original length. (After Carlson and Johnson.)

beginning of a series of complete muscle twitches is known as *treppe* (the German word for staircase). The magnitude of the first few twitches increases in a stepwise manner. Although this response is still not well understood, it has been suggested that a progressive buildup of calcium in the sarcoplasm by the successive stimuli could account for it. The calcium buildup would increase the propulsive energy by increasing the number of myosin-actin linkages.

The following phenomena are also observed if the stimulations are continued at a constant rate: After treppe the magnitude of the contractions levels off. As the stimulations are continued, the contractions weaken. This state of *fatigue*, brought about by depletion of nutrients and oxygen and the accumulation of waste products (especially lactic acid), eventually leads to a complete absence of response. As the state of fatigue sets in, the muscle fails to relax completely after each contraction. This condition is known as *con-*

tracture. The term contracture is also used clinically to describe a partially contracted state of muscle (see p. 176).

An important factor governing the force with which a muscle contracts is its initial length. Maximum force is obtained when a muscle is stretched to its approximate resting length in its normal attachments in the body. At this length there is a maximum overlap between thin filaments and the myosin heads. If in the laboratory preparation weights are added to the muscle lever, stretching the muscle, the work performed when the muscle contracts (load × distance lifted) will increase to an optimum load and decrease as more weights are added.

The optimum temperature at which muscles perform their best work is 37° C (98.6° F) in man. As the temperature rises above this level, excitability is lost, the muscle finally entering a state of heat rigor, or permanent shortening.

COMPARISON OF ISOMETRIC AND ISOTONIC CONTRACTION. In the foregoing descriptions of muscle contraction, the tension developed was utilized to perform work in moving a load some distance. This occurs normally when walking, climbing, lifting objects, or turning the head. If a muscle does not shorten as it contracts, the tension may be utilized for such actions as holding an object in a fixed position or maintaining posture against the force of gravity. According to the classification introduced by Adolf Fick in the nineteenth century, the contraction is called *isotonic* when the muscle shortens against a constant load and *isometric* when it does not shorten. An isometric twitch curve following a single stimulus, showing a rise in tension to a peak as the muscle contracts and a fall as it relaxes (Fig. 8–9), is recorded in the laboratory by attaching one end of a muscle to a rigid rod and the other end to the stationary lever

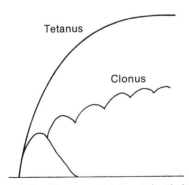

Tetanus

Clonus

Figure 8–8. Clonus and tetanus in skeletal muscle. Tetanus occurs at stimulation rates between about 30 to 100 stimuli per second, depending upon the muscle (the required stimulation rate is lower for slowly contracting than for rapidly contracting muscles).

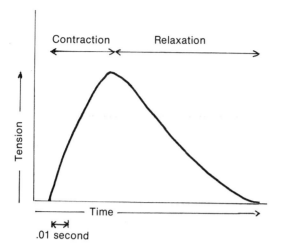

Figure 8–9. Illustration of the rise and fall in tension during a single isometric twitch. Tension is recorded by attaching one end of the muscle to a rigid rod and the other to the fixed lever of an electronic force transducer. A brief latent period occurs after stimulation before the onset of the contraction.

of an electronic force transducer. A volley of stimuli at high frequency will produce, just as it does in an isotonic contraction, a fusion of summated twitches in a sustained contraction called tetanus. Tension rises to a maximum, which is maintained for the duration of the stimulation. Maximum tension is obtained when the length of the stimulated muscle is very close to its length in the body.

CONTRACTION TIMES OF MUSCLES AND MOTOR UNITS. Muscles differ considerably in the speed of their contractions. For example, the contraction times of the lateral rectus, gastrocnemius and soleus of the cat (determined as the time required to reach peak tension in an isometric twitch) are, respectively, 7.5, 40, and 90 milliseconds. These contraction times correlate with normal functions: rapid eye movements (lateral rectus), moderately rapid movements in walking and running (gastrocnemius), and prolonged supportive action (soleus). Traditionally, certain muscles have been described, on the basis of appearance and speed of contraction, as either (1) red, slow-contracting, and having a preponderance of small-diameter, reddish fibers; and (2) white, fast-contracting, and having a preponderance of large-diameter, pale fibers. Most muscles fall somewhere between the two extremes, and the proportions of the two basic fiber types vary considerably from one muscle to another. It has also been observed that the motor units of a muscle can be distinguished on the basis of contraction times and other characteristics. In the gastrocnemius muscle of cats it has been possible to correlate contraction times and other properties of three types of motor units with their histochemical profiles. Fibers of fast-contracting units, which also fatigue rapidly, are of large diameter, have few capillaries and mitochondria, and contain an abundance of glycogen. Their apparent dependence upon anaerobic glycolysis could explain their rapid fatigue. Large-diameter fibers also have an extensive sarcoplasmic reticulum. Since this would allow rapid release and uptake of large amounts of calcium ions, it is consistent with their faster contraction. Fibers of slow-contracting, fatigue-resistant units have small diameters, a rich capillary supply, many mitochondria and little glycogen. This profile suggests a high capacity for aerobic energy pathways. Small-diameter fibers also contain large amounts of the oxygen-carrying heme protein myoglobin. This characteristic and the presence of cytochromes (also heme proteins) in the abundant mitochondria, as well as the vascularity of these fibers, account for the description of small fibers as red, as distinguished from the large, white fibers. The fibers of the third group of motor units in the cat's gastrocnemius muscle, described as fast-contracting and fatigue-resistant, are of variable diameter and liberally supplied with capillaries. Their glycogen and mitochondrial content suggests utilization of both aerobic and anaerobic pathways.

Smooth Muscle

Smooth muscle is found in the digestive and respiratory tracts and other hollow structures, such as the urinary bladder and blood vessels. Other locations include the iris and ciliary muscle of the eye and the piloerector muscles of the skin. Since the contraction in smooth muscle is ordinarily not induced at will, it is called *involuntary* muscle. Each smooth muscle cell, also called a fiber, contains a single large nucleus and is smaller than the fiber of skeletal muscle, usually ranging in length from 20 to 200 micrometers and in diameter from 2 to 6 micrometers. The banding, or cross-striation, effect noted in skeletal muscle is absent in the smooth muscle fiber.

The smooth muscle of hollow structures such as the small intestine is grouped into an inner circular layer and an outer longitudinal layer. Simultaneous contraction of the two layers results in a reduction in both the circumference and length of the tubular structure.

Although the fiber arrangement and function of smooth muscle varies somewhat from organ to organ, two types are generally described. In the first, cells are found in rolled sheets, with the cell membranes of adjacent fibers in close contact. Relatively few nerve terminals are present. This pattern is found in most hollow organs of the body. This type of smooth muscle, known as *visceral* or *unitary* smooth muscle, exhibits the property of *automaticity* — it contracts in the absence of nerve stimulation. The function of the nerve supply (by the autonomic nervous system) is to regulate the rate and degree of contraction. The electrical impulses, whether of external or internal origin, pass from one fiber to another via membrane junctions known as *nexuses*, also called *gap junctions* (the same name as communicating junctions in epithelial tissue). Visceral smooth muscle produces a relatively slow contraction but permits greater extensibility. In the other arrangement, the smooth muscle pattern is less well organized but the fibers are separate and, by and large, independently innervated. This type, called *multiunit* smooth muscle, is found chiefly where finer gradations of contractions occur, such as in the iris and the ciliary muscle of the eye and the piloerector muscles of the skin. This type of smooth muscle is not characterized by automaticity.

Thick and thin filaments apparently are not so regularly arranged in smooth muscle as in striated muscle. Nevertheless, the contraction of smooth muscle is believed to occur in a way that is similar to contraction in skeletal muscle.

Cardiac Muscle

Cardiac, or heart, muscle is involuntary muscle, possessing the striated appearance of voluntary muscle. The striations result from the same arrangement of thick and thin filaments as in skeletal muscle. The mechanism of contraction of the two types of muscle is essentially the same. Cardiac muscle fibers have a single, centrally placed nucleus and are branched at their ends (Fig. 8–10). Muscle fibers are functionally linked at their branched ends by junctional specializations with interdigitations of cell membrane called

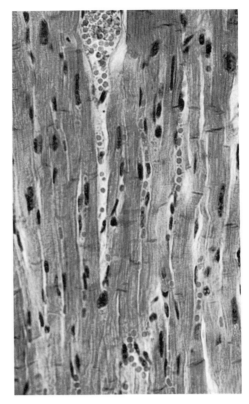

Figure 8–10. Photomicrograph of human cardiac muscle. Branching fibers with central nuclei are functionally linked by intercalated discs, which can be seen as dense transverse lines forming a steplike pattern. (From Leeson, C. R., and Leeson, T. S.: Histology. 4th ed., Philadelphia, W. B. Saunders Co., 1981.)

intercalated discs. The resulting three-dimensional network, once thought to be a single multinucleated mass of cytoplasm (a syncytium), is generally referred to as a *functional syncytium*. Two such functional syncytia are present in the heart. The walls and septum of the atria, the upper chambers of the heart, compose one and the walls and septum of the ventricles, the lower chambers of the heart, compose the other.

An important characteristic of cardiac muscle cells is the slow return of the membrane to a resting state following excitation by an electrical impulse. During the recovery period it is insensitive, or *refractory*, to another impulse (this condition contrasts sharply with the very brief refractory period of skeletal muscle). The long refractory period of cardiac muscle prevents tetanization, which, of course, would interfere with its rhythmic pumping action.

The heart will continue to beat (although

at a different rate) even when its nerve supply is cut. The intrinsic beat is generated by electrical impulses arising from the *"pacemaker,"* a concentration of specialized neuromuscular tissue in the right atrium. This neuromuscular tissue is also responsible for the rapid conduction of the impulse throughout the ventricles. (The properties of the neuromuscular tissue of the heart are discussed in more detail in the chapter on the circulation.) The functional syncytial arrangement of cardiac muscle and the presence of neuromuscular tissue make it possible for the upper and lower chambers to contract en masse. Regulation of the heart rate is accomplished by the action of the autonomic nervous system on the pacemaker (see Chapter 11 for additional information).

DISORDERS OF MUSCLE

Disease of muscle originates in the nerve supply, the vascular supply or the connective tissue sheaths. The major symptoms of muscular disorders are paralysis, weakness, pain, atrophy, spasm, and cramps.

A condition in which a muscle shortens its length in the resting state is known as a *contracture*. Contractures occur when an individual remains in bed for prolonged periods and the muscles are not properly exercised. Eventually, the muscles readjust to the resting length of a flexed arm or leg. Contractures are treated by the painful and slow procedure of exercising and relengthening the muscle. Contractures can be prevented by keeping the body in correct alignment when resting and by periodically exercising the muscles. Muscular exercise can be either active (by the patient himself), or passive (by someone else).

Myalgia refers to muscular pain; *myositis* is the term used to describe inflammation of muscular tissue. *Fibrositis* is an inflammation of the connective tissue within a muscle, particularly near a joint. Usually a combination of fibrositis and myositis, *fibromyositis*, is present. Such a condition is commonly known as rheumatism, lumbago, or charley horse.

Two other entities affecting the muscle are *muscular dystrophy* and *myasthenia gravis*. Muscular dystrophy occurs most often in males and is a slowly progressive disorder ending in complete helplessness. In muscular dystrophy, the child begins to walk clumsily and tends to fall. Examination reveals pseudohypertrophy of some muscle groups and wasting of others. The term pseudohypertrophy is employed because the muscles feel large owing to the deposition of fat.

Myasthenia gravis is characterized by the weakness and easy fatigability of muscles. It is caused by an impairment of conduction of the normal impulse at the myoneural junction of striated muscle as a result of a decrease in the number of receptors for acetylcholine on the muscle membrane at the junctions. This decrease is believed to be due to an autoimmune response (destruction of a natural substance by the body's immunological defense system). Neostigmine, a drug serving to interfere with cholinesterase (an enzyme that destroys acetylcholine) is given for therapy. Surgical removal of the thymus (if enlarged) has been beneficial, possibly because it reduces the autoimmune response.

In *atrophy* the muscle fibers degenerate because of disuse, as when limbs are placed in casts. Muscles can become a fraction of their normal size; within six months to two years the fibers are actually replaced by fibrous connective tissue. Stimulation of nerves with an electric current keeps muscular tissue viable until full muscular activity returns. (A reverse condition, *hypertrophy of use*, is a normal event and refers to the increase in size of exercised muscle due to an increase in the diameters of individual muscle fibers, with an increase in the number of their myofibrils.)

Muscles act in an orderly fashion, and the performance of even the slightest movement demands the cooperative effort of many muscles. The cerebellum of the brain is devoted largely to coordinating muscular activity. If a muscle becomes paralyzed, the sequence for coordination is disrupted and other muscles are unable to act in sequence; this may lead to muscular atrophy.

INTRAMUSCULAR INJECTION

The importance of a proper site for intramuscular injection is recognized by those who have experienced the pain resulting when a poor site is selected for injection. The ideal site is deep within the muscle, and away from major nerves and arteries. The best sites are the vastus lateralis, the deltoid, and the gluteal muscles.

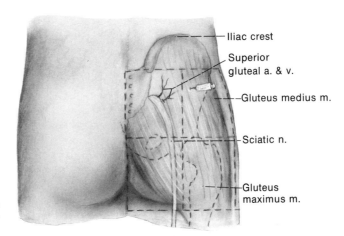

Labels in figure:
Iliac crest
Superior gluteal a. & v.
Gluteus medius m.
Sciatic n.
Gluteus maximus m.

Figure 8–11. Intramuscular injection in the gluteal region should be in the upper outer quadrant.

The gluteal region has become the most common site for intramuscular injection. The area best suited is the upper and outer quadrant (Fig. 8–11). The student should remember that the gluteal region extends to the anterior superior iliac spine. This should be used as a landmark when defining the quadrants. When the upper outer quadrant is used, there is little danger of the needle piercing the sciatic nerve or the superior gluteal artery.

The deltoid muscle is thick and extends from the clavicle, acromion, and spine of the scapula to the deltoid tuberosity of the humerus (Fig. 8–12). Owing to the nonyielding tendinous septa in the upper and lower regions of this muscle, only a small area in the center provides a satisfactory site for injection. This site is found 2 cm below the acromion. The gluteal region is preferred, since it has a greater muscle mass, permitting injection of larger volumes of fluid.

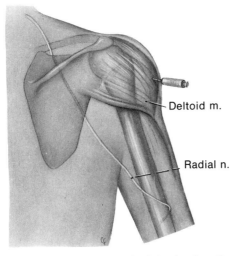

Labels in figure:
Deltoid m.
Radial n.

Figure 8–12. Intramuscular injection into the deltoid, two to three fingerbreadths below the acromion.

INTRODUCTION TO THE ANATOMY AND ACTIONS OF SKELETAL MUSCLES

Tables 8–1 through 8–15 include most of the important muscles of the body. They list the origin and insertion of each muscle and its principal action and innervation. The **origin** is the more fixed attachment of a muscle that serves as a basis of action. The movable attachment where the effects of movement are produced is the **insertion**. Frequently the action of a muscle can be altered by reversal of the origin and insertion. For example, the latissimus dorsi extends, adducts, and rotates the arm (back-stroke of the crawl in swimming) when the humerus is the insertion, and raises the trunk and pelvis (pulling the body up in rope climbing) when the humerus is the origin. The action of a muscle may also vary depending upon whether it contracts on one or both sides of the body or whether all or a part of the muscle contracts. Taking the sternocleidomastoid as an example, contraction on both sides will flex the head, whereas contraction on one side will turn the head to the opposite side. In the case of the deltoid muscle, it abducts, flexes or extends the arm, depending upon whether the whole muscle, the anterior fibers, or the posterior fibers contract.

Most voluntary muscles are not inserted directly into bone but rather through the medium of a strong, tough, nonelastic, fibrous cord called a *tendon*. Tendons vary in length from a fraction of an inch to more than one foot. Muscles may have one of these connective tissue cords, consisting largely of closely packed bundles of white collagenous fibers, attached to each of the extremities. If the tendon is wide, thin, and flat it is called an *aponeurosis*. Tendons and aponeuroses are continuous with the endo-, peri-, and

177

epimysium of muscle and the periosteum of bone, an arrangement which firmly harnesses muscle to bone.

It should be remembered that muscles are named according to *action* (e.g., adductor and extensor); according to *shape* (quadratus); according to *origin* and *insertion* (sternocleidomastoid); according to number of *divisions* (triceps, with three heads, each adjacent to a separate origin, and digastric, with two bodies); according to *location* (tibialis and radialis); and according to *direction of fibers* (transversus).

Muscles vary in the arrangement of their fiber bundles. In most muscles the bundles are approximately parallel and pass in a line of pull from the origin to the insertion. Muscles having this arrangement of bundles may be *quadrilateral* (flat and short), *straplike* (flat and long), or *fusiform* (L. *fusus*, spindle; L. *forma*, shape). In straplike muscles the fibers may run the entire length of the muscle or between transverse, tendinous intersections positioned at intervals along the length of the muscle. In other muscles the bundles are oblique to the line of pull, often joining a central tendon in a featherlike arrangement (from both sides in the *bipennate* form, from one side in the *unipennate* form). In *multipennate* muscles the bundles converge on many tendons in a complex fashion. Pennate muscles contract with greater force but for shorter distances than muscles with a parallel arrangement of fibers. In another, less common *radial* arrangement, bundles of fibers converge on a common tendon from a wide area.

Muscles which bend a limb at a joint are called *flexors*. Muscles which straighten a limb at a joint are called *extensors*. If the limb is moved away from the midline of the body, an *abductor* is at work; if the limb is brought toward the midline, *adductors* are responsible. There are also muscles *rotating* the involved limb. In movements of the ankle, muscles of *dorsiflexion* turn the foot upward, while muscles of *plantar flexion* bring the foot toward the ground. In movements of the hand, turning the forearm so that the palm of the hand faces upward is called *supination*, and turning it to bring the palm facing the ground is *pronation*. *Levators* raise a part of the body; *depressors* lower it.

In performing a given movement, such as bending the arm at the elbow, the muscles executing the actual movement are known as the *prime movers* or *agonists*. Muscles

straightening the elbow are *extensors*, also called *antagonists*. The agonist muscle, or flexor, must relax for the extensor muscle, or antagonist, to perform. *Synergists* are muscles assisting the agonist. They hold a joint crossed by the tendon of the prime mover in the best possible position for effective action.

When muscles contract across joints, movement is accomplished by a system of levers. A bone acts as a **lever** (a rigid piece) that is turned about a **fulcrum** (a joint) by a **force** (contracting muscle or muscles), thereby moving a **load** (body part and possibly an added weight). There are three main classes of levers (Fig. 8–13). In the first class the fulcrum is located between the applied force and the load (as in using a crowbar). In the second and third classes the fulcrum is at one end of the lever. In second class levers the load is between the fulcrum and the force (as in a wheelbarrow), whereas in third class levers the force is applied between the fulcrum and the load (as in shoveling snow). The law of levers states that the force multiplied by the length of the force arm (distance from the force to the fulcrum) is equal to the load multiplied by the length of the load arm (distance from the load to the fulcrum). Hence, if the force arm is longer than the load arm, it is possible to move a heavy load with a weak force, thereby gaining what is called "mechanical advantage." Under these circumstances the force acts over a relatively long distance, moving a load a relatively short distance. In bringing about movements in the body, however, the objective is to move a body part a comparatively long distance with a muscular contraction acting over a short (and, hence, not awkward) distance rather than to obtain mechanical advantage. Therefore, the force arm is generally much shorter than the load arm. In Figure 8–13 this principle is illustrated in the action of the biceps brachii, a third class lever (the most commonly occurring class in the body), and the triceps brachii, a first class lever. There is a difference of opinion as to whether a second class lever (which always provides mechanical advantage because of the position of the load) exists anywhere in the body. Lifting the heel off the ground to stand on one's toes by the action of the calf muscles, principally the gastrocnemius, also illustrated in Figure 8–13, is described by some anatomists as an example of a lever of this class.

Text continued on page 188

Table 8–1 MUSCLES OF THE FACE AND SCALP°

MUSCLE	ORIGIN	INSERTION	FUNCTION	INNERVATION
Epicranius (Occipitofrontalis) Occipitalis	Occipital bone and mastoid portion of temporal bone	Galea aponeurotica (epicranial aponeurosis)	Draws scalp backward	Facial
Frontalis	Galea aponeurotica	Muscles above orbit and nose	Draws scalp forward, elevates eyebrows, and wrinkles skin of forehead	Facial
Orbicularis oculi (L. *orbicularis*, circular; L. *oculus*, eye)	Medial aspects of frontal and maxillary bones and medial palpebral ligament	Fibers encircle orbit and pass across eyelid to interlace laterally (forming the lateral palpebral raphe)	Closes eyelids	Facial
Orbicularis oris (L. *os*, mouth)	Muscle fibers surrounding the mouth	Skin at angle of mouth	Closes and puckers lips; compresses lips against teeth	Facial
Zygomaticus minor	Zygomatic bone	Muscles of upper lip	Draws upper lip upward and outward	Facial
Levator labii superioris (L. *levare*, to raise)	Inferior margin of orbit	Muscles of upper lip	Elevates upper lip	Facial
Levator labii superioris alaeque nasi	Frontal process of maxilla	Greater alar cartilage; skin of ala of nose and lateral part of upper lip	Raises upper lip; dilates nostril	Facial
Buccinator (L., trumpeter)	Posterior portion of alveolar processes of maxilla and mandible	Orbicularis oris at angle of mouth	Compresses cheek and retracts angle of mouth	Facial
Zygomaticus major	Zygomatic bone	Orbicularis oris	Pulls angle of mouth upward and backward when laughing	Facial
Mentalis (L. *mentum*, chin)	Incisive fossa of mandible	Skin of chin	Raises and protrudes lower lip, as in doubt or disdain and in drinking	Facial

°See Figures 8–14 to 8–16.

Table 8–2 MUSCLES OF MASTICATION°

MUSCLE	ORIGIN	INSERTION	FUNCTION	INNERVATION
Masseter (G. *maseter*, chewer)	Zygomatic bone and adjacent portions of maxilla	Angle and lateral surface of ramus of mandible	Raises mandible, closing jaws	Trigeminal
Temporalis	Temporal fossa of skull and from deep surface of temporal fascia	Coronoid process of mandible	Raises mandible, closing jaws; posterior fibers draw protruding mandible backward	Trigeminal
Medial pterygoid	Medial surface of lateral pterygoid plate of sphenoid; palatine bone; tuberosity of maxilla	Medial surface of ramus and angle of mandible	Raises mandible, closing jaws; acting with lateral pterygoid on same side, pulls mandible to one side; the medial and lateral pterygoids on both sides act together to bring lower jaw forward	Trigeminal
Lateral pterygoid (Two-headed)	Upper head from greater wing of sphenoid; lower head from lateral surface of pterygoid plate of sphenoid	Front of neck of mandible; capsule and disc of temporomandibular joint	Depresses mandible, opening jaws (see also medial pterygoid)	Trigeminal

°See Figures 8–17 and 8–18.

Table 8–3 MUSCLES MOVING THE TONGUE*

MUSCLE	ORIGIN	INSERTION	FUNCTION	INNERVATION
Genioglossus (G. *geneion*, chin; G. *glōssa*, tongue)	Internal surface of mandible near symphysis	Hyoid bone; inferior surface of tongue	Depresses and thrusts tongue forward	Hypoglossal
Styloglossus	Styloid process of temporal bone	Side of tongue	Draws tongue upward and backward	Hypoglossal
Hyoglossus	Body of hyoid	Side of tongue	Depresses tongue	Hypoglossal

*See Figure 8–19.

Table 8–4 SUPRA AND INFRAHYOID MUSCLES OF THE NECK*

MUSCLE	ORIGIN	INSERTION	FUNCTION	INNERVATION
Suprahyoid				
Digastric	Anterior belly: mandible; posterior belly: mastoid process of temporal bone	Hyoid	Raises hyoid or depresses mandible, opening mouth	Trigeminal and facial
Mylohyoid	Mandible	Body of hyoid	Raises mouth floor; raises hyoid or depresses mandible, opening mouth	Trigeminal
Geniohyoid	Internal surface of mandible near symphysis	Hyoid	Elevates, draws hyoid forward; depresses mandible, opening mouth	First cervical spinal nerve via hypoglossal
Stylohyoid	Styloid process	Body of hyoid	Draws hyoid upward and backward	Facial
Infrahyoid				
Sternohyoid	Manubrium	Body of hyoid	Depresses hyoid	Branches from ansa cervicalis
Omohyoid	Superior border of scapula	Lateral border of hyoid	Depresses hyoid	Branches from ansa cervicalis
Sternothyroid	Manubrium	Thyroid cartilage	Depresses larynx	Branches from ansa cervicalis
Thyrohyoid	Thyroid cartilage	Hyoid	Depresses hyoid or raises larynx	First cervical spinal nerve via hypoglossal

*See Figures 8–19 to 8–22.

Table 8–5 MUSCLES MOVING THE HEAD AND SHOULDER GIRDLE*

MUSCLE	ORIGIN	INSERTION	FUNCTION	INNERVATION
Sternocleidomastoid	Two heads, one from the sternum, the other from the clavicle	Mastoid process of temporal bone and lateral half of superior nuchal line of occipital bone	One side rotates head to opposite side; both sides flex head and neck	Spinal accessory
Splenius capitis	Lower half of ligamentum nuchae; spinous processes of 7th cervical and upper 3 or 4 thoracic vertebrae	Mastoid process of temporal bone; occipital bone	Both sides extend head; one side turns head to same side	Lateral branches of the dorsal rami of the middle cervical spinal nerves
Trapezius	Occipital bone; ligamentum nuchae; spinous processes of 7th cervical to 12th thoracic vertebrae	Acromion and spine of scapula; lateral third of clavicle	Raises and pulls shoulders backward; rotates scapula; extends head or draws it to opposite side if one side contracts	Spinal accessory

Table continued on following page

Table 8–5 MUSCLES MOVING THE HEAD AND SHOULDER GIRDLE° (*Continued*)

MUSCLE	ORIGIN	INSERTION	FUNCTION	INNERVATION
Levator scapulae (L. *levare*, to raise)'	Upper 4 or 5 cervical vertebrae	Vertebral border of scapula	Elevates scapula	3rd and 4th cervical and dorsal scapular
Rhomboideus major	Spines of 2nd to 5th thoracic vertebrae	Vertebral border of scapula	Moves scapula backward	Dorsal scapular
Rhomboideus minor	Spinous processes of last cervical and 1st thoracic vertebrae	Vertebral border of scapula at root of spine	Moves scapula backward	Dorsal scapular
Pectoralis minor†	Upper margins and outer surfaces of 3rd to 5th ribs; fasciae covering intercostals	Medial border of coracoid process of scapula	Depresses shoulder and rotates scapula downward	Anterior thoracic
Serratus anterior†	Outer surfaces and superior borders of upper 8 or 9 ribs; fasciae covering intercostals	Ventral surface of vertebral border of scapula	Moves scapula forward and away from spine	Long thoracic

°See Figures 8–20 to 8–28.
†See Figure 8–60 for pectoralis minor and Figure 8–62 for serratus anterior.

Table 8–6 MUSCLES MOVING THE VERTEBRAL COLUMN°

MUSCLE	ORIGIN	INSERTION	FUNCTION	INNERVATION
Erector spinae (Sacrospinalis)				
Iliocostalis			Extend and bend vertebral column laterally	Dorsal rami of upper lumbar, thoracic and lower cervical spinal nerves
lumborum	Iliac crest	Angles of lower 6 or 7 ribs		
thoracis	Upper border of angles of 6 lower ribs	Angles of 6 upper ribs		
cervicis	Angles of 1st 6 ribs	Transverse processes of 4th to 6th cervical vertebrae		
Longissimus			Extend and bend vertebral column laterally; capitis extends head or, if one side only contracts, turns head to same side	Dorsal rami of lumbar, thoracic and lower cervical spinal nerves
thoracis	Transverse processes of lumbar vertebrae and thoracolumbar fascia	Transverse processes of all thoracic vertebrae; lower 9 or 10 ribs		
cervicis	Transverse processes of upper 4 or 5 thoracic vertebrae	Transverse processes of 2nd to 6th cervical vertebrae		
capitis	Transverse processes of upper 4 or 5 thoracic vertebrae	Mastoid process of temporal bone		
Spinalis			Extend vertebral column; capitis extends head or turns head slightly to one side if one side only contracts	Dorsal rami of thoracic and cervical spinal nerves
thoracis	Spinous processes of upper lumbar and lower thoracic vertebrae	Spines of upper thoracic vertebrae		
cervicis	Spinous processes of upper 2 thoracic and 7th cervical vertebrae	Spinous process of axis		
capitis	Spinous processes of upper thoracic and 7th cervical vertebrae	Occipital bone		

°See Figure 8–28.

Table 8–7 MUSCLES MOVING THE HUMERUS*

MUSCLE	ORIGIN	INSERTION	FUNCTION	INNERVATION
Coracobrachialis (L. *brachium*, arm)	Coracoid process of scapula	Middle and medial surface of humerus	Flexes, adducts arm	Musculocutaneous
Pectoralis major (L. *pectoralis*, of the breast)	Anterior surface of sternal half of clavicle; sternum; aponeurosis of external oblique; costal cartilages of upper 6 ribs	Lateral border of bicipital groove of humerus	Adducts, flexes, rotates arm medially	Anterior thoracic
Teres major	Posterior aspect of lateral border of scapula	Medial border of bicipital groove of humerus	Adducts, extends, rotates arm medially	Lower subscapular
Teres minor	Dorsal surface of lateral border of scapula	Greater tuberosity of humerus	Rotates arm laterally; steadies head of humerus in glenoid cavity	Axillary
Deltoid	Lateral third of clavicle; acromion and spine of scapula	Deltoid tuberosity on lateral surface of shaft of humerus	Abducts arm; flexes and medially rotates arm (anterior portion); extends and laterally rotates arm (posterior portion)	Axillary
Supraspinatus (L. *supra*, above)	Fossa superior to spine of scapula	Greater tuberosity of humerus	Abducts arm	Suprascapular
Infraspinatous (L. *infra*, below)	Infraspinatus fossa on posterior aspect of scapula	Greater tubercle of humerus	Rotates arm laterally; steadies head of humerus in glenoid cavity	Suprascapular
Latissimus dorsi (L. *latissimus*, widest)	Spinous processes of lower 6 thoracic and lumbar vertebrae and sacrum; posterior part of crest of ilium; outer surfaces of lower 4 ribs	Bicipital groove of humerus	Extends, adducts, rotates arm medially; raises trunk and pelvis	Thoracodorsal
Subscapularis	Subscapular fossa	Lesser tubercle of humerus	Rotates arm medially; steadies head of humerus in glenoid cavity	Subscapular

*See Figures 8–23 to 8–27 and 8–29 to 8–31.

Table 8–8 MUSCLES MOVING THE FOREARM*

MUSCLE	ORIGIN	INSERTION	FUNCTION	INNERVATION
Brachialis (L. *brachium*, arm)	Lower half of anterior surface of humerus	Tuberosity and coronoid process of the ulna	Flexes forearm	Musculocutaneous and radial
Triceps brachii (three-headed)		Olecranon of the ulna	Extends forearm	Radial
Long head	Axillary border of scapula below glenoid cavity			
Lateral head	Lateral and posterior surfaces of shaft of humerus			
Medial head†	Posterior surface of shaft of humerus below lateral head			
Biceps brachii (two-headed)		Tuberosity of radius; deep fascia of medial forearm via bicipital aponeurosis	Flexes forearm; supinates forearm and hand; long head helps steady head of humerus in glenoid cavity	Musculocutaneous
Long head	Upper margin of the glenoid cavity of scapula			
Short head	Coracoid process of scapula			

Table continued on following page

Table 8–8   MUSCLES MOVING THE FOREARM° (*Continued*)

MUSCLE	ORIGIN	INSERTION	FUNCTION	INNERVATION
Anconeus (G. *agkōn*, elbow)	Posterior surface of lateral epicondyle of humerus	Olecranon and dorsal surface of the ulna	Extends forearm	Radial
Brachioradialis	Lateral supracondyloid ridge of humerus	Lower end of radius	Flexes forearm	Radial
Supinator	Lateral epicondyle of humerus; shaft of ulna; radial ligament of elbow	Anterior and lateral surfaces of shaft of radius	Supinates forearm and hand	Posterior interosseous
Pronator teres	Medial epicondyle of humerus and coronoid process of the ulna	Middle of lateral surface of shaft of radius	Pronates forearm and hand	Median
Pronator quadratus	Lower part of anterior surface of the ulna	Lower part of anterior surface of radius	Pronates forearm and hand	Anterior interosseous

°See Figures 8–32 to 8–36, 8–39 to 8–44, and 8–47.
†Medial head of triceps not shown in figures.

Table 8–9   MUSCLES MOVING THE WRIST°

MUSCLE	ORIGIN	INSERTION	FUNCTION	INNERVATION
Flexor carpi radialis (G. *karpos*, wrist)	Medial epicondyle of humerus	Bases of 2nd and 3rd metacarpals	Flexes, abducts wrist (see text)	Median
Flexor carpi ulnaris	Medial epicondyle of humerus and upper two-thirds of dorsal border of ulna	Pisiform, hamate, and 5th metacarpal	Flexes, adducts wrist (see text)	Ulnar
Extensor carpi radialis brevis	Lateral epicondyle of humerus	Base of 3rd metacarpal bone	Extends, abducts wrist (see text)	Radial
Extensor carpi radialis longus	Lower third of lateral supracondylar ridge of humerus	Base of 2nd metacarpal bone	Extends, abducts wrist (see text)	Radial
Extensor carpi ulnaris	Lateral epicondyle of humerus	Base of 5th metacarpal bone	Extends, adducts wrist (see text)	Radial
Palmaris longus	Medial epicondyle of humerus	Palmar aponeurosis	Flexes wrist	Median
Extensor digitorum communis	Lateral epicondyle of humerus	Extensor tendon to each finger derived from the common extensor tendon	Extends wrist and fingers	Posterior interosseous

°See Figures 8–39 to 8–43, 8–46, and 8–48 to 8–50.

Table 8–10   MUSCLES MOVING THE THUMB°

MUSCLE	ORIGIN	INSERTION	FUNCTION	INNERVATION
Flexor pollicis longus (L. *pollex*, thumb)	Anterior surface of body of radius	Base of distal phalanx of thumb	Flexes phalanges of thumb	Anterior interosseous
Flexor pollicis brevis	Flexor retinaculum;† tubercle of trapezium	Base of proximal phalanx of thumb	Flexes proximal phalanx of thumb; continuing to act, it flexes metacarpal and, in cooperation with opponens pollicis, rotates it medially	Median and ulnar

Table continued on following page

Table 8–10. MUSCLES MOVING THE THUMB* (*Continued*)

MUSCLE	ORIGIN	INSERTION	FUNCTION	INNERVATION
Extensor pollicis longus	Lateral side of dorsal surface of ulna	Base of 2nd phalanx of thumb	Extends phalanges of thumb	Radial
Extensor pollicis brevis	Dorsal surface of radius; interosseous membrane	Dorsal surface of proximal phalanx of thumb	Extends proximal phalanx of thumb; continuing to act, it helps extend metacarpal	Posterior interosseous
Adductor pollicis	Capitate; trapezoid; 2nd and 3rd metacarpals	Ulnar side of base of 1st phalanx of thumb	Adducts thumb	Ulnar
Abductor pollicis longus	Posterior surfaces of radius and ulna	Radial side of base of 1st metacarpal bone	Abducts, extends thumb	Posterior interosseous
Abductor pollicis brevis	Flexor retinaculum;† scaphoid; trapezium	Lateral surface of base of proximal phalanx of thumb	Abducts thumb	Median
Opponens pollicis	Tubercle of trapezium; flexor retinaculum†	Radial side of 1st metacarpal	Flexes and rotates 1st metacarpal medially, opposing thumb	Median

*See Figures 8–40 to 8–44, 8–46 to 8–48, and 8–50 to 8–53.
†The flexor retinaculum is a strong, ligamentous band crossing the front of the wrist.

Table 8–11   MUSCLES MOVING THE FINGERS*

MUSCLE	ORIGIN	INSERTION	FUNCTION	INNERVATION
Flexor digitorum profundus	Anterior and medial surface of shaft of ulna; depression on medial side of coronoid process	Bases of distal phalanges of fingers	Flexes distal phalanx of each finger; may also assist in flexing wrist	Ulnar and median
Flexor digiti minimi brevis	Hamate; flexor retinaculum (see footnote of Table 8–10)	Ulnar side of base of proximal phalanx of little finger	Flexes little finger	Ulnar
Interossei, dorsal	Adjacent sides of metacarpal bones	Proximal phalanges and dorsal digital expansions† of fingers	Abduct fingers	Ulnar
Flexor digitorum superficialis	Humeroulnar head: medial epicondyle of humerus and coronoid process of ulna; radial head: anterior border of radius	Middle phalanges of fingers	Flexes middle and then proximal phalanges; may also flex wrist	Median
Extensor indicis	Dorsal surface of shaft of ulna; interosseous membrane	Phalanges of index finger	Extends index finger	Posterior interosseous
Interossei, palmar	2nd, 4th, and 5th metacarpal bones	Dorsal digital expansions† of index, ring, and little fingers	Adduct fingers	Ulnar
Abductor digiti minimi	Pisiform bone; flexor carpi ulnaris tendon	Medial surface of base of proximal phalanx of little finger	Abducts little finger	Ulnar
Opponens digiti minimi	Hamate; flexor retinaculum (see footnote of Table 8–10)	Ulnar side of 5th metacarpal	Flexes and laterally rotates 5th metacarpal, deepening palm and assisting in opposing little finger to thumb	Ulnar

*See Figures 8–37 to 8–45 and 8–47 to 8–53.
†The dorsal digital expansions are small aponeuroses covering the dorsal surface of each proximal phalanx, blending in their centers with the extensor digitorum tendons.

Table 8–12 MUSCLES OF THE ABDOMINAL WALL*

MUSCLE	ORIGIN	INSERTION	FUNCTION	INNERVATION
External oblique	Lower 8 ribs	Anterior half of outer lip of iliac crest; linea alba; pubis	Compresses abdominal contents; assists in flexing or bending vertebral column to one side	Ventral rami of lower 6 thoracic spinal nerves
Internal oblique	Inguinal ligament,† via iliac fascia; iliac crest; lumbodorsal fascia	Costal cartilages of lower 3 or 4 ribs; linea alba; pubis via conjoint tendon‡	Compresses abdominal contents; assists in flexing or bending vertebral column to one side	Ventral rami of lower 6 thoracic and 1st lumbar spinal nerves
Transversus abdominis	Lateral third of inguinal ligament;† anterior three-fourths of the inner lip of iliac crest; lumbodorsal fascia; inner surface of cartilages of lower 6 ribs	Linea alba; pubis via conjoint tendon‡	Compresses abdominal contents	Ventral rami of lower 6 thoracic and 1st lumbar spinal nerves
Rectus abdominis	Crest of pubis and ligaments covering symphysis pubis	Cartilages of 5th, 6th, and 7th ribs	Flexes or bends vertebral column to one side; assists in compressing abdominal contents	Ventral rami of lower 6 thoracic spinal nerves

*See Figures 8–54 to 8–60 and 8–65 to 8–67.

†The inguinal ligament is the lower border of the aponeurosis of the external oblique; it stretches from the anterior superior iliac spine to the pubic tubercle.

‡The conjoint tendon is formed by the lower parts of the aponeuroses of the transversus abdominis and internal oblique.

Table 8–13 MUSCLES OF RESPIRATION*

MUSCLE	ORIGIN	INSERTION	FUNCTION	INNERVATION
Diaphragm	Xiphoid process; costal cartilages of lower 6 ribs; lumbar vertebrae	Central tendon	Pulls central tendon downward to increase vertical diameter of thorax	Phrenic
External intercostals (11) (L. *costa*, rib)	Lower border of a rib	Upper border of a rib below origin	Raise ribs during inspiration	Intercostal
Internal intercostals (11)	Ridge on inner surface of a rib	Upper border of a rib below origin	Depress ribs during forced expiration	Intercostal
Scaleni (anterior, medial, and posterior scalenus)	Transverse processes of 2nd to 7th cervical vertebrae	1st 2 ribs	Raise 1st 2 ribs during deep inspiration; bend vertebral column to one side or the other	Branches of ventral rami of most cervical spinal nerves

*See Figures 8–57 to 8–64.

Table 8–14 MUSCLES MOVING THE HIP AND KNEE JOINTS*

MUSCLE	ORIGIN	INSERTION	FUNCTION	INNERVATION
Iliopsoas			Flexes thigh or trunk	
Psoas major	Transverse processes of lumbar vertebrae	Lesser trochanter of femur		Ventral rami of 1st 3 lumbar spinal nerves
Iliacus	Margin of iliac fossa; sacrum	Fibers converge into lateral side of tendon of psoas major		Femoral
Gluteus maximus	Posterior gluteal line of ilium and posterior surface of sacrum and coccyx	Gluteal tuberosity of femur and iliotibial tract†	Extends flexed thigh; extends trunk	Inferior gluteal

Table continued on following page

Table 8-14   MUSCLES MOVING THE HIP AND KNEE JOINTS* (*Continued*)

MUSCLE	ORIGIN	INSERTION	FUNCTION	INNERVATION
Gluteus medius	Lateral surface of ilium	Lateral surface of greater trochanter of femur	Abducts thigh; anterior fibers rotate thigh medially; tilts pelvis when one foot is lifted so as to prevent sagging on the unsupported side	Superior gluteal
Gluteus minimus	Lateral surface of ilium	Anterior surface of greater trochanter of femur	Same as gluteus medius	Superior gluteal
Tensor fasciae latae	Anterior part of iliac crest; lateral surface of anterior superior iliac spine	Iliotibial tract†	Steadies pelvis on femur and femur on tibia	Superior gluteal
Adductor longus	Pubic crest	Linea aspera of femur	Adducts, flexes thigh	Obturator
Adductor brevis	Inferior ramus of pubis	Linea aspera of femur	Adducts thigh	Obturator
Adductor magnus	Ischial tuberosity; ischio-pubic ramus	Linea aspera of femur; medial condyle of femur	Adducts, extends thigh	Sciatic and obturator
Obturator externus	Pubis; ischium; superficial surface of obturator membrane	Trochanteric fossa of femur	Rotates thigh laterally	Obturator
Pectineus	Pubis	Femur distal to lesser trochanter	Flexes, adducts thigh	Femoral and accessory obturator
Hamstrings			Flex leg; extend thigh or trunk	
Biceps femoris Long head	Tuberosity of ischium	Lateral side of head of fibula and lateral condyle of tibia		Tibial
Short head	Lateral lip of linea aspera of femur	Same as long head		Peroneal
Semitendinosus	Tuberosity of ischium	Upper medial surface of tibia		Tibial
Semimembranosus	Tuberosity of ischium	Medial condyle of tibia		Tibial
Popliteus	Lateral condyle of femur	Posterior surface of shaft of tibia	Rotates tibia medially or femur laterally	Tibial
Gracilis (L., slender)	Body of pubis and pubic arch	Medial surface of shaft of tibia	Flexes and medially rotates leg	Obturator
Sartorius (L. *sartor*, a patcher, tailor)	Anterior superior iliac spine	Upper part of medial surface of tibia	Flexes and laterally rotates thigh	Femoral
Quadriceps femoris (four heads)				
Rectus femoris (L. *rectus*, straight)	Anterior inferior iliac spine; groove above the acetabulum	Base of patella, continuing into tuberosity of tibia; condyles of tibia	Extend leg; rectus femoris assists in flexing hip joint	Femoral
Vastus lateralis	Greater trochanter and linea aspera of femur			
Vastus medialis	Medial lip of linea aspera of femur; inter-trochanteric line			
Vastus intermedius	Ventral surface of femur			

*See Figures 8–69 to 8–85.

†The iliotibial tract, or band, is the thickened portion of the deep fascia of the thigh, called the fascia lata because of its wide extent (L. *latus*, wide). It extends from the iliac crest to the lateral condyle of the tibia.

Table 8-15   MUSCLES MOVING THE FOOT AND TOES°

MUSCLE	ORIGIN	INSERTION	FUNCTION	INNERVATION
Gastrocnemius (G. *gastroknēmia*, calf of the leg)	Medial head from medial condyle of femur; lateral head from lateral condyle of femur	Calcaneus, jointly with soleus, via tendo calcaneus	Plantar flexes foot; flexes leg	Tibial
Soleus	Posterior aspect of head of fibula and medial border of tibia	With gastrocnemius into calcaneus via tendo calcaneus	Plantar flexes foot	Tibial
Tibialis posterior	Interosseous membrane between tibia and fibula; posterior surface of tibia and fibula	Three cuneiforms; cuboid; navicular; 2nd, 3rd, and 4th metatarsals	Inverts foot; assists in plantar flexion of foot	Tibial
Tibialis anterior	Lateral condyle and upper portion of lateral surface of shaft of tibia	Undersurface of medial cuneiform and base of 1st metatarsal	Dorsiflexes and inverts foot	Deep peroneal
Peroneus tertius (G. *peronē*, fibula)	Lower third of medial surface of fibula	Dorsal surface of base of 5th metatarsal	Dorsiflexes foot	Deep peroneal
Peroneus longus	Head and lateral surface of shaft of fibula	Lateral side of 1st metatarsal and medial cuneiform	Everts foot	Superficial peroneal
Peroneus brevis	Lower two-thirds of lateral surface of shaft of fibula	Tuberosity at base of 5th metatarsal	Everts foot	Superficial peroneal
Plantaris	Lateral condyle of femur	Calcaneus	Plantar flexes foot	Tibial
Flexor hallucis brevis (L. *hallex*, the great toe)	Cuboid; 3rd cuneiform	Base of proximal phalanx of great toe	Flexes great toe	Medial plantar
Flexor hallucis longus	Posterior surface of fibula	Base of distal phalanx of great toe	Flexes great toe; plantar flexes foot	Tibial
Extensor hallucis longus	Fibula and interosseous membrane	Dorsal surface of base of distal phalanx of great toe	Extends great toe; dorsiflexes foot	Deep peroneal
Interossei, dorsal	Surfaces of adjacent metatarsal bones	Proximal phalanges and dorsal digital expansions† of 4 lateral toes	Abduct toes	Lateral plantar
Flexor digitorum longus	Posterior surface of shaft of tibia	Distal phalanges of 4 lateral toes	Flexes toes; plantar flexes foot	Tibial
Extensor digitorum longus	Medial surface of fibula; lateral condyle of tibia; interosseous membrane	Extensor tendon to each of 4 lateral toes derived from common extensor tendon	Extends toes; dorsiflexes foot	Deep peroneal
Flexor digitorum brevis	Medial tuberosity of calcaneus; plantar fascia	Middle phalanges of 4 lateral toes	Flexes toes at proximal interphalangeal joint	Medial plantar
Abductor hallucis	Medial tuberosity of calcaneus; plantar fascia	Medial surface of base of proximal phalanx of great toe	Abducts, flexes great toe	Medial plantar
Abductor digiti minimi	Medial and lateral tubercles of calcaneus; plantar fascia	Lateral surface of base of proximal phalanx of little toe	Abducts little toe	Lateral plantar

°See Figures 8–86 to 8–105.
†The dorsal digital expansions of the foot are formed in the same way as those of the hand (see footnote to Table 8–11).

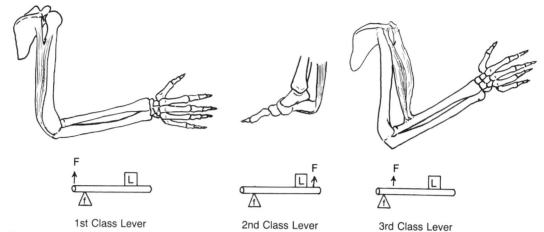

1st Class Lever   2nd Class Lever   3rd Class Lever

Figure 8–13. Examples of the action of muscles by a system of levers in which the bone (or group of bones), acting as a rigid bar, or lever, turns around a joint, functioning as a fulcrum (f), when a contracting muscle, the force (F), moves a part of the body, the load (L). *First class lever:* Extension of the forearm by the triceps brachii. *Second class lever:* Although not all anatomists agree that there are legitimate examples of second class levers in the body, some cite lifting the heel off the ground to stand on one's toes as an example. *Third class lever:* Flexion of the forearm by the biceps brachii. The third class lever is the most common in the body.

MUSCLES OF THE FACE AND SCALP
(Table 8–1 and Figs. 8–14 to 8–16)

The muscles of the face and scalp move the lips, cheeks, eyelids, nose, scalp, and skin of the forehead. Many are used primarily as muscles of facial expression. A number of them, among other things, play roles in articulation and mastication. All of these muscles insert, not into bone, but rather into the skin, sometimes blending with other muscles. Some do not take origin from bone either.

Sphincter-type muscles surround the eyes and mouth. The **orbicularis oculi** encircles the orbit and occupies the eyelids. Its contraction closes the eyelids. It also draws the skin of the forehead, temple, and cheek medially, creating folds which may become permanent, as the so-called "crow's feet." The **orbicularis oris** surrounds the mouth and consists in part of fibers derived from neighboring muscles, especially the buccinator. Contraction of its superficial fibers closes and puckers the lips; contraction of its deeper fibers compresses the lips against the teeth.

The orbicularis oris and other muscles acting on the lips are involved in articulation and mastication as well as facial expression.

The **buccinator** is a deep cheek muscle extending from the posterior portions of the alveolar processes of the maxilla and mandible forward to the corner of the mouth. Contraction of the buccinators compresses the cheeks against the teeth, an action that can aid mastication by preventing food from passing to the sides of the mouth. Compression of the cheeks can also force air between the lips, which accounts for the muscle's name (buccinator is the Latin word for a trumpeter).

Covering the dome of the skull is the **epicranius** muscle, which consists of the *frontalis*, overlying the frontal bone, the *occipitalis*, overlying the occipital bone, and a connecting aponeurosis, the *galea aponeurotica*. The occipitalis draws the scalp backward; the frontalis draws the scalp forward or elevates the eyebrows and wrinkles the skin of the forehead, a common facial expression, often a part of registering interest or surprise.

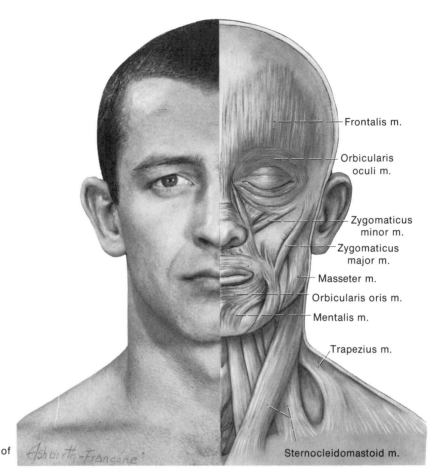

Figure 8–14. Muscles of the face, superficial layer.

Frontalis m.

Orbicularis oculi m.

Zygomaticus minor m.

Zygomaticus major m.

Masseter m.

Orbicularis oris m.

Mentalis m.

Trapezius m.

Sternocleidomastoid m.

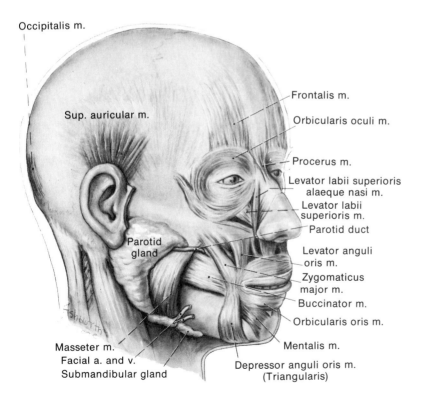

Occipitalis m.

Sup. auricular m.

Frontalis m.

Orbicularis oculi m.

Procerus m.

Levator labii superioris alaeque nasi m.

Levator labii superioris m.

Parotid duct

Parotid gland

Levator anguli oris m.

Zygomaticus major m.

Buccinator m.

Orbicularis oris m.

Masseter m.
Facial a. and v.
Submandibular gland

Mentalis m.

Depressor anguli oris m. (Triangularis)

Figure 8–15. Muscles of the face, deep layer.

189

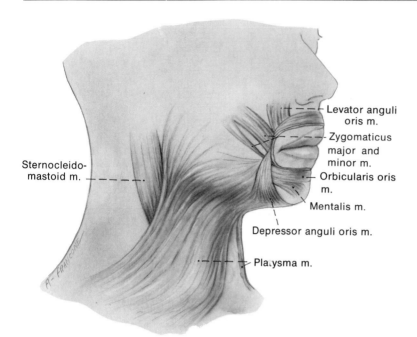

Sternocleido-
mastoid m.

Levator anguli
oris m.

Zygomaticus
major and
minor m.

Orbicularis oris
m.

Mentalis m.

Depressor anguli oris m.

Platysma m.

Figure 8–16. Superficial muscles of the neck and muscles around the mouth.

MUSCLES OF MASTICATION
(Table 8–2 and Figs. 8–17 and 8–18)

The muscles of mastication include the temporalis, masseter, and the medial and lateral pterygoids. The **temporalis** and **masseter** raise the mandible, closing the jaws and occluding the teeth. The **medial pterygoid** assists in this action. The **lateral pterygoid** depresses the mandible, opening the jaws. When the lateral and medial pterygoids on the same side contract together, they pull the mandible to one side. Side-to-side grinding movements are brought about by alternating contractions of these two muscles, first on one side and then on the other. When the lateral and medial pterygoids on both sides contract together, the lower jaw is brought forward.

MUSCLES MOVING THE TONGUE
(Table 8–3 and Fig. 8–19)

The tongue has two groups of muscles: (1) *intrinsic*, lying entirely within it, and (2) *extrinsic*, which insert into it and have attachments on the mandible, hyoid bone and styloid process of the temporal bone. Contraction of the intrinsic muscles (in each half, the superior and inferior longitudinal, the transverse and the vertical) changes the shape of the tongue. Contraction of the extrinsic mus-

cles, the **genioglossus,** the **hyoglossus,** and the **styloglossus,** pulls the tongue upward, downward, forward, or backward. One other muscle, the *palatoglossus*, which is primarily associated with the region of the soft palate, also inserts into the tongue (on its side). It pulls the back of the tongue upward. Its contraction also narrows the opening (isthmus of fauces) between the mouth and the oropharynx.

SUPRAHYOID AND INFRAHYOID MUSCLES OF THE NECK
(Table 8–4 and Figs. 8–19 to 8–22)

The *suprahyoid* muscles, the **digastric, stylohyoid, mylohyoid,** and **geniohyoid,** raise the hyoid bone. When the hyoid is fixed, three of them (the digastric, mylohyoid, and geniohyoid) depress the mandible, opening the jaws. This action is secondary to depression of the mandible by the lateral pterygoids, assisting when there is resistance or when it is necessary to open the mouth wide. The *infrahyoid* muscles, the **sternohyoid, omohyoid, sternothyroid** and **thyrohyoid,** as a group lower the hyoid bone; hence they are antagonists of the suprahyoid muscles. They hold the hyoid in place when the contractions of three of the suprahyoid muscles are opening the jaws. The two groups of muscles can also cooperate in fixing the hyoid bone when the tongue is moved.

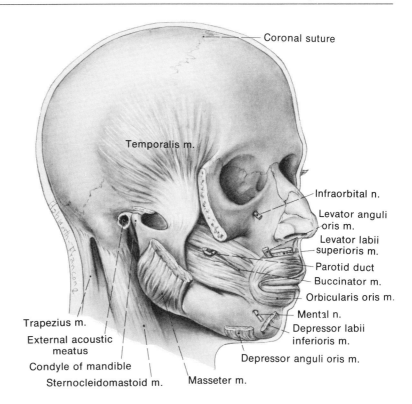

Figure 8–17. Muscles of mastication.

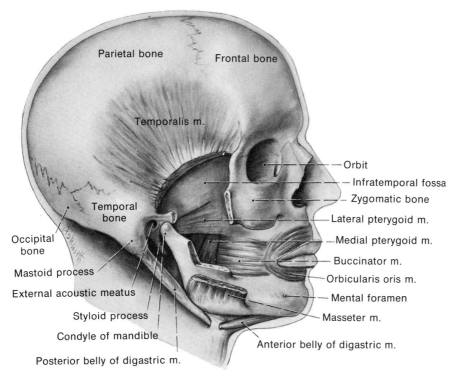

Figure 8–18. Muscles of the head within the skull. The temporalis, masseter, zygoma, and part of the mandible have been removed.

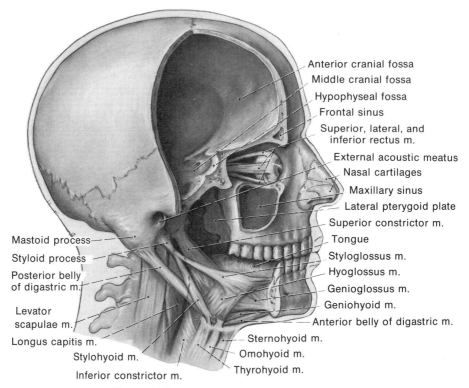

Anterior cranial fossa
Middle cranial fossa
Hypophyseal fossa
Frontal sinus
Superior, lateral, and
  inferior rectus m.
External acoustic meatus
Nasal cartilages
Maxillary sinus
Lateral pterygoid plate
Superior constrictor m.
Tongue
Styloglossus m.
Hyoglossus m.
Genioglossus m.
Geniohyoid m.
Anterior belly of digastric m.
Sternohyoid m.
Omohyoid m.
Thyrohyoid m.

Mastoid process
Styloid process
Posterior belly
of digastric m.
Levator
scapulae m.
Longus capitis m.
Stylohyoid m.
Inferior constrictor m.

Figure 8–19. Muscles of the tongue and throat.

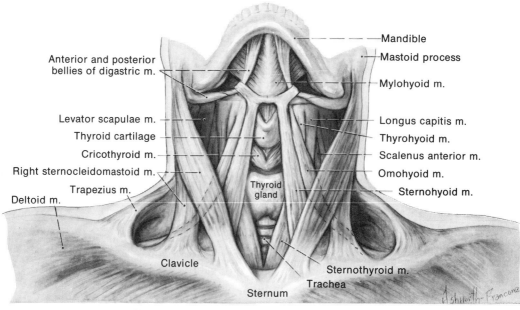

Anterior and posterior
bellies of digastric m.

Levator scapulae m.
Thyroid cartilage
Cricothyroid m.
Right sternocleidomastoid m.
Trapezius m.
Deltoid m.

Mandible
Mastoid process
Mylohyoid m.
Longus capitis m.
Thyrohyoid m.
Scalenus anterior m.
Omohyoid m.
Sternohyoid m.

Thyroid
gland

Clavicle
Sternothyroid m.
Trachea
Sternum

Figure 8–20. Muscles of the neck, superficial layer.

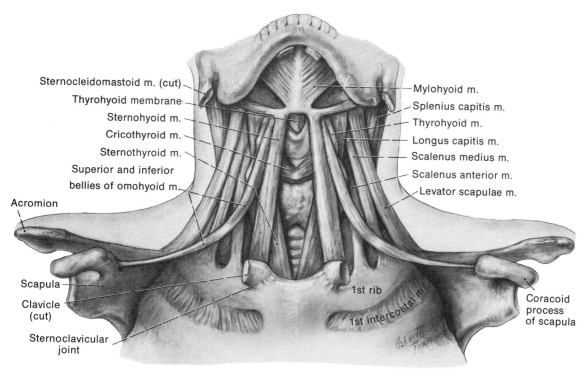

Sternocleidomastoid m. (cut)
Thyrohyoid membrane
Sternohyoid m.
Cricothyroid m.
Sternothyroid m.
Superior and inferior
bellies of omohyoid m.
Acromion
Scapula
Clavicle
(cut)
Sternoclavicular
joint

Mylohyoid m.
Splenius capitis m.
Thyrohyoid m.
Longus capitis m.
Scalenus medius m.
Scalenus anterior m.
Levator scapulae m.
Coracoid
process
of scapula
1st rib
1st intercostal m.

Figure 8–21. Second layer of muscles of the neck.

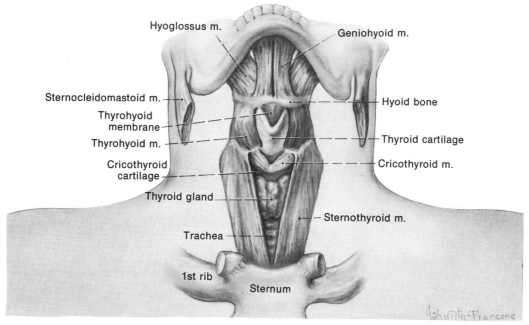

Hyoglossus m.
Sternocleidomastoid m.
Thyrohyoid
membrane
Thyrohyoid m.
Cricothyroid
cartilage
Thyroid gland
Trachea
1st rib
Sternum

Geniohyoid m.
Hyoid bone
Thyroid cartilage
Cricothyroid m.
Sternothyroid m.

Figure 8–22. Deep muscles of the neck.

MUSCLES MOVING THE HEAD AND SHOULDER GIRDLE
(Table 8–5 and Figs. 8–20 to 8–28 and 8–57)

The muscles moving the head have attachments on the shoulder girdle, vertebrae, and sternum. The **sternocleidomastoid**, a muscle of the neck region, has two heads, one arising from the sternum, the other from the clavicle; it inserts into the temporal and occipital bones. When it contracts on one side, the head is rotated to the opposite side. Contraction on both sides draws the head forward and downward, generally accompanied by flexion of the neck, as in eating. The **trapezius**, a back muscle, has attachments leading from the occipital bone and vertebrae to the scapula and clavicle. When the head is fixed, the trapezius moves the shoulders; when the shoulders are fixed, it moves the head, contraction on both sides extending it, contraction on one side turning it to the opposite side. Other muscles moving the head include the **splenius capitis** and the upper parts of two of the columns of the erector spinae (the *longissimus capitis* and the *spinalis capitis*, listed in Table 8–6). These muscles extend the head if both sides contract or, if one side contracts, turn it to the same side.

A number of muscles moving the shoulder girdle have origins on the vertebral column or ribs and insert into the scapula. An important function of these muscles (and of the trapezius, mentioned above, which also has attachments on the scapula) is to steady and adjust the position of the scapula (which

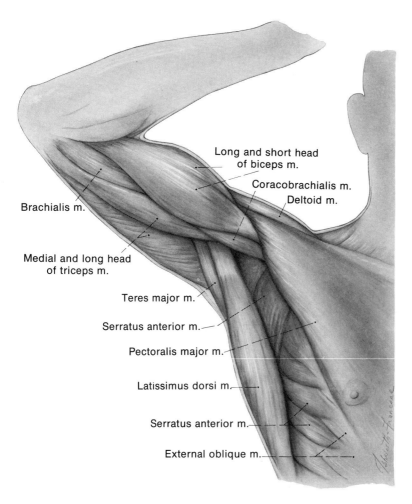

Long and short head of biceps m.

Coracobrachialis m.

Deltoid m.

Brachialis m.

Medial and long head of triceps m.

Teres major m.

Serratus anterior m.

Pectoralis major m.

Latissimus dorsi m.

Serratus anterior m.

External oblique m.

Figure 8–23. Muscles in the region of the axilla when the arm is raised.

articulates with the clavicle at its lateral end but is free on its other borders) during active use of the arms.

A variety of scapular movements can be produced by the concerted actions of two or more muscles acting on it. For example, the trapezius acts with the **levator scapulae** to raise the scapula or to support a weight on the shoulder, and with the **rhomboideus major** and **rhomboideus minor** to pull it backward, bracing the shoulder; acting with the **serratus anterior**, the principal movement is forward rotation of the scapula so that the arm can be raised above the head from the side. The rhomboids and levator scapulae acting together with the **pectoralis minor** rotate the scapula so as to depress the point of the shoulder.

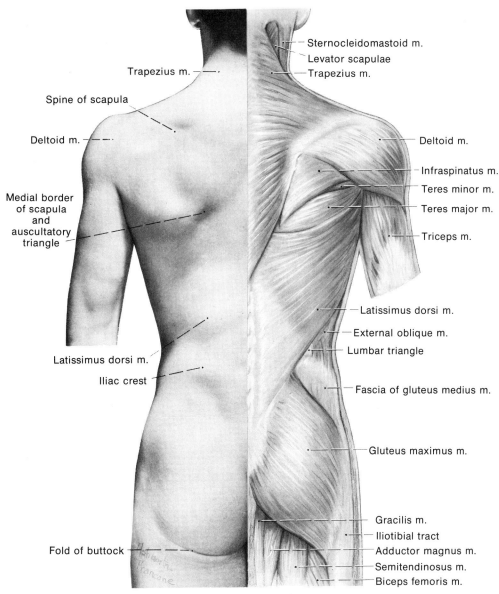

Figure 8–24. Muscles of the back.

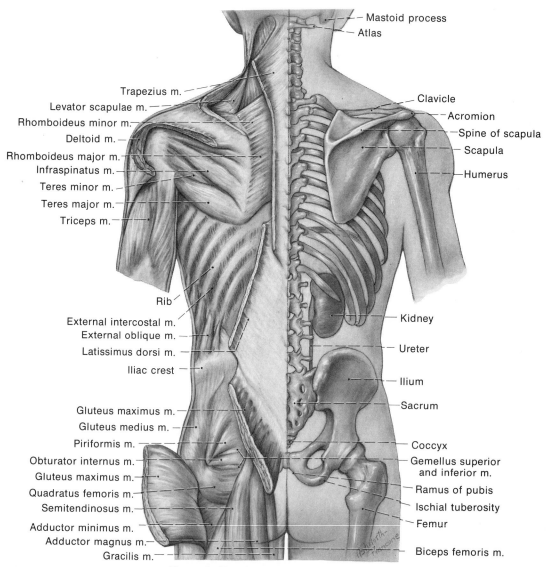

Mastoid process
Atlas
Trapezius m.
Levator scapulae m.
Rhomboideus minor m.
Deltoid m.
Rhomboideus major m.
Infraspinatus m.
Teres minor m.
Teres major m.
Triceps m.
Clavicle
Acromion
Spine of scapula
Scapula
Humerus
Rib
External intercostal m.
External oblique m.
Latissimus dorsi m.
Iliac crest
Kidney
Ureter
Ilium
Sacrum
Gluteus maximus m.
Gluteus medius m.
Piriformis m.
Obturator internus m.
Gluteus maximus m.
Quadratus femoris m.
Semitendinosus m.
Adductor minimus m.
Adductor magnus m.
Gracilis m.
Coccyx
Gemellus superior and inferior m.
Ramus of pubis
Ischial tuberosity
Femur
Biceps femoris m.

Figure 8–25. Deep muscles of the back.

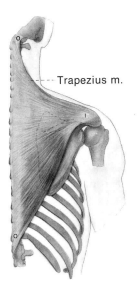

Trapezius m.

Figure 8-26A.

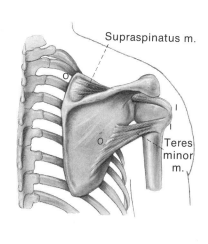

Supraspinatus m.

Teres minor m.

Figure 8-26B

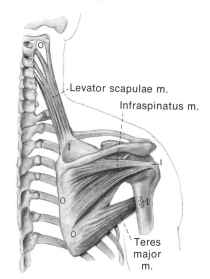

Levator scapulae m.

Infraspinatus m.

Teres major m.

Figure 8-26C

KEY
O = origin
I = insertion

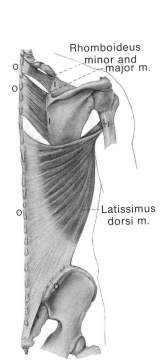

Rhomboideus minor and major m.

Latissimus dorsi m.

Figure 8-27

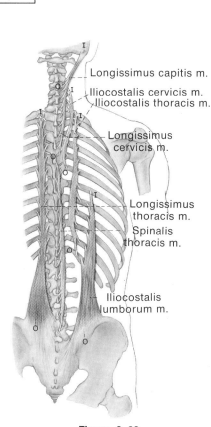

Longissimus capitis m.

Iliocostalis cervicis m.
Iliocostalis thoracis m.

Longissimus cervicis m.

Longissimus thoracis m.

Spinalis thoracis m.

Iliocostalis lumborum m.

Figure 8-28

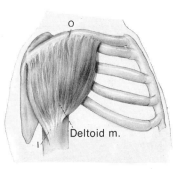

Deltoid m.

Figure 8-29

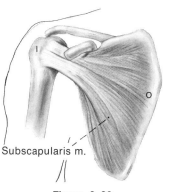

Subscapularis m.

Figure 8-30

MUSCLES MOVING THE VERTEBRAL COLUMN
(Table 8–6 and Fig. 8–28)

The vertebral column is controlled and kept erect largely by a group of deep muscles of the back extending from the pelvis to the skull. Prominent among these is the **erector spinae**, which is split into three columns: the *iliocostalis* (lateral), the *longissimus* (intermediate), and the *spinalis* (medial). Each of these has three parts, a lower, middle, and upper, called from below upward lumborum, thoracis, and cervicis in the iliocostalis and thoracis, cervicis, and capitis in the other two columns. The longissimus is the largest of the columns; the spinalis is somewhat indistinct and the cervicis part of it is frequently absent. In each part the muscles extend from their origins on the vertebrae, pelvis, or ribs upward several segments to their insertions on the vertebrae, ribs, or skull. The erector spinae extends the vertebral column. The lateral and intermediate columns also bend the vertebral column to one side if the muscles on one side only contract. The capitis parts, which have attachments on the skull, extend or turn the head to one side. The efficient action of the erector spinae, as well as of other long muscles of the vertebral column, is helped by the action of short muscles deep to the erector spinae, some of which (the interspinales, the intertransversarii, and the rotatores) have attachments on adjacent vertebrae. These short muscles prevent buckling of the vertebral column when the long muscles contract. Both rotation and extension of the vertebral column are produced by another column of muscles (the semispinales thoracis and cervicis), which extend obliquely upward from the transverse processes to the spinous processes of vertebrae.

Some of the abdominal muscles, especially the *rectus abdominis* and, to a lesser extent, the oblique muscles (listed in Table 8–12), act on the vertebral column. They flex the column or, if the muscles on one side only contract, bend it to one side. Lateral movement of the vertebral column is also brought about by the scaleni (listed in Table 8–13).

MUSCLES MOVING THE HUMERUS
(Table 8–7 and Figs. 8–23 to 8–27 and 8–29 to 8–31)

Most of the muscles moving the humerus have their origins on the scapula, and all insert on the proximal end of the humerus.

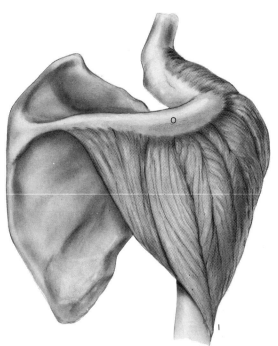

Figure 8–31. Posterior view of right deltoid. O = origin, I = insertion.

One, the thick, triangular deltoid muscle, has attachments on the clavicle as well. Two do not arise from the scapula. One of these, the pectoralis major, a muscle of the chest region, has attachments on the sternum, costal cartilages, and clavicle; the other, the latissimus dorsi, a broad, flat, triangular muscle of the back, has attachments on the thoracic and lumbar vertebrae, pelvis, and lower ribs.

The **latissimus dorsi** has a powerful action. It adducts, extends, and, since it inserts on the anterior side of the humerus, medially rotates the humerus. Closely related to the latissimus dorsi is the **teres major**, a muscle arising from the dorsal surface of the scapula which also inserts into the anterior surface of the humerus and has the same action as the latissimus dorsi. If the arms are raised and fixed, as when rope climbing, the latissimus dorsi will raise the trunk and pelvis.

The **pectoralis major** adducts, medially rotates, and flexes the humerus. If the raised arm is fixed, the pectoralis major will assist the latissimus dorsi in raising the trunk.

The anterior fibers of the **deltoid**, acting with the pectoralis major, flex the arm. Its posterior fibers cooperate with the latissimus dorsi and teres major during extension of the arm. Acting as a whole, the deltoid abducts the arm, aided in this saction by the **supraspinatus.** As mentioned in the description of the muscles moving the shoulder girdle, in order to raise the arm above the head by abduction, the scapula must be rotated in a forward direction (by the combined actions of the trapezius and serratus anterior). In the early stages of abduction it is necessary to prevent the head of the humerus from sliding upward in the glenoid cavity. This is accomplished by the actions of the **infraspinatus and teres minor**, which have attachments on the dorsal surfaces of the scapula and humerus (and are also lateral rotators of the humerus), and of the **subscapularis,** which extends from the ventral surface of the scapula to the ventral surface of the humerus (and also medially rotates the humerus).

MUSCLES MOVING THE FOREARM
(Table 8–8 and Figs. 8–32 to 8–36, 8–39 to 8–44, and 8–47)

The muscles moving the forearm act on the elbow joint to flex or extend the forearm,

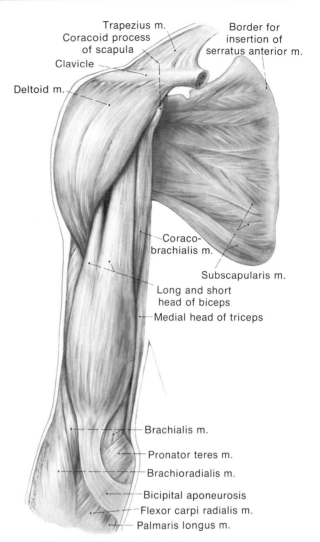

Figure 8–32. Muscles of the shoulder and the upper right arm, anterior view.

on the proximal radioulnar joint to supinate or pronate the forearm and hand, or on both joints. Two of these muscles, the biceps brachii (both heads) and the triceps brachii (long head), cross the shoulder joint, but their actions on the humerus are minimal.

The **biceps brachii** flexes the forearm, effectively when the forearm is supinated and weakly when it is pronated. Flexion of the forearm is also brought about by contraction of the **brachialis**, which acts as well from the prone as from the supine position, and of the **brachioradialis**, which acts best from the semipronated position. The biceps brachii is also a supinator, becoming active when this movement is rapid or when resistance is encountered, conditions under which its powerful action reinforces the action of the **supinator** muscle (which acts alone when the movement is slow or unopposed).

The **triceps brachii** extends the forearm. Ordinarily this movement is produced by the medial head with little assistance from the lateral or long heads. However, when the movement is carried out against resistance, as in doing push-ups, the lateral and long heads become more active. Assisting the triceps brachii in extension of the forearm is the **anconeus** muscle.

The principal pronator of the forearm, the **pronator quadratus**, has its only attachments on the ulna and radius. The pronator quadratus is assisted by the action of the **pronator teres** only during rapid or forceful movements.

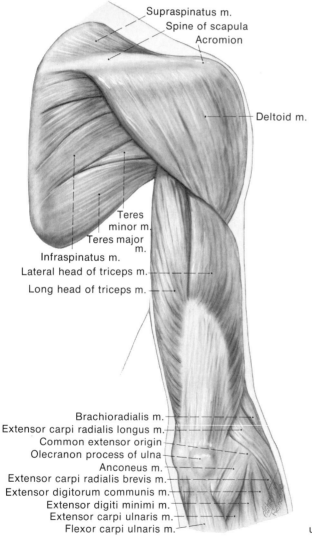

Supraspinatus m.
Spine of scapula
Acromion
Deltoid m.
Teres minor m.
Teres major m.
Infraspinatus m.
Lateral head of triceps m.
Long head of triceps m.
Brachioradialis m.
Extensor carpi radialis longus m.
Common extensor origin
Olecranon process of ulna
Anconeus m.
Extensor carpi radialis brevis m.
Extensor digitorum communis m.
Extensor digiti minimi m.
Extensor carpi ulnaris m.
Flexor carpi ulnaris m.

Figure 8–33. Muscles of the shoulder and upper arm, posterior view.

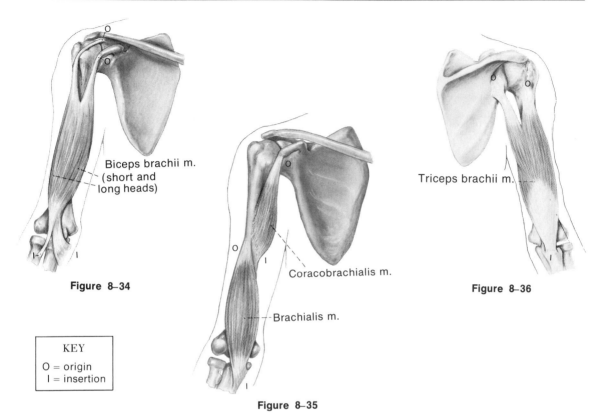

O
O
Biceps brachii m.
(short and
long heads)
I
I

Figure 8–34

O
O
I
Coracobrachialis m.
Brachialis m.
I

Figure 8–35

O
O
Triceps brachii m.
I

Figure 8–36

KEY
O = origin
I = insertion

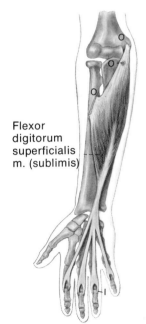

O
O
O
Flexor
digitorum
superficialis
m. (sublimis)
I

Figure 8–37

O
Flexor
digitorum
profundus
m.
Lumbrical m.
I

Figure 8–38

O
Brachioradialis
m.
O
Flexor
carpi
ulnaris m.
O
Flexor
digiti
minimi
brevis m.
I
I
O
I

Figure 8–39

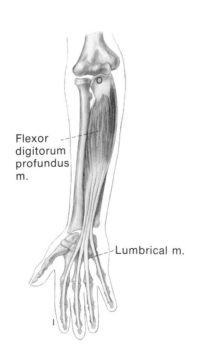

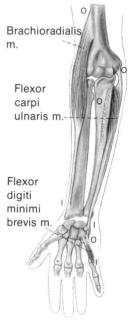

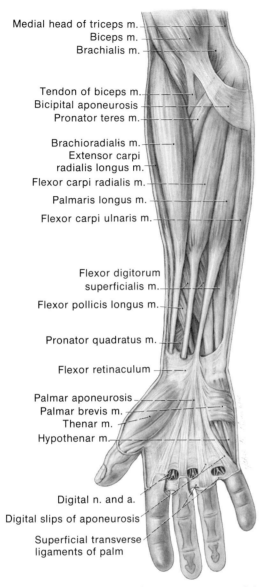

Medial head of triceps m.
Biceps m.
Brachialis m.

Tendon of biceps m.
Bicipital aponeurosis
Pronator teres m.

Brachioradialis m.
Extensor carpi
radialis longus m.
Flexor carpi radialis m.
Palmaris longus m.
Flexor carpi ulnaris m.

Flexor digitorum
superficialis m.
Flexor pollicis longus m.

Pronator quadratus m.

Flexor retinaculum

Palmar aponeurosis
Palmar brevis m.
Thenar m.
Hypothenar m.

Digital n. and a.

Digital slips of aponeurosis

Superficial transverse
ligaments of palm

Figure 8–40. Muscles of the palmar aspect of the
right hand and forearm.

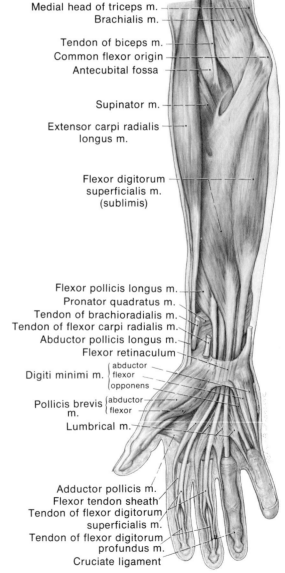

Medial head of triceps m.
Brachialis m.

Tendon of biceps m.
Common flexor origin
Antecubital fossa

Supinator m.

Extensor carpi radialis
longus m.

Flexor digitorum
superficialis m.
(sublimis)

Flexor pollicis longus m.
Pronator quadratus m.
Tendon of brachioradialis m.
Tendon of flexor carpi radialis m.
Abductor pollicis longus m.
Flexor retinaculum

Digiti minimi m. { abductor
flexor
opponens

Pollicis brevis { abductor
m. { flexor

Lumbrical m.

Adductor pollicis m.
Flexor tendon sheath
Tendon of flexor digitorum
superficialis m.
Tendon of flexor digitorum
profundus m.
Cruciate ligament

Figure 8–41. Second layer of muscles of the right
hand and forearm, palmar aspect.

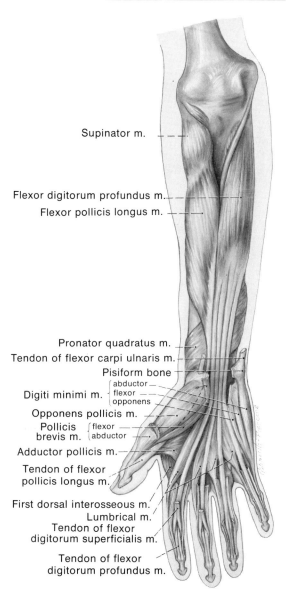

Supinator m.

Flexor digitorum profundus m.
Flexor pollicis longus m.

Pronator quadratus m.
Tendon of flexor carpi ulnaris m.
Pisiform bone
Digiti minimi m. {abductor / flexor / opponens}
Opponens pollicis m.
Pollicis {flexor / abductor}
brevis m.
Adductor pollicis m.
Tendon of flexor
pollicis longus m.

First dorsal interosseous m.
Lumbrical m.
Tendon of flexor
digitorum superficialis m.

Tendon of flexor
digitorum profundus m.

Figure 8–42. Deep muscles of the right forearm and hand, palmar surface.

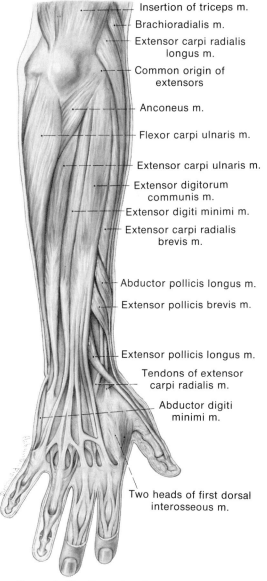

Insertion of triceps m.
Brachioradialis m.
Extensor carpi radialis
longus m.
Common origin of
extensors
Anconeus m.
Flexor carpi ulnaris m.
Extensor carpi ulnaris m.
Extensor digitorum
communis m.
Extensor digiti minimi m.
Extensor carpi radialis
brevis m.
Abductor pollicis longus m.
Extensor pollicis brevis m.
Extensor pollicis longus m.
Tendons of extensor
carpi radialis m.
Abductor digiti
minimi m.
Two heads of first dorsal
interosseous m.

Figure 8–43. Posterior view of the right forearm and hand, showing the superficial muscles.

MUSCLES MOVING THE WRIST
(Table 8–9 and Figs. 8–39 to 8–43, 8–46, and 8–48 to 8–50)

The muscles moving the wrist extend from the distal end of the humerus to the hand, inserting mainly into the metacarpals. One of the prime movers of the wrist, the **extensor digitorum communis**, is an extensor of the fingers as well as of the wrist. Five of the muscles are attached to the metacarpal bones on either the radial or ulnar side of the hand. This group — the **flexor carpi radialis**, the **flexor carpi ulnaris**, the **extensores carpi radialis** (**brevis** and **longus**) and the **extensor carpi ulnaris** — forms a set that acts in dif-

ferent combinations to produce different movements. Together the flexors on the radial and ulnar sides flex the wrist; the extensors on the two sides act together to extend the wrist; the flexor on the radial side, acting together with the extensors on the same side, abducts the wrist; the flexor and extensor on the ulnar side act together to adduct the wrist. The extensors on the two sides function together in another way, namely, as synergists when the fingers are flexed to grasp objects or to make a fist. A number of the flexors of the fingers cross the wrist joint, and extension of the wrist is necessary to limit their action to the fingers. Furthermore, a strong grasp is not possible unless the wrist is extended.

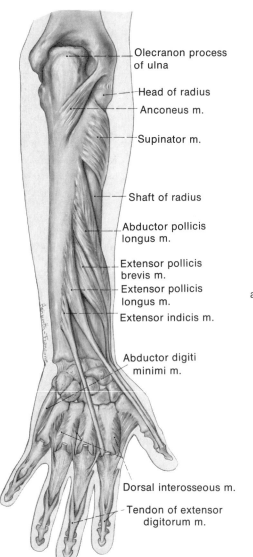

Olecranon process of ulna

Head of radius

Anconeus m.

Supinator m.

Shaft of radius

Abductor pollicis longus m.

Extensor pollicis brevis m.

Extensor pollicis longus m.

Extensor indicis m.

Abductor digiti minimi m.

Dorsal interosseous m.

Tendon of extensor digitorum m.

Figure 8–44. Deep layer of muscles of the right forearm and hand, posterior view.

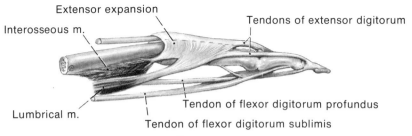

Extensor expansion

Interosseous m.

Tendons of extensor digitorum

Lumbrical m.

Tendon of flexor digitorum profundus

Tendon of flexor digitorum sublimis

Figure 8–45

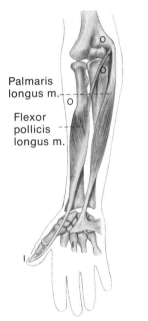

Palmaris longus m.

Flexor pollicis longus m.

Figure 8–46

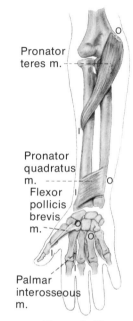

Pronator teres m.

Pronator quadratus m.

Flexor pollicis brevis m.

Palmar interosseous m.

Figure 8–47

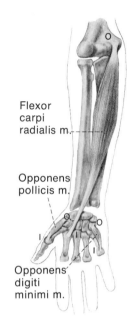

Flexor carpi radialis m.

Opponens pollicis m.

Opponens digiti minimi m.

Figure 8–48

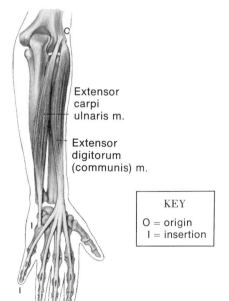

Extensor carpi ulnaris m.

Extensor digitorum (communis) m.

KEY

O = origin
I = insertion

Figure 8–49

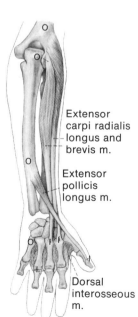

Extensor carpi radialis longus and brevis m.

Extensor pollicis longus m.

Dorsal interosseous m.

Figure 8–50

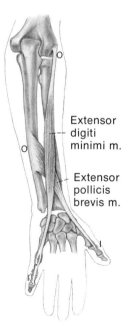

Extensor digiti minimi m.

Extensor pollicis brevis m.

Figure 8–51

MUSCLES MOVING THE THUMB AND FINGERS
(Tables 8–10 and 8–11 and Figs. 8–37 to 8–53)

The fingers and thumb can be flexed and extended at their interphalangeal joints and flexed, extended, abducted, and adducted at their metacarpophalangeal joints (as well as circumducted by a combination of these four movements). The thumb differs from the fingers by having one rather than two interphalangeal joints and in that the metacarpal with which it articulates is freely movable at the carpometacarpal (saddle) joint (which can be rotated as well as flexed, extended, abducted, adducted, and circumducted). Flexion and medial rotation of the first metacarpal makes it possible to easily touch the tip of each finger with the tip of the thumb, a movement called *opposition* or *apposition*.

A number of the muscles moving the thumb and fingers originate on the forearm. Those arising from the hand, the intrinsic muscles of the hand, are generally placed into three groups: (1) those of the thumb, which form the *thenar eminence*, a fleshy prominence on the radial side of the base of the palm; (2) those of the little finger, which form the *hypothenar eminence*, a lesser prominence on the ulnar side of the palm;

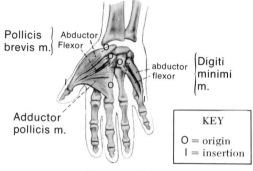

Figure 8–53

and (3) a group composed of the interosseous and lumbrical muscles; the former either abduct or adduct the fingers and, acting with the lumbricals, flex the fingers.

The muscles that move the thumb, the *pollices* (L. *pollex*, thumb), are listed separately in Table 8–10.

MUSCLES OF THE ABDOMINAL WALL
(Table 8–12 and Figs. 8–54 to 8–60 and 8–65 to 8–67)

Four large, flat muscles, the **external oblique**, the **internal oblique**, the **transversus abdominis**, and the **rectus abdominis**, form the abdominal wall. The two oblique and the transversus muscles, named for the direction of their fibers, wrap around most of the abdomen, the aponeuroses of their left and right sides blending in the midline to form a raphe, or seam, called the *linea alba* (L. *linea*, line; L. *albus*, white). The external oblique is the outermost muscle, the transversus the innermost. The rectus abdominis is a straplike muscle extending the length of the center of the abdomen, its left and right sides separated by the linea alba. It is situated between the aponeuroses of the oblique and transversus muscles, which form the so-called rectus sheath (the aponeurosis of the internal oblique splits, one layer joining the aponeurosis of the external oblique above the rectus abdominis, the other layer joining the aponeurosis of the transversus below the rectus abdominis).

The abdominal muscles provide firm pressure on the abdominal organs, holding them in place and protecting them. The ten-

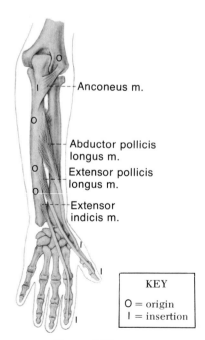

Anconeus m.

Abductor pollicis longus m.

Extensor pollicis longus m.

Extensor indicis m.

KEY
O = origin
I = insertion

Figure 8–52

sion of the oblique muscles, particularly the internal oblique, is principally responsible for this. The abrupt contraction of these muscles, especially of the obliques, raising the intra-abdominal pressure, aids respiration (moving the diaphragm upward during forced expiration), defecation, urination, vomiting, and parturition (childbirth). Contraction of the rectus abdominis flexes the vertebral column; contraction on only one side bends the vertebral column to that side. The oblique muscles have the same actions on the vertebral column, but to a lesser extent.

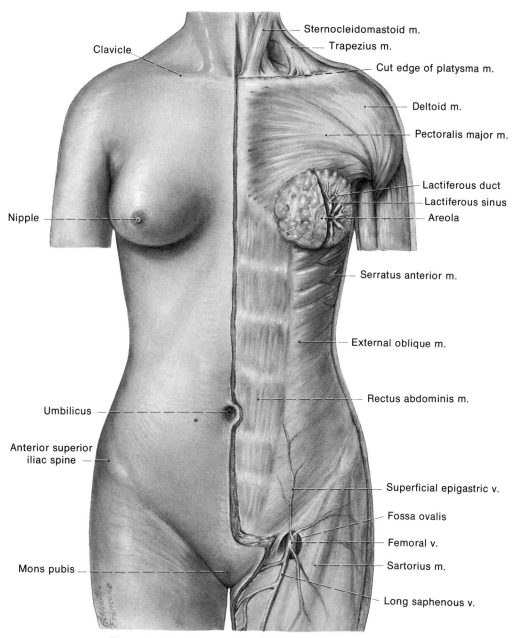

Figure 8–54. Muscles of the anterior surface of the female.

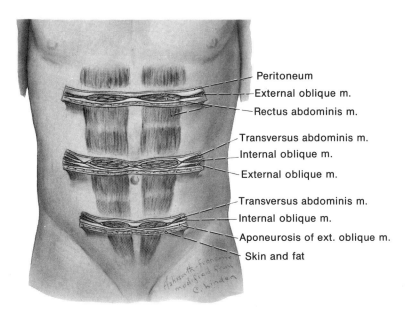

Peritoneum

External oblique m.

Rectus abdominis m.

Transversus abdominis m.

Internal oblique m.

External oblique m.

Transversus abdominis m.

Internal oblique m.

Aponeurosis of ext. oblique m.

Skin and fat

Figure 8–55. Diagram of rectus muscles and sheaths of fascia enveloping them. The muscles have been cut to show the layers of fascia and peritoneum.

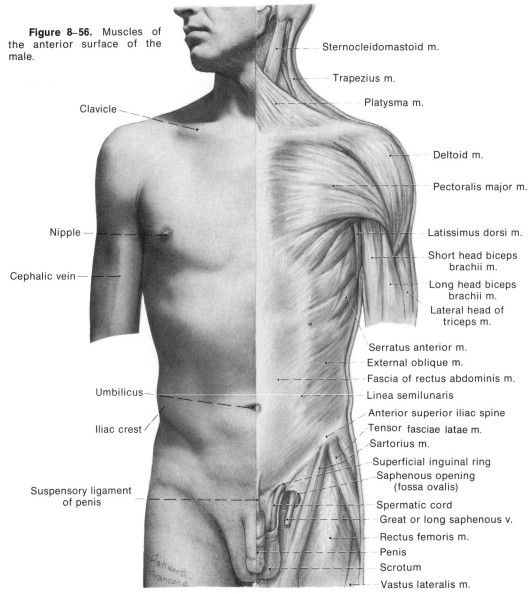

Figure 8–56. Muscles of the anterior surface of the male.

Sternocleidomastoid m.

Trapezius m.

Platysma m.

Clavicle

Deltoid m.

Pectoralis major m.

Latissimus dorsi m.

Short head biceps brachii m.

Nipple

Long head biceps brachii m.

Cephalic vein

Lateral head of triceps m.

Serratus anterior m.

External oblique m.

Fascia of rectus abdominis m.

Umbilicus

Linea semilunaris

Anterior superior iliac spine

Iliac crest

Tensor fasciae latae m.

Sartorius m.

Superficial inguinal ring

Saphenous opening (fossa ovalis)

Suspensory ligament of penis

Spermatic cord

Great or long saphenous v.

Rectus femoris m.

Penis

Scrotum

Vastus lateralis m.

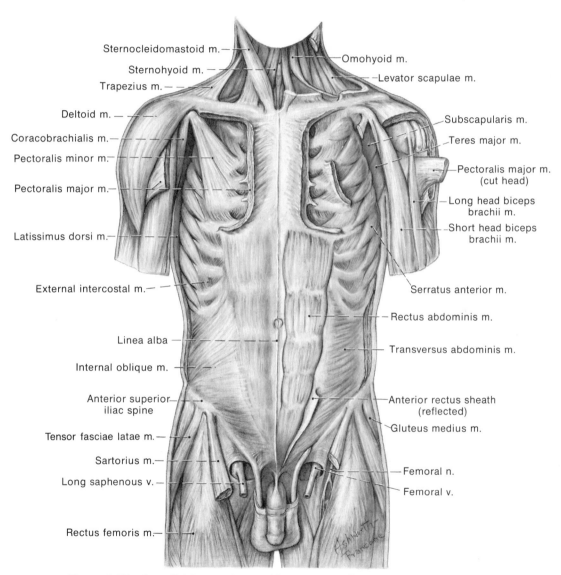

Sternocleidomastoid m.

Sternohyoid m.

Trapezius m.

Deltoid m.

Coracobrachialis m.

Pectoralis minor m.

Pectoralis major m.

Latissimus dorsi m.

External intercostal m.

Linea alba

Internal oblique m.

Anterior superior iliac spine

Tensor fasciae latae m.

Sartorius m.

Long saphenous v.

Rectus femoris m.

Omohyoid m.

Levator scapulae m.

Subscapularis m.

Teres major m.

Pectoralis major m. (cut head)

Long head biceps brachii m.

Short head biceps brachii m.

Serratus anterior m.

Rectus abdominis m.

Transversus abdominis m.

Anterior rectus sheath (reflected)

Gluteus medius m.

Femoral n.

Femoral v.

Figure 8–57. Superficial musculature; skin and pectoralis major have been removed.

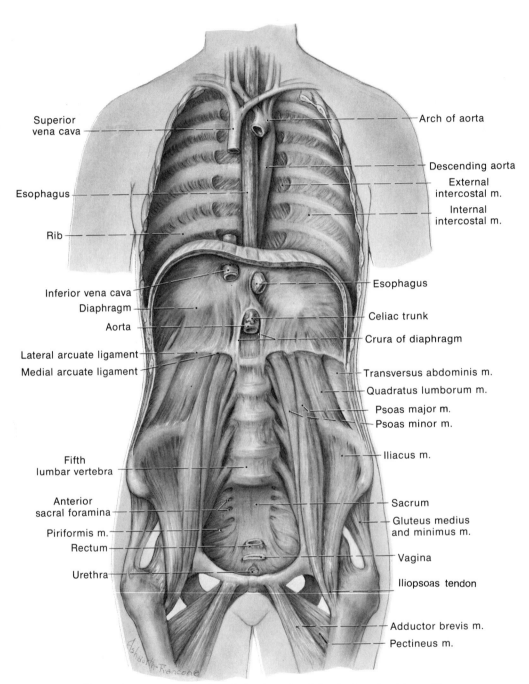

Superior
vena cava

Esophagus

Rib

Inferior vena cava

Diaphragm

Aorta

Lateral arcuate ligament

Medial arcuate ligament

Fifth
lumbar vertebra

Anterior
sacral foramina

Piriformis m.

Rectum

Urethra

Arch of aorta

Descending aorta

External
intercostal m.

Internal
intercostal m.

Esophagus

Celiac trunk

Crura of diaphragm

Transversus abdominis m.

Quadratus lumborum m.

Psoas major m.

Psoas minor m.

Iliacus m.

Sacrum

Gluteus medius
and minimus m.

Vagina

Iliopsoas tendon

Adductor brevis m.

Pectineus m.

Figure 8–58. Deep muscles of the thoracic, abdominal, and pelvic cavities.

MUSCLES OF RESPIRATION
(Table 8–13 and Figs. 8–57 to 8–64)

The **diaphragm**, a dome-shaped muscle separating the thoracic from the abdominal cavity, is the principal muscle of respiration. Since its fibers converge into a tendinous region near the center of the dome, called the *central tendon*, the dome is pulled downward when the muscle contracts during inspiration. Also contracting during inspiration are the **external intercostals.** Contraction of these muscles raises the ribs, mainly at their sternal ends (which are lower than their vertebral ends), thereby increasing the anterior-posterior dimension of the thorax. The bucket-handle–like upward motion of the ribs also increases the lateral dimension of the thorax. In quiet breathing these two muscles alternately contract and relax. In deep inspiration they contract more forceful-ly and accessory muscles become active, principally the **sternocleidomastoids** (listed in Table 8–5), which raise the sternum and thorax when the head is fixed, and the **scaleni**, which raise the first two ribs when their attachments on the cervical vertebrae are fixed. If very forceful inspiration becomes necessary, other muscles may be called into action, among them the *pectoralis major* muscles (Table 8–7) and the *pectoralis minor* muscles (Table 8–5), which raise the ribs if the shoulders and arms are fixed. As indicated, expiration is a passive process. However, in forced expiration the *abdominal muscles*, especially the obliques, and the *internal intercostals* contract. Contraction of the abdominal muscles raises the intra-abdominal pressure, forcing the relaxing diaphragm upward, higher than its resting position. The action of the internal intercostals, which is opposite to that of the external intercostals, reduces the size of the thorax.

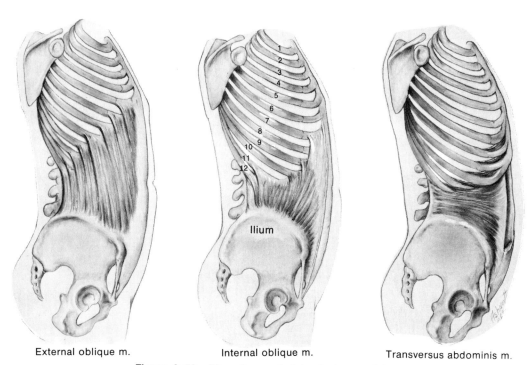

External oblique m.   Internal oblique m.   Transversus abdominis m.

Figure 8–59. Three layers of abdominal musculature.

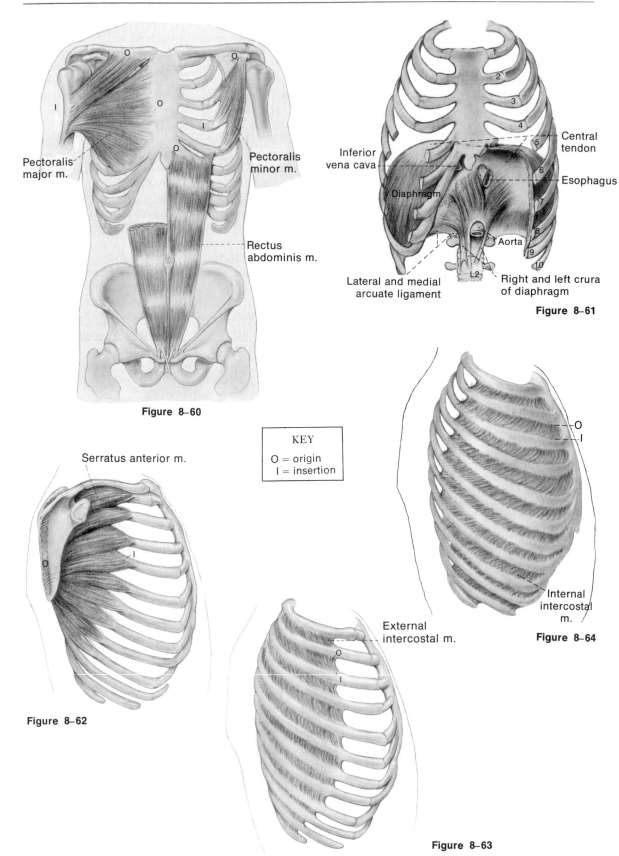

Pectoralis major m.

Pectoralis minor m.

Rectus abdominis m.

Figure 8–60

Inferior vena cava

Central tendon

Diaphragm

Esophagus

Aorta

Lateral and medial arcuate ligament

Right and left crura of diaphragm

L2

Figure 8–61

Serratus anterior m.

KEY
O = origin
I = insertion

Figure 8–62

External intercostal m.

Internal intercostal m.

Figure 8–64

Figure 8–63

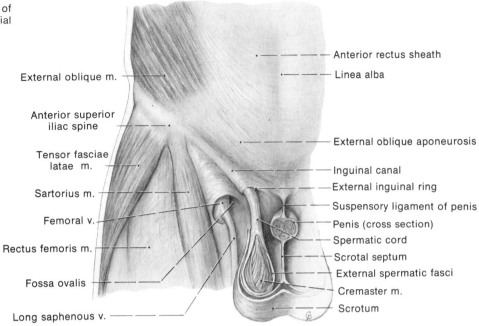

Figure 8–65. Muscles of the inguinal region, superficial layer.

External oblique m.

Anterior superior iliac spine

Tensor fasciae latae m.

Sartorius m.

Femoral v.

Rectus femoris m.

Fossa ovalis

Long saphenous v.

Anterior rectus sheath

Linea alba

External oblique aponeurosis

Inguinal canal

External inguinal ring

Suspensory ligament of penis

Penis (cross section)

Spermatic cord

Scrotal septum

External spermatic fasci

Cremaster m.

Scrotum

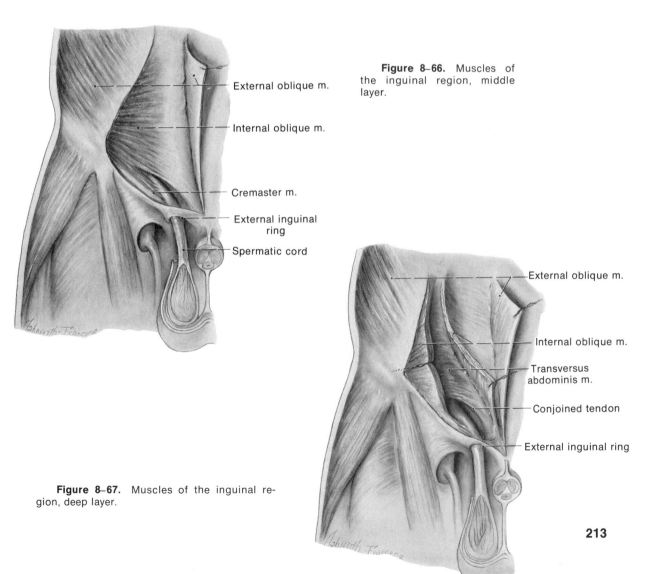

External oblique m.

Internal oblique m.

Cremaster m.

External inguinal ring

Spermatic cord

Figure 8–66. Muscles of the inguinal region, middle layer.

External oblique m.

Internal oblique m.

Transversus abdominis m.

Conjoined tendon

External inguinal ring

Figure 8–67. Muscles of the inguinal region, deep layer.

213

MUSCLES MOVING THE HIP AND KNEE JOINTS
(Table 8–14 and Figs. 8–69 to 8–85)

The principal flexor of the hip joint, the **iliopsoas**, has two parts: the *psoas major* muscle, arising from the lumbar region of the vertebral column, and the *iliacus* muscle, arising from the ilium. The two insert together on the femur. When the pelvis is fixed, the iliopsoas flexes the thigh. Acting from below when the thigh is fixed, the powerful contraction of the iliopsoas will flex the trunk against resistance, as in doing sit-ups.

The **gluteus maximus**, the largest and most superficial muscle of the buttock, is an extensor of the hip joint. When the pelvis is fixed, it extends the thigh, principally bringing it in line with the trunk from the flexed position. It extends the trunk when the thigh is fixed. Acting with the **hamstrings** (a group of muscles on the posterior surface of the femur which cross the hip and knee joints) it draws the trunk upward from a stooped position. The extensors of the hip joints play an important role in maintaining an erect posture. The hamstrings immediately respond to any action that carries the body forward (such as swaying at the ankles, forward arm swinging, or bending at the hips) by contracting vigorously. The gluteus maximus muscles come into play when more powerful extensor activity is needed. They assist the hamstrings in preventing the forward momentum of the trunk from flexing the hip joints during bipedal locomotion, becoming of primary importance when it is strenuous, as in running. (Anthropologists have pointed out that the development of a powerful gluteus maximus — which has a weak action in apes and monkeys — is an important adaptation for bipedal locomotion.) The hamstrings function not only as extensors of the hip joint but also act on the knee joint as flexors.

The **gluteus medius** and **minimus** muscles play a very special role in bipedal locomotion. In quadrupedal primates these two muscles, because of the shape and orientation of the pelvis, are extensors of the hip joint. In humans, on the other hand, these two muscles, acting from a fixed pelvis, can abduct the thigh, but their chief function is to stabilize the pelvis when one foot is lifted off the ground in the course of bipedal gait. When this occurs, contraction of the gluteus medius and minimus muscles on the supporting side tilts the pelvis so as to counteract the tendency of the pelvis to sag on the unsupported side. Paralysis of these two muscles, the most serious muscular disorder of the hip, causes an ungainly, lurching gait.

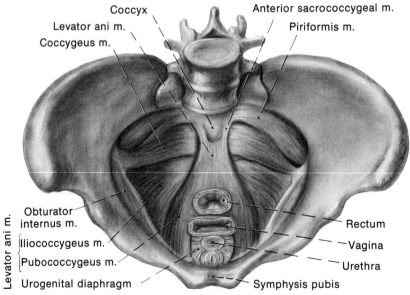

Figure 8–68. Muscles of the pelvic floor.

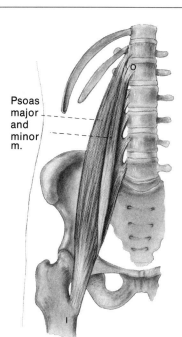

Psoas major and minor m.

O

I

Figure 8–69

KEY

O = origin
I = insertion

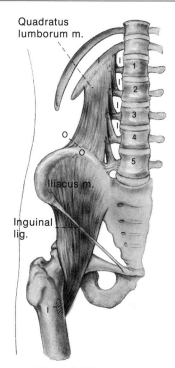

Quadratus lumborum m.

1
2
3
4
5

O
O

Iliacus m.

Inguinal lig.

I

Figure 8–70

Gluteus maximus m.

Figure 8–71

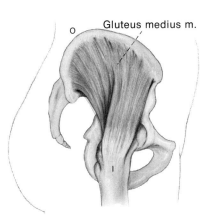

O

Gluteus medius m.

I

Figure 8–72

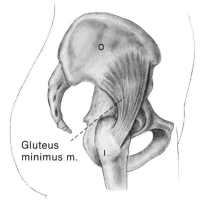

O

Gluteus minimus m.

I

Figure 8–73

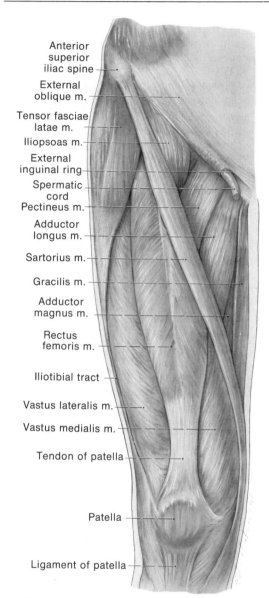

Figure 8–74. Superficial muscles of the right upper leg, anterior surface.

Anterior superior iliac spine
External oblique m.
Tensor fasciae latae m.
Iliopsoas m.
External inguinal ring
Spermatic cord
Pectineus m.
Adductor longus m.
Sartorius m.
Gracilis m.
Adductor magnus m.
Rectus femoris m.
Iliotibial tract
Vastus lateralis m.
Vastus medialis m.
Tendon of patella
Patella
Ligament of patella

The principal extensor of the leg, the **quadriceps femoris,** covers most of the anterior and lateral surfaces of the femur. Three of its four divisions, namely, the *vastus lateralis,* the *vastus medialis* and the *vastus intermedius,* arise from the femur; the fourth, the *rectus femoris,* arises from the pelvis (hence is also a flexor of the hip). The tendons of all four divisions blend to form a single, strong quadriceps tendon (tendon of patella) attached to the base of the patella.

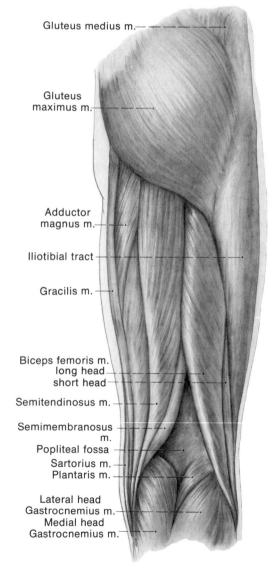

Gluteus medius m.
Gluteus maximus m.
Adductor magnus m.
Iliotibial tract
Gracilis m.
Biceps femoris m. long head
short head
Semitendinosus m.
Semimembranosus m.
Popliteal fossa
Sartorius m.
Plantaris m.
Lateral head Gastrocnemius m.
Medial head Gastrocnemius m.

Figure 8–75. Superficial muscles of the right upper leg, posterior surface.

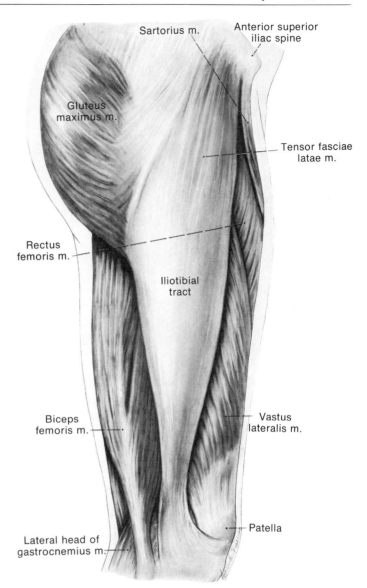

Figure 8–76. Lateral view of superficial muscles of the right upper leg.

Fibers of the tendon pass over the patella to blend with the ligament of the patella, which may be regarded as a continuation of the tendon of the muscle and which inserts into the tuberosity of the tibia. The muscle has additional insertions on the condyles of the tibia.

The **sartorius**, a straplike muscle extending obliquely from the anterior superior iliac spine to the medial surface of the tibia at its proximal end, is the longest muscle in the body. It flexes the thigh and leg (the only muscle to flex both) and rotates the thigh laterally. With these movements on both sides, the legs can be crossed in the traditional tailor fashion, which accounts for the muscle's name (L. *sartor*, patcher, tailor).

The **popliteus** is a short muscle at the back of the knee extending from the lateral condyle of the femur to the posterior surface of the tibia. It medially rotates the tibia or, acting from a fixed tibia, rotates the femur laterally. It is generally regarded as the muscle that "unlocks" the knee joint at the onset of flexing the fully extended knee. In knee flexion while crouching, it may assist the action of the posterior cruciate ligament in preventing forward dislocation of the femur.

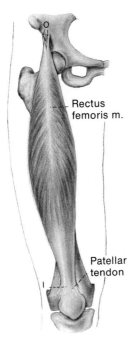

Rectus femoris m.

Patellar tendon

Figure 8–77

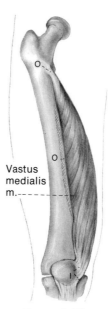

Vastus medialis m.

Figure 8–78

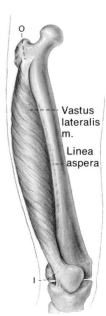

Vastus lateralis m.

Linea aspera

Figure 8–79

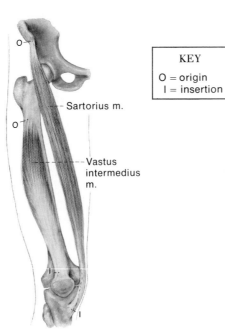

Sartorius m.

Vastus intermedius m.

Figure 8–80

KEY

O = origin
I = insertion

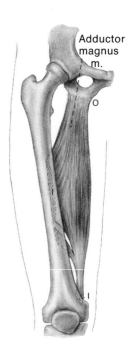

Adductor magnus m.

Figure 8–81

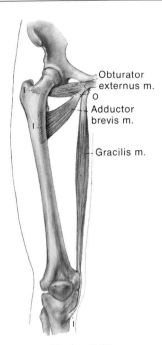

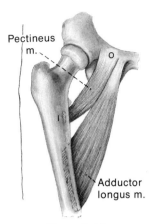

Figure 8-83

Figure 8-82

KEY

O = origin
I = insertion

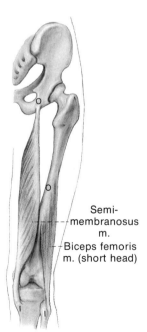

Figure 8-84

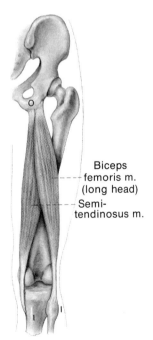

Figure 8-85

MUSCLES MOVING THE FOOT AND TOES
(Table 8–15 and Figs. 8–86 to 8–105)

The **gastrocnemius** and **soleus** muscles, which form the thick, fleshy posterior part of the leg (the calf), are the principal plantar flexors of the foot. The tendons of these two muscles join to form the *tendo calcaneus (Achilles' tendon)*, the thickest and strongest tendon in the body. The gastrocnemius, which arises from two heads on the femur, also flexes the knee. The three-part muscular mass formed by the gastrocnemius and soleus

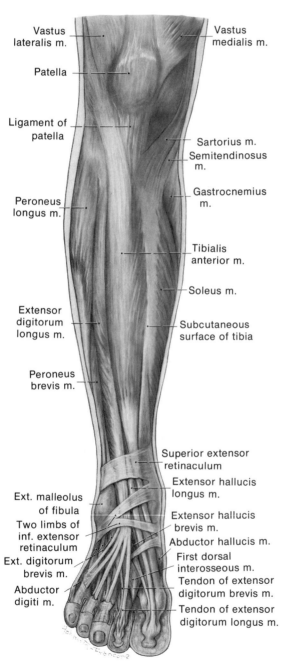

Figure 8–86. Superficial muscles of the right lower leg and foot, anterior surface.

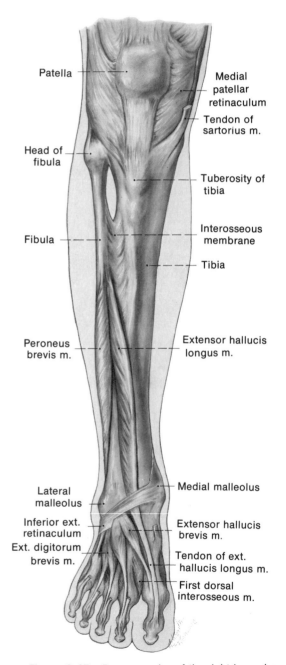

Figure 8–87. Deep muscles of the right lower leg and foot.

with its common insertion into the calcaneus is sometimes referred to as the *triceps surae*.

The **tibialis anterior** is a dorsiflexor of the foot. It also inverts the foot and is especially active when the two movements are combined in walking. Acting with the tibialis anterior in dorsiflexion of the foot are the **extensor digitorum longus**, which also extends the four lateral toes, and the **extensor hallucis longus**, which also extends the great toe (*hallex* is the Latin word for the great toe; hence the hallucis muscles are those that move the great toe).

Eversion of the foot is brought about mainly by the **peroneus longus** and **peroneus brevis**. The tendon of the peroneus longus crosses the sole of the foot obliquely and may be involved in stabilizing the arches when the heel is lifted off the ground.

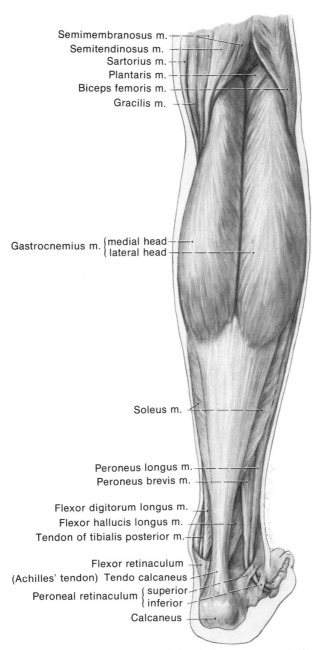

Figure 8–88. Superficial muscles of the right lower leg, posterior view.

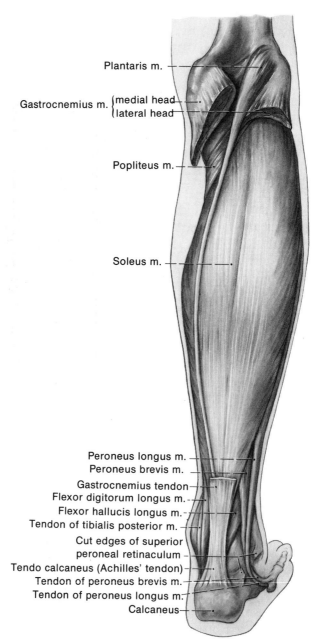

Plantaris m.

Gastrocnemius m. {medial head
{lateral head

Popliteus m.

Soleus m.

Peroneus longus m.
Peroneus brevis m.
Gastrocnemius tendon
Flexor digitorum longus m.
Flexor hallucis longus m.
Tendon of tibialis posterior m.
Cut edges of superior
peroneal retinaculum
Tendo calcaneus (Achilles' tendon)
Tendon of peroneus brevis m.
Tendon of peroneus longus m.
Calcaneus

Figure 8–89. Second layer of muscles of the right lower leg and foot, posterior view.

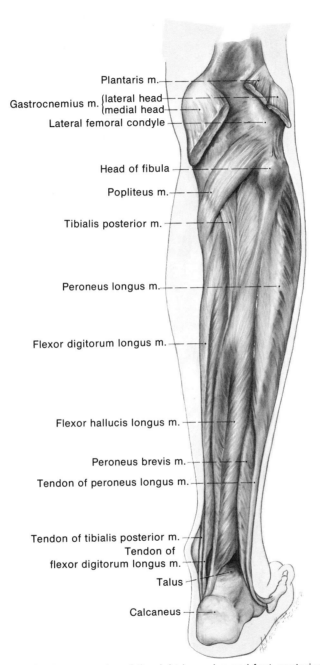

Plantaris m.

Gastrocnemius m. {lateral head
{medial head

Lateral femoral condyle

Head of fibula

Popliteus m.

Tibialis posterior m.

Peroneus longus m.

Flexor digitorum longus m.

Flexor hallucis longus m.

Peroneus brevis m.

Tendon of peroneus longus m.

Tendon of tibialis posterior m.

Tendon of
flexor digitorum longus m.

Talus

Calcaneus

Figure 8–90. Deep muscles of the right lower leg and foot, posterior view.

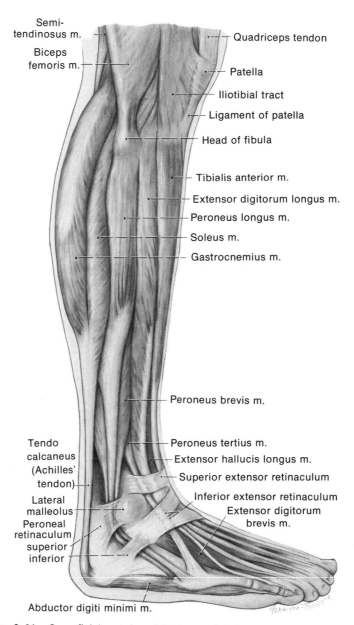

Semi-
tendinosus m.

Biceps
femoris m.

Quadriceps tendon

Patella

Iliotibial tract

Ligament of patella

Head of fibula

Tibialis anterior m.

Extensor digitorum longus m.

Peroneus longus m.

Soleus m.

Gastrocnemius m.

Peroneus brevis m.

Tendo
calcaneus
(Achilles'
tendon)

Peroneus tertius m.

Extensor hallucis longus m.

Superior extensor retinaculum

Inferior extensor retinaculum

Extensor digitorum
brevis m.

Lateral
malleolus

Peroneal
retinaculum
superior
inferior

Abductor digiti minimi m.

Figure 8–91. Superficial muscles of the lower right leg and foot, lateral view.

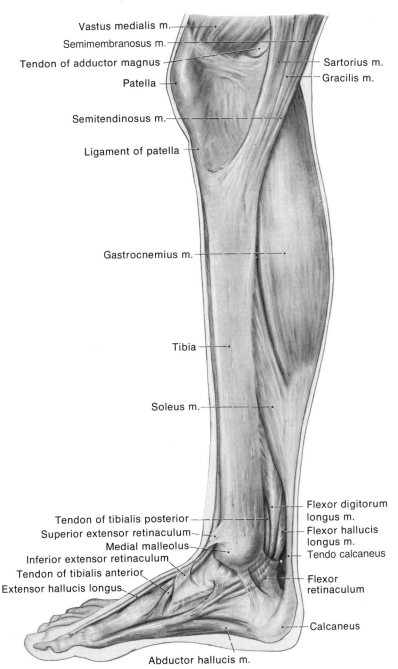

Vastus medialis m.
Semimembranosus m.
Tendon of adductor magnus
Patella
Semitendinosus m.
Ligament of patella
Sartorius m.
Gracilis m.
Gastrocnemius m.
Tibia
Soleus m.
Tendon of tibialis posterior
Superior extensor retinaculum
Medial malleolus
Inferior extensor retinaculum
Tendon of tibialis anterior
Extensor hallucis longus
Flexor digitorum longus m.
Flexor hallucis longus m.
Tendo calcaneus
Flexor retinaculum
Calcaneus
Abductor hallucis m.

Figure 8–92. Superficial muscles of the lower right leg and foot, medial view.

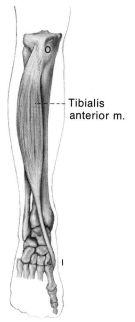

Tibialis anterior m.

Figure 8–93

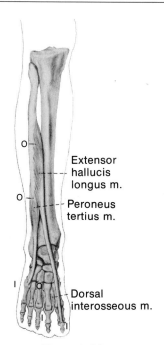

Extensor hallucis longus m.

Peroneus tertius m.

Dorsal interosseous m.

Figure 8–94

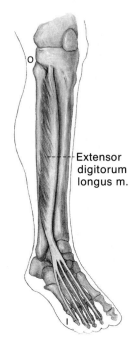

Extensor digitorum longus m.

Figure 8–95

KEY
O = origin
I = insertion

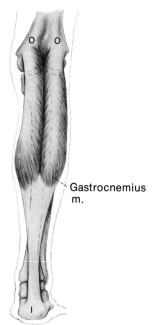

Gastrocnemius m.

Figure 8–96

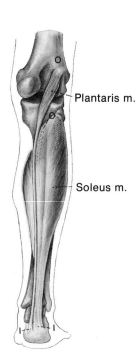

Plantaris m.

Soleus m.

Figure 8–97

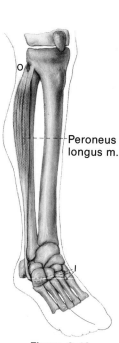

Peroneus longus m.

Figure 8–98

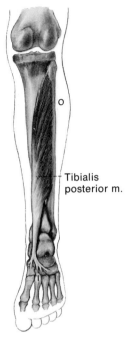

Figure 8–99

Tibialis posterior m.

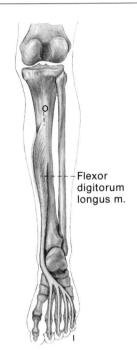

Figure 8–100

Flexor digitorum longus m.

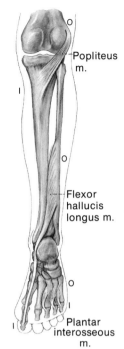

Popliteus m.

Flexor hallucis longus m.

Plantar interosseous m.

Figure 8–101

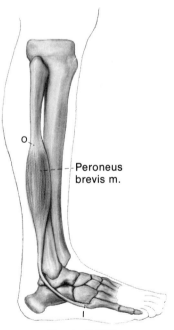

Peroneus brevis m.

Figure 8–102

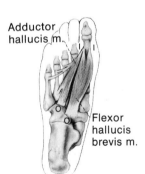

Adductor hallucis m.

Flexor hallucis brevis m.

Figure 8–103

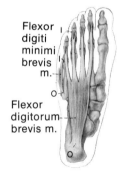

Flexor digiti minimi brevis m.

Flexor digitorum brevis m.

Figure 8–104

KEY

O = origin
I = insertion

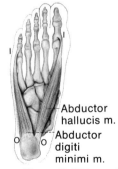

Abductor hallucis m.

Abductor digiti minimi m.

Figure 8–105

SUMMARY

THE MUSCULAR SYSTEM

The three types of muscle are skeletal, smooth, and cardiac.

Skeletal Muscle

1. Structure and Nomenclature

a. Skeletal muscle is also called *striated muscle* because, when it is examined under the light microscope, alternating dark and light bands are seen, and *voluntary muscle* because it is subject to voluntary control.

b. A muscle is composed of bundles (*fasciculi*) of muscle fibers, each a long, narrow, multinucleated cell bounded by a membrane called the *sarcolemma.*
   (1) Each muscle fiber is made up of *myofibrils*, composed of thick and thin filaments.
      (a) *The thick filaments consist largely of the protein* myosin.
      (b) *The thin filaments contain three proteins:* actin (*the principal one*), troponin, *and* tropomyosin. *The thin filaments are attached to a transverse structure (referred to as the Z line) and overlap the thick filaments.*
   (2) This arrangement of the filaments gives rise to the banded appearance of the myofibrils.
      (a) *The thick filaments are the dark, or A, bands.*
      (b) *The thin filaments, where they do not overlap the thick filaments, are the light, or I, bands.*

c. Connective tissue called *endomysium, perimysium,* and *epimysium* surrounds the fibers, fasciculi, and whole muscle, respectively.

2. Mechanism of Contraction

a. When a muscle contracts, the thin filaments slide toward the centers of the thick filaments.
   (1) In the electron microscope this is seen as a shortening of the I band and a decrease in the distance between Z lines (the length of a sarcomere).
   (2) Rotation of the heads of myosin molecules (which face opposite ends of the thick filaments) apparently provides the propulsive force for the sliding of the thin filaments.

b. The contraction is triggered by the release of calcium from the sarcoplasmic reticulum.
   (1) Calcium combines with the troponin component of the thin filament, which functions as a latch (apparently by holding tropomyosin in a position that blocks the myosin binding site on actin), preventing the interaction of ATP-activated myosin heads and actin. Calcium binding releases the latch.
   (2) When myosin and actin interact, the energized state of the myosin heads breaks down, providing the propulsive force for pulling the thin filaments.

3. Transmission of the Electrical Impulses to the Sarcoplasmic Reticulum

a. A single nerve fiber, as a result of terminal branching, innervates on the average about 150 muscle fibers; these muscle fibers and the innervating nerve fiber constitute a *motor unit.*

b. The transmission of an electrical impulse from a nerve fiber branch to a muscle fiber at the neuromuscular junction is mediated by *acetylcholine* released from the neuronal terminal.

c. The impulse traveling along the muscle fiber membrane reaches the sarcoplasmic reticulum via the T tubules, invaginations of the muscle fiber membrane.

d. The arrival of the impulse activates the release of calcium from the sarcoplasmic reticulum, thereby triggering contraction of the muscle fiber.

4. Energy Sources for Skeletal Muscle Contraction

a. During *moderate exercise* the sources of energy are stored ATP, ATP synthesized from creatine phosphate and ATP produced by the oxidation of fatty acids and glucose taken up from the blood.

Oxygen consumption rises sharply.

b. During *strenuous exercise*, additional ATP is supplied by the anaerobic breakdown of muscle glycogen to lactic acid.

c. The *oxygen debt* (the amount of oxygen consumed above the resting level after exercise) is small following moderate exercise and represents replenishment of the approximately half-depleted stores of ATP and creatine phosphate.

   (1) Following strenuous exercise, part of the glycogen and possibly all of the ATP and creatine phosphate must be replaced, and the oxygen debt is large.

5. **Principles of Muscular Contraction**

a. The *all-or-none principle* states that a stimulus strong enough to elicit a response will produce maximum contraction of a motor unit. The weakest stimulus that will initiate contraction is known as the *threshold stimulus*.

   (1) Two subthreshold stimuli applied in rapid succession may be equivalent to a threshold stimulus (summation of stimuli).

b. Application of stimuli of increasing strength will excite nerve fibers with higher thresholds which will activate the muscle fibers of their motor units and increase the force of contraction of a muscle.

c. Stimulating a muscle before it relaxes will increase the magnitude of the response.

   (1) A volley of stimuli at high frequency will cause a sustained contraction of increased magnitude (phenomenon known as *tetanus*).

   (2) Continued stimulation will result in weak contractions (*fatigue*) and incomplete relaxation (*contracture*).

d. Initial length of a muscle affects the force of contraction.

   (1) It is maximum when stretched to its approximate resting length in its normal attachments in the body.

e. When a muscle shortens against a constant load, the contraction is called *isotonic*. It is called *isometric* when it does not shorten.

f. *Red muscle fibers* — those with small diameters, a rich capillary supply, large amounts of myoglobin, many mitochondria, and little glycogen — fatigue less readily and contract more slowly than *white muscle fibers* — those with large diameters, few capillaries and mitochondria, an abundance of glycogen, and an extensive sarcoplasmic reticulum.

Smooth Muscle

1. **Smooth muscle has no cross-striations and each cell has a single large nucleus.**

   a. Since contraction is not induced at will, it is called *involuntary muscle*.

2. **Smooth muscle is found in hollow structures, such as the digestive and urinary tracts, and other locations, such as the iris and ciliary muscle of the eye.**

3. **Visceral, or unitary, smooth muscle, found in most hollow structures, contracts in the absence of nerve stimulation.**

   a. Few nerve terminals are present.
   b. The fibers are in close contact.
   c. Electrical impulses pass from fiber to fiber via membrane junctions.

4. **Multiunit smooth muscle, found where finer gradations of contractions occur, such as in the iris, does not contract in the absence of nerve stimulation.**

   a. The fibers are by and large independently innervated.

5. **Although thick and thin filaments are not so regularly arranged in smooth as in skeletal muscle, the contraction mechanism is believed to be similar.**

Cardiac Muscle

1. **Cardiac muscle, the muscle of the heart, has a striated appearance, resulting from the same arrangement of thick and thin filaments as in skeletal muscle.**

2. **Its fibers have a single nucleus and are functionally linked at their branched ends by junctional specializations called intercalated discs.**

   a. This creates two **functional syncytia** — two atria forming one, two ventricles the other.

3. The heartbreat does not depend upon its nerve supply.

   a. Special neuromuscular tissue initiates the beat and is responsible for the rapid transmission of electrical impulses throughout the heart.

Intramuscular Injection

1. The proper site for intramuscular injection is one that avoids major nerves and blood vessels. The three areas best suited for intramuscular injection are:

   a. The upper outer quadrant of the gluteal area.
   b. The vastus lateralis.
   c. The deltoid muscle, at least 2 cm below the acromion.

Introduction to Anatomy and Actions of Skeletal Muscles

1. Muscles are named according to action, shape, origin and insertion, number of divisions, location, or direction of fibers.

2. The origin is the stationary attachment of the muscle to the skeleton. The insertion is the movable attachment of the muscle.

3. Muscle is usually attached to bone indirectly by means of tendons, consisting of strong, nonelastic fibrous tissue.

4. Prime movers execute an action, while antagonists must relax for the action to occur.

5. Synergists assist the prime movers and act to reduce excess and unnecessary motion.

6. Muscles contracting across joints produce movements by a system of levers. There are three classes of levers. The third class is the most common in the body; the second class is rare or, according to some anatomists, nonexistent.

REVIEW QUESTIONS

1. Describe or draw the fasciculi, fibers, endomysium, perimysium, and epimysium of a skeletal muscle. What is the contractile unit of a muscle fiber? What accounts for the striated appearance of muscle fibers?
2. Explain the sliding filament model of muscular contraction. How does calcium trigger the contraction?
3. How does moderate exercise differ from strenuous exercise with respect to the sources of muscular energy and the size of the oxygen debt? How is the difference in oxygen debt accounted for?
4. Define the following phenomena observed during the contraction of an isolated muscle: summation of twitches, tetanus, treppe, fatigue, and contracture. In what type of contraction is work done? In what type of contraction is tension utilized to hold an object in a fixed position?
5. Distinguish between the muscle fibers of muscle units that contract slowly and are resistant to fatigue and fibers in units that contract rapidly and fatigue rapidly.
6. Compare the characteristics of skeletal, smooth, and cardiac muscle.

Unit 3 □ INTEGRATION AND METABOLISM

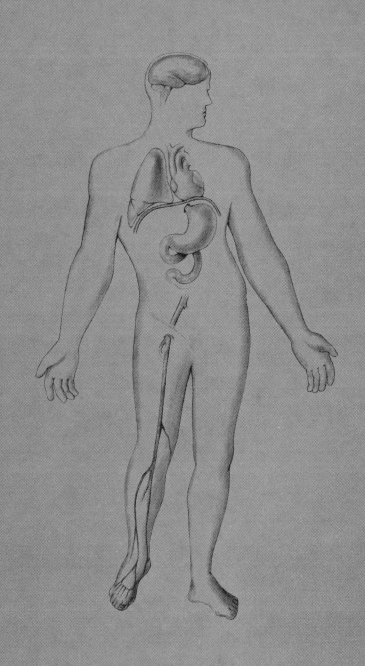

9

The Nervous System

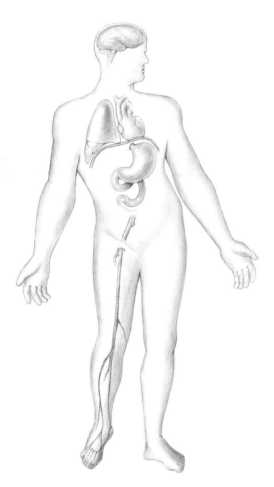

Objectives

The aim of this chapter is to enable the student to:

☐ Describe the structure of neurons and distinguish between the different types.

☐ Describe the changes in membrane permeability that give rise to a propagated nerve impulse.

☐ Outline the succession of events in neuromuscular and synaptic transmission and identify the principal differences between the two types of transmission.

☐ Explain how receptors function and how sensations are identified.

☐ Identify the principal parts of the brain and the major functions of each.

☐ Describe the meninges of the brain and spinal cord.

☐ Describe the origin, function, and circulation of cerebrospinal fluid.

☐ Outline the principal features of the spinal cord.

☐ Describe the anatomy and distribution of the spinal and cranial nerves.

☐ Outline the anatomical characteristics and principal functions of the sympathetic and parasympathetic divisions of the autonomic nervous system.

☐ Describe reflex action and enumerate the principal differences between stretch and withdrawal reflexes.

☐ Outline the pathways for the perception of somesthetic sensations.

☐ Discuss the different types of pain and the modulation of pain.

☐ Describe the pathways for motor function and distinguish between the pyramidal and extrapyramidal systems, both structurally and functionally.

☐ Explain the role of the limbic system in governing emotions.

☐ Explain the physiological basis for long-term as opposed to short-term memory.

☐ Describe the functions of the language areas of the brain.

Throughout history the complexities of the human body have stimulated the imagination. Each mystery solved merely reveals the multiple avenues of complex organizational patterns intimately involved in the function of the living, thinking human being. Perhaps even more fascinating than molecular biology itself is the knowledge of man's ability to comprehend, learn, and act as an individual organism — not only to grasp the wonder of the world, but to question and study it. Man's awareness of his environment is made possible by the integrated functioning of the nervous system, a group of tissues composed of highly specialized cells possessing the characteristics of excitability and conductivity. The nervous system, in association with the endocrine system, not only creates an awareness of the environment but makes it possible for the human body to respond to environmental changes with the necessary precision.

DIVISIONS OF THE NERVOUS SYSTEM

For descriptive purposes, the nervous system can be divided into two parts: the central nervous system and the peripheral nervous system. The **central nervous system** includes the *brain* and *spinal cord*, enclosed in the cranium and the vertebral canal. The **peripheral nervous system** includes 12 pairs of *cranial nerves* and their branches and 31 pairs of *spinal nerves* and their branches. The peripheral nervous system provides input to the central nervous system from *sensory receptors* and output from it to *effectors* (muscles and glands). Communicating networks within the central nervous system and various brain centers which process incoming sensory information make possible the appropriate unconscious or conscious response to sensory input. For convenience, peripheral efferent nerve fibers distributed to smooth muscle, cardiac muscle, and glands are referred to as the *autonomic nervous system*.

TYPES OF CELLS IN THE NERVOUS SYSTEM

The nervous system is composed of a special tissue containing two major types of cells: <u>neurons,</u> the active conducting elements, and <u>neuroglia</u> (G. *glia*, glue), the supporting elements.

Neurons

The basic unit of the nervous system is the neuron, or nerve cell, which conducts an electrical impulse from one part of the body to another. The neuron itself consists of a cell body (perikaryon), containing a single nucleus, and processes transmitting impulses to and from the cell body (Fig. 9–1).

Neurons have two types of processes: **axons** and **dendrites.** An axon is a single, elongated, cytoplasmic extension carrying nerve impulses *away* from the cell body. The axon substance, or axoplasm, is jellylike. The axon itself has a smooth outline, is of constant diameter, is sheathed, and terminates in more minute branches, which form junctions with effectors and other neurons. There is only one axon per neuron, but side branches, called *collaterals*, may arise along the course of an axon.

The dendrites (G. *dendron,* tree) are processes that carry impulses *toward* the cell body. The word dendrite describes the manner in which the processes appear in true

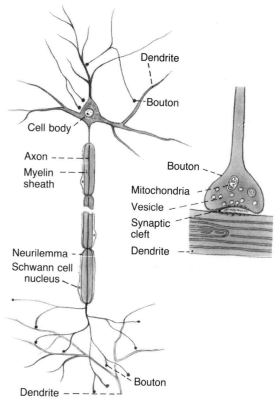

Figure 9–1. Nerve cell showing branching processes ending in boutons. Detail of synapse between bouton and dendrite on right.

* ASTROCYTES

dendrites — numerous, short, branching, and thickened at their point of origin. True dendrites are unsheathed and their surfaces have spinelike projections (dendrite spines) that are the principal sites of junctions between dendrites and axon terminals, where nerve impulses are transmitted from the latter to the former. Sensory neurons (those conducting sensory information to the central nervous system) have a single process that bifurcates a short distance from the cell body. One branch (the *peripheral process*) runs from a receptor to the cell body located just outside the central nervous system. The other (the *central process*, or axon) runs from the cell body to the central nervous system (Fig. 9–2). The peripheral process has the smooth surface, is sheathed, and is in other respects histologically similar to axons. *Sensory neurons, therefore, do not have true dendrites,* although the peripheral process is sometimes called a dendrite because it conducts impulses to the cell body.

♣ **Cytoplasmic Organelles.** Located in the cell body are the *endoplasmic reticulum* and associated *ribosomes* (collectively called *Nissl bodies*), the Golgi apparatus, mitochondria, and lysosomes. True dendrites have a similar organelle composition but lack the Golgi apparatus and have lesser amounts of endoplasmic reticulum. Ribosomes and the Golgi apparatus are lacking in axons. Nissl bodies characteristically respond to injury of a nerve fiber by breaking up into a powderlike mass and dispersing with a loss of affinity to stains, a change called chromatolysis. Also present throughout the neuron are *microtubules* (about 250 Å in diameter), *No* *neurofilaments* (also called intermediate filaments, and about 100 Å in diameter), and *microfilaments* (about 40 Å in diameter). These organelles play a role in transporting neuronal substances, especially neurotransmitters or enzymes needed for their synthesis (see below), from the cell body to axon terminals. They also appear to be involved in nerve fiber growth. In tissue culture studies of axon growth, the microtubules (and probably also the neurofilaments) form a necessary "scaffolding" and the microfilaments (com-

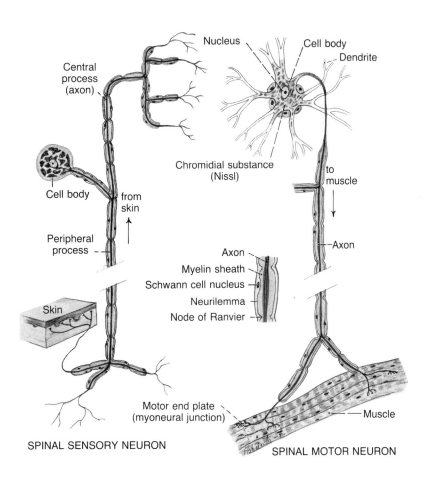

Figure 9–2. Motor and sensory neurons.

SPINAL SENSORY NEURON

SPINAL MOTOR NEURON

posed of neural actin, structurally similar to the actin of muscle) seem to act as contractile "probes" at the growing tip. Drugs destroying these structures prevent growth.

✸ The Nerve Fiber. The term *nerve fiber* refers to any long neuron process, such as an axon or peripheral process of a sensory neuron. All fibers of the peripheral nervous system have a wrapping outside the cell membrane formed by accessory cells of the peripheral nervous system called **Schwann cells.** Fibers less than about one micrometer in diameter have a thin wrapping. In the case of the larger-diameter fibers, repeated wrappings form a thick sheath called *myelin*. When this sheath is formed, the bulk of the cytoplasm of the Schwann cell is expelled as it wraps around a segment of the nerve fiber, so that what remains is a tightly wound spiral of Schwann cell membrane with occasional clefts of cytoplasm (Fig. 9–3). The outermost wrapping, containing the flattened nuclei of the Schwann cells and the greater part of their cytoplasm, is referred to as the *neurilemma* or *sheath of Schwann*. Myelin covers the entire fiber except at its termination, which is enveloped by the neurilemma, and at periodic constrictions called *nodes of Ranvier*, where the neurilemma dips inward with fingerlike processes to cover the fiber. Segments between nodes are called *internodes*, each formed by a single Schwann cell. Fibers wrapped in a myelin sheath are called *myelinated fibers*. The small-diameter fibers, which lack the multilayered myelin sheath, are called *nonmyelinated fibers*. Some anatomists refer to the thin wrapping of Schwann cells around a small-diameter fiber as its neurilemma.

In the central nervous system, where Schwann cells are absent, the myelin sheath is formed by accessory cells called **oligodendroglia.** However, there is an important difference between myelin formed by oligoden-

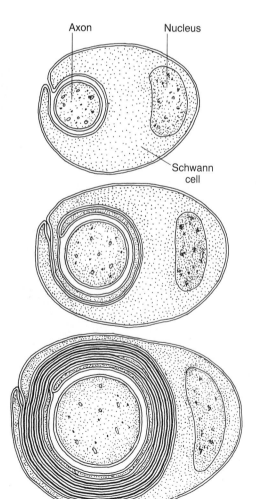

Axon   Nucleus

Schwann cell

Figure 9–3. Schematic representation of the formation of the myelin sheath of a peripheral nerve fiber. Myelinization begins during the embryologic development of the nervous system. In the peripheral nervous system the process is largely completed at birth, although it continues as the nervous system expands. (Myelinization in the brain and spinal cord, on the other hand, is far less complete at birth.) The myelin sheath of a peripheral nerve fiber is formed by accessory cells of the nervous system, called Schwann cells, each of which wraps its compacted, flattened cell-surface membrane around the axon. As myelinization proceeds, the axon increases in diameter and successive Schwann cell wrappings are added. The outermost wrapping, containing the nucleus and most of the cytoplasm, is called the neurilemma. (See also Figure 9–4.)

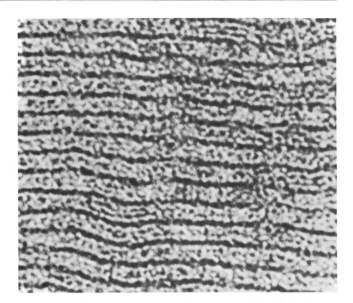

Figure 9–4. Electron micrograph of part of a myelin sheath showing dense period lines (formed by the near fusion of the cytoplasmic faces of the Schwann cell membrane) alternating with less dense lines (formed by the apposition of the external surface of the Schwann cell membrane). (From Warwick and Williams: Gray's Anatomy, 35th British Ed., London, Longman Group Ltd., 1973.)

droglia and Schwann cells. A whole oligodendroglial cell does not wrap itself around a segment of a neuron fiber; rather, it sends out processes (the average number may be as high as 40), each of which wraps around a segment of an adjacent fiber. Hence, these fibers lack an outer, nucleus-containing wrapping (neurilemma).

Myelin is about 80 per cent lipid and is an effective insulator. It increases the rate at which impulses are conducted along nerve fibers, a property described below under "Saltatory Conduction."

Schwann Cells and Nerve Fiber Regeneration. Schwann cells play an essential role in nerve fiber regeneration. When a nerve fiber is damaged or cut, the part connected to the cell body sends out new sprouts, but the part distal to the cut undergoes degenerative changes (initially described by Augustus Volney Waller in 1852 and known as _Wallerian degeneration_). The axon swells and fragments, the myelin breaks up, and the disintegrating material is removed by macrophages. At the same time, Schwann cells proliferate, and a re-formed neurilemma joins the proximal end of the neuron to provide what has been called "contact guidance" for the growing tip of the axon. When growth is completed, the Schwann cells form a new myelin sheath (Fig. 9–5).

Damaged fibers of the central nervous system (as well as of the optic nerve, which also does not have Schwann cells) cannot repair themselves. The oligodendroglial cells do not regenerate after injury to the nerve fiber, and other glial cells in the damaged region, known as _astrocytes,_ proliferate to form a dense tangle of processes that blocks regrowth of the fiber. Attempts have been made in experiments with laboratory animals to overcome this blockage by replacing the damaged parts of spinal cords with grafts of peripheral nerve tissue containing Schwann cells. Only limited regrowth, however, has been observed.

Classification of Neurons. Neurons differ in size of cell body; length, size, and number of dendrites; length and size of axon; and number of branches from the axon terminals.

NEURONS CLASSIFIED ACCORDING TO STRUCTURE. Structurally, neurons are commonly described as _unipolar, bipolar,_ and _multipolar._ This classification depends on the number of processes extending from the cell body. A unipolar neuron has only one process. True unipolar neurons, those with a single axon, are rare, except in the embryo. Sensory neurons that have one process which divides in two a short distance after leaving the cell body are also classified as unipolar, although some authors describe them as _pseudounipolar,_ since they develop from embryological bipolar cells and function as bipolar cells. Bipolar neurons have only two processes, one conducting impulses to the cell body (not a true dendrite, although often called one), the other an axon; such cells are found in the retina of the eye and in the

MOTION (handwritten)

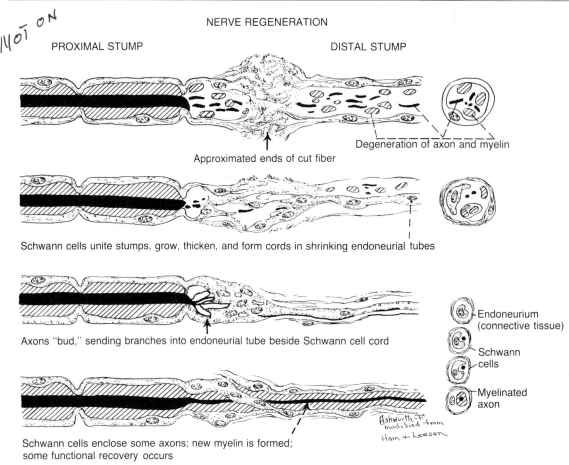

NERVE REGENERATION

PROXIMAL STUMP   DISTAL STUMP

Degeneration of axon and myelin

Approximated ends of cut fiber

Schwann cells unite stumps, grow, thicken, and form cords in shrinking endoneurial tubes

Axons "bud," sending branches into endoneurial tube beside Schwann cell cord

Endoneurium (connective tissue)

Schwann cells

Myelinated axon

Ashworth-F. modified from Ham & Leeson (handwritten attribution)

Schwann cells enclose some axons; new myelin is formed; some functional recovery occurs

Figure 9–5. Schematic drawing of nerve regeneration.

olfactory epithelium. Multipolar neurons have many true dendrites and a single axon. The majority of neurons in the brain and spinal cord are multipolar.

★ NEURONS CLASSIFIED ACCORDING TO FUNCTION. There are three classes of neurons entering into the formation of nerve pathways. *Sensory*, or *afferent* (L. *afferre*, to carry to), neurons convey impulses from the skin or other sense organs to the central nervous system (spinal cord and brain). *Motor*, or *efferent* (L. *efferre*, to carry away), neurons carry impulses away from the central nervous system to muscles and glands. The third class consists of neurons which lie entirely within the central nervous system. These neurons receive input from sensory neurons and communicate with one another or with motor neurons. They are of two types: those with long axons which form tracts connecting different parts of the nervous system, and those with short axons which form local

visceral somatic AFFerent EFFerent (handwritten marginalia)

circuits within a given region of the central nervous system. Some authors refer to all neurons located entirely within the central nervous system as *interneurons* or *internuncial neurons*. Others restrict these terms to the short-axon type. The short-axon neurons (also known as ~~Golgi type II neurons~~, in distinction from the long-axon ~~Golgi type I~~ neurons) play important roles in information processing. Frequently this involves inhibitory processes. For example, in one kind of inhibitory interaction, lateral inhibition, which occurs in sensory pathways, maximally excited neurons may reduce the activity of less-excited adjacent neurons via inhibitory interneurons, thereby "sharpening" sensory patterns. One special type of interneuron lacks an axon and apparently conducts impulses in both directions via dendritelike processes. The amacrine cell of the retina and the granule cell of the olfactory bulb are examples of cells of this type.

COM FOR ASSOC NE (handwritten marginalia)

Accessory Cells

The nonnervous elements consist of blood vessels, connective tissue, and supporting cells known collectively as neuroglia. Schwann cells, which form the myelin sheath and neurilemma of fibers of the peripheral nervous system, have already been described. Mention has also been made of oligodendroglia, which form the myelin sheath of fibers of the central nervous system. Other accessory cells of the central nervous system are *astrocytes,* *microglia,* and *ependymal cells.*

← PART OF RETICULO SYSTEM
PART OF ENDOTHELIO
FOR
N. S.

Astrocytes (G. *astron,* star) are so named because their processes are star shaped (Fig. 9–6). Some of the processes have terminal expansions in contact with blood vessels. The capillaries of the central nervous system are relatively impermeable and constitute a so-called "blood brain barrier" (demonstrated by injecting certain dyes, such as trypan blue, which will stain all tissues but those of the central nervous system). It has been suggested that astrocytes, which occupy the space between capillaries and neurons, control the transport of substances between the blood stream and neurons.

Microglia, unlike all other cells of the nervous system, develop from the embryonic mesoderm (which gives rise, among other things, to connective tissue, muscles, and the vascular system) rather than the ectoderm (from which the epidermis and neural tube develop). Microglia function as phagocytic cells.

Ependymal cells line the ventricles (cavities) of the brain and the central canal of the spinal cord. In the embryo these cells are columnar and ciliated, but in the adult are cuboidal in shape with few cilia.

✗ The Nerve Impulse

Neurons function to conduct signals from one part of the body to another. The capacity for selective permeability to ions is a function of the cell membrane, and it is this property of the nerve cell which is involved in the transmission of the nerve impulse. In the resting state the interior of the nerve fiber is negative to the exterior by approximately 70 to 90 millivolts. This difference in potential across the membrane is called the **resting membrane potential** of the nerve fiber. In general terms, the origin of the resting membrane potential is accounted for as follows: The active transport of positively charged sodium ions to the outside of the cell (the so-called sodium pump) with the reciprocal transfer of positively charged potassium ions to the inside maintains a high concentration of sodium outside and a high concentration of potassium inside the cell. Diffusion of sodium and potassium across the cell membrane in response to the concentration gradients created by the active transport mechanism results in the "leaking" of sodium back into and potassium out of the cell. However, the cell membrane is much more permeable to potassium than to sodium. Very little inward diffusion of sodium occurs, and the greater outward diffusion of potassium creates a deficit of positive charges on the inner surface of the membrane that is responsible for the resting membrane potential (Fig. 9–7). The relatively high permeability of the membrane to potassium is accounted for by the presence in the membrane of a class of permanently open channels (proteins functioning as such) selectively permeable to potassium.

When a stimulus is applied to a nerve

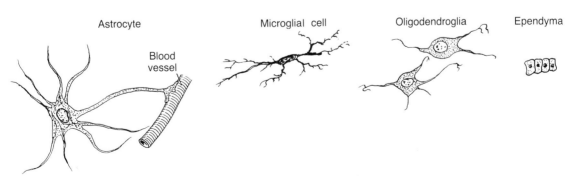

Astrocyte   Microglial cell   Oligodendroglia   Ependyma

Blood vessel

Figure 9–6. Neuroglial cells of the central nervous system.

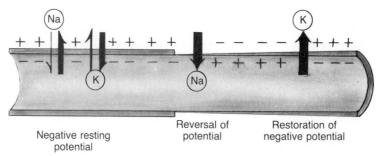

Negative resting
potential

Reversal of
potential

Restoration of
negative potential

Figure 9–7. Schematic representation of the events responsible for the resting membrane potential of a nerve fiber and the action potential. Sodium is actively pumped out of and potassium moves into the cell interior. Some inward diffusion of sodium and outward diffusion of potassium occurs as a result of the concentration gradients created by the active transport mechanism. The more rapid outward diffusion of potassium gives rise to the negative resting potential. A stimulus opens the sodium channels, flooding the interior with sodium, reversing the membrane potential. Closing of the sodium channels is followed by opening of the potassium channels and a rapid outflow of potassium, which returns the membrane potential to negative. This transitory reversal of potential, called the action potential or nerve impulse, is propagated along the membrane.

cell, an impulse, a transient reversal of the membrane potential, is transmitted along the nerve fiber. This comes about as follows: The stimulus causes changes in the conformation of membrane proteins functioning as sodium and potassium ion channels that are closed in the resting state. This results first in opening of the sodium channels and a rapid inflow of sodium, which changes the membrane potential locally from negative to positive (the *spike potential*). This is followed by closing of the sodium channels and opening of the potassium channels. A rapid outflow of potassium returns the membrane potential to negative. These changes, the so-called **action potential,** can be recorded with an oscilloscope and are illustrated in Figure 9–8. The local disturbance stimulates the adjacent regions of the nerve fiber, and the action potential sweeps along the fiber. (In the body the stimulus is normally received at one end of the neuron and is propagated in one direction, but if a nerve fiber is artificially stimulated in the middle the action potential will be transmitted in both directions.)

For a brief period following stimulation of a nerve fiber it will not respond to a new stimulus. The interval of complete unresponsiveness is called the *absolute refractory period*. The absolute refractory period is followed by a *relative refractory period*, during which time a stronger than minimum effective stimulus will lead to the transmission of a nerve impulse. For a large mammalian myelinated nerve fiber the absolute refractory period ranges from .4 to 1 millisecond. Excitability gradually returns to about 95 per cent of the resting level in from 10 to 30 milliseconds.

The absolute refractory period corresponds to a period when the inflow of sodium ions is completely inactivated. The sodium channel protein apparently has three conformations. In the resting state the conformation is closed. A stimulus changes it to an open conformation. This change from a closed to an open conformation is terminated after a brief interval by a process called *sodium inactivation*. The closed conformation in the inactivated state is different from the resting

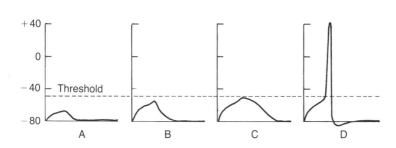

Figure 9–8. The potential changes in the interior of the nerve fiber of a squid, recorded on an oscilloscope, following subthreshold and threshold stimuli. Subthreshold stimuli of increasing strength cause successively greater, brief, nonpropagated, upward deflections (A, B, and C). A threshold stimulus gives rise to the so-called action potential (the propagated impulse), showing a sharp rising phase (spike potential) and rapid descent (D).

state conformation, and until the channel returns to the resting state it will not respond to a new stimulus.

ationby ✗ **All-or-None Principle.** The transmission of a nerve impulse by a nerve fiber is said to work on an all-or-none principle. This means that nerve fibers will not transmit an impulse unless the stimulus has a certain strength (the *threshold* of the nerve fiber). If the threshold is reached, the impulse is maximal. Each type of nerve fiber sends an impulse of only one strength — its characteristic impulse. A stronger stimulus does not lead to a larger impulse.

A stimulus just strong enough to lead to a propagated impulse is called a *threshold stimulus*. A *subthreshold stimulus* will cause the internal potential to become briefly less negative, deflecting the voltage upward (Fig. 9–8). Only when the threshold voltage of the nerve fiber is reached will the sodium influx be of sufficient magnitude to cause the sharp spike potential and propagated impulse.

Different nerve fibers have different thresholds — some will fire only with very strong stimulation, others with very weak stimulation, but all fibers work characteristically and on the all-or-none firing principle.

No ➤ **Chronaxie and Excitability of Nerve Fibers.** To be effective, a stimulus must be of sufficient duration and intensity. The stronger the current, the shorter the time required to excite a fiber (Fig. 9–9). The time required for a current twice the minimum effective voltage (the rheobase) to excite a fiber is called *chronaxie* and is used as a convenient measure of the relative excitability of nerve fibers — the shorter the chronaxie, the greater the excitability.

✗ **Saltatory Conduction.** Myelin is resistant to the flow of ions, and the thick myelin sheath of myelinated fibers prevents continuous passage of impulses along the length of the fiber. Ion flow at nodes of Ranvier sets up potential differences between nodes, and the impulse jumps from one node to another. This process, called *saltatory conduction* (L. *saltatorius*, of dancing), greatly increases the transmission velocity of nerve impulses.

Transmission of the Impulse at the Neuromuscular Junction *will lecture on*

As mentioned in the description of skeletal muscle in Chapter 8, a motor neuron branches terminally and innervates from a few to more than a thousand muscle fibers depending upon the precision of the muscular action. The junction at which the axon branch and muscle fiber meet is known as the *neuromuscular junction,* also called the *myoneural junction* or *motor end plate.* In most muscles the junction is situated at the midpoint of the fiber and consists of several expanded endings of an axon branch arranged in a group. Each expanded ending

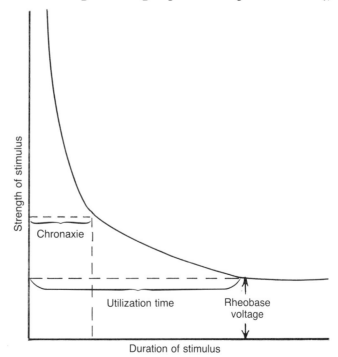

Figure 9–9. Relationship between the intensity of a current and the time it must flow to reach threshold and excite a fiber. Since the time required (utilization time) for the minimum effective voltage (rheobase) to excite is difficult to measure, chronaxie, the time a current of twice the rheobase must flow to excite, is taken as a measure of excitability.

contains mitochondria and vesicles that store a chemical mediator (see below) and projects into an invagination of the muscle fiber membrane (synaptic trough). The space between an ending and an invaginated muscle fiber membrane is called the *synaptic cleft*. Folds in the bottom of the muscle fiber membrane (subneural clefts) increase the surface area for stimulation (Fig. 9–10).

In the 1930's Sir Henry Dale and colleagues made the important discovery that the transmission of electrical impulses from nerve to muscle requires the intervention of a specific chemical mediator, **acetylcholine.** A nerve impulse causes the sudden release of a large amount of acetylcholine from vesicles in which it is stored in the axon branch endings into the synaptic clefts. The release of acetylcholine is apparently triggered by the influx of calcium into the axon branch

endings. This leads to the fusion of the acetylcholine-containing vesicles with the membrane of the axon branch endings and discharge of acetylcholine (a process called exocytosis). Acetylcholine diffuses across the synaptic clefts and is bound by a receptor protein embedded in the membrane of the muscle fiber. According to recent research findings this receptor is an ion channel that is "gated" by acetylcholine. Upon binding acetylcholine it undergoes a change in conformation that opens the channel to the passage of sodium and potassium ions. A sudden influx of sodium and outflow of potassium is associated with a reduction in the difference in potential across the cell membrane (making the membrane potential less negative). This change is called the **end plate potential** *NO* **(EPP)** and, when it reaches a critical level (the threshold of the muscle fiber), it is the

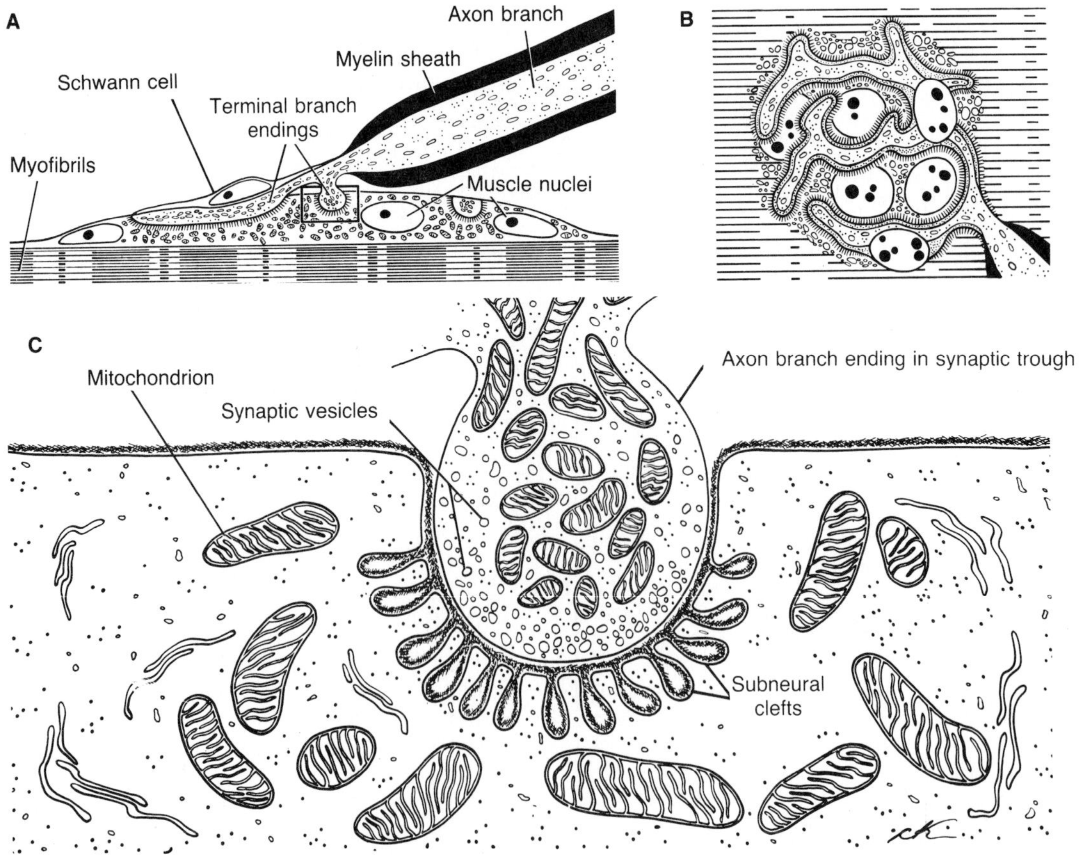

Figure 9–10. Schematic representation of the motor end plate as seen by light and electron microscopy. *A,* Longitudinal section as seen in the light microscope. *B,* Surface view as seen in the light microscope. *C,* Appearance in the electron microscope of the area represented by the rectangle in *A.* (From Bloom, W., and Fawcett, D. C.: *Textbook of Histology,* 10th ed., Philadelphia, W. B. Saunders Co., 1975.)

stimulus for generating an action potential, which is propagated along a muscle fiber in the same way an action potential is propagated along a nerve fiber. The action of acetylcholine is halted by the enzyme *acetylcholinesterase,* located on the membrane of the muscle fiber, which splits acetylcholine into acetic acid and choline.

In the 1950's it was demonstrated by Bernard Katz and Paul Fatt that even in the absence of stimulation the end plate region is not entirely at rest. Randomly occurring subthreshold **miniature end plate potentials** NO → **(MEPP)** resulting from the spontaneous, intermittent release of acetylcholine can be recorded. The effect of a stimulus is to greatly increase the release of acetylcholine. The amount released following a stimulus is sufficient to induce an action potential in the muscle fiber.

Certain drugs, such as *methacholine, nicotine,* and *carbachol,* mimic the effect of acetylcholine at the neuromuscular junction. However, because these drugs either are not or are very slowly destroyed by acetylcholinesterase, their actions persist. Moderate doses induce a state of muscular spasm, but high doses cause paralysis because the receptor protein becomes unresponsive to chemical mediators.

Neuromuscular transmission can be blocked by <u>curare,</u> which has a greater affinity for the receptor protein than acetylcholine. Poisoning with this drug can cause death as a result of paralysis of the muscles of respiration.

Synaptic Transmission
ONLY whaTS lecTured 6 N IN CLASS

Signals are passed from one neuron to another at specialized junctions called **synapses.** Most often transmission is from the axon terminal of one neuron to the dendrites or cell body of another, synapse occurring most frequently between axon terminals and dendrites. (Other, less common, types of synapses involved in information transfer include axon on axon, dendrite on axon, dendrite on dendrite, and dendrite on cell body.)

Before an axon makes synaptic connections, it gives rise to many branches, each of which ends in a knoblike expansion called a *presynaptic knob, bouton,* or *presynaptic terminal* (Fig. 9–1). A presynaptic knob is separated from the membrane of a postsynaptic neuron by a *synaptic cleft* (about 200 Å

wide) and contains mitochondria and vesicles filled with a *neurotransmitter,* a chemical mediator that alters the permeability of the postsynaptic membrane. The arrival of a nerve impulse at the presynaptic terminal leads to the discharge of the neurotransmitter into the synaptic cleft just as it does at the axon branch endings at the neuromuscular junction. However, whereas the vesicles in the axon endings at the neuromuscular junction contain only acetylcholine, which always has an excitatory effect on the postsynaptic membrane, the vesicles of presynaptic knobs contain any one of a number of neurotransmitters which may exert either excitatory or inhibitory actions. Furthermore, it is not unusual for the action of a given neurotransmitter to be excitatory at some synapses and inhibitory at others. When a neurotransmitter diffuses across the synapse, it is bound by a receptor protein in the membrane of the postsynaptic neuron. The receptor may, as is the case with the acetylcholine receptor at the neuromuscular junction, function as a chemically gated ion channel, assuming an open conformation when a specific neurotransmitter is bound. Some receptors, on the other hand, appear to function by a more elaborate mechanism which current research suggests often involves the formation of cyclic AMP, functioning as a "second messenger" (see Chapter 2, page 39) in mediating the action of the neurotransmitter.

The effect of an excitatory neurotransmitter is to bring about ion flows that make the membrane potential less negative, producing what is called the **excitatory postsynaptic potential (EPSP).** An excitatory postsynaptic potential produced by discharge of the neurotransmitter from a single presynaptic knob will not reach the threshold for initiating an action potential in the postsynaptic neuron. To reach the threshold a summing of many excitatory postsynaptic potentials must occur. This may be accomplished by the discharge of the neurotransmitter from a number of presynaptic knobs simultaneously, a process called *spatial summation.* Converging neural pathways, which result in the innervation of a single neuron by the terminal branches of many neurons, make possible spatial summation by input from many presynaptic neurons. A summing of excitatory postsynaptic potentials may also be brought about by the discharge of the neurotransmitter from presynaptic knobs in rapid succession, a process called *temporal summation.*

When the membrane potential of the post-synaptic neuron is made less negative than the resting membrane potential, but not sufficiently so to reach the threshold for firing, the neuron is said to be *facilitated*. In this state the neuron is more responsive to weak input signals than it would otherwise be. The resting potential of a motoneuron, for example, is −70 millivolts. Threshold potential is approximately −60 millivolts. It is facilitated if the membrane potential is between −70 and −60 millivolts.

The effect of inhibitory neurotransmitters on the postsynaptic membrane is the reverse of excitatory neurotransmitters. They cause ion flows (usually an outflow of potassium ions or inflow of chloride ions) that make the membrane potential more negative (hyperpolarized). This change is called the **inhibitory postsynaptic potential (IPSP).**

Synaptic inhibition can also be caused by a reduction in the release of an excitatory neurotransmitter from presynaptic terminals, an action called **presynaptic inhibition.** Interneuron terminals overlying excitatory presynaptic terminals apparently release a neurotransmitter that acts on these terminals (an example of an axon on axon synapse).

Synaptic response is influenced by diverging and converging neural pathways. *Divergence* refers to the innervation of many neurons by the terminal branches of a single neuron. *Convergence* is the innervation of a single neuron by the terminal branches of many neurons. In diverging pathways the signals may be amplified or sent to separate parts of the nervous system. A significant consequence of convergence is that a single neuron can receive input from widely scattered regions of the nervous system. What a neuron will do in response to its various inputs is determined by the *algebraic summing of excitatory and inhibitory signals converging upon it.* It is perhaps apparent that convergence provides an important mechanism for the correlation and evaluation of information by the central nervous system.

Although a number of substances have been tentatively identified as neurotransmitters, only two, acetylcholine and norepinephrine, meet all of the criteria used by researchers for classification as such. These criteria are the presence of enzymes for its synthesis, a mechanism for termination of its action, reaction with a receptor site upon release, and identification of a response.

Among the substances that do not meet all of these criteria but that are commonly accepted as neurotransmitters are dopamine, serotonin, gamma aminobutyric acid (regarded as the most common inhibitory neurotransmitter in the brain), glycine (concentrated in certain parts of the spinal cord, where it is inhibitory), glutamic acid, and aspartic acid.

All of the substances listed above are either simple compounds or individual amino acids. In recent years a new class of compounds, the neuropeptides, has become a neurotransmitter candidate. As a rule these peptides are also found in the intestinal tract or pituitary gland. Some are well-known hormones, such as secretin, gastrin, cholecystokinin (gastrointestinal hormones), ACTH, vasopressin (pituitary hormones), thyrotropin-releasing hormone, and luteinizing hormone–releasing hormone (hypothalamic hormones). Another, substance P, has a long history (it was isolated from the brain and intestines more than 50 years ago) and in recent years has been intensively studied as a transmitter of pain signals in the spinal cord. Two others, the enkephalins and endorphins, have aroused a great deal of excitement because of their morphinelike properties. Studies with some of these neuropeptides suggest that they do not function as neurotransmitters in the usual sense, but as neuromodulators — altering a neuron's response to a neurotransmitter. It has been observed that some neurons contain one or more neuropeptides in addition to a traditional small-molecule neurotransmitter. This appears to violate the rule, generally accepted for many years, that any given neuron releases only one neurotransmitter. It is possible, however, that the rule is one neurotransmitter per neuron plus one or more neuromodulators.

Neurotransmitters are continuously synthesized in synaptic knobs or the neuronal cell body. The neurotransmitters or enzymes required for their synthesis are transported from the cell body along the fiber to the knobs. Excessive neuronal stimulation will eventually deplete the store of transmitter substance, thereby causing cessation of synaptic transmission. This *fatigue* serves as a protective device, as in limiting the duration of an epileptic seizure.

There is evidence that the number of presynaptic terminals may actually increase with prolonged repetitive stimulation. It has been postulated that these physical changes may in part form the basis of memory.

✗ Acidosis and alkalosis affect synaptic transmission by decreasing or increasing excitability. A decrease in pH from the normal of 7.4 to 7.0 depresses neuronal activity, as in severe diabetic coma. An increase in pH from 7.4 to 7.8 often results in convulsions owing to increased excitability.

✗ Sensory Receptors *Know what each functions for & where located*

Input by sensory neurons to the central nervous system providing information about changes in the external and internal environment depends upon the existence of *receptors*. A receptor is a peripheral ending of a sensory neuron, or a structure or organ innervated by a sensory neuron, that is especially sensitive (but not exclusively) to a given kind of stimulus (called the *adequate stimulus*). Receptors vary in complexity from the free nerve endings sensitive chiefly to pain to the highly complicated organs for vision and hearing. Stimulation of a receptor causes changes that induce a localized potential in sensory neurons, called the *generator potential*, which, if it reaches a critical (threshold) amplitude, generates a propagated action potential.

Each sensory neuron transmits impulses to the central nervous system that will be identified as a specific kind of sensation, such as pain, touch, and sound. Since each sensory neuron functions simply as a transmitter of nerve impulses, it is perhaps apparent that the identification of the sensation depends upon the connections made by the sensory pathways in the brain. From this it also follows that no matter how the sensory neuron is stimulated (by the adequate stimulus or otherwise) the sensation perceived will be the same. A greater than threshold stimulus to a receptor will not increase the magnitude of the propagated action potential (all-or-none law), but it will increase the frequency of the impulses. Increasing the intensity of the stimulus also excites more receptors (partly because of different receptor thresholds).

Receptors are difficult to classify, and several somewhat conflicting classification schemes have haphazardly arisen. The broadest classification distinguishes two principal types, receptors for the *general senses* distributed throughout the body and receptors for the *special senses* in the head region, namely, sight, hearing, taste, smell, and equilibrium (receptors for the last-named sense are located in the inner ear). The general senses include pain, touch, pressure, cold, warmth, and the kinesthetic sense (the perception of the position and movement of parts of the body made possible by receptors in tendons and tissues in and around joints). All of the foregoing receptors provide input that is consciously perceived. Other general receptors can detect bodily changes that are not consciously perceived but that play vital roles in maintaining homeostasis. These include receptors for arterial pressure (in the aorta and the carotid sinus), arterial oxygen (in the aortic and carotid bodies), arterial carbon dioxide (in the medulla of the brain and the aortic and carotid bodies), blood temperature, osmotic pressure, and glucose concentration (in the hypothalamus).

Among other terms frequently encountered in descriptions of sensory receptors are the following: *Proprioceptors* — receptors of vital importance for locomotor and postural responses, including kinesthetic receptors, the muscle spindle, and equilibrium receptors in the inner ear. *Somesthetic receptors* (G. *soma*, the body; G. *aisthetikos*, of perception) — frequently used to describe general body receptors for consciously perceived sensations. *Exteroceptors* — receptors responding to stimuli from the external environment, from a distance or on the body surface. *Interoceptors* — receptors responding to stimuli from the internal environment, excluding muscles, tendons, and joints.

Equilibrium
Unconcious
Kinesthesia

The simplest sensory receptors are *free nerve endings* — undifferentiated peripheral endings of sensory nerve fibers. All pain receptors are of this type. Although the largest proportion of free nerve endings are receptors for pain, functionally different free nerve endings apparently exist, not distinguishable anatomically, which are sensitive to crude touch, pressure, itch, and temperature. *Meissner's corpuscles* (Fig. 9–11), receptors for discrete touch, are especially numerous in the upper dermis of the hands, feet, lips, and nipples, and in the mucous membrane of the tip of the tongue. Other touch receptors include *Merkel's discs*, found in great numbers in the deepest epidermal layer of fingertips, and the end organs of hair (basketlike arrangements of nerve fibers around hair follicles). *Pacinian corpuscles* are very large receptors sensitive to deep pressure. They are widely distributed in such areas as the deep layers of the skin and under

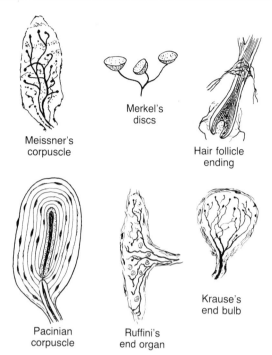

Meissner's corpuscle

Merkel's discs

Hair follicle ending

Pacinian corpuscle

Ruffini's end organ

Krause's end bulb

Figure 9–11. Six sensory receptors. The muscle spindle is shown in Figure 9–68.

mucous and serous membranes. *Krause's end bulbs*, found in the upper dermis, and *Ruffini's end organs*, found deep in the dermis and other connective tissues, have traditionally been described as cold and warmth receptors, respectively. However, careful examination of regions of the skin where response to cold or warmth has been aroused does not reveal specific receptors of this kind. These structures, especially Ruffini's end organs, may function as receptors for touch and pressure. Ruffini's end organs are also located in joint capsules, where they are kinesthetic receptors. Other kinesthetic receptors are the *Golgi tendon receptors* and Pacinian corpuscles in tissues in and around joints.

A characteristic property of receptors is their *adaptation to stimulation*. This means that the frequency of impulses declines with the continued application of a stimulus of constant strength. Consequently, the sensation decreases in intensity and may disappear. In the case of *rapidly adapting receptors*, such as the Pacinian corpuscle and some of the touch receptors, namely, the hair receptors and Meissner's corpuscles, the impulses are extinguished within a second or less. Such receptors can provide information

about changes in or movement of stimuli. Pacinian corpuscles, for example, which adapt to extinction within a few hundredths of a second, can detect high frequency vibrations. *Poorly adapting receptors* adapt slowly and not to extinction. Pain receptors are an example of poorly adapting receptors that continue to transmit impulses as long as they are stimulated. Other poorly adapting receptors are the muscle spindle, Ruffini's end organs, Merkel's discs and the receptors for blood pressure, oxygen, and carbon dioxide.

Classification of Nerve Fibers

Nerve fibers can be classified according to diameter (including the myelin sheath) and velocity of conduction. Type A fibers are myelinated and are subclassified (from the largest and fastest conductors to the smallest and slowest conductors) as A-α, A-β, A-γ and A-δ. Type B fibers are also myelinated but are slightly smaller than the A-δ fibers, and are the preganglionic fibers of the autonomic nervous system (see page 294). Type C fibers are very small, nonmyelinated fibers with the slowest conduction rates.

Impulses from the primary sensory endings of muscle spindles are transmitted by A-α fibers (diameter, 13–20 μ; velocity, 70–120 meters/sec.). Receptors for discrete touch (Meissner's corpuscles and Merkel's discs), deep pressure, and kinesthesia are innervated by A-β fibers (diameter, 8–13 μ; velocity, 40–70 meters/sec.). Reception for cold is associated with A-δ fibers (diameter, 1–4 μ; velocity, 5–15 meters/sec.) and for warmth with C fibers (diameter, 0.2–1 μ; velocity, 0.5–1.5 meters/sec.). Pain is transmitted by two kinds of fibers: A-δ fibers, which transmit "fast" pain, and C fibers, which transmit "slow" pain. Pain is frequently sensed in two phases — an immediate, sharp, localized, painful sensation followed by a more diffuse burning sensation that may persist and become unbearable. The former is associated with A-δ fibers, the latter with C fibers. Aching pain, arising from deep structures and the viscera (often felt on the body surface), is also transmitted by C fibers.

Motor Fibers. Motoneuron fibers, whose branches terminate at the neuromuscular junction, are type A-α. Efferent fibers innervating the muscle spindle are A-γ. These fibers (so-called gamma efferents) control the sensitivity of the muscle spindle (see page 301 for details). As mentioned, preganglionic fibers of the autonomic nervous system are type B. Postganglionic autonomic fibers are type C.

✗ CENTRAL NERVOUS SYSTEM

The *central nervous system*, as mentioned in the beginning of this chapter, includes the brain and spinal cord (Fig. 9–12). It is divided grossly into gray and white matter. **Gray matter** is so called because of its appearance and the preponderance of nerve cell bodies and true dendrites. **White matter**, on the other hand, is composed chiefly of myelinated nerve fibers — white in gross appearance — and few, if any, nerve cell bodies. In the spinal cord an H-shaped central region of gray matter is surrounded by white matter. In the brain the gray matter is broken into clumps or is present as a surface layer (cortex) of the cerebrum and cerebellum.

The term **nucleus,** when applied to the nervous system, designates a mass of gray matter in any part of the brain or spinal cord. **Ganglion** also means a cluster of nerve cell bodies and dendrites, but usually refers to those cells located outside the brain and spinal cord.

THE BRAIN

The first mention of the term *brain* is found in the Egyptian scrolls of papyrus. Historically, the Greeks did not have a word for the brain. Owing to rhythmic movements which seemed closely related with what occurred in the mind, they placed its location in the midriff, since the rhythm of breathing is closely related to mental states.

The word brain actually refers to that part of the central nervous system contained within the skull. It is the most complex and largest mass of nervous tissue in the body and contains literally billions of nerve cells. It has been estimated that an electron tube computer would have to be the size of a New York City skyscraper to contain the equipment in the 3 pounds or so of the human brain.

The weight of the brain is an indication of growth which, in early life, depends on enlargement of cells and their processes, an increase in the neuroglial constituents, and myelinization of the nerve fibers. The average weight of the human brain in the adult is approximately 1380 grams in the male and 1250 grams in the female. The brain grows rapidly up to the fifth year of life and stops growing after the age of 20. During old age, the weight of the brain decreases. When fully developed, the brain is a large organ filling the cranial cavity and applied closely to the inner wall of the skull. The brain is subdivided into three major areas (Fig. 9–13) which are, in turn, composed of subdivisions. These areas, arising during embryological development (Fig. 9–14), are the forebrain (prosencephalon), midbrain (mesencephalon), and hindbrain (rhombencephalon).

✗ I. Forebrain (prosencephalon)
   A. Cerebrum (telencephalon)
      1. Gray matter (cerebral cortex, the covering)
      2. White matter (core)
   B. Diencephalon
      1. Thalamus   *know Relationship to 3rd ventricle*
      2. Hypothalamus
II. Midbrain (mesencephalon)

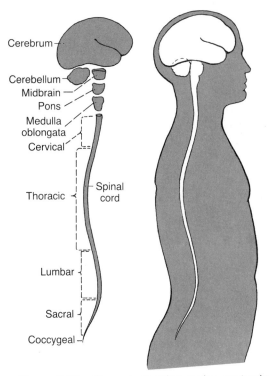

Figure 9–12. Diagram showing major anatomic divisions of the central nervous system.

Cerebrum

Cerebellum
Midbrain
Pons
Medulla oblongata
Cervical

Thoracic

Spinal cord

Lumbar

Sacral

Coccygeal

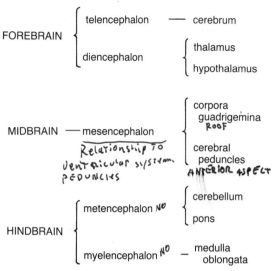

FOREBRAIN
- telencephalon — cerebrum
- diencephalon
  - thalamus
  - hypothalamus

MIDBRAIN — mesencephalon
- corpora guadrigemina *ROOF*
- cerebral peduncles *ANTERIOR ASPECT*

Relationship to Ventricular system. PEDUNCLES

HINDBRAIN
- metencephalon *NO*
  - cerebellum
  - pons
- myelencephalon *NO* — medulla oblongata

Figure 9–13. Major subdivisions of the brain.

III. Hindbrain (rhombencephalon)
A. Pons
B. Medulla
C. Cerebellum

The term *brain stem* refers to those parts of the brain remaining after removal of the cerebrum and cerebellum.

Forebrain

#Cerebrum *ALL ON EXAM*

The cerebrum (Figs. 9–15 to 9–17) is the largest portion of the brain, representing approximately seven-eighths of its total weight. Nerve centers governing all sensory and motor activities, as well as poorly defined areas which determine reason, memory, and intelligence, are located in the cerebrum.

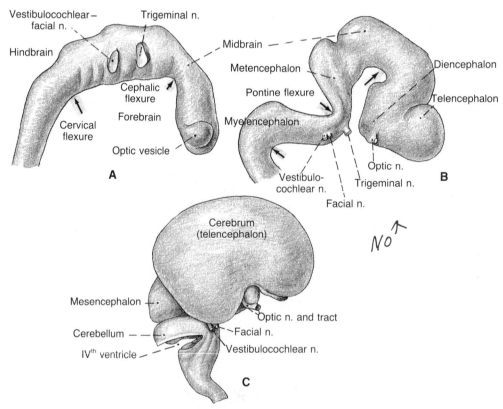

NO↑

Figure 9–14. *Embryologic development of the brain.* Three primary brain vesicles can be recognized: the forebrain (prosencephalon), the midbrain (mesencephalon), and the hindbrain (rhombencephalon). *A* and *B* show development at about 3 weeks and 6 weeks, respectively. Ultimately the forebrain subdivides into the telencephalon and the diencephalon, the midbrain remains the mesencephalon, and the rhombencephalon becomes the metencephalon and myelencephalon. *C* shows the brain at approximately 11 weeks of development.

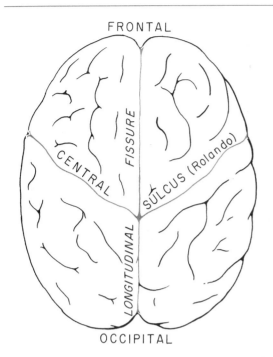

Figure 9–15. Major fissures of the brain, superior view.

With the increase in brain size occurring during embryonic development, the area of cortical gray matter expands out of all proportion and volume to the white matter upon which it rests. As a result, the surface rolls and folds upon itself. Each bulge produced in this manner is called a **gyrus** or convolution. These gyri do not occur haphazardly but are present in a distinguishable pattern. If the intervening furrow is shallow, it is called a **sulcus**; if it is deep, it is referred to as a **fissure**.

The *longitudinal fissure*, extending from the posterior aspect to the anterior border of the cerebrum, almost completely divides it into two **cerebral hemispheres**. Each hemisphere, with a full set of centers for sensory, motor, and other activities, appears to be the mirror image of the other. However, the cerebrum is not fully symmetrical in its functioning. For example, most people favor the right hand, whose movements are for the most part controlled by the left hemisphere, and language ability in most people resides mainly in the left hemisphere.

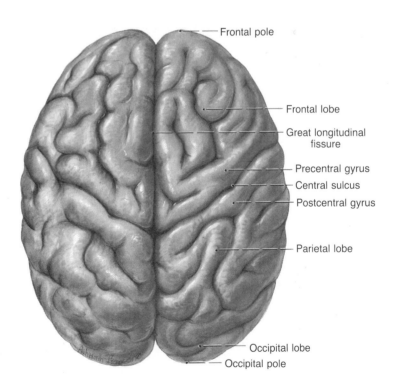

Figure 9–16. Superior view of the brain.

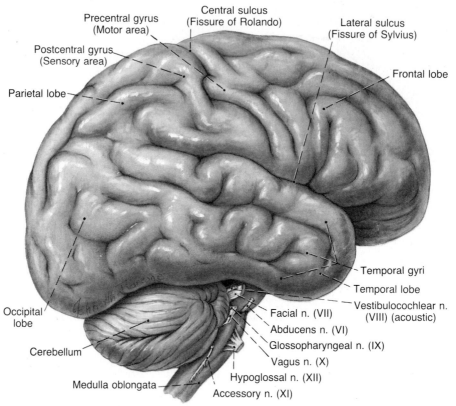

Figure 9–17. Right side of the brain showing cerebrum, cerebellum, and spinal cord. Several cranial nerves are seen.

Fiber tracts connecting the two hemispheres are called **commissural fiber tracts** The *corpus callosum* (the "great cerebral commissure") is the largest of the commissural tracts (Figs. 9–18 and 9–19). Its size and position suggest that its function is crucial to the proper performance of the cerebrum. If the corpus callosum is divided in two, an organism with two mental units is created, each with its own will competing for control over the whole. The corpus callosum allows information to be passed from one hemisphere to the other.

Association fiber tracts connect parts of the same hemisphere. They may be short, connecting adjoining gyri, or long, connecting distant gyri. Connecting the cortex with other parts of the brain and the spinal cord are **projection fiber tracts.**

Each hemisphere possesses six major sulci (Figs. 9–20 and 9–21).

The *lateral sulcus* (fissure of Sylvius) sweeps backward above the temporal lobe and continues over the superolateral surface almost horizontally backward.

The *central sulcus* (fissure of Rolando) commences at the midpoint of the superior border and extends inferiorly toward the lateral sulcus, separating the frontal and parietal lobes.

The *sulcus cinguli* is a prominent sulcus on the medial surface of the hemisphere, extending anteroposteriorly parallel to the corpus callosum.

The *calcarine sulcus* and the *parieto-occipital sulcus* traverse the posterior part of the medial surface of the hemisphere, converging (the parieto-occipital from above, the calcarine from below) to meet a short distance from the posterior end of the corpus callosum.

The *collateral sulcus* runs parallel to the medial border.

Cerebral Cortex. The cerebral cortex is the gray outer layer of the cerebrum (Fig. 9–22). Even before knowledge of the microscopic anatomy of the cortex was available, feeble attempts were made to discern the function of the cerebral cortex. During the Renaissance, for instance, physicians spec-

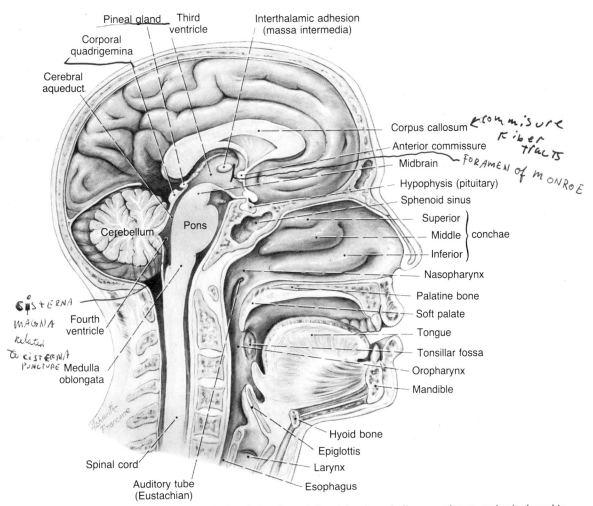

Pineal gland Third ventricle

Corporal quadrigemina

Interthalamic adhesion (massa intermedia)

Cerebral aqueduct

Corpus callosum *Kommisure Fiber tracts*

Anterior commissure

Midbrain *FORAMEN of MONROE*

Hypophysis (pituitary)

Sphenoid sinus

Cerebellum   Pons

Superior

Middle } conchae

Inferior

Nasopharynx

Palatine bone

CISTERNA MAGNA Related to CISTERNA PUNCTURE

Fourth ventricle

Soft palate

Tongue

Tonsillar fossa

Oropharynx

Mandible

Medulla oblongata

Spinal cord

Hyoid bone

Epiglottis

Auditory tube (Eustachian)

Larynx

Esophagus

Figure 9–18. Sagittal section through the head showing relationship of cerebellum, cerebrum, and spinal cord to other parts of the head and neck.

ulated as to the nature of the "seat of intelligence." One of the earliest truly revealing insights into the organization of the cortex was the recognition in the second half of the 19th century, as a result of clinical and experimental observations, that the cortex can be divided into regions having different functions. Paul Broca in the 1860's correlated injury to a specific region of the cortex (third frontal gyrus in the left hemisphere) with a loss of speech. In 1870 Gustav Fritsch and Eduard Hitzig reported that electrical stimulation of the cerebral cortex of dogs just anterior to the central sulcus elicited muscle twitches on the side of the body opposite the site of stimulation. Three years later similar observations were made in monkeys. These experiments confirmed a conclusion already

drawn by the British neurologist Hughlings Jackson, who had noted that an irritative lesion in the cerebral cortex on one side of the brain could cause epileptic movements on the opposite side of the body. (At that time the notion that the cerebral cortex had anything to do with movements of the body was startling, since it was generally believed that the cerebral cortex was exclusively the repository of thoughts.) Gradually an accumulation of experimental and clinical findings, especially correlations of the kind made by Broca between injury to a specific part of the brain and a given defect, such as numbness or blindness, led to the charting of the most obvious functional areas.

In 1909 K. Brodmann described six cell layers of the cerebral cortex and divided the

Associate Broca with speech

Brodmann – mapping Areas

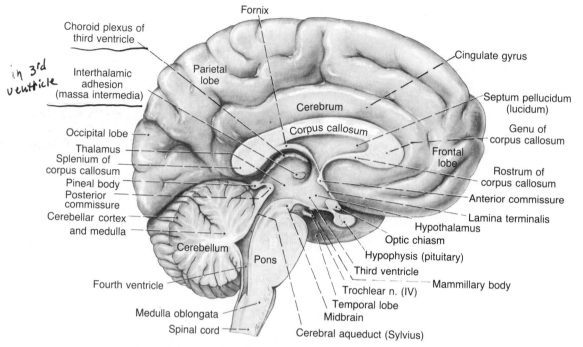

in 3rd ventricle

Figure 9–19. Sagittal view of the left half of the brain and spinal cord.

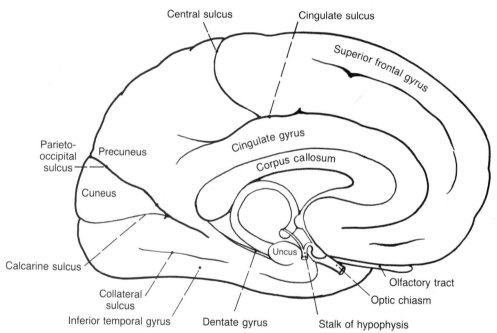

Figure 9–20. Major landmarks of the medial portion of the left cerebral hemisphere.

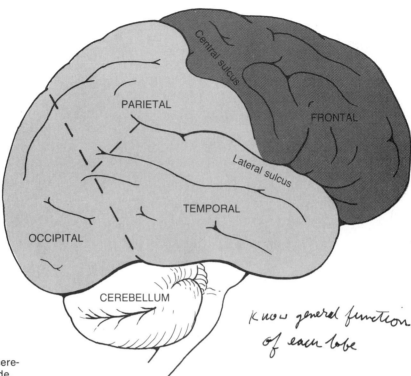

Central sulcus

PARIETAL

FRONTAL

Lateral sulcus

TEMPORAL

OCCIPITAL

CEREBELLUM

Know general function of each lobe

Figure 9–21. Lobes of the cerebral cortex, lateral view, right side.

cortex into 52 areas (each designated by number) on the basis of variations in these layers (Fig. 9–23). Brodmann maps provided convenient reference guides to the cortex and are still used today to identify specific cortical areas, especially when there is an approximate correspondence between functional areas and Brodmann-numbered areas.

Division of the cortex into *lobes* is also a convenience, since they serve as useful reference points for discussion. These lobes bear the name of the overlying bones of the skull, and include the frontal, parietal, temporal, and occipital lobes (Figs. 9–21 and 9–22).

FRONTAL LOBE. The frontal lobe includes all the cortex lying anterior to the central sulcus and above the lateral sulcus. **Areas 4 and 6** of Brodmann, the major motor areas, are located in this lobe. *Area 4*, referred to by some authors as the motor cortex or primary motor cortex, is a band of cortex just anterior to the central sulcus occupying most of the precentral gyrus. Discrete movements involving an individual muscle or a small number of muscles are initiated by stimulating specific loci in this area (this is

the region examined by Fritsch and Hitzig in their pioneering studies published in 1870). Wilder Penfield and colleagues at the Montreal Institute of Neurology mapped this area in humans by electrical stimulation during neurosurgery. The parts of the body are in a general way represented in an inverted order, and the amount of cortex represented is proportional to the dexterity with which the movement is performed (Fig. 9–24). *Area 6*, called the premotor cortex by some authors, is immediately anterior to area 4. Since areas 4 and 6 are closely related functionally and are linked by intracortical fibers, some authors refer to the two areas collectively as the precentral motor area. Area 6, however, appears to be more concerned with gross rather than delicate, precise movements, which depend upon the integrity of area 4.

Histologically, areas 4 and 6 are characterized by a preponderance of large *pyramidal cells* (named for the shape of their cell bodies) and a small number of *granule cells* (so named because of their small size). The very largest of the pyramidal cells (discovered by the Russian anatomist Vladimir Betz

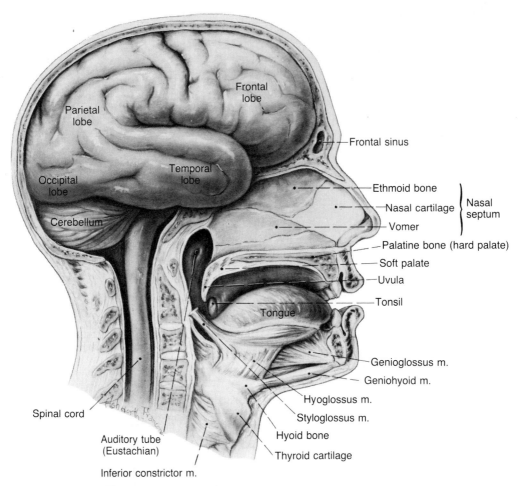

Figure 9–22. Sagittal section through the head (brain intact).

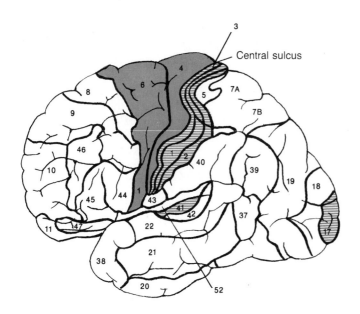

Figure 9–23. Superolateral view of the left cerebral hemisphere showing the areas designated numerically by Brodmann based upon differences in the appearance of cell layers of the cortex in these areas. The areas colored red (4 and 6) correspond approximately to the major motor areas. The areas corresponding approximately to the major sensory areas have red lines: somatosensory (3, 1 and 2); visuosensory (17); and auditosensory (41).

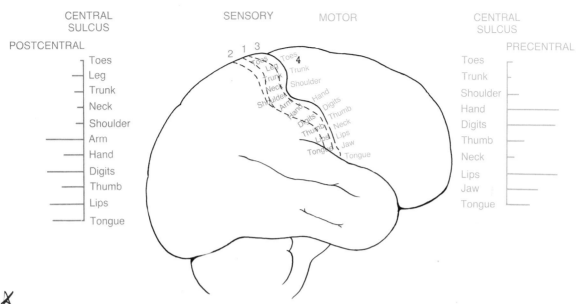

CENTRAL SULCUS

SENSORY   MOTOR

CENTRAL SULCUS

POSTCENTRAL

PRECENTRAL

Toes
Leg
Trunk
Neck
Shoulder
Arm
Hand
Digits
Thumb
Lips
Tongue

Toes
Trunk
Shoulder
Hand
Digits
Thumb
Neck
Lips
Jaw
Tongue

Figure 9–24. Lateral view of the brain showing the representation of the parts of the body in the somesthetic and primary motor areas. The amount of brain surface related to a specific part of the body is proportional not to the size of the body part but to sensory discrimination or dexterity in its use, as illustrated diagrammatically.

in 1874 and known as the *giant cells of Betz*) are concentrated in area 4. The axons of the pyramidal cells are the principal output of the motor cortex (the pathways for motor function are described on page 309).

Another area concerned mainly with motor activity, called the *supplementary motor area*, occupies the major part of the medial wall of the frontal lobe. Its function has not been well defined.

The region of the frontal lobe just anterior to area 6 and not sharply differentiated from it, corresponding approximately to area 8 of Brodmann, is known as the *frontal eye field*. Stimulation here causes the eyes and head to turn away from the side stimulated. Opening and closing of the eyelids and dilation of the pupils may also be elicited.

Also located in the frontal lobe is Broca's speech area, which corresponds approximately to area 44 of Brodmann (see page 317 for a discussion of the cortical mechanisms for speech and language comprehension).

Much of the cerebral cortex in front of areas 8 and 44 is known as the prefrontal cortex, also referred to as the orbitofrontal cortex. This area is concerned with emotional behavior and subtle kinds of mental processing (for a discussion of this area, see page 316).

PARIETAL LOBE. This lobe extends from the central sulcus about four-fifths of the way around the cortex and joins the occipital lobe at the posterior aspect of the brain. Located in the parietal lobe are *areas 3, 1, and 2* of Brodmann, a band of cortex in the postcentral gyrus (behind the central sulcus) which receives sensory input for touch, pressure, temperature, and kinesthesia from all parts of the body and is known as the *somesthetic area*. Electrical stimulation of specific loci in this area in conscious patients undergoing surgery arouses sensations (usually described as tingling) in localized parts of the body, usually opposite to the side of the brain stimulated. By means of such stimulation this area has been mapped and, as in the case of the primary motor area, the parts of the body are represented in general in an inverted order. The amount of cortical representation is proportional to the sensory discrimination in the particular part of the body.

The histological features of the somesthetic cortex are the opposite of the motor cortex — it has a large number of granule cells and few pyramidal cells.

TEMPORAL LOBE. This lobe lies beneath the lateral sulcus. The primary sensory receptive area for auditory impulses (the *au-*

ditosensory area), which coincides with *area 41* of Brodmann, is found in the temporal lobe. Inferior and posterior to the auditosensory area are the correlative areas for auditory input (including Wernicke's language area, described on page 317).

General functions → OCCIPITAL LOBE. The occipital lobe occupies the posterior segment of the cerebral hemisphere. Actually no true separation exists between the occipital lobe and the parietal and temporal lobes, although the parieto-occipital sulcus is considered the anterior margin. Area 17, the primary cortical sensory area for vision (the *visuosensory area*), and adjacent areas 18 and 19, correlative areas for visual sensory information, are found in the occipital lobe.

know what it is PROJECTION AREAS. Portions of the cortex that have become specialized for dispatch of motor directives (principally areas 4 and 6) and for reception of sensory messages (including areas 3, 1, and 2, somatosensory; 41, auditosensory; and 17, visuosensory) have traditionally been called *projection areas*. Some authors object to this designation because the projection of fibers from or to the cortex is not limited to these classically described projection areas. On the other hand, since they are the major cortical input and output areas, they perhaps should in

some way be distinguished from the remainder of the cortex. It has also become apparent that the postcentral somatosensory area contributes to motor projection tracts and the precentral motor area receives sensory projection fibers. Nonetheless, the designations sensory and motor are in accord with the basic functions of these areas, although some authors refer to the two areas together as the sensorimotor cortex.

know what it is ASSOCIATION AREAS. The brain must possess memory to relate information of the moment with that of the past and to recognize its significance. This involves functional correction, repeated exchanges of data, and synthesis of data. Such elaborate functions of the cortex are performed by the association areas. More than three-fourths of the cerebral cortex is occupied by association areas. Although these areas also receive and give rise to projection fibers, their principal function is to integrate information received from various sources.

The Basal Ganglia
← what it Does ← Parkinsons diseas

The basal ganglia (Figs. 9–25 and 9–26) are four paired masses of gray matter embedded in the white matter of the cerebral hemispheres. The basal ganglia include the cau-

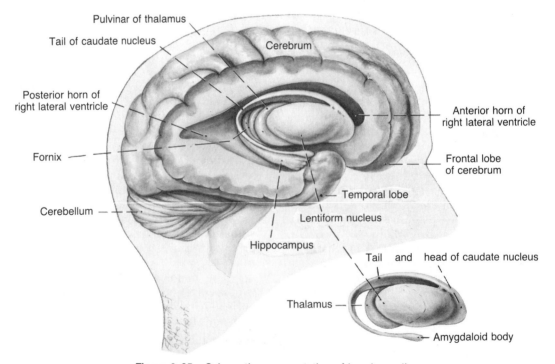

Figure 9–25. Schematic representation of basal ganglia.

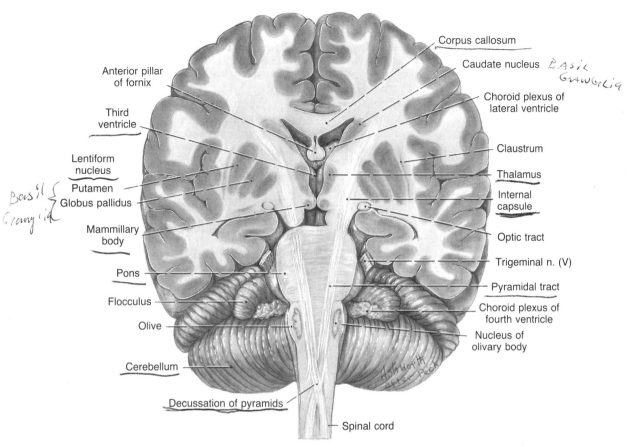

Basal Ganglia (handwritten, right of "Caudate nucleus")

Basil Ganglia (handwritten, left of "Putamen/Globus pallidus")

Corpus callosum
Caudate nucleus
Choroid plexus of lateral ventricle
Claustrum
Thalamus
Internal capsule
Optic tract
Trigeminal n. (V)
Pyramidal tract
Choroid plexus of fourth ventricle
Nucleus of olivary body

Anterior pillar of fornix
Third ventricle
Lentiform nucleus
Putamen
Globus pallidus
Mammillary body
Pons
Flocculus
Olive
Cerebellum
Decussation of pyramids
Spinal cord

Figure 9–26. Frontal or coronal section through the brain showing basal ganglia and brainstem. Note decussation of the corticospinal (pyramidal) tract just prior to entering the spinal cord.

date nucleus (medial portion) and the putamen and globus pallidus (lateral portion), collectively called the lentiform nucleus. These nuclei, together with the white matter separating them, constitute the *corpus striatum* (Latin for striped body), so named for its banded appearance. The large mass of fibers constituting the white matter is called the *internal capsule*. It contains fibers leading to and from the cerebral cortex that connect the cortex to the rest of the brain and spinal cord. Fibers fanning out from the internal capsule to various parts of the cortex are known as the *corona radiata*. If a small blood vessel in the area ruptures (not uncommon in this region), an interference with the efferent tracts descending from the cortex can occur, with resultant paralysis. The basal ganglia play an important role in the control of motor function, and injury to them produces either unilateral or bilateral signs, including tremor, rigidity, and uncontrolled,

aimless movements. The functions of the basal ganglia are further discussed in the description of the extrapyramidal system on page 311. *Know what its relation is in studying the brain*

NO

Electroencephalograms (EEG) — Electrical Activity of the Cerebral Cortex

Human brain cells generate electrical potentials that can be measured through the skull and are the basis of electroencephalography, a clinical diagnostic procedure used as an aid in diagnosis of epilepsy, brain tumor, hemorrhage, and other disorders. The electroencephalogram is recorded by placing electrodes on the individual's head. The EEG varies from the asynchronous, high frequency, low voltage waves of the mentally active or excited state (*beta waves*; 15–60 cycles/sec., 5–10 microvolts) through the more rhythmic, lower frequency, higher voltage activity of the relaxed state (*alpha waves*;

8–10 cycles/sec., about 50 microvolts) to the slow, large waves of deep sleep (synchronized cortical activity — *delta waves*; 1–5 cycles/sec., 20–200 microvolts). (Alpha, beta, and delta waves are illustrated in Fig. 9–27.) The alpha rhythm of the inattentive brain, usually recorded with the eyes closed, will be replaced by beta activity by simply opening the eyes in bright light. Slow, large waves are seen in the awake state only in early childhood. Their occurrence in adults other than during sleep is an indication of some brain disorder.

In the course of a night's sleep, episodes occur during which the eyes dart back and forth (although the muscles are in general relaxed), dreaming occurs, and the EEG shows characteristics of the awake state (beta-type activity) and light sleep (rhythms slower than alpha, faster than delta — sometimes called theta waves). Hence, it is generally recognized that there are two kinds of sleep: (1) **REM sleep** (for rapid eye movements) and (2) **non-REM,** or **NREM, sleep** (divided into four progressively deeper stages, each associated with a characteristic EEG pattern). The sleeper during REM episodes has been likened to an almost motionless spectator at a theater, scanning the scene with back and forth eye movements. Occasionally, body movements, usually related to dream content, are observed during REM sleep. NREM and REM sleep alternate through the night, REM sleep adding up to a total of about one and a half hours, that is, about 20 per cent of a normal night's sleep. REM sleep apparently serves some essential function because, when sleep is monitored and subjects are awakened at the start of REM episodes for several successive nights so as to reduce the total REM sleep time, the subjects will catch up on their REM sleep during the recovery period. REM sleep time increases by about 25 per cent during the first night of the recovery period and gradually returns to normal on succeeding nights. Curtailment of REM sleep produces anxiety, irritability, and increased appetite. These symptoms disappear when REM sleep is no longer interrupted.

Sleep and the wakeful state appear to depend upon a balance between two opposing systems. One, the *reticular activating system* (pages 260 and 305), is responsible for arousal and maintaining the awake state. The other, a series of so-called *hypnogenic zones* in the medulla, pons, midbrain, hypothalamus and thalamus, appears to be responsible for inducing sleep, according to some authorities by inhibiting the reticular activating system.

The Diencephalon

The thalamus and hypothalamus constitute the diencephalon and are located in the forebrain along with the cerebrum.

The Thalamus. The *thalamus*, a paired structure, consists of large masses of gray matter located below the corpus callosum, joined in the midline by the *intermediate mass* (interthalamic adhesion). It is a relay center for all kinds of sensory impulses (except olfactory impulses) as they travel from the peripheral sensory receptors to the sensory areas of the cerebral cortex. The crude identification of stimuli as pain, variation of temperature, or touch is the result of thalamic integrations. (For further details see description of sensory pathways to the brain on page 303.)

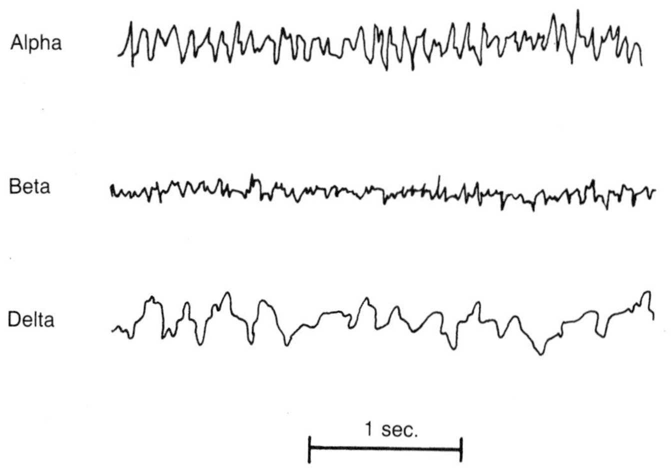

Alpha

Beta

Delta

1 sec.

Figure 9–27. Principal types of normal EEG waves.

Besides its sensory activities, the thalamus is functionally interrelated with the major motor centers. It occupies a position between the cerebral motor cortex and the cerebellum, and also between the cerebral motor cortex and the basal ganglia, and relays efferent impulses from these centers to the motor cortex. Impulses passing from the hypothalamus to the prefrontal area of the cerebral cortex also are relayed in the thalamus and serve in the integration of emotional behavior. (Emotional behavior is further discussed on page 314.)

> **The Hypothalamus** (Fig. 9–19). The hypothalamus lies beneath the thalamus. Mainly through studies of laboratory animals, the hypothalamus has been found to be concerned with the regulation of peripheral autonomic nervous system discharges accompanying behavior and emotional expression (page 299). In addition, the hypothalamus has centers for regulating body water and electrolyte concentrations (page 529), body temperature (page 515), and feeding activities (page 507). It also manufactures hormones of the neurohypophysis (posterior pituitary gland) and controls secretion by both the posterior and the anterior pituitary, and thus has an important role in regulating endocrine functions and in maintaining normal sexual behavior and reproduction (page 545). The pituitary gland is attached to the hypothalamus by a narrow stalk, the *infundibulum.* The area of the hypothalamus adjacent to the infundibulum is called the *tuber cinereum*. In the posterior part of the hypothalamus is a pair of rounded *mammillary bodies.*

Mesencephalon (Midbrain)

The midbrain is found between the forebrain and the hindbrain. Several nuclear masses are located on its posterior surface, the tectum (Latin for roof), above the cerebral aqueduct (Fig. 9–18). Four of these nuclear masses are present as small elevations: the upper two, or *superior colliculi*, are involved in visual reflexes, especially the coordination of tracking movements (described in Chapter 10, on page 337), and the lower two, or *inferior colliculi*, are associated with hearing. The four are known collectively as the *corpora quadrigemina.* Two large, diverging stalks emerging ventrally from each half of the cerebrum form the anterior part of the midbrain. The stalks are called *cerebral pe-duncles;* they constitute the main motor connection between the forebrain and the hindbrain. The midportion of the mesencephalon, known as the *tegmentum,* contains important efferent and afferent pathways. The tegmentum also contains the *red nucleus,* which is connected with the cerebellum. This nucleus is involved in motor movement and postural reflex patterns.

Hindbrain

Cerebellum (Fig. 9–26). The cerebellum occupies the posterior cranial fossa. It is separated from the cerebral hemispheres by the *tentorium cerebelli* (see p. 261).

The cerebellum is oval in shape, with a central constriction and lateral expanded portions. The constricted central portion is called the *vermis* (Latin for worm) and the lateral expanded portions the *hemispheres*. The cerebellum resembles the cerebrum in structure, with the gray matter forming a layer of cortex placed on the surface rather than centrally located, as in the spinal cord. Cross section of the cerebellum reveals its patterns of folds and fissures outlined by white matter, which led anatomists of the medieval period to give the cerebellar white matter the name *arbor vitae* (Latin for tree of life).

The cerebellum is divided into lobes by deep and distinct fissures. These lobes include the anterior, posterior, and flocculonodular lobes. The *anterior* and *posterior lobes* are concerned with the function of movement; the *flocculonodular lobe* is concerned with the function of equilibrium. The cerebellum is connected by afferent and efferent pathways with all other parts of the central nervous system. In general, the cerebellum greatly aids the motor cortex of the cerebral hemispheres in the *integration* of voluntary movement. The role of the cerebellum is further discussed on page 311.

The Pons (Figs. 9–19 and 9–26). The pons lies anterior to the cerebellum and between the midbrain and medulla. On its ventral surface is a midline groove for the basilar artery. As the name implies, the pons is a bridgelike structure, consisting almost entirely of white matter linking the various parts of the brain and serving as a relay station from the medulla to the higher cortical centers. There are also several important nuclear groups for the cranial nerves.

✗ Medulla Oblongata (Fig. 9–19). The medulla oblongata is continuous with the spinal cord on one end and with the pons on the other. It lies ventral to the cerebellum, and its posterior aspect forms the floor of the fourth ventricle (the ventricles of the brain are described on this page). On the ventral surface of the medulla are the *pyramids,* which, as the name implies, are pyramid-shaped tracts. These tracts are a posterior continuation of a portion of the tracts that constitute the cerebral peduncles of the midbrain (other tracts of the cerebral peduncles lead to the cerebellum via the pons). The pyramidal tracts are the pathways for initiating skillful movements of skeletal muscles (see discussion of the pyramidal system on page 310). Two prominent nuclei, the *nucleus gracilis* and *nucleus cuneatus,* are located on the posterior portion of the medulla. It is in these nuclei that fibers from the corresponding tracts in the cord (described on page 304) synapse. Externally, the medulla resembles the upper part of the spinal cord. Consequently, it is often called the spinal bulb; but the medulla is thicker than the cord and consists of central gray matter broken into more or less distinct nests of cell bodies, or nuclear masses, with columns of white matter interwoven among the nuclei. All the afferent and efferent tracts of the spinal cord are represented in the medulla, and many of these decussate, or cross, from one side to the other, whereas others terminate. The medulla has a number of vital regulatory and reflex centers, including those controlling the circulatory system (page 386), breathing (page 464), swallowing (page 496), vomiting (page 497), coughing, and sneezing (page 467).

Reticular Formation. Scattered throughout the area of the midbrain, pons, medulla, hypothalamus, and thalamus are numerous large and small neurons related to each other by small processes. These neurons and their fibers constitute the reticular formation. They are not often collected into distinct nuclei; but the lateral reticular and inferior olivary nuclei are exceptions in that they are readily identified as nuclear groups. The reticular formation is capable of modifying the reflex activity of the spinal neurons. It is essential for cortical activities, such as initiating and maintaining wakefulness; hence it is often called an activating system. Injury to this system can result in unconsciousness. (The functions of the retic-

ular formation are further explained in connection with the description of sensory and motor pathways on pages 305 and 310.)

Ventricles of the Brain

At an early stage, the embryonic central nervous system is a hollow *neural tube.* The brain develops as an expansion of the superior end of this tube with the formation of cavities, called *ventricles,* continuous with the central canal of the spinal cord, the remnant of the embryonic neural tube. The ventricular system (Figs. 9–28 to 9–30) includes two lateral ventricles, the third ventricle, the cerebral aqueduct, and the fourth ventricle. The **lateral ventricles** are inside the cerebral hemispheres. Each possesses a posterior, anterior, and inferior portion (horn). The posterior horn extends into the occipital lobe, the anterior horn into the frontal lobe, and the inferior horn into the temporal lobe. The lateral ventricles are separated from each other by a thin, translucent partition, the *septum pellucidum* (Fig. 9–19). Each lateral ventricle communicates with the third ventricle by way of an **interventricular foramen** (foramen of Monro — foramen is the Latin word for opening). The **third ventricle** is a small, slitlike cavity in the center of the diencephalon continuous with the **cerebral aqueduct of Sylvius,** a canal which passes lengthwise through the midbrain between the cerebral peduncles and the corpora quadrigemina to connect the third and fourth ventricles. The **fourth ventricle** lies between the cerebellum on the posterior side and the pons and medulla on the anterior side.

Meninges

Three membranes collectively known as the meninges (singular, meninx) provide protection to the brain and spinal cord (Fig. 9–31). From outside in, these are the dura mater, arachnoid, and pia mater.

Dura Mater. The dura matter (Latin for hard mother), the outer meninx, is made of dense fibrous tissue. There are two portions of the dura, cranial and spinal. The cranial dura is arranged in two layers, closely connected except where they separate to form sinuses for the passage of venous blood. The outer *endosteal layer* is adherent to the bones of the skull and forms the internal periosteum. This layer terminates at the foramen

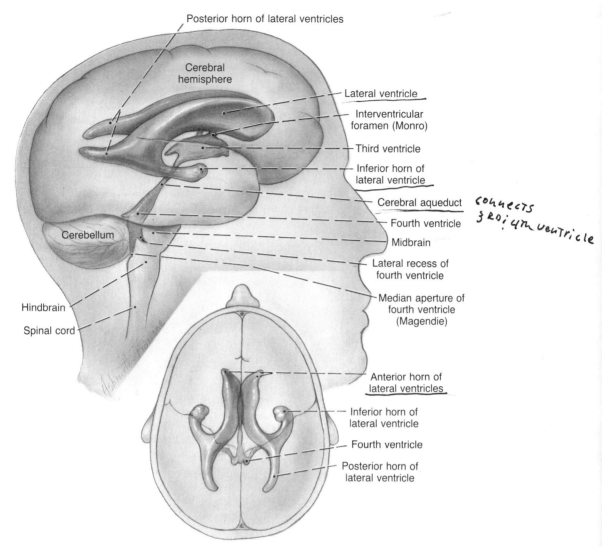

Posterior horn of lateral ventricles

Cerebral hemisphere

Lateral ventricle

Interventricular foramen (Monro)

Third ventricle

Inferior horn of lateral ventricle

Cerebral aqueduct *connects 3rd; 4th ventricle*

Fourth ventricle

Midbrain

Cerebellum

Lateral recess of fourth ventricle

Median aperture of fourth ventricle (Magendie)

Hindbrain

Spinal cord

Anterior horn of lateral ventricles

Inferior horn of lateral ventricle

Fourth ventricle

Posterior horn of lateral ventricle

Figure 9–28. Ventricular system, lateral and superior views.

magnum, and its place is taken by the periosteal lining of the vertebral canal. The inner, or *meningeal*, layer covers the brain and sends numerous prolongations inward for support and protection of the different lobes of the brain. The inner layer becomes continuous with the spinal dura mater.

Four extensions of the meningeal dura project into the cranial cavity: the falx cerebelli (between the two cerebellar hemispheres), the falx cerebri (in the longitudinal fissure separating the two cerebral hemispheres), the tentorium cerebelli (separating the cerebellum from the cerebrum), and the diaphragma sellae (overlying the pituitary gland). These projections also form the venous sinuses, situated between the endosteal and meningeal layers of the dura, which return blood from the brain to the blood

stream (the veins of the brain open into the sinuses).

The Arachnoid. The arachnoid is a delicate serous membrane located between the dura and pia. As the name implies, it has the microscopic appearance of a spider web. The cranial portion invests the brain loosely and, with the exception of the longitudinal fissure, it passes over the various convolutions and sulci and does not dip down into them. The spinal portion is tubular and surrounds the cord loosely. The **subarachnoid space** between the arachnoid and the pia is occupied by thin, delicate connective tissue trabeculae and intercommunicating channels in which cerebrospinal fluid is contained. Along the base of the brain, the pia and the arachnoid are separated to form the arachnoid cisternae.

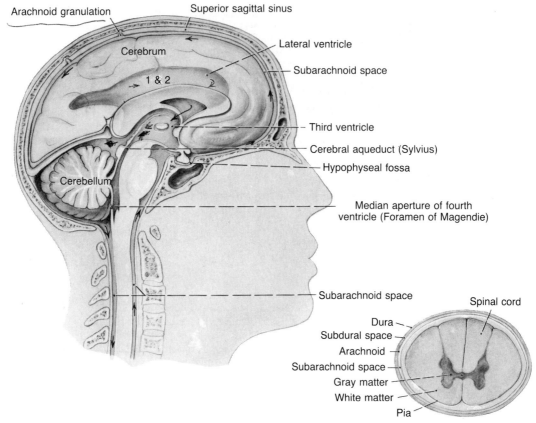

Figure 9–29. Circulation of cerebrospinal fluid in brain and spinal cord.

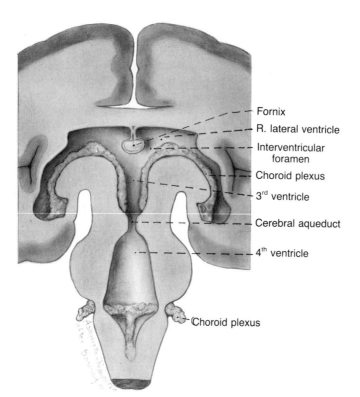

Figure 9–30. Diagrammatic representation of the ventricles of the brain. (From Basmajian, J. V.: *Primary Anatomy,* Sixth Edition, Baltimore, The Williams & Wilkins Co., 1970.)

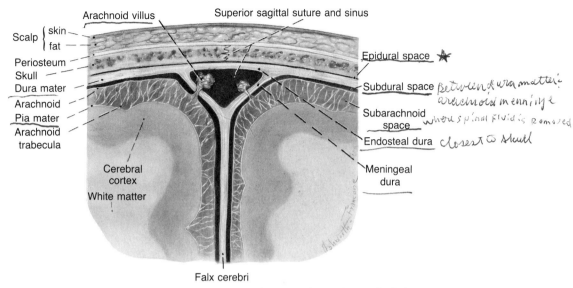

Scalp { skin / fat
Periosteum
Skull
Dura mater
Arachnoid
Pia mater
Arachnoid trabecula
Arachnoid villus
Superior sagittal suture and sinus
Cerebral cortex
White matter
Epidural space ✦
Subdural space *Between dura matter & arachnoid meninge*
Subarachnoid space *where spinal fluid is removed*
Endosteal dura *closest to skull*
Meningeal dura
Falx cerebri

Figure 9–31. Coronal section of skull, brain, meninges, and superior sagittal sinus.

The Pia Mater. The pia mater is a vascular membrane consisting of a plexus of fine blood vessels held together by areolar connective tissue. The cranial portion invests the surface of the brain and dips down between the convolutions; the spinal portion is thicker, less vascular, and closely adherent to the entire surface of the spinal cord, sending processes into the ventral fissure.

The pia mater extends below the spinal cord (which ends in a conelike formation, the conus medullaris, at about the second lumbar vertebra) as a slender filament called the **filum terminale** (Fig. 9–32). The filum terminale is surrounded at the upper two-thirds of its length by tubular extensions of the arachnoid and dura mater and is fused at its terminal third with an investing sheath of dura mater, called the coccygeal ligament, which blends with the periosteum of the coccyx. Cerebrospinal fluid (see below) can be conveniently obtained by tapping the subarachnoid space between the third and fourth lumbar vertebrae (Fig. 9–39).

Cerebrospinal Fluid

Cerebrospinal fluid (Fig. 9–29) *circulates within the ventricles, the central canal of the spinal cord and also within meshes of the subarachnoid space.* It is colorless, with a composition similar to that of lymph. It consists of water with traces of protein, glucose, lymphocytes and even some hormones.

The volume of cerebrospinal fluid is about 150 ml. The fluid serves as a water jacket to guard the brain and spinal cord against injury. It also provides buoyant support, and it has been calculated that a brain weighing 1500 grams in air weighs only 50 grams as it floats in the cerebrospinal fluid.

Cerebrospinal fluid is continuously formed in all four ventricles by active secretion, principally from the capillaries of the **choroid plexuses** (pouchlike projections of the pia mater into the ventricles covered with the ependymal lining of the ventricles). The fluid circulates (Fig. 9–29) from each lateral ventricle through an interventricular foramen into the third ventricle and then passes through the cerebral aqueduct into the fourth ventricle and spinal canal. It flows into the subarachnoid space from the fourth ventricle via three foramina — one medial aperture *(foramen of Magendie)*, and two lateral apertures *(foramina of Luschka)*. Cerebrospinal fluid drains from the subarachnoid space into the superior sagittal sinus through projections of the arachnoid into the sinus called **arachnoid villi** (Fig. 9–31).

NO **Hydrocephalus** (Fig. 9–33). Hydrocephalus is a condition that occurs when blockage of circulation of cerebrospinal fluid increases pressure on the surface of the brain or cord. It is not common for an increased formation of fluid to be responsible for this condition except in a tumor of the choroid plexus. Congenital hydrocephalus is spoken

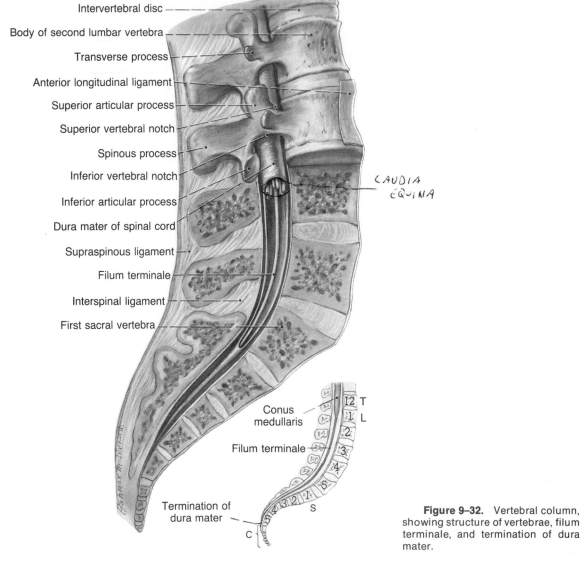

Intervertebral disc

Body of second lumbar vertebra

Transverse process

Anterior longitudinal ligament

Superior articular process

Superior vertebral notch

Spinous process

Inferior vertebral notch

Inferior articular process

Dura mater of spinal cord

Supraspinous ligament

Filum terminale

Interspinal ligament

First sacral vertebra

CAUDIA EQUINA

Conus medullaris

Filum terminale

T
L
S
C

Termination of dura mater

Figure 9–32. Vertebral column, showing structure of vertebrae, filum terminale, and termination of dura mater.

of as either communicating or noncommunicating, depending on whether there is transmission of fluid between the ventricles and subarachnoid spaces. Obstruction of the flow of fluid is probably the commonest cause of hydrocephalus. If this obstruction occurs before the time the sutures of the skull ordinarily close, the increased intracranial pressure produces an expansion of the brain and its coverings, with the entire head increasing progressively in size. The soft bones of the infant's skull are pushed apart, and compression of the cortex results, until only a paper-thin ribbon of cerebral tissue remains. Despite marked depression of the cerebral cortex, the nerve cells frequently show a remarkable capacity for survival.

Following closure of the sutures, the brain can no longer yield to increasing hydrocephalus, and changes in brain tissue are then more destructive.

The signs and symptoms of hydrocephalus can be evident at the time of birth. The head enlarges, the anterior fontanelle bulges, and the suture lines of the skull separate. The veins of the scalp dilate, becoming prominent.

Surgical treatment consists of shunting the cerebrospinal fluid from one compartment into another in the normal fluid pathways, or from the cerebrospinal fluid compartments to some other area of the body where it can be absorbed. One of the techniques is described in Figure 9–34.

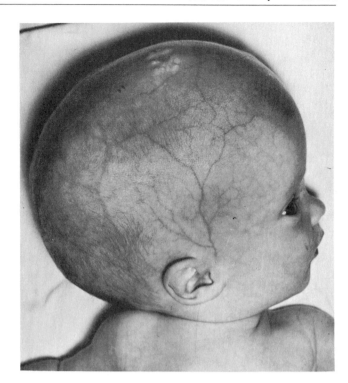

Figure 9–33. Child, age 4 months, with hydrocephalus.

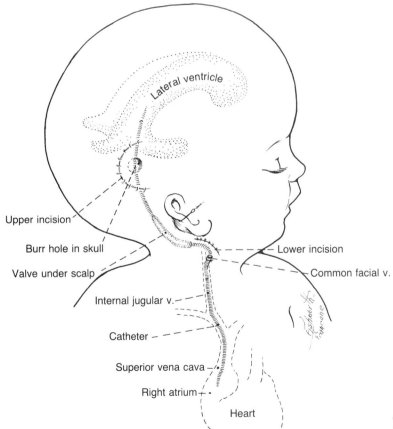

Upper incision

Burr hole in skull

Valve under scalp

Internal jugular v.

Catheter

Superior vena cava

Right atrium

Lateral ventricle

Lower incision

Common facial v.

Heart

Figure 9–34. Operative procedure for hydrocephalus in which a catheter drains the ventricular system into the right atrium.

Disorders Involving the Brain

NO **Meningitis.** Meningitis is an infection of the meninges. The diagnosis depends on a history of infection, the so-called meningeal signs (such as stiffness of the neck), and abnormalities in the spinal fluid. In small infants, manifestations of mild meningitis are sometimes masked for several days, with the symptoms suggesting an upper respiratory infection.

NO **Traumatic Head Injuries.** A common injury is one in which a rapidly moving blunt object strikes the head or the head is flung against a hard surface. Such blunt head injuries almost always result in at least brief loss of consciousness and, even though the skull is not penetrated or bone fragments driven into the cavity, the brain may suffer gross damage, e.g., contusion, laceration, hemorrhage, swelling, herniation. Crushing injuries or injury from high-velocity missiles may produce severe and often fatal damage without immediate loss of consciousness.

Concussion is defined as a transient state of paralysis of nervous function or loss of consciousness. Even when consciousness is not lost, in a few days symptoms may arise, including headache, dizziness, loss of self-confidence, nervousness, fatigue, inability to sleep, and depression. No account has been given of the mechanism of these symptoms.

Other symptoms may occur that are an indication of some process in addition to concussion; symptoms include delayed traumatic collapse, seizures, monoplegia or paraplegia, coma or acute drowsiness, confusion, or headache. The bases of these symptoms can be several, ranging from contusion, laceration, and local or generalized edema to epidural or subdural hemorrhage and hematomas.

Interestingly, many patients who suffer actual skull fractures do not have serious or prolonged disorder of cerebral function. On the other hand, in fatal head injuries autopsy may reveal an intact skull in 20 to 30 per cent of cases.

NO **Seizure Disorders.** Seizure disorders are a manifestation of an abnormal discharge of nerve impulses from some part or focus of the brain. Seizures may be due to a temporary, self-limiting condition resulting, for instance, from a head injury; a reversible condition such as hypocalcemia; or a permanent, abnormal condition in the brain which may

or may not be accounted for by a demonstrable lesion. When the seizures are of a recurring type, the disorder is commonly known as epilepsy. Four kinds of epilepsy are generally described: grand mal, petit mal, psychomotor, and Jacksonian.

In **grand mal** attacks there is a sudden loss of consciousness and a generalized convulsion. Many patients experience a forewarning sensation (aura), which is different for each individual and may be, among other things, auditory, visual, or cutaneous. The convulsion occurs in two stages. In the first, tonic muscular contractions (without relaxation) occur, often twisting the facial features and distorting the position of the body. These are followed after a few seconds by clonic contractions — jerky movements, usually violent. During the clonic stage the EEG waves are high voltage and synchronous, of lower frequency than the delta rhythm.

Petit mal seizures are characterized by a momentary suspension of consciousness. The individual stares blankly into space, and there are no convulsive movements. Just before the attack the EEG shows large, slow waves (delta rhythm frequency), each large wave followed by a sharp spike.

In **psychomotor** seizures the individual makes automatic, stereotyped movements, such as smacking of the lips, while in a trancelike state. There is a feeling of unreality, sometimes causing the person to feel that what he sees or hears at the moment has been experienced in the past. There is no general convulsion. This type of seizure is usually caused by a disturbance in the temporal lobe.

Jacksonian seizures are caused by well-defined focal lesions. Clonic convulsive movements occur in a localized region of the body on the side opposite the site of the lesion. They generally spread by a progressive "march" to adjacent parts, as from a finger to the entire arm. After this, the spreading of the convulsion may come to a halt or continue — on one side of the body only or until a generalized convulsion occurs.

Spinal Cord *all on exam*

The spinal cord, lodged within the vertebral canal, is directly continuous superiorly with the medulla oblongata (see Fig. 9–18). It

stroke is on test

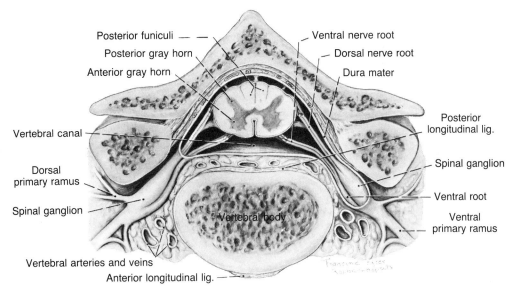

Figure 9–35. Relation of spinal cord and nerves to vertebra.

begins at the foramen magnum (at the point of the uppermost rootlet of the first cervical nerve). In its growth, the spinal cord lags behind the growth of the vertebral column after the third embryonic month. As a result, the cord in the adult terminates at the junction of the first and second lumbar vertebrae. The **conus medullaris** is the tapered lower end of the spinal cord lying opposite the first segment of the lumbar region (Fig. 9–32). Descending from the apex of the conus med-

ullaris to the coccyx is the filum terminale (page 263).

The spinal cord is flattened dorsoventrally and exhibits two swellings along its length — the **cervical** and **lumbar enlargements.** These enlargements are produced by the greater number of nerve fibers at these levels.

Cross Section of the Spinal Cord (Figs. 9–35 to 9–38). In cross section, the spinal cord reveals an outer region of **white matter** and

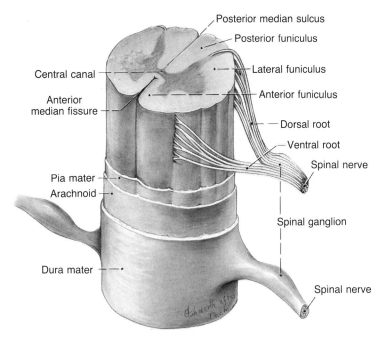

Figure 9–36. Section of spinal cord illustrating formation of a spinal nerve and layers of meninges.

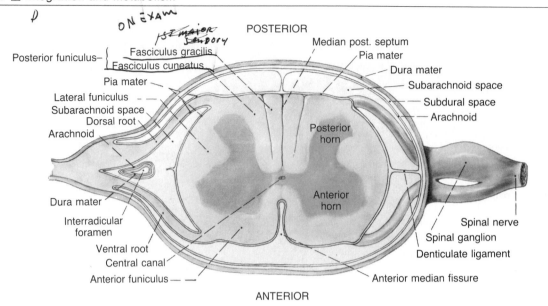

[handwritten annotations: "ON EXAM", "1ST MAJOR SENSORY"]

Figure 9–37. Cross section of spinal cord illustrating meningeal coverings.

an inner region of **gray matter** arranged in the form of the letter *H*. The transverse bar of the H is the gray commissure connecting the two lateral masses of gray matter. There is a minute canal in the center of the cord — all that remains of the cavity of the neural tube. This opens into the fourth ventricle at its upper end and terminates blindly in the central canal of the filum terminale.

Several longitudinal furrows groove the cord along its length. The deep *anterior median fissure* and the shallow *posterior median sulcus* (from which the posterior median septum deeply penetrates the cord) divide

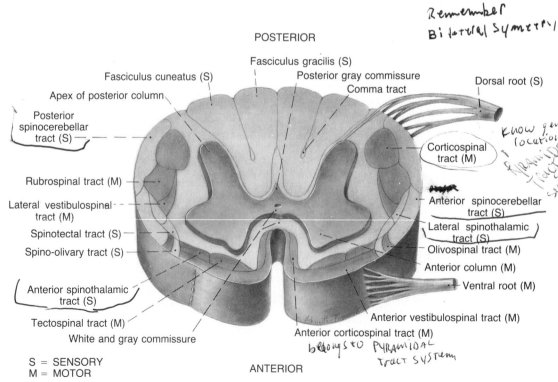

[handwritten annotations: "Remember Bilateral Symmetry", "Know general location", "Pyramidal Tract System", "belongs to PYRAMIDAL Tract System"]

S = SENSORY
M = MOTOR

Figure 9–38. Major ascending and descending tracts of the spinal cord.

the spinal cord into two symmetrical halves. The attachments of the dorsal and ventral roots of the spinal nerves (Fig. 9–36), coinciding with the posterolateral sulcus and anterolateral sulcus, respectively, mark the division of the white matter in each half of the spinal cord into three segments — the **posterior, lateral** and **anterior columns**, or **funiculi**. Each column has a number of bundles (fasciculi) of fibers, termed **tracts**. Some tracts are ascending, providing sensory input to the brain; others are descending, carrying motor signals from the brain to the spinal cord. Still others (intersegmental) begin in one region of the spinal cord and end in another. The name of the tract often indicates the column in which it travels, its origin, and termination. For example, the lateral spinothalamic tract has fibers that arise from cell bodies within the

spinal cord, travel in the lateral column and make connections with neurons in the thalamus. The tracts of major functional significance are discussed in subsequent sections (pages 303 and 310).

An **anterior**, or **ventral, horn** and a **posterior**, or **dorsal, horn** (called anterior and posterior gray columns by some anatomists) are found on each half of the gray matter. The anterior horn contains cell bodies from which motor fibers of the spinal nerves arise. The posterior horn contains cell bodies from which afferent ascending fibers pass to the brain after synapsing with sensory fibers from the spinal nerves. The gray matter also contains, among other things, a great number of neurons connecting impulses from one side of the cord to the other, and from one level of the cord to another.

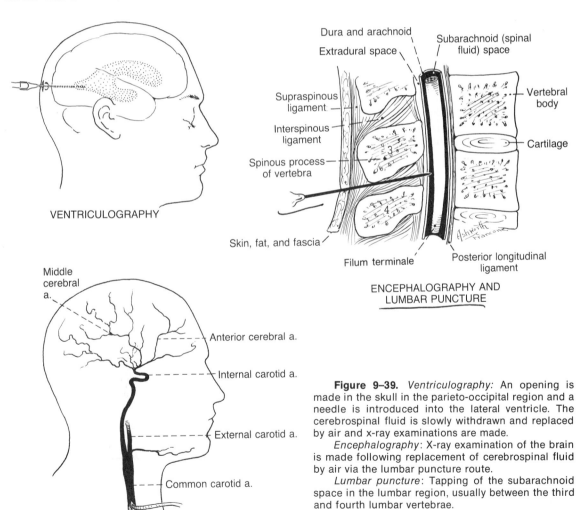

VENTRICULOGRAPHY

CEREBRAL ANGIOGRAPHY

Figure 9–39. *Ventriculography:* An opening is made in the skull in the parieto-occipital region and a needle is introduced into the lateral ventricle. The cerebrospinal fluid is slowly withdrawn and replaced by air and x-ray examinations are made.

Encephalography: X-ray examination of the brain is made following replacement of cerebrospinal fluid by air via the lumbar puncture route.

Lumbar puncture: Tapping of the subarachnoid space in the lumbar region, usually between the third and fourth lumbar vertebrae.

Cerebral angiography: X-ray examination of the vascular system of the brain is made after the injection of radiopaque material into the common carotid artery.

Special Examinations of the Nervous System (Fig. 9–39)

No — Only know lumbar puncture

Examination of the spinal fluid is often necessary. The fluid is obtained with the patient lying on his side. The tap, or *lumbar puncture,* is best performed between the third and fourth lumbar vertebrae. If the puncture has been performed without trauma, clear fluid is obtained.

Intracranial tumors can produce a distortion of the ventricles of the brain. The ventricles are outlined by removing a small area of bone and then injecting air through a needle inserted into the posterior horn of the lateral ventricle (*ventriculography*) or by injecting air into the lumbar subarachnoid space (*encephalography*).

In *cerebral angiography,* visualization of the intracranial blood vessels is accomplished by injecting radiopaque media into the carotid or vertebral arteries. With proper timing, both the arterial and venous phases of circulation can be outlined.

Computerized axial tomography (CAT) is an ingenious x-ray diagnostic technique that distinguishes far smaller density differences between tissues than conventional x-rays and produces an image representing x-ray absorption at a great many projection angles. The x-ray beams of the CAT scanner, after passing through the body's tissues, strike a sensitive crystal detector, generating electronic signals that are transmitted to a computer. The computer reconstructs an image, displayed on a screen, in which each color or shade represents a tissue of specific density. The technique makes it possible to pinpoint such defects as tumors, blood clots, and hemorrhage sites with extraordinary accuracy. The first instruments were designed for head scanning. Most machines in current use can do body scanning as well.

PERIPHERAL NERVOUS SYSTEM: SPINAL AND CRANIAL NERVES

SPINAL NERVES

A **nerve** is a group of bundles of nerve fibers outside the spinal cord or brain. Thirty-one pairs of nerves called spinal nerves (Fig. 9–40) arise from the spinal cord along almost its entire length and emerge from the vertebral canal through the intervertebral foramina. In a transverse section of a spinal nerve, large numbers of closely packed fibers, some myelinated and some nonmyelinated, can be seen by ordinary microscopy. These are grouped into small bundles called fascicles, each surrounded by a dense sheath, the *perineurium.* From the perineurium, strands of connective tissue called *endoneurium* extend into the spaces between the individual nerve fibers, surrounding each fiber and binding together the fibers of a bundle. The *epineurium* forms a protective covering for the entire nerve unit. (See Fig. 9–41.)

Attached to each segment of the spinal cord on either side are a **dorsal root** containing fibers of sensory neurons and a **ventral root** containing fibers of motor neurons. Each dorsal root presents a *spinal ganglion* near or within the intervertebral foramen. Just distal to the ganglion, the dorsal root combines with the corresponding ventral root to form a spinal nerve. The cell bodies of sensory neurons lie in the spinal ganglia. The cell bodies of motor neurons lie in the ventral horns of the spinal cord.

The 31 pairs of spinal nerves are named for the region of the vertebral column through which they exit. There are eight pairs of cervical spinal nerves, 12 thoracic, five lumbar, five sacral and one coccygeal. The first cervical spinal nerve, which often lacks a dorsal root, emerges between the atlas and the skull. The second to seventh cervical nerves leave the vertebral canal above the corresponding vertebrae; the eighth nerve leaves the vertebral canal below the seventh cervical vertebra. Thereafter, the nerves exit below their corresponding vertebrae. Because, as mentioned, the spinal cord is shorter than the vertebral column, the dorsal and ventral roots must descend progressively greater distances as they emerge further along the length of the cord in order to reach the appropriate intervertebral foramen before forming a spinal nerve. The roots arising from the terminal portion are drawn down to a collection called the **cauda equina** (Latin for horse's tail).

Many of the larger branches given off by the spinal nerves bear the same names as the artery they accompany or the part they supply. Thus, the radial nerve passes from the radial side of the forearm in company with the radial artery. The intercostal nerves pass

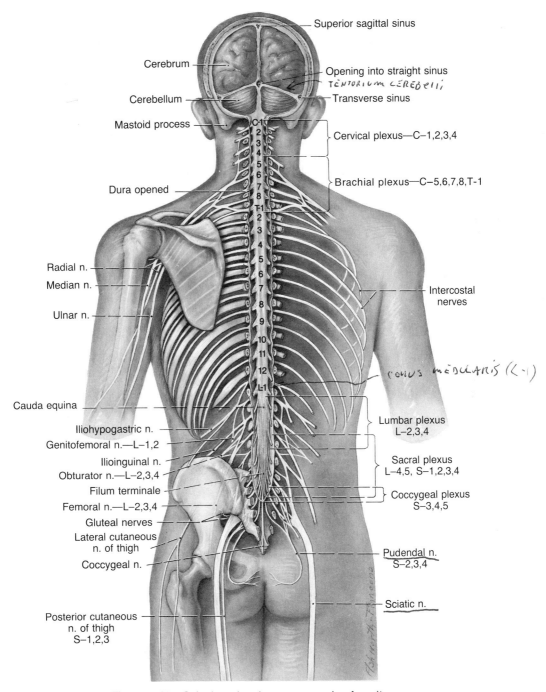

Figure 9–40. Spinal cord and nerves emerging from it.

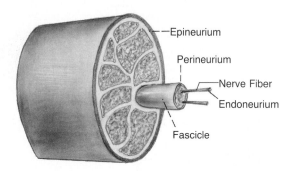

Epineurium

Perineurium

Nerve Fiber

Endoneurium

Fascicle

Figure 9–41. Diagrammatic representation of a peripheral nerve.

between the ribs in company with the intercostal arteries.

Soon after a spinal nerve leaves the cord, it branches in four directions. The *meningeal ramus* (L. *ramus,* branch) carries nerve fibers to and from the meninges of the spinal cord and the intervertebral ligaments. The *dorsal ramus* carries nerve fibers serving the muscles and skin of the back of the head, neck and trunk; the ventral and lateral parts of these structures as well as the upper and lower extremities are served by the usually larger and more important *ventral ramus.* The fourth branch belongs to the autonomic nervous system and has two portions, a *white ramus* and a *gray ramus.* (See section under Autonomic Nervous System.)

The **dorsal rami** extend backward through their transverse processes and, with the exception of those of the first cervical, fourth and fifth sacral, and coccygeal, divide into medial and lateral branches. The nerve supply by the dorsal rami is segmentally arranged and located from the back of the head to the coccyx. The dorsal ramus of C-1, called the *suboccipital nerve,* is larger than the ventral ramus. It supplies the deep muscles of the back of the neck. The dorsal ramus of C-2, also larger than the ventral ramus, supplies the skin of the back of the head and neck and the deep muscles of the neck. Its medial division is called, because of its size and major distribution, the *greater occipital nerve.*

The **ventral rami,** serving a more widespread area of the body than the dorsal rami, are segmentally arranged in the thoracic region only. Here the ventral rami of the first eleven thoracic nerves become the intercostal nerves, while the ventral ramus of the last thoracic nerve, below the bottom rib, becomes the subcostal nerve. These nerves serve the muscles and skin of the thorax and upper abdomen. In the cervical, lumbar and sacral regions *plexuses,* interlacing networks of nerves, arise from the ventral rami from which, in turn, *peripheral nerves* take their origin.

will talk conceptualize this

Plexuses (Figs. 9–40 and 9–42 and Tables 9–1 through 9–4)

Cervical Plexus. The first plexus formed is the *cervical plexus,* derived from the ventral rami of C-1, 2, 3, and 4. The branches of the cervical plexus can be divided into two groups: (1) superficial, or cutaneous, distributed to the skin, and (2) deep, distributed for the most part to muscles. The cutaneous nerves include the *lesser occipital, great auricular, anterior (transverse) cutaneous,* and *supraclavicular.* These nerves supply the skin behind the ear and on the auricle, angle of the jaw, shoulder, lateral and anterior regions of the neck, and upper thorax (Table 9–1). The major deep nerve is the *phrenic,* which extends through the thorax to supply the large musculature of the diaphragm (Fig. 9–43). Other deep branches of the cervical plexus are distributed to a group of muscles attached to the vertebral column functioning as flexors of the head and neck and to some of the muscles in the hyoid region. Nerve fibers arising from the first five cervical segments of the spinal cord form the spinal portion of the accessory nerve (11th cranial nerve — see page 291).

Brachial Plexus. The *brachial plexus* extends downward and laterally to pass over the first rib and behind the middle third of the clavicle to enter the axilla (armpit). It is derived from the ventral rami of nerves C-5, 6, 7, and 8, as well as T-1, and provides the entire nerve supply for the upper extremities. The ventral rami, constituting the roots of the plexus, form three trunks (upper, middle, and lower), each of which splits into an anterior and posterior division. A lateral and a medial

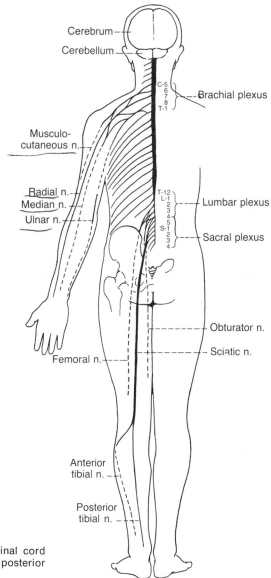

Cerebrum

Cerebellum

C-5
6
7
8
T-1

Brachial plexus

Musculo-
cutaneous n.

Radial n.

Median n.

Ulnar n.

T-12
L-1
2
3
4
5
S-1
2
3
4

Lumbar plexus

Sacral plexus

Obturator n.

Sciatic n.

Femoral n.

Anterior
tibial n.

Posterior
tibial n.

Figure 9–42. Branches of spinal cord as seen on left side of body only, posterior view.

Table 9–1   CERVICAL PLEXUS

NERVE	ORIGIN	INNERVATION
Lesser occipital	C–2	Skin over lateral part of occipital region
Great auricular	C–2, 3	Skin over angle of jaw, parotid gland, posteroinferior half of lateral and medial aspects of auricle, and mastoid region
Anterior (transverse) cutaneous	C–2, 3	Supplies skin about the hyoid bone and the thyroid cartilage (ventral and lateral parts of the neck from chin to sternum)
Supraclavicular	C–3, 4	Skin of shoulder, most lateral regions of the neck, and upper part of breast
Phrenic	C–3, 4, 5	Diaphragm

Table 9–2 BRACHIAL PLEXUS

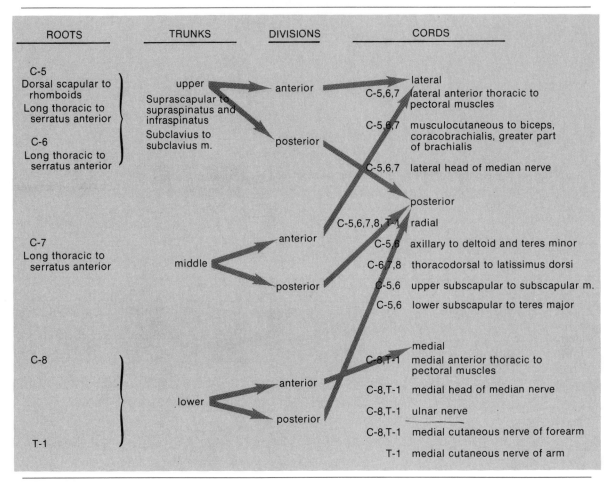

Table 9–3 LUMBAR PLEXUS

NERVE	ORIGIN	INNERVATION
Iliohypogastric	L–1	Skin of buttocks and anterior abdominal wall
Ilioinguinal	L–1	Skin of pubis, inguinal region, upper medial part of thigh, root of penis and upper part of scrotum (mons pubis and adjoining part of labium majus in female)
Genitofemoral	L–1, 2	Skin of scrotum and upper anterior part of thigh
Lateral cutaneous of thigh	L–2, 3	Skin of lateral surface of thigh
Obturator	L–2, 3, 4	Supplies adductor muscles of thigh and gracilis. Cutaneous branch is distributed to the inner surface of the thigh
Femoral	L–2, 3, 4	Motor branches to quadriceps femoris, sartorius and pectineus muscles. Cutaneous branches supply skin of hip region, anterior aspect of thigh and medial aspect of leg and foot

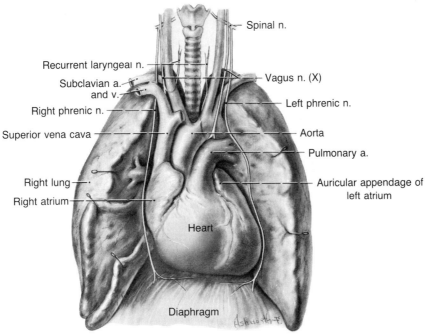

Right phrenic n.

Subclavian a. and v.

Recurrent laryngeal n.

Spinal n.

Vagus n. (X)

Left phrenic n.

Superior vena cava

Aorta

Pulmonary a.

Right lung

Right atrium

Auricular appendage of left atrium

Heart

Diaphragm

Figure 9–43. Contents of thoracic cavity, illustrating positions of phrenic nerve.

cord are formed from the anterior divisions; a posterior cord is formed from the posterior divisions (Table 9–2 and Fig. 9–44). Nerves of the brachial plexus may arise from one or more than one root, trunk, or cord. Arising from roots are the *dorsal scapular nerve* (from C-5), which supplies the rhomboideus muscles, and the *long thoracic nerve* (from C-5, 6, and 7), which supplies the serratus anterior muscle. The large *suprascapular nerve,* which supplies the supraspinatus and infraspinatus muscles, arises from the upper trunk, as does the small nerve to the subclavius muscle. Important nerves arising from the cords of the brachial plexus are the following (Figs. 9–44 and 9–45).

A. Lateral cord
1. The *musculocutaneous nerve* supplies the biceps brachii, coracobrachialis, and brachialis. It is the sensory supply for the skin on the outer side of the forearm.
2. The *median nerve* (including a medial head from the medial cord) supplies flexor muscles of the wrist (except for the flexor carpi ulnaris) and most of the flexors and abductors of the fingers and thumb.

B. Medial cord
The *ulnar nerve* innervates the flexor carpi ulnaris and the medial half of the flexor digitorum profundus in the forearm, as well as the muscles of the hand, except those supplied by the median nerve. If injured, it gives rise to a sensation of "pins and needles" in the area of its sensory distribution — the skin on the medial aspect of the elbow, wrist, and hand.

C. Posterior cord
1. The *circumflex (axillary) nerve* supplies the branch to the teres minor, and terminates by innervating the deltoid and the skin over it.
2. The *radial nerve* spirals around the back of the humerus, supplying the triceps. It innervates all the muscles of the back of the forearm, and sensory branches serve the skin on the back of the forearm and hand. The radial nerve lies close to the humerus and can be seriously injured in fractures of the midshaft of the bone.

Lumbar Plexus. The ventral rami of the lumbar segments 1, 2, 3, and the greater part of 4 form the *lumbar plexus.* The lumbar

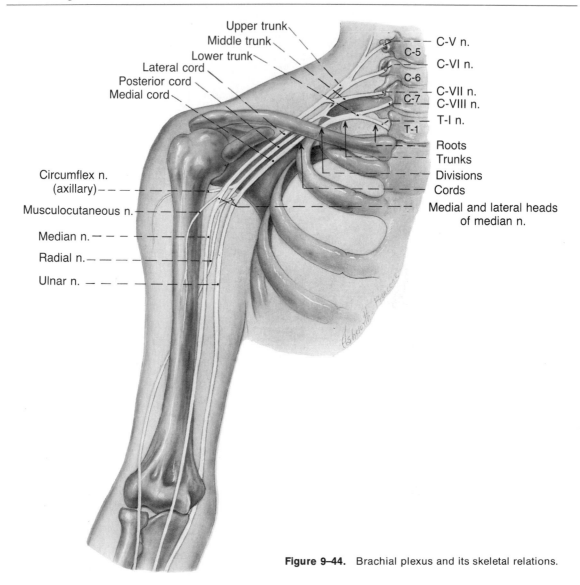

Upper trunk
Middle trunk
Lower trunk
Lateral cord
Posterior cord
Medial cord

C-V n.
C-5
C-VI n.
C-6
C-VII n.
C-7
C-VIII n.
T-1
T-I n.

Roots
Trunks
Divisions
Cords

Circumflex n.
(axillary)

Musculocutaneous n.

Median n.

Radial n.

Ulnar n.

Medial and lateral heads
of median n.

Figure 9–44. Brachial plexus and its skeletal relations.

plexus is situated on the inside of the posterior abdominal wall. Three important nerves in this plexus are (Fig. 9–46):

1. The *femoral nerve* is the largest of the group, with the widest distribution. Motor branches supply muscles of the thigh (flexors) and leg; cutaneous branches supply the skin of the anterior thigh, the hip, and the leg. The largest branch of the femoral nerve, the superficial *saphenous nerve*, extends into the foot, serving the skin on the medial aspect of the leg and foot.

2. The *lateral cutaneous nerve of the thigh* supplies the skin on the lateral half of the thigh.

3. The *genitofemoral nerve* supplies the scrotum and the skin of the upper anterior part of the thigh (not shown in Fig. 9–46).

Sacral Plexus. The *sacral plexus* is formed on the anterior aspect of the sacrum by the ventral rami of part of L-4, all of L-5, S-1, 2, and 3, and part of S-4. It gives rise to the largest nerve in the body, the sciatic nerve. The branches of the sacral plexus include the following (Fig. 9–46):

1. The *sciatic nerve*, formed from L-4 and 5 and S-1, 2, and 3, is located deep in the gluteus maximus muscle and travels down the posterior aspect of the thigh, dividing into two terminal branches — the *tibial* and

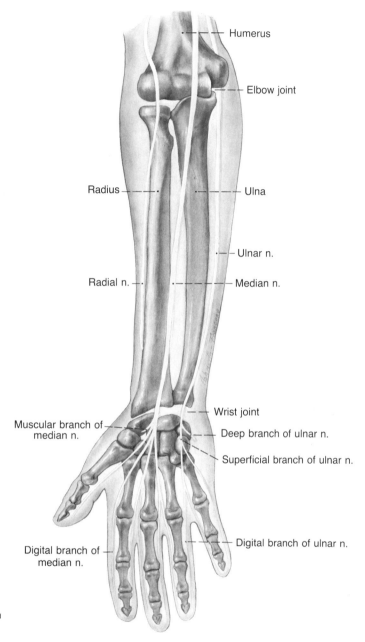

Humerus

Elbow joint

Radius

Ulna

Ulnar n.

Radial n.

Median n.

Wrist joint

Muscular branch of
median n.

Deep branch of ulnar n.

Superficial branch of ulnar n.

Digital branch of ulnar n.

Digital branch of
median n.

Figure 9–45. Nerves of right forearm
and hand (palmar view.)

common peroneal nerves. The common
peroneal innervates the skin and muscles on
the anterior and lateral surfaces of the leg and
the dorsum of the foot. The tibial innervates
the posterior muscles and the skin of the
leg.

2. The *pudendal nerve* is formed by the
rami of S-2, 3, and 4, and supplies the muscles of the external genitalia, the skin of the
perineum, and the anal sphincter.

The fifth sacral and coccygeal nerves are

unimportant in man. In animals, these two
spinal nerves supply the tail.

Dermatomes. The areas of the skin
served by each pair of spinal nerves have
been mapped. A strip of skin supplied by one
pair of spinal nerves is called a *dermatome*
(Fig. 9–47). Overlap between adjoining dermatomes minimizes damage to any one
nerve. One of the procedures used to prepare
these maps in humans entailed stimulation of
the sensory roots of individuals in surgery

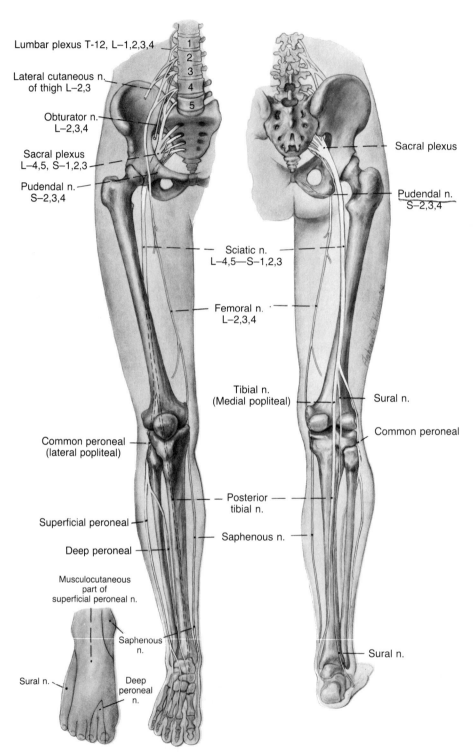

Lumbar plexus T-12, L–1,2,3,4

Lateral cutaneous n. of thigh L–2,3

Obturator n. L–2,3,4

Sacral plexus L–4,5, S–1,2,3

Pudendal n. S–2,3,4

Sacral plexus

Pudendal n. S–2,3,4

Sciatic n. L–4,5—S–1,2,3

Femoral n. L–2,3,4

Tibial n. (Medial popliteal)

Sural n.

Common peroneal

Common peroneal (lateral popliteal)

Posterior tibial n.

Superficial peroneal

Saphenous n.

Deep peroneal

Musculocutaneous part of superficial peroneal n.

Saphenous n.

Sural n.

Sural n.

Deep peroneal n.

Figure 9–46. Anterior and posterior views of the right leg and foot, showing lumbar and sacral plexuses and the regions supplied. Inset shows areas of the foot supplied by the nerves.

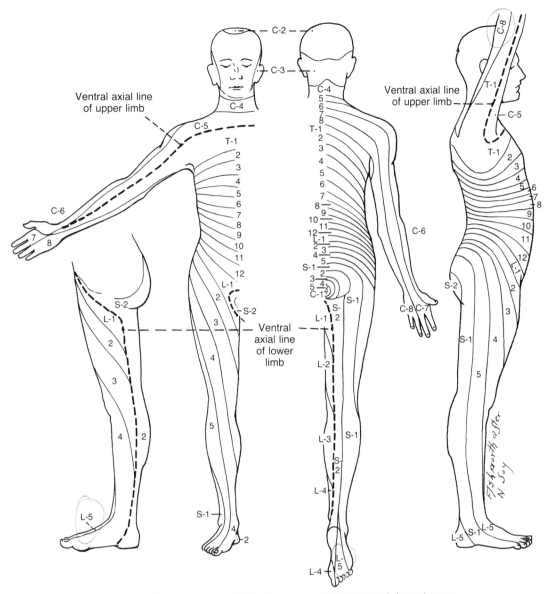

Figure 9–47. Cutaneous distribution of spinal nerves and dermatomes.

Table 9–4 SACRAL PLEXUS

NERVE	ORIGIN	INNERVATION
Sciatic		
Tibial	L–4 to S–3	Muscles and skin of back of leg
Common peroneal	L–4 to S–2	Skin and muscles of anterior and lateral aspect of leg and dorsal surface of foot
Superior gluteal	L–4 to S–1	Gluteus medius and minimus and tensor fasciae latae
Inferior gluteal	L–5 to S–2	Gluteus maximus
Posterior cutaneous of thigh	S–1, 2, 3	Skin of lateral part of perineum, lower buttock and back of thigh and leg

and observing the resulting vasodilation. Data obtained from cases of herpes zoster, a painful condition caused by a viral infection, usually in a single dorsal root ganglion, have also been used to map dermatomes.

NO ### Peripheral Nerve Injury

When a peripheral nerve is injured, nerve fibers distal to the point of injury undergo changes originally described by Waller in 1852 (see page 237 for a description of the degeneration and regeneration of a nerve fiber). Sympathetic fibers of the autonomic nervous system regenerate most rapidly. A return of function in peripheral nerve injury can be recognized initially by an improvement in color of the skin. Sensory function returns next. This is shown initially by sensitivity of the paralyzed muscle to pressure or pinching, and is followed by a return of protopathic (perceiving only coarser stimuli) sensitivity to pain, pressure, heat, and cold. Epicritic sensibility (perceiving fine variations of touch and temperature) returns next, followed by sensitivity to joint movement and touch localization. The last function to return is motor. Finally, actual muscle contraction occurs.

The most accurate motor tests for injury to the median and ulnar nerves at the wrist are those involving the actions of the small muscles of the hand. If a patient is asked to oppose the tip of the thumb to the tip of the little finger without flexion of the distal phalanx of the thumb or little finger, a perfectly adequate and accurate test for median nerve function will have been employed. Function of the ulnar nerve distal to damage at the wrist can be tested by having the patient abduct and adduct the extended fingers. If the patient is unable to extend the wrist when the hand lies flat upon the table, the radial nerve has been injured.

location, Names, where they go generally

✗ ## CRANIAL NERVES (Figs. 9–48 to 9–63 and Table 9–5)

The cranial nerves are 12 pairs of symmetrically arranged nerves attached to the brain. Each leaves the skull through a foramen at its base. The site where the fibers composing the nerve enter or leave the brain surface is usually termed the *superficial origin* of the nerve; the more deeply placed region from which the fibers arise or around which they terminate is called the *deep origin* of the nerves. The cell bodies of sensory neurons are located in ganglia just outside the brain (except those of the olfactory nerve, which are located in the nasal mucous membrane, and of the optic nerve, which are located in the retina); the cell bodies of motor neurons are located in nuclei within the brain.

The cranial nerves include the olfactory (I), optic (II), oculomotor (III), trochlear (IV), trigeminal (V), abducens (VI), facial (VII), vestibulocochlear (acoustic) (VIII), glossopharyngeal (IX), vagus (X), accessory (XI), and hypoglossal (XII) (Table 9–5).

A number of the cranial nerves are, like spinal nerves, mixed nerves, containing both motor and sensory fibers. Cranial nerves I (olfactory), II (optic), and VIII (vestibulocochlear), however, carry only sensory fibers (from the nose, eye, and ear, respectively). Cranial nerves III (oculomotor), IV (trochlear), and VI (abducens), which supply the eye muscles, XI (accessory), and XII (hypoglossal), which innervates the tongue, have been described as purely motor nerves although, according to some anatomists, they also contain fibers from muscle proprioceptors.

The **olfactory nerve** (I), serving the function of smell, is formed by about 20 bundles of nerve fibers leading from the olfactory area of the nasal mucous membrane, where the cell bodies are located (the neurons are the olfactory receptors), to the olfactory bulb above each nasal cavity. In the olfactory bulb, synaptic connections are made with neurons whose axons pass backward as the olfactory tract (Fig. 9–51). In testing for smell, each naris should be separately examined for the presence of the sense of smell. A complete absence of this sense is called *anosmia*.

The **optic nerve** (II), conducting visual impulses, is composed of more than one million nerve fibers, or approximately 38 per cent of all the cranial nerve fibers (Fig. 9–52).

Visual impulses are received through the rods and cones and are transmitted (via bipolar neurons) to the ganglion cells, which constitute one of the layers of the retina. The axons of the ganglion cells converge (upon the optic disc) to form the optic nerve for each eye. The two optic nerves unite after their entrance into the cranial cavity to form the optic chiasm. From this point the nerves continue as the optic tracts.

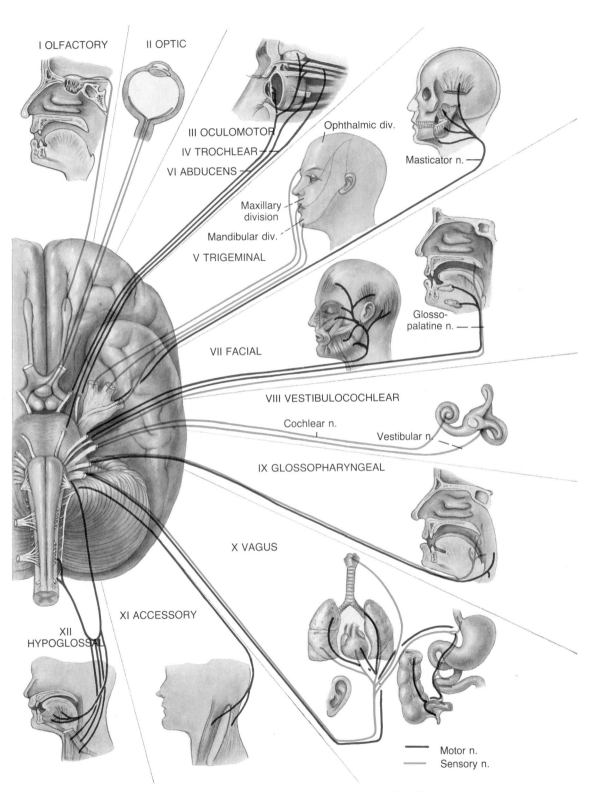

I OLFACTORY

II OPTIC

III OCULOMOTOR

IV TROCHLEAR

VI ABDUCENS

Ophthalmic div.

Masticator n.

Maxillary division

Mandibular div.

V TRIGEMINAL

VII FACIAL

Glosso-palatine n.

VIII VESTIBULOCOCHLEAR

Cochlear n.

Vestibular n.

IX GLOSSOPHARYNGEAL

X VAGUS

XI ACCESSORY

XII HYPOGLOSSAL

Motor n.
Sensory n.

Figure 9–48. Distribution of cranial nerves. (After Netter.)

Table 9–5 CRANIAL NERVES

NUMBER	NAME	SUPERFICIAL ORIGIN	EXIT FROM SKULL	FUNCTION
I	Olfactory	(Extends from nasal mucosa to olfactory bulb)	Cribriform plate of ethmoid	Sensory: olfactory (smell)
II	Optic	(Extends from retina to optic chiasm)	Optic foramen	Sensory: vision
III	Oculomotor	Midbrain	Superior orbital fissure	Motor: external muscles of eyes except lateral rectus and superior oblique; levator palpebrae superioris Parasympathetic: sphincter of pupil and ciliary muscle of lens
IV	Trochlear	Roof of midbrain	Superior orbital fissure	Motor: superior oblique muscle
V	Trigeminal			
	Ophthalmic branch	Ventral surface of pons	Superior orbital fissure	Sensory: cornea; nasal mucous membrane; skin of face and scalp
	Maxillary branch	Ventral surface of pons	Foramen rotundum	Sensory: skin of face; mucous membrane of mouth and nose; teeth
	Mandibular branch	Ventral surface of pons	Foramen ovale	Motor: muscles of mastication Sensory: skin of face; mucous membrane of mouth; teeth
VI	Abducens	Lower margin of pons	Superior orbital fissure	Motor: lateral rectus muscle

	Nerve	Origin	Opening in skull	Function
VII	Facial	Lower margin of pons	Stylomastoid foramen	Motor: muscles of facial expression Sensory: taste, anterior two-thirds of tongue Parasympathetic: lacrimal, submandibular, and sublingual glands
VIII	Vestibulocochlear Vestibular	Groove between pons and medulla oblongata	Internal auditory meatus	Sensory: equilibrium
	Cochlear	Groove between pons and medulla oblongata	Internal auditory meatus	Sensory: hearing
IX	Glossopharyngeal	Medulla oblongata	Jugular foramen	Motor: stylopharyngeus muscle Sensory: taste, posterior one-third of tongue; pharynx; branch of the carotid sinus and carotid body Parasympathetic: parotid gland
X	Vagus	Medulla oblongata	Jugular foramen	Sensory: external meatus, pharynx, larynx, aortic sinus, and thoracic and abdominal viscera Motor: pharynx and larynx Parasympathetic: thoracic and abdominal viscera
XI	Accessory	Medulla oblongata and upper 5 cervical segments of spinal cord	Jugular foramen	Motor: trapezius and sternocleidomastoid muscles; muscles of pharynx and larynx
XII	Hypoglossal	Anterior lateral sulcus between olive and pyramid	Hypoglossal canal	Motor: muscles of tongue

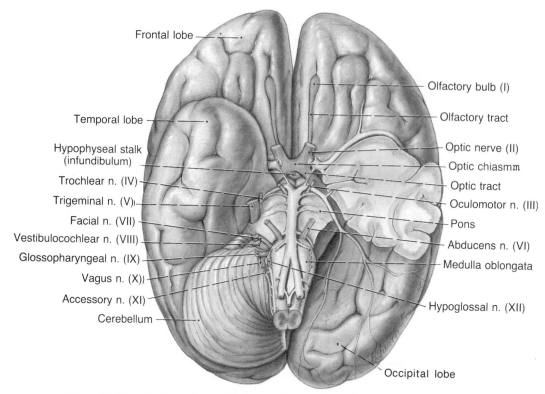

Figure 9–49. Inferior surface of the brain showing sites of exit of the cranial nerves.

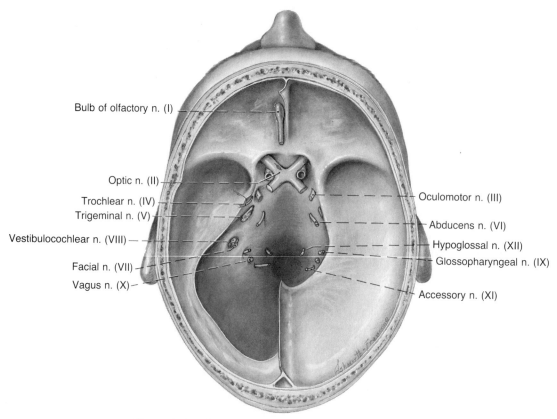

Figure 9–50. Sites of exit of cranial nerves from the skull.

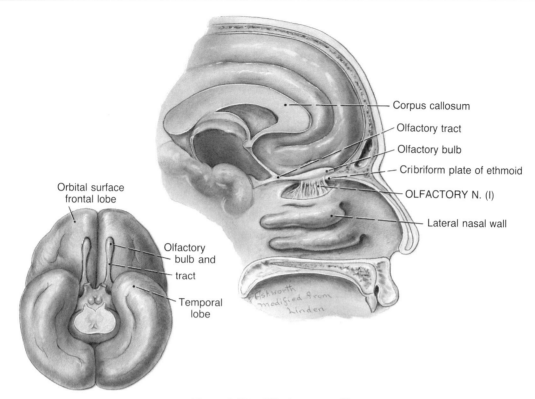

Figure 9–51. Olfactory nerve (I).

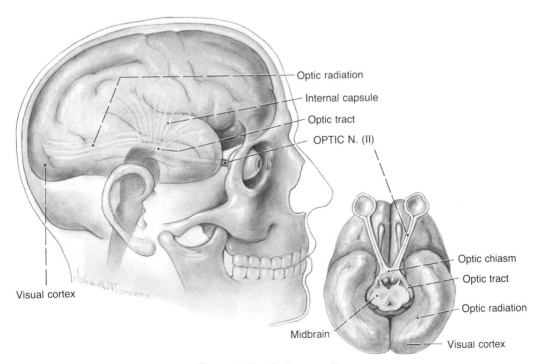

Figure 9–52. Optic nerve (II).

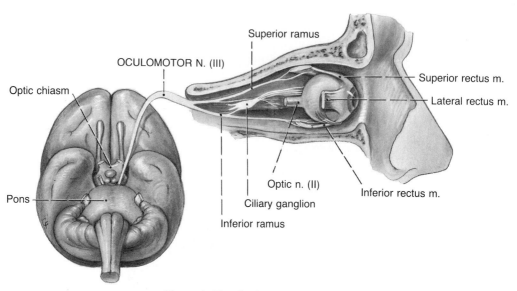

Figure 9–53. Oculomotor nerve (III).

The **oculomotor nerve** (III), predominantly motor, contains efferent nerves affecting four of the six external muscles that move the eye (Fig. 9–53). It also supplies fibers to the levator palpebrae superioris muscle, which raises the eyelid. The patient with third nerve damage complains of blurred vision or of seeing two objects instead of one (diplopia). Weakness of the extraocular muscles is determined by the patient's holding his head without moving it and following the examiner's fingertips with his eyes. The oculomotor nerve also contains efferent fibers belonging to the autonomic nervous system (page 299) that synapse with fibers leading to the smooth muscles of the eyes (iris and ciliary muscles).

The smallest of the cranial nerves, the **trochlear nerve** (IV), contains efferent fibers supplying the superior oblique muscle of the eye (Fig. 9–54). Its integrity is examined by checking movements of the eye.

The **trigeminal nerve** (V), the largest of the cranial nerves, is the general sensory nerve of the face, nose, mouth, forehead, and the top of the head, and motor nerve to the jaw muscles of mastication. It consists of three divisions: ophthalmic, maxillary, and mandibular (Fig. 9–55). The trigeminal nerve conducts efferent fibers to the muscles of mastication via the mandibular branch. It is also composed of afferent fibers located in the skin of the face and anterior scalp, mucous membrane of the mouth and nasal cavities, and meninges. Injury to the trigeminal nerve produces a loss of sensation to light touch and temperature on the corresponding half of the face. In addition to this loss of sensation, the cornea and the conjunctiva (a mucous membrane lining the exposed surface of the eyeball) are insensitive, as are the mucous membranes of the corresponding side of the nose, mouth, and anterior two-thirds of the tongue. When the motor portion of the trigeminal nerve is affected, the masseter and other muscles of mastication are paralyzed and subsequently atrophy. The motor portion of the trigeminal nerve is tested by asking the patient to clench his teeth. The examiner feels the masseters to determine the strength of contraction. Examination of the sensory portion is conducted by evaluating the corneal (blink) reflex and sensitivity of the skin of the face.

Trigeminal neuralgia is perhaps the most agonizing of all benign afflictions of man. The maxillary and mandibular divisions of the fifth nerve are the usual sites of this disorder. The tic, or muscle twitch, of trigeminal neuralgia is characteristic. Pain is excruciatingly explosive and stabbing in quality and is present over the area of distribution of the involved division. It is usually so severe that the facial muscles on the affected side develop a spasm; hence the term **tic douloureux.** Initially the attacks are brief, lasting

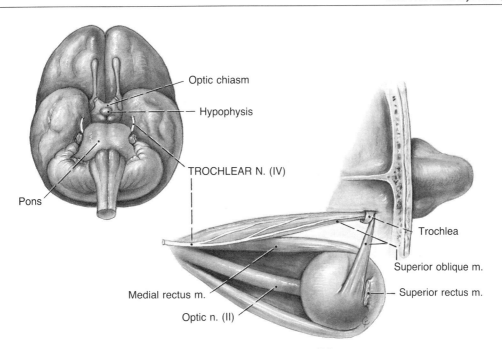

Figure 9–54. Trochlear nerve (IV).

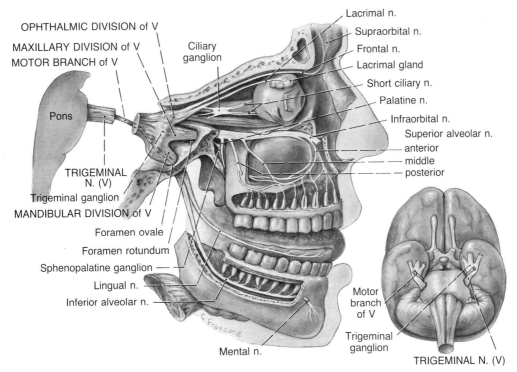

Figure 9–55. Trigeminal nerve (V).

from a few seconds to two minutes. Invariably, the patient becomes aware of trigger zones which, if touched, set off pain. These are usually located in the region of the mouth or upper lip. Eventually, the attacks may become more frequent, producing almost continuous paroxysms of pain. The cause of trigeminal neuralgia is unknown. Treatment includes division of the sensory root of the fifth nerve, but only after a trial with drugs, to which many patients respond.

The **abducens nerve** (VI), composed of efferent fibers supplying the lateral rectus muscle of the eyeball, serves the function of lateral movement of the eye (Fig. 9–56).

The **facial nerve** (VII), principally a motor nerve, contains efferent fibers found in the muscles of the face and scalp (Fig. 9–57). The facial nerve serves the function of facial expression. It also contains efferent fibers of the autonomic nervous system which lead to activation of the lacrimal (tear) and submandibular and sublingual (salivary) glands. It includes afferent fibers from the mucous membranes of the anterior two-thirds of the tongue, serving the function of taste.

When the seventh nerve is injured or diseased as it leaves the pons, the resulting paralysis gives the face a one-sided appearance, and the paralyzed side is flat and motionless. A loss of taste may occur in the anterior two-thirds of the tongue in the presence of damage to the facial nerve. In peripheral damage, such as occurs in **Bell's palsy** or injury to the facial nerve in the bony canal, all the muscles of facial expression are paralyzed. The patient cannot wrinkle his forehead or close his upper eyelid. In a central lesion, only the facial muscles below the eyelids are paralyzed.

The facial nerve is examined by asking the patient to wrinkle his forehead, to frown, to whistle, or to close his eyelids tightly. By these various simple maneuvers, muscles innervated by the facial nerve are tested and weakness or paralysis of the nerve is easily detected. The sensory function of the nerve is evaluated by asking the patient to protrude his tongue and by rubbing sugar, salt, or quinine onto the tongue to check for taste.

The **vestibulocochlear (acoustic) nerve** (VIII) (Fig. 9–58) serves the functions of hearing and equilibrium. There are two divisions — the *cochlear* division, concerned with hearing, and the *vestibular* division, concerned with equilibrium. The fibers form-

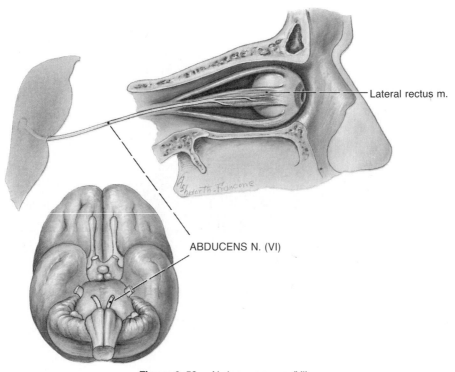

Figure 9–56. Abducens nerve (VI).

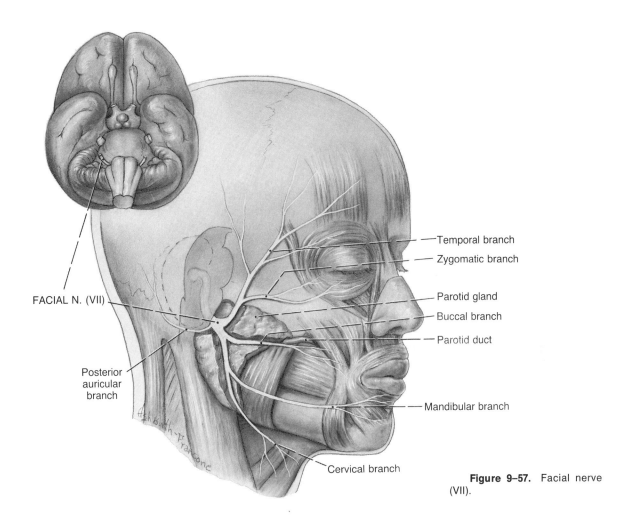

FACIAL N. (VII)

Temporal branch
Zygomatic branch
Parotid gland
Buccal branch
Parotid duct
Mandibular branch

Posterior auricular branch

Cervical branch

Figure 9–57. Facial nerve (VII).

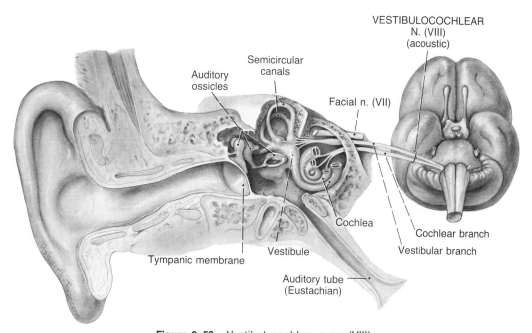

VESTIBULOCOCHLEAR N. (VIII) (acoustic)

Auditory ossicles
Semicircular canals
Facial n. (VII)

Cochlea
Cochlear branch
Vestibular branch

Tympanic membrane
Vestibule

Auditory tube (Eustachian)

Figure 9–58. Vestibulocochlear nerve (VIII).

ing the cochlear division come from the spiral ganglion of the cochlea; the fibers forming the vestibular division come from the vestibular ganglion, located in the internal auditory meatus (both ganglia are composed of bipolar neurons from which a central fiber passes to the brain and a peripheral fiber to the internal ear). Injury to the vestibular portion of the acoustic nerve produces symptoms that include vertigo (a sensation of whirling movement) and nystagmus (involuntary rapid eye movements).

The **glossopharyngeal nerve** (IX) is formed by five or six small fibrous bundles emerging from the medulla oblongata (Fig. 9–59). The ninth nerve serves the function of general sensation and taste for the posterior one-third of the tongue. It also contains sensory fibers from the mucous membrane of the pharynx, the carotid body, and the carotid sinus. Motor fibers innervate the stylo-

pharyngeus muscle, which aids in movement of the pharynx. The glossopharyngeal nerve also carries fibers of the autonomic nervous system leading to innervation of the parotid gland, a large salivary gland in front of the ear.

The **vagus nerve** (X) (Fig. 9–60) contains motor fibers innervating the pharyngeal and laryngeal muscles and sensory fibers from the pleura, aortic sinus, and thoracic and abdominal viscera. The vagus nerve is also an important part of the autonomic nervous system, containing fibers that lead to innervation of the heart, pancreas, and smooth muscles of the lungs and digestive tract.

The vagus nerve is routinely tested by observing pharyngeal muscles, which is accomplished by asking the patient to phonate and say "ah." Under normal circumstances, the soft palate and uvula will be pulled up in the midline. In the case of weakness of one

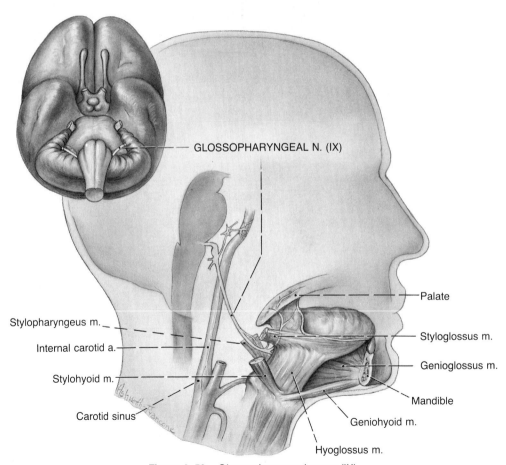

Figure 9–59. Glossopharyngeal nerve (IX).

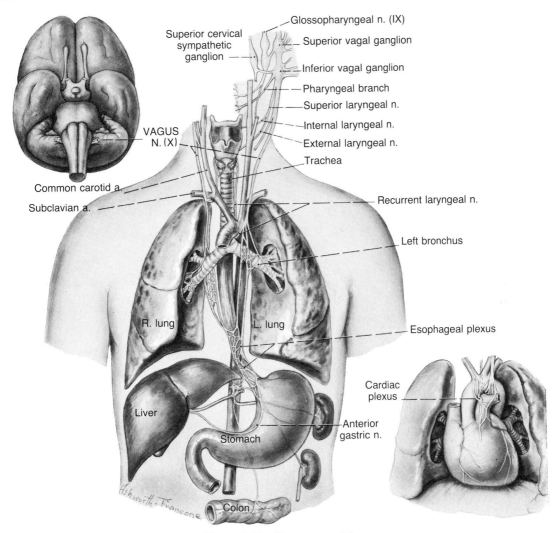

Figure 9–60. Vagus nerve (X).

side, the palate will be pulled to the healthy side upon phonation, while the diseased side droops.

ASSOCIATED with VAGUS

The <u>*recurrent laryngeal nerve*</u> (Fig. 9–61), which takes its origin from the vagus nerve, is of particular importance in clinical medicine; when the thyroid gland is abnormal and removal indicated, damage to this nerve sometimes occurs. Damage to the recurrent laryngeal nerve results in hoarseness.

The **accessory nerve** (XI) (Fig. 9–62) consists of two parts: a cranial (bulbar) portion and a spinal portion. The spinal portion is composed of fibers arising from the upper five segments of the spinal cord, which join the cranial portion after passing up through the foramen magnum as a common trunk. The two portions separate after traveling together for only a short distance. The cranial part joins the vagus nerve, and its fibers leading to the muscles of the pharynx and larynx are distributed through branches of the vagus nerve. Fibers of the spinal portion innervate the trapezius and sternocleidomastoid muscles, which permit movement of the head and shoulders.

Weakness of the trapezius muscle is determined by having the patient raise his shoulders against resistance. Weakness of the sternocleidomastoid muscle is ascertained by asking the patient to turn his head to the right and left against resistance of the examiner's hand.

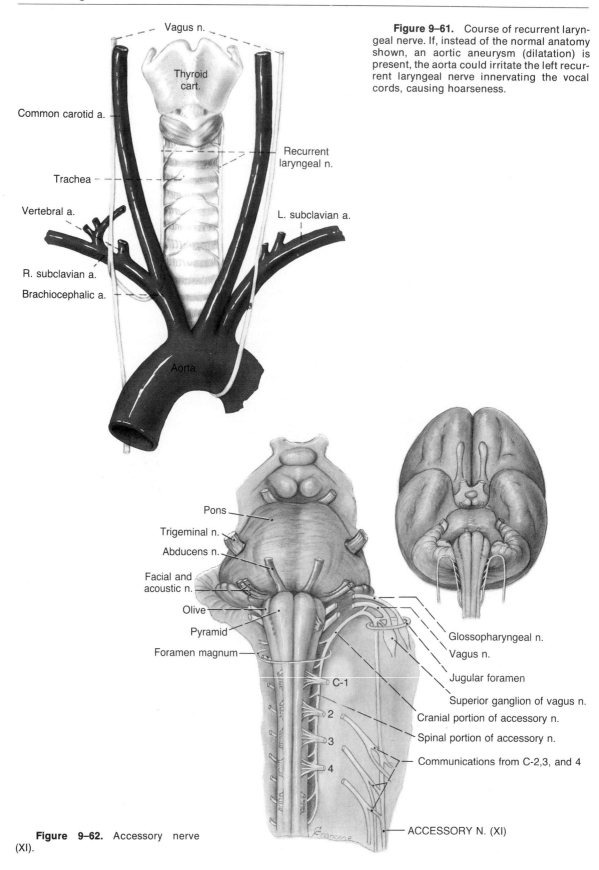

Figure 9–61. Course of recurrent laryngeal nerve. If, instead of the normal anatomy shown, an aortic aneurysm (dilatation) is present, the aorta could irritate the left recurrent laryngeal nerve innervating the vocal cords, causing hoarseness.

Vagus n.

Thyroid cart.

Common carotid a.

Recurrent laryngeal n.

Trachea

Vertebral a.

L. subclavian a.

R. subclavian a.

Brachiocephalic a.

Aorta

Pons

Trigeminal n.

Abducens n.

Facial and acoustic n.

Olive

Pyramid

Foramen magnum

C-1

2

3

4

Glossopharyngeal n.

Vagus n.

Jugular foramen

Superior ganglion of vagus n.

Cranial portion of accessory n.

Spinal portion of accessory n.

Communications from C-2,3, and 4

ACCESSORY N. (XI)

Figure 9–62. Accessory nerve (XI).

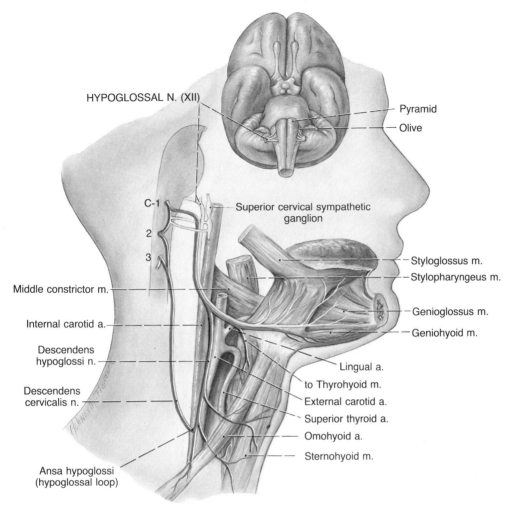

HYPOGLOSSAL N. (XII)

Pyramid

Olive

C-1

Superior cervical sympathetic ganglion

2

3

Styloglossus m.

Stylopharyngeus m.

Middle constrictor m.

Genioglossus m.

Internal carotid a.

Geniohyoid m.

Descendens hypoglossi n.

Descendens cervicalis n.

Lingual a.

to Thyrohyoid m.

External carotid a.

Superior thyroid a.

Omohyoid a.

Sternohyoid m.

Ansa hypoglossi (hypoglossal loop)

Figure 9–63. Hypoglossal nerve (XII).

The **hypoglossal nerve** (XII) supplies muscles of the tongue, allowing movement of the tongue (Fig. 9–63). The function of the hypoglossal nerve can be determined by having the patient protrude his tongue. When there is injury to this nerve, the tongue will deviate toward the side of the injury.

ts given to us all on test
Dr. RADTKEs maTerial

✶ AUTONOMIC NERVOUS SYSTEM

As mentioned in the beginning of this chapter, efferent peripheral nerve fibers distributed to smooth muscle, cardiac muscle, and glands (exocrine and some endocrine) are generally described as belonging to the autonomic nervous system. Since autonomic nerves also carry sensory fibers from the viscera, some authors include these afferent pathways as part of the autonomic nervous system.

The autonomic nervous system, among other things, helps to control arterial pressure, gastrointestinal motility and secretion, urinary output, sweating, body temperature, and various other functions. The overall function of the autonomic nervous system seems to be to maintain homeostasis.

Anatomically, the efferent pathway of the autonomic nervous system is unique in the following way: Whereas a skeletal muscle is innervated by a neuron with its cell body in the central nervous system and its axon extending without interruption to the muscle, smooth muscle, the heart, and glands are innervated by a 2-neuron chain — a *preganglionic neuron* with its cell body in the central nervous system and axon extending to a ganglion outside the central nervous system, and a *postganglionic neuron* with its cell body in a ganglion and axon extending to the muscle or gland. The ganglion, in effect, serves as a synaptic center between pre- and postganglionic neurons.

Autonomic Subdivisions

The autonomic nervous system may be divided, both functionally and structurally, into the sympathetic and parasympathetic nervous divisions.

The **sympathetic**, or **thoracolumbar, division** of the autonomic nervous system arises from all the thoracic and the first three lumbar segments of the spinal cord. The **parasympathetic**, or **craniosacral, division** of the autonomic nervous system arises from the third, seventh, ninth, and tenth cranial nerves, and from the second, third, and fourth sacral segments of the spinal cord. Generally speaking, the actions of the sympathetic division are directed toward mobilizing the body's energies for dealing with an increase in activity, whereas the actions of the parasympathetic division conserve body energies. Most organs are innervated by both divisions, and the effects of each are opposite. For example, the heart's action is increased by sympathetic stimulation and decreased by parasympathetic stimulation. The sympathetic system is the more primitive, sometimes exerting a mass action fortified by epinephrine and norepinephrine from the adrenal medulla. This type of mass discharge has been picturesquely described as preparing an animal for "fight or flight." Sympathetic responses include, among others, constriction of blood vessels in the skin and abdominal region (shifting blood to the brain), increase in the rate and force of contraction of the heart, dilation of the bronchial tree, decreased motility of the digestive tract, inhibition of the urinary bladder, and increase in the release of glucose into the blood stream. The parasympathetic system is more advanced structurally and functionally, and its actions are never as generalized as the sympathetic responses. Its actions on the smooth muscles of the gut and digestive glands, increasing motility and secretion, and on the iris, constricting the pupil to protect the eye from intense sunlight, are often cited as examples of the conservative and restorative function of the parasympathetic system. The actions of the autonomic nervous system are summarized in Table 9–6.

Pharmacological (Cholinergic or Adrenergic) Classification of Fibers. The transmission of impulses at the neuromuscular junction and at synapses by chemical transmitters was described in the beginning of this chapter. It is a matter of historical interest that it was in the autonomic nervous system that the action of transmitters was first discovered. In 1921 Otto Loewi reported that the rate of contraction of a frog's heart was slowed when it was perfused with fluid which had first perfused another heart that had been slowed by stimulation of the vagus (a parasympathetic) nerve. Obviously, some substance, which Loewi called "Vagusstoffe," released by the first heart, slowed the second one. In the same way, Loewi demonstrated that stimulation of the cardiac accelerator (a sympathetic) nerve caused the release of a substance, which he called "Acceleransstoffe," that increased the heart rate. It was later established that Loewi's Vagusstoffe was acetylcholine and his Acceleransstoffe was norepinephrine.

Acetylcholine is released at all postganglionic nerve endings of the parasympathetic system. It is also the neurotransmitter liberated at preganglionic endings of both the sympathetic and parasympathetic systems. Norepinephrine is released at the terminals of sympathetic postganglionic neurons except those innervating sweat glands, which release acetylcholine. On the basis of the neurotransmitter liberated, autonomic nerve fibers are called either *cholinergic* (releasing acetylcholine) or *adrenergic* (releasing norepinephrine, also called noradrenalin). These adjectives are also applied to pharmacological agents that cause effects similar to those produced by acetylcholine and norepinephrine.

As a result of studies of the excitatory and inhibitory effects of norepinephrine, epinephrine, and a number of other adrenergic agents, it has been concluded that there are two types of adrenergic receptors. These have been designated *alpha receptors* and *beta receptors*. Norepinephrine has its most

USE Dr. RADTKES KNOW IT ALL CHART

Table 9-6 FUNCTIONS OF THE AUTONOMIC NERVOUS SYSTEM

ORGAN	SYMPATHETIC STIMULATION	PARASYMPATHETIC STIMULATION
Eye Iris	Stimulates radial fibers (dilates pupil)	Stimulates circular fibers (constricts pupil)
Ciliary muscle	Inhibits (flattens lens—weak action)	Stimulates (bulges lens)

Salivary glands
  (parotid, sublingual,
    submaxillary)
	Vasoconstriction may diminish secretion	Stimulates copious secretion high in enzyme content

Lacrimal glands		Stimulates secretion
Sweat glands	Copious sweating (cholinergic)	

Heart
  SA node
  Muscle
	Increased rate
	Increased force of contraction
		Decreased rate

Lungs Bronchi	Dilation	Constriction

Stomach
  Wall
  Glands
	Decreased motility and tone
	Stimulates secretion of alkaline juice with low enzyme activity
		Increased motility and tone
		Stimulates secretion of acid juice with high enzyme activity

Intestine
  Wall
  Anal sphincter
Pancreas
	Decreased motility and tone
	Contraction
	Vasoconstriction may diminish secretion
		Increased motility and tone
		Inhibition
		Stimulates secretion of pancreatic enzymes

Suprarenal gland Medulla	Secretion of epinephrine	

Urinary bladder
  Wall
  Sphincter
	Inhibition
	Excitation
		Excitation
		Inhibition

Penis	Ejaculation	Erection (vasodilation)
Arrector pili muscles of hair follicles	Contraction	

Arterioles
  Splanchnic region and
    skin
  Skeletal muscles
    Baro- and chemoreceptor
     response
    Responses to exercise
     and alarm
	Constriction
	
	Constriction
	
	Dilation	

pronounced effect on alpha receptors; epinephrine has an approximately equal effect on each type. Among the actions associated with alpha receptors are constriction of blood vessels in the skin and abdominal region, relaxation of the smooth muscle of the intestine, and contraction of the radial fibers of the iris (dilating the pupil). Actions associated with beta receptors include dilation of blood vessels in skeletal muscles and the coronary circulation, increase in the rate and force of contraction of the heart, and relaxation of the smooth muscle of the bronchi and their branches.

OUTFLOW AND DISTRIBUTION OF SYMPATHETIC FIBERS

Preganglionic Neurons. The cell bodies of sympathetic preganglionic neurons are located in the lateral horn of the first thoracic to the third lumbar segments of the spinal cord. Each axon leaves the cord through a ventral root and enters a spinal nerve, which it immediately leaves via a **white ramus communicans** (preganglionic fibers are myelinated) to pass into a **paravertebral ganglion.** The paravertebral ganglia are found on either side of the vertebral column, close to the bodies of the vertebrae. They form a series of 22 to 26 ganglia (usually no more than 23) connected together in a chain or trunk extending from the base of the skull to the coccyx (Fig. 9–64). Some pregan-

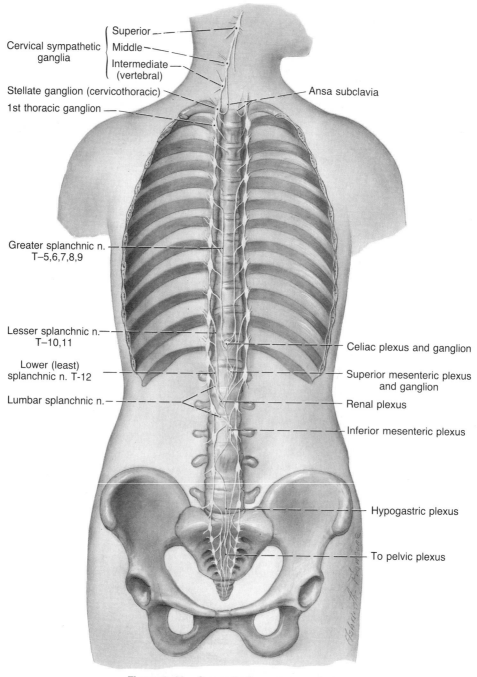

Figure 9–64. Sympathetic nervous system.

glionic fibers synapse in these ganglia (immediately or after passing up or down the sympathetic chain); others continue to *prevertebral (collateral) ganglia*, located mainly in the abdominal and pelvic cavities near the aorta and its branches, or to smaller, more peripherally located ganglia; still others reach and supply cells in the medulla of the suprarenal (adrenal) glands (Fig. 9–65). Three large prevertebral ganglia, named according to their positions near their respective arteries, are the celiac, superior mesenteric, and inferior mesenteric. Preganglionic fibers leading to the prevertebral ganglia form the *splanchnic nerves*. The principal splanchnic nerves arising from the thoracic region are the greater, lesser, and least splanchnic nerves (Fig. 9–66).

Postganglionic Neurons. Some postganglionic fibers arising from cell bodies in paravertebral ganglia pass back into spinal nerves via a **gray ramus communicans** (postganglionic fibers are nonmyelinated), and by traveling with these nerves supply, in the regions served by spinal nerves, smooth muscle of blood vessels in the skin and skeletal muscles, arrector pili muscles of hair follicles and sweat glands. Those that do not pass back into spinal nerves supply mainly the thoracic viscera (including fibers in the cardiac nerves, which function as augmenters of the activity of the heart) and the major part of the head and neck regions, including the smooth muscles of the eyes and eyelids, blood vessels of the skin and skeletal muscles, sweat glands, and arrector pili muscles (many fibers reaching their destinations via branches of cranial nerves).

Since only thoracic and upper lumbar spinal nerves have white rami carrying preganglionic fibers whereas all spinal nerves have gray rami carrying postganglionic fibers, it follows that postganglionic neurons whose fibers are in gray rami of cervical, lower lumbar, and sacral spinal nerves have synapsed with preganglionic fibers that have ascended or descended the sympathetic chain. In the cervical part of each sympathetic chain there are three ganglia: a superior (probably formed by a fusion of four ganglia), middle (which may be fused with the superior ganglion), and inferior, or stellate (probably formed by a fusion of the lower two cervical and first thoracic ganglia). Preganglionic fibers concerned with supplying the upper extremities arise from the second to seventh thoracic spinal segments and synapse mainly in the inferior cervical ganglion, from where postganglionic fibers pass in gray rami to spinal nerves of the brachial plexus.

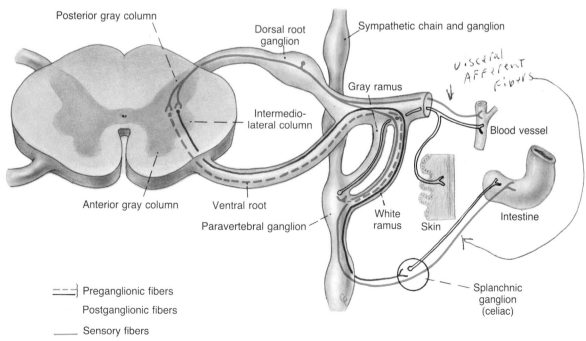

Figure 9–65. Pathways for distribution of sympathetic fibers.

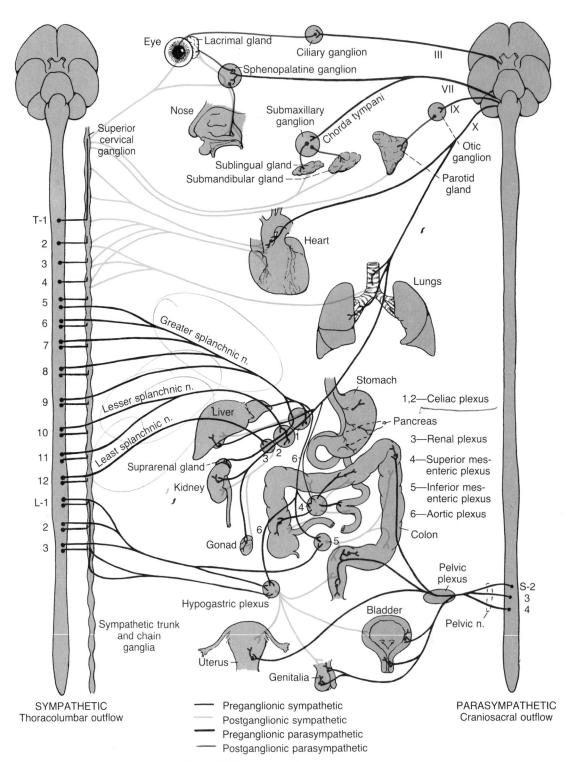

Figure 9–66. Autonomic nervous system.

Postganglionic fibers supplying the greater part of the head and neck regions arise chiefly from cell bodies in the superior cervical ganglion which have made synaptic connections with preganglionic fibers that have ascended from the upper five (upper three for the most part) thoracic segments. Interruption of preganglionic input into the superior cervical ganglion or postganglionic outflow from it produces *Horner's syndrome* (first described by the Swiss ophthalmologist Johann Horner), which includes drooping of the upper eyelid (ptosis), small pupil, and absence of sweating on the affected side of the head and neck.

Postganglionic fibers arising from cell bodies in prevertebral or other outlying ganglia principally serve the abdominal and pelvic viscera. These fibers form the great *plexuses* found in close relation to major arteries. The so-called "solar plexus," located in the abdomen alongside the celiac artery, is another name for the *celiac plexus*. This plexus contains postganglionic fibers derived from the celiac ganglion as well as some preganglionic parasympathetic fibers.

OUTFLOW AND DISTRIBUTION OF PARASYMPATHETIC FIBERS

The cell bodies of preganglionic parasympathetic neurons are located in the brain stem and in the second, third, and fourth sacral segments of the spinal cord. Their axons are long and synapse in the cranial part with postganglionic neurons in four ganglia in the head (Fig. 9–66) and in the sacral part with postganglionic neurons in minute ganglia lying near or within the walls of the innervated organs. **Cranial preganglionic fibers** exit via the third (oculomotor), seventh (facial), ninth (glossopharyngeal), and tenth (vagus) cranial nerves. They synapse with postganglionic neurons whose fibers innervate the following organs: oculomotor — iris and ciliary muscles of the eyes; facial — salivary glands (submaxillaries and sublinguals) and lacrimal glands; glossopharyngeal — salivary glands (parotids); and vagus — thoracic, abdominal, and pelvic viscera.

The **sacral preganglionic fibers** leave the spinal cord via the ventral roots, branching off to proceed peripherally as the *pelvic nerve*, which enters into the formation of the *pelvic plexus* (Fig. 9–66), from which branches lead to the parasympathetic ganglia. Sacral postganglionic fibers innervate the lower colon, rectum, bladder, and reproductive organs.

The craniosacral, or parasympathetic, nervous system can be surgically altered in treatment of various disease states. The vagus nerves are divided for the treatment of duodenal ulcer. When the vagus nerves are divided, there is an important influence on hydrochloric acid secretion by the stomach. This results in the elimination of the cephalic phase of gastric secretion (see Chapter 14) with diminished production of hydrochloric acid by the parietal cells.

CONTROL OF THE AUTONOMIC NERVOUS SYSTEM

The hypothalamus is an important center for regulation and integration of both sympathetic and parasympathetic activity. Its widespread connections include the cerebral cortex, thalamus, medulla oblongata, and spinal cord. The medulla oblongata has centers that regulate the activity of the heart and the degree of constriction of blood vessels, and the hypothalamus mediates modifying effects on these centers. Many attempts have been made to identify discrete sympathetic and parasympathetic centers in the hypothalamus by stimulating specific areas in animals. The results have not been entirely consistent, although according to some authors sympathetic control tends to reside in the lateral and posterior regions and parasympathetic control in the medial and anterior regions.

ASPECTS OF THE FUNCTIONAL ORGANIZATION OF THE NERVOUS SYSTEM

To understand how the nervous system functions it is necessary to examine pathways for sensory input to specific parts of the central nervous system, interconnections between functional regions of the central nervous system, and efferent pathways leading to specific actions. This section describes aspects of the functional organization of the nervous system from the simple to the complex, and includes discussions of reflexes, sensory perception, motor function, emotional behavior, and language.

Reflex Action

A reflex action is an involuntary response to a sensory stimulus. A well-known example is the patellar reflex, or knee jerk. Many actions are partially voluntary and partially reflex. For example, a mixture of volition and reflex activity is involved in the act of swallowing. In general the numerous and diverse reflexes involved in a specific behavior pattern are so interrelated that the result is one continuous smooth and well-directed action, each reflex merging with the next in rapid sequence. Reflex actions are often thought of as machinelike, but they are also purposeful, in general serving to protect the body. For instance, the reflexive contraction of the pupil of the eye when illuminated by bright light serves to protect the retina.

The following elements are involved in a typical spinal cord reflex arc (Fig. 9–67):

1. A receptor.
2. A sensory neuron.
3. Synapse in the spinal cord between sensory and internuncial neurons (with the exception of the stretch reflexes, such as the knee jerk, described below).
4. Synapse between internuncial and motor neurons.
5. Junction between motor neuron and skeletal muscle.

It should be borne in mind that sensory neurons forming part of reflex arcs usually also make other synaptic connections including, if the sensation is consciously perceived, with neuronal pathways leading to the sensory cortex. In addition, internuncial neurons are usually not simply links in a single reflex arc, but have connections with other groups of internuncial neurons, thus making very complex reflex arcs possible.

Much of our knowledge of reflex action has come from studies of spinal cord reflexes in animals whose spinal cords have been transected. Two spinal cord reflexes that have been intensively studied are the stretch reflex, typified by the knee jerk, and the flexor reflex, also called the withdrawal reflex, in which withdrawal of a limb brought about by muscle flexion occurs in response to stimulation of pain, or *nociceptive* (L. *nocere*, to hurt; L. *capere*, to take), receptors (although almost any stimulus may elicit this response). *this to 303 relates to lecture packet*

The **stretch reflex,** also called the *myotatic reflex* (G. *mys*, muscle; G. *tasis*, a stretching), is a monosynaptic reflex and employs only two types of neurons — sensory and motor. A method used clinically to evaluate the state of the stretch reflexes is to check the knee jerk or other muscle jerks by striking, for instance, the patellar tendon with a reflex hammer. Striking the tendon produces a rapid stretching of the muscle that is picked up by the muscle spindle receptors. The signal then travels to the cord, and a motor neuron is triggered to stimulate the muscle.

The stretch reflex plays an essential role in maintaining normal posture and is most pronounced in the *antigravity muscles,* such as the elevators of the jaw and the extensors of the neck, back, knee, and ankle. The reflex response to stretching the muscles by the force of gravity maintains, without conscious

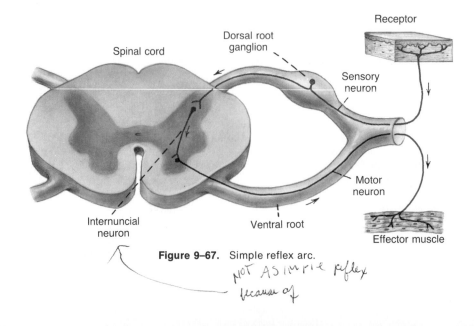

Figure 9–67. Simple reflex arc.

NOT AS simple reflex because of

effort, an upright body and head and a closed jaw. Skeletal muscle tone, the steady state of partial contraction normally exhibited by all skeletal muscles, is dependent upon the integrity of the stretch reflex. Interrupting sensory input from muscle spindles to the spinal cord by cutting the dorsal roots will cause a muscle to become almost flaccid.

Muscle tone is also governed by excitatory and inhibitory impulses from the brain that act on motor neurons as well as on neurons that control the sensitivity of the muscle spindle, called **gamma efferents.** This action makes possible continuous adjustments in muscle tone for maintaining balance and support. The gamma efferents are so called because their fibers are Type A gamma (small diameter — see page 246) as distinguished from the Type A alpha fibers of the motor neurons, which stimulate muscle contraction, and of the primary sensory neurons of the muscle spindle. The spindle itself is composed of muscle fibers (called *intrafusal fibers)* of smaller diameter than the regular muscle fibers, surrounded by a capsule. The central portion of the muscle spindle fibers is innervated by sensory endings sensitive to stretch, the end portions by gamma efferents (Fig. 9–68). When a muscle is stretched, the entire lengths of the spindle fibers are stretched and the sensory endings are stimulated, triggering reflex muscular contraction. Stimulation of muscle fibers by gamma efferents causes the ends to contract. This stretches the central, noncontractile region and thus has the same effect on the sensory

endings as stretching the muscle. Consequently, muscle tone is increased. Decreased stimulation by gamma efferents has the opposite effect. The spindle fibers are innervated by two types of sensory neurons, namely, those forming **primary,** or **annulospiral, endings** and those forming secondary, or "flower spray," endings. The annulospiral endings respond very strongly to a change in length and adapt rapidly; the secondary endings respond less strongly to a change in length and do not readily adapt.

Excessive stretching of a muscle, which could tear it, will inhibit the stretch reflex as a result of what is known as the *reverse myotatic reflex.* The receptors for this reflex (the *Golgi tendon organ)* respond to excessive stretch by triggering an inhibitory reflex arc presumably formed by sensory fibers from the receptor leading to inhibitory internuncial neurons which synapse with motor neurons.

The **flexor,** or **withdrawal, reflex** differs from the stretch reflex in a number of ways. The stretch reflex is, as mentioned, monosynaptic and its effect is circumscribed; that is, only the muscle that was stretched contracts. The withdrawal reflex, on the other hand, is diffuse, involving a complex network of synapses between sensory neurons and internuncial neurons, which in turn interconnect with other internuncial neurons in more than one segment of the cord both ipsilaterally (on the same side — L. *ipse,* self; L. *latus,* side) and contralaterally (on the opposite side — L. *contra,* against). Thus, stepping on a nail will normally cause withdrawal of the entire lower extremity with flexion of the knee and thigh. In addition, the opposite limb will be extended, giving rise to the *crossed extension reflex.* Furthermore, when the flexors causing the withdrawal are stimulated, the antagonists, the extensors, are inhibited and relax. Likewise, with the associated crossed extension reflex, stimulation of the extensors on the opposite side is accompanied by inhibition of the flexors. This phenomenon, inhibition of an antagonist when a prime mover contracts, is called *reciprocal innervation.* Another characteristic of withdrawal reflexes not displayed by stretch reflexes is a phenomenon called *after discharge,* the continuation of a response after the stimulation ends. The existence of alternate pathways in flexor responses (so-called parallel and reverberating circuits, illustrated in Fig. 9–69) can account for this.

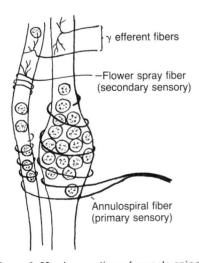

Figure 9–68. Innervation of muscle spindle.

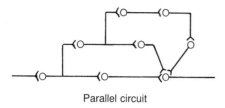

Parallel circuit

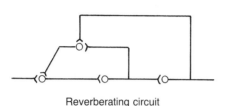

Reverberating circuit

Figure 9–69. Parallel and reverberating neuronal circuits.

Mention was made in the discussion of stretch reflexes of excitatory and inhibitory impulses from higher centers acting on spinal cord neurons. Normal reflex activity of the spinal cord depends upon these discharges, the net effect of which is normally excitatory. Their interruption by transection of the cord causes what is known as **spinal shock,** a condition in which, among other things, almost all spinal reflexes below the transection are completely abolished. In frogs, reflex activity returns to normal in minutes. Dogs and cats recover in days. Humans require months for recovery, and even then the reflex responses are generally abnormal and may be weak, excessive, or spasmodic. One of the responses seen in humans after accidental cord transection or damage to certain motor tracts (the pyramidal tracts — see page 310) is the *Babinski reflex,* an abnormal response to stimulation of the sole of the foot. The normal response to stimulation of the sole of the foot, called the *plantar reflex,* is plantar flexion of the toes. The sign of Babinski (observed in infants before they learn to walk as well as in cases of damage to the nervous system) is dorsiflexion of the big toe and fanning out of the others. Midbrain transection between the superior and inferior colliculi (decerebrate preparation) has a quite different effect from spinal transection. Muscle tone, especially of the antigravity muscles, is increased, producing a condition known as **decerebrate rigidity.** This occurs because inhibition of stretch reflexes by signals from the inhibitory area of the reticular

formation is lost, whereas facilitation of stretch reflexes by signals from the facilitatory area of the reticular formation is intensified (the facilitatory area becomes hyperactive because it is no longer subject to inhibition from higher brain levels, probably the cerebellum, basal ganglia, and cerebral cortex). The increased muscle tone results principally from stimulation of the gamma efferents of the muscle spindles.

In some reflexes involving sensory input and motor outflow in spinal nerves the coordinating centers are in the brain. One especially important group of reflexes of this type is the *tonic neck reflexes,* which bring about postural changes in the limbs in response to bending or rotation of the head that tend to provide support in the direction of the head movement. Turning or bending the head to the right, for example, will increase the tone of the extensors on the right side and of the flexors on the left.

A classification of reflexes useful in clinical work distinguishes superficial, deep, visceral, and pathological reflexes. *Superficial reflexes* are those produced by stimulation on the surface of the body. The withdrawal and plantar reflexes, previously mentioned, are examples, as are the corneal reflex, i.e., blinking of the eye when the cornea is touched, and the abdominal reflex, in which light scratching of the skin of a quadrant of the abdomen results in contraction of the muscles of that quadrant. *Deep reflexes* are stretch reflexes, previously described, tested by tapping the tendon of a muscle. Examples of *visceral reflexes* are the carotid sinus reflex, in which exerting pressure on the carotid sinus produces a fall in blood pressure, and the pupillary reflex — constriction of the pupil when a light is shined into the eye. *Pathological reflexes* are those not normally present, such as the previously described Babinski reflex.

While reflexes in themselves serve many important functions, such as avoiding injury, keeping the body and head upright, preventing excessive changes in blood pressure (by altering the diameter of arterioles and changing the rate and contractile force of the heart), and emptying the bladder, the question may be asked: Do they play roles other than those that can be clearly identified? It has been suggested that they do, or at least that sets of circuits involved in reflex responses constitute "prefabricated" units for building volitional movements, such as walking and performing athletic feats. It has been argued in support of this view that since, for the most part, fibers descending from the motor cortex synapse only with internuncial neurons, it is at least in theory possible for this to occur.

Pathways for Conscious Sensory Perception

must know

The pathways for sensations that are consciously perceived lead to the cerebral cortex. The sensory cortical projection areas are illustrated in Figure 9–23. Areas 3, 1, and 2, in the **postcentral gyrus** of the parietal lobe, are the receptive areas for touch, pressure, temperature, pain, and kinesthesia (see page 245) from all parts of the body and head. Area 17, in the occipital lobe, is the sensory receptive area for vision; area 41, in the temporal lobe, is the cortical area for hearing. The area for equilibrium is believed to be closely associated with the area for hearing. The sensory projection area for taste is in the parietal lobe, for smell in the orbitofrontal area. All consciously perceived sensory impulses, except those for smell, are relayed through the **thalamus**. The thalamus is responsible for a primitive, or *protopathic*, sensibility — a crude awareness of the kind of sensation, whether the sensation is pleasant or unpleasant, and its general location. Discriminatory sensibility is dependent upon the cerebral cortex. The specific pathways for the special senses are described in Chapter 10. Described below are the pathways for touch, pressure, temperature, pain, and kinesthesia. These sensations are often called the *somesthetic sensations*, and their cortical projection region in the postcentral gyrus is generally referred to as the *somesthetic cortex*.

The pathways for somesthetic sensations usually involve three neurons. The sensory neuron is the first-order neuron and leads from a receptor to the gray matter of the spinal cord or to nuclei in the brain. The second-order neuron passes to the thalamus and the third-order neuron to the somesthetic cortex.

Pathways for Pain, Temperature, and Crude Touch and Pressure from the Body. The fibers of sensory (first-order) neurons transmitting pain, temperature, and crude touch and pressure sensations enter the cord through the dorsal root and make synaptic connections with second-order neurons that give rise to the **spinothalamic tracts.** Fibers forming the spinothalamic tracts decussate (cross) and ascend to the thalamus in the lateral column (*lateral spinothalamic tract* — Fig. 9–70) and anterior column (*anterior spinothalamic tract*). It is usually stated that the lateral spinothalamic tract transmits chiefly pain and temperature sensations, whereas the anterior spinothalamic tract transmits chiefly crude touch and pressure. However, some authors point out that the separation of sensory information is

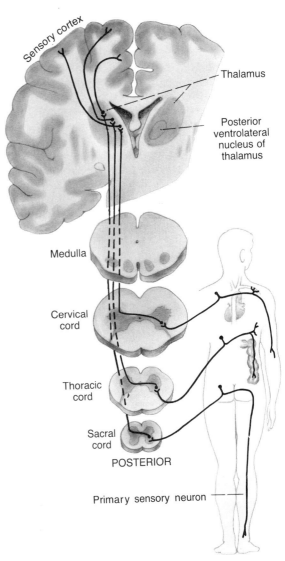

Figure 9–70. Lateral spinothalamic tract (pathway for pain and temperature.)

not sufficiently clear-cut to warrant this conventional functional division. The second-order neurons synapse in the thalamus with third-order neurons that convey impulses principally to the somesthetic cortex.

Some fibers that arise and travel with the spinothalamic tracts in the lateral and anterior columns do not reach the thalamus. These fibers terminate in the reticular formation, where many make synaptic connections with neurons whose fibers project to the thalamus. Since the fibers ascending to the reticular formation (*spinoreticular fibers*) do not form a discrete tract, many authors refer to them and the spinothalamic fibers as constituting the **anterolateral pathway** or **system.**

Diffuse, burning pain, as opposed to pricking pain, often has emotional or strongly aversive dimensions. According to some investigators, there is a neural basis for this phenomenon. It is believed that in the thalamus the terminus for fibers transmitting burning pain (from either the uninterrupted spinal tracts or from the reticular formation) is in the medial (intralaminar) region, whereas fibers conveying pricking pain terminate in the more lateral regions. Fibers transmitting burning pain also ascend from the reticular formation to the hypothalamus. Neurons in the medial thalamus and in the hypothalamus have a widespread cortical influence. Intractable pain is of the burning type. It has been reported that surgically created lesions in the intralaminar region of the thalamus relieve certain kinds of intractable pain without impairing other sensations.

Pathways for Discriminatory Touch and Pressure and for Kinesthesia from the Body. The pathways for discriminatory touch and pressure sensations and for kinesthesia from the body involve the fibers of first-order neurons that ascend the spinal cord in the dorsal column, often called the **dorsal column pathway** or **system.** The sensory neuron fibers forming the dorsal columns pass up the cord to nuclei in the medulla on the same side that they enter the cord in two tracts, the *fasciculus gracilis* and the *fasciculus cuneatus* (Fig. 9–71). In the medulla the first-order neurons synapse with neurons that cross to the opposite side and ascend to the thalamus in a broad band of fibers called the *medial lemniscus.* Third-order neurons project principally to the somesthetic cortex.

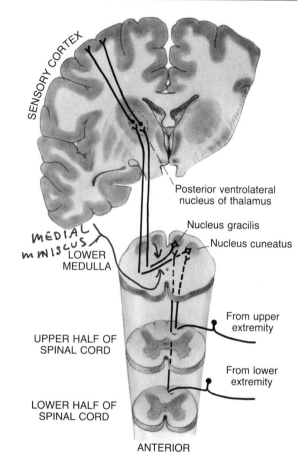

Figure 9–71. Fasciculi gracilis and cuneatus of dorsal funiculus (pathway for kinesthesia and discriminatory tactile sensations).

Although tactile sensations are transmitted by both the spinothalamic tracts and dorsal columns, only those transmitted via the dorsal columns provide precise localization, discrete two-point discrimination, and an awareness of fine gradations of intensity and of vibratory sensations.

Somesthetic Sensory Input from the Head. The fifth (trigeminal) cranial nerve carries sensory fibers for touch, pressure, pain, and temperature in the head and kinesthesia for the muscles of mastication (which are supplied by motor branches of the fifth cranial nerve). According to some anatomists, kinesthetic sensations for the facial and ocular muscles are also transmitted by the fifth cranial nerve; others say that kinesthetic sensations for the muscles of the head are in general mediated by cranial nerves supplying motor branches to them.

These pathways also involve first-, second- and third-order neurons, fibers of the third-order neurons projecting from the thalamus to the somesthetic cortex. All fibers enter the pons. Those mediating principally pain and temperature descend as the *spinal tract of the trigeminal nerve* to make synaptic connections in the *nucleus of the spinal tract*, the greater number no lower than the medulla, but some as far down as the first cervical segment of the spinal cord. Fibers transmitting tactile sensations and kinesthesia ascend to make synaptic connections in the *principal sensory nucleus* (tactile sensations mainly) and the *mesencephalic nucleus* (kinesthetic sensations). The majority of the second-order neurons cross before ascending to the thalamus. Some, however, ascend on the same side.

Representation in the Somesthetic Cortex. Since somesthetic sensations from the body are transmitted by tracts that decussate, either in the cord or the medulla, the postcentral gyrus of each cerebral hemisphere receives input from the opposite side of the body. The greater part of the input from the head is also to the opposite cerebral hemisphere. The representation of the different parts of the body and head in the postcentral gyrus is illustrated in Figure 9–24. The size of the cortical area on this topographical map is proportional to the number of incoming fibers from a given part of the body. Thus the area for the fingers, which have a high concentration of receptors at their tips, is larger than the area for the entire trunk.

Determination of the shape, size, texture and weight of an object requires integration of sensory input in the somesthetic cortex. Further integration in the somesthetic association areas adjacent to the postcentral gyrus makes it possible to identify a particular object, for example, a knife or a pencil. Synthesis of sensory data and the relation of information of the moment with that of the past in the association areas is necessary for the recognition of the nature and use of an object.

Role of the Reticular Activating System. In the late 1940's H. W. Magoun and Giuseppe Moruzzi discovered that electrical stimulation of parts of the reticular formation (see page 260) awakened a drowsing cat. The direct stimulation of the sensory cortex had been shown to have no such effect. Magoun and Moruzzi therefore concluded that the reticular formation, among other things, functions as an alarm to awaken the brain and so named it the *reticular activating system*. Since then it has been found that projections to the reticular formation provide input for all types of sensations. Just about any sensory input to the reticular activating system can initiate a general stimulation of the entire cerebral cortex and other parts of the brain. With experience, the reticular formation comes to be discriminating in its response to different stimuli, so that, for example, sounds of traffic will not cause a city dweller to be aroused but the smell of smoke may. The reticular activating system receives not only sensory input but also input from various parts of the cerebrum. This can account for the observation that activities such as whistling, conversation, and movement can help maintain a wakeful state. Destruction of the reticular activating system will produce a permanent comatose state.

Aspects of the Physiology of Pain

As described in the section on sensory receptors, painful stimuli are received at naked nerve endings and are carried through myelinated A-delta fibers (fast, sharp, localized pain) and nonmyelinated C fibers (slow, burning, diffuse pain).

Stimuli effective in arousing the sensation of pain vary to some degree for each tissue. The very existence of pain impulses arising from the viscera was debated until it was shown that adequate stimuli for pain originating in the heart or digestive tract, for example, are different from those producing pain in the skin. Skin is sensitive to cutting and burning, whereas this type of stimulation does not give rise to distress when applied to the stomach or intestine. Pain in the digestive tract is produced by distention or spasm of the smooth muscle, as well as by chemical irritation of an inflamed mucosa. Severe pain can occur in skeletal muscle when the blood supply is reduced — the basis of a condition known as *intermittent claudication* (pain in the leg, particularly the calf, induced by walking and reduced by rest, associated with arterial disease of the lower extremities).

Ischemia (reduction in oxygen supply), the only proved cause of pain in the heart muscle, is responsible for *angina pectoris* (chest pain transmitted to the left shoulder and arm, usually caused by physical exertion or emotional stress in individuals with narrowed coronary arteries) and the pain of myocardial infarction (blockage of a coronary artery to the heart with death of heart muscle).

Most pain impulses from the viscera are carried by fibers running in sympathetic nerves. These fibers enter the cord through the dorsal roots by way of the white rami communicans (Fig. 9–65). A few visceral pain impulses are transmitted by sacral parasympathetic and cranial nerves.

Referred Pain (Fig. 9–72). When pain is aroused by stimulation of afferent endings in the viscera, it is usually referred to some other skin area, a fact of great diagnostic importance.

Afferent nerves from the viscera terminate in the spinal cord segment which supplies the particular viscus involved. Those areas to which pain from various organs is referred have been mapped out; they indicate to the physician the internal source of

irritation. For example, the sensory fibers from the heart terminate in the third cervical through the fifth thoracic cord segments, and pain arising in the heart as a result of ischemia is not localized specifically to the region of the heart, but to those superficial structures whose sensory nerves also terminate in these spinal segments. Therefore, the pain felt under the upper sternum usually radiates to the skin of the left shoulder and arm. It is believed that the pain is referred to the skin of the arm and shoulder because ascending second-order neurons receiving impulses from the skin of the arm and shoulder also receive signals from the heart.

Parietal Pain. Pain from the viscera may spread to the parietal layer of the peritoneum, pleura or pericardium, each of which is innervated by spinal nerves. Parietal pain is, in contrast to true visceral pain, sharp and localized directly over the painful organ.

Phantom Limb Pain. Following an amputation, the patient can retain the amputat-

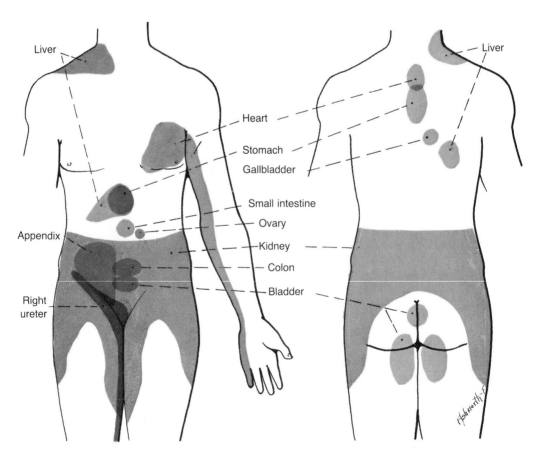

Figure 9–72. Areas of referred pain, anterior and posterior views.

ed limb as a part of his body image. This is a reflection of the association established between stimuli from the periphery and the cortical area of representation. Stimuli continue to arise from the severed sensory nerves and are interpreted centrally as arising for example, from the hand. Yet the patient mistakenly feels that his pain is imaginary, since he knows his hand was amputated. Pain of this kind places additional psychological burdens on the patient who believes he is imagining things his reason tells him cannot exist. It is important to explain to this type of patient that the sensation of pain is real and not a figment of his imagination. The sensation can be defined clearly, and the patient will say that his arm is twisted or that his thumb is being pushed backward. The cortical image of the amputated extremity can remain fixed in the same position as when amputation occurred. This is particularly true in traumatic amputations.

The management of phantom limb pain is more effective if measures are taken to prevent it rather than treat it once the condition has been established. If pain is due to a surgical amputation, anesthetic infiltration of the nerve bundles at the site of amputation should be performed before surgery. In this way, the surgeon can probably minimize the locking or painful image in the patient's consciousness.

Headache. Headache is one of the most common of all symptoms and can occur in the absence of definite pathology or as a manifestation of serious illness. Most headaches are transient, but a few are chronic, occurring over a period of months, years, or a lifetime. A headache can result from stimulation of any pain-sensitive structure in the head. Most commonly headaches are associated with dilation of cranial blood vessels or with contraction of skeletal muscles of the head and neck.

Headaches that occur only occasionally may be caused by fatigue, eyestrain, hunger, or overindulgence in alcohol. Headaches persisting for weeks or months without relief, except in intensity, are often associated with constant or periodic emotional tension. Another type of chronic headache is *migraine* — recurrent headache, usually concentrated on one side of the head, sometimes accompanied by nausea and often preceded by premonitory sensory disturbances, or aura. The aura may be visual (flashing or spinning lights), auditory (ringing in the ears), or cutaneous (numbness or tingling sensations). Migraine occurs in about 10 per cent of the population, most commonly in women, and it runs in families.

The pain of migraine is associated with dilation of blood vessels primarily in the area of distribution of the external carotid artery. Many neurologists believe that a vasomotor regulatory defect is responsible for the disorder. The migraine attack is preceded by vasoconstriction, and the vasodilation, it has been proposed, is triggered by the release of serotonin from blood platelets in the constricted blood vessels. Until recently there has been no satisfactory drug candidate for long-term treatment of migraine. The most effective drugs are either addictive (ergotamine tartrate) or have serious side effects. A most promising new candidate is propranolol, a drug used to treat heart disease patients, which seems to be much more effective than any other drug and yet has fewer side effects. (The clue to the drug's antimigraine action was the report by cardiac patients who also had migraine that taking propranolol relieved their migraine.) Propranolol is believed to be effective because it blocks the beta, or vasodilator, receptors of cranial blood vessels.

Regulation of Pain

It is generally recognized that the perception of pain can be influenced by such things as anxiety, thought processes, past experience, and the application of liniments or irritants to the skin. These alterations in pain perception can be accounted for by the modulation of synaptic transmission at several levels in the pathway for transmitting pain impulses from the periphery to the brain. It is recognized that synaptic transmission can be depressed in the *substantia gelatinosa* of the spinal cord, the locus of the first relay station in the anterolateral pathway. It is believed that here interneurons receiving input from nonpain sensory nerve fibers and from fibers descending from the cerebral cortex and subcortical regions of the brain act as "gatekeepers" over the flow of pain signals by presynaptic inhibition of transmission from pain fibers to neurons sending pain signals to the brain. This proposed action by interneurons of the substantia gelatinosa is known as the **gate control theory.** A possible physiological basis for pain gating is the interaction between the _enkephalins_, short-chain, morphinelike neuropeptides, and _substance P,_ a neuropeptide released at the terminals of pain fibers. Enkephalins inhibit the release of substance P from these terminals. It has been proposed that depression of the synaptic transmission of pain impulses occurs when signals reaching interneurons in the substantia gelatinosa from the surface of the body or from the brain trigger the release of enkephalins at interneuron fiber terminals, suppressing the release of substance P at the endings of sensory neuron fibers mediating pain. As a result, the excitability of the neurons receiving synaptic input from pain fibers, which convey pain signals to the brain, is reduced. Modulation of synaptic transmission of pain impulses could occur by a similar mechanism at supraspinal levels.

Other substances besides the enkephalins appear to be involved in the control of pain. For example, it has been reported that relief from intractable pain (pain not responsive to medication) by electrical stimulation (of the periventricular gray matter with implanted electrodes) and by acupuncture is associated with the accumulation in the cerebrospinal fluid of the long-chain, morphinelike neuropeptides known as _endorphins._

Special Treatment of Chronic Pain. Pain for most people is self-limiting and can be relieved by medication. A headache will disappear without treatment. If relief is needed, it can be provided by taking an aspirin. The pain of bruises, burns, or surgery will vanish as healing proceeds. There is, however, a group of people for whom recurrent episodes of intractable pain is a chronic condition. Among the victims of such pain are those suffering from: (1) certain kinds of headaches; (2) phantom limb pain; (3) terminal cancer pain; (4) causalgia — burning pain that can occur after damage to nerves following sudden injury, such as a bullet wound, and which usually, but not always, gradually disappears; (5) neuralgia — pain along the course of a peripheral nerve, generally without apparent cause (the most common form is trigeminal neuralgia, or _tic douloureux_); and (6) disorders of joints, especially arthritis. Among the variety of techniques currently employed to treat chronic pain are electrical stimulation, acupuncture, and surgery. In some cases, complete and

permanent relief is obtained. Sometimes the pain is reduced from an unbearable to a tolerable level. Too often, unfortunately, relief is either unobtainable or temporary.

The use of **electrical stimulation** to treat chronic pain can be traced to the first century, when victims of gout, among others, were exposed to shock from electric eels. Acceptance of the gate control theory of pain has led to a reintroduction of electrical stimulation to treat pain in recent years. The most commonly used instrument for this purpose is the _transcutaneous stimulator_. Electrodes are taped to the skin over the spine or painful area and are switched on or off at will by the patient.

The Chinese practice of **acupuncture** (L. _acus_, needle) — the insertion and twirling of needles at specific sites on the body surface — was introduced into this country in 1972. Since then it has found increasing acceptance as a technique for treating chronic pain. Presumably acupuncture relieves pain in much the same way as electrical stimulation. It has been pointed out that the acupuncture points shown in traditional Chinese atlases are located close to clusters of peripheral nerves.

Surgery for controlling pain involves interrupting the transmission of pain impulses in three main areas of the nervous system: (1) the autonomic nervous system; (2) peripheral nerves, spinal roots and the spinal cord; and (3) the brain. Sympathectomies are performed in various locations. The most frequently performed operation in the parasympathetic nervous system is interruption of the vagus nerve. In a _rhizotomy_ (G. _rhiza_, root; G. _tomē_, a cutting) a sensory nerve root is divided. The anterolateral region of the spinal cord is sectioned to interrupt the spinothalamic tracts in an operation known as _anterolateral cordotomy_. As mentioned earlier, it has been reported that relief from some forms of intractable pain can be obtained by surgically created lesions in the intralaminar region of the thalamus.

A distinction must be drawn between the sensations of pain and the response of the patient to pain. Severing tracts connecting the anterior frontal cortex with subcortical areas of the brain (prefrontal lobotomy) will alter the patient's reaction to pain, so that relief is obtained even though pain is still felt. Since operations on the frontal cortex are associated with severe personality changes, this type of surgery is now generally avoided.

Organic Sensations

Organic sensations include sensations such as hunger (appetite, hunger pangs, and hunger drive), thirst, urination and defecation urges, nausea, and sex sensation.

The nature of the internal conditions leading to the various components of hunger is still quite a mystery. *Appetite* is the longing for a preferred food substance, and is associated with conditioned reflexes such as salivation and secretion of stomach juices. Food preferences are determined by previous experience, genetic factors, and dietary deficiencies. Specific hungers often occur when the body needs certain substances. *Hunger pangs* can occur as the result of strong stomach contractions, although the hunger drive can clearly operate in the absence of these contractions, which may be only a by-product of the physiological state of the individual. Animals without stomachs exhibit a desire for food more often than do normal animals. Lowered blood sugar level apparently is an important factor in creating desire for food. This factor operates through centers in the hypothalamus, which contains more blood vessels than any other part of the nervous system and receives circulatory, chemical, sensory, and neural stimuli. The hypothalamus plays an important role in the control of other drives such as thirst and sex. In the case of thirst, the intensity of the drive is related to the water deficit. Thus, a dehydrated individual will consume enough water to replace his water deficit within about 30 minutes. It is thought that concentration of salt and other chemical substances in the body fluids, as well as the total amount of fluid present in the body, helps to determine thirst.

Nausea is a disagreeable sensation in the epigastrium which may or may not be associated with vomiting, and which is carried by both the vagus nerve and by sympathetic nerves. The vomiting center is in the reticular formation of the medulla. This center is the site of action of the so-called *emetic* drugs, which cause vomiting.

The sensation of *air hunger* is a result of excess carbon dioxide accumulation in the lungs. Although oxygen is a constant requirement of the body, the body cannot readily respond directly to oxygen lack. However, as oxygen is used up, carbon dioxide collects in the lungs, causing great discomfort unless the reflex breathing mechanisms are able to again substitute oxygen for carbon dioxide. When oxygen starvation occurs in an atmosphere lacking excess carbon dioxide — for example at high altitudes — a kind of intoxication results. The individual may undergo memory impairment and paralysis or may shout or burst into tears. At the same time he feels confident of his abilities and does not realize the seriousness of his condition. There is evidence that partial oxygen starvation brings out emotional reactions which are normally held under voluntary control.

Consciousness of *fatigue* impels human beings to seek rest. Everybody is aware of how desperate the need for sleep can become. As a result of prolonged exercise, the chemistry of the blood is altered in several ways. An elevated concentration of lactic acid in muscles presumably stimulates the nervous system directly or activates certain receptors. In sleepiness, it may be that nerve and brain centers are directly stimulated by chemical conditions in the body. The story of fatigue is complicated by the fact that it sometimes seems to result not from physical exertion but from boredom, worry, or frustration.

Pathways for Motor Function *As D. scussed in class*

The parts of the cerebral cortex most concerned with movement are Brodmann areas 4 and 6 (see page 253). It should be noted, however, that the lines around motor areas are not always clearly drawn. Muscular contractions, for example, can be elicited by stimulation of the postcentral sensory area (the somesthetic cortex — Brodmann areas 3, 1, and 2), and, as mentioned, some authors speak of the pre- and postcentral motor and sensory areas as the sensorimotor cortex. Area 19 reprocesses visual sensory information and is, therefore, described as an association area of the visual cortex. Yet, if area 19 is stimulated in an experimental animal, the eyes will turn away from the side stimulated.

Distinction Between the Pyramidal and Extrapyramidal Systems *As covered in class*

Two major motor pathways can be distinguished anatomically and functionally. They are (1) the pyramidal (corticospinal) pathway, and (2) the extrapyramidal pathway.

The Pyramidal (Corticospinal) Tracts. The fibers of the pyramidal, or corticospinal, tracts descend without interruption from the cerebral cortex to the spinal cord. These tracts initiate voluntary movements of skeletal muscles, especially those involving discrete movements of the limbs, particularly individual finger movements. The term pyramidal has two origins. These tracts were originally called the "pyramidal" system because they include the axons of the giant pyramidal cells of Betz (page 253), which at one time were thought to be the only fibers in the corticospinal tracts and now are estimated to account for about 3 to 4 per cent of the total number. The pathway also became known as pyramidal because in passing through the medulla it forms structures called pyramids because of their shape. Many corticospinal fibers arise from area 4; others (estimated as two-thirds of the corticospinal fibers) arise from area 6, areas 3, 1, and 2 (the somesthetic cortex), and other cortical areas. At the lower border of the medulla, most of the fibers cross and descend in the posterior part of the lateral column as the *lateral corticospinal tract*. A few fibers descending in the lateral column do not cross to the opposite side. A variable number of fibers, usually no more than 10 per cent, descend uncrossed in the *ventral corticospinal tract*, but then cross just before terminating. As a result of the crossing, the pyramidal pathway initiates movements, for the most part, on the opposite side of the body. Most of the fibers of the corticospinal tracts synapse with interneurons that connect to motor neurons in the ventral horn (it has been estimated that about 5 per cent of the corticospinal fibers synapse directly with motor neurons). Fibers extending from the cerebral cortex to nuclei of cranial nerves that initiate discrete movements of muscles supplied by cranial nerves form the *corticobulbar tracts*. It is believed that in this pathway cortical control over certain muscles is bilateral, particularly the muscles of the lips, tongue, jaws, and larynx.

Extrapyramidal Pathway. Other motor pathways are collectively called "extrapyramidal." This system, in contrast to the corticospinal and corticobulbar pathways, does not lead from the cerebral cortex without interruption to motor neuron stations, but comprises an incompletely worked out multisynaptic network interconnecting various parts of the cerebral cortex with subcortical structures, including the thalamus, basal ganglia, cerebellum, reticular formation, and red nucleus, giving rise to certain recognized tracts projecting from subcortical centers to the spinal cord and brain stem. The extrapyramidal system apparently initiates certain kinds of voluntary movement (see below); regulates and coordinates the action of the pyramidal system to ensure smoothness of movement; is responsible for certain automatic movements; is concerned with posture and unconscious adjustments of muscle tone; and controls breathing and various visceral functions, such as the heart rate, gastrointestinal motility and activities involving basic drives. The major pathways to the spinal cord, called the **reticulospinal tracts**, arise from the reticular formation, a part of the brain that receives information of widespread origin. These tracts descend in the anterior and lateral columns. Since some fibers are crossed and others uncrossed, the reticular formation exerts bilateral control over motor function. Other extrapyramidal tracts descending to the spinal cord include the *rubrospinal tract* (from the red nucleus), the *vestibulospinal tracts* (from the vestibular nuclei), and the *tectospinal tract* (from the superior colliculus). Some extrapyramidal tracts have bulbar divisions controlling motor neurons of cranial nerves. The vestibular nuclei receive major input from the vestibular branch of the eighth cranial nerve (which mediates equilibrium) and from the cerebellum. The vestibulospinal tracts are believed to be major regulators of the tone of antigravity muscles and, therefore, of the erect posture. The red nucleus receives input principally from the cerebellum and motor cortex. The rubrospinal tract, arising from the red nucleus, is regarded as functionally antagonistic to the vestibulospinal tract because it modulates the tone of flexor muscles. The tectospinal tract apparently coordinates movements of the head and neck in connection with visual responses.

Some investigators have concluded from experimental and clinical observations that the voluntary movements initiated by the extrapyramidal system are chiefly coordinated movements involving muscles on both sides of the body, such as bowing, kneeling, walking, rolling, sitting down, standing up, and turning. One of the most interesting approaches to identifying the kinds of voluntary movements associated with the extrapyramidal system is the analysis of the **apraxias,** disorders in the execution of certain types of movements on command that can be explained by damage to fibers linking the language areas in the left cerebral hemisphere (see page 317) with cerebral motor areas. These disorders usually affect the left side of the body because of injury to the corpus callosum, with the disruption of tracts connecting the left and right cerebral hemispheres. Such patients, upon command to "show me how you comb your hair," can usually carry out the command with the right arm but not the left because the command cannot reach the motor areas in the right hemisphere which initiate voluntary movements via the pyramidal system on the left side of the body. However, commands to walk backwards, kneel, or bend the head down can be executed because the extrapyramidal system on one side of the brain controls the involved muscles of the neck and body on both sides.

The various types of automatic movements initiated by the extrapyramidal system include arm swinging while walking, gesticulating, and facial expressions such as smiling or frowning in response to emotional stimuli. A good illustration of the difference between facial movements executed deliberately by action of the pyramidal system and automatically by action of the extrapyramidal system in response to emotional stimuli is the difference between the artificial "pyramidal" smile produced when posing for a photograph and the natural "extrapyramidal" smile produced in response to an amusing remark.

✗ **Roles of the Basal Ganglia and the Cerebellum.** As mentioned, two important regulatory centers of the extrapyramidal system are the basal ganglia and the cerebellum. These parts of the brain exercise control over the motor cortex via pathways relayed through the thalamus. Loss of such control as

a result of lesions in the basal ganglia can cause coarse tremors of resting muscles or aimless movements such as involuntary, rapid jerks (chorea, as in St. Vitus' dance) or slow, involuntary, writhing movements (athetosis). Rigidity, due to reduction of inhibitory impulses acting on stretch reflexes, is often seen in damage to the basal ganglia. **Parkinson's disease,** a disorder affecting the elderly associated with degeneration of parts of the basal ganglia, is characterized by tremor of the extremities at rest (which disappears with activity), rigidity (involving flexor as well as extensor muscles), hypokinesia (limited, slow movement), and a poverty of expressive, automatic movements. The common denominator of this condition appears to be a loss of neurons projecting from the substantia nigra (a midbrain structure regarded as a functional part of the basal ganglia system) to the caudate nucleus and putamen of the basal ganglia (see Fig. 9–73) that release the neurotransmitter dopamine (3,4 dihydroxyphenylethylamine). Since dopamine is unable to pass the blood-brain barrier, Parkinsonism is currently treated by administration of a precursor of dopamine that does pass the blood-

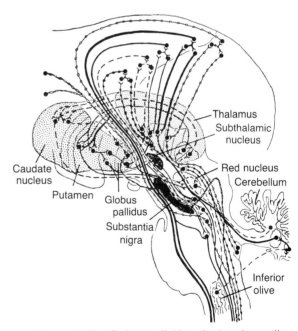

Figure 9–73. Pathways linking the basal ganglia with related structures of the brain stem, thalamus, and cerebral cortex. (From Jung and Hassler: Handbook of Physiology, Sec. I, Vol. II. The Williams & Wilkins Co., 1960.)

brain barrier, namely, L-dopa (3,4 dihydroxyphenylalanine).

The cerebellum functions, in part, by comparing (unconsciously) sensory input (from proprioceptors providing information about the action of skeletal muscles, receptors in the internal ear detecting changes in the position and rates of rotation of the head, and receptors for touch, vision, and hearing) with input from the motor cortex and then sending inhibitory signals to the motor cortex that promote smooth, coordinated motor activity. Major input to the cerebellum from touch receptors in the skin and proprioceptors sensing muscular activity comes from the *dorsal spinocerebellar tract* (Fig. 9–74), which arises from Clarke's nucleus, located in the thoracic or upper lumbar region of the spinal cord (where fibers, and collaterals of fibers, ascending in the dorsal column pathway make synaptic contact with second-order neurons of Clarke's nucleus, whose axons form the tract); from the *ventral spinocerebellar tract* (mainly fibers of second-order neurons that have crossed to the opposite side of the spinal cord after connections have been made with first-order neurons); and from the dorsal column pathway relayed through the medulla. Sensory input to the cerebellum comes not only via the pathways from the various aforementioned receptors but also from the somesthetic, visual, auditory, and equilibrium areas of the cerebral cortex.

A general term used to describe uncoordinated motor activity, such as is manifested in cerebellar disease, is **ataxia**. Specific disorders caused by cerebellar malfunction include (1) *disequilibrium*, with a drunkenlike gait; (2) *intention tremor*, such as increased shaking of the hand while eating as the fork approaches the mouth; (3) *adiadochokinesis* (G. *a*, absence; G. *diadochos*, succeeding; G. *kinēsis*, motion), extreme difficulty with successive movements, such as alternating pronation and supination; (4) *dysmetria* (G. *dys*, hard, bad; G. *metron*, a measure), the inability to judge the extent of movements, so that the individual cannot touch an examiner's fingertips without overshoot (hyperme-

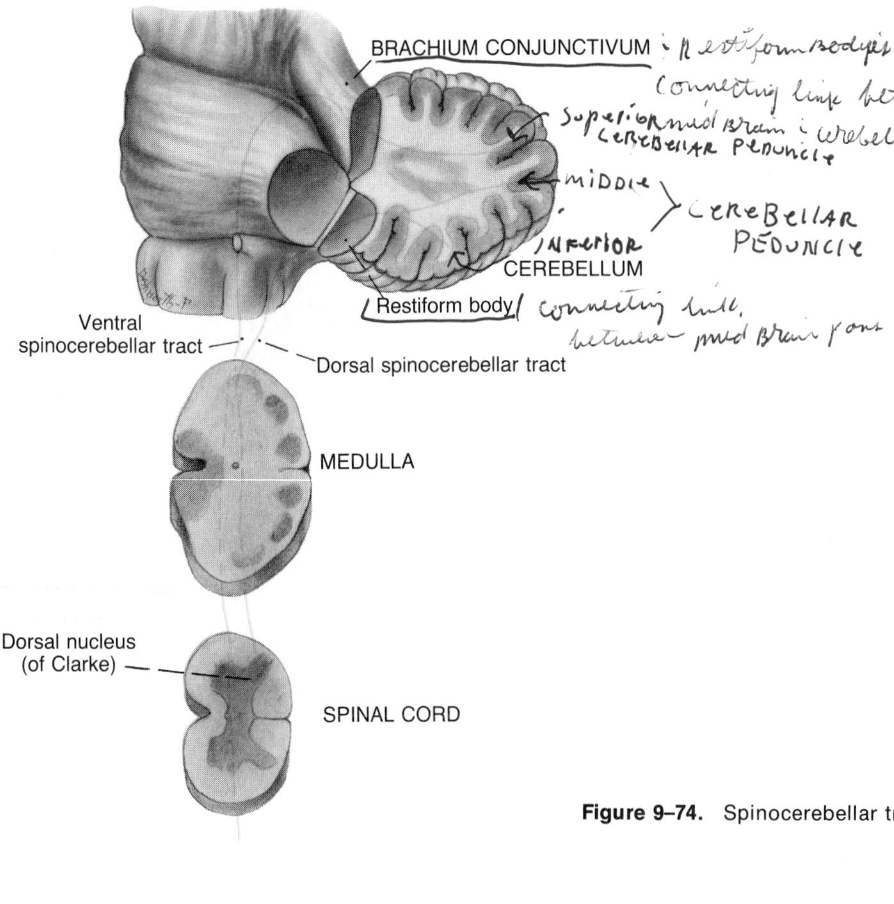

Figure 9–74. Spinocerebellar tracts.

tria) or undershoot (hypometria) or carry out a simple act, such as lifting a glass of water, without reducing it to a number of independent, uncoordinated movements (decomposition of movement); and (5) *hypotonia*.

A technique for controlling epileptic seizures currently under study, which was developed as a result of an understanding of cerebellar function, involves the use of electrodes implanted in the cerebellum. As mentioned, inhibitory signals from the cerebellum to the cerebral cortex prevent inappropriate movements. When an epileptic experiences warning signals of an approaching seizure, the cerebellum can be stimulated to block the seizure.

ABNORMALITIES OF MOTOR AND SENSORY FUNCTION

Paralysis *Know terms as in class*

Paralysis is a complete loss of voluntary motor function. *Paresis* means incomplete paralysis. Types of paralysis include *monoplegia*, paralysis of a single extremity; *hemiplegia*, paralysis of one side of the body; *paraplegia*, paralysis of both lower extremities; and *quadriplegia*, paralysis of all four extremities.

Paralysis may be either spastic or flaccid. With flaccid paralysis there is a loss of muscle tone; with spastic paralysis there is increased muscle tone in the patient's limbs. Spastic paralysis follows damage to parts of the extrapyramidal system, removing the inhibitory controlling influences on the stretch reflex. Although voluntary movement is lost in spastic paralysis, reflex movement can be elicited. The deep reflexes are increased and the superficial reflexes are diminished or absent (see page 302). There is no muscle atrophy. If tested electrically, muscles react normally to stimulation. A gradually developing lesion in the spinal cord damaging the descending motor pathways will usually also produce spastic paralysis. Flaccid paralysis usually results from damage to lower motor neurons. (Lower motor neurons are those with cell bodies in the ventral horn and fibers extending directly to skeletal muscles, as distinguished from the so-called upper motor neurons, which descend from the brain to the spinal cord.) Destruction of the lower motor neurons causes a total loss of muscle tone and

later a wasting of the innervated muscles. This is part of the condition referred to as lower motor lesion.

Infantile Paralysis (Poliomyelitis). Poliomyelitis is caused by a virus that damages the anterior horn cells of the cord and the motor nuclei of the cranial nerves. It is characterized by flaccid paralysis of the lower motor neuron type without sensory disturbances. Today infantile paralysis is not often seen because of the immunization program instituted about 20 years ago.

Degeneration of Areas of the Spinal Cord

Multiple Sclerosis. Multiple sclerosis is a disease of the central nervous system characterized by a patchy demyelinization in multiple areas followed by replacement of the myelin by scarlike plaques (formed by overgrowths of astrocytes) that interrupt and distort the flow of nerve impulses. The disease is generally diagnosed between the ages of 20 and 40, and the incidence is higher in females than males. The symptoms vary and involve both sensory and motor systems. They include, among other things, numbness, muscular weakness, disturbances in vision, loss of coordination, spasticity, hand tremors, impaired speech, and paralysis. Spontaneous periods of remission, sometimes lasting months or years, are common, but the course is generally progressive. There is no specific treatment. Research findings in recent years suggest that the disease is caused by a viral infection that provokes, in genetically susceptible individuals, an autoimmune response in which the myelin sheath is attacked by the body's own immune system.

Syringomyelia. Syringomyelia is a condition of the spinal cord in which there is excessive multiplication of the neuroglia (gliosis) in the central gray substance accompanied by formation of cysts. First affected are fibers mediating pain and temperature where they make synaptic contact with cells of the posterior horn. The result is a loss of these sensations on the side of the diseased segments. The sensations of touch, pressure, and kinesthesia are unaffected until later in the disease. So long as the disease does not damage the white substance, the effects are limited and have a segmental distribution. Involvement of descending motor pathways will cause a spastic paralysis below the level of the lesion.

Tabes Dorsalis. This is a disease caused by syphilis in which the fibers of the dorsal roots are attacked at their point of entry into the spinal cord. The principal symptom is ataxia (failure of muscular coordination). In addition, since individuals with this condition are unaware of the rate, force, direction, and extent of movement of the limbs, they must watch their feet when walking to avoid staggering. Stereognosis, the ability to identify an object with the eyes closed, is also lost in tabes dorsalis. Among other symptoms are loss to a variable degree of all sensations and so-called "lightning pains" — sudden attacks of severe pain, usually localized to an area supplied by one or more spinal segments (most common in the abdomen and lower extremities).

Brain Centers and Pathways for Emotional Experiences and Behavior ΛΙΟ

One of the first physiologists to propose that specific parts of the brain are concerned with emotional experiences and responses was James W. Papez (rhymes with capes). In part on the basis of the observation that rabies, a disease causing severe emotional disturbances, seemed to damage parts of an area of the cerebral cortex referred to as the rhinencephalon (G. *rhis*, nose; G *enkephalos*, brain) because it apparently receives olfactory impulses, Papez suggested that centers for emotions were located in this region of the brain. The **hippocampus,** a curved elevation of cortex on the floor of the inferior horn of the lateral ventricle, and the **parahippocampal gyrus** form important parts of this region. Papez also drew upon the work of Bard, Cannon, and others who demonstrated the roles of the thalamus and hypothalamus in autonomic responses accompanying emotional states in animals, and in 1937 proposed that interconnections among a group of structures forming part of what is now called the limbic system play a key role in governing emotions. The term "limbic," derived from *limbus*, Latin for border, describes the ring-like border around the top of the brain stem formed by the cortical areas of this system, now well established as an important regulator of emotional experiences and behavior. Starting with the ventral surface of the frontal

lobe beneath the septum pellucidum, the limbic cortex continues up and over the corpus callosum as the **cingulate gyrus,** and then posteriorly and ventrally as the parahippocampal gyrus (Fig. 9–75). This part of the cortex belongs to the oldest part of the cerebrum, the *paleocortex* (G. *palaios*, old, ancient). Among other subcortical structures of the limbic system, in addition to the **thalamus** and **hypothalamus,** is the **amygdala,** a group of nuclei adjacent to the hippocampus. The "Papez circuit" traces an important pathway of the limbic system. This circuit runs from the hippocampus to the mammillary body of the hypothalamus via tracts below the corpus callosum called the fornix. From there the circuit continues to the thalamus by way of the mammillothalamic tract and to the cingulate gyrus via the internal capsule and corona radiata. A tract called the cingulum then runs from the cingulate gyrus back around to the hippocampus. Stimulation of various parts of the limbic system can arouse pleasant or unpleasant feelings or cause different kinds of emotionally directed responses. The hypothalamus, as mentioned earlier, contains areas for controlling the autonomic system and important parts of the endocrine system and for regulating such functions as body temperature, feeding behavior, volume of body fluids, and electrolyte concentrations. Strategically situated in the center of the limbic system, it serves as an intermediary for bringing about emotional effects of the limbic system on these vegetative functions. Stimulation of the amygdala, which has reciprocal connections with all parts of the limbic system, especially the hypothalamus, induces many effects that can be initiated by stimulation of the hypothalamus, as well as various patterns of behavior, including those involving basic drives. Stimulation of the cortical regions of the limbic system can evoke autonomic responses similar to those observed upon stimulation of the hypothalamus or amygdala, but the underlying role of these cortical areas, it is believed, is to function as association areas, correlating immediate with past information of an emotional nature so as to give meaning to emotional experiences.

An important pathway concerned with the recognition of the quality of sensory input, especially those sensations that are pleasurable, and with governing emotionally inspired responses, especially those whose

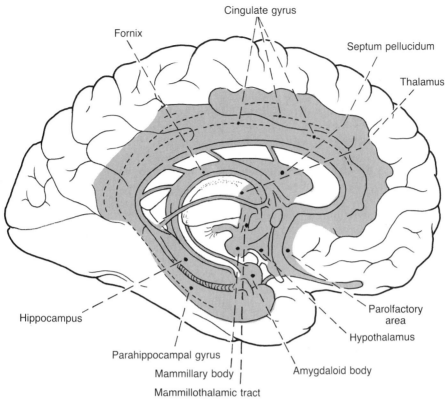

Figure 9–75. The limbic system, shown by the shaded areas of the diagram. (Modified from Williams and Warwick: Gray's Anatomy, 36th Brit. Ed., W. B. Saunders Co., 1980.)

consummation satisfies basic needs and brings pleasure, is the *medial forebrain bundle.* This pathway is both ascending and descending and interconnects the reticular formation, hypothalamus, and the septal region of the cortex. Located along the course of the medial forebrain bundle, especially in the ventromedial nuclei of the hypothalamus, are the so-called *pleasure centers,* apparently concerned with the satisfaction of basic drives. These centers, a part of what has been called the reward system, can be demonstrated by implanting electrodes in the brain of an animal and allowing it to self-stimulate these sites by pressing a lever. Lever pressing rates as high as 5000 times per hour have been recorded. If the particular center stimulated satisfies hunger, food deprivation will increase the rate of lever pressing, and giving the animal a choice between pressing a lever to receive food or an electrical stimulus will generally result in selection of the stimulus.

The neurotransmitters norepinephrine and dopamine and the short-chain, mor-

phinelike neuropeptides known as enkephalins (assumed to be either neurotransmitters or modulators of the action of neurotransmitters) have been implicated in the functioning of the reward system of the brain. Many investigators believe that there is a link between abnormal reward mechanisms and the primary symptoms of **schizophrenia,** which have been described as a poverty of emotional responses or inappropriate responses to people or the environment. Two models of schizophrenia, both linking a malfunctioning of the reward system to the fundamental symptoms of the disorder, have been proposed. According to one, a degeneration of norepinephrine pathways of the reward system as a consequence of the destructive effect of an abnormal metabolite formed during the synthesis of norepinephrine leads to a reduction of the perception of pleasure and of behavior that would normally provide a pleasurable reward, and is responsible for the withdrawal from reality into fantasy and other abnormal emotional responses. The other model proposes that hyperactivity of the reward system brought about by an increase in the sensitivity or number of dopamine receptors causes the disruption of normal emotional responses.

Much of the frontal lobe anterior to the motor association areas seems to be involved in emotional as well as certain kinds of mental functions. This area, which embraces parts of the limbic cortex, is referred to as the **prefrontal cortex.** It is also known as the *orbitofrontal cortex*, since it includes the orbital aspect of the frontal lobe. One of the most famous cases in the annals of medicine has to do with damage principally to this part of the brain. In 1848 Phineas Gage, a railroad construction foreman, had a tamping iron blown through the anterior pole of his brain, entering his left eye and emerging from the center of his head. He lived for 12 years after the accident but underwent severe changes in personality. According to the description by his physician, "He is fitful, irreverent, indulging at times in the grossest profanity (which was not previously his custom), manifesting but little deference to his fellows . . . at times pertinaciously obstinate yet capricious and vacillating, devising many plans for future operation which are no sooner arranged than they are abandoned. . . . His mind was radically changed, so that his friends and acquaintances said he was no longer Gage."

Among the prominent features of damage to the anterior part of the frontal lobe are subtle disturbances in mental processes that interfere with the ability to concentrate and categorize information. A characteristic susceptibility to distraction makes it difficult to perform mental processes requiring a sequence of thoughts. Associated with these difficulties are an absence of continuity of behavior, lack of foresight, poor judgment, and an inability to anticipate or plan for future events on the basis of past experience.

In the early 1930's it was discovered that ablation of the anterior frontal cortex (prefrontal lobectomy) or severing tracts connecting the anterior frontal cortex with the deeper portions of the brain (prefrontal lobotomy) alleviated the symptoms of experimental neurosis in monkeys. This led to the introduction of prefrontal lobotomy in 1935 by a Portuguese neurosurgeon, Egar Moniz, to treat humans, especially those with anxiety neurosis or manic-depressive psychosis. This operation become very popular (about 50,000 were performed), but unfortunately it created a large population of emotional vegetables. The introduction of tranquilizers called a halt to this form of surgery. The current approach to psychosurgery is to destroy selective areas of the limbic system. The most prevalent operation is *cingulotomy,* performed principally to relieve intractable pain and depression. Another is *amygdalotomy,* used to treat individuals subject to outbursts of uncontrollable violence. This new approach has aroused considerable controversy. Opponents argue that our present knowledge of brain function is inadequate to justify such surgical intervention and that any form of surgery could have a general blunting effect on emotions and thought processes.

Memory

Memory is the capacity to recall acquired information or what one has experienced. This function is performed by association areas throughout the brain. Memory traces apparently are not localized in any specific part of the brain, although at least one part, the hippocampus, seems to play a special role in memory (see below).

A distinction is often made between *short-term* and *long-term* memory. Short-term memory has traditionally been studied by asking a subject to immediately recall a sequence of digits (analogous to remembering a telephone number long enough to dial it). The length of the sequence recalled is a measure of the short-term memory span. To study long-term memory a subject might be asked to commit to memory a list of words or other material. Hours, days, or weeks later the subject's recall of the memorized material is measured. Memory has been studied in animals by training animals to perform tasks in which short-term memory is utilized and testing for retention of the task some time later as evidence for long-term memory.

One conclusion drawn from experiments with animals is that long-term, but not short-term, memory involves relatively permanent chemical or structural changes, or both, in the nervous system. In one of the first of such studies, goldfish were trained to move away from a light to avoid a shock. If a drug blocking protein synthesis was injected before a series of trials, the goldfish mastered the task but failed to remember it, as untreated goldfish did, days later. Consolidation of long-term memory apparently occurs within a short time after training, since goldfish injected with the inhibitory drug immediately after training forgot the task, whereas those injected one hour afterwards remembered it. Similar experiments performed with mice and rats have consistently supported the view that protein synthesis is involved in long-term memory. The synthesis of protein, it is believed, signifies changes occurring at synaptic terminals. Possibly alterations in membrane structure take place, or an increase in the size or number of terminals might accompany protein synthesis.

In the 1950's clinical observations were made of a patient who underwent surgery for the treatment of epilepsy which called attention to the critical importance of the hippocampus for the establishment of new long-term memories. The patient's hippocampus and some associated structures in the temporal lobe were destroyed on both sides of the brain. Afterwards he retained, to a large degree, skills and knowledge acquired prior to the operation but was unable to retain any new information for more than a short interval. This profound *anterograde amnesia* did not improve with time. The patient could attend to ongoing events and, with effort, recall numbers of a few digits for several minutes, but the long-term memory deficit was so severe he could not even recognize people who visited him regularly. (Such radical surgery has not been performed again, but comparable memory losses have been observed following operations on one side of the brain of patients who had unsuspected damage on the other side.) To explain the effects of hippocampal lesions on memory, it has been suggested that the hippocampus plays an essential role in initiating long-term memory storage in many parts of the brain (a process some investigators have called the "now print" mechanism). The authors of a recent book on the hippocampus have proposed that the hippocampus establishes a cognitive map of relationships between words or events in carrying out its role in memory.

Language Areas of the Brain

Since language disorders are for the most part associated with damage to the left cerebral hemisphere, it is assumed that in most people the areas controlling language are located in the left side of the brain. This phenomenon, specialization of one side of the brain for a given function, is called **cerebral dominance.** More than 95 per cent of right-handed individuals are described as left hemisphere dominant for language. About 60 to 70 per cent of left-handers are also said to show language dominance in the left hemisphere, the remainder being equally divided between those having language represented bilaterally and those having a language dominant right hemisphere (so-called "reversed" language dominance).

Most of our understanding of the functions of the parts of the brain concerned with language have come from careful study of language disorders in individuals suffering brain damage caused by occlusion of blood vessels, followed by postmortem examination of their brains.

The ability to speak requires the cooperation between two language areas. Lesions in either one can cause *aphasia* (G. *a*, not; G. *phasis*, speech), a general term for language disorders resulting from brain damage in which verbal output is linguistically incorrect. These areas are generally referred to as (1) **Broca's area** (area 44), located in the frontal lobe anterior to the region in the primary motor cortex governing movement of the mouth, tongue, and vocal cords, and (2) **Wernicke's area,** situated in the temporal lobe adjacent to the primary auditory area (Fig. 9–76).

Paul Broca, writing in the 1860's, was the first person to relate speech disorders to specific brain lesions. Broca also established that the damage was almost always on the left side of the brain in the area of the frontal lobe now generally referred to by his name. About 10 years later Carl Wernicke described aphasias resulting from damage to the left temporal lobe. Wernicke established that there were differences between Broca's type of aphasia and those he described. Furthermore, Wernicke described a theoretical model, now generally accepted, to account for both kinds of aphasia.

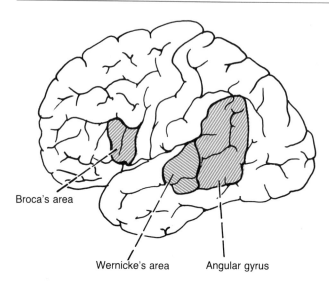

Broca's area

Wernicke's area   Angular gyrus

Figure 9–76. Language areas of the brain.

An individual with lesions in Broca's area has almost normal language comprehension but speaks slowly, with great effort, in incomplete sentences with poor syntax. According to Wernicke's model, Broca's area is the center for programming the muscles responsible for speech production. Individuals with lesions in Wernicke's area may appear to speak normally, but their language comprehension is deficient (both written and spoken, since written language is learned in reference to spoken language) and their speech is lacking in meaningful content. Wernicke's area can be described as the locus for the comprehension of language. Tracts connect Wernicke's and Broca's areas, and when a person speaks an auditory pattern in Wernicke's area is relayed to Broca's area, where the muscles involved in speech are coordinated for articulation. If the tracts connecting Wernicke's area with Broca's area are interrupted, language comprehension is retained, but speech is abnormal.

In the 1890's another important language area was discovered, the **angular gyrus,** located between Wernicke's area and the visual areas of the occipital lobe. This area appears to contain programs that link Wernicke's area to the visual cortex. Lesions in this area cause *alexia* (G. *lexis,* word), the inability to read with comprehension, and *agraphia* (G. *graphein,* to write), the inability to write with meaningful content. Damage to this area does not disturb speech or comprehension of the spoken language. Alexia occurs with this kind of brain damage because to read with understanding the visual

pattern in the visual association area must be converted by programs in the angular gyrus to an auditory pattern in Wernicke's area. Agraphia occurs because to write intelligibly programs in the angular gyrus must convert the auditory pattern in Wernicke's area to a visual one in the visual association cortex.

When the brain receives visual sensations, everything in the left field of vision is transmitted to the right occipital lobe and everything in the right field is transmitted to the left lobe. (For details of the sensory pathways from the eyes to the brain, see page 336.) Therefore, damage to the corpus callosum, interrupting passage of visual information from the right occipital lobe to the angular gyrus ·and Wernicke's area in the left hemisphere, will make it impossible to comprehend reading matter in the left field of vision.

O N   T E S T

✗ **Special Functions of the Right Cerebral Hemisphere**

The left cerebral hemisphere, as we have seen, plays the dominant role in language functions. It is also specialized for analytical and sequential processing of nonlinguistic information. The right hemisphere, on the other hand, seems to be specialized for processing information that can be visualized or perceived as a whole. Thus, identifying an object by feel is more dependent upon the right than the left hemisphere. A curious example of analytical processing by the left hemisphere and holistic processing by the right hemisphere is the observation that trained musicians identify melodies better with the right ear (which transmits more sound to the left hemisphere) than the left, whereas the reverse is true for nonmusicians. Musicians apparently identify a melody by analyzing its components; nonmusicians perceive the melody as a whole.

SUMMARY

THE NERVOUS SYSTEM

Divisions

The nervous system is divided for descriptive purposes into the **central nervous system** (the brain and spinal cord) and the **peripheral nervous system** (12 pairs of cranial nerves and their branches and 31 pairs of spinal nerves and their branches).

Neurons

1. **Specialized for the conduction of nerve impulses, consisting of a cell body containing a nucleus and processes transmitting impulses to and from the cell body.**

2. **The processes are of two types: dendrites and axons.**

   a. **Dendrites** are a group of short, unsheathed processes arranged like branches of a tree that transmit impulses to the cell body.

   b. The **axon** is a single, elongated, sheathed process conducting impulses away from the cell body. Side branches arising along the course of an axon are called collaterals.

Nerve Fibers

1. **Any single, elongated neuronal process (such as an axon or a peripheral process of a sensory neuron) is called a nerve fiber.**

   a. All peripheral nerve fibers have a wrapping formed of accessory cells of the nervous system called Schwann cells.

      (1) *Myelinated fibers* have multiple wrappings of Schwann cell membrane which form a thick sheath called myelin. The outermost wrapping, containing the nuclei of the Schwann cells and most of the cytoplasm, is called the neurilemma.

      (2) *Unmyelinated fibers* have a thin Schwann cell wrapping, called by some anatomists the neurilemma of these fibers.

      (3) Myelin is an effective insulator, and in myelinated fibers impulses jump from one node of Ranvier (gaps in the myelin sheath covered by neurilemma) to another (saltatory conduction), greatly increasing transmission velocity.

   b. In fibers of the central nervous system the myelin sheath is formed by accessory cells, called oligodendroglia, which send out processes, each wrapping around a segment of a nerve fiber.

   c. Schwann cells are essential for regeneration of damaged nerve fibers; hence, fibers of the central nervous system, where Schwann cells are absent, cannot regenerate.

The Nerve Impulse

1. **In the resting state a difference in potential of approximately 70 to 90 millivolts across the cell membrane (interior negative to the exterior) is called the** *resting membrane potential.*

   a. This resting membrane potential results from the active transport of sodium ions to the exterior of the cell with the reciprocal transfer of potassium to the interior, and the more rapid "leaking" of potassium to the exterior.

2. **When membrane permeability is altered by a stimulus, a rapid inflow of sodium changes the interior potential locally from negative to positive; a halt to the inflow of sodium and rapid outflow of potassium returns the interior potential to negative. This** *action potential* **sweeps along the nerve fiber.**

3. **Transmission of the nerve impulse operates on the "all-or-none" principle:**

   a. If a stimulus is strong enough to excite a fiber (threshold stimulus), a maximal impulse is transmitted. Different nerve fibers have different thresholds.

Transmission of Impulses at the Neuromuscular Junction

1. The junction between the terminal branching portions of a motor neuron and the membrane of a muscle fiber is called the neuromuscular junction or motor end plate. Here several expanded endings of a nerve fiber branch are separated from an invagination of the muscle fiber membrane by a space called the synaptic cleft.

   a. Excitation of a muscle fiber by a motor neuron at the neuromuscular junction is brought about by an increase in the rate of release from vesicles in the motor neuron terminals of a chemical mediator, acetylcholine, which crosses the synaptic cleft and induces changes in membrane permeability which give rise to the so-called end plate potential. When the end plate potential reaches the threshold of the muscle fiber, it is the stimulus for generating an action potential along the muscle fiber.

Synaptic Transmission

1. Signals are passed from one neuron to another at junctions called synapses. The most common type is between axon branch terminals of presynaptic neurons and the dendrites and cell bodies of postsynaptic neurons. A synaptic cleft separates a presynaptic terminal (also called a presynaptic knob or bouton) from the membrane of the postsynaptic neuron.

   a. At the synapse an excitatory or inhibitory neurotransmitter is released by the presynaptic cell. The former, after diffusing across the synaptic cleft, induces an excitatory postsynaptic potential, the latter an inhibitory potential. Summation of a number of excitatory potentials is necessary for generation of an action potential in the postsynaptic cell; usually, whether an action potential is generated depends upon the algebraic sum of excitatory and inhibitory potentials.

Sensory Receptors

1. Receptors are sensory neuron endings or specialized structures or organs particularly sensitive (but not exclusively) to a specific stimulus.

   a. Identification of the sensation takes place in the brain.

2. The simplest receptors are free nerve endings sensitive principally to pain. The most complex are the organs for vision and hearing.

3. General sensory receptors, in addition to free nerve endings, include Meissner's corpuscles (touch), Merkel's discs (touch), Pacinian corpuscles (pressure), and Ruffini's end organs (kinesthesia).

4. Receptors such as kinesthetic receptors in tendons and joints, the muscle spindle, and the equilibrium receptors of the middle ear, all of which play a vital role in locomotor and postural responses, are generally referred to as proprioceptors.

Central Nervous System

1. **Brain**

   a. The three developmental divisions of the brain are the forebrain, which includes the cerebrum and the diencephalon (thalamus and hypothalamus); the midbrain; and the hindbrain, which includes the pons, medulla, and cerebellum.

      (1) **Cerebrum**

         (a) *Represents seven-eighths of weight of brain; responsible for discriminatory identification of and integration of sensory information, memory, reasoning, use of language, emotional behavior, and initiation of movement; surface layer of gray matter (cerebral cortex) greatly expanded by convolutions, or gyri.*

         (b) *Longitudinal fissure divides cerebrum into two hemispheres, each divided for convenience into four major lobes bearing names of overlying bones of skull: frontal, parietal, temporal, and occipital; frontal lobe contains areas for initiating movement, parietal lobe for perception of somesthetic sensations (tactile, temperature, pain, and kinesthesia), temporal lobe for the perception of sound, occipital lobe for the perception of visual sensations; associa-*

tion areas adjacent to sensory areas and spread throughout cortex correlate data and relate past and present data to give it significance.

(c) *Commissural tracts connect two hemispheres (largest is corpus callosum); association tracts connect parts of same hemisphere; projection tracts connect cortex with other parts of brain and spinal cord.*

(d) *Imbedded in white matter of cerebrum are two pairs of nuclei (caudate and lentiform), collectively called basal ganglia, which play important role in controlling motor activity; between each nucleus is a large mass of white matter (internal capsule) which contains fibers leading to and from cerebral cortex that connect cortex to rest of brain and spinal cord.*

(2) **Thalamus**

(a) *Paired mass of gray matter situated below corpus callosum.*

(b) *Relay center for sensory impulses (except olfactory) from peripheral receptors to cerebral cortex; responsible for crude awareness of sensation (protopathic sensibility).*

(c) *Processes and relays coordinating motor impulses from the basal ganglia and cerebellum to the cerebral motor cortex.*

(d) *Relay and integration center for emotional behavior.*

(3) **Hypothalamus**

Involved in the regulation of body temperature, feeding activities, concentration and volume of extracellular fluid, autonomic nervous system responses, endocrine functions.

(4) **Midbrain**

(a) *Four rounded masses, superior and inferior colliculi (collectively called corpora quadrigemina), form roof (tectum) of posterior surface of midbrain; superior colliculi coordinate tracking move-*

ments of eyes; inferior colliculi are associated with hearing.

(b) *Two large bundles of fibers derived from internal capsule, called cerebral peduncles, form anterior part of midbrain; bundles contain major cerebral motor system (many fibers continuing posteriorly as corticospinal, or pyramidal, tracts); other fibers lead to pons, where connections are made to cerebellum.*

(5) **Cerebellum**

(a) *Like cerebrum, cerebellum has surface layer (cortex) of gray matter; outline of white matter surrounding deep folds and fissures of gray matter is known as arbor vitae.*

(b) *Functions principally as integration center for promoting smooth, coordinated, voluntary movements; receives input from proprioceptors and receptors for touch, vision, and hearing as well as from motor cortex; then sends inhibitory signals to motor cortex that prevent inappropriate movements.*

(6) **Pons**

(a) *Lies anterior to cerebellum between midbrain and medulla.*

(b) *Bridgelike structure consisting almost entirely of white matter, linking various parts of brain.*

(7) **Medulla Oblongata**

(a) *Continuous with spinal cord through foramen magnum.*

(b) *Ventrally are pyramids (corticospinal tracts).*

(c) *Posteriorly are two prominent nuclei, gracilis and cuneatus, where corresponding tracts (pathway for discriminatory touch and kinesthesia) synapse.*

(d) *Contains centers for regulating cardiovascular functions, maintaining and controlling breathing, and coordinating swallowing, vomiting, coughing, and sneezing reflexes.*

(8) **Reticular Formation**
 (a) *Diffusely scattered neurons throughout area of medulla, pons, and midbrain.*
 (b) *Receives afferent projections providing all types of sensory input and is essential for arousal and maintaining wakefulness (in this respect known as reticular activating system).*
 (c) *Contains centers for facilitating or inhibiting stretch reflexes.*
 (d) *As part of extrapyramidal system, is site of origin of reticulospinal tracts leading to spinal motor neurons.*

b. **Ventricles of the brain**
 Four cavities, or ventricles, of the brain are continuous with the central canal of the spinal cord: two lateral ventricles, one in each hemisphere, one (third) in the diencephalon, and one (fourth) anterior to the cerebellum.

c. **Meninges of the brain**
 (1) **Dura mater** (outermost): Dense fibrous tissue consisting of two layers, an outer (endosteal dura), which forms the internal periosteum of the cranial bones, and an inner (meningeal dura). Extensions of the meningeal dura form four partitions: falx cerebelli, falx cerebri, tentorium cerebelli, and diaphragma sellae.
 (2) **Arachnoid** (middle meninx): A loose, delicate membrane with microscopic appearance of a spider web.
 (3) **Pia mater** (inner meninx): A vascular membrane.

d. **Cerebrospinal fluid**
 (1) Circulates within ventricles, central canal of spinal cord, and subarachnoid space of brain and spinal cord (between arachnoid and pia mater), serving as protective jacket and providing buoyancy for brain.
 (2) Continuously formed in ventricles, principally by choroid plexuses (pouchlike projections of pia mater into ventricles, covered with ependyma). Circulates from lateral ventricles through foramina of Monro into third ventricle, passes through cerebral aqueduct into fourth ventricle (and spinal canal), then passes through three foramina into subarachnoid space. It drains into the superior sagittal sinus (a separation between endosteal and meningeal dura) through arachnoid villi (projections of arachnoid into sinus).

2. **Spinal Cord**

 a. Extends from foramen magnum to second lumbar vertebra.
 b. Central H-shaped core of gray matter surrounded by white matter.
 c. Meningeal dura, arachnoid, and pia mater of brain continuous with spinal meninges. Slender extension of pia mater below spinal cord is called filum terminale. Cerebrospinal fluid samples obtained by tapping the subarachnoid space below spinal cord between third and fourth lumbar vertebrae.

Peripheral Nervous System: Spinal and Cranial Nerves

1. **Spinal Nerves**

 a. Thirty-one pairs: 8 cervical, 12 thoracic, 5 lumbar, 5 sacral, and 1 coccygeal.
 b. Formed by junction of a dorsal (sensory) root and a ventral (motor) root. Cell bodies of sensory neurons lie in spinal (dorsal root) ganglia. Cell bodies of motor neurons lie in ventral gray horn of spinal cord.
 c. Dorsal and ventral roots descending from terminal end of spinal cord to reach appropriate intervertebral foramen are drawn into collection called cauda equina.
 d. Shortly after a spinal nerve is formed from a dorsal and ventral root, it branches into:
 (1) A meningeal ramus.
 (2) A dorsal ramus, serving muscles and skin of the back of head, neck, and trunk.
 (3) A ventral ramus, serving ventral part of these structures as well as upper and lower extremities.
 e. In the cervical, lumbar, and sacral regions the ventral rami give rise to interlacing nerve networks (plexuses) from which peripheral nerves arise.

2. Cranial Nerves

a. Twelve pairs. Names in order from I to XII: olfactory, optic, oculomotor, trochlear, trigeminal, abducens, facial, vestibulocochlear, glossopharyngeal, vagus, accessory, and hypoglossal.

b. For distribution and function, see Table 9–5.

Autonomic Nervous System

1. Efferent nerve fibers distributed to smooth muscle, the heart, and glands are, for convenience, referred to as the autonomic nervous system.

2. Distinctive anatomical feature — in this system a 2-neuron chain leads to an effector.

a. A preganglionic neuron with cell body in central nervous system and axon extending to ganglion outside central nervous system.

b. A postganglionic neuron with cell body in ganglion and axon extending to muscle or gland.

3. Divisions

a. **Sympathetic** (thoracolumbar): Preganglionic neuron cell bodies in lateral horn of first thoracic to the third lumbar segments of the spinal cord.

  (1) Axons pass (via white ramus) to paravertebral ganglia.

    (a) *Pass through to prevertebral ganglia in abdomen and pelvis.*

    (b) *Synapse in paravertebral ganglia with the postganglionic neurons whose axons return to spinal nerves (via gray ramus).*

    (c) *Synapse in paravertebral ganglia with the postganglionic neurons whose axons do not return to spinal nerves and serve the head region and thoracic viscera.*

b. **Parasympathetic** (craniosacral): Cell bodies of preganglionic fibers in brain and second, third, and fourth sacral segments of spinal cord.

  (1) Axons are long and synapse with postganglionic fibers in four ganglia in head (cranial part) or in minute ganglia lying near or within the walls of innervated organs (sacral part).

  (2) Cranial preganglionic axons travel with following nerves: oculomotor, facial, glossopharyngeal, and vagus.

4. Pharmacological Classification of Fibers

a. Nerve fibers of the autonomic system are classified on the basis of the neurotransmitter released at nerve endings as cholinergic (releasing acetylcholine) or adrenergic (releasing norepinephrine, also called noradrenalin).

  (1) Preganglionic fibers are cholinergic.

  (2) Postganglionic fibers of the parasympathetic system are cholinergic.

  (3) Postganglionic fibers of the sympathetic system are adrenergic (except those innervating sweat glands, which are cholinergic).

5. Distribution and Functions: See Figure 9–66 and Table 9–6.

Functional Organization of Nervous System

1. Reflexes

a. A reflex is an involuntary response to a stimulus such as withdrawal of a limb (by flexion) in response to an irritating stimulus, contraction of a muscle in response to the stretching of it, constriction of the pupil in response to light, and dilation or constriction of arterioles in response to changes in blood pressure.

b. A simple spinal cord reflex arc includes:

  (1) A receptor

  (2) A sensory neuron

  (3) Synapse in spinal cord between sensory and internuncial neurons (with exception of stretch reflex)

  (4) Synapse between internuncial and motor neurons

  (5) Junction between motor neuron and skeletal muscle

2. Pathways for Conscious Perception of Somesthetic Sensations

a. Cortical projection: areas 3, 1, and 2 in postcentral gyrus of parietal lobe. On topographical map, size for each part of body is proportional to number of projected fibers.

b. Pain, temperature, and crude touch and pressure: spinothalamic tracts (antero-lateral pathway). First-order neuron to spinal cord, second-order (after decussation) to thalamus, third-order to post-central gyrus.

c. Discriminatory touch and pressure and kinesthesia: dorsal column pathway (fasciculi gracilis and cuneatus). First-order neuron to medulla, second-order (after decussation) to thalamus, third-order to post-central gyrus.

3. Pathways for Motor Function

a. The portions of the cerebral cortex most concerned with movement are areas 4 and 6. On topographical map, cortical representation of given part of body in area 4 is proportional to dexterity of movements.

b. Distinction between pyramidal and extrapyramidal systems
   (1) Pyramidal system (corticospinal tracts): Tracts descend from cerebral cortex without interruption to spinal motor neurons and initiate skilled movements of skeletal muscles.
   (2) Extrapyramidal system: Network interconnecting various parts of cerebral cortex and several subcortical centers (including thalamus, basal ganglia, and cerebellum) with major pathways to spinal motor neurons arising from reticular formation (reticulospinal tracts). Functions include:
      (a) *Initiating certain kinds of voluntary movement.*
      (b) *Regulating action of pyramidal system to produce smooth, coordinated movements.*
      (c) *Bringing about automatic movements (smiling, gesticulating).*
      (d) *Making unconscious adjustments in posture and muscle tone.*
      (e) *Controlling visceral functions and activities involving basic drives.*

4. Brain Areas for Emotional Expression

a. Interconnected group of structures known as limbic system plays key role in governing emotions.

b. Among parts of brain included in system are hippocampus, parahippocampal gyrus, cingulate gyrus, amygdala, thalamus, and hypothalamus.

5. Language Areas of Brain

a. In most people the cortical language areas are located in the left cerebral hemisphere (cerebral dominance).

b. These areas are
   (1) **Broca's area** in frontal lobe (center for programming muscles used in speech)
   (2) **Wernicke's area** in temporal lobe (locus for language comprehension)
   (3) **Angular gyrus,** which links Wernicke's area and the visual cortex.

REVIEW QUESTIONS

1. What forms the central nervous system; the peripheral nervous system?
2. Describe the following parts of a neuron: cell body, dendrites, axon.
3. What is the function of Schwann cells?
4. Distinguish between myelinated and nonmyelinated nerve fibers.
5. How does the formation of the myelin sheath differ in the central and peripheral nervous systems? Explain why fibers of the central nervous system do not regenerate.
6. Briefly discuss: the nerve impulse; the all-or-none principle; transmission of impulses at the neuromuscular junction; synaptic transmission.
7. Name the lobes of the cerebrum. Explain Brodmann's division of the cerebral cortex. In what lobes and in what Brodmann areas are the following found: (1) the major motor areas; (2) the somesthetic cortex; (3) the auditosensory area; (4) the visuosensory area?
8. List the principal functions of the basal ganglia, thalamus, hypothalamus, cerebellum, and medulla oblongata.
9. Give the location of each of the four ventricles of the brain.
10. Name the meninges of the brain in order from outside in.
11. Where is the cerebrospinal fluid? Trace the path of a drop of cerebrospinal fluid from a lateral ventricle to the arachnoid villi.

12. Describe the cross section of the spinal cord.
13. Distinguish between the dorsal and ventral roots of a spinal nerve.
14. How many pairs of spinal nerves are there? How are they named?
15. Name the four major plexuses and give their levels of origin.
16. Name the 12 pairs of cranial nerves and give the principal function of each.
17. Briefly describe the structural and functional differences between the sympathetic and parasympathetic divisions of the autonomic nervous system. Which fibers are cholinergic; which are adrenergic?

18. Distinguish between the spinothalamic (anterolateral) and dorsal column pathways for somesthetic sensations.
19. List the principal structural and functional differences between the pyramidal and extrapyramidal motor pathways.
20. What parts of the brain form the limbic system? What is its importance?
21. What is meant by cerebral dominance? Briefly describe the language functions of Broca's area, Wernicke's area, and the angular gyrus. Distinguish between aphasia caused by lesions in Broca's area and Wernicke's area. Explain how lesions in the angular gyrus cause alexia and agraphia.

10
Special Senses

Objectives

The aim of this chapter is to enable the student to:

☐ Describe the receptors for each of the special senses — vision, hearing, equilibrium, olfaction, and taste — and explain how each functions.

☐ Illustrate and interpret some of the common abnormalities of vision and hearing.

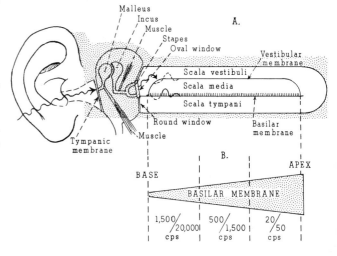

VISION

External Structures of the Eye

The external structures of the eye are the *orbital cavity*, the *extrinsic ocular muscles*, the *eyelids*, the *conjunctiva*, and the *lacrimal apparatus* (Figs. 10–1 through 10–4).

The Orbital Cavity. The orbital cavity contains the eyeball and is a bony, cone-shaped region in the front of the skull lined with fatty tissue to cushion the eyeball. The bones forming the orbital cavity are fragile and thin. The bone at the rim of the orbit is thicker to protect the eye from injury (see Chapter 6).

Extrinsic Ocular Muscles (Figs. 10–3 and 10–4 and Table 10–1). Six extrinsic, or external, muscles connect the eyeball to the orbital cavity and provide rotary movement and support. These muscles are four straight (rectus) muscles (*superior, inferior, lateral,* and *medial)* and two oblique muscles (*superior* and *inferior).*

The Eyelids. The eyelids, or *palpebrae,* are two movable "curtains" located anterior to the eyeball; they protect the eye from dust, intense light, and impact. The **palpebral fissure** is the interval between the eyelids. The *canthus* is the corner, or angle, at which the lids meet. Situated at the inner canthus is the lacrimal caruncle (L. *caruncula,* a little piece of flesh), a small, reddish mass consisting of an island of skin containing sebaceous glands and a few slender hairs. The free margins of the eyelids are surmounted by eyelashes, which protect the eye from dust and perspiration.

A plate of condensed fibrous tissue, the *tarsus,* is located at the free edge of each eyelid, giving the lid substance and shape. The tarsal plate contains tarsal (*Meibomian)* glands opening onto the lid margin. These glands, a modified form of sebaceous glands, secrete an oily substance onto the eyelids.

Conjunctival Membrane. The conjunctiva, a thin layer of mucous membrane, lines the inner surface of each eyelid and is reflected over the exposed surface of the eyeball as a protective cover. The apposed conjunctival membranes slide past each other when the eyelids open and close.

Lacrimal Apparatus. The eye is cleansed and lubricated by the lacrimal (L. *lacrima,* a tear) apparatus, which consists of (a) the lacrimal gland, which secretes a fluid known as tears, and its excretory ducts, through which the fluid reaches the surface of the eye; and (b) the lacrimal canaliculi, lacrimal sac and nasolacrimal duct, through which the fluid is drained into the nasal cavity (Fig. 10–2).

The *lacrimal gland* is located in a depression of the frontal bone at the upper and outer angle of the orbit. Approximately 12 ducts lead from each gland to the surface of the conjunctiva of the upper lid, where they deposit the lacrimal fluid.

The *lacrimal canaliculi* are two ducts extending from the inner angle of the eyelid and emptying into the lacrimal sac. Orifices known as the *puncta lacrimalia,* positioned at the inner canthus of the eye, open into these canals.

The *lacrimal sac* is located at the inner angle of the eyelids in a groove at the junc-

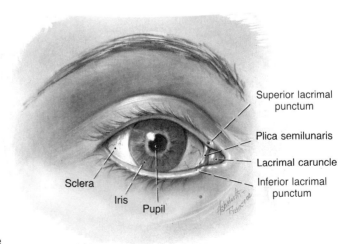

Superior lacrimal punctum

Plica semilunaris

Lacrimal caruncle

Inferior lacrimal punctum

Sclera

Iris

Pupil

Figure 10—1. External appearance of the eye and surrounding structures.

Table 10–1 MUSCLES OF THE EYE

MUSCLE	ORIGIN	INSERTION	FUNCTION	INNERVATION
Superior rectus	Apex of orbital cavity	Upper and central portion of eyeball	Rolls eyeball upward and somewhat medially	Oculomotor
Inferior rectus	Apex of orbital cavity	Lower central portion of eyeball	Rolls eyeball downward and somewhat medially	Oculomotor
Medial rectus	Apex of orbital cavity	Midway on medial side of eyeball	Rolls eyeball medially	Oculomotor
Lateral rectus	Apex of orbital cavity	Midway on lateral portion of eyeball	Rolls eyeball laterally	Abducens
Superior oblique	Apex of orbital cavity	Between superior and lateral recti of eyeball	Rotates eyeball downward and laterally	Trochlear
Inferior oblique	Orbital plate of maxilla	Between superior and lateral recti of eyeball	Rotates eyeball upward and laterally	Oculomotor

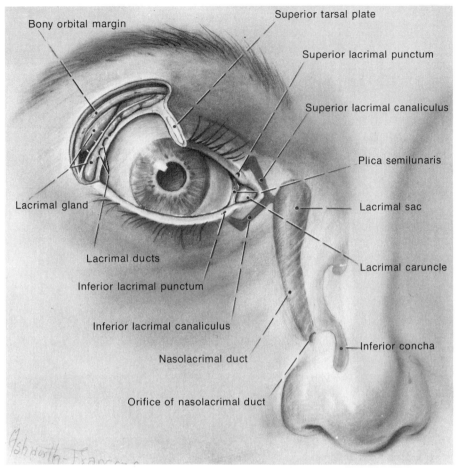

Figure 10–2. Lacrimal apparatus in relation to the eye.

tion of the lacrimal bone with the frontal process of the maxilla. The lacrimal sac is an enlargement of the upper end of the nasolacrimal duct.

The *nasolacrimal duct* extends from the lacrimal sac to the inferior meatus of the nose.

Fluid secreted by the lacrimal gland washes over the eyeball and is swept up by the blinking action of the eyelids. Contrac-

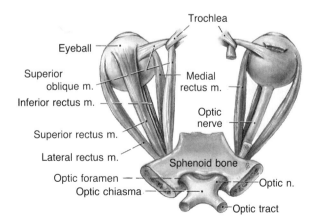

Figure 10–3. Extrinsic muscles of the eye. (Inferior oblique m. not shown. See Figure 6–19.)

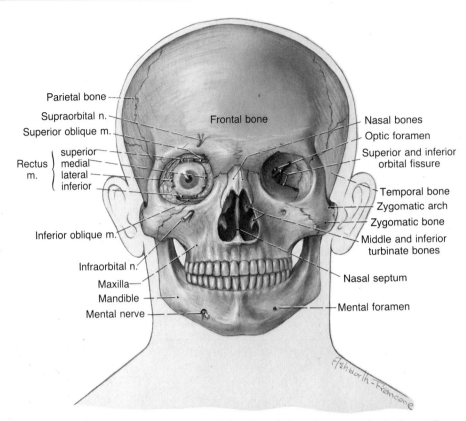

Figure 10–4. Anterior view of the skull showing relation of eye muscles to the orbit.

tion of the lacrimal part of the obicularis oculi muscle (pars lacrimalis) as the eyelids close during blinking dilates the lacrimal sac, pulling fluid from the edges of the lids along the lacrimal canaliculi into the lacrimal sac. When the lids open and the pars lacrimalis is relaxed, the lacrimal sac constricts, forcing fluid into the lacrimal duct. Gravitational force, in turn, moves the fluid down the nasolacrimal duct into the inferior meatus of the nose. Thus, the eyeball is continually irrigated by a gentle stream of fluid which prevents it from becoming dry and inflamed and has a bactericidal action because of the presence of an enzyme, lysozyme, which breaks down the cell walls of many bacteria.

Internal Structures of the Eye

Layers of the Eyeball. The wall of the eyeball is composed of three layers. The outer consists of the **sclera**, a fibrous protective coat, and **cornea**, a transparent tissue serving as a refracting surface. The middle is composed of the **choroid**, a vascular, pigmented layer, **ciliary body**, and **iris**. The inner is the **retina**, a layer containing visual receptor cells (Fig. 10–5).

THE OUTER LAYER. The *sclera* (G. *sklēros*, hard), or white of the eye, forms the fibrous external support of the eyeball. It covers the posterior three-fourths of the eyeball, joining with the transparent cornea covering the anterior portion of the eyeball.

The *cornea* extends anteriorly from the sclera. It is approximately 10 to 11 mm in diameter. The function of the cornea is similar to that of a photographic lens. It is the principal refracting medium of the eye, bending light rays to help focus them on the retina. When looking at a distant object, the cornea accounts for three-fourths of the eye's focusing capacity. Its focusing power, however, is fixed, and adjusting the focus to view objects at different distances is accomplished by changing the curvature of the lens (described below in the section on the lens).

THE MIDDLE LAYER. The *choroid*, the

membranous lining inside the sclera, is high-ly vascular and darkly pigmented. This pig-mentation prevents the internal reflection of light.

The *ciliary body* is the anterior continua-tion of the choroid, appearing triangular in section with its apex extending from the choroid and its base surrounding the iris. The ciliary muscle portion governs the convexity of the lens. Ciliary processes, folds of a richly vascular tissue covered with epithelium pro-jecting internally from the anterior portion of the ciliary body, produce the aqueous humor, which fills the anterior and posterior chambers of the eye (see below).

The *iris*, attached to the ciliary body, is a diaphragm located anterior to the lens and posterior to the cornea. It has a circular open-ing in its center (the pupil) regulating the amount of light admitted to the interior of the eyeball. Circular and radiating muscle fibers are present in the iris. The circular fibers contract the pupil in strong light and near vision; the radial fibers dilate the pupil in dim light and far vision.

THE INNER LAYER. The *retina* is the photoreceptive layer of the eye. It translates light waves into neural impulses. It has no anterior portion, extending forward only as far as the posterior part of the ciliary body.

Eye Humors

The **aqueous humor** fills the anterior cavity of the eye (that portion of the eye in front of the lens), which is subdivided into an **anterior chamber** (in front of both the lens and iris) and a **posterior chamber** (between the lens and iris). Aqueous humor is secreted by the ciliary processes and is drained into the venous system by a ring-shaped sinus, the sinus venosus sclerae (**canal of Schlemm**), located within the sclera (Fig. 10–6). Defec-tive outflow of fluid increases the intraocular pressure, a condition called glaucoma. Se-vere glaucoma may cause blindness as a result of compression of the arteries leading to the optic nerve (where it is formed at the optic disc), reducing the necessary blood supply. The aqueous humor nourishes the lens and cornea, which do not possess a blood supply of their own.

The **vitreous humor**, a soft, jellylike ma-terial, fills the posterior cavity of the eye (the portion behind the lens) and maintains the spherical shape of the eyeball.

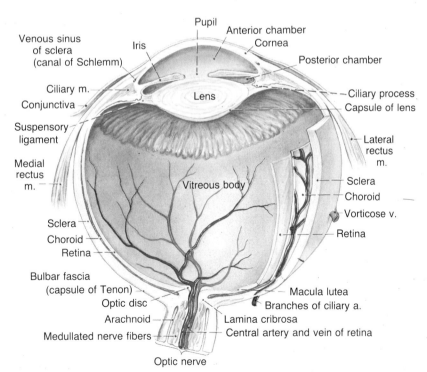

Figure 10–5. Midsagittal section through the eyeball showing layers of retina and blood supply. (After Leder-le.)

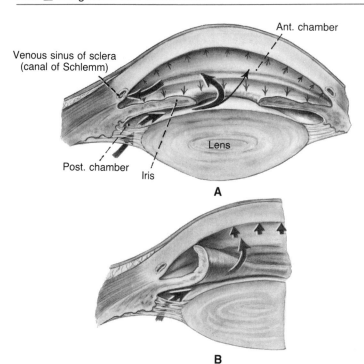

A

B

Figure 10–6. *A,* Normal movement of the aqueous humor through posterior chamber, anterior chamber and out the canal of Schlemm. *B,* Blockage of fluid flow causing fluid retention, resulting in acute glaucoma.

The Lens

The **lens**, lying immediately posterior to the iris, is a biconvex, crystalline body enclosed in a transparent *capsule*. From this capsule, suspensory ligaments extend out radially to sites of attachment in a region marked by ridges (striae) where the apex of the ciliary body meets the choroid. Adjusting the tension of the *suspensory ligaments* changes the shape of the lens to keep the object continually focused on the retina. For near vision the lens bulges; for distant vision it flattens. When the ciliary muscle of the eye is relaxed, the suspensory ligaments are tensed by their attachments, and tension transmitted to the lens capsule keeps the lens relatively flat. Under these conditions the eye focuses the approximately parallel light rays coming from distant objects (beyond 20 feet) on the retina. To focus diverging light rays from close objects, the curvature of the lens must be increased, thereby increasing its refractive power (ability to bend light rays). The process of focusing the image on the retina is called *accommodation*. Accom-

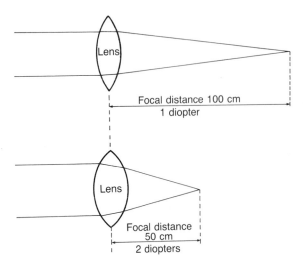

Figure 10–7. Diagrammatic representation of the refractive power of a lens. A lens that brings parallel rays of light to a focus at a distance of 100 cm has a refractive power of 1 diopter. A lens that brings parallel rays to a focus at half that distance has a refractive power of 2 diopters.

modation for near vision is brought about by contraction of the ciliary muscle. This draws the ring of insertions of the suspensory ligaments forward and inward. The tension on the suspensory ligaments and lens capsule is eased, and the intrinsic elasticity of the lens causes the lens (principally its anterior surface) to become more convex.

The unit used to express the refractive power of any optical system is the diopter. A lens with a focal distance of 100 cm (focusing parallel rays of light at a point 100 cm from its center) has a refractive power of 1 diopter. The shorter the focal distance, the greater the refractive power; thus, lenses having focal distances of 50 and 10 cm have refractive powers of 2 (100/50) and 10 (100/10) diopters, respectively (Fig. 10–7). When the lens is accommodated for distant vision, the refractive power of the eye is approximately 60 diopters (about three-fourths accounted for by the cornea, about one-fourth by the lens). In young children accommodation for near vision can increase the optical power of the eye by approximately 14 diopters (lens power increasing from about 15 to about 29 diopters). Unfortunately, the lens' power of accommodation declines with age, and at 45 to 50 years of age is usually no more than 2 diopters, at which time reading glasses are commonly worn.

Physiology of Vision

For conscious reception of a visual image, the image must be formed on the retina and transformed into nerve impulses which are relayed to the sensory projection areas in the occipital lobes.

As mentioned, the focusing of the image on the retina by the lens is called accommodation. Regulation of the amount of light admitted through the action of the iris and alignment of the visual axes of the two eyes are reflexes associated with this act. Thus, when the eyes are accommodating for near vision the lens becomes more convex, the eyes converge (keeping the image in the same place on each retina), and the pupils constrict (increasing the depth of focus).

Function of the Retina. When the image is formed on the retina, the photosensitive cells of the retina (the **rods** and **cones**) translate the light energy into nervous impulses. Each eye contains approximately 6 million cones and 120 million rods. The majority of cones are massed together in a small area called the *macula lutea*, within which is a small region called the **fovea centralis**, containing only cone cells. The concentration of cones diminishes away from the macula, whereas the concentration of rods reaches a maximum about 4 mm from the fovea. The fovea is the central focusing point for the optic system of the eye. Since rods are absent in the fovea centralis, it is considered a "blind spot" in dim light (Fig. 10–8).

Rods are sensitive to dim light and function in night vision. They contain a photosensitive chemical called **rhodopsin**, a combination of *retinal* (vitamin A aldehyde) and a specific type of protein, an *opsin*. When light is absorbed by rhodopsin, retinal changes

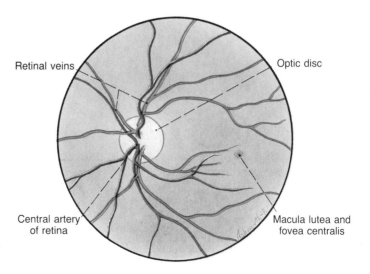

Figure 10–8. Retina of the normal eye as seen through the ophthalmoscope.

from the *cis* form (containing a bent chain), which has the property of forming a stable combination with opsin, to the *trans* form (containing a straight chain), transforming the opsin-retinal union into an unstable one. This leads to a reaction sequence which produces a number of unstable intermediates and ends with the separation of retinal from opsin. Regeneration of rhodopsin from retinal and opsin involves the return of retinal from the *trans* to the *cis* form (a process catalyzed by the enzyme retinal isomerase), which then combines with opsin. The cycle of rhodopsin breakdown and regeneration does not necessarily go through a stage of detachment of retinal from opsin. By the action of light, some of the *trans* retinal of intermediate products is converted back to the *cis* form, and rhodopsin is regenerated (Fig. 10–9). It has been suggested that during the initial stages of the rhodopsin cycle ionized segments of opsin are exposed which attack the rod cell membrane and produce a change in electrical potential.

When rod cells are functioning in dim light, no measurable reduction in the concentration of rhodopsin in the retina occurs. Rhodopsin disappears when the retina is exposed to bright light. It is regenerated under reduced illumination. This regeneration of rhodopsin is part of the adjustment of the eyes to dim light, a process called *dark adaptation*, which involves the iris (an increase in the diameter of the pupil) as well as the retina. Dark adaptation requires about 30 minutes. For many years it was believed that the only change occurring in the retina during this interval is the accumulation of rhodopsin. Current research suggests that, although rhodopsin regeneration is critical to dark adaptation, neurophysiological mechanisms, not well understood but possibly in-

cluding alterations in bipolar cell responses, may also be involved.

As indicated in the bottom part of Figure 10–9, retinal is formed from vitamin A (retinol) and is in turn converted to vitamin A. A severe deficiency in vitamin A results in a shortage of retinal and therefore rhodopsin, causing *night blindness* — the inability to see in dim light.

Rods are slender cells consisting of an inner segment (facing the interior of the eyeball) and an outer segment composed of stacked, rhodopsin-containing discs. The outer segment is continually renewed by the shedding and replacement of discs. The inner segment synthesizes new rhodopsin. Discs are assembled at the base of the outer segment, from where they migrate to the tip and are shed. Epithelial cells adjacent to the rods phagocytize the shed discs.

The photochemistry of color vision (daylight vision) involves cones. Three types of cones have been identified, each containing a different pigment maximally sensitive to red, blue, or green light (Fig. 10–10). Normal color vision depends upon the combination of these colors in the sensory cortex. In the most common forms of *color blindness* the individual cannot distinguish between red and green because of a lack of either the red-sensitive or green-sensitive pigment. Since the genes for color blindness are recessive and sex-linked (carried only on the X chromosome), this condition is much more rare in females than males.

Nerve Pathways for Vision (Figs. 10–11 and 10–12). Signals generated by the rods and cones are relayed to **bipolar cells** which in turn make synaptic connections with **ganglion cells** whose fibers form the optic nerve. In the fovea, the region of maximum visual acuity, there is little overlap in the synaptic connections between receptor and bipolar cells and between bipolar and ganglion cells. In the periphery, on the other hand, the overlap is considerable and a single ganglion cell receives input from several cone cells and as many as hundreds of rod cells. The intensity of the ganglion cells' response can be modified by two types of neurons, namely, **horizontal cells** and **amacrine cells** (Fig. 10–11), both of which carry inhibitory signals across the retina. The principal function of horizontal cells apparently is to mediate communication between bipolar cells and a group of receptor cells in the outer ring of a

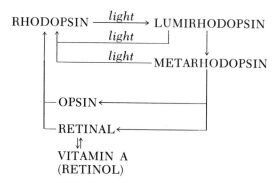

Figure 10–9. Rhodopsin cycle.

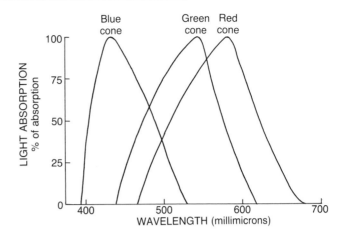

Figure 10–10. Sensitivity curves for the three color receptive cones of the human retina.

ganglion cell's field. Input from horizontal cells reduces the magnitude of the bipolar cells' response. This has the effect of heightening the contrast between concentric regions of ganglion cell fields. Amacrine cells connect to bipolar and ganglion cells and to each other. Their inhibitory action also heightens the contrast between concentric regions of ganglion cell fields. However, whereas horizontal cells respond to sustained illumination, amacrine cells respond to changes in illumination — "turning on" or "turning off" — and have their effect on ganglion cells that are also responding to changes in illumination.

The circular area in the retina seen through the ophthalmoscope where the axons of ganglion cells converge to form the optic nerve is called the *optic disc.* An absence of rods and cones at this point accounts for the

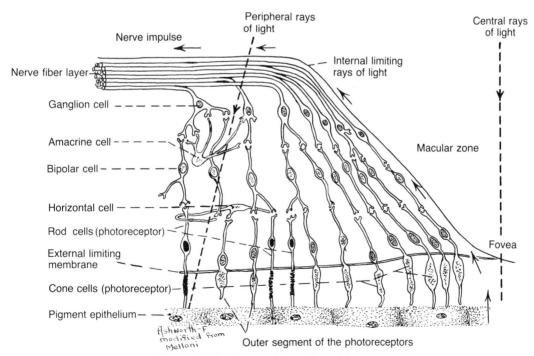

Figure 10–11. Layers of the retina of the eye.

blind spot in the field of vision. The optic nerve perforates the sclera at the optic disc to create a sievelike structure, the *lamina cribrosa*. The optic nerve extends from the disc to the **optic chiasm**, where the fibers undergo partial decussation — fibers arising from the nasal half of each retina cross; those from the temporal half do not. From the chiasm, the

fibers (now called the *optic tracts*) continue to the lateral geniculate bodies of the **thalamus**. From the lateral geniculate bodies, fibers arise, passing through the posterior limbs of the *internal capsule* and into the visual cortical areas of the **occipital lobes**.

As illustrated in Figure 10–12, when the eyes are fixed on a point in the field of vision,

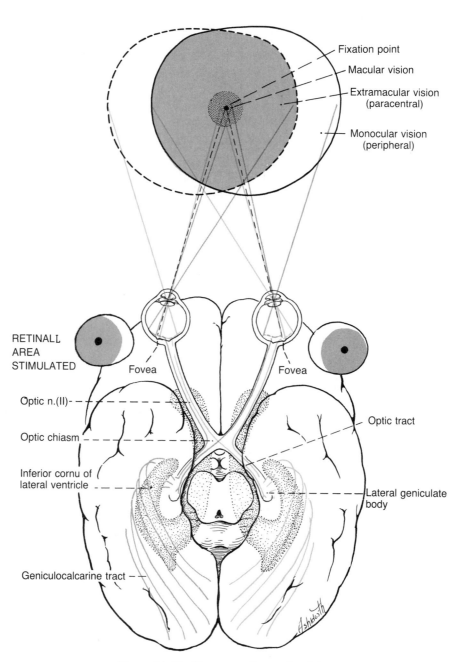

Figure 10–12. Nervous pathways for vision.

objects to the left of this point form an image to the right of the fovea on each retina. This is the temporal half of the right retina and the nasal half of the left retina. Since nerve fibers arising from the nasal half of the retina cross in the optic chiasm, *stimuli in the left field of vision of both eyes excite the right visual cortex*. The reverse is true for the right field of vision of both eyes.

Not all optic tract fibers lead to the thalamus. Those forming part of the pathway for the *pupillary reflex* (constriction of the pupil in response to light) pass to the **pretectal region** (between the corpora quadrigemina and the thalamus). Synaptic connections are made here with neurons whose axons lead to nuclei of the oculomotor nerve, which carries parasympathetic fibers leading to the smooth muscles of the eye. Other optic tract fibers terminate in the **superior colliculus**, which also receives input from the visual cortex and the auditory and somesthetic systems (from both the periphery and cerebral cortex). The principal role of the superior colliculus is to coordinate tracking movements of the eyes — eye movements in response to moving visual, auditory, or tactile stimuli. Experimentally produced lesions in the superior colliculus of monkeys impair the efficiency of these movements.

Binocular Vision. Man's eyes are arranged so that the visual fields of the two eyes overlap to a considerable extent (Fig. 10–12), with each eye receiving a slightly different view. The difference between the two views, called *binocular parallax*, leads to a disparity between the retinal images of the third dimension of an object, which makes possible the perception of depth. Points on each retina forming identical images equidistant from the fovea are called *corresponding points*. Figure 10–13 illustrates how the images of the flat surface of an object lie on corresponding points, whereas the images of the third dimension do not — they lie on what are called *disparate retinal points*. The disparity is responsible for three-dimensional vision. The processing of binocular information to synthesize a three-dimensional picture takes place in the visual cortex and involves specific neurons sensitive to disparate left and right retinal images.

Binocular vision is maintained through nervous and muscular coordination of eye movements. If the muscles are not coordinated, *strabismus* results. In strabismus, the visual axes of the eyes are not parallel. The brain cannot cope with the excessive disparity, and double vision (diplopia) results.

Abnormalities of the Eye

The focusing properties of the eye are often imperfect, causing nearsightedness (myopia), farsightedness (hyperopia), oldsightedness (presbyopia), and uneven focusing in different planes (astigmatism). Other abnormalities of the eye include cataracts, corneal opacity, inflammations of the conjunctiva (conjunctivitis), and styes.

Myopia results from an abnormally long distance between the cornea and lens, or lens and retina, or too powerful a lens, and is a

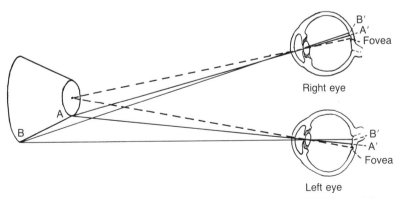

Figure 10–13. Disparity between the two retinal images of the third dimension of an object, which gives rise to binocular depth perception, is illustrated in this drawing. The images of the bottom of the bucket lie on corresponding retinal points; that is, the distance from the fovea to A′, representing point A on the left side of the bottom of the bucket, is the same on both retinas. The images of the top of the bucket lie on disparate retinal points; that is, the distance from the fovea to B′, representing point B on the left side of the top of the bucket, is not the same on each retina.

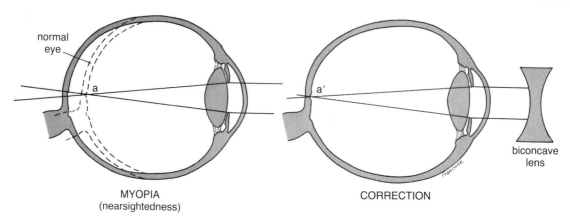

Figure 10–14. Myopia, or nearsightedness; note how the image focuses in front of the retina. A biconcave lens is used as a corrective device for this condition—*a* indicates incorrect point of focus; *a'* indicates focus after correction.

condition in which the image of a distant object (beyond 20 feet, at which distance light rays entering the eye are almost parallel) focuses in front of the retina. Myopic individuals cannot see distant objects clearly without the aid of glasses. By use of a concave lens of proper power, the position of the image is moved farther back to focus on the retina (Fig. 10–14). **Hyperopia** (farsightedness) is the opposite condition, resulting from an abnormally short distance between the cornea and lens, or lens and retina, or a weakened lens; in hyperopia the image of a distant object focuses behind the retina. In the normal condition, the ciliary muscle is relaxed when the image of a distant object is focused on the retina. In the farsighted condi-

tion, however, near vision accommodation must be carried out to focus distant objects on the retina. Furthermore, the near point (i.e., the nearest point at which objects are seen distinctly) is farther away from the eyes in hyperopic than in normal or myopic individuals. Hyperopia is corrected by use of a convex lens of proper power to move the image forward and focus it on the retina (Fig. 10–15). **Presbyopia** (G. *presbys*, old man; G. *ōps*, eye) occurs with increasing age. In presbyopia, the lens gradually loses its elasticity, interfering with correct accommodation, so that the near point is a yard or more away from the eye; consequently, older individuals need a convex lens to clearly see objects less than a yard away.

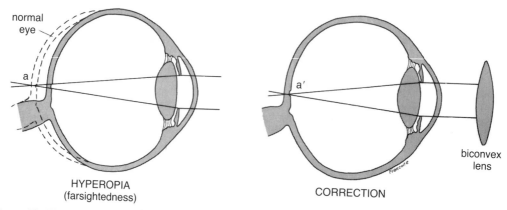

Figure 10–15. Hyperopia, or farsightedness; note how the image focuses behind the retina. A biconvex lens is used as a corrective device for this condition—*a* indicates incorrect point of focus; *a'* indicates focus after correction.

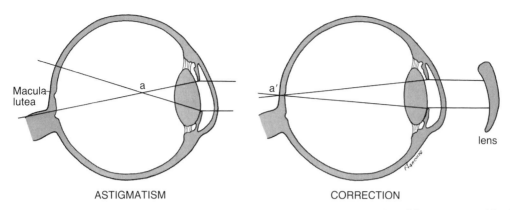

Macula lutea

a

a'

lens

ASTIGMATISM

CORRECTION

Figure 10–16. Astigmatism: uneven focusing of the image resulting from distortion of the curvature of the lens or cornea — *a* indicates incorrect point of focus; *a'* indicates focus after correction.

Astigmatism (G. *a-*, not; G. *stigma*, a point) is a visual defect resulting from distortion of the curvature of the cornea or lens of the eye. It is corrected by a cylindrical lens placed in the proper axial position (Fig. 10–16).

Cataract (Fig. 10–17) is a lens opacity — a region in which light scattering causes a loss of transparency — usually the result of an aging process, which obscures vision. The light is scattered when it encounters a region where there is an abrupt change in the concentration of lens protein. *Nuclear cataracts,* those formed in the core of the lens, arise as a result of a gradual change in protein structure which leads to the formation of huge aggregates of protein molecules. *Cortical cataracts,* those formed in the outer layers of the lens, generally arise from a disruption of lens fibers (elongated epithelial cells). Cataract formation may be accelerated or initiated, among other things, by specific diseases, inherited metabolic disorders, drugs, or exposure to x-rays and other forms of radiation. The primary symptom of cataract is a progressive, painless loss of vision. The degree of this loss depends on the location and the extent of the opacity. Nearsightedness develops in the early stages of nuclear cataract (usually as a result of changes in the refractive index of the lens) so that some elderly patients may discover that they can read without glasses (second sight). Pain is absent unless the cataract swells.

Frequent eye examinations and change of eye glass prescriptions will help maintain useful vision during development of a cataract. Removal of the lens is necessary when useful vision is lost. After a cataract lens is surgically removed (Fig. 10–18), strong glasses must be worn to correct the very farsighted condition of a lensless (aphakic) eye. Corrective glasses for a single eye cause the image on the retina of the lensless eye to

Figure 10–17. The transmission of light through a normal lens to stimulate the retinal fovea, and the blockage of light to that area by the opacity of the lens in the condition known as cataract.

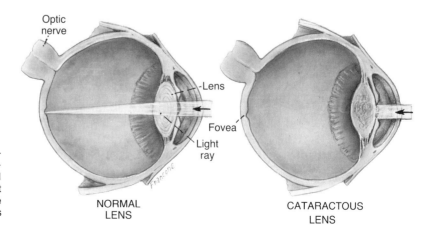

Optic nerve

-Lens

Fovea

Light ray

NORMAL LENS

CATARACTOUS LENS

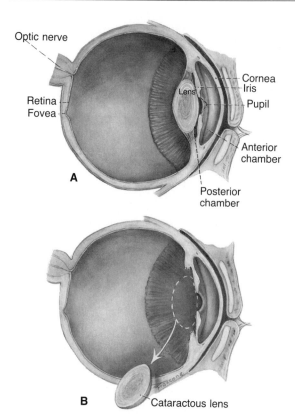

A

Optic nerve

Retina
Fovea

Lens

Cornea
Iris

Pupil

Anterior
chamber

Posterior
chamber

B Cataractous lens

Figure 10–18. *A,* Cataractous changes of the lens in relation to other structures of the eye. *B,* Removal of the lens from surrounding structures as in cataract surgery. After surgery, glasses or contact lenses must be worn.

be more than 10 per cent larger than the image in the normal eye. Since the brain cannot fuse two such images, surgery may not be performed until both cataract lenses must be removed; if only one lens is removed, contact lenses that avoid excessive magnification are used.

Injuries or infections of the cornea can lead to *corneal opacity,* causing blindness. A corneal transplant is a method of treatment. In a successful transplant, the transparency of the graft will persist. Homotransplants of the cornea are tolerated, since the cornea of the eye lacks blood and lymph vessels. Blood and lymph vessels are necessary for graft rejection. If corneal tissue is transplanted to another area, such as under the skin, it will be destroyed. If skin is transplanted to the anterior chamber of the eye, it will survive.

Conjunctivitis (inflammation of the conjunctiva) is the most common infection of the eye. It can be caused by irritation from dust, pollen, bacteria, or viruses, and is character-

ized by inflammation and an increased flow of tears. The conjunctival membrane takes on a pink or fiery red color. Mild cases will clear spontaneously if further irritation of the eye is prevented.

A **stye** is an inflammation of a sebaceous gland of the eyelid.

AUDITORY AND EQUILIBRIUM SENSES

When sound is produced, the atmosphere is disturbed by sound waves (compressions and rarefactions of air created by a vibrating object) radiating from the source. Sound waves impinge on the eardrum (tympanic membrane), and the membrane vibrates at the same frequency as the source creating the sound. Sound vibrations are carried from the tympanic membrane to the inner ear to be transformed into nerve impulses.

The inner ear also contains end organs concerned with equilibrium. These are of two types: (a) those sensitive to the pull of gravity (providing information about the position of the head) and to linear acceleration and deceleration of the head, and (b) those sensitive to angular acceleration and deceleration (changes in the rate of rotation) of the head.

Structures of the Ear

The ear consists of three portions: an external, middle, and inner ear (Figs. 10–19 to 10–21).

External Ear. The auricle (ear flap) of the external ear collects sound waves and transmits them through the *external acoustic meatus,* or *auditory canal,* to the **tympanic membrane.** The external auditory canal is an S-shaped structure about 2½ cm in length, lined with numerous glands secreting a yellow, waxy substance, *cerumen.* Cerumen lubricates and protects the ear.

Middle Ear. The middle ear (tympanic cavity) is a tiny cavity in the temporal bone. Within it are the three auditory ossicles: the **malleus** (hammer), **incus** (anvil), and **stapes** (stirrup). Two small muscles, the *stapedius* and *tensor tympani,* are also found in the middle ear. The stapedius muscle is attached to the stapes, and the tensor tympani muscle to the handle of the malleus.

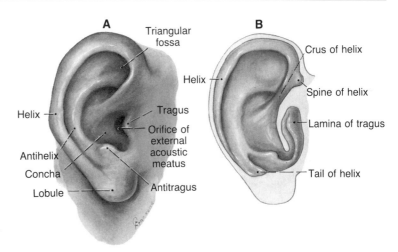

Figure 10–19. *A,* External ear. *B,* Cartilage portion of ear.

The middle ear has five openings — the opening covered by the tympanic membrane; the opening of the *auditory*, or *Eustachian*, *tube*, which connects the middle ear with the nasopharynx and through which outside air can enter; the opening into the mastoid cavity; and the openings into the inner ear (round and oval windows). Three functions have been ascribed to the middle ear. The first function is to transmit energy from sound vibrations in the air column of the external acoustic meatus across the middle ear into the fluid contained within the *cochlea* (the central hearing apparatus). The bones of the middle ear pick up the vibrations from the tympanic membrane and transmit them across the middle ear to the *oval window* (the opening to the inner ear). The second function is to reduce the amplitude of vibrations accompanying loud sounds of low frequency (see below under "Reflex Contraction of Middle Ear Muscles"). The third function of the middle ear is to equalize air pressure on both sides of the tympanic membrane via the auditory tube to prevent the membrane from rupturing.

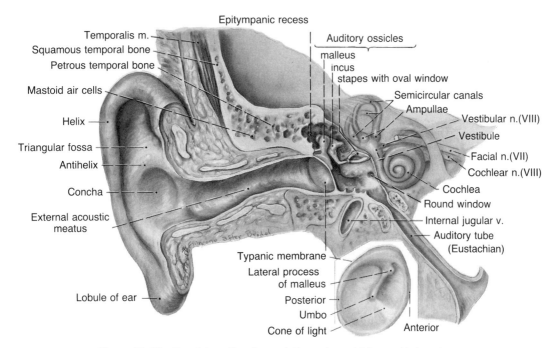

Figure 10–20. Frontal section through the outer, middle, and internal ear.

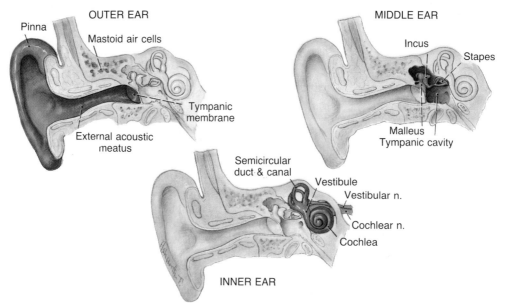

Figure 10–21. Three divisions of the ear.

The Inner Ear. The inner ear consists of bony and membranous labyrinths. The bony labyrinth, composed of a series of canals hollowed out of the temporal bone, is filled with perilymph. The membranous labyrinth, lying entirely within the bony labyrinth, is filled with endolymph. The **bony labyrinth** consists of the *cochlea*, containing the organ of hearing, and the *vestibule* and *semicircular canals*, containing the organs of equilibrium (Fig. 10–22). The **membranous labyrinth** consists of the *cochlear duct* within the cochlea, the *utricle* and *saccule* within the vestibule, and the *semicircular ducts* within the semicircular canals. Those portions of the inner ear concerned with equilibrium are collectively called the **vestibular apparatus.**

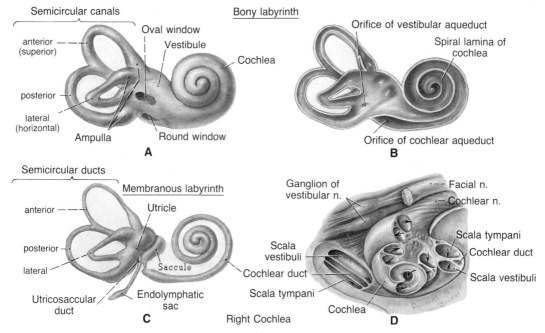

Figure 10–22. Bony *(A, B)* and membranous *(C, D)* labyrinths of the inner ear.

Physiology of Equilibrium

The utricle and saccule contain receptors (often referred to as the *otolith organs*) sensitive to gravity and to linear acceleration and deceleration of the head. The receptors are located in a small, thickened area in the walls of the utricle and saccule, called the *macula*, which receives the fibers of the eighth cranial nerve. This area contains *hair cells*, and the ultrafine hairs, or cilia, of these cells project into a gelatinous membrane known as the otoconial or otolithic membrane because it contains microscopic crystals of calcium carbonate called *otoconia* (G. *ōtikos*, of the ear; G. *konis*, dust) or *otoliths* (G. *lithos*, stone). The otoconia add mass to the membrane, thereby increasing its response to gravity or to inertial forces when the head is linearly accelerated or decelerated. Under resting conditions, the pull of gravity exerted on the otoconial membrane bends the hairs of the hair cells; the direction of bending will vary with head position. Bending of hairs sets up impulses in sensory neuron fibers innervating the hair cells. Since the hairs are oriented in various directions, the pattern of stimulation will vary with head position, and a given pattern will apprise the brain of the orientation of the head, thereby helping maintain static equilibrium. The otolith organs also help maintain equilibrium during linear acceleration and deceleration. Thus, a sudden movement forward has the effect of a backward pull on the otoconial membrane, changing the direction of the bending of the hairs. The resulting sensation is one of falling backward, which leads to a compensatory leaning forward.

There are three semicircular canals in each ear at right angles to each other, each enclosing a semicircular duct which contains receptors sensitive to angular acceleration and deceleration. When the head is bent forward 30 degrees, the lateral canal (Fig. 10–22) is in a horizontal plane and the superior and posterior canals are in vertical planes, one projecting forward 45 degrees, the other backward 45 degrees. Within the dilated portion (*ampulla*) at the base of each semicircular duct (near the junction with the utricle) is an elevated area, called the crista (the Latin word for crest), containing a gelatinous dome (the *cupola*) into which the hairs of *hair cells* project. As the head begins to rotate, inertia of the *endolymph* in the semi-circular ducts is equivalent to movement of the endolymph in the direction opposite to the rotation. As a result, the cupola "moves," bending the embedded hairs in the direction opposite to the rotation. At the cessation of rotation, fluid inertia causes bending of the hairs in the same direction as the ceased rotation. Bending of the hairs in a specific direction — toward the utricle in the case of the horizontally oriented lateral ducts, away from the utricle in the case of the vertically oriented superior and posterior ducts — has an excitatory effect; bending of the hairs in the opposite direction has an inhibitory effect. The right and left horizontal canals function as a pair — rotation to the right excites the canal on the right side and inhibits the one on the left (and vice versa). The anterior (superior) canal on one side and the posterior canal on the other side also function as a pair and are so oriented that whenever one is excited the other is inhibited.

Nerve Pathways for Equilibrium. The hair cells of the organs of equilibrium are innervated by nerve fibers of the *vestibular branch of the eighth cranial nerve.* These fibers arise from the cell bodies of bipolar neurons of the vestibular ganglion, located in the internal auditory meatus. Most of the central fibers of these neurons terminate in the vestibular nuclei, situated at the boundary of the pons and medulla. The connections made from this point are widespread and include fibers to the spinal cord (medial vestibulospinal tracts to the cervical and thoracic regions and lateral vestibulospinal tracts to all regions), cerebellum, reticular formation, nuclei of the third, fourth, and sixth cranial nerves and to the sensory projection area for equilibrium in the temporal lobe (relayed through the thalamus). Branches of the eighth cranial nerves also pass directly to the cerebellum.

Signals transmitted by the vestibulospinal tracts are important for maintaining the tone of antigravity muscles. The interconnections between the vestibular nuclei, reticular formation, and cerebellum play a vital role in making reflexive adjustments in muscle tone (via impulses sent through the reticulospinal and vestibulospinal tracts) to maintain equilibrium as the body falls to one side, forward or backward. Nerve impulses passing from the vestibular nuclei to the reticular formation also form part of the activating input of the reticular formation (see page 305).

The arrival of equilibrium impulses in the cerebral cortex makes possible conscious awareness of equilibrium sensations. This input becomes essential for conscious orientation of the head in the absence of visual or tactile clues. Thus, individuals with congenital defects of the vestibular apparatus may drown in deep water, since the defect prevents orientation by labyrinth receptors, and orientation by sight or touch is not possible.

Input from the vestibular apparatus to the nuclei of cranial nerves III, IV, and VI (through the cerebellum as well as the vestibular nuclei) makes possible automatic eye movements that stabilize the gaze when the head is suddenly turned, thereby maintaining a stable image on the retina. This mechanism can be demonstrated by holding one's hand about 12 inches in front of the face and fixing the gaze upon the palm as the head is shaken from side to side about three times per second. If the vestibular system is functioning normally, the creases in the palm will remain distinct because each time the head is turned the semicircular canals signal the ocular muscles to turn the eyes in the opposite direction. If the reverse test is performed — shaking the hand from side to side while the head is held still — the creases in the palm will be blurred. Thus, visual information must be supported by the vestibular mechanism for satisfactory stabilization of the gaze.

A special case of the stabilization of the gaze is the alternating eye movements, called *nystagmus* (G. *nystagmos*, drowsiness), that occur when a person is rapidly rotated, consisting of a slow phase in the direction opposite to the rotation and a rapid phase in the direction of the rotation. The slow component, which tends to maintain the gaze at a fixed point, is initiated by the semicircular canals. The pathway for the quick "reset" component is unknown. The nystagmus will disappear if the rotation is continued for a while at a constant rate. When clinical tests are performed to observe nystagmus, the subject is usually rotated in a special (Bárány) chair at the rate of once every two seconds with the eyes closed. Postrotational nystagmus movements, which are opposite to those occurring during rotation (slow component in the *same* direction as the rotation), are examined. In addition, for the brief interval that the nystagmus lasts, the subject has the sensation of rotating in a direction opposite to the rotation in the chair and, if asked to stand up or walk, will tend to fall in the direction of the rotation.

Physiology of Hearing

Sound is a sensation produced when vibrations initiated in the external environment strike the tympanic membrane. The amplitude of a wave determines loudness, whereas pitch is correlated with the frequency, or number of waves per unit of time — the greater the amplitude, the louder the sound; the greater the frequency, the higher the pitch.

The unit used to measure the intensity of sound above the normal threshold of hearing is the *decibel*, or 1/10 of a bel. Since the decibel is a measure of relative intensity on a logarithmic scale, a 50-decibel (5-bel) sound (average for normal conversation) is 10^3, or 1000, times louder than a 20-decibel (2-bel) sound (a whisper). The sound of a power lawn mower, approximately 90 decibels, is 10^4, or 10,000, times louder than normal conversation.

Sound frequencies audible to the human ear range from 20 to 20,000 cycles/sec. The frequency range for most speech sounds is between 300 and 3000 cycles/sec. The threshold of hearing varies with the pitch of the sound, the greatest sensitivity occurring between 1000 and 3000 cycles/sec.

The cochlea, which contains the organ of hearing, is coiled two and one-half times in the shape of a snail shell about a central axis of bone (Figs. 10–22 to 10–24). Three compartments compose the hollow cochlea. The upper passage, or *scala vestibuli*, ends at the oval window; the lower passage, or *scala tympani*, ends at the round window. These two passages connect at the apex of the spiral; both contain perilymph. A third passage, the *cochlear duct*, filled with endolymph, lies between the scala vestibuli and the scala tympani.

The cochlear duct is bounded above by the *vestibular membrane* and below by the basilar membrane. The **basilar membrane** has tightly stretched fibers; the shorter fibers are located at the base, and the longer ones at the apex. The **organ of Corti** (Fig. 10–24), the organ of hearing, lies on the basilar membrane; it contains numerous receptor hair cells which mediate the transformation of the vibrations of the basilar membrane into nerve impulses (see below).

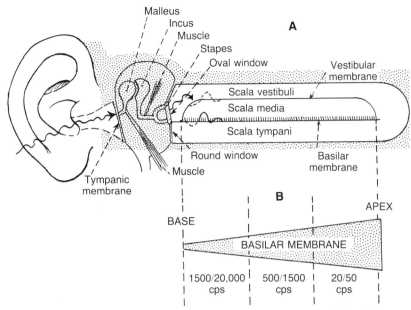

Figure 10–23. *A,* Movement of fluid in the cochlea set up by sound waves reaching the tympanic membrane. *B,* High frequency; vibration causes basilar fibers close to the oval window to vibrate; fibers toward the apex are some 12 times longer and are influenced by sounds producing fewer waves or cycles per second (CPS). (From McNaught, A. B., and Callander, R.: *Illustrated Physiology.* Edinburgh, Churchill Livingstone, 1970.)

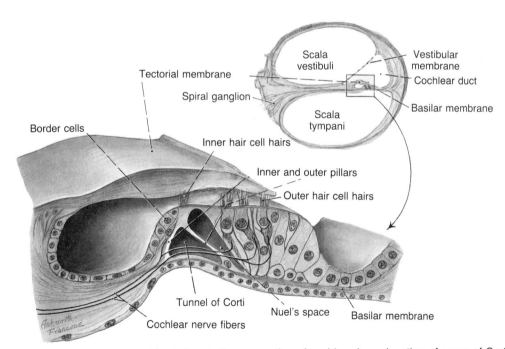

Figure 10–24. Spiral organ of Corti. Insert of cross section of cochlea shows location of organ of Corti.

Sound waves entering the acoustic meatus create vibrations in the tympanic membrane. The ossicles of the middle ear, in turn, carry these vibrations to the *oval window*. Vibrations in the oval window set up sound waves in the perilymph which travel through the thin vestibular membrane to the endolymph of the cochlear duct. The waves pass through the basilar membrane to the perilymph of the scala tympani and are dissipated against the membrane of the round window. Each sound wave sets up a traveling wave in the basilar membrane which increases in amplitude as it moves toward the apex of the cochlear duct. Maximum vibration of the basilar membrane occurs at the point on the membrane at which the frequency of vibrations is the same as the frequency of the vibrations of the sound generating the traveling wave. After reaching the maximum, the amplitude drops off sharply. *High frequency sounds cause maximum vibration of the basilar membrane at the base of the cochlear duct* (near the stapes, where the fibers are shorter and stiffer); *low frequency sounds cause maximum vibration near the apex.* Movements of the basilar membrane result in bending of the hairs of the hair cells (a shearing motion between the ends of the hairs and the tectorial membrane). This induces a change in electrical potential in these cells and release of a neurotransmitter that sets up nerve impulses in auditory nerve fibers.

The sound waves meet resistance as they pass from air to the aqueous medium of the inner ear. However, because the vibrations collected by the tympanic membrane are transferred to the much smaller oval window, the vibrations are amplified, and this amplification system largely overcomes the impedance between air and the aqueous environment of the inner ear. If sound waves entered the cochlea directly at the oval window, hearing sensitivity would be reduced by about 30 decibels.

Reflex Contraction of Middle Ear Muscles. The transmission of sound through the middle ear is affected by contraction of the stapedius and tensor tympani muscles. Contraction of the stapedius (which inserts into the stapes) stiffens and resists the motion of the chain of middle ear ossicles. Contraction of the tensor tympani (which inserts into the handle of the malleus) increases the tension on the tympanic membrane as it pulls the

membrane inward. These actions weaken the transmission of low frequency sounds. For many years, a visible movement of the tympanic membrane in both ears following a loud sound was described as a sound-provoked tympanic reflex. It is now recognized that this response occurs only as a part of a more general startle, or defensive, reaction (identified by contraction of the head and neck muscles and grimacing) to unexpected or especially intense sounds. On the other hand, repeated pure tones of 70 decibels or more above threshold in individuals with normal hearing *always* cause bilateral contraction of the stapedius. For this reason, this response of the stapedius is now generally referred to as the *acoustic* or *stapedius reflex.* According to classical theory, reflex contraction of the middle ear muscles protects the inner ear from damage by loud sounds. An alternative function for the stapedius reflex has been suggested — reduction of the masking by loud low frequency sounds of sounds of other frequencies.

Nerve Pathways for Hearing. The sensory nerve fibers of the *cochlear division of the eighth cranial nerve,* which innervate the hair cells of the organ of Corti, take origin from the cell bodies of bipolar neurons of the spiral ganglion of the cochlea. The central fibers of these neurons travel to the dorsal and ventral cochlear nuclei in the medulla, where they synapse. From here the pathway continues through a number of stations to the auditory cortical area in the upper part of the **temporal lobe.** The intermediate points include the superior olivary nucleus in the pons, the nucleus of the lateral lemniscus, the inferior colliculus, and the medial geniculate body of the thalamus (the lateral lemniscus is the name of the ascending pathway from the superior olivary nucleus to the thalamus). All fibers synapse in the medial geniculate body; most also synapse in the superior olivary nucleus and the inferior colliculus. In addition, some synaptic connections are made in the nucleus of the lateral lemniscus. As a result of partial decussation at several points (principally via the trapezoid body, which connects the cochlear nuclei with the opposite superior olivary nuclei, and also through the commissure of Probst, which links the nuclei of the lateral lemniscus, and through the inferior collicular commissure), the auditory cortex receives bilateral input. Each ear, however, has greater representation at all levels on the opposite side of the brain. The reticular activating system (see page 305), the superior colliculus (see page 337), and the cerebellum (see page 312) also receive input from the auditory system.

Sound Localization. Determining the direction from which sound is coming requires sound reception by both ears and depends, for the most part, upon differences in the intensity and time of arrival of sound at the two ears. The ear on the side of the sound receives a more intense and earlier stimulus. Sound localization does not involve conscious judgment on the part of the listener. In studies with cats, intensity and time cues have been related to neural responses. Presenting a sound to one ear only will excite more neural activity in the brain on the opposite side. The same observation is made when a more intense sound is presented to one ear than to the other. When a sound is delivered to one ear just before it is delivered to the other, a greater response is recorded in the brain on the side opposite the ear receiving the earlier signal. The principle of sound localization by a difference in intensity has been used to identify malingerers claiming to be deaf in one ear. For example, if a tone is presented simultaneously to both ears through earphones, but more intensely to the left ear, a normal person will say the sound is coming from the left. An individual deaf in the left ear will hear the sound in the right ear. A person feigning deafness in the left ear

will say he does not hear any sound. This test clearly shows that sound localization does not require a comparison of separate sensations aroused in two ears. A single localized sound is heard.

Hearing Impairment

Any portion of the auditory apparatus can be affected by disease or injury, leading to partial or total deafness. **Conduction hearing impairment** is caused by interference with the transmission of sound vibrations through the external or middle ear. Vibrations may be weakened or blocked by the accumulation of wax in the external ear, by perforation or hardening of the tympanic membrane, or by adhesions of the bones of the middle ear. In *otosclerosis*, ossification around the footplate of the stapes blocks the transmission of sound to the oval window. **Sensorineural hearing impairment** results from a congenital deficiency, injury, or disease of the organ of Corti or of the auditory nerve. Long exposure to loud sounds is a common cause of sensorineural hearing impairment. In this type of deficiency the hearing loss is usually greater for the high than for the low frequencies.

The extent of hearing loss at various frequencies can be determined with an audiometer, an instrument through which pure tones are delivered through earphones, starting with the intensity at each frequency that

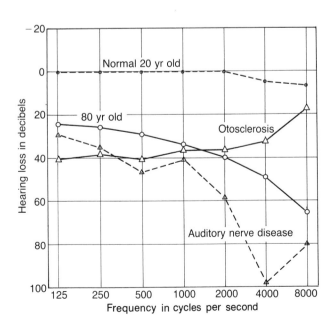

Figure 10–25. Combined audiogram showing three types of abnormalities.

is barely audible to a person with normal hearing. The number of decibels each tone must be raised before a subject can hear it, a measure of the hearing loss for that frequency, is plotted to obtain a record called an **audiogram** (Fig. 10–25). Audiograms may also be obtained by bone conduction tests, in which a vibrator delivering pure signals is placed on the skull, usually on the mastoid prominence behind the ear. Bone conduction audiograms aid in the diagnosis of hearing impairment, since the pathway of the vibrations to the inner ear bypasses the external acoustic meatus and the middle ear.

If an individual's hearing impairment is sensorineural, the audiograms obtained by air and bone conduction will show approximately equal hearing losses. On the other hand, if the individual has a conduction hearing loss, only the audiogram obtained by air conduction will reveal the impairment — the bone conduction audiogram will be normal or near normal. Another difference between individuals with conduction hearing impairment and those with sensorineural impairment is how they perform in speech discrimination tests. In these tests the subject is asked to repeat phonetically balanced words heard well above threshold through a loudspeaker. Individuals with conduction hearing impairment generally score 100 per cent in such tests, whereas subjects with sensorineural impairment score considerably below 100 per cent, often 60 per cent or less. Because of this deficiency, individuals with sensorineural hearing impairment will find that hearing aids, although helpful, will not restore speech comprehension to normal.

OLFACTORY SENSE (SENSE OF SMELL)

Receptor Cells

Less is known about the sense of smell than about the more complex senses. Receptors for smell are located in the *olfactory* (L. *olfacere,* to smell) *epithelium,* an area about 2.5 cm square in each nostril located in the roof of the nasal cavity (Fig. 10–26). The olfactory epithelium contains supporting cells and actual olfactory cells.

Olfactory cells are bipolar neurons with their cell bodies in the mucosal epithelial layer. At the mucosal surface they divide into many fine hairlike processes, or cilia, which

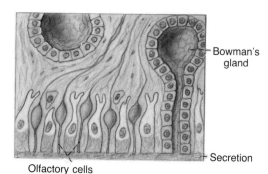

Bowman's gland

Secretion

Olfactory cells

Figure 10–26. Olfactory epithelium showing supporting cells and olfactory cells.

lie uncovered except for a thin layer of mucus; nowhere else in the body are nerve endings so exposed. The axons of the olfactory cell bodies pass through the *cribriform plate* of the *ethmoid bone* as fibers of the *olfactory nerve* to the *olfactory bulb* above each nasal cavity (Fig. 9–51, page 285). Here synaptic connections are made with neurons (principally mitral cells) whose axons form the *olfactory tract.* The exact route these axons follow is uncertain, but the primary olfactory area is now believed to be in the lateroposterior part of the orbitofrontal cortex.

Physiology of Olfaction

In order for a substance to arouse the sensation of smell it must first of all be volatile so that it can be carried by eddy currents to the olfactory epithelium. A relatively high water and lipid solubility is characteristic of substances with strong odors. Water solubility is necessary for the substance to dissolve in the layer of mucus covering the olfactory cells. Lipid solubility presumably aids penetration of the membranes of the receptor cells.

A number of theories have been presented attempting to explain the mechanism of smell. An underlying assumption of many of these theories is that some kind of interaction occurs between odoriferous molecules and the membranes of the olfactory cells, possibly with specific receptors, which alters permeability of the membranes and induces a nerve impulse.

Although olfactory receptors are sensitive to exceedingly low concentrations of odor-producing substances, the differential sensitivity of olfaction is considered to be poor. According to most reports, the concentration of an odor-producing substance must be changed by about 30 per cent before a difference can be detected. In a recent study, however, in which fluctuations in the concentrations of stimulants were reduced to a minimum, changes in concentration, in some cases as low as 5 per cent, could be detected. Comparable visual discrimination threshold is a 1 per cent change in light intensity. Maximum odor intensity is achieved with a 50-fold increase above the threshold concentration. This is a small range compared with most sensory systems.

Humans can distinguish between 2000 and 4000 different odors. Evidence indicates that the direction from which the odor comes can be detected by the slight difference in the time of arrival of odoriferous molecules in the two nostrils.

Sniffing. That portion of the nasal cavity containing the olfactory receptors is poorly ventilated. The amount of air reaching this region is greatly increased by sniffing, thereby increasing the intensity of the odor.

Receptors for smell adapt quickly at first — about 50 per cent in the first second — and slowly thereafter. Nevertheless, after a minute or more of continuous stimulation by a specific odor, the ability to recognize the odor is lost. Central mechanisms are believed to be involved in this phenomenon. If another odor is immediately smelled, adaptation to the first in no way seems to impair the sensing of the second.

Many attempts have been made to classify odors, but none helps to explain the physiology of smell. Each substance causes its own particular sensation. A multitude of distinct odors can be recognized, and individual odors in a mixed smell can be distinguished.

GUSTATORY SENSE (SENSE OF TASTE)

Receptor Cells

Like the sense of smell, the sense of taste provides a chemical sensitivity for an organism, enabling it to decide if particles should be ingested or rejected. The specialized structures for the reception of taste are the **taste buds**. Approximately 9000 of these structures are found on the tongue. Taste

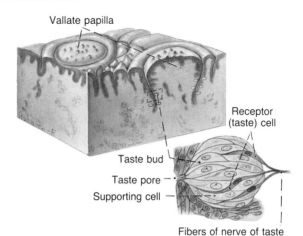

Figure 10–27. Taste bud and section from tongue showing where it is found.

buds are onion-shaped receptors containing a tiny pore opening onto the surface of the tongue. They measure 50 to 70 micrometers in diameter and consist of supporting cells and five to 18 *hair cells*, or gustatory (L. *gustare*, to taste) receptors. The hairs project into the taste pore. The buds are found in numerous small projections (*papillae*) on the tongue. The large papillae forming a V-line on the posterior portion of the tongue are *vallate papillae*. The *fungiform papillae*, more numerous and smaller, are located chiefly on the tip and sides of the tongue (Fig. 10–27).

Physiology of Taste

Only when a substance is in solution can it stimulate the gustatory hairs. Substances arousing taste sensations are believed to alter in some way the ionic permeability of the hair membranes and thereby evoke a change in electrical potential. Receptor potentials of the taste cells then generate impulses in the endings of the sensory neurons innervating taste cells.

Taste studies in animals and humans have demonstrated the existence of functionally distinct types of taste receptor cells (with no corresponding histological difference). Taste buds show sensitivity to combinations of four primary taste sensations — *sweet, salty, sour,* and *bitter*. Their distribution on the tongue gives rise to maximum sensitivity to sweet taste at the tip, sourness at the sides,

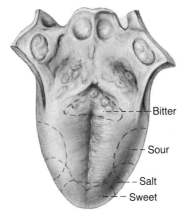

Bitter

Sour

Salt

Sweet

Figure 10–28. Taste areas of the tongue.

bitterness at the back, and salty taste at the tip and sides (Fig. 10–28).

Intensity of discrimination is relatively crude — a 30 per cent change in concentration is necessary for discrimination to occur.

Acids taste sour, the sourness being generally proportional to the hydrogen ion concentration. A salty taste is produced principally by the cation of salts. Sweet substances are usually organic and include sugars, alcohols, and aldehydes. Bitter-tasting substances are frequently organic also, and include chemicals classified as alkaloids, such as quinine, caffeine, and nicotine. Flavor is accomplished when a variety of tastes is synthesized from the four basic taste components. Many substances are identified by combinations of gustatory and olfactory sensations, aided also by touch, pressure, temperature, and pain sensations.

The sense of taste has been found to be an important factor in nutrition. Animals deprived of the sense of taste suffer from malnutrition even when an adequate diet is available to them.

Most special senses are supplied by a single nerve extending from the receptor to the brain; however, taste is made possible by multiple nerves. It is served by the chorda tympani branch of the *facial nerve* (VII) for the front of the tongue, the *glossopharyngeal nerve* (IX) for the back of the tongue, and the *vagus nerve* (X) for the deeper recesses of the throat and pharynx. Axons of these nerves lead to taste nuclei in the medulla. From here second-order neurons pass to the thalamus, where synaptic connections are made with

neurons whose fibers lead to the projection area for taste in the parietal lobe (the lower end of the somesthetic area of the postcentral gyrus). Taste fibers also pass to the reticular formation and to nuclei in the medulla serving salivatory reflexes.

SUMMARY

SPECIAL SENSES

Vision

1. **External Structures of the Eye**

   a. Orbital cavity (contains eyeball)
   b. Extrinsic ocular muscles (provide support for and control movement of eyeball)
   c. Eyelids (give protection)
   d. Conjunctiva (line each eyelid and exposed surface of eyeball)
   e. Lacrimal apparatus (lubricates eye)

2. **Internal Structures of the Eye**

   a. Layers of the eyeball
      (1) Outer layer (consists of sclera posteriorly, cornea anteriorly)
      (2) Middle layer (consists of choroid posteriorly, ciliary body [containing the ciliary processes and ciliary muscle] and iris anteriorly)
      (3) Inner layer (consists of retina)
   b. Fluid media of the eye
      (1) Aqueous humor (fills anterior and posterior chambers of anterior cavity of eyeball, nourishes lens and cornea)
      (2) Vitreous humor (fills posterior cavity, maintains spherical shape of eye)

3. **Accommodation**

   a. Cornea is principal refracting medium of eye, accounting for three-fourths of focusing power when viewing distant objects.
   b. Focusing on objects closer than 20 feet from eyes involves increasing convexity of lens. This is accomplished by contracting the ciliary muscle, which draws the insertions of the suspensory ligaments forward and inward, easing tension on the suspensory ligaments and lens capsule.

c. Accommodation for near vision includes, in addition to focusing image on retina, contraction of circular fibers of iris (constricting pupil) and aligning visual axes of eyes.

d. Accommodation for far vision involves relaxation of ciliary muscles, contraction of radial fibers of iris (dilating pupil) and aligning visual axes.

4. Physiology of Vision

a. Retina changes image focused on it into nerve impulses.

b. Retina contains rods sensitive to dim light and cones sensitive to bright light. Cones function in color vision.

c. Rods and cones are receptor cells having photosensitive chemicals that undergo changes to initiate nerve impulse.

d. After initiation, nerve impulses are relayed via bipolar cells to ganglion cells, axons of which form optic nerve.

e. Horizontal and amacrine cells transmit inhibitory signals across retina to heighten contrast in visual field.

f. Stimuli in left field of vision of both eyes excite right visual cortex in occipital lobe, and vice versa.

5. Binocular Vision

Disparity between left and right retinal images of third dimension of an object, resulting from different views seen by each eye (binocular parallax), is synthesized by brain into three-dimensional picture.

6. Abnormalities of the Eye

a. Problems of focus include nearsightedness (myopia), farsightedness (hyperopia), oldsightedness (presbyopia), and uneven focusing in different planes (astigmatism).

b. Other abnormalities include cataract, an alteration in concentration of protein fibers of lens, causing light scattering; corneal opacity; and conjunctivitis, an inflammation of the conjunctiva.

Auditory Sense

1. **Sound vibrations in air cause eardrum (tympanic membrane) to vibrate; vibrations in turn are conveyed to inner ear and transformed into nerve impulses.**

2. Structure of the Ear

a. **External ear:** Auricle collects sound waves and directs them through external acoustic meatus to tympanic membrane.

b. **Middle ear** includes malleus, incus, and stapes. These three bones transmit sound vibrations from tympanic membrane to inner ear and reduce amplitude of large vibrations. Pressure on both sides of tympanic membrane is equalized by way of auditory, or Eustachian, tube.

c. **Inner ear** has bony labyrinth consisting of cochlea, containing organ of Corti, end organ of hearing, and semicircular canals and vestibule, containing organs for balance of body. Within cochlea is membranous cochlear duct. Organ of Corti rests on floor of cochlear duct, formed by the basilar membrane.

3. Physiology of Hearing

a. Sound waves cause tympanic membrane to vibrate.

b. Bones of middle ear transmit these vibrations to oval window of inner ear, which in turn transmits vibrations to perilymph of passageway (scala vestibuli) above cochlear duct.

c. As vibrations pass through endolymph of cochlear duct to perilymph in passageway (scala tympani) below cochlear duct, vibrations are set up in basilar membrane — high frequency sounds causing maximum displacement of basilar membrane at base of cochlea, low frequency at apex.

d. Vibrations of basilar membrane bend hairs of hair cells of organ of Corti, initiating changes in electrical potential, followed by the release of a neurotransmitter that stimulates nerve fibers of the cochlear branch of the eighth cranial nerve.

e. As result of partial decussation of fibers at several stations in pathway from medulla to cerebrum, auditory cortex receives bilateral input, but each ear has greater representation on opposite side.

Equilibrium

1. **The utricle and saccule (portions of the membranous labyrinth located in the**

vestibule) contain receptors sensitive to gravity and to linear acceleration and deceleration of the head, consisting of ultrafine hairs of hair cells projecting into a gelatinous membrane weighted with crystals of calcium carbonate (otoconia). Gravitational pull on the otoconial membrane bends the hairs, initiating nerve impulses; the direction of bending will vary with head position, informing the brain of the orientation of the head. During linear acceleration and deceleration the force exerted against the otoconial membrane will change the direction of bending of the hairs.

2. In the ampulla, at the base of each of three semicircular ducts (inside each semicircular canal), are receptors for angular acceleration and deceleration consisting of a gelatinous membrane (the cupola) into which the hairs of hair cells project. The hairs are bent in the direction opposite to the direction of head rotation, and bending in specific directions has an excitatory or inhibitory effect on neural activity.

3. The hair cells of the organs of equilibrium are innervated by fibers of the vestibular branch of the 8th cranial nerve.

Olfactory Sense

Olfactory receptor cells are bipolar neurons with their cell bodies in the olfactory epithelium. Their axons become the olfactory nerve.

Gustatory Sense

1. Approximately 9000 taste buds, the receptors for taste, are found on the human tongue in the fungiform and vallate papillae. Hairs of taste cells project from a taste bud through a pore to the surface of a papilla.

2. Taste buds are sensitive to combinations of four primary tastes—sweet, salty, sour, and bitter—and their distribution results in maximum sensitivity to sweet taste at the tip of the tongue, sourness at the sides, bitterness at the back, and salty taste at the tip and sides.

REVIEW QUESTIONS

1. List the functions of the five external structures of the eye. Describe the structure of the lacrimal apparatus.
2. Name the major components of the three layers of the eyeball.
3. What is the principal refracting medium of the eye? Describe how accommodation for near vision occurs.
4. Explain the cause of glaucoma.
5. Distinguish between the functions of rods and cones. Describe the rhodopsin cycle.
6. Differentiate myopia, hyperopia, presbyopia, and astigmatism.
7. List the principal components of the outer, middle, and inner ear.
8. Distinguish between the functions of the equilibrium receptors in the saccule and utricle and those in the semicircular canals.
9. How does sound produce nerve impulses? Distinguish between conduction and sensorineural hearing impairment.
10. Describe the receptors for the olfactory and gustatory senses.

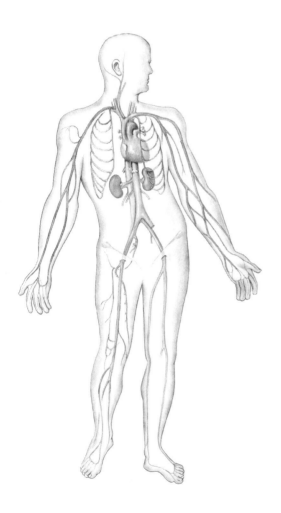

11

The Circulatory System

Objectives

The aim of this chapter is to enable the student to:

☐ Describe the major components of blood and distinguish between the functions of the different types of blood cells.

☐ List, in sequence, the basic steps in blood clotting.

☐ Describe the basic organization of the circulatory system.

☐ Enumerate the steps of the cardiac cycle.

☐ Explain the origin of the heartbeat.

☐ Describe an ECG.

☐ Name and describe the difference in structure and function of the different types of blood vessels.

☐ List the major factors governing arterial blood pressure and explain the role of the medullary vasomotor and cardiac centers in regulating blood pressure.

☐ Name the major vessels of the circulatory system.

☐ Explain the unique features of the circulation through the liver.

☐ Describe coronary heart disease and some of the congenital defects of the cardiovascular system.

In 1628, after nine years of careful observation, William Harvey published the first scientific treatise demonstrating the continuous circulation of blood. Since that time, a great deal of physiologic and biochemical data on the circulatory system has accumulated. The circulatory system nourishes every part of the body. The fluid bathing the body tissues is derived from the blood; the pump circulating the blood is the heart; the tubes through which the blood flows are the blood vessels.

BLOOD

The Nature of Blood

Although blood appears homogeneous, if a thin layer is placed under a microscope, its heterogeneous character becomes obvious. If blood is centrifuged or allowed to stand, it separates into two distinct fractions. Usually less than half consists of "formed" ele-

ments — **red blood cells,** which are involved in the transport of respiratory gases; **white blood cells,** which combat infection; and **platelets,** which play an essential role in blood clotting (Figs. 11–1 and 11–2). These normally constitute 38 to 52 per cent of the total blood volume. The remainder is the straw-colored fluid, the **plasma.** The *hematocrit* (G. *haima,* blood; G. *krinein,* to separate) is the percentage of "formed" elements by volume. Thus, if the percentage of "formed" elements is 45, the hematocrit is 45.

Blood Plasma

Blood plasma is a straw-colored liquid composed of water (about 91 per cent) and chemical compounds (about 9 per cent), mainly protein. The total plasma volume and ratio of plasma to formed elements are held constant by the homeostatic mechanisms of the body. *Serum* differs from plasma in that it is the fluid remaining after formation of a blood

Table 11–1   CONSTITUENTS OF BLOOD IN NORMAL AND ABNORMAL STATES

CONSTITUENT	NORMAL LEVEL	ALTERATIONS IN DISEASE STATES
Total bilirubin	Less than 1 mg/100 ml	Increased in hemolytic anemia and in obstruction to biliary flow, such as a stone in the common bile duct
Calcium	4.5–5.5 mEq/l	Increased in hyperparathyroidism; decreased in hypoparathyroidism
Total cholesterol	140–250 mg/100 ml	Increased in hypothyroidism; decreased in hyperthyroidism and starvation
Fibrinogen	0.2–0.4 gm/100 ml	Increased in severe infections; decreased in primary liver disease and malnutrition
Glucose	70–110 mg/100 ml	Increased after meals and in diabetes mellitus; decreased in Addison's disease
Nonprotein nitrogen (NPN)	20–35 mg/100 ml	Includes urea, uric acid, creatinine, ammonia, and amino acids; increased in disease of the kidneys
Protein-bound iodine (PBI)	3–7 mg/100 ml	Increased in hyperthyroidism; decreased in hypothyroidism
Phosphate	3–4.5 mg/100 ml	Increased in renal disease and hypoparathyroidism, as well as in Addison's disease; decreased in vitamin D deficiency and hyperparathyroidism
Potassium	3.5–5.0 mEq/l	Increased in Addison's disease and diseases of the kidney; decreased after diarrhea, and with administration of adrenocortical hormones
Total protein Albumin Globulin	6–8.6 gm/100 ml 3.2–4.5 gm/100 ml 2.3–3.5 gm/100 ml	Decreased in diseases of the kidney and liver, and in malnutrition; globulin is elevated in chronic infection
Sodium	140–148 mEq/l	Increased in diseases of the kidney; decreased in Addison's disease
Uric acid	2.6–7 mg/100 ml	Increased in kidney disease and gout

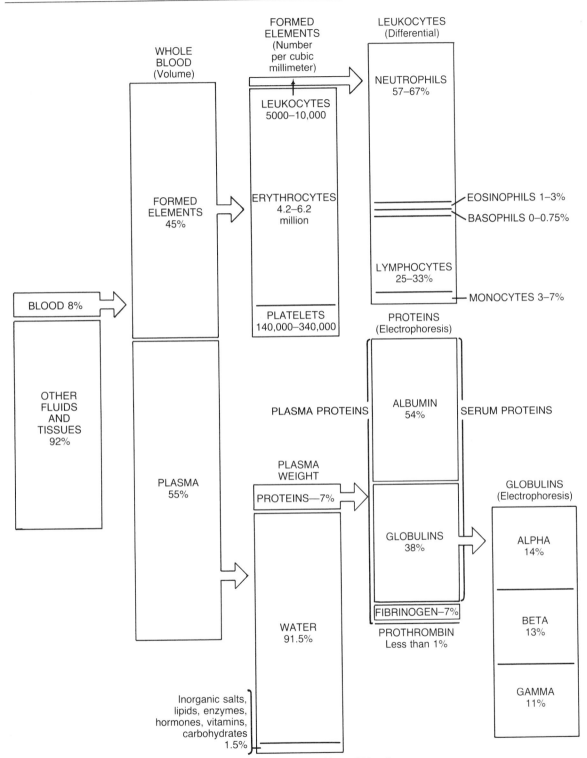

Figure 11–1. Composition of blood.

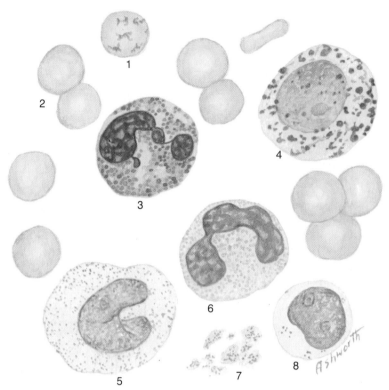

Figure 11–2. Blood cells: 1, reticulocyte; 2, erythrocyte; 3, eosinophil; 4, basophil; 5, monocyte; 6, neutrophil; 7, platelets; and 8, lymphocyte. Numbers correspond to those in Figure 11–3, illustrating the stages of blood cell formation.

clot and, therefore, does not contain a number of the clotting factors present in plasma. Plasma can be maintained only if an anticoagulant is added to keep clotting from occurring. (See Table 11–1 for constituents of blood plasma and Table 11–2 for characteristics of blood.)

The four major plasma proteins are *albumin, globulin, fibrinogen,* and *prothrombin.* Albumin is important in maintaining the osmotic equilibrium of the blood. Since albumin cannot readily pass through the capillary wall, it remains in the blood stream and

exerts an osmotic pressure, attracting water from the tissue spaces back into the blood stream. If plasma protein, particularly serum albumin, leaks from the capillaries as a result of injury, such as a severe burn, water cannot be retained and the blood volume drops. If the loss is severe, shock results. Treatment necessary to counteract this state includes the intravenous injection of serum albumin.

Globulin is important because it contains antibodies involved in the body's immune mechanism. If globulin is examined by *electrophoresis,* it can be separated into three groups: alpha, beta, and gamma. The gamma globulin is the antibody fraction.

The electrophoretic method used in separating the plasma proteins involves placing the serum or plasma in an electric field, causing the negatively charged protein molecules existing as ions in plasma to migrate toward the positive electrode. The protein molecules move at different speeds, depending on size, shape, and charge, and eventually become separated from each other.

Fibrinogen and prothrombin are important in the process of coagulation and will be discussed subsequently.

Table 11–2 CHARACTERISTICS OF BLOOD

CHARACTERISTIC	NORMAL VALUE
Specific gravity	Males, 1.057 Females, 1.053
Average blood volume	69 ml/kg of body weight
Viscosity (relative to water)	Whole, 3.5–5.4 Plasma, 1.9–2.3
pH	Arterial, 7.39 Venous, 7.35
Arterial oxygen content	Total, 20.3 ml oxygen/100 ml of blood In plasma, 0.3 Combined with hemoglobin, 20.0

Blood Cell Formation

All blood cells originate from undifferentiated **stem cells** called hemocytoblasts. Primitive cells of each family have similar morphologic characteristics. As primitive cells change to the more mature cell forms, they undergo alterations in nuclear and cytoplasmic characteristics: cells decrease in size; the relative and absolute size of the nucleus decreases (in the erythrocytic series, the nucleus actually disappears); and the intensity of the stain taken up by the cytoplasm diminishes (Fig. 11–3).

The first recognizable blood cells in the human embryo, forming in islands within the *mesenchyme* of the yolk sac, originate from hemocytoblasts. During the second month of intrauterine life, the liver assumes a major role in the formation of blood cells. During the fifth month, the spleen is the dominant producer, but this activity rapidly subsides. At birth, some *hematopoietic* (formation of blood) activity may remain in the liver but none is occurring in the spleen.

Development of blood cells within the bones commences during the fifth month of fetal life. Blood-forming elements appear initially in the centers of bone marrow cavities; the blood-forming centers later expand to occupy the entire marrow space. This widely dispersed blood cell formation continues until puberty, when the marrow in all the ends of the long bones becomes less cellular and more fatty, giving rise to yellow bone marrow, in which most of the hematopoietic tissue has been replaced by fat. In the adult, only the **red bone marrow,** located principally in the skull, vertebrae, ribs, sternum, and pelvis, retains hematopoietic activity. The total productive bone marrow in the adult is about 1400 gm. In elderly individuals, areas of bone marrow, once occupied by active cell production, become fat laden. This helps explain the difficulty elderly individuals experience in regenerating lost blood.

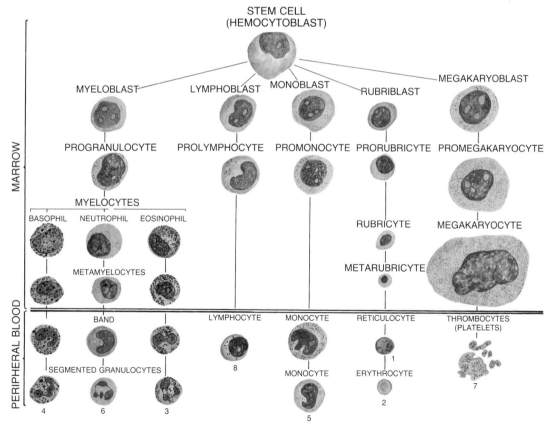

Figure 11–3. Stages in the formation of the peripheral blood cells. Numbered cells correspond to cell types in Figure 11–2.

Types of Blood Cells

Erythrocytes

Red blood cells, or *erythrocytes* (G. *erythros,* red; G. *kytos,* cell), transport oxygen (almost all of the oxygen in blood is bound to hemoglobin in red blood cells) and play a key role in the transport of carbon dioxide (see Chapter 13 for a discussion of the chemistry of gas transport). Just before a red cell reaches maturity, the nucleus is extruded. The mature red blood cell has the shape of a **biconcave disc,** resembling a doughnut with a thin central portion instead of a hole. This shape provides a large absorptive surface, the total surface area of erythrocytes representing approximately 3200 square meters, or 1500 times the surface of the human body. The diameter of red blood cells is approximately 7 micrometers. They are elastic and increase in size as the pH of the blood diminishes. Thus the erythrocyte is larger in venous blood than in arterial.

The number of red cells per cubic millimeter of blood can be determined by counting a limited number of cells spread on a ruled microscopic slide, the hemocytometer. The red cell count is approximately 5,400,000 cells per cubic millimeter in males and 4,700,000 per cubic millimeter in females. Muscular exercise and emotional states are associated with a temporary increase in the number of red cells. The increase occurs from the expulsion of stores of blood in the spleen and liver.

Regulation of Red Blood Cell Production. Red blood cell production, or *erythropoiesis* (G. *poiēsis,* production), is regulated by **erythropoietin,** also called erythropoietic stimulating factor (ESF). Erythropoietin is responsible for the increase in the rate of production of red blood cells by any condition that reduces the oxygen supply to the tissues *(hypoxia).* Hypoxia causes the concentration of erythropoietin to rise to detectable levels in the blood. After a person ascends to a high altitude, for example, the concentration of erythropoietin in the blood rises daily and the rate of erythrocyte formation rises sharply after two days to a maximum in five days. Erythropoietin also controls the rate of red blood cell production under normal conditions. The best evidence for this is the observation that the injection of antibodies to erythropoietin into mice essentially abolishes erythropoiesis. Erythropoie-

tin is formed in the blood by the action of an enzyme released principally from the kidneys called *renal erythropoietic factor (REF).* REF cleaves a portion of a plasma protein to produce the active substance. For many years it was believed that erythropoietin acted by stimulating the stem cell. Recent findings, however, indicate that it acts rather on an erythropoietin-sensitive progeny of the stem cell. To cite one example, in studies with mice injected with a known number of stem cells after destruction of their bone marrow by irradiation, the effect of erythropoietin on the rate of red blood cell production could be accounted for only if it acted not on the stem cell but on a greater number of proliferating progeny.

HEMOGLOBIN. Hemoglobin, contained in the red cells, plays an essential role in oxygen transport. It is formed during the manufacture of the red blood cells in the bone marrow. Each red blood cell contains approximately 280 million hemoglobin molecules. The hemoglobin molecule consists of four protein chains, each of which enfolds an oxygen-carrying nonprotein group called *heme.* The major hemoglobin of the human adult, called hemoglobin A, is composed of two *alpha* chains, each containing 141 amino acids, and two *beta* chains, each containing 146 amino acids, and is symbolically represented as $\alpha_2\beta_2$. A small fraction of the hemoglobin normally found in human blood (hemoglobin $A_2 — \alpha_2\delta_2$) has two *alpha* and two *delta* chains. The major fetal hemoglobin (hemoglobin $F — \alpha_2\gamma_2$) consists of two *alpha* and two *gamma* chains. The delta and gamma chains have the same number of amino acids as beta chains. Heme is a complex of iron and protoporphyrin (a ring structure with a framework of four groups called pyrroles, each containing four carbons and a nitrogen). Each iron atom can take up one molecule of oxygen. Hemoglobin carries over 98 per cent of the oxygen transported by the blood; less than 2 per cent is carried in simple solution in the plasma. The normal levels for hemoglobin are 15 gm per 100 ml in males and 13 to 14 gm per 100 ml in females.

Destruction of Erythrocytes. The life span of erythrocytes is approximately 80 to 120 days. When their usefulness is impaired by age, the red cells are destroyed by the macrophages of the *reticuloendothelial system,* especially of the spleen. Two to ten million red cells are destroyed each second;

yet, because of replacement, the number of circulating cells remains remarkably constant. When red cells are destroyed, hemoglobin is set free and broken down into its components, heme and the protein globin. The heme decomposes into its constituents, protoporphyrin and iron. The iron is utilized to form new erythrocytes or, if an excess of iron exists in the body, it is brought to the bone marrow, spleen, and liver for storage. Protoporphyrin is converted to *bilirubin,* which is carried to the liver and excreted with the bile. It is the bilirubin that gives bile its golden-yellow color.

HEMOLYSIS AND CRENATION OF RED BLOOD CELLS. *Hemolysis in vitro* (in a vessel outside the body) is the rupture of red cell membranes and resultant liberation of hemoglobin from the red corpuscles. It may result from osmotic forces such as would result from the injection of distilled water, or by mechanical stress as in heating or freezing. Hemolysis is characterized by a red tinge to the serum or plasma from which the red blood cells have been separated.

Crenation is a shriveling of the cell, noted when the cells are placed in a salt solution of high concentration. The fluid within the cell passes into the surrounding medium. Crenation does not alter the integrity of the cell wall and hemoglobin does not escape, thus differentiating it from hemolysis.

Anemias. Anemia is a condition characterized by a deficiency in the amount of oxygen carried by red blood cells to the tissues. It is most commonly caused by a decrease in the rate of formation of red blood cells, an increase in their rate of destruction, or a reduction in hemoglobin synthesis. When red blood cell production is reduced as a result of damage to the red bone marrow, the condition is called hypoplastic anemia or, in severe cases, **aplastic anemia** (in this condition the number of platelets and white blood cells is also reduced). Bone marrow can be destroyed by, among other things, radiation, infections, and drugs, especially some used in cancer chemotherapy. In **pernicious anemia** there is a reduction in the formation of red blood cells because of a deficiency in vitamin B_{12}, known as the maturation factor. The underlying cause of this condition is a failure of the stomach to produce enough "intrinsic factor," a glycoprotein that facilitates the absorption of vitamin B_{12} from the small intestine into the blood stream. The red blood cell count is very low in pernicious anemia and the cells produced are large (*macrocytic*), oddly shaped, and fragile.

Hemolysis *in vivo* (in the body) refers to a shortened life span of red blood cells, whatever the cause may be, and whether or not rupture (by agents such as cobra venom, for example) occurs intravascularly. Anemias brought about by a reduced life span of erythrocytes, therefore, are called **hemolytic anemias.** A number of hereditary diseases exist in which structural abnormalities in the red blood cells lead to their premature removal from the circulation, principally by the spleen. One such is **sickle cell anemia,** an unusual condition caused by an abnormality in the structure of the protein portion of hemoglobin (substitution of valine for glutamic acid in the sixth position of the beta chains). In this disease, when the oxygen concentration in the blood is lowered following the release of oxygen from the red blood cells, the abnormal hemoglobin molecules aggregate and distort the cells into various bizarre shapes, including the originally described crescent, or sickle, shape. Because the sickle cell is rigid, it causes clogging of the capillaries (an event associated with severe bouts of pain), which leads to the early destruction of the cells. Individuals with so-called *sickle cell trait* (heterozygous individuals with one normal and one sickle cell gene) have normal as well as sickle cell hemoglobin and are generally free from symptoms of the disease, although a below-normal concentration of oxygen in the blood, such as occurs at a high altitude, may provoke sickling and painful crises. Since individuals with sickle cell trait are relatively resistant to malaria, in a population exposed to malaria they have a selective advantage over homozygous individuals — those with either two normal or two sickle cell genes. This advantage maintains a high frequency of the sickle cell gene in populations throughout the world where malaria is prevalent.

A group of disorders of hemoglobin synthesis, the **thalassemias,** may also give rise to the premature destruction of red blood cells. These anemias, common in Greece and the Mediterranean coastal region, result from an absence of or decreased synthesis of one or more globin chains (with continued normal production of the others). The unbalanced hemoglobins are unstable and precipitate within the red blood cells. As a consequence, the cells are destroyed. The degree of anemia varies from mild to severe; the severe forms are usually fatal.

Insufficient hemoglobin synthesis occurs in **iron deficiency anemia.** In this type of anemia the number of red blood cells may be almost normal, but the individual cells are much smaller and pale *(microcytic, hypochromic),* owing to a lack of sufficient hemoglobin. Iron deficiency anemia usually follows chronic blood loss. When the supply of iron becomes depleted because of increased red blood cell formation to compensate for the blood loss, hemoglobin production is diminished and anemia results. This deficiency may also occur when the demand for iron is unusually great, as during infancy, adolescence, or pregnancy.

Leukocytes (Table 11–3)

Three general types of white blood cells, or *leukocytes* (G. *leukos,* white), are found in blood: **granulocytes** (cells with numerous granules) and the nongranular forms, namely, **lymphocytes** and **monocytes.** *Neutrophils,* the most numerous of the granulocytes, are phagocytic, functioning in the destruction of pathogenic microorganisms and other foreign matter. The granules, it was established in the 1960's, are actually lysosomes, organelles containing digestive enzymes (see Chapter 3, pages 52 and 57). At wound or infected sites the number of invading neutrophils rises to a peak in 24 hours. Neutrophils and two other subtypes of granulocytes (Fig. 11–2) are classified on the basis of the staining properties of their granules. *Basophils* are readily stained with the basic dye methylene blue, *eosinophils* with the red acid dye eosin, and neutrophils only weakly with both types of dye. Eosinophils apparently phagocytize antigen-antibody complexes (see Chapter 12). The function of basophils is still uncertain.

Lymphocytes are a somewhat heterogeneous group of cells important in the process of immunity, producing antibodies and other agents involved in the immune process; all have essentially the same staining characteristics. Monocytes possess a relatively large amount of cytoplasm and a round or kidney-shaped nucleus. They function as phagocytes, becoming transformed into macrophages after invading infected sites, where their numbers reach a peak in 48 hours.

Diseases Involving Abnormalities of the White Cell Series. Many diseases are characterized by a change in the number of circulating leukocytes. An increase in the white cell count, generally indicating an acute infection, is called **leukocytosis. Leukopenia,** a reduction in the number of white cells, occurs occasionally in viral diseases.

The total white cell count ranges from 5000 to 10,000 per cubic millimeter; however, it may be as high as 500,000 per cubic millimeter in *leukemia.* Leukemia is characterized by an uncontrolled proliferation of leukocytes which generally resemble immature cells and are usually nonfunctional. The type of leukocyte involved differentiates the varieties of leukemia — granulocytic, lymphocytic, and monocytic.

Table 11–3   WHITE BLOOD CELLS (LEUKOCYTES)

TYPE	NUMBER/MM³	FUNCTION	INCREASED COUNT	DECREASED COUNT
Neutrophil	3000–6000 (57–67%)	Phagocytosis	Pyrogenic infections; leukemia	Toxic reactions such as occur with the administration of certain drugs
Eosinophil	150–300 (1–3%)	Phagocytosis of antigen-antibody complexes	Allergy; parasitic infections; leukemia	Administration of adrenocortical hormones
Basophil	0–100 (0.5–1%)	Exact function unknown	Leukemia	Unknown
Lymphocyte	1500–3000 (25–33%)	In immune response	Infectious mononucleosis; chronic infections; viral infections; leukemia	Adrenocortical hormones
Monocyte	100–600 (3–7%)	As a macrophage	Tuberculosis; protozoal infection; leukemia; infectious mononucleosis	No known cause

Infectious mononucleosis is a benign disease associated with an increase in mononuclear leukocytes. It usually occurs in children and young adults, and is believed to be caused by a virus. The patient with infectious mononucleosis evidences a slightly elevated temperature, enlarged lymph nodes, fatigue, and a sore throat.

Platelets

Platelets, or thrombocytes (G. *thrombos*, lump), are cytoplasmic fragments of giant, multinucleated red bone marrow cells called *megakaryocytes* (Fig. 11–3) and play a role in hemostasis (G. *stasis*, a standing), the process of checking bleeding. They are about half the size of erythrocytes, number from 140,000 to 340,000 per cubic millimeter of blood, are irregular in shape, and are capable of ameboid movement. Although the platelet is a fragment of a cell, it is rich in ATP and contains many of the organelles normally present in cells (Fig. 11–4). Platelets clump together to form a plug in the initial phase of controlling bleeding. This process is accelerated by thrombin, an enzyme involved in blood clotting. Clumping is followed by the retraction of platelet pseudopods with en-

meshed fibrin and blood cells to produce a hard clot (for details, see below). A deficiency in platelets causes a tendency to bleed. One such condition is known as *idiopathic thrombocytopenic purpura* (ITP). Idiopathic means cause unknown; thrombocytopenia means low platelet count; purpura (Latin for purple) is a condition in which hemorrhages (G. *rhēgnynai*, to burst) occur in the skin and mucous and serous membranes, most commonly of pinhead size (petechiae). It has been suggested that individuals with this disorder produce antibodies that destroy their own platelets. Since spontaneous petechiae occur in platelet-deficient individuals, it has been inferred that platelets are not only involved in the blood clotting process but also in some way help maintain the integrity of capillary walls.

Hemostasis

Three separate mechanisms are involved in hemostasis: platelet clumping, or agglutination (L. *agglutinare*, to glue), contraction of blood vessels, and formation of a fibrin clot. When a vessel larger than a capillary is cut or damaged, platelets rapidly accumulate at the

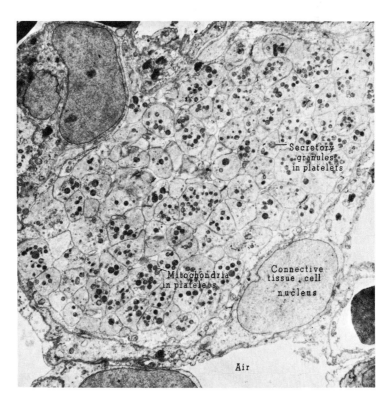

Figure 11–4. A lung capillary containing numerous blood platelets (Magnified 12,000×).

site of injury and adhere to the vascular wall (to the collagen of the subendothelium). The aggregate of platelets forms a temporary plug capable of arresting the bleeding in small arteries and veins. Simultaneously with platelet agglutination, vasoconstriction of muscle-containing vessels occurs. Shortly after the appearance of the initial aggregate, platelets fuse into a dense, structureless mass. The mass forms a temporary solid seal at the site of injury. When a platelet agglutination occurs, a second type of vasoconstriction takes place affecting the injured vessel and many neighboring vessels. This is the result of the release of serotonin from platelets. Only after the sequence of platelet change does actual coagulation, or clotting, occur, completing the process of hemostasis.

Mechanism of Coagulation. The formation of the **fibrin clot,** generally referred to as blood coagulation, is the most complex of the hemostatic mechanisms. Formation of insoluble fibrin from the soluble protein *fibrinogen* is brought about by the action of **thrombin.** Thrombin is a proteolytic enzyme — it removes two pairs of low molecular weight peptides from each molecule of fibrinogen to form molecules of fibrin monomer. Many monomers polymerize to produce fibrin threads. The enzymatic action of fibrin stabilizing factor (further binding the monomers covalently) strengthens the threads.

The clot is now a meshwork of randomly distributed fibrin threads that will trap blood cells, platelets, and plasma.

A few minutes after the clot has formed, it begins to contract, apparently as a result of the contraction of platelet pseudopods that adhere to the fibrin meshwork. Most of the plasma is thus expelled from the clot within 30 to 60 minutes. As the clot retracts, the edges of the broken blood vessel are pulled together, thus contributing to the ultimate state of hemostasis.

Thrombin, the enzyme responsible for the formation of fibrin, is not present in the blood stream. It is formed from an inactive precursor, *prothrombin,* by the action of *prothrombin activator,* also called prothrombin-converting principle. The production of prothrombin activator is initiated in two ways, via (1) a pathway designated **extrinsic,** triggered by the release of a lipoprotein *(thromboplastin)* from injured tissue, and (2) a pathway designated **intrinsic,** which does not require contact with injured tissue. The intrinsic pathway can be triggered by surface contact with glass, which contains an agent that activates a blood protein known as clotting factor XII, or the *Hageman factor.* In the body the intrinsic pathway is thought to be initiated by the adhesion of platelets to the broken surfaces of blood vessels. Figure 11–6 illustrates the intrinsic and extrinsic pathways leading to a formation of prothrombin activator. Because of the stepladder sequence of the intrinsic pathway, it has been described as a waterfall or cascade. Deficiencies in the intrinsic pathway are associated with a number of hereditary bleeding diseases.

Calcium ions appear necessary for the operation of both the intrinsic and extrinsic

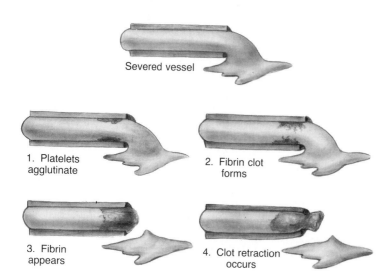

Severed vessel

1. Platelets agglutinate

2. Fibrin clot forms

3. Fibrin appears

4. Clot retraction occurs

Figure 11–5. Formation of clot following injury.

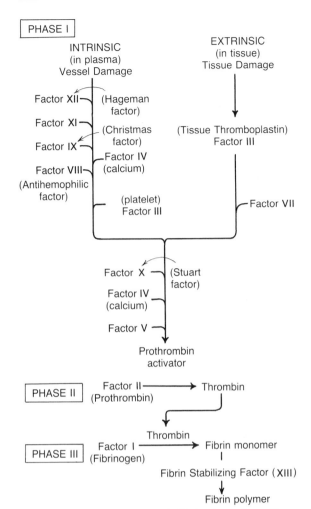

PHASE I

INTRINSIC
(in plasma)
Vessel Damage

EXTRINSIC
(in tissue)
Tissue Damage

Factor XII — (Hageman factor)

Factor XI —
(Christmas factor)

Factor IX —
Factor IV (calcium)

Factor VIII —
(Antihemophilic factor)

(Tissue Thromboplastin)
Factor III

(platelet)
Factor III

Factor VII

Factor X — (Stuart factor)

Factor IV (calcium)

Factor V

Prothrombin activator

PHASE II — Factor II ————→ Thrombin
(Prothrombin)

Thrombin

PHASE III — Factor I ————→ Fibrin monomer
(Fibrinogen)
|
Fibrin Stabilizing Factor (XIII)
↓
Fibrin polymer

Figure 11–6. Phases of fibrin formation. Two pathways, intrinsic and extrinsic, lead to the activation of Stuart factor, which interacts with other clotting factors to form what is known as prothrombin activator, an enzyme that converts prothrombin to thrombin by splitting prothrombin into two fragments, one of which is active thrombin. Thrombin, a proteolytic enzyme, removes two pairs of peptides from fibrinogen to form the so-called fibrin monomer. Many monomers polymerize to produce insoluble fibrin threads. The threads are strengthened by the enzymatic action of fibrin stabilizing factor.

processes. However, these ions do not actually enter into any of the reactions. They simply act as cofactors, causing reactions to take place. Factor III of the intrinsic pathway, released from platelets, is a phospholipid. Factors V through XII are plasma proteins. Prothrombin and factors VII, IX, and X, proteins similar to prothrombin, require vitamin K for their synthesis, which takes place in the liver.

A malfunction or absence of any of the clotting factors causes some degree of bleeding tendency. The most frequently implicated factor is VIII, the antihemophilic factor. Individuals with **hemophilia** synthesize an abnormal, functionally defective form of the clotting factor. Since this condition is transmitted as a sex-linked recessive trait, it is only rarely seen in females.

Thrombosis is clotting in blood vessels. A clot, or *thrombus* (G. *thrombos,* lump), forming in the blood vessels of the leg or arm may be associated with local damage; if it should block the blood supply to the heart or brain, it can be fatal. A *thromboembolus* (G. *embolos,* plug) is a clot that has become dislodged from its place of origin and has lodged elsewhere in the body.

Anticlotting Factors. *Heparin* occurs naturally in the body tissues, although it has rarely been demonstrated in blood. It reduces the ability of blood to clot by activating a plasma protein called antithrombin, which inhibits the actions of clotting factors IX, X, XI, and XII as well as of thrombin. Heparin is produced by *mast cells,* found in most organs of the body, and is employed clinically to prevent the enlargement of thrombi in patients.

The fibrinolytic system involves the digestion of fibrin clots into a number of soluble fragments. Fibrinolysis is mediated by an enzyme called *plasmin,* or *fibrinolysin,* present in the body in the form of the active precursor, *plasminogen.* Plasminogen, a widely distributed globulin, is converted enzymatically to plasmin, a *proteolytic* enzyme capable of digesting the fibrin.

Dicumarol is a drug clinically employed as an anticoagulant. It inhibits the manufacture of clotting factors II (prothrombin), VII, IX, and X by its inhibitory action on vitamin K, which is necessary for their synthesis.

Hemostasis in Capillaries. The control of capillary bleeding is made possible by a different mechanism. Capillary constriction does not play a significant role, since capillaries do not contain contractile tissue. Also, plugs of aggregated platelets have not been shown to develop in severed capillaries. It has been suggested that capillary bleeding may be arrested by adhesion of the endothelial walls of the capillary, aided by torn connective tissue fibers and pressure of tissue fluids.

Blood Grouping

The safe administration of blood from donor to recipient requires typing and cross-matching. These procedures are necessary, since a patient receiving blood incompatible with his own can experience a serious or fatal reaction. The systems of classification are based on the presence of specific *antigens (agglutinogens)* in the red cells. An antigen is a substance or a part of a cell, normally foreign to the body, possessing a chemical group that induces an immune response on the part of immunologically active lymphocytes that includes, among other things, the production of *antibodies*. Antibodies combine with the offending antigens as the first step in inactivating them (for further details, see Chapter 12). The primary classification systems are ABO and Rh (Table 11–4).

ABO Grouping. Blood groups are named for the antigens (mainly protein) contained in the red cells. In each case the blood contains antibodies (also called agglutinins) to antigens *not* present in the blood as well as immunological cells that can produce more of these antibodies. Thus, type A blood has anti-B agglutinins; type B, anti-A agglutinins; type O, both agglutinins; and type AB, neither. The reason for the presence of these antibodies is uncertain. However, since few, if any, are present at birth, it has been suggested that their production is caused by the entry into the body of A and B antigens in food or in other ways. Blood typing is based upon the clumping, or agglutination, of a given type of red blood cells in a blood specimen brought about by the agglutinins in a sample of antiserum.

It is perhaps apparent that, when giving a blood transfusion, blood cannot be donated that contains antigens not present in the recipient's blood. Such blood is alien to the recipient, whose blood contains antibodies that will cause agglutination and hemolysis of the donor's red blood cells. Thus, individuals with type A blood cannot accept a transfusion of blood types B or AB; type B individuals cannot accept A or AB blood; and type O individuals cannot accept A, B, or AB blood. Individuals with AB blood, whose blood contains both A and B antigens, are universal recipients. Type O individuals, whose blood contains neither¹ antigen, are universal donors.

Rh Factor. The Rh factor, so named because it was first found in the blood of the rhesus monkey, is a system consisting of 12 antigens. Of these, "D" is the most antigenic; the term Rh positive, as it is generally employed, refers to the presence of antigen D. The Rh negative individual does not possess the D antigen, and consequently forms anti-D antibodies when injected with D positive cells. Anti-D agglutinin does not occur naturally in the blood.

The initial transfusion of Rh positive blood into an Rh negative individual may merely sensitize the recipient and cause the development of agglutinins without the occurrence of severe symptoms; however, once sensitized, the recipient will probably experience a severe reaction to subsequent infusions of Rh positive blood.

The same reaction may occur when an Rh negative mother has an Rh positive baby. If at the time of delivery some of the infant's blood enters the mother's blood stream, she

Table 11–4   BLOOD GROUPING

TYPE	PERCENTAGE OF POPULATION	RED CELL ANTIGENS (Agglutinogens)	PLASMA ANTIBODIES (Agglutinins)
ABO			
A	41%	A	Anti-B
B	10%	B	Anti-A
AB	4%	A, B	
O	45%	°	Anti-A, anti-B
Rh (D)			
Positive	85%	Rh	
Negative	15%		†

°Type O blood is sometimes called the "universal donor," since it does not contain agglutinogens A or B.
†Anti-Rh does not occur naturally in blood, but will result if an Rh negative individual is given Rh positive blood.

may become sensitized. This could cause a problem with a subsequent Rh positive fetus. Antibodies produced as a result of the initial sensitization could enter the circulation of the fetus and cause agglutination and hemolysis. The infant with this condition, called **erythroblastosis fetalis,** might be born dead or with hemolytic anemia. During the 1960's it was discovered that this could be avoided by giving the mother a shot of Rh antibodies from 24 to 72 hours after giving birth to an Rh positive child. This treatment prevents the development of antibodies by the mother's immune system.

BASIC DIVISIONS OF THE CIRCULATORY SYSTEM

The basic divisions of the circulatory system are (1) the **heart,** a muscular pump consisting of two receiving chambers (atria) and two pumping chambers (ventricles) and (2) two closed circuits (Fig. 11–7), the **pulmonary circuit,** carrying oxygen-poor blood from the heart (right ventricle) to the respiratory (alveolar) surfaces of the lungs and oxygenated blood back to the heart (left atrium), and the **systemic circuit,** carrying oxygen-rich blood from the heart (left ventricle) to all parts of the body except the respiratory surfaces of the lungs and oxygen-poor blood back to the heart (right atrium). When the ventricles contract, blood is propelled simultaneously into both circuits (these circuits are considered in more detail in a later section). The *arteries*, which receive this blood at high pressure and velocity and conduct it throughout the body, are thickly walled with elastic fibrous tissue and a wrapping of muscle cells. The arterial tree terminates in short, narrow, muscular vessels called *arterioles*, from which blood enters simple endothelial tubes known as *capillaries*. These microscopically thin capillaries are permeable to oxygen, carbon dioxide, vital cellular nutrients, hormones, and waste products, and serve as the site for the exchange of substances between the blood stream and the interstitial fluid surrounding the body cells.

From the capillaries, the blood, moving more slowly and under low pressure, enters small vessels called *venules*, which converge to form *veins*, ultimately guiding the blood back to the heart.

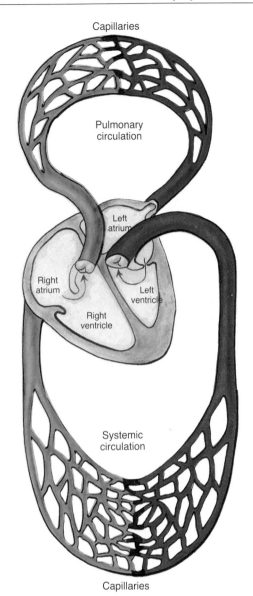

Figure 11–7. Schematic drawing showing relationship between systemic and pulmonary circulatory circuits. Observe that in this drawing of the pulmonary circuit the veins are colored red and the arteries blue to denote the higher level of oxygenation of the blood in the pulmonary veins.

THE HEART (Fig. 11–8)

The heart is a four-chambered, hollow, muscular organ lying between the lungs in the middle mediastinum. Approximately two-thirds of its mass is to the left of the midline. It is about the size of a man's fist,

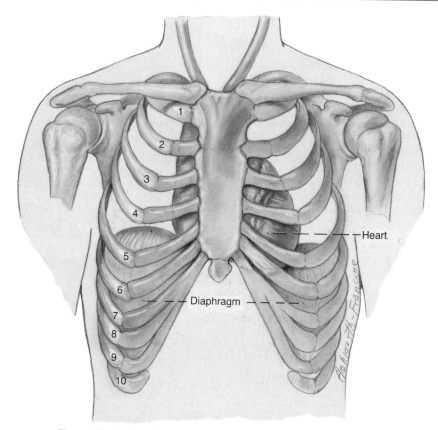

Figure 11–8. Relationship of the heart and diaphragm to rib cage.

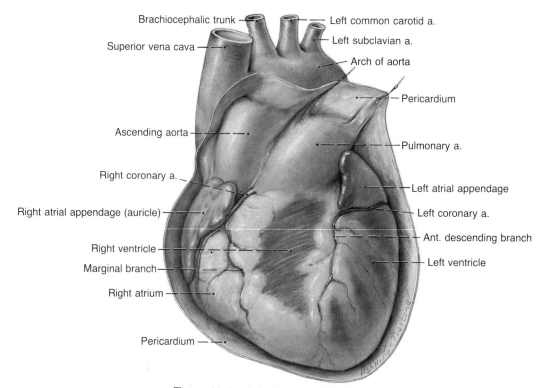

Figure 11–9. Anterior view of the heart.

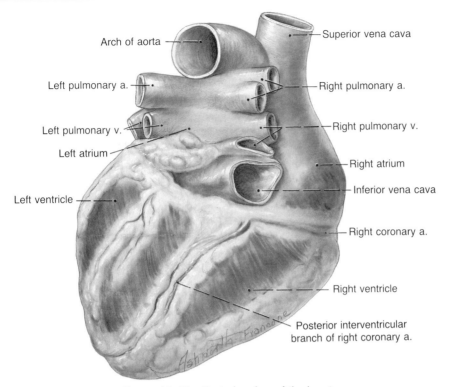

Arch of aorta

Left pulmonary a.

Left pulmonary v.

Left atrium

Left ventricle

Superior vena cava

Right pulmonary a.

Right pulmonary v.

Right atrium

Inferior vena cava

Right coronary a.

Right ventricle

Posterior interventricular branch of right coronary a.

Figure 11–10. Posterior view of the heart.

and in the normal male weighs approximately 300 gm. The heart is shaped like an inverted cone, with its apex pointed downward (Figs. 11–9 and 11–10).

Structure

The structures of the heart include the *pericardium*, the sac enclosing the chambers;

valves; and *arteries*, which supply blood to the heart muscle.

Pericardium. The pericardium (Figs. 11–11 and 11–12) is an invaginated sac consisting of an **external fibrous coat** and an **internal serous membrane.** The outer, or parietal, layer of the serous membrane (called the *parietal pericardium*) lines the fibrous coat. The inner, or visceral, layer of the serous membrane (the *visceral pericar-*

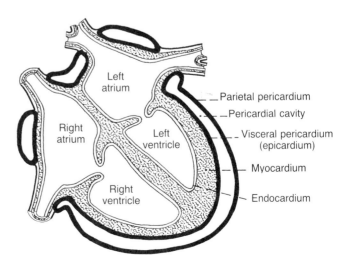

Left atrium

Right atrium

Left ventricle

Right ventricle

Parietal pericardium

Pericardial cavity

Visceral pericardium (epicardium)

Myocardium

Endocardium

Figure 11–11. Heart wall and pericardium. (Note the thickened left ventricular wall.)

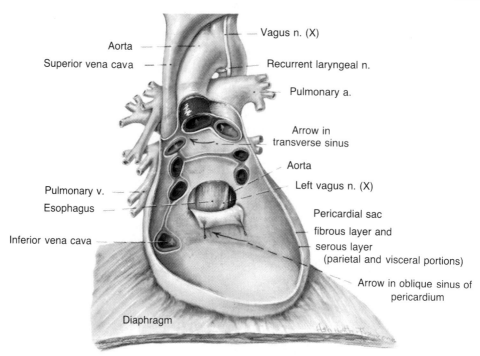

Aorta

Superior vena cava

Pulmonary v.

Esophagus

Inferior vena cava

Diaphragm

Vagus n. (X)

Recurrent laryngeal n.

Pulmonary a.

Arrow in
transverse sinus

Aorta

Left vagus n. (X)

Pericardial sac
fibrous layer and
serous layer
(parietal and visceral portions)

Arrow in oblique sinus of
pericardium

Figure 11–12. The heart has been removed from the pericardial sac to show the relations of the blood vessels, esophagus, and vagus nerve.

dium) adheres to the heart and becomes the outermost layer of the heart, the *epicardium.*

Ten to 15 ml of pericardial fluid is normally found between the parietal pericardium and the visceral pericardium. With every heartbeat this serous fluid lubricates the two membranes as their surfaces glide over each other. Pericarditis is an inflammation of the pericardium and may result from viral or bacterial infection or cancerous growth.

Wall of the Heart. The wall of the heart consists of three distinct layers — the **epicardium** (external layer, the visceral pericardium), the **myocardium** (middle muscular layer), and the **endocardium** (inner layer of endothelium). Coronary vessels supplying arterial blood to the heart traverse the epicardium before entering the myocardium, the layer responsible for the ability of the heart to contract. The myocardium consists of interlacing bundles of cardiac muscle fibers (for a description of cardiac muscle, see Chapter 8, page 175). Cardiac muscle has a high concentration of mitochondria (also called sarcosomes) and, like red skeletal muscle, depends primarily on aerobic metabolism. Its principal fuel is fatty acids derived from the blood stream. The bundles of muscle fibers

are so arranged as to result in a wringing type of movement, efficiently squeezing blood from the heart with each beat (Fig. 11–13). The thickness of the myocardium varies according to pressure generated to move blood to its destination. The myocardium of the left ventricle is, therefore, thickest; the myocardium of the right ventricle is moderately thickened, while the atrial walls are relatively thin.

Forming the inner surface of the myocardial wall is a thin layer of endothelial tissue which forms the endocardium. This layer lines the cavities of the heart, covers the valves and small muscles associated with opening and closing the valves, and is continuous with the lining membrane of the large blood vessels. Inflammation of the endocardium is called *endocarditis.*

Chambers of the Heart. The heart is divided into right and left halves, with each half subdivided into two chambers. The upper chambers, the *atria,* are separated by the *interatrial septum;* the lower chambers, the *ventricles,* are separated by the *interventricular septum.* The atria serve as receiving chambers for blood from the various parts of the body, the ventricles as pumping chambers.

The **right atrium** constitutes the right

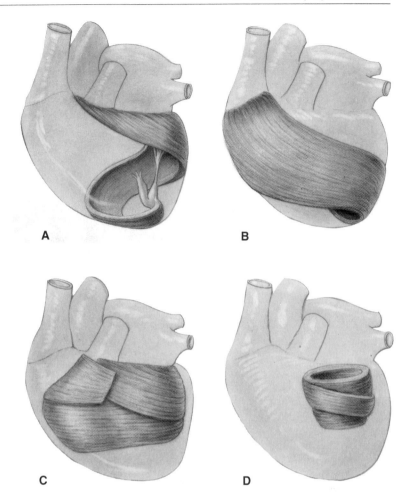

Figure 11–13. *A* and *B* illustrate the superficial muscle layer of the heart winding around both ventricles. *C* shows the middle myocardial layer winding around only the upper 3/4 of both ventricles, whereas the inner layer is present only around the left ventricle (*D*).

superior portion of the heart. It is a thin-walled chamber receiving blood from all tissues except the lungs. Three veins empty into the right atrium: the superior and inferior venae cavae, bringing blood from the upper and lower portions of the body, and the coronary sinus, draining blood from the heart itself. Blood flows from the atrium to the right ventricle.

The **right ventricle** constitutes the right inferior portion of the heart. The pulmonary artery carrying blood to the lungs leaves from the superior surface of the right ventricle.

The **left atrium** constitutes the left superior portion of the heart. It is slightly smaller than the right atrium, with a thicker wall. The left atrium receives the four pulmonary veins draining oxygenated blood from the lungs. Blood flows from the left atrium into the left ventricle.

The **left ventricle** constitutes the left inferior portion of the heart. The walls of this chamber are three times as thick as those of the right ventricle. Blood is forced through the aorta to all parts of the body except the lungs.

Valves of the Heart. There are two types of valves located in the heart: the **atrioventricular valves,** located between the atria and ventricles (*tricuspid* on the right side; *bicuspid,* or *mitral,* on the left), and the **semilunar valves** (*pulmonary* and *aortic*), located between the ventricles and the pulmonary artery (right side) and aorta (left side) (Figs. 11–14 to 11–17).

William Harvey, in his treatise *Exercitatio de Motu Cordis et Sanguinis in Animalibus* (Essay on the Motion of the Heart and Blood in Animals), published in 1628, in which he described for the first time the continuous circulation of the blood, made particular note of how the arrangement of the heart's valves allows blood to flow through the heart in one direction only. Insofar as

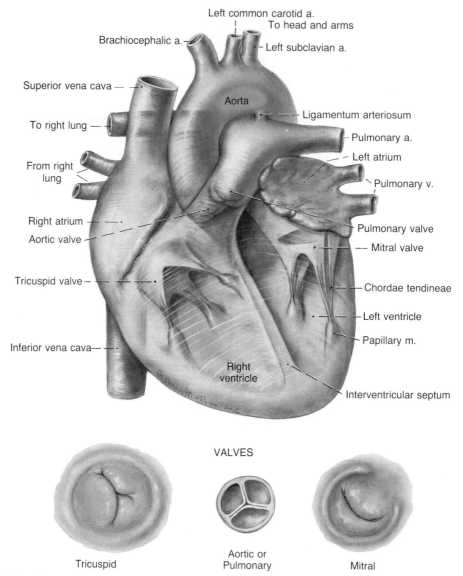

VALVES

Tricuspid

Aortic or
Pulmonary

Mitral

Figure 11–14. Schematic "transparent" drawing of the heart showing the relations of the various heart valves.

the heart performs as a pump to drive blood through the blood vessels, the atrioventricular valves are **inlet valves.** They open into the ventricles, allowing blood to enter these pumping chambers when their muscular walls relax. The semilunar valves are **outlet valves.** When the ventricles contract, they open into the pulmonary artery and aorta, and blood is propelled into these vessels.

The atrioventricular valves are thin, leaf-like structures. The tricuspid valve, guarding the right atrioventricular opening, is so called because it consists of three irregularly shaped flaps (or cusps) formed mainly of

fibrous tissue and covered by endocardium (Figs. 11–14 and 11–15). These flaps are continuous with each other at their bases, creating a ring-shaped membrane surrounding the margin of the atrial opening. Their pointed ends project into the ventricle and are attached by cords called the *chordae tendineae* to small muscular pillars, the *papillary muscles*, within the interior of the ventricles. The bicuspid, or mitral, valve, guarding the left atrioventricular opening, is so named because it consists of two flaps and resembles a bishop's miter. The mitral valve is attached in the same manner as the tricuspid, but it is

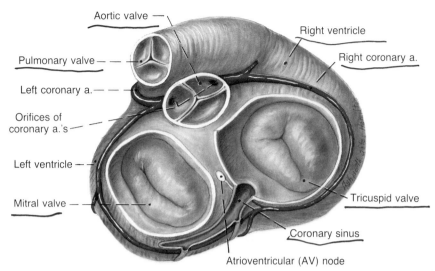

Aortic valve —
Right ventricle
Pulmonary valve — —
Right coronary a.
Left coronary a.— —
Orifices of coronary a.'s
Left ventricle —
Mitral valve —
Tricuspid valve
Coronary sinus
Atrioventricular (AV) node

Figure 11–15. A view of the heart from above, showing the valves, coronary arteries, and sinus.

stronger and thicker, since the left ventricle is a more powerful pump.

When the ventricle contracts, blood is forced backward, passing between the flaps and walls of the ventricles. The flaps are thus pushed upward until they meet and unite, forming a complete partition between the atria and ventricles. The expanded flaps of the valves resist any pressure of the blood which might force them to open into the atria because they are restrained by the chordae tendineae and papillary muscles.

Each semilunar valve consists of three pockets of tissue attached at the point at which the pulmonary artery and aorta leave the ventricles (Figs. 11–14 and 11–15). Their closure prevents backflow of blood into the ventricles.

Valves are associated with leaving the heart.

SVC—superior vena cava
RPA—right pulmonary artery
RA —right atrium
IVC —inferior vena cava
LPA —left pulmonary artery
LA —left atrium
LV —left ventricle
RV —right ventricle
AV —aortic valve
PV —pulmonary valve
MV —mitral valve
TV —tricuspid valve

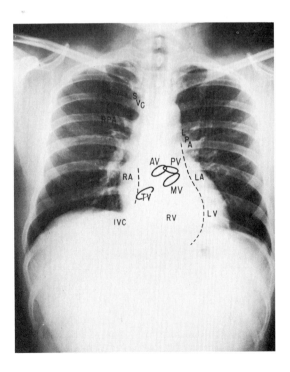

Figure 11–16. X-ray of anterior aspect of thoracic region.

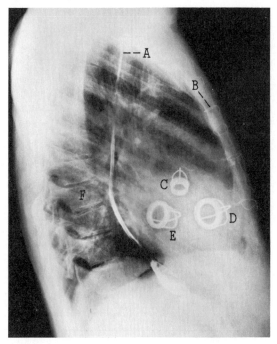

Figure 11–17. Three artificial valves implanted in a patient's heart by Dr. A. Starr of the University of Oregon Medical School. *A*, esophagus; *B*, wire sutures in sternum; *C*, aortic valve; *D*, tricuspid valve; *E*, mitral valve; and *F*, vertebral column.

Blood Supply to the Heart. Owing to the presence of the watertight lining of the heart (the endocardium) and the thickness of its muscle walls, it is necessary for the heart to possess a vascular system of its own. Two arteries, the **left** and **right coronary arteries,** branch from the aorta as it leaves the heart and curl back across the chambers of the heart, sending twigs through the muscular walls (Fig. 11–18).

These vessels are the first branches of the aorta and are so named because they form a crown around the base of the heart. The left coronary artery branches immediately. The anterior descending branch supplies blood to the anterior part of the left ventricle and a small part of the anterior and posterior portions of the right ventricle. The circumflex branch supplies blood to the left atrium and upper front and rear of the left ventricle. The branches of the right coronary artery supply blood to the right atrium and ventricle and portions of the left ventricle.

Blood is drained from the heart principally into the right atrium by way of the **coronary sinus,** which collects blood from the coronary veins (Fig. 11–19). About 25 per

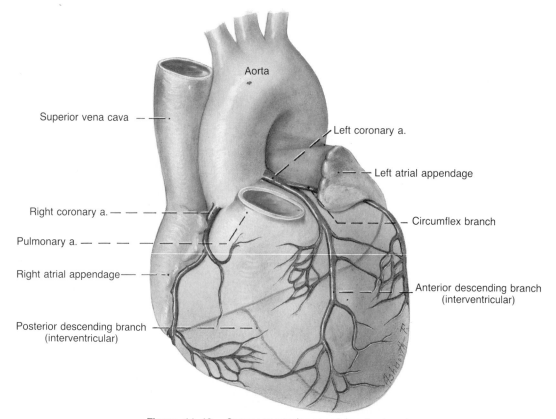

Figure 11–18. Coronary arteries supplying the heart.

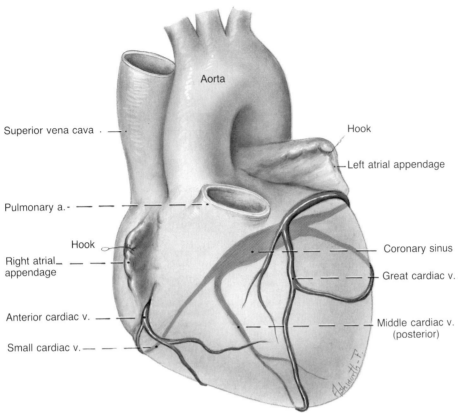

Superior vena cava

Aorta

Hook

Left atrial appendage

Pulmonary a.

Hook

Coronary sinus

Right atrial appendage

Great cardiac v.

Anterior cardiac v.

Middle cardiac v. (posterior)

Small cardiac v.

Figure 11–19. Venous drainage of the heart.

cent of the blood drains directly into the ventricles via deep channels, the arterioluminal, the arteriosinusoidal, and the Thebesian vessels.

Cardiac Cycle

The heart exhibits a definite rhythmic cycle of ventricular contraction (**systole**) and relaxation (**diastole**). Figure 11–20 shows the pressure alterations in the left heart and aorta during the cycle. The cycle is generally divided into eight phases: isovolumetric contraction, maximum ejection, reduced ejection, protodiastole, isovolumetric relaxation, rapid filling, reduced filling, and atrial contraction. The isovolumetric phase (the beginning of systole) is initiated by the spread of electrical excitatory impulses through the ventricle, causing it to contract. Ventricular pressure rises, and as soon as it exceeds atrial pressure the atrioventricular valve (already almost closed by eddy currents reflected from the ventricular wall) closes. (Bulging of the

AV valve into the atrium during closure is responsible for the "C" wave of the atrial pressure curve.) The pressure in the ventricle, contracting as a closed chamber, rises steeply, and when it exceeds aortic pressure the aortic valve opens. Blood flows from the left ventricle into the aorta, rapidly at first (*maximum ejection* phase) and then more slowly (*reduced ejection* phase). The outflow of blood begins to slow following the fall in ventricular pressure below aortic pressure, the negative pressure gradient gradually reducing the rate of flow. Blood flow comes to a halt as the systolic phase of the cycle ends.

The diastolic portion of the cycle is generally regarded as beginning when the ejection of blood from the ventricle ceases just prior to the closure of the aortic valve. This phase of the cycle is called *protodiastole* (G. *prōtos*, first). Closure of the aortic valve is brought about by a momentary reversal of blood flow, and the beginning of the next phase, *isovolumetric relaxation*, is marked by the incisura (L. *incidere*, to cut) — a notch in the aortic pressure curve resulting from a

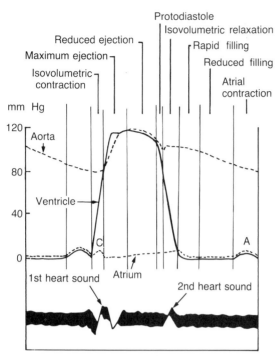

Figure 11–20. Pressure changes in the left ventricle, left atrium, and aorta and the principal heart sounds during the cardiac cycle.

transient rise in pressure as reverse blood flow bounces off the aortic valve. During the isovolumetric phase the pressure in the ventricle, relaxing as a closed chamber, falls abruptly. When the ventricular pressure falls below the atrial pressure, the atrioventricular valve opens and ventricular filling commences, the filling occurring rapidly at first (*rapid filling* phase), then more slowly (*reduced filling,* or *diastasis,* phase). *Atrial contraction* (the final phase of diastole) produces a slight increase of pressure in the two chambers (noted as the "A" wave in the atrial pressure curve). Under normal conditions, atrial contraction makes a minor contribution to ventricular filling, the major part occurring early in diastole when the blood accumulated in the atrium rapidly flows into the ventricle following the opening of the AV valve. However, if ventricular filling is incomplete because of a narrowed atrioventricular valve opening, pumping of blood through the narrowed opening by atrial contraction provides a margin of safety.

The entire cardiac cycle lasts about 0.8 second. Systole normally occupies about 30 per cent of the cycle. The principal effect of increasing the heart rate on the cycle is to decrease the length of diastole. The phases of the cardiac cycle are summarized in Table 11–5.

Heart Sounds. Closure of the heart valves is associated with an audible sound. The first sound occurs when the mitral and tricuspid valves close, marking the approximate beginning of systole, the second with the closing of the pulmonic and aortic semilunar valves following the end of systole (Fig. 11–20). These characteristic heart sounds appear to be caused principally by the vibration of the valves and walls of the heart and major vessels around the heart. The first sound, "lub," is soft, low pitched, and relatively long. The second sound, "dup," is shorter, sharper, and higher pitched than the first and coincides with the incisura of the aortic pressure curve.

The first heart sound is followed, after a short pause, by the second. A pause about twice as long comes between the second sound and the beginning of the next cycle. The clinician takes the interval between the first and second sound as an approximate measure of the length of systole.

Narrowing of the openings (stenosis) by calcification of the valves, for example, or incomplete closure of the valves (insufficiency) can create abnormal sounds called **murmurs.** Murmurs caused by narrowed openings can be explained by the increase in velocity of blood flow through the constricted openings and the resulting turbulence. Collision of blood moving in opposite directions contributes to murmurs caused by incomplete closure of AV valves.

Cardiac Output

The volume of blood ejected per beat is known as the *stroke volume.* Stroke volume times the number of beats per minute is called the *minute volume* or *cardiac output.* Under resting conditions, cardiac output approximates 5 liters per minute — an amazing fact considering that the total blood volume of an average man is only 5 to 6 liters. The average volume of blood ejected by the heart per beat is 60 to 70 ml. The output of the heart depends on venous return, cardiac rate, and the force of cardiac contraction.

Venous Return. Cardiac output increases with an increase in venous return.

Table 11–5 THE CARDIAC CYCLE

PHASE	EVENTS IN THE LEFT SIDE OF THE HEART AND AORTA
Isovolumetric contraction	Ventricular contraction begins; AV valve closes; ventricular pressure rises steeply
Maximum ejection	Begins with opening of aortic valve; ejection of blood from ventricle is rapid, accounting for the greater part of the outflow
Reduced ejection	Outflow of blood from the ventricle gradually comes to a halt
Protodiastole	Interval just prior to aortic valve closure when ejection of blood from the ventricle has ceased
Isovolumetric relaxation	Interval between closure of the aortic valve and opening of the AV valve; ventricular pressure falls rapidly; incisura in aortic pressure curve is seen at the beginning of this phase
Rapid filling	Opening of AV valve is followed by rapid flow of blood into the ventricle, filling of ventricle occurring chiefly during this interval
Reduced filling	Filling of ventricle declines
Atrial contraction	Completes filling of ventricle; atrial contraction followed immediately by onset of ventricular contraction, beginning another cycle

Venous return is influenced by the following factors: contraction of skeletal muscles squeezing the veins, forcing the blood to move; increased negative pressure in the pleural cavity with inspiration; and higher pressure in the capillaries than in the veins, forcing the blood toward the heart. Gravity aids the venous return from areas that are above the level of the heart. With a decreased blood volume, as in hemorrhage, venous return is lowered. Dilatation of the vessels, particularly the veins, allows for pooling of blood and a consequent drop in venous return.

Heart Rate. In the resting individual with a constant venous return, the normal frequency of the heart provides sufficient diastolic time for both venous filling and recovery of the cardiac muscle. When the venous return is increased (with no increase in heart rate), a two- or threefold increase in stroke volume and cardiac output results. Increasing the heart rate without a concurrent increase in venous return has only a limited effect upon cardiac output because, as mentioned, as the heart rate increases, the duration of diastole and, therefore, filling of the ventricles decreases. A moderate increase in rate will cause some increase in output because the largest volume of blood enters the ventricles during the initial rapid inflow period of diastole. Increasing the heart rate from 70 to 90 beats per minute can increase the cardiac output by about 20 per cent. Further increases in rate will not significantly increase cardiac output. Very high rates (above about 140 beats per minute), in fact, will decrease cardiac output because of a pronounced decrease in ventricular filling and stroke volume.

Force of Cardiac Contraction. The force of the heart contraction depends on the initial length of the fibers, the length of the diastolic pause, the oxygen supply, and the integrity and mass of the myocardium.

Starling's law of the heart states that "the energy of contraction is proportional to the initial length of the cardiac muscle fiber"; that is, the greater the initial length of the muscle fibers in the heart, the more forceful the contraction. When venous return is relatively great, this tends to expand the heart and, consequently, to stretch the muscle fibers prior to each beat. As Starling's law states, the muscle fibers actually have the property that the more they are stretched (within reasonable physiological limits) prior to contraction, the more forceful will be that contraction. Since increased venous return necessitates that the heart do more work in pumping this added amount of blood, the "increased stretch–increased contraction strength" property of the muscle fibers serves as an automatic regulator so that the heart can keep up naturally with its workload, which is supplied in this case by the venous return. This interesting property of a muscle fiber to contract more strongly when it is stretched prior to contraction is a property of all striated muscle and not simply of cardiac muscle. There are limits to this stretch response, however, and if venous return is excessive and the fibers overstretched, a weakened contraction will result, with diminished cardiac output; consequently, the heart will not empty adequately. The force of heart contraction is also diminished if the diastolic phase is too short and there is inadequate filling.

The Heartbeat

The heart is inherently rhythmic. This was apparently recognized by the Greek anatomist Erasistratus in the third century B.C. In 1890 Newell Martin of Johns Hopkins University demonstrated that the heart of a mammal will continue to beat (although at a different rate) when cut off completely from its nerve supply. The function of the nerve supply is to regulate the beat and make possible homeostatic control of the heart rate.

The heartbeat is generated by specialized neuromuscular tissue of the heart. It has been shown by cell culture techniques that cardiac tissue is actually composed of two functionally different types of cells, corresponding in the intact heart to muscle cells specialized for contraction and neuromuscular cells specialized for initiating and conducting the electical impulses that cause the heart to contract. Individual cells of the latter type beat rhythmically in culture. The neuromuscular tissue of the heart consists of (a) the **sinoatrial (SA) node,** called the pacemaker because the heartbeat is generated by electrical impulses arising spontaneously from it; (b) the **atrioventricular (AV) node;** and (c) the **Purkinje system,** which includes the left and right branches of the AV bundle (bundle of His) and the peripheral Purkinje network (see Fig. 11–21).

The *sinoatrial node* is a small mass of tissue embedded in the wall of the right atrium close to the point of entry of the superior vena cava. As an impulse is generated in the SA node, it immediately spreads through the atrial muscle in a ripple pattern similar to that of waves generated when a stone is thrown into a pool of water and initiates its contraction. Impulses from the SA to the AV node are preferentially conducted by pathways (called internodal tracts) consisting apparently of a mixture of fibers similar to Purkinje fibers and ordinary muscle fibers. The AV node is located beneath the endocardium of the right atrium at the base of the interatrial septum. To permit sufficient time for complete atrial contraction before subsequent simultaneous contraction of the ventricles, the impulse is delayed slightly in its passage through the AV node. The fibers which leave this node constitute the *Purkinje system.* These fibers pass into the interventricular septum, where right and left bundle branches project downward beneath the endocardium on either side of the septum. They then curve around the tip of the ventricular chambers and back toward the atria along the lateral walls. These fibers terminate in the ventricular muscle, and excitation in the muscle fibers is initiated.

The average normal heart rate is about 70 beats per minute. Rates from 60 to 100 are considered normal. A too rapid rate is called *tachycardia* (G. *tachys,* swift); a too slow rate is called *bradycardia* (G. *bradys,* slow).

The spontaneous origin of electrical impulses at the SA node can be explained by the unstable resting membrane potential of nodal cells due to a leakage of sodium into these cells (see Chapter 9, page 239, for a description of the nerve impulse). In recordings of electrical potential at the SA node this is seen as a gradual upward deflection in voltage, called the **prepotential.** Each time threshold voltage is reached, an impulse is initiated.

If the SA node is not functioning normally, there are other potential pacemakers (ectopic foci) available. They are the AV node, the ventricular pacemaker, and the atrial pacemaker. Usually it is the AV node that takes over the initiation of impulses, establishing a heart rate of about 60 beats per minute, with the atria and ventricles contracting simultaneously. Patients have been known to survive 20 to 30 years with the AV node acting as pacemaker.

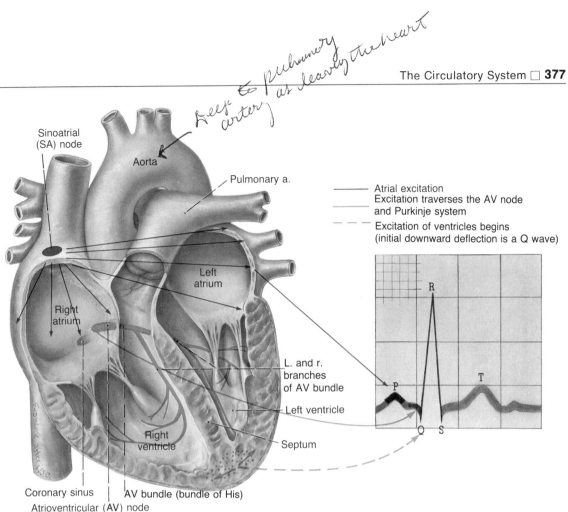

deep to pulmonary cortex) as clearly the heart

Sinoatrial
(SA) node

Aorta

Pulmonary a.

—— Atrial excitation
Excitation traverses the AV node
and Purkinje system
- - - Excitation of ventricles begins
(initial downward deflection is a Q wave)

Left
atrium

Right
atrium

R

L. and r.
branches
of AV bundle

P

T

Left ventricle

Right
ventricle

Septum

Q   S

Coronary sinus | AV bundle (bundle of His)
Atrioventricular (AV) node

Figure 11–21. Conducting system of the heart showing source of electrical impulses produced on electrocardiogram.

Nervous Control of the Heart

Adjustments in the heart rate to maintain homeostasis and meet the demands of changing conditions are made possible by innervation of the SA node by the *sympathetic* and *parasympathetic* divisions of the autonomic nervous system. Increased stimulation of sympathetic nerves increases the release of *norepinephrine* by the nerve endings and increases the impulse rate of the SA node. Increased stimulation of the vagus (parasympathetic) nerve increases the release of *acetylcholine* by nerve endings and decreases the impulse rate at the SA node. The vagus nerve exerts a strong, continuous restraining action on the heart. In dogs, this can be demonstrated by blocking the action of the vagus nerve with atropine. The result is about a 2½-fold increase in heart rate. Massive vagal stimulation can stop the heart for several seconds. Stimulation of the vagus

nerve also delays conduction through the AV node; sympathetic stimulation has the reverse effect. The atria are supplied by both sympathetic and parasympathetic nerves, the ventricles largely by sympathetic nerves (Fig. 11–22). Consequently, control over the force of the contraction of the heart is exercised primarily by the sympathetic system. This action is especially important during exercise. (Mechanisms governing the activity of the heart via the cardiac centers in the medulla are described on page 387.)

Effect of Ions on Heart Function. Potassium and calcium have a marked influence on impulse transmission within cardiac muscle. In addition, calcium ion concentration is important in the contractile process. The concentration of ions in extracellular fluids also affects cardiac function.

Excess potassium ions in extracellular fluid, in addition to slowing the heart rate, cause the heart to dilate and become flaccid.

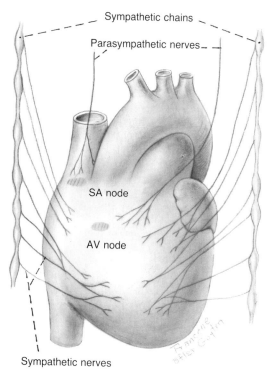

Sympathetic chains

Parasympathetic nerves

SA node

AV node

Sympathetic nerves

Figure 11–22. The cardiac nerves.

There is general weakness of cardiac muscle. This weakening of the strength of contraction is caused by a decreased resting membrane potential.

Calcium ions in excess produce just the opposite effect; the heart goes into spastic contraction. This is believed to be caused as the excess calcium ions excite the process of cardiac contraction. Conversely, a deficiency causes cardiac weakness. There is, however, little danger of excess calcium ions within the extracellular fluid in cardiac muscle because excess calcium is precipitated as salts in bone before a dangerous level is reached in the heart.

Presumably due to an increased permeability of muscle membrane to ions, temperature may also affect heart function. Heart rate increases as temperature increases and, conversely, decreases as temperature decreases.

The Electrocardiogram (Figs. 11–23 and 11–24). As an impulse travels along the cardiac muscle fibers, an electric current is generated by the flowing ions. This current spreads into the fluids around the heart and a minute portion actually flows to the surface of the body. An *electrocardiogram* is a record of

this electrical activity as measured by a *galvanometer.* Electrodes are placed on the surface of the body at various points, depending on the type of information desired. The standard ECG consists of 12 separate recordings from 12 separate leads (6 limb, 6 chest). Each lead is a particular combination of electrode attachments. Historically, only three limb leads (so-called standard limb leads devised by Einthoven in 1908) were used (and are still used today for prehospital evaluation). They are: Lead I, right arm and left arm; Lead II, right arm and left leg; and Lead III, left arm and left leg. An electrocardiogram has the prime function of assessing the ability of the heart to transmit the cardiac impulse. Each portion of the cardiac cycle produces a different electrical impulse, causing the characteristic deflections of an ECG recording needle. The deflections, or *waves,* on the recording apparatus are, in order, the *P wave,* the *QRS complex,* and the *T wave.* As a wave of excitation (reversal of electrical charges across the cell membranes) passes over the atria, the impulse is recorded as the P wave. As it continues on through the ventricles, it is registered as the QRS complex. The T wave is caused by currents generated as the ventricles return to the resting state. This recovery process is completed in the muscle of the ventricles about 0.25 second after excitation. There are, therefore, both excitation and recovery waves represented in the ECG.

The atria return to the resting state at the same time that the ventricles are excited. The atrial recovery wave is, therefore, obscured by the larger QRS wave.

SINUS ARREST AND SINOATRIAL BLOCK. In sinus arrest the SA node temporarily fails to send its impulses, but normal rhythm is eventually restored. The ECG shows extended T-P intervals (missed cycles). In sinoatrial block there is a persistent failure of the SA node to activate the atria at alternate beats or after a series of beats, frequently leading to a pattern of extended T-P intervals. If the AV node takes over as pacemaker, a regular beat pattern is reestablished at the new rate with inverted P waves.

ATRIOVENTRICULAR BLOCK (HEART BLOCK). Atrioventricular block is an impairment in the conduction of impulses from the atrium to the ventricle. The disturbance is located in the atrioventricular node and

ELECTROCARDIOGRAM

The wave of excitation spreading through the heart wall is accompanied by electrical changes.
The record of these changes is an ELECTROCARDIOGRAM (ECG)

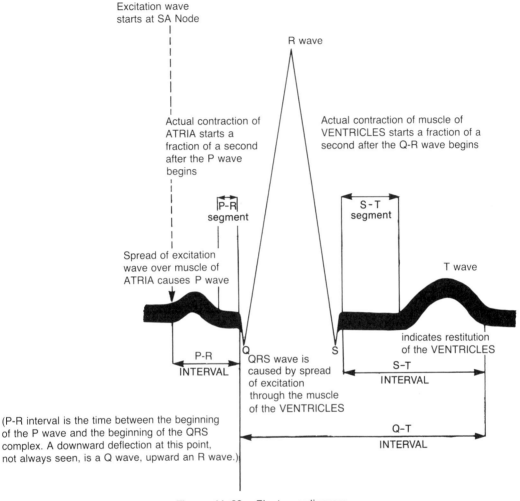

Excitation wave starts at SA Node

R wave

Actual contraction of ATRIA starts a fraction of a second after the P wave begins

Actual contraction of muscle of VENTRICLES starts a fraction of a second after the Q-R wave begins

P-R segment

S-T segment

Spread of excitation wave over muscle of ATRIA causes P wave

T wave

indicates restitution of the VENTRICLES

P-R INTERVAL

Q

QRS wave is caused by spread of excitation through the muscle of the VENTRICLES

S

S-T INTERVAL

(P-R interval is the time between the beginning of the P wave and the beginning of the QRS complex. A downward deflection at this point, not always seen, is a Q wave, upward an R wave.)

Q-T INTERVAL

Figure 11–23. Electrocardiogram.

usually indicates myocardial disease. In the first degree block, a delay in atrioventricular conduction occurs. The delay is indicated by a prolonged P-R interval in the electrocardiogram. Second degree atrioventricular block is recognized by the "dropped beat," that is, when it takes two or more atrial impulses to stimulate ventricular response (QRS). Thus, in second degree heart block with a 2:1 atrioventricular response, a ventricular rate one-half that of the atrial rate will be recorded on the ECG. Complete atrioventricular

block (third degree block) represents a total dissociation of the atrial and ventricular rhythms. The ventricle sets its own rhythm with an ectopic pacemaker located in the atrioventricular node, the bundle of His, or Purkinje fibers.

BUNDLE BRANCH BLOCK. Bundle branch block occurs when electrical impulses are blocked to the right or left bundle of His; this causes one ventricle to contract after the other, resulting in a double peak in the QRS wave.

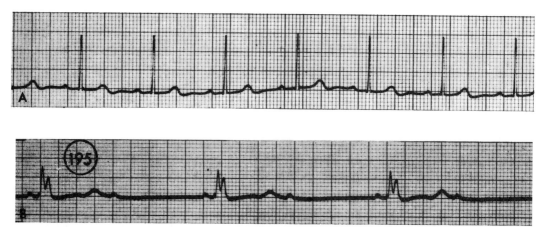

Figure 11–24. An electrocardiogram. *A*, Normal. *B*, Heart block (there is only one ventricular contraction for every two atrial contractions).

ATRIAL FLUTTER. In this cardiac disturbance, regular atrial rhythm is 240 to 360 beats per minute. Atrial flutter is usually indicative of severe damage to the heart muscle. It is encountered occasionally in normal hearts, but occurs mostly in patients with heart disease. Since the atrioventricular node cannot respond to each impulse, a 2:1, 3:1, or 4:1 rhythm develops. This means that the atrioventricular node and ventricle respond to only one out of two, three, or four atrial impulses. Thus, the electrocardiogram can show an atrial rate of 240 and a ventricular rate of 120.

ATRIAL FIBRILLATION. In atrial fibrillation, the excitation wave passes through the atrial musculature more rapidly and irregularly than in atrial flutter. The atrioventricular node is bombarded by numerous impulses generated at multiple atrial foci. Atrial fibrillation is characterized by an irregularity of the rhythm and strength of the ventricular beat. Some beats are too weak to be felt as a pulsation in the peripheral arteries because too little blood is ejected from the ventricles owing to inadequate ventricular filling from short diastole. Thus, the observer can count a rate of 140 beats per minute at the cardiac apex with a stethoscope and palpate only 110 beats per minute at the wrist — a pulse deficit of 30. This pulse deficit represents the ventricular contractions which are too weak to transmit the pulse wave peripherally. Blood pressure determination in such cases is inaccurate, since it varies with the strength of the beat. Weak beats are not caused by myocardial weakness. They are caused by an inadequate diastolic filling period and, thus, by a reduced stroke volume.

OTHER ABNORMALITIES OF CARDIAC RHYTHM. Spasmodic supraventricular tachycardia is the commonest *arrhythmia* (any variation in the normal heart beat). It usually occurs in young adults but can occur at any age and often is not associated with severe heart disease. The heart rate is between 100 and 200 with a regular rhythm.

In *ventricular fibrillation*, the rapid stimuli from multiple ventricular ectopic foci cause tremulous contractions that lack propulsive force, and blood circulation ceases; death generally follows within minutes. Ventricular fibrillation can occur immediately after a severe heart attack, as damage to heart muscle causes disturbances in excitation.

Ventricular tachycardia is a pathological condition usually seen in patients with coronary artery disease and results from a ventricular ectopic pacemaker blocking a normal pattern from the SA node. Quick treatment is necessary, as the ventricular rate is too fast for proper functioning.

Ventricular flutter is caused by a single ventricular ectopic focus which has a rate of 200 to 300 beats per minute. It is easily seen on an ECG, having the appearance of a smooth sine wave. Patients with ventricular flutter can deteriorate rapidly into ventricular fibrillation.

Since the QRS wave represents the passage of an excitation process through the ventricle, any pathology causing abnormal impulse transmission will alter the shape, voltage, or duration of the QRS complex.

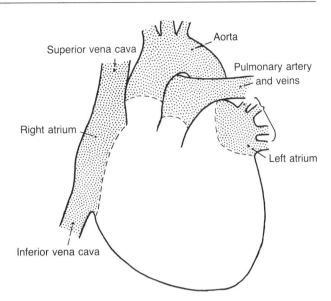

Figure 11–25. Diagrammatic representation showing anastomoses in heart transplant. (Shaded areas are recipient.)

Closed Cardiac Massage

When the heart stops, the procedure of choice for maintaining circulation is closed cardiac massage. Closed cardiac massage must be started as soon as possible after the heart stops. If as long as four minutes is allowed to elapse, there can be irreversible damage to the brain.

In performing closed cardiac massage, the patient should be placed on a firm surface. Cardiac massage should not be undertaken with the patient lying on a soft bed.

The individual performing the massage positions himself at a right angle to the trunk of the patient, with one hand on top of the other, and places the heel of the hand over the lower half of the patient's sternum (but not on the xiphoid process), applying pressure vertically about once every second (Fig. 11–26). The sternum should move approximately two inches toward the vertebral column. At the completion of each maneuver, the hands do not leave the chest, but are completely relaxed to permit full chest expansion. An assistant should perform mouth-to-mouth (or

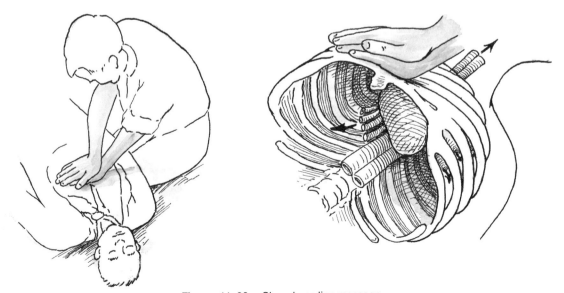

Figure 11–26. Closed cardiac massage.

mouth-to-nose) ventilation (Chapter 13, page 471) after every five heart compressions. If an assistant is not available, the rescuer should quickly ventilate the lungs three times and follow with 15 heart compressions. After this, a cycle of two ventilations followed by 15 compressions should be maintained.

BLOOD VESSELS

The blood vessels consist of a closed system of tubes functioning to transport blood to all parts of the body and back to the heart. As in any biological system, structure and function of the vessels are so closely related one cannot be discussed without bringing into account the other. It should be noted that the inner surface of the entire circulatory system consists of endothelium (the descriptive term for a single layer of squamous epithelium in the heart and blood and lymphatic vessels). Additional layers are specializations.

Arteries. Arteries transport blood to the various body tissues under high pressure exerted by the pumping action of the heart. The heart forces blood into these elastic tubes, which recoil, sending blood on in pulsating waves. It is, therefore, imperative that they possess strong, elastic walls to insure fast, efficient blood flow to the tissues.

The wall of an artery consists of three layers (Fig. 11–27 and Table 11–6). The in-nermost, the *tunica intima,* is bounded on the inner surface by smooth endothelium and on the other side by elastic fibers, the *internal elastic lamina,* which in medium-sized and small arteries is thick and clearly delineated. Between the endothelium and elastic lamina are a small number of smooth muscle cells surrounded by extracellular components of connective tissue. The *tunica media,* or middle coat, consists of smooth muscle cells having a circular arrangement intermingled with elastic fibers and small amounts of noncellular connective tissue elements. In larger vessels, the tunica media is thicker and composed primarily of elastic fibers. As arteries become smaller, the number of elastic fibers decreases and the number of smooth muscle fibers increases. The outer limiting layer is the *tunica adventitia,* a connective tissue with collagenous and elastic fibers. In large arteries the adventitia is a relatively thin coat. In medium-sized and small arteries it may be thicker than the tunica media, and a concentration of elastic fibers adjacent to the tunica media forms a distinct *external elastic lamina.* Arteries (and veins) with a diameter greater than 1 mm are supplied with small, nutrient blood vessels, called the *vasa vasorum,* which form a dense capillary network in the adventitia and penetrate the outer part of the media. The remainder of these arteries (or veins) are nourished by diffusion from the blood being transported.

Table 11–6   STRUCTURE OF BLOOD VESSELS

VESSEL	OUTER LAYER: TUNICA ADVENTITIA	MIDDLE LAYER: TUNICA MEDIA	INNER LAYER: TUNICA INTIMA
Large arteries (elastic)	Relatively thin layer, consisting of connective tissue	Layer consists largely of elastic fibers with some smooth muscle	Inner surface of endothelium, outer zone an elastic lamina, connective tissue matrix components and small number of smooth muscle cells in between
Medium and small arteries (muscular)	Thick layer, consisting of connective tissue	Fewer elastic fibers, more smooth muscle	Similar to large arteries, but elastic lamina more distinct
Arterioles	Thin	Consists of muscular tissue	Layer composed mainly of endothelium
Capillaries	Absent	Absent	Endothelial layer one cell thick
Veins	Layer of connective tissue	Thin; little muscle and few elastic fibers	Endothelial lining with scant connective tissue matrix components

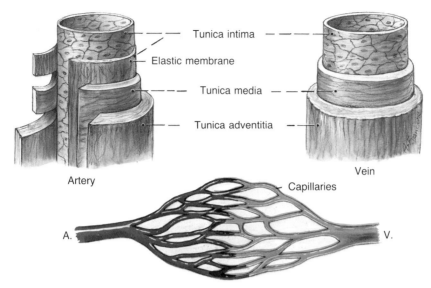

Tunica intima

Elastic membrane

Tunica media

Tunica adventitia

Artery

Vein

Capillaries

A.   V.

Figure 11–27. Component parts of arteries and veins.

Arterioles. The transition from artery to *arteriole* is gradual, marked by a progressive thinning of the vessel wall and a decrease in the size of the lumen, or passageway. The tunica intima consists of an endothelial lining bounded by patches of elastic fibers. The elastic fibers become scantier as the caliber of the arterioles decreases, finally disappearing in the smallest vessels. The tunica media of larger arterioles is composed of a few circularly arranged layers of smooth muscle cells. As the vessels become smaller, the number of layers of muscle cells decreases, and in the smallest diameter vessels the media is a single layer of spiraling smooth muscle cells. The adventitia of arterioles is relatively thin and there is no external elastic lamina.

The arterioles, as the last branches of the arterial system, must act as control valves through which blood is released into the capillaries. The muscular wall of arterioles is capable of undergoing large changes in caliber, thereby vastly altering blood flow to the capillaries. Blood flow is, therefore, directed to tissues which require it most.

Metacapillaries. *Metacapillaries* (G. *meta*, between), called *metarterioles* by some authors, are intermediate in structure between the smallest arterioles and the capillaries. In many tissues true capillaries arise from these vessels as well as from arterioles. Metacapillaries have a larger caliber than true capillaries, and consist of endothelium

and spiraling smooth muscle cells scattered at intervals along their lengths. They are sometimes called "thoroughfare channels" because they connect arterioles and venules (see below) and major capillary networks arise from them (Fig. 11–28). The flow of blood from metacapillaries into capillary networks is regulated by precapillary sphincters, each a ring of smooth muscle surrounding a capillary where it branches from a metacapillary. Opening and closing of these sphincters alternately irrigates different capillary networks.

Capillaries. The focal point of the entire cardiovascular system is the network of some 10 billion microscopic capillaries functioning to provide a method whereby fluids, nutrients, oxygen, carbon dioxide, and wastes are exchanged between the blood and interstitial spaces. Capillaries are simply thin endothelial tubes, usually surrounded by a basement membrane, serving to maintain the integrity of the vessel. They have an average diameter of from 7 to 9 micrometers (similar to that of a red blood cell).

A single capillary unit consists of a branching and anastomosing network of vessels, each averaging 0.5 to 1 mm in length. The number of capillaries in active tissue, such as muscle, liver, kidneys, and lungs, is greater than the number in less metabolically active tissues, such as tendons and ligaments.

The endothelium of capillaries may be

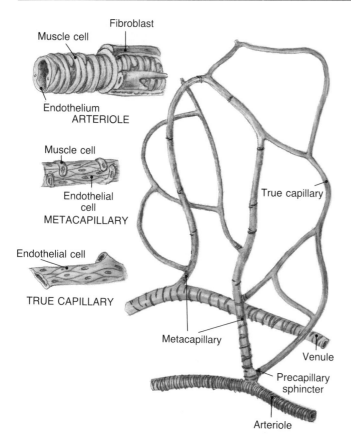

Muscle cell
Fibroblast
Endothelium
ARTERIOLE

Muscle cell
Endothelial cell
METACAPILLARY

Endothelial cell
TRUE CAPILLARY

True capillary

Metacapillary

Venule

Precapillary sphincter

Arteriole

Figure 11–28. Diagrammatic representation of a portion of a capillary bed typical of many tissues. Blood flows into the bed through an arteriole and out through a venule. Connecting the arteriole and venule is a metacapillary, from which blood flows into true capillaries. Precapillary sphincters regulate the flow of blood from the metacapillary into the true capillaries.

(a) *continuous,* as in skeletal muscle, the skin, and the lungs, with no interruptions in the endothelial layer; (b) *fenestrated* (L. *fenestra,* window), as in the intestine, the pancreas, and the glomerulus of the kidney, containing a continuous layer of endothelial cells but with pores (which may be covered by a thin diaphragm) penetrating the cells; and (c) *discontinuous,* as in the liver, with gaps between cells. The discontinuous type are called *sinusoids.* Their walls are, in part, formed by *phagocytes.* In the continuous and fenestrated types the walls are completely surrounded by basement membrane.

The permeability of capillaries varies from one region to another in the body. How substances are transported across capillary walls is still under intensive study. It is generally believed that exchange can occur both between and through endothelial cells. In continuous capillaries, *pinocytotic vesicles* apparently play a transport role, taking up substances on one side of the cell and discharging them on the other (see Chapter 3, page 57, for a description of pinocytosis). It also seems likely that in fenestrated capillaries the pores are sites of transfer.

The distribution of fluid between the blood stream and the interstitial space is governed largely by the balance between the *hydrostatic pressure* of the blood, which forces fluid out of the capillaries, and the *osmotic pressure* (see Chapter 3, page 56) of blood, created principally by the concentration of plasma proteins (albumin, chiefly), which draws fluid into the capillaries. The osmotic pressure of blood is approximately 25 mm of mercury. The hydrostatic pressure exceeds the osmotic pressure on the arterial side of capillaries and is lower on the venous side. Thus, the balance of flow is outward at the arterial end, inward at the venous end. A severe loss of fluid from the blood stream can occur as a result of a reduction in osmotic pressure (as in starvation, which leads to a reduction in blood protein synthesis in the liver) or an increase in capillary hydrostatic pressure (as when the return of venous blood to the heart is impaired). When the increase in volume of interstitial fluid can be recognized by a clinician, the condition is called **edema.**

Venules. These vessels collect blood from the capillary beds. A venule consists of an endothelial tube supported by a small amount of collagenous tissue and, in a larger venule, by smooth muscle fibers between the endothelium and connective tissue as well. As venules continue to increase in size they begin to show the characteristic wall structure of arteries but are much thinner.

Veins. Veins function to conduct blood from the peripheral tissues to the heart. Veins, like arteries, have three coats. The tunica intima is thin and generally has no distinct internal elastic lamina. The tunica media contains much less muscle and fewer elastic fibers than the tunica media of arteries. The adventitia is the best developed of the three coats. The tunica adventitia is composed chiefly of connective tissue. Blood pressure in these vessels is extremely low compared with that in the arterial system, and blood must exit at an even lower pressure, creating a need for a special mechanism whereby blood will be kept moving on its return to the heart rather than being allowed to pool and create more resistance to capillary flow. To achieve this, most veins possess a unique system of **valves** formed by paired semilunar folds in the tunica intima which open toward the heart. They serve to direct the flow of blood to the heart, particularly in an upward direction, preventing backflow when closed (Fig. 11–29). Movement of blood in veins toward the heart is brought about largely by the massaging action of contracting skeletal muscles and by the pressure gradient created by breathing when the

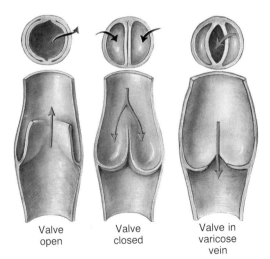

Valve   Valve   Valve in
open   closed   varicose
                 vein

Figure 11–29. Veins contain bicuspid valves which open in the direction of blood flow, but prevent regurgitation of flow when pockets become filled and distended.

pressure in the thoracic cavity decreases and the pressure in the abdominal cavity increases during inspiration. Insufficiency of the valves can cause veins to become **varicose,** that is, swollen with accumulated blood, knotted, and tortuous. The veins lose their elasticity as a result of the continuous distention. Varicosity commonly occurs in the superficial veins of the lower extremities, which are subject to strain when the individual stands for long periods of time. It is thought that there is a genetic predisposition to the development of varicose veins. Pregnancy and obesity hasten their development.

Veins tend to follow a course parallel to that of arteries but are present in greater number. Their lumina are larger than those of arteries and the walls thinner.

BLOOD PRESSURE

Basic Principles

Blood pressure is pressure exerted by the blood against the walls of the vessels. The term applies to arterial, capillary, and venous pressure. Usually it indicates pressure existing in the large arteries — commonly measured at the brachial artery just above the elbow. The blood pressure is highest in the brachial artery at the time of contraction of the ventricles (ventricular systole). This level is known as the **systolic pressure.** Pressure during ventricular diastole (relaxation of the ventricles) is called **diastolic pressure** and is principally the result of force exerted by the elastic rebound of the arterial wall. Blood pressure is usually expressed as a fraction — for example, as 120/80, in which 120 in mm of mercury represents systolic pressure and 80, diastolic pressure. The difference between the systolic and diastolic pressure is the **pulse pressure.**

Blood pressure is subject to fluctuations. In general, the healthy individual has a systolic pressure of 100 to 120 mm of mercury and a diastolic pressure of 60 to 80 mm of mercury. The upper limits of normal blood pressure are usually defined as 160 mm of mercury systolic and 95 mm diastolic. Pressures above this level (hypertension) shorten life expectancy.

A simple model of the cardiovascular system may help to visualize the major fac-

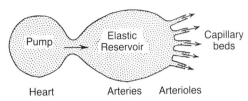

Figure 11–30. Schematic representation of arteries as an elastic reservoir with inflow from the heart and drainage through arterioles into capillary beds. Inflow and outflow rates determine the average pressure in the reservoir.

tors governing arterial blood pressure. If, as is illustrated in Figure 11–30, the large arteries are regarded as a blood chamber acting as an elastic reservoir, pressure builds up as it overfills. Increasing the inflow (cardiac output) into the reservoir and/or decreasing the outflow (drainage through the arterioles into the capillary beds) from the reservoir will raise the average arterial pressure. Decreasing cardiac output and/or increasing drainage will lower the average arterial pressure. Arteriolar drainage is altered largely by decreasing (constricting) or increasing (dilating) the diameter of arterioles. These relationships are generally expressed as follows: BP = CO × R, where BP is the arterial pressure, CO the cardiac output, and R the *peripheral resistance* — the resistance of blood flow through the arterioles. The elasticity of the arterial walls has a considerable influence on arterial pressure. Expansion of the arteries reduces the build-up of systolic pressure. Elastic recoil prevents the diastolic pressure from falling to too low a value. If the elasticity of the large arteries is diminished, the systolic pressure will be abnormally high and the diastolic pressure abnormally low.

The magnitude of systolic pressure largely depends upon the amount of blood ejected from the ventricle, the level of pre-existing diastolic pressure, and the elasticity of the aorta. The diastolic pressure is influenced chiefly by the duration of diastole and the peripheral resistance; the longer the duration of diastole, the lower the diastolic pressure.

It should be apparent that by constricting or dilating arterioles in specific areas of the body, such as skeletal muscles, the skin, and the abdominal region, it is possible not only to regulate the blood pressure but also to alter the distribution of blood in various parts of the body. It is perhaps also apparent that

the number of capillary beds open at any one time also affects arteriolar drainage — closing most of them down would obviously reduce drainage. The low pressure in the pulmonary circuit (about one-sixth the pressure in the systemic circuit) is, in part, accounted for by the large number of open capillary beds in the respiratory surfaces of the lungs. In addition, pulmonary arterioles have thinner muscular coats and larger diameters than arterioles of the systemic circuit.

Figure 11–31 illustrates the blood pressure, blood velocity, and cross-sectional area in each segment of the vascular tree. Note that the greatest fall in blood pressure, about 50 mm of mercury, occurs during the passage of blood through the arterioles. In this portion of the circulation, blood is flowing through a vast number of minute vessels, representing a larger total cross-sectional area than the arteries. The energy loss from friction as the blood passes through numerous vessels of small diameter is considerable. This dissipation of energy accounts for the drop in pressure. The pressure continues to fall progressively as blood flows through the capillary networks and the veins. It can also be seen from the curves for blood velocity and the vascular cross-sectional area in Figure 11–31 that velocity declines in the arterioles and capillaries as the cross-sectional area increases in these regions. Velocity increases in the veins as the cross-sectional area decreases in this portion of the vascular tree. This phenomenon is analogous to the common observation that a river runs slowly where it is wide and rapidly where it is narrow.

Regulation of Arterial Blood Pressure and the Distribution of Blood

Vasomotor and Cardiac Centers in the Medulla. Arterial blood pressure and the distribution of blood in the circulatory system are principally controlled by modifying the activity of the **vasomotor** (L. *vas*, a vessel) and **cardiac centers,** located in the medulla. The vasomotor center consists of two parts, one called the "pressor area," the other called the "depressor area." Electrical stimulation of the pressor area causes vasoconstriction, thereby raising blood pressure; stimulation of the depressor area inhibits the vasoconstriction activity of the pressor area,

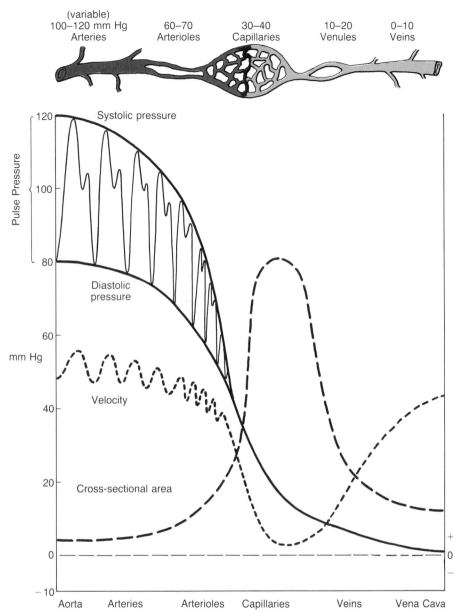

Figure 11–31. Blood pressure, blood velocity, and cross-sectional area of the vascular tree in various segments of the circulatory system. (Modified from Zoethout and Tuttle: *Textbook of Physiology*, twelfth edition. St. Louis, The C. V. Mosby Co., 1955.)

causing vasodilation, thereby lowering blood pressure. These responses are brought about by regulation of the tone of vascular smooth muscle, mainly of arterioles, acting through the sympathetic division of the autonomic nervous system. Spontaneous activity of the vasomotor center (it continues to discharge nerve impulses even when deprived of all incoming nerve signals) maintains a partial state of contraction of vascular smooth mus-

cle, called the *vasomotor tone,* which can be increased or decreased by a variety of inputs to the center, such as from receptors in blood vessels monitoring changes in blood pressure or from higher levels of the nervous system, especially the hypothalamus.

Two cardiac centers, the *cardioinhibitor center* and the *cardioaccelerator center,* govern the activity of the heart. The cardioinhibitor center acts through the parasympathetic division of the autonomic nervous system (vagus nerve); the cardioaccelerator center acts through the sympathetic division. The changes in the activity of the heart are apparently brought about by reciprocal variations in the activity of these centers. Thus, a decrease in heart rate results from an increase in the activity of the cardioinhibitory center and a decrease in the activity of the cardioaccelerator center, and vice versa. Changes in the activity of the cardioinhibitory center seem to have a more pronounced effect on heart rate than changes in the activity of the cardioaccelerator center. These centers also influence the force of contraction of the heart, parasympathetic stimulation decreasing and sympathetic stimulation increasing the force of contraction. However, changes in the force of contraction are mediated largely via the sympathetic nerve fibers. Just as input to the vasomotor center from other parts of the nervous system modifies the activity of the vasomotor center, so does it increase or decrease the activity of the cardiac centers.

The Baroreceptor Reflex. A fundamental mechanism for regulating blood pressure is a reflexive adjustment to deviations in blood pressure itself initiated by *baroreceptors* (also called *pressoreceptors*), receptors sensitive to stretch located in the walls of a number of large arteries, especially in the *aortic arch* and the *carotid sinuses* (slight enlargements at the bifurcation of each common carotid artery into the internal and external carotid arteries). A rise in blood pressure increases the rate of impulse transmission from these receptors to the vasomotor and cardiac centers in the medulla. The principal response is vasodilation of arterioles in the abdominal region (including the spleen, liver, intestine, pancreas, stomach, and kidneys), skin, and skeletal muscles, lowering blood pressure toward normal. Conversely, a fall in blood pressure causes reflex vasoconstriction and a rise in blood pressure. Changes in heart rate are also induced by the baroreceptor reflex — a rise in pressure decreasing the heart rate, a fall in pressure increasing the heart rate. However, the adjustments in blood pressure are due mainly to the changes in peripheral resistance brought about by vasoconstriction or vasodilation. Since the baroreceptor reflex continuously and rapidly prevents large deviations from normal blood pressure, the nerves innervat-

ing the baroreceptors of each carotid sinus (the *sinus nerve,* a branch of the glossopharyngeal nerve) and the aortic arch (the *aortic nerve,* a branch of the vagus nerve) are called "buffer nerves." This buffer action is of critical importance upon assuming an upright from a supine posture, when blood tends to pool in the lower part of the body. The baroreceptor response prevents postural hypotension and maintains an adequate flow of blood to the brain; a deficient response can cause unconsciousness.

The baroreceptors are not operative below 60 mm Hg and are most sensitive in the normal blood pressure range. Another characteristic of these receptors is that they adapt to long-term changes in blood pressure. Thus, if an individual becomes hypertensive, the receptors are reset so as to maintain the higher blood pressure. If the hypertension is corrected, the control level will be reset downward.

The Chemoreceptor Reflex. Chemoreceptors sensitive to oxygen deficiency (and to a lesser extent to elevated carbon dioxide concentration and reduced pH) are in the aortic and carotid bodies, located, respectively, along the arch of the aorta and adjacent to each carotid sinus (near the bifurcation of each common carotid artery). A fall in oxygen concentration elicits a reflex increase in blood pressure by acting on the vasomotor center and causing vasoconstriction, especially in the limbs and intestine. This reflex, unlike the baroreceptor reflex, which is most active in the normal range of blood pressure, does not become operative until the blood pressure falls below 60 to 70 mm Hg (remaining active down to about 40 mm Hg). It is, therefore, a mechanism for controlling blood pressure when, as a consequence of a pronounced fall in blood pressure, the flow of blood and hence the delivery of oxygen to vital organs, particularly the brain and heart, approach dangerously low levels.

The Effect of Reduced Blood Flow to the Brain on the Vasomotor Center: the CNS Ischemic Response. When, as a result of a very large fall in blood pressure, the brain becomes ischemic (lacking sufficient blood flow to maintain normal metabolism), the vasomotor center becomes highly active, and an intense peripheral vasoconstriction causes a pronounced rise in blood pressure. This response is believed to be brought about by a rise in the concentration of carbon dioxide, which accumulates because of a delayed removal by slowly moving blood, and has a strong excitatory effect on the vasomotor center. This so-called *central nervous system (CNS) ischemic response,* like the chemoreceptor response, becomes operative when the fall in blood pressure approaches a danger point. Since it is not activated until the pressure falls below 40 to 50 mm Hg, it has been called a "last resort" response to hypotension.

The Renin-Angiotensin and the Renin-Angiotensin-Aldosterone Responses. A fall in the pressure of the blood flowing through the kidneys initiates a sequence of events that results in the formation of the body's most powerful vasoconstrictor, *angiotensin II;* the widespread vasoconstriction which follows its formation raises blood pressure. The first step in the sequence leading to the formation of angiotensin II is the release by the kidneys of an enzyme called *renin,* which acts on a protein found in blood to produce angiotensin I, which is in turn converted to angiotensin II (see Chapter 15 for further details). Angiotensin II has another action which raises blood pressure — it stimulates the release from the adrenal gland of the hormone *aldosterone,* which increases the reabsorption of sodium from the kidney tubules to the blood stream, leading to water retention and an expansion of blood volume.

The renin-angiotensin and renin-angiotensin-aldosterone mechanisms act more slowly in bringing about changes in blood pressure than the baroreceptor, chemoreceptor, and CNS ischemic responses. The baroreceptor reflex is the most rapidly acting — responding immediately and having a maximum effect within just a few seconds. The chemoreceptor and CNS ischemic responses also occur within seconds, exerting maximum effect in about half a minute. The effect of the renin-angiotensin control mechanism is observable after a few minutes, while it takes several hours for the renin-angiotensin-aldosterone mechanism to influence blood pressure.

Cardiovascular Changes in Anticipation of and During Exercise and in the Alarm Defense Response. Exercise produces a pattern of cardiovascular changes (which begin before the exercise starts) that is basically the same as the pattern characteristic of a reaction to emotional stress, often referred to as the *alarm defense response.* In both cases, signals from the cerebral cortex, particularly the motor cortex and probably parts of the limbic system, activate the hypothalamus, which coordinates the response. The circulatory changes include vasoconstriction in the abdominal region and skin, vasodilation in skeletal muscles, and an increase in heart rate and the force of the heart's contraction. Vasoconstriction and augmentation of the activity of the heart are mediated by the medullary vasomotor and cardiac centers. The pathway by which vasodilation in skeletal muscles is induced is anatomically and physiologically distinct from the vasomotor center pathway — it leads from the hypothalamus to the spinal cord and involves sympathetic vasodilator fibers (acting, it is believed, on beta, or vasodilator, receptors). These circulatory adjustments are supported by the release of epinephrine and norepinephrine from the adrenal medulla. Suppression of the baroreceptor reflex prevents diminution of these cardiovascular changes by the rise in blood pressure. Contributing to the greatly increased blood supply to active muscles is a local response — relaxation of the precapillary sphincters. Overheating in the course of the exercise may elicit dilation of arterioles in the skin to increase heat loss from the surface of the body. This is one of the homeostatic adjustments, mediated by the hypothalamus, called forth to regulate body temperature (see Chapter 14).

Blood Pressure Measurement

Blood pressure is measured with a *sphygmomanometer* (G. *sphygmos,* pulse; G. *manos,* rare, thin; G. *metron,* a measure). The pressure of blood within the artery is balanced by an external pressure exerted by air contained in a cuff applied externally around the arm. Actually, what is measured is the pressure within the cuff. The steps employed in determining blood pressure with a sphygmomanometer are the following:

1. The cuff is wrapped securely around the arm above the elbow.

2. Air is pumped into the cuff with a rubber bulb until pressure in it is sufficient to stop the flow of blood in the brachial artery. At this point, the brachial pulse disappears. Pressure within the cuff is shown on the scale of the sphygmomanometer.

3. The observer places a stethoscope over the brachial artery just below the elbow and gradually releases the air from within the cuff. The decreased air pressure permits the blood to flow, filling the artery below the cuff. Faint tapping sounds corresponding to the heartbeat are heard. When the sound is first noted, the air pressure from within the cuff is recorded on the scale. This pressure is equal to the systolic blood pressure.

4. As the air in the cuff is further released, the sounds become progressively louder. Then the sounds change in quality from loud to soft and finally disappear. At the point where the sounds change from loud to soft, the manometer reading corresponds to the diastolic pressure.

The American Heart Association recommends that, when a wide difference exists between the point at which the sound becomes dull and muffled and the point at which the sound completely disappears, the level at which the sound completely disappears should also be recorded as diastolic blood pressure. As mentioned, blood pressure is expressed as a ratio — 120/80, for example, representing 120 mm Hg systolic and 80 mm Hg diastolic.

Hypertension

Blood pressure greater than 140/90 is generally considered to be abnormal and is associated with a greater incidence of strokes, heart disease, and kidney failure. According to a report released in 1979 by the National Heart, Lung and Blood Institute, 35 million Americans, or one in six, have what is called *definite hypertension,* defined as blood pressure above 160/95, and another 25 million have *borderline hypertension,* defined as blood pressure between 140/90 and 160/95. In a small percentage of cases, the hypertension is secondary to clinical conditions involving specific organs. This type is called *secondary hypertension.* Among the causes of secondary hypertension are kidney disease and narrowing of the arteries leading to the kidneys (reducing the pressure of the blood flowing to the kidneys and hence the release of renin—see page 389). Excess secretion of aldosterone (the hormone promoting sodium, and hence water, retention by the kidneys) in disorders of the adrenal gland is another cause of secondary hypertension.

In the vast majority of cases (85 to 95 per cent) the cause of hypertension is unknown.

This type is called *primary* or *essential hypertension.* Heredity appears to be a factor in essential hypertension — the child of a hypertensive parent has twice as much chance of developing hypertension as a child whose parents have normal blood pressure. Some investigators believe that individuals genetically predisposed to hypertension have a deficiency in kidney function, specifically a slight impairment of the ability to secrete sodium, which leads to a gradual overfilling of the vascular beds, an increase in cardiac output, and a rise in blood pressure. Other investigators have postulated that the sympathetic division of the autonomic nervous system of individuals genetically predisposed to hypertension overresponds to emotional stress, causing repeated bouts of increased cardiac output and high blood pressure. It is postulated that an increase in cardiac output, which is accompanied by increased muscle blood flow in individuals reacting to stressful stimuli, provokes vasoconstriction in vascular beds where the blood flow exceeds the metabolic needs of the tissues so as to return the blood flow to normal levels (a response referred to as autoregulation). Long-term vasoconstriction may result in thickening of vascular walls, causing a permanent increase in peripheral resistance and chronic hypertension.

Pulse

An impulse can be felt over an artery lying near the surface of the skin. The impulse is secondary to alternate expansion and contraction of the arterial wall resulting from the beating heart. When the heart ejects blood into the aorta, its impact on the elastic walls creates a pressure wave continuing along the arteries. This impact is the pulse. All arteries have a pulse, but it is most easily felt where the vessel approaches the surface of the body. The pulse is readily distinguished at the following locations (Fig. 11–32).

1. Radial artery: on radial side of wrist.

2. External maxillary (facial) artery: at the point of crossing the mandible.

3. Temporal artery: at the temple above and to the outer side of the eye.

4. Carotid artery: on the side of the neck.

5. Brachial artery: on the inner side of the biceps.

6. Femoral artery: in the groin.

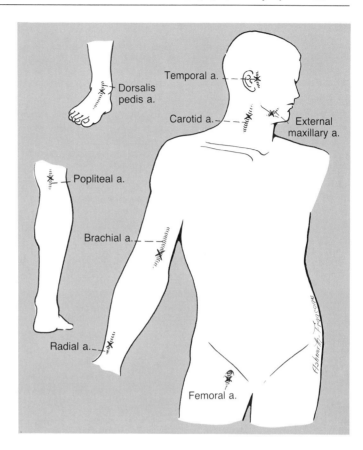

Figure 11–32. The pulse is readily distinguished at any of the indicated pressure points.

7. Popliteal artery: behind the knee.

8. Dorsalis pedis artery: anterosuperior aspect of the foot.

The radial artery is most commonly used to check the pulse. Several fingers should be placed on the artery just proximal to the wrist joint. More than one fingertip is preferable because of the large, sensitive surface available to palpate the pulse wave. During palpation of the pulse, certain data should be recorded, including the number of pulses per minute, the force and strength of the pulse, and the tension offered by the artery to the finger. Normally, the interval between pulses is of equal length. Irregularity occurs when there is abnormal cardiac rhythm, such as in atrial fibrillation. In this condition, as previously noted, there is a pulse deficit, with the rate counted at the apex being greater than that counted at the radial artery of the wrist.

Blood Volume

The normal adult has a blood volume of approximately 5 liters. Normal blood volume may be reduced by a loss of whole blood in hemorrhage, a deficiency of red cells (anemia), or a loss of plasma. Dilation of the arterioles, venules, and capillaries traps blood in the periphery of the vascular system, causing a diminished available blood volume without actual blood loss. An increase in blood volume occurs in certain diseases but is usually less marked than blood loss.

The integrity of the endothelial membrane of the capillaries is a vital factor in maintaining normal blood volume. Many factors alter the permeability of the capillaries. When the endothelium is injured, its permeability to plasma proteins is increased, leading to a loss of fluid into the interstitial spaces. Damage to the endothelium can occur from many factors, including toxins and hypoxia (oxygen deficiency).

Shock

The term *shock* has a variety of meanings, but in medicine it generally refers to a state of the circulatory system in which there is insufficient flow of blood to the tissues throughout the body. If this condition is caused by a diseased or damaged heart failing to pump with sufficient force, it is called *cardiogenic shock*. All other forms of shock are produced by (1) a reduction in blood volume or (2) an increase in vascular capacity brought about by vasodilation, so that the volume of blood, even if normal, underfills the system. Either of these conditions (or some combination of both) leads to a decrease in venous return and, consequently, in cardiac output and arterial pressure. The reduction in circulatory activity tends to produce a vicious cycle of deterioration by causing vascular and tissue damage which in turn leads to further decreases in cardiac output and blood pressure and to further tissue damage. Unless the trend is reversed, death soon results. The common signs of shock in the early stages include apprehension, cold skin, cyanosis of the fingertips, and reduced blood pressure.

Shock produced by a reduction in blood volume is called *hypovolemic shock*. Hemorrhage is the most obvious cause of this type of shock. Hypovolemic shock may also result from, among other things, severe burns, which cause the loss of plasma into the interstitial fluid compartment in the area of the burned tissue, and vomiting or diarrhea, which bring about dehydration (the loss of body fluid in all compartments). *Anaphylactic shock* occurs following a particular kind of allergic reaction (see Chapter 12, page 440) as a result of widespread vasodilation and hence an increase in vascular capacity, as well as the loss of fluid from the blood stream due to an increase in capillary permeability. In *neurogenic shock* there is an increase in vascular capacity (with no change in blood volume), the vasodilation resulting from a loss of vasomotor tone. This type of shock may be caused by, among other things, deep general anesthesia (depressing the vasomotor center), high spinal anesthesia (blocking sympathetic outflow to the periphery), damage to the brain or spinal cord, and fainting. *Septic shock* is produced by a widely disseminated infection and is generally associated with the release of toxins which cause vasodilation and have a depressant effect on the heart. There also may be loss of plasma from the capillaries. This type of shock is most commonly seen during hospitalization for serious illness or surgery.

Shock has been divided into three phases: (1) *compensated,* in which the body's compensatory mechanisms maintain adequate blood flow to the vital organs and the patient recovers without treatment; (b) *progressive,* in which the compensatory mechanisms do not halt the fall in blood pressure, but the patient responds to treatment and recovers; and (c) *irreversible,* when blood transfusion and other therapy fail to bring about recovery.

The mechanisms controlling blood pressure have been described in earlier sections of this chapter. As indicated, an acute fall in blood pressure will first activate the baroreceptor reflex, quickly followed by the chemoreceptor and CNS ischemic responses if the pressure falls to dangerously low levels. Within minutes the renin-angiotensin vasoconstriction mechanism contributes to the recovery process. Over a long period of time the renin-angiotensin-aldosterone mechanism participates in combatting shock. If, in spite of the action of the body's compensatory mechanisms and therapeutic measures undertaken, shock progresses to the irreversible stage, this means that the circulatory system is unable to sustain a temporary recovery of blood pressure and cardiac output brought about by transfusion or other intervention because the heart cannot pump with sufficient force. The principal causes of this condition appear to be (1) deterioration of heart muscle because of oxygen deficiency resulting from a diminished coronary blood flow and (2) depression of cardiac contractility by one or more toxic substances — generally referred to as the *myocardial depressant factor(s) (MDF)* — released into the blood stream from the abdominal region. Activation of proteolytic enzymes by hypoxia is the primary trigger for MDF formation, and it has been suggested that the pancreas is the principal site of its formation.

Coronary Heart Disease

Coronary heart disease, the major cause of death in the United States, occurs when the coronary arteries become so narrowed by *atherosclerosis* (localized areas of thickened tunica intima associated with the accumulation of smooth muscle cells and lipids, principally cholesterol) that they are unable to deliver sufficient blood to the heart muscle to meet its demands for oxygen. A primary sign of this condition is *angina pectoris*, periodic severe pain in the chest generally radiating to the left shoulder and down the inner side of the arm, usually precipitated by physical exertion or emotional stress. In a heart attack the pain is caused by *myocardial infarction,* death of a part of the heart muscle due to total blockage of one of the coronary arteries or its branches. Whether or not the victim survives depends largely upon the amount of heart muscle destroyed. The occlusion, it is generally believed, is caused by the formation of a blood clot (thrombus) over the atherosclerotic lesion, or plaque, but there is reason to believe that in some cases the plaque itself may cause complete blockage.

Atherosclerotic plaques (see Fig. 11–33) develop most commonly in the aorta and in the coronary, cerebral, iliac, and femoral arteries, especially at junctions. The lesion begins with the accumulation of smooth muscle cells in the intima. Only occasional smooth muscle cells are seen in the intima of children's arteries, but they accumulate slowly with age, even in "normal" arteries. Once the development of a lesion is initiated, the number of smooth muscle cells increases rapidly as they divide, migrate from the tunica media through the internal elastic lamina into the intima, and continue to multiply. As the lesion progresses, smooth muscle cells become filled with lipids (called foam cells when this happens). In the initial phase, a raised area of intima, called a fatty streak, appears. Following this, a thick, fibrous plaque takes form, consisting of a fibrous cap composed of foam cells embedded in a matrix of elastic fibers and other connective tissue components (all synthesized by foam cells) overlying extracellular lipids and cell debris. In the advanced, or complicated, lesion the plaques become calcified.

A key to understanding atherosclerosis is answering the question: "What initiates the proliferation of smooth muscle cells?" Two theories currently under investigation propose different answers to this question. The older, the response to injury theory, proposes that damage to the endothelium, possibly induced by mechanical forces or chemicals, is followed by penetration of the arterial wall by a substance released from platelets that are aggregating at the site of injury that stimulates the proliferation of smooth muscle cells. According to the opposing monoclonal hypothesis, the accumulation of smooth mus-

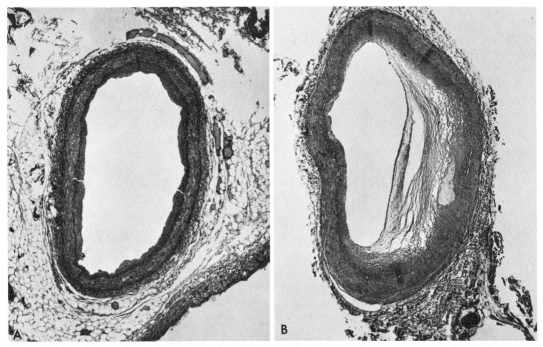

Figure 11–33. These photomicrographs show (*A*) a normal artery seen in cross section and (*B*) a diseased artery in which the channel is partially occluded by atherosclerosis. (By permission: David M. Spain, M.D., previously published: Scientific American, August, 1966.)

cle cells is a result of the multiplication of a single mutant smooth muscle cell freed from the usual constraints on cell division. The latter theory is based on the observation that in some individuals two forms of an enzyme (glucose-6-phosphate dehydrogenase) are equally distributed between smooth muscle cells of the tunica intima, yet in almost all atherosclerotic plaques of such individuals all of the smooth muscle cells have the same form of the enzyme (be it one or the other).

Hypertension, a high concentration of low density plasma lipoproteins (which apparently carry cholesterol to tissues), a low concentration of high density lipoproteins (which appear to be involved in the removal of cholesterol from tissues), and cigarette smoking are major coronary risk factors. Proponents of the response to injury theory argue that hypertension can damage endothelial cells, and that cigarette smoking, by impairing lung function and the oxygen-carrying capacity of hemoglobin (the carbon monoxide in cigarette smoke combines with hemoglobin more readily than oxygen), reduces the supply of oxygen to arterial tissue, a condition that stimulates the proliferation of smooth muscle cells. Proponents of the monoclonal hypothesis argue that substances in cigarette smoke and derivatives of cholesterol enhance the rate of mutation, and that individuals with hypertension are more susceptible to the action of mutagens than people with normal blood pressure (the incidence of cancer is also higher in hypertensive individuals).

Aneurysm

An aneurysm (G. *aneurysma*, dilatation) is a dilatation of the wall of an artery, forming a blood-filled sac. It occurs most frequently in the descending aorta, and eventually may rupture, causing hemorrhage and death. One or more of the following symptoms may be associated with an aortic aneurysm in the thoracic region: chest pain, labored breathing, and a change in voice quality due to irritation of the recurrent laryngeal nerve. An aneurysm in the abdominal aorta may cause severe abdominal or pelvic pain. A congenital defect in a cerebral artery known as berry aneurysm is the most common cause of subarachnoid hemorrhage.

Stroke

A stroke, also known as a cerebrovascular accident (CVA), is an interruption of blood supply to a portion of the brain. The most common cause is occlusion of an artery by *thrombosis* (formation of a thrombus — a blood clot within a vessel). Thrombosis is usually secondary to atherosclerosis, the atherosclerotic plaque serving as the initiating site for the formation of the thrombus. Other causes include *thromboembolism* — blockage of an artery by a blood clot (or fragment) that has broken loose from its site of origin — and *hemorrhage* due to rupture of an artery. Hemorrhagic stroke is most likely to occur in hypertensive individuals, and the ruptured artery is usually one that has become vulnerable because of atherosclerotic changes or the presence of an aneurysm. Although a stroke may occur without warning, in most patients it is preceded by transient decreases in blood supply to a portion of the brain — so-called *transient ischemic attacks (TIA's)*. The symptoms of these warning episodes are the same as those of a major stroke and depend upon the part of the brain affected. There may be weakness, paralysis, sensory disturbances, or difficulty in speech or writing. However, the symptoms disappear within 24 hours (usually within six hours).

Congenital Defects of the Cardiovascular System

The most common congenital defects are patent ductus arteriosus, ventricular septal defects, atrial septal defects, the so-called tetralogy of Fallot, and coarctation of the aorta (Fig. 11–34).

Patent ductus arteriosus is a condition characterized by the presence of a channel joining the left pulmonary artery to the aorta. This occurs normally in the fetus, and usually the patent ductus closes within a few weeks after birth. If it does not close, it must be closed surgically.

Septal defects are small holes within the septum between the atria or ventricles. Small openings usually cause little difficulty; large openings can result in death shortly after birth. Septal defects are closed directly, while maintaining general circulation by means of a heart-lung machine.

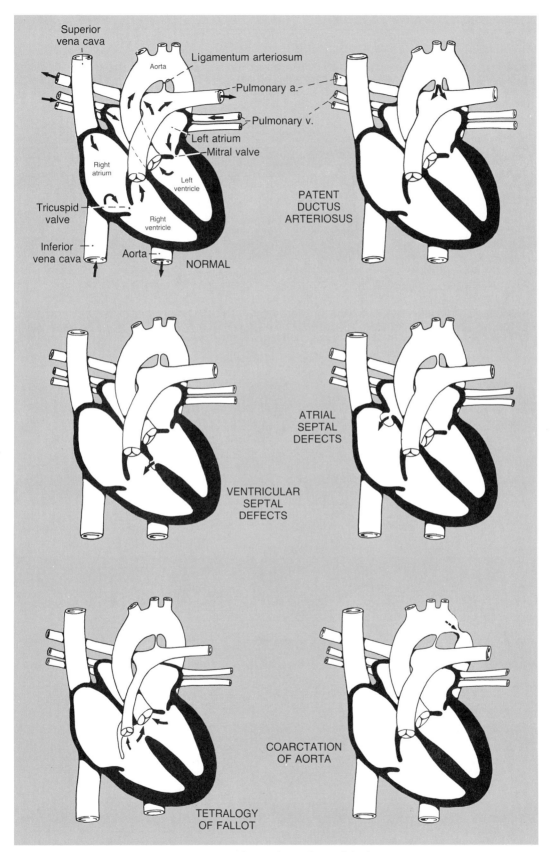

Superior
vena cava

Ligamentum arteriosum

Aorta

Pulmonary a.

Pulmonary v.

Left atrium

Mitral valve

Right
atrium

Left
ventricle

Tricuspid
valve

Right
ventricle

Inferior
vena cava

Aorta

NORMAL

PATENT
DUCTUS
ARTERIOSUS

VENTRICULAR
SEPTAL
DEFECTS

ATRIAL
SEPTAL
DEFECTS

TETRALOGY
OF FALLOT

COARCTATION
OF AORTA

Figure 11–34. Congenital defects of the heart.

395

Tetralogy of Fallot is a bizarre combination of defects including pulmonary stenosis (valvular or subvalvular narrowing), ventricular septal defect, enlargement of the right ventricle, and apparent displacement of the aorta to the right. The result of this combination of defects is that much of the blood does not flow through the pulmonary system. The most characteristic feature is severe cyanosis, or a bluish appearance of the skin, because of a lack of oxygenated blood. A common procedure for increasing pulmonary blood flow is to shunt the blood from the systemic circulation to the pulmonary circulation; this is accomplished by joining the subclavian artery or aorta to the pulmonary artery. Currently, tetralogy of Fallot is frequently treated by a direct attack, using the heart-lung machine and correcting the abnormalities.

Coarctation of the aorta is a congenital defect involving a drastic narrowing of the aorta. It causes an increased workload on the left ventricle. If severe, collateral circulation develops. A pressure 10 to 15 mm Hg higher in the right than the left brachial artery might indicate coarctation between the right and left subclavian arteries. The condition is corrected either by removing the constricted portion and joining the two open ends of the aorta or by substituting a plastic portion for the removed part of the aorta.

Techniques Employed to Evaluate the Heart and Vascular System

Right Heart Catheterization. Right heart catheterization is performed by inserting a catheter (a long tube) into the antecubital vein (at the elbow), the saphenous vein, or

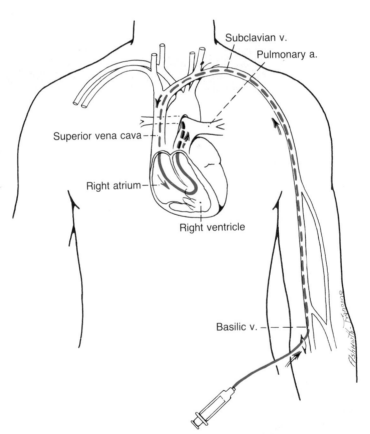

Figure 11–35. Right heart catheterization.

the femoral vein. The catheter, which is opaque to x-ray, is advanced into the right atrium, right ventricle, and pulmonary artery under fluoroscopy. This procedure, by measuring pressure and oxygen saturation in the right heart chamber, is used to diagnose valvular abnormalities of the right side of the heart (Fig. 11–35).

Left Heart Catheterization. Left heart catheterization is accomplished by introducing a catheter into the brachial or femoral artery and advancing it through the aorta across the aortic valve and into the left ventricle. Mitral and aortic valvular defects and myocardial disease can be evaluated by this technique.

Circulation Time. The circulation time between two points in the cardiovascular system is measured by injecting an indicator substance into one area of the circulation and recording its arrival time at another. Arm to lung circulation time is measured by timing

the appearance of ether in the lung after its injection into a peripheral vein. Arm to tongue circulation is measured by injecting a substance such as calcium gluconate or Decholin into the antecubital vein and recording the time until the patient tastes this material. Circulation time depends on the velocity of blood flow and the dimensions of the circulatory pathway involved. A high cardiac output is generally associated with a reduced circulation time. A low cardiac output accompanying venous congestion usually has a prolonged circulation time.

Angiocardiography. (See Figs. 11–36 to 11–39). X-ray outlines of the cardiac chambers and great vessels are provided by rapidly injecting x-ray opaque material through an arm vein or through a catheter threaded into the right or left side of the heart. This procedure is followed by a series of rapid exposures to x-ray or to x-ray movies called cineangiography. Angiocardiography

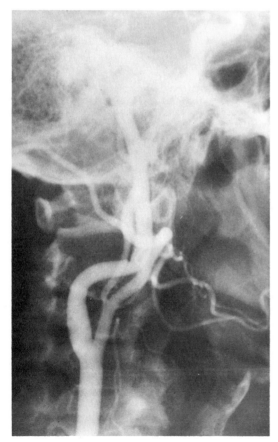
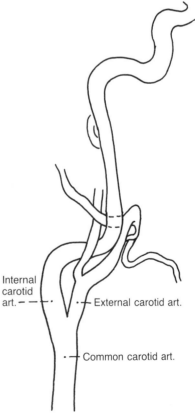

Internal carotid art.

External carotid art.

Common carotid art.

Figure 11–36. Angiograph for common carotid study.

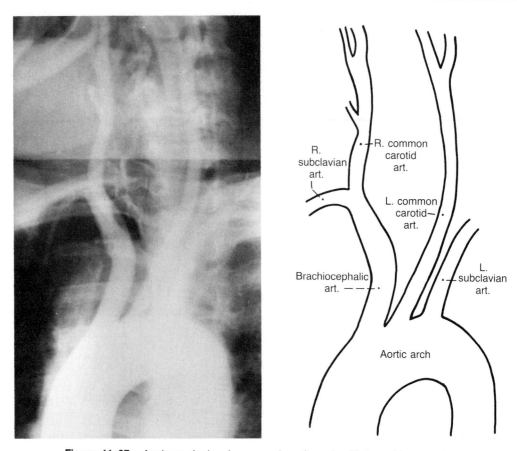

Figure 11–37. Angiograph showing normal aortic arch with branching arteries.

permits direct visualization of the cardiac chambers and great vessels. By outlining abnormal circulatory pathways it provides one of the best methods of detecting the site and extent of congenital abnormalities of the heart. It can also be used to study arteries and veins.

Vein to Artery Graft. The accurate diagnosis of peripheral and coronary arterial disease or damage, coupled with the development of new surgical techniques, has led to more frequent use of vein grafts in the repair of damaged arteries. These grafts can be obtained from various parts of the vascular system and are used to replace the damaged or diseased portion of the artery. This procedure is being utilized more and more as treatment of circulatory occlusions of the heart caused by conditions such as atherosclerosis.

Central Venous Catheterization. In order to alleviate vein irritation and discomfort caused by long-term venous therapy the relatively sophisticated technique of central venous catheterization has been recently developed. The procedure involves positioning a large-gauge needle in the subclavian, internal jugular, or external jugular vein and passing a catheter through the needle into the vein and, subsequently, into the superior vena cava. In this way a rapid and convenient method is provided to monitor central venous pressure and provide a route for parenteral alimentation, long-term intravenous therapy with anti-coagulant solutions, and rapid infusion of large volumes of fluid. It provides an immediate route for emergency treatment of conditions such as cardiac arrest, for temporary placement of a pacemaker, or for obtaining pulmonary arteriographs.

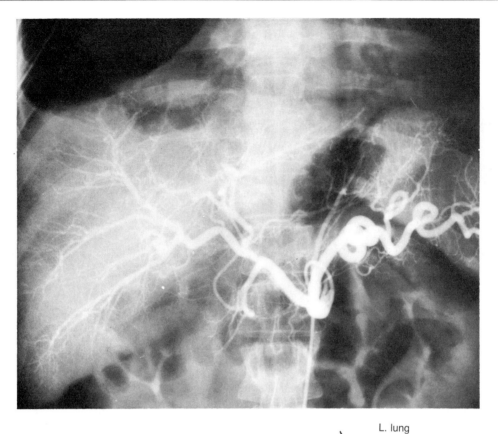

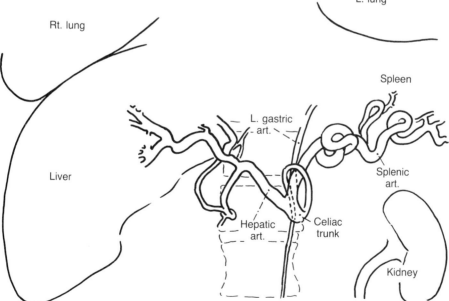

Figure 11–38. Normal celiac angiograph with normal hepatic, left gastric, and splenic branches. The liver, kidneys, and spleen are all well seen in their relationship to one another. In this particular angiograph the patient was noted to have right lung collapse with mass. Lung cancer was diagnosed with no evidence of liver metastases.

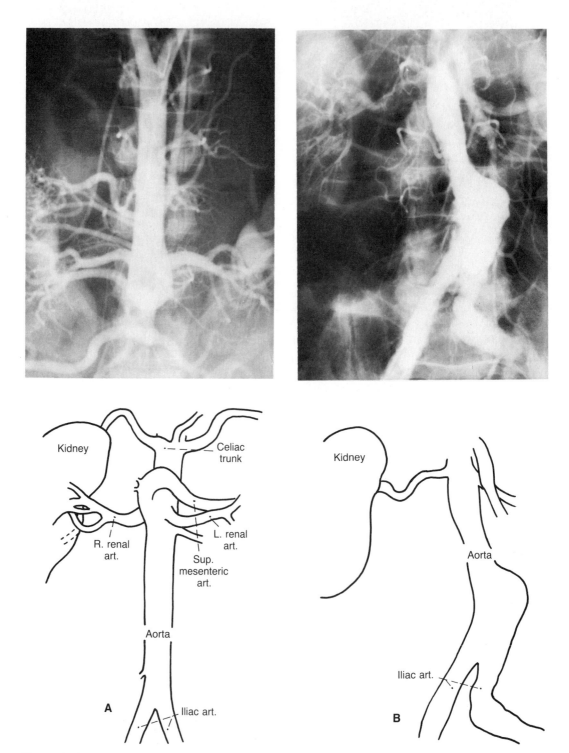

Figure 11–39. *A*, An aortogram and iliac study on a young patient. *B*, For comparison, an aortogram from a 69-year-old male with severe atherosclerosis is shown. The aorta and iliacs are dilated and irregular.

PULMONARY AND SYSTEMIC CIRCUITS

As mentioned in the beginning of the chapter, blood is pumped from the heart into two circuits: pulmonary and systemic. These are described in more detail in this section (see Figs. 11–40 to 11–60). Special consideration is also given to the circulation through the liver and brain and to the fetal circulation.

Text continued on page 407

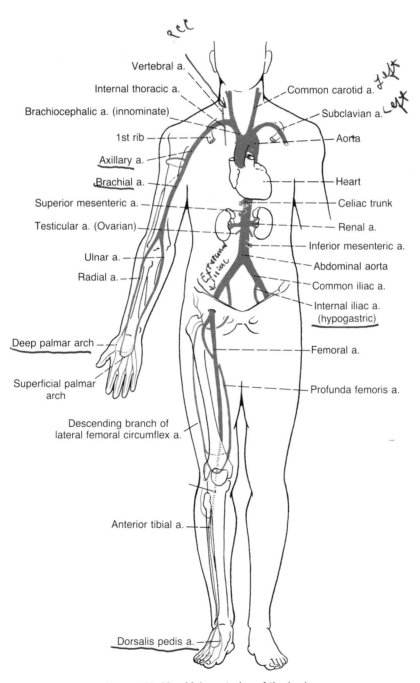

Figure 11–40. Major arteries of the body.

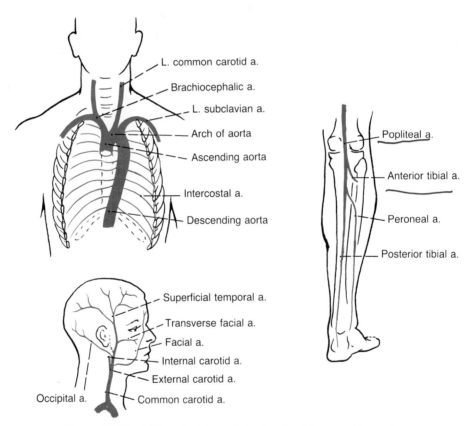

Figure 11–41. Major arterial supply to the chest, face, and lower leg.

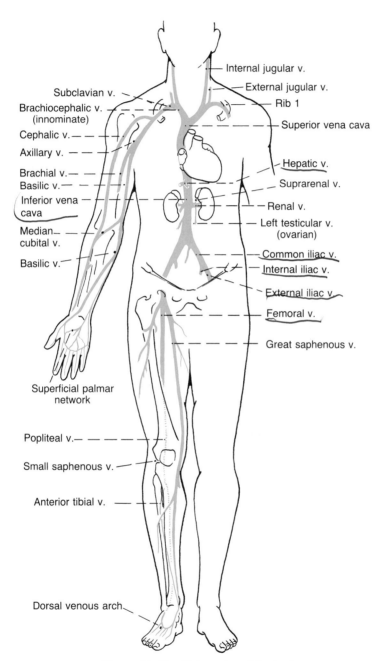

Internal jugular v.

External jugular v.

Subclavian v.

Brachiocephalic v. (innominate)

Rib 1

Superior vena cava

Cephalic v.

Axillary v.

Hepatic v.

Brachial v.

Basilic v.

Suprarenal v.

Inferior vena cava

Renal v.

Left testicular v. (ovarian)

Median cubital v.

Common iliac v.

Basilic v.

Internal iliac v.

External iliac v.

Femoral v.

Great saphenous v.

Superficial palmar network

Popliteal v.

Small saphenous v.

Anterior tibial v.

Dorsal venous arch

Figure 11–42. Major veins of the body.

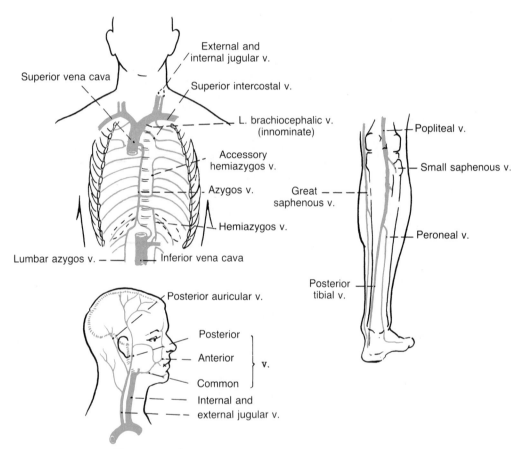

Figure 11–43. Major veins of the chest, face, and lower leg.

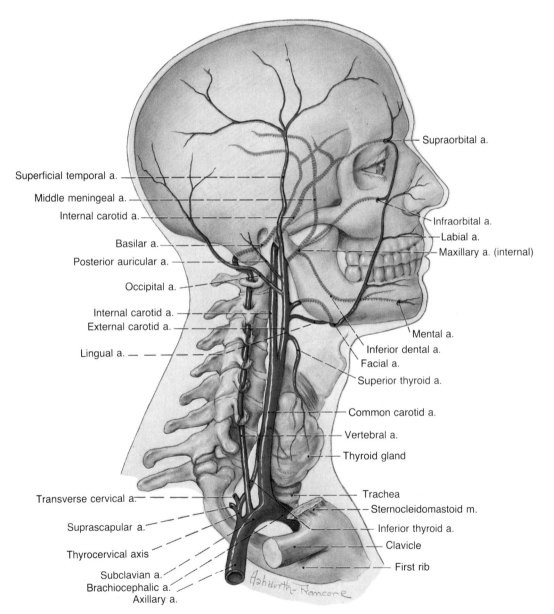

Figure 11–44. Arterial supply to the head and neck.

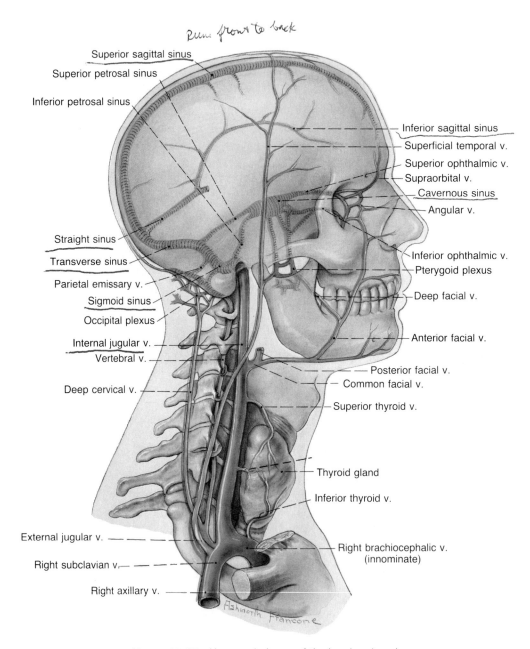

Superior sagittal sinus

Superior petrosal sinus

Inferior petrosal sinus

Runs front to back

Inferior sagittal sinus

Superficial temporal v.

Superior ophthalmic v.

Supraorbital v.

Cavernous sinus

Angular v.

Straight sinus

Transverse sinus

Parietal emissary v.

Sigmoid sinus

Occipital plexus

Internal jugular v.

Vertebral v.

Deep cervical v.

Inferior ophthalmic v.

Pterygoid plexus

Deep facial v.

Anterior facial v.

Posterior facial v.

Common facial v.

Superior thyroid v.

Thyroid gland

Inferior thyroid v.

External jugular v.

Right subclavian v.

Right axillary v.

Right brachiocephalic v. (innominate)

Figure 11–45. Venous drainage of the head and neck.

Pulmonary Circulation

The pulmonary system carries blood from the right ventricle to the respiratory surfaces of the lungs and back to the left atrium. The pulmonary trunk, originating from the superior surface of the right ventricle, passes upward beside the route of the aorta. Between the fifth and sixth thoracic vertebrae, the trunk divides into two branches — the right and left pulmonary arteries — which enter the right and left lungs, respectively. After entering the lungs, the branches subdivide, finally emerging as capillaries. Capillaries surround air sacs (alveoli), pick up oxygen, and release carbon dioxide. Gradually, the capillaries unite, assuming the characteristics of veins. Veins join to form pulmonary veins, which carry oxygenated blood from the lungs to the left atrium.

An embolus (a bit of matter, such as a blood clot, air, tumor cells, fat, or clumps of bacteria, carried in the blood stream until lodged in an artery) obstructing a pulmonary artery or one of its large branches often results in death. Frequently, the patient will recover if the main pulmonary artery is not involved. If the major pulmonary artery is obstructed, cardiac output falls suddenly, the skin becomes pale because of intense vasoconstriction, the blood pressure drops, and the patient manifests evidences of shock. There is usually an increased heart rate.

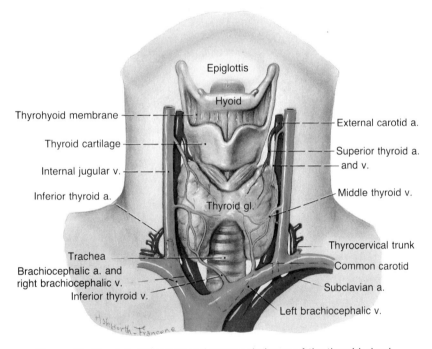

Figure 11–46. Arterial supply and venous drainage of the thyroid gland.

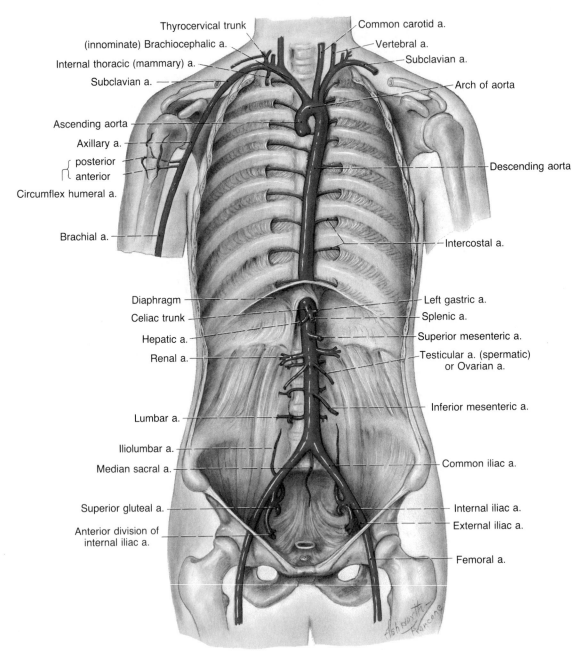

Thyrocervical trunk

(innominate) Brachiocephalic a.

Internal thoracic (mammary) a.

Subclavian a.

Ascending aorta

Axillary a.

posterior
anterior

Circumflex humeral a.

Brachial a.

Diaphragm

Celiac trunk

Hepatic a.

Renal a.

Lumbar a.

Iliolumbar a.

Median sacral a.

Superior gluteal a.

Anterior division of
internal iliac a.

Common carotid a.

Vertebral a.

Subclavian a.

Arch of aorta

Descending aorta

Intercostal a.

Left gastric a.

Splenic a.

Superior mesenteric a.

Testicular a. (spermatic)
or Ovarian a.

Inferior mesenteric a.

Common iliac a.

Internal iliac a.

External iliac a.

Femoral a.

Figure 11–47. The aorta and its major branches.

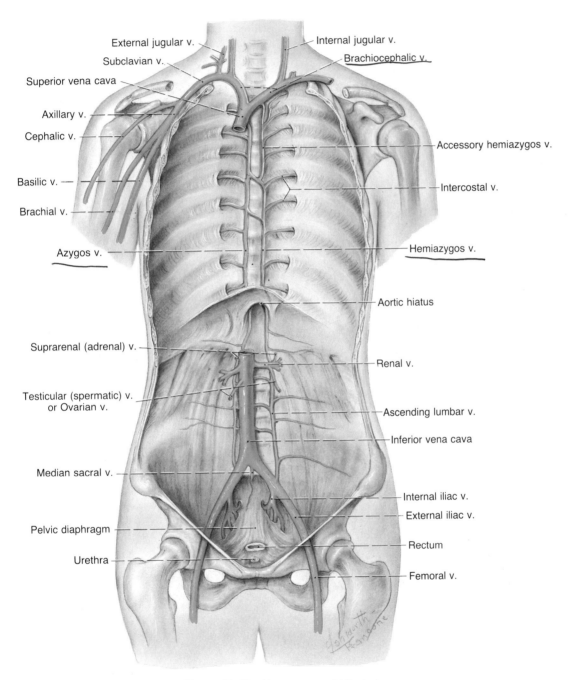

External jugular v.

Subclavian v.

Superior vena cava

Axillary v.

Cephalic v.

Basilic v.

Brachial v.

Azygos v.

Suprarenal (adrenal) v.

Testicular (spermatic) v. or Ovarian v.

Median sacral v.

Pelvic diaphragm

Urethra

Internal jugular v.

Brachiocephalic v.

Accessory hemiazygos v.

Intercostal v.

Hemiazygos v.

Aortic hiatus

Renal v.

Ascending lumbar v.

Inferior vena cava

Internal iliac v.

External iliac v.

Rectum

Femoral v.

Figure 11–48. Vena cava and tributaries.

Systemic Circulation

The systemic circulation carries oxygen, nutrients, and wastes for the entire body, including the bronchial tree (nonrespiratory portion) of the lungs. All systemic arteries spring from the aorta. The aorta emerges from the superior surface of the left ventricle, passes upward beside the pulmonary artery as the *ascending aorta*, and then turns to the left as the *aortic arch*, passing over the pulmonary artery and then progressing downward as the *descending aorta* (Fig. 11–52). The descending aorta, lying close to the ver-

tebral bodies, passes through the diaphragm to the level of the fourth lumbar vertebra. It terminates by dividing into the two common iliac arteries. The descending aorta is divided into the thoracic segment (above the diaphragm) and the abdominal segment (below the diaphragm). Major arteries of the body spring from the aorta. They are described in Figures 11–61 to 11–64.

The veins emerge from the capillaries. All veins of the systemic circulation flow into either the inferior or superior vena cava, which in turn empties into the right atrium. The major veins of the body are described in Figures 11–61 to 11–64.

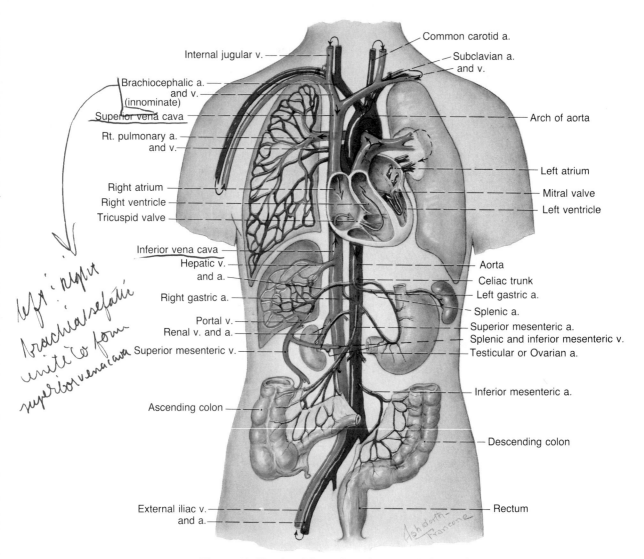

left i right
brachiacefalic
unite to form
superior vena cava

Figure 11–49. Arterial supply and venous drainage of organs.

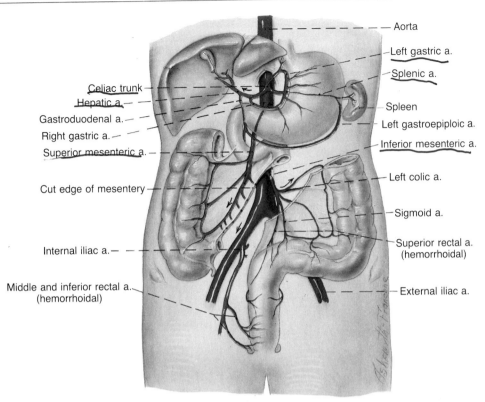

Figure 11-50. Arterial supply to the abdominal viscera.

Aorta

Left gastric a.

Splenic a.

Spleen

Left gastroepiploic a.

Inferior mesenteric a.

Left colic a.

Sigmoid a.

Superior rectal a.
(hemorrhoidal)

External iliac a.

Celiac trunk

Hepatic a.

Gastroduodenal a.

Right gastric a.

Superior mesenteric a.

Cut edge of mesentery

Internal iliac a.

Middle and inferior rectal a.
(hemorrhoidal)

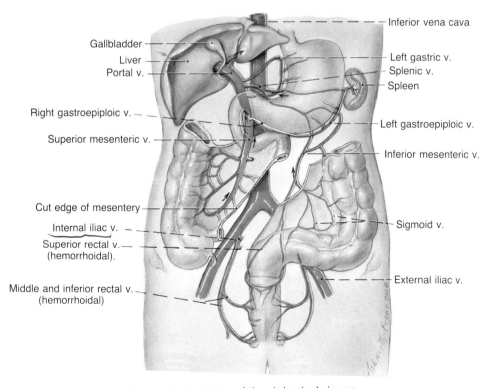

Figure 11-51. Veins of the abdominal viscera.

Inferior vena cava

Gallbladder

Liver

Portal v.

Left gastric v.

Splenic v.

Spleen

Right gastroepiploic v.

Left gastroepiploic v.

Superior mesenteric v.

Inferior mesenteric v.

Cut edge of mesentery

Internal iliac v.

Superior rectal v.
(hemorrhoidal)

Sigmoid v.

Middle and inferior rectal v.
(hemorrhoidal)

External iliac v.

Circulation Through the Liver

Blood flowing to the liver comes from the hepatic artery (20 per cent) and the hepatic portal vein (80 per cent); blood leaving the liver flows through the hepatic veins, which empty into the inferior vena cava. The hepatic arterial blood supplies oxygen requirements for the liver. The hepatic portal circuit is unique in that blood from the intestines, stomach, spleen, and pancreas first passes through the liver before entering the vena cava and going to the heart. This type of circulation, in which blood from one or more organs circulates through another before returning to the heart, is referred to in a general way as a *portal system*. Another example of this is the flow of venous blood from the hypothalamus to the neurohypophysis, or posterior pituitary gland (described in Chapter 16). Substances in the hepatic portal blood are processed by the liver; agents such as fibrinogen and prothrombin are added to the blood in the liver.

Text continued on page 421

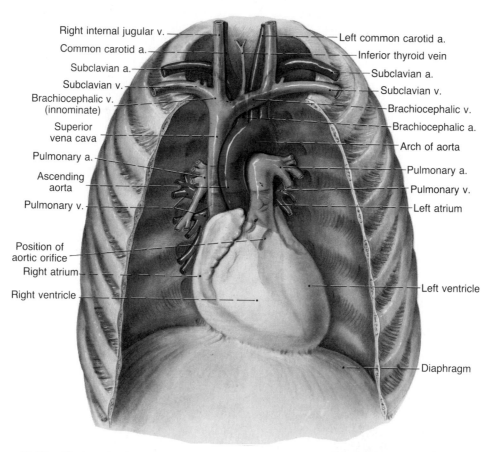

Figure 11–52. The heart in situ, showing its relation to the chest cavity and diaphragm with the major arteries and veins of the chest.

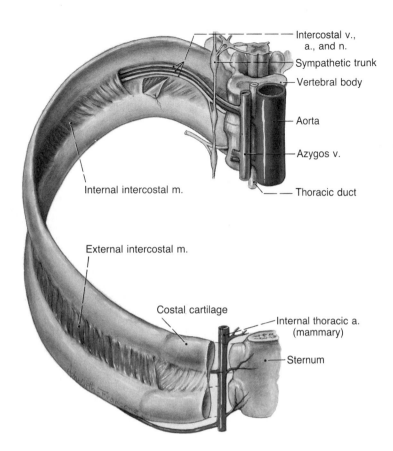

Figure 11–53. Artery, vein, and nerve supply to a rib.

Intercostal v., a., and n.

Sympathetic trunk

Vertebral body

Aorta

Azygos v.

Thoracic duct

Internal intercostal m.

External intercostal m.

Costal cartilage

Internal thoracic a. (mammary)

Sternum

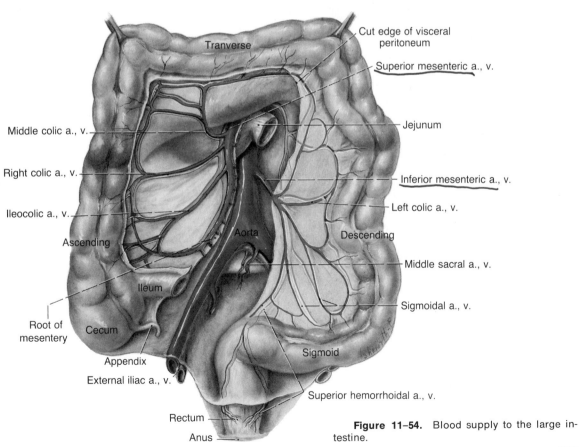

Cut edge of visceral peritoneum

Tranverse

Superior mesenteric a., v.

Middle colic a., v.

Jejunum

Right colic a., v.

Inferior mesenteric a., v.

Ileocolic a., v.

Left colic a., v.

Ascending

Aorta

Descending

Middle sacral a., v.

Ileum

Sigmoidal a., v.

Root of mesentery

Cecum

Sigmoid

Appendix

External iliac a., v.

Superior hemorrhoidal a., v.

Rectum

Anus

Figure 11–54. Blood supply to the large intestine.

413

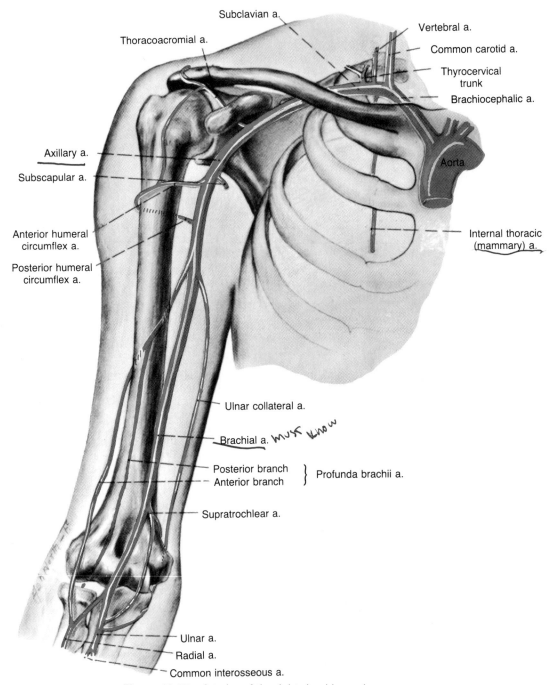

Figure 11–55. Arteries of the right shoulder and upper arm.

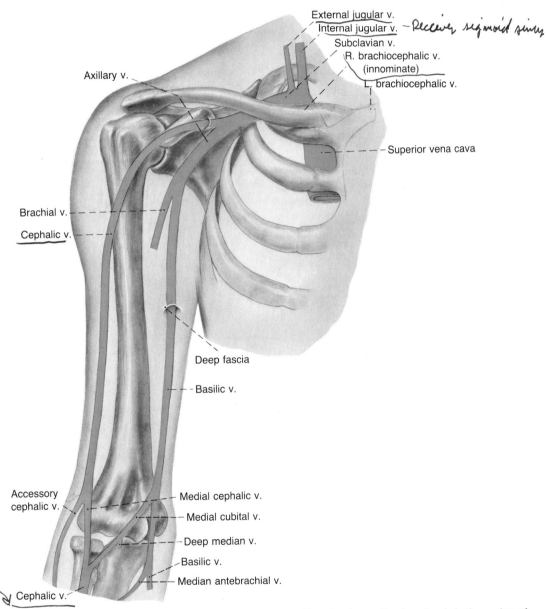

External jugular v.

Internal jugular v. — *Receives sigmoid sinus*

Subclavian v.

R. brachiocephalic v.
(innominate)

L. brachiocephalic v.

Axillary v.

Superior vena cava

Brachial v.

Cephalic v.

Deep fascia

Basilic v.

Accessory
cephalic v.

Medial cephalic v.

Medial cubital v.

Deep median v.

Basilic v.

Median antebrachial v.

*Know
where
it
empties*

Cephalic v.

Figure 11–56. Veins of the right shoulder and upper arm. The basilic vein pierces the deep fascia in the region of the middle of the arm.

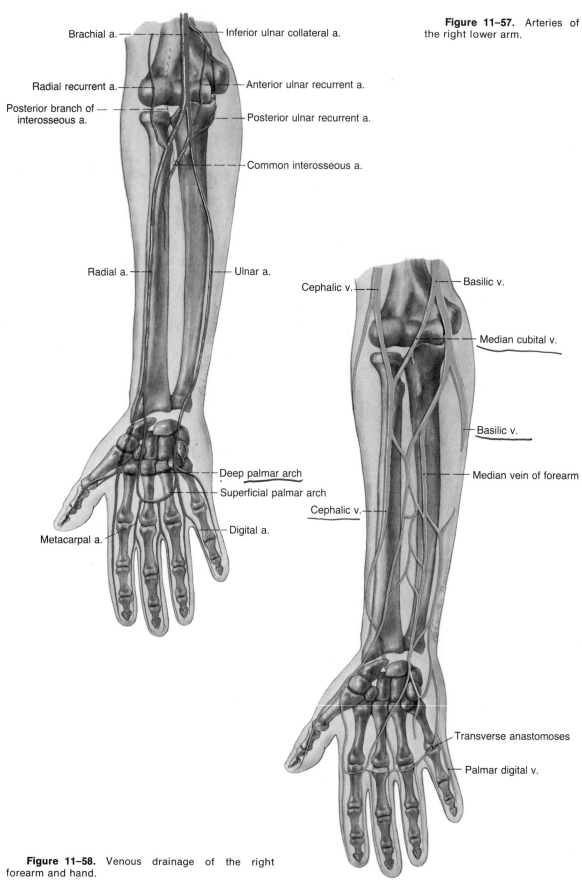

Brachial a.
Inferior ulnar collateral a.
Radial recurrent a.
Anterior ulnar recurrent a.
Posterior branch of interosseous a.
Posterior ulnar recurrent a.
Common interosseous a.
Radial a.
Ulnar a.
Deep palmar arch
Superficial palmar arch
Metacarpal a.
Digital a.

Figure 11–57. Arteries of the right lower arm.

Cephalic v.
Basilic v.
Median cubital v.
Basilic v.
Median vein of forearm
Cephalic v.
Transverse anastomoses
Palmar digital v.

Figure 11–58. Venous drainage of the right forearm and hand.

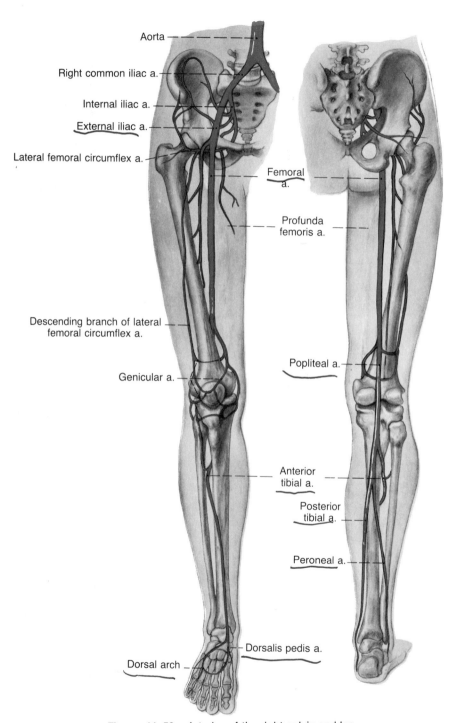

Figure 11–59. Arteries of the right pelvis and leg.

Aorta

Right common iliac a.

Internal iliac a.

External iliac a.

Lateral femoral circumflex a.

Femoral a.

Profunda femoris a.

Descending branch of lateral femoral circumflex a.

Genicular a.

Popliteal a.

Anterior tibial a.

Posterior tibial a.

Peroneal a.

Dorsalis pedis a.

Dorsal arch

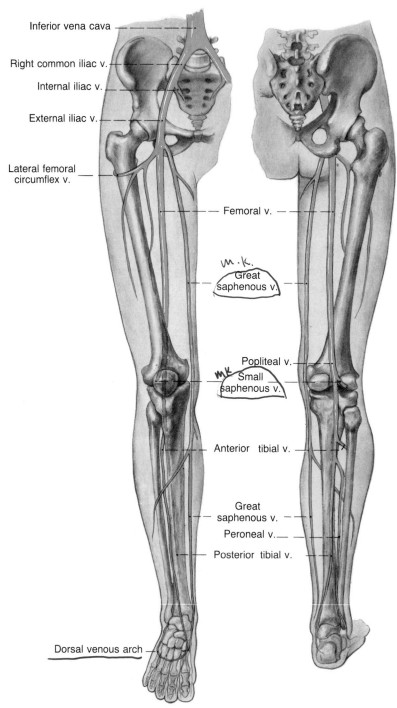

Figure 11–60. Veins of the right pelvis and leg.

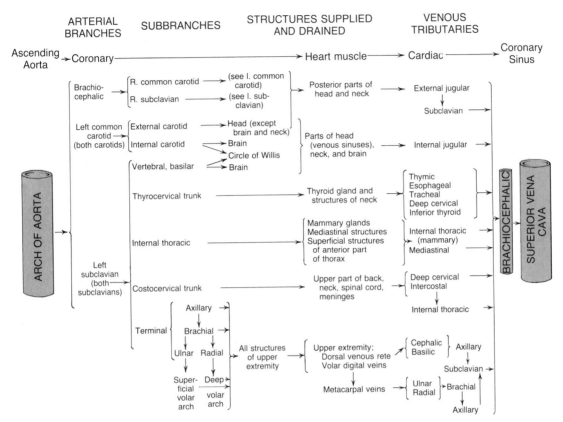

Figure 11-61. Branches of the arch of the aorta and tributaries of the superior vena cava.

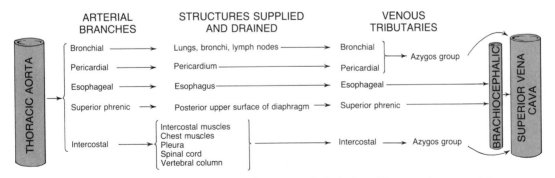

Figure 11-62. Branches of the thoracic aorta and tributaries of the superior vena cava.

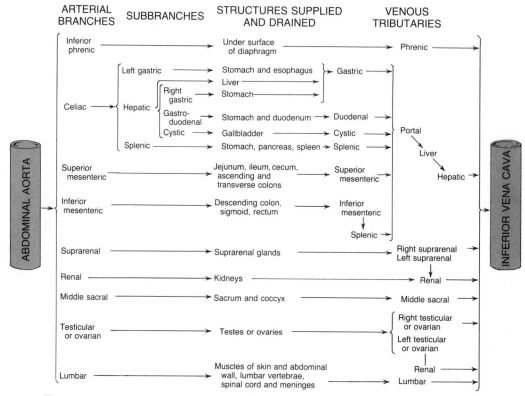

Figure 11–63. Branches of the abdominal aorta and tributaries of the inferior vena cava.

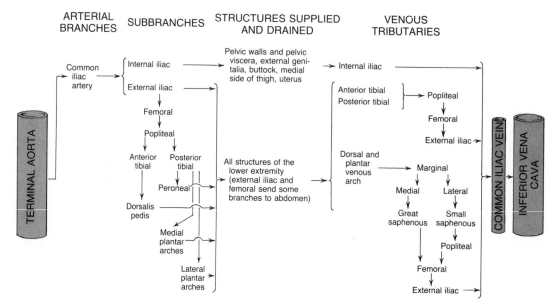

Figure 11–64. Branches of the terminal aorta and tributaries of the inferior vena cava.

Vascular Supply to the Brain (Figs. 11–66 to 11–68)

The intracranial contents receive arterial blood from the internal carotid and vertebral arteries. Venous drainage is via the cerebral veins and dural venous sinuses. The diploic and emissary veins are communications between the intracranial and extracranial venous channels.

Importance of Oxygen Supply to the Brain. It is not possible to overemphasize the importance of a constant oxygen supply to the body and especially to the brain. The nervous system actually consumes oxygen at a very slow rate. However, this consumption goes on at all times, and neural damage can occur after a few minutes of severe oxygen lack (hypoxia). In fact, temporary asphyxia at birth often causes serious damage to the brain, resulting in mental retardation and other abnormalities, such as epileptic seizures and paralysis. In a recent study of 40,000 births, feeblemindedness was found to be many times more common among children who suffered any anoxia at birth than among their siblings who had normal births.

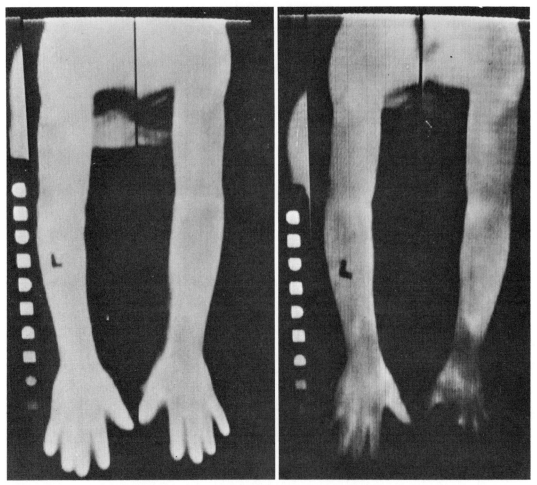

Figure 11–65. Effect of nicotine on the circulation is seen in thermograms of a man's arms before he smoked (*left*) and 15 minutes after he smoked a cigarette *(right)*. Nicotine has constricted blood vessels, reducing the amount of blood in the arms and lowering their temperature. (By permission: J. Gershon-Cohen, M.D. Previously published Scientific American, February 1967.)

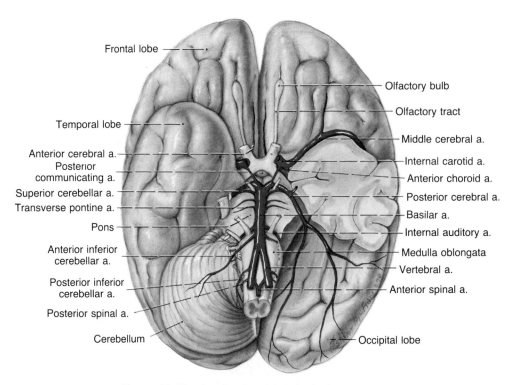

Frontal lobe

Olfactory bulb

Olfactory tract

Temporal lobe

Middle cerebral a.

Anterior cerebral a.

Internal carotid a.

Posterior communicating a.

Anterior choroid a.

Superior cerebellar a.

Posterior cerebral a.

Transverse pontine a.

Basilar a.

Pons

Internal auditory a.

Anterior inferior cerebellar a.

Medulla oblongata

Vertebral a.

Posterior inferior cerebellar a.

Anterior spinal a.

Posterior spinal a.

Cerebellum

Occipital lobe

Figure 11-66. Arteries supplying the brain, ventral view.

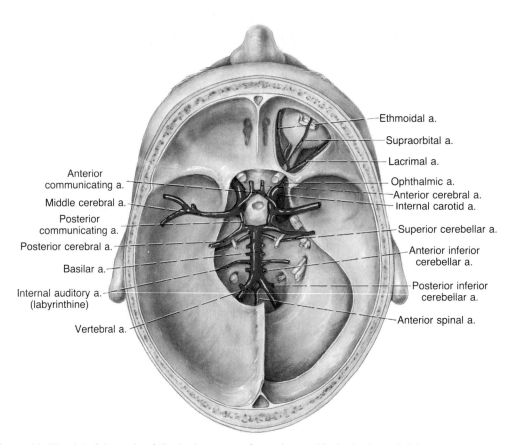

Ethmoidal a.

Supraorbital a.

Lacrimal a.

Anterior communicating a.

Ophthalmic a.

Anterior cerebral a.

Middle cerebral a.

Internal carotid a.

Posterior communicating a.

Superior cerebellar a.

Posterior cerebral a.

Anterior inferior cerebellar a.

Basilar a.

Internal auditory a. (labyrinthine)

Posterior inferior cerebellar a.

Anterior spinal a.

Vertebral a.

Figure 11-67. Arterial supply of the brain as seen from above with the brain and right tentorium cerebelli removed.

Arterial Supply. The *internal carotid arteries* arise from the common carotid arteries, which bifurcate at the level of the thyroid cartilage, enter the carotid canal in the skull, pass along the anterior border of the tympanic cavity, and turn medially to pierce the dural lining on the side of the sphenoid bone. The internal carotid artery gives origin to the ophthalmic artery and the anterior and middle cerebral arteries.

The *vertebral artery* arises from the subclavian, passes through the foramina in cervical vertebrae, perforates the dura mater between the atlas and occipital bone, and bends upward and medially in front of the medulla. Before uniting anteriorly at the lower margin of the pons to form the basilar artery, the vertebral arteries give rise to the posterior inferior cerebellar arteries. The anterior inferior cerebellar and superior cerebellar arteries arise from the basilar artery.

The *basilar artery*, in turn, bifurcates to form two posterior cerebral arteries. This system is connected to the internal carotids by the posterior communicating arteries, while the anterior communicating artery serves to join the anterior cerebral arteries. Thus, the circle of Willis, a site of aneurysms, is formed by the two posterior cerebral arteries, the two anterior cerebrals, the two internal carotid arteries, and the posterior and anterior communicating arteries.

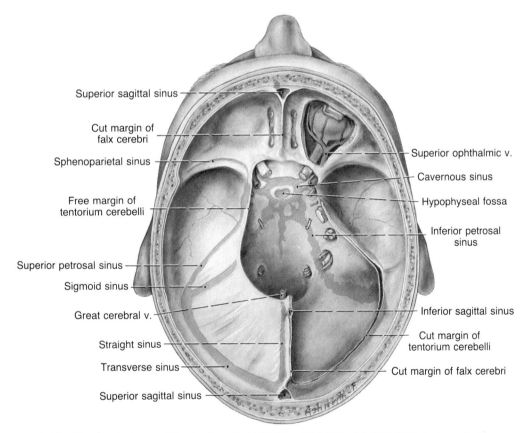

Figure 11–68. Venous drainage of the brain and meninges with brain and right tentorium cerebelli removed.

Fetal Circulation

The circulatory system of the fetus differs from that of the adult in that the lungs and alimentary canal of the fetus are nonfunctional and, therefore, receive only a minimal blood supply from the fetal heart. Another basic difference stems from the fact that the fetal heart must pump relatively large amounts of deoxygenated blood back to the placenta, from which it originally receives oxygenated blood. The primary features dis-

tinguishing fetal from adult circulation can be seen in Table 11–7 and Figures 11–69 and 11–70.

The oxygenated blood from the placenta enters the fetus by way of the umbilical vein. It then passes through the ductus venosus into the inferior vena cava, mainly bypassing the liver. From the inferior vena cava, the blood enters the right atrium of the beating fetal heart. At this point about two-thirds of this oxygenated (placental) blood is deflected directly into the left atrium, passing through

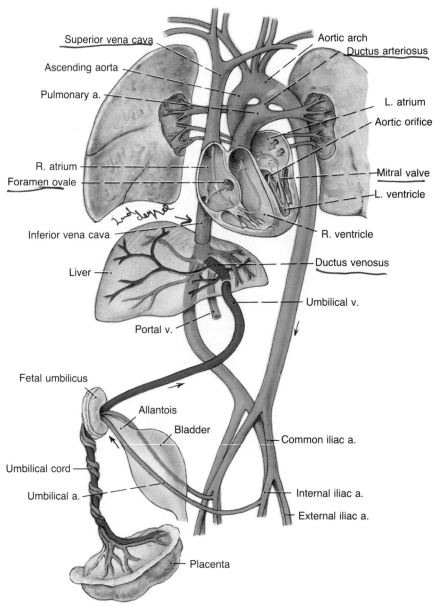

Figure 11–69. Circulatory system of the fetus. (For comparison with adult circulation, see Figure 11–70.)

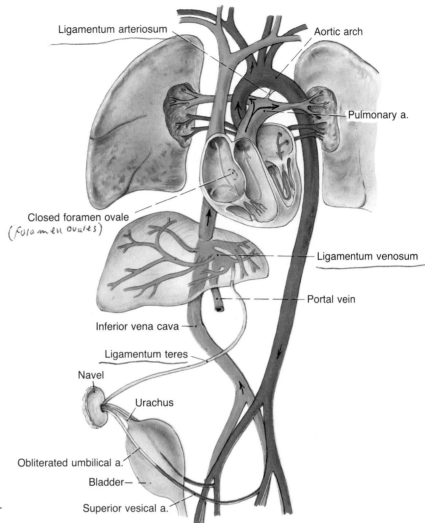

Ligamentum arteriosum

Aortic arch

Pulmonary a.

Closed foramen ovale
(*Foramen ovales*)

Ligamentum venosum

Portal vein

Inferior vena cava

Ligamentum teres

Navel

Urachus

Obliterated umbilical a.

Bladder

Superior vesical a.

Figure 11–70. Adult circulation.

What could be improved upon?

Table 11–7 DIFFERENCES IN ADULT AND FETAL CIRCULATION

STRUCTURE	FUNCTION IN FETUS	FUNCTION IN ADULT
Two umbilical Arteries Umbilical artery	Joins fetus to placenta	Atrophies to become the lateral umbilical ligament
Umbilical vein	*Joins Placenta to fetus* Joins fetus to placenta	Becomes the round ligament of the liver (ligamentum teres)
Ductus venosus	Vessel connecting the umbilical vein to the inferior vena cava	Becomes a fibrous cord (ligamentum venosum) embedded in the wall of the liver
Foramen ovale	An opening between the two atria	Closes shortly after birth
Ductus arteriosus	Blood vessel connecting the pulmonary artery with the aorta	Closes and atrophies after birth, becoming the ligamentum arteriosum

the foramen ovale. This portion of the oxygenated blood, which has been deflected directly to the left side of the heart, bypassing the right side, moves then from the left atrium into the left ventricle, is pumped out the aorta, and is channeled primarily to the head and upper extremities.

The remaining original oxygenated blood in the right atrium is mixed with the deoxygenated blood returning through the superior vena cava from the head and upper extremities. This mixture is primarily deflected into the right ventricle. From the right ventricle this blood is pumped out into the large pulmonary artery. A small portion of the blood circulates through the lungs. The largest portion, however, flows through the ductus arteriosus into the aorta. It enters the aorta distal to the point at which the blood to the head leaves. This basically independent stream of blood from the right ventricle then moves down the descending branch of the aorta. Some of the blood supplies the lower areas of the body. The remainder returns to the placenta via the umbilical arteries.

At birth, changes are the result of inflation of the lungs, permitting routing of the blood through the pulmonary system instead of the umbilical vessels. The changes are described in Table 11–7.

SUMMARY

THE CIRCULATORY SYSTEM

Blood

1. Composed of plasma and cells—red blood cells, white blood cells, and platelets.

2. Blood cell formation (hematopoiesis) in the adult occurs in the red bone marrow, located principally in the skull, vertebrae, ribs, sternum, and pelvis. All blood cells originate from undifferentiated cells called stem cells.

3. Red Blood Cells

   a. Function in the transport of respiratory gases (oxygen and carbon dioxide). Almost all of the oxygen in the blood is carried by hemoglobin.
   b. Production is under the control of erythropoietin, a substance formed in the blood by the action of an enzyme released principally by the kidney called renal erythropoietic factor.
   c. Life span is about 80 to 120 days. Aged cells are destroyed principally in the spleen. Their destruction gives rise to the bile pigment bilirubin.
   d. A decrease in red blood cells or their oxygen transport capacity results in anemia. It is most commonly caused by
      (1) A decrease in the rate of formation of red blood cells (as in pernicious anemia)
      (2) Insufficient hemoglobin synthesis (as in iron deficiency anemia)
      (3) Increased rate of destruction of red blood cells (as in sickle cell anemia)

4. White Blood Cells (Leukocytes)

   a. Three general types: granulocytes, lymphocytes, and monocytes.
   b. Neutrophils, the most numerous granulocytes, are phagocytic; the granules are lysosomes.
   c. Lymphocytes function in the immune response.
   d. Monocytes become transformed into macrophages at sites of infection.

5. Platelets (Thrombocytes)

   Cytoplasmic fragments of megakaryocytes; essential for normal blood clotting.

6. Blood Coagulation (Clotting)

   a. In the initial phase, platelets clump and fuse to form a temporary seal at the site of injury.
   b. Retraction of platelet pseudopods with enmeshed fibrin produces a hard clot.
   c. Thrombin promotes clumping of platelets and functions as an enzyme, converting fibrinogen, a soluble protein, into thrombin monomers, which assemble into insoluble fibrin threads.
   d. Active thrombin is formed from an inactive precursor, prothrombin, by the action of prothrombin activator.
   e. Two pathways, extrinsic and intrinsic, lead to the formation of prothrombin activator.

7. Blood Grouping

   a. ABO series
      (1) Blood types A, B, AB, and O are named for the antigens contained in the red blood cells.

(2) Type O individuals have no antigens and are, therefore, universal blood donors.

(3) Type AB individuals, with antigens A and B, are universal blood recipients.

b. Rh factor: Problem arises if offspring of an Rh negative mother is Rh positive and, at the time of delivery, infant's blood enters the blood stream of the mother. Antibodies produced by mother could cause hemolytic anemia in subsequent Rh positive fetus or the infant might be born dead.

Divisions of the Circulatory System

The circulatory system consists of (1) the heart, a muscular pump with two receiving and two pumping chambers, and (2) two closed circuits, the pulmonary circulation, carrying blood from the right ventricle to the respiratory surfaces of the lungs and back to the left atrium, and the systemic circulation, carrying blood from the left ventricle to the remaining parts of the body and back to the right atrium.

Structure of the Heart

1. Pericardium

Fibroserous sac enclosing heart. Pericardial fluid between parietal pericardium (lining fibrous pericardial coat) and visceral pericardium (lining heart) lubricates membranes.

2. Wall

a. Epicardium (external), the visceral pericardium
b. Myocardium (middle), the cardiac muscle
c. Endocardium (inner), the endothelium

3. Chambers

a. Right and left atria (receiving chambers)
b. Right and left ventricles (pumping chambers)

4. Valves

a. Atrioventricular (bicuspid, left; tricuspid, right) open from atria into ventricles
b. Semilunar (pulmonary and aortic) open from ventricles into pulmonary artery and aorta

5. Blood Supply

a. Right and left coronary arteries (first branches of aorta)
b. Drained principally by coronary sinus into right atrium

Cardiac Cycle

1. **Rhythmic cycle of contraction (systole) and relaxation (diastole).**

2. **During systole, when ventricular pressure rises above aortic and pulmonary pressure, blood is ejected from ventricles; during diastole, when ventricular pressure falls below atrial pressure, blood flows into the ventricles.**

3. **The interval between the first and second heart sounds is an approximate measure of length of systole (ordinarily half as long as diastole).**

   a. First sound (low pitch) associated with closure of atrioventricular valves
   b. Second (higher pitch) associated with closure of semilunar valves

Cardiac Output

1. **Stroke volume (volume ejected per beat) times beats per minute is called cardiac output. Under resting conditions it is approximately 5 liters per minute.**

2. **As venous return increases, stretched cardiac muscle fibers contract more forcefully, enabling the heart to effectively eject a larger volume of blood.**

3. **Increasing the heart rate with no increase in venous return has limited effect on cardiac output because shortened diastole reduces filling of ventricles.**

The Heartbeat

1. **The heart is intrinsically rhythmic — it beats when isolated from its nerve supply.**

2. **The generation and spread of electrical impulses responsible for the heartbeat is the function of specialized neuromuscular tissue: the SA node, AV node, and Purkinje system.**

   a. The beat arises in the SA node (pacemaker)
   b. The impulse spreads through the atria, initiating their contraction, to the AV node

c. The Purkinje system, arising from the AV node, distributes the impulse to all parts of the ventricles, initiating ventricular muscle excitation and contraction

3. **The electrocardiogram is a record of the spread of electrical activity through the muscle of the heart.**

   a. The P wave registers excitation of the atria, the QRS complex, the spread of activity through the ventricles
   b. The T wave records the recovery in the ventricles

4. **Innervation of the SA node by the autonomic nervous system makes possible homeostatic regulation of the heart rate. Parasympathetic (vagus nerve) stimulation decreases, sympathetic stimulation increases, the heart rate.**

Structure of the Walls of Blood Vessels

1. **Arteries**

   a. Tunica intima — endothelium on luminal surface; bounded externally by elastic lamina; small number of smooth muscle cells and connective tissue matrix components in between
   b. Tunica media — smooth muscle intermingled with elastic fibers and connective tissue matrix components, elastic fibers predominating in large arteries, smooth muscle in smaller arteries
   c. Tunica adventitia — fibroelastic connective tissue

2. **Arterioles**

   a. Tunica intima — endothelial lining bounded by patches of elastic fibers which become scantier as the arterioles become smaller, disappearing in the smallest
   b. Tunica media — a few layers of spiraling smooth muscle cells, reduced to a single layer in the smallest arterioles
   c. Tunica adventitia — relatively thin

3. **Capillaries—thin endothelial tubes.**

4. **Venules—endothelium surrounded by collagenous tissue and, in larger venules, by smooth muscle fibers as well**

5. **Veins—three coats similar to those of arteries, but much thinner, and valves which open toward the heart and prevent backflow when closed.**

6. **Arteries and arterioles conduct blood from the heart to capillaries, where nutrients pass to the tissues and wastes to the blood; venules and veins carry blood from the capillaries to the heart.**

Blood Pressure

1. **Usually expressed as the ratio of systolic pressure in mm Hg to diastolic pressure in mm Hg. Average normal ratio is 120/80. Hypertension usually defined as ratio exceeding 160/95.**

2. **Increasing cardiac output and/or peripheral resistance (resistance of blood flow through the arterioles) increases average arterial pressure and vice versa. Peripheral resistance is altered by constriction or dilatation of arterioles.**

3. **Expansion of elastic walls of arteries reduces buildup of systolic pressure; elastic recoil of arteries prevents excessive fall in diastolic pressure.**

4. **The major centers for regulating peripheral resistance and the rate and force of contraction of the heart are the vasomotor and cardiac centers of the medulla.**

   a. The vasomotor center consists of a "pressor area" and a "depressor area" — electrical stimulation of the former causes vasoconstriction; of the latter, vasodilation by inhibition of vasoconstriction. Spontaneous activity of the vasomotor center maintains a partial state of contraction of vascular smooth muscle (the vasomotor tone) by acting through the sympathetic division of the autonomic nervous system. This tone can be increased or decreased by a variety of inputs to the center.
   b. The heart is regulated by reciprocal variations in the activity of two cardiac centers: the cardioinhibitor center (parasympathetic) and cardioaccelerator center (sympathetic).
   c. A fundamental regulatory mechanism mediated by the vasomotor and cardiac centers is the baroreceptor reflex, involving receptors sensitive to stretch in the aortic arch and carotid sinuses. A rise in blood pressure, increasing the rate of impulses from the baroreceptors to the medullary centers, causes vasodilation in the abdominal region, skin, and skeletal muscles, lowering blood

pressure; a fall in pressure has the reverse effect. Changes in heart rate (a rise in pressure decreasing it, a fall in pressure increasing it) also occur. Oxygen deficiency triggers the chemoreceptor reflex. These receptors are located in the aortic and carotid bodies, and the response, vasoconstriction by action on the vasomotor center, raises blood pressure. Ischemia in the brain (which increases the concentration of carbon dioxide) excites the vasomotor center and induces intense vasoconstriction and a rise in blood pressure (so-called CNS ischemic response). The baroreceptor reflex is most active in the normal range of blood pressure. The chemoreceptor and CNS ischemic responses are activated at below-normal pressures.

REVIEW QUESTIONS

1. Briefly describe the functions of red blood cells, white blood cells, and platelets.
2. How is the production of red blood cells regulated?
3. Describe three types of anemia.
4. In what way do the intrinsic and extrinsic pathways of blood clotting differ? In what way are they the same?
5. Explain the danger of an Rh negative mother giving birth to an Rh positive baby.
6. Distinguish between the pulmonary and systemic circuits of the circulation.
7. Describe the structure of the walls of the heart.
8. Explain the functions of the heart valves.
9. Briefly describe the phases of the cardiac cycle.
10. What does the neuromuscular tissue of the heart consist of? What is its function?
11. Name and explain the origin of each of the waves of an electrocardiogram.
12. Outline the principal structural features of arteries, arterioles, metacapillaries, capillaries, venules, and veins.
13. Describe and explain the importance of the vasomotor and cardiac centers of the medulla.
14. Describe each of the following: the baroreceptor reflex, the chemoreceptor reflex, and the CNS ischemic response.
15. Briefly discuss the cardiovascular changes that occur in anticipation of and during exercise. Distinguish between those changes that involve the vasomotor center and those that do not.

12
The Lymphatic System

Objectives

The aim of this chapter is to enable the student to:

- [ ] List the components of the lymphatic system.
- [ ] Follow the course of lymph from the intercellular space to the blood stream.
- [ ] Explain the functions of the lymphatic system.
- [ ] Describe the organs related to the lymphatic system.
- [ ] Distinguish between the B cell and T cell immune systems.

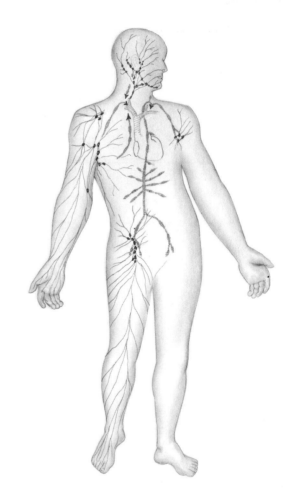

COMPONENTS OF THE LYMPHATIC SYSTEM

Originating in the tissue spaces of the body is an entirely separate vessel system serving as an accessory system for the flow of fluid from tissue spaces into the circulation. This is called the *lymphatic system*.

The lymphatic system consists of lymph capillaries, lymphatic vessels, lymphatic ducts, and lymph nodes. Lymph capillaries originate as microscopic blind ends and converge to form larger and larger vessels, which drain into two main trunks, the *thoracic duct*, which empties into the left subclavian vein at its junction with the internal jugular vein, and the *right lymphatic duct*, which empties into the right subclavian vein at its junction with the right internal jugular vein (Fig. 12–1). Lymph nodes, situated at intervals in the course of the lymphatic vessels, are especially numerous along the main tributaries that empty into the thoracic duct or right lymphatic duct.

The fluid in the lymphatic vessels is called **lymph** (L. *lympha*, water). Its composition is similar to that of plasma, except for the low concentration of proteins. Lymph contains large numbers of white cells, particularly lymphocytes. It is generally a clear liquid, but lymph from the small intestine becomes milky after a meal. The milky appearance results from the presence of chylomicrons, spherical particles manufactured from digested lipids (see Chapter 14). Such lipid-laden lymph is called *chyle*.

FUNCTIONS OF THE LYMPHATIC SYSTEM

The lymphatic system has three main functions:
1. *Conservation of plasma proteins and fluid*. The lymph circulation returns to the blood stream vital substances, chiefly proteins, that have leaked out of the capillaries along with accumulated interstitial fluid.
2. *Defense against disease*. The lymphatic system protects the body against disease-producing microorganisms and other invading foreign substances in two ways:
   a. By *phagocytosis*. Macrophages lining the channels (sinuses) of lymph nodes phagocytize and digest foreign matter.
   b. By the *immune response*. Two types of lymphocytes in lymph nodes proliferate in response to contact with foreign substances, giving rise to specialized cells that manufacture antibodies or to cells that inactivate the invading agent by other means. (The immune response is described in a separate section at the end of this chapter.)
3. *Lipid absorption*. Intestinal lymphatics are the pathways for the absorption of digested lipids from the alimentary canal.

LYMPHATICS

Lymph Capillaries. Lymph capillaries, the smallest conducting vessels of the lymphatic system, are thin-walled tubes composed of a single layer of overlapping endothelial cells attached by anchoring filaments to the surrounding connective tissue. The interior overlapping edges of the cells seem to act as valves, forming openings into the capillaries through which fluid can enter and, when closed by backflow, preventing outflow.

Lymph Vessels. Lymph vessels, into which the lymph capillaries drain, have three-layered walls similar to the walls of veins, and valves, more numerous than in veins, which permit lymph to flow in only one direction. These valves give lymph vessels a characteristic beaded appearance.

Lymph is propelled along lymph vessels by the massaging action of skeletal muscles on the vessels, pressure changes secondary to breathing (decreasing in the thorax and increasing in the abdomen during inspiration), and the contraction of stretched smooth muscle of the vessel walls, providing an intrinsic pumping mechanism. Each segment of a vessel between valves functions as an independent pump as it stretches upon filling and contracts to force lymph forward into the next section, which in turn contracts. Other factors contributing to the flow of lymph include the continuous formation of new lymph pushing old lymph forward and the pulsations of arteries.

Thoracic Duct. The thoracic duct, the largest lymph vessel in the body, is the common trunk of all the lymph vessels of the body except those of the upper surface of the

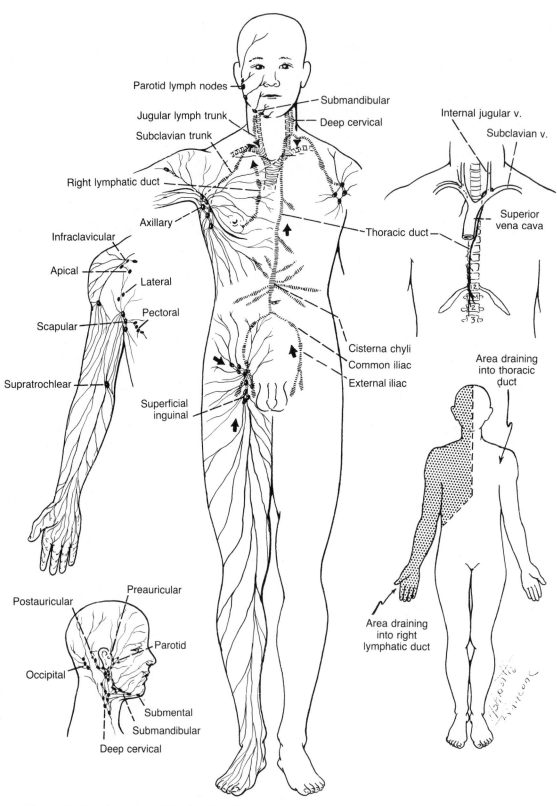

Parotid lymph nodes

Jugular lymph trunk

Subclavian trunk

Right lymphatic duct

Axillary

Infraclavicular

Apical

Lateral

Pectoral

Scapular

Supratrochlear

Superficial inguinal

Submandibular

Deep cervical

Internal jugular v.

Subclavian v.

Superior vena cava

Thoracic duct

Cisterna chyli

Common iliac

External iliac

Area draining into thoracic duct

Area draining into right lymphatic duct

Postauricular

Preauricular

Parotid

Occipital

Submental

Submandibular

Deep cervical

|||||||||| Deep collecting channels and their lymph nodes

Superficial collecting channels and their lymph nodes

Figure 12–1. The lymphatic system and drainage.

432

right lobe of the liver, the right lung and pleura, the right side of the heart, the right arm, and the right side of the head, neck, and thorax. It originates in the abdomen at the upper end of the *cisterna chyli*, an elongated sac located in the right lumbar region of the abdominal cavity under the diaphragm. The cisterna is a receiving area for lymph from the right lumbar, left lumbar, and intestinal trunks. The right and left lumbar trunks convey lymph from the lower extremities, testes or ovaries, walls and viscera of the pelvis, kidneys, suprarenal glands, and deep lymphatics of the abdominal walls. The intestinal trunks carry lymph from the stomach, spleen, pancreas, a major portion of the liver, and the intestine. The thoracic duct ascends to the right side of the lower thoracic vertebral bodies. It is located between the thoracic aorta and the azygos vein. At the level of the aortic arch, the thoracic duct crosses obliquely to the left and continues superiorly, lying to the left side of the esophagus. The thoracic duct arches laterally behind the left carotid sheath at the root of the neck and enters the left subclavian vein at its junction with the left internal jugular vein.

Right Lymphatic Duct. The right lymphatic duct is a vessel one-half inch in length lying on the scalenus anterior muscle. It joins the right subclavian vein at its junction with the right internal jugular vein. The right lymphatic duct returns lymph from the upper surface of the right lobe of the liver, the right lung and pleura, the right side of the heart, the right arm, and the right side of the head, neck, and thorax.

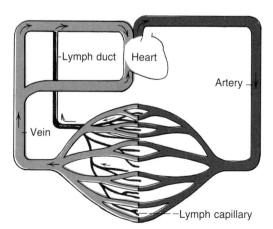

Figure 12–2. Diagrammatic representation of lymphatic system, showing its relationship to the circulatory system.

IMPORTANCE OF LYMPH FLOW

It has been estimated from studies in dogs with radioactively labeled plasma proteins that in one day 50 per cent or more of the total plasma protein is lost from the capillaries and returned to the blood stream by the lymphatic circulation. Furthermore, the amount of fluid filtered from the capillaries is greater than the amount reabsorbed. Inadequate lymph drainage can lead to an excessive accumulation of fluid in the interstitial space, a condition called edema. Some **lymphedemas** (edemas resulting from deficient lymph drainage) can cause gross disfiguring. An example is *elephantiasis*, a specific lymphedema resulting from blockage of lymph vessels. In a form of elephantiasis common in the tropics, the blockage follows invasion by a parasitic roundworm (filaria).

LYMPH NODES

Lymph nodes are small, oval bodies found at intervals in the course of the lymphatic vessels. Each node consists of lymphatic tissue enclosed in a fibrous connective tissue capsule (Fig. 12–3). Extensions of the capsule, called *trabeculae*, project into the interior of the node. On one side of the node there is a depression, called the *hilum*, where blood vessels enter and leave. The outer region, or *cortex*, of the node is characterized by the presence of densely packed lymphocytes, generally forming isolated masses called nodules. These nodules constitute colonies which during active periods have distinct central areas (germinal centers), appearing lighter in stained sections, that contain rapidly dividing cells. The number of nodules varies in accordance with the level of antigenic stimulation (see the description of the immune response at the end of this chapter). In the *medulla* of the node — the inner region and area around the hilum — the lymphocytes are more loosely arranged, forming irregularly branched strands (cords).

Lymph passes through several groups of nodes before entering the blood. It enters the nodes through several afferent vessels at different points on the periphery, passes through a system of channels, called sinuses (first through cortical sinuses and then through medullary sinuses), and leaves through one or two efferent channels at the

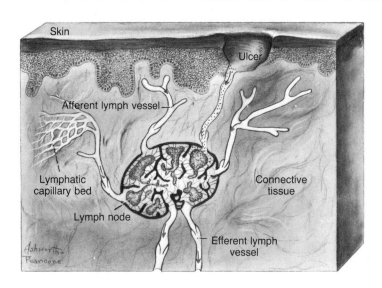

Figure 12–3. Diagrammatic drawing of a lymph node in the area of an infected ulcer.

hilum. As mentioned, the sinuses, lined with macrophages, act as filtering beds for removing potentially harmful matter before it can enter the blood stream. Functioning in this way, the lymph nodes are part of the **reticuloendothelial system** (see Chapter 4, page 88).

Lymph nodes usually appear in groups, among which are the following: (1) *deep cervical*, which lie along the carotid sheath (fascia enclosing the common carotid artery, jugular vein, and vagus nerve) and drain lymph from all of the vessels of the head and neck (either directly or after passage through outlying groups of lymph nodes); (2) *axillary*, in the armpits, which receive all of the lymph directly or indirectly from the upper extremities, as well as (directly or indirectly) lymph from the mammary glands and the skin and muscles of the chest, back, and lower part of the back of the neck; (3) *tracheobronchial*, which are grouped around the thoracic part of the trachea and the bronchi, include some of the largest nodes in the body, and drain the lungs and heart; (4) *preaortic*, lying directly anterior to the abdominal aorta, which receive lymph from outlying groups of nodes draining the gastrointestinal tract, liver, pancreas, and spleen, including the more than 100 lymph nodes of the mesentery (a fold of peritoneum attaching the intestine to the posterior abdominal wall); and (5) *inguinal*, in the groin, which receive (directly or indirectly) most of the lymph from the lower extremities, the external genitalia, and anterior abdominal wall.

CLINICAL CONSIDERATIONS

Lymph nodes filter products resulting from bacterial and nonbacterial inflammation and prevent the products from entering the general circulation. This process often produces tenderness and swelling in nodes of an infected area. If bacteria in an area drained by a node become too numerous, they may attack the node itself, resulting in an abscess (a localized collection of pus in a cavity formed when tissue disintegrates).

Lymphangitis is an inflammation of a lymphatic vessel in which narrow red streaks may be seen in the skin extending from the infected area to the draining group of lymph nodes. These streaks represent inflamed subcutaneous lymph vessels.

Lymph node enlargement may be local or widespread and may be accompanied by signs of acute inflammation, including heat and tenderness. As a result of inflammation, nodes may fuse with one another instead of remaining discrete. Causes of lymph node enlargement include infection, allergy, leukemia, lymphomas (tumors of lymphoid tissue, such as Hodgkin's disease, one of the most common cancers of the lymph nodes), and spread of malignancy from elsewhere in the body.

One feature of the lymphatic system is its significance in the spread of tumors. Carcinoma, cancer arising in epithelial tissues, occasionally produces a secondary growth in regional lymph nodes. Many of these secondary growths (metastases) result from tumor emboli detaching from the point of origin and lodging in nodes of the lymphatic vessels. In general, if the tumor has reached the lymph nodes at the time of surgery, the outlook for survival of the patient is less favorable.

RELATED ORGANS

Three organs closely related to the lymphatic system are the spleen, tonsils, and thymus. All of these organs are composed largely of lymphoid tissue, a specialized form of connective tissue characterized by a framework of reticular tissue (see Chapter 4, page 87) and the presence of lymphocytes.

Spleen

Location and Structure. The spleen is a soft, vascular, oval body, 5 inches long and 3 inches wide, weighing approximately 7 ounces. It lies in the left upper abdomen beneath the diaphragm and behind the lower ribs and costal cartilages (Fig. 12–4).

The splenic hilum is the site of entrance and exit of the vessels of the spleen. The body of the spleen has a covering, called the capsule, consisting of fibroelastic tissue and occasional smooth muscle cells. The capsule is almost completely surrounded by peritoneum, which forms its outer (serous) coat. Extensions of the capsule, the trabeculae, pass into the interior and divide the organ into a number of incomplete compartments. The splenic tissue, or pulp, is of two kinds — *white pulp* and *red pulp*. White pulp consists of lymphoid tissue that forms a sheath around arterioles supplying the compartments. Here and there dense accumulations of lymphocytes along the sheaths form nodules which, as in lymph nodes, may show active germinal centers. The red pulp consists of numerous venous sinuses separating networks of reticular tissue. From birth to early adulthood, the white pulp forms the greater part of the spleen. Thereafter, the white pulp progressively atrophies and the red pulp becomes the predominant tissue.

Functions. The spleen has four major functions.

1. *Blood destruction.* Old red blood cells, having reached their normal life span of approximately 120 days, are destroyed in all parts of the reticuloendothelial system, including the lymph nodes and spleen. The spleen, however, is the major site of erythrocyte destruction.

2. *Immunologic function.* The spleen, along with other lymphoid tissues, participates in the immune response (described in the following section).

3. *Blood storage.* The spleen serves as a reservoir for blood or, more specifically, for red blood cells, as most of the plasma is returned to the circulation, whereas RBC are enmeshed in the splenic pulp. Marked contraction of the spleen occurs during muscular exercise, thereby releasing RBC to aid in oxygen transport to active muscles. The spleen undergoes rhythmic variations in size in response to physiologic demands, such as exercise and hemorrhage, and thus influences the volume of circulating blood. The elastic nature of the spleen's framework allows the spleen to vary its size considerably, an increase in blood expanding it, elas-

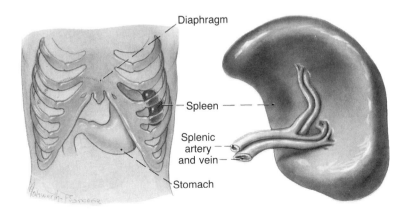

Figure 12–4. The spleen and its relation to the stomach and rib cage.

Diaphragm

Spleen

Splenic artery and vein

Stomach

tic recoil contracting it. The volume of stored blood may vary from 1000 to as little as 50 ml.

4. *Blood filtration.* The spleen, serving as a part of the body's reticuloendothelial defense mechanism, filters microorganisms from the blood.

An individual can survive with no apparent disability if the spleen has been removed; however, diseases affecting the spleen may profoundly affect several important body functions.

Tonsils

Several groups of tonsils, forming a ring of lymphoid tissue, guard the entrance of the alimentary and respiratory tracts from invasion by microorganisms. The components of this ring are the palatine tonsils, nasopharyngeal tonsil (adenoids), and lingual tonsil (Figs. 12–5 and 12–6). The lymphoid tissue of the tonsils is arranged in nodules, which may have germinal centers.

The **palatine tonsils,** known more commonly as the "tonsils," are two oval masses of lymphoid tissue, each attached to the side wall of the throat between the palatoglossal arch (mucus-covered projection of the palatoglossus muscle extending from the soft palate to the tongue) and the palatopharyngeal arch (mucus-covered projection of the pala-

topharyngeus muscle extending from the soft palate to the pharynx). The tonsils are larger in children than in adults.

The **nasopharyngeal tonsil,** or **adenoids,** is a mass of lymphoid tissue located in the nasal pharynx extending from the roof of the nasal pharynx to the free edge of the soft palate (Fig. 12–6).

The **lingual tonsil** is an accumulation of lymphoid tissue found on the dorsum of the tongue posterior to the vallate papillae (Fig. 12–6; see also Fig. 14–5).

Chronic infection of the tonsils is not so common as was once suspected. The term "chronic tonsillitis" is frequently misused to indicate any type of sore throat occurring when the tonsils are still present. With tonsillitis, enlargement and tenderness of the anterior cervical lymph nodes are common. The tonsils may be enlarged and red or covered with pus. If both tonsils and adenoids are infected, the lymph nodes of the posterior triangle of the neck enlarge.

Fewer tonsillectomies and adenoidectomies are being performed today than were done 40 years ago. This is because recent knowledge indicates that removal of tonsils and adenoids may not significantly lower the incidence of upper respiratory infection unless the tonsils themselves have been infected. Tonsils may also be important in the development of immune bodies; however, true recurrent infection of the tonsils is still an indication for their removal by operation.

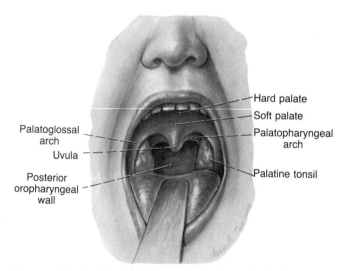

Figure 12–5. Relationship of tongue, uvula, and palatine tonsils.

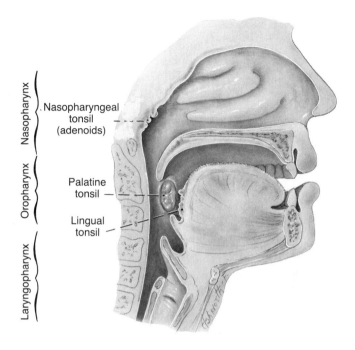

Nasopharynx

Oropharynx

Laryngopharynx

Nasopharyngeal tonsil (adenoids)

Palatine tonsil

Lingual tonsil

Figure 12-6. The nasopharyngeal tonsil extends from the roof of the nasal pharynx to the free edge of the soft palate; the palatine tonsils are attached to the side walls of the back of the mouth between the anterior and posterior pillars; the lingual tonsils are located on the dorsum of the tongue from the vallate papillae of the tongue to the epiglottis.

Thymus

The thymus is a flat, pinkish-gray, two-lobed organ lying high in the chest anterior to the aorta and posterior to the sternum (Fig. 12–7). In the thymus the lymphoid tissue is not arranged in nodules.

This organ plays a critical role in the development of part of the immune system (see below). It is relatively large in relation to body size during fetal life and the first two years after birth. It increases in size until puberty and then begins to atrophy.

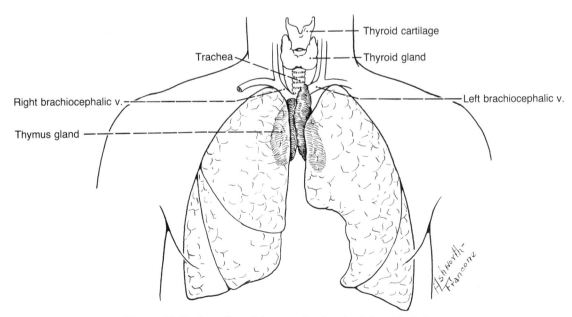

Thyroid cartilage

Thyroid gland

Trachea

Right brachiocephalic v.

Left brachiocephalic v.

Thymus gland

Figure 12-7. Location of thymus gland and relationship to lungs.

THE IMMUNE RESPONSE

The immune response not only resists invasion by infectious microorganisms but also functions to identify and destroy whatever can be described as "nonself," including transplanted organs and malignant cells. Two immune systems can be distinguished; in each a different population of lymphocytes is activated and a different agent combats the invasion. In one, the **B cell system,** the response is mediated by proteins called **antibodies;** in the other, the **T cell system,** the response is mediated by **specialized cells** sensitized to foreign substances. The former response is called *humoral immunity*, the latter *cellular* or *cell-mediated immunity*. The B cell system is most effective against acute bacterial infections, such as those caused by streptococci, pneumococci, some influenza bacilli, and meningococci. The T cell system is most active in combating chronic bacterial infections, such as tuberculosis, as well as fungi and some viruses. Cell-mediated immunity is also especially active against malignant cells and the cells of transplanted organs.

B and T lymphocytes have a common parent cell, namely, the *stem cell* of the red bone marrow (see Chapter 11, page 357). T cells are so named because they are dependent upon the *thymus gland* for their differentiation, that is, transformation from precursors to mature T cells. Newborn mice surgically deprived of a thymus have a deficiency in cell-mediated immunity; most will, for example, accept skin grafts from mice of other strains that would be quickly rejected by normal mice. A mutant strain of mice lacking a thymus (hairless, so-called "nude" mice) do not form T cells but manufacture antibodies. Likewise, children born without a thymus lack a T cell system but have a fairly normal B cell system (DiGeorge syndrome). It has been postulated on the basis of these and other observations that during the period in which the immune system is taking form — mainly before and shortly after birth — forerunners of T cells pass from the bone marrow to the thymus, where they develop into mature T cells which then migrate to other lymphoid organs. Some investigators believe that B cell differentiation occurs in a presently unknown site equivalent to the bursa of Fabricius (after which B cells were named), a lymphoid organ located at the posterior end of the gastrointestinal tract of birds that is essential for the development of their B cells. Other investigators, who are of the opinion that there is no mammalian equivalent to the bursa of Fabricius, take the term B cell to mean bone marrow derived. B and T cells are found in lymph, the lymphoid tissue of lymphoid organs, mainly the lymph nodes and spleen, and diffuse lymphoid tissue found in various locations, especially in the digestive and respiratory tracts.

The triggering agents of the immune response are called **antigens.** These are large molecules, such as proteins or polysaccharides, and are generally surface components of foreign substances. Antigens provoke the same response in B and T cells: rapid cell division, with the formation of distinct *clones* (colonies of cells arising from a single parent cell) in lymphoid tissue. The cells produced by successive cell divisions become more and more specialized. The end result of B cell proliferation is the formation of cells, called **plasma cells,** that manufacture (at a rate of about 2000 per second) identical antibodies constructed to combine selectively with the triggering antigen. The specialized cells formed in T cell clones are sensitive to and capable of binding the triggering antigen. B cell response to many antigens requires assistance from T cells. In such cases antibodies will not be produced unless "helper" T cells are present. Another T cell, the "suppressor" T cell, which inhibits the initiation or expression of the response of both B and T cells to antigens, plays an important role as a modulator of the immune response. Macrophages are also involved in the immune response, functioning in the induction of the response by a process that has been described as "antigen presentation," that is, uptake of antigens (outside as well as within lymphoid tissue) and delivery to B and T cells. Antigen presentation seems to be a general requirement for T cell activation and activation of B cells when helper T cells are required.

At one time it was generally believed that antigens entered antibody-producing cells and acted as templates for molding antibodies into complementary shapes. This "instructive" theory has been discarded in favor of the "selection" theory first proposed by Sir Macfarlane Burnet in the 1950's. According to the **selection theory,** the antigen simply selects cells endowed with genes coded for the synthesis of matching antibodies. The selection is accomplished by a "fit" between patches on the antigens called *antigenic determinants* and binding sites on receptors (glycoproteins) on the surface of B cells. The receptors apparently are antibody molecules with antigen-combining sites identical to the combining sites of antibodies later synthesized by plasma cells.

Since antibodies are proteins classified as globulins (gamma group — see Chapter 11, page 356) and have immunological properties, they are called **immunoglobulins.** There are five classes of immunoglobulins, designated IgM, IgG, IgA, IgD, and IgE. IgG is the most common, accounting for about 70 per cent of the circulating antibodies. IgG consists of four protein chains, two heavy and two light (Fig. 12–8). Each half, one heavy and one light chain, is identical to the other half. (This basic four-chain unit is common to all antibodies, but in some classes the units combine into multiunit forms.) At one end of each chain the amino acid sequence varies from one IgG antibody to another. These *variable regions* provide two antigen-binding sites. The diversity of amino acid sequences in the variable regions makes possible the wide range of configurations necessary for binding a great variety of antigens. The variable regions then confer **antigen-binding specificity.** The amino acid sequence

of the remaining portion of each chain is the same in all IgG antibodies. This *constant region* determines the class of the antibody and is responsible for functional properties of antibodies other than antigen binding. For example, a segment of the constant region of IgG binds a family of serum enzymes known as **complement,** thereby initiating a sequence of reactions capable of destroying cells.

The term complement was originally meant to indicate that these blood proteins helped antibodies defend against infectious organisms. As it turned out, the antibody's role in this method of attack is to identify the invading agent as foreign and activate and bind complement. The complement reaction sequence leads to the formation of surface lesions that can kill the invading cell. In addition, some complement products attract *phagocytes* (neutrophils and macrophages) to the scene. Others promote binding of these phagocytic cells to the invading cells. Still others stimulate the release of histamine by mast cells. Histamine increases the permeability of capillaries, facilitating penetration of phagocytes into the region where the immune response is in progress. These actions increase the susceptibility of invading microorganisms to phagocytosis (the process of facilitating phagocytosis is called *opsonization*). Activation of the complement system is the antibody's most commonly used defense mechanism. Other, direct actions include rupturing cell membranes, inducing agglutination (clumping) of antigenic agents, covering toxic sites, and causing the precipitation of antigens by the formation of insoluble antigen-antibody complexes.

Promoting phagocytosis seems to be the principal means by which sensitized cells derived from T cells combat invading agents. After binding to antigens they release a substance (*chemotactic factor*) that attracts macrophages and another (*migration inhibitory factor*) that keeps macrophages in the vicinity. Sensitized lymphocytes also release a cytotoxic substance (*lymphotoxin*) that can kill a variety of target cells. The most unusual action of sensitized lymphocytes is the release of a substance (*transfer factor*) that, in some unknown manner, confers on other lymphocytes the capability of attacking the specific antigenic agent they themselves are attacking.

Immunological Memory. One of the distinctive features of the immune response

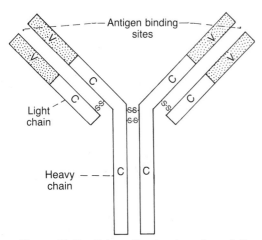

Figure 12–8. Schematic drawing of an IgG antibody showing the arrangement of two heavy and two light polypeptide chains. Chains are divided into a variable (V) portion, in which the amino acid sequence varies from one IgG antibody to another, and a constant (C) portion, in which the amino acid sequence is the same for all IgG antibodies.

is immunological memory — the ability of individuals who have recovered from an infection to respond more effectively and vigorously to reinfection. This is explained, in large part, by the formation (in clones of B and T cells during the first attack) of so-called *memory cells*, which give rise to clones of their own when the infectious agent reappears some time later. In effect, the first encounter with an antigen greatly expands cells to be selected during a subsequent invasion.

Immunological Tolerance and Autoimmune Diseases. The immune system, as we have seen, distinguishes between self and nonself. The lack of response by the immune system to self is referred to as *self-tolerance*. It has been postulated that self-tolerance develops in the fetus as a result of the destruction, following contact with native, potentially antigenic substances, of autoreactive lymphocytes. An observation made in a pair of fraternal twins who shared a common placental circulation is consistent with this view (such twins, a rarity, have two blood groups, their own and that of their twin). These twins accepted skin cross-grafting as if they were identical, rather than fraternal, twins.

Occasionally the tolerance mechanism goes awry and the immune system attacks one's own tissues. When this happens, the resulting disorder is called an *autoimmune disease*. It has been suggested that in some cases the autoimmunity may arise because tolerance fails to develop in the first place. Isolation of some substances from the circulation, as in the interior of the thyroid gland, may keep them from making contact with lymphocytes during the time the immune system is developing. If, for some reason, such a substance later gains access to the body fluids, it may act as an antigen and stimulate an immune response. A number of thyroid diseases do, in fact, appear to result from autoimmunity. Some autoimmune diseases may be caused by viruses. Multiple sclerosis is thought to be one. A number of hypotheses have been advanced to explain how this could come about. It has been suggested, for example, that a viral infection might unmask or release a potential, hidden antigen or that a viral antigen could combine with a cell-surface protein to form a new, alien substance.

Allergen-Reagin Reactions. IgE, one of the classes of antibodies, is responsible for certain types of allergic reactions, especially in genetically susceptible individuals. The basic responses are the same as those seen in the hypersensitive state in animals, called *anaphylaxis*, induced by injection of an antigen. Allergic reactions of this type occur in, among others, hay fever, asthma, and hives, and following bee stings or the injection of certain drugs. IgE antibodies are called *reagins;* antigens that react with reagins are called *allergens*. Reagins have the property of adhering to mast cells, and if, following initial exposure to allergens, which sensitize the individual, the same allergens re-enter the body and interact with reagins affixed to mast cells, the mast cells rupture, releasing histamine and other substances. If massive amounts of histamine pass into the circulation, the resulting widespread vasodilation and increased capillary permeability may be responsible for sudden death from shock. Associated with generalized histamine release and preceding vascular collapse and shock are, among other symptoms, diffuse reddening of the skin, hives, and respiratory distress due to swelling and obstructive secretions in the airway. One of the anaphylactic substances released by mast cells causes spasm of bronchiolar smooth muscle.

INTERFERON

It is generally recognized that the principal defender against a first attack by a virus is not the immune response, which takes days to become maximally effective, but rather the production and release by virus-infected cells of a small protein called *interferon* that acts on other cells to render them resistant to viral infection. (Since a number of interferons have been identified, interferon is a generic name for a class of proteins, all having similar antiviral activity.) When interferon leaves the cell that produced it, it binds to surface receptors on a nearby uninfected cell where it triggers the synthesis of enzymes that act to inhibit viral protein synthesis, thereby preventing any virus entering that cell from multiplying and killing it. Interferon's antiviral activity is very broad — it protects against essentially all viruses — but it exerts its protective effect only on cells of the same species that produced it. Interferon manufactured in the laboratory from cultured human cells has been tested with good results in clinical trials against a number of viral infections, including chronic hepatitis. It has also been observed that interferon causes partial regression of some animal and human cancers. Testing interferon has been limited by a small supply, but large-scale production by recombinant DNA technology (see Chapter 3) should soon relieve the shortage.

SUMMARY

THE LYMPHATIC SYSTEM

Components of Lymphatic System and Lymph Flow

1. Blind end lymph capillaries, into which interstitial fluid flows, branch throughout the intercellular space and converge to form larger and larger lymph vessels. Eventually two main trunks are formed, the thoracic duct, which empties into the left subclavian vein, and the right lymphatic duct, which empties into the right subclavian vein.

2. Valves in lymphatic vessels allow lymph to flow in only one direction—from the tissue spaces to the blood stream. Lymph is propelled largely by the massaging action of skeletal muscles, pressure changes accompanying breathing, and contraction of stretched smooth muscle of vessel walls.

3. Lymph is similar in composition of plasma except for the low concentration of proteins.

4. Lymph passes through groups of lymph nodes before reaching the blood stream.

Functions of Lymphatic System

1. Returns to the blood stream protein and fluid lost from the capillaries.

2. Defense against disease

   a. Phagocytic action of macrophages in lymph nodes.
   b. Immune response by lymphocytes in lymph nodes.

3. Lipid absorption.

Immune Response

1. Function of lymphocytes in lymphoid tissue, especially the lymph nodes.

2. Two immune systems, the B cell system (humoral immunity) and the T cell system (cell-mediated immunity), can be distinguished. Both B and T cell lymphocytes respond to specific antigens by rapidly dividing to form clones. Plasma cells formed in B cell clones produce antibodies, which combine with the triggering antigens and initiate events that lead to the destruction of these antigens. Specialized antigen-sensitive cells produced in T cell clones bind to the invading antigens and initiate events that lead to their elimination.

3. Both B and T cells are derived from a common parent cell, the stem cell of the red bone marrow. T cell differentiation is dependent on the thymus; B cell differentiation may occur in the equivalent of the bursa of Fabricius of birds or in the bone marrow.

4. The B cell system is most effective against acute bacterial infections (including those caused by streptococci, pneumococci, and meningococci). The T cell system is most active against chronic bacterial infections (such as tuberculosis) as well as fungi and some viruses. Cell-mediated immunity is also especially active against cancer and organ transplants.

REVIEW QUESTIONS

1. Describe the three major functions of the lymphatic system.
2. Name the two major lymph ducts and list the areas drained by each. What is the cisterna chyli?
3. Describe the major functions of lymph nodes, the spleen, and the thymus.
4. Define the following: B cell, T cell, plasma cell, antigen, antibody, complement. allergen, reagin.
5. Briefly explain immunological memory and immunological tolerance.
6. Explain how interferon combats viral infections.

13
The Respiratory System

Objectives

The aim of this chapter is to enable the student to:

- Describe the structures forming the upper respiratory tract and the divisions of the bronchial tree within the lungs.
- Describe the structure and function of the alveoli of the lungs.
- Explain the importance of the surfactant coating of the alveoli.
- Explain the roles of the diaphragm and external intercostal muscles in breathing.
- Outline the pressure changes in the thorax and lungs during inspiration and expiration.
- Define the different types of abnormal breathing.
- Discuss the factors influencing the efficiency of breathing.
- Describe the mechanisms of oxygen and carbon dioxide transport in the blood.
- Explain how a normal respiratory rhythm is maintained.
- Discuss the regulation of pulmonary ventilation.
- Describe the characteristics of several respiratory disorders.

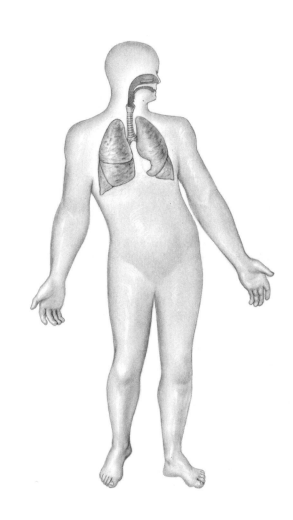

HISTORY

The rising and falling of the chest proved mysterious to the Greeks and Romans as they observed the changes in rate and rhythm during excitement and fear. To them, air was an intangible, divine spirit known as "pneuma," presumably entering the body at birth and leaving it at death. Aristotle actually believed that respiratory activity cooled the blood. Five hundred years later, in A.D. 170, Galen showed that the arteries were filled with blood and that the lungs added and removed something from the blood. In addition, Galen recognized several of the respiratory muscles and nerves. Circulation of the blood was traced through the lungs in the sixteenth century by Realdo Colombo. In 1774, Scheele, a Swedish chemist, and Priestley, working independently, isolated oxygen. Shortly thereafter, Lavoisier named it and discovered its function in combustion. By means of an ice calorimeter, he and Laplace demonstrated that respiration is a form of combustion.

GENERAL FUNCTION AND ANATOMY

The term respiration is defined as the union of oxygen with food in the cells, with the subsequent release of energy for work, for heat, and for the release of carbon dioxide and water. The respiratory system functions to supply oxygen for the metabolic needs of the cells and to remove one of the waste materials of cellular metabolism, carbon dioxide. This involves the process of *external respiration*, absorption of O_2, and removal of CO_2 from the lungs, and *internal respiration*, gaseous exchanges between the cells of the body and their fluid medium. The *nose, pharynx, larynx, trachea,* and *bronchi* are parts of the upper respiratory tract, an open passage leading from the exterior to the lungs. In the lungs, the successive divisions of the bronchial tree (the smaller bronchi, *bronchioles*, and *alveolar ducts*) lead to the **alveoli,** the functional units of the lungs. Gaseous exchange between blood and air occurs only in the alveoli. Approximately 20 million alveoli are present at birth. This number increases to about 300 million during the first 6 to 10 years of life with no change in the number of conducting airways.

The Nose

The term nose includes the external nose, that part of the upper respiratory tract that protrudes from the face, and the nasal cavity; only a small part of the nasal cavity is in the external nose, most of it lying over the roof of the mouth. Figures 13–1 and 13–2 show the location of cartilage and bones in the nose. The septal cartilage forms the anterior part of the nasal septum, which divides the nasal cavity into two lateral halves. The lateral cartilages are winglike expansions of the septal cartilages. The alar cartilages are U-shaped and are located on the sides of the nose below the lateral cartilages. The alar, lateral, and septal cartilages form the cartilaginous framework of the external nose; the nasal bones and parts of the maxillary and frontal bones form its bony framework. The external openings of the nasal cavities are called the anterior nares or nostrils.

The bony roof of the nose consists of an anterior portion, the frontal bones; a middle portion, the cribriform plate of the ethmoid; and a posterior portion, parts of the sphenoid and vomer bones. The floor of the nose is formed by the maxillary and palatine bones.

The nasal cavity is composed of two wedge-shaped cavities separated by a septum formed largely by the perpendicular plate of the ethmoid bone, the vomer bone, and the septal cartilage (Fig. 13–1). The crests of the nasal bones form a small part of the superior aspect of the septum; the crests of the maxilla and palatine bones complete the inferior aspect. (See pages 121–124 for supplemental diagrams.)

The lateral wall of the nose has three bony projections, the superior, middle, and inferior conchae, or turbinates, beneath which lie the superior, middle, and inferior meatuses (air passages), respectively. Each concha is covered by a thick mucous membrane, functioning to warm and moisten air (Fig. 13–3).

The anterior portion of the nasal cavity is lined with a thick layer of *stratified squamous epithelium* containing sebaceous glands. The spongy conchae increase the amount of tissue surface within the nose, and the respiratory epithelium of the conchae secretes mucus. Mucous membranes also filter out bacteria and dust particles. Air must be warmed; otherwise the tissue lining the respiratory tract functions poorly. Absence of

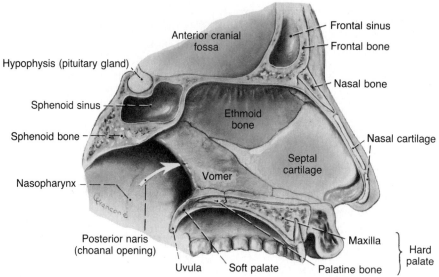

Figure 13–1. Sagittal section through nose showing components of nasal septum.

moisture for even a few minutes destroys the cilia of the respiratory epithelium.

The nose filters substances in two ways. (1) Vibrissae (the hairs that can be seen in the nose) filter out the coarsest bodies, such as insects. (2) Air currents passing over the moist mucosa in curved pathways deposit fine particles, such as dust, powder, and smoke, against the wall. These fine particles are subsequently conveyed to the pharynx and swallowed.

The mucous membrane of the nose continues anteriorly with the skin lining the vestibule and posteriorly with the mucous membrane of the nasopharynx. The posterior part of the nasal cavities and the nasopharynx

are lined with *pseudostratified ciliated columnar epithelium.* The cilia wave back and forth about 12 times per second and help the mucus to clean the air. The superior portion of the nose is lined with neuroepithelial tissue containing olfactory cells, which function in the sensation of smell.

The Paranasal Sinuses (Figs. 13–4 and 13–5)

Paranasal sinuses are air-containing spaces communicating with the nasal cavity and lined with a mucous membrane. Although they are paired, they are commonly asymmetrical. The paired sinuses include the *maxillary, frontal, ethmoid,* and *sphenoid sinuses.* The primary function of paranasal sinuses is to lighten the bones of the skull. Secondarily, they function to provide mucus for the nasal cavity and act as resonant chambers for the production of sound.

The maxillary sinuses are the largest of the paranasal sinuses. Each is located in the maxilla and opens into the middle meatus. The frontal sinuses, located in the frontal bone superior and medial to the orbit of the eye, empty into the middle meatus. The ethmoid air cells are numerous, irregularly shaped air spaces that open into the middle and superior meatuses.

The sphenoid sinus is in the sphenoid bone. It is located posterior to the eye, be-

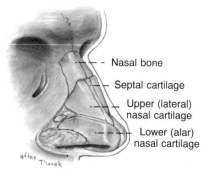

Figure 13–2. The lower portion of the external nose has a cartilaginous rather than a skeletal framework, consisting of a septal cartilage, two lateral cartilages, and a series of smaller cartilages.

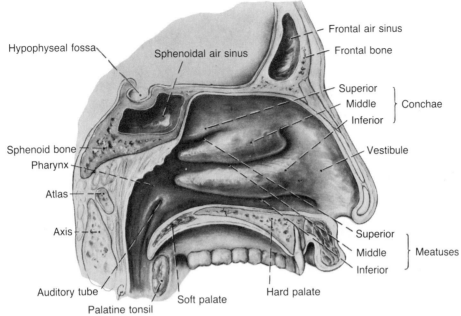

Figure 13–3. Nasal septum removed, showing lateral aspect of nasal cavity with conchae (turbinates).

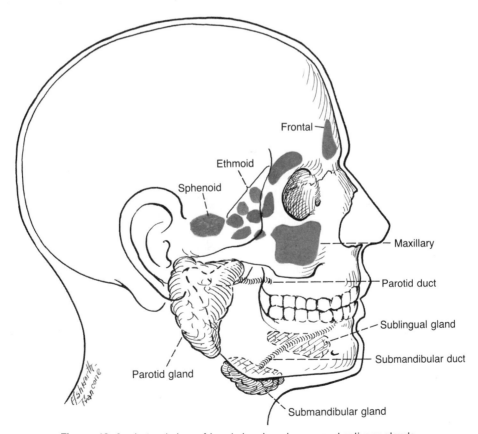

Figure 13–4. Lateral view of head showing sinuses and salivary glands.

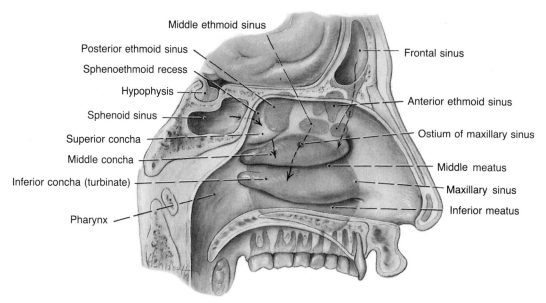

Figure 13–5. Sagittal section of the nasal cavity showing anatomy of the sinuses and direction of normal drainage. Note that drainage from frontal, maxillary, and anterior sinuses is into the middle meatus, while the posterior ethmoid and sphenoid sinuses drain into the superior meatus.

hind the upper portion of the nasal cavity. An infection of the sphenoid sinus can damage vision because of its proximity to the optic nerve. Drainage from the sphenoid sinus is into the superior meatus.

The nasolacrimal duct extends from the eye to the inferior meatus and drains the lacrimal secretions which constantly bathe the surface of the eye (see Chapter 10).

The Pharynx

The pharynx is a musculomembranous tube, 5 inches in length, extending from the base of the skull to the esophagus. The posterior aspect abuts against the cervical vertebrae. The pharynx is divided into three parts — nasal, oral, and laryngeal.

The *nasopharynx* lies behind the nose; the *oropharynx* lies behind the mouth. The nasopharynx and oropharynx are separated by the soft palate, a membranous sheet of muscle covered by mucous membrane. The *laryngopharynx* lies below the hyoid bone and behind the larynx.

There are four openings into the nasopharynx — two from the auditory (Eustachian) tubes and two from the nose, the *posterior nares*. The oropharynx has a single

opening, called the *isthmus of the fauces*, which communicates with the mouth. The laryngopharynx opens into the larynx and esophagus.

The pharyngeal tonsil (adenoids) lies in the rear wall of the nasopharynx near the posterior nares. If it becomes enlarged, it can obstruct the posterior nares (see Figure 12–6). When an individual has enlarged adenoids, mouth breathing and a nasal or plugged quality to the voice develop. The lingual tonsil is located in the oropharynx at the base of the tongue. The palatine tonsils are located in the isthmus of the fauces, the opening between the mouth and the oropharynx (but generally included as part of the oropharynx), bounded by the palatopharyngeal and the palatoglossal arches (mucus-covered projections of the palatopharyngeus and palatoglossus muscles, the former extending from the soft palate to the lateral walls of the pharynx, the latter extending from the soft palate to the tongue — see Figures 12–5 and 14–5). The palatine tonsils are commonly referred to as "the tonsils" and are removed when the patient has a tonsillectomy (see Chapter 12). The pharynx serves as a passage for two systems — the respiratory and the digestive. It also assumes an important function in the formation of sound, particularly in the creation of vowel sounds.

The Larynx

The larynx, or "voice box" (Figs. 13–6 and 13–7), connects the pharynx with the trachea. Its opening is at the base of the tongue. The larynx is broad superiorly and shaped like a triangular box. It joins the trachea inferiorly, where it is narrower and round. It consists of nine cartilages united by extrinsic and intrinsic muscles as well as by ligaments.

There are three paired and three unpaired cartilages of the larynx:

Unpaired	*Paired*
Thyroid	Arytenoid
Cricoid	Cuneiform
Epiglottic	Corniculate

The *thyroid* cartilage is the largest cartilage in the larynx. It is formed by a pair of quadrangular laminae which fuse in front at an angle to form a prominence called the *laryngeal prominence* or "Adam's apple." The angle is greater in men (about 90°) than in women (about 120°), and the male Adam's apple is more prominent. Consequences of this greater thyroid angle in the male are longer vocal folds (see below) and a lower-pitched voice.

The leaf-shaped *epiglottis* is attached to the superior border of the thyroid cartilage. It has a hinged, doorlike action at the entrance to the larynx. During swallowing, it acts as a lid to help prevent aspiration of food into the trachea. The *cricoid* cartilage is the most inferior of the nine laryngeal cartilages; it is

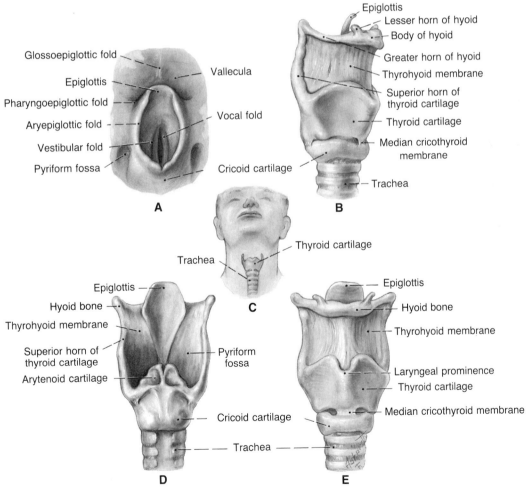

Figure 13–6. The larynx as viewed from above (A), from the side (B), in relation to the head and neck (C), from behind (D), and from the front (E).

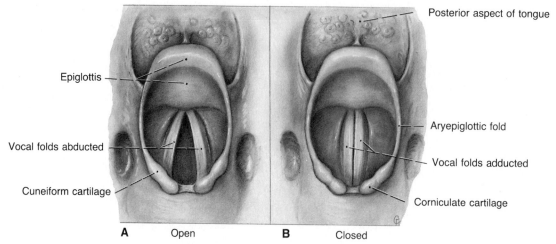

Epiglottis

Vocal folds abducted

Cuneiform cartilage

A　Open

Posterior aspect of tongue

Aryepiglottic fold

Vocal folds adducted

Corniculate cartilage

B　Closed

Figure 13–7. Superior view of vocal cords.

shaped like a signet ring with the signet facing posteriorly. The pyramid-shaped *arytenoid cartilages* are small and are attached to the superior portion of each cricoid lamina. The *corniculate cartilages* are small cones of elastic tissue, each articulating with the apex of an arytenoid cartilage. These cartilages serve to prolong the arytenoid cartilages backward and medially and provide attachments for the aryepiglottic folds (folds of mucus membrane stretching forward to each side of the epiglottis). The *cuneiform cartilages* are small, elongated, club-shaped cartilages situated in the aryepiglottic folds in front of the corniculate cartilages.

Located in the laryngeal cavity are a pair of **vocal folds** (true vocal cords) and a pair of **ventricular folds** (false vocal cords). Each vocal fold is a sharp, white fold of mucous membrane stretching between the thyroid cartilage in front to the vocal process of the arytenoid cartilage behind. Each ventricular fold is a thick, pink fold of mucous membrane enclosing a narrow band of fibrous tissue; it stretches from the thyroid cartilage to the anterolateral surface of the arytenoid cartilage. The portion of the laryngeal cavity above the ventricular folds is called the *vestibule*; the portion between the ventricular folds above and the vocal folds below is called the *ventricle*. The space between the vocal folds is known as the **rima glottidis** or **glottis.**

Musculature of the Larynx. Two sets of muscles are found in the larynx, extrinsic and intrinsic. The extrinsic muscles take origin in structures surrounding the larynx and func-

tion to move the larynx. The intrinsic muscles are located within the larynx proper. These muscles open and close the glottis during inspiration and expiration. They close the laryngeal aperture and glottis during swallowing and regulate the tension of the vocal folds in the production of sound. Both the intrinsic and extrinsic muscles are composed of striated muscle fibers.

Movements of the mobile arytenoid cartilages by muscles which insert into the muscular process of each arytenoid cartilage open and close the glottis. The muscular process, the rounded, prominent lateral angle of the base of the arytenoid cartilage, projects backward and laterally. The vocal process, to which each vocal fold is attached, is the forward-projecting, pointed anterior angle of the base of the arytenoid cartilage. Contraction of the *posterior cricoarytenoid muscles* pulls the muscular processes of the two arytenoid cartilages closer together, drawing the vocal processes and attached vocal folds further apart, widening the opening of the glottis. Contraction of the *lateral cricoarytenoid muscles* has the opposite effect and closes the glottis.

The *cricothyroid muscles* are the principal tensors of the vocal folds. Their contraction pulls the narrow anterior arch of the cricoid cartilage upward, tilting the upper part of the broad posterior lamina dorsally, thereby forcing the arytenoid cartilages backward. They also move the thyroid cartilage forward. These actions increase the distance between the points of attachment of the vocal folds on the thyroid and arytenoid cartilages.

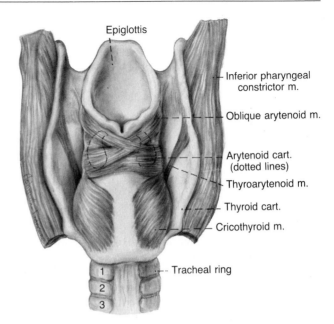

Epiglottis

Inferior pharyngeal
constrictor m.

Oblique arytenoid m.

Arytenoid cart.
(dotted lines)

Thyroarytenoid m.

Thyroid cart.

Cricothyroid m.

Tracheal ring

1
2
3

Figure 13–8. Muscles of the larynx.

The *thyroarytenoid muscles* pull the arytenoid cartilages forward, relaxing the vocal folds.

Nerve Supply of the Larynx. The larynx is supplied by branches of the vagus nerve, the *recurrent laryngeal* and *superior laryngeal nerves*. The recurrent laryngeal has both sensory and motor branches and supplies all of the muscles of the larynx except the cricothyroid muscle. The superior laryngeal nerve is chiefly sensory but, since one of the muscles it serves is the cricothyroid, the vocal folds cannot be tensed if it is interrupted and the voice is deepened. If the recurrent laryngeal nerves are interrupted, the vocal folds become fixed in the so-called "cadaveric" position (also their position during quiet breathing) — neither closed, as during vocalization, nor wide open, as during deep inspiration. If the recurrent laryngeal nerve is interrupted on one side only, the vocal fold on the opposite side will be drawn across the midline toward the stationary vocal fold; hence, vocalization (see below) is possible, but the timbre of the sound is altered, changing the quality of the sound.

The Production of Vocal Sounds. Investigators of vocalization by humans have described the component parts of the sound-generating system as an instrument consisting of the lungs (a power supply); the vocal folds (an oscillator); and the larynx, pharynx, and mouth (a resonant chamber, called the vocal tract, analogous to the body of a violin).

Sound is produced when, with the glottis closed, the expulsion of air from the lungs causes a rapid, repeated opening and closing of the glottis that feeds a train of air pulses into the vocal tract. In general, the greater the lung pressure and the thinner, shorter, tauter the vocal folds, the higher the frequency of vibration of the vocal folds and emission of air pulses, and the higher the pitch. The sounds so generated are transformed into speech by the movements of the articulators — the lips, jaws, and tongue.

The Trachea

The trachea, or "windpipe," is a cylindrical tube about 4 to 5 inches in length. The trachea is flattened posteriorly where it comes into contact with the esophagus. It extends from the level of the sixth cervical vertebra to the fifth thoracic vertebra and divides into two primary bronchi. The inferior portion of the trachea is crossed by the arch of the aorta. The thyroid gland lies anterior to the second, third, and fourth tracheal rings.

The trachea consists of four layers: a mucous membrane (mucosa); submucosa; a layer containing cartilage, fibrous connective tissue, and smooth muscle; and an outer covering of connective tissue, the adventitia. The inner layer (mucous membrane) is composed of a *pseudostratified ciliated columnar epithelium* with mucus-secreting goblet cells, anchored by a basement membrane to an underlying connective tissue. These cilia sweep inhaled particles deposited on the mucous film to the pharynx to be swallowed. The submucosa is loose connective tissue containing glands and fat cells. In the third layer, about 20 horseshoe-shaped hyaline cartilages form incomplete rings around the trachea, preventing its total collapse. The posterior gaps in the rings are bridged by interlacing bundles of smooth muscle. A dense connective tissue with elastic and collagenous fibers fills the spaces between the rings of cartilage. The adventitia is a loose connective tissue containing blood vessels and autonomic nerves.

Function of the Trachea. The trachea functions as a simple passageway for air to reach the lungs; occasionally it becomes occluded, either from swelling of the mucosal lining, accumulated secretions, or aspirations of material into it. Occlusion of the trachea necessitates either a tracheotomy (Fig. 13–9) or a tracheostomy. The term *tracheotomy* means merely an opening into the trachea. *Tracheostomy* is a procedure in which the trachea is brought to the skin or a tube is placed into it to keep it open for a period of time. A tracheotomy or tracheostomy is performed to provide an airway when there is an obstruction at or above the level of the larynx. Symptoms of laryngeal obstruction are frightening and include difficult respiration (dyspnea) and inspiratory stridor (a harsh, high-pitched sound often heard in laryngeal obstructions).

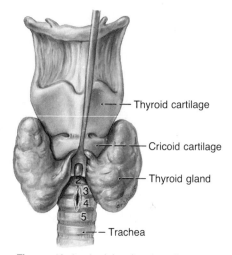

Figure 13–9. Incision for a tracheotomy.

The Bronchi and Branches

The two **primary bronchi**, each supplying a lung, split from the trachea at the level of the superior border of the fifth thoracic vertebra. The right bronchus differs from the left in that it is shorter and wider and takes a more vertical course. Foreign bodies from the trachea usually enter the right bronchus because of these characteristics. The primary bronchi lie posterior to the pulmonary vessels with the left behind the aorta. Each primary bronchus divides into three right and two left **secondary**, or **lobar, bronchi,** which supply the lobes of the lungs (superior, middle, and inferior in the right lung; superior and inferior in the left). The secondary bronchi in turn divide into **tertiary**, or **segmental, bronchi,** each of which is distributed to a unit of the lung called a *bronchopulmonary segment* (Fig. 13–10). The segmental bronchi continue to divide into successively smaller branches. Fine branches, now called **bronchioles**, enter basic units of the lung called *lobules*. Each bronchiole divides upon entering a lobule into several **terminal bronchioles**, each of which further subdivides into two or more **respiratory bronchioles.** The respiratory bronchioles open into **alveolar ducts**, from which alveoli arise (see below).

Those portions of the primary bronchi external to the lungs have essentially the same structure as the trachea but are of smaller diameter. Within the lungs the bronchial cartilages assume a platelike shape, and some completely encircle the bronchi. As the bronchi become narrower, the amount of cartilage decreases and no longer forms complete rings. The cartilage finally disappears at the bronchioles. With the decrease in cartilage there is a concomitant increase in smooth muscle, which is intermingled with numerous elastic fibers.

The pseudostratified ciliated columnar epithelium of the trachea continues into the bronchi, changing to simple ciliated columnar epithelium in the bronchioles and to cuboidal ciliated, without goblet cells, in the smaller terminal bronchioles. The epithelium becomes less ciliated as it approaches the alveolar ducts. Alveolar ducts are simply thin tubes composed of a single layer of squamous epithelium surrounded by fibroelastic tissue. The ducts open into **alveoli**, generally arranged in clusters, each cluster forming an alveolar sac (Figs. 13–11 and 13–12). Smooth

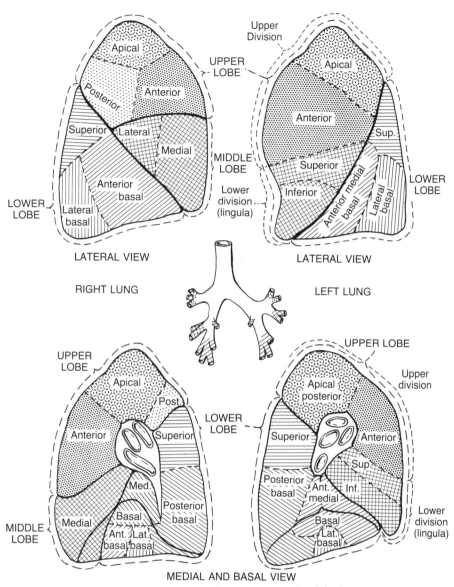

Figure 13-10. Bronchopulmonary segments of the lungs.

muscle cells surround the openings. Three types of cells are found in alveoli: (1) thin *squamous epithelial cells*, known as type I cells, forming an almost continuous lining around the alveolar spaces; (2) slightly more numerous *cuboidal epithelial cells*, known as type II cells or granular pneumocytes, lying behind the surface epithelial cells or bulging between them (occupying less than 3 per cent of the alveolar surface), which secrete a substance that reduces surface tension (discussed in the following section); and (3) *macrophages*, active phagocytic cells (see below). Underlying these cells is a basal lamina (filamentous collagenous fibers) adjacent to a framework of reticular and elastic fibers (alveolar septa) housing the *alveolar capillary network*, embedded in a protein-polysaccharide ground substance. An important function of the alveolar macrophages is to clear the lungs of inhaled particles that have not been eliminated by the mucociliary system of the respiratory passages that sweeps particles to the pharynx to be swallowed. These cells migrate around the alveoli engulfing particles, and laden macro-

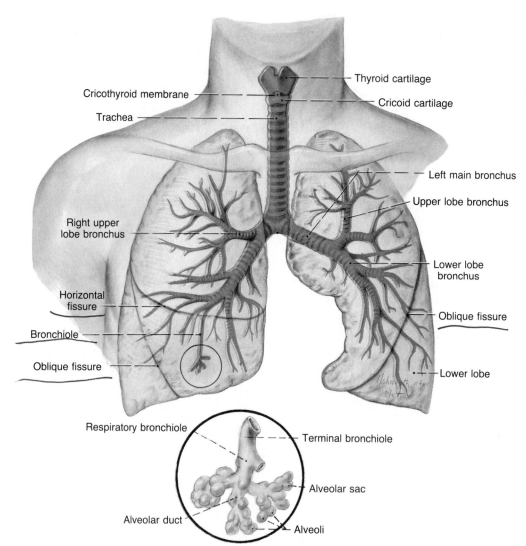

Figure 13–11. Distribution of bronchi within the lungs. Enlarged inset shows detail of alveolar ducts opening into clusters of alveoli, each cluster an alveolar sac.

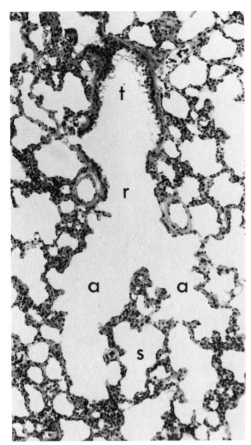

Figure 13–12. Section of a lung showing a terminal bronchiole (t) leading into a respiratory bronchiole (r), which divides into two alveolar ducts (a). Alveolar sacs (s) and alveoli are also seen. (Magnified 75×.) (From Leeson, C. R., and Leeson, T. S.: Histology. 3rd ed., Philadelphia, W. B. Saunders Co., 1976.)

The Thoracic Cavity. The thoracic cavity is separated from the abdomen by the diaphragm, a large sheet of muscle. The center of the cavity contains other structures between the lungs which are enclosed in an oblong, wide area called the *mediastinum* (Fig. 13–13). The mediastinum is bounded anteriorly by the sternum, posteriorly by the bodies of the 12 thoracic vertebrae, superiorly by the thoracic inlet, and inferiorly by the diaphragm. The sides of the mediastinum are formed by the mediastinal pleura. Contents of the mediastinal space include the pericardium (with the enclosed heart), aortic arch, thymus, vagus nerve, esophagus, trachea, and numerous blood vessels. Each lung is enveloped by a serous membrane called the pleura. One layer of this membrane, known as the *visceral pleura*, covers the surface of the lung. The other layer, called the *parietal pleura*, is in close contact with the diaphragm and interior border of the chest. Between the visceral and parietal pleurae is a potential space, the *pleural cavity*, which contains a fluid for lubrication. The normal pleural arrangement allows for respiration with minimal friction, but when the pleura is inflamed (pleurisy) breathing becomes painful.

phages leave the lungs via the lymphatics or blood or by migrating to the so-called mucociliary escalator. Heavy smoking considerably impairs clearance by macrophages. In one recent study it was found that about one year after inhaling magnetic dust (magnetite) smokers retained about 50 per cent of the dust deposited in the lungs, whereas nonsmokers retained only 10 per cent.

The nerves supplying the trachea and bronchi are derived from the vagus by way of the recurrent laryngeal branch and from the sympathetic division of the autonomic nervous system. The arterial supply to the trachea is from the inferior thyroid arteries; the arterial supply to the bronchioles comes from the bronchial arteries, which take origin from the aorta.

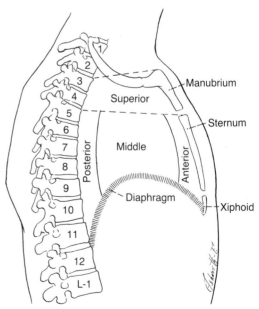

Figure 13–13. Subdivisions of the mediastinum.

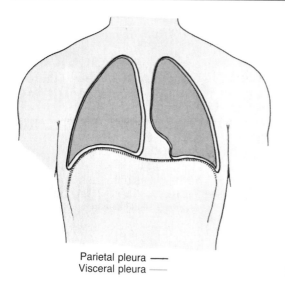

Parietal pleura ——
Visceral pleura ——

Figure 13–14. Lungs and associated visceral and parietal pleurae.

The Lungs. The lungs (Figs. 13–14 to 13–17) are cone-shaped organs which completely fill the pleural spaces, extending from the diaphragm to about 1½ inches above the clavicle. The part of the lung above the clavicle is called the *cupula.* The medial surface of each lung is concave around the mediastinum. The primary bronchi and pulmonary arteries enter a slit in each lung called the *hilum* via the root of the lungs — the only real connection of the lungs with the body itself.

The lungs are divided by fissures (Fig. 13–11). The *oblique* and *horizontal fissures* divide the right lung into superior, middle, and inferior lobes. On the left side, there is only an oblique fissure, dividing the left lung into superior and inferior lobes. Smaller units of the lungs, the bronchopulmonary segments, are recognized, each supplied by a single segmental bronchus (Fig. 13–10).

The adult lung is a spongy mass, frequently blue-gray in color because of inhaled dust and soot in the respiratory lymphatics.

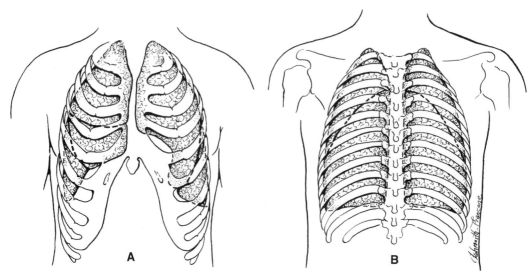

A   B

Figure 13–15. Relation of lungs to thorax anteriorly (A) and posteriorly (B). Dashed lines indicate fissures and lobes of lungs.

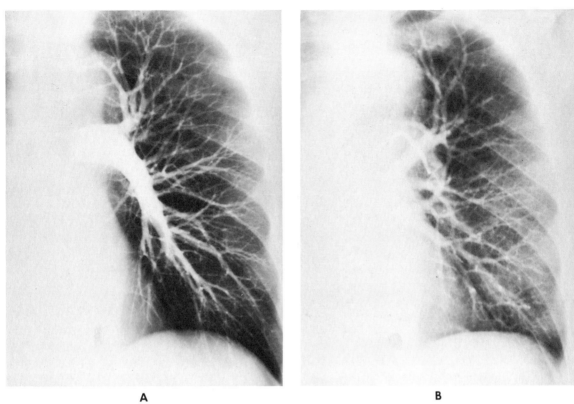

Figure 13–16. *A*, Angiograph of pulmonary arterial system. *B*, Angiograph of pulmonary venous system.

In contrast, the lung of a baby is pink, since no foreign material has yet entered. Prior to the age of three weeks, some of the pulmonary tissue can be incompletely filled with air. At birth, the lungs are filled with fluid; when the first breath is taken, the lungs begin to become spongy, eventually filling with air to a degree similar to that found in the adult.

The interior of the lung is by far the most extensive body surface in contact with the environment. In the normal adult, this area is approximately the size of a tennis court. Normal life processes require about 1 square meter of lung surface for each kilogram of body weight.

The alveoli of the lungs (Fig. 13–18) are coated with a surface-active substance, or **surfactant** (a lipoprotein in which the active components are phospholipids), which lowers surface tension. *Surface tension* in the lungs (resulting from the contraction of the thin layer of water moistening alveolar surfaces at the air-water interface) is a powerful force, accounting for about one-half to two-

thirds of the lungs' elastic recoil. The surfactant prevents lung collapse from excessive surface tension. It also equalizes surface tension as the alveoli expand and contract — surface tension increases as the radii of the alveoli decrease, but this is counterbalanced by the thickening of the surfactant layer, which decreases surface tension. By the same token, differences between large and small alveoli in surfactant concentration bring about an even distribution of surface tension among alveoli of different sizes. Recent investigations have shown that fetal type II alveolar epithelial cells begin to manufacture surfactant about two months before birth. A deficiency in surfactant in premature infants can cause what is known as the **respiratory distress syndrome** (RDS) — extreme difficulty with inhalation because of the decrease in expandability of the lungs or, in serious cases, massive lung collapse. RDS is also called hyaline membrane disease because leakage of fluid in this condition gives the alveoli a glassy, pink coating.

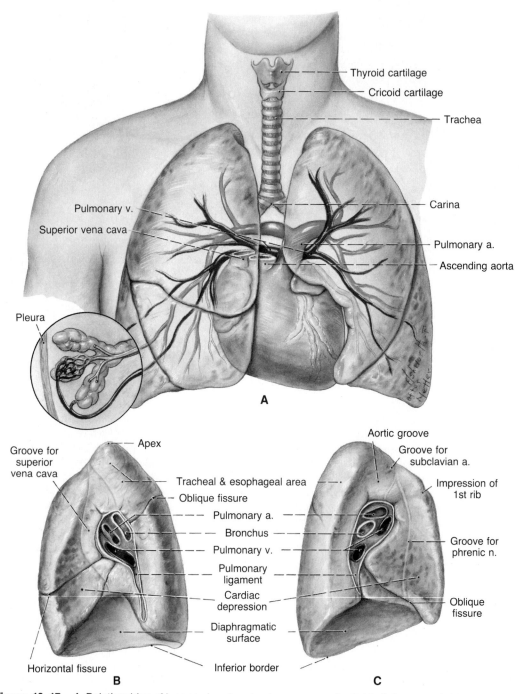

Figure 13–17. *A*, Relationships of lungs to heart and pulmonary vessels. *B*, Medial aspect of right lung. *C*, Medial aspect of left lung.

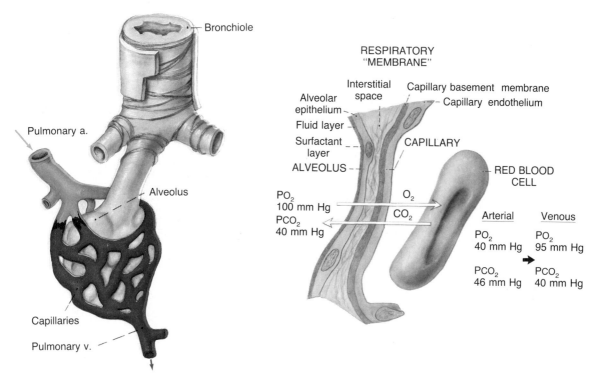

RESPIRATORY
"MEMBRANE"

Interstitial
Alveolar   space   Capillary basement membrane
epithelium   Capillary endothelium

Fluid layer

Surfactant   CAPILLARY
layer

ALVEOLUS

PO_2
100 mm Hg O_2 RED BLOOD
PCO_2 CELL
40 mm Hg CO_2

                                Arterial   Venous

                                PO_2 PO_2
                                40 mm Hg   95 mm Hg

                                PCO_2 PCO_2
                                46 mm Hg   40 mm Hg

Bronchiole

Pulmonary a.

Alveolus

Capillaries

Pulmonary v.

Figure 13–18. Basic microscopic functional unit of the lung. (Courtesy of Roche Laboratories.)

RESPIRATION

Mechanics of Breathing

Quiet breathing is accomplished by the alternate contraction and relaxation of the *diaphragm* and *external intercostal muscles.* Most of the air movement is accounted for by the action of the diaphragm.

Inspiration. When the diaphragm contracts, it descends and elongates the thoracic cavity (Fig. 13–19). The contraction of the external intercostal muscles raises the ribs at the sternal end. This action forces the sternum outward, increasing the anterior-posterior diameter of the thorax (Fig. 13–19). In addition, as the ribs swing upward (in a manner similar to the motion of a bucket handle), the lateral diameter of the thorax increases. As the thorax enlarges, cohesion between the visceral and parietal pleurae causes both layers to expand, thereby enlarging the lungs. This reduces the pressure within the lungs (intrapulmonic pressure).

Intrapulmonic pressure reaches a minimum at the midpoint of inspiration (approximately −2 mm Hg, that is, 2 mm Hg below atmospheric pressure — see Fig. 13–20). The reduction in intrapulmonic pressure causes air to rush into the lungs. At the end of inspiration the pressure between the lungs and atmosphere is equalized (Fig. 13–20).

Expiration. Expiration during quiet breathing is a passive process, occurring as the diaphragm and external intercostal muscles relax. The thoracic cavity returns to its resting size and the lungs recoil. As mentioned, the surface tension of fluid lining the alveoli causes a continuous tendency of the alveoli to contract, accounting for about one-half to two-thirds of the lungs' elastic recoil. Rebound of elastic fibers accounts for the remainder. Recoil contraction of the lungs increases intrapulmonic pressure (it reaches a maximum of about +4 mm Hg at the midpoint of expiration), forcing air out of the lungs. At the end of expiration the pressure between the lungs and atmosphere is equalized (Fig. 13–20).

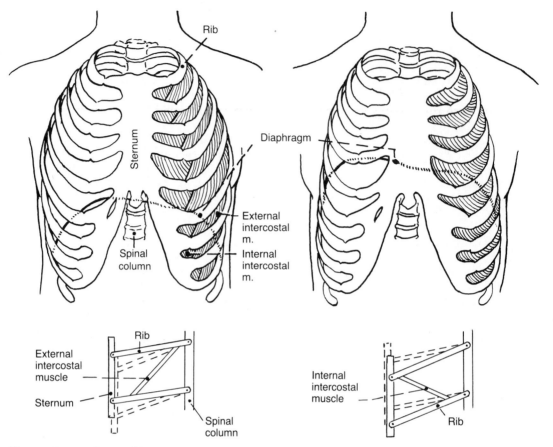

Figure 13–19. Thorax with associated actions during respiration. During quiet breathing, only inspiration is an active process — contraction of the diaphragm, the major respiratory muscle, and the external intercostals enlarges the thorax. The internal intercostals are among the muscles contracting during forced expiration.

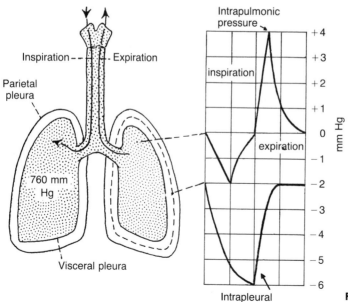

Figure 13–20. Changes in intrathoracic and intrapulmonic pressures during respiration.

Deep Breathing. During quiet breathing, about 500 ml of air is inhaled and exhaled. At least 80 per cent of the air movement is brought about by the contraction and relaxation of the diaphragm. Forceful inspiration not only requires stronger contractions by the diaphragm and external intercostals but also calls forth the use of accessory muscles, principally the sternocleidomastoids, which lift the upper sternum, and the scaleni, which lift the first two ribs. Deep breathing may involve forced expiration, which, unlike quiet expiration, is an active process. Contraction of the muscles of the abdominal wall forces the abdominal contents against the diaphragm, raising it. Contraction of the internal intercostals reduces the diameter of the thorax by an action opposite to that of the external intercostals.

Intrapleural Pressure. At all times, the intrapleural, or intrathoracic, pressure is negative (Fig. 13–20). The negative pressure is maintained because the tendency of elastic recoil to contract the lungs is opposed by the tendency of the chest wall to resist lung contraction. In effect, two coiled springs are pulling in opposite directions, thereby maintaining a negative pressure. If air enters the potential space (pleural cavity) between the visceral and parietal pleurae, as may occur in chest wounds, the condition is called **pneumothorax.** Separation of the visceral and parietal layers of the pleura eliminates the counterforce acting against the lungs' elastic recoil. Consequently, the lungs collapse. Since the two pleural cavities are not connected, the pneumothorax is usually unilateral; however, the increased pressure on the opened side pushes the mobile mediastinum toward the uninvolved side, exerting pressure on the normal lung and decreasing its ability to expand.

Types of Breathing

Normal, quiet breathing is known as *eupnea. Apnea* is a temporary cessation of breathing. *Dyspnea* is difficult breathing. *Orthopnea* is the inability to breathe easily in a horizontal position. *Hyperpnea* is an increased depth of breathing. *Tachypnea* is excessively rapid and shallow breathing.

Lung Volumes

The normal resting lung volume in a man of average size is about 3 liters. Normal inspiration increases this volume by approximately 500 ml. Forced maximum inspiration raises this to about 6 liters. Forced maximum expiration lowers the lung volume to approximately 1 liter. The lung volumes are divided as follows (Fig. 13–21):

Vital capacity (VC) — the largest volume of air that can be expired after a maximal inspiration or the largest volume that can be inspired after maximal expiration.

Residual volume (RV) — the air remaining in the lungs even after maximal forced expiration.

Total lung capacity (TLC) — the total volume of air in the lungs upon maximal inhalation, including residual volume.

Tidal volume (TV) — the amount of air inspired or expired with each breath at rest or during any stated activity. The average figure at rest for an adult male is 500 ml. Of this, about 350 ml reaches the alveoli. The remaining 150 ml moves in and out of the so-called **dead space** — the nose, pharynx, larynx, trachea, and bronchial tree — and serves no useful purpose.

Inspiratory capacity (IC) — the volume capable of being inspired at the end of a quiet expiration.

Inspiratory reserve volume (IRV) — the volume capable of being inspired after quiet inspiration (inspiratory capacity less tidal volume).

Expiratory reserve volume (ERV) — the volume capable of being expired at the end of a quiet expiration.

Functional residual capacity (FRC) — expiratory reserve volume plus residual volume.

It will be noted that "capacities" consist always of two or more "volumes." The volumes and capacities are primarily dependent on the size and build of the individual. They change with body position, for the most part decreasing when the individual assumes a recumbent position and increasing when he stands. This is caused by abdominal pressure on the diaphragm during recumbency, along with a decrease in pulmonary volume in this position, thus decreasing the space available for air.

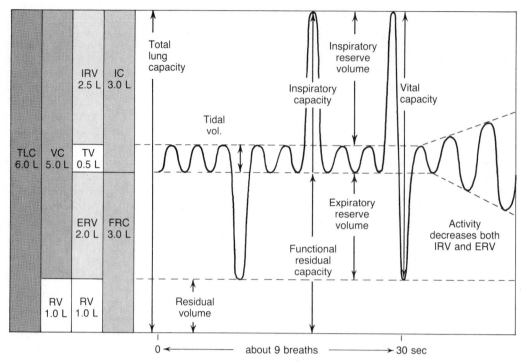

Figure 13–21. Spirometric graph showing respiratory capacities and volumes.

Ventilation

The volume of air exchanged in one minute (minute respiratory volume) is termed *ventilation*. Normal ventilation, representing a tidal volume of 500 ml and a respiratory rate of 12 breaths per minute, is approximately 6 liters per minute. *Maximum breathing capacity* is generally taken as the maximum ventilation during an interval of 12 seconds. The maximum breathing capacity of a young male adult is about 125 to 170 liters per minute.

Clinical Spirometry

Clinically, respiratory volumes and capacities are recorded graphically by using a spirometer (Fig. 13–21 is actually such a record). The record is obtained by having the patient breathe in and out of the spirometer; movements are translated to the moving drum of a kymograph by means of a pen. Spirometry is an initial step in the physiologic evaluation of a patient with labored respiration. A reduction in vital capacity generally indicates a loss of functioning lung tissue

or a decrease in *compliance* (expandability, defined specifically as the change in lung volume induced by unit change in distending pressure). In some diseases, such as pneumonia, cancer, and tuberculosis, both compliance and the amount of functioning tissue are reduced. If the impairment in maximum breathing capacity is greater than the impairment in vital capacity, increased airway resistance, such as occurs in asthma, is indicated. Increased airway resistance can also be detected by measuring the *timed vital capacity*. A normal individual, when exhaling maximally, can expel at least 75 per cent of the vital capacity in one second, 85 per cent in two seconds, and 95 per cent in three seconds. In patients with constricted airway passages, these percentages will be reduced.

The Economy of Energy Expenditure for Breathing

Normally, most of the work of breathing expands the lungs, overcoming elastic recoil (referred to as elastic work). Some work overcomes airway resistance, and a small amount overcomes tissue viscous resistance (resistance of nonelastic tissues to a change in shape). It has been calculated that providing adequate alveolar ventilation with a minimum expenditure of energy is accomplished by breathing at a rate of 15 breaths per minute, exchanging 500 ml of tidal air. Shallow, rapid breathing reduces elastic work, but this type of breathing is not maximally efficient because it increases the proportion of useless dead space ventilated. Breathing deeply and slowly fails to achieve maximum economy because, although it increases alveolar ventilation, it also increases elastic work considerably and, in addition, increases energy expenditure by using expiratory muscles to increase intrapulmonary pressure.

Normal, quiet breathing uses about 2 to 3 per cent of the body's total energy output. Heavy exercise increases the work of breathing about 25-fold but only approximately doubles the proportion of the total energy used. Diseases that reduce lung compliance or airway resistance, on the other hand, can increase the proportion of work used for breathing to about one-third or more of the total energy expended. A workload increase of this magnitude can be the cause of death in such diseases.

GAS TRANSPORT

In considering gas transport, Dalton's law of partial pressures comes into play. According to this law, the partial pressure of a gas in a mixture of gases is related directly to the concentration of that gas and the total pressure of the mixture (the sum of the partial pressures of all the gases in the mixture). Alveolar air contains 14 per cent oxygen, 5.6 per cent carbon dioxide, and 80.4 per cent nitrogen. In order to calculate the partial pressure of each gas in this mixture, barometric pressure (760 mm Hg at sea level) must be corrected for the pressure exerted by water vapor (47 mm Hg) in alveolar air. Thus, the partial pressure (PO_2) of oxygen in alveolar air is equal to $.14 \times (760 - 47)$. This comes to almost 100 mm Hg. The partial pressure of carbon dioxide (PCO_2) in alveolar air, calculated in the same manner, is 40 mm Hg.

The partial pressure of a gas in a liquid is proportional to the amount of gas dissolved in the liquid. The amount dissolved is directly related to the partial pressure of the gas in the environment. A gas will diffuse into a liquid from a gaseous mixture over the liquid. For this reason, the blood flowing through the lungs tends to equilibrate its gaseous partial pressure with that of the alveolar air, that is, the PO_2 and PCO_2 of the blood leaving the lungs are nearly equal to the PO_2 and PCO_2 of the alveolar air.

Oxygen Transport. The partial pressure principle would explain the transport of 0.3 ml of oxygen per 100 ml in arterial blood. This, however, is well below the level necessary to sustain life. There must be another method of oxygen transport in the blood. This other mechanism is the transport of oxygen as *oxyhemoglobin*. The chemical combination of oxygen with hemoglobin to form oxyhemoglobin accounts for 97 per cent of the oxygen delivered to the tissues. Hemoglobin consists of four polypeptide chains, each wrapped around a nonprotein, iron-containing group called *heme*. Each iron atom can loosely bind one oxygen molecule. Normal blood contains 15 grams of hemoglobin per 100 ml of blood, and each gram is capable of combining with 1.34 ml of oxygen. Thus, if hemoglobin in the blood stream were completely saturated with oxygen, the total amount of oxygen bound to hemoglobin would be 1.34×15, or about 20 ml of oxygen per 100 ml of blood (commonly expressed as 20 volumes per cent). The degree to which hemoglobin combines with oxygen is determined by the partial pressure of oxygen, and a partial pressure of 100 mm Hg, the partial pressure of oxygen in blood leaving the lungs, is sufficient to almost saturate hemoglobin — hemoglobin in blood leaving the lungs is about 97 per cent saturated. Hence, this blood contains approximately 19.4 ml of oxygen ($.97 \times 20$) bound to hemoglobin per 100 ml of blood (19.4 volumes per cent). As first noted by Christian Bohr, K. A. Hasselbach, and August Krogh in 1904, the relationship between hemoglobin saturation and the partial pressure of oxygen (determined in a series of glass containers called microtonometers containing blood to which different concentrations of oxygen were added) gives rise to an S-shaped, or *sigmoid*, curve, known as the oxygen-hemoglobin dissociation curve (this is so because the binding of oxygen by one iron atom causes structural changes in hemoglobin that increase the affinity of the remaining iron atoms for oxygen). The curve rises relatively slowly at first, then steepens, and finally flattens out as it approaches complete saturation (Fig. 13–22).

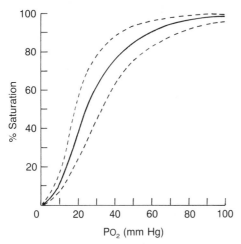

Figure 13–22. Oxygen-hemoglobin dissociation curves. The solid line is the dissociation curve determined at a carbon dioxide partial pressure of 40 mm Hg. An increase in Pco_2 shifts the curve to the right, a decrease shifts it to the left. Curve to the right determined at Pco_2 of 90 mm Hg, curve to the left determined at Pco_2 of 20 mm Hg.

A curve of this shape is well suited to hemoglobin's physiological role as a vehicle for transporting oxygen from the lungs to the tissues. A reduction in the Po_2 of arterial blood would have to be substantial before it has much effect on hemoglobin saturation. Thus, if one ascends to a moderately high altitude of 7500 feet, the partial pressure of oxygen in blood leaving the lungs will be reduced from 100 to about 60 mm Hg because of the low barometric pressure and partial pressure of oxygen in the inhaled air; yet the hemoglobin in this blood will be approximately 90 per cent saturated and will be carrying about 18 ml of oxygen (.9 × 20) per 100 ml of blood, not a great deal less than the 19.4 ml per 100 ml of blood it carries at sea level. The steeper part of the curve at lower partial pressures of oxygen means that when the blood arrives at the tissue capillaries, where oxygen is leaving the blood (and the Po_2 of blood falls on the average — varying from tissue to tissue — to about 40 mm Hg), hemoglobin surrenders a relatively large amount of oxygen for a small drop in Po_2. At rest, about 5 ml of oxygen per 100 ml of blood is released to the tissues. During strenuous exercise, two to three times this amount is released in the capillaries of active muscle, where the Po_2 may fall to as low as 20 mm Hg. The unloading of oxygen from hemo-

globin in exercising muscle is facilitated by rises in carbon dioxide concentration, acidity, and temperature (see below).

One of the important properties of hemoglobin is its response to changes in carbon dioxide concentration or pH. Increases in carbon dioxide concentration or decreases in pH reduce the affinity of hemoglobin for oxygen; hence, hemoglobin becomes less saturated with oxygen at all partial pressures of oxygen, shifting the oxygen-hemoglobin dissociation curve to the right (Fig. 13–22). Decreases in CO_2 concentration or increases in pH have the reverse effect — hemoglobin becomes more saturated with oxygen at all partial pressures of oxygen, shifting the curve to the left. These shifts, known as the *Bohr effect*, favor uptake of oxygen in the capillaries of the respiratory surfaces of the lungs (where CO_2 is leaving the blood) and the release of oxygen in the tissues (where CO_2 is entering the blood). The Bohr effect is especially useful during exercise — the rise in the production of carbon dioxide and metabolic acids provokes even greater increases in oxygen release from hemoglobin. Exercising muscle also benefits from the effect of temperature on the oxygen-hemoglobin dissociation curve, since a rise in temperature shifts the curve to the right, and the temperature of active muscle often increases by as much as 3 to 4 degrees.

Carbon Dioxide Transport. When carbon dioxide diffuses from the tissues to the blood (increasing the concentration of carbon dioxide in blood from about 48 to 52 volumes per cent, Pco_2 increasing from 40 to 46 mm Hg), about 70 per cent is transported as **bicarbonate ions**, about 20 per cent bound to the protein of hemoglobin (in combination with NH_2 groups, forming what is known as **carbaminohemoglobin**) and about 10 per cent in solution. The formation of bicarbonate ions occurs in the following manner. In the red blood cells, the enzyme **carbonic anhydrase** catalyzes the formation of carbonic acid:

$$H_2O + CO_2 \rightarrow H_2CO_3$$

Carbon acid dissociates into hydrogen and bicarbonate ions:

$$H_2CO_3 \rightarrow H^+ + HCO_3^-$$

Without the help of carbonic anhydrase, little

carbonic acid and bicarbonate would be formed (carbonic anhydrase increases the rate of carbonic acid formation 5000-fold). After the bicarbonate ions are formed inside the RBC most of them diffuse out of the red cells into the plasma and an equal number of chloride ions (Cl^-) diffuse into the cells in exchange. This shifting of chloride ions into the cell to satisfy the ionic equilibrium is referred to as the *chloride shift*. Thus, as the bicarbonate content of the plasma increases, the chloride content decreases.

While these processes are occurring, oxygen is being released from oxyhemoglobin and, since deoxyhemoglobin is a weaker acid than oxyhemoglobin, it combines with hydrogen ions released by the dissociation of carbonic acid. Deoxyhemoglobin also binds carbon dioxide much more readily than oxyhemoglobin and, as mentioned, about 20 per cent of the carbon dioxide in blood is transported bound to amino groups of the protein of hemoglobin as carbaminohemoglo-

bin. The exchange of respiratory gases in the tissues is summarized in Figure 13–23.

When venous blood reaches the lungs, carbon dioxide diffuses out of the plasma into the alveoli as the processes described above are reversed: Oxygenation of hemoglobin results in the release of hydrogen ions, which combine with bicarbonate ions, and the carbonic acid formed by this reaction is split into carbon dioxide and water (the reaction between CO_2 and water, catalyzed by carbonic anhydrase, is reversible, and in the lungs, where CO_2 is leaving the blood stream, the equilibrium of the reaction shifts so as to favor the breakdown of carbonic acid). In addition, carbon dioxide is liberated from carbaminohemoglobin as oxyhemoglobin is formed. About 4 ml of carbon dioxide per 100 ml of blood is released from the blood stream to the alveoli during the passage of blood through the respiratory surfaces of the lungs. Figure 13–24 summarizes the exchange of respiratory gases in the lungs.

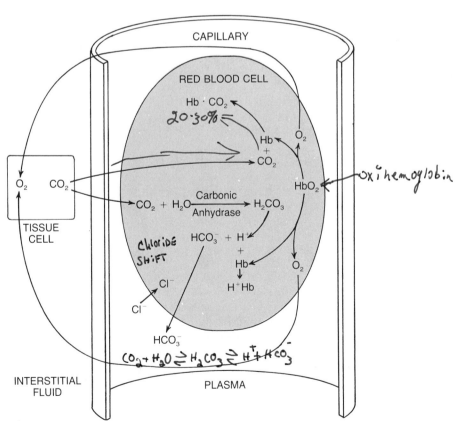

Figure 13–23. Exchange of respiratory gases in the tissues.

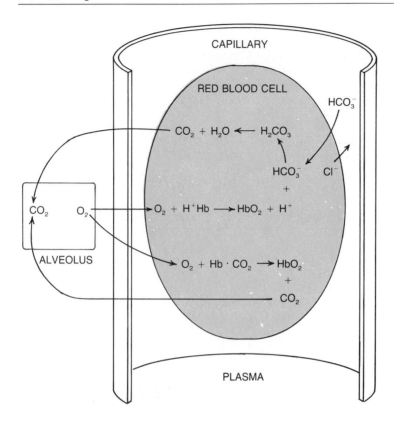

NOT ON EXAM

Figure 13-24. Exchange of respiratory gases in the lungs.

CONTROL OF RESPIRATION

Maintaining the Normal Respiratory Rhythm: Brain Centers and the Hering-Breuer Reflex

The diaphragm and other muscles of respiration are voluntary and can be controlled at will. However, normal breathing continues involuntarily even in an unconscious state, and removal of all parts of the brain above the pons does not significantly alter the respiratory rhythm.

Neurogenic mechanisms controlling respiration are located in the reticular substance of the medulla oblongata and pons. The area in the medulla is generally referred to as the **respiratory center**. Respiratory control areas in the pons are known as the *pneumotaxic center* and the *apneustic center*. Of paramount importance is the medullary respiratory center, consisting of bilateral, overlapping inspiratory and expiratory centers. If this center is destroyed, breathing ceases altogether.

The basic automatic rhythm of respira-

tion is established by the medullary respiratory center. However, the normal timing of the alternating rhythm — on the average an inspiratory phase of two seconds and expiratory phase of three seconds — depends largely upon the regulatory action of inhibitory inputs to the respiratory center from the lungs as they expand and from the pneumotaxic center. The regulation of the respiratory cycle by expansion of the lungs is known as the **Hering-Breuer reflex**, first described in 1868 by Hering and Breuer, who observed that inflation of the lungs arrested inspiration, expiration then following. The lungs contain stretch receptors which, when activated by expansion of the lungs, transmit impulses via the vagus nerve to the respiratory center that inhibit inspiration, thereby preventing further inflation.

Under normal conditions, the Hering-Breuer reflex plays the dominant role in maintaining the normal respiratory pattern. It is apparently supported by the *pneumotaxic reflex*, which occurs as the pneumotaxic center receives discharges from the respiratory center during inspiration and returns impulses that inhibit inspiration. Section of the vagus nerve or removal of the pneumotaxic center in animals causes deep, slow breathing. The influence of the apneustic center on respiration can be demonstrated in some animals by eliminating both the vagus nerve and the pneumotaxic center. This elicits cramping of the inspiratory muscles (contractions lasting several seconds) caused by discharges from the apneustic center, no longer subject to inhibitory influences from the pneumotaxic center and vagus nerve. This type of response is often called apneusis. How important the apneustic center is in humans, however, is uncertain.

Regulation of Pulmonary Ventilation

A distinction can be made between establishing and regulating a normal respiratory rhythm and adjusting ventilation by modifying the activity of the respiratory center so as to maintain normal concentrations of carbon dioxide, oxygen, and hydrogen ions in the blood or altering ventilation to meet the demands of changing conditions, such as exercising strenuously or living at high altitudes. Changes in blood levels of carbon dioxide, hydrogen ions, and oxygen induce changes in ventilation that tend to counter the changes in blood chemistry so as to keep the carbon dioxide and oxygen concentrations and pH within a narrow range. Ordinarily, these interactions in turn keep ventilation within narrow limits. However, during exercise or following ascent to a high altitude, additional mechanisms cause substantial increases in ventilation.

Site of Action of Carbon Dioxide, Hydrogen Ions, and Oxygen on Ventilation

Under normal conditions, the primary regulator of pulmonary ventilation are changes in the carbon dioxide concentration in the blood (and accompanying changes in pH — see below). At normal blood levels, oxygen has only a slight effect on ventilation. The primary site of action of carbon dioxide and hydrogen ions is the respiratory center in the medulla or the immediate vicinity. A rise in carbon dioxide and hydrogen ion concentrations increases ventilation, a fall depresses it. A decrease in oxygen concentration increases ventilation by stimulat-

ing chemoreceptors in the *carotid and aortic bodies* (located near the bifurcation of the common carotid arteries into the internal and external carotids and in the aortic arch), which in turn transmit signals to the medullary respiratory center. Although a reflexive increase in ventilation in response to an increase in the carbon dioxide concentration in blood flowing to the carotid bodies can be demonstrated, some investigators have inferred from the experimental evidence that ordinarily the increase in ventilation induced by the action of CO_2 on the respiratory center prevents a rise in CO_2 to levels that would provoke a response from the peripheral chemoreceptors. On the other hand, some researchers have concluded from studies in animals with denervated chemoreceptors that about 10 to 20 per cent of the regulation of pulmonary ventilation in the resting state arises from stimulation of peripheral chemoreceptors. The peripheral receptor response to CO_2 undoubtedly assumes a more important role in respiratory control during sleep, when short periods of apnea may occur in normal individuals, especially infants, apparently because the medullary respiratory center is less responsive to CO_2. Under these conditions CO_2 rises to levels that are more likely to activate the chemoreceptors. A deficiency in the carotid body chemoreceptor response has, in fact, been implicated in the so-called **sudden infant death syndrome** (crib death). It is the general consensus that in most cases the cause of death of these infants is a failure of respiratory control — breathing fails to start after a prolonged period of apnea. Prolonged episodes of apnea during sleep and a depressed respiratory response to increased levels of inhaled CO_2 have been observed in apparently healthy babies who later died in their sleep — victims of the sudden infant death syndrome. In one study, postmortem examination revealed that more than half of 56 victims had underdeveloped carotid bodies (in humans, the aortic bodies are believed to be of minor importance as respiratory chemoreceptors).

Quantitative Aspects of the Effects of Carbon Dioxide, Hydrogen Ions, and Oxygen on Ventilation

Carbon Dioxide and Hydrogen Ions. Inspired air normally contains about 0.04

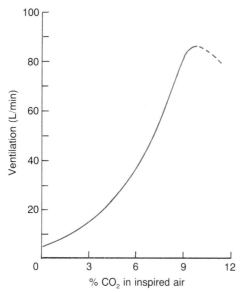

Figure 13–25. Effect of carbon dioxide on ventilation. Carbon dioxide becomes intolerable when the percentage in inspired air exceeds 10 per cent.

per cent carbon dioxide. Inhaling air with 4 per cent carbon dioxide, on the average, doubles ventilation (Fig. 13–25). Concentrations of up to 10 per cent CO_2 induce further increases in ventilation until a maximum of about 80 liters per minute is reached. Further increases in carbon dioxide concentration depress ventilation and cause considerable discomfort and dizziness. In terms of partial pressure, an increase in P_{CO_2} from 40 mm Hg (normal arterial level) to 42.5 mm Hg doubles ventilation. A rise to 60 mm Hg increases ventilation 10-fold. Lowering P_{CO_2} depresses respiration. The threshold value for P_{CO_2} is very close to 40 mm Hg. Lowering the carbon dioxide concentration below this causes apnea.

Since, as described earlier, carbon dioxide produces hydrogen ions by dissociation of carbonic acid, the question has been raised as to whether carbon dioxide itself stimulates respiration or whether it is the hydrogen ions that are responsible for this action. It is generally agreed that both influence the activity of the respiratory center. It has also been shown that an increase in the concentration of metabolic acids in the blood increases ventilation when carbon dioxide levels are not rising. The effects of carbon dioxide and acidity are additive; that is, the effects may summate or cancel one another.

Oxygen. Lowering the concentration of oxygen in inhaled gas mixtures below the approximately 21 per cent normally present in the atmosphere does not consistently increase ventilation until the oxygen levels are reduced to about 10 to 12 per cent. Usually a measurable increase in ventilation is not observed until the P_{O_2} in blood falls below approximately 60 mm Hg. The response to a reduction in oxygen concentration is limited because the increase in ventilation induced by the lowering of P_{O_2} in blood blows off carbon dioxide. The reduction in carbon dioxide concentration in the blood decreases ventilation, braking the stimulatory effect of the reduced oxygen concentration on ventilation. Hence, in order to demonstrate the stimulatory effect of reduced oxygen concentrations per se on ventilation, it is necessary to hold the blood P_{CO_2} constant by adding CO_2 to the inhaled gas mixtures. When this is done, a slight increase in ventilation is observed when the blood P_{O_2} is lowered from 100 to 80 mm Hg. Further reductions in P_{O_2} produce more substantial increases in ventilation — approximately a doubling at 60 mm Hg and a tripling at 40 mm Hg. At 20 mm Hg, it may be five times higher than normal.

One of the physiological adjustments that take place when an individual ascends to a very high altitude is a decided increase in ventilation in response to the reduced oxygen content of the rarefied atmosphere. Ventilation promptly increases to a moderate degree and continues to increase gradually over a period of a week to levels substantially above normal *despite the pronounced fall in blood CO_2* induced by the hyperventilation. This acclimatization is associated with a greater responsiveness of the respiratory center to CO_2 so that a low concentration of CO_2 in the blood has only a slight depressant effect on ventilation.

Effect of Exercise on Ventilation

During strenous exercise, ventilation can increase as much as 15- to 20-fold. At one time, some respiratory physiologists believed that the increase in carbon dioxide production during exercise was responsible for the increase in ventilation. However, an increase of P_{CO_2} in arterial blood usually is not observed during exercise — the increase in ventilation prevents its accumulation in the blood. A number of observations indicate that the increase in ventilation results principally from stimulation of the respiratory center by reflexes originating in proprioceptors in the joints of the body and impulses transmitted from the motor area of the cerebral cortex.

Other Factors Affecting Ventilation

Blood pressure also influences ventilation. A sudden drop of arterial pressure brings about an increase in ventilation, and a sudden rise in pressure brings about a decrease in ventilation. These effects are elicited from baroreceptors (described in Chapter 11) in the aortic arch and carotid sinuses that reflexively stimulate or inhibit the respiratory center, and the respiratory response helps stabilize blood pressure. Thus, the increase in ventilation following a drop in blood pressure increases the return of venous blood to the heart, thereby raising blood pressure. (Venous return increases because deeper inspirations increase the pressure gradient between the abdominal and thoracic cavities.) With a rise in blood pressure, the reverse occurs. The effects of changes in blood pressure on ventilation, however, are observed only when the fall or rise in pressure is abrupt and pronounced.

Different sensory stimuli can also elicit reflex respiratory effects. For example, severe pain usually causes increased ventilation, and a sudden cold stimulus brings about temporary apnea. Another stimulus, that of stretching the anal sphincter, increases ventilation. Stretching the anal sphincter is sometimes employed to stimulate respiration during emergencies.

Age is another factor influencing ventilation. At birth, normal ventilation is about 500 ml per minute, with a respiratory rate of about 33 breaths per minute and a tidal volume of 15 ml. Ventilation increases to about 6 liters per minute in the adult (rate, 12 breaths per minute; tidal volume, 500 ml). This means that infants ventilate about 200 ml per minute per kilogram as compared with about half this amount per kilogram in adults.

RESPIRATORY PHENOMENA

Cough. A *cough* is a mechanism for clearing obstructions of the airway. Usually it is a reflex response to irritation of the respiratory passages in which impulses transmitted to the medulla trigger an automatic sequence of events. During coughing, forcible expiratory effort against the closed glottis first raises the air pressure in the chest. The glottis then suddenly opens, reducing pressure in the trachea and large bronchioles to atmospheric level. The high pressure still remaining in the air spaces around the trachea collapses its posterior wall. As a result, air passes out through a much narrower trachea with a great force and velocity, blowing out foreign material and mucus with it.

Sneeze. A *sneeze* might be described as an upper respiratory cough. In the preparatory stages more and more air is inspired, and at the climax air is expelled with explosive force. During a sneeze the glottis is wide open and air meets its chief resistance in the mouth or nasal passages, so that the expiratory blast serves to clear the passages of the nose or mouth just as the cough clears the bronchi and trachea.

Yawn. *Yawning* aids respiration by more completely ventilating the lung. In ordinary breathing apparently not all of the alveoli of the lungs are equally ventilated; some actually periodically close. The blood passing through collapsed alveoli enters the arterial system without being oxygenated and dilutes the average oxygen content. Collapsed alveoli are opened by the long, deep inspiration of the yawn.

Hiccup. A *hiccup* is an abnormal response serving no known useful purpose. It is a spasmodic contraction of the diaphragm, resulting from stimulation either in the diaphragm itself or in the respiratory center of the brain, and caused by substances in the blood or by local circulatory abnormalities. The vocal cords usually open during inspiration (vocalization is produced normally only during expiration) and are apparently closed during the hiccup; the vibrations produce the characteristic sound. Persistent hiccups can generally be halted by inhalation of air containing 5 to 7 per cent carbon dioxide.

Cheyne-Stokes Breathing. *Cheyne-Stokes breathing* is a type of periodic breathing; that is, breathing characterized by alternating intervals of breathing and apnea. During the breathing period of Cheyne-Stokes breathing, the depth of respiration increases gradually to a maximum and then decreases rapidly. The use of narcotics, brain damage, and chronic heart failure are among the causes of Cheyne-Stokes breathing. Narcotics and brain damage apparently alter the sensitivity of the respiratory center. Higher than normal concentrations of carbon dioxide are needed to initiate respiration, but small increases in concentration provoke an excessive response. An episode of hyperventilation lowers the carbon dioxide concentration, reducing the activity of the respiratory center. Breathing becomes shallower and ceases because the center fails to respond rapidly enough to the rise in the concentration of carbon dioxide. Heart failure may cause Cheyne-Stokes breathing because of a delay in the flow of blood from the heart to the brain. Carbon dioxide fails to reach the respiratory center in time to prevent apnea. Cheyne-Stokes respiration often occurs as the respiratory pattern in premature infants. In normal adults, a few cycles of Cheyne-Stokes breathing may follow voluntary hyperventilation.

COMMON RESPIRATORY DISORDERS

The most important respiratory disorders are those in which the blood fails to become oxygenated (Fig. 13–26). Nearly all respiratory problems tend toward hypoxia. Hypoxia is sometimes manifested in *cyanosis*. This term refers to the fact that the skin, mucous membranes, and nail beds turn blue because of an increased presence of deoxygenated hemoglobin in the capillaries.

Emphysema. Emphysema, a condition characterized by a breakdown of alveolar walls and loss of elasticity of the lungs, usually is the final stage of a lung disease which causes chronic bronchiolar obstruction. It has become one of the most common respiratory diseases, primarily because it occurs more frequently in heavy smokers than in nonsmokers. One factor recently implicated in the development of emphysema is damage to the elastic fiber network of the alveolar wall by the enzyme elastase. Normally the lungs are protected against such damage by a circulating antielastase. However, in cigarette smokers there is an imbalance between elastase and antielastase activity as a result of (1) suppression of antielastase activity, (2) more neutrophils (which release elastase) in the lungs, and (3) secretion of elastase by macrophages (those of nonsmokers do not secrete this enzyme). The likelihood of bronchiolar obstruction is increased in cigarette smokers because terminal bronchioles are narrowed by hyperplasia (an increase in the number

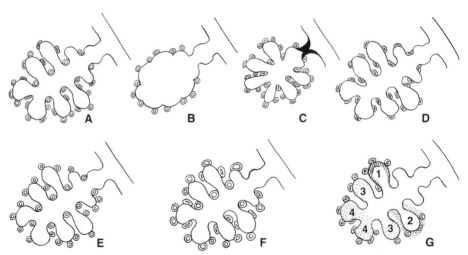

Figure 13–26. Area for gas exchange in the alveoli. *A*, Normal arrangement of alveoli clustered about an alveolar duct (about half the alveolar capillaries are open, and half are closed). *B*, Destruction of alveolar septa and about half the total available number of capillaries. *C*, Obstruction of bronchiole and decreased area for gas exchange with no decrease in potential alveolocapillary contact surface. *D*, Obstruction of the pulmonary circulation (no alveolocapillary blood flow). *E*, Increase in the number of open capillaries, as might occur in exercise. *F*, Capillary enlargement, as might occur in chronic mitral stenosis. *G*, Longer paths for diffusion due to (1) thickening of alveolar epithelium, (2) tissue separating alveolar capillary from alveolar epithelium, (3) beginning pulmonary edema, and (4) nonventilated alveoli filled with edema fluid or exudate.

of cells) and the secretion of mucus is increased. Plugging of bronchioles with mucus often traps air in the alveoli, causing them to become overextended, and, if an individual happens to cough, the sudden rise in pressure may rupture alveolar walls, especially those damaged by the action of elastase. The physiological effects of emphysema include increased airway resistance, with increased effort expended in breathing, and greatly decreased diffusing capacity. Hypoxia, hypercapnia (increased CO_2 concentration in the blood), and acidosis are observed, and pulmonary hypertension is induced, owing to the decrease in the number of pulmonary capillaries.

Atelectasis. Atelectasis (G. *atelēs*, imperfect; G. *ektasis*, extension) is the term used to describe any condition that causes collapse of alveoli in a localized region, an entire lung, or both lungs. The respiratory distress syndrome (described on page 455) is one example of atelectasis. Common causes of atelectasis are a chest wound that permits air to leak into the pleural cavity and blockage of a primary bronchus or one of the smaller bronchial tubes following general anesthesia given for major surgery.

Bronchiectasis. Bronchiectasis is characterized by dilatation of the bronchi. It results from three factors: (1) flaccidity of the bronchial walls following chronic inflammation of the bronchial tree; (2) increase in the distending forces, as from long, continued coughing; and (3) traction on the walls, as from fibrous tissue formation in the lung secondary to an inflammatory disease such as pneumonia. The symptoms of bronchiectasis are coughing, voluminous sputum, and labored respiration on exertion. Pertussis immunization is helping to decrease the incidence of bronchiectasis.

Asthma. Substances in the air, such as pollen, may cause an allergic reaction when inspired, creating localized edema in the walls of the small bronchioles, secretion of thick mucus into their lumens, and spasms of their smooth muscular walls (see discussion of allergen-reagin reactions in Chapter 12). There is evidence that the allergic spasm of smooth muscle may be intensified by a decrease in opposing relaxation because of a decreased responsiveness of bronchiolar smooth muscle to epinephrine. Some investigators believe the hyposensitivity to epinephrine is caused by a deficiency of epinephrine receptors (β-adrenergic type—see Chapter 9, page 294) as a result of their destruction by an autoimmune response. The spasms greatly increase airway resistance. Since during expiration the rise in intrathoracic pressure compresses smaller bronchi and bronchioles, airway resistance is greater during expiration than inspiration. Therefore, asthmatics may inspire adequately but expiration is difficult and prolonged. Over an extended period the lungs become increasingly distended; with long-standing asthma, the chest adopts a barrel-shaped appearance. In children asthma is commonly caused by sensitivities to food; in adults it is frequently caused by sensitivities to pollen. An asthmatic attack can be precipitated by an emotional crisis as well as by an allergen.

Pneumonia. Pneumonia is an inflammation of the alveoli and supportive tissues, usually with an accumulation of fluid and blood cells in the alveoli. The most common type is bacterial pneumonia and is usually caused by pneumococci.

The disease begins as an infection within the alveoli of one part of the lungs. The alveolar membrane becomes edematous and highly porous, to the point of allowing red blood cells and white blood cells to pass out of the blood into the alveoli. Therefore, the infected alveoli progressively fill with fluid and cells, and the infection spreads as bacteria extend to other alveoli.

Reduction in the total available surface area of respiratory membrane therefore occurs. As in many other pulmonary diseases, carbon dioxide is adequately excreted, but oxygenation of the blood is diminished. This is caused by the fact that carbon dioxide passes through the alveolar walls about 20 times as readily as does oxygen. Pneumonia occurs most frequently in young children and in the aged. It is commonly classified according to the causative microorganism, for example, as pneumococcal, streptococcal, staphylococcal, or Friedländer's (Klebsiella pneumoniae).

Tuberculosis. In tuberculosis, the tubercle bacilli invade the lungs, and initially there is acute inflammation in the area of the bacilli, with accumulation first of neutrophils and later macrophages. If the bacteria are destroyed, healing may occur without scarring. If immediate healing does not occur, the lesion may undergo early necrosis, sometimes leading to massive cavity formation.

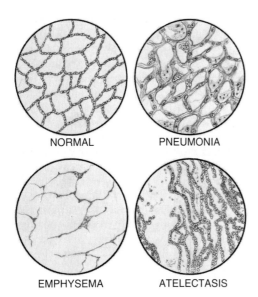

NORMAL PNEUMONIA

EMPHYSEMA ATELECTASIS

Figure 13–27. Histologic sections of normal and diseased alveoli.

More frequently, the lesion is invaded by epithelioid cells and fibroblasts, and the characteristic *tubercle* is produced, containing tubercle bacilli, leukocytes, macrophages, epithelioid cells, and fibroblasts. Older tubercles may be surrounded by a thick, fibrous capsule. These lesions may heal and calcify following penetration and replacement of the tubercles by fibrous tissue. If the bacilli continue to multiply, necrosis occurs in the center of the tubercle, producing a soft, necrotic material having the consistency and appearance of cheese (so-called caseous tubercle). Caseous tubercles may enlarge by extension or fusion with other tubercles. Eventually, the caseous material may be discharged into the bronchioles, leaving cavities. Tuberculosis may reduce considerably the amount of functional lung tissue. In addition, the fibrosis decreases lung compliance. Consequently, vital capacity and maximum breathing capacity are diminished.

Pulmonary Edema. Pulmonary edema influences respiration in much the same way as pneumonia. It is caused by an insufficiency of the left heart in pumping blood received from the lungs to the rest of the body, causing blood to back up into the pulmonary circulation. This is generally the result of cardiac insufficiency caused by poor blood supply to the muscles of the heart, but can also be caused by mitral or aortic valvular disease.

Infarction of the Lungs. The commonest source of pulmonary infarction is an embolus from the right atrium or from the lower extremities and pelvis which eventually obstructs a branch of the pulmonary artery. The symptoms of pulmonary infarction are a sudden onset of labored respiration, often with collapse of the lung and a bloody sputum. Characteristically, the onset is acute and can be followed rapidly by death.

Air Embolism. Air embolism is an unusual complication which occasionally follows the opening of a large vein in the neck during a surgical operation or the accidental injection of large volumes of air with blood transfusions. In the dog it is necessary to introduce 90 ml of air to produce death; however, the administration of even a small amount of air into the pulmonary vein — for example, as little as 1 ml — can cause death, since it frequently lodges in the brain.

Sinusitis. Sinusitis in the acute stage is manifested by pain referred to the maxillary and frontal sinuses. The nose is plugged, and nasal and postnasal mucus discharges occur. In the chronic form of sinusitis, the postnasal discharge becomes persistent.

General Signs and Symptoms

Signs and symptoms associated with respiratory disturbances include the following. A productive cough — or for that matter, a nonproductive cough — is a symptom common to disease of the trachea, bronchi, bronchioles, or pulmonary parenchyma, whether infectious or the result of tumor. *Hemoptysis,* or blood-streaked sputum, accompanies disease of the lung. Involvement of the pleura by infection or tumor is associated with pain intensified by respiration and coughing.

Spontaneous pneumothorax is characterized by pain and breathlessness. Breathlessness is a common symptom in pulmonary disease whenever there is decreased vital capacity below the normal minimum for the particular patient. This might be caused by pulmonary consolidation, emphysema, or disease of the heart.

ARTIFICIAL RESPIRATION

Mouth-to-Mouth Resuscitation

In 1958 the American Medical Association published a symposium concluding that mouth-to-mouth resuscitation was superior to all other means of artificial respiration. It is currently believed that mouth-to-mouth resuscitation is the only technique assuring adequate ventilation in all cases. The subject is placed in a supine position; the rescuer, behind the subject, grasps the subject's lower jaw and lifts it vertically upward. The rescuer then places his mouth over the subject's mouth, pinching the nostrils shut at the same time, and exhales until it can be seen that the chest has expanded. The rescuer's mouth is then removed to allow the subject to exhale. The cycle is repeated approximately 12 to 15 times per minute (Fig. 13–28).

Iron Lung

The *tank respirator* (iron lung) is the apparatus that first made prolonged artificial respiration a practical matter. The patient is placed into a rigid tank from which only his head protrudes, and an airtight seal is made around his neck. To provide inspiration the bellows is expanded, so that the pressure in the tank becomes subatmospheric. Pressure in the patient's upper airway is atmospheric, so that the air flows along the trachea into the lungs. This flow of air continues until the lungs are sufficiently inflated for the elastic resistance of the lungs and the paralyzed chest wall to equalize the difference between atmospheric pressure and the pressure within the tank. The intrathoracic pressure lies between the pressure in the trachea and that within the tank, its precise level depending on the elastic resistance of the lungs and chest wall. The principal use of the tank respirator is for patients with weakness of the respiratory muscles, such as sometimes occurs in poliomyelitis. The disadvantage of a tank respirator is that it is cumbersome and the patient is rather inaccessible to other forms of treatment and diagnosis. Iron lungs are infrequently used today.

Mechanical Respirator Therapy

Mechanical respirators are used intermittently or continuously for assisting or controlling breathing. Basically, there are two types. Pressure-cycle respirators inflate the lungs to a predetermined pressure; inspiration ceases and expiration begins when this pressure is reached. Acute respiratory distress is treated primarily with a volume-controlled respirator which delivers a predetermined volume of air with each inspiration. The Bennett respirator is shown in Figure 13–29.

Intermittent Positive Pressure Respiration

Most medical centers in the United States currently use different pieces of equipment for *intermittent positive pressure respiration* (Fig. 13–29). This is administered through an endotracheal tube passed into the nose or mouth. The larynx will not tolerate the presence of a tube for extended periods of time, and 24 hours is probably as long as it should be left in place. For long term intermittent positive pressure respiration, it is necessary to introduce gas into the lungs through a tracheostomy. When the patient is ill, a tracheostomy tube with an inflated cuff is usually employed to make an airtight seal with the walls of the trachea. This serves two purposes — prevention of saliva, vomit, or other foreign material from passing into the chest, and prevention of air which is blown into the chest from leaking through the nose

ARTIFICIAL RESPIRATION
MOUTH-TO-MOUTH (MOUTH-TO-NOSE) METHOD

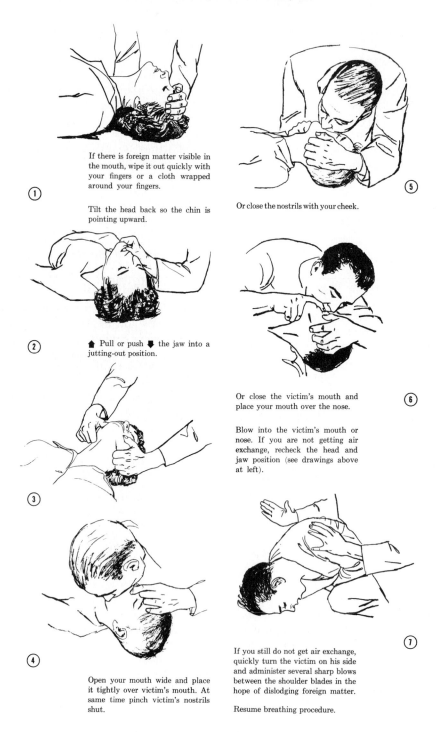

① If there is foreign matter visible in the mouth, wipe it out quickly with your fingers or a cloth wrapped around your fingers.

Tilt the head back so the chin is pointing upward.

② ⬆ Pull or push ⬇ the jaw into a jutting-out position.

④ Open your mouth wide and place it tightly over victim's mouth. At same time pinch victim's nostrils shut.

⑤ Or close the nostrils with your cheek.

⑥ Or close the victim's mouth and place your mouth over the nose.

Blow into the victim's mouth or nose. If you are not getting air exchange, recheck the head and jaw position (see drawings above at left).

⑦ If you still do not get air exchange, quickly turn the victim on his side and administer several sharp blows between the shoulder blades in the hope of dislodging foreign matter.

Resume breathing procedure.

THE AMERICAN NATIONAL RED CROSS

Figure 13–28. Mouth-to-mouth respiration. (Courtesy of the American National Red Cross.)

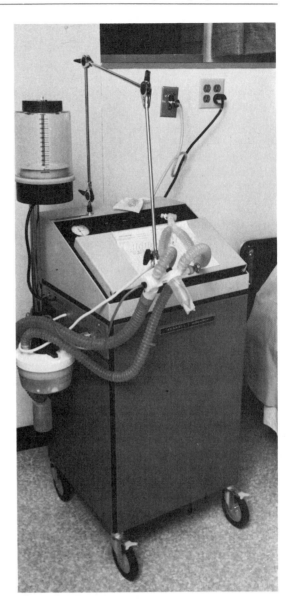

Figure 13–29. Artificial respirator.

and mouth. The tracheostomy tube is connected to the tubing from a respirator which, during inspiration, provides pressure above atmospheric pressure. Air passes into the chest until the pressure in the airway is balanced by the elastic resistance of the lungs and chest wall. The intrathoracic pressure is raised but remains less than the pressure in the airway. The intrathoracic pressure is, therefore, higher than atmospheric pressure applied to the trunk, limbs, and veins, so that intermittent positive pressure respiration impedes the venous return during inspiration in precisely the same way as the tank respirator. The principal use of intermittent positive pressure respiration is for the patient who not only requires artificial respiration but also needs a tracheostomy.

SUMMARY

THE RESPIRATORY SYSTEM

Components and Function of the Respiratory System

1. Exchange of respiratory gases between the blood and air (uptake of oxygen, elimination of carbon dioxide) takes place in the alveoli of the lungs.

2. The nose, pharynx, larynx, trachea, and primary bronchi form an open passage, the upper respiratory tract, leading from the exterior to the lungs. In the lungs the primary bronchi subdivide into lobar and segmental bronchi, bronchioles, and alveolar ducts. The latter lead into the alveoli.

Nasal Cavity

1. Divided by a septum into right and left halves.

2. In each half superior, middle, and inferior meatuses lie below the superior, middle, and inferior conchae (turbinates).

3. Openings: anterior nares to outside; posterior nares to nasopharynx.

Pharynx

1. Musculomembranous tube lined with mucous membrane.

2. Nasopharynx (behind the nose) has four openings: two auditory (Eustachian) tubes, two posterior nares.

3. Oropharynx (behind mouth) has one opening: the isthmus of the fauces.

4. Laryngopharynx (behind larynx) has two openings: into larynx and esophagus.

5. Contains pharyngeal tonsil (adenoids) in nasopharynx, palatine tonsils at junction of oral cavity and oropharynx, and lingual tonsil at base of tongue.

Larynx

1. Nine cartilages

   a. Unpaired: thyroid (Adam's apple), cricoid (signet ring), and epiglottis (lid to larynx).
   b. Paired: arytenoid, cuneiform, and corniculate.

2. A pair of vocal folds (true vocal cords) extend from the thyroid cartilage to the arytenoid cartilages. The space between the folds, the *rima glottidis*, or *glottis*, is widened by contraction of the posterior cricoarytenoid muscles and closed by contraction of the lateral cricoarytenoid muscles. The cricothyroid muscles are the principal tensors of the vocal folds. In phonation, long, lax cords give low-pitched voice; short, tense cords give high-pitched voice.

Trachea

1. Tube four to five inches long from larynx to bronchi containing 15 to 20 horseshoe-shaped cartilages. Openings of the "horseshoes" face posteriorly and are bridged by smooth muscle; spaces between cartilages filled with elastic and collagenous fibers.

2. Tracheotomy: opening into trachea; tracheostomy: tube into trachea.

Bronchi and Branches

1. Primary bronchi formed by branching of trachea; right primary bronchus shorter, wider, more vertical.

2. Successive divisions: three right and two left secondary (lobar) bronchi; tertiary, or segmental, bronchi, which are distributed to the bronchopulmonary segments and which divide into successively smaller and smaller branches, the finest branches called bronchioles; terminal bronchioles arising from a bronchiole immediately after the bronchiole enters a lung lobule; respiratory bronchioles, subdivisions of terminal bronchioles; alveolar ducts, which arise from respiratory bronchioles.

Alveoli

1. Arranged in clusters, each cluster called an alveolar sac.

2. Cells

   a. Thin squamous epithelial: single layer forms an almost continuous lining.
   b. Type II epithelial (cuboidal): secrete surfactant that coats alveoli, lowering surface tension (deficiency in surfactant in premature infants can cause respiratory distress syndrome).
   c. Macrophages.

Mechanics of Breathing

1. Inspiration: accomplished actively — contractions of diaphragm and external intercostals enlarge thorax and expand lungs. Lowered intrapulmonic pressure causes air to move into the lungs (action of diaphragm accounting for most air movement).

2. Expiration: accomplished passively — relaxation of diaphragm and external intercostals allows elastic recoil of lungs to force air out of the lungs.

Ventilation (Minute Respiratory Volume)

1. Normally, at rest, approximately 6 liters per minute, representing a tidal volume (volume of air inspired or expired with each breath) of 500 ml and a respiratory rate of 12 breaths per minute.

2. Shallow, rapid breathing decreases efficiency because it increases the proportion of air moving in and out of the dead space (nose, pharynx, larynx, trachea, and bronchial tree).

3. Deep, slow breathing is not maximally effective because it increases the work required to expand the lungs (overcoming elastic recoil) and requires the use of expiratory muscles.

Oxygen Transport in Blood

1. Ninety-seven per cent of the oxygen delivered to the tissues is carried by hemoglobin.

2. The relationship between the partial pressure of oxygen and the per cent saturation of hemoglobin with oxygen is described by a sigmoid curve. Hemoglobin in blood leaving the lungs, where the P_{O_2} is about 100 mm Hg, is about 97 per cent saturated; P_{O_2} can drop to 60 mm Hg and the hemoglobin will still be almost 90 per cent saturated. As blood passes through the tissues, where the P_{O_2} drops on the average to about 40 mm Hg, hemoglobin surrenders about 5 ml of oxygen per 100 ml of blood.

3. An increase in carbon dioxide concentration or decrease in pH increases oxygen release by hemoglobin.

Carbon Dioxide Transport in Blood

1. When carbon dioxide passes from the tissues to the capillaries, the concentration of carbon dioxide in the blood increases on the average from 48 to 52 ml of carbon dioxide per 100 ml of blood.

2. About 70 per cent of the carbon dioxide is transported as bicarbonate ions (made possible by the enzymatic action of carbonic anhydrase in red blood cells), about 20 per cent is transported bound to hemoglobin, and the remainder is transported in solution.

Maintenance of Normal Respiratory Rhythm

1. The basic automatic breathing rhythm is dependent upon the respiratory center in the medulla. Breathing ceases if this center is destroyed.

2. The depth and pattern of the breathing cycle is regulated by the Hering-Breuer reflex, which involves inhibition of inspiration by expansion of the lungs.

Regulation of Ventilation

1. Accumulation of carbon dioxide in the blood increases ventilation principally by directly stimulating the respiratory center. A reduction in carbon dioxide concentration has the reverse effect. Under normal conditions, change in the carbon dioxide concentration in the blood is the primary regulator of ventilation.

2. Reduced oxygen concentration in the blood increases ventilation by stimulating chemoreceptors in the carotid bodies, which in turn stimulate the respiratory center. This reflex is effective at very high altitudes because, as a result of acclimatization, the reduced concentration of CO_2 in the blood induced by hyperventilation has only a slight depressant effect on respiration.

3. During exercise, ventilation is increased as a result of stimulation of the respiratory center by reflexes arising from proprioceptors in joints and impulses transmitted from the cerebrum.

REVIEW QUESTIONS

1. List the structures through which air passes from the nose to the alveoli.
2. Name the three paired and three unpaired laryngeal cartilages. Describe the structural differences between the male

and female thyroid cartilage and one consequence of this difference. Describe the vocal folds. What is the name of the space between the vocal folds?

3. Name the three types of cells found in alveoli. Which type almost completely surrounds the alveolar spaces? Which type secretes a surfactant? Of what importance is the secretion of surfactant?

4. Contraction of what muscle accounts for most of the air movement during respiration? During quiet breathing, is expiration active or passive? Describe the changes in intrapulmonic and intrapleural pressure during inspiration and expiration.

5. Define the following terms: tidal volume, vital capacity, inspiratory reserve volume, inspiratory capacity, and ventilation.

6. Explain how the shape of the oxygen-hemoglobin curve suits the physiological function of hemoglobin.

7. How is most of the carbon dioxide transported in the blood? What are the other means of carbon dioxide transport? What is the role of the enzyme carbonic anhydrase in carbon dioxide transport?

8. Describe the Hering-Breuer reflex.

9. Which has a more pronounced effect on respiration: changes in blood levels of carbon dioxide or of oxygen?

10. Do changes in carbon dioxide concentration act principally on or near the respiratory center in the medulla or via carotid and aortic body chemoreceptor reflexes? How do changes in carbon dioxide concentration affect ventilation?

11. Does a fall in oxygen concentration increase ventilation by acting centrally on the medulla or on peripheral chemoreceptors?

12. How does ascending to very high altitudes affect ventilation? How can the change in ventilation be accounted for?

14

The Digestive System and Metabolism

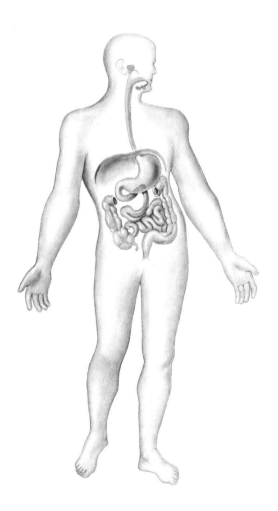

Objectives

The aim of this chapter is to enable the student to:

□ Describe the components of the digestive system and its associated structures.

□ Distinguish between the four layers of the digestive tract.

□ Identify the unique anatomical features of the small intestine.

□ List the sequence of events in swallowing.

□ Describe the motility of the separate parts of the gastrointestinal tract.

□ Outline the steps in the digestion of carbohydrate, protein, and fat.

□ Discuss the regulation of the secretions of the digestive glands.

□ Describe the absorption of the products of digestion and identify their sites of absorption.

□ Explain the function of bile in absorption and digestion.

□ Summarize the functions of the liver.

□ Describe the disposition of the major foodstuffs following their absorption.

□ Briefly discuss the regulation of food intake.

□ Explain what is meant by the basal metabolic rate.

□ Describe the mechanisms of the regulation of body temperature.

HISTORY

The history of medicine gives an interesting account of the ideas and events leading to our present state of knowledge of the digestive system. In the early nineteenth century many physical and chemical theories of digestion were entertained but only meagerly substantiated or correlated. The detailed workings of the gastrointestinal system as a whole were largely a matter of dispute — even in the reliable textbooks of the period, one of which contained William Hunter's amusing remark: "Some physiologists will have it that the stomach is a mill, that it is a fermenting vat, and others, again, that it is a stew-pan; but, in my view of the matter, it is neither a mill, a fermenting vat, nor a stew-pan; but a stomach, gentlemen, a stomach."

There was little factual knowledge concerning the relation between structure and function in the digestive system until 1833, when a significant advance was made with the publication of William Beaumont's "Experiments and Observations on the Gastric Juice and the Physiology of Digestion." The subject of this study was Alexis St. Martin, a Canadian voyageur who had been accidentally wounded by a discharge of a musket. The shot "entered posteriorly, and in an oblique direction, forward and inward, literally blowing off integuments and muscles the size of a man's hand, fracturing and carrying away the anterior half of the sixth rib, fracturing the fifth, lacerating the lower portion of the left lobe of the lungs, the diaphragm, and perforating the stomach."

After surgical repair and healing, there remained an aperture 2½ inches in circumference in both the wall of the stomach and the side of the patient. Beaumont attempted to close this wound but failed; subsequently, the natural protrusion of the layers of the stomach in a sort of fistula (an abnormal passage leading from the abdominal wall to one of the hollow abdominal organs) produced a permanent valve, which prevented the escape of gastric contents even when the stomach was full, but which could easily be depressed to permit the entrance of a tube or other instrument and the introduction of food substances. The interior of the stomach could be seen with the naked eye.

Realizing the unique opportunity presented, Beaumont conducted a series of experiments between 1825 and 1833, during which time St. Martin enjoyed normal, robust health. The most important of Beaumont's pioneering results contain concepts accepted as fundamental today.

ANATOMY

The digestive system (Figs. 14–1 and 14–2) consists of (1) a long, muscular tube

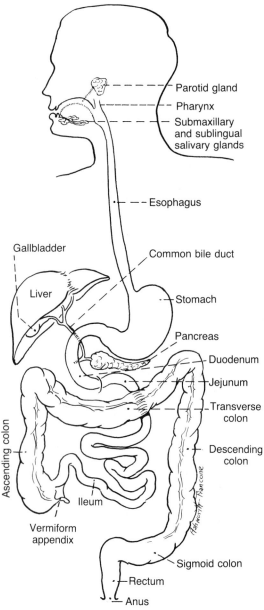

Figure 14–1. The digestive system and its associated structures.

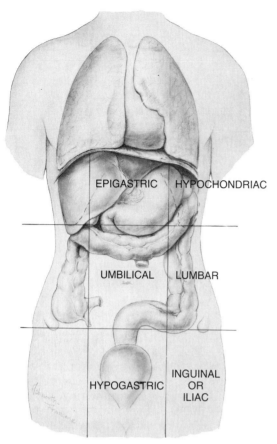

Figure 14–2. Regions of the abdomen and underlying viscera.

beginning at the lips and ending at the anus, including the mouth, pharynx, esophagus, stomach, and small and large intestine; and (2) certain large glands located outside the digestive tube, including the salivary glands, liver, gallbladder, and pancreas — all of which empty their secretions into the tube. The major functions of the digestive system are the digestion and absorption of ingested food and the elimination of solid wastes.

Lips

The lips have an outer surface covered by skin. The red, free margins represent a zone of transition from skin to mucous membrane. The epithelium of the inner surface of the lip is stratified squamous and is similar to the epithelium found on the inner surface of the cheek, pharynx, and esophagus. The substance of the lip consists of striated muscle fibers with fibroelastic connective tissue.

Cheeks

The cheeks, or side walls of the mouth, lined by *stratified squamous epithelium,* contain several accessory muscles of mastication, notably the buccinators, which prevent food from escaping the chewing actions of the teeth.

Teeth

Two sets of teeth make their appearance during the lifetime of an individual — the **deciduous,** or **temporary** (milk), **teeth** and the **permanent teeth.** Both sets begin their development *in utero,* the deciduous teeth at about the seventh fetal week, the permanent teeth at about the fourth month. The *deciduous set* consists of 20 teeth, 5 in each quadrant: 2 *incisors, 1 canine,* and 2 *molars.* The deciduous teeth erupt on the average between 6 and 24 months after birth and are usually shed between the ages of 6 and 12. There are 32 *permanent teeth* in a full set, 8 in each quadrant: 2 *incisors, 1 canine, 2 premolars,* and 3 *molars* (Figs. 14–3 and 14–4). The incisors, canines, and premolars replace the deciduous teeth (the premolars succeeding the deciduous molars), and the molars occupy new positions in the expanded adult jaw. Eruption of the third molars, or wisdom teeth, is delayed until after the age of 18, and one or more are absent in up to 25 per cent of some populations (the percentage varying from one population to another).

Solid food must be reduced to small particles before it can effectively undergo chemical changes in the digestive tract. The teeth accomplish this function by the process of *mastication.* Each type of tooth is adapted to its function — chisel-shaped incisors for cutting; canines with a single cusp, or high point (hence also called cuspids), for tearing; and premolars (bicuspids), which have two cusps, and molars, which have multiple cusps (most commonly four or five), for grinding. Faulty teeth can cause indigestion or malnutrition.

All teeth are constructed on the following basic plan (Fig. 14–3): Each is divided into two principal parts, (1) the **crown,** the exposed portion, and (2) the **root** (or roots), the portion embedded in the *alveolus* (bony socket) of the maxilla or mandible. The region of junction of the crown and root is called the *neck.* (The incisors, canines, and

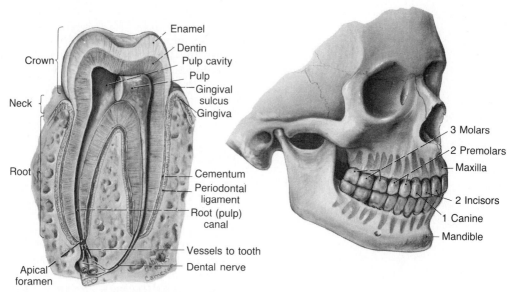

Figure 14–3. Midsagittal view of molar tooth, vertical position.

most premolars have a single root; the first and second lower molars have two roots, the first two upper molars generally have three; the third molars often have no more than one root.) The bulk of the tooth is composed of *dentin* (L. *dens,* tooth), a substance similar to bone in composition but harder and more compact. The dentin surrounds a central cavity, called the *pulp cavity,* which consists of an expanded upper *pulp chamber* and a narrow *pulp,* or *root, canal(s)* with an opening(s) at the end called the *apical foramen.* The pulp cavity is filled with a soft, vascular

connective tissue called pulp (from which it takes its name) that supplies nutrients and sensory innervation for pain for the tooth. The dentin of the crown is covered with *enamel,* the hardest substance in the body, composed mainly of calcium phosphate. *Cementum,* a bonelike tissue, covers the dentin of the root. The tooth is suspended in its socket by the *periodontal ligament,* or *membrane,* a relatively soft, fibrous connective tissue (modified periosteum). Collagen fibers of the periodontal ligament (known as Sharpey's fibers) are anchored in the cementum and buried in the alveolar bone. The suspension provided by the periodontal ligament allows each tooth a slight degree of movement (not possible in the rigidly attached teeth of nonmammalian vertebrates) so that a shifting, presumably to place the teeth in the most effective chewing position, can occur. The periodontal ligament also acts as a shock absorber, furnishes nutrients to the cementum and alveolar bone, and contains nerve endings sensitive to pressure, providing information to the brain during mastication. The *gingiva,* or *gum,* the mucous membrane surrounding the neck and lower part of the crown of the tooth like a collar, covers the periodontal ligament and crest of the alveolar bone. The gingiva can be distinguished from the rest of the oral mucosa in a healthy mouth by its pale pink color and stippled appearance. The gingival epithelium (stratified squamous) dips toward the root of the tooth before it attaches to the enamel so as to form a

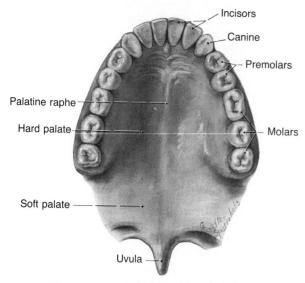

Figure 14–4. Roof of mouth with adult teeth.

shallow groove, the *gingival sulcus,* around each tooth.

Blood vessels and nerves enter the pulp cavity through the apical foramen. Nerve fibers terminate as free nerve endings at the periphery of the pulp close to a layer of cells (odontoblasts) underlying the dentin on the surface of the pulp. Each odontoblast has one or more cytoplasmic processes extending into fine canals in the dentin, known as *dentinal tubules,* which extend from the pulpal surface to the periphery of the dentin. It is assumed that pain reception (all effective stimuli to the dentin and pulp are perceived as pain) occurs by triggering impulses in odontoblast processes which are then somehow transmitted to the nerve fibers (although alternative mechanisms, such as stimulation of nerve endings by changes in fluid pressure, have been proposed).

Dental caries (L. *caries,* decay) is localized, progressive disintegration of teeth by acids (mainly lactic acid) produced by bacterial fermentation of carbohydrates. Cavities formed, if untreated, enlarge and destroy most of the tooth. The responsible bacteria concentrate on specific tooth sites in the form of an adherent, gelatinous mat known as a bacterial plaque, most commonly on the occlusal (biting) surfaces and interproximally (between the teeth where they touch). The plaque is usually deposited on a film, called the pellicle, a product of saliva that coats the tooth surface. The early lesion can be seen as a white or brown spot beneath the plaque, produced by demineralization of the enamel. In the late stage, when cavities have formed, bacteria occupy the decalcified dentinal tubules. Animal, epidemiological, and clinical studies support the view that sucrose (table sugar) is the most cariogenic carbohydrate in our modern diet. A small percentage of the population is caries resistant, apparently because of hereditary factors. Although research has not identified any specific mechanism for hereditary caries resistance, one consistent difference between caries-susceptible and caries-resistant individuals has been demonstrated: acid production by plaques (allowed to develop an appreciable thickness by not brushing teeth for three days) is much lower in resistant than susceptible subjects. Some component in saliva is believed to be responsible for the difference between the two groups. The importance of saliva, in general, as a caries-controlling factor is clearly demonstrated when its production is disturbed: tooth decay becomes rapid and rampant.

Dental caries is at least partially preventable by ingesting fluoride. In this country fluoridation of public water supplies has been found to reduce caries by 50 to 60 per cent. Dietary fluoride supplements or topical application of fluoride is recommended for children in communities without natural or artificial fluoridation of water.

Periodontal disease, also known as pyorrhea, is an inflammation of the gingiva and periodontal ligament caused by the bacteria of dental plaques deposited on teeth at the gum line. Initially, the gingival sulcus enlarges into a deep pocket, and as the disease progresses the inflammation extends into the deeper structures. In the advanced stages, erosion of cementum and bone occurs. When the eroded cementum can no longer anchor Sharpey's fibers, the tooth will no longer be held in its socket. The loss of teeth as a result of periodontal disease generally occurs in adulthood — by the age of 35 it overtakes dental caries as the leading cause of lost teeth.

Tongue

The floor of the mouth contains the tongue, a highly movable structure divided in half by the median fibrous septum, the bulk of each half composed of two sets of muscles, *intrinsic muscles* (superior and inferior longitudinal, transverse, and vertical), lying entirely within the tongue, and *extrinsic muscles* (with origins in the mandible, styloid process of the temporal bone, and hyoid bone), which pull the tongue up, down, forward, and back. A fold of mucous membrane, the *frenulum,* attaches the tongue to the floor of the mouth. If the frenulum is too short, it may restrict the movements of the tongue (tongue-tie condition). The tongue functions to mix saliva with food and to keep the mass pressed between the teeth for chewing before it pushes the food backward for swallowing. Numerous taste buds are scattered over the surface of the tongue (Fig. 14–5).

The palate, or roof of the mouth, consists of two parts: an anterior portion, the hard palate, formed by the maxillary and palatine bones; and a posterior portion, the soft palate,

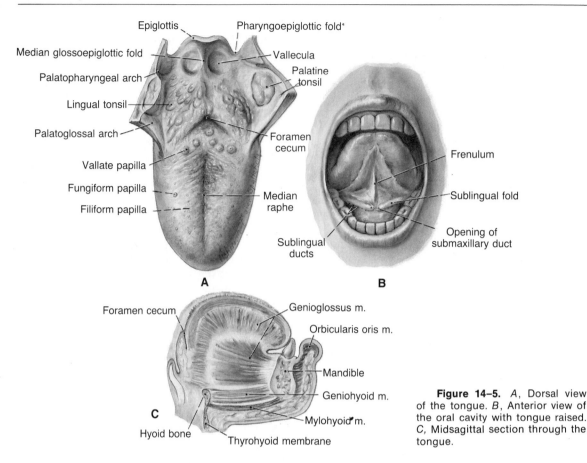

Figure 14–5. *A*, Dorsal view of the tongue. *B*, Anterior view of the oral cavity with tongue raised. *C*, Midsagittal section through the tongue.

composed of muscles ending in a free projection called the *uvula*. The opening of the pharynx lies behind the uvula (Fig. 14–4).

Pharynx

The pharynx is the portion of the digestive tract serving as a passageway for both the respiratory and digestive systems. It permits an individual to breathe through his mouth even if the nasal passages are obstructed. The pharynx has longitudinal and circular muscle layers of the striated type. The circular muscles are called constrictors.

Layers of the Wall of the Digestive Tract

A basic histologic plan is seen throughout the remainder of the digestive tract, although there are individual features peculiar to each region. In general the wall of the digestive tract is composed of the following layers:

Mucous Membrane, or Mucosa. This is the innermost layer of the digestive tract. It is composed of a superficial *epithelium* resting on a basement membrane and an underlying support of connective tissue, the *lamina propria*, with a thin arrangement of smooth muscle fibers, the *muscularis mucosae*, beneath the lamina propria. Glandular cells of the mucosa secrete digestive juices and mucus. Only mucus is secreted in the esophagus and colon. Accumulations of lymphoid tissue are often found in supporting connective tissue.

Submucosa. This layer is composed of areolar connective tissue with numerous lymphatics, blood vessels, and a nerve plexus known as the *submucous* or *Meissner's plexus*. It is found between the mucous and muscular layers and acts to compensate for changes in size of the digestive tube during the passage of food.

Muscular Layer, or Muscularis Externa. This consists of smooth muscle fibers in two distinct sections. The inner circular layer, when contracted, narrows the lumen of the tube. The longitudinally arranged fibers of the outer layer serve to shorten the tube by their contraction. Between the two layers is a plexus of nerves called the *myenteric plexus* or *Auerbach's plexus.*

Serous Layer, or Serosa. This outermost covering is the *visceral peritoneum,* the layer of the peritoneum deflected over the viscera and completely surrounding most of them (see Chapter 4, page 85). The parietal layer of the peritoneum *(parietal peritoneum)* lines the abdominal wall. The two layers of the peritoneum are in contact, and the potential space between them is called the peritoneal cavity (in the male it is a closed sac; in the female the free ends of the uterine tubes open into it).

Esophagus

The esophagus is a long, straight tube communicating in a direct path with the stomach. Passage of food is facilitated by ordinary gravitational forces, as well as by the type and arrangement of muscles in the tube itself. The esophagus extends from the pharynx to the stomach for a distance of about 10 inches. It is posterior to the trachea and anterior to the vertebral column; it passes through the diaphragm in front of the aorta to enter the stomach.

Although the esophagus is similar to the remaining portions of the digestive tract, there are a few differences. For instance, the epithelium of the esophagus is *stratified squamous,* whereas the epithelium of the stomach and intestine is columnar. The muscular layer of the upper third of the esophagus is striated, and that of the lower third is smooth. A transitional zone exists in the middle and contains both striated and smooth muscle. The outer covering of the esophagus is not serous but is a layer of connective tissue (the adventitia).

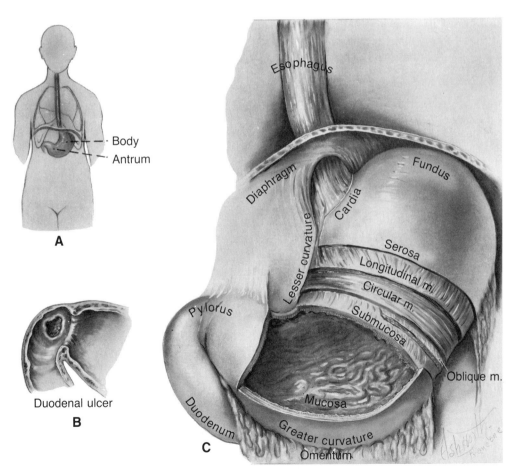

Figure 14–6. *A,* Anatomic position of esophagus and stomach. *B,* Duodenal ulcer. *C,* Anterior view of the stomach with portion of the anterior wall removed. (Note the various layers which make up the stomach wall.)

Stomach

The stomach, the most dilated portion of the digestive tract, lies under the diaphragm just below the costal margin in the upper abdomen. It serves mainly as a storage and mixing chamber for food prior to passage into the duodenum (the first part of the small intestine), but some digestion takes place, and the mixed, partially digested food is reduced to a semifluid mass.

The stomach consists of three parts: the *fundus,* an upper portion ballooning toward the left; a *body,* the central portion; and the *pyloric portion* (antrum), a relatively constricted portion at the terminal end just before the entrance into the duodenum (Fig. 14–6).

The wall of the stomach is composed of the same three layers found in other regions of the digestive tract, with certain modifications. The stomach, in addition to having an external longitudinal and an underlying circular layer of smooth muscle, has an oblique layer located inside the circular one. The musculature is heavier in the pyloric portion than in the rest of the stomach. The circular muscle layer is thickened in the pyloric region to form the *pyloric sphincter.*

The *cardia* is the opening between the esophagus and the stomach. It does not refer to any anatomical structure. The *pylorus* is the opening between the stomach and the duodenum. It too, strictly speaking, does not refer to an anatomical structure, although it is often used to designate the entire pyloric portion.

When the stomach is empty, the mucosa is thrown into prominent folds called *rugae* which flatten out when the stomach is full. The epithelium is *simple columnar.* Densely packed gastric glands, numbering about 35 million, open at the surface via *gastric pits.* These glands are branched tubular and penetrate the lamina propria all the way to the muscularis mucosae.

Folds of peritoneum, called *omenta,* extend from the stomach to other abdominal organs. The *greater,* or *great, omentum* drops down over the intestine from the greater curvature of the stomach and passes upward to the transverse colon of the large intestine (Fig. 14–7 and Fig. 1–8). It contains an abundance of fat and serves as an insulating cover-

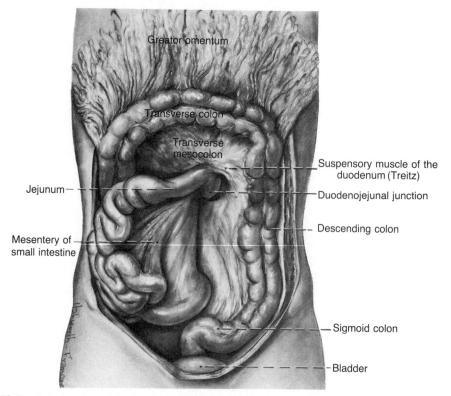

Figure 14–7. Anterior view of the intestine with greater omentum raised. The small intestine has been retracted to show the junction of the duodenum and jejunum.

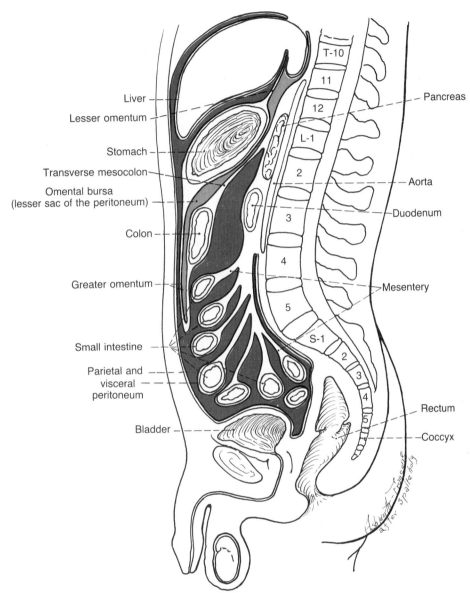

Figure 14–8. Midsagittal section through the trunk showing the mesentery of the small intestine (mesentery proper), mesentery of the colon (mesocolon — transverse portion shown), and the greater and lesser omenta, all formed by folds of peritoneum. The mesentery proper and transverse mesocolon are attached to the posterior abdominal wall. The greater omentum drops down over the intestine from the greater curvature of the stomach and passes upward to fuse with the visceral peritoneum of the transverse colon and the anterior layer of the transverse mesocolon. The lesser omentum passes from the lesser curvature of the stomach to the liver. The omental bursa (lesser sac of the peritoneum), enclosed by the greater and lesser omenta and other portions of the peritoneum, is colored blue. The greater sac of the peritoneum, the main part of the peritoneal cavity, between the visceral and parietal layers of the peritoneum, is colored red. The omental bursa and greater sac of the peritoneum communicate via an opening situated between the liver and duodenum (epiploic foramen).

ing; it may also limit the spread of infection. The *lesser omentum* extends from the lesser curvature of the stomach to the liver (Fig. 1–10).

Small Intestine

The small intestine extends from the distal end of the pyloric sphincter to the cecum, the first portion of the large intestine. It is approximately 18 feet in length and is divided into three portions: the *duodenum, jejunum,* and *ileum.* The duodenum, named because it is about equal in length to the breadth of 12 fingers, is the shortest, widest, and most fixed portion of the small intestine. It receives secretions of the liver and pancreas. The junction between the duodenum and jejunum is demarcated by a fibromuscular band arising from the diaphragm (containing striated muscle fibers in its upper part, elastic tissue in the middle, and, generally, smooth muscle in the lower part) known as the suspensory muscle of the duodenum (Treitz's muscle) (Fig. 14–7). The duodenum is supplied by branches of the celiac artery and the remainder of the small intestine by branches of the superior mesenteric artery.

The intestine, both small and large, is anchored to the abdominal wall (or to the pelvic wall in the case of the pelvic, or sigmoid, portion of the large intestine) by folds of peritoneum collectively called the *mesenteries* (Fig. 14–8). The mesentery of the small intestine (the mesentery proper) extends from the jejunum and ileum to the abdominal wall. (The duodenum, which has no mesentery, is relatively fixed to the posterior abdominal wall and covered with peritoneum on most of its anterior surface.) The mesentery of the colon of the large intestine (see below) is called the mesocolon (consisting of transverse and sigmoid portions; ascending and descending portions are also occasionally present).

Histologically, the wall of the small intestine is typical of the digestive tract as a whole, but is distinguished by the following specializations of the mucosa which increase its surface area: (1) **Circular folds (plicae circulares),** large, permanent, transverse folds of the entire thickness of the mucosa containing a core of submucosa (Fig. 14–9), usually extending about one-half to two-thirds (occasionally completely) around the circumference of the lumen (interior passageway). (2) **Villi,** fingerlike projections of mucosa into the lumen containing blood vessels and a centrally located lymphatic vessel (the central lacteal). (3) **Microvilli,** numerous cylindrical processes on the free surface of the epithelial cells, forming the so-called *brush,* or *striated, border* (Fig. 14–10). Tubular glands, known as the *crypts of Lieberkühn,* are found in the mucosa between the villi. In the duodenum, *Brunner's glands* (which secrete a mucus high in bicarbonate content) are located in the submucosa. *Simple columnar epithelium* lines the small intestine (Fig. 14–9). The cells of the epithelium are interspersed with mucus-secreting *goblet cells.* The occurrence of these cells increases toward the caudal end of the digestive tube.

Large Intestine

The large intestine, approximately 1.5 meters (5 feet) long, extends from the end of the ileum to the anus and is divisible into the *cecum, colon, rectum,* and *anal canal.* It differs from the small intestine in several ways, including its greater width and the following characteristics (Fig. 14–11):

1. There are no villi on the surface of the mucosa.

2. In the cecum, colon, and upper rectum the glands are of greater depth, are more closely packed, and contain many goblet cells.

3. The longitudinal muscle layer of the cecum and colon forms three conspicuous bands called *taeniae coli.*

4. Many appendices epiploicae, or pouches of fat-filled peritoneum, are apparent along the free border of the colon.

The cecum, or first portion of the large intestine, is an elongated pouch situated in the right lower portion of the abdomen. Attached to its base is a slender tube, the vermiform (wormlike) process, or appendix, which has a cavity communicating with the cecum. When infection occurs in the appendix, it is usually secondary to some obstruction of the appendix producing damage and inflammation. Appendicitis is treated by removing the appendix to prevent rupture and peritonitis (inflammation of the peritoneum).

The *ascending colon* extends upward from the cecum on the right posterior abdominal wall to the undersurface of the liver just

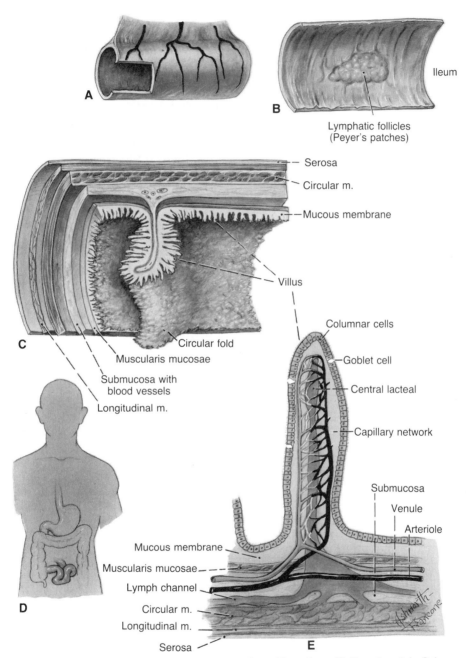

Figure 14–9. *A,* Segment of small intestine. *B,* Interior view of intestine with Peyer's patch. *C,* Layers composing intestinal wall. *D,* Anatomic position showing stomach and large and small intestines. *E,* Midsagittal section through villus.

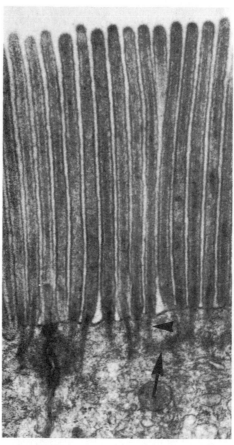

Figure 14–10. Electron micrograph of the microvilli of the brush border on the free surface of a duodenal columnar cell. Bundles of filaments in the core of the villi penetrate into the cytoplasm (arrow) and blend with the filamentous terminal web (arrow) of the apical cytoplasm. (From Leeson, C. R., and Leeson, T. S.: Histology. 3rd ed., Philadelphia, W. B. Saunders Co., 1976.)

anterior to the right kidney. The *transverse colon* overlies the coils of the small intestine and crosses the abdominal cavity from right to left below the stomach.

The *descending colon* begins near the spleen, passing downward on the left side of the abdomen to the iliac crest to become the *sigmoid,* or *pelvic, colon,* so called because of its S-shaped course within the pelvic cavity.

The transverse and sigmoid colons are completely surrounded by peritoneum and have mesenteries (the transverse and sigmoid mesocolons). The cecum is usually surrounded by peritoneum. The ascending and descending colons are generally covered by peritoneum on the anterior surface and sides only, but occasionally may be completely invested by peritoneum and then possess mesocolons.

The *rectum* lies on the anterior surface of the sacrum and coccyx and terminates in the narrow *anal canal,* which opens to the exteri-

or at the *anus* (Fig. 14–12). Intestinal glands are absent in the anal canal, and about 2.5 cm above the anus the epithelium changes from columnar to stratified squamous, which is continuous with the epidermis at the anal orifice. The circular smooth muscle of the anal canal is thickened to form the *internal sphincter.* Bundles of skeletal muscle surrounding the canal form the *external sphincter.* Vertical folds, the *anal columns* (columns of Morgagni), can be seen in the anal canal, each containing an artery and vein, the latter being subject to enlargements known as *hemorrhoids* (Fig. 14–13). Hemorrhoids are either internal or external and can cause bleeding and pain. An external hemorrhoid is covered by skin and an internal one by mucosa. Factors predisposing to hemorrhoids include constipation, increased intra-abdominal pressure (as in pregnancy) and a general hereditary weakness of the vein wall.

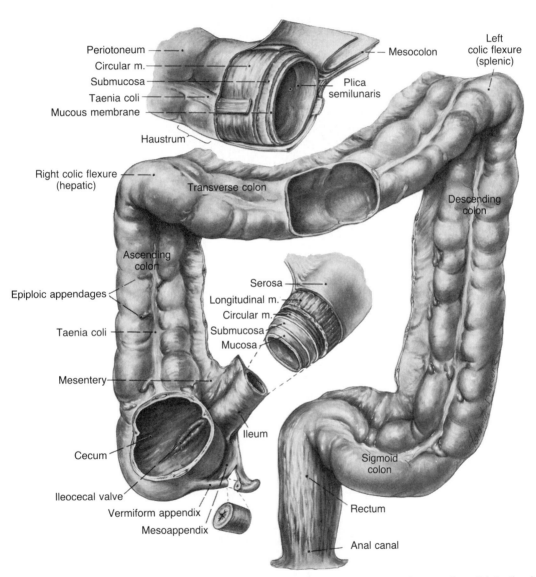

Figure 14–11. Position and structure of the large intestine. The walls of both the large and small intestine have been enlarged and dissected to show their various layers.

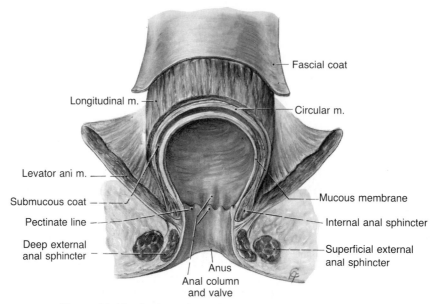

Figure 14–12. Anal canal and the various layers of the rectum.

ACCESSORY STRUCTURES

The pancreas, liver, and gallbladder, derivatives of that portion of the digestive tube which forms the small intestine, and the salivary glands, derivatives of the cranial portion of the foregut, are intimately associated with the physiology of digestion. The salivary glands secrete digestive enzymes into the mouth that initiate carbohydrate digestion. The pancreas secretes digestive enzymes that act on all three major foodstuffs — carbohydrates, fat, and protein. Bile, secreted by the liver, is essential for the normal absorption of digested lipids. The gallbladder concentrates and stores bile. The duodenum receives pancreatic juice via the pancreatic duct and bile via the common bile duct.

Salivary Glands. There are three pairs of salivary glands: parotid, submaxillary, and sublingual. The *parotid glands* are located in the subcutaneous regions of the cheek, anterior and inferior to the ears. The parotid duct opens just opposite the second upper molar. Each *submaxillary gland* is located in the floor of the mouth close to the angle of the

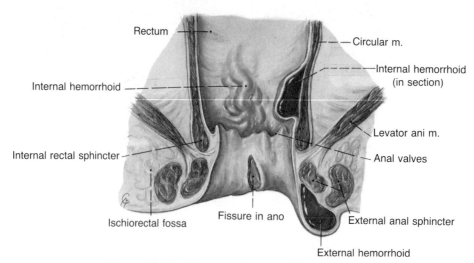

Figure 14–13. Common disorders of the anal canal.

jaw. The submaxillary duct opens laterally to the point at which the frenulum attaches to the tongue. The *sublingual gland* is located under the mucous membrane of the floor of the mouth, just lateral to the tongue. Several sublingual ducts open either near the tongue or into the submaxillary duct (Fig. 14–5).

Pancreas

The pancreas is a large, lobulated gland resembling the salivary glands in structure (Fig. 14–14). It has both exocrine and endocrine functions, secreting externally through a duct and internally into the blood or lymph, respectively. Pancreatic juice, a digestive juice, is the product of the exocrine pancreas. The secretions are collected by the major **pancreatic duct** and emptied into the duodenum.

Pancreatic secretion is under the control of the hormones *secretin* and *cholecystokinin-pancreozymin (CCK-PZ)*, which are released from the duodenal mucosa and carried to the pancreas by the blood. They func-

tion in pH regulation and digestion, respectively.

Liver

The liver is the largest organ in the body and is located in the upper part of the abdominal cavity under the dome of the diaphragm (Fig. 14–15). Its superior surface, in contact with the diaphragm, is smooth and convex. The inferior surface is concave and exhibits impressions marking the point at which the liver is in contact with the abdominal viscera. Blood is transported to the liver from the digestive tract, spleen, and pancreas via the portal vein and from the aorta via the hepatic artery. The portal vein and hepatic artery enter the liver through a region called the porta hepatis; both the artery and vein are accompanied by bile ducts and lymphatic vessels (Fig. 14–16). The portal vein and hepatic artery repeatedly branch, making the liver a highly vascularized organ.

The liver is demarcated into four lobes. The two main lobes are the right and left,

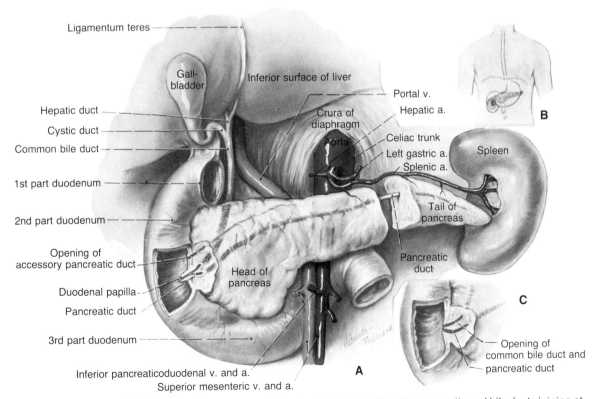

Figure 14–14. *A*, Relationship of the pancreas to the duodenum, showing the pancreatic and bile ducts joining at the duodenal papilla. A section has been removed from the pancreas to expose the pancreatic duct. *B*, Anatomic position of the pancreas. *C*, Common variation.

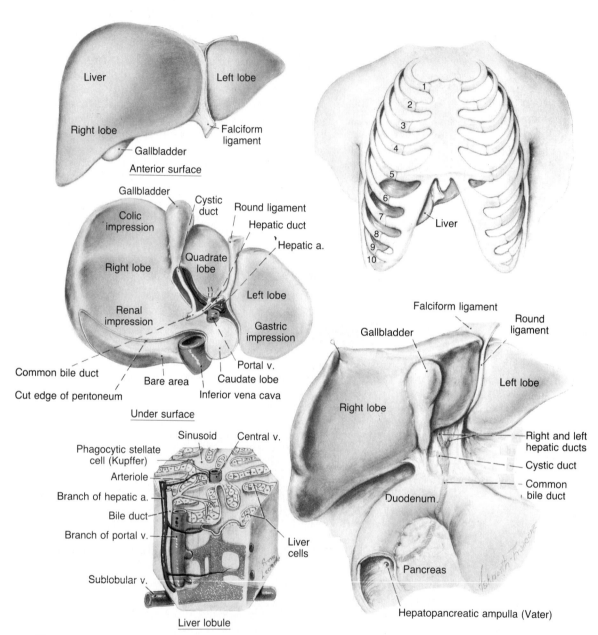

Figure 14–15. The liver, its normal location, relationships, and unit structure. (Liver lobule section courtesy of Lederle Laboratories.)

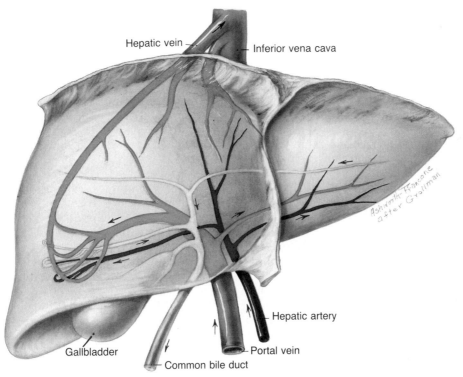

Figure 14–16. Hepatic portal system of the liver.

separated by the falciform ligament. The main right lobe is subdivided into a right lobe proper, the quadrate lobe, and the caudate lobe. The liver cells of a lobule are arranged around a *central vein* in irregular, branching, interconnecting plates *(hepatic laminae)* that form a spongelike architecture. Between the plates is an extensive communicating system of cavities *(hepatic lacunae)* which contain blood sinusoids. The sinusoids are lined with endothelial-type cells and phagocytic (Kupffer) cells, and are separated from the plates of liver cells by a narrow space known as the *space of Disse.* The sinusoids convey blood to the central vein from branches of the portal vein and hepatic artery, which are situated adjacent to the liver lobule (accompanied by a small bile duct) in the interlobular connective tissue. Blood flows from the central veins via interlobular veins into the hepatic veins, which drain into the inferior vena cava.

Bile canaliculi form a three-dimensional network between liver cells (the boundaries of these minute channels are formed by the cell membranes of the liver cells — no endothelial lining is present). Bile secreted by the liver cells drains from the bile canaliculi into

the bile ducts at the periphery of the lobules via small ductules (canals of Hering). Bile leaves the liver in the two main ducts (the right and left hepatic ducts), which unite to form a single duct, generally referred to as the *hepatic duct* (but also called the common hepatic duct or hepatic duct proper). The hepatic duct is joined by the *cystic duct* from the gallbladder to form the **common bile duct,** which passes obliquely through the duodenal wall, joining the pancreatic duct to open into the duodenum at the *duodenal papilla,* or *ampulla of Vater* (Fig. 14–14).

In relation to digestion and absorption of food, the major function of the liver is the production of *bile.* It is formed in a volume of 500 to 1000 ml daily, and is concentrated by the gallbladder. The most important constituents of bile are the *bile acids,* which are synthesized in the liver from cholesterol and secreted as conjugated **bile salts.** These bile salts are formed by conjugation (combination) of the bile acids with the amino acid glycine or taurine (ethanolaminesulfonic acid), and the conjugated bile acids combined with sodium or potassium are the bile salts. Cholic acid, for example, one of the principal bile acids, conjugated with glycine or taurine forms glycocholic or taurocholic acid, which, combined with sodium, are the bile salts sodium glycocholate and sodium taurocholate. Bile salts combine with the end products of lipid digestion to form water-soluble complexes, thereby greatly facilitating the absorption of these digestive products from the small intestine (for further details, see page 504).

Other constituents of bile include phospholipids, cholesterol, inorganic salts, and the major bile pigment, bilirubin (the waste product of red blood cell destruction — see Chapter 11, page 359). Bilirubin is prepared for excretion into the bile by conjugation with glucuronic acid (a derivative of glucose). This converts bilirubin from a lipid-soluble to a water-soluble form. The rate of conjugation of bilirubin is generally low in newborn infants because of a deficiency of the responsible enzyme, glucuronyl transferase (adult activity is not reached until about the tenth day of life). A severe deficiency, most common in premature infants, may lead to a pronounced elevation in the level of unconjugated bilirubin in the blood and serious damage to the brain, a condition called *kernicterus.*

Bile is secreted continuously, but secretion increases after meals. Presumably this increase is due mainly to the stimulatory action of bile salts discharged from the gallbladder and subsequently reabsorbed from the small intestine into the portal blood. The duodenal hormone secretin also increases the output of bile by the liver.

The liver, although considered a structural and functional part of the digestive system, functions in many activities not directly concerned with the process of digestion. Among these are hematopoiesis and coagulation, phagocytosis, and detoxification. The liver produces erythrocytes in the embryo — and in some abnormal states in the adult. It also synthesizes prothrombin, fibrinogen, and other clotting factors which are necessary for coagulation of blood. The liver destroys old and worn-out erythrocytes and removes bacteria and foreign bodies from the blood via its Kupffer cells, which are a part of the reticuloendothelial system (see Chapter 4). It functions in detoxification by changing the nitrogenous waste, ammonia, into the less toxic urea. Enzyme systems in the liver also inactivate drugs and detoxify various environmental chemicals, such as insecticides, dyes, and food additives. The chemical transformations include oxidation (the principal mechanism), reduction, hydrolysis, and conjugation (chemical combination with a substance such as glucuronic acid, as described above for bilirubin).

The influences of the liver on nutrition include storage of glycogen; storage of vitamins A, D, E, and K, as well as B_{12} and certain other water-soluble vitamins; and metabolism of carbohydrates, fats, and proteins.

Cirrhosis is a disease of the liver representing a progressive degeneration and inflammation of the liver; it is characterized by an increase in connective tissue and scar tissue formation throughout the liver lobules.

Alcoholism is the most common cause of cirrhosis. Although malnutrition is common in alcoholics, and malnutrition does impair liver function, biopsy studies with human volunteers have demonstrated that the consumption of alcohol with nutritionally optimal diets causes the accumulation of fat in the liver (the characteristic "fatty liver," the first and reversible phase of the disease) and ultrastructural changes in the liver cell. Animal studies suggest that acetaldehyde, one of the metabolic products of alcohol, may have a direct toxic effect on the liver cell and that hydrogen, another product of alcohol metabolism, may contribute to hepatic fat accumulation. These observations raise doubts about a once widely held belief that malnutrition is the primary cause of alcoholic cirrhosis. In the usual sequence of events in the disease, the engorgement of the liver cells with fat interferes with their normal function and causes cell death. The necrosis triggers an inflammatory process (alcoholic hepatitis). In some cases death occurs at this stage. In the final stage fibrous scars, the hallmark of cirrhosis, disrupt the architecture of the liver cell and interfere with the flow of blood to and from the liver. Backup pressure in the portal system can lead to excessive fluid loss in the abdominal cavity (*ascites*). The accumulation of ammonia and other toxic substances in the blood as a result of decreased liver function can cause hepatic coma and death.

Gallbladder

The gallbladder is a saclike structure attached to the inferior surface of the liver and serving as a reservoir for bile. The cystic duct of the gallbladder joins the ductal system from the liver to form the common bile duct (Fig. 14–17).

Bile consists chiefly of water, salts of bile acids, pigments, inorganic salts, cholesterol, and phospholipids. Water, chloride, and bicarbonates are absorbed in the gallbladder, increasing the relative concentrations of the other constituents of bile.

Contraction of the gallbladder with expulsion of bile into the duodenum is stimulated by a hormonal mechanism. The presence of certain foodstuffs — particularly fat in the duodenum — causes release of the hormone *cholecystokinin-pancreozymin*, which then reaches the gallbladder via the blood and brings on contraction. Gallbladder contraction occurs within 30 minutes following a meal.

Gallstones (cholelithiasis). Gallstones are composed of the constituents of bile that have precipitated and formed into crystals. The incidence of gallstones increases with age and is twice as common among women as men. In about 90 per cent of the cases, cholesterol is the major or sole constituent of the stones. Calcium is sometimes an important component, and bilirubin predominates in some stones.

Gallstones are formed in the gallbladder, but an abnormal composition of the bile secreted by the liver appears to be principally responsible for their formation. Since bile salts solubilize cholesterol by the formation of micelles (see Chapter 2, page 39), the ratio of cholesterol to bile salts is a critical factor in the formation of most gallstones.

It has been observed that most gallbladder patients have a smaller pool of bile acids in general and often much less *chenodeoxycholic acid* in particular. These findings have led to the introduction at the Mayo Clinic of so-called "cheno" therapy — ingestion of capsules of chenodeoxycholic acid. This treatment, which is quite successful, literally dissolves the gallstones.

Jaundice is a yellowish discoloration of the skin, mucous membrane, and body fluids because of an excess of biliary pigment. The most common type is *obstructive jaundice,* which is caused by internal occlusion of the bile duct by gallstones or by a growth such as a tumor. *Hemolytic jaundice* is a form of jaundice that results from an abnormally rapid formation of bile pigments following hemolysis (destruction of red blood cells). *Hepatic jaundice* is impaired excretion of bile due to damage to the hepatic cells.

Cholecystitis is an inflammation of the gallbladder. A patient with cholecystitis will experience intermittent attacks of severe pain, most often after heavy meals. Belching is a common finding with cholecystitis, as is intolerance to fats and leafy vegetables.

MOTOR ACTIVITIES OF THE DIGESTIVE TRACT

Swallowing. The process of swallowing (deglutition) is divided into three stages:

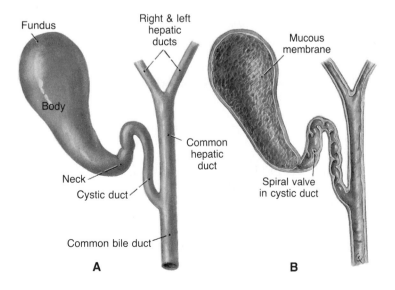

Figure 14–17. *A,* External view of the gallbladder. *B,* Sagittal section through the gallbladder.

Fundus

Right & left hepatic ducts

Mucous membrane

Body

Common hepatic duct

Neck

Cystic duct

Spiral valve in cystic duct

Common bile duct

A

B

buccal, pharyngeal, and esophageal. In the buccal phase the ground, rounded mass of food mixed with saliva, called the *bolus* (Latin for choice bit), passes through the oral cavity into the pharynx. In the pharyngeal phase the bolus passes through the pharynx into the esophagus, and in the esophageal phase it passes through the esophagus into the stomach. Only the buccal phase is under voluntary control. In this stage, the tongue is pulled backward and up against the hard and soft palates, forcing the bolus into the oral pharynx. As the bolus passes into the pharynx, it stimulates receptors surrounding the entrance to the oral pharynx which transmit impulses to the *swallowing center* located in the medulla near the respiratory center (Fig. 14–18). Signals from this center initiate a number of automatic responses. The soft palate is raised and pushed against the posterior wall of the pharynx, thereby preventing regurgitation of food through the nose. The larynx is pulled upward and forward. This movement, in combination with the backward movement of the tongue, draws the larynx under the base of the tongue and places the epiglottis in a horizontal position above the laryngeal opening. The aryepiglottic folds are adducted, as are the true and

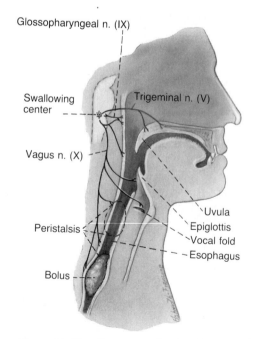

Figure 14–18. Movement of bolus down esophagus. The trigeminal nerve controls the muscles of mastication; the glossopharyngeal nerve, the stylopharyngeus muscle; and the vagus nerve, esophageal peristalsis.

Glossopharyngeal n. (IX)

Swallowing center

Trigeminal n. (V)

Vagus n. (X)

Peristalsis

Bolus

Uvula
Epiglottis
Vocal fold
Esophagus

Figure 14–19. Peristalsis.

false vocal cords. This closes the larynx, and food passes to one side or the other of the epiglottis into the pharynx (or over the end of the epiglottis if large quantities of fluid are swallowed). During this time, discharges from the swallowing center inhibit respiration.

When the bolus enters the pharynx, reflex contraction of the superior constrictor muscle of the pharynx initiates a rapid **peristaltic** (G. *peristaltikos*, clasping and compressing) **wave** propelling food down the pharynx toward the esophagus. Relaxation of the so-called upper esophageal, or pharyngoesophageal, sphincter (a short zone at the pharynx-esophagus junction in the region of the cricopharyngeus muscle) allows food to enter the esophagus. The peristaltic wave (comparable to constricting one's fingers around a tube and sliding them toward one end [see Fig. 14–19]) continues into the esophagus and sweeps the bolus toward the stomach. Before the wave reaches the stomach, a slow wave of relaxation above the stomach opens the lower esophageal sphincter. This sphincter is anatomically indistinguishable from the rest of the esophagus but physiologically represents a segment of the esophagus about 5 cm above the stomach that remains constricted until reflexively relaxed as the peristaltic wave approaches. Its constriction prevents reflux of gastric contents into the esophagus. A relaxed sphincter, a condition called *chalasia*, is sometimes seen in infants but rarely in adults.

Peristalsis in the esophagus is largely a vagal reflex; that is, fibers in the vagus nerve conduct impulses from the esophagus to the swallowing center and back again to initiate peristalsis when food reaches the esophagus. Since the muscular layer of the upper third of the esophagus is skeletal muscle, severing branches of the vagus nerve innervating the esophagus interferes with swallowing. However, in time, the intrinsic excitability of the smooth muscle of the lower portion of esophagus becomes adequate under these circumstances to trigger peristaltic waves when gravity forces food into the lower regions of the esophagus.

Peristalsis in the Stomach

Accumulation of food in the stomach initiates peristaltic waves in the stomach that serve to mix the contents and, as the mixture becomes fluid, to gradually empty the stomach by forcing fluid through the pylorus into the duodenum. The murky, semifluid mass of partially digested food that passes along the digestive tract is called **chyme** (G. *chymos*, juice).

Each peristaltic wave begins as a slight constriction, usually near the midpoint of the body of the stomach. The wave becomes progressively deeper as it travels toward the pylorus and ends with a contraction of the pyloric sphincter. A new wave begins every 20 seconds, and each wave lasts about one minute. Thus, three waves at a time travel down the stomach. The powerful contractions of the muscles in the pyloric portion of the stomach (which has been described as functioning somewhat like the gizzard of birds) are largely responsible for pulverizing the stomach contents. The rate of emptying is determined largely by the strength of the contractions. Relaxation of the sphincter, of course, permits gastric contents to pass through the pylorus, but the narrow pylorus resists the passage of fluid, so the strength of the peristaltic contraction determines the amount of chyme that is expelled into the duodenum in each cycle. Contraction of the sphincter at the end of each cycle prevents regurgitation of duodenal contents into the stomach.

Feedback from the duodenum is an important regulator ·of gastric emptying. Two control mechanisms are involved, one *neuronal*, the other *hormonal*. Both have **inhibitory** effects on gastric motility. The neuronal mechanism, known as the *enterogastric* (G. *enteron,* intestine; G. *gastēr,* belly) *reflex* is mediated by the vagus nerve (through central connections in the medulla). The reflex is activated, among other things, by acids, the products of protein digestion, hypo- or hypertonic fluids, and a building up of pressure in the duodenum. Hormonal feedback inhibition of gastric motility is elicited largely by the accumulation of fat in the duodenum. This stimulates the release of a hormone (which has never been isolated in

pure form) called *enterogastrone* from the mucosa of the duodenum which is transported by the blood stream to the stomach, where it exerts an inhibitory effect on gastric contractions. Cholecystokinin-pancreozymin, the duodenal hormone that acts principally on the gallbladder (stimulating its contraction) and pancreas (stimulating enzyme secretion), also inhibits gastric emptying. The delay in stomach emptying induced by these feedback mechanisms protects the duodenum against overloading and excessive acidity and allows more time for the digestive processes in the duodenum to proceed.

Vagal reflexes are important for maintaining effective gastric peristalsis during digestion. Following section of the vagus nerve (vagotomy), peristaltic pressure may be insufficient for normal gastric emptying. Another cause of inadequate emptying of the stomach is *pylorospasm*, a congenital condition in infants but rarely seen in adults. Actually, the abnormality in congenital infant pylorospasm is not sustained contraction of the pyloric sphincter but rather hypertrophy of the pyloric muscle. Some clinicians, therefore, prefer to describe the condition as pyloric stenosis.

Hunger Contractions. When the stomach has been empty for a long time, so-called "hunger" contractions may occur. They are usually rhythmic, strong, peristaltic contractions lasting 20 seconds with no pause between successive contractions. Shorter, nonrhythmic contractions may also occur. Very strong contractions sometimes fuse to produce a sustained spasm lasting two to three minutes. At one time some physiologists believed that hunger pangs were the primary regulator of appetite. However, although some individuals describe hunger in terms of these contractions, others never experience them. Furthermore, surgical section of the vagus nerve, which eliminates hunger contractions, fails to diminish the sensation of hunger in patients who before surgery consistently felt these hunger pangs. Hunger, for these individuals, simply became the diffuse feeling it is with most people.

Vomiting

Vomiting is a reflex coordinated by a center in the medulla (called the *vomiting center*) which has the effect of emptying the upper gastrointestinal tract. Stimuli within the alimentary canal, especially the duodenum, may activate the vomiting center, as may stimuli from various other parts of the body. Nauseating odors or sights, seasickness, and emotional upset can trigger vomiting. Drugs such as apomorphine may induce vomiting by acting directly on the vomiting center. The sequence of events in vomiting is as follows: (1) Strong, sustained contractions occur in the upper small intestine; (2) the pyloric sphincter contracts; (3) the pyloric portion of the stomach contracts. These three responses, occurring one after the other, fill the fundus and body of the stomach, which are relaxed and dilated. This is followed by (4) relaxation of the lower and upper esophageal sphincters and (5) inspiration and closure of the glottis. Contraction of the abdominal muscles and diaphragm then compresses the stomach, evacuating its contents.

Segmenting Contractions and Peristalsis in the Small Intestine

Contractions of the small intestine are of two types — peristalsis and those known as segmenting. The latter are rhythmic contractions occurring along a section of the intestine which divide it into small segments, giving it the appearance of a chain of sausages. When the rings of constriction relax, new contractions form rings in the middle of the previously formed segments, thereby forming new segments in different positions (Fig. 14–20). Intestinal contents are mixed by the repeated segmentations. In addition, the contractions travel toward the distal end of the intestine and help move the contents down the intestinal tract. The segmenting contractions occur at a rate of 11 per minute in the duodenum and eight to nine per minute in the ileum. In the regions between, the rates exhibit a gradient with highest activity toward the duodenum, lowest toward the ileum.

Peristaltic waves are usually superimposed upon the segmenting contractions and, as they travel along the intestine, sweep the contents toward the distal end. Ordinarily the waves occur at regular intervals and travel for varying distances.

Peristaltic contractions, characteristic of many tubular structures of the body, have one feature in common — the constricted ring moves in one direction only. These structures are intrinsically polarized. As mentioned, parasympathetic (vagal) stimulation increases the intensity of the peristaltic contractions by smooth muscle of the alimentary canal, but surgical section does not abolish them. Paralysis of the myenteric nerve plexus, however, does eliminate peristalsis.

Ileocecal Valve and Movements of the Large Intestine

The lower end of the ileum projects as an invagination into the cecum, forming what is known as the ileocecal valve, which functions to permit gradual passage of small amounts of intestinal contents into the cecum while at the same time preventing regurgitation from the colon into the ileum. While digestion is in progress, the valve opens rhythmically, each time allowing the injection of about 15 ml of fluid into the cecum. Ingestion of food intensifies ileal peristalsis and increases the frequency of opening of the ileocecal valve (so-called *gastroileal reflex*).

The principal type of colon contraction is similar to the segmenting contractions of the small instestine. A distinguishing feature of these contractions is the outward bulging of the segments between constricted rings into sacs called *haustra* as a result of the contraction of longitudinal muscle at the same time the circular muscle contracts. This type of contraction serves primarily to *mix* colon contents, but may contribute to propulsive action by traveling in an analward direction. Of much less frequent occurrence than these mixing contractions are peristaltic contractions called *mass movements*. Mass movements generally occur no more than two or three times a day, most commonly shortly after or during a meal. This response to eating is referred to as the *gastrocolic reflex*. The mass movement wave is characteristically prolonged, lasting two to four minutes, and has the effect of rapidly transferring the contents of the proximal colon to the distal colon. Since such movements are often followed by a desire to defecate, it is assumed they can be strong enough to move the colon contents into the rectum.

Figure 14–20. Rhythmic segmenting contractions.

Defecation

The rectum is normally empty until just prior to defecation — the fecal mass is stored in the sigmoid (pelvic) colon. The desire to defecate arises when, usually as a result of mass movement, feces are forced into the rectum, raising rectal pressure. Rectal pressoreceptors can distinguish between the increases in pressure resulting from feces, liquid, or gas. Defecation is preceded by voluntary relaxation of the external sphincter and compression of the abdominal contents by straining efforts. These actions give rise to stimuli that support and augment the *defecation reflex*, which is responsible for evacuating the rectum. The defecation reflex is initiated by distention of the rectum. When this occurs, impulses are transmitted to the reflex centers in the spinal cord (sacral and lumbar segments) and brain (hypothalamus). Return signals to the colon, rectum, and anus trigger intense peristaltic contractions of the colon (the entire colon may be involved) and rectum, and relaxation of the internal anal sphincter. Voluntary control over the external anal sphincter either allows defecation to proceed or inhibits it. If an individual repeatedly ignores the defecation reflex, reconditioning of the reflex occurs with the end result that rectal distention is no longer followed by an urge to defecate; consequently, feces are retained in the rectum and colonic stasis, or *constipation*, ensues.

DIGESTION

The process of digestion involves the enzymatic breakdown of food into products that can be absorbed from the intestinal tract into the blood stream. The major foods are **carbohydrates, fats,** and **proteins.** The principal carbohydrate in food is *starch* — plant polysaccharides constructed from glucose units. Among other dietary carbohydrates are *glycogen* (so-called "animal starch"), *sucrose* (table sugar), a disaccharide consisting of glucose and fructose, and *lactose* (milk sugar), a disaccharide composed of glucose and galactose.

Digestion begins in the mouth with the enzymatic action of **ptyalin,** salivary amylase (G. *amylon,* starch). Ptyalin hydrolyzes (splitting with the addition of water) starch (and glycogen) into the disaccharide *maltose*

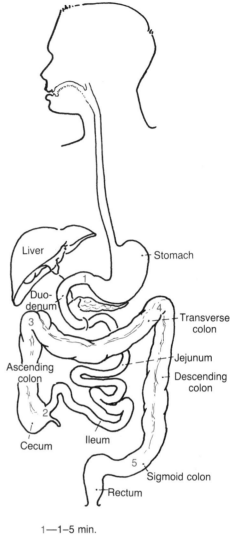

1—1–5 min.
2—4½ hrs.
3—6½ hrs.
4—9½ hrs.
5—12–24 hrs.

Figure 14–21. The time required for food substances to reach various portions of the digestive tract.

(composed of two glucose units). However, food does not remain in the mouth long enough for more than a small percentage of dietary starch to be converted to maltose. The enzymatic action of ptyalin continues in the stomach for as long as several hours until the contents are mixed with gastric secretions. When this occurs, the acid mixture of the stomach inactivates ptyalin. About 30 to 60 per cent of the ingested starch is degraded to maltose before the action of ptyalin is halted.

In the stomach the only digestive process of any consequence initiated is the hydrolysis of proteins. The enzyme **pepsin** splits proteins into derivative proteins (*proteoses* and *peptones*), *polypeptides* and a relatively few free amino acids.

In the small intestine enzymes delivered to the duodenum in pancreatic juice and intestinal enzymes continue the digestion of starch and protein. In addition, **pancreatic lipase** is responsible for the digestion of most of the dietary fat, splitting fat into *monoglycerides, fatty acids,* and some free *glycerol.* Proteins and the products of pepsin digestion are split into individual amino acids by the actions of the pancreatic proteolytic enzymes **trypsin, chymotrypsin** and **carboxypeptidases** and a number of **intestinal peptidases** (including aminopeptidase and tetra-, tri-, and dipeptidases). The end product of the digestive action of **pancreatic amylase** on starch is maltose, the same product formed by the action of ptyalin. **Intestinal maltase** splits maltose into two *glucose* molecules. Other intestinal enzymes digest sucrose and lactose. **Intestinal sucrase** splits sucrose into *glucose* and *fructose;* **intestinal lactase** degrades lactose into *glucose* and *galactose.* Table 14–1 summarizes the digestion of carbohydrates, proteins, and fat. A description of the control of the secretion of digestive enzymes and further details of the digestive process in the mouth, stomach, and intestine appear in the following sections.

Salivary Secretions

Salivary secretions are of two types: (1) *serous secretion*, a clear solution containing the digestive enzyme ptyalin, and (2) *mucous secretion*, a thick, viscous solution containing mucus. The secretion of the parotid gland is serous. Submaxillary secretion is both serous and mucous; sublingual secretion is mucous only. The binding and lubricating properties of mucus facilitate mastication, the formation of the bolus, and swallowing. Saliva is secret-

Table 14–1   DIGESTION OF CARBOHYDRATES, PROTEINS, AND FAT

	CARBOHYDRATES	PROTEINS	FAT
Mouth	*Ptyalin (salivary amylase)* initiates digestion, splitting starch and glycogen into the disaccharide maltose.		
Stomach	Continued action of ptyalin.	*Pepsin* initiates digestion, splitting proteins into derivative proteins (proteoses and peptones) and polypeptides.	
Small intestine	*Pancreatic amylase* splits starch and glycogen into maltose. Disaccharidases of the small intestine split maltose, sucrose, and lactose into their constituent monosaccharides: *Maltase* splits maltose into two glucose molecules. *Sucrase* splits sucrose into fructose and glucose. *Lactase* splits lactose into galactose and glucose.	Pancreatic enzymes *trypsin* and *chymotrypsin* (both, like pepsin, endopeptidases — cleaving peptide bonds in the interior region of proteins) split proteins and the products of pepsin digestion into peptides. *Peptidases* (all intestinal enzymes except two pancreatic carboxypeptidases°) split peptides into amino acids.	*Pancreatic lipase* splits fat into monoglycerides, fatty acids, and some free glycerol (to a minor extent, a lipase of the small intestine also splits fat).

°Carboxypeptidases split off carboxyl-terminal amino acids from peptides as opposed to aminopeptidases, which split off amino-terminal amino acids.

Table 14–2 GASTROINTESTINAL HORMONES

HORMONE	SOURCE	STIMULUS FOR PRODUCTION	ACTION
Gastrin	Mucosa of pyloric portion of stomach	Nerve stimulation by way of vagus nerve; distention and chemical stimulation by food in the stomach	Stimulates the secretion of an acid-rich digestive juice by the gastric glands
Enterogastrone	Duodenal mucosa	Principally fat in the duodenum	Inhibits gastric secretion and motility
Secretin	Duodenal mucosa	Principally acid in the duodenum	Stimulates secretion of watery pancreatic juice containing bicarbonate
Cholecystokinin-pancreozymin (CCK-PZ)	Duodenal mucosa	Products of protein digestion and fat in the duodenum	Stimulates the production of an enzyme-rich pancreatic juice; stimulates contraction of the gallbladder
Villikinin	Mucosa of the small intestine	Chyme in the intestine	Stimulates movements of the intestinal villi

ed continuously and is greatly increased by appetite-arousing stimuli. About 1 to 1.5 liters of saliva are secreted daily.

Salivary secretion is **exclusively under nervous control.** The control center for salivation, a group of nuclei between the medulla and pons, is stimulated by a variety of sensations. Thus, the taste, smell, or sight of food activates the center, and impulses conducted by parasympathetic nerve fibers (in the seventh and ninth cranial nerves) stimulate salivary secretion. Foods arousing pleasant sensations provoke a copious secretion. Those arousing unpleasant sensations cause far less secretion and may even inhibit salivation to the extent that swallowing is made difficult.

The characteristics and the actual volume of saliva are related to the type of food ingested. For example, acid substances and dry foods produce a large volume of thin, watery saliva; milk or cold water produces a smaller volume of viscous saliva. The enzymatic content of saliva varies with the stimulus. Meat and weak acids stimulate the production of similar volumes of saliva, but the enzyme content is greater with meat than with weak acids.

During periods of dehydration when the body has lost large quantities of fluid, salivary secretion is reduced or suppressed completely. This may also occur at times of emotional stress. Irritation of the esophageal, gastric, and duodenal mucous membranes reflexively stimulates salivary secretion. Thus, excessive salivation may be an early warning sign of disease of the upper digestive tract.

Gastric Secretion

The gastric glands are tubular (usually branched tubular) and are of two different types: (1) **pyloric glands** and a small number surrounding the opening of the esophagus, called **cardiac glands**, in which *mucus-secreting cells* predominate; and (2) **main gastric glands** (also called fundic glands), located throughout the body and fundus of the stomach, containing three principal kinds of cells — *chief, or zymogenic, cells,* which secrete *pepsinogen* (the precursor of the proteolytic enzyme pepsin), *parietal, or oxyntic, cells* (G. *oxynein,* to make acid), which secrete *hydrochloric acid,* and *mucus-secreting cells.* The chief cells are located mainly in the lower part (referred to as the body or base) of these glands. The mucus-secreting cells line the neck. The oxyntic cells are scattered throughout the glands, but are most numerous in the neck region, and appear to lie behind or between the other cell types, bulging into the underlying connective tissue. The mucus secreted by the glandular mucus-secreting cells is different from the mucus secreted by the surface epithelial cells of the stomach. The secretion of the latter cells is thicker and more viscous, and is largely responsible for the thick, tenacious layer of mucus that protects the stomach lining from the acidity and proteolytic action of gastric juice.

A characteristic of proteolytic enzymes in the gastrointestinal tract is their synthesis as inactive precursors, called *zymogens*, which are stored in granules within the glandular cells. Synthesis in this form and storage in granules protect the cells from self-destruction. Pepsinogen, following its secretion, is transformed into pepsin upon contact with acid by a process known as *autoactivation*. In the initial step, a fragment is split off one end to produce active pepsin, which then catalyzes further activation at a rapidly accelerating rate.

Three phases of the secretion of digestive juice by gastric glands in response to a meal are generally described: *cephalic, gastric,* and *intestinal*. Each phase is named according to where the stimuli initiating the secretion arise.

Cephalic Phase. The cephalic phase is induced by the sight, smell, taste, or thought of food. The nerve impulses eliciting secretion are conducted to the stomach by way of the vagus nerve (its section abolishes this phase of secretion). The secretion of gastric juice is triggered *directly* by stimulation of the gastric glands and *indirectly* by stimulating the release of the hormone **gastrin** from specialized epithelial cells (so-called G cells) in the pyloric portion of the stomach. Gastrin is absorbed into the blood stream and transported to the gastric glands, where it acts principally on the acid-secreting oxyntic cells and also to some extent on the pepsinogen-secreting chief cells. Vagal stimulation of the secretion of gastric juice by gastric glands and of gastrin by G cells acts through local nerve circuits in the stomach wall.

Gastric Phase. When food enters the stomach, distension by the bulk of the meal and chemical stimuli induce gastric juice secretion. In this phase, too, this secretion involves direct stimulation of the gastric glands and indirect stimulation by activating the release of gastrin. The secretion of both gastric juice and gastrin by food in the stomach is brought about by short, so-called intramural (L. *intra*, within; L. *murus*, wall) reflexes and long, vagovagal reflexes (in which impulses are conducted to the brain and back to the stomach by fibers of the vagus nerve). The cephalic and gastric phases overlap considerably in time and interact so as to produce a greater secretion than either could alone.

Intestinal Phase. The presence of certain digestive products in the upper part of the small intestine also stimulates secretion of gastric juice. This phase, of lesser importance than the first two, is believed to be mediated by an as yet unidentified hormone released by the duodenum that acts on the stomach.

Inhibition of Gastric Secretion. The interplay between stimulation and inhibition of gastric secretion determines the activity of the gastric glands at any one time. Two inhibitory mechanisms have been well established: one operates through the stomach, the other through the duodenum.

The presence of a strong acid in the antrum of the stomach results in a decrease in gastric secretion. A pH of 2.0 or less inhibits the release of gastrin from the antrum and thereby decreases the secretion of an acid-rich gastric juice. (Strong acids also inhibit gastric emptying — protecting the duodenum from excess acidity.) Fat, acid, or hypertonic solutions in the duodenum stimulate the release of hormones that inhibit gastric secretion. One of these, referred to as enterogastrone, which is released principally by fat, was mentioned earlier in connection with duodenal feedback inhibition of gastric motility. Others include cholecystokinin-pancreozymin (the principal functions of which are stimulation of pancreatic enzyme secretion and gallbladder contraction) and secretin (the principal action of which is stimulation of bicarbonate secretion by the pancreas), which reduce acid-rich gastric secretion by inhibiting the response of the gastric glands to gastrin. Although cholecystokinin-pancreozymin and secretin do not appear to be released in sufficient amounts to independently inhibit gastric secretion, each one augments the action of the other. Hence, it is possible that together they play a role in inhibiting the secretion of an acid-rich gastric juice.

Despite all the mechanisms for inhibiting oversecretion of hydrochloric acid and damage to the mucosal wall of the stomach and duodenum from this acid, **peptic ulceration** frequently occurs. A peptic ulcer is an ulcer in either the stomach or the duodenum caused in part by the action of gastric juice. The major goal of both medical and surgical treatment of peptic ulcer is to reduce the production of hydrochloric acid by the parietal cells of the stomach. Medical reduction of parietal cell secretion involves neutralizing the acid after secretion by ingestion of antacids or by the use of anticholinergic drugs to block the stimuli for the secretion of acids.

Until a few years ago, the principal surgical means of reducing acidity was to remove the major portion of the stomach secreting hydrochloric acid. Now, the principal aim of surgical treatment is to reduce the stimuli for acid secretion. This is accomplished by cutting the vagus nerves and by removing the gastrin-producing pyloric gland area (antrum). Sectioning the vagus nerves, as mentioned, is associated with an impairment of gastric emptying; when this operation is employed, the surgeon must perform a concomitant drainage procedure, allowing the pylorus to drain freely into the duodenum, or must actually join the stomach to the jejunum to aid gastric emptying after surgery.

Pancreatic Secretion

As described above, enzymes in pancreatic juice continue the process of starch and protein digestion in the small intestine. Virtually all of the fat entering the duodenum is undigested. Only a small amount of butterfat is digested in the stomach by gastric lipase (a tributyrase). The bulk of the dietary fat is digested by pancreatic lipase. Intestinal lipase contributes to some extent to fat digestion. The importance of pancreatic lipase for normal fat digestion is made plain by the observation that the principal consequence of pancreatic exocrine insufficiency is excess fat excretion in feces (steatorrhea). Pancreatic juice also contains nucleases, which split nucleic acids into nucleotides; phospholipases, which digest phospholipids; and cholesterol esterase, which hydrolyzes cholesterol esters (splitting off the long-chain fatty acid portion).

The proteolytic enzymes trypsin, chymotrypsin, and carboxypeptidases are secreted as inactive precursors. *Trypsinogen* is converted to trypsin by the action of *enterokinase*, an enzyme secreted by the small intestine, and by an autoactivation process. Trypsin converts *chymotrypsinogen* and *procarboxypeptidases* to their active forms.

Pancreatic secretion, like gastric secretion, is regulated by both neural and hormonal mechanisms. *Vagal stimulation* of the pancreas occurs at the same time as the cephalic and gastric phases of gastric secretion. Two hormones secreted by the duodenum, *secretin* and *cholecystokinin-pancreozymin*, act on the exocrine pancreas. The exocrine pancreas contains two types of secretory cells. One type (acinar cells) secretes *enzymes*. The other type (intralobular duct cells) secretes *water and bicarbonate*. Secretin acts on duct cells to induce the secretion of water and bicarbonate. Vagal stimulation and cholecystokinin-pancreozymin induce the secretion of enzymes by activating acinar cells. Hydrochloric acid is the most effective stimulus for the release of secretin. Induction of the release of bicarbonate by secretin protects the duodenum against peptic ulceration and creates a favorable pH for the activity of pancreatic enzymes. Fats and the products of protein digestion are the most effective stimuli for the release of cholecystokinin-pancreozymin.

Intestinal Enzymes

The enzymes of the small intestine complete the digestion of protein and carbohydrate. The disaccharidase maltase splits maltose, derived from the digestion of starch and glycogen by salivary and pancreatic amylases, into two glucose molecules. Other intestinal disaccharidases, sucrase and lactase, split the dietary disaccharides sucrose and lactose into their constituent monosaccharides. A number of intestinal peptidases split peptides into amino acids. In the initial stages of protein digestion, the proteinases, also called endopeptidases — first pepsin in the stomach and then the pancreatic enzymes trypsin and chymotrypsin in the small intestine — cleave peptide bonds in the interior regions of proteins and polypeptides. The peptides produced by the actions of these enzymes are reduced to amino acids by a number of peptidases — all intestinal enzymes except carboxypeptidases A and B, which have been isolated from pancreatic juice. The intestinal peptidases include aminopeptidase and tetra-, tri-, and dipeptidases.

Enzymes of the small intestine also degrade nucleotides. Nucleotidases remove the phosphate group from nucleotides, and nucleosidases split the resulting nucleosides into their constituents — a pentose and a purine or pyrimidine base.

The secretion of the intestinal mucosa, presumably derived from the crypts of Lieberkühn, the intestinal glands, is a thin fluid of neutral pH, largely devoid of enzymes. It is rapidly reabsorbed, and the resulting circulation of this fluid helps maintain optimum conditions for digestion and absorption. The intestinal lumen also contains cellular debris, a source of enzymes, arising from the dissolution of cells continuously shed at the tips of the intestinal villi. Cell division at the base of the crypts and migration of new cells up the villi continuously replace shed cells.

The duodenum contains special glands in the submucosa, called Brunner's glands, which secrete mucus. The ducts of these glands open into the crypts of Lieberkühn. Their secretion, as well as the secretion of mucus by mucosal goblet cells, is an important protective mechanism against ulceration.

ABSORPTION

The absorption of the end products of digestion occurs almost exclusively in the small intestine. Although some glucose, alcohol, and water are absorbed in the stomach, the amount so absorbed is negligible. Organic nutrients are not absorbed from the large intestine, but significant amounts of water and salts are.

The site of absorption in the small intestine is the columnar cells of the villi. Each villus contains a *rich capillary plexus* beneath the basement membrane and a large lymphatic vessel, called the *central lacteal*, in the core (Fig. 14–9). Thin smooth muscle fibers continuous with the muscularis mucosae and arranged in bundles around the central lacteal are also present in the lamina propria of the villus. Their contraction is especially important for maintaining the flow of lymph. Simple sugars, amino acids, short-chain fatty acids (derived from butterfat), and glycerol are absorbed into the capillary network and transported to the liver via the *hepatic portal vein* (Fig. 14–22). The major products of lipid digestion are absorbed as chylomicrons (see below) into the central lacteal and carried via the intestinal lymphatics to the *thoracic duct,* which empties into the left subclavian vein just above the heart (Fig. 14–22).

The simple sugars glucose and galactose are absorbed by active transport, whereas fructose appears to be absorbed by facilitated diffusion. The active absorption of glucose and galactose is apparently coupled to the active transport of sodium. Inhibition of active sodium transport interferes with the absorption of these sugars. At one time it was generally believed that maltose, sucrose, and lactose were completely hydrolyzed to simple sugars in the intestinal lumen. A number of observations, however, indicate that some of these disaccharides are hydrolyzed by enzymes located in the microvillus membrane of the brush border. For example, it has been found that when preparations of hamster small intestine are incubated with sucrose solutions glucose accumulates within the epithelium to a concentration 20 times that of glucose in the incubation medium. In addition, the maltase, sucrase, and lactase activity of the mucosa is located primarily in the brush border membrane.

In humans the activity of lactase is maximal immediately after birth. Thereafter it declines, reaching a minimum in most children after one and one-half to three years. High lactase activity in human adults is found only in dairying cultures, where milk consumption is traditionally high. Adults, other than those of milk-drinking populations, are intolerant to excessive amounts of dietary lactose. Apparently, lactose tolerance is transmitted genetically and as a dominant trait. **Lactose intolerance** in infants is of clinical importance. The consequences of intolerance are bloating, belching, flatulence, cramps, and explosive diarrhea. Two processes cause these symptoms: (1) the osmotic effect of lactose in the colon draws water into the lumen, and (2) fermentation of lactose by colon bacteria generates organic acids and carbon dioxide.

The absorption of amino acids also involves active transport mechanisms. The bulk of the ingested protein is hydrolyzed to amino acids, and the absorption of protein occurs for the most part as amino acids. Some intact peptides, however, are absorbed and hydrolyzed intracellularly.

The efficient absorption of lipids is made possible by the formation of a clear solution containing the digested products. This is accomplished by the formation of polymolecular aggregates called **micelles**, composed of monoglycerides, free fatty acids, cholesterol, and bile salts. The formation of these micelles requires the presence of bile salts. In

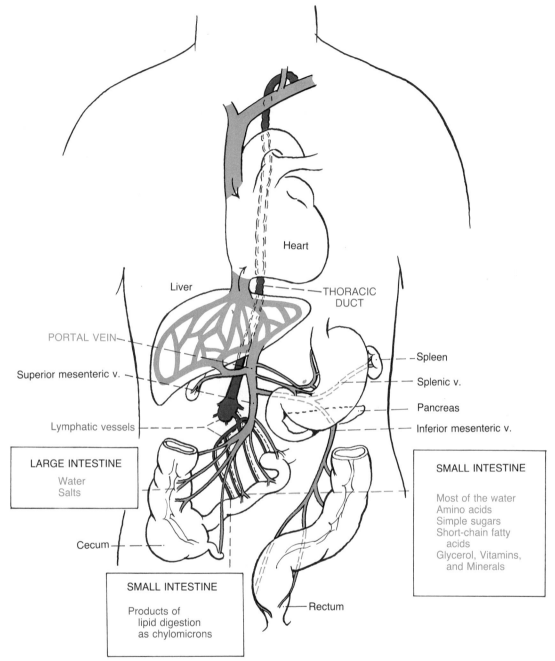

Figure 14–22. Major sites of absorption of the products of digestion.

their absence the absorption of fat is greatly reduced and the absorption of cholesterol is completely abolished.

When fat is undergoing digestion, pancreatic lipase acts at the interface of fat droplets and the water medium in which the droplets are suspended. As the digestion proceeds, two distinct phases can be distinguished — a clear phase containing micelles and an oily phase containing tri- and diglycerides. The formation of the clear phase not only provides a medium for absorption but also accelerates digestion by removing the end products of digestion from the site of enzyme action. When the micellar lipid products are absorbed, the bile salts return to the lumen for reuse in the formation of new micelles. At the lower end of the ileum, bile salts are absorbed into the blood stream, transported to the liver, and then resecreted into the bile duct. As a result of this so-called *enterohepatic circulation*, bile salts are used over and over again for micelle formation.

After monoglycerides enter the intestinal cell, some are hydrolyzed to fatty acids and glycerol. Triglycerides are then resynthesized. Two pathways for triglyceride synthesis have been demonstrated: direct esterification of monoglycerides and from glycerol phosphate (derived almost entirely from the degradation of glucose, via dihydroxyacetone phosphate) and fatty acids. At the same time, some of the diglycerides formed as an intermediate product during triglyceride synthesis are converted to phospholipids, and two-thirds of the cholesterol (essentially all is taken up by the intestinal cell in the unesterified form) is esterified with long-chain fatty acids. Following this, the lipids are packaged by the intestinal cell in the form of transport vehicles, namely, lipoproteins known as **chylomicrons** (a term coined in 1920 by Simon Gage to describe microscopic particles in chyle, the descriptive term for fat-laden intestinal lymph). Chylomicrons are spherical particles ranging from about 100 to 500 nanometers in diameter containing a core of neutral lipid (triglycerides and esterified cholesterol) surrounded by a membranelike coat of protein and phospholipid (unesterified cholesterol is in both the core and the outer coat). Triglycerides account for more than 90 per cent of the weight of chylomicrons, protein less than 1 per cent. As mentioned, chylomicrons pass into the central lacteal of the villus and travel in intestinal lymph to the thoracic duct. Movement of lymph in lacteals is facilitated by the contraction of the muscularis mucosae and the smooth muscle fibers of the villi. Continuous lashing movements and rhythmic shortening and lengthening of the villi have the effect of "milking" the villi, propelling lymph toward the thoracic duct. Movement of the villi is triggered by a local reflex and a hormone called *villikinin* in response to chyme in the intestine. After chylomicrons enter the blood stream, they are taken up largely by adipose tissue fat depots, such as those in the subcutaneous layer of the skin and in the abdominal region.

Water and various electrolytes are ab-

sorbed in both the small and large intestines. Electrolytes are absorbed most rapidly in the proximal portions of the small intestine because of the larger surface area and greater membrane permeability. It is also known that monovalent ions, such as sodium, potassium, chloride, and bicarbonate, are absorbed more readily than the polyvalent ions, such as calcium, magnesium, and sulfate. Sodium is absorbed by an active transport mechanism. Potassium and chloride ions are passively absorbed in response to concentration gradients. Calcium is absorbed by an active process requiring the presence of vitamin D (see Chapter 6, page 111). The parathyroid hormone plays a regulatory role in calcium absorption.

Most dietary iron is organically complexed and released during digestion. The absorption of iron occurs in the small intestine, and it enters the intestinal cell by an active transport process. Within the intestinal cell it appears to be transported in association with a compound of low molecular weight (possibly a complex with amino acids), and is in equilibrium with iron stored as ferritin (iron bound to a protein called apoferritin). When iron passes out of the intestinal cell to be transported in the blood stream, it is picked up by a globulin (transferrin). When the body's iron stores are depleted, the absorption of iron is increased. The major site of the control of absorption seems to be at the point of transfer of iron from the intestinal cell to the blood, but the mechanism is poorly understood. Animal studies suggest that an inhibitor in plasma, present in high concentrations in the iron-loaded state and virtually absent in the iron-deficient state, may regulate absorption. Since the concentration of ferritin in plasma varies inversely with iron absorption, it has been suggested that plasma ferritin may be the inhibitor responsible for controlling iron absorption.

The absorption of water occurs by the simple physical process of osmosis.

Malabsorption Syndromes

General consequences of malabsorption syndromes include weight loss, disturbances of acid-base balance, impaired calcium absorption, and vitamin deficiencies. Patients with a malabsorption syndrome show diarrhea, weight loss, and weakness. Among the underlying mechanisms producing abnormal absorption can be included insufficient intestinal surface area, alteration in bowel motility, alterations in the autonomic nervous system, deficiencies in digestive enzymes, and diseases of the bowel lining.

Intravenous Hyperalimentation (Parenteral Alimentation)

There are periods of time during patient care when the gut cannot and should not be used for feeding purposes, and nutrition supplied via the veins becomes necessary. Intravenous hyperalimentation is employed in an attempt to meet the patient's nutritional requirements by concentrating nutrients as much as possible in order to stay within a daily fluid limit of about 2000 ml and to develop a delivery system that will avoid injury to the vascular system by a hypertonic solution. The most appropriate solution contains 20 per cent dextrose, 5 per cent protein, and 5 per cent minerals and vitamins. This solution is delivered into a relatively large, high-flow vessel such as the superior vena cava.

REGULATION OF FOOD INTAKE

It has been observed that individuals with tumors of the hypophysis that are encroaching upon the hypothalamus tend to become obese. In addition, destructive lesions in the hypothalamus, generally caused by vascular thrombosis, often result in severe inanition (L. *inanis*, empty), a pathological state due to lack of food. In animals two centers in the hypothalamus involved in controlling food intake have been identified. Destruction of the ventromedial hypothalamic nucleus (the so-called "satiety center") in rats, cats, and monkeys causes hyperphagia (G. *hyper,* over; G. *phagein*, to eat) and obesity. Destruction of the lateral hypothalamus nuclei (called the "feeding center") results in a cessation of feeding (aphagia). It has been suggested that when the desire for food is satisfied the satiety center inhibits the feeding center; if the satiety center is destroyed control over feeding is lost. The satiety center concentrates glucose and responds to increases in blood glucose levels with increased electrical activity. Drugs that reduce appetite, such as amphetamines, also increase the electrical activity of the satiety center. It is generally believed that the activity of the satiety center is also influenced by input from peripheral receptors. There is some reason to believe that feedback mechanisms developed early in life may permanently affect feeding habits. It has been found, for example, that overfed infants develop a greater number of fat cells in fat depots than normally fed infants. The number remains constant — weight-reducing regimens reduce the amount of fat in the cells but not the number of cells. This might explain why overfed infants tend to be overweight all their lives.

NUTRITIONAL REQUIREMENTS, METABOLISM, AND THE DISPOSITION OF MAJOR FOODSTUFFS

Organic Nutrients

Food supplies fuel for the cells' energy needs and the ingredients for manufacturing essential cell constituents. The body requires not only food in bulk but also specific food substances it cannot make. For example, the cells of the body lack the ability to manufacture all of the amino acids needed for protein synthesis. Those that cannot be synthesized must be obtained preformed in ingested food; such amino acids are called *essential amino acids*. The adult human probably requires eight essential amino acids. These are tryptophan, lysine, methionine, threonine, phenylalanine, leucine, isoleucine, and valine. Histidine and arginine, called essential amino acids by some authors, are actually synthesized in the body, but only in amounts sufficient to meet the demands of maintenance, not growth and repair.

The body is also unable to synthesize two polyunsaturated fatty acids, linoleic and linolenic acid (18-carbon fatty acids containing two and three double bonds, respectively). These *essential fatty acids* must be obtained from plant foods. Immature rats deprived of these two fatty acids display severe pathological signs, grow poorly, and die prematurely. Humans with a congenital inability to absorb dietary fat as chylomicrons (due to a failure to synthesize the protein portion of chylomicrons) develop neurological symptoms, possess crenated red blood cells and have a limited life span. It is assumed that some of these conditions result from a deficiency of essential fatty acids. Since essential fatty acids are components of cell membrane phospholipids, it is believed that disorders associated with a deficiency of essential fatty acids are partly accounted for by a failure of cell membranes to function normally. It has also been suggested that the consequences of essential fatty acid deficiency may be due in part to the inability to synthesize a group of derivatives of polyunsaturated fatty acids, called *prostaglandins*, which affect a wide range of physiological processes. (The principal precursor for the synthesis of prostaglandins is arachidonic acid, a 20-carbon fatty acid that has four double bonds and is formed from linoleic acid.) Prostaglandins have been described as "hormonelike" or "local hormones" because they are produced in the cells of many tissues and exert their effect at or near sites of synthesis. They were originally found in human seminal fluid and identified as substances that could stimulate the contraction of the smooth muscle of the uterus and lower blood pressure. Among other actions of prostaglandins are: decreasing gastric acid secretion, increasing salt and water clearance by the kidneys, regulating the secretion of certain hormones, modulating synaptic transmission by norepinephrine, and regulating the aggregation of platelets. Although, as mentioned, it has been suggested that some of the consequences of essential fatty acid deficiency may be due in part to failure to synthesize prostaglandins, it is not known how any particular disorder can be related to prostaglandin lack.

Vitamins, by definition, are essential organic nutrients required in trace amounts to maintain good health. Their usual source is food, but some can be synthesized in the body. Vitamins have widely divergent properties and many function as components of coenzymes. They can be separated into two groups by virtue of their solubility characteristics. The fat-soluble vitamins are A, D, E, and K; the water-soluble vitamins include the B-complex, C, and compounds with related activity (see Table 14–3).

Metabolism of Foodstuffs

The chemical processing of foodstuffs is called *metabolism*. The term metabolism includes two major phases — *anabolism* and *catabolism*. Anabolism is the process of building complex molecules from simpler ones. Catabolism is the reverse process. Catabolism is accompanied by the release of energy and its storage as adenosine triphosphate (ATP). In Chapter 3 (page 58) we described the production of ATP by the oxidative degradation of fatty acids and glucose to carbon dioxide and water via the citric acid (Krebs) cycle and by the anaerobic breakdown of glucose to lactic acid. ATP is also produced by the oxidative breakdown of amino acids via the Krebs cycle. The catabolism of amino acids occurs mainly in the liver; the kidneys are also significantly active. In the initial steps of the breakdown of amino acids, the amino groups are removed. This occurs largely by *transamination* — the transfer of the α, or primary, amino group (attached to the carbon next to the carboxyl group) of an amino acid to an α-keto acid (having oxygen double-bonded to the carbon next to the carboxyl group), usually α-ketoglutaric acid, converting the amino acid to an α-keto acid and the α-ketoglutaric acid to glutamic acid. Glutamic acid may undergo *deamination* — splitting off the amino group, re-forming α-ketoglutaric acid, and producing ammonia (the ammonia is combined with carbon dioxide, forming urea, in a sequence of reactions that take place in the liver, known as the urea cycle). For the greater number of amino acids, the pathway leading to entry into the Krebs cycle is via the formation of acetyl-CoA; others enter as one or another compound of the cycle. Acetyl-CoA formation may be direct or indirect via pyruvic acid or acetoacetyl-CoA (Fig. 14–23). Amino acids that give rise to pyruvic acid or compounds of the Krebs cycle are called *glucogenic* because, as illustrated in Figure 14–23, pyruvic acid and oxaloacetic acid, an intermediate of the Krebs cycle, are in the pathway leading to the synthesis of glucose. In the period following the absorption of a meal, the breakdown of muscle protein to amino acids that are transported to the liver and converted to glucose is a fundamental mechanism for maintaining normal blood sugar (see the following section for further details). Amino acids that give rise to acetoacetyl-CoA (or directly to acetyl-CoA, which can give rise to acetoacetyl-CoA by condensation of two molecules of acetyl-CoA) are called *ketogenic* because free acetoacetic acid (formed by removal of coen-

Table 14–3 VITAMINS

VITAMIN	SOURCE	FUNCTION	DEFICIENCY
Fat-Soluble			
A	Yellow fruits and vegetables, leafy green vegetables, fish liver oil, milk, butter, eggs	Essential for maintenance of normal epithelium; synthesis of rhodopsin for night vision	Night blindness; keratinization of epithelium of respiratory, digestive, and genitourinary tracts and in eyes (tear duct damage can lead to eye infection [xerophthalmia] and blindness)
D	Exposure to sunshine; fish liver oil	Facilitates absorption of calcium and phosphorus from the intestine; utilization of calcium and phosphorus in bone development	Rickets in children; osteomalacia in adults
E	Lettuce, whole wheat, spinach, vegetable and plant oils	Antioxidant; essential for reproduction in rats; no definite function has been determined in humans	Sterility in rats; no known effect on humans
K	Liver, cabbage, spinach, tomatoes	Synthesis by the liver of prothrombin and other blood clotting factors	Impaired mechanism of blood coagulation
Water-Soluble			
B_1 (thiamine)	Whole grain cereals, eggs, pork, bananas, apples	Coenzyme in metabolism of carbohydrate as thiamine pyrophosphate; maintains normal appetite and absorption	Beriberi (peripheral nerve degeneration leading to muscle atrophy and heart failure)
B_2 (riboflavin)	Liver, meat, milk, eggs, fruit	Constituent of 2 coenzymes (FMN, FAD) involved in oxidation-reduction reactions	Cheilosis (cracks at corners of mouth); lesions of cornea
B_6 (pyridoxine)	Whole grain cereal, yeast, milk, eggs, fish, liver	Coenzyme (as pyridoxal phosphate) in amino acid metabolism	Dermatitis; irritability; convulsions in infants
Niacin	Liver, fish, tomatoes, yeast, peanut butter	Constituent of 2 coenzymes (NAD, NADP) involved in oxidation-reduction reactions	Pellagra (skin lesions, diarrhea, dementia)
B_{12}	Liver, kidneys, milk, eggs, cheese	Maturation of erythrocytes	Pernicious anemia
Pantothenic acid	Egg yolk, lean meat, kidneys, skimmed milk, yeast	A constituent of coenzyme A	Fatigue; impaired coordination
Folic acid	Leafy green vegetables, liver	Coenzyme in transfer of 1-carbon groups	Macrocytic anemia
Biotin	Liver, eggs, milk; synthesized by bacteria in the intestinal tract	Coenzyme serving as carrier of carbon dioxide for carboxylation reactions in fatty acid synthesis	Fatigue; depression; nausea; dermatitis; muscle pains
C (ascorbic acid)	Citrus fruits, tomatoes, green vegetables, potatoes	Hydroxylation of proline in synthesis of collagen and other hydroxylation reactions	Scurvy (extreme weakness, swollen and bleeding gums, poor wound healing, hemorrhaging under the skin, weak bones)

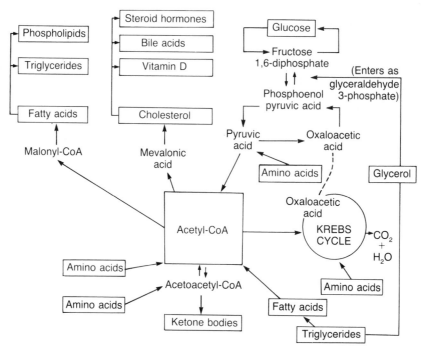

Figure 14–23. Catabolic and anabolic pathways. The oxidation of fatty acids and glucose produces acetyl-CoA, which may enter the Krebs cycle to be converted to carbon dioxide and water. Many amino acids also give rise to acetyl-CoA; others are directly converted to compounds of the Krebs cycle. Acetyl-CoA is also the biosynthetic precursor of fatty acids and cholesterol. The pathway for the synthesis of fatty acids from acetyl-CoA is completely different from the pathway by which fatty acids are degraded. Malonyl-CoA, a key intermediate in the synthesis of fatty acids, is a 3-carbon compound formed from acetyl-CoA and bicarbonate. When fatty acids are synthesized, 2-carbon units of malonyl-CoA are successively added to acetyl-CoA and a growing fatty acid chain (growing as a result of the addition of these 2-carbon units). Since the carbon added as bicarbonate to form malonyl-CoA is lost as carbon dioxide each time the chain is elongated, all of the carbons of the synthesized fatty acids are derived from acetyl-CoA. Biosynthesis of glucose from pyruvic acid occurs in part by a reversal of the degradative sequence (all steps between fructose 1,6-diphosphate and phosphoenol pyruvic acid are reversible; the steps between phosphoenol pyruvic acid and pyruvic acid and two of the three steps between glucose and fructose 1,6-diphosphate are not). Note that oxaloacetic acid is not only a compound of the Krebs cycle but also is in the pathway of the synthesis of glucose from pyruvic acid.

zyme A from acetoacetyl-CoA, a process called deacylation) is one of the so-called ketone bodies (the other ketone bodies, β-hydroxybutyric acid and acetone, are derived from acetoacetic acid). Normally the concentration of ketone bodies in the blood is very low, but during prolonged fasting and in diabetes the concentrations of acetoacetic acid and β-hydroxybutyric acid may reach high levels because they are produced in large amounts in the liver as a result of the excessive breakdown of fatty acids (to acetyl-CoA, followed by condensation of two molecules of acetyl-CoA, deacylation of the acetoacetyl-CoA thus formed to acetoacetic acid, and reduction of acetoacetic acid to β-hydroxybutyric acid). Since the liver does not utilize ketone bodies, they pass into the

blood stream (the utilization of ketone bodies by nonhepatic tissues is discussed in the following section).

Figure 14–23, illustrating the major catabolic and anabolic pathways, draws attention to the central role of acetyl-CoA as a biochemical intermediate. It is formed by the oxidation of glucose, fatty acids and many amino acids, and is a biosynthetic precursor of fatty acids (by a sequence that is totally different from the degradative sequence), from which triglycerides and phospholipids are formed, and of cholesterol, which in turn is the precursor of other steroids, such as bile acids, steroid hormones (estrogens, androgens, progesterone, and adrenal steroids), and vitamin D (formed in skin exposed to sunlight from 7-dehydrocholesterol).

Disposition of the Major Foodstuffs Following Their Absorption

During the time a meal is being absorbed, almost all of the body's energy needs are supplied by the breakdown of glucose. As mentioned, the greater part of the dietary fat is transported by chylomicrons to the fat depots. This stored fat remains untapped during the first few hours after eating. Glucose and amino acids are transported to the liver in the hepatic portal vein. A large proportion of the glucose is taken up by the liver and either utilized or converted to glycogen for storage. Glucose passing out of the liver is taken up by the working tissues, especially the brain and skeletal muscles. Amino acids taken up by the liver are used to manufacture proteins, especially the many blood proteins.

Some are converted to glucose and glycogen. All of the dietary glucose and amino acids in excess of the body's needs and the liver's capacity to store glycogen (which is limited) are converted to fat and transported (in the form of lipoproteins known as *very low density lipoproteins*) to the fat depots.

About three to four hours after eating a meal, two events take place: (1) the concentration of fatty acids in the blood stream rises, and (2) the concentration of amino acids in the blood stream rises. The increase in blood levels of fatty acids is caused by the hydrolysis of triglycerides in the fat depots and the release of fatty acids into the blood stream. These fatty acids are transported (bound to plasma albumin) principally to skeletal muscle, the heart, and the liver (Fig. 14–24). In the postabsorptive period, working tissues,

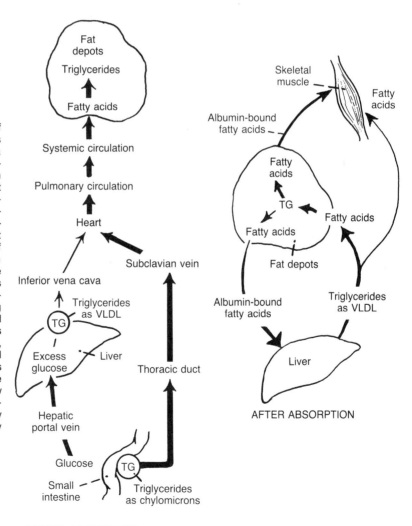

Figure 14–24. Transport of triglycerides (fat) and fatty acids during and after the absorption of a meal. During absorption, chylomicrons transport triglycerides from the small intestine to the fat depots, and very low density lipoproteins (VLDL) transport triglycerides synthesized from excess glucose (and amino acids) to the fat depots. Following hydrolysis of these triglycerides (by lipoprotein lipase) the released fatty acids are taken up by adipose tissue cells and new triglycerides are synthesized. About four hours after eating a meal, triglycerides are hydrolyzed in the fat depots and the fatty acids are transported, bound to albumin, principally to the liver and skeletal muscle. (and the heart). Excess fatty acids received by the liver are returned to the depots as very low density lipoproteins. Some triglyceride fatty acids of very low density lipoproteins are also taken up by skeletal muscle (and the heart.)

except the brain, rely to a great extent upon fatty acids for their energy needs. The liver receives considerably more fatty acids than it can use and returns the excess to the fat depots in the form of very low density lipoproteins. Some of the excess fatty acids transported by very low density lipoproteins are also taken up by skeletal muscle and the heart.

The rise in amino acid concentration in the blood is accounted for by the breakdown of protein in skeletal muscle and the transport of the released amino acids to the liver, where they are converted to glucose. The conversion of amino acids to glucose, a process known as *gluconeogenesis*, is essential for maintaining normal blood glucose levels in the postabsorptive period because the demands of the brain for glucose exceed the ability of the liver to maintain blood sugar levels by degrading stored glycogen. Normally, glucose is the brain's exclusive fuel; it requires between 100 to 150 grams per day. The liver stores less than 100 grams of glycogen. Since part of this store is held in reserve for emergency needs and about a third of the glucose released by the liver in the postabsorptive period is consumed by organs other than the brain, the liver's supply of glycogen is insufficient for an overnight fast. Gluconeogenesis becomes an important source of blood glucose a few hours after a meal.

If a fast is prolonged for a week or more, a number of adjustments are made to conserve body protein. The most important change is a shift by the brain from the exclusive use of glucose for fuel to the consumption of the ketone bodies β-hydroxybutyric acid and acetoacetic acid as a primary source of energy. These ketone bodies accumulate in the circulation during fasting as a result of the excessive breakdown of fatty acids in the liver. It has been estimated that after prolonged fasting they provide about 55 per cent of the brain's energy needs (the amount utilized apparently varying considerably from one area of the brain to another), amino acids about 15 per cent, and glucose about 30 per cent. Another adaptive response is the use by other working tissues of proportionately more fatty acids and less glucose to supply their energy requirements.

Plasma Lipoproteins. Lipids are transported in plasma by four classes of lipoproteins. Two have been described — chylomicrons, which transport dietary fat from the small intestine via the intestinal lymphatic vessels and the thoracic duct to the blood stream to be deposited mainly in the fat depots, and very low density lipoproteins (VLDL), which function mainly in transporting endogenous (G. *endon*, within; G. *genesthai*, from *gignesthai*, to be produced) fat to the fat depots from the liver following its synthesis (1) from excess glucose and amino acids during the absorption of a meal, and (2) in the postabsorptive period, using excess fatty acids transported to the liver. The other two classes of plasma lipoproteins are known as *low density lipoproteins* (LDL) and *high density lipoproteins* (HDL). These two classes of lipoproteins appear to function principally as vehicles for transporting cholesterol.

The average protein content of high density, low density and very low density lipoproteins is 50, 25, and 10 per cent, respectively. Chylomicrons in lymph have, on the average, less than one per cent protein, but acquire additional protein from high density lipoproteins upon passing into the blood stream, increasing their average protein content to about 2.5 per cent. One of these proteins (which is also transferred to very low density lipoproteins) activates an enzyme, known as *lipoprotein lipase*, that is essential for the tissue uptake of the triglyceride fatty acids of chylomicrons and very low density lipoproteins. This enzyme is released from tissue cells and hydrolyzes triglycerides at the surface of the capillary endothelium. This is followed by cellular uptake of the released fatty acids and resynthesis of triglycerides (by combination of the fatty acids with α-glycerophosphate derived from glucose). An extremely high concentration of chylomicrons in plasma is found in individuals with an inherited deficiency of lipoprotein lipase. The blood of some of these patients has been described as resembling cream of tomato soup.

The action of lipoprotein lipase on chylomicrons and very low density lipoproteins leads to a loss of about 95 per cent of the triglycerides of these lipoproteins. A small amount of cholesterol is also taken up along with fatty acids, but the greater part of the cholesterol is delivered to the liver (chiefly in the form of so-called chylomicron remnants) or incorporated into low density lipoproteins (mainly by way of so-called intermediate density lipoproteins derived from very low density lipoproteins).

HEAT PRODUCTION AND BASAL METABOLIC RATE

Chemical energy is used to perform work. The categories of work energy are mechanical, electrical, and chemical. Chemical energy is transformed to work in the form of mechanical energy when a muscle shortens. It is transformed in the form of electrical energy when a nerve impulse is transmitted, and provides chemical energy during synthetic reactions. During the buildup of complex molecules, chemical energy is stored at the expense of energy supplied by the breakdown of other molecules. The body is only 20 per cent efficient in converting chemical energy to work energy. The remainder appears as thermal energy, or heat. Much work energy is ultimately converted to heat. Thus, a considerable amount of mechanical work of the heart is converted to heat in overcoming friction as blood passes through the circulatory system. When a muscle shortens, much of the energy overcomes viscosity, and friction again generates heat.

Thus, it is apparent that most of the chemical energy of the body is ultimately converted to heat, either directly from chemical reactions or indirectly from work energy. When no external work, such as lifting a load or exercising, is being done, essentially all metabolic energy ultimately appears as heat. With strenuous physical exertion about three-fourths of the increase in metabolic energy above the resting level appears as heat, the remainder as work.

Basal Metabolic Rate. Basal metabolism and basal metabolic rate (BMR) are the terms applied to the utilization of energy occurring in a fasting and resting individual. Basal metabolic rate is determined clinically 12 to 18 hours after the last meal, usually in the morning following a normal period of sleep. During the test period, no voluntary muscle movement should occur. The room temperature is comfortable and the patient is physically and mentally at rest. The energy exchange so determined is that required to maintain the vital activities of the body. The units of BMR are usually given in Calories per square meter of body surface per hour. A calorie (spelled with a small c) is the amount of heat required to raise 1 gram of water 1° C. A Calorie (large C), the unit used for expressing basal metabolism, is equal to 1000 calories. Surface area is taken into consideration because tall, slender individuals have a higher surface-to-volume ratio than short, stocky individuals and, therefore, generally have a higher metabolic rate to compensate for the greater heat loss from the body surface. Determinations of BMR most commonly are based on oxygen consumption. For each liter of oxygen consumed an average of 4.825 Calories of heat are produced under basal conditions. Thus, if an individual consumes 12.5 liters of oxygen per hour (corrected to standard conditions), this would be 12.5 × 4.825, or about 60 Calories per hour. If this individual is five feet (152.4 cm) tall and weighs 120 pounds (54.5 Kg), there would be a surface area of 1.5 square meters (Fig. 14–25). The BMR of this individual would be 60/1.5, or 40 Calories per square meter per hour.

FACTORS INFLUENCING BMR. When a resting individual ingests food, heat production is increased above the basal level. This increased heat production produced simply from eating is known as the *specific dynamic action* of foods and varies with the type of food ingested. Protein has a greater specific dynamic action than either fat or carbohydrate. For example, if proteins are fed to an animal in an amount possessing a heat value equivalent to the basal metabolism, heat production will be raised by 30 per cent. Thus, feeding 100 Calories to an animal with a basal metabolism of 100 Calories per day will increase the heat production to 130 Calories per day. The extra heat is generated by the combustion of body constituents. The specific dynamic action of fats and carbohydrate amounts to 4 and 6 per cent, respectively. The higher specific dynamic action of protein is believed to be associated with deamination and urea formation.

Other factors influencing the total exchange of energy in the living organism include age and sex (Table 14–4), temperature, and muscular exercise. Thyroid hormones exert a considerable influence on the rate at which cellular oxidation occurs, and excesses and deficits of circulating thyroid hormones modify the metabolic rate. Certain other substances, such as male sex hormones, growth hormone, epinephrine, and norepinephrine,

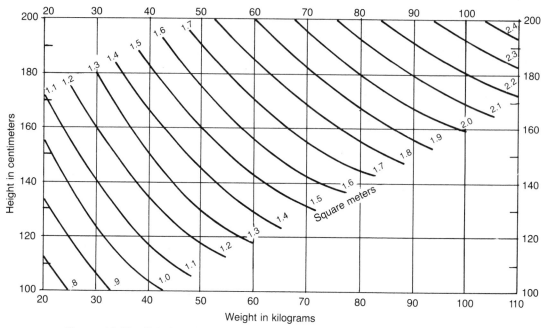

Figure 14–25. Relation of height and weight to body surface area. (After DuBois.)

increase the metabolic rate because of their stimulating effect on cellular activity.

Temperature Regulation

Mammals and birds are *homeothermic*, or warm-blooded, animals, which means that they are capable of maintaining a nearly constant internal body temperature. If the body temperature varies with environmental changes, the term *poikilothermic*, or cold-blooded, is employed.

Table 14–4 BASAL METABOLIC RATE
(Calories/sq. meter/hr.)

AGE (Years)	MALES	FEMALES
10–12	49.5	45.8
12–14	47.8	43.4
14–16	46.0	41.0
16–18	43.0	38.5
18–20	41.0	37.6
20–30	40.5	36.8
30–40	39.5	36.5
40–50	38.0	35.3
50–60	36.9	34.4
60–70	35.8	33.6
70–80	34.5	32.6

Metabolism continuously supplies heat, and heat is continuously lost from the body. Heat loss occurs through (1) radiation, conduction, and convection from the surface of the body, (2) evaporation of water from the skin and lungs, (3) warming of inspired air, and (4) urination and defecation. Heat loss by routes (1), (3), and (4) occurs only when the environment is cooler than the body. Routes (1) and (2), except for evaporation of water from the lungs, are subject to physiological control, and adjustments in heat loss by these routes are among the mechanisms utilized by a temperature regulating center in the hypothalamus (see below) to maintain a normal body temperature.

Radiation refers to the exchange of heat between the body and surrounding objects with which it is not in contact. Heat (in the form of infrared rays) is radiated from the body surface to cooler objects and to the body from warmer objects. At normal room temperature, about 60 per cent of the heat lost from the body is accounted for by radiation. The amount of cooling by radiation (and by conduction and convection) varies with the temperature difference between the surface of the body and the surroundings, and this difference can be increased or decreased by altering the flow of blood in the skin, thereby changing its temperature — increasing blood flow by inducing dilation of cutaneous blood vessels when it is necessary to lose heat, decreasing flow by cutaneous vasoconstriction to conserve heat.

Conduction refers to the transfer of heat to an object in contact with the body. Ordinarily, it accounts for a small fraction of the heat lost from the body.

Heat loss by *convection* means heat transfer by conduction to air which then rises and is replaced by air that is unheated by contact with the skin. Heat loss by convection is small unless air movement is increased, for example, by wind or a fan.

Heat loss by *evaporation* — heat expended to change water to water vapor — accounts for about 30 per cent of the total body heat loss at ordinary room temperature. About two-thirds of this loss is from the skin, the remainder from the lungs. Until the body is overheated, heat loss by evaporation of water from the skin does not involve sweating but rather occurs as a result of the simple diffusion of water through the skin, a process called *insensible perspiration*. However, the secretion of sweat (by the eccrine sweat glands — see Chapter 5) at higher environmental temperatures dramatically increases the proportion of heat lost by the evaporation of water from the skin; when the temperature of the environment reaches 95° F, evaporation of water, mainly from the skin, accounts for almost all of the heat loss. Cooling by evaporation from the skin is greatly aided by dry, moving air.

Heat loss by the warming of inspired air and through the urine and feces generally accounts for about 3 per cent of the total heat loss.

The control of body temperature (apart from voluntary behavioral adjustments) is made possible by the activity of the *temperature regulating center in the hypothalamus*. This center is sensitive to changes in temperature of the blood and also receives input from nerve fibers innervating temperature receptors in the skin. The hypothalamic center integrates input from these two sources — one providing information about the internal, or core, temperature, the other providing information about the temperature of the surface of the body — and initiates appropriate adjustments in heat production and heat dissipation when the temperature deviates too far from normal. When it becomes necessary to raise body temperature,

heat production is increased and heat is conserved by constriction of cutaneous blood vessels so as to decrease the circulation of blood in the skin and by the absence of sweating. An increase in heat production is brought about principally by increasing the metabolism of skeletal muscle; initially muscle tension is increased (which may raise the overall heat production as much as 50 per cent) and then shivering is induced (which, if intense, may raise heat production as much as three times above normal). The release of hormones from the adrenal medulla (epinephrine and norepinephrine) and thyroid gland (thyroxine and triiodothyronine) also plays a role in the production of heat in response to cold. (Hormonally induced heat production is referred to by some investigators as nonshivering thermogenesis, abbreviated NST.) Epinephrine and norepinephrine (their release is controlled by the sympathetic nervous system) bring about an immediate but short-lived increase in cellular metabolism and heat production. Thyroid hormones (their release is controlled by way of a hypothalamic hormone acting on the anterior pituitary gland, which in turn controls the thyroid gland — see Chapter 16) bring about a gradual rise in metabolic rate and heat production. Their effect requires several weeks to reach a maximum, during which time the thyroid gland increases in size. The generation of heat as a result of the release of thyroid hormones is regarded as an adaptive response to chronic cold exposure.

When overheating necessitates an increase in heat loss, sweat glands are stimulated and cutaneous blood vessels are dilated so as to increase the flow of blood through the skin.

The abnormally high temperature of a *fever* is accounted for by a change in what is called the "set point" of the hypothalamic temperature regulating center by the action of fever-producing agents (bacterial toxins, for example) called *pyrogens*. There is reason to believe that the action of pyrogens is mediated by prostaglandins (see page 508). Aspirin, an antipyretic (fever-reducing) drug, inhibits the synthesis of prostaglandins, and injecting prostaglandins directly into the hypothalamus induces fever.

Temperature is a valuable barometer of disease. The figure 98.6° F is usually quoted as the normal mouth temperature; however, in the normal individual there is some fluctuation. Upon awakening in the morning, the basal temperature can be as low as 97° F. This temperature usually rises during the day to reach 99° F in the latter part of the afternoon. The temperature of the environment, unless extreme, does not greatly influence body temperature, since the regulating mechanisms for heat gain and loss maintain a homeothermic state. The body temperature is lowest in the female at the time of menstruation. In the aged, the temperature is usually lower than during the younger years.

Temperature can be determined most accurately rectally. The rectal temperature is approximately 0.9° F higher than oral temperature. With a fever the difference is reduced between rectal and oral temperatures. In taking an oral or rectal temperature, the thermometer should be allowed to remain in place for at least 2 minutes. The drinking of hot or cold fluids prior to taking the temperature will cause erroneous results.

HEAT EXHAUSTION. Heat exhaustion, or heat collapse, is characterized by sweating, weakness, reduced blood pressure, rapid pulse, usually a normal body temperature, and the general findings of circulatory collapse. The victim's skin is pale, cold, and clammy. The onset of heat exhaustion is often preceded by a prolonged period of physical exertion in a hot and humid environment. Large unreplaced losses of salt and water are the most important factors in the development of heat exhaustion. Treatment should be directed toward restoring the body fluid (by intake of water and salt) and temperature to normal and re-establishing vasomotor tone. It is important to remove the patient to a cool environment.

HEAT CRAMPS. Occasionally associated with profuse sweating are heat cramps, a condition not so serious as heat exhaustion. They generally occur following strenuous exercise, not necessarily in a hot environment, and are characterized by painful spasms of the arms and legs in individuals who otherwise appear to be in satisfactory condition. Dilution of body fluids as a result of the replacement of lost water but not salt is responsible for the cramps. Heat cramps can usually be relieved by having the patient drink a salt solution prepared by dissolving one teaspoon of table salt in a quart of water.

HEATSTROKE. Heatstroke, or sunstroke, is characterized by high fever, delirium, and profound coma and occurs primarily in individuals over the age of 60. The victims are often in a hot, humid environment. The high relative humidity impedes the evaporation of sweat, and body temperature rises with an increase in the rate of sweating. Somewhere in this vicious cycle, sweat glands cease to function and body temperature rises to alarming levels because of absorption of heat from the environment. The reason for this sudden failure of thermal regulation is unknown. The major signs of heatstroke, in addition to a very high body temperature, are a hot, dry, flushed skin, rapid breathing, and a fast, full, bounding pulse. Heatstroke is a medical emergency because the patient, if untreated, may lapse into a coma and die. Treatment is directed primarily toward reducing body temperature.

SUMMARY

THE DIGESTIVE SYSTEM

Anatomy

Consists of (1) an alimentary canal — a long, muscular tube beginning at the lips and ending at the anus, including the mouth, pharynx (oral and laryngeal portions), esophagus, stomach, and small and large intestine, and (2) accessory glands that empty secretions into the tube — salivary glands, pancreas, liver, and gallbladder.

1. Teeth

  a. Crown projects above the gum, root below. Dentin (bulk of tooth) surrounds pulp cavity. Enamel covers dentin of crown; cementum covers dentin of root and anchors tooth to periodontal ligament.

  b. Each quadrant of mouth has eight teeth — two incisors, one canine, two premolars, and three molars.

2. Esophagus

  a. Mucous membrane lined with stratified squamous epithelium rather than simple columnar epithelium, as in stomach and intestine.

  b. Muscular layer of upper third, striated; lower third, smooth; middle, both striated and smooth.

  c. Segment above stomach (indistinguishable anatomically from remainder of esophagus) functions as sphincter, remaining closed until reflexively relaxed as peristaltic wave approaches.

3. Stomach

a. Consists of upper fundus, central body, and constricted lower pyloric portion (antrum).
b. Musculature contains an oblique inner layer of smooth muscle in addition to external longitudinal and underlying circular smooth muscle layers found elsewhere in digestive tract.
c. Thick circular muscle in pyloric portion forms pyloric sphincter.
d. Openings: cardia, between esophagus and stomach; pylorus, between stomach and duodenum.

4. Small Intestine

a. Divided into duodenum, jejunum, and ileum.
b. Surface area, serving absorptive function, increased by:
  (1) Circular folds (plicae circulares)—permanent, transverse folds
  (2) Villi (fingerlike projections)
  (3) Microvilli (processes on free surface of epithelial cells that form the brush border).
c. Invagination of ileum into cecum (the first part of the large intestine) forms ileocecal valve, which opens rhythmically during digestion, permitting gradual emptying of ileum and preventing regurgitation.

5. Large Intestine

a. Extends from the end of the ileum to the anus and is divisible into the cecum, colon, rectum, and anal canal. The major part is the colon, which consists of ascending, transverse, descending, and sigmoid portions.
b. The longitudinal muscle of the cecum and colon forms three conspicuous bands (taeniae coli).
c. Thickened circular smooth muscle of anal canal forms the internal anal sphincter. Surrounding skeletal muscle forms the external sphincter.

6. Salivary Glands

a. Three pairs (parotid, submaxillary, and sublingual), with ducts opening into the mouth.
b. Two types of secretions:
  (1) Serous containing ptyalin (enzyme initiating digestion of starch)
  (2) Mucous—viscous, containing mucus, which facilitates mastication

7. Pancreas

a. Two types of secretory cells in exocrine pancreas:
  (1) Enzyme-secreting (acinar cells)
  (2) Bicarbonate-and-water-secreting (intralobular duct cells)
b. Pancreatic duct empties pancreatic juice into duodenum.

8. Liver and Gallbladder

a. Bile secreted by liver is essential for normal absorption of digested lipids. Bile salts combine with products of lipid digestion to form water-soluble complexes (micelles) which are absorbed by intestinal cells.
b. Gallbladder concentrates and stores bile.
c. Hepatic duct, formed from bile duct system of liver, joins cystic duct of gallbladder to form common bile duct, which empties into duodenum.

Motility of Digestive Tract

1. Swallowing

a. In buccal stage (voluntary) bolus pushed toward pharynx.
b. In pharyngeal and esophageal stages (involuntary) bolus passes through pharynx into esophagus and through esophagus into stomach.
c. Reflexes raise soft palate, raise larynx, adduct aryepiglottic folds and true and false vocal cords, and inhibit respiration. When food enters the pharynx, reflex contraction of the superior constrictor muscle initiates peristalsis, propelling the food, and relaxation of the upper and lower esophageal sphincters allows food to pass first into the esophagus and then into the stomach.

2. Peristalsis in Stomach

a. Mixes contents and forces chyme through pylorus.
b. Three waves (each beginning every 20 seconds near midpoint of stomach, last-

ing about one minute, and ending with contraction of pyloric sphincter) travel down stomach at one time.

c. Rate of emptying determined largely by strength of contractions.

d. Feedback from duodenum regulates gastric emptying. Two control mechanisms, one neuronal (enterogastric reflex), the other hormonal (mediated mainly by enterogastrone), inhibit gastric motility.

3. Contractions of the Small Intestine

a. Segmenting: Rhythmic contractions along a section dividing it into segments; primarily mixing action.

b. Peristaltic waves superimposed upon segmenting contractions.

c. Ingestion of food increases ileal peristalsis and frequency of opening of ileocecal valve (gastroileal reflex).

4. Contractions of Large Intestine

a. Simultaneous contraction of circular and longitudinal muscle, forming haustra.

b. Infrequent (usually two or three times daily at most) mass movements transferring contents from proximal to distal colon and into rectum. Most commonly occur shortly after a meal (gastrocolic reflex).

5. Defecation Reflex

a. Distention of rectum triggers intense peristaltic contractions of colon and rectum and relaxation of internal anal sphincter.

b. Reflex preceded by voluntary relaxation of external sphincter and compression of abdominal contents.

Digestion

1. Mouth

a. **Enzymatic action:** Initiation of the digestion of carbohydrate by ptyalin, which splits starch into the disaccharide maltose. Action in mouth slight, but continues in stomach until acid medium inactivates ptyalin.

b. **Regulation:** Exclusively nervous — impulses transmitted from center in medulla (activated principally by taste, smell, or sight of food) to salivary glands by parasympathetic nerve fibers.

2. Stomach

a. **Enzymatic action:** Initiation of protein digestion by pepsin, producing proteoses, peptones, and polypeptides. Pepsinogen (secreted by chief cells) converted to pepsin by autoactivation process in presence of acid (secreted by parietal cells).

b. **Regulation**
   (1) *Cephalic phase* (abolished by sectioning vagus nerve): Initiated by taste, sight, or smell of food; secretion stimulated directly or indirectly by the hormone gastrin. Gastrin, released from so-called G cells in the pyloric region of the stomach, stimulates the secretion of an acid-rich gastric juice.
   (2) *Gastric phase*: Initiated by food in stomach; secretion triggered directly or indirectly, as in cephalic phase.
   (3) *Intestinal phase*: Initiated by digestive products in upper small intestine; mediated by hormone released by duodenum acting on stomach.
   (4) *Inhibition:* Strong acid in antrum inhibits gastrin release. Fat, acid, or hypertonic salt solutions in duodenum stimulate release of hormones which inhibit gastric secretion.

3. Intestine

a. **Enzymatic action:** Fat digestion and continuation of carbohydrate and protein digestion.
   (1) Pancreatic lipase splits fat into monoglycerides, fatty acids, and glycerol.
   (2) Pancreatic amylase converts starch and glycogen into maltose. Intestinal disaccharidases split maltose, sucrose, and lactose into their constituent monosaccharides.
   (3) Pancreatic enzymes trypsin and chymotrypsin (both endopeptidases) split proteins and the products of pepsin digestion into peptides. Peptidases (all intestinal enzymes except two carboxypeptidases from the pancreas) split peptides into amino acids.

b. **Regulation of pancreatic secretion:** By vagus nerve during cephalic and gastric phases of gastric secretion and by two duodenal hormones—cholecystokinin-pancreozymin and secretin. Vagus stimulation and cholecystokinin-pancreozymin stimulate enzyme secretion; secretin stimulates bicarbonate secretion.

Absorption

1. Occurs almost exclusively in the small intestine.

2. Simple sugars, amino acids, short-chain fatty acids, and glycerol are absorbed into blood stream via capillary network of villi. Products of lipid digestion are absorbed as chylomicrons into intestinal lymphatics via central lacteal of villi.

Disposition of Major Foodstuffs

Absorbed fat, carried by chylomicrons, passes from thoracic duct into venous system; greater part taken up by fat depots and stored. Glucose and amino acids are transported to liver via hepatic portal vein; a portion is utilized and a portion passes to other tissues. Any excess that cannot be stored in liver as glycogen is converted to fat and transported as very low density lipoproteins to fat depots. During absorption of meal, glucose provides almost all of body's energy needs. In postabsorptive period, fatty acids supply most of body's energy requirements; blood glucose (normally exclusive source of energy for brain) is maintained by conversion of amino acids (derived from muscle protein) into glucose in liver.

Basal Metabolic Rate

Basal metabolic rate refers to energy production under basal conditions (resting in a comfortably warm environment 12 to 18 hours after a meal), usually expressed as Calories per square meter of body surface per hour. It is most commonly measured by rate of oxygen consumption (for every liter of oxygen consumed, an average of 4.825 Calories of heat are produced under basal conditions).

Temperature Regulation

Hypothalamus contains center for regulating body temperature which is sensitive to changes in blood temperature and also receives input from temperature receptors in the skin. This center mediates homeostatic adjustments—sweating, changes in blood flow through skin, shivering, and the release of epinephrine and norepinephrine from the adrenal medulla and thyroxine and triiodothyronine from the thyroid (nonshivering thermogenesis).

REVIEW QUESTIONS

1. Name the teeth in a quadrant of the mouth of a deciduous and of a permanent set of teeth. Describe the structure of a tooth. What causes loosening of teeth in periodontal disease?
2. Describe the four layers of the wall of the digestive tract and the distinguishing histological features of the small intestine.
3. Distinguish between peristalsis and segmenting contractions in the small intestine.
4. Outline the steps in the digestion of carbohydrates, proteins, and fat. Give the source and describe the action of each of the responsible enzymes.
5. Describe the control of the three phases of gastric secretion and of pancreatic secretion.
6. Discuss the roles of chylomicrons and very low density lipoproteins in the disposition of dietary and endogenous fat.

15
The Urinary System

Objectives

The aim of this chapter is to enable the student to:

☐ Describe the gross external and internal structure of the kidney.

☐ Describe the microanatomy of the kidney and the nephron.

☐ Distinguish between the two principal stages of urine formation.

☐ Explain how a hypertonic urine is formed.

☐ Discuss the role of aldosterone in regulating blood and urine volume.

☐ Explain how the kidneys help maintain the buffering capacity of the body fluids.

☐ Describe the structure and function of the ureters, urinary bladder, and urethra.

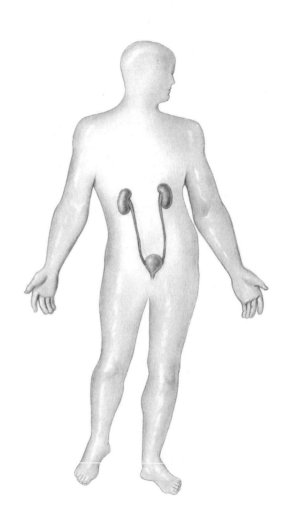

During the Egyptian era, 5000 years ago, the diagnosis of diabetes was actually made when the physician tasted the urine for sweetness. Later, during the Middle Ages, disease in general was evaluated by visually examining the urine. Medical reports during this time frequently stated that "the pulse was normal, the urine normal, yet the patient died." Urine became an accurate clue to body function only after the perfection of the microscope.

The urinary system is one of the four excretory pathways of the body; the others are the large intestine, the skin, and the lungs. It consists of two kidneys, which produce urine; two ureters, which convey urine to the bladder; and the urethra, which discharges urine from the bladder. Regulation of the concentration of substances excreted in the urine enables the body to control the concentration of substances in the blood so as to maintain homeostasis of the body fluids.

KIDNEYS

Gross Anatomy (Figs. 15–1 and 15–2)

In the newborn the kidneys are about three times as large in proportion to body weight as in the adult. The weight of each kidney ranges from 125 to 170 grams in the adult male and from 115 to 155 grams in the adult female.

The kidneys are bean-shaped organs lying behind the parietal peritoneum against the muscles of the posterior abdominal wall, just above the waistline (Figs. 15–1 and 15–2).

Since the kidneys are in contact with the diaphragm above, they move slightly with this structure during respiration.

The upper poles of the kidneys are on a level with the upper border of the twelfth thoracic vertebra; their lower poles extend to the level of the third lumbar vertebra. The right kidney is usually slightly lower than the left, possibly because of its close relationship to the liver. Anteriorly, the right kidney is covered by the suprarenal gland, the hepatic flexure of the colon, the descending portion

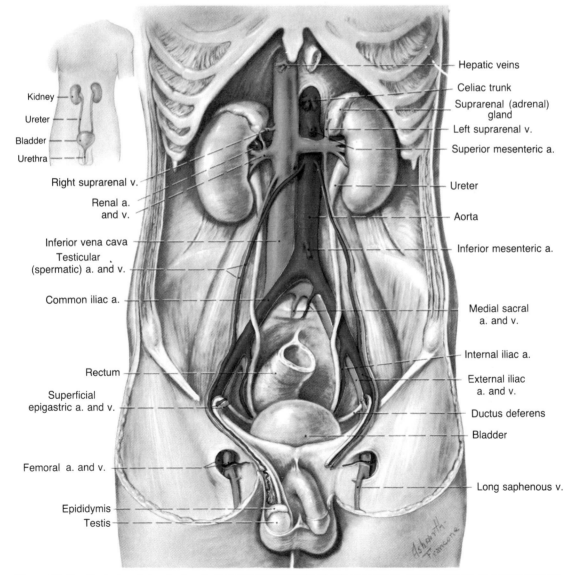

Figure 15–1. Posterior abdominal wall, showing relationship of urinary system, genital system, and great vessels.

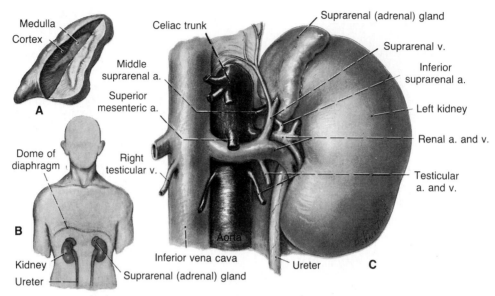

Figure 15–2. *A,* Suprarenal gland sectioned to show the medulla. *B,* Anatomic position of kidneys and suprarenal glands. *C,* Anterior aspect of left kidney, showing adrenal gland and vascular supply.

of the duodenum, and the liver. The' suprarenal gland, splenic flexure of the colon, stomach, pancreas, jejunum, and spleen are related to the anterior surface of the left kidney.

There are three capsules surrounding each kidney: the true capsule, the surrounding perirenal fat, and the renal fascia. The *true capsule* of the kidney, the capsule proper, is a smooth, transparent, fibrous membrane closely applied to the surface. Normally it can be readily stripped from the organ. Adipose tissue, *perirenal fat*, surrounds the capsule proper and is in turn enclosed by the renal fascia, a thin, fibrous layer which anchors the kidney to the surrounding structures and helps maintain the normal position of the organ.

When the kidney is inflamed, the renal tissue becomes adherent to the true capsule and cannot be removed without tearing the organ. If the adipose capsule or the renal fascia is deficient, ptosis (dropping) of one or both kidneys can occur.

External Structure. Each kidney has a convex lateral border and a concave medial border. At the medial surface the renal artery, vein, and nerves, as well as lymphatic vessels, enter and leave the concave surface through a notch called the *hilum*. The cavity located at the hilum is a saclike collecting portion called the *pelvis*, representing the upper, expanded portion of the ureter.

Internal Structure (Fig. 15–3). In cross section, the kidney exhibits an inner darkened area, the *medulla*, and an outer pale area, the *cortex*. The medulla consists of from eight to 12 *renal pyramids*, with apices converging into projections known as papillae, which in turn are received by cavities (*calyces*) of the pelvis. The cortex consists of a peripheral layer extending from the capsule to the bases of the pyramids and *renal columns* traversing the area between the pyramids. It is divided into lobules composed of convoluted and radiant portions.

VASCULAR SUPPLY. The primary branches of the renal artery give rise to *lobar arteries*, usually one for each pyramid, which branch into *interlobar arteries*. These extend to the boundary of the cortex and medulla of the kidney, where they divide into *arcuate arteries*, arching across the bases of the pyramids. *Interlobular arteries* extend from the arcuate arteries into the convoluted portion of the cortex. Fine branches, the afferent arterioles, enter the glomerular capillary networks of the renal corpuscles (see below). An efferent arteriole leaves each glomerulus. Most efferent arterioles are short and branch to form capillary networks around the cortical tubules of the cortex and medulla. (Efferent arterioles that follow a different course will be described later in connection with the process of concentrating urine.) The capillary networks converge and lead into the interlob-

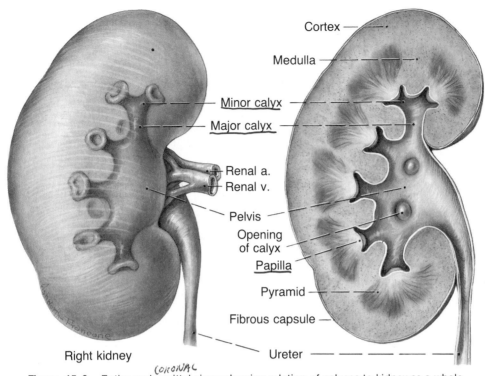

Cortex

Medulla

Minor calyx

Major calyx

Renal a.
Renal v.

Pelvis

Opening
of calyx

Papilla

Pyramid

Fibrous capsule

Right kidney

Ureter

CORONAL

Figure 15–3. Entire and ~~sagittal~~ views showing relation of calyces to kidney as a whole.

ular and medullary veins, which, in turn, empty their contents into the arcuate veins between the cortex and the medulla. The arcuate veins converge to form interlobar veins, joining to empty into the renal vein. The *renal vein* leaves the kidney at the hilum, draining into the inferior vena cava.

INNERVATION OF THE KIDNEYS. The kidneys receive a rich supply of sympathetic, vasoconstrictor fibers extending from the fourth thoracic to the fourth lumbar segment of the spinal cord. Afferent fibers from the renal pelves and ureters assume an important role in pain of renal origin.

Microscopic Anatomy

The functioning renal unit is called the **nephron** (Figs. 15–4 and 15–5). Each kidney contains about one million nephrons, each consisting of a renal corpuscle and tubule. The *renal corpuscle*, or Malpighian body, consists of a **glomerulus**, a tuft of capillaries derived from the afferent arteriole, resting in a cuplike depression of the tubule called the *glomerular capsule* or **Bowman's capsule**. The capillaries of the glomerulus unite to form the outgoing efferent arteriole (of considerably smaller diameter than the afferent arteriole). The glomerular capillaries are thus uniquely situated between two arterioles. Extending from Bowman's capsule is a long tubule consisting of a **proximal convoluted tubule,** a **loop of Henle**, and a **distal convoluted tubule** which opens into a **collecting duct** along with a number of other distal tubules. The tubules give a striated appearance to the medulla, and the renal corpuscles give a fine granular appearance to the cortex. Urine is discharged at the apex of the medullary pyramid into the calyces of the pelvis and then flows down the ureter.

The point at which a portion of the distal convoluted tubule comes in contact with the afferent arteriole is called the *juxtaglomerular apparatus*, secreting renin, an enzyme of importance in regulating sodium and water retention and blood pressure.

The epithelium of Bowman's capsule is of the squamous type and consists of an outer (parietal) layer lining the capsule and an inner (visceral) layer covering the glomerulus. The cells of the visceral layer have interdigitating processes. The proximal convoluted tubule is lined with cuboidal epithelium.

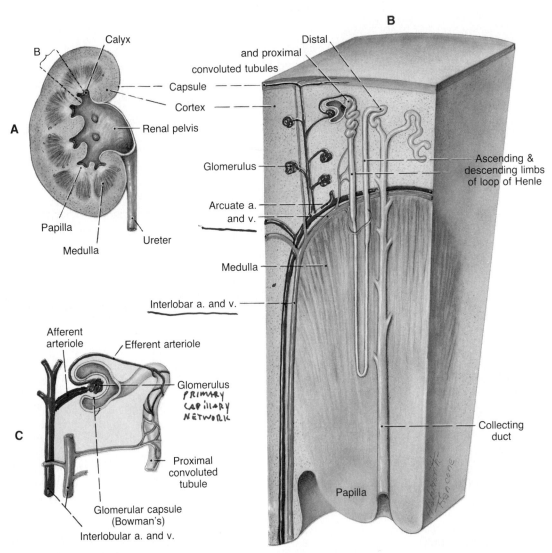

Figure 15–4. *A,* Sagittal section through kidney showing gross structure (note pelvis, calyces, medulla, cortex). *B,* Nephron and its relationship to medulla and cortex. The dotted lines in *A* show the area of the kidney from which this section was taken. *C,* Magnified view of nephron.

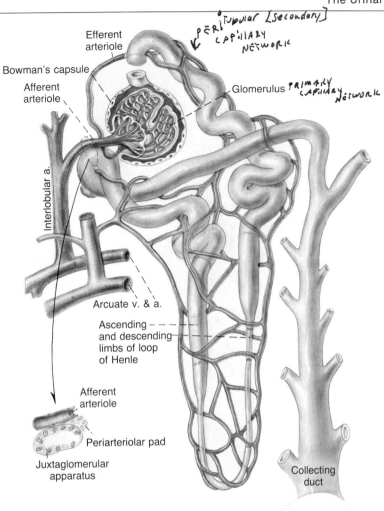

Efferent arteriole

PERITUBULAR [Secondary] CAPILLARY NETWORK

Bowman's capsule

Afferent arteriole

Glomerulus PRIMARY CAPILLARY NETWORK

Interlobular a.

Arcuate v. & a.

Ascending and descending limbs of loop of Henle

Afferent arteriole

Periarteriolar pad

Juxtaglomerular apparatus

Collecting duct

Figure 15–5. Detail of nephron showing vascular supply and juxtaglomerular apparatus.

This changes to squamous epithelium as the loop of Henle dips down into the medulla (the portion with a small diameter is known as the thin segment). A transition from squamous to cuboidal epithelium occurs in the straight, ascending, thick limb. The cuboidal epithelium continues into the distal convoluted tubule and the proximal portion of the collecting duct. Columnar epithelium lines the distal part of the collecting duct.

Kidney Regeneration

Renal reserve is dependent on the regenerative capacity of the kidney. When one kidney is removed, the opposite organ undergoes an enlargement because of an increase in size of the contained nephrons rather than an increase in total number of nephrons.

Only 25 per cent of the total renal mass is necessary for survival of the individual. The epithelium of the renal tubules can regenerate after injury — for example, in poisoning due to mercury; however, the entire nephron does not regenerate.

Kidney Transplantation (Fig. 15–6)

To date, more than 15,000 homologous kidney transplants have been done on patients dying of renal failure. The best results in homotransplantation occur when the donor is closely related to the recipient; 80 to 90 per cent survive for two years or longer. Whether the kidney comes from a close relative or from a cadaver, the recipient must take immunosuppressive drugs for the rest of his or her life to prevent rejection. Kidney trans-

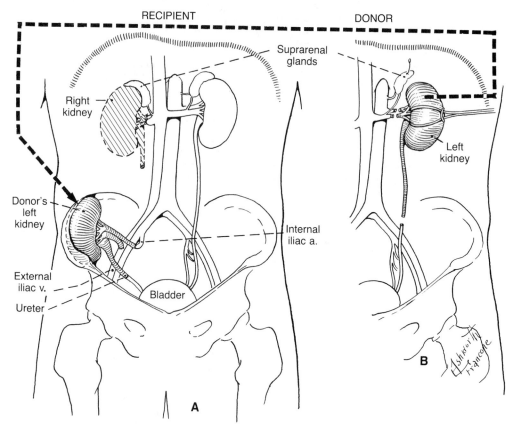

Figure 15–6. *A* illustrates kidney transplanted to right pelvis. *B* shows kidney of donor.

plants between identical twins may function for years.

It should be noted, however, that even in transplants between identical twins the cause of damage to the original kidney may subsequently affect the transplanted kidney; despite acceptance of the transplant, the patient dies owing to recurrence of the disease.

Another problem in transplantation of the kidney is one of logistics, particularly of preservation of the kidney prior to transplantation. In general, sub-zero preservation is probably superior to preservation above zero, but no organ can be successfully frozen and remain alive. The freezing point of an entire kidney has been depressed to 6 degrees below zero C without the kidney actually freezing (soft state), and the kidney has been retransplanted as an autologous kidney (from the same animal to the same animal). When the opposite kidney is removed, the stored kidney sustains life as the only remaining kidney.

Physiology of Urine Formation

Urine Composition (Table 15–1). Urine is 96 per cent water, in which salts, toxins, pigments, hormones, and wastes from protein metabolism are dissolved. It is a complex, aqueous solution of inorganic and organic substances. The urinary output is approximately 1500 ml daily, 60 gm of which are solutes.

Mechanism of Urine Formation and Excretion. There are primarily two stages in the elaboration of urine by the kidney, the glomerular stage (formation of primitive urine by filtration) and the tubular stage, with the successive or simultaneous processes of reabsorption (from the tubular lumen to the blood) and secretion (from the blood to the tubular lumen). Except for its absence of proteins, the glomerular filtrate is almost identical in composition to plasma. Reabsorption and secretion markedly change the composition of the filtrate. These two processes provide mechanisms for eliminating or

Table 15–1   COMPOSITION OF URINE

Solutes 60 gm daily	Organic wastes 35 gm	Urea	30 gm
		Creatinine	1–2 gm
		Ammonia	1–2 gm
		Uric acid	1 gm
		Others	1 gm
	Inorganic salts° 25 gm	Chloride	Sodium
		Sulfate	Potassium
		Phosphorus	Magnesium

° Sodium chloride is the chief inorganic salt in urine.

conserving substances in accordance with the body's requirements. Thus, nutritionally valuable substances are completely or almost completely reabsorbed, and waste products are not absorbed, poorly absorbed, or secreted. In addition, the reabsorption and secretion of a number of substances are continuously regulated in order to maintain their normal concentrations in the body fluids.

GLOMERULAR FILTRATION. The glomerulus acts as a semipermeable membrane permitting a protein-free filtrate of plasma to pass through to Bowman's capsule. The barrier between the capillary lumen and the cavity of Bowman's capsule through which the glomerular filtrate must pass consists of three layers: (1) a fenestrated epithelium (perforated with pores—see Chapter 11, page 384) of the glomerular capillaries, (2) a basement membrane, and (3) the epithelium of Bowman's capsule (visceral layer), which contains clefts called "slit pores" (each bridged by a thin membrane) formed by interdigitating foot processes (pedicels) projecting from the arms (trabeculae) of starfish-shaped epithelial cells.

The glomerular filtrate has a pH of approximately 7.4 with a specific gravity of 1.010. Normal levels of various substances exist in the following concentrations:

glucose	80 mg/100 ml
urea nitrogen	15 mg/100 ml
sodium	140 mEq/l
chloride	100 mEq/l
bicarbonate	27 mEq/l
potassium	4.5 mEq/l

As can be seen, the filtrate produced is similar to plasma without plasma proteins. The process of glomerular filtration is essentially a passive one, similar to the movement of

substances from the vascular capillary to the interstitial spaces.

As mentioned, blood is supplied to the glomerulus by an afferent arteriole. The glomerular capillaries unite to form an outgoing efferent arteriole, which gives rise to the peritubular capillary network. The resistance of the narrow efferent arteriole to the flow of blood is an important factor in maintaining a high glomerular pressure (while at the same time creating a low pressure in peritubular capillaries, a condition favorable for tubular reabsorption). The filtration pressure represents the glomerular blood (hydrostatic) pressure less the glomerular osmotic pressure and capsular hydrostatic pressure. According to recent estimates, the glomerular filtration pressure is approximately 10 mm Hg (Fig. 15–7).

Approximately 1200 ml of blood (containing 650 ml of plasma), or 24 per cent of the total cardiac output, passes through the kidney per minute. Of this, the fluid filtered from all glomeruli of both kidneys into Bowman's capsules amounts to about 125 ml per minute. This *glomerular filtration rate* varies directly with the filtration pressure.

Tubular Reabsorption and Secretion. The final composition of urine is determined to a much greater extent by tubular reabsorption than by tubular secretion. Secretion is, however, the principal determinant of the concentration of potassium ions in the urine, and the synthesis and secretion of hydrogen ions by tubular cells play an important role in regulating the acid-base balance in the body fluids (described later). Reabsorption and secretion can occur by both active and passive processes.

Substances actively reabsorbed include sodium ions, glucose, amino acids, and acetoacetate, beta-hydroxybutyrate, calcium,

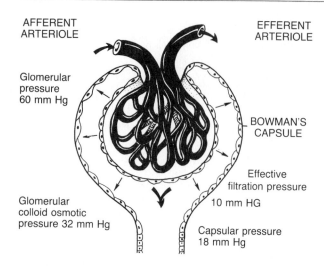

AFFERENT ARTERIOLE

EFFERENT ARTERIOLE

Glomerular pressure 60 mm Hg

BOWMAN'S CAPSULE

Effective filtration pressure 10 mm HG

Glomerular colloid osmotic pressure 32 mm Hg

Capsular pressure 18 mm Hg

Figure 15–7. The normal filtration pressure is about 10 mm of mercury. Glomerular hydrostatic pressure (60 mm Hg) minus glomerular colloid osmotic pressure (32 mm Hg) minus capsular pressure (18 mm Hg) equals filtration pressure, 10 mm Hg. The passage of substances in and out of the tubule varies in different portions of the tubule and collecting duct.

phosphate, and sulfate ions. Most of the reabsorption occurs in the proximal tubules, in which the absorptive surface is greatly increased by the presence of numerous microvilli on the free surface of the cuboidal epithelial cells. The active transport of *sodium ions* accounts for the greater part of the oxygen consumption of the kidney. This process not only restores most of the sodium temporarily lost in the glomerular filtrate but, by its electrical effect, also leads to the reabsorption of *chloride ions* accompanying the sodium ions. (It is well established that passive reabsorption of chloride in response to an electrical gradient occurs in the proximal tubules; there is also evidence for the active reabsorption of chloride in some segments of the nephrons, particularly across the thick part of the ascending limbs of the loops of Henle.) The active transport of sodium also provides the principal driving force for the passive reabsorption of *water* by osmosis. Since sodium salts make up 90 per cent of the solute in the body fluids, under normal conditions the amount of sodium reabsorbed determines the amount of water reabsorbed. Usually about 99 per cent of the fluid is reabsorbed and about 1 ml of urine is formed per minute. *Glucose* and *amino acids* are normally completely reabsorbed from the proximal tubule. However, *glycosuria* (glucose in the urine) will occur if the concentration of the glucose in the plasma exceeds about 300 mg per 100 ml. At this concentration, the carrier system for tubular glucose transport is apparently saturated, and all of the filtered glucose in excess of this concentration appears in the urine.

Urea, the most abundant substance in the urine, is passively reabsorbed in consequence of the concentration gradient created by the reabsorption of water. However, since a much smaller proportion of urea than water is reabsorbed, the concentration of urea in urine is 60 to 70 times greater than in plasma.

Potassium is about 12 times more concentrated in urine than in plasma. It is both reabsorbed and secreted. The secretory process accounts for the elevated urine concentration. Most of the reabsorption of potassium occurs in the proximal tubules, apparently passively. Secretion takes place in the distal tubules and collecting ducts by a passive process involving an exchange of potassium for sodium ions. The active reabsorption of sodium provides the driving force, with potassium ions diffusing into the lumen in response to the electrical gradient created by the outflow of sodium. This exchange process is opposed by the reabsorption of small amounts of potassium by active transport.

Another ion that is both secreted and reabsorbed by the tubules (by active processes) is urate (the negative ion of uric acid, the end product of the metabolism of purines, the base components of nucleic acids). There is some uncertainty about the relative contribution to the urine of unreabsorbed urate as opposed to urate secreted into the tubules (uric acid is about 14 times more concentrated in urine than in plasma), but it is generally believed that secretion is the chief source.

The proximal tubule actively secretes certain waste products such as *para-aminohippuric acid*, drugs such as *penicillin*, and a number of substances administered for diagnostic purposes, such as *Diodrast* (iodopyracet — used for x-ray of the kidney).

Clearance. The efficiency with which the kidney excretes any substance is often expressed as its clearance. Clearance represents the volume of plasma that is cleared of a given substance each minute. In the case of a substance such as *inulin* (a polymer of fructose), which is neither reabsorbed nor secreted by the tubules, the volume of plasma cleared of it per minute is the same as the volume of plasma filtered per minute (glomerular filtration rate). If 125 ml of plasma per minute is filtered and 1 ml of urine per minute is excreted, inulin would be 125 times more concentrated in urine than in plasma, and inulin clearance could be calculated as $125/1 \times 1$, or 125 ml per minute. In general terms, the ratio of urine to plasma concentration (each expressed as mg/ml) multiplied by the volume of urine per minute (ml/min) represents the clearance of any substance (subscript x), which may be expressed as follows: $C_x = U_x/P_x \times V$. By comparing the clearance of a substance with inulin clearance, it can be determined whether the particular substance undergoes a net reabsorption or a net secretion. A clearance lower than inulin's means that a net reabsorption of the substance (lowering the ratio of urine to plasma concentration) has occurred; a higher value means a net secretion has occurred. The clearance of a substance, such as glucose, that is completely reabsorbed and not secreted is zero. The clearance of a substance that is completely secreted and not reabsorbed is equal to the total plasma flow through the kidney.

Alteration of Urine Concentration and Volume

The ability of the kidney to form urine either much more concentrated (hypertonic) or much more dilute (hypotonic) than plasma has intrigued physiologists for many years. There are two aspects to this function. One is the *regulatory mechanism*, the other the *concentrating mechanism*. Regulation of the concentration of urine is accomplished by the *antidiuretic hormone* (ADH), secreted by the neurohypophysis (posterior pituitary gland). This hormone is synthesized in the hypothalamus and stored in the neurohypophysis.

When fluid loss exceeds fluid intake, osmoreceptors in the hypothalamus respond to the rise in the osmotic pressure of the plasma by stimulating the release of ADH by the neurohypophysis. ADH greatly increases the permeability of the collecting ducts, and probably to some extent the distal tubules, to water (see Chapter 16, page 547, for a discussion of the synthesis and mechanism of action of ADH). Normally, about 80 per cent of the water is reabsorbed before the urine reaches the distal tubule, and the fluid entering it is hypotonic. Hypertonic urine can be formed by reabsorption of water from the distal regions of the tubular system only if ADH is present. When the body fluids become diluted following the intake of a large volume of water, ADH is not secreted and a dilute, voluminous urine is secreted.

The steps in the formation of a concentrated or dilute urine are illustrated in Figure 15–8. As mentioned, most of the tubular reabsorption occurs in the proximal tubule. As the filtrate passes through this segment, it is reduced to about one-third of its original volume, remaining essentially isotonic. Since this reduction in volume occurs whether the urine formed is concentrated or dilute, the term *obligatory water reabsorption* is applied to the reabsorption of water in this

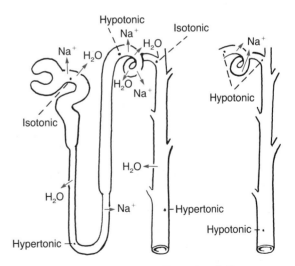

Formation of concentrated urine (in presence of ADH)　　Formation of dilute urine (in absence of ADH)

Figure 15–8. Schematic representation of the formation of concentrated and dilute urine, showing the transfer of sodium (Na^+) and water (H_2O) from the tubules to the interstitial fluid and the changes in tonicity of tubular fluid.

portion of the kidney in distinction to the variable water reabsorption in the distal segments, generally referred to as *facultative water reabsorption.*

The concentration of the medullary interstitial fluid increases from the cortical to the papillary end, where the concentration is up to eight times greater than in plasma. This condition arises because the ascending limb of the loop of Henle has a very low permeability to water, and, as fluid ascends, sodium chloride is removed while water remains behind. The descending loop of Henle is highly permeable to water; therefore, fluid leaving the proximal tubule becomes progressively more concentrated as it descends the loop of Henle and loses water, acquiring approximately the same osmotic pressure as the surrounding fluid, and then becomes progressively more dilute as a result of the removal of salt as it ascends, entering the distal convoluted tubule as a hypotonic solution. If ADH is absent, the active reabsorption of sodium chloride from the distal tubule and collecting duct with little water removal further dilutes the fluid and a large volume of hypotonic urine is excreted. If ADH is present, water is removed from the distal regions of the tubular system so that the fluid entering the medullary portion of the collecting duct will be isotonic, and it becomes progressively more concentrated as it flows through the medullary portion of the collecting duct, forming a relatively small volume of hypertonic urine.

It is perhaps apparent that the formation of a hypertonic urine depends upon the maintenance of a hypertonic medullary interstitial fluid. This means that the sodium chloride transferred from the ascending limb of the loop of Henle to the interstitial fluid of the medulla must not be immediately carried away by the blood stream. This does not happen because of the countercurrent flow of blood through the medulla. Each efferent arteriole arising from a glomerulus near the junction of the cortex and medulla (juxtamedullary glomeruli) divides into a group of descending, straight vessels (**descending vasa recta**). These vessels supply a capillary network which then gives rise to ascending, straight vessels (**ascending vasa recta**) that enter the venous system. As blood flows down the vasa recta, the plasma becomes progressively more concentrated. In the ascending vasa recta, salt passes from the plasma to the interstitial fluid. In effect, the vasa recta functions as a **countercurrent exchanger** as salt is transferred from the ascending to the descending vessels (Fig. 15–9). The important point is that the recirculation of salt through the interstitial fluid of the medulla maintains the high osmotic pressure of this fluid.

Effect of Aldosterone on Sodium and Water Retention. Adrenal steroid hormones, particularly aldosterone, are important regulators of blood and urine volumes. Aldosterone increases sodium reabsorption in the distal convoluted tubules and collecting ducts (by increasing the synthesis of a protein involved in active sodium transport),

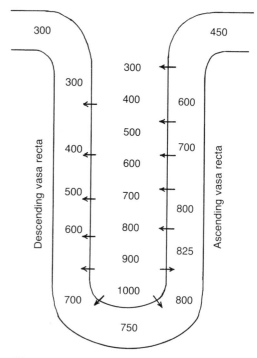

Figure 15–9. Diagrammatic representation of the recirculation of sodium salts (arrows) through the medullary interstitial fluid via the countercurrent exchanger mechanism of the loop of the vasa recta. Sodium salts passing into the blood of the descending vasa recta are partially returned to the interstitial fluid from the ascending vasa recta. The values for the concentrations of the tubular and interstitial fluid are in milliosmols. (A 1-osmolal solution contains 1 mole of a solute per kilogram of water, which depresses the freezing point 1.86° C. A milliosmol is 1/1000 of an osmol. The milliosmolality of a given solution is defined as the freezing point depression divided by 0.00186.) The concentration of the medullary interstitial fluid can be seen to increase from 300 milliosmols at the cortical end to 1000 milliosmos at the papillary end.

which in turn leads to an increase in water reabsorption. Changes in blood volume or pressure influence aldosterone secretion via the renin-angiotensin system. *Renin*, an enzyme, is released by the juxtaglomerular apparatus of the kidney (page 523) in response to a reduction in the volume or pressure of the blood flowing through the kidney. Its activity leads to the formation in the blood of *angiotensin II*, an octapeptide that stimulates the secretion of aldosterone. Angiotensin II is produced in two stages. In the first stage, *angiotensin I*, a decapeptide, is formed by the action of renin on a plasma protein (called renin substrate); in the second, angiotensin I is split (by angiotensin I converting enzyme) upon passage through a number of organs, especially the lungs. Angiotensin II also causes widespread vasoconstriction. This action and the expansion of the blood volume by angiotensin II raise blood pressure. The sodium- and, hence, water-retaining effect of aldosterone is the target of a number of useful diuretics that function by blocking the action of aldosterone in the kidneys.

Renal Regulation of Acid-Base Balance

Hydrogen ions are synthesized and secreted by the cells of the proximal and distal convoluted tubules, the collecting ducts, and the thick portion of the loops of Henle. The **secretion of hydrogen** is accompanied by the **restoration of bicarbonate** to the blood. This helps maintain the buffering capacity of the body fluids. The most abundant buffer in the extracellular fluids is the sodium bicarbonate 1-carbonic acid system (see Chapter 17, page 582, for a general discussion of buffer systems). Strong acids derived from dietary sources and metabolic processes react with bicarbonate (using hydrochloric acid as an example) as follows:

$$HCl + NaHCO_3 \rightarrow NaCl + H_2CO_3$$
$$H_2CO_3 \rightarrow H_2O + CO_2$$

These reactions result in the conversion of a strong acid to a weak one, namely, carbonic acid, and the dissociation of carbonic acid into carbon dioxide, which is expired, and water. At the same time, however, one mole of bicarbonate is lost from the extracellular fluid for each mole of acid reacting with the buffer system. The bicarbonate must be replaced in order to maintain the buffering capacity of the body fluids.

Renal cells produce bicarbonate and hydrogen ions by a reversal of the above reaction sequence. Carbon dioxide, derived from the blood or metabolic reactions in the tubular cell, combines with water in the presence of the enzyme carbonic anhydrase to form carbonic acid, which ionizes to form bicarbonate and hydrogen ions. Following this, the hydrogen ions are secreted into the tubular lumen in exchange for sodium ions. The sodium and bicarbonate ions are transferred to the blood, thereby replenishing the depleted bicarbonate. (This sequence is shown in Figure 15–10.) The secreted hydrogen ions react with constituents of the tubular fluid as follows:

1. With bicarbonate ions (usually combined with sodium) to form carbonic acid, which in turn dissociates into carbon dioxide and water. The water becomes part of the tubular fluid; the carbon dioxide diffuses out of the tubular lumen and may be utilized to regenerate bicarbonate. The net result is the removal of sodium bicarbonate from the tubular fluid.

2. With dibasic phosphate (Na_2HPO_4), form-

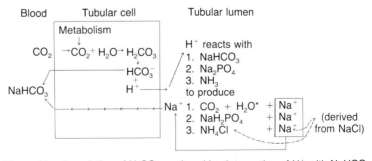

Figure 15–10. Chemical reaction sequences leading to the secretion of hydrogen ions in exchange for sodium ions, the replenishment of blood sodium bicarbonate, and the formation of titratable acid (NaH_2PO_4) and ammonium ions.

*Formed by dissociation of H_2CO_3 produced by the reaction of H^+ with $NaHCO_3$.

ing monobasic phosphate (NaH$_2$PO$_4$), which is excreted in the urine. The released sodium is exchanged for the secreted hydrogen that reacted with the dibasic phosphate.

3. With ammonia (which is continuously formed in the tubular cell, for the most part from the amino acid glutamine) to form ammonium ions (NH$_4^+$). The ammonium ions are excreted in the urine, largely in combination with chloride ions.

It should be apparent that, when hydrogen ions react with bicarbonate ions, the carbonic acid formed disappears from the tubular fluid as carbon dioxide, and hydrogen ions do not accumulate. Hydrogen reacting with dibasic phosphate and other weak acids, however, will appear in the excreted urine as what is called the *titratable acid* (determined by the amount of alkali required to titrate the urine to the pH of plasma). When the concentration of bicarbonate in the plasma and glomerular filtrate is high (above about 28 mEq per liter), bicarbonate, but not titratable acid, will appear in the excreted urine. When the plasma concentration of bicarbonate is low, the secreted hydrogen ions will neutralize all of the available bicarbonate in the tubular fluid, and the urine will contain titratable acids or ammonium ions but no bicarbonate. The urine normally is slightly acid (pH approximately 6.0).

URINALYSIS

The normal volume of urine voided in one day is between 1000 and 1500 ml, being less in summer and more in winter. An adult voids on the average of five to nine times daily, the volume each time being between 100 and 300 ml.

A urinalysis properly done will reveal the presence of renal disease, give clues as to the nature of the disease if present, provide a valuable tool in following the progression of disease, and give an immediate assessment of renal function.

Freshly voided urine is usually transparent and the color varies from a pale to dark yellow. Upon inspection, color variations may exist which indicate the following:

(a) Yellow-brown to deep olive green, produced by increased bilirubin content;

(b) Red hues, produced by blood, foods such as beets, and some drugs such as phenolphthalein found in some laxatives;

(c) Brown-black, produced by old blood.

Upon shaking, white foam indicates the presence of bile salts and pigment, a small amount of which is normal. An increased amount of foam will, however, be indicative of excess amounts of protein in the urine.

Fresh urine normally has a characteristic aromatic odor which develops into the pungent odor of ammonia upon standing. Certain ingested substances, such as asparagus, create characteristic odors, while the sweet smell of acetone or acetoacetic acid is recognized in diabetic ketosis. Heavily infected kidneys may produce urine which has a particularly unpleasant odor.

The concentration of urine (or the number of particles of solute dissolved in a unit of urine water) is usually determined by testing for specific gravity, the normal range of which is from 1.003 to 1.030. In an individual with healthy kidneys, this test will provide information about the state of hydration of the patient (if the urine is highly concentrated, the patient is dehydrated). Specific gravity tests will also determine the presence of parenchymatous renal disease, and will help distinguish between acute renal failure and dehydration.

Testing the urine for pH, which is normally very close to 6.0, can reveal such problems as infection with urea-splitting organisms, with the liberation of ammonia causing the urine to be more alkaline.

Glucose, protein, or sediment (cellular elements such as RBC, WBC, yeast, epithelial cells, and casts, crystals, and bacteria) in the urine are all indicative of particular disease states or problems. Testing for these substances involves microscopic examination of stained material.

Congenital Malformations

Polycystic Kidney Disease. Polycystic kidney disease is a hereditary disorder characterized by the distribution of hundreds of fluid-filled cysts of widely differing sizes throughout both kidneys. Two forms are recognized: a relatively rare infantile form, in which the inheritance is autosomal recessive, and an adult form, in which the inheritance is autosomal dominant. The infantile form is generally discovered shortly after birth and is rapidly fatal. It is believed that in this form of the disease the cysts result from a failure of the fusion of the renal collecting ducts and tubules.

Horseshoe Kidney. From the initial position in the pelvis, the kidneys normally ascend to the lumbar region. On occasion they join each other during the ascent, usually at their lower poles. These fused kidneys are known as a "horseshoe kidney" and occur about once in every 1000 births. Fused kidneys are capable of normal function, but stones are slightly more common because of the angulation of the ureter, which results in stasis of the urinary flow.

Disorders Associated with the Kidneys

Uremia. Uremia is the term used for a retention in the blood of normal constituents of urine and the symptom complex associated with this condition. There may be, among other things, headache, nausea, vomiting, hypertension, anemia, and coma. Uremia may develop rapidly due to acute renal failure or gradually with chronic renal failure.

Renal Failure: Acute and Chronic. *Acute renal failure* is a sudden, severe loss of kidney function. Characteristic of this condition is a urinary output of less than 400 ml per day. Among the more common causes are: (1) tubular necrosis, which might result from renal ischemia (diminution of blood supply), for example, as a consequence of shock or from an overdose of a nephrotoxin such as bichloride of mercury; (2) acute inflammation of the glomeruli (glomerulonephritis — see below); and (3) obstruction of urinary outflow, as by calculi (stones) in the urinary tract. *Chronic renal failure* is generally caused by a progressive kidney disease, such as pyelonephritis (see below) or chronic glomerulonephritis.

One of the serious complications of renal failure is the cardiotoxic effect of elevated blood potassium (hyperkalemia), resulting in arrhythmias and, in high concentrations, cardiac arrest and death. The anemia which usually accompanies renal failure is believed to be caused mainly by insufficient production of renal erythropoietic factor (see Chapter 11, page 358). A reduced calcium concentration in bone, causing structural weakness, often occurs in chronic renal failure. The principal cause of this condition is a deficiency in the formation of the active form of vitamin D_3, which is necessary for the normal absorption of calcium from the small intestine (the kidneys are responsible for the second stage of the hydroxylation of vitamin D_3 to 1,25-dihydroxyvitamin D_3 — see Chapter 6, page 111).

Glomerulonephritis. Acute glomerulonephritis (inflammation of the glomeruli) generally develops during the first two decades of life 10 to 20 days after an acute respiratory infection as a result of an antigen-antibody reaction. Most patients recover spontaneously; in only 2 per cent does the disease become chronic.

Pyelonephritis. Pyelonephritis, an inflammation of the kidney and its pelvis that begins in the pelvis and extends into the renal tissue, is caused by actual invasion by bacteria, usually ascending from the ureter. Most often the responsible microorganisms are colon bacilli originating from fecal contamination of the urinary tract.

Nephrosis. Nephrosis, also called the nephrotic syndrome, is characterized by loss of protein, especially albumin, into the urine, resulting in edema and a reduction in blood volume. This condition may accompany other symptoms of renal disease or occur without any other abnormality of kidney function. The latter form of the syndrome, called idiopathic nephrosis, has a much higher incidence in children than adults. The cause of the loss of albumin into the urine (albuminuria) is an increase in glomerular permeability. This has been attributed by various investigators to (1) a loss of negative charge in the pores of the capillary endothelium or basement membrane so that the negatively charged albumin permeates more readily, and/or (2) an increase in the size of the slit pores of the glomerular epithelium or of the pores in the capillary endothelium.

Dialysis

Hemodialysis (Fig. 15–11) exploits the simple principle of diffusion. A semipermeable membrane is interposed between the blood of the patient and a specially prepared solution called the dialysate. The changes that follow depend on the characteristics of the membrane and the composition of the dialysate as compared with that of the blood. If there is a relatively high level of any substance in the blood of a patient and none in the dialysate, that substance will diffuse

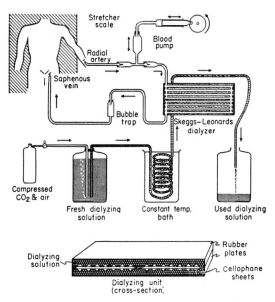

Figure 15–11. Schematic diagram of the Skeggs-Leonards artificial kidney.

from the patient into the solution. Urea, potassium, phosphate, and other substances present in high concentrations in the uremic patient can thus be removed by hemodialysis.

A model of an artificial kidney shown in Figure 15–11 includes a steel tube 2 feet deep and 2 feet in diameter. In the center is a spiral of cellophane tubing connected to plastic tubes which carry the blood from the patient to be purified in the dialysate and then back again to the patient. Microscopic pores are present in the cellophane tubing. Substances with a molecular weight of less than 5000 can pass through these pores.

It is now possible by hemodialysis to keep patients alive without any functioning kidney tissue for as long as 10 years or more.

URETERS

The ureters are two tubes, one for each kidney, which function to convey urine from the kidneys to the bladder. Each begins as a number of cuplike divisions of the renal pelvis known as *calyces*, joining to form two or three short tubes which unite into the funnel-shaped, dilated renal pelvis. The ureter proper passes from the pelvis to the posterior aspect of the urinary bladder. Each

is 25 to 30 cm in length, 4 to 5 mm in diameter, and consists of outer fibrous, middle muscular, and inner mucous layers. Contraction of the muscular layer produces characteristic peristaltic waves beginning at the renal pelvis and ending at the bladder.

Narrowed areas along the course of the ureter are of practical importance, since stones are likely to lodge at these points. The first narrowed area is at the junction of the ureter and renal pelvis; the next is at the point at which the ureter crosses the iliac artery; the third is at the position of entrance of the ureter into the bladder wall. At all three of these regions the lumen is sufficiently narrowed so that stones frequently become lodged.

The location of the ureter in the female is of particular interest, since its proximity to the uterus and cervix predisposes it to injury during surgery of the uterus. The female ureter lies close to the unattached border of the ovary on the lateral wall of the pelvis and enters the base of the broad ligament crossed by the uterine artery. As it approaches the bladder it lies adjacent to the cervix, where it can be injured in removal of the uterus (hysterectomy).

A double ureter is not an uncommon abnormality; it can be either partial or complete. If two completely separate ureters exist on one side, the two ureteral orifices are usually present on the same ureteric ridge. Occasionally the ureter is ectopic — that is, opening into an abnormal location such as the urethra itself or the vagina. An ectopic ureter can cause incontinence (continuous dripping), especially when its opening into the urogenital tract occurs below the sphincter of the bladder. Ectopic ureter should be considered in the young female child with enuresis (page 535).

URINARY BLADDER

The urinary bladder (Figs. 15–12 and 15–13) lies posterior to the symphysis pubis; it is separated from the rectum by the seminal vesicles in the male and by the vagina and uterus in the female. The superior surface of the bladder is covered by peritoneum. Laterally the bladder is supported by the levator ani musculature, and posteriorly it rests on the obturator internus muscle.

Basically, the bladder consists of two

parts—a small triangular area near the mouth of the bladder called the *trigone*, on which both the ureters and urethra open; and the *detrusor muscle* (smooth muscle of bladder wall), forming the principal portion of the body.

The trigonal muscle extends inferiorly on the floor of the proximal urethra and anchors the ureters as the bladder fills. The detrusor muscle encircles the vesical neck and also extends inferiorly adjacent to the proximal urethra.

The wall of the bladder is composed of four layers (from within outward): *mucosal*, *submucosal*, *muscular*, and *serosal*. Transitional epithelium lines the mucosal layer.

Micturition

The bladder, serving as a reservoir for urine, gradually fills and becomes distended. In the distended state, the muscular wall contracts and the pressure within the bladder increases. The normal capacity of the bladder is from 300 to 350 ml. As the volume increases, the tension rises. When the pressure within the bladder reaches 18 cm of H_2O, stretch and tension receptors are stimulated, producing the desire to urinate. Voluntary control can be exerted until the bladder pressure increases to 100 cm of H_2O, at which point involuntary micturition begins. It is currently believed that the entire urethra in the female and the prostatic and membranous urethra in the male function as the internal sphincter of the bladder. Circular skeletal muscle of the urogenital diaphragm, located a few centimeters below the bladder and through which the urethra passes, forms an external sphincter. When the fluid volume reaches about 150 ml, impulses are transmitted via the pelvic nerves to the micturition spinal reflex center in the sacral region of the spinal cord, but the return of impulses to the bladder (via preganglionic parasympathetic fibers in the pelvic nerves to ganglia in the bladder wall, and then via postganglionic fibers to the body of the detrusor muscle and the urethra) is blocked by inhibitory signals from the brain. When this inhibition is voluntarily lifted, the internal sphincter relaxes, and contraction of the detrusor muscle expels urine from the bladder. Urine in the urethra triggers the transmission of impulses to the spinal center, inducing reflexive relaxation of the external sphincter by decreasing the rate

of impulses traveling in motor neurons (in the pudendal nerves) to the external sphincter, which normally is tonically contracted. Voiding is accelerated by contraction of the diaphragm and abdominal wall.

Enuresis. Enuresis (involuntary bedwetting during sleep by a child over 3 years of age) can be caused by many factors, including local irritation of the bladder and urethra and emotional instability. When the child possesses a normal mental capacity and does not have actual disease, the outlook is favorable. The habit of voiding voluntarily should be established in children by the third year.

URETHRA

The male urethra is a narrow musculomembranous tube extending from the bladder to the external urethral meatus (Figs. 15–12 and 15–13). It follows a tortuous course for a distance of approximately 8 inches and is divided into three portions: prostatic, membranous, and cavernous.

The first part, the *prostatic urethra*, about 3 cm in length, commences at the bladder neck (outlet of the bladder) and traverses the prostate to the two-layered triangular ligament. The *membranous urethra*, about 1 cm in length, lies between the two layers of the triangular ligament, connecting the penile and prostatic urethrae. The *cavernous urethra* (penile portion), about 15 cm long, extends from the triangular ligament to the urethral orifice (see Chapter 18, pages 597 and 599, for supplemental diagrams).

The urethral wall consists of three layers: mucosal, submucosal, and muscular. The prostatic urethra is lined with transitional epithelium. Pseudostratified columnar epithelium lines the remaining portions except for the terminal dilation of the penile urethra (fossa navicularis), which is lined with stratified squamous epithelium.

The urethra serves as the distal portion of the urinary tract for eliminating urine from the body; additionally, the male urethra is the terminal portion of the reproductive tract, serving as a passageway for semen.

The female urethra, which serves only a urinary function, is about 4 cm in length and is supported by the anterior wall of the vagina. The urethra adjacent to the bladder is lined with transitional epithelium, the remainder largely with stratified squamous epi-

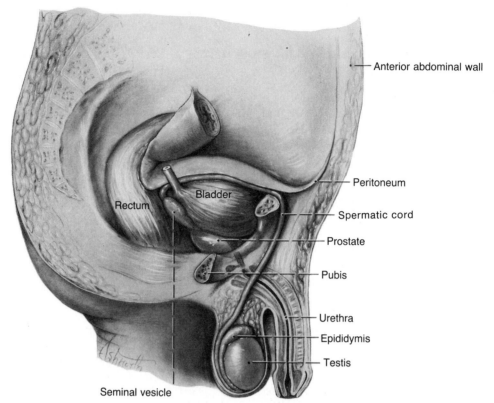

Figure 15–12. Sagittal section through the male pelvis.

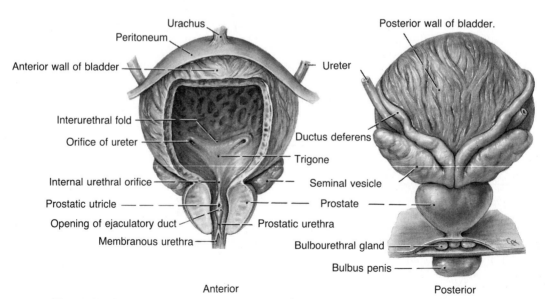

Figure 15–13. Internal and external aspects of the urinary bladder and related structures.

thelium. Skene's glands open into the urethra just within the external urinary meatus. The female urethra is generally recognized as being surrounded by a complex network of glands and ducts that form ideal foci for chronic infection. The epithelial lining of the female urethra is subject to hormonal influence and takes part in the general atrophy of the adjacent vaginal mucosa in the post-menopausal period. The urethral meatus is bathed by vaginal, uterine, and rectal discharges throughout life, exposing the delicate urethral structures to irritation and bacterial invasion.

SUMMARY

THE URINARY SYSTEM

Gross Anatomy

1. The kidneys are two bean-shaped organs, retroperitoneal in position, situated on the musculature of the posterior abdominal wall at the level of the twelfth thoracic and first three lumbar vertebrae. The right kidney is slightly lower than the left.

2. Three renal capsules surround the kidney: the capsule proper, perirenal fat, and the renal fascia.

3. External Structure

The hilum is a notch on the concave surface of the kidney where the renal vessels and nerves enter and leave the kidney substance.

4. Internal Structure

   a. Inner layer called the medulla.
   b. Outer layer called the cortex.
   c. The renal pyramids are triangle-shaped wedges of medulla with apices projecting as papillae and ending in calyces of the pelvis of each ureter.
   d. Renal columns are inward extensions of cortex between the pyramids.

5. Vascular Supply

   a. Primary branches of the renal artery give rise to lobar arteries, which branch into interlobar arteries extending to the boundary of the cortex and the medulla, where they divide into arcuate arteries.

   b. Interlobular arteries extend from the arcuate arteries into the superficial part of the cortex.

Microscopic Anatomy

1. Arterial blood enters Bowman's capsule via an afferent arteriole to form a capillary tuft called the glomerulus. Bowman's capsule, together with the glomerulus, forms the renal corpuscle.

2. The complete functional unit of the kidney is the nephron, composed of the renal corpuscle and its tubular extensions — proximal convoluted tubule, loop of Henle, and distal convoluted tubule which empties into a collecting duct.

3. Blood leaves the glomerulus via an efferent arteriole that gives rise to the peritubular capillaries.

Urine Formation

1. Urine formed in two stages:

   a. Glomerular filtration
   b. Tubular reabsorption and secretion

2. About 125 ml per minute of the approximately 650 ml per minute of plasma flowing through the glomeruli is filtered into Bowman's capsules. The filtrate is almost identical to plasma in composition except for the absence of plasma proteins.

3. Tubular reabsorption and secretion, in accordance with the body's needs, markedly change the composition of the filtrate; reabsorption to a greater extent than secretion determines the final composition of urine.

4. Reabsorption of sodium by active transport is followed by the passive reabsorption of water. Glucose and amino acids are normally completely reabsorbed by active processes. Urea is passively reabsorbed but is 60 to 70 times more concentrated in urine than in plasma.

5. Potassium, about 12 times more concentrated in urine than in plasma, is both reabsorbed and secreted, secretion (by a process involving sodium-potassium exchange) accounting for the high urine concentration. Certain waste products and drugs are eliminated by active secretion.

Formation of Concentrated Urine

1. Dependence on ADH

a. ADH increases the permeability of the collecting ducts and probably the distal convoluted tubules to water.

b. When fluid loss causes concentration of the plasma, hypothalamic osmoreceptors stimulate the release of ADH from the neurohypophysis.

2. Impermeability of ascending loop of Henle to water concentrates medullary interstitial fluid. Countercurrent exchange system of descending and ascending vasa recta maintains hypertonicity of medullary fluid, permitting urine to become concentrated (if ADH is present) by the removal of water from the distal regions of the tubular system.

Regulatory Action of Aldosterone

Aldosterone, a hormone secreted by the adrenal cortex, increases reabsorption of sodium, and consequently of water. Its release occurs as follows:

a. Reduction in the volume or pressure of the blood flowing through the kidneys stimulates the release of renin, an enzyme, from the juxtaglomerular apparatus of the kidneys.

b. Renin initiates the formation in the blood of angiotensin II, which triggers aldosterone secretion.

Renal Regulation of Acid-Base Balance

The action of carbonic anhdrase in tubular cells results in the formation of hydrogen and bicarbonate ions. Hydrogen is secreted into the tubular lumen in exchange for sodium, and sodium bicarbonate is transferred to the blood, replenishing the bicarbonate lost following its reaction with strong acids. Secreted hydrogen ions react with:

a. Bicarbonate, forming carbon dioxide and water;

b. Dibasic phosphate, forming monobasic phosphate; and

c. Ammonia, forming ammonium ions.

Ureters

1. Location and Structure

a. Retroperitoneal, extending from the kidneys to the posterior part of the bladder.

b. Ureters begin in the kidney as several calyces, which unite to form a pelvis.

c. The walls are of smooth muscle with a mucous lining and a fibrous outer layer.

2. Function

Collect urine and convey it to the bladder.

Urinary Bladder

1. Location and Structure

a. Posterior to symphysis pubis.

b. Bladder consists of trigone, with three openings (one urethral, two for ureters), and detrusor musculature.

2. Function

a. Storage of urine.

b. Reservoir that expels urine from the body. Process of urination is called voiding or micturition. This occurs as follows:

(1) When the fluid volume in the bladder reaches about 150 ml, signals are transmitted to micturition reflex center in sacral region of spinal cord.

(2) When inhibition from brain is lifted, return impulses trigger relaxation of internal urethral sphincter and contraction of detrusor muscle. Urine in urethra causes reflexive relaxation of external urethral sphincter.

Urethra

1. Location and Structure

a. Musculomembranous tube lying behind symphysis pubis and extending through prostate gland, triangular ligament and penis in male.

b. Lies anterior to vagina in female.

2. Function

a. Male: passageway for expulsion of urine and semen.

b. Female: passageway for expulsion of urine from the body.

REVIEW QUESTIONS

1. How does the composition of the glomerular filtrate differ from that of plasma? What processes change the composition of the filtrate?

2. What is the meaning of the term clearance? What is the clearance of glucose? Under what circumstances is the clearance of a substance the same as the glomerular filtration rate?
3. Explain how a dilute or concentrated urine is formed.
4. What is the action of aldosterone on the kidneys? How do changes in blood volume or pressure regulate the release of aldosterone?
5. How does the action of carbonic anhydrase in tubular cells lead to the replenishment of sodium bicarbonate lost from body fluids when it reacts with strong acids?
6. Describe the process of micturition.

16
The Endocrine System

Objectives

The aim of this chapter is to enable the student to:

- ☐ Define the term hormone and discuss the origin of the modern concept of endocrine function.
- ☐ Distinguish between the mechanisms of action of the major classes of hormones.
- ☐ Describe the anatomical relationship between the hypothalamus and hypophysis.
- ☐ Discuss the interrelation between the hypothalamus and the endocrine system.
- ☐ Locate and describe each endocrine gland. Summarize the actions of the hormones secreted by each endocrine gland.
- ☐ Describe the disorders of endocrine glands.

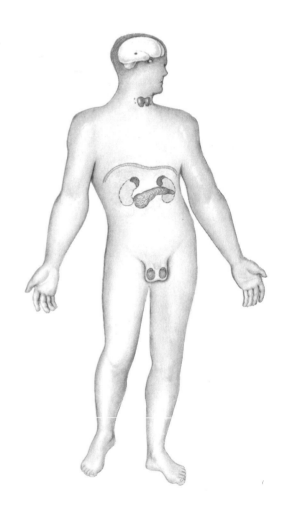

TERMINOLOGY AND GENERAL FUNCTIONS

Introduction

The endocrine system is composed of a diverse group of tissues which function to produce and release into the blood stream substances known as **hormones**, a term derived from the Greek word *hormaein* — to excite. The hormones are usually released in very low concentrations and transported to their sites of action elsewhere in the body, where they exert regulatory effects on cellular processes. Hormones may act upon the cells of specific organs, referred to as *target organs*, or upon cells widely distributed throughout the body. Cellular processes regulated by hormones include the permeability of cell membranes, the activity of specific enzyme systems, and gene transcription, leading to the synthesis of enzymes and other proteins.

The first experiment demonstrating an endocrine function was performed in 1849 by A. A. Berthold at the University of Göttingen. Berthold observed that the atrophy of the comb and loss of male behavior in cockerels following castration could be prevented by grafting a testis into the abdominal cavity. He concluded that the testis released something into the circulation that maintained male secondary sexual characteristics and behavior. However, these observations went unnoticed for many years, and about 40 years elapsed before it became generally understood that the ductless glands function by releasing "chemical messengers" into the blood.

The origin of the modern concept of endocrine function can be traced to events

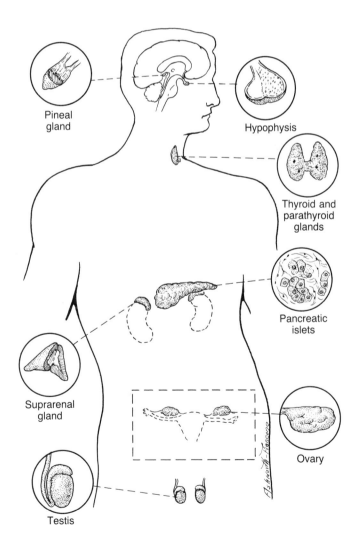

Figure 16–1. Location of eight glands of internal secretion.

Table 16-1 GLANDS OF INTERNAL SECRETION

GLANDS	LOCATION
1. Hypophysis (pituitary)	Sella turcica of the sphenoid bone
2. Thyroid	Neck, with one lobe on each side of the trachea
3. Parathyroids (four)	Posterior aspect of the thyroid gland
4. Pancreatic islets	Scattered throughout the pancreas
5. Suprarenal glands (two)	Superior to each kidney
6. Ovaries (two)	In pelvis, one on each side of the uterus
7. Testes (two)	One in each side of the scrotal sac
8. Pineal	Above the superior colliculi of the midbrain

that led to an understanding of the function of the thyroid gland. In 1883 three Swiss surgeons surgically removed enlarged thyroids (goiters) from 46 patients to relieve pressure on the trachea. The operation relieved the mechanical stress but caused the most extreme form of symptoms frequently seen in endemic goiter (especially prevalent in certain mountainous regions, such as the Alps, and now known to be due to a deficiency in dietary iodine). These symptoms included a low basal metabolic rate and a lethargic state of mind. This observation, and the duplication in thyroidectomized animals of certain signs (such as stunted growth) of infant endemic goiter (cretinism), suggested that the thyroid gland produces a substance necessary for normal development and health. By 1890, hypothyroid patients were being treated successfully by adding sheep's thyroid to their diet. The success of the substitution therapy refuted the view that the function of the thyroid and other ductless glands is to remove hypothetical noxious substances from the blood. This "detoxification theory" had been widely accepted as an explanation for syndromes described for diseased states of the adrenals, pancreas, and parathyroids, as well as the thyroid.

The view that endocrine glands regularly release into the blood stream substances necessary for the normal development and function of other parts of the body was clearly stated in 1891 by Brown-Séquard and D'Arsonval. At the beginning of the 20th century the understanding of endocrine function was further advanced by the discovery that a hormone may be secreted in response to a specific stimulus and be the mediator of a specific response. Such was the case with the intestinal hormone secretin, which, as described in Chapter 14, is secreted in response to acid in the duodenum and stimulates the exocrine pancreas. In 1902 Bayliss and Starling prepared an extract of the intestinal mucosa which, when injected into an animal, caused the secretion of pancreatic juice. Bayliss and Starling proposed the term *hormone* to identify this and similar substances.

The release of a hormone is frequently triggered by a change in the concentration of some substance in the body fluids. The effect of the hormone is corrective; the stimulus is eliminated, leading to a reduction of the secretion. Such a sequence is characteristic of a negative feedback homeostatic control system. Hormones, then, perform a number of functions — they coordinate body activities, control growth and development, and maintain homeostasis. In addition, the endocrine system interacts with the nervous system to bring about various responses to changes in the external and internal environment.

Listed below are the endocrine glands that will be discussed in this chapter and their secretions:

1. **Hypothalamus:**
   Thyrotropin-releasing hormone (TRH)
   Corticotropin-releasing factor (CRF)
   Gonadotropin-releasing hormone (GnRH)
   Growth hormone–releasing factor (GHRF)
   Growth hormone release–inhibiting hormone (GHRIH, also called somatostatin)
   Prolactin release–inhibiting factor (PIF)
   Prolactin–releasing factor (PRF)
   Melanocyte-stimulating hormone–releasing factor (MRF)
   Melanocyte-stimulating hormone release–inhibiting factor (MIF)
   (According to custom, those substances in this listing that have had their structures determined are referred to as

hormones; those that have not are referred to as factors.)

2. **Hypophysis** (pituitary gland)
   a. Adenohypophysis (anterior pituitary gland):
      Thyroid-stimulating hormone (TSH, also called thyrotropin)
      Adrenocorticotropic hormone (ACTH)
      Follicle-stimulating hormone (FSH)
      Luteinizing hormone (LH)
      Prolactin
      Growth hormone (GH)
      Melanocyte-stimulating hormone (MSH)
   b. Neurohypophysis (posterior pituitary gland): Antidiuretic hormone (ADH) and oxytocin. These hormones are synthesized in the hypothalamus and transported to the neurohypophysis via nerve fibers.
3. **Thyroid:** Thyroxine, triiodothyronine, and calcitonin.
4. **Parathyroid:** Parathyroid hormone.
5. **Adrenal**
   a. Adrenal cortex: Cortisol and aldosterone.
   b. Adrenal medulla: Epinephrine and norepinephrine. The adrenal medulla, innervated by preganglionic sympathetic nerve fibers, functions as a component of the sympathetic nervous system.
6. **Islets of Langerhans of the pancreas:** Insulin and glucagon.
7. **Ovary:** Estrogens and progesterone.
8. **Testis:** Testosterone.
9. **Pineal gland:** Melatonin.
10. **Placenta:** Human chorionic gonadotropin, estrogens, progesterone, and human placental lactogen.

Mechanism of Hormone Action

Hormones can be divided into two major classes: (1) *proteins, peptides, and derivatives of amino acids,* and (2) *steroids,* all synthesized from cholesterol. Steroid hormones are the hormones of the adrenal cortex, the female sex hormones (estrogens and progesterone), and the male sex hormones (androgens, principally testosterone). All other hormones listed in the preceding paragraph belong to the first-mentioned class. Many hormonal actions can be described in terms of distinctly different mechanisms common to hormones of each class as follows:

Protein, Peptide, and Amino Acid Derivative Hormones. A series of observations in the late 1950's and early 1960's with hormones of this class led to the first unifying concept for hormonal action. It was found that a number of these hormones exert some of their actions via a "second messenger," **cyclic AMP** (cyclic 3′,5′-adenosine monophosphate). In the first step the hormone binds to a receptor protein on the surface of the cell membrane. This binding increases the activity of an enzyme in the membrane called *adenylate cyclase,* which converts the abundant ATP in the cytoplasm in contact with the inner side of the membrane to cyclic AMP. Cyclic AMP then induces a change in some cellular process. This may involve changing the rate of enzymatic reactions, altering membrane permeability, or stimulating the release of stored hormones. The first cellular process shown to be mediated by cyclic AMP (by Earl Sutherland and colleagues) was the acceleration of the breakdown of glycogen to glucose in the liver cell by epinephrine and glucagon. Sutherland and co-workers observed that incubating either hormone with a membrane-containing fraction of cells produced a substance, later identified as cyclic AMP, that stimulated glycogenolysis in the cytoplasmic cell fraction, thus mimicking the hormonal action on the intact cell. The sequence of events worked out to account for these observations is illustrated in Figure 16–2. Cyclic AMP has been shown to be the mediator of the actions of a considerable number of other hormones, including the hypothalamic releasing factors and hormones, thyroid-stimulating hormone, adrenocorticotropic hormone, follicle-stimulating hormone, luteinizing hormone, antidiuretic hormone, parathyroid hormone, and secretin.

In recent years it has been reported that some polypeptide hormones, including insulin, prolactin, growth hormone, and gonadotropins, can penetrate into cells. There is considerable disagreement about where these hormones go and what they do when they get inside cells. One possible effect of polypeptide hormones after entering cells is exerting long-term effects on metabolism or cell growth. Such a view is especially favored by a number of investigators studying the action of insulin, the most intensively studied of the polypeptide hormones and a hormone whose long-term effects are poorly understood.

The mechanism of action of the thyroid hormones at the cellular level has also been the subject of much study over the past several years. Considerable evidence has accumulated suggesting that the initiation of the major effects of triiodothyronine and to a lesser extent thyroxine involves binding of these hormones to specific nuclear receptors (which belong to a class of nonhistone proteins believed to play a role in regulating gene expression) followed by the stimulation of gene transcription, that is, formation of messenger RNA containing instructions for the synthesis of specific proteins.

Steroid Hormones. Steroid hormones function by entering target cells and binding to receptor proteins in the cytoplasm, which then enter the nucleus and activate specific genes. Note that, in distinction to the process described for the thyroid hormones, the first step is *binding of a hormone to a receptor in the cytoplasm.* Receptor proteins consist of two subunits, each of which binds one hor-

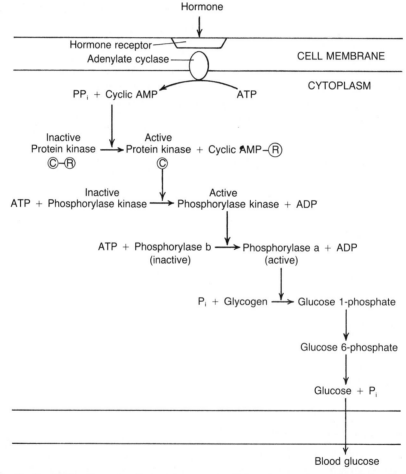

Figure 16–2. Cyclic AMP acting as a "second messenger" for glucagon or epinephrine in the stimulation of glycogen breakdown in the liver cell to yield blood glucose. Binding of the hormone to a receptor on the outer surface of the membrane in some way activates adenylate cyclase, an enzyme located on the inner surface of the membrane that converts ATP into cyclic AMP. Cyclic AMP activates protein kinase, an enzyme consisting of a regulatory subunit (R) to which cyclic AMP binds and a catalytic subunit (C) inhibited by the regulatory subunit. The regulatory subunit dissociates from the catalytic subunit when cyclic AMP binds to it. The active subunit catalyzes the phosphorylation of inactive phosphorylase kinase to form active phosphorylase kinase. This enzyme, in turn, catalyzes the phosphorylation of phosphorylase *b* (inactive form) to phosphorylase *a* (active form), which then catalyzes the breakdown of glycogen to glucose 1-phosphate, from which glucose 6-phosphate and finally free blood glucose are formed. Stimulation of glycogen breakdown in the liver was the first hormonal action found to be mediated by cyclic AMP.

mone molecule. The binding alters the receptor protein in some way, enabling the complex to migrate into the nucleus, where one of the receptor subunits binds to a chromosomal protein. The unbound subunit dissociates from the bound subunit and interacts with DNA. The result is an increase in gene transcription, producing messenger RNA, which contains coded information for the synthesis of proteins. The activity of these proteins, most of which apparently function as enzymes, is responsible for the effect of the hormone on the target cell. Receptor proteins have been identified in target tissues of all the known steroid hormones.

Hypothalamus

Hormones of the Hypothalamus Acting on the Adenohypophysis. In the 1940's it was discovered that the hypothalamus synthesizes and secretes hormones (called *releasing* and *release-inhibiting hormones or factors*) that control the secretion of the hormones of the adenohypophysis (anterior pituitary gland). These hormones are transported to the adenohypophysis by a portal system which forms a direct vascular link between the hypothalamus and the adenohypophysis. The pituitary gland is connected to the hypothalamus by a stalk. *Portal vessels* arising from capillaries in the *median eminence* of the hypothalamus, adjacent to the pituitary stalk, pass down the stalk into the adenohypophysis (Fig. 16–3). Specialized neurosecretory cells in various parts of the hypothalamus synthesize the hypothalamic hormones. The nerve endings of these cells terminate on capillaries in the median eminence, and the hormones liberated at these endings are absorbed by these capillaries and carried to the anterior pituitary gland, where they stimulate or inhibit the release of anterior pituitary hormones.

Secretion of two of the major anterior pituitary hormones — namely, prolactin, which governs milk production, and growth hormone, which governs, among other things, general body growth — is subject to both stimulatory and inhibitory control by corresponding releasing and release-inhibiting hypothalamic hormones or factors. There are corresponding releasing but not release-inhibiting hormones or factors for the other major anterior pituitary hormones. These hormones — namely, thyrotropin, adrenocorticotropic hormone, and the two gonadotropins (follicle-stimulating hormone and luteinizing hormone, for which there is a single hypothalamic releasing hormone) — control the functions of the thyroid, adrenal cortex, ovaries, and testes, and the hormones of the target organs exert feedback control over the secretion of these pituitary hormones. It has been suggested that the absence of feedback by hormones from target organs could explain the dual system (one stimulatory and

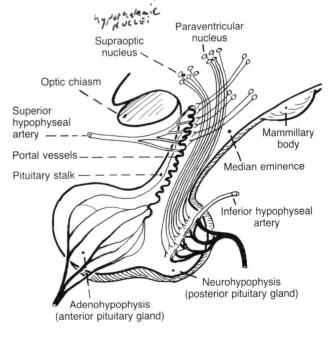

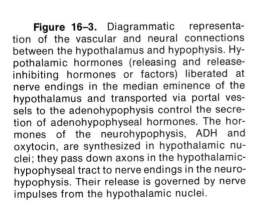

Figure 16–3. Diagrammatic representation of the vascular and neural connections between the hypothalamus and hypophysis. Hypothalamic hormones (releasing and release-inhibiting hormones or factors) liberated at nerve endings in the median eminence of the hypothalamus and transported via portal vessels to the adenohypophysis control the secretion of adenohypophyseal hormones. The hormones of the neurohypophysis, ADH and oxytocin, are synthesized in hypothalamic nuclei; they pass down axons in the hypothalamic-hypophyseal tract to nerve endings in the neurohypophysis. Their release is governed by nerve impulses from the hypothalamic nuclei.

one inhibitory) of hypothalamic regulation of prolactin and growth hormone secretion. (There are also hypothalamic releasing and release-inhibiting factors regulating the secretion of the melanocyte-stimulating hormone, a hormone of minor importance in humans — see below.) The names and abbreviations of all the releasing and release-inhibiting hormones and factors are listed on page 542.

Three of these hypothalamic hormones have been isolated in pure form and have had their structures determined (and, as mentioned before, are named as hormones rather than factors). These are thyrotropin-releasing hormone (a modified tripeptide), gonadotropin-releasing hormone (a decapeptide), and growth hormone release-inhibiting hormone, also called somatostatin (a tetradecapeptide). Using radioimmunoassay developed with synthetic hormone preparations, the distribution of these hormones in the brain has been determined. Although they are found in highest concentration in the hypothalamus, significant amounts of all three are found in other parts of the brain. About 70 per cent of the thyrotropin-releasing hormone in the rat brain, in fact, is located outside the hypothalamus. It has been suggested that thyrotropin-releasing hormone functions in extrahypothalamic regions of the brain as a modulator of neurotransmission. In studies with humans, thyrotropin-releasing hormone has been found to have a mood-elevating effect under certain conditions in depressed individuals.

Considerable amounts of somatostatin are found in the pancreas and stomach, and some investigators have suggested that it is synthesized by these organs as well as by the brain. The hormone appears to be involved in the regulation of pancreatic and gastric secretion — it inhibits the secretion the hormones glucagon, insulin (by the pancreas), and gastrin (by the stomach).

Neural Control of the Neurohypophysis and Adrenal Medulla by the Hypothalamus. Long before it was discovered that the hypothalamus secretes releasing and release-inhibiting hormones and factors it was known that neurosecretory cells of the *supraoptic* and *paraventricular nuclei* of the hypothalamus manufacture two hormones (**ADH** and **oxytocin**) that pass down their axons in the hypothalamic-hypophyseal tract in the pituitary stalk to nerve endings in the neurohypophysis, where they are stored (Fig. 16–3). These hormones are released from the neurohypophysis into the blood stream upon stimulation by impulses arising in the hypothalamic nuclei.

The hypothalamus controls the secretion of epinephrine and norepinephrine by the adrenal medulla by a direct nerve pathway: Fibers passing down the spinal cord synapse with preganglionic neurons whose fibers lead to the adrenal medulla.

The hypothalamus, then, exerts direct nervous control over the secretions of the neurohypophysis and adrenal medulla and, via portal blood vessels, hormonal control over the secretions of the adenohypophysis. In earlier chapters it has been noted that the hypothalamus contains, among others, centers for regulating body temperature and the volume of body fluids and is linked by nerve circuits to almost all parts of the brain. Utilizing input from other parts of the brain and information received from the blood passing through it, the hypothalamus continuously regulates almost the entire endocrine system. Ordinarily, these interactions contribute to normal development and health. Disturbed emotional states, however, may have the opposite effect. For example, poor growth in children deprived of normal parental affection (a condition called deprivation dwarfism) is apparently in large measure a consequence of a hormonal deficiency, especially of growth hormone, due to undersecretion (or oversecretion in the case of somatostatin) of hypothalamic releasing factors or hormones.

HYPOPHYSIS (PITUITARY GLAND)

The hypophysis is a mass of tissue about 1 cm in diameter, weighing approximately 0.8 gm in the adult. It consists of two basic divisions: the *adenohypophysis,* or *anterior pituitary gland,* and the *neurohypophysis,* or *posterior pituitary gland,* and, as mentioned, is connected by a stalk with the hypothalamus of the brain. The adenohypophysis is embryologically derived from the oral ectoderm, whereas the neurohypophysis is a downgrowth from the floor of the diencephalon of the forebrain. The adenohypophysis is divisible into a pars anterior and pars intermedia. In humans, the pars intermedia is rudimentary.

Neurohypophysis (Posterior Pituitary Gland)

The neurohypophysis, as described above, does not actually produce any hormones, but functions in storing two hormones in terminal endings of neurons whose cell bodies are located in the supraoptic and paraventricular nuclei of the hypothalamus. The two hormones, oxytocin and ADH, are synthesized and packaged into secretory granules in the neuronal cell bodies (either as finished products or as hormone precursors that are processed during axonal transport) and transported along the axons to the nerve endings. Release of the hormones from the secretory granules in the nerve endings is governed by nerve impulses from the hypothalamic nuclei. Both hormones are octapeptides. Six of the eight amino acids in the two molecules are identical, which explains why each exhibits to some extent the major actions of the other.

Antidiuretic Hormone (ADH). The major action of ADH (also known as *vasopressin*) is to reduce the volume and increase the concentration of urine by increasing the permeability of the collecting ducts and distal convoluted tubules of the kidneys to water, thereby allowing greater amounts of water to be reabsorbed from the tubules into the blood stream (see Chapter 15, page 529). This action is mediated by cyclic AMP, and recent studies suggest that protein phosphorylation reactions are involved. In electron micrographs of freeze-fractured cell membranes of rat collecting ducts, particle aggregation is seen following ADH administration, and it has been proposed that these changes represent the formation of water channels. In high concentration, ADH constricts arterioles, raising arterial blood pressure. This response may have physiological significance during severe hemorrhage. The rate of release of ADH from the neurohypophysis is governed by the concentration of the plasma and blood volume. According to some studies, cells in the supraoptic nuclei of the hypothalamus (the principal source of ADH) function as osmoreceptors, increasing or decreasing in size in response to changes in the concentration of the extracellular fluid. In any case, excess water loss, increasing the concentration of the plasma, results in the transmission of nerve impulses to the neurohypophysis, an increase in ADH release and,

consequently, conservation of water. Hemorrhage resulting in a loss of 10 per cent of the blood volume will also stimulate the release of ADH. A 25 per cent reduction in blood volume causes up to a 50-fold increase in the secretion of ADH. Low-pressure receptors in the left atrium appear to be the principal receptors in this response.

The most important disorder associated with a deficiency of the neurohypophysis is **diabetes insipidus**, a disease caused by a diminished production of antidiuretic hormone. Deficiency of ADH prevents the reabsorption of water by the kidneys and leads to the excretion of large volumes of urine — up to 20 liters a day.

Oxytocin (pitocin). The primary function of oxytocin is to influence the lactating breast to release milk from the glandular cells into the ducts. This is brought about by contraction of the myoepithelial cells in the alveoli of the mammary glands. Initially, suckling by the infant is the stimulus for the release of oxytocin. Impulses from the breast are transmitted to the hypothalamic nuclei, which trigger oxytocin release from the neurohypophysis (Fig. 16–4).

Oxytocin also stimulates the uterus to contract at the time of childbirth. It acts on the smooth muscle of the pregnant uterus to

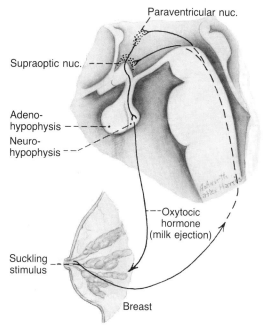

Figure 16–4. Interrelationships of hypothalamus, neurohypophysis, and breast.

maintain labor. Commercial forms of oxytocin are sometimes employed to increase uterine contraction and decrease hemorrhage following delivery. Although the sequence of events during parturition is uncertain, it is known that stimulation of the pregnant uterus initiates nerve impulses that pass to the hypothalamus and induce an increase in the secretion of oxytocin, and that during labor the concentration of oxytocin in the blood increases.

Adenohypophysis (Anterior Pituitary Gland)

The major cell types composing the anterior lobe of the hypophysis can be easily recognized by simple staining techniques. These are chromophils, which accept stains, and chromophobes, which do not accept stains. Chromophobes constitute 20 to 28 per cent of the cells of the adenohypophysis. Chromophils are subdivided into basophils, accepting basic dyes, and acidophils, accepting acid dyes. The *basophils* produce thyroid-stimulating hormone, follicle-stimulating hormone, and luteinizing hormone; the

acidophils produce growth hormone and prolactin; the *chromophobes* probably produce adrenocorticotropic hormone.

The major hormones of the adenohypophysis, with the exception of growth hormone, control the activities of specific target glands — the thyroid, adrenal cortex, ovaries, testes, and mammary glands. All adenohypophyseal hormones are proteins.

Thyroid-Stimulating Hormone (TSH). The thyroid-stimulating hormone (also called *thyrotropin*) regulates the size and function of the thyroid gland, promoting tissue growth and the production and secretion of thyroid hormones (thyroxine and triiodothyronine). Removal of the hypophysis (hypophysectomy) causes degenerative changes in the thyroid gland and considerable, but not complete, loss of function. Severing the connection between the anterior pituitary and the hypothalamus or transplanting the pituitary gland to another part of the body has a similar, but less pronounced, effect on the thyroid as a result of a reduction in the amount of thyrotropin secreted by the anterior pituitary in the absence of thyrotropin-releasing hormone. The blood levels of thyroxine and triiodothyronine are

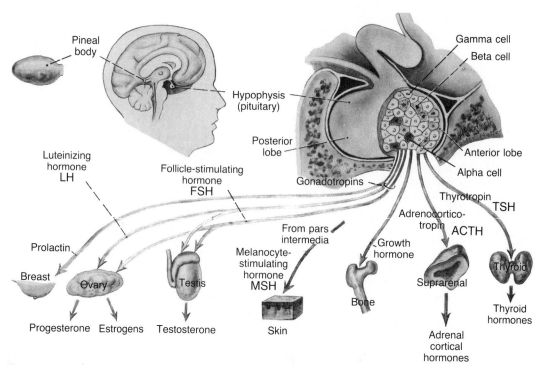

Figure 16-5. The adenohypophysis produces several hormones, some controlling the activity of other endocrine glands (thyroid, adrenal cortex, and gonads).

regulated by a negative feedback mechanism. A rise in plasma concentrations of these thyroid hormones reduces the secretion of thyrotropin by the anterior pituitary, and the subsequent decrease in the secretion of thyroid hormones lowers the concentration of thyroid hormones in the blood. Conversely, a fall in plasma thyroid hormones increases thyrotropin secretion, leading to a rise in plasma thyroid hormones. As mentioned, transplanting the pituitary gland to another site in the body reduces thyrotropin secretion; yet the thyroid hormones retain negative feedback control over the secretion of thyrotropin. Thus, the basic negative feedback mechanism is intact, but operates as though at a lower set point.

Adrenocorticotropic Hormone (ACTH). The adrenocorticotropic hormone, also called *adrenocorticotropin*, regulates the growth and function of the middle (*zona fasciculata*) and inner (*zona reticularis*) zones of the adrenal cortex, the regions that synthesize and secrete cortisol and similar steroid hormones (and small amounts of androgens). ACTH exerts almost no control over the thin outer region (*zona glomerulosa*) of the adrenal cortex, where aldosterone is synthesized. In hypophysectomized animals, the secretion of cortisol falls to subnormal levels, whereas the secretion of aldosterone remains nearly normal. ACTH secretion is considerably reduced if corticotropin-releasing factor is absent, as when the connection between the anterior pituitary and hypothalamus is interrupted. A negative feedback mechanism regulates the blood levels of cortisol just as it does the blood levels of thyroid hormones. A rise in plasma cortisol reduces ACTH secretion; this leads to a reduction in adrenal cortisol secretion and a fall in plasma cortisol. A fall in plasma cortisol results in an increase in ACTH secretion followed by an increased secretion of cortisol and a rise in plasma cortisol.

Gonadotropic Hormones. *Follicle-stimulating hormone* (FSH) stimulates the growth of the ovarian follicles in females and spermatogenesis in males (a process that also requires the action of testosterone).

Luteinizing hormone (LH) is also called *interstitial cell–stimulating hormone* (ICSH) in the male. It controls the testicular production of testosterone. In the female, LH acts synergistically with FSH to promote maturation of the ovarian follicle, and the midcycle surge in LH secretion triggers ovulation (following which the ruptured follicle is converted to the corpus luteum, from which luteinizing hormone derives its name).

Testosterone blood levels are regulated by a negative feedback system — a rise in plasma testosterone decreases LH secretion, which, in turn, reduces testosterone secretion; a fall in plasma testosterone increases LH secretion, which provokes an increase in testosterone secretion. Testosterone has little effect on the secretion of FSH. However, it has been found that an extract of the testes free of testosterone or other steroids depresses FSH blood levels. It is believed that a hormonal substance in this extract, called "inhibin," regulates FSH secretion. The rise in FSH observed in individuals with damaged epithelium of the seminiferous tubules of the testes has been attributed to a deficiency in inhibin secretion.

The feedback mechanism controlling the secretion of estrogens, progesterone, and the gonadotropins during the menstrual cycle is described in Chapter 18.

Prolactin. Prolactin contributes to the development of the mammary glands (which is governed principally by estrogens and progesterone in the presence of growth hormone) and stimulates the synthesis of milk (which begins a day or two after parturition) in conjunction with other hormones, including insulin and cortisol. There is some evidence that in males the stimulation of testosterone secretion by luteinizing hormone is facilitated by prolactin. Its release from the adenohypophysis is controlled principally by prolactin release–inhibiting factor (PIF). The secretion of prolactin is normally kept at a very low level by PIF, but immediately after childbirth the release of PIF is apparently suppressed, and prolactin secretion rises dramatically. A prolactin-releasing factor has also been identified. It has been observed, however, that section of the pituitary stalk in animals results in a severalfold increase in prolactin secretion (the secretion of all other hormones of the adenohypophysis is greatly decreased by this procedure).

Growth Hormone. Growth hormone, also called *somatotropin*, accelerates growth, increasing the size of all organs and promoting the growth of bone before closure of the epiphyses. It increases protein formation, decreases carbohydrate utilization, and increases the mobilization of fat for energy use.

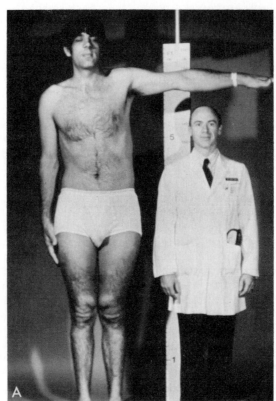

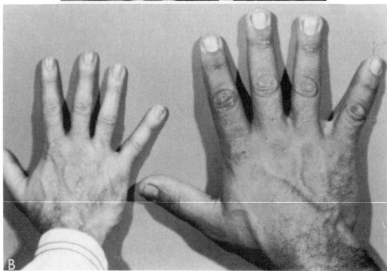

Figure 16–6. Gigantism with acromegaly in a male aged 28. *A*, Height approximately 7 feet, 6 inches. *B*, Hand of same individual as compared to normal-sized hand.

Some of the specific actions of growth hormone follow:

1. Growth hormone increases the length of bones by increasing the formation and release by the liver of a substance known as *somatomedin*, which stimulates the proliferation of cartilage cells at the epiphyseal disc, or growth plate. This widens the disc, and growth is proportional to the widening.

2. Growth hormone enhances protein synthesis by increasing the uptake of amino acids by cells and by increasing the incorporation of amino acids into protein. Insulin has similar effects on protein formation, and the presence of insulin is necessary for the expression of the anabolic action of growth hormone, and for its growth-promoting activity in general.

3. Growth hormone treatment increases blood sugar. Injection of the hormone into animals decreases glucose uptake by cells (particularly skeletal and heart muscle) and the oxidation of glucose by these cells. These actions are opposite and antagonistic to the actions of insulin.

4. Growth hormone increases the transport of fatty acids from fat depots, principally to skeletal muscle, the heart, and the liver, by accelerating the hydrolysis of triglycerides in the depots. (It has been suggested that since fatty acids interfere with the uptake and oxidation of glucose, growth hormone impairment of glucose utilization is in part the result of its lipid-mobilizing action.)

Low blood sugar levels stimulate the release of growth hormone. Thus the hormone may help to augment the use of fat for energy during fasting.

An underproduction of growth hormone in childhood results in **dwarfism.** The pituitary dwarf is generally a well-proportioned but small person. If there is an overproduction of growth hormone in children before the epiphyses of the long bones close, **gigantism** results (Fig. 16–6).

In the adult, overproduction of growth hormone results in **acromegaly.** Since bones cannot increase in length after the closure of the epiphyses in the adult, cancellous bones increase in thickness. As a result of acromegaly, the feet and hands become large and spadelike, while the bones of the face and skull become thicker. Hyperglycemia and glycosuria frequently occur. An acidophilic tumor is usually responsible for the condition.

Melanocyte-Stimulating Hormone (MSH). The melanocyte-stimulating hormone causes darkening of the skin (presumably by stimulating the epidermal melanocytes, which manufacture the dark pigment, melanin), but this effect is observed only when hypersecretion of the hormone occurs, as in Addison's disease (see below). (In amphibians, the melanocyte-stimulating hormone rapidly darkens the skin by dispersing melanin granules, which are concentrated around the nucleus of the melanin-producing cells in the absence of the hormone.) Recent studies with rats and humans suggest that the melanocyte-stimulating hormone may have extrapigmentary actions, particularly on the central nervous system. It appears to improve attention focusing, especially upon visual stimuli.

A summary of hypophyseal hormones is included in Table 16–2.

THE THYROID GLAND

The human thyroid (Fig. 16–7) is composed of two lobes lying on either side of the trachea and connected in the midline by a thin isthmus extending over the anterior surface of the trachea. In the adult, the thyroid weighs from 20 to 30 grams. It is encapsulated by two layers of connective tissue — the outer one continuous with the cervical fascia and the inner one intimately adherent to the surface of the gland itself.

The ancients assigned the thyroid gland such functions as serving as a vascular shunt for cerebral circulation and beautifying the neck, especially when it enlarged into a "goiter."

Microscopic Anatomy of the Thyroid

The thyroid has a remarkable capacity to store secretions, as is reflected in its histology (which differs from other endocrine glands, in which the cells are arranged in sheets between blood vessels). Normally, the thyroid is composed of *follicles* of uniform size, each, in effect, a separate gland, and each about the diameter of a pinhead (Fig. 16–8). The sacs do not have external openings, but are richly supplied with minute blood and lymph vessels bringing supplies of iodine and carrying away thyroid hormones. In the

Table 16–2 HYPOPHYSEAL HORMONES

NAME AND SOURCE	SYNONYMS	FUNCTION
Adenohypophysis (anterior lobe)		
TSH	Thyroid-stimulating hormone; thyrotropin	Stimulates thyroid growth and secretion.
ACTH	Adrenocorticotropic hormone; adrenocorticotropin; corticotropin	Stimulates adrenocortical growth and secretion
Growth Hormone	Somatotropin	Accelerates body growth
FSH	Follicle-stimulating hormone	Stimulates growth of ovarian follicles in the female and spermatogenesis in the male
LH	Luteinizing hormone; interstitial cell-stimulating hormone, ICSH (in the male)	Stimulates ovulation in the female and production of testosterone in the male
Prolactin		Stimulates synthesis of milk
MSH	Melanocyte-stimulating hormone	Hypersecretion causes darkening of skin
Neurohypophysis (posterior lobe)		
Antidiuretic Hormone (ADH)	Vasopressin	Promotes water retention by way of the renal tubules and stimulates smooth muscle of blood vessels
Oxytocin		Stimulates release of milk and contraction of smooth muscle in the uterus

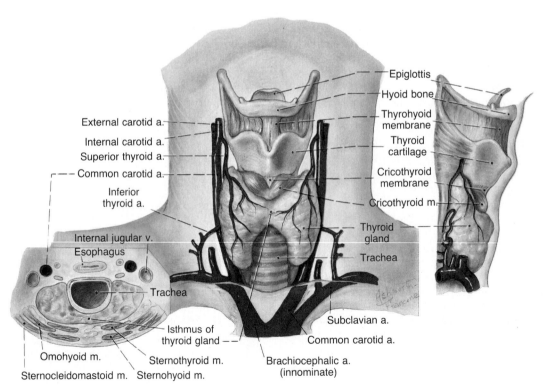

Figure 16–7. Plate of thyroid gland showing its blood supply and relations to trachea; in cross section, anterior, and right lateral views.

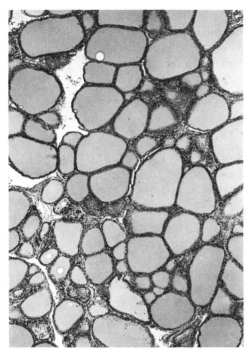

Figure 16–8. Photomicrograph of the thyroid gland showing normal follicles, each lined with simple cuboidal epithelium and filled with colloid. Magnification 50 ×. (From Leeson, C. R., and Leeson, T. S.: Histology. 4th ed., Philadelphia, W. B. Saunders Co., 1981.)

healthy gland the follicle consists of a single, approximately spherical layer of cuboidal cells surrounding a cavity filled with a substance known as *colloid*. Colloid itself is a homogeneous substance giving the gland its most distinguishing histologic characteristic. It is the storage product of the secretory epithelium. In iodine deficiency follicles become distended with colloid and the cells lining the follicles become flattened. When the thyroid overacts, colloid stores become depleted and the epithelium assumes a columnar shape. The stroma (delicate fibrous tissue), located between the follicles, is denser in some areas than in others, creating fibrous septa traversing the gland.

Physiology of the Thyroid

The thyroid is one of the most sensitive organs of the body. During puberty, pregnancy, and physiologic stress it increases in size, becoming more active. Changes in activity and size normally occur during the menstrual cycle. Two hormones responsible for the major functions of the thyroid gland have been chemically defined. These are thyroxine (T_4, for the four iodine atoms attached to the thyronine nucleus) and triiodothyronine (T_3, for three iodine atoms). The thyroid secretes about 10 times as much thyroxine as T_3. However, since a portion of the circulating T_4 is converted to T_3 by partial deiodination in the liver, kidneys, and other tissues and since T_3 is much more active than T_4, many investigators believe that most of the biological activity of these hormones is mediated by T_3.

The synthesis of the thyroid hormones involves the following steps: (1) Uptake by thyroid cells of iodine as sodium or potassium iodide from the blood. This is an active transport process and is often called the "thyroid pump." (2) Oxidation of iodide (I^-) to form what is known as "active" iodine. (3) Combination of "active" iodine with the amino acid tyrosine (bound to the giant protein molecules thyroglobulin, the principal substance of colloid) to form monoiodotyrosine (MIT) and diiodotyrosine (DIT). This apparently occurs on the cell membrane at the cell-colloid interface. (4) T_3 is then formed by combination of MIT and DIT, thyroxine by combination of two molecules of DIT. (The structure of tyrosine and its iodinated derivatives are shown in Fig. 16–9.)

To be released from the gland, the hormones must be split from thyroglobulin by a proteolytic enzyme. This occurs in thyroid cells following pinocytosis of colloid and fusion of colloid-containing vesicles with lysosomes. MIT and DIT that do not combine to form thyroid hormones are also split off from thyroglobulin during the enzymatic cleaving of the hormones from thyroglobulin and then enzymatically deiodinated. The deiodination serves the important function of conserving thyroidal iodine for recycling. A congenital absence of thyroid deiodinase causes iodine deficiency.

Thyroid-stimulating hormone promotes the uptake of iodide and all steps in the synthesis and release of the thyroid hormones. Following their secretion, thyroxine and T_3 are transported in the blood for the most part bound to proteins. Measurement of plasma-protein–bound iodine (PBI) is an index of thyroid function.

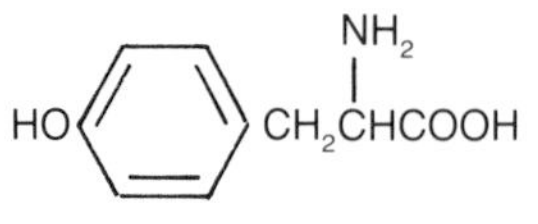

Tyrosine

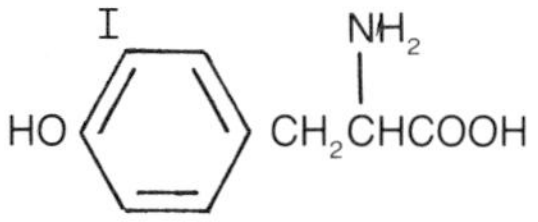

Monoiodotyrosine (MIT)

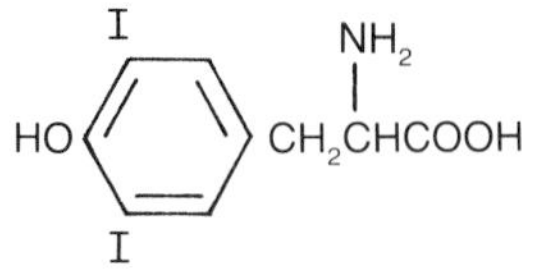

Diiodotyrosine (DIT)

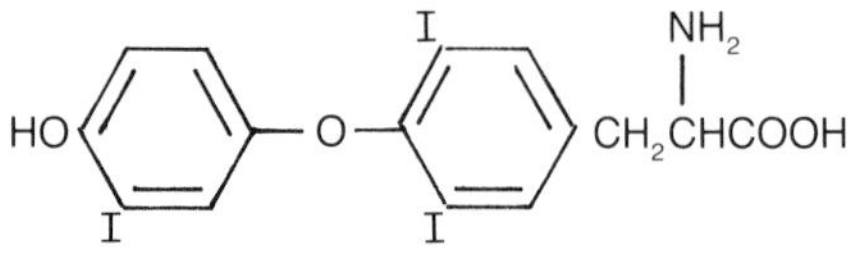

Triiodothyronine (T3)

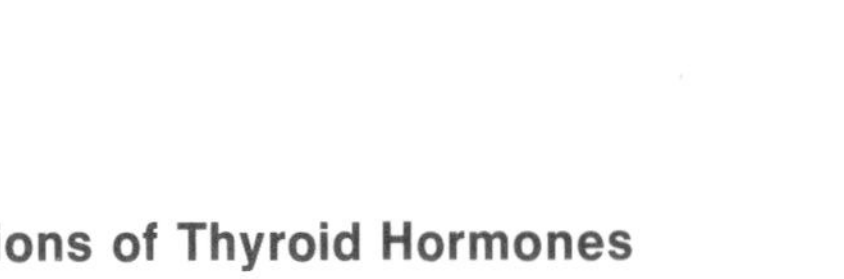

Thyroxine (T4)

Figure 16–9. Tyrosine and compounds formed by its iodination in the thyroid gland, including the thyroid hormones T_3 and thyroxine.

Actions of Thyroid Hormones

Although the thyroid hormones exert many effects on almost all tissues of the body, the basic cellular mechanism by which these hormones act is still poorly understood. In general, thyroid hormones promote growth and differentiation and increase oxidative metabolism. In 1895, Adolf Magnus-Levy demonstrated that the thyroid gland regulates the *basal metabolic rate* (BMR—defined in Chapter 14, page 513). He observed a low basal oxygen consumption in hypothyroid patients and was able to correct the deficiency by administering a thyroid extract. Hyperthyroid individuals have a high BMR.

Thyroid hormones have a "permissive action" on growth hormone secretion and function. In the absence of thyroid hormones, growth hormone is not secreted normally and does not have its normal growth-promoting actions. During growth, the action of thyroid hormones on protein metabolism is primarily anabolic. These hormones increase synthesis in almost all tissues of the body, and growth hormone cannot exert its normal effect on tissue and body growth unless they are present. In hyperthyroid adults, on the other hand, the catabolic effect of thyroid hormones on protein metabolism predominates.

The thyroid hormones are specifically required for the normal development of the central nervous system. This requirement, as well as the need for thyroid hormones for normal growth, is evident in children called cretins, who are hypothyroid from infancy. Such children are dwarfed and mentally retarded. (See Chapter 6, page 112, for a brief description of the action of thyroid hormones on bone.)

In the hyperthyroid condition, catabolic effects of thyroid hormones on carbohydrate and fat metabolism are apparent. The oxidation of glucose is increased, and fatty acids are mobilized from the fat depots and oxidized by active tissues at an increased rate. Thyroid hormones actually accelerate all aspects of carbohydrate metabolism, including absorption of glucose from the small intestine into the blood and its entry into tissue cells. Synthesis of glucose from noncarbohydrate precursors is also increased.

Thyroid hormones also augment the catabolism of cholesterol. In the hypothyroid state the reverse condition, a reduced catabolism of cholesterol and fat, is observed, and elevated blood lipids are a characteristic feature. The concentration of the cholesterol-rich plasma low density lipoproteins is especially high in hypothyroid individuals. Since elevated levels of plasma low density lipoproteins, as has been noted (Chapter 11, page 394), accelerate the development of atherosclerosis, this disease is generally seen in prolonged hypothyroidism.

Goiter. Goiter (*L. guttur*, throat) is the descriptive term for any enlarged thyroid, whether it be secreting too little, too much, or normal amounts of thyroid hormones. At one time, in certain areas of the world where the

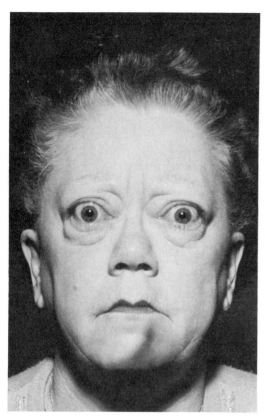

Figure 16–10. Exophthalmos. Note startled appearance and loss of eyebrows.

iodide content of the soil was so low that the drinking water and locally grown food did not provide sufficient iodide for the synthesis of normal amounts of thyroid hormones, significant proportions of the populations had goiters. Goiters of this type, known as *endemic goiters*, develop because the low blood levels of iodine induce hypersecretion of TSH. The TSH-stimulated thyroids enlarge, the follicles becoming engorged with colloid. Many individuals with endemic goiters have sufficient amounts of circulating thyroid hormones for the maintenance of normal health; many others do not. *Toxic goiter* refers to a clinical hyperthyroid state. This type of goiter is often called *exophthalmic* (L. *ex*, out of; G. *ophthalmos*, eye) *goiter* because most patients have prominent, protruding eyes.

Increased Secretion of Thyroid Hormones. Hyperthyroidism was first described by the Irish physician Robert Graves in 1835, and is usually called *Graves' disease.* In this condition the patient becomes excitable and nervous, exhibiting a moist skin, rapid pulse, elevated metabolic rate, intol-

erance to heat, weight loss, increased appetite, tremor of the hand, and exophthalmos (Fig. 16–10). It now appears that Graves' disease is a curious autoimmune disorder. The blood of these patients contains antibodies that combine with receptors for thyroid-stimulating hormone on the cell-surface membranes of thyroid cells and *mimic the action of TSH,* causing massive secretion of thyroid hormones.

The treatment of hyperthyroidism is well established. A physician can choose among the alternatives of surgery, actually removing large segments of the thyroid, administration of radioactive iodine to destroy segments of the gland, or the use of antithyroid drugs to block the production of thyroid hormones.

Reduced Secretion of Thyroid Hormones. The severe form of hypothyroidism in adults is known as *myxedema* because of the edematous, puffy thickening of the skin, especially below the eyes and of the lips, fingers, and legs (Fig. 16–11). An accumulation of mucoprotein in the subcutaneous tissue, which absorbs fluid, is responsible for the thickening. The characteristic clinical signs of myxedema include a low basal meta-

Figure 16–11. Myxedema. Note thick lips, baggy eyes, loss of hair, and dry skin.

bolic rate, lethargy, slowing of the mental faculties, cool and dry skin, low heart rate and blood pressure, weight gain, and loss of hair. Adult hypothyroidism is most commonly seen in endemic goiter and an autoimmune disease of the thyroid gland known as *Hashimoto's disease*.

As mentioned, untreated thyroid deficiency in infancy results in *cretinism*, a condition characterized by stunted growth and mental retardation. Normal changes in body proportion fail to occur. Formation and eruption of teeth are delayed, and the child exhibits a broad face with large tongue and mouth. The condition may be caused by a congenital absence of the thyroid gland or failure to synthesize thyroid hormones because of a genetic enzymatic defect, or it may be the childhood form of endemic goiter. The diagnosis of hypothyroidism can be made by clinical findings, the thyroidal radioactive iodine (I^{131}) uptake, and measurement of serum-protein–bound iodine. Hypothyroidism is treated by the oral administration of thyroxine or thyroid extract.

Cancer of the Thyroid. Cancer of the thyroid occurs in all age groups. Thirty years ago it was relatively common in infants following x-ray administration to the neck to combat an enlarged thymus. Treatment of thyroid carcinoma consists of surgical removal of the gland, or destruction by large doses of x-ray. Treatment with radioactive iodine holds hope for some patients in whom thyroid cancer has spread to other parts of the body.

Calcitonin. In the 1960's it was discovered that the thyroid produces another hormone, one that rapidly lowers blood calcium. The hormone, called calcitonin or thyrocalcitonin, is a polypeptide containing 32 amino acids and is synthesized by the parafollicular, or C, cells of the thyroid, located in the interstitial tissue between the follicles. Its action is opposite to that of the parathyroid hormone. High blood calcium stimulates its release, and it inhibits bone resorption and the liberation of calcium, thereby lowering blood calcium.

THE PARATHYROID GLANDS

The parathyroid glands were unknown to the medical profession until 1880, when they were described by a Swedish anatomist. Surgeons have learned that the accidental removal of these structures at the time of a thyroidectomy results in a serious condition known as tetany.

The parathyroid glands are yellowish or reddish-tan, flattened, oval bodies, 6 mm in length and 3 to 4 mm in breadth; usually four in number, they are located on the posterior aspect of the lobes of the thyroid (Fig. 16–12). On histologic section, the parathyroid gland consists of two epithelial cell types: *chief* and *oxyphil*. The chief cell is more numerous and has a large vesicular, centrally placed nucleus embedded in a faintly staining cytoplasm containing glycogen. The oxyphil cell, characterized by eosinophilic granulation, does not contain glycogen, and is slightly larger than the chief cell. Parathyroid hormone is produced by the chief cells. The function of the oxyphil cells, which appear after puberty, is unknown.

Physiology of the Parathyroids

The parathyroid gland secretes parathyroid hormone, a protein consisting of a single polypeptide chain composed of 84 amino acids. Its function is closely linked with the homeostatic regulation of the calcium ion concentration of body fluids, and secretion of the hormone is governed by a negative feedback system. Low blood calcium increases the secretion of the parathyroid hormone. The hormone raises blood calcium, principally by increasing bone resorption (Chapter 6, page 113). It also increases the reabsorption of calcium from the kidneys and, by stimulating the formation of 1,25-dihydroxyvitamin D_3 in the kidneys (Chapter 6, page 111), it increases the absorption of calcium from the small intestine (the hormone's action on vitamin D_3 in the kidneys is indirect — it decreases phosphate reabsorption from the kidneys, and the lowered plasma phosphate apparently stimulates the conversion of 25-hydroxyvitamin D_3 to the more reactive 1,25-dihydroxyvitamin D_3). Elevated levels of blood calcium decrease the secretion of parathyroid hormone. As mentioned, high blood calcium is also the stimulus for the secretion of calcitonin by the thyroid gland, a hormone that promptly lowers blood calcium by inhibiting bone resorption.

Calcium serves four major functions: bone formation, coagulation of blood, maintenance of normal cell permeability, and main-

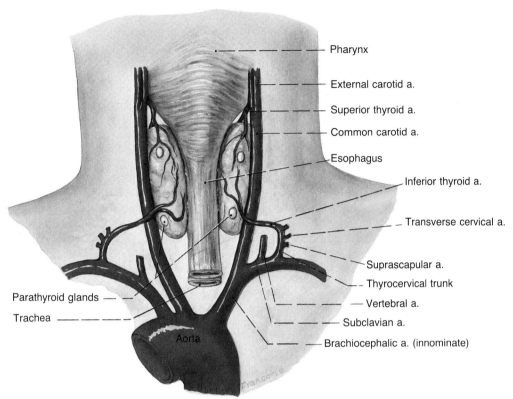

Pharynx

External carotid a.

Superior thyroid a.

Common carotid a.

Esophagus

Inferior thyroid a.

Transverse cervical a.

Suprascapular a.

Thyrocervical trunk

Vertebral a.

Subclavian a.

Brachiocephalic a. (innominate)

Parathyroid glands

Trachea

Aorta

Figure 16–12. Posterior view of the neck and thyroid gland, showing the approximate location of the parathyroid glands.

tenance of normal neuromuscular irritability.

Although calcium is present in all body fluids, 99 per cent is contained in bone. The normal adult requirement is 1 gram per day. During periods of rapid growth, this requirement may increase to approximately 2 grams per day.

Diseases of the Parathyroid Glands

Hypoparathyroidism (Tetany). The findings associated with parathyroid underactivity include a drop in serum calcium and a rise in serum inorganic phosphorus. With parathyroid deficiency the urinary excretion of calcium initially rises owing to a decrease in calcium reabsorption by the kidneys, but later falls as plasma calcium declines. Common symptoms of parathyroid deficiency are increased excitability of the musculature to mechanical stimulation and fibrillary twitchings followed by jerky muscular contractions. The neuromuscular symptoms become more severe as the calcium

level of the blood falls. Tetany is encountered following accidental removal or injury of the parathyroid glands when the thyroid has been surgically treated. One remaining parathyroid is thought to be sufficient to prevent the occurrence of tetany. Treatment of hypoparathyroidism must be considered from the point of view of acute and chronic phases. In the acute phase, which frequently occurs in the postoperative period following removal of the parathyroid with the thyroid, treatment is aimed at preventing muscle spasm and convulsions. This is accomplished by restoring the serum calcium level to normal by the intravenous injection of calcium salts.

During the chronic stage of hypoparathyroidism the major goal of treatment is to maintain the serum calcium level at normal so as to prevent the symptoms and signs of tetany and to avoid future complications, including cataracts. Vitamin D is given to enhance the absorption of calcium by the small intestine. Oral calcium salts are also of value.

Hyperparathyroidism. The basic problem in hyperparathyroidism is excess circulating parathyroid hormone, leading to increased serum calcium levels (hypercalcemia). Calcium is precipitated in the urinary tract and results in the formation of kidney stones. These in turn may cause obstruction of the ureter with accompanying pain and infection. Excess parathyroid hormone causes excess resorption of bone, producing pain, tenderness, fracture, and deformity. X-ray evidence of demineralization of bones is present; if the disease is severe or of long standing, bone cysts can occur. The laboratory findings in hyperparathyroidism include an increase in urinary calcium and phosphate. Hyperparathyroidism is usually caused by a parathyroid tumor. Treatment consists of surgical removal of the tumor.

SUPRARENAL (ADRENAL) GLANDS

There are two suprarenal glands, one superior to each kidney. Each resembles an admiral's cocked hat in shape and each is about 1½ inches in length and ½ inch in diameter. The suprarenal gland varies in weight in different age groups, the average in the adult being about 4 grams. Each suprarenal gland has a cortex, or outer portion, and a medulla, or inner portion. The cortex and medulla are different in both origin and function: the cortex is derived from the mesoderm in close association with the developing gonads, whereas the medulla is neuroectodermal in origin.

Suprarenal Cortex

The cortex of the suprarenal gland is deep yellow in color and occupies three-quarters of the total width of the suprarenal gland in cross section. From the surface inward its component layers are the *zona glomerulosa*, the *zona fasciculata*, and the *zona reticularis*.

Three general types of substances are secreted by the cortex: mineralocorticoids, represented principally by *aldosterone;* glucocorticoids, represented chiefly by *cortisol (hydrocortisone);* and sex hormones (androgens of low potency and very small amounts of estrogens). The mineralocorticoids and glucocorticoids are the major hormones. To some extent they share the same functions, but each has its own primary activity. The mineralocorticoids function primarily in influencing sodium and potassium urinary excretion. The glucocorticoids, among other things, have important metabolic actions, are essential for a normal response to stress, and have anti-inflammatory and antiallergic activity.

In 1856 Brown-Séquard demonstrated that rabbits died if their adrenal glands were removed. Subsequently, it was found that high sodium and low potassium diets could prevent death.

Mineralocorticoids. Aldosterone (Fig. 16–13) is the principal natural mineralocorticoid and is the most active substance known to promote sodium retention. It is secreted by the outer zone, or zona glomerulosa, of the cortex.

The daily rate of aldosterone secretion in humans varies from 70 to 200 micrograms on a normal salt diet, compared with the secretion of 25 mg of cortisol daily. The secretion of aldosterone can increase up to 900 micrograms per day in the face of severe sodium restriction. Aldosterone is an important link in the regulation of water and electrolyte metabolism. It increases the renal reabsorption (in the distal tubules and collecting ducts) of sodium and, consequently, the passive reabsorption of water (see Chapter 15, page 530). Deficiency in aldosterone secretion results in a marked reduction in plasma volume. Since reabsorption of sodium from the distal tubules and collecting ducts of the kidneys is accompanied by the secretion of potassium into these regions of the renal tubular system, high potassium levels in the blood are a consequence of insufficient aldosterone secretion. This has a toxic effect on the heart, causing weak contractions and arrhythmia. Aldosterone also exerts extrarenal effects on electrolyte metabolism, decreasing sodium and increasing potassium concentration in saliva and sweat.

An understanding of the role of sodium in the cause of edema has led to the use of agents to block the renal tubular activity of aldosterone.

Regulation of the secretion of aldosterone by the renin-angiotensin system was described in Chapter 15 (page 531). The secretion of aldosterone is also governed by slight changes in plasma potassium. An increase in potassium concentration of less than 1 mEq/liter will induce a pronounced increase in aldosterone secretion.

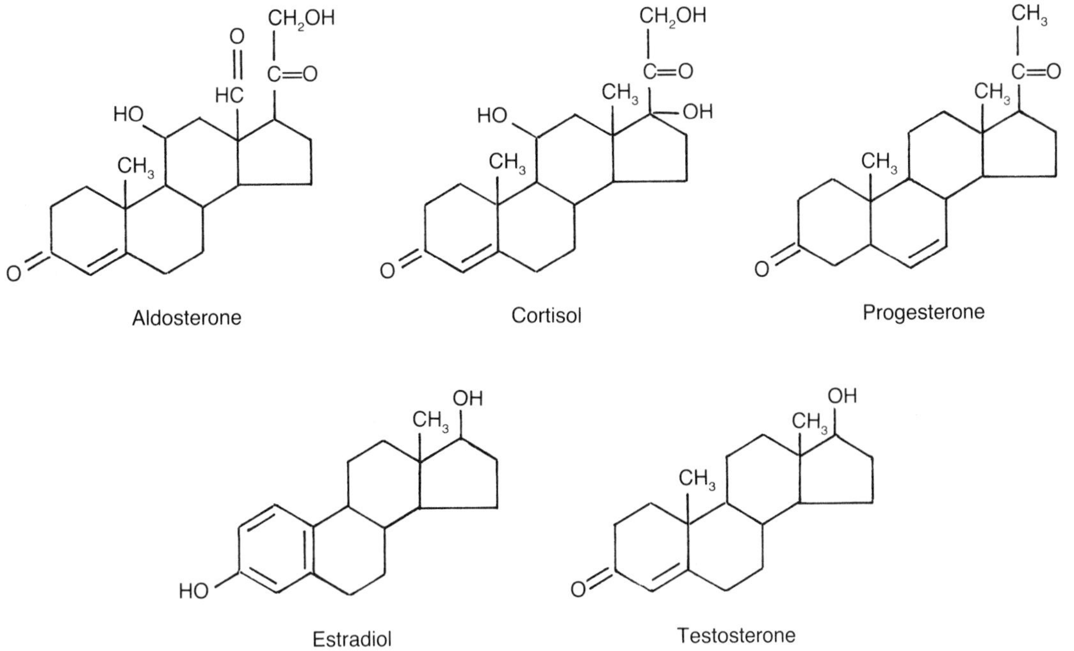

Figure 16–13. Major steroid hormones: aldosterone (mineralocorticoid) and cortisol (glucocorticoid), secreted by the adrenal cortex; progesterone, secreted by the corpus luteum and placenta; estradiol (estrogen), secreted by the ovarian follicles, corpus luteum, and placenta; testosterone (androgen), secreted by the testes. All are synthesized from cholesterol (see Figure 2–12 on page 38).

Glucocorticoids. Glucocorticoids influence the metabolism of glucose, protein, and fat. The term glucocorticoid refers to the action of these hormones in raising blood sugar. Cortisol is the principal glucocorticoid and is formed by the zona fasciculata and zona reticularis. Although there are several glucocorticoids secreted by the cortex, 90 per cent of the total activity is represented by cortisol.

Metabolic Actions of Glucocorticoids. Glucocorticoids decrease the cellular uptake and incorporation of amino acids into proteins in skeletal muscle and increase the uptake and utilization of amino acids in the liver. Since the catabolism of skeletal muscle protein, releasing amino acids, is not depressed (and according to some investigators is increased by glucocorticoids), the net effect is to increase the *mobilization of amino acids* from skeletal muscle to the liver. The most striking metabolic action of glucocorticoids in the liver is to increase *gluconeogenesis* (the synthesis of "new" glucose from such precursors as lactic acid, glycerol, and certain

amino acids). Amino acids are the major substrate for gluconeogenesis, and the combined actions of glucocorticoids — accelerating the mobilization of amino acids from skeletal muscle to the liver and increasing gluconeogenesis in the liver — greatly increase glucose production by the liver. Glucocorticoids apparently enhance gluconeogenesis by stimulating the synthesis of a number of enzymes required for this process. (Because the stimulatory effect of certain hormones, glucagon especially, epinephrine for another, cannot be expressed in the absence of glucocorticoids, it is sometimes stated that glucocorticoids have a "permissive action" on gluconeogenesis.) The effect of glucocorticoids on gluconeogenesis accounts, in part, for their tendency to raise the level of blood glucose. Glucocorticoids have another action that raises blood glucose — they decrease the uptake and oxidation of glucose by skeletal muscle cells.

Glucocorticoids increase the *mobilization of fatty acids* from the fat depots to active tissues. It appears they do this by augmenting the actions of a number of other hormones, including growth hormone, ACTH, and epinephrine, that accelerate the mobilization of fatty acids by increasing lipolysis (cleavage of triglycerides, forming fatty acids and glycerol) in adipose tissue.

Requirement of Glucocorticoids for a Normal Response to Stress. Stress of almost any kind, such as injury, burns, cold, pain, or fright, will cause an immediate, pronounced rise in ACTH blood levels, followed within minutes by an increase in the secretion of glucocorticoids. The ability of the body to cope normally with the stress depends upon glucocorticoid secretion. Why this is so is still not clear. It has been suggested that the requirement of glucocorticoids for the optimal actions of norepinephrine and epinephrine on arterioles and the heart (Chapter 11) is of importance in responding to stress. The muscular weakness and fatigue caused by glucocorticoid insufficiency may be partly accounted for by this action. Mobilization of fatty acids and amino acids may also have a role in dealing with stress. The amino acids can be utilized not only for gluconeogenesis but also for protein synthesis.

Anti-inflammatory and Antiallergic Effects of Glucocorticoids. Glucocorticoids in high concentrations have the following actions: (1) stabilization of lysosomal enzymes; (2) depression of the vasodilator action of histamine; (3) reduction of capillary permeability; (4) impairment of the migration of phagocytes; and (5) causing atrophy of lymphoid tissue and, in consequence, a reduction in the number of circulating lymphocytes and antibodies. Because of these actions, glucocorticoids are used to treat a number of diseases, such as rheumatoid arthritis, in which the damage is caused by the inflammatory reaction, as well as allergic disorders, such as hay fever, allergic dermatitis, and asthma, in which inflammation or other consequences of anaphylactic responses (see Chapter 12, page 440) have disturbing effects. In rheumatoid arthritis, stabilization of the lysosomal enzymes, thereby preventing the release of destructive enzymes, appears to be the major factor in alleviating the painful consequences of the disease. In some anaphylactic allergic responses, administration of cortisol has a life-saving effect by preventing death from shock. On the other hand, the anti-inflammatory and antiallergic actions of glucocorticoids can have harmful

consequences in individuals with hypersecreting suprarenal glands. Patients with Cushing's syndrome (see below), for example, are abnormally susceptible to infectious diseases and suffer from poor wound healing because of a depressed inflammatory response.

Effect of Glucocorticoids on Blood Cells. Glucocorticoids apparently play a permissive role in the production of red blood cells. Deficiency in glucocorticoids often results in anemia; hypersecretion of glucocorticoids usually causes polycythemia. High concentrations of glucocorticoids also cause a rapid destruction of eosinophils. Eosinopenia is one of the diagnostic features of excessive secretion of glucocorticoids.

Circadian Rhythm in Glucocorticoid Secretion. There is a daily rhythm in the secretion of glucocorticoids: plasma cortisol levels are at a peak in the early morning and at a low late in the evening. Such a rhythm is called circadian (from the Latin meaning approximately a day) because it normally coincides with the 24-hour light-dark cycle. The rhythm in the secretion of glucocorticoids is the result of a circadian rhythm in the secretion of ACTH.

Androgens. Androgens produce masculinization. The most important androgen is testosterone, which is secreted by the testes. Suprarenal androgens are of minor importance, except when excessive secretion by an androgen-producing tumor has an intense masculinizing effect. This can cause a child or even an adult female to take on an adult masculine appearance, including growth of the clitoris to resemble a penis, growth of a beard, deepening of the voice, and increased muscular strength.

Abnormalities of Suprarenal Cortex Function. *Addison's disease* (described by Thomas Addison, 1855), a relatively rare disorder most common in middle life, occurs equally in both sexes. Addison's disease is a deficiency of function of the suprarenal cortex, with insufficient production of both glucocorticoids and mineralocorticoids, resulting in an incapacity of the renal tubules to adequately reabsorb sodium, accompanied by retention of potassium, and in metabolic defects. The loss of sodium, and chloride along with it, results in the excretion of large volumes of water. The plasma volume is reduced, followed by a drop in blood pressure. (If aldosterone secretion ceases alto-

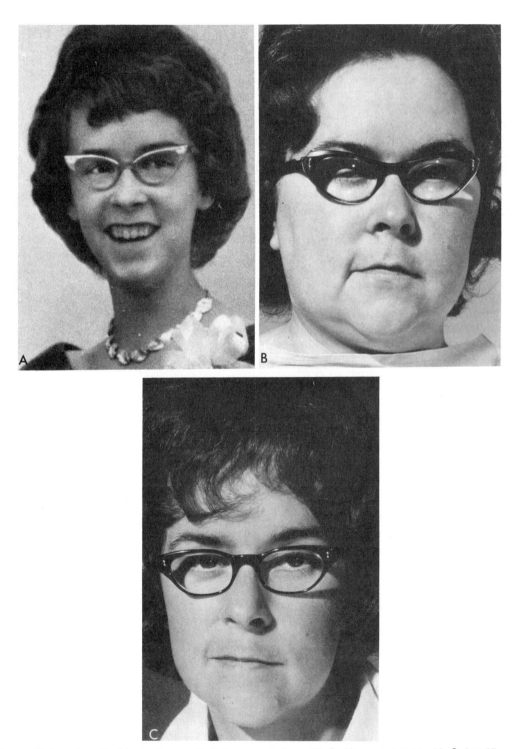

Figure 16–14. True Cushing's disease. *A,* Before onset at age 18. *B,* After onset at age 26. *C,* Age 27, one year after adrenalectomy.

gether, the patient will die in shock within 4 days to 2 weeks unless treated with mineralocorticoids or given salt therapy.)

Other characteristic symptoms of Addison's disease include slow heart rate, abnormal electrocardiogram, muscular weakness, hypoglycemia, and gastrointestinal disturbances. Pigmentation of the skin and mucosa is another diagnostic feature. The excessive melanin deposition is caused by a lack of suprarenal feedback to the hypophysis, with a resultant increased secretion of ACTH and melanocyte-stimulating hormone. The outlook for patients with this disease is favorable with adequate substitution of suprarenal cortical hormones.

Cushing's disease (first described by Harvey Cushing in 1932), a primary disorder of the adenohypophysis, involves excess production of ACTH with resulting suprarenal hyperfunction (Fig. 16–14). The adrenal cortex can, however, be hyperfunctional without stimulation from the adenohypophysis (as in suprarenal tumors). The term *Cushing's syndrome* is generally applied to the clinical signs characterizing both types of adrenocortical hyperfunction. Most of the abnormalities result from a chronic excess of cortisol; androgen excess accounts for others. The patient exhibits nitrogen loss; wasting of muscles and loss of strength; hyperglycemia; decreased fat in the limbs; and excess fat in the face ("moon face"), abdomen, buttocks, and shoulders ("buffalo torso"). In women, excess facial hair (hirsutism), acne, and menstrual abnormalities are frequent findings. Although the sodium-retaining effect of cortisol is low compared with aldosterone, it is sufficient (because of the high cortisol levels in these patients) to cause hypertension, which may be aggravated by cortisol's enhancement of the vasoconstricting action of epinephrine and norepinephrine. As a result of the stimulatory effect of glucocorticoids on the brain, mental aberrations may also occur, ranging from euphoria to depression. If the cause of Cushing's syndrome is a pathological condition of the adenohypophysis, treatment is aimed at reducing the overproduction of ACTH. In many patients, irradiation of the adenohypophysis is successful in returning the secretion of ACTH to normal. If the hypersecretion of ACTH cannot be readily corrected, a bilateral surgical adrenalectomy may be performed followed by steroid replacement therapy for the rest of the patient's life. When an adrenal tumor is respon-

sible for the syndrome, the only satisfactory treatment is surgical removal.

Suprarenal Medulla

Whereas the hormones of the cortex are steroids, those of the medulla, epinephrine and norepinephrine, belong to a class of compounds called *catecholamines*. They are formed from the amino acid tyrosine (Fig. 16–15). The medulla is composed of irregular masses of cells separated by sinusoidal-type

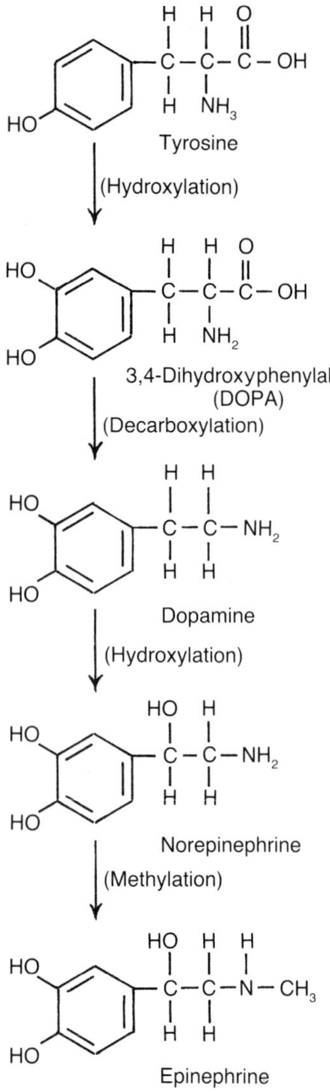

Figure 16–15. Steps in the synthesis of norepinephrine and epinephrine from tyrosine.

vessels. Adrenomedullary extracts are composed of both epinephrine and norepinephrine with constant proportions characteristic for a given species. The human medulla usually secretes four times as much epinephrine as norepinephrine.

The adrenal medulla is not essential for life, but functions in conjunction with the sympathetic nervous system to help the individual meet certain types of emergency situations. The hormones are released upon stimulation by preganglionic nerve endings, and their actions support and prolong sympathoadrenal responses. The major effects are cardiovascular and metabolic. The overall effect of the two hormones on the cardiovascular system is to increase the heart rate and force of ventricular contraction, constrict arterioles in the skin and abdominal region, and dilate arterioles in skeletal muscle. Norepinephrine acts principally as a vasoconstrictor; epinephrine is more potent as a stimulator of the heart. The metabolic effects of the hormones include stimulating the breakdown of glycogen in the liver and skeletal muscle and gluconeogenesis in the liver (actions of epinephrine principally), and mobilizing fatty acids from the fat depots. The release of glucose from the liver into the circulation causes a rise in blood sugar. Table 9–6, p. 295, lists the actions of the sympathetic nervous system. Essentially the same responses are brought about by the release of epinephrine and norepinephrine from the adrenal medulla.

PANCREATIC ISLETS

The pancreatic islets of Langerhans, constituting about 2 per cent of the glandular tissue, are scattered throughout the pancreas (Fig. 16–16). The islets secrete two polypeptide hormones, *insulin* and *glucagon*.

Structure of the Islets. The pancreatic islets of the human contain at least three cell types, *alpha*, *beta*, and *delta*, distinguished on the basis of histologic characteristics. Insulin is formed by the beta cells of the islets, and glucagon by the alpha cells. Recent studies suggest that the delta cells produce somatostatin, which, as mentioned earlier in this chapter (in the section describing hypothalamic hormones), has the property of inhibiting the secretion of glucagon and insulin. It has been proposed that somatostatin acts lo-

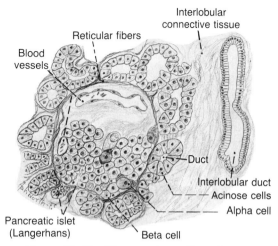

Figure 16–16. Microscopic section of pancreas showing a pancreatic islet (of Langerhans).

cally to suppress the secretory activity of the alpha and beta cells, but under what circumstances is a matter of conjecture.

Insulin

In 1889, von Mering and Minkowski removed the pancreas from a dog to see whether it would survive without pancreatic digestive juice. The dog developed glycosuria and other symptoms strikingly similar to human diabetes. Thus it was discovered that the pancreas has other than digestive functions. Sometime later it was observed that when a dog's pancreatic duct was ligated, the pancreas shriveled but the animal did not develop diabetes. Examination of the atrophied pancreas revealed that the acinar (exocrine) tissue degenerated (as a result of the accumulation of digestive enzymes) but the islets, for the most part, remained normal in appearance. Apparently the islet tissue secreted some substance that prevented diabetes. In 1921, Frederick Banting, a Canadian surgeon, reasoned that the many attempts to extract an antidiabetic hormone from fresh pancreas failed because the digestive enzymes destroyed it. He, therefore, in collaboration with a young graduate student named Charles Best, tied off the pancreatic ducts of a number of dogs and waited for the acinar tissue to atrophy. Best prepared an extract of the pancreas tissue, which they injected into depancreatized dogs. The extract lowered blood sugar and brought about recovery from

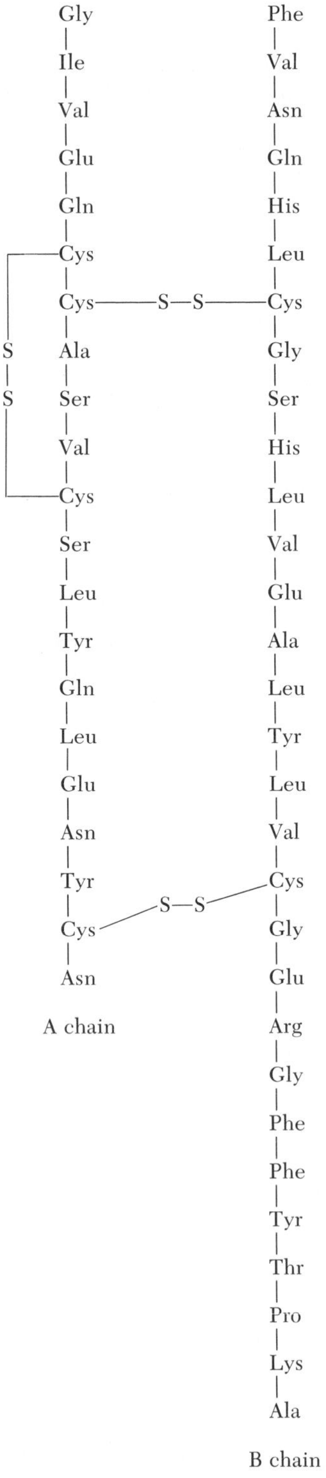

Gly
|
Ile
|
Val
|
Glu
|
Gln
|
Cys
|
Cys————S—S————Cys
|
Ala
|
Ser
|
Val
|
Cys
|
Ser
|
Leu
|
Tyr
|
Gln
|
Leu
|
Glu
|
Asn
|
Tyr
|
Cys
|
Asn

A chain

Phe
|
Val
|
Asn
|
Gln
|
His
|
Leu
|
Cys
|
Gly
|
Ser
|
His
|
Leu
|
Val
|
Glu
|
Ala
|
Leu
|
Tyr
|
Leu
|
Val
|
Cys
|
Gly
|
Glu
|
Arg
|
Gly
|
Phe
|
Phe
|
Tyr
|
Thr
|
Pro
|
Lys
|
Ala

B chain

Figure 16–17. The amino acid sequence of bovine insulin. It consists of two polypeptide chains — the A chain, with 21 amino acids, and the B chain, with 30 — crosslinked by two disulphide bridges. This was the first protein to have its amino acid sequence determined.

the diabetic state. Following this discovery, procedures were developed for preparing an active extract of pancreas from just-slaughtered cattle, using techniques that checked the action of the digestive enzymes. In January of 1922 Banting and Best successfully treated a 14-year-old boy who was terminally ill with diabetes with a bovine pancreatic hormonal preparation given the name insulin.

Insulin, it is now known, consists of 51 amino acids arranged in two polypeptide chains connected by two disulphide bridges. In the 1950's Sanger and colleagues determined the complete amino acid sequence of bovine insulin (Fig. 16–17).

The overall effect of insulin on intermediary metabolism is to (1) increase the utilization and decrease the production of glucose, (2) increase the storage and decrease the mobilization and oxidation of fatty acids, and (3) increase the formation of protein (increasing cellular uptake of amino acids and the synthesis of protein from amino acids).

One of the earliest observed actions of insulin is its enhancement of the uptake of glucose in many nonhepatic tissues, especially skeletal muscle and adipose tissue. In skeletal muscle, when high levels of insulin and glucose promote the rapid influx of glucose into the cells, increased amounts of glucose are utilized for glycogen synthesis and oxidation to carbon dioxide and water. (Growth hormone and glucocorticoids inhibit the uptake and oxidation of glucose in skeletal muscle, thus opposing the effect of insulin.)

In adipose tissue high levels of insulin and glucose result in a rapid conversion of glucose to fatty acids and the esterification of fatty acids to triglycerides. During the absorption of a meal, the levels of insulin, glucose, and chylomicron triglycerides are high, creating optimal conditions for triglyceride synthesis in adipose tissue: insulin increases the activity in adipose tissue of lipoprotein lipase (an enzyme that acts at the capillary endothelium to hydrolyze triglycerides of chylomicrons and very low density lipoproteins — see Chapter 14), promoting the uptake of plasma triglyceride fatty acids, and there is an abundance of α-glycerophosphate derived from glucose (glucose is the only source of α-glycerophosphate in adipose tissue, since the cells cannot phosphorylate glycerol), which combines with the fatty acids released from plasma triglycerides or synthesized from glucose. At the same time, insulin inhibits lipolysis (the cleavage of triglycerides, releasing fatty acids) in adipose tissue cells by its antagonistic effect on several other hormones that increase lipolysis. The lipolytic action of a number of hormones, including epinephrine, ACTH, TSH, and glucagon, is mediated by cyclic AMP — these hormones increase the activity of adenylate cyclase, the enzyme that converts ATP to cyclic AMP, which acts as a "second messenger" (see page 543). Insulin apparently opposes this effect by decreasing the level of cyclic AMP, possibly by increasing the activity of an enzyme (phosphodiesterase) that degrades cyclic AMP. As mentioned earlier, growth hormone and glucocorticoids increase lipolysis in adipose tissue, hence opposing the action of insulin. Growth hormone also increases the production of cyclic AMP, but slowly, apparently by stimulating new enzyme formation.

Insulin inhibits the production of glucose in the liver by opposing the stimulatory actions of glucagon and epinephrine on glycogenolysis (the breakdown of glycogen) and gluconeogenesis ("new" glucose synthesis, mainly from amino acids). The level of cyclic AMP is raised by glucagon and epinephrine and lowered by insulin. Insulin also diminishes the supply of substrates for gluconeogenesis from other tissues — amino acids from skeletal muscle (where insulin promotes amino acid uptake and protein synthesis) and glycerol from adipose tissue (where insulin reduces the release of glycerol by lipolysis). It was noted earlier that glucocorticoids increase gluconeogenesis by stimulating the synthesis of gluconeogenic enzymes; thus here again, the actions of insulin and glucocorticoids are opposite.

Since cyclic AMP inhibits glycogen synthesis, insulin, by lowering the concentration of cyclic AMP, increases glycogen synthesis. Other actions of insulin in the liver include increasing the oxidation of glucose and its conversion to fatty acids.

The primary regulator of insulin secretion is the level of blood glucose. At the fasting level, secretion is at a minimum, and secretion increases in response to a rise in blood sugar. Amino acids and three gastrointestinal hormones, gastrin, secretin, and cholecystokinin-pancreozymin, also increase insulin secretion. After eating a meal, the blood level of insulin is high as a result of the release of the gastrointestinal hormones into the blood and the absorption of glucose and amino acids. As a consequence of the elevated levels of insulin, glucose, and amino acids, the depleted stores of glycogen (in the liver especially) and protein (principally in skeletal muscle) are replaced. In addition, adipose tissue fat stores are replenished. The production of glucose in the liver and lipolysis in adipose tissue are inhibited. The oxidation of glucose is stimulated, and during this period glucose is utilized almost exclusively for energy.

In the postabsorptive period the blood level of insulin drops. In the liver, as a result of the reduction in the restraining influence of insulin, the stimulating effect of glucagon and epinephrine on glycogenolysis and (with the permissive action of glucocorticoids) on gluconeogenesis predominates, and the production of glucose rises. The greater part of the glucose produced is derived from gluconeogenesis, with amino acids from the breakdown of skeletal muscle providing the chief substrate for the glucose synthesis (when insulin levels are low, there is a net release of amino acids from skeletal muscle). Glucose uptake by muscle and adipose tissue is reduced. The brain, which does not require insulin for any of its metabolic functions, is the major consumer of the blood glucose. Lipolysis in adipose tissue increases and fatty acids are mobilized from fat depots. With the exception of the brain, the active tissues utilize fatty acids as the major source of energy in the postabsorptive period.

When insulin is lacking, as in severe **diabetes mellitus** (G. *diabainein,* to pass through; L. *mellitus,* of honey), the uptake of glucose by muscle and adipose tissue is depressed, glucose production in the liver is unrestrained (amino acids released from skeletal muscle providing a steady source of substrate for gluconeogenesis), and fatty acids are rapidly mobilized from the depots. The liver, incapable of oxidizing to carbon dioxide the amount of fatty acids it receives (or get rid of the excess as very low density lipoproteins — see Chapter 14), produces large amounts of acetoacetic acid and other ketone bodies (β-hydroxybutyric acid, enzymatically derived from acetoacetic acid and comprising about 70 per cent of the ketone bodies, and acetone, apparently arising by spontaneous decarboxylation of acetoacetic acid). These ketone bodies accumulate in the blood stream, a condition called *ketosis*, and, since acetoacetic acid and β-hydroxybutyric acid are moderately strong acids, a state of *acidosis* develops. Diabetics also have elevated levels of plasma very low density lipoproteins.

If the condition is untreated, glucose levels will rise to values as high as 400 to 800 mg per 100 ml of blood. The extreme *hyperglycemia* leads to pronounced *glycosuria* and excretion of large volumes of water *(polyuria)* accompanying the glucose (osmotic diuresis). The patient also exhibits dehydration, polydipsia (excessive thirst), polyphagia (increased eating), weight loss, and wasting of muscles. The acidosis stimulates deep, rapid breathing (Kussmaul breathing). The usual terminal sequence is severe dehydration, decreased plasma volume, peripheral circulatory failure, coma, and death (see description of hypertonic dehydration in Chapter 17, page 577).

It should be apparent that the symptoms expressed by a lack of insulin are a consequence of an imbalance between the metabolic actions of insulin and the opposing actions of several other hormones. In 1931, long before the hormonal interrelations described above were recognized, Houssay and Biasotti demonstrated that removal of the hypophysis from a depancreatized dog (so-called *Houssay animal*) caused a marked amelioration of the symptoms of diabetes, a phenomenon that can be accounted for in large part by a loss of growth hormone and ACTH and a greatly reduced secretion of glucocorticoids. This discovery stimulated the worldwide investigations that led to an appreciation of the integrated action of insulin and antagonistic hormones in metabolic regulation.

Distinction Between Juvenile-Onset and Maturity-Onset Diabetes. Diabetes resulting from an insufficient secretion of insulin, known as juvenile-onset diabetes, can be distinguished from another form of the disease called maturity-onset diabetes. In maturity-onset diabetes the blood levels of insulin are generally normal or above normal. Juvenile-onset diabetes begins abruptly (hence also called acute-onset diabetes), most often in young people, and the entire range of symptoms usually appears immediately. Insulin treatment is essential. Maturity-onset diabetes, on the other hand, starts slowly, generally in older people, and the symptoms are milder. This form can usually be treated by dietary regulation.

The defect in maturity-onset diabetes has been described as a reduced sensitivity to the effects of insulin, a phenomenon generally called *insulin resistance*. It has been observed that monocytes from individuals with maturity-onset diabetes bind about 50 per cent as much insulin as monocytes from healthy individuals and that these cells have a lower than normal number of *insulin-binding receptors*. Similar observations have been made with human erythrocytes. Since the major effects of insulin are apparently initiated by the binding of the hormone to receptor sites on the cell surface, a deficiency in insulin binding could be responsible for the diabetic condition.

In both forms of diabetes, especially the maturity-onset form, individuals have an inherited predisposition to the development of the disease. A number of epidemiological and animal studies have suggested that the juvenile-onset form is initiated by certain types of viral infections (including mumps and German measles) and that the development of the disease is dependent upon a genetic susceptibility to pancreatic damage resulting from these infections. In 1978 a direct link was established between juvenile-onset diabetes and a viral infection: a Coxsackie virus isolated by cell culture technique from the pancreas of a child who developed severe diabetes after the onset of an influenzalike illness and died shortly thereafter induced diabetes upon injection into a susceptible strain of mice.

Complications of Long-Standing Diabetes. Although successful treatment of the primary metabolic derangements of diabetes has greatly prolonged the life of diabetics, major complications arise in individuals who have had the disease for a long period of time. Many investigators believe that these complications, which include damage to the retina of the eye, renal failure, cataracts, disturbances in peripheral nerve function, and poor peripheral circulation, which may lead to gangrene, are a consequence of imperfect control of blood glucose. Chemical changes involving glucose itself may be responsible for the abnormalities. It has been observed, for example, that *cataract formation* in the lenses of diabetic rats is associated with the accumulation of sorbitol in lens cells. Sorbitol is enzymatically formed in lens cells when the concentration of glucose is high. It is very slowly metabolized and does not leak out of cells. The accumulation of sorbitol increases the osmotic pressure in the cells; this draws in water, causing swelling and disruption of lens fibers. Cataract formation in diabetic rats can be prevented with drugs that inhibit aldose reductase, the enzyme that converts glucose to sorbitol. Studies with diabetic rats also suggest that sorbitol accumulation may contribute to the deterioration of the myelin sheaths of peripheral nerve fibers.

Diabetic retinopathy is the leading cause of blindness in this country among individuals between the ages of 20 and 46. This condition results from the destruction of tiny blood vessels in the eye. In the more severe form, known as proliferative retinopathy, new blood vessels grow on the surface of the retina and protrude into the vitreous humor. These vessels eventually rupture and bleed into the vitreous humor. Finally, scar tissue forms in association with the new vessels, which may pull on the retina, detaching it from the choroid. The chance of becoming blind from proliferative retinopathy can be reduced by a treatment called photocoagulation, in which intense bursts of light from a xenon arc lamp or argon laser fuse and destroy new blood vessels.

Damage to small blood vessels in diabetics also contributes to poor peripheral circulation and to changes in kidney glomeruli that can cause renal failure. A characteristic feature of blood vessel damage is a thickening of the basement membrane. Some investigators believe that the underlying cause of this change is excessive nonenzymatic attachment of glucose to membrane proteins, altering their configurations (nonenzymatic binding of glucose to proteins is a normal process but is assumed to cause tissue damage when excessive).

The belief that controlling blood glucose more precisely will delay or prevent the long-term complications of diabetes has stimulated research on artificial pancreases which will automatically inject insulin in response to fluctuations in the patient's blood glucose. One approach is the development of a system consisting of a sensor of blood glucose concentration, a minicomputer that determines the amount of insulin (or, sometimes, glucose) to be administered, and a pump that delivers insulin or glucose into the blood stream.

Glucagon

Glucagon, the specific hormone produced by the pancreatic islets in the alpha cells, is a straight-chain polypeptide consisting of 29 amino acids. Measurable amounts of glucagon are present in circulating blood. The blood level of glucagon rises in response to *hypoglycemia*. The actions of glucagon have been described in the foregoing discussion of insulin. Glucagon, it has been noted, increases gluconeogenesis and glycogenolysis in the liver and lipolysis in adipose tissue.

OVARIES

The ovaries are two small glands located in the pelvic portion of the female abdomen and attached to the broad ligament. The outer layer of the ovaries consists of a specialized epithelium which produces the ova. Two types of hormones are secreted by the ovaries, estrogens and progesterone (see Chapter 18, page 618, for a description of their actions).

TESTES

The testes are two small, ovoid glands suspended from the inguinal regions by the spermatic cords and surrounded and supported by the scrotum. Two major types of specialized tissue are found in testicular substance—tubules containing germinal epithelium functioning in the formation of spermatozoa and interstitial cells of Leydig producing testosterone. (The functions of testosterone are described in Chapter 18, page 616).

PINEAL GLAND

The human pineal gland is a small, conical organ, gray in color, lying at about the middle of the brain. It is attached anteriorly to the posterior wall of the third ventricle by the pineal stalk, located above the superior colliculi of the midbrain. The pineal is less than 1 cm in its longest diameter and weighs approximately 0.1 to 0.2 gram. It is not a functionless vestige, as had been previously believed. It synthesizes melatonin, a hormone that exerts inhibitory effects on the gonads. Prepubertal tumors associated with increased pineal secretion delay sexual development. Reduced pineal function causes precocious puberty. Recent evidence suggests that melatonin may act on the hypothalamus and adenohypophysis to modify the synthesis of gonadotropins and other adenohypophyseal hormones.

In a number of species, including humans, secretion of melatonin by the pineal gland follows a daily (circadian) rhythm, reaching a peak at night and a low in the daytime. In rats, the activity of the enzyme N-acetyltransferase, which is involved in the synthesis of melatonin from serotonin, also displays a circadian rhythm (the peak at night 30 to 50 times higher than the daytime low). In rats kept in constant darkness, the rhythm of enzyme activity "runs free" for a period slightly longer than 24 hours. The suprachiasmatic nucleus of the hypothalamus has been implicated as the central regulator of this enzyme activity, and environmental lighting can affect the oscillatory mechanism via the retinohypothalamic tract, which terminates in the suprachiasmatic nucleus. In the rat, the pineal gland is extensively innervated by sympathetic nerve fibers (with cell bodies in the superior cervical ganglia). Norepinephrine released at these endings increases N-acetyltransferase activity and melatonin synthesis; during the night, more norephinephrine is released than during the day. The norepinephrine rhythm, in turn, sets the rhythm for the enzyme activity — interruption of sympathetic innervation abolishes the enzyme rhythm and enzyme activity remains at its low, daytime level. Continuous exposure of rats to light also eliminates the rhythm. As a consequence, the ovaries increase in weight and the estrus cycle is accelerated.

PLACENTA

The placenta has been recognized as an endocrine organ since the earliest days of this century, when it was noted that the ovaries of pregnant women could be removed after 3 or 4 months of gestation without terminating pregnancy. Human chorionic gonadotropin (HCG), estrogens, progesterone, and human placental lactogen (HPL) are secreted by the placenta.

Production of human chorionic gonadotropin begins when implantation occurs, and reaches a peak at about the ninth week of gestation. The hormone keeps the corpus luteum of the ovary intact and secreting progesterone and estrogens which, if stopped, would cause termination of pregnancy as a result of the loss of support for the uterine endometrium. The life span of the corpus luteum is about 10 weeks, at which time progesterone and estrogen secretion by the placenta is sufficient to maintain pregnancy.

Placental secretion of progesterone and estrogens increases during the course of pregnancy, reaching a high peak just before birth. The high levels of estrogens during pregnancy cause growth of the muscles of the uterus, increased vascular supply to the uterus, growth of the breasts, and enlargement of the external sex organs and vaginal opening (in preparation for birth). Progesterone promotes the development of the decidua of the uterus, which not only is essential for implantation of the fertilized ovum, but also plays a role in supplying nutrition to the young embryo. Progesterone also contributes to breast growth and decreases the contractility of the uterine musculature, allowing expansion for growth of the fetus and preventing spontaneous abortion.

Secretion of human placental lactogen begins about the fifth week of pregnancy. The hormone has prolactin activity and appears to induce a number of metabolic changes, including accelerated lipolysis, decreased glucose uptake, and increased gluconeogenesis.

Hormone-Producing Tumors of Nonendocrine Origin

Since all cells are capable of synthesizing proteins, it is not surprising that cancers have been found which secrete hormones indistinguishable from pituitary hormones. For example, oat cell carcinomas of the lung frequently produce ACTH. In turn, Cushing's syndrome results from ACTH stimulation of the suprarenal glands. Nearly all of the hormones of the pituitary gland have now been linked with cancers of various organs.

SUMMARY

THE ENDOCRINE SYSTEM

General Functions

Endocrine glands directly release into the blood stream substances called hormones that have a regulatory effect on cellular processes in other parts of the body. Hormones may act upon the cells of specific organs, called target organs, or upon cells widely distributed throughout the body.

Mechanisms of Hormone Action

1. *Via a "second messenger":* Many hormones classified as proteins, peptides, or amino acid derivatives activate an enzyme (adenylate cyclase) in the cell membrane that converts cytoplasmic ATP to cyclic AMP. Cyclic AMP, acting as a second messenger, induces a change in some cellular process.

2. *Gene activation:* Steroid hormones (adrenal cortical hormones and male and female sex hormones) bind a cytoplasmic receptor protein, which migrates into the nucleus and induces gene transcription, leading to the synthesis of proteins, most of which function as enzymes.

Hypothalamus

1. Secretes hormones, known as releasing and release-inhibiting hormones or factors, which control the secretion of the hormones of the adenohypophysis.

2. Synthesizes the hormones of the neurohypophysis, ADH, and oxytocin. These hormones, manufactured in neuronal cell bodies in the hypothalamus, are transported along axons to the neurohypophysis. Release of these hormones from the neurohypophysis is governed by nerve impulses from the hypothalamus.

3. Controls the secretion of epinephrine and norepinephrine by the adrenal medulla via direct nerve pathways.

Hormones of the Neurohypophysis

1. **ADH:** Increases the permeability of the collecting ducts and distal convoluted tubules of the kidneys to water. In high concentration, constricts arterioles.

2. **Oxytocin:** Stimulates the release of milk from the mammary glands. Stimulates contraction of the uterus at the time of childbirth.

Hormones of the Adenohypophysis

1. *Thyroid-stimulating hormone:* Stimulates thyroid growth and synthesis and secretion of thyroxine and T_3.

2. *Adrenocorticotropic hormone:* Stimulates growth of middle and inner layers of adrenal cortex and hormonal production and secretion by these layers (cortisol chiefly).

3. *Follicle-stimulating hormone:* Stimulates development of ovarian follicles in females and spermatogenesis in males.

4. *Luteinizing hormone:* Triggers ovulation. In males (also called interstitial cell-stimulating hormone) stimulates production and secretion of testosterone.

5. *Prolactin:* Contributes to the development of the mammary glands and stimulates milk synthesis.

6. Growth hormone

   a. Accelerates growth, increasing the size of all organs.

   b. Increases proliferation of cartilage cells at the growth plate of long bones.

   c. Increases amino acid uptake and protein synthesis by body cells generally.

   d. Increases blood glucose by decreasing glucose uptake and oxidation in skeletal and heart muscle particularly.

   e. Increases mobilization of fatty acids from the fat depots.

Hormones of the Thyroid Gland

1. *Thyroxine* (T_4) and *triiodothyronine* (T_3)

   a. Raise BMR.

   b. Exert anabolic action on protein metabolism during growth and a permissive action on the effects of growth hormone on tissue growth. Catabolic effect on protein metabolism predominates in hyperthyroid adults.

   c. Required for normal development of the central nervous system.

   d. Accelerate all phases of glucose metabolism, including absorption from the small intestine, uptake by tissue cells, and oxidation.

  e. Increase mobilization and oxidation of fatty acids and the catabolism of cholesterol.

  f. Abnormalities
    (1) Hypothyroidism: myxedema (adults), cretinism (infants).
    (2) Hyperthyroidism: Graves' disease.

2. *Calcitonin:* Lowers blood calcium by inhibiting bone resorption; secreted in response to high blood calcium.

Parathyroid Hormone

1. Raises blood calcium principally by increasing bone resorption; secreted in response to low blood calcium.

2. Deficiency of hormone causes tetany.

Major Hormones of the Adrenal Cortex

1. *Aldosterone* (principal mineralocorticoid): Regulates fluid and electrolyte balance by increasing the reabsorption of sodium by the kidney tubules.

2. *Cortisol* (principal glucocorticoid)

  a. Increases mobilization of amino acids from skeletal muscle to the liver.
  b. Increases gluconeogenesis in the liver.
  c. Decreases uptake and oxidation of glucose by skeletal muscle.
  d. Increases mobilization of fatty acids from fat depots.
  e. Required for a normal response to stress.
  f. Exerts anti-inflammatory and antiallergic actions.
  g. Abnormalities
    (1) Hyposecretion: Addison's disease.
    (2) Hypersecretion: Cushing's syndrome.

Hormones of the Adrenal Medulla

Epinephrine and norepinephrine: Function in conjunction with sympathetic nervous system (preganglionic sympathetic nerve fibers innervate adrenal medulla) in certain types of emergency situations.

Hormones of Pancreatic Islets

1. *Insulin*

  a. Increases glucose uptake by skeletal muscle and its utilization for oxidation and glycogen synthesis.
  b. Increases glucose uptake by adipose tissue and triglyceride synthesis.
  c. Inhibits lipolysis in adipose tissue.
  d. Increases utilization of glucose in the liver, stimulating oxidation, glycogen synthesis, and conversion to fatty acids.
  e. Reduces production of glucose in the liver by inhibiting gluconeogenesis and glycogenolysis.
  f. Increases cellular uptake of amino acids and protein synthesis.
  g. Diabetes
    (1) Juvenile-onset: insulin insufficiency.
    (2) Maturity-onset: insulin resistance (possibly result of reduced number of insulin-binding receptors).

2. *Glucagon*

  a. Increases gluconeogenesis and glycogenolysis in the liver.
  b. Increases lipolysis in adipose tissue.

Hormone of Pineal Gland

Melatonin: **Exerts inhibitory effect on endocrine functions of gonads.**

Hormones of the Placenta

1. *Human chorionic gonadotropin:* Maintains corpus luteum of the ovary.

2. *Estrogens* and *progesterone:* See Chapter 18.

REVIEW QUESTIONS

  1. What class of hormones binds to a receptor protein in the cytoplasm after entering the cell? What happens after the hormone binds to the receptor?
  2. What substance functions as a "second messenger" for hormone action? How is it formed? To what group do the hormones belong that act via this second messenger?
  3. Where are the releasing and release-inhibiting hormones or factors synthesized? How do they reach their destinations and what are their actions?
  4. Name and list the principal actions of the hormones of the neurohypophysis and

adenohypophysis. Where are the hormones of the neurohypophysis synthesized and how do they reach the neurohypophysis?

5. What are the actions of glucagon, epinephrine, and insulin on glycogenolysis and gluconeogenesis in the liver?

6. What is the action of insulin on the uptake of glucose by skeletal muscle and adipose tissue?

7. What are the actions of epinephrine, ACTH, glucagon, growth hormone, glu-cocorticoids, and insulin on lipolysis in adipose tissue?

8. What are the actions of glucocorticoids and insulin on the mobilization of amino acids from skeletal muscle to the liver?

9. Distinguish between juvenile-onset and maturity-onset diabetes.

10. Name the hormones that are hypersecreted and those that are hyposecreted in the following endocrine disorders: Myxedema, Graves' disease, Addison's disease, Cushing's syndrome.

17

Fluids and Electrolytes

Objectives

The aim of this chapter is to enable the student to:

☐ Identify the two major factors controlling distribution of water between the vascular and interstitial compartments of the extracellular fluid.

☐ Describe the pathways of exchange of water between the body and the external environment, and the control mechanisms involved.

☐ Differentiate and describe the three types of hypertonic dehydration.

☐ Define the state of water excess, or intoxication, indicating its symptoms and possible etiology.

☐ Distinguish between the various types of edema.

☐ Discuss the treatment of burns in stages and relative to degree and scope.

☐ Explain the mechanisms of potassium, magnesium, phosphate, and chloride balance.

☐ Identify and explain the actions of the major buffer systems.

☐ Differentiate between respiratory and metabolic acidosis and alkalosis in terms of etiology, symptoms, and treatment.

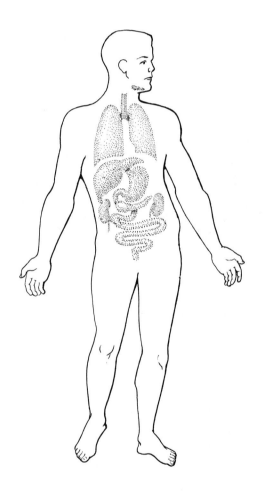

INTRODUCTION

The nineteenth century physiologist Claude Bernard first advanced the concept that there exists within higher organisms a purposeful tendency toward the constancy of the internal fluid environment of the body.

After Bernard, understanding of the role of body electrolytes increased only slowly. More recently, practical methods for the exact analysis of electrolytes in body fluids and radioisotope techniques for determining the volume of the different types of body fluids have been associated with a markedly increased knowledge.

Body fluids have been "compartmentalized" by physiologists to help define their distribution. Fluids are in the *extracellular space* (outside cell membranes) or in the *intracellular space* (within cell membranes). The extracellular space is further divided into a *vascular*, or *plasma*, *compartment* (within blood vessels) and an *interstitial compartment* (between cells) (Fig. 17–1).

What percentage, then, by weight of an animal is represented by water? An early human embryo is 97 per cent water; a newborn infant, 77 per cent water. Water constitutes 60 to 70 per cent of the weight of an adult male and slightly less of an adult female. Since fat is essentially free of water, the less fat present, the greater the percentage of body weight due to water.

Body water diffuses throughout the body without recognizing anatomic boundaries. For instance, water passes in a continuous manner across the connective tissue surface of the capillaries. If all the water molecules

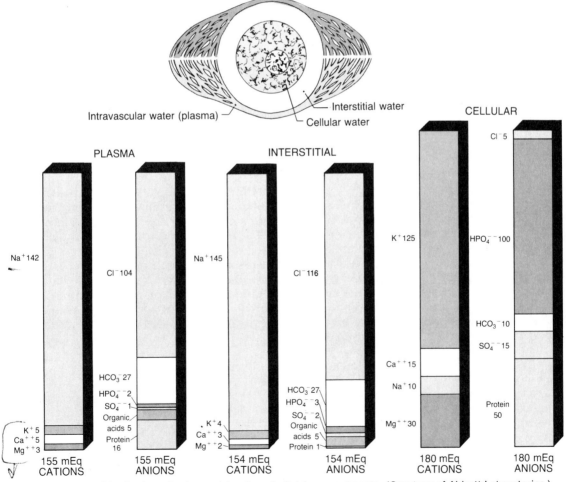

Figure 17–1. Distribution of anions and cations in fluid compartments. (Courtesy of Abbott Laboratories.)

in the blood were suddenly labeled, perhaps only one-half of the labeled molecules would be present in the blood 1 minute later.

Distribution and Movement of Water. In the human body about 60 to 70 per cent of the lean body weight is water; some three-quarters of this is contained within the cells, while the remaining quarter is in the extracellular fluid. The extracellular fluid is divided into two compartments, the interstitial fluid lying between the cells and outside the vascular system, and the plasma and lymph water moving within the vascular and lymphatic systems. The interstitial compartment contains about three-fourths of the extracellular fluid.

The distribution of water between the cell and the internal environment of the body is controlled by the effective osmotic pressure across the cell membrane, which in turn depends primarily on the relative concentrations of sodium and potassium between the cell and the extracellular fluid. The cell membrane is relatively impermeable to sodium and the cell actively transports this cation out of the cell so as to maintain its internal concentration at a very low level. Potassium moves into the cell to maintain an electrochemical equilibrium, and as a result reaches a high concentration within the cell. Negatively charged ions (anions) balance these positively charged ions (cations) inside and outside the cell. The anions within the cell are primarily phosphate and protein; those outside are primarily chloride and bicarbonate.

If the concentration of water in the extracellular fluid increases, the concentration of sodium falls, and there is a net movement of water into the cells. If the concentration of water in the extracellular fluid decreases, the concentration of sodium increases and there is a net movement of water out of the cells. The effective osmotic pressure across the cell membrane can be temporarily altered or reversed in certain abnormal or disease situations that produce unusually high concentrations of glucose, urea, or other substances in the extracellular fluids.

Two main factors control the distribution of water between the vascular and interstitial compartments of the extracellular fluid — the effective osmotic pressure across the capillary membrane and the hydrostatic pressure of the blood in the capillary. Because of the different permeability characteristics of the capillary membrane, the solute that creates the effective osmotic pressure is the concentration of plasma proteins in the vascular fluid (plasma), a concentration which is much greater than that in the interstitial fluid (7 gm per 100 ml vs. 1 gm per 100 ml). In other words, the concentration of water is greater in the interstitial fluid than in the plasma, causing water to diffuse from the interstitial fluid into the vascular fluid of the capillary. This general osmotic tendency is opposed by the greater hydrostatic pressure in the capillary, which produces a net flow of water out of the capillary into the interstitial fluid. More specifically, there is an outflow of fluid from the arterial end of the capillary and an inflow in the venous end, so that there is a constant circulation of water and the substances dissolved in it between the fluids surrounding the cells and the blood. However, the system is not perfectly balanced — more fluid is filtered from the capillaries than is returned. Lost fluid, along with protein that leaks out of the capillaries, is returned to the blood stream by the lymphatic circulation.

Exchanges of Water with the External Environment

Water is taken into the body through the mouth and absorbed from the gastrointestinal tract. It is lost from the body to the external environment through the skin, respiratory tract, kidneys and, to a slight extent, the gastrointestinal tract. Generally speaking, the most important variable controlling the total water content of the body is water intake, being adjusted or controlled to balance whatever is lost. The most important exception is a mechanism which permits the body to reduce the loss of water through the kidneys to a minimum when a deficit occurs and environmental water is not readily available for ingestion (Fig. 17–2).

Water Loss

Water lost through the respiratory tract and skin is not under any direct control related to the content of water in the body. Loss of water from the respiratory tract is a consequence of the moist nature of the membranes of the tract. Water naturally evaporates from them to the inhaled dry (drier) air

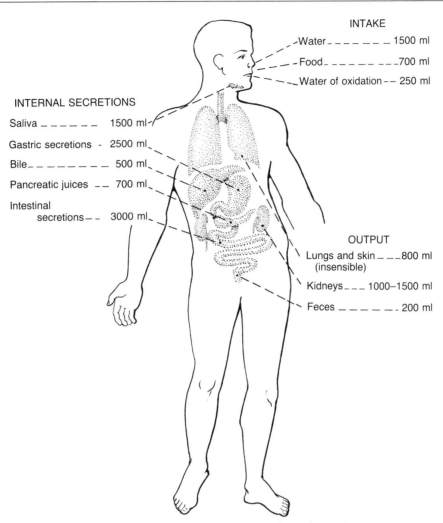

INTAKE
Water _ _ _ _ _ _ _ 1500 ml
Food _ _ _ _ _ _ _ 700 ml
Water of oxidation _ _ 250 ml

INTERNAL SECRETIONS
Saliva _ _ _ _ _ _ 1500 ml
Gastric secretions - 2500 ml
Bile _ _ _ _ _ _ _ 500 ml
Pancreatic juices _ _ 700 ml
Intestinal
secretions _ _ 3000 ml

OUTPUT
Lungs and skin _ _ _ 800 ml
(insensible)
Kidneys _ _ _ 1000–1500 ml
Feces _ _ _ _ _ _ 200 ml

Figure 17–2. Balance between intake and output.

and is exhaled and lost to the body. The rate of loss varies directly with the dryness and temperature of the inspired air and the depth and rate of ventilation. Rate of ventilation varies directly with the production of carbon dioxide and this, in turn, is proportional to the metabolic rate. Thus, an increased water loss from respiratory evaporation aids in the loss of heat produced by increased metabolism. It is important to note here that in this mechanism the control of water loss is sacrificed to the control of exchanges of carbon dioxide and heat, which have even greater priority in the homeothermic animal.

Likewise, no direct control system operates to govern loss of water from the skin. In humans, there is constant diffusion of water through the skin which, under normal conditions, immediately evaporates. In response to an increase in body temperature, central control mechanisms cause a marked increase in the secretion of sweat, enhancing the evaporative loss of heat. The loss of water by this route may reach dramatic proportions in humans (e.g., 2 liters per hour). This is another example of the priority of body temperature regulation over that of body water.

Sweat contains about one-half the concentration of sodium present in the extracellular fluid (although it approaches isotonicity with the body fluids as the rate of sweating increases), so that a loss of sweat tends to increase the concentration of sodium in the internal environment. Loss of water from the respiratory tract has an even greater tendency, per volume of water lost, to increase internal sodium concentration, since pure water is lost by this route. However, because of the loss of sodium in sweating it is necessary to ingest salt (NaCl) when replacing this water; otherwise the extracellular fluid becomes hypotonic, which produces various uncomfortable and potentially dangerous effects.

When solid foods or hypertonic solutions are ingested, water moves into the lumen of the upper gastrointestinal tract because of the effective osmotic gradient between the internal environment and the contents of the lumen. This movement continues until the contents of the lumen are isotonic with the fluids of the body and results in a temporary dehydration of the internal environment and the cells. This water is later reabsorbed from the lower tract through a reversal of the osmotic forces as the foodstuffs and salts are absorbed. Only a very small portion of this water is lost in the feces.

Some substances which cannot be absorbed (e.g., the osmotic cathartics such as magnesium sulfate) create a continuing osmotic pressure in the tract, leading to retention of water and its loss in the stool. Vomiting and diarrhea can result in sizable losses of fluid from the body. Even though this lost fluid is isotonic with the fluids of the body, it differs significantly in specific composition from the extracellular fluid owing to the selective secretion of ions in different parts of the tract. Vomiting results in a greater loss of hydrogen than sodium, whereas diarrhea usually results in a greater loss of potassium than sodium ions.

The kidneys excrete water both as a vehicle for other materials and as "free" water. They are the only organs in the body that function to adjust water loss so as to balance water intake. The excretion of free water is influenced by feedback mechanisms that can appreciate both the concentration and volume of water in the extracellular fluids. Aldosterone, a hormone of the adrenal cortex, and ADH, a hormone of the neurohypophysis, are involved in this process. The actions and regulation of the secretion of these hormones have been described in Chapters 15 and 16.

It is important to remember that the movement of water in and out of the kidney tubules is always caused by osmotic forces. Thus, if there is a solute in the tubular urine that cannot be reabsorbed or if the quantity of solutes in the urine exceeds the maximum rate of reabsorption that the tubular cells can achieve for those solutes, the substances will remain in the lumen and create an effective osmotic pressure that will retain water and thus increase the urine flow and water loss to the body. An example of such an effect is the osmotic diuresis caused by intravenous infusion of mannitol or inulin, whose molecules are small enough to pass the glomerular filter but are too large to be reabsorbed from the tubule. As a result, these substances cause water retention in the tubule and marked diuresis.

The feedback control systems of the kidneys can go only so far in maintaining homeostasis of the internal environment. The uncontrollable loss of water through the lungs and skin continues, and the kidneys themselves are always obliged to excrete sufficient water to meet the minimum osmotic requirements of the solutes that they excrete. Therefore, although these controls operate well in the immediate control of the water economy of the body, the long-term maintenance of this economy depends upon the intake of water.

Water Intake

Under normal circumstances, water enters the body only through the mouth and gastrointestinal tract. It may do so as water *per se,* as the vehicle in various fluid mixtures, and as the water contained in solid food. Another source of water to the body is metabolic water produced in the oxidation of foodstuffs. The specific sensory mechanisms of the feedback control of water content by water intake are rather complex and sophisticated, and their detailed description is beyond the scope of this discussion. Some general statements, however, may be valuable. The receptors that provide information to the central nervous system for water intake control include, on the positive side, those sensitive to changes in the effective osmotic pressure and to the volume of the internal environment or its vascular component, and probably those sensitive to increases in peripheral and central temperature (in anticipation of water loss through perspiration) and to oral and pharyngeal dehydration (dryness of the mouth and throat). On the negative side are those receptors sensitive to gastric distention and other learned gastrointestinal cues for metering intake. In addition to these, the control system for water intake behavior is influenced by information reflecting the priority of other demands on the animal's behavior.

Water Deficiency

The excessive loss of water from the body can cause electrolyte loss ranging from very light to very heavy. Dehydration is classified by the *resultant* concentration of electrolytes in the extracellular fluids. Accordingly, there is hypotonic, hypertonic, and isotonic dehydration of the extracellular space. The cellular space normally responds osmotically to the condition realized in the extracellular space. The clinical definition of dehydration is a water deficiency of 6 per cent or more of total body water. During the first few days of continuing dehydration the primary loss is of extracellular fluid. When 25 per cent or more of the volume of the extracellular fluid has been lost, the signs and symptoms of dehydration appear: (1) dry skin, parched tongue, and sunken eyeballs; (2) output of less than 500 ml of urine in 24 hours; (3) specific gravity of urine greater than 1.030; and (4) recent weight loss.

Hypertonic Dehydration (Table 17–1)

Three general conditions may lead to hypertonic dehydration:

First, hypertonic dehydration develops from water deprivation together with excessive water loss, typically through the lungs and skin, as on a hot day. This leads to a sharp rise in the hematocrit, with values as high as 65 per cent, and parallel increases in sodium ion concentration. These parallel increases in

Table 17–1 CLINICAL SIGNS OF HYPERTONIC DEHYDRATION

	HEMATOCRIT	ELECTROLYTES
Desiccation ("true" dehydration)	Very high (parallel)	Very high
Diabetic and uremic dehydration	Very high (>)	High
Solute loading	Very high (<)	Extremely high

hematocrit and sodium concentrations reflect a loss of "pure" water and are sometimes referred to as desiccation or "true" dehydration; that is, the primary loss is water. Endogenous water diffuses out of the tissue cells but not in sufficient volume to offset the continuing loss from the skin and lungs. Urine becomes scanty and highly concentrated. Eventually, delirium, convulsions, and coma or shock develop. The net effect is cellular dehydration and hypertonic extracellular fluid.

Diabetic or uremic dehydration is distinct from the true desiccation and develops from the accumulation of an excessive amount of hypertonic nonelectrolytes in the extracellular fluid, such as glucose or urea. Water is lost in the attempt to deal with this excess of nonelectrolyte solute; the water loss is in excess of salt loss, but the marked elevation of sodium concentration, as occurs in true desiccation, does not develop.

Despite the differences, both of these disorders should be treated similarly. Blood and interstitial fluid volumes and osmolarity must be restored. This is achieved by administering a sufficient volume of water by mouth or a .45 per cent sodium chloride solution intravenously.

The third type of hypertonic dehydration occurs with the administration of excessive amounts of solute by mouth or vein. When the extracellular space is overloaded with more solute than the kidneys can take care of, large amounts of water are excreted in an attempt to rid the body of excess solute. In true desiccation the concentrations of the various electrolytes parallel the rise in the hematocrit, but in "solute loading" the hematocrit lags behind the serum electrolyte values, which can become extreme. Cellular dehydration occurs from the osmotic pull of the hypertonic extracellular fluid, and large volumes of water are excreted into the urine, which has a fixed specific gravity. This solute diuresis persists despite intensive antidiuretic stimulation from the pituitary and adrenal glands.

Treatment consists in immediate cessation of the "solute loading" by mouth, tube, or vein and administration of generous volumes of water. Diabetics should be given supplements of insulin, and uremic patients should be allowed time for their kidneys to unload the excess solute.

Hypertonic dehydration may also develop in a number of other disorders, for instance, when swallowing is difficult or impossible, as occurs in debilitated, comatose, or dysphagic patients; in patients whose kidneys are not able to concentrate water normally owing to a lack of ADH, as in diabetes insipidus; in diarrhea, when excessive water is lost with relatively small losses of electrolytes; and in burn cases, especially with open treatment.

Hypotonic Dehydration

Hypotonic dehydration is normally dealt with under the more general heading of *water intoxication,* which deals with all conditions leading to hypotonic extracellular fluid. It is worth mentioning here, however, that fasting with normal water intake — the effect opposite to solute loading over time — will lead to a hypotonic extracellular fluid with normal water levels. Similarly, a loss of sweat with water but not salt replacement can lead to hypotonic extracellular fluid.

Water Intoxication

Water intoxication results from overloading the extracellular space with hypotonic fluid. The onset of water intoxication may be either acute or chronic but is usually preceded by a period of antidiuresis. The continued infusion of water eventually produces diuresis, but with excretion of larger quantities of sodium with the water. This compounds the problem, producing a very low serum sodium, even more so than was caused by the original dilution. Potassium levels usually remain around normal in such cases.

The development of symptoms of water intoxication actually depends upon the rate of infusion and the rate of renal excretion of hypotonic water. Symptoms appear when there is a rapid fall in serum sodium. Clinical features of water intoxication are weakness, lethargy, vomiting, drowsiness, edema, weight gain, coma, and convulsions.

All these signs and symptoms are readily reproduced by low serum sodium concentrations and cerebral edema. The brain is a unique organ in the body in that it is only slowly permeable to sodium ions. After an excess of hypotonic solution has been given to a patient, the brain becomes relatively

hypertonic. Cerebral cells take up water but lose very few sodium ions. *Waterlogging of the neural cells* produces delirium, coma, and convulsions. Fundamentally, water intoxication is characterized by an excess of hypotonic extracellular fluid and a relative hypertonicity of the tissue cells, which subsequently produces cellular overhydration.

Treatment consists of withholding all fluid intake and allowing the body time to rid itself of excess extracellular water by way of the lungs, the skin, and the kidneys. When coma or convulsions are present, a hypertonic saline solution in small volumes may be given, such as 250 ml of a 3 per cent NaCl solution. Urea and mannitol infusions are also useful for dehydrating the brain.

Compulsive water drinking leads to water intoxication when the patient receives more water than his kidneys can excrete, which is about 13 ml per minute. Water intoxication may also occur when ADH secretion is excessive (this can occur as a result of fear, pain, or in acute infections such as pneumonia; as a result of most anesthetics or analgesics such as morphine and Demerol; or as a result of acute stress, such as trauma or major surgery). The postoperative period of excessive ADH secretion is usually 12 to 36 hours.

It should always be kept in mind that an abnormal retention of water may serve a useful purpose, such as sustaining the plasma volume in adrenal insufficiency. In approaching treatment of fluid imbalances generally, the etiology of the disturbance should be determined as rapidly as possible, and it should be ascertained that the homeostatic mechanisms which regulate body fluid composition are normal. It is important in planning fluid therapy to know the sodium, potassium, calcium, CO_2, chloride, pH, nonprotein nitrogen, and glucose concentrations of the plasma and the hemoglobin concentration or hematocrit of whole blood. The lab data occasionally reveal the presence of markedly abnormal solute concentrations which, if not treated properly, may lead to symptomatic solute defects and death.

Edema

When the volume of interstitial fluid has been increased to the point of being recognizable by clinical examination, edema is said to be present. This ranges from about 10 to 15 per cent increase in fluid content. Edema is of four fundamental types. One type is produced by a lowering of serum albumin concentration. If the level of serum albumin falls below 2.5 to 3 grams per 100 ml, there is increased filtration into the interstitial space at the arterial end of the capillaries and diminished return into the capillaries at the venous end. This condition, leading to accumulation of fluid in the interstitial space, is characteristic of nephrosis (see Chapter 15). It is also seen in protein starvation, although other factors found in this condition may be contributory.

A second type of edema is produced by damage to the capillary endothelium, allowing passage of fluid with a high protein content into the interstitial space. This sets up a new net osmotic pull toward the interstitial space, leading to the interstitial fluid build-up. This mechanism is involved in the production of blisters, hives, and localized inflammation when local damage to capillaries is produced by toxins, trauma, histaminelike substances, or exposure to cold.

The third type is produced by increased venous pressure. This type of edema is seen with use of the tourniquet, in varicose veins, and, supposedly, in congestive heart failure. That increased venous pressure occurs in cardiac decompensation is generally recognized, but some doubt has been cast on the primary importance of this fact in the production of edema. Many believe that renal retention of sodium produced by forward failure of the heart is the primary phenomenon which leads to retention of water, then to increased venous pressure, then to edema. The increased venous pressure, in any case, acts to impede return of fluid to the vascular compartment from the interstitial space.

Obstruction of the lymphatics produces *lymphedema,* in which fluid and protein accumulate in the interstitial space as a result of insufficient lymph drainage. Furthermore, interstitial protein accumulation draws large amounts of fluid from the capillaries.

Treatment of Burns

A burned area will exude large amounts of plasma. Thus, the individual with a severe burn presents a difficult problem in fluid and electrolyte therapy. Fluid requirements in burned patients are related to the degree of burn and to the total area of skin involved. This area must be carefully measured and is usually expressed as a percentage of total body surface, which can be conveniently expressed by the *rule of nines.* In this rule, the head equals 9 per cent of the surface area; each arm, 9 per cent; the anterior trunk, 18 per cent; the posterior trunk, 18 per cent; each lower extremity, 18 per cent; and the genitalia, 1 per cent (see Fig. 17–3).

Burns produce three characteristic features: (1) loss of plasma volume; (2) elevation of the hematocrit; and (3) oliguria (diminished quantity of urine). A basic feature is the loss of plasma to a third space, the area of burned tissue into which water, electrolytes, and protein translocate. Because of increased capillary permeability, water, electrolytes,

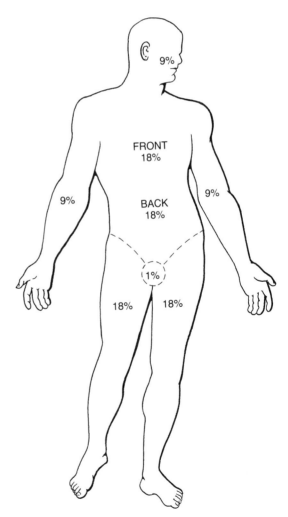

Figure 17–3. The *rule of nines* is a convenient method for rapidly estimating the percentage of surface area loss following a burn.

and protein move from the vascular space into this third space. The protein loss is less than the water and electrolyte loss. Consequently, the plasma volume shrinks, the hematocrit rises, and the concentration of total protein increases. The net result is desalting, deproteinating, and dehydrating of the normal extracellular space owing to losses of water, electrolytes, and proteins into the burned tissues. The prerenal losses of water, especially into the burned tissues, evoke oliguria.

Endogenous water leaves the cells to replace the water lost from the extracellular space. Potassium moves along with this water into the interstitial space. Sodium then moves into the cells to maintain electrochemical balance. The net effect is a cellular K/Na exchange. In patients with oliguria, anuria, or adrenal insufficiency, the serum potassium level can increase to dangerous levels, leading to cardiac arrhythmias and diastolic arrest. More generally, the total body sodium and potassium concentrations drop because of extravasation of sodium and potassium ions into the third space, renal excretion, and cellular K/Na exchange.

Patients with less than 10 per cent of their body burned may require fluid therapy only for maintenance needs, whereas if more than 20 per cent of the skin surface is involved extensive fluid therapy may be required. In severe burns, in which the various volume control mechanisms fail to maintain blood pressure, shock will quickly ensue. The fluid treatment of burns, then, begins by combating shock with intravenous fluids, continually monitoring venous pressure to determine the proper infusion rate. One must also guard against administering an excessive amount of fluid, which can result in cardiac failure and pulmonary edema. Again, the most expedient method of avoiding hypervolemia is to determine the venous pressure repeatedly.

Combating shock also involves replacement of the proper amounts of colloids and salts as well as water. Dextran, albumin, plasma, saline, or blood also may be used for this purpose. A practical formula for fluid replacement consists of using 1 ml of fluid for each percentage area of burn per pound of body weight. The total volume lost should be replaced within 24 hours after burning, and of this volume 40 per cent should be colloid and 60 per cent electrolyte solution.

Hyperkalemia sometimes develops in the early stages of burns when there is renal failure and an outflow of potassium from the destroyed cells. Several days following a burn the fluid which accumulated in the interstitial space may suddenly be reabsorbed, and acute overexpansion of the vascular system may occur. Sodium and water intake should be restricted during this period.

Regulation of Electrolyte Balance

Mechanisms regulating sodium and calcium balance have been described in the chapters on the urinary and endocrine systems. The following is a brief account of the mechanisms by which the concentrations and distribution of potassium, magnesium, phosphates, and chlorides are regulated.

Potassium Balance

Potassium is the major cation in the intracellular fluid and is important in regulation of intracellular fluid volume, neuromuscular irritability, and hydrogen ion concentration. When potassium moves out of the cell, sodium and hydrogen ions move into the cell. When extracellular concentrations of sodium and hydrogen become excessive, they are carried into the cells osmotically, and potassium moves out of the cells. Extracellular acidosis then causes potassium leakage from the cells and a high serum potassium; alkalosis has the opposite effect.

Normally, potassium is ingested in the diet and is excreted by the kidneys. But the body's mechanisms for conserving potassium are not as efficient as those for sodium. Some potassium is lost in the urine even when the intake of potassium is low. The rate of excretion of potassium is controlled by aldosterone, ADH, and the acid-base balance of the body. A high extracellular potassium concentration will increase aldosterone secretion, the feedback mechanism being just the opposite of that for sodium (a low extracellular sodium stimulates secretion of aldosterone). When the production of aldosterone is stimulated, sodium will be actively retained while potassium will be excreted. The renal tubules can excrete either potassium or hydrogen ions in exchange for the sodium they reabsorb. Therefore, if the kidneys excrete more hydrogen ions, fewer potassium ions will be excreted. Potassium may also be lost through gastrointestinal tract disturbances such as vomiting and diarrhea.

Magnesium Balance

Most of the body's magnesium is intracellular, like potassium. Magnesium activates the enzyme systems needed to produce cellular energy by the breakdown of ATP to adenosine diphosphate (ADP). It also activates phosphatase, the enzyme that catalyzes essential chemical reactions of the liver and bone.

Most of the intracellular magnesium is bound to proteins and is not osmotically active (ionized), and each cell seems to have responsibility for the integrity of its internal magnesium concentration. Extracellular magnesium is only about one-tenth the intracellular content, and this concentration is maintained by the kidneys, apparently in direct relation to plasma concentration; that is, as plasma magnesium concentration increases, renal excretion of magnesium increases, and vice versa. Intestinal absorption of magnesium is rather poor, which serves to make various magnesium salts excellent laxatives, for instance, milk of magnesia, magnesium citrate, and magnesium sulfate. The lack of more precise controls over magnesium concentration seems apparent from the fact that in the presence of poor renal function administration of magnesium compounds as laxatives leads to a high blood concentration of magnesium.

There are similarities between the actions of magnesium and calcium. There are also curious differences between these two ions. A low serum magnesium or calcium increases neuromuscular irritability, and a high concentration of these ions has a reverse effect. Magnesium narcosis, produced by injecting a magnesium preparation, can be promptly antagonized by the parenteral administration of calcium. However, the toxic effects of hypomagnesia can be aggravated by calcium or phosphorus in the diet.

Phosphates

Intracellular phosphate concentration, which seems to be controlled by the individual cells, is many times the extracellular concentration. Within the cells phosphates are involved in high energy systems (e.g., ATP) and are necessary for the formation of nucleic acids.

The concentration of phosphate in the extracellular fluid is regulated by two related but partially independent mechanisms. Parathyroid hormone stimulates the osseous tissue to give up calcium phosphate to solution, but the feedback regulation is dependent on calcium concentration and not phosphate. The kidneys are stimulated by parathyroid hormone to excrete phosphate. The resulting fall in plasma phosphate tends to promote bone resorption, facilitating the effect of the parathyroid hormone on bone. The overall effect of the parathyroid hormone is a sharp rise in plasma calcium and a small lowering of plasma phosphate for a shorter duration. The ultimate regulators of phosphate concentration in the extracellular fluid, then, are the kidneys. Normally, phosphate is excreted in the urine, only a small amount appearing in the stool.

Chloride Balance

Chloride is mainly an extracellular ion; however, it diffuses readily between the intracellular and extracellular compartments. The ease with which chloride diffuses makes it particularly valuable in regulating osmotic pressure differences between fluid compartments and in the regulation of acid-base balance. A prime example of the role of chloride is seen in the *chloride-bicarbonate shift*. When bicarbonate ion is formed from carbonic acid, the concentration of bicarbonate ion increases in the red blood cells. Bicarbonate ions diffuse into the plasma. However, the potassium in the red blood cell, which electrically balances the bicarbonate ion in the cell, cannot pass as easily into the plasma. As a result, when bicarbonate ions diffuse out of the red blood cell, other negative ions must diffuse inward to take their place. The negative ion in greatest abundance in the plasma chloride, therefore, enters the cell at the time the bicarbonate diffuses outward.

Consequently, as CO_2 leaves the tissues and enters the blood, bicarbonate ion shifts from the red blood cells into the plasma, and chloride ion shifts from the plasma into the red blood cells. As a result, the content of chloride in *venous* red blood cells is slightly higher than the content of chloride in *arterial* red blood cells, the opposite being true of the plasma.

Similarly, chloride responds to changes in protein concentrations of the various fluid compartments to maintain the electrical and osmotic gradients necessary for cellular functioning. Chloride also functions in compensating for other electrolyte imbalances. Because of its great osmotic ability it is, in effect, the first line of defense in the event of electrolyte imbalances.

Intake of chloride in the diet is usually in combination with sodium and, as a general rule, the regulation and behavior of chloride in the body is directly related to sodium regulation and behavior. Chloride may be lost from the kidneys, gastrointestinal tract, and skin. Chloride reabsorption by the kidneys is in direct proportion to sodium reabsorption and, in effect, the adrenocortical hormones, especially aldosterone, which increase reabsorption of sodium, also have the same consequence for chloride. Other factors affecting sodium concentration, like potassium increases, usually have a like effect on chloride concentrations. Gastrointestinal loss of chloride, on the other hand, is most severe in vomiting, where the concentrated HCl of the stomach is lost. Sodium chloride is lost through the skin in sweating.

Acid-Base Regulation

The problem of regulating acid-base balance is essentially one of preventing alterations in hydrogen ion concentration secondary to the continuous formation and expulsion of the acid end products of metabolism.

The acidity of a solution is determined by the concentration of hydrogen ions (H^+). Acidity is conveniently expressed by the symbol pH. Neutral solutions have a pH of 7. The pH of a strongly basic, or alkaline, solution may be as high as 14, while that of an acidic solution can be less than 1. The pH of extracellular fluid in health is maintained at a level between 7.35 and 7.45. To prevent acidosis or alkalosis, several special control systems are available in the body: (1) All the body fluids contain buffer systems which prevent excessive changes in hydrogen ion concentration. (2) The respiratory center is stimulated by changes in the carbon dioxide

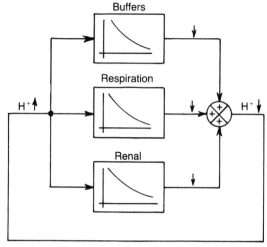

Figure 17–4. The regulation of acid-base balance. (From Milhorn, H. T., Jr.: The Application of Control Theory to Physiological Systems. Philadelphia, W. B. Saunders Co., 1966.)

and hydrogen ion concentrations to alter pulmonary ventilation, which affects the rate of carbon dioxide removal from the body fluids. Since carbon dioxide forms a weak acid in solution, its removal lowers the hydrogen ion concentration. (3) The kidneys also respond to changes in hydrogen ion concentration by excreting either an acid or an alkaline urine.

These three control systems operate together in the maintenance of body fluid pH (Fig. 17–4). The buffer system can act within a fraction of a second, whereas the respiratory system takes 1 to 3 minutes to readjust the hydrogen ion concentration after a sudden change. The kidneys, although the most powerful of all acid-base regulatory systems, require from several hours to a day to readjust the hydrogen ion concentration.

Buffer Activity

A solution that has a tendency to resist changes in its pH when treated with strong acids or bases is called a *buffer*. A buffer solution contains a weak acid or base and a salt of this acid or base. In biological fluids the bicarbonate–carbonic acid system, the phosphate system, the hemoglobin-oxyhemoglobin system, and the proteins act as the principal buffers in the regulation of pH.

The Bicarbonate–Carbonic Acid System

The sodium bicarbonate (NaHCO$_3$)–carbonic acid (H$_2$CO$_3$) buffer system is present in all body fluids (Fig. 17–5). It should be noted that carbonic acid is a weak acid; that is, it binds its hydrogen ions strongly. If a strong acid (one that is loosely attached to H) such as hydrochloric acid is added, it reacts almost immediately with the bicarbonate to form carbonic acid and sodium chloride. The system operates by changing the strong acid into a weak acid and successfully prevents a major change in pH. The fact that the carbonic acid can easily be reduced to carbon dioxide and water and removed from the body through respiration greatly enhances the combined efficiency of these mechanisms in responding to changes in hydrogen ion concentration.

Summary equations:

$$HCl + NaHCO_3 \rightarrow H_2CO_3 + NaCl$$
$$H_2CO_3 \rightarrow H_2O + CO_2$$

If a strong base such as sodium hydroxide is added, the carbonic acid reacts immediately with it to form sodium bicarbonate and water. Again the buffer mechanism has prevented a major change in pH by changing a strong base into the less alkaline sodium bicarbonate.

Summary equation:

$$NaOH + H_2CO_3 \rightarrow NaHCO_3 + H_2O$$

The Phosphate System

The phosphate buffer system is composed of NaH$_2$PO$_4$ and Na$_2$HPO$_4$ and functions very much like the bicarbonate buffer system.

Summary equations:

$$HCl + Na_2HPO_4 \rightarrow NaH_2PO_4 + NaCl$$
$$NaOH + NaH_2PO_4 \rightarrow Na_2HPO_4 + H_2O$$

In the first reaction the introduction of a strong acid leads to its conversion to a weak acid and NaCl. In the second reaction the strong base is converted to a less alkaline Na$_2$HPO$_4$ and water. The phosphate buffer system has a potential capacity and efficiency very much like that of the bicarbonate system. However, its concentration in the extracellular fluid is only one-sixth that of the bicarbonate buffer system; it should also be kept in mind that the actual capacity and efficiency of the bicarbonate system are

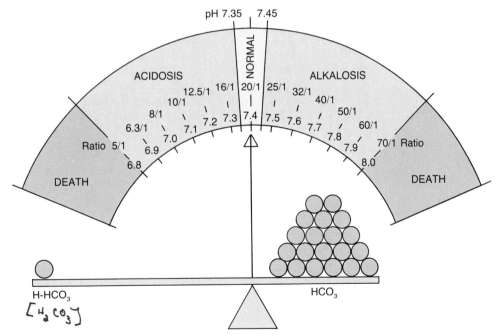

Carbonic acid in a ratio of 1:20 with bicarbonate salt maintains a normal body pH

Figure 17–5. Acidosis and alkalosis showing ratio between carbonic acid and bicarbonate ion.

greatly augmented by the respiratory expulsion of carbon dioxide. In urine and possibly in intracellular fluid, in which CO_2 concentration is higher, inorganic phosphate plays an important role as a buffer.

With the usual meat-containing diet, the urine is somewhat more acid than the blood. NaH_2PO_4 is formed when excess hydrogen ions combine in the kidney tubules with Na_2HPO_4. The NaH_2PO_4 then passes into the urine, and the sodium ion is absorbed from the tubules in place of the hydrogen ion, the result being to buffer the urine while allowing large quantities of hydrogen ion to be expelled.

The Protein Buffer System

The most abundant buffer of the body consists of proteins of the cells and plasma. The protein buffer system operates in precisely the same manner as that of the bicarbonate system. However, unlike simpler buffers, the buffer effect of proteins is not concentrated at some specific pH, but rather exhibits some buffer action over nearly the entire pH scale. This is because proteins are composed of several different kinds of amino acids, each of which has its own specific acid-base properties. The two major groups that allow proteins to act as both acid and base buffers are first, the —COOH group, which can dissociate into —COO^- and H^+, and second, the common —NH_3OH group, which can dissociate into —NH_3^+ and OH^-.

Summary equations:

$$^+NH_3-Pr-COOH + 2OH^- \rightarrow$$
$$NH_2-Pr-COO^- + 2H_2O$$

$$NH_2-Pr-COO^- + 2H^+ \rightarrow {}^+NH_3-Pr-COOH$$

Hemoglobin-Oxyhemoglobin System

Both hemoglobin and oxyhemoglobin are proteins and act as weak acids, with oxyhemoglobin being slightly more acidic. In the venous blood, where carbonic acid (dissolved CO_2) concentration is relatively high, the deoxyhemoglobin buffers the increase in hydrogen ion from carbonic acid formed in the red blood cell. The deoxyhemoglobin is, of course, a weaker acid than carbonic acid or this would not occur. Deoxyhemoglobin

being partially in the form of a potassium salt, the reaction occurs as follows.

Summary equation:

$$K_2Hb + H_2CO_3 \rightarrow HKHb + KHCO_3$$

In the arterial blood, in which the carbonic acid concentration is significantly less than in the venous blood, oxyhemoglobin, which is more acidic than carbonic acid, operates to offset the loss of hydrogen ions from the loss of carbonic acid (CO_2) that occurs from respiratory ventilaton.

Summary equations:

$$HKHb + O_2 \rightarrow KHbO_2 + H^+$$
$$H^+ + NaHCO_3 \rightarrow H_2CO_3 + Na^+$$

The hemoglobin-oxyhemoglobin system is perhaps best understood as a "second level" buffer system, since it, in effect, buffers the bicarbonate-carbonic acid buffer system in the blood.

Respiratory Regulation of Acid-Base Balance

The carbon dioxide and hydrogen ion concentrations can affect the rate of alveolar ventilation by a direct stimulating action of both CO_2 and H^+ on the respiratory center in the medulla oblongata. The respiratory system operates as a feedback control for regulating carbon dioxide and hydrogen ion concentrations; that is, when such concentrations rise above normal, the respiratory system is stimulated to become more active and, as a result, carbon dioxide is removed at an increased rate and its concentration decreases in the extracellular fluids, thus reducing the hydrogen ion concentration back toward normal. Conversely, if a decrease in carbon dioxide and hydrogen ion concentrations occur, the respiratory center becomes depressed, alveolar ventilation decreases, and carbon dioxide and hydrogen ion concentrations build toward normal. This regulatory system is, of course, dependent on the fact that the carbon dioxide concentration in the atmosphere being breathed is much lower than that in body fluids. The overall "buffering power" of the respiratory system is approximately two times as great as that of all the chemical buffers combined; that is, about two times as much acid or base can normally be buffered by this mechanism as by the chemical buffers.

Renal Regulation of Acid-Base Balance

When the hydrogen ion concentration changes from normal, the kidneys tend to compensate for this excess by excreting hydrogen ion and returning bicarbonate to the plasma and extracellular fluid. The mechanisms by which the kidneys accomplish this are described in Chapter 15, page 531.

CLINICAL CONSIDERATIONS

Sodium Depletion and Imbalance

The effects of pure sodium depletion are strikingly different from those of pure water depletion. These two clinical states form the extremes of the range of fluid-electrolyte depletion in the body. Initially, water is lost in amounts comparable to sodium loss, thus maintaining a normal concentration of plasma sodium at the expense of extracellular fluid volume. With advancing sodium depletion, the relative water loss decreases and, consequently, the sodium concentration in the extracellular fluid (plasma) begins to decrease. Most patients with clinical sodium depletion (and hyponatremia) are first seen at this stage.

With the extracellular fluid gaining in hypotonicity, osmotic forces begin drawing water into the cells. The hematocrit and plasma protein concentration rise, and there is poor venous filling; hence, cardiac output diminishes and blood pressure falls. With severe sodium depletion, hypovolemia induces tachycardia; selective vasoconstriction may lead to diminished circulation through the skin and extremities, leading to cold limbs and dehydration fever, and also through the kidneys, leading to oliguria or anuria. These volume effects do not account for some of the changes observed in sodium depletion, such as muscle cramps, gastric atony with anorexia, and sometimes vomiting.

Clinical sodium depletion has been observed in numerous disease conditions. A low intake of sodium does not in itself lead to significant sodium depletion. The important causes are abnormal losses in gastrointestinal secretions, urine, and sweat. Losses of gastrointestinal secretions by diarrhea, vomiting, aspiration, or discharge from fistulae are the most common causes of severe sodium depletion, which is usually complicated by alkalosis or acidosis, depending on the relatively higher or lower losses of hydrogen ions.

Urinary losses are especially critical in that they are more likely to go unrecognized for a time than are gastrointestinal losses. Polyuria does not in itself lead to sodium depletion and, conversely, the absence of polyuria does not exclude the possibility of urinary loss of sodium. A common cause of sodium depletion through urinary loss is in solute loading — usually with glucose or urea. Lack of aldosterone to stimulate sodium reabsorption, as in Addison's disease, is another mechanism of loss.

The diagnosis of sodium depletion depends mainly on a knowledge of its causes and of the different clinical pictures which it may produce. Biochemical studies are of limited value in diagnosis, because the sodium concentration in the plasma *does not* reflect the true picture in many cases; the sodium balance may have been affected by changes in the water balance and by shifts of sodium into or out of cells and possibly bone.

Treatment of sodium depletion depends on its degree. For minor depletion, the addition of extra salt to the diet is effective both in treatment and in prevention. When sodium depletion is of moderate degree, as in diabetic coma, treatment with 0.9 per cent saline intravenously is satisfactory; the amount needed is commonly about 2 to 3 liters. When there is a complicating acidosis, part of the sodium should be given as bicarbonate or lactate. For severe sodium depletion, hypertonic 5 per cent saline produces a rapid restoration of plasma volume and renal circulation. Much of the dilution that occurs apparently comes from the excess intracellular water that builds up during depletion. Acidosis and alkalosis, which are common in severe cases stemming from gastric or intestinal losses, necessitate combining lactate with the hypertonic saline solution.

Two general thoughts should be kept in mind: (1) a low serum sodium is not in itself an indication for treatment with sodium salts; and (2) when diagnosis of sodium depletion is clear, the net treatment is to increase body sodium.

Acidosis

Acidosis may be defined as an excess of hydrogen ion within the body. The term is not synonymous with acidemia, which means an excessive concentration of hydrogen ion in the plasma. For instance, an increase in respiration may maintain a normal hydrogen ion concentration in the plasma even when excessive hydrogen ion is being produced in metabolism. The state of acidosis without acidemia has been referred to as *compensated* acidosis; this is not a stable situation and tends to break down into *uncompensated* acidosis if the cause of hydrogen ion excess persists. Since the buffers, the respiratory system, and the kidneys all operate to. maintain homeostasis of the pH of the various compartments, when one system malfunctions, leading to an imbalance somewhere, then compensation occurs in terms of the activity of the other systems. For instance, retention of CO_2 (potential hydrogen ion) in early respiratory failure can be compensated for by increased renal retention of bicarbonate, but with continued or increasing respiratory failure, acidemia is added to acidosis. There are many causes of acidosis, but they may be conveniently grouped under two major headings — respiratory acidosis and metabolic acidosis (Fig. 17–6).

Respiratory Acidosis. Respiratory acidosis is characterized by a primary rise in Pco_2, and invariably results from some form of respiratory failure. Acute respiratory acidosis usually stems from acute airway obstruction or central nervous system (CNS) depression, such as that from barbiturate poisoning. Chronic respiratory acidosis usually stems from chronic obstructive lung disease.

Nonrespiratory compensation mechanisms operate primarily to increase the bicarbonate concentration in the extracellular fluid so as to reestablish the normal 20:1 bicarbonate to carbonic acid ratio. Carbon dioxide diffuses into the red blood cells, where it can be buffered. This will result in a chloride shift, liberating increased amounts of bicarbonate into the extracellular fluid. The kidneys will increase their formation of ammonia, increase their excretion of hydrogen ion, and retain more bicarbonate. The increased Pco_2 will stimulate increased respiration, which will eliminate more of the carbon dioxide where this is possible. It is important to note that the nonrespiratory

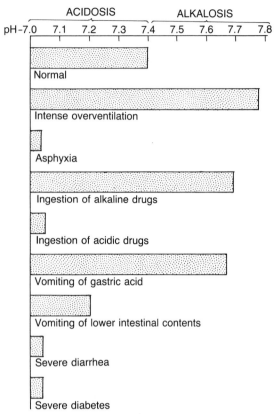

Figure 17–6. pH of the body fluids in various acid-base disorders.

compensations are activated by the low pH of the blood, so that, as the blood pH increases, these mechanisms become less and less active, even though the Pco_2 may still remain high. Patients whose acidosis is relatively well compensated, as evidenced by a nearly normal pH, should not be treated overzealously. Lowering their Pco_2 too rapidly leaves them with a sizable bicarbonate excess and shifts their acid-base balance into acute alkalosis.

Patients in acidosis usually complain of weakness and headache. CO_2 narcosis and CNS depression are marked by a decreased level of consciousness. In severe respiratory acidosis there may be cardiac arrhythmias and coma. Sodium lactate given intravenously may save the life of a patient with acute respiratory acidosis. However, more generally, establishing satisfactory ventilation and/or working to correct the basic disorder are first steps.

Metabolic Acidosis. Metabolic acidosis may occur from either abnormal metabolism, as in diabetic or lactic acidosis, or from impaired excretion, as in uremic acidosis. These conditions lead to an accumulation of acid metabolites in the blood stream. Some conditions lead to excessive loss of bicarbonate, as in chronic renal disease, in which the kidneys are unable to reabsorb tubular bicarbonate to the blood stream. Severe diarrhea or prolonged intestinal suction can also result in a loss of base and, consequently, metabolic acidosis. A third general cause of metabolic acidosis is the ingestion of acid or acid-producing substances. Ammonium chloride is an acid-producing salt, since the liver converts the ammonium to neutral urea, leaving chloride to circulate in the blood stream. Since chloride and bicarbonate are in relative balance in the blood, this increase in chloride causes a decrease in bicarbonate and results in acidosis. Ingestion of household metal polishes, laundry bleaches, or methyl alcohol, frequently used as a fuel for chafing dishes or fondue pots, will produce metabolic acidosis.

Respiratory compensation is produced by rapid breathing, which blows off CO_2 at an increased rate and results in a shift in the bicarbonate–carbonic acid ratio toward the alkaline. In severe cases this hyperventilation of metabolic acidosis is called Kussmaul breathing, although in extreme cases, when the pH has fallen to 7, these Kussmaul respirations may disappear. The kidneys compensate for metabolic acidosis by retaining more bicarbonate while increasing the formation of ammonia and elimination of hydrogen ion.

Patients with metabolic acidosis usually complain of general malaise, weakness, and headache. Nausea and vomiting may occur, as may hypotension, cardiac arrhythmias and, in severe cases, coma.

In the treatment of metabolic acidosis the goals are to halt the metabolic disturbance that produced the acidosis and to replace the electrolytes that have been lost. Alkalinizing salts such as sodium bicarbonate or sodium lactate are usually administered only to patients in severe metabolic acidosis (pH 7.2 or below). Alkalinizing solutions are dangerous because they may complicate matters by causing metabolic alkalosis. Ordinarily the acid-base balance will automatically return to normal when the metabolic disturbance has been corrected and the specific electrolytes have been replaced.

Alkalosis

The normal course of metabolism tends toward an excess of hydrogen ion, to be disposed of by the kidneys and, less directly, by the lungs. The more common metabolic disturbances tend to increase hydrogen ion production; and impaired renal and pulmonary function tends to produce acidosis by restricting the elimination of hydrogen ion. It is, therefore, not surprising to find that alkalosis is seldom a spontaneous state, but arises from the imposition of alkali loads on the body or from the excessive activity of normal lungs. These two mechanisms correspond to metabolic and respiratory alkalosis (Fig. 17–6).

Respiratory Alkalosis. Respiratory alkalosis is characterized by a primary fall in PCO_2 caused by persistent hyperventilation. The cause of the hyperventilation may be anxiety, pulmonary embolism, congestive heart failure, cirrhosis of the liver, CNS injury to breathing centers, or severe infection.

The kidneys compensate for the increased alkalinity by retaining hydrogen and chloride and by increasing their excretion of sodium, potassium, and bicarbonate. There may be a slowing of the rate of respiration, but this compensatory mechanism depends upon removal of the cause of hyperventilation.

The patient usually complains of dizziness and becomes apprehensive. There is numbness and tingling in the fingers and toes. There may be palpitations and tremors. In severe cases there may be signs of tetany. Only if the respiratory alkalosis is uncompensated should one undertake to restore the PCO_2 to normal. When the alkalosis is compensated, restoring carbon dioxide to normal without also giving sodium bicarbonate is almost certain to bring acidemia.

Metabolic Alkalosis. Administration of excessive amounts of sodium bicarbonate or sodium salts of other organic acids such as sodium lactate may produce metabolic alkalosis. The loss of chlorides as hydrochloric acid in persistent vomiting may result in high circulating levels of sodium bicarbonate, causing alkalosis. Another possible cause is excess excretion of acid or potassium into the urine, which may result from vigorous mercurial diuretic therapy or from hyperadrenocorticism, such as occurs in Cushing's disease or steroid therapy.

The symptoms and signs of metabolic alkalosis are vague, but may include weakness, mental dullness, tetany, and paralytic ileus.

Treatment consists of restoration of volume and ionic depletions. It is particularly important to treat severe deficits of body potassium and chloride. Patients with severe losses of stomach contents (unless they have liver failure) may be saved by adding ammonium chloride to the IV solution to counteract the high bicarbonate levels. Electrolytes in urine or gastric fluid loss should be measured and total losses carefully estimated.

SUMMARY

FLUIDS AND ELECTROLYTES

Significance of Fluid and Electrolyte Balance

The maintenance of balance between the three major fluid compartments—the plasma, interstitial fluid, and intracellular fluid—in terms of the relative distribution of the total body water and electrolytes is involved in homeostasis.

Distribution and Movement of Water

1. Of the lean body weight 60 to 70 per cent is water, with about three-fourths contained in the cells and one-fourth in the extracellular fluid.

2. Distribution of water between the intracellular and extracellular spaces depends primarily on the effective osmotic gradients between these compartments. The regulation of sodium and potassium ions is most important in developing and maintaining these gradients.

3. The two main factors controlling distribution of water between the vascular and interstitial compartments of the extracellular fluid are:

   a. The effective osmotic pressure across the capillary membrane, which depends primarily on the plasma protein concentration.
   b. Hydrostatic pressure of the blood in the capillary.

Exchanges of Water with the External Environment

1. Water is taken into the body through the mouth and absorbed from the gastrointestinal tract.

2. Water is lost from the body through the skin, lungs, kidneys, and gastrointestinal tract.

3. The most important variable controlling the total water content is water intake, being adjusted or controlled to balance whatever is lost.

Water Loss to the External Environment

1. Water loss from the skin and lungs is not under any direct control related to the content of body water.

   a. Loss from the lungs is due to their necessarily moist nature. Rate of loss varies with dryness of air and rate of ventilation.
   b. Rate of loss from the skin depends upon regulation of body temperature.
   c. Loss from the lungs is pure water and loss from the skin is usually hypotonic, with sodium chloride concentration of about one-half that found in the extracellular fluid.

2. Water moves into the upper gastrointestinal tract in response to ingested solids and hypertonic solutions and is reabsorbed almost totally in the lower tract with absorbed nutrients. Only a very small portion of this water is lost in the feces.

3. The kidneys excrete water both as a vehicle for other materials and as "free" water.

Water Deficiency

1. There are three types of dehydration classified by the *resultant* concentration of electrolytes in the extracellular fluid: hypertonic, hypotonic, and isotonic.

2. Hypertonic dehydration is distinguished into three types.

   a. Hypertonic dehydration from water deprivation together with excessive water loss.
   b. Diabetic or uremic dehydration.
   c. The type which occurs with the administration of excessive amounts of solute by mouth or vein.

Water Intoxication

1. Water intoxication results from the overloading of the extracellular space with hypotonic fluid.

2. Symptoms appear with a rapid fall in serum sodium.

Edema

1. When the volume of interstitial fluid has been increased to the point of being recognizable by clinical examination (about 10 to 15 per cent), edema is said to be present.

2. Edema is of four fundamental types.

   a. Lowering of the plasma albumin concentration, which alters the effective osmotic gradient between the plasma and interstitial compartments.
   b. Damage to the capillary endothelium, allowing passage of protein into the interstitial space, which sets up a new osmotic gradient, pulling water into the interstitial space. This mechanism is involved in blisters, hives, and localized inflammation.
   c. Increased venous pressure, which opposes the return of fluid to the vascular compartment from the interstitial space.
   d. Obstruction of the lymphatics produces lymphedema, in which fluid and protein accumulate in the interstitial space.

Treatment of Burns

1. Burns produce three characteristic features: loss of plasma, elevation of the hematocrit, and oliguria.

2. Plasma is lost to a third space, the area of burned tissue into which water, electrolytes, and protein translocate.

3. A net K/Na exchange occurs as endogenous water leaves the intracellular space to replace water lost from the extracellular space and takes potassium with it; the potassium is replaced in the cells by sodium.

   a. The potassium levels in the extracellular space can reach dangerous levels in this K/Na exchange, particularly in oliguria, anuria, or adrenal insufficiency.

   b. More generally, the body experiences a drop in total body sodium and potassium concentration, with renal excretion and extravasation of sodium and potassium into the third space.

4. In severe burns the volume control mechanisms fail to maintain blood pressure, and shock may quickly ensue. Administration of intravenous fluid combats this problem. However, excessive fluid can result in cardiac failure and pulmonary edema. Venous pressure must be continually monitored.

5. A practical formula for replacement of fluids consists of using 1 ml of fluid for each percentage area of burn per pound of body weight.

6. Hyperkalemia may develop in the early stages when there is renal failure and an outflow of potassium from destroyed cells.

7. Several days after the burn, the fluid of the third space may suddenly be reabsorbed and acute overexpansion of the vascular system may occur. Sodium and water intake should be restricted during this period.

Potassium Balance

1. Potassium is the major cation of the intracellular fluid and is important in regulation of intracellular fluid volume, neuromuscular irritability, and hydrogen ion concentration.

2. When potassium moves out of the cells, sodium and hydrogen move in. When sodium and hydrogen become excessive in the extracellular fluid and are osmotically forced into the cells, potassium moves out.

3. The feedback mechanism between potassium and aldosterone is just the opposite of that of sodium.

4. Potassium may also be lost through gastrointestinal tract disturbances such as vomiting and diarrhea.

Magnesium Balance

1. Magnesium is primarily an intracellular cation.

   a. Magnesium activates enzyme systems in the energy cycle and also activates phosphatase, the enzyme that catalyzes reactions in the liver and bone.

b. Most intracellular magnesium is bound to protein and is not osmotically active (ionized).

2. Extracellular magnesium is only about one-tenth of the intracellular content.

a. Extracellular magnesium concentration is maintained by the kidneys.

3. Intestinal absorption of magnesium is rather poor, which serves to make magnesium salts excellent laxatives.

4. There are similarities between the actions of magnesium and calcium; also there are curious differences.

a. A low serum magnesium or calcium increases neuromuscular irritability and a high concentration of either has the opposite effect.
b. Magnesium narcosis is antagonized by parenteral administration of calcium.
c. However, hypomagnesemia can be aggravated by calcium or phosphorus in the diet.

Phosphate Balance

1. The regulation of phosphate concentrations is closely related to that of calcium.

2. Intracellular phosphate concentration is many times the extracellular concentration.

3. Phosphates within the cells are involved in high energy systems (e.g., ATP) and are necessary for formation of nucleic acids.

4. Two related, but partially independent, mechanisms regulate extracellular phosphate concentration.

a. Parathyroid hormone stimulates osseous tissue to give up calcium phosphate to solution, but the feedback regulation depends on calcium, not phosphate.
b. The kidneys are stimulated by the parathyroid hormone to excrete phosphate and are the ultimate regulators of extracellular phosphate concentration.

5. Normally, phosphate is excreted in the urine, only a small amount appearing in the stool.

Chloride Balance

1. Chloride is mainly an extracellular anion; however, it diffuses readily between the intracellular and extracellular compartments.

2. Because it easily traverses the cell membrane, chloride is important in regulating both osmotic pressure and acid-base balance.

a. The chloride-bicarbonate shift occurs when bicarbonate ion concentration increases in the red blood cells because of carbonic acid formation. Bicarbonate diffuses into the plasma, and chloride diffuses into the cell from the plasma.
b. As a result, the content of chloride in *venous* red blood cells is slightly higher than that in *arterial* red blood cells.
c. Chloride also responds to changes in protein concentration in various fluid compartments to maintain electrical and osmotic gradients.

3. Chloride may be lost from the kidneys, gastrointestinal tract, and skin.

a. Chloride reabsorbed by the kidneys is in direct proportion to sodium reabsorption, so that chloride reabsorption is affected by the same factors controlling sodium reabsorption, especially aldosterone.
b. Gastrointestinal loss is most severe in vomiting, when the concentrated HCl of the stomach is lost.
c. Sodium chloride is lost through sweating.

Acid-Base Regulation

1. Regulation of acid-base balance is essentially a problem of preventing alterations in hydrogen ion concentration secondary to the continuous formation and expulsion of the acid end products of metabolism.

2. The acidity or alkalinity of a solution is determined by the concentration of hydrogen ions.

a. Acidity is expressed as pH.
b. The pH of normal extracellular fluid is between 7.35 and 7.45.

3. To prevent acidosis or alkalosis, several special control systems are available in the body.

a. All body fluids contain buffer systems which prevent excessive changes in hydrogen ion concentration.
b. The respiratory center is stimulated by

changes in CO_2 and H^+ concentrations to alter the rate of pulmonary ventilation and thus CO_2 is removed from body fluids. About two times as much acid or base can be buffered by this mechanism as by all the chemical buffers combined.

c. The kidneys excrete either acidic or alkaline urine in response to changes in hydrogen ion concentration.

4. The buffers act within a fraction of a second, the respiratory system takes 1 to 3 minutes, and the kidneys, although the most powerful, require from several hours to a day to readjust the hydrogen ion concentration.

Buffer Activity

1. A buffer solution contains a weak acid or base and a salt of this acid or base.

2. The bicarbonate-carbonic acid buffer system is contained in all body fluids.

a. When a strong acid (HCl) is added, it reacts with the bicarbonate to form weak carbonic acid and sodium chloride.

b. When a strong base (NaOH) is added, it reacts with the carbonic acid to form sodium bicarbonate and water.

c. The actual capacity and efficiency of this buffer system are greatly augmented by the respiratory expulsion of carbon dioxide.

3. The phosphate buffer system acts almost identically to the bicarbonate buffer system.

a. A strong acid is converted into a weak acid and sodium chloride.

b. A strong base is converted into the less alkaline Na_2HPO_4 and water.

c. The potential capacity and efficiency of the phosphate and bicarbonate buffer systems are similar.

d. The concentration of phosphate in the extracellular fluid is only about one-sixth that of bicarbonate.

e. The phosphate system also plays an important role in aiding excretion of hydrogen ion in the urine.

4. The protein buffer system is the most abundant and operates the same as the bicarbonate system.

a. Unlike the other systems, the buffer effect of proteins covers the whole pH scale.

b. This breadth of action is due to the variety of amino acids composing the proteins, each of which has its own specific acid-base properties.

c. The two major groups involved in protein buffering are the —COOH group, which dissociates to give off a hydrogen ion, and the common —NH_3OH, which dissociates to give off a hydroxyl ion.

Sodium Depletion and Imbalance

1. Pure sodium depletion is the extreme opposite of pure water depletion (desiccation).

2. With increasing sodium depletion (and hypotonicity), osmotic forces begin drawing water into the cells.

a. The hematocrit and plasma protein concentration rise, and there is poor venous filling; hence, cardiac output diminishes and blood pressure falls.

b. With severe sodium depletion, hypovolemia induces tachycardia; selective vasoconstriction may lead to diminished circulation through the skin, extremities, and kidneys, leading to cold limbs and to oliguria or anuria.

3. Clinical sodium depletion has been observed in numerous disease conditions.

a. Loss of gastrointestinal secretions by diarrhea, vomiting, aspiration, or discharge from fistulae is common and is usually complicated by alkalosis or acidosis.

b. Urinary losses are especially critical because they are easily overlooked. Solute loading with glucose or urea is a cause of sodium depletion, as is lack of aldosterone, as found in Addison's disease.

Acidosis

1. Acidosis may be defined as an excess of hydrogen ion in the body. The term is *not* synonymous with acidemia, which means an excess of hydrogen ion in the plasma.

2. The state of acidosis without acidemia has been referred to as *compensated* acidosis; this is not a stable situation and tends to break down into *uncompensated* acidosis if the cause of hydrogen ion excess persists.

Respiratory Acidosis

1. Respiratory acidosis is characterized by a primary rise in Pco_2, and invariably results from some form of respiratory failure.

Metabolic Acidosis

1. Metabolic acidosis may occur either from abnormal metabolism, as in diabetic or lactic acidosis, or from impaired excretion, as in uremic acidosis.

2. Respiratory compensation is produced by rapid breathing, which blows off CO_2 at an increased rate.

Alkalosis

1. Alkalosis results either from the imposition of alkali loads on the body or from excessive activity of the lungs.

Respiratory Alkalosis

1. Respiratory alkalosis is characterized by a primary fall in Pco_2 due to persistent hyperventilation.

Metabolic Alkalosis

1. Administration of excessive amounts of sodium bicarbonate or sodium salts of other organic acids such as sodium lactate may produce metabolic alkalosis.

REVIEW QUESTIONS

1. Approximately what percentage of the body weight is water? Is the greater part of the body water in the intracellular or extracellular space? Where is most of the extracellular water located?
2. What are the two main factors that control the distribution of water between the vascular and interstitial compartments of the extracellular fluid?
3. Is the control of water loss from the skin related to the content of body water? If not, to what is water loss from the skin related? Do any other organs besides the kidneys adjust water loss to balance water intake?
4. Define the term edema. Describe four types of edema.
5. List the three characteristic features of burns.
6. List some of the causes of respiratory acidosis and metabolic acidosis.

Unit 4 □
REPRODUCTION

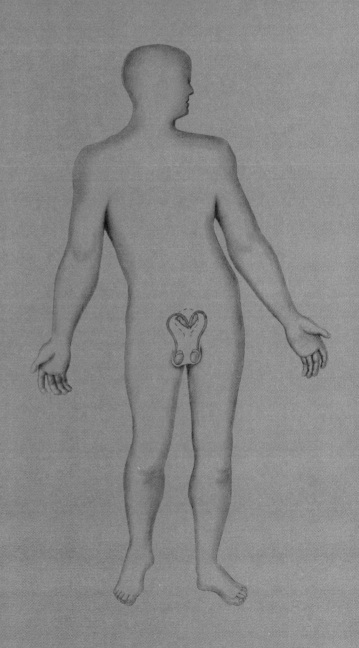

18

The Reproductive System

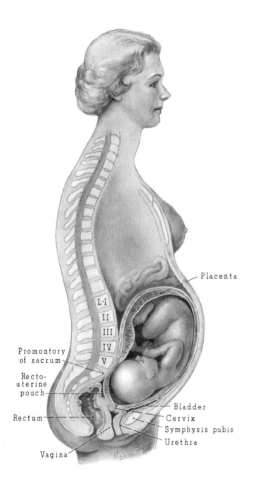

Placenta

L-I

II

III

IV

V

Promontory of sacrum

Recto-uterine pouch

Rectum

Vagina

Bladder

Cervix

Symphysis pubis

Urethra

Objectives

The aim of this chapter is to enable the student to:

☐ Describe the anatomy of the external and internal organs and associated structures of the male reproductive system and explain their functions.

☐ Summarize the congenital abnormalities related to the development of the penis and descent of the testes.

☐ Describe the anatomy of the external and internal organs and associated structures of the female reproductive system and explain their functions.

☐ Describe the structure and functions of the mammary glands.

☐ Describe the processes of spermatogenesis and oogenesis.

☐ Outline and discuss in stages: ovulation, fertilization, and implantation.

☐ Summarize the three stages of the menstrual cycle and discuss menstrual problems and menopause.

☐ Describe the interrelations between estrogens, progesterone, and gonadotropins during the menstrual cycle.

☐ Summarize the functions of androgens, estrogens, and progesterone.

☐ Name and describe briefly the different layers of the placenta and discuss its overall functions.

☐ Describe the stages of labor.

HISTORICAL DEVELOPMENT

Many early scientific explanations of reproduction were more mystical than scientific. Hippocrates believed that "seeds from all parts of the male and female bodies flowed together to unite and form the fruit." Aristotle opined that the male factor provided movement and the female factor provided substance, with the sex of the baby depending upon which factor predominated. In 1672 de Graaf observed the follicles of an ovary and mistakenly thought they were ova. The actual ovum was not seen until 1827, when von Baer traced its course along the uterine tube into the uterus. Spermatozoa were so named because they were originally thought to be "small parasitic animals." In 1853 fertilization was properly described as the entry of the spermatozoon into the ovum; however, the vast knowledge at our disposal today concerning reproduction came about largely as the product of investigation during the last five decades.

MALE REPRODUCTIVE SYSTEM

External Organs (Figs. 18–1 to 18–3)

Scrotum and Penis. The scrotum and penis are the external male organs of reproduction. The scrotum is a pouch which hangs behind the penis and is suspended from the pubis. It is a continuation of the abdominal wall and is divided by a septum into two sacs, each containing and supporting one of the testes with its *epididymis*, or connecting tube. After adolescence the skin of the scrotum is more heavily pigmented than the covering of the general body, and is covered with sparse hair. Scattered in the subcutaneous tissue of the scrotum are fibers of smooth muscle (the dartos layer). The fibers of the dartos layer contract in the presence of reduced ambient or body temperature and give a more wrinkled appearance to the scrotum. This contraction of the dartos causes the testes to be positioned close to the perineum (region between the thighs at the lower end of the trunk; see Fig. 18–3), where they can absorb body heat and maintain a temperature compatible with the viability of spermatozoa. Under conditions of normal temperature, muscle fibers are relaxed, the

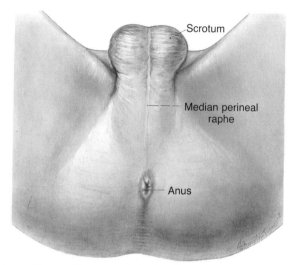

Figure 18–1. Superficial view of the male perineum (subject in supine position with thighs fully abducted.)

scrotum is pendulous, and the walls are relatively free from wrinkles.

The penis, the male organ of copulation, is a flaccid structure when not stimulated. It is attached to the anterior and lateral walls of the pubic arch in front of the scrotum and is composed of three longitudinal columns of erectile tissue (capable of considerable enlargement when engorged with blood) surrounded by nonfatty subcutaneous tissue and covered with skin (Fig. 18–4). Two of the longitudinal columns, the **corpora cavernosa penis**, are located dorsally and form the greater part of the penis. They run together as a pair, surrounded by a common fibrous envelope and separated only by a median fibrous septum. *Trabeculae* continuous with the fibrous envelope and consisting of collagenous, elastic, and smooth muscle fibers divide each corpus cavernosum penis into *cavernous spaces*. These spaces are lined with endothelium and constitute blood sinuses. The third longitudinal column, known as the **corpus spongiosum** or **corpus cavernosum urethrae**, is situated ventrally and is traversed by the cavernous, or penile, portion of the urethra. Its fibrous envelope and trabeculae are thinner and more elastic and the cavernous spaces smaller than those of the corpora cavernosa penis. At its distal end, the corpus spongiosum suddenly expands, forming the *glans penis*, upon which the urethral orifice is located. The skin of the penis is thinner and, like that of the scrotum, more

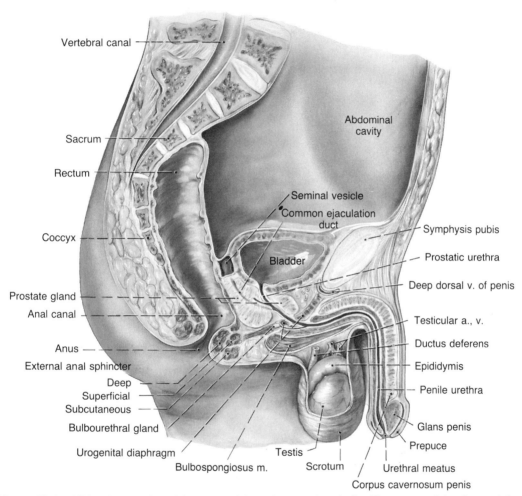

Figure 18–2. Midsagittal section of the male pelvis and external genitalia. (The course of the ductus deferens is shown in Figure 15–12.)

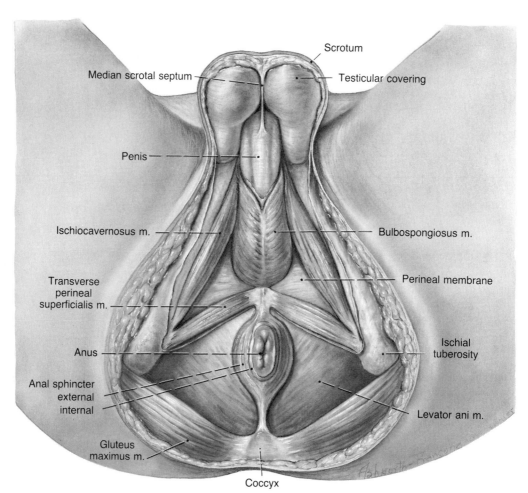

Figure 18–3. Male perineum with skin and superficial fascia removed.

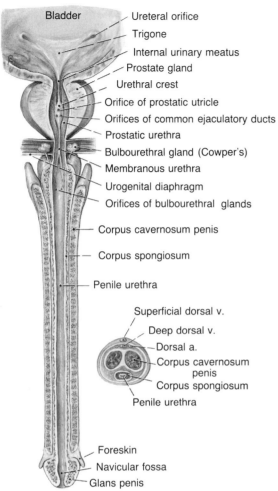

Figure 18-4. Section through the bladder, prostate gland, and penis.

highly pigmented than the skin of the remainder of the body. It is covered with hair only at the base. Terminally, the skin folds inward and backward upon itself, overhanging the glans penis as the *prepuce*, or *foreskin*. In current practice, this foreskin may be removed in newborn boys by the simple surgical procedure known as circumcision (Fig. 18–5).

The phenomenon of *erection* occurs with sexual stimulation. Parasympathetic stimulation causes the arteries supplying the penis to dilate, and a large quantity of blood under pressure enters the cavernous spaces of the erectile tissue. As these spaces expand, they compress the veins supplying the penis, thus retaining all the entering blood. This causes the penis to become firm and erect and facilitates its penetration into the female vagina during sexual intercourse. When the arteries

constrict, more blood leaves the penis than enters, and the organ returns to its flaccid state.

The penis may be the site of several abnormalities noted at birth (Fig. 18–5). Two of these are *hypospadias* and *epispadias*. Malformations of the urethral groove and urethral canal sometimes create abnormal openings either on the ventral surface of the penis (hypospadias) or on the dorsal surface (epispadias). Such abnormalities are generally associated with a failure of normal descent of the testes and with malformations of the urinary bladder. Both hypospadias and epispadias should be surgically corrected.

PHIMOSIS. When the orifice of the prepuce is too narrow to permit retraction over the glans penis, the condition is known as phimosis. Phimosis prevents cleanliness and permits accumulation of secretions under the prepuce, favoring the development of secondary bacterial infection. Circumcision obviates phimosis and possibly protects against the development of tumors by lessening the accumulation of secretions, minimizing the tendency to irritation and infection.

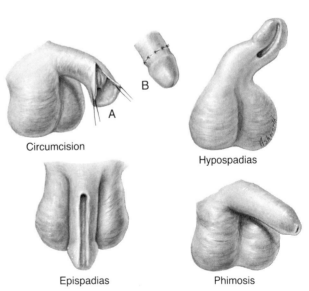

Circumcision

Hypospadias

Epispadias

Phimosis

Figure 18-5. In *circumcision* the prepuce is removed. *A* shows incision in the prepuce. Closure of the wound after removal of the prepuce is shown in *B*.

The penis may be the site of several abnormalities at birth. Among these are *hypospadias,* in which the urethral opening is on the ventral surface of the penis; *epispadias,* in which the urethral opening appears on the dorsal surface; and *phimosis,* in which the orifice of the prepuce is too narrow to permit retraction over the glans penis.

Internal Organs

The internal organs of reproduction in the male can be divided into three groups. First there are the male gonads, or testes. The second group consists of a series of ducts, including the epididymis, ductus deferens, and ejaculatory duct. The third group of internal organs are the accessory glands: seminal vesicles, prostate, and bulbourethral (Cowper's) glands.

Testes. The testes correspond to the ovaries in the female. Each is an oval organ about 2 inches in length, lying within the abdominal cavity in early fetal life. About 2 months prior to birth the testes leave the abdomen and descend into the scrotum.

Occasionally the testes do not descend, but remain in the abdomen, giving rise to a condition known as *cryptorchism* (G. *kryptos*, hidden; G. *orchis*, testis); this can happen unilaterally or bilaterally. The cause of this condition is poorly understood. In a small percentage of cases it is believed to be a hereditary abnormality; but in most instances it is an isolated anatomic abnormality or mechanical obstruction to descent. When cryptorchism is discovered before the age of puberty, the testes are usually normal in size but in an abnormal location. When the condition is discovered at or after the age of puberty, the testes have already commenced to atrophy and decrease in size.

The fetal testis is preceded in its descent from the abdomen into the scrotum by an invaginating process of the peritoneum, called the processus vaginalis, from which the *tunica vaginalis*, the outer covering of the testis, is derived. The tunica vaginalis is reflected onto the inner surface of the scrotum, hence may be described as having vis-

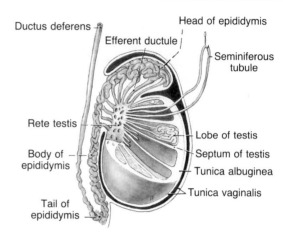

Figure 18–7. Diagram of a section of the male testis showing detail of a seminiferous tubule.

ceral and parietal layers. Beneath the tunica vaginalis is a fibrous investment of the testis known as the *tunica albuginea* (Fig. 18–6), consisting of fibroelastic connective tissue containing scattered smooth muscle cells, especially in the region adjacent to the epididymis. At its posterior border the tunica albuginea is reflected into the testis, forming an incomplete vertical septum known as the *mediastinum testis*. Fibrous septa extend into the substance of the testis, dividing it into about 250 wedge-shaped lobes. Each lobe contains from one to three narrow, coiled tubes known as **seminiferous tubules** (Fig. 18–7). If uncoiled, a tubule would measure about two feet in length. Male reproductive cells at different stages of development are found within these tubules. The maturing spermatozoa are usually seen in the center of the tubule and the premature spermatogonia and primary spermatocytes at the periphery of the tubule nearer the germinal epithelium.

In addition to reproductive cells, supportive and nutritive cells known as *Sertoli cells* are found in the testis. These cells supply nutrients to the spermatozoa. *Interstitial cells of Leydig* are scattered in the intertubular tissue and are responsible for the production of male hormones.

The seminiferous tubules unite to form a series of larger, straight ducts, which in turn form a network known as the *rete testis*. About 20 small, coiled ductules, the *efferent ductules*, leave the upper end of the rete testis, perforate the tunica albuginea, and open into the epididymis (Fig. 18–7).

Epididymis. The epididymis is the first

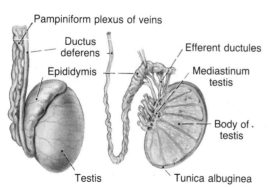

Figure 18–6. Male testis, entire and sectioned views.

part of the duct system of the testis. It is a coiled tube lying on the posterior aspect of the testis and extending for about 1½ inches from an enlarged upper end (the head) downward (as the body) to the tail. About 16 feet of tube are coiled within this short distance.

Ductus Deferens. Each ductus deferens is a continuation of the epididymis and has been described as "the excretory duct of the testis." It consists of an inner mucous layer, a middle muscular layer, and an outer fibrous layer. It ascends along the posterior border of the testis to enter the abdomen through the *inguinal canal,* an oblique passageway through the abdominal wall about an inch and a half in length extending between an opening in the aponeurosis of the external oblique muscle called the subcutaneous or external inguinal ring and an opening in the transversalis fascia (the deep internal fascia of the abdomen) called the abdominal or internal inguinal ring. Between the testis and the internal inguinal ring the ductus deferens lies within the **spermatic cord** (Figures 8–65 and 8–66), a structure which contains, in addition to the ductus deferens, nerves, blood vessels, and lymphatics. From the internal inguinal ring the ductus deferens crosses the bladder and ureter to the medial side of the seminal vesicle (where it is joined by the duct of the seminal vesicle to form the ejaculatory duct — see below). (The course of the ductus deferens can be seen in Figure 15–12.)

Seminal Vesicles. There are two seminal vesicles, membranous pouches lying posterior to the bladder near its base, each

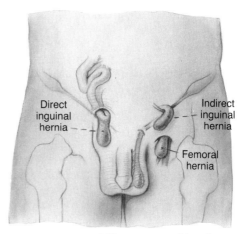

Figure 18–9. Different types of hernias.

consisting of a single tube coiled upon itself. The seminal vesicles secrete a thick, nutrient-containing fluid. The tube of each seminal vesicle ends in a straight, narrow duct joining the ductus deferens to form the **ejaculatory duct.** The ejaculatory duct is a tube about 1 inch in length penetrating the base of the prostate gland and opening into the prostatic portion of the urethra (Fig. 18–8).

Prostate. The prostate gland is a conical body about the size of a chestnut lying inferior to the bladder, with much of its base, or superior surface, in contact with the bladder, and its apex facing downward (Fig. 18–4). It surrounds the first inch of the urethra and secretes a thin, milky, alkaline fluid which aids in maintaining the viability of sperm cells. In older men a progressive enlargement of the prostate commonly obstructs the urethra and interferes with the passage of urine. This condition calls for the surgical removal of a part of the prostate gland. The prostate is also a frequent site of cancer in elderly men.

Bulbourethral Glands. The bulbourethral glands (Cowper's) are two glands, each about the size of a pea, located inferior to the prostate on either side of the urethra (Fig. 18–4). These discharge a lubricating mucous secretion prior to ejaculation which also becomes part of the semen.

The **male urethra** is a tubelike organ responsible for transmitting both semen and urine. It extends from the internal urethral orifice in the urinary bladder to the external urethral orifice at the distal end of the penis (see Chapter 15).

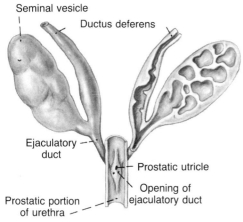

Figure 18–8. Seminal vesicle and related parts. On the left the vesicle and duct are intact; the right side is sectioned to show internal detail.

FEMALE REPRODUCTIVE SYSTEM

External Organs

Vulva. The external female reproductive organs (Fig. 18–10) are collectively known as the vulva, which includes the mons pubis, labia majora, labia minora, clitoris, vestibular glands, and hymen (see Fig. 18–11).

MONS PUBIS AND LABIA MAJORA. The most anterior of the anatomic structures of the vulva is the mons pubis (mons veneris), a firm, cushionlike elevation of adipose tissue over the symphysis pubis, covered by pubic hair. The labia majora are two rounded folds of adipose tissue with overlying skin; they extend from the mons pubis downward and backward to encircle the vestibule (see below). The outer surfaces of these folds are covered with hair, whereas the inner surfaces, containing sebaceous follicles, are smooth and moist. The labia majora are united anteriorly by a fold of skin, the anterior

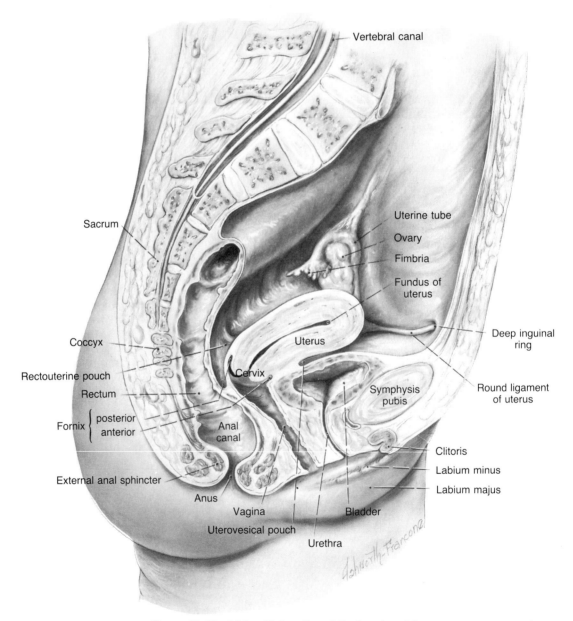

Figure 18–10. Midsagittal section of the female pelvis.

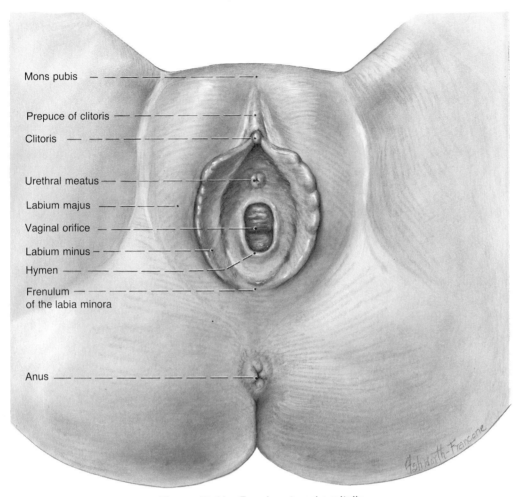

Mons pubis

Prepuce of clitoris

Clitoris

Urethral meatus

Labium majus

Vaginal orifice

Labium minus

Hymen

Frenulum
of the labia minora

Anus

Figure 18–11. Female external genitalia.

commissure. They are not united posteriorly although the ends together with the connecting skin are called the posterior commissure. The labia majora are homologues of the scrotum in the male.

LABIA MINORA. The labia minora are two folds of skin lying medial to the labia majora. Anteriorly, the labia minora divide into two layers. The upper folds join just in front of the clitoris to form the *prepuce* of the clitoris, while the lower folds are attached to the inferior aspect of the glans of the clitoris to form its *frenulum.* Posteriorly, the labia minora become less distinct, but the ends usually appear to be joined by a transverse fold of skin called the *frenulum of the labia minora.*

VESTIBULE. The vestibule of the vagina is the cleft between the labia minora. Situated within the cleft of the vestibule are

the hymen, the vaginal orifice, the urethral orifice, and the openings of the vestibular glands. Between the vaginal orifice and the frenulum of the labia minora is a shallow depression called the *vestibular fossa.* The urethral orifice is an opening 4 to 6 mm in diameter, located about 1 inch posterior to the clitoris and immediately anterior to the vaginal orifice. Multiple small *paraurethral glands* (Skene's) surround the orifice and are homologous to the prostate in the male. These glands open by way of a pair of ducts into the vestibule at the sides of the urethral orifice.

The vaginal orifice occupies the greater portion of the posterior two-thirds of the vestibule. On either side of the vaginal orifice, deep within the perineal tissues, are the two *greater vestibular glands* (Bartholin's glands) (Fig. 18–12). Each opens into the

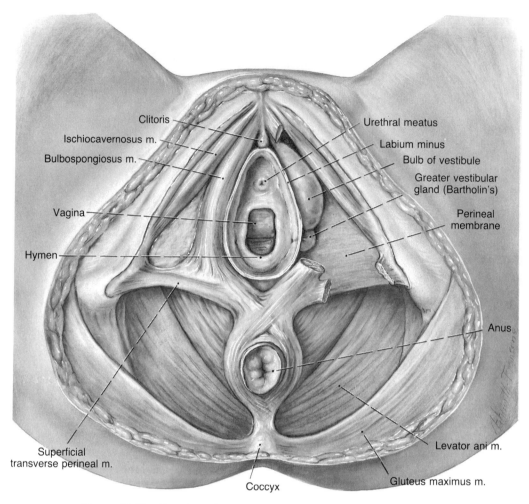

Figure 18–12. Female perineum with skin and superficial fascia removed.

vestibule by means of a duct placed laterally in a groove between the hymen and the labium minus. The greater vestibular glands, homologous to the bulbourethral glands in the male, elaborate a mucous secretion which acts as a lubricant during sexual intercourse.

CLITORIS. The clitoris is a pea-shaped projection of erectile tissue, nerves, and blood vessels occupying the apex of the vestibule anterior to the vagina. It is partially covered by the anterior ends of the labia minora and is highly sensitive to tactile stimulation. The clitoris is important in the sexual excitation of the female and represents the homologue of the penis in the male, but it is not traversed by the urethra.

HYMEN. The hymen is a thin fold of vascularized mucous membrane separating the vagina from the vestibule. It can be entirely absent or can cover the vaginal orifice partly or completely. If the hymen completely covers the vaginal orifice, it is known as an imperforate hymen. Anatomically, neither its absence nor presence can be considered a criterion for virginity.

Perineum. The perineum is the inferior outlet of the pelvis, bounded anteriorly by the symphysis pubis, anterolaterally by the inferior rami of the pubis and the ischial tuberosities, and posteriorly by the tip of the bony coccyx. When the thighs are fully abducted, the perineum assumes a diamond shape which is further divided into anterior and posterior regions by a line drawn between the two ischial tuberosities. The triangle anterior to the line is called the *urogenital triangle* and contains the external

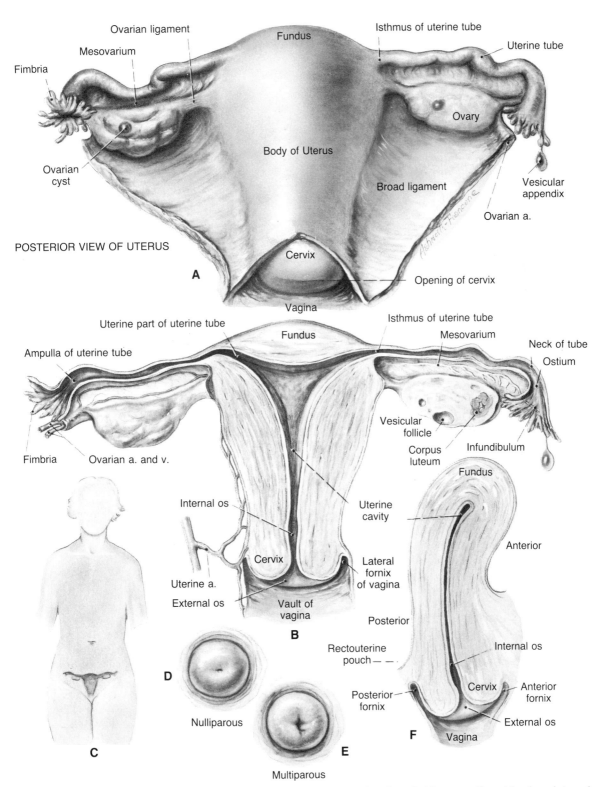

Figure 18–13. Female organs of reproduction. *A*, Uterus, posterior view. *B*, Uterus sectioned to show internal structure. *C*, Position in body. *D* and *E*, Shape of cervix before and after childbirth. *F*, Right lateral sagittal view.

urogenital organs. The triangle posterior to the line is the rectal triangle, containing the anus.

The perineal structures are sometimes torn during childbirth. Tears can extend from the vaginal orifice posteriorly through the perineum and damage the anal sphincters. To avoid this danger an incision is deliberately made in the perineum just prior to the passage of the fetus through the vagina. This incision (episiotomy) allows enough room for the infant to pass and thus minimizes perineal damage.

Internal Organs

Vagina. The internal organs of reproduction (Fig. 18–13) include the vagina, uterus, uterine tubes, and ovaries. The vagina is a tubular canal 4 to 6 inches in length, directed upward and backward and extending from the vestibule to the uterus. It is situated between the bladder and the rectum. The vaginal wall consists of an internal membranous lining and a muscular layer capable of constriction and enormous dilatation, separated by a layer of erectile tissue. The mucous membrane, consisting of stratified squamous epithelium, forms thick, transverse folds and is kept moist by cervical secretions (the cervix is the lower part of the uterus). The vaginal walls are normally folded in close apposition to each other, forming a collapsed tube. The vagina serves as part of the birth canal and represents the female organ of copulation.

Uterus. The uterus is a pear-shaped, thick-walled, muscular organ suspended in the anterior part of the pelvic cavity above the bladder and in front of the rectum. In its normal state it measures about 3 inches in length and 2 inches in width. The lower end of the uterus projects into the vagina; this portion, called the *cervix*, corresponds to the stem end of an inverted pear. The *corpus*, or *body, of the uterus* is superior to the cervix. The uterine tubes enter into the upper end of the uterus, one on each side. The *fundus* is the uppermost, rounded portion of the organ, lying between the two uterine tubes. The uterus, tilted forward and projecting above the bladder from behind, is freely movable; consequently, its position varies with the state of distention of the bladder and rectum (Fig. 18–10). The uterine cavity is normally

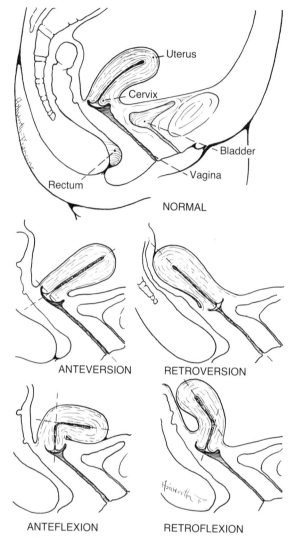

Figure 18–14. Normal and abnormal positions of the uterus.

triangular and flattened anteroposteriorly, making the cavity appear as a mere slit when it is observed from the side.

The uterus is covered with a layer of peritoneum and is attached to both sides of the pelvic cavity by means of a double sheet of peritoneum, or *broad ligaments*, through which the uterine arteries course (Fig. 18–15). The principal supports of the uterus, the *cardinal ligaments*, lie in the base of the broad ligaments. There are also two *round ligaments*, attached on either side and near the uterine tubes, which hold the uterus in its anterior position. The two *uterosacral ligaments* are fibrous bands curved along the floor of the pelvis from the junction of the

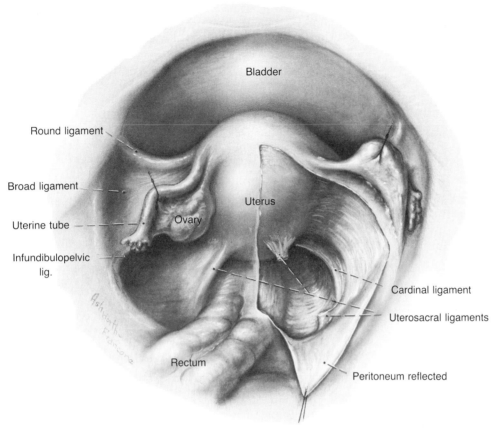

Figure 18–15. View from above and behind of uterine structures as they are seen in the pelvic cavity. The peritoneum has been reflected on the right side, and the uterosacral ligament has been cut to expose the cardinal ligament found in the base of the broad ligament.

cervix and corpus to the sacrum. The uterosacral ligaments aid in supporting the uterus and in maintaining its position.

The wall of the uterus consists of three layers. The outer layer is a peritoneal investment of the organ, continuous on each side with the peritoneum of the broad ligament. The middle layer, **myometrium** (G. *mys,* muscle; G. *mētra,* womb), a thick, muscular layer, consists of bundles of interlaced, smooth muscle fibers embedded in connective tissue. The myometrium in turn is subdivided into three ill-defined but intertwining muscular layers, the middle of which contains many large blood vessels. It is this intertwining arrangement of muscles that presses against the blood vessels and stops them from bleeding after delivery.

During pregnancy, there is a marked increase in the thickness of the myometrium. This occurs not only because of hypertrophy (actual enlargement of existing fibers) but also because of the addition of new fibers

derived from transformation and division of mesenchymal cells. The inner coat of the uterine wall is the mucous membrane, or **endometrium**. It consists of an epithelial lining and connective tissue called the endometrial stroma. The stroma supports the tubular epithelial glands opening into the uterine lumen. Two types of arteries supply blood to the endometrium. The straight arteries supply the deeper layer and the coiled type supplies the superficial layer. The coiled arteries undergo progressive changes during the menstrual cycle and are sloughed during menstruation.

Uterine Tubes. The uterine (Fallopian) tubes are two flexible, trumpet-shaped, muscular tubes approximately 4½ inches in length, extending from the fundus of the uterus on either side toward the pelvic brim. Each uterine tube is suspended by a fold of the broad ligament called the *mesosalpinx* (salpinx means tube). The wall of the tube is composed of the same three layers as the uterus — mucous, smooth muscle, and serous layers. The mucous, or internal, layer is lined with ciliated columnar epithelium and is continuous with the epithelium of the uterus as well as with the peritoneum in the abdominal cavity. The muscular coat consists of a circular inner layer and a discontinuous longitudinal outer layer. One end of the tube, the *isthmus*, opens into the uterine cavity and is continuous with the *ampulla*. The ampulla is the dilated, central part of the tube curving over the ovary, and is in turn continuous with the *infundibulum*, a trumpet-shaped expansion of the tube which opens into the abdominal cavity (Fig. 18–13).

The infundibulum is surrounded by fingerlike projections, or *fimbriae*. The fimbriated portion of the uterine tube curves about the ovary and is adjacent to but not necessarily in direct contact with it. When an ovum is expelled from the ovary, the fimbriae work like tentacles to draw the ovum into the tube, where fertilization may occur. Then, by muscular peristaltic contractions and ciliary activity, the tube conducts the ovum to the uterine cavity.

Ovaries. The ovaries, often referred to as the primary reproductive organs of the female, are two oval-shaped structures about 1½ inches in length; they are located in the upper part of the pelvic cavity, one on each side of the uterus. Each ovary is suspended from the broad ligament of the uterus by the *mesovarium*, a fold of peritoneum, and is anchored to the uterus by the ovarian ligament. The infundibulopelvic, or suspensory, ligament of the ovary extends from its upper pole to the pelvic wall.

A thin layer of cuboidal cells, the germinal epithelium, covers each ovary. The inner structure, or stroma, of the ovary consists of a meshwork of spindle-shaped cells, connective tissue, and blood vessels. Minute follicles at various stages of development are present within each ovary. The ova develop within these follicles. The two major functions of ovaries are development and expulsion of the female ova and elaboration of female sex hormones.

Mammary Glands

The two mammary glands, or breasts, are accessory reproductive organs. The breasts of postpartum women secrete milk available for nourishment of the newborn. Each breast is located anterior to the pectoral muscles and extends as a convex structure from the lateral margin of the sternum to the anterior border of the axilla (Fig. 18–16).

The mammary papilla, or nipple, containing the openings of the milk ducts, is located near the center of each breast. A wider circular area of pigmented skin, known as the *areola*, surrounds each nipple. There are from 15 to 20 lobes of glandular tissue arranged radially within the breast, each embedded in adipose tissue and drained by its own lactiferous duct. The dilated portion (lactiferous sinus) of each duct, situated under the areola, serves as a reservoir for milk. In the fully developed mammary glands with milk-secreting potential, the lobes are composed of a number of lobules consisting of clusters of rounded alveoli which open into small branches of the lactiferous ducts. The alveolar luminal lining constitutes the secretory surface from which milk arises.

Development of the Mammary Glands and Lactation. At birth, the mammary glands consist almost entirely of lactiferous ducts; no alveoli are present. Little change in this condition occurs until puberty, at which time, under the influence of estrogens, conspicuous growth and branching of the duct system occurs along with extensive deposition of fat. Small, solid, spheroidal masses of cells are formed at the ends of the smallest branches of the ducts. These are potential alveoli; true secretory alveoli develop only during pregnancy when a rising output of estrogens and progesterone (by the corpus luteum and later the placenta) causes marked alterations in the mammary glands — estrogens stimulating further expansion of the duct system and supporting adipose tissue, progesterone stimulating the development of alveoli. Although it is the specific actions of estrogens and progesterone that are primarily responsible for the development of the mammary glands, other hormones, especially growth hormone and prolactin, are also necessary for their normal development. The mammary glands of nonpregnant women are subject to fluctuations associated with the rise and fall of hormonal secretions during the menstrual cycle. Many women notice fullness, tightness, heaviness, and, occasionally, pain in the breasts just before the onset of menstruation.

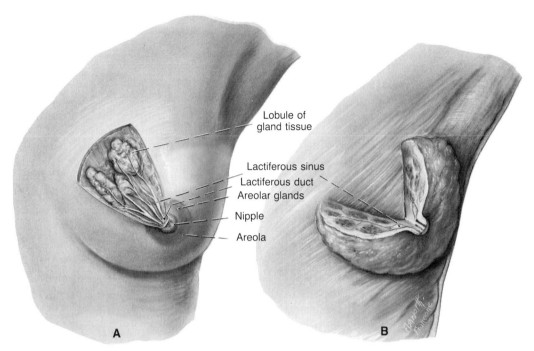

Lobule of
gland tissue

Lactiferous sinus
Lactiferous duct
Areolar glands

Nipple

Areola

Figure 18–16. The female breast. *A*, The skin has been partly removed to show the underlying structures. *B*, A section has been removed to show the internal structures in relation to the muscles.

The secretion formed by the mammary glands toward the end of pregnancy and until milk production (lactation) begins about one to three days after childbirth is called *colostrum*. Colostrum, produced at a much lower rate than milk, contains about the same amount of protein and lactose as milk, but almost no fat. The onset of lactation is preceded by a dramatic rise in blood prolactin, caused apparently by suppression of the secretion of prolactin release-inhibiting factor (see Chapter 16), possibly due to the sudden loss of placental progesterone and estrogens. Prolactin is principally responsible for the initiation of lactation, but other hormones, including insulin and glucocorticoids, play roles in milk production.

SUCKLING STIMULUS. There is a well-recognized nervous factor in the maintenance of normal milk secretion — that is, the suckling stimulant to the mother's breast by the infant. Suckling by the newborn stimulates nerve endings at the nipple, and impulses are carried through the hypothalamic region to the neurohypophysis. There, oxytocin is released and taken by the blood to the mammary glands. Oxytocin causes contrac-

tion of the myoepithelial cells surrounding the milk-producing cells of the alveoli, forcing milk into the lactiferous ducts to be made available to the infant. It has been shown that failure of the ejection reflex eventually leads to lactation failure.

PHYSIOLOGIC PROCESSES RELATED TO REPRODUCTION

Spermatogenesis

Spermatogenesis is the production of spermatozoa. It takes place in the seminiferous tubules of the testes when sexual maturity is reached.

In the embryo original, or *primordial*, germ cells differentiate and appear in the region in which the reproductive organs form. As the primordial germ cells multiply by mitotic cell division, some differentiate and form the youngest male gametes, or *spermatogonia*. Others are organized to form the seminiferous tubules, in which young germ cells grow and develop. The designated spermatogonia then multiply several times and enter a growth period. After birth, through infancy and childhood, these remain in a relatively inactive state. At the time of sexual maturity they again become active when spermatogenesis — the formation of spermatozoa from spermatogonia — is initiated. This usually occurs between the ages of 12 and 15 in the adolescent male.

Spermatogenesis may be divided into three major phases: (1) formation of primary spermatocytes from spermatogonia; (2) meiotic division of spermatocytes, producing haploid spermatids; and (3) differentiation of spermatids into spermatozoa.

In the first phase, **spermatogonia** (often referred to as stem cells) undergo mitotic division to give rise to two populations of cells. One represents a reservoir of spermatogonia. The other continues to divide, the last generation of cells becoming transformed into **primary spermatocytes** by enlarging and undergoing other morphological changes in preparation for meiosis. In the first meiotic division (reduction division), each primary spermatocyte produces two cells, called **secondary spermatocytes,** each containing one set of double-stranded chromosomes. Each of these, in turn, undergoes a second meiotic division, forming two **spermatids,** each of which contains a single set of chromosomes. Thus, four haploid spermatids arise from each primary spermatocyte (see Chapter 3, page 65, for a more complete description of meiosis). The spermatids gradually become transformed into **spermatozoa.** During this transformation the spermatids remain attached to Sertoli cells, which presumably supply nutrients and other substances necessary for bringing about the differentiation of the spermatids into spermatozoa.

About 10 to 11 weeks are required for the formation of the highly specialized spermatozoa from the primitive spermatogonia. The spermatozoon is often described as being tadpole shaped. It consists of an oval head, containing a nucleus; a middle piece, or body, of cytoplasm (separated from the head by a narrow neck); and a long tail, which aids in motility by its lashing movement (Fig. 18–17). The head is capped by a structure called the **acrosome,** derived from the Golgi apparatus, which contains digestive enzymes used, among other things, to aid in penetrating the surrounding investments of the ovum. The midsection contains numerous mitochondria.

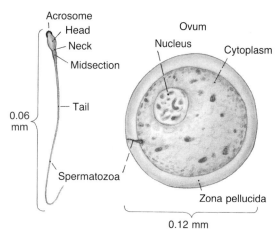

Figure 18–17. Size relations of sperm and ovum.

Spermatozoa released from Sertoli cells in the seminiferous tubules are still functionally immature; that is, they are immotile and lack the ability to effect fertilization. They acquire motility and the ability to fertilize during passage (about two weeks) through the epididymis, in a process called *maturation.* The final phase of maturation, called *capacitation,* is a period of conditioning believed to involve activation of acrosomal enzymes. In a number of lower animals, capacitation has been shown to occur in the female reproductive tract. Whether or not some degree of capacitation also occurs in the human female reproductive tract is uncertain.

During ejaculation, the spermatozoa present in each ductus deferens and the epididymal tails are transported by contractions of the smooth muscles of these structures and of the ejaculatory ducts into the urethra. The secretions of the seminal vesicles and prostate gland are also injected into the urethra at this time, these secretions and those of the bulbourethral glands (contributed prior to ejaculation) together with the spermatozoa forming the reproductive fluid known as *semen.* The accumulation of the semen in the urethra ends the first stage of ejaculation and triggers the second stage — propulsion of the semen through the urethra and out the urethral meatus by contractions of skeletal muscles surrounding the base of the penis, to be deposited during coitus in the vagina close to the cervix.

The most important factors influencing fertility are the actual number of spermatozoa (sperm count), the percentage of abnormal forms, and spermatozoal motility. It has been estimated that a sperm count of over 20 million sperm per ml in an ejaculate of 3 to 5 ml is required for normal fertility. Men with lower sperm counts are not necessarily infertile, but are less fertile than men with higher counts.

Oogenesis. Oogenesis (G. *ōion,* egg; G. *genesis,* production) is the development of the ovum, which takes place within the ovary. As in the male, the female primordial germ cells are derived from the germinal epithelium in the embryo. These multiply and form primitive ova, or **oogonia.** As in spermatogenesis, the mitotic division of the oogonia results in daughter cells with a diploid number (46) of chromosomes. The cells formed in the final mitotic division enter a period of growth and are transformed into **primary oocytes** with the diploid number of chromosomes. All ova produced by the female during reproductive life are derived from primary oocytes already present in the ovaries at birth.

When sexual maturity is reached, meiotic division of the primary oocytes occurs, with the production in the first, or reduction, division of cells containing one set (23) of double-stranded chromosomes. Here, unlike the corresponding stage of spermatogenesis, the division of the cytoplasm is unequal, producing the large and functional **secondary oocyte** and the small, nonfunctional first *polar body,* which usually undergoes rapid degeneration but which can occasionally divide to form two functionless cells. During the second, or mitotic, division of meiosis the secondary oocyte divides, again unequally, to produce a **mature ovum** and a second polar body. Thus, from each primary oocyte only one mature haploid ovum is produced (while each primary spermatocyte gives rise to four mature spermatozoa) (see Fig. 18–18).

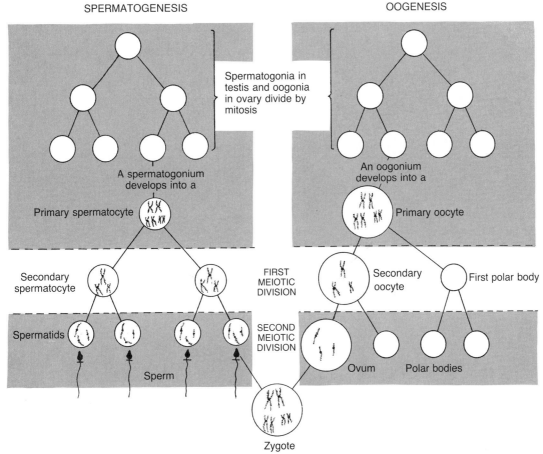

SPERMATOGENESIS   OOGENESIS

Spermatogonia in testis and oogonia in ovary divide by mitosis

A spermatogonium develops into a

Primary spermatocyte

An oogonium develops into a

Primary oocyte

Secondary spermatocyte

FIRST MEIOTIC DIVISION

Secondary oocyte

First polar body

Spermatids

SECOND MEIOTIC DIVISION

Ovum   Polar bodies

Sperm

Zygote

Figure 18–18. Gametogenesis.

The mature ovum is large in comparison to the spermatozoon (Fig. 18–17). It is nonmotile and barely visible to the naked eye. The nucleus of the ovum is surrounded by cytoplasm containing a small quantity of nutritive material in the form of yolk granules.

FOLLICLE MATURATION AND OVULATION. When the primary oocytes are formed, each is surrounded by a single layer of cells derived from the germinal epithelium. A primary oocyte (in prophase I of meiosis) and its surrounding layer of cells (called granulosa cells) are known as a **primary follicle** (see Fig. 18–19). About 400,000 primary follicles are present in the ovaries when the reproductive period of the female begins. At the onset of puberty, when the secretion of large amounts of follicle-stimulating hormone (FSH) commences, a mature ovum develops from a primary oocyte approximately once every 28 days. Changes in the ovary associated with the regular development of

ova are referred to as the *ovarian cycle.* (Changes taking place in the uterine endometrium at the same time are known as the menstrual cycle.) During an ovarian cycle a group of follicles undergo growth and development, but only one reaches maturity and ovulates; all others degenerate (a process called *atresia,* forming what are called *atretic follicles*). Growth of a follicle is characterized by (1) proliferation of granulosa cells; (2) formation of a capsule of connective tissue from the ovarian stroma around the follicle (consisting of an inner cellular layer, the theca interna, and an outer fibrous layer, the theca externa); (3) completion of the first meiotic division with the formation of a secondary oocyte (the second meiotic division [of oocyte] is arrested at metaphase, and this is the condition at ovulation and fertilization); and (4) expulsion of the first polar body.

As the follicle develops, a cavity soon appears, separating the mass of proliferating

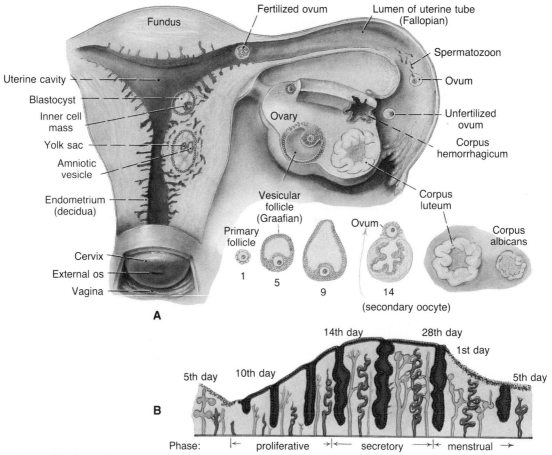

Figure 18–19. *A,* Physiologic processes of the ovary and uterus, showing ovulation, transportation of the ovum, and implantation. *B,* Cyclic menstrual changes in the uterine endometrium.

granulosa cells into two parts. The cavity, or antrum, is filled with fluid (liquor folliculi) believed to be secreted by the cells of the follicle. The oocyte becomes pressed to one side of what at this stage is called the *vesicular follicle* and is separated from the surrounding layer of cells by a transparent membrane known as the *zona pellucida*. A mound of cells surrounding the oocyte, known as the *cumulus oophorus,* projects into the antrum. The follicle becomes distended by an accumulation of contained fluid and moves outward to the surface of the ovary. Once a month, usually about the middle of a 28-day menstrual cycle, the process of ovulation occurs. The follicle ruptures and the ovum (more precisely, the secondary oocyte), surrounded by a ring of granulosa cells called the **corona radiata,** slowly oozes out of the ovarian surface in a stream of follicular fluid. *Ovulation is initiated by a steep rise in the release of luteinizing hormone (LH)* from the adenohypophysis. Rupture of the follicle is *not* caused by an increase in intrafollicular pressure arising from the accumulation of fluid within the antrum. On the contrary, ovulation is preceded by a slight fall in intrafollicular pressure. The cause of rupture is an increase in distensibility and reduction in breaking strength of the follicular wall (theca externa). This appears to occur as follows: LH (with cyclic AMP acting as a second messenger) stimulates the secretion of progesterone by follicular tissue. Progesterone, in turn, induces the production of an enzyme (collagenase) that weakens the framework of the theca externa.

Once ovulation has occurred, definite changes take place within the ovary. First there is minimal hemorrhage into the ruptured follicle, forming a blood clot, the *corpus hemorrhagicum*. Then the cells of the ruptured follicle undergo alteration and create a mass known as the **corpus luteum** (yellow body), which absorbs the corpus hemorrhagicum. The corpus luteum secretes large amounts of progesterone and lesser amounts of estrogens. If fertilization occurs, the corpus luteum continues to function until about the third month of pregnancy, when the placenta takes over its function and it begins to slowly degenerate. It is still present in the ovary at the time of birth. If fertilization does not occur, the corpus luteum degenerates and menstruation follows (described later). The location of the old corpus luteum is marked by an area of white scar tissue in the ovary known as the *corpus albicans.*

Fertilization

After its discharge from the ovary, the ovum (secondary oocyte, actually) begins a six- to eight-day journey, with its destination, the uterus, more than 3 inches away. It does not have any means of locomotion and must be transported through the uterine tube by peristaltic contractions of smooth muscles and by the activity of cilia present in the tube.

Fertilization normally occurs when the ovum is about one-third of the way down the tube. Spermatozoa reach this point five minutes after coitus. Of the hundreds of millions of spermatozoa usually ejaculated, only tens of thousands enter the cervix. Of these, only a few thousand reach the body of the uterus, and only a few hundred travel the remaining distance. The mechanisms by which the spermatozoa make the complete trip so rapidly are still uncertain.

When the sperm reaches the ovum, it releases acrosomal enzymes, including hyaluronidase, which aid in dispersal of the corona radiata, and a proteolytic enzyme utilized in penetrating the zona pellucida. Normally only one sperm enters the ovum. As soon as penetration has occurred, the sperm sheds its tail and the chromosomal material forms the male *pronucleus*. Simultaneously, the ovum becomes impenetrable to other spermatozoa and prevents fertilization by several sperm.

The presence of the male pronucleus induces the secondary oocyte to proceed with the second meiotic division, and it casts off the second polar body. The male and female pronuclei come together and join into one. The union of the two gametes restores the chromosome number to 46, and the fertilized ovum (also known as the *zygote*) begins its first cleavage in the process of development.

Menstrual Cycle and the Menopause

The Menstrual Cycle. The menstrual cycle commences at the age of puberty (menarche) and continues until the menopause, approximately 40 years later. The day of onset of the menstrual flow is considered the first day of the cycle. The cycle ends on the last day prior to the next menstrual flow. Normally the cycle is 28 days in duration, but it can vary from 22 to 35 days. Three phases of the menstrual cycle are distinguished — menstrual, proliferative, and secretory (see Fig. 18–19).

MENSTRUAL PHASE. The menstrual phase lasts from the first day to about the fifth day of the cycle. Menstruation occurs when the expectation of implantation of the blastocyst (described later) following fertilization is not fulfilled. The endometrial lining is destroyed and is rebuilt for the next possible implantation. When the ovum is not fertilized, the corpus luteum regresses; the subsequent fall in the blood levels of progesterone and estrogens is followed by the disintegration of the uterine endometrium. This is preceded by intermittent constriction of the coiled arteries, which causes anoxia and results in shriveling of the superficial (functional) layer of the endometrium. Necrotic tissue is shed, and this is followed by rupture of surface vessels. The entire functional layer is eventually sloughed, leaving only the deep (basal) layer intact (Fig. 18–19).

PROLIFERATIVE PHASE. The proliferative phase, characterized by estrogen stimulation, begins at about the fifth day of the cycle and extends through ovulation, which usually occurs near the midpoint of the cycle (14 days *before* the onset of menstruation). The endothelium thickens as estrogen secretion rises. There is rapid growth of glands and supporting connective tissue (stroma). Coiled arteries grow into all but the superficial third of the regenerating tissue.

The ovulatory process is initiated by a sharp rise in the secretion of luteinizing hormone. Conspicuous changes do not occur in the endometrium at this point. A distinct rise in basal body temperature occurs a day or so after ovulation and remains high until the onset of the next menstrual period. The presence of progesterone accounts for this temperature rise.

SECRETORY PHASE. During the secretory (progestational) phase, progesterone levels rise; there is a concomitant but lesser rise in estrogens. The endometrium differentiates into a secretory type of tissue capable of fulfilling the requirements for implantation of the embryo. The glands hypertrophy and take on a coiled and tortuous appearance.

This further thickens the endometrium. Coiled arteries grow almost to the surface of the endometrium. If implantation does not occur, the corpus luteum decreases in functional activity, degenerative changes are observed in the uterine endometrium, and the menstrual phase starts again.

If fertilization and implantation occur, secretion of human chorionic gonadotropin maintains the corpus luteum; hence, the secretion of progesterone and estrogens is uninterrupted and menstruation does not occur (see Chapter 16, page 568, for a description of placental hormones).

Menstrual Problems. Amenorrhea (absence of menstruation), infrequent or irregular menstruation, prolonged menstruation, and dysmenorrhea (see below) are the most frequent menstrual problems.

Absence of menstruation after the age of 16 is rarely normal. On the other hand, menstrual irregularity, characterized by scanty or heavy flow at intervals of several months or less than 28 days, is quite common during adolescence. It is usually associated with failure of ovulation. The first adolescent cycles may be anovulatory, in which it is believed a follicle develops, becomes cystic, and degenerates, menstruation nevertheless occurring.

Dysmenorrhea, or painful menstruation, the most common menstrual problem, is sometimes caused by pathological conditions such as fibroid tumors of the uterus. Usually, however, it occurs with no obvious cause, a condition known as *primary dysmenorrhea.* Recent research findings have disclosed a probable physiological basis for primary dysmenorrhea, namely, overproduction by the uterus of prostaglandins (locally acting, hormonelike substances — see Chapter 14, page 508). In the uterus, prostaglandins, by triggering muscular contractions, appear to play a critical role in the initiation of both menstruation and labor. Prostaglandins normally rise sharply toward the end of the menstrual cycle. At the same time, the concentration of progesterone, which in high concentration checks the action of prostaglandins, falls. In women with primary dysmenorrhea, the production of prostaglandins by the uterus is excessive — their concentration in menstrual fluid is two to three times higher than normal. The concentration is highest when menstrual pain is most severe, on the first or second day of menstruation. Associated with the increased prostaglandin concentration is a higher than normal resting uterine pressure between muscular contractions. This slows the flow of blood to uterine muscle, and a resulting oxygen deficiency causes pain. In clinical trials, dysmenorrhea has been successfully treated with drugs that inhibit prostaglandin synthesis.

Menopause. The cessation of menstruation is called menopause. It usually occurs between the ages of 50 and 55, and is apparently associated with an impairment of follicular maturation. Several years before menopause, the menstrual cycles may become irregular, both shortening and lengthening, and the menstrual flow may vary from very light to very heavy. Anovulatory cycles may occur.

Associated with menopause are two major symptoms: (1) *flushes*, reddening of the face and a sensation of warmth, sometimes lasting for hours, centered in the head, neck, and upper part of the thorax (these may appear years prior to the actual cessation of menstruation); and (2) *flashes*, brief, intense suffusions of heat over the entire body, accompanied by reddening of the face and sweating (these may continue for a number of years after menopause). These symptoms can be accounted for by a drop in estrogen production. The intense flash episodes have been described as a manifestation of an estrogen withdrawal syndrome because women with gonadal dysgenesis, who have never been exposed to normal estrogen levels and do not experience flashes, will experience them for the first time if estrogen is administered for several months and then discontinued. In a recent study of postmenopausal women, it was observed that the flash episodes are synchronized to sudden rises in the blood levels of luteinizing hormone. Luteinizing hormone release itself is not responsible for initiating the flashes (they occur in hypophysectomized women), and the authors of the study concluded from their observations and those of other investigators that

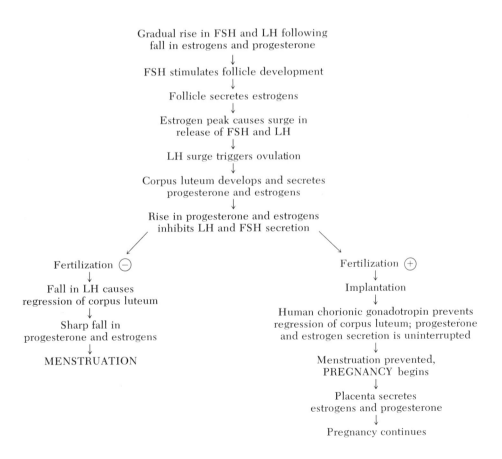

Figure 18–20. Hormonal interrelations during the menstrual cycle and hormonal changes following prevention of the initiation of a new cycle by implantation.

flashes are brought about by some change in an estrogen-sensitive area of the brain that also controls the pulsatile release of the hypothalamic gonadotropin-releasing hormone, which in turn causes the pulsatile secretion of luteinizing hormone.

Hormonal Interrelations During the Menstrual Cycle

The interrelation between the secretion of estrogens and progesterone and the secretion of gonadotropins during the menstrual cycle is illustrated in Figures 18–20 and 18–21. The gradual rise in the secretion of follicle-stimulating hormone (FSH) and luteinizing hormone (LH) by the anterior pituitary gland at the beginning of the cycle is a negative feedback response to the decline in plasma estrogens and progesterone follow-

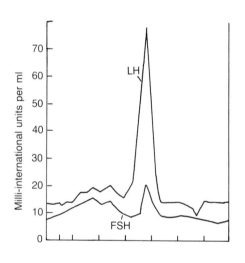

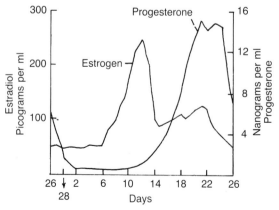

Figure 18–21. Typical changes in plasma concentrations of follicle-stimulating hormone (FSH), luteinizing hormone (LH), estradiol, and progesterone during a 28-day menstrual cycle.

ing the degeneration of the corpus luteum toward the end of the cycle. The rising level of FSH stimulates the development of the ovarian follicle, and the growing follicle secretes estrogens. Clearly inconsistent with negative feedback control is the preovulatory surge in gonadotropin secretion, especially luteinizing hormone (the LH surge triggering ovulation), immediately following the steep rise in the secretion of estrogens by the maturing follicle. This phenomenon is accounted for largely by an increase in the responsiveness of the anterior pituitary gland to gonadotropin-releasing hormone, which is induced by the peak in plasma estrogens (the hypothalamic releasing hormones are described in Chapter 16). Following ovulation, the corpus luteum (which develops from the remains of the ruptured follicle) secretes progesterone and estrogens. Negative feedback accounts for the fall in plasma levels of FSH and LH in the postovulatory period during the time the concentrations of progesterone and estrogens are rising. The fall in the concentration of LH in the plasma causes the regression of the corpus luteum, which, in turn, leads to a sharp fall in plasma progesterone and estrogens, initiating menstruation. If fertilization and implantation occur, the cycle is interrupted because the secretion of human chorionic gonadotropin (see Chapter 16) maintains the corpus luteum, thereby preventing the drop in plasma progesterone and estrogens. Secretion of progesterone and estrogens by the placenta is sufficient to maintain pregnancy when the corpus luteum becomes nonfunctional (at about the tenth week of pregnancy).

Birth control pills take advantage of the pronounced inhibitory effect of progesterone on the secretion of LH. The most commonly used pills contain a synthetic progesterone and a very small amount of synthetic estrogen. Taking the pills for 21 consecutive days, beginning with the fifth day of the cycle, effectively inhibits the preovulatory surge in LH, thereby preventing ovulation.

Functions of Androgens

Testosterone, the principal and most potent androgen, is formed by the interstitial cells of Leydig within the seminiferous tubules of the testes. (The structure of testosterone and of other major steroid hormones is shown in Figure 16–13.) During embryological development, testosterone is responsible for **sexual differentiation.** Whether or not testes or ovaries develop is determined by the X and Y sex chromosomes. If a sperm bearing an X chromosome fertilizes an ovum (producing a zygote with two X chromosomes), ovaries will develop; if a sperm bearing a Y chromosome fertilizes an ovum (producing a zygote with one X and one Y chromosome), testes will form. (For a description of human chromosomes, see Chapter 3, page 65.) Secretion of testosterone by the embryonic testicular cells of Leydig leads to the formation of the male duct system, accessory organs, and external genitalia (regression of the primordial Müllerian ducts, from which the uterine tubes and uterus are formed, is induced by a hormone produced by the embryonic Sertoli cells of the testes called the Müllerian inhibiting factor). In the absence of masculinization by the testes, the female reproductive organs and genitalia develop. In other words, male sexual differentiation is imposed upon the natural inclination of the embryo (without hormones from either gonad) toward female development.

In target areas which give rise to the external genitalia and the prostate gland (the urogenital tubercle, from which the penis is formed; the urogenital swelling, from which the scrotum is formed; and the urogenital sinus, from which the prostate is formed), testosterone apparently functions as a prehormone — it is enzymatically converted to dihydrotestosterone, the active hormone in these regions. The need for dihydrotestosterone for the differentiation of some embryonic tissues is strikingly illustrated in infants born with an inherited deficiency in 5α-reductase, the enzyme that converts testosterone to dihydrotestosterone. This is a rare disorder but is observed in many families in an isolated village in the Dominican Republic. At birth, the affected males have ambiguous external genitalia — a labialike scrotum, a blind vaginal pouch, and a clitorislike phallus — and, before the disorder became obvious to the villagers, were raised as girls (masculination occurs at puberty — see below). (Individuals of this type, having a male genetic constitution and gonads and external genitalia more female than male in appearance, are referred to as male pseudohermaphrodites — true hermaphrodites have the gonads of both sexes.)

It is generally believed that the development of the interstitial cells of Leydig in the embryo and the secretion of testosterone by these cells are induced by human chorionic gonadotropin. After birth the cells of Leydig appear to regress and hormone secretion by the testes is at a bare minimum until puberty. At this time, the secretion of gonadotropins increases and the cells of Leydig are activated by luteinizing hormone (the regulation of testosterone secretion by LH is described in Chapter 16). The increase in testosterone secretion at puberty is responsible for the pronounced growth of the external and internal reproductive organs and the appearance of the *secondary sexual characteristics,* including deepening of the voice (mainly due to structural changes of the larynx and vocal folds), greatly increased muscular development, and the male hair pattern. Testosterone also promotes protein anabolism throughout the body, increases the formation of red blood cells, accelerates the deposition of bone matrix, and, to a slight extent, increases sodium and water retention by the kidneys.

An intriguing question raised by the study of the 5α-reductase–deficient males described above is: Do sex hormones play a role in shaping gender identity? The most widely held contemporary view is that gender identity is determined by how the child is raised. The investigators of the 5α-reductase–deficient males have questioned this traditional concept. As mentioned, the affected males were raised as girls. However, at puberty they became masculinized and almost all of them switched to male gender identity. (Masculinization of these individuals occurs at puberty despite the deficiency in 5α-reductase activity: their voices deepen, they develop a typical male build with a substantial increase in muscle mass, the phallus enlarges to become a functional penis [a change so striking they were called guevedoces, meaning penis at 12, by the townspeople], and the testes descend into a well-formed scrotum [normal spermatogenesis—a process requiring testosterone as well as follicle-stimulating hormone activity—occurring]. The only exceptions to normal masculinization are scanty or absent beard, lack of temporal recession of the hairline, and a small or absent prostate gland.) The authors of the report on these individuals suggest that exposure to testosterone *in utero* shapes gender identity. The implication is that the gender change can be ascribed to the effect of testosterone on the fetal brain and further stimulation of the brain at puberty. A number of investigators, reluctant to accept the hypothesis that prenatal exposure to testosterone affects gender identity, do say, however, that fetal exposure to androgens can have subtle effects on behavior. Supporting such a view is a study by a group of psychologists of girls born with adrenal hyperplasia, a condition in which an enzyme defect of the adrenal cortex exposes the fetus to huge amounts of androgens. After birth, the masculinized external genitalia of the children studied were surgically feminized and adrenal androgens were suppressed to normal levels by treatment with corticosteroids. The psychologists observed these girls from infancy to puberty and concluded that they were significantly different from a control group of girls. They typically displayed more intense outdoor play, greater association with male peers, and were identified by themselves and others as tomboys. They also spent less time in doll play and other "mother rehearsal" roles.

Functions of Estrogens

Estrogens are secreted by the developing ovarian follicle and later by the corpus luteum. During pregnancy they are secreted by the placenta.

Estrogens are responsible for the increased growth of the uterus and vagina at puberty; development of secondary sex characteristics, such as the female figure; and repair of the endometrium following menstruation.

Estrogens exercise partial control over breast development and function. In pregnancy and puberty, estrogens stimulate the formation of ducts in the mammary glands. Estrogens also tend to increase the motility of the uterus and its sensitivity to oxytocin. In this respect its action is opposite to that of progesterone. Toward the end of pregnancy the ratio of estrogens to progesterone increases. This change is believed to be partly responsible for the increased contractility of the uterus at that time. Other actions of estrogens include slightly increasing sodium and water reabsorption by the renal tubules and increasing matrix formation in bone. Diminished secretion of estrogens produces irregularity of the menses and underdevelopment or atrophy of the breast and uterus.

Functions of Progesterone

Progesterone is secreted by the corpus luteum and placenta. It converts the already partially thickened uterine endometrium into a secretory structure specialized for the process of implantation, it is responsible for development of the milk-secreting cells of the mammary glands during pregnancy, and it decreases the motility of the uterus. Diminished secretion of progesterone leads to menstrual irregularities in nonpregnant women and spontaneous abortion in pregnant women.

Chromosomal Abnormalities

Abnormalities in the number of human sex chromosomes can arise as a result of a phenomenon called *nondisjunction* —failure during meiosis of a pair of chromosomes to separate in the first division or failure of two strands of an individual chromosome to separate in the second division. As a result, gametes with an excess or absence of X or Y chromosomes can be produced. Chromosomal abnormalities resulting from fertilization with such gametes are likely to have adverse effects on development. Individuals with the following chromosomal patterns have been described: XO, XXX, XXY, XXXY, XXXXY, and XYY. The YO genotype is apparently lethal.

Individuals with the XO pattern have female genitalia. However, the ovaries regress after the third month *in utero,* and at puberty only remnant structures (so-called streak gonads, devoid of germ cells) are present. Stature is short, and maturation does not occur at puberty. Other congenital defects, such as malformation of the aorta, deafness, and mental deficiency, may be observed. This symptom complex is referred to as Turner's syndrome.

Individuals with the XXY pattern have the genitalia of the normal male, and testosterone production at puberty is often sufficient for the development of male characteristics; however, seminiferous tubules are abnormal. Individuals with this genotype tend to be tall, and frequently suffer from speech and language difficulties. This disorder is known as Klinefelter's syndrome. A number of individuals with XXX patterns have been reported; this is associated with oligomenorrhea (scanty menstruation), sometimes sterility, and a higher than normal incidence of mental deficiency. The rare individuals with XXXY and XXXXY chromosomal patterns have testes and masculine characteristics.

The XYY genotype has received considerable public attention because of its association with an elevated crime rate and the suggestion that the extra Y chromosome contributes to "aggressive tendencies." In one recent study, however, it was concluded, on the basis of a careful analysis of the records, that, although XYY males do have a higher rate of criminal convictions, the crimes generally are not acts of aggression against other individuals. Males with an XYY genotype are usually tall and score lower than average on intelligence tests.

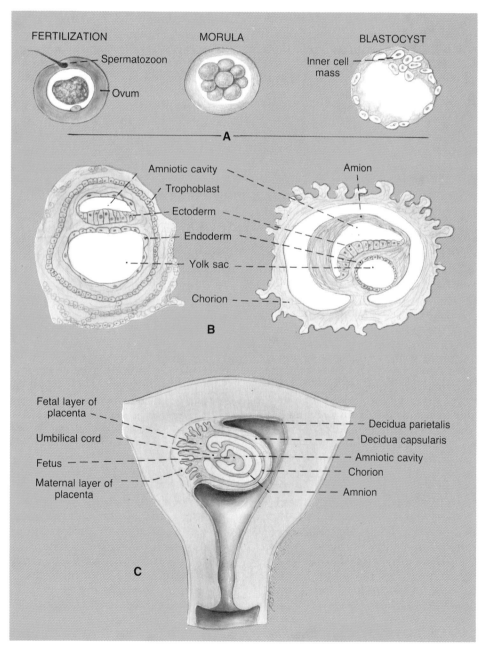

Figure 18–22. *A*, Early cell division. *B*, Developing blastocyst after implantation. *C*, Frontal section of pregnant uterus showing fetal membranes.

Embryology (Fig. 18–22)

In its broadest terms, the science of embryology deals with the study of the embryo (a term denoting the juvenile stage of an animal while it is contained within the maternal body). However, in humans many call the developing young an embryo until organogenesis is completed at 12 to 14 weeks; others call it an embryo until 20 weeks or 1000 gm weight is reached. After that time and until birth it is referred to as the fetus.

Cleavage. Immediately following fertilization, the zygote begins to undergo rapid cell division, or mitosis. First two, four, then eight cells and so forth are formed, each containing 46 chromosomes. The 16-cell stage is reached about 96 hours after ovulation. This process of cell division is called cleavage.

At first the cells, called **blastomeres,** form a solid sphere; the cell mass is known as the **morula.** Successive cleavages produce cells of smaller size, so that the developing morula is only a little larger than the original zygote. As the cells of the morula continue to multiply, they form a hollow ball of cells known as the **blastocyst.** Differentiation of these cells continues to take place, forming one group of cells lying externally, known as the **trophoblast,** and another internally, forming the *inner cell mass* (embryoblast, or formative mass), which gives rise to two layers, the *ectoderm* and *endoderm.* Hollow spheres begin to appear on either side of the ectoderm and endoderm; it is in the region of attachment of these two layers, now called the *embryonic disc,* that the future embryo will develop. A third layer of cells, the *mesoderm,* begins to develop and spread out between the ectoderm and endoderm. Specific tissues will be derived from these three primary germ layers. The ectoderm develops into the epidermis and its appendages (nails, hair, etc.) and the·tissues of the nervous system. The connective tissues, muscle tissues, bone tissues, and tissues of the vascular and lymphatic systems are derived from the mesoderm. The epithelial lining of the digestive tract and its derivatives develops from the endoderm. Further details of the embryology of the various systems of the body are beyond the scope of this book.

Twinning. Identical twins arise from a single ovum fertilized by a single sperm. At some early stage, a separation into two parts occurs, each becoming a separate embryo. If the separation occurs at the two-cell stage, each embryo can have separate membranes. If separation does not occur until the formation of the inner cell mass, then both embryos usually have a single placenta. Identical twins are also known as *monozygotic* or *uniovular twins.* Fraternal twins, also known as *dizygotic* or *biovular twins,* result from the fertilization of two separate ova, both released at approximately the same time. Generally, each developing individual has his own membranes and placenta.

Implantation. Six to eight days after fertilization, the *blastocyst,* having traveled down the uterine tube, enters the uterus and becomes embedded in the endometrium on the posterior wall of the fundus. This process is called *implantation.* The lining of the uterus has been thickened in preparation for about three weeks. The trophoblast burrows into the endometrial lining and carves out a nest for the blastocyst, which then sinks into the underlying connective tissue. The uterine vessels and glands in the penetrated area disrupt; the fluid thus formed furnishes nourishment for the implanted blastocyst. The epithelium heals over, and the embryo develops within the tissues of the uterine wall — not in the cavity, as occurs in most lower animals.

Fetal Membranes and the Placenta

Amnion. The amnion, the innermost of the fetal membranes (Fig. 18–23), is derived from the inner layer of the trophoblast reinforced by mesodermal cells. It appears at an early stage as a small sac with an amniotic cavity covering the dorsal surface of the embryo. The amnion gradually enlarges to completely surround the embryo, coming into apposition with the inner surface of the chorion. The amniotic cavity is filled with amniotic fluid bathing the embryo. This serves to cushion the fetus against possible injury, to maintain the constancy of its temperature, and to furnish a medium in which the developing individual can readily move.

Chorion. The chorion is the outermost covering of the growing embryo, providing both nourishment and protection. The embryo is connected with the connective tissue layer of the chorion by the forerunner of the umbilical cord. The villous portion of the

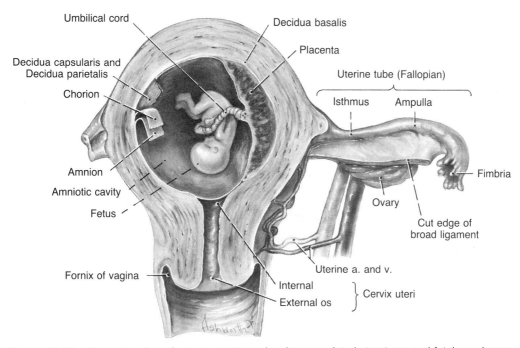

Figure 18–23. Frontal section of pregnant uterus showing associated structures and fetal membranes.

chorion, in which fetal blood vessels develop, forms the fetal part of the placenta.

The Decidua. The decidua is the mucous membrane of the uterus that has undergone certain changes under the influence of progesterone to prepare it for implantation and nutrition of the ovum. It is usually divided into three parts: the *decidua basalis,* that portion beneath the embryo between the chorionic vesicle and the myometrium of the uterus that forms the maternal part of the placenta; the *decidua capsularis,* a thin layer of endometrium covering the embryo, which expands as the embryo grows, obliterating the uterine lumen; and the *decidua parietalis,* the remaining part of the uterine endometrium, which lines the uterus and initially is separated from the decidua capsularis, but later is in contact with it.

The Placenta. The placenta is the structure in the wall of the uterus to which the embryo is attached by means of the umbilical cord (Fig. 18–24) and through which it receives nutrition, exchanges respiratory gases,

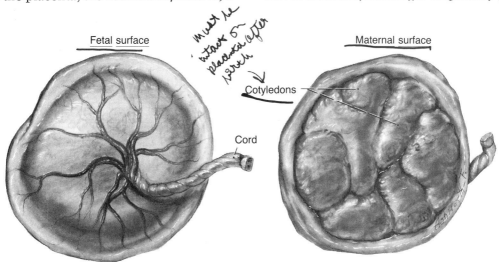

Figure 18–24. Placenta (fetal and maternal surfaces).

and eliminates wastes. The placenta develops from the chorion of the embryo and the decidua basalis of the uterus. By the third month of pregnancy, it is completely formed by the infiltration of the villi of the chorion into the decidua basalis. These villi enlarge, multiply, and branch to the point that each is bathed in a pool of maternal blood.

Actually, there is no exchange of blood between the fetal and maternal portions of the placenta. The maternal placenta receives its blood from the uterine arteries, and blood is returned by way of the uterine veins. The fetal placenta is bathed in maternal blood and receives nutrients ingested by the mother by diffusion through the villi. Oxygen from the mother's blood also diffuses into the blood of the fetus. The waste products diffuse from the fetal blood and are eliminated by the excretory organs of the mother. Thus, the placenta forms the only means by which the nutritional, respiratory, and excretory functions of the fetus are possible.

The placenta also serves as an effective barrier against most diseases of bacterial origin; however, viruses and some blood-borne diseases such as syphilis affect the fetus. Antibodies are transmitted by the mother to the developing embryo and fetus to build up immunity against various diseases. (For discussion of the Rh factor, see Chapter 11.) This immunity is necessary during the first few months of life before the time when the infant can produce its own antibodies.

The mature placenta is a circular disc 8 inches in diameter and nearly 1 inch in thickness, weighing approximately 1 pound. The fetal surface is smooth and glistening, beneath which can be seen many large vessels. The maternal surface is red and flesh-like. At delivery, after the fetus is born, the placenta becomes detached from the uterus and is the "afterbirth" (Fig. 18–24).

Disorders of Pregnancy

Abortion generally refers to any interruption of pregnancy before the end of the 20th week or when the fetus weighs less than 500 grams. Abortion can be either spontaneous or induced. When infection occurs, the process is known as a septic abortion. Women who abort repeatedly are said to be habitual abortors. Termination of pregnancy after the 20th week and prior to the 28th week or when the

weight of the fetus is between 500 and 999 grams is called *immature labor*. Termination between the 28th through the 36th week is called *premature labor*.

Ectopic Pregnancy. Occasionally the fertilized ovum becomes implanted in the uterine tube, a serious condition known as an *ectopic pregnancy*. Ectopic pregnancy includes all cases in which the fertilized ovum becomes implanted at a site other than the decidua of the normal uterine cavity. The most common site for this to occur is the uterine tube, but there are also other regions, such as the ovary, cervix, broad ligament, and peritoneal cavity. The uterine tube must either expel the ovum from its implantation cavity in the tubal mucosa into its lumen (tubal abortion), or the tube must give way (tubal rupture). This mishap frequently occurs before the embryo reaches the age of six weeks; it endangers the life of the mother.

Laboratory Diagnosis of Pregnancy

Most pregnancy tests are designed to detect the presence of human chorionic gonadotropin (HCG) in a sample of urine. In the past, this was done with biological tests. Today, simpler, faster, and less expensive test tube and slide tests based upon immunological principles are generally used.

One of the most widely used biological tests was to inject mice subcutaneously with acidified urine from the patient and on the fifth day examine the ovaries of the mouse for the presence of corpora hemorrhagica or corpora lutea, a positive sign that HCG is present and the patient is pregnant.

In the immunological test tube procedure, the presence of HCG in the urine is detected by its inhibition of the agglutination of HCG-coated red cells or latex particles (which serve as the antigens) with antibodies to HCG (anti-HCG rabbit serum). When the urine to be tested is added to the antiserum prior to the addition of the HCG-coated red cells or latex particles, HCG present in the urine neutralizes the antiserum so that it will not agglutinate the HCG-coated cells or particles; hence, the test is positive if no agglutination occurs. In the slide test, a drop of urine is mixed with a drop of antiserum on a glass slide. Two drops of HCG-coated latex particles are added and the slide is rocked for

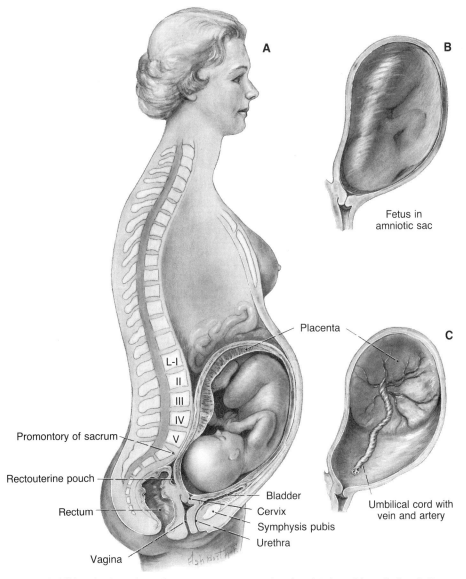

about two minutes. As in the test tube procedure, the absence of agglutination indicates pregnancy.

Calculation of Term

On the assumption that the gestation period totals 280 days from the beginning of the last menstrual period, the date of delivery is estimated by adding one year and seven days to the date of the last menstrual period and subtracting three months.

Labor

The mechanisms involved in the onset of labor are complex and poorly understood. It is certain that labor is not initiated by a single event; it must be regarded as a consequence of many developments occurring during the course of gestation. The uterus is relatively quiescent during gestation, but, as labor approaches, there are signs of increasing myometrial irritability. There is also increased sensitivity of the uterine musculature to oxytocin, in preparation for the forceful muscular contractions required to expel the fetus.

Figure 18–25. *A,* Midsagittal section of a pregnant woman showing fetal position. *B,* Amniotic sac with fetus. *C,* Placenta in uterus with fetus removed.

The hormones generated from the placenta and ovaries are known to play key roles in determining the onset of labor. Progesterone exerts a pregnancy-stabilizing effect. Labor cannot occur until its influence is effectively diminished. Estrogens promote rhythmic contractility of the uterus. It is probably·significant that estrogens increase in amount until the end of gestation, when secretion diminishes. It is also believed that prostaglandins (the locally acting, hormone-like substances mentioned earlier in connection with dysmenorrhea) produced by the uterus play an important role in initiating labor. These substances stimulate uterine contraction, but their action is inhibited by a high concentration of progesterone. When plasma progesterone falls at term, prostaglandins can exert their effect on the uterine muscle.

Oxytocin from the neurohypophysis is known to exert a powerful effect on uterine contractility and is believed to play a role in labor. Labor is a complicated process involving not only uterine contractions but also softening of the cervical canal, relaxation of the pubic ligaments, and contractions of the abdominal muscles. Abdominal contraction is thought to be a reflex response to stimulation of the cervical canal. It has been claimed that at the end of pregnancy softening of the cervical canal is brought about by a placental hormone called relaxin and relaxation of the pubic ligaments is brought about largely by estrogens and progesterone.

The stages of labor are conveniently described in three phases (Fig. 18–26). In the first stage, there are regular contractions, rupture of the ·membranes, and a progressive dilatation of the cervix. The obstetrician follows the course of labor by frequent examinations. Complete dilatation of the cervix is synonymous with the cervical dilatation of 10 cm. The second stage extends from the time of complete cervical dilatation to delivery. In the third stage, the "afterbirth" is delivered.

A dependable sign of impending labor is the so-called "show." This is the vaginal discharge of a small amount of blood-tinged mucus representing the extrusion of mucous blood which has filled the cervical canal during pregnancy. It is a late sign, and labor usually ensues within 24 hours. The quantity of blood escaping with the mucus (show) amounts to only a few milliliters. Any substantial loss of blood at this time should be regarded as suggestive of an abnormal condition.

True labor must be distinguished from false labor. In true labor the pains occur at regular intervals; the intervals gradually shorten, and the intensity of pain increases. "Show" has occurred and the cervix dilates.

In false labor, pains occur at irregular intervals; the intervals remain long; the contractions increase in intensity and then fade away. There is no show, and the cervix remains undilated.

Contraception

There are many and varied methods utilized in the prevention of pregnancy. Mechanical means by which contraception is achieved with varying degrees of success include the use of the condom, diaphragm, and the intrauterine device (IUD). This latter device is simply a coil or loop placed within the uterus, the function of which is believed to prevent implantation of the fertilized ovum.

Physiologic or chemical means of contraception include the rhythm method, douching, suppositories, foams, and the contraceptive pill.

Oral contraceptives, as mentioned in the discussion of the hormonal interrelations during the menstrual cycle, block ovulation and are usually taken for 21 consecutive days of each cycle. The rhythm method is useful only for women with regular periods, whose day of ovulation can be predicted with reasonable confidence. As a rule, ovulation occurs 14 days before the onset of menstruation. Thus, women with 22-, 28-, and 34-day cycles will ovulate on the eighth, fourteenth, and twentieth day, respectively. An ovum may be fertilized within 24 hours after ovulation, but spermatozoa retain their motility for up to five days. To avoid pregnancy, it is advisable to refrain from intercourse for six days before and three days after the day of ovulation.

VENEREAL DISEASE

When penicillin was introduced during World War II, it was predicted that the two major venereal diseases of that time, syphilis and gonorrhea, would ultimately be eradi-

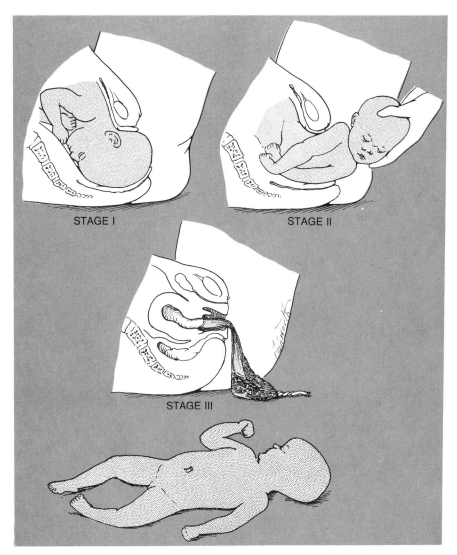

STAGE I

STAGE II

STAGE III

Figure 18–26. The stages of labor can be described as follows. The first stage is characterized by regular contractions, rupture of the membranes and a progressive dilatation of the cervix; the second stage extends from the time of complete cervical dilatation to delivery; during the third stage the "afterbirth" is delivered.

cated. This has not occurred. In fact, there has been a worldwide resurgence of venereal disease.

Gonorrhea (G. *gonē*, seed; G. *rhoia*, flow) is an infectious inflammation of the urethra, also generally involving, in the female, the paraurethral (Skene's) glands, the greater vestibular (Bartholin's) glands, and the cervix (in the adult female the squamous epithelium of the vagina is resistant to the invading gonococcus). In the male, the typical onset (two to ten days after sexual contact) consists of acute anterior urethritis (inflammation of the penile portion of the urethra) associated with a purulent (pus-containing) discharge and also a burning sensation upon urination. The inflammation may ascend to involve the membranous and prostatic portions of the urethra, prostate gland, seminal vesicles, epididymes, and bladder. Damage to the tubal structures may cause sterility and require surgery for relief of symptoms. In women, the infection initially involves the urethra and adjacent glandular structures, and later tends to progress to the cervix. Characteristic symptoms include urinary frequency, dysuria, and purulent urethral and vaginal discharges. However, more than 50 per cent of the infected women remain asymptomatic except for slight dysuria (a considerably lower percentage of men are asymptomatic). The infection may ascend above the cervical canal and produce pelvic inflammatory disease (PID), a term applied to all pelvic infections above the cervix. Damage to the uterine tubes can lead to sterility.

Mechanical prophylaxis by means of a condom provides the only reliable protection against infection. Penicillin is the preferred drug for treatment. However, beginning in the late 1950's penicillin-resistant strains began to appear which necessitated ever-increasing penicillin dosages, and in 1976 a new strain, resistant to any amount of penicillin, emerged. When penicillin treatment fails, the antibiotic of second resort is spectinomycin.

Syphilis is a disease with an early infectious phase and a late chronic tendency. It is caused by a motile spirochete and is acquired through sexual contact. Syphilis is divided into three stages: primary, secondary, and tertiary. Primary syphilis is diagnosed by finding the primary lesion, or chancre, at the inoculation site. Primary lesions generally develop within three weeks after infection; the incubation period varies from 10 to 90 days. Chancres (usually painless ulcers) occur most commonly in the genital area, but extragenital involvement, such as of the rectum or lips, has been reported. The chancres usually heal spontaneously.

In secondary syphilis the manifestations appear six to eight weeks after the chancre and remain for two to six weeks. Secondary syphilis is characterized by a generalized skin rash.

The secondary stage is followed by a quiescent (latent) period of variable length, during which time symptoms are absent. Although the disease seems to be arrested, pregnant women can transmit the disease to their offspring during this period (called pre-natal or congenital syphilis). The subsequent course of the disease is varied — some individuals proceed to a spontaneous cure; some, although not cured, remain asymptomatic; while others develop late complications of tertiary syphilis, the most serious of which involve the brain, spinal cord, or cardiovascular system. Typical late complications include personality changes, the ataxic gait of tabes dorsalis, and aortic aneurysm.

Penicillin is the drug of choice, but only early treatment is effective.

Herpes progenitalis is manifested by "cold sore"–like lesions around the male and female genital organs, often accompanied by fever and muscle aches. It is caused by a virus and spread by sexual contact. In about 90 per cent of the cases, the agent is herpes simplex II, one of two known types of the herpes simplex virus (the other, herpes simplex I, causes herpes facialis—characterized by cold sores around the mouth chiefly — and accounts for about 10 per cent of the genital infections). The genital sores heal within a few weeks and the victim feels fine. However, the virus persists in a latent form and many individuals have periodic recurrences of the disease. The chief danger of genital herpes is to infants born during the time their mothers have an active infection. The mortality rate for infected newborns is high, and three-quarters of the survivors will suffer blindness or brain damage. Therefore, if sores are found close to the time of delivery, a Caesarean section should be performed to avoid infecting the infant during passage through the birth canal. Herpes progenitalis is now the major venereal disease worldwide for both men and women. Although treatment to date has not been effective, some new drugs currently being tested look promising.

SUMMARY

THE REPRODUCTIVE SYSTEM

Male Reproductive System

1. External Organs

  a. Scrotum: pouch supporting testes.
  b. Penis: male organ of copulation; it contains three columns of erectile tissue — two dorsal (corpora cavernosa penis), one ventral (corpus cavernosum urethrae, or corpus spongiosum).
  c. Congenital abnormalities of penis: hypospadias and epispadias.
  d. Clinical consideration of penis: circumcision and phimosis.

2. Internal Organs of the Male Reproductive Tract

  a. Male gonads: testes
    (1) Structure and location: 250 wedge-shaped lobes containing coiled seminiferous tubules.

(2) Contain reproductive cells and supportive (Sertoli) cells inside tubules, as well as interstitial cells between tubules.

(3) Congenital defect: cryptorchism.

b. Series of ducts

(1) Epididymis: a coiled tube lying on posterior aspect of testis.

(2) Ductus deferens: continuous with epididymis and joins duct of seminal vesicle to form ejaculatory duct.

(3) Ejaculatory duct: opens into urethra.

(4) Urethra: transmits semen and urine.

c. Accessory glands adding secretions to semen

(1) Seminal vesicles: membranous pouches lying posterior to the bladder; secrete thick, nutrient-containing fluid.

(2) Prostate gland: surrounds first part of urethra; secretes a thin, milky, alkaline fluid.

(3) Bulbourethral glands: located below prostate; discharge lubricating mucous secretion prior to ejaculation.

Female Reproductive System

1. External Organs: Vulva

a. Mons pubis: adipose tissue over symphysis pubis.

b. Labia majora: rounded folds of adipose tissue extending downward from mons pubis to encircle vestibule; homologous to scrotum.

c. Labia minora: two smaller folds medial to labia majora.

d. Vestibule: cleft between the labia minora within which the vaginal and urethral orifices are situated. The ducts of the paraurethral (Skene's) glands open at the sides of the urethral orifice; the duct openings of the greater vestibular (Bartholin's) glands are lateral to the vaginal orifice.

e. Clitoris: a small projection of erectile tissue at the apex of the vestibule; homologous to penis.

f. Hymen: mucous membrane separating vagina from vestibule; can be present or absent in virginity.

2. Internal Organs

a. Vagina: tubular canal

(1) Structure: three layers.

(2) Location: between bladder and rectum.

(3) Function: forms part of birth canal and represents female organ of copulation; capable of constriction and enormous dilatation.

b. Uterus

(1) Location: above bladder and in front of rectum.

(2) Consists of three parts: cervix, corpus, and fundus.

(3) Supporting ligaments

(a) *Cardinal ligaments: principal support of uterus.*

(b) *Broad ligaments: to both sides of pelvic cavity.*

(c) *Round ligaments: hold uterus in forward, tilted position.*

(d) *Uterosacral ligaments: help support and maintain position of uterus.*

(4) Wall of uterus: divided into three layers

(a) *Outer serous layer of peritoneum.*

(b) *Middle muscular layer, myometrium, divided into three ill-defined, intertwining layers, the middle of which contains many large blood vessels.*

(c) *Inner mucous layer, endometrium, subject to regulation by ovarian hormones and is involved in menstruation and implantation; superficial layer sloughs during menstruation.*

c. Uterine tubes: pair of flexible, muscular tubes

(1) Location: extend from upper angle of uterus on either side toward sides of pelvis.

(2) Attachment: suspended by peritoneal fold, the mesosalpinx.

(3) Structure: three layers, mucous, smooth muscle, and serous; mucous layer is lined with ciliated epithelium.

(4) Infundibula with fimbriae open into abdominal cavity.

(5) Function: to convey ovum to uterus by muscular contraction and ciliary action. Fertilization takes place in uterine tube.

d. Ovaries: primary reproductive organs of female
  (1) Location: in upper part of pelvic cavity on each side of uterus.
  (2) Attachment: each suspended from broad ligament by peritoneal fold, mesovarium; anchored to uterus by ovarian ligament.

3. Mammary Glands

a. Location: anterior to pectoral muscles of chest.
b. Structure: convex structures of adipose tissue and ducts
  (1) Nipple of each breast surrounded by circular area of pigmented skin (areola).
  (2) Fifteen to 20 lobes arranged radially within each breast, embedded in adipose tissue.
  (3) Each lobe has its own lactiferous duct.
c. Development of mammary glands and lactation
  (1) At birth glands consist almost entirely of lactiferous ducts.
  (2) Estrogens at puberty stimulate the growth and branching of lactiferous ducts. Small, solid, spheroidal masses of cells at the ends of the smallest ducts are potential alveoli.
  (3) During pregnancy estrogens promote further expansion of the duct system and supporting adipose tissue, and progesterone stimulates the development of alveoli.
  (4) The secretion formed toward the end of pregnancy and prior to lactation after childbirth is called colostrum.
  (5) Lactation is initiated within about one to three days after childbirth by a steep rise in plasma prolactin.
  (6) Suckling by the infant maintains milk secretion: the stimulus is conducted through the hypothalamus and neurohypophysis to release oxytocin, which causes the contraction of myoepithelial cells surrounding the alveoli.

Spermatogenesis: Production of Spermatozoa

1. Formation of primary spermatocytes from spermatogonia.

2. Formation from each spermatocyte of two secondary spermatocytes in first meiotic division and four haploid spermatids in second meiotic division.

3. Differentiation of spermatids into spermatozoa.

Oogenesis and Ovulation

1. Ova produced during reproductive life of female derived from primary oocytes present at birth.

2. About 400,000 primary follicles (each a primary oocyte surrounded by a layer of granulosa cells) are present in ovaries at the onset of the reproductive life of the female.

3. Meiotic divisions occur with unequal distribution of cytoplasm, forming one large, mature ovum and nonfunctional polar bodies.

4. FSH initiates follicle maturation; first meiotic division occurs prior to ovulation.

5. Ovulation triggered by sharp rise in LH blood levels.

Fertilization

1. Transportation of ovum: peristalsis and ciliary flagellation.

2. Site of fertilization: one-third of the way down uterine tube.

3. Penetration of ovum (actually secondary oocyte) by spermatozoon initiates second meiotic division.

4. Union of male and female pronuclei forms diploid zygote.

Menstrual Cycle and Menopause

1. Menstrual cycle normally requires 28 days, and three phases are distinguished:
  a. Menstrual — day 1 to about day 5: sloughing of superficial endometrium.
  b. Proliferative (characterized by estrogen stimulation) — day 5 to 14: rebuilding of endometrium.
  c. Secretory (characterized by progesterone stimulation) — day 14 to 28: preparation for implantation.

2. Menstrual problems
  a. Absence of, infrequent or irregular, and prolonged menstruation.
  b. Dysmenorrhea (painful menstruation).

3. Menopause, permanent cessation of menstrual activity, usually occurs between ages 50 and 55. Its chief symptoms are:

a. Flushes over head, neck, and upper thorax, sometimes lasting hours.
b. Flashes — brief suffusions of heat over entire body, accompanied by sweating.

Hormonal Interrelations During Menstrual Cycle

1. Rise in FSH and LH at beginning of cycle follows decline in estrogen and progesterone blood levels (negative feedback response).

2. Steep rise in estrogen secretion by maturing follicle causes surge in gonadotropin secretion, especially LH (largely due to increased sensitivity of adenohypophysis to gonadotropin-releasing hormone).

3. LH induces ovulation.

4. Corpus luteum secretes progesterone and estrogens.

5. Rise in concentration of progesterone and estrogens causes fall in LH and FSH secretion (negative feedback response).

6. Fall in LH causes regression of corpus luteum and decline in progesterone and estrogen blood levels.

7. Pronounced inhibition of LH secretion by progesterone utilized in birth control pills to block ovulation.

Functions of Testosterone (Principal Androgen, Secreted by Interstitial Cells of Leydig)

1. Induces sexual differentiation during embryological development.

2. Stimulates growth of genitalia and appearance of secondary sex characteristics at puberty.

3. Promotes protein anabolism.

4. Accelerates deposition of bone matrix.

Functions of Estrogens (Secreted by Ovarian Follicle, Corpus Luteum, and, During Pregnancy, by Placenta)

1. Stimulate growth of uterus and vagina and development of secondary sex characteristics at puberty.

2. Induce repair of endometrium following menstruation.

3. Promote growth of duct system of mammary glands.

4. Increase motility of uterus and its sensitivity to oxytocin.

5. Accelerate matrix formation in bone.

Functions of Progesterone (Secreted by Corpus Luteum and, During Pregnancy, by Placenta)

1. During the postovulatory period converts partially thickened uterine endometrium to a secretory structure suitable for implantation.

2. Promotes growth of mammary gland alveoli during pregnancy.

3. Decreases motility of the uterus.

Cleavage: Cell Division of an Embryo

1. Morula stage with blastomeres.

2. Blastocyst: a hollow ball of cells with a thin layer of cells called the trophoblast.

3. Implantation at blastocyst stage.

4. Twinning
a. Identical (monozygotic, or uniovular) twins arise from a single fertilized ovum; at some stage a separation into two parts occurs, each becoming a separate embryo.
b. Fraternal (dizygotic, or biovular) twins arise from the fertilization of two separate ova.

Embryology: Science Dealing with the Developing Embryo

Three germ layers develop in the embryo, from which specific tissues are eventually derived:

1. Ectoderm: epidermis and tissues of the nervous system.

2. Mesoderm: connective and muscular tissues.

3. Endoderm: lining of the digestive tract and its derivatives.

Placenta

1. Formed about the third month of pregnancy by infiltration of villi of chorion into the decidua basalis of the uterus.

2. It is the structure to which the embryo is attached by the umbilical cord and through

which, without actual exchange of blood, it receives nutrients, exchanges respiratory gases, and eliminates wastes.

Labor

1. Three stages of labor: period of progressive cervical dilatation, complete cervical dilatation to delivery, and delivery of "afterbirth."

2. Show: vaginal discharge of blood-tinged mucus.

3. True labor: pains at regular intervals, intervals shorten, pain increases, show, and cervix dilates.

4. False labor: no show, pains at irregular intervals, contractions increase in intensity and then fade away, and cervix undilated.

REVIEW QUESTIONS

1. Name the three columns of erectile tissue of the penis. How do they function? Which of the columns encloses the urethra?

2. In what structure of the testis does spermatogenesis take place? Name the series of ducts through which spermatozoa pass to reach the urethra. Name the accessory glands that contribute to the formation of semen.

3. List and describe the external organs of the female reproductive system.

4. List the internal organs of the female reproductive system. Give the locations of the cervix and the infundibulum.

5. Describe the changes in the structure of the mammary glands at puberty and during pregnancy. For what changes are estrogens and progesterone responsible? What hormone initiates lactation? Describe how the suckling stimulus promotes milk secretion.

6. Describe the principal changes occurring in the uterus in the phase before and the phase after ovulation. What triggers ovulation? How does implantation prevent the initiation of a new cycle?

7. List the major functions of androgens.

8. Define the following: amnion, chorion, decidua, and placenta.

Appendix A
Prefixes, Suffixes, and Combining Forms

a-, ab-	from, away
a-, an-	without, lack, not
ad-	to, toward
adeno-	gland
adip-	fat
-algia	pain
amphi-	both, of both kinds
amyl-	starch
andro-	man
angi-	vessel
ante-	before
anti-	against
apo-	away from, detached
arachno-	spider
arthro-	joint
-ase	enzyme
auto-	self
bi-	two
-blast	germ, sprout
brachi-	arm
brachy-	short
brady-	slow
carbo-	carbon
cardi-	heart
cephal-	head
cerebro-	brain
chol-	bile
chondr-	cartilage
chromo-	color
circum-	around
-cle	small
con-	with, together
contra-	against, in opposition
cortico-	rind, bark

costo-	rib
cuti-	skin
cyst-	bladder
cyt-	cell
de-	remove
dermat-	skin
di-	twice
dia-	through, between
dis-	denoting separation
dys-	bad, difficult
e-	out of, from
ecto-	on outside
-emia	denoting condition of the blood
endo-	within
entero-	intestine
epi-	upon, above, over
erythro-	red
eu-	good
ex-, exo-	outside, out of
galact-	milk
gastr-	stomach
-genesis	origination, development
glosso-	tongue
-gnosis	cognition
gyn-	woman
gyr-	ring, circle
hem-	blood
hemi-	half
hepat-	liver

hetero-	different		-opia	defect of the eye
homeo-	alike		-osis	a condition, a process
homo-	same		osteo-	bone
hydro-	water		oto-	ear
hyper-	above, excessive		ovi-	egg
hypo-	below, deficient			
hystero-	uterus			
			para-	beside, near, beyond
			patho-	disease
in-	into, not		peri-	around
infra-	below, beneath		phago-	eating, feeding
inter-	between		phlebo-	vein
intra-	within		pneumato-	air
iso-	equal, like		poly-	many
-itis	inflammatory disease		post-	behind, after
			pre-	before, in front of
			pro-	before, in front of
juxta-	nearness		psycho-	mind
			pulmo-	lung
kerat-	horn			
			retro-	backward, behind
			rhin-	nose
labio-	lip		-rrhea	flow
leuk-	white			
lip-	fat			
-lysis	dissolution, detachment		sarc-	flesh
			scler-	hard
			semi-	half
macro-	large		somat-, -some	body
mal-	bad, ill		spermat-	seed, germ
mega-	large, great		sub-	under, deficient
megalo-			super-	above, upon, excessive
melan-	black, dark-colored		supra-	above, upon
mening-	membrane		syn-	with, together
meso-	middle			
mono-	one, single		tachy-	swift
myo-	muscle		trans-	across, through
			tri-	three
			tropho-, -trophy	nutrition
necro-	dead			
nephr-	kidney			
neuro-	nerve		-ule	small
			ultra-	beyond, excess
			uni-	one
-oid	resembling			
oligo-	scant, sparse			
-oma	tumor, swelling		vaso-	vessel
ophthalmo-	eye			

Appendix B
Metric Units and U.S. Equivalents

Nomenclature for Metric Units

m = *milli* = 0.001 = 10^{-3} meter or gram or liter (thousandth)
μ = *micro* = 0.000,001 = 10^{-6} meter or gram or liter (millionth)
n = *nano* = 0.000,000,001 = 10^{-9} meter or gram or liter (billionth)
p = *pico* = 0.000,000,000,001 = 10^{-12} meter or gram or liter (trillionth)
For example:
mm = millimeter = 10^{-3} meter (=10^7 Å)
μm = micrometer = 10^{-6} meter (also, μ = micron)
nm = nanometer = 10^{-9} meter (also, millimicron = mμ)
Å = angstrom = 10^{-10} meter (= 0.1 nm; 10 Å = 1 nm)
pm = picometer = 10^{-12} meter
pg = picogram = 10^{-12} g
ppm = μg/cc (ml); μg/g

Linear Measure

1 centimeter (cm) = 0.3937 inch
1 inch = 2.54 cm
1 meter (m) = 39.37 inches

Weights

1 gram (g) = 0.03527 ounce
1 ounce = 28.3495 grams
1 kilogram (kg) = 2.2046 pounds
1 pound = 0.4536 kilogram

Liquid measure

1 liter (l) = 1.0567 quarts
1 quart = 0.9464 liter
1 gallon = 3.7856 liters

Temperature

Degrees Celsius (°C) (Centigrade)	Degrees Fahrenheit (°F)
100	212
90	194
80	176
70	158
60	140
50	122
40	104
37	98.6
30	86
20	68
10	50
0	32

$$°C = (5/9 \ °F) - 32$$
$$°F = (9/5 \ °C) + 32$$

Suggested Additional Reading

BASIC CHEMISTRY AND THE CHEMICAL CONSTITUENTS OF LIVING MATTER

Doty, P.: Proteins. Scientific American, September, 1957.
Eyre, D. R.: Collagen: molecular diversity in the body's protein scaffold. Science 207:1315–1322, 1980.
Kamen, M.: A universal molecule of living matter. Scientific American, August, 1958.
Marshall, E.: NAS study on radiation takes the middle road. Science 204:711–714, 1979.
Masterton, W. L., Slowinski, E., and Stanitski, C. L.: Chemical Principles. 5th Ed., Philadelphia, Saunders College Publishing, 1981.
McGilvery, R. W.: Biochemistry: A Functional Approach. 2nd Ed., Philadelphia, W. B. Saunders Co., 1979.
Mortimer, C. E.: Chemistry: A Conceptual Approach. 4th Ed., New York, D. Van Nostrand Co., 1979.
Phillips, D. C.: The three-dimensional structure of an enzyme molecule. Scientific American, November, 1966.
Routh, J. I., Eyman, D. P., and Burton, D. J.: A Brief Introduction to General, Organic and Biochemistry. 2nd Ed., Philadelphia, W. B. Saunders Co., 1976.
Sackheim, G. I., and Schultz, R. M.: Chemistry for the Health Sciences. 3rd Ed., New York, Macmillan Publishing Co., Inc., 1977.
Sharon, N.: Carbohydrates. Scientific American, November, 1980.

THE CELL

Bretscher, M. S.: Membrane structure: some general principles. Science 181:622–629, 1973.
Buffaloe, N. D., and Throneberry, J. D.: Concepts of Biology. Englewood Cliffs, N. J., Prentice-Hall, Inc., 1973.
Chambon, P.: Split genes. Scientific American, May, 1981.
deDuve, C.: The lysosome. Scientific American, May, 1963.
DeRobertis, E. D. P., Saez, F. A., and DeRobertis, E. M. F., Jr.: Cell Biology. 7th Ed., Philadelphia, Saunders College Publishing, 1980.
Fox, F. C.: The structure of cell membranes. Scientific American, February, 1972.
Gilbert, W., and Villa-Komaroff, L.: Useful proteins from recombinant bacteria. Scientific American, April, 1980.
Kornberg, A.: The synthesis of DNA. Scientific American, October, 1968.
Marx, J. L.: Restriction enzymes: prenatal diagnosis of genetic disease. Science 202:1068–1069, 1978.
Mitchell, P.: Keilin's respiratory chain concept and its chemiosmotic consequences (Nobel lecture). Science 206:1148–1159, 1979.
Olins, D. E., and Olins, A. L.: Nucleosomes: The structural quantum in chromosomes. American Scientist 66:704–711, 1978.
Palade, G.: Intracellular aspects of the process of protein synthesis (Nobel lecture). Science 189:347–357, 1975.

TISSUES

Arey, L. B.: Human Histology. 4th Ed., Philadelphia, W. B. Saunders Co., 1974.
Bloom, W., and Fawcett, D. W.: A Textbook of Histology. 10th Ed., Philadelphia, W. B. Saunders Co., 1975.

635

Leeson, T. S., and Leeson, C. R.: A Brief Atlas of Histology. Philadelphia, W. B. Saunders Co., 1979.
Lentz, T. L.: Cell Fine Structure. Philadelphia, W. B. Saunders Co., 1971.
Odland, G., et al.: Human wound repair. J. Cell Biol. 39:135–151, October, 1968.
Schafer, J. A.: Water transport in epithelia. Symp. Federation Proc. 38:119–160, 1979.
Staehelin, L. A., and Hull, B. E.: Junctions between living cells. Scientific American, May, 1978.
Tanzer, M. L.: Cross-linking of collagen. Science 180:561–566, 1973.

SKIN

Braverman, I. M.: Skin Signs of Systemic Disease. 2nd ed. Philadelphia, W. B. Saunders Co., 1981.
Epstein, E., and Epstein, E. Jr. (Eds.): Skin Surgery. 4th Ed., Springfield, Charles C Thomas, 1977.
Montagna, W.: Advances in Biology of Skin. Twelve Volumes. New York, Appleton-Century Crofts, 1972.
Pillsbury, D. M., and Heaton, C. L.: A Manual of Dermatology. 2nd Ed., Philadelphia, W. B. Saunders Co., 1980.
Scheuplein, R. J., et al.: Permeability of the skin. Physiol. Rev. 51:702–747, 1971.
Sundell, B.: Principles of skin grafting in burns. Ann. Chir. Gynaecol. Fenn. 60:5–8, 1971.
Tregear, R.: Physical Functions of Skin. New York, Academic Press, 1966.

THE SKELETAL SYSTEM

Bourne, G. W.: The Biochemistry and Physiology of Bone. 2nd Ed., Four Volumes. New York, Academic Press, 1972 (Vols. 1-3), 1974 (Vol. 4).
Harris, W. H., and Heaney, R. P.: Skeletal Renewal and Metabolic Bone Disease. Boston, Little, Brown and Co., 1970.
Kolata, G. B.: Vitamin D: Investigations of a new steroid hormone. Science 187:635–636, 1975.
Marx, J. L.: Osteoporosis: New help for thinning bones. Science 207:628–630, 1980.
Morey, E. R., and Baylink, D. J.: Inhibition of bone formation during space flight. Science 201:1138–1141, 1978.
Napier, J.: The antiquity of human walking. Scientific American, April, 1967.
Vaughan, J. M.: The Physiology of Bone. Oxford, Clarendon Press, 1970.

THE ARTICULAR SYSTEM

Crawford, T. B., Adams, D. S., Cheevers, W. P., and Cork, L. C.: Chronic arthritis in goats caused by a retrovirus. Science 207:997–999, 1980.
Evans, F. G. (Ed.): Studies in the Anatomy and Function of Bone and Joints. New York, Springer-Verlag, 1966.
Herring, G. M.: The chemical structure of tendon, cartilage, dentin and bone matrix. Clin. Orthop. 60:261–299, 1968.
Larson, C. B., and Gould, M.: Orthopedic Nursing. 8th Ed., St. Louis, C. V. Mosby Co., 1974.
Rancho Los Amigos Hospital Staff Ass'n.: Bones, Joints and Muscles of the Human Body: A Programmed Text for Physical Therapy Aides. Riverside, N.J., Glencoe Press, 1970.
Ziff, M.: Pathophysiology of rheumatoid arthritis. Federation Proc. 32:131–133, 1973.

THE MUSCULAR SYSTEM

Basmajian, J. V., and Macconaill, M. A.: Muscles and Movements: A Basis for Human Kinesiology. Baltimore, Williams & Wilkins, 1977.
Bendall, J. R.: Muscles, Molecules and Movement. New York, American Elsevier, 1969.
Bethlem, J.: Myopathies. New York, J. B. Lippincott Co., 1977.
Close, R. I.: Dynamic properties of mammalian skeletal muscles. Physiol. Rev. 52:129–197, 1972.
Cohen, C.: The protein switch of muscle contraction. Scientific American, Nov., 1975.
Hoyle, G.: How is muscle turned on and off? Scientific American, April, 1970.
Huxley, H. E.: The mechanism of muscular contraction. Science 164:1356–1366, 1969.
Laki, K.: Contractile Proteins & Muscle. New York, Marcel Dekker, 1971.
Margaria, R.: The sources of muscular energy. Scientific American, March, 1972.
Podolsky, R. J.: Muscle activation: The current status. Federation Proc. 34:1374–1378, 1975.
Stanley, E. F., and Drachman, D. B.: Effect of myasthenic immunoglobulin on acetylcholine receptors of intact mammalian neuromuscular junctions. Science 200:1285–1287, 1978.
Vandenburgh, H., and Kaufman, S.: In vitro model for stretch-induced hypertrophy of skeletal muscle. Science 203:265–268, 1979.

THE NERVOUS SYSTEM

Axelrod, J.: Neurotransmitters. Scientific American, June, 1974.
Barr, M. L.: The Human Nervous System. 3rd Ed., New York, Harper and Row, 1979.
Easton, T. A.: On the normal use of reflexes. American Scientist 60:591–599, 1972.

Epstein, B. S.: The Spine: A Radiological Text & Atlas. 4th Ed., Philadelphia, Lea and Febiger, 1976.
Geschwind, N.: The organization of language and the brain. Science 170:940–944, 1970.
Geschwind, N.: The apraxias: neural mechanisms of disorders of learned movement. American Scientist 63:188–195, 1975.
Greenough, W. T.: Experimental modification of the developing brain. American Scientist 63:37–46, 1975.
Holden, C.: Pain, dying, and the health care system. Science 203:984–985, 1979.
Hornykiewicz, O.: Parkinson's disease: From brain homogenate to treatment. Federation Proc. 32:183–190, 1973.
Hubel, D. H.: The brain. Scientific American, Sept., 1979.
Lasek, R.: Axonal transport and the use of intracellular markers in neuroanatomical investigations. Federation Proc. 34:1603–1611, 1975.
Morell, P., and Norton, W. T.: Myelin. Scientific American, May, 1980.
Noback, C. R., and Demarest, R. J.: The Human Nervous System: Basic Principles of Neurobiology. 3rd Ed., New York, McGraw-Hill Book Co., 1980.
O'Keefe, J., and Nadel, L.: The Hippocampus as a Cognitive Map. New York, Clarendon (Oxford University Press), 1978.
Ruch, T. C., and Patton, H. D.: Physiology and Biophysics, Vol. 1: The Brain and Neural Function. Philadelphia, W. B. Saunders Co., 1979.
Schwartz, J. H.: The transport of substances in nerve cells. Scientific American, April, 1980.
Wallace, P.: Neurochemistry: unraveling the mechanism of memory. Science 190:1076–1078, 1975.
Wise, C. D., and Stein, L.: Dopamine-β-hydroxylase deficits in the brains of schizophrenic patients. Science 181:344–347, 1973.

SPECIAL SENSES

Barber, G. W.: Physiological chemistry of the eye. Arch. Ophthalmol. 87:72–106, 1972.
Cain, W. S.: Differential sensitivity for smell: "noise" at the nose. Science 195:796–798, 1977.
Davis, H., and Silverman, R. S.: Hearing and Deafness. 4th Ed., New York, Holt, Rinehart and Winston, 1978.
Fisher, K. D., Carr, C. J., Huff, J. E., and Huber, T. E.: Dark adaptation and night vision. Federation Proc. 29:1605–1638, 1970.
Gordon, B.: The superior colliculus of the brain. Scientific American, Dec., 1972.
Harper, R.: Human Senses in Action. Baltimore, Williams & Wilkins Co., 1972.
Parker, D. E.: The vestibular apparatus. Scientific American, Nov., 1980.
Pettigrew, J. D.: The neurophysiology of binocular vision. Scientific American, Aug., 1972.
Schneider, B., Trehub, S. E., and Bull, D.: High-frequency sensitivity in infants. Science 207:1003–1004, 1980.
Sewell, W. F., Norris, C. H., Tachibana, M., and Guth, P. S.: Detection of an auditory nerve–activating substance. Science 202:910–912, 1978.
Siegel, M.: Optics and visual physiology. Arch. Ophthalmol. 86:100–112, 1971.
Sinclair, J. G.: Reflections on the role of receptor systems for taste and smell. Int. Rev. Neurobiol. 14:159–171, 1971.
Somjen, G. G.: Sensory coding in the mammalian nervous system. New York, Plenum Publishing Corp., 1975.
Wilentz, J. S.: Senses of Man. New York, Apollo Editions, 1971.

THE CIRCULATORY SYSTEM

Adolph, E. F.: The heart's pacemaker. Scientific American, March, 1967.
Bank, A., Mears, J. G., and Ramirez, F.: Disorders of human hemoglobin. Science 207:486–493, 1980.
Berne, R. M., and Levy, M. N.: Cardiovascular Physiology. 3rd Ed., St. Louis, C. V. Mosby Co., 1977.
Edsall, J. T.: Hemoglobin and the origins of the concept of allosterism. Federation Proc. 39:226–235, 1980.
Henry, J. P., and Meehan, J. P.: Circulation: An Integrative Physiological Study. Chicago, Year Book Medical Publishers, 1971.
Holmes, W. L.: Blood Cells as a Tissue. New York, Plenum Publishing Corp., 1971.
Kaplan, N. M.: The control of hypertension: a therapeutic breakthrough. American Scientist 68:537–545, 1980.
Kolata, G. B.: Atherosclerotic plaques: competing theories guide research. Science 194:592–594, 1976.
Lefer, A. M., and Glenn, T. M.: Toxic factors in shock. Symp. Federation Proc. 37:2717–2740, 1978.
Maugh, T. H.: A new understanding of sickle cell emerges. Science 211:265–267, 1981.
Ratnoff, O. D., and Bennett, B.: The genetics of hereditary disorders of blood coagulation. Science 179:1291–1298, 1973.
Ross, R., and Harker, L.: Hyperlipidemia and atherosclerosis. Science 193:1094–1100, 1976.

Rossi, E. C.: The function of platelets in hemostasis. Med. Clin. North Am. 56:25–33, 1972.

Weber, K. T., and Janicki, J. S.: Cardiac mechanics. Symp. Federation Proc. 39:131–207, 1980.

THE LYMPHATIC SYSTEM

Cooper, M. D., and Lawton, A. R.: The development of the immune system. Scientific American, Nov., 1974.

Elues, M. W.: The Lymphocytes. Chicago, Year Book Medical Publishers, 1972.

Marx, J. L.: Antibody structure: now in three dimensions. Science 189:1075–1076, 1114, 1975.

Mayer, M. M.: The complement system. Scientific American, Nov., 1973.

Mayerson, H. S. (Ed.): Lymph and the Lymphatic System: Proceedings Conference on Lymph and the Lymphatic System. Springfield, Charles C Thomas, 1968.

Paul, W. E., and Benacerraf, B.: Functional specificity of thymus-dependent lymphocytes. Science 195:1293–1300, 1977.

Rose, N. R., and Milgrom, F. (Eds.): Principles of Immunology. New York, Macmillan Publishing Co., Inc., 1979.

THE RESPIRATORY SYSTEM

Avery, M. E., Wang, N., and Taeusch, H. W., Jr.: The lung of the newborn infant. Scientific American, April, 1973.

Campbell, F. J., et al. (Eds.): The Respiratory Muscle: Mechanics and Neural Control. 2nd Ed., Philadelphia, W. B. Saunders Co., 1970.

Cherniack, R., et al.: Respiration in Health and Disease. 2nd Ed., Philadelphia, W. B. Saunders Co., 1972.

Cohen, D., Arai, S. F., and Brain, J. D.: Smoking impairs long-term dust clearance from the lung. Science 204:514–516, 1979.

Comroe, J. H., Jr.: The lung. Scientific American, Feb., 1966.

Crofton, J., and Douglas, A.: Respiratory Diseases. 2nd Ed., Philadelphia, F. A. Davis Co., 1975.

Fraser, R. G., and Paré, J. A. P.: Organ Physiology: Structure and Function of the Lung. 2nd Ed., Philadelphia, W. B. Saunders Co., 1977.

Murray, J. F.: The Normal Lung: The Basis for Diagnosis and Treatment of Pulmonary Disease. Philadelphia, W. B. Saunders Co., 1976.

Naeye, R. L.: Sudden infant death. Scientific American, April, 1980.

Pace, N.: Respiration at high altitude. Federation Proc. 33:2126–2132, 1974.

Safar, P.: Respiratory Therapy: Resuscitation and Intensive Care. Philadelphia, F. A. Davis Co., 1972.

Slonin, N. B., and Hamilton, L. H.: Respiratory Physiology. 3rd Ed., St. Louis, C. V. Mosby Co., 1976.

Sundberg, J.: The acoustics of the singing voice. Scientific American, March, 1977.

THE DIGESTIVE SYSTEM AND METABOLISM

Davenport, H. W.: Physiology of the Digestive Tract: An Introductory Text. 4th Ed., Chicago, Year Book Medical Publishers, 1977.

Davidson, C. S. (Ed.): Problems in Liver Diseases. New York, Thieme-Stratton, Inc., 1979.

Fredrickson, D. S.: Plasma lipoproteins and apolipoproteins. Harvey Lectures, Series 68:185–237, 1973.

Johnson, L. R.: Gastrointestinal hormones: physiological implications. Symp. Federation Proc. 36:1929–1951, 1977.

Kassel, B., and Kay, J.: Zymogens of proteolytic enzymes. Science 180:1022–1027, 1973.

Kretchner, N.: Lactose and lactase. Scientific American, Oct., 1972.

Mandel, I. D.: Dental caries. American Scientist 67:680–688, 1979.

Mayer, J.: Human Nutrition: Its Physiological, Medical and Social Aspects. Springfield, Charles C Thomas, 1979.

Munro, H. N.: Iron absorption and nutrition. Symp. Federation Proc. 36:2015–2032, 1977.

Rubin, E., and Lieber, C. S.: Experimental alcoholic hepatitis: a new primate model. Science 182:712–713, 1973.

Young, V. R., and Scrimshaw, N. S.: The physiology of starvation. Scientific American, Oct., 1971.

THE URINARY SYSTEM

Atherton, J. C.: Renal physiology. Br. J. Anaesth. 42:236–245, 1972.

Brenner, B. M.: Renal handling of sodium. Symp. Federation Proc. 33:13–36, 1974.

Brenner, B. M., and Rector, F. C. (Eds.): The Kidney. 2nd Ed., Two Volumes. Philadelphia, W. B. Saunders Co., 1981.

Hamburger, J., Richet, G., and Grunfeld, J. P.: Organ Physiology: Structure and Function of the Kidney. Philadelphia, W. B. Saunders Co., 1971.

Kaye, D. (Ed.): Urinary Tract Infection and Its Management. St. Louis, C. V. Mosby Co., 1972.

Leaf, A., and Cotran, R. S.: Renal Pathophysiology. 2nd Ed., New York, Oxford University Press, 1980.

Mitchell, J. P.: Urology for Nurses. Baltimore, Williams & Wilkins Co., 1970.

Rouiller, C., and Muller, A. (Eds.): The Kidney: Morphology, Biochemistry, Physiology. Four Volumes. New York, Academic Press, 1969 (Vols. 1 and 2), 1971 (Vols. 3 and 4).

THE ENDOCRINE SYSTEM

Brownstein, M. J., Russell, J. T., and Gainer, H.: Synthesis, transport, and release of posterior pituitary hormones. Science 207:373–378, 1980.

Fawcett, D. W., et al.: The ultrastructure of endocrine glands. Recent Progr. Hormone Res. 25:315–380, 1969.

Greep, R. O., and Astwood, E. B. (Eds.): Handbook of Physiology: Section 7: Endocrinology. Seven Volumes. Baltimore, Williams & Wilkins, 1972–1976.

Hamwi, G. J.: Nutrition and diseases of the endocrine glands. Amer. J. Clin. Nutr. 23:311–329, 1970.

Kolata, G. B.: Blood sugar and the complications of diabetes. Science 203:1098–1099, 1979.

Locke, W., and Schally, A. V. (Eds.): Hypothalamus & Pituitary in Health & Disease. Springfield, Charles C Thomas, 1972.

Maugh, T. H.: Diabetes: epidemiology suggests a viral connection. Science 188:347–351, 1975.

Notkins, A. L.: The causes of diabetes. Scientific American, Nov., 1979.

O'Malley, B. W., and Schrader, W. T.: The receptors of steroid hormones. Scientific American, Feb., 1976.

Oppenheimer, J. H.: Thyroid hormone action at the cellular level. Science 203:971–979, 1979.

Schally, A. V., Kastin, A. J., and Arimura, A.: Hypothalamic hormones: the link between brain and body. American Scientist 65:712–719, 1977.

Sutherland, E. W.: Studies on the mechanism of hormone action (Nobel lecture). Science 177:401–408, 1972.

Zatz, M., and Brownstein, M. J.: Intraventricular carbachol mimics the effects of light on the circadian rhythm in the rat pineal gland. Science 203:358–360, 1979.

FLUIDS AND ELECTROLYTES

Goldberger, E.: Primer of Water, Electrolyte and Acid-Base Syndromes. 6th Ed., Philadelphia, Lea and Febiger, 1980.

Maxwell, M. H., and Kleeman, C. R.: Clinical Disorders of Fluid and Electrolyte Metabolism. 2nd Ed., New York, McGraw-Hill Book Co., 1972.

Mikal, S.: Homeostasis in Man. Boston, Little, Brown and Co., 1967.

Searcy, R. L.: Diagnostic Biochemistry. New York, McGraw-Hill Book Co., 1969.

Share, L., et al.: Regulation of body fluids. Ann. Rev. Physiol. 34:235–260, 1972.

Sundell, B.: Evaluation of fluid resuscitation in the burned patient. Ann. Chir. Gynaecol. Fenn. 60:192–195, 1971.

Wedeen, R. P., et al.: Mechanisms of edema and the use of diuretics. Pediat. Clin. North Amer. 18:561–576, 1971.

THE REPRODUCTIVE SYSTEM

Beaconsfield, P., Birdwood, G., and Beaconsfield, R.: The placenta. Scientific American, August, 1980.

Brackett, B. G.: Mammalian fertilization in vitro. Federation Proc. 32:2065–2068, 1973.

Casper, R. F., Yen, S. S. C., and Wilkes, M. M.: Menopausal flushes: a neuroendocrine link with pulsatile luteinizing hormone secretion. Science 205:823–825, 1979.

Catt, K. J.: IV Reproductive endocrinology. Lancet 1:1097–1104, 1970.

Colman, L., and Colman, A. D.: Pregnancy: The Physiological Experience. Henden and Henden, 1972.

Ehrhardt, A. A., and Meyer-Bahlburg, H. F. L.: Effects of prenatal sex hormones on gender-related behavior. Science 211:1312–1318, 1981.

Field, J. (Ed.): Handbook of Physiology. Section 7, Vols. 2 and 3. Baltimore, Williams & Wilkins Co., 1972.

Imperato-McGinley, J., Guerrero, L., Gautier, T., and Peterson, R. E.: Steroid 5α-reductase deficiency in man: an inherited form of male pseudohermaphroditism. Science 186:1213–1215, 1974.

Kolata, G. B.: Infertility: promising new treatments. Science 202:200–203, 1978.

Kolata, G. B.: Sex hormones and brain development. Science 205:985–987, 1979.

Marx, J. L.: Dysmenorrhea: basic research leads to a rational therapy. Science 205:175–176, 1979.

Newton, N., and Newton, M.: Psychologic aspects of lactation. N. Engl. J. Med. 277:1179, Nov. 30, 1967.

Page, E. W., Villee, C. A., and Villee, D. B.: Human Reproduction: Essentials of The Core Content of Reproductive Obstetrics, Gynecology and Prenatal Medicine. 3rd Ed., Philadelphia, W. B. Saunders Co., 1981.

Rhodes, P.: Reproductive Physiology for Medical Students. Baltimore, Williams & Wilkins Co., 1969.

Rondell, P.: Follicular processes in ovulation. Federation Proc. 29:1875–1879, 1970.

Segal, S. J.: The physiology of human reproduction. Scientific American, Sept., 1974.

Shearman, R. P. (Ed.): Human Reproductive Physiology. Oxford, Blackwell Scientific Publications, 1972.

ADDITIONAL REFERENCES

Best and Taylor's Physiological Basis of Medical Practice. 10th Ed., edited by J. R. Brobeck. Baltimore, Williams & Wilkins Co., 1979.

Crouch, J. E.: Functional Human Anatomy. 3rd Ed., Philadelphia, Lea and Febiger, 1978.

Cunningham, D. J.: Textbook of Anatomy. Edited by G. J. Romanes; 11th Ed., Oxford, Oxford University Press, 1972.

Downman, C. B. B. (Ed.): Modern Trends in Physiology. New York, Appleton-Century Crofts, 1972.

Ganong, W. F.: Review of Medical Physiology. 9th Ed., Los Altos, California, Lange Medical Publications, 1979.

Gray's Anatomy. 36th Brit. Ed. Edited by P. L. Williams and R. Warwick. London, Longman Group Ltd., 1981.

Guyton, A. C.: Textbook of Medical Physiology. 6th Ed., Philadelphia, W. B. Saunders Co., 1981.

Leeson, C. R., and Leeson, T. S.: Histology, 4th Ed., Philadelphia, W. B. Saunders Co., 1981.

Lehninger, A. L.: Biochemistry. 2nd Ed., New York, Worth Publishers, Inc., 1975.

Watson, J. E.: Medical-Surgical Nursing and Related Physiology. 2nd Ed., Philadelphia, W. B. Saunders Co., 1979.

Glossary

abdomen (ab′dō-men): the portion of the body lying between the diaphragm and the pelvis.

abduct (ab-dukt′): to draw away from the median line.

ablation (ab-lā′shun): removal of a part, especially by cutting.

absorption (ab-sorp′shun): the taking up of fluids or other substances by the skin, mucous surfaces, or vessels.

accommodation (ah-kom″o-da′shun): focusing of the image on the retina by the lens.

acetabulum (as″e-tab′u-lum): the large, cup-shaped cavity with which the head of the femur articulates.

acetylcholine (as″ĕ-til-ko′lēn): a neurotransmitter released at the neuromuscular junction, synapses, and parasympathetic postganglionic nerve endings.

Achilles' tendon (ah-kil′ēz): another name for the tendo calcaneus, the powerful tendon at the back of the heel shared by the gastrocnemius and soleus muscles (also collectively called the triceps surae).

acid (as′id): sour, having properties opposed to those of the alkalis; characterized by excess hydrogen ions, giving it a pH less than seven.

acidophils (ah-sid′o-fils): acid-staining cells, especially those of the adenohypophysis, which produce growth hormone and prolactin.

acidosis (as″ĭ-dō′sis): a pathologic condition resulting from accumulation of acid or loss of base in the body and characterized by increase in hydrogen ion concentration (decrease in pH).

acinus (ass′i-nus): a saccular terminal division of a compound gland.

acromegaly (ak″ro-meg′ah-le): overproduction of growth hormone in adults.

acromion (ah-krō′me-on): outward extension of the scapula forming the point of the shoulder.

acrosome (ak′ro-sōm): a cap on the sperm head with enzymatic function.

active transport: any movement of particles across a membrane against the concentration gradient, thus requiring an expenditure of energy.

Addison's disease (ad′ĭ-sonz): deficiency of suprarenal cortex functions.

adduct (ah-dukt′): to draw toward a center or toward a median line.

adenohypophysis (ad″ē-no-hi-pof′ĭ-sis): the anterior portion of the hypophysis (pituitary gland).

adenoid (ad′ĕ-noid): generally, anything referring to glands; usually used in the plural for the nasopharyngeal tonsil.

641

adenosine triphosphate, ATP (ah-den′o-sin): a nucleotide with two additional phosphate groups found in all cells and serving as a direct source of energy for cellular processes.

adhesion (ad-hē′zhun): abnormal union of two surfaces.

adiadochokinesis (ah-di″ah-do″ko-ki-nē′sis): inability to perform rapidly alternating movements.

adipose (ad′ĭ-pos): of a fatty nature; fat.

ad libitum (ad-lib′i-tum): freely; as much as wanted.

adrenal (ad-rē′nal): suprarenal glands, located above the kidneys.

Adrenalin (ah-dren′ah-lin): trademark for a preparation of epinephrine.

adrenergic (ad″ren-er′jik): activated or transmitted by norepinephrine; a term applied to those nerve fibers that liberate norepinephrine.

adventitia (ad′ven-tish′e-ah): the outermost covering of a structure but not forming an integral part of it.

aerobic (ā-er-o′bik): growing only in the presence of molecular oxygen.

afferent (af′er-ent): conveying toward a center.

agglutination (ah-gloo″tĭ-nā′shun): a joining together; an aggregation of suspended particles.

agglutinin (ah-gloo′tĭ-nin): antibody which clumps a particular antigen.

agglutinogen (ag″loo-tin′o-jen): antigen stimulating the production of an agglutinin.

agraphia (ah-graf′e-ah): inability to write with meaningful content.

albumin (al-bū′min): plasma protein largely responsible for the osmotic pressure of blood.

aldosterone (al″do-ster′ōn): the principal mineralocorticoid secreted from the cortex of the adrenal glands.

alexia (ah-lek′se-ah): inability to read with comprehension.

alimentary (al″e-men′tar-e): pertaining to food or nutritive material.

alkaline (al′kah-līn): basic, see **base.**

alkalosis (al″kah-lo′sis): a condition in which there is an excessive proportion of alkali in the blood.

alveolus (al-ve′o-lus): a small cavity; air saccule in the lungs; bony socket of a tooth; terminal saccule of a compound gland.

ameboid movement (ah-mē′boid): movement of an ameba or leukocyte by protrusion of a footlike structure, or movement similar to it.

amenorrhea (a-men″o-rē′ah): absence of menstruation.

amine (a-mēn′): any organic compound containing nitrogen.

amino acid (a-mē′nō): an organic compound with an NH_2, and a COOH group in its molecule, and having both acid and basic properties. Amino acids are the structural units from which proteins are built.

amniocentesis (am″ne-o-sen-tē′sis): transabdominal perforation of the uterus to obtain a sample of amniotic fluid.

amnion (am′ne-on): the thin, transparent, silvery, and tough inner membrane which protects the embryo in the uterus during pregnancy.

amorphous (ah-mor′fus): having no definite form; shapeless.

amphiarthrosis (am″fe-ar-thro′sis): form of articulation permitting little motion.

ampulla (am-pŭl′lah): a saclike dilatation of a tube or duct.

amylase (am′ĭ-lās): an enzyme that hydrolyzes starch to maltose.

anabolism (ah-nab′o-lizm): any constructive process in which simple substances are converted by living cells into more complex compounds, such as conversion of simple compounds into protoplasm.

anaerobic (an″ā-er-o′bik):   growing only in the absence of oxygen.

analgesia (an″al-jē′ze-ah):   loss of sensitivity to pain.

anaphylaxis (an″ah-fi-lak′sis):   a state of hypersensitivity in animals to an allergen caused by the prior injection of the same allergen in which the characteristic allergic response, which includes spasm of smooth muscle, vasodilation and increased capillary permeability, involves interaction between allergens and reagins (IgE antibodies fixed to mast cells).

anastomosis (ah-nas″to-mō′sis):   a surgical connection between vessels or between parts of a tube, such as the stomach to the small intestine.

androgen (an′dro-jen):   any hormone that possesses masculinizing activity.

anemia (ah-nē′me-ah):   condition in which oxygen transport by red blood cells is deficient.

anesthesia (an″es-thē′ze-ah):   loss of sensation.

aneurysm (an′u-rizm):   a sac filled with blood formed by the dilatation of the wall of an artery or of a vein.

angina (an-jī′nah):   any disease characterized by spasmodic choking or suffocative pain.

angina pectoris (an′jī-nah pec′to-ris):   periodic severe pain in the chest radiating to the left shoulder and down the inner side of the arm, usually precipitated by physical exertion or emotional stress.

angiocardiography (an″je-o-kar″di-og′rah-fe):   roentgenography of the heart and great vessels after intravenous injection of opaque fluid.

annulus (an′u-lus):   ringlike or circular structure.

anorexia (an″o-rek′se-ah):   lack or loss of the appetite for food.

anosmia (an-oz′me-ah):   absence of sense of smell.

anoxia (an-ok′se-ah):   reduction of oxygen in body tissues below physiologic levels.

antagonistic muscle (an-tag′o-nist-ik):   muscle which acts in opposition to the action of another muscle.

anterior: situated in front of or in the forward part.

antibody (an′tĭ-bod″e):   agglutinin; a protein (serum globulin) synthesized by an animal in response to an antigen which has entered the body.

antigen (an′tĭ-jen):   agglutinogen; a substance which, on gaining access to the blood stream, stimulates the formation of specific antibodies.

antrum (an′trum):   a cavity or chamber, especially one within a bone.

anuria (ah-nu′re-ah):   absence of excretion of urine.

aorta (ā-or′tah):   the main vessel rising from the left ventricle of the heart from which the systemic arterial circulation proceeds.

aperture (ap′er-chūr):   an opening or orifice.

apex (ā-peks):   the top or the pointed extremity of a conical part.

aphagia (ah-fā′je-ah):   nonfeeding.

aphasia (ah-fā′ze-ah):   defect or loss of the power of expression by speech.

aplastic (hypoplastic) anemia (ā-plas′tik ah-ne′me-ah):   reduced RBC formation caused by damage to the red bone marrow.

apnea (ap-nē′ah):   a transient cessation of breathing.

apneusis (ap-nu′sis):   breathing characterized by cramping of inspiratory muscles.

aponeurosis (ap″o-nu-ro′sis):   a flattened, expanded tendon.

appendage (ah-pen′dij):   a thing or part affixed or attached.

apraxia (ah-prak′se-ah):   inability to carry out purposeful movements in the absence of paralysis or other motor sensory impairment.

aqueduct (ak′we-dukt″):   a channel in a body structure or organ, especially a canal for the conduction of liquid.

aqueous humor (a′kwe-us hū′mor):   fluid produced in the eye, occupying the anterior and posterior chambers of the anterior cavity.

arachnoid (ah-rak′noid):   the middle of the three coverings (meninges) of the brain.

areola (ah-re′o-lah):   minute space in a tissue; the pigmented ring around the nipple.

areolar (ah-re′o-lar):   pertaining to or containing areolae; containing minute interspaces.

arrhythmia (ah-rith′me-ah):   any variation from the normal rhythm of the heartbeat.

arteriole (ar-te′re-ōl):   a very small artery.

artery (ar′ter-e):   a vessel through which the blood passes away from the heart to the various parts of the body.

arthritis (ar-thrī′tis):   inflammation of a joint.

arthrosis (ar-thrō′sis):   a joint or articulation.

articular (ar-tik′u-lar):   of or pertaining to a joint.

articulation (ar-tik″u-lā′shun):   the site of union or junction between two or more bones in the skeleton.

ascites (ah-sī′tēz):   accumulation of serous fluid in the abdominal cavity.

asphyxia (as-fik′se-ah):   loss of consciousness because of deficient oxygen supply.

aspirate (as′pĭ-rāt):   to remove fluids or gases from a cavity by suction.

asthenia (as-thē′ne-ah):   bodily weakness.

asthma (az′mah):   an allergic reaction to inspired foreign substances that creates localized edema in the walls of the small bronchioles, secretion of thick mucus, and spasms of the bronchiole walls.

astigmatism (ah-stig′mah-tizm):   defective curvature of refractive surfaces of the eye; as a result a ray of light is not focused sharply on the retina, but is spread over a diffuse area.

astrocyte (as′trō-sīt):   star-shaped cell, especially of the neuroglia.

ataxia (ah-tak′se-ah):   loss of muscle coordination.

atelectasis (at″e-lek′tah-sis):   incomplete expansion of the lungs at birth; lung collapse.

athetosis (ath″e-to′sis):   slow, involuntary, writhing movements.

atony (at′o-ne):   lack of normal tone or strength.

atrium (ā′tre-um):   a chamber or cavity; usually either one of the upper chambers of the heart.

atrophy (at′ro-fe):   a wasting away or diminution in the size of a cell, tissue, organ, or part.

audiogram (aw′de-o-gram″):   the record of a test of pure sound tones used to determine the extent of hearing loss.

auricle (aw′re-kl):   the flap of the ear.

autoimmune disease (aw″to-im-mūn′):   the attack by the immune system on one's own tissues.

autonomic (aw″to-nom′ik):   self-controlling; functionally independent.

autophagy (aw-tof′ah-je):   the eating of one's own flesh; nutrition of the body by the consumption of its own tissues.

autosome (aw′to-sōm):   any ordinary chromosome as distinguished from a sex chromosome.

axial (ak'se-al):   of, or pertaining to, the axis of a structure or part.

axilla (ak-sil'ah):   armpit.

axolemma (ak-so-lem'ah):   the surface membrane of an axon.

axon (ak'son):   neuronal process conducting impulses away from the cell body.

B cell system: immunity mediated by proteins (antibodies) to combat acute bacterial infections.

Babinski reflex (bah-bin'skē):   abnormal response to sole of foot stimulation after damage to motor tracts or spinal cord transection.

bacteriophage (bak-te're-o-fāj″):   bacterial virus; an agent that parasitizes a bacteria.

baroreceptors (bar″o-re-sep'tors):   receptors responding to change in blood pressure, located in the aortic arch and internal carotid arteries.

Bartholin's glands (bar'to-linz) (greater vestibular glands):   between the labia minora and the hymen.

basal ganglia (bā'sal gang'gle-ah):   4 paired masses of gray matter embedded in the white matter of the cerebral hemispheres and concerned with regulating motor activity.

base: nonacid; characterized by excess OH ion and a pH greater than 7.

bel: a unit for measuring loudness of sound.

benign (be-nīn'):   not malignant; not life-threatening.

biceps (bī'seps):   a muscle having two heads.

bifurcate (bī-fur'kāt):   forked; divided into two like a fork.

bilateral (bī-lat'eral):   pertaining to both sides of the body.

bile (bīl):   a fluid secreted by the liver and poured into the intestines. It aids in the absorption and digestion of fat.

bilirubin (bil″e-roo'bin):   red pigment in the bile.

biliverdin (bil″e-ver'din):   green pigment in the bile.

binocular (bin-ok'u-lar):   the visual field produced by two eyes.

binocular parallax (par'ah-laks):   the difference in the view of an object seen by each eye, making possible depth perception.

biovular, binovular (bī-ov'u-lar, bin-ov'u-lar):   pertaining to or derived from two distinct ova.

bipennate (bi″pen'āt):   said of muscles whose fibers are arranged on each side of a tendon, like the barbs on the shaft of a feather.

blastocyst (blas'to-sist):   a modified blastula; that is, a stage in the development of the embryo when the cells are arranged in a single layer to form a hollow sphere.

blastomere (blas'to-mere):   any one of the cells into which the fertilized ovum divides.

BMR (basal metabolic rate):   the exchange of energy occurring in a fasting and resting individual.

bolus (bō'lus):   a rounded food mass of soft consistency.

bone shaft: the body (diaphysis) of a long bone.

boutons (bōo'tuns):   presynaptic terminals.

Bowman's capsule (bo'manz):   the glomerular capsule; the cuplike depression of the tubular system of a nephron that surrounds a tuft of capillaries.

brachial (brā-ke-al):   pertaining to the arm.

bradycardia (brād″e-kar'de-ah):   abnormal slowness of the heartbeat, as evidenced by slowing of the pulse rate to 60 per minute or less.

Broca's area (bro′kahz): area of the brain for programming speech muscles.

bronchiole (brong′ke-ōl): one of the finer subdivisions of the branched bronchial tree of the lungs.

bronchus (brong′kus): either one of the two main branches of the trachea.

Brunner's glands (brun′erz): glands of the duodenum which secrete a mucus high in bicarbonate content.

buccal (buk′al): pertaining to the cheek.

buffer (buf′er): a substance in a fluid medium which lessens the change in hydrogen or hydroxyl ion concentration when an acid or base is added.

bursa (bur′sah): sac or saclike cavity filled with a viscid fluid situated at places in the tissue at which friction would otherwise develop.

calculus (kal′ku-lus): stone formed in various parts of the body, principally in ducts, hollow organs, and cysts.

Calorie (kal′o-re): equal to 1000 calories.

calorie: a unit of heat, being the amount of heat required to raise 1 gram of water 1° C.

calyx (kā′liks): a cup-shaped organ or cavity.

canaliculus (kan″ah-lik′u-lus): a small canal or channel.

cancellous (kan′se-lus): of a reticular, spongy, or latticelike structure.

capacitation (kah-pas′i-tā-tion): the final stage of maturation of sperm cells.

capillary (kap′ĭ-lar″e): any one of the minute vessels that connect the arterioles and the venules, forming a network in nearly all parts of the body.

carbohydrate (kar″bo-hī′drāt): originally defined as an organic compound containing carbon, hydrogen, and oxygen in which the latter two are in the same proportion as in water, but not all compounds now described as carbohydrates fit this definition; includes sugars and glycogen.

carcinoma (kar″si-nō′mah): a malignant new growth made up of epithelial cells tending to infiltrate the surrounding tissues.

carotid (kah-rot′id): principal artery on each side of the neck.

carpal (kar′pal): of or pertaining to the wrist.

casein (kā′se-in): principal protein of milk.

catabolism (kah-tab′o-lizm): any process by which complex substances are converted by living cells into simpler compounds.

catalyst (kat′ah-list): a substance which changes the velocity of a reaction but does not form part of the final product.

cataract (kat′ah-rakt): an opacity of the eye lens.

cation (kat′i-on): ion carrying a positive charge.

caudal (kaw′dal): denoting a position more toward the tail.

cecum (sē′kum): a dilated pouch that is the first portion of the large intestine.

celiac (sē′le-ak): pertaining to the abdomen.

cementum (sē-men′tum): a layer of bony tissue covering the root of a tooth.

centimeter (sen′ti-me″ter): a unit of linear measure of the metric system, being 1/100 meter, or about 2/5 inch.

cephalic (sĕ-fal′ik): pertaining to the head or superior end of the body.

cerebellum (ser″e-bel′um): division of the brain concerned with coordination of movements, located behind the cerebrum and above the pons and fourth ventricle.

cerebral cortex (ser'e-bral):   the gray matter covering the cerebrum.

cerebral dominance (dom'ĭ-nans):   specialization of one side of the brain.

cerumen (sĕ-roo'men):   waxlike secretion found within the external meatus of the ear.

cervix (ser'viks):   the neck or any necklike part; usually, the lower end of the uterus.

chancre (shang'kur):   the lesion (usually an ulcer) formed at the primary site of inoculation; usually refers to the initial lesion of syphilis.

chemoreceptor (kem'o-re-sep-tor):   a receptor adapted for excitation by chemical substances.

Cheyne-Stokes breathing (chān'stōks):   breathing characterized by alternating intervals of stertorous respiration and apnea.

chiasm (kī'azm):   an X-shaped crossing.

cholelithiasis (kō″le-li-thi'ah-sis) (gallstones):   crystals of bile in the gallbladder.

cholesterol (kō-les'ter-ol):   the most common steriod; present in bile, blood, and various tissues and the precursor of steroid hormones, vitamin D, and bile acids.

cholesterol esterase (es'ter-ās):   an enzyme which hydrolyzes cholesterol esters.

cholinergic (kō'lin-er'jik):   a term applied to those nerve fibers which liberate acetylcholine.

cholinesterase (kō″lin-es'ter-ās):   a substance which hydrolyzes acetylcholine.

chorea (ko-rē'ah):   the ceaseless occurrence of a wide variety of rapid, jerky, but well-co-ordinated movements, performed involuntarily.

chorion (kor'ee-on):   the outermost fetal membrane, serving a protective and nutritive function.

choroid plexuses (kor'oyd plek'suses):   pouchlike projections of pia mater into the ventricles which secrete cerebrospinal fluid.

chromatid (krō-mah-tid):   one of the two spiral filaments making up a chromosome which separate in cell division, each going to a different pole of the dividing cell.

chronaxie (krō'nax-e):   measure of nerve fiber excitability, specifically the time required for twice the minimum voltage (rheobase) to cause excitation.

chyle (kīl):   the milky fluid taken up by the lacteals from the food in the intestine after digestion.

chylomicron (kī″lo-mī'kron):   a lipid particle (largely triglyceride) with a protein-phospholipid coat absorbed into the intestinal lymphatics and found in the blood during the digestion of fat.

chyme (kīm):   semifluid, homogeneous, creamy material produced by the gastric digestion of food.

chymotrypsin (kī″mo-trip'sin):   a protein-degrading enzyme secreted by the pancreas as the inactive precursor chymotrypsinogen.

cilia (sil'e-ah):   minute, hairlike processes attached to the free surface of a cell.

cirrhosis (sir-rō'sis):   a disease of the liver in which there is degeneration of the liver cells and increase of connective tissue.

cisterna (sis-ter'nah):   an enclosed space serving as a reservoir for lymph or other body fluid. The *cisterna chyli* is the elongated sac from which the thoracic duct arises.

cleavage (klēv'ij):   mitotic segmentation of the zygote into blastomeres.

clone (klōn):   a group of cells arising by cell division from a single parent cell.

coagulation (kō-ag″u-lā'shun):   process of changing into a clot or being changed into a clot.

coarctation (ko″ark-tā'shun):   a condition of stricture or contracture.

cochlea (kŏk'le-ah):   anything having a spiral form; part of the inner ear.

coenzyme (kō-en'zīm):   a nonprotein substance actuating an enzyme.

collagen (kŏl′ah-jen):   the main supportive protein of connective tissue.

collateral (kŏ-lăt′er-al):   accompanying; running by the side of; accessory.

colloid (kŏl′oid):   a state of matter in which particles, collectively called the disperse phase, are distributed in what is termed the dispersion medium; the particles range in size from 1 to 100 nanometers, larger than those of a true solution, but not large enough to settle out on standing.

colostrum (ko-lŏs′trum):   the secretion of the mammary glands prior to lactation.

coma (kō′mah):   profound unconsciousness.

commissure (kŏm′ĭ-shoor):   the bond of fibers joining corresponding opposite parts, mainly in the brain and spinal cord.

concha (kong′kah):   a structure resembling a shell in shape.

condyle (kon′dīl):   a rounded projection on a bone, usually for articulation with another bone.

congenital (kon-jen′ĭ-tal):   existing at birth.

conjugation (kon″ju-gā′shun):   the act of joining together; in biology, the union of one organism with another for an exchange of nuclear material.

contraceptive (kon″trah-sep′tiv):   any device used to prevent conception.

contraction (kon-trak′shun):   a shortening, as of a muscle in the normal response to a nervous stimulus.

contralateral (kon″trah-lat′er-al):   situated on or pertaining to the opposite side.

convoluted (kon′vo-lūt-ed):   rolled together or coiled.

coracoid (kor′ah-koid):   like a raven's beak in form.

corium (kō′re-um):   the true skin, or the dermis.

coronary (kor′o-na-re):   encircling in the manner of a crown; a term applied to vessels, nerves, and ligaments.

corpus (kor′pus):   the body as a whole, or the main part of any organ.

corpus albicans (al′bĭ-kanz):   scar tissue in the ovary.

corpus callosum (kah-lo′sum):   largest of the commissural tracts which connect the two brain hemispheres.

corpus luteum (lū′te-um):   a yellow mass in the ovary formed by a Graafian follicle which has matured and discharged its ovum.

corpuscle (kor′pus-l):   any small mass or body.

cortex (kor′teks):   the outer layer of an organ, as distinguished from its inner substance.

costal (kos′tal):   pertaining to a rib or ribs.

crenation (kre-nā′shun):   the passage of the fluid within a cell into the surrounding medium, causing the cell to shrivel.

cretinism (krē′tin-izm):   a chronic condition due to congenital lack of thyroid secretion.

cribriform (krib′ri-form):   perforated like a sieve with small apertures.

cricoid (krī′koid):   ring-shaped.

cruciate (kroo′she-āt):   shaped like a cross.

crypt (krĭpt):   a minute, tubelike depression opening on a free surface.

cryptorchism (krĭp-tor′kizm):   failure of the testes to descend into the scrotum.

crypts of Lieberkühn (le′ber-kĭn):   glands of the small intestine.

crystalloid (kris′tal-loid):   a noncolloid substance which in a solvent passes readily through animal membranes.

cubital (kū′bĭ-tal):   pertaining to the forearm or elbow.

cupula (ku′pu-lah):   the portion of the lung above the clavicle.

Cushing's disease (koosh′ingz):   an excess of ACTH, resulting in adrenal cortex hyperfunction.

cutaneous (kū-ta′ne-us):   pertaining to the skin.

cyanosis (si″ah-no′sis):   a bluish appearance of the skin or nails secondary to deficient oxygenation of blood.

cytology (sī-tol′o-je):   the study of cells.

cytoplasm (sī′to-plazm″):   the protoplasm of a cell exclusive of that of the nucleus.

dead space: the air contained within the nose, pharynx, larynx, trachea, and bronchial tree.

deamination (de-am″ĭ-nā′shun):   a chemical reaction in which the amino group is split from an amino acid.

decibel (des′ĭ-bel):   1/10 of a bel.

decidua (de-sid′u-ah):   the mucous membrane lining of the uterus preparatory to implantation of the zygote.

deciduous (de-sĭd′u-us):   not permanent; cast off at maturity.

decussation (dē″kus-sa′shun):   a crossing over, particularly a band of nerves fibers crossing the median plane of any part of the central nervous system.

deglutition (dē″gloo-tish′un):   the act of swallowing.

deltoid (del′toid):   having a triangular outline.

dendrite (den′drīt):   a branched and tree-shaped protoplasmic process from a nerve cell which conducts impulses toward the cell body.

dental caries (kar′ēz):   disintegration of teeth by acids produced by bacterial fermentation of carbohydrates.

dentate (den′tāte):   having teeth or projections like saw teeth on the edges.

dentin (den′tin):   the chief tissue of the teeth; surrounds the tooth pulp.

deoxyhemoglobin (de-ok″se-hē″mo-glo′bin):   oxygen-free hemoglobin.

deoxyribonucleic acid, DNA (de-ok″si-rī″bo-nu-klē′ic):   nucleic acid present in chromosomes of the nuclei of cells. It is the chemical basis of heredity and the carrier of genetic information.

dermatome (der′mah-tōm):   a strip of skin supplied by one pair of spinal nerves.

dermis (der′mis):   the true skin, or corium; the second, major layer, beneath the epidermis.

dextrose (deks′trōs):   glucose, a monosaccharide, the principal blood sugar.

diabetes (di″ah-bē′tĕz):   a condition marked by a habitual discharge of an excessive quantity of urine and by excessive thirst; two major types are diabetes insipidus and diabetes mellitus.

diabetic retinopathy (di″ah-bet′ik ret″ĭ-nop′ah-the):   deterioration of tiny blood vessels in the eye.

dialysis (dī-al′ĭ-sis):   the process of separating crystalloids and colloids in solution by the difference in their rates of diffusion through a semipermeable membrane; crystalloids pass through readily, colloids slowly or not at all.

diaphragm (di′ah-fram):   a musculotendinous partition, especially that which separates the thorax and abdomen.

diaphysis (di-af′ĭ-sis):   the shaft of a long bone.

diarthrosis (di″ar-thrō′sis):   a freely movable articulation.

diastole (dī-as′tō-lē):   the relaxation and dilation of the ventricles of the heart, during which time they fill with blood.

diencephalon (dī'en-sef'ah-lon):   the posterior division of the prosencephalon of the brain.

diffusion (dĭ-fū'zhun):   net transfer of a substance from a region of high to a region of low concentration as a result of random motion of particles.

diplopia (dĭ-plō'pe-ah):   the seeing of single objects as double.

disaccharide (dī-sak'ah-rīd):   any one of a class of sugars which yield two monosaccharides upon hydrolysis; includes sucrose, lactose, and maltose.

distal (dis'tal):   remote, farther from any point of reference.

diuresis (dī"u-rē'sis):   increased excretion of urine.

diuretic (dī"u-ret'ik):   increasing the volume of urine; an agent that increases the volume of urine.

diverticulum (dī"ver-tik'u-lum):   a pouch or pocket from a main cavity or tube.

dorsal (dor'sal):   denoting a position toward the back or posterior.

dorsum (dor'sum):   the back.

dropsy (drop'se):   accumulation of serous fluid in a body cavity or tissues.

duct: a tube for the passage of excretions or secretions.

dura mater (du'rah mā'ter):   the outermost, toughest, and most fibrous of the three meninges of the brain.

dwarfism (dwarf'izm):   smallness due to underproduction of growth hormone.

dysfunction (dis-funk'shun):   partial disturbance, impairment, or abnormality of the functioning of an organ.

dysmenorrhea (dis"men-o-re'ah):   painful menstruation.

dysmetria (dis-met're-ah):   inability to judge extent of self-movements.

dyspnea (disp-nē'ah):   difficult or labored breathing.

dystrophy (dis'tro-fe):   defective nutrition; defective development or degeneration.

dysuria (dis-u're-ah):   difficult or painful urination.

"ear drum":   the tympanic membrane.

ectoderm (ek'to-derm):   the outermost of the three primary germ layers of an embryo.

ectopic (ek-top'ik):   not in the normal place or position, as ectopic pregnancy—implantation of the fertilized ovum in a place other than the uterus.

edema (e-dē'mah):   the presence of an abnormally large volume of fluid in the interstitial spaces of the body.

efferent (ef'er-ent):   conveying away from the center.

electrocardiogram (e-lek"tro-kar'de-o-gram):   a graphic record of the electric current produced by the excitation of heart muscle.

electroencephalogram (e-lek"tro-en-sef'ah-lo-gram):   the graphic record of the electrical activity of the brain.

electrolyte (e-lek'tro-līt):   any solution conducting electricity by means of its ions.

electrophoresis (e-lek"tro-fo-rē'sis):   the movement of charged particles suspended in a liquid on various media (e.g., paper, starch, agar) under the influence of an applied electric field.

embolus (em'bo-lus):   clot or other plug brought by the blood from another vessel and forced into a smaller one so as to obstruct circulation.

embryo (em'bre-o):   the early or developing stage of any organism; in humans, the organism in its first two months of existence in the womb.

emesis (em'e-sis):   vomiting.

emphysema (em″fĭ-sē′mah): respiratory disorder characterized by increased airway resistance and distention and rupture of the pulmonary alveoli.

empyema (em″pī-ē′mah): accumulation of pus in a cavity of the body, especially in the chest.

encephalon (en-sef′ah-lon): the brain.

endemic goiter (en-dem′ic goi′ter): goiter peculiar to certain regions produced by hypersecretion of TSH due to insufficient dietary iodine.

endocardium (en″do-kar′de-um): inner heart layer (endothelium).

endocrine (en′do-krin): secreting internally; applied to organs functioning to secrete substances into the blood or lymph, producing an effect on another organ or part.

endoderm (en′do-derm): innermost of the three germ layers of an embryo.

endogenous (en-doj′e-nus): developing or originating within the organism, or arising from causes within the organism.

endometrium (en″do-mē′tre-um): mucous membrane that lines the cavity of the uterus.

endomysium (en″do-mis′e-um): the connective tissue sheath surrounding each muscle fiber.

endoneurium (en″do-nu′re-um): connective tissue in a nerve surrounding the individual fibers of a bundle, binding them together.

endoplasmic reticulum (en-dō-plaz′mik re-tik′ū-lum): network of tubules and vesicles in cytoplasm.

endosteum (en-dos′te-um): membranous layer of connective tissue lining marrow cavities and spaces of bones.

enuresis (en″u-rē′sis): involuntary urination.

enzyme (en′zīm): a protein capable of accelerating or producing by catalytic action some change in a specific substrate.

ependymal cells (e-pen′dĭ-mal): cells that line the cavities of the brain and central canal of the spinal cord.

epicardium (ep″i-kar′de-um): external heart layer (visceral layer of pericardium).

epidermis (ep″i-der′mis): the outermost and nonvascular layer of the skin; it is composed of five distinct layers.

epigastrium (ep″ĭ-gas′tre-um): the upper middle region of the abdomen, located within the sternal angle.

epimysium (ep″ĭ-mis′e-um): the fibrous sheath surrounding an entire muscle.

epineurium (ep″ĭ-nu′re-um): the connective tissue covering of a nerve.

epiphysis (e-pif′ĭ-sis): a segment of bone separated from the long bone early in life by a piece of cartilage, but later becoming part of the larger bone.

epithelium (ep″ĭ-thē′le-um): one of the four major types of tissues; consisting of closely packed cells covering internal and external surfaces of the body, including the lining of the vessels, and forming glands.

erythrocyte (e-rith′ro-sīt): red blood cell, shaped like a biconcave disc.

erythropoiesis (e-rith″ro-poi-ē′sis): the production of red blood cells.

essential amino acids: tryptophan, lysine, methionine, threonine, phenylalanine, leucine, isoleucine, and valine, which cannot be synthesized in the body and must be obtained in the diet.

essential fatty acids: linoleic and linolenic acid (unsaturated fatty acids with two and three double bonds, respectively), which cannot be synthesized in the body.

esterification (es-ter″ĭ-fi-kā′shun): the process of converting an acid into an ester.

ethmoid (eth′moid): cribriform; sievelike.

etiology (ē″tĭ-ol′o-je): the study of cause, especially of disease.

eupnea (ūp-nē′ah):   normal respiration.

evagination (ē-vaj″ĭ-nā′shun):   an outpouching of a layer or part.

eversion (ē-ver′zhun):   a turning inside out.

excoriation (eks-ko″re-ā′shun):   a superficial loss of substance, such as is produced on the skin by scratching.

exocrine (ek′so-krin):   applied to glands which deliver secretions to an epithelial surface, directly or through ducts.

excretory (eks′kre-to-re):   pertaining to discharge of waste products from the body.

expiration (eks″pĭ-ra′shun):   expelling air from the lungs.

extrapyramidal (eks″trah-pi-ram′ĭ-dal):   outside the pyramidal tracts.

extravasation (eks-trav″ah-sa′shun):   escape of fluid from its proper place, as blood into tissue spaces after rupture of a vessel or urine after rupture of the bladder or urethra.

extrinsic (eks-trin′sik):   originating outside.

facilitation (fah-sil″ĭ-ta′shun):   increased ease in carrying out an action; augmented response at synapse due to simultaneous or prior stimulation.

fascia (fash′e-ah):   subcutaneous adipose tissue (superficial fascia) and various arrangements of connective tissue penetrating between individual or groups of muscles and surrounding other structures, such as nerves and blood vessels.

fascicle (fas′ĭ-k′l):   a small bundle or cluster, especially of nerve or muscle fibers.

febrile (feb′ril):   pertaining to fever.

fenestrated (fen′es-trāt″ed):   pierced with one or more openings.

fertilization (fer-ti-li-zā′shun):   union of ovum and spermatozoon.

fetus (fē′tus):   the developing young in the uterus after the end of the second month.

fiber (fi′ber):   an elongated, threadlike structure of organic tissue.

fibrillation (fi-brĭ-lā′shun):   a local quivering of muscle fibers; usually refers to spasmodic contraction of the cardiac muscle.

fibrin (fi′brin):   a whitish, insoluble protein formed from fibrinogen, important in the clotting of blood.

fibrinogen (fi-brin′o-jen):   a soluble protein in the blood plasma which, by the action of thrombin, is converted into fibrin, thus producing clotting of the blood.

fibroblast (fi′bro-blast):   connective tissue cell that synthesizes the matrix of connective tissue proper.

filiform (fil′ĭ-form):   thread-shaped.

filtration (fil-trā′shun):   the passage of liquid and solutes through a semipermeable membrane under pressure.

filum terminale (fi′lum ter′min-ah-le):   the portion of pia mater extending below the spinal cord.

fimbria (fim′bre-ah):   any fringelike structure.

fissure (fish′ūr):   any cleft or groove, normal or otherwise.

fistula (fis′tchu-lah):   a deep tract, often leading to an internal hollow cavity.

follicle (fol′ĭ-kl):   a small excretory or secretory sac or gland.

foramen (fo-rā′men):   a natural hole or passage, especially one into or through bone.

fossa (fos′ah):   a pit or depression.

fovea (fō′ve-ah):   a fossa, or cup; applied to various depressions in the structure of the body, such as the fovea centralis.

frenulum (fren′u-lum): a small fold of skin or mucous membrane, especially one that limits the movements of an organ or part of an organ.

fundus (fun′dus): the base or part of a hollow organ most remote from the entrance.

funiculus (fu-nik′u-lus): one of the three main divisions of the white matter of the spinal cord.

fusiform (fū′sĭ-form): spindle-shaped.

galactose (gah-lak′tos): a monosaccharide obtained from lactose, or milk sugar.

gametes (gam′ēts): sex cells.

gamma efferents (gam′mah ef′er-ents): neurons which control the sensitivity of the muscle spindle.

gamma globulin (glob′u-lin): the fraction of plasma globulin (one of the major classes of proteins in plasma), separated by electrophoresis, containing antibodies.

ganglion (gang′gle-on): a collection or mass of nerve cells.

gene (jēn): the biologic unit of heredity; self-reproducing and located in a definite position on a particular chromosome.

geniculate (je-nik′u-lāt): bent, like a knee.

genitalia (jen″ĭ-tā′le-ah): the reproductive organs.

genu (jēn′yoo): the knee, or any structure bent like a knee.

germ layers: three primary layers of cells in an embryo from which the organs and tissues develop. They are the ectoderm, mesoderm, and endoderm.

gestation (jes-tā-shun): pregnancy.

gland: an organ that produces a specific product or secretion.

globin (glō′bin): the protein constituent of hemoglobin.

glomerulus (glo-mer′u-lus): a coil or cluster of capillaries projecting into Bowman's capsule, a cuplike depression at the origin of a renal tubule.

glossal (glos′al): pertaining to the tongue.

glucagon (gloo′kah-gon): a hormone produced by the pancreas in response to hypoglycemia that raises blood sugar.

glucocorticoid (gloo″ko-kor′tĭ-koid): a hormone of the adrenal cortex having mainly metabolic actions.

gluconeogenesis (gloo″ko-nē″o-jen′e-sis): the synthesis of "new" glucose from substrates such as amino acids and lactic acid.

glucose (gloo′kōs): a monosaccharide, the principal blood sugar.

gluteal (gloo′te-al): pertaining to the buttocks.

glycogen (glī′ko-jen): a polysaccharide which is the chief carbohydrate storage material in animals.

glycosuria (glī″ko-su′re-ah): glucose excreted in the urine.

goblet cell: a form of epithelial cell containing mucin and bulged out like a goblet.

goiter (goi′ter): enlargement of the thyroid gland, causing a swelling in the front part of the neck.

gonad (gon′ad): ovary or testis.

Graafian follicle (graf′e-an): small, spherical, vesicular sac embedded in the cortex of the ovary which contains a developing ovum.

granulocyte (gran′u-lo-sīt): a granular leukocyte, either a neutrophil, basophil, or eosinophil.

Graves' disease (grāvz): hyperthyroidism.

groin: the depression between the abdomen and thigh; also called the inguinal region.

gustatory (gus'tah-to"re):   pertaining to the sense of taste.

gyrus (jī'rus):   a convoluted ridge.

haploid (hap'loid):   having single (not paired) chromosomes.

haustra (haws'trah):   sacculations in the colon.

helix (hē'liks):   anything having a spiral form.

hematocrit (he-mat'o-krit):   volume percentage of erythrocytes in whole blood.

hematopoiesis (hem"ah-to-poi-e'sis):   the formation and development of blood cells.

heme (hēm):   the oxygen-transporting complex of hemoglobin composed of iron and proto-porphyrin.

hemiparesis (hem"e-par-e'sis):   muscular weakness of one side of the body.

hemocytoblast (hē"mo-sī'to-blast):   undifferentiated stem cell which gives rise to all blood cells.

hemoglobin (hē"mo-glo'bin):   the oxygen-carrying red pigment of the red blood corpuscles.

hemolysis (he-mol'i-sis):   the destruction of red blood cells and the liberation of hemoglobin.

hemolytic anemia (hē"mo-lit'ik):   anemia due to shortened *in vivo* survival of the erythrocytes and inability of the bone marrow to compensate for their decreased life span.

hemophilia (hee"mo-fil'e-ah):   a disorder in blood clotting, transmitted as a sex-linked recessive trait, caused by a defective clotting factor.

hemorrhage (hem'or-ij):   a copious escape of blood; bleeding.

hemostasis (hē"mo-stā'sis):   the checking of the flow of blood through any part or vessel.

heparin (hep'ah-rin):   an anticoagulant found mainly in the liver.

hermaphrodite (her-maf'ro-dīt):   an individual containing gonads of both sexes.

hernia (her'ne-ah):   protrusion of a loop or knuckle of an organ or tissue through an abnormal opening.

hilus, hilum (hī'lus, hī'lum):   depression where vessels enter an organ.

histology (his-tol'o-je):   that part of anatomy dealing with the minute structure, composition, and function of the tissues.

homeostasis (ho"me-o-stā'sis):   a tendency to uniformity or stability in an organism.

homogeneous (ho"mo-jē'ne-us):   having the same nature or qualities; of uniform character in all parts.

homologous (ho-mol'o-gus):   corresponding in structure, position, and origin. In transplantation, tissues or organs are exchanged between two nonidentical individuals of the same species.

horizontal cell: neuron carrying signals across the retina.

hormone (hor'mōn):   a substance produced in one part of the body, most commonly an endocrine gland, that is transported in the blood to another part, often a specific target organ, where it exerts a regulatory action.

Horner's syndrome: symptom complex resulting from interruption of sympathetic nerve supply to the head and neck, including ptosis (drooping of upper eyelid), small pupil, and absence of sweating.

hyaline (hī'ah-lĭn):   glassy; transparent or nearly so.

hydrocephalus (hī"dro-sef'ah-lus):   a condition characterized by abnormal accumulation of cerebrospinal fluid in the cranial vault; also called hydrocephaly.

hydrolysis (hī-drol'ĭ-sis):   decomposition with the addition of water.

hydrostatic (hī"dro-stat'ik):   pertaining to a liquid in a state of equilibrium.

hyoid (hī'oid): U-shaped bone between the root of the tongue and the larynx.

hypercapnia (hī"per-kap'ne-ah): abnormally high blood CO_2 concentration.

hyperemia (hī"per-ē'me-ah): increased blood in a part.

hyperglycemia (hī"per-gli-sē'me-ah): concentration of glucose in the blood above the normal level.

hyperphagia (hī"per-fā'je-ah): ingestion of a greater than optimal quantity of food.

hyperplasia (hī"per-plā'ze-ah): an increase in the size of a tissue or organ owing to an increase in the number of cells.

hyperpnea (hī"perp-nē'ah): abnormal increase in the depth and rate of the respiratory movements.

hypertension (hī'per-ten'shun): abnormally high tension, especially high blood pressure.

hypertonic (hī"per-ton'ik): having an osmotic pressure greater than that of a physiologic salt solution or other solution with which it is compared.

hypertrophy (hī-per'tro-fe): the enlargement or overgrowth of an organ or part due to an increase in size of its constituent cells.

hypochondriac (hī"po-kon"dre-ak): pertaining to the upper lateral region of the abdomen below the lowest ribs.

hypodermic (hī-po-der-mik): applied beneath the skin.

hypoglycemia (hī"po-gli-sē'me-ah): concentration of glucose in the blood below the normal limit.

hypophysis (hī-pof'ĭ-sis): the pituitary gland.

hypothalamus (hī"po-thal'ah-mus): the portion of the diencephalon which forms the floor and part of the lateral wall of the third ventricle; exerts control over visceral activities, water balance, temperature, sleep, etc.

hypotonic (hī-po-ton'ik): having an osmotic pressure lower than that of a physiologic salt solution or other solution with which it is compared.

hypoxia (hī-pox'se-ah): reduced oxygen level in the tissues.

impermeable (im-per'me-ah-b'l): not permitting a passage, as for fluid.

implantation (im"plan-tā'shun): attachment of the blastocyst to the epithelial lining of the uterus.

inanition (in"ah-nish'un): the physical condition which results from complete lack of food.

inclusion (in-klu'zhun): that which is enclosed, especially referring to any particle or foreign substance included within a cell.

incus (ing'kus): the anvil; the middle of the three ossicles of the ear.

infarction (in-fark'shun): process leading to the development of an infarct—an area of necrosis of tissue due to complete interference with blood flow.

inferior (in-fe're-or): situated below.

inflammation (in"flah-mā'shun): a series of reactions produced in the tissues by an irritant, marked by an erythema with exudation of serum and leukocytes.

infundibulum (in"fun-dib'u-lum): a funnel-shaped structure or passage.

ingestion (in-jes'chun): the act of taking food, medicine, etc., into the body by mouth.

inguinal (ing'gwĭ-nal): pertaining to the groin.

inhalation (in"hah-lā'shun): the drawing of air or other vapor into the lungs.

insertion: place of attachment of a muscle to the bone which it moves.

in situ (in sī'tu): in the normal place or confined to the site of origin without invasion of neighboring tissues.

inspiration (in″spĭ-ra′shun):   breathing air into the lungs.

intercellular (in″ter-sel′u-lar):   situated between the cells of any structure.

intercostal (in″ter-kos′tal):   situated between the ribs.

interstitial (in″ter-stish′al):   pertaining to or situated in the spaces or gaps of a tissue.

intima (in′tĭ-mah):   innermost.

intravascular (in″trah-vas′ku-lar):   within the blood vessels.

intrinsic (in-trin′sik):   situated within or pertaining exclusively to a part.

invaginate (in-vaj′ĭ-nāt):   to infold so as to form a pocket or channel.

in vitro (in vī′tro):   within a glass; observable in a test tube.

in vivo (in vī′vo):   within the living body.

involution (in″vo-lu′shun):   retrograde or degenerative change.

ion (ī′on):   an atom or a group of atoms having a positive or negative charge.

ipsilateral (ip″sĭ-lat′er-al):   pertaining to the same side.

irritability (ir″ĭ-tah-bil′ĭ-te):   the quality of responding to stimuli.

ischemia (is-kē′me-ah):   local and temporary deficiency of blood, chiefly due to contraction of a blood vessel.

isotonic (ī″so-ton′ik):   having the same osmotic pressure as a physiologic salt solution.

isthmus (is′mus):   the neck or constricted part of an organ.

keratin (ker′ah-tin):   an insoluble protein which is the principal constituent of hair and nails; contains large amounts of sulfur.

kinesthesia (kin″es-thē′ze-ah):   "muscle sense"; sense of position and movement of body parts.

Kupffer cells (koop′fer):   cells of the liver involved with destruction of erythrocytes and removal of bacteria and foreign bodies from the blood.

labium (lā′be-um):   a lip or lip-shaped organ.

lacrimal (lak′rĭ-mal):   pertaining to tears.

lactation (lak-tā′shun):   the production of milk by the mammary glands.

lacteal (lak′te-al):   pertaining to milk; any one of the intestinal lymphatics that take up chyle.

lactiferous (lak-tif′er-us):   producing or conveying milk.

lactose (lak′tōs):   a disaccharide obtained from milk.

lacuna (lah-ku′nah):   a small pit, hollow, or depression.

lamella (lah-mel′ah):   a thin leaf or plate, as of bone.

lamina (lam′ĭ-nah):   a thin, flat plate or layer.

larynx (lar′inks):   the voice-box, located at the top of the trachea.

lateral: denoting a position toward the side and farther away from the median plane.

lemniscus (lem-nis′kus):   a secondary pathway in the central nervous system which usually decussates and terminates in the thalamus.

lesion (le′zhun):   an alteration of structure or of functional capacity due to injury or disease.

leukocyte (lū′ko-sīt):   a white blood cell, the two major types of which are granular and nongranular.

leukopenia (lū″ko-pē′ne-ah):   a reduction of white cells.

ligament (lig'ah-ment): any tough, fibrous band connecting bone or supporting viscera.

limbic (lim'bik): pertaining to a border or margin.

lipid (lip'id): fat and fatlike compounds having in common the property of insolubility in water and solubility in fat solvents.

lipoprotein lipase (lĭp"o-prō'te-in lĭp'ās): an enzyme essential for the tissue uptake of the triglycerides of chylomicrons and very low density lipoproteins.

liter (lē'ter): the volume occupied by 1 kilogram of pure water at its temperature of maximum density and under standard atmospheric pressure. It is the equivalent of 1.0567 quarts liquid measure.

lobotomy (lo-bot'o-me): incision into a lobe, e.g., a prefrontal lobotomy.

loin: the lateral and posterior region of the body between the thorax and the pelvis.

lumbar (lum'bar): pertaining to the loins.

lumen (lu'men): the space inside of a tube or tubular organ.

lymph: transparent liquid found in the lymphatic vessels.

lymphedema (lim"fe-dē'mah): edema resulting from deficient lymph drainage.

lymphocyte (lim'fo-sīt): one of the two kinds of nongranular leukocytes; two types, B cells and T cells, function in the immune response.

lysosome (lī'so-sōm): cytoplasmic particle containing hydrolyzing enzymes.

macrocyte (mak'ro-sīt): an abnormally large erythrocyte, i.e., one from 10 to 12 microns in diameter, found in the blood in certain anemias, especially pernicious anemia.

macrophage (mak'ro-fāj): a phagocytic cell that belongs to the reticuloendothelial system.

macroscopic (mak"ro-skop'ik): visible with the unaided eye or without the microscope.

macula (mak'u-lah): a spot.

malignant (mah-lig'nant): virulent; tending to go from bad to worse.

malleus (mal'e-us): the largest of the auditory ossicles; also called the hammer.

maltose (mawl'tōs): a disaccharide present in malt, malt products, and sprouting seeds; it is formed by the hydrolysis of starch and is converted into glucose by the enzyme maltase.

mammary (mam'er-e): pertaining to the breast.

mammillary (mam'ĭ-ler"e): like or pertaining to a nipple.

mandible (man'dĭ-bl): the horseshoe-shaped bone forming the lower jaw.

manometer (mah-nom'e-ter): an instrument for measuring the pressure or tension of liquids or gases.

manubrium (mah-nu'bre-um): uppermost portion of the sternum.

mastication (mas"tĭ-kā'shun): the chewing of food.

mastoid (mas"toid): breast-shaped, as the mastoid process of the temporal bone.

matrix (mā'triks): the ground substance in which cells are embedded.

meatus (me-ā'tus): a passage or channel, especially the external opening of a canal.

medial: pertaining to the middle; nearer the median plane.

mediastinum (mē"de-as-tī'num): partition separating adjacent parts; the space in the center of the chest between the two pleural cavities.

medulla (me-dul'ah): the central portion of an organ as contrasted with its cortex.

megakaryocyte (meg"ah-kar'e-o-sīt): the giant cell of bone marrow which gives rise to blood platelets.

meiosis (mī-ō'sis): a special type of cell division occurring during the maturation of sex cells by which the normal diploid number of chromosomes is reduced to a single (haploid) set.

melanocyte (mĕ-lan′o-sīt):   the epidermal cell which synthesizes melanin.

membrane (mem′brān):   a thin layer of tissue covering a surface or dividing a space or organ; the enclosure of a cell or cell organelle.

memory cells: those cells that give rise to clones of their own upon reappearance of the same infectious agent.

menarche (me-nar′ke):   onset of menstruation.

meninges (me-nin′jēs):   three membranes which cover and protect the brain and spinal cord. The innermost membrane is pia mater (pī-ah mā′ter); the middle membrane is arachnoid mater (ah-rak′noid); the outermost membrane is dura mater (du′rah).

menopause (men′o-pawz):   cessation of menstruation in the human female, occurring usually between the ages of 50 and 55.

menstrual cycle (men′stroo-al):   cyclic changes in the uterus beginning at puberty and ending at menopause in which a period of partial shedding of the uterine endometrium follows a period of endometrial growth in preparation for a possible pregnancy.

menstruation (men″stroo-ā′shun):   partial sloughing of the uterine endometrium accompanied by bleeding which normally recurs, usually at approximately 4-week intervals, in the absence of pregnancy during the reproductive period of the female.

mesencephalon (mes″en-sef′ah-lon):   the midbrain.

mesenchyme (mes′eng-kīm):   the network of embryonic connective tissue in the mesoderm from which are formed the connective tissues of the body and also the blood vessels and lymphatic vessels.

mesentery (mes′en-ter″e):   peritoneal fold attaching the intestine to the posterior abdominal wall.

mesoderm (mes′o-derm):   the middle layer of the three primary germ layers of the embryo, lying between the ectoderm and endoderm.

mesothelium (mes″o-thē′le-um):   a layer of flat cells which in the adult forms a squamous-celled layer of epithelium covering the surface of all serous membranes.

metabolism (mĕ-tab′o-lizm):   the sum total of all of the chemical reactions occurring in cells, including those providing energy and those resulting in the synthesis of structural components of cells and matrices, reserve energy stores, and substances, such as hormones, that perform various special functions.

metachromatic (met″ah-krō-mat′ik):   tissue in which different elements take on different colors with the same dye.

metastasis (mĕ-tas′tah-sis):   the transfer of disease from one organ or part to another not directly connected to it.

meter (mē′ter):   the basic unit of linear measure of the metric system, equivalent to 39.371 inches.

methylation (meth″ĭ-lā′shun):   the process of substituting a methyl group for a hydrogen atom.

micelles (mī-sels′):   molecular aggregates containing one or more amphipathic substances which form at a critical micellar concentration and are water soluble.

microglia (mī-krog′le-ah):   a type of neuroglia with a phagocytic action.

microvilli (mī″kro-vil′ī):   processes on the free surface of epithelial cells.

micturition (mik″tu-rish′un):   the passage of urine.

mineralocorticoid (min″er-al-o-kor′ti-koid):   a hormone of the adrenal cortex particularly effective in causing the retention of sodium and the loss of potassium.

mitochondria (mī″to-kon′dre-ah):   cell organelles that produce most of the cell's ATP; known as the powerhouse of the cell.

mitosis (mī-to′sis): cell division producing two daughter cells with the same number of chromosomes as the parent cell.

mitral (mī′tral): shaped somewhat like a miter (a headdress worn by bishops); pertaining to the mitral, or bicuspid, valve—the AV valve on the left side of the heart.

monosaccharide (mon″o-sak′ah-rīd): a simple sugar which cannot be hydrolyzed into sugars of lower molecular weight; common examples are dextrose (glucose) and fructose.

monovular (mon-ov′u-lar): pertaining to or derived from a single ovum.

morbid (mor′bid): pertaining to disease.

morphology (mor-fol′o-je): a study of the shape and structure of living organisms.

morula (mor′u-lah): the cleaving ovum during the stage in which it forms a solid, mulberrylike mass of cells.

motile (mō′til): capable of spontaneous movement.

motor neuron: efferent neuron that carries impulses away from the brain and spinal cord to muscles and glands.

mucosa (mu-kō′sah): a mucous membrane, one which lines tracts and cavities opening to the exterior, consisting of a surface layer of epithelium and underlying connective tissue.

myelin sheath (mī′e-lin): sheath around nerve fibers; in peripheral nerves formed by multiple wrappings of Schwann cell membranes.

myocardium (mī″o-kar′de-um): the muscular substance of the heart muscle.

myoepithelial cells (mī″o-ep″ĭ-thē′le-al): epithelial cells with contractile properties found in the secretory units of the mammary, sweat, lacrimal, and salivary glands.

myopia (mī-ō′pe-ah): nearsightedness; a defect in vision characterized by the focusing of parallel rays in front of the retina.

myosin (mī′o-sin): a protein forming the thick filaments of the myofibril of a muscle fiber.

myotatic reflex (mī″o-tat′ik): stretch reflex.

nares (na′rēz): the external openings into the nasal cavities; plural of naris.

navicular (nah-vik′u-lar): boat-shaped.

necrosis (nĕ-kro′sis): death of a cell or of a group of cells.

nephron (nef′ron): basic functional unit of the kidney; consisting of the renal corpuscle with its Bowman's capsule and the long tubule extending from the capsule.

nerve: bundle of nerve fibers outside the brain or spinal cord.

neurilemma (nu″rĭ-lem′mah): the outermost wrapping of myelin of a peripheral nerve fiber, containing the nuclei of Schwann cells and most of their cytoplasm.

neuroglia (nu-rog′le-ah): supporting cells of nervous tissue; neuroglia and neurons are the two types of nerve cells.

neurohypophysis (nu″ro-hī-pof′ĭ-sis): the posterior portion of the hypophysis (pituitary gland).

neuron (nu′ron): a nerve cell.

nodule (nod′ūl): a small node.

norepinephrine (nor″ep-ĭ-nef′rin): a neurotransmitter released at synapses and sympathetic postganglionic nerve endings; also a hormone secreted by the suprarenal medulla.

nuchal (nu′kal): pertaining to the back of the neck.

nucleotide (nu′kle-o-tīd): molecular unit from which nucleic acids are synthesized, consisting of a 5-carbon sugar, phosphate group, and nitrogenous base.

nucleus (nu′kle-us): a spheroid body within a cell, distinguished from the rest of the cell by its denser structure and by containing chromosomes; a collection of nerve cell bodies in the central nervous system.

nulliparous (nul-lip′ah-rus): having never given birth to a child.

occiput (ok′-sĭ-put): the back part of the head.

odontoid (o-don′toid): like a tooth.

olecranon (o-lek′rah-non): curved process of the ulna at the elbow.

olfactory (ol-fak′to-re): pertaining to the sense of smell.

oligodendroglia (ol″ĭ-go-den-drog′le-ah): type of neuroglia; gives rise to the myelin sheath of nerve fibers of the central nervous system.

oliguria (ol″i-gu′re-ah): diminished quanitity of urine.

ophthalmic (of-thal′mik): pertaining to the eye.

organelle (or″gan-el′): one of the minute, specialized structures of cells concerned with the functions of metabolism, locomotion, etc.

orifice (or′ĭ-fis): the entrance or outlet of any body cavity.

orthopnea (or″thop-ne′ah): inability to breathe easily except in an upright position.

osmosis (os-mo′sis): the net transfer of water, when two solutions are separated by a membrane, from the more dilute solution (where the water molecules are in higher concentration) to the more concentrated solution.

osseous (os′e-us): of the nature or quality of bone; bony.

osteoblast (os′te-o-blast): a cell which arises from a fibroblast and which, as it matures, is associated with the production of bone.

ovulation (ov′u-lā′shun): rupture of an ovarian follicle with the release of a secondary oocyte (immature ovum).

oxygen debt (ok′sĭ-jen): following exercise, the amount of oxygen consumed above the basal oxygen consumption level.

oxyhemoglobin (ok″se-hē″mo-glo′bin): hemoglobin combined with oxygen.

oxyntic (oks-in′tik): secreting an acid substance.

Pacinian corpuscles (pah-sin′e-an): receptors of deep pressure.

palate (pal′at): roof of the mouth.

palliative (pal′e-ā″tiv): affording relief but not cure.

palpebrae (pal′pe-brē): eyelids.

papilla (pah-pil′ah): a small, nipple-shaped projection or elevation.

parasympathetic (par″ah-sim″pah-thet′ik): craniosacral division of the autonomic nervous system; in general, it is concerned with restorative processes, such as slowing the heart rate.

parenchyma (par-eng′kĭ-mah): the tissue of an organ performing its special function as distinguished from the supporting tissue.

parenteral (par-en′ter-al): outside of the intestine; not via the alimentary canal; a subcutaneous, intravenous, or intramuscular injection.

paresthesia (par″es-thē′ze-ah): perverted sensation of burning, prickling, or tingling.

parietal (pah-rī′ĕ-tal): of or pertaining to the walls of a cavity.

Parkinson's disease: a disorder affecting the elderly, associated with degeneration of parts of the basal ganglion, characterized by tremor, rigidity, and hypokinesis.

parotid (pah-rot′id): situated near the ear, as the parotid gland.

parous (par′ous):   having borne a child.

paroxysm (par′ok-sizm):   a fit, attack, or sharp increase in intensity of a disease, occurring at intervals.

parturition (par″tu-rish′un):   labor; the act of giving birth to a child.

pathology (pah-thol′o-je):   the study of disease, especially the structural and functional changes in tissues and organs of the body which are caused by disease.

pectineal (pek-tin′e-al):   pertaining to the pubic bone.

pectoral (pek′to-ral):   pertaining to the breast or chest.

peduncle (pe-dung′kl):   a narrow part acting as a support; a large nerve fiber tract interconnecting parts of the brain, especially extending from the cerebellum.

pelvis (pel′vis):   any basinlike structure, particularly the basin-shaped ring of bone at the posterior extremity of the trunk.

pendulous (pen′du-lus):   hanging loosely.

pennate (pen′āt):   like a feather.

pepsin (pep′sin):   a proteolytic enzyme of the stomach secreted as an inactive precursor, pepsinogen.

pericardium (per″ĭ-kar′de-um):   the fibroserous sac that surrounds the heart.

perichondrium (per″ĭ-kon′dre-um):   the connective tissue membrane covering the surface of a cartilage.

perikaryon (per″ĭ-kar′e-on):   the main protoplasmic mass of a cell; the cell body, as distinguished from the nucleus and the processes.

perimysium (per″ĭ-mis′e-um):   the connective tissue enclosing a fascicle of skeletal muscle fibers.

perineurium (per″ĭ-nu′re-um):   the connective tissue sheath surrounding each bundle of fibers in a peripheral nerve.

periosteum (per″ĭ-os′te-um):   the tough fibrous membrane surrounding the bone.

peripheral (pĕ-rif′ar-al):   situated at or near the outward part or surface.

peristalsis (per″ĭ-stal′sis):   the movement by which the alimentary canal or other tubular organs provided with both longitudinal and circular muscle fibers propel their contents. It consists of a wave of contraction passing along the tube.

pernicious anemia (per-nish′us):   macrocytic anemia involving a pronounced reduction in red cell production due to vitamin B_{12} deficiency based on a defect in gastric secretion.

peroneal (per″o-nē′al):   pertaining to the fibula or to the outer side of the leg.

petechia (pe-tē′ke-ah):   a minute, rounded spot of hemorrhage on a surface such as the skin, mucous membrane, etc.

petrous (pet′rus):   hard; stony.

phagocyte (fag′o-sīt):   any cell ingesting microorganisms, foreign particles, or other cells.

phagocytosis (fag″o-si-to′sis):   the engulfing of microorganisms, other cells, and foreign particles by phagocytes.

phrenic (fren′ik):   pertaining to the diaphragm.

pia mater (pī′ah mā′ter):   the innermost of the three meninges, or membranes, of the brain and spinal cord.

pilomotor (pī″lo-mo′tor):   causing movement of hair.

pineal (pin″e-al):   shaped like a pine cone; referring to the pineal gland, or epiphysis cerebri.

pinocytosis (pī″no-sī-to′sis):   the engulfing of liquid globules by cells by a process in which minute incuppings, or invaginations, are formed in the surface of a cell and close to form vesicles containing extracellular material.

piriform (pir′ĭ-form):   pear-shaped.

pisiform (pī′sĭ-form):   like a pea in shape and size.

plantar (plan′tar):   pertaining to the sole of the foot.

plantar reflex: flexion of toes in response to stroking the sole of the foot.

plasma (plaz′mah):   the fluid portion of the blood in which the corpuscles are suspended.

plasmin (fibrinolysin) (plaz′min):   an enzyme capable of digesting fibrin clots. It is formed from plasminogen (a globulin) by enzyme action.

plasmolysis (plaz-mol′ĭ-sis):   contraction or shrinking of the protoplasm of a cell due to the loss of water by osmotic action.

platelet (plāt′let):   a circular or oval disc found in the blood of all mammals, concerned with the coagulation of blood.

pleura (ploor′ah):   membranous sac which encloses the lungs and lines the chest cavity. Parietal pleura lines the chest cavity, and visceral pleura adheres closely to the lungs.

plexus (plek′sus):   a network, especially of nerves, veins, or lymphatics.

plica (plī′kah):   a fold.

pneumothorax (nu″mo-tho′raks):   an accumulation of air or gas in the pleural cavity which may occur spontaneously or as a result of trauma or a pathological process, or be introduced deliberately.

polar body: a nonfunctional cell formed during oogenesis.

polycythemia (pol″e-sī-thē′me-ah):   excess in the number of red corpuscles in the blood.

polydipsia (pol″e-dip′se-ah):   excessive thirst.

polymer (pol′ĭ-mer):   a compound, usually of high molecular weight, formed by the combination of simpler molecules.

polymorphonuclear (pol″e-mor″fo-nu′kle-ar):   having a nucleus deeply lobed or so divided that it appears to be multiple.

polyphagia (pol″e-fā′je-ah):   increased eating.

polysaccharide (pol″e-sak′ah-rīd):   one of a group of carbohydrates which upon hydrolysis yield more than two molecules of simple sugar; e.g., glycogen, dextrin.

pons: a bridge connecting parts of an organ; the convex white eminence situated at the base of the brain.

popliteal (pop-lit′e-al):   pertaining to the posterior surface of the knee.

posterior (pos-tēr′e-or):   situated behind or toward the rear.

precursor (pre-kur′sor):   anything that precedes another or from which another is derived.

presbyopia (pres″be-ō′pe-ah):   oldsightedness; impairment of the ability to accommodate for near vision.

primordium (prī-mor′de-um):   the earliest discernible indication during embryonic development of an organ or part.

prolapse (pro-laps′):   the falling down of an organ or other part.

proliferation (pro-lif″er-a′shun):   the reproduction or multiplication of similar forms, especially of cells.

pronate (prō′nāt):   to turn the forearm so that the palm faces downward or to the back.

protopathic (pro″to-path′ik):   primitive, nondiscriminatory sensibility.

protoplasm (pro′to-plazm):   the essential material of all plant and animal cells; the only known form of matter in which life is manifest.

protuberance (pro-tu′ber-ans):   a projecting part, process, or swelling.

proximal (prok′sĭ-mal):   nearest; closer to any point of reference.

pterygoid (ter'ĭ-goid):   shaped like a wing.

ptosis (tō'sis):   prolapse of an organ or part.

ptyalin (tī'ah-lin):   a salivary amylase which splits starch into maltose.

puberty (pu'ber-te):   the age at which the reproductive organs become functionally operative and secondary sex characteristics develop.

Purkinje system (pur-kin'je):   the fibers leaving the AV (atrioventricular) node.

purulent (pū'ru-lent):   containing, consisting of, or forming pus.

pylorus (pī-lor'us):   the opening between the stomach and the duodenum.

racemose (ras'e-mōs):   resembling a bunch of grapes.

ramus (rā'mus):   a branch, as of an artery, bone, nerve, or vein.

receptor: a sensory nerve terminal or a specialized structure especially sensitive to a particular kind of stimulus to which it readily responds.

reduction: the addition of hydrogen to a substance; more generally, the loss of positive charges and the gaining of electrons.

reflex (re'fleks):   an involuntary response to a stimulus.

refraction (re-frak'shun):   the bending of a ray of light as it passes from one medium into another of different density.

renal (rē'nal):   pertaining to the kidney.

renin (rē'nin):   an enzyme secreted by the kidney that initiates the formation of angiotensins in plasma.

resorption (re-sorp'shun):   the loss of substance through physiologic or pathologic means.

respiration (res-pi-rā'shun):   inspiration and expiration of air via the lungs.

reticuloendothelial (re-tik″u-lo-en″do-thē'le-al):   connective tissue cells carrying on the process of phagocytosis.

reticulum (re-tik'u-lum):   a network, especially a protoplasmic network in cells.

retina (ret'ĭ-nah):   the innermost, light-receptive layer of the eyeball.

Rh factor: a factor first isolated in rhesus monkey blood, consisting of 12 antigens; Rh positive refers to presence of antigen D.

ribonucleic acid, RNA (rī″bo-nu-klē'ic):   nucleic acid playing role in protein synthesis.

ribosome (rī'bo-sōm):   dense aggregation of RNA and protein, usually attached to the endoplasmic reticulum; the site of protein synthesis.

rigor mortis (rig'or mor'tis):   stiffening of a dead body.

rostral (ros'tral):   having to do with a beaklike appendage.

ruga (roo'gah):   a ridge, wrinkle, or fold.

saccharide (sak'ah-rīd):   one of a series of carbohydrates, including the sugars.

saccule (sak'ūl):   a little sac.

sagittal (saj'ĭ-tal):   a plane or section parallel to the long axis of the body.

salpinx (sal'pinks):   a tube, especially the uterine or auditory tube.

saltatory conduction (sal'tah-to″re):   conduction in nerve fiber in which an impulse jumps from one node to another.

sarcolemma (sar″ko-lem'ah):   muscle fiber membrane.

sarcoma (sar-kō'mah):   a tumor, often malignant, arising from connective or nonepithelial tissue.

Schwann cell (shvon): special cell forming the myelin sheath of peripheral nerve fibers.

sciatic (sī-at′ik): pertaining to the ischium.

sclera (sklē′rah): the tough, white, outermost layer of the eyeball, covering approximately the posterior three-fourths of its surface.

sebum (sē′bum): the secretion of sebaceous glands.

semen (sē′men): thick, whitish secretion of the reproductive organs of the male; it consists of spermatozoa and secretions from several accessory organs.

semilunar (sem″ĭ-lu′nar): resembling a crescent or half-moon.

senescence (se-nes′ens): the process or condition of growing old.

sensory neuron (sen′so-re): afferent neuron that carries impulses from receptors in the skin or from other sensory structures to the brain and spinal cord.

septum (sep′tum): a dividing wall or partition.

serous (sēr′us): pertaining to, characterized by, or resembling serum.

serratus (ser-ra′tus): saw-toothed.

Sertoli cells (ser-to′lē): supporting cells of the seminiferous tubules which, among other things, supply nutrients and other substances necessary for the formation of spermatozoa.

serum (sēr′um): plasma minus clotting substances.

sickle cell anemia: abnormality in the protein portion of hemoglobin causing misshaping of the RBC's and premature rupture.

sigmoid (sig′moid): shaped like a letter S.

sinoatrial node (sī″no-ā′tre-al) (pacemaker): neuromuscular tissue in the right atrium which generates electrical impulses that initiate the heartbeat.

sinus (sī′nus): a recess, cavity, or hollow space.

skeleton (skel′ĕ-ton): the bony framework of the higher vertebrate animals.

Skene's glands (skēnz): paraurethral glands.

somatic (so-mat′ik): pertaining to the framework of the body, as distinguished from the viscera.

spasticity (spas-tis′ĭ-te): increased muscle tone producing stiffness.

spermatozoa (sper″mah-to-zo′ah): the mature male sex cells.

sphenoid (sfē′noid): wedge-shaped.

sphincter (sfingk′ter): a ringlike muscle enclosing a natural orifice; for example, the anal sphincter.

sphygmomanometer (sfig″mo-mah-nom′e-ter): instrument for measuring blood pressure in the arteries.

splanchnic (splangk′nik): pertaining to the viscera.

sputum (spu′tum): matter ejected from the mouth, usually saliva mixed with mucus and other substances from the respiratory tract.

squamous (skwā′mus): scaly or platelike.

stapes (stā′pēz): the innermost of the ossicles of the ear, shaped somewhat like a stirrup.

stasis (stā′sis): a stoppage of the blood or any other body fluid in any part.

stenosis (ste-no′sis): narrowing or stricture of a duct or canal.

stereognosis (ster″e-og-no′sis): ability to identify an object by means of tactile and kinesthetic sensations.

steroid (ster′oyd): term applied to any one of a large group of substances chemically related to sterols; includes sterols, D vitamins, bile acids, certain hormones, etc.

stimulus (stim′u-lus):   any agent, act, or influence producing a reaction in a receptor.

stratum (strā′tum):   a layer.

striated (strī′āt-ed):   striped; provided with streaks or lines.

stroma (stro′mah):   the supporting connective tissue or framework of an organ.

subcutaneous (sub″ku-tā′ne-us):   beneath the skin.

substrate (sub′strāt):   a substance upon which an enzyme acts.

sulcus (sul′kus):   a groove, trench, or furrow.

superior: situated above.

supinate (sū′pĭ-nāt):   to turn the forearm so that the palm faces upward or to the front.

suprarenal (su″prah-re′nal):   situated above the kidney; the suprarenal gland is the adrenal gland.

surfactant (sur-fak′tant):   a lipoprotein which lowers surface tension in the lungs.

suture (sū′chūr):   a form of articulation characterized by the presence of a thin layer of fibrous tissue uniting the margins of the contiguous bones; found only in the skull.

sympathetic: thoracolumbar division of the autonomic nervous system; in general concerned with the expenditure of energy; for example, accelerating the heart rate.

synapse (sin′aps):   junctional region between two adjacent neurons, forming the place at which the nerve impulse is transmitted from one neuron to another.

synarthrosis (sin″ar-thro′sis):   a form of articulation permitting no movement.

syncytium (sin-sit′e-um):   a multinucleate mass of protoplasm produced by the merging of cells.

syndrome (sin′drōm):   a group of symptoms and signs occurring together in such a way as to indicate the existence of a common cause.

synovial fluid (sĭ-no′ve-al):   viscous fluid which is secreted by the synovial membrane to lubricate the joints.

synthesis (sin′thĕ-sis):   putting together parts to form a more complex whole.

systemic (sis-tem′ik):   pertaining to or affecting the body as a whole.

systole (sis′tō-lē):   contraction of the ventricles of the heart.

T cell system: cell-mediated immune system especially effective in combatting chronic bacterial infections, fungi, and some viruses.

tachycardia (tak″e-kar′de-ah):   excessive rapidity in the action of the heart.

tachypnea (tak″ip-ne′ah):   excessively rapid and shallow breathing.

tegmentum (teg-men′tum):   a covering.

tendon (ten′dun):   the fibrous cord of connective tissue in which the fibers of a muscle end and by which a muscle is attached to a bone or other structure.

tension (ten′shun):   the condition of being stretched.

thorax (thō′raks):   the chest; that portion of the trunk above the diaphragm and below the neck.

thrombin (throm′bin):   the enzyme derived from prothrombin which converts fibrinogen to fibrin.

thrombocyte (throm′bo-sīt):   a blood platelet.

thromboembolus (throm″bo-em′bo-lus):   a dislodged blood clot that has resettled in an area different from that in which it was formed.

thrombus (throm′bus):   a clot in a blood vessel or in one of the cavities of the heart formed by coagulation of the blood and remaining at the point of its formation.

tidal volume: the volume of air inspired or expired with each breath.

tonus (tō′nus):   the slight, continuous contraction of muscles which in skeletal muscles aids in the maintenance of posture and the return of blood to the heart.

toxic (tok′sik):   harmful to the body; poisonous.

trabecula (trah-bek′u-lah):   a supporting or anchoring strand of connective tissue, as such a strand extending from a capsule into the substance of the enclosed organ; one of the plates or spicules of cancellous bone.

tracheostomy (trā″ke-os′to-me):   a process in which a tracheal tube is placed to facilitate breathing in cases of obstruction.

tracheotomy (trā″ke-ot′o-me):   the operation of cutting into the trachea.

tract: a region, principally one of some length; a collection or bundle of nerve fibers in the central nervous system having the same origin, function, and termination.

trauma (traw′mah):   a wound or injury.

trigone (tri′gon):   a small triangular area near the mouth of the bladder between the openings of the two ureters and the urethra.

trochlear (trok′le-ar):   resembling a pulley.

trophic (trof′ik):   of or pertaining to nutrition.

trypsin (trip′sin):   a protein-degrading enzyme secreted by the pancreas as an inactive precursor, trypsinogen.

tubercle (tu′ber-kl):   a nodule or small eminence.

tunica (tu′ni-kah):   a membrane or other structure covering or forming a layer of a body part or organ.

tympanum (tim′pah-num):   the middle ear.

ulcer (ul′ser):   a loss of substance on a cutaneous or mucous surface causing gradual disintegration and necrosis of the tissues.

umbilicus (um″bĭ-li′kus):   the round, depressed scar on the abdomen marking the site of attachment of the umbilical cord in the fetus; the navel.

unilateral (u″nĭ-lat′er-al):   pertaining to only one side of the body.

urea (u-re′ah):   the chief nitrogenous constituent of the urine, produced in the liver from ammonia (derived chiefly from deamination of amino acids) and carbon dioxide.

uremia (u-rē′me-ah):   retention in the blood of urinary constituents due to kidney failure and the symptoms resulting therefrom.

utricle (u′tre-kl):   a little sac.

vagina (vah-ji′nah):   a sheathlike structure; usually the canal between the vulva and uterus of a female.

vagus (vā′gus):   "wandering"; designating the tenth cranial nerve.

vallate papilla (val′āt pah-pil′ah):   largest papilla (nipplelike projection or elevation) of the tongue.

valve: a membranous fold in a canal or passage which prevents the reflux of its contents.

varicose (var′ĭ-kōs):   swollen, knotted, and tortuous blood vessels.

vas: a vessel.

vascular (vas′ku-lar):   pertaining to or full of vessels.

vasoconstriction (vas″o-kon-strik′shun):   diminution of the diameter of vessels, especially constriction of arterioles, leading to decreased flow of blood to a part.

vasodilation (vas″o-di-la′shun):   dilation of a vessel, especially dilation of arterioles, leading to increased supply of blood to a part.

vasomotor (vas″o-mo′tor):   regulating the contraction (vasoconstriction) and expansion (vasodilation) of blood vessels.

vastus (vas′tus):   wide; of great size.

vein: vessel which conveys blood to or toward the heart.

ventilation (ven″tĭ-lā′shun):   the volume of air exchanged in one minute.

ventral (ven′tral):   denoting a position more toward the belly surface than some other object of reference.

ventricle (ven′trĭ-kl):   any small cavity.

venule (ven′ul):   vessel of similar function to veins but of smaller size.

vermiform (ver′mĭ-form):   shaped like a worm.

vestibule (ves′tĭ-būl):   a space or cavity at the entrance to a canal, especially that of the ear.

viable (vī′ah-bl):   capable of living in the environment outside the mother's body.

villus (vil′us):   a minute, elongated projection from the surface of a mucous membrane or other membrane.

viscera (vis′er-ah):   the internal organs.

viscous (vis′kus):   pertaining to sticky or gummy fluid which flows with difficulty.

vitamin (vī′tah-min):   a general term for a number of unrelated organic substances that occur in many foods in small amounts and that are necessary for the normal metabolic functioning of the body.

vitreous humor (vit′re-us hu′mor):   transparent, gelatinlike substance filling the posterior cavity of the eye (behind the lens).

volar (vo′lar):   pertaining to the palm or sole.

Wernicke's area (ver′ni-kez):   area of the brain for language comprehension.

xiphoid (zif′oid):   shaped like a sword.

zygote (zī′gōt):   a fertilized egg.

zymogen (zī′mo-jen):   the inactive precursor of an enzyme.

Index

Note: Page numbers in *italics* refer to illustrations.
Page numbers followed by t refer to tables.

Tricarboxylic acid cycle. See *Krebs cycle*.
Triceps brachii muscle, 182t, 200, 201
Triceps muscle, *18, 19*
  lateral head of, *10, 208*
  long head of, *194*
  medial head of, *194, 202*
Tricuspid valve, 369, *370, 371, 410*
Trigeminal nerve (V), 257, 282t, *284, 286–288, 287, 292*
  branches of, 282t, *287*
Trigeminal neuralgia, clinical manifestations of, 286, 288
Triglyceride(s), composition and functions of, 35, *36*
  transport of, 511–512, *511*
Trigone, of urinary bladder, 535, *536*
Triquetrum, *140,* 141
Trochlea, of humerus, 138, *139, 140*
Trochlear nerve (IV), 252, 282t, *284, 286, 287*
Trochlear notch, of ulna, 138
Trophoblast(s), 620
Tropocollagen, secondary structure of, *32*
Tropomyosin, 168
  in muscle contractions, 170, *171*
Troponin, 168
  in muscle contractions, 170, *171*
Trunk, bones of, 130–138. See also specific bone.
Trypsin, in digestion, 500, 500t
Tryptophan, RNA code words for, 71t
Tuber cinereum, 259
Tubercle(s), of humerus, 138
Tuberculosis, pathophysiology of, 469–470
Tunica adventitia, 382, 382t, *383*
Tunica albuginea, of testis, 600, *600*
Tunica intima, 382, 382t, *383*
Tunica media, 382, 382t, *383*
Tunica vaginalis, of testis, 600, *600*
Turbinate bone(s), middle and inferior, *330*
Twinning, 620
Tympanic membrane, 340, *341, 342*
Tyrosine, RNA code words for, 71t

Ulcer(s), decubitus, etiology of, 104
  dermal, *103*
  duodenal, *483*
  peptic, manifestations of, 502–503
Ulna, 116t, *117, 118, 140*
  coronoid process of, *140*
  head of, *140*
  olecranon process of, *200, 204*
  position in pronation and supination, *153*
  structure of, 138
  styloid process of, *140,* 141
Ulnar artery, *401, 414, 416*
Ulnar collateral artery, *414, 416*
Ulnar collateral ligament, *151*

Ulnar nerve, 271, 273, 274t, 275, 276, 277
  branches of, 277
Ulnar recurrent artery(ies), *416*
Ulnar styloid process, *140*
Umbilical artery, *424*
Umbilical cord, *621*
Umbilical vein, *424*
Umbilicus, *10, 11, 207, 208*
Umbo, of ear, *341*
Uncus, 252
Urachus, *425, 536*
Uracil, in nucleic acids, 69, *69, 70*
Urea, tubular reabsorption of, 528
Uremia, manifestations of, 533
Ureter, *15, 16, 19, 196, 521, 522, 523, 524,* 534
  orifice of, *536*
Urethra, *17, 214, 521,* 535, *536, 537*
  male, 601
Uric acid, blood levels of, 354t
Urinalysis, 532
Urinary bladder, *13, 14, 15, 16, 484, 485, 521,* 534–535, *536*
Urinary system, composition of, 14–15
Urinary tract, 520–539
  congenital malformation of, 532–533
  historical aspects of, 520
  water loss through, 576
Urination, mechanics of, 535
Urine, characteristics of, 532
  composition of, 526, 527t
  concentration and volume of, alteration of, 529–531, *529*
  formation and excretion of, 526–527
    glomerular filtration in, 527
    tubular reabsorption and secretion in, 527–528
  pH of, 27t
Urogenital diaphragm, *214, 597, 599*
Urogenital triangle, of female perineum, 604
Urticaria, clinical manifestations and etiology of, 104
Uterine tube, *15,* 602, 605, 607–608, *607*
  ampulla of, *605*
Uterosacral ligament, of uterus, 606, *607*
Uterovesical pouch, *602*
Uterus, *15,* 602, *605,* 606
  abnormal positions of, 606, *606*
  broad ligament of, *15*
  ligaments of, 605, *606, 607*
  round ligament of, *15*
  walls of, 607
Utricle, of ear, 342, *342*
Utriculosaccular duct, of ear, *342*
Uvula, *254, 436, 444, 482*

Vagal ganglion, 291, *292*
Vagina, *17, 214,* 602, *604, 605,* 606
Vagus nerve (X), 250, 283t, *284,* 290–291, *291, 368*

Valine, RNA code words for, 71t
  structure of, *31*
Vallate papilla, of tongue, *349, 482*
Vallecula, *447, 482*
Vasa recta, in regulation of urine concentration, 530, *530*
Vasa vasorum, 382
Vasomotor center, of medulla, in regulation of arterial blood pressure, 386–388
Vasopressin, actions of, 547
Vastus intermedius muscle, 186t, 216, *218*
Vastus lateralis muscle, *10,* 186t, *208,* 216, *216, 217, 218, 220*
Vastus medialis muscle, 186t, 216, *216, 218, 220, 225*
Vein(s), graft to arteries, in management of coronary artery disease, 398
  major, *403*
  structure of, *383, 385*
  valves of, 385, *385*
  varicose, manifestations of, 385
Vena cava. See *Inferior vena cava* and *Superior vena cava.*
Venereal disease(s), gonorrhea, 625–626
  herpes progenitalis, 626
  syphilis, 626
Ventilation, 460
  age and, 467
  blood pressure and, 467
  effects of exercise on, 466–467
  pulmonary, regulation of, 465
  sensory stimuli and, 467
  site of action of carbon dioxide, hydrogen and oxygen in, 465
  quantitative aspects of, 465–466, *466*
Ventral cavity, 8, *9*
Ventral nerve root, of spinal cord, 267, *270*
Ventral primary ramus, of spinal cord, 267
Ventral ramus, of spinal nerve, 272
Ventricle, left, 367, 369, *370, 371, 377, 410, 412*
  right, 367, 369, *370, 371, 377, 410, 412*
Ventricular fibrillation, characteristics of, 380
Ventricular flutter, characteristics of, 380
Ventricular fold(s), of larynx, 448
Ventricular system, of brain, 260, *261, 262*
Ventricular tachycardia, characteristics of, 380
Ventriculography, *269, 270*
Venule(s), structure of, 384–385, *384*
Vertebra(e). See also specific vertebrae.
  articulation between, *155*
  articulation with ribs, 134, *134*
  body, of, 130
  cervical, relationship to skull and face, *123*
  fifth lumbar, *17*